The Princeton Review

PrincetonReview.com

THE BEST 366 COLLEGES

2008 Edition

By Robert Franek,
Tom Meltzer, Christopher Maier, Erik Olson,
Julie Doherty, and Eric Owens

Random House, Inc., New York
2008 Edition

The Princeton Review, Inc.
2315 Broadway
New York, NY 10024
E-mail: bookeditor@review.com

© 2007 by The Princeton Review, Inc.

ISBN   978-0-375-76621-3

Publisher: Robert Franek
Editors: Adrinda Kelly, Adam Davis, Laura Braswell
Director, Production Editorial: Christine LaRubio
Copy Editor: Meave Shelton
Director, Print Production: Scott Harris
Director, Data Collection: Ben Zelevansky

Printed in the United States of America.

9 8 7 6 5 4 3 2 1

2008 Edition

FOREWORD

Every year, about two million high school graduates go to college. To make sure they end up at the *right* school, they spend several billion dollars on the admissions process. This money pays for countless admissions officers and counselors, a bunch of standardized tests (and preparation for them), and many books similar to—but not as good as—this one.

It's expensive because most admissions professionals have a thing about being in control. As a group, colleges resist almost every attempt to standardize or otherwise simplify the process. Admissions officers want you to believe that every admissions decision that they render occurs within systems of weights, measures, and deliberations that are far too complex for you to comprehend. They shudder at the notion of having to respond to students and their parents in down-to-earth language that might reveal the arbitrary nature of a huge percentage of the admissions and denials that they issue during each cycle. That would be admitting that good luck and circumstance play a major part in many successful applications. So, in flight from public accountability, they make the process a lot more mysterious than it needs to be.

Even the most straightforward colleges hide the information you would want to know about the way they'll evaluate your application: What grades and SATs are they looking for? Exactly how much do extracurricular activities count? What percentage of the aid that they give out is in loans and what percentage is in grants?

We couldn't get answers to these questions from many colleges. In fact, we couldn't get answers to *any* questions from some schools. Others who supplied this information to us for earlier editions of this guide have since decided that they never should have in the first place. After all, knowledge is power.

Colleges seem to have the time and money to create beautiful brochures that generally show that all college classes are held under a tree on a beautiful day. Why not just tell you what sort of students they're looking for and what factors they'll use to consider your application?

Until the schools demystify the admissions process, this book is your best bet. It's not a phone book containing every fact about every college in the country. And it's not a memoir written by a few graduates describing their favorite dining halls or professors. We've given you the facts you'll need to apply to the few hundred best schools in the country, and we offer enough information about them—which we gathered from more than 120,000 current college students—to help you make a smart decision about which school to attend.

As complicated and difficult as the admissions process is, we think you'll love college itself—especially at the schools listed in this book.

Good luck in your search.

John Katzman
June 2007

ACKNOWLEDGMENTS

Each year we assemble an awe-inspiringly talented group of colleagues who work together to produce our guidebooks; this year is no exception. Everyone involved in this effort—authors, editors, data collectors, production specialists, and designers—gives so much more than is required to make *The Best 366 Colleges* an exceptional student resource guide. This new edition yields the essentials of what prospective college students really want: The most honest, accessible, and pertinent information about the colleges they are considering attending for the next four years of their lives. My sincere thanks go to the many who contributed to this tremendous project. I am proud to note here that we have again successfully provided an uncompromising look into the true nature of each profiled college or university based on the opinions of each institution's current students. I know our readers will benefit from our collective efforts.

A special thank you goes to our authors, Tom Meltzer, Christopher Maier, Erik Olson, Julie Doherty, and Eric Owens, for their dedication in sifting through tens of thousands of surveys to produce the essence of each school profiled. Very special thanks go to Adrinda Kelly, Adam Davis, and Laura Braswell for their editorial commitment and vision. They met the challenges of this book head on; I am grateful for their thoughtful and careful reading.

A warm and special thank you goes to our Student Survey Manager Jen Adams, who works exceptionally well with school administrators and students alike. Jen is in the trenches every day, and her spirit never wavers.

My continued thanks go to our data collection pros, Ben Zelevansky and Perry Medina, for their successful efforts in collecting and accurately representing the statistical data that appear with each college profile. A sincere thank-you goes to Ben Zelevansky for all the detailed work he completed for data generation and presentation.

The enormousness of this project and its deadline constraints could not have been realized without the calm presence of our production team, Scott Harris, Director of Print Production; Christine LaRubio, Director of Production Editorial; and Meave Shelton, Copy Editor. Their unconditional dedication, focus, and most important, careful eyes, continue to inspire and impress me. They deserve great thanks for their flexible schedules and uncompromising efficiency.

Special thanks also go to Jeanne Krier, our Random House publicist, for the work she has done on this book and the overall series since its inception. Jeanne continues to be my trusted colleague, media advisor, and friend. I would also like to make special mention of Tom Russell and Nicole Benhabib, our Random House publishing team, for their continuous investment and faith in our ideas.

Last, I thank John Katzman, Mark Chernis, and Young Shin for their steadfast confidence in this book and our publishing department, and for always being the champions of student opinion. It is a pleasure to work with each of you.

Again, to all who contributed so much to this publication, thank you for your efforts; they do not go unnoticed.

Robert Franek
VP—Publisher
Lead Author—*The Best 366 Colleges*

CONTENTS

PART I INTRODUCTION

GETTING INTO SELECTIVE COLLEGES: A GUIDE FOR HIGH SCHOOL STUDENTS

This is a guide to the nation's 366 most academically outstanding institutions, so it's no surprise that many of them may be selective in their admissions. If you're like any one of the 2,000,000 (and growing!) high school students who apply to college each year, you're probably wondering what admissions officers at these schools are looking for in an applicant. What exactly does it take to get into a selective college? To be sure, high grades in challenging courses are just the beginning. To get into most of the colleges in this book, you will need to:

- Earn high grades
- Enroll in challenging courses
- Prepare for the SAT or the ACT, and SAT Subject Tests
- Polish your writing skills
- Plan ahead for those letters of recommendation you'll need by establishing great relationships with your teachers and advisors
- Focus on activities, community service, and/or after-school or summer employment that show commitment over a long period of time and allow you to demonstrate leadership skills

Here's a brief primer in what you should be doing year by year in high school to prepare yourself for admission to *your* "Best" college. For a detailed guide on how you can make the most of your high school years and segue those experiences into a successful college application, check out our new book: *The Road to College: The High School Student's Guide to Discovering Your Passion, Getting Involved, and Getting Admitted.* Pick it up at PrincetonReview/bookstore.com.

Freshman Year

It's easier to finish well in high school if you start off that way. Concentrate on your studies and work hard to earn good grades. Get to know your teachers and ask for their help if you are having trouble in a subject (or even if you just really enjoy it and want to learn more). They'll most certainly want to help you do your best. Odds are, there is an honor roll at your school: Make it a goal to get on it. And if your grades are so good that you qualify for membership in the National Honor Society, pat yourself on the back and don't think twice about accepting the invitation to join.

Make it a point to meet your guidance counselor to begin thinking about colleges you may be interested in and courses and admission tests they require. Also work on building your vocabulary to get an early start on prepping for the SAT and ACT. Sign up for the Princeton Review's Vocab Minute on PrincetonReview.com. Consider participating in the National Vocabulary Championship (www.WinWithWords.com).

The Princeton Review is a proud partner of this contest with the Game Show Network, now in its second year. Last year, winners walked away with over $100,000 in prizes and Princeton Review services. To learn how you can enter, visit WinWithWords.com.

Read a Good Book!

Your vocabulary and reading skills are key to doing well on the SAT and ACT. You can do some early prep for both tests by reading good books. Here are some fiction and non-fiction books we love by great authors you may not have encountered before.

- *The Curious Incident of the Dog in the Night-Time: A Novel* by Mark Haddon
- *A Heartbreaking Work of Staggering Genius* by Dave Eggers
- *Life of Pi* by Yann Martel
- *Reading Lolita in Tehran* by Azar Nafisi
- *White Teeth* by Zadie Smith

For extra practice building your vocabulary, check out our *Word Smart* books. Full of mnemonic tricks, they make learning even the toughest vocabulary a breeze.

Sophomore Year

As a sophomore, you'll need to stay focused on your studies. You'll also want to choose one or more extracurriculars that interest you. Admissions Officers look favorably on involvement in student government, student newspaper, varsity sports, and community service. But don't overload your schedule with activities just to rack up a long list of extracurriculars that you hope will impress admissions officers. Colleges would much rather see you focus on a few worthwhile extracurriculars than divide your time among a bunch of different activities that you're not passionate about. If you didn't earn strong grades during your freshman year, start doing so this year. Scope out the Advanced Placement course offerings at your school. You'll want to sign up for as many AP courses as you can reasonably take, starting in your junior year. Our test-prep series, *Cracking the AP*, can help give you a leg up on passing the AP exams and gaining college credit while in high school, and Admissions Officers will want to see that you've earned high grades in challenging classes.

Your sophomore year is when you'll have an opportunity to take the PSAT. Given every October, the PSAT is a shortened version of the SAT. It is used to predict how well students may do on the SAT and it determines eligibility for National Merit Scholarships. While your PSAT scores won't count until you retake the test in your junior year, you should approach this as a test run for the real thing. Check out our book, *Cracking the PSAT /NMSQT* for more info. It has two full-length practice tests and tips on how to score your best on the test.

What Should You Do This Summer?

Ahhh, summer. The possibilities seem endless. You can get a job, intern, travel, study, volunteer, or do nothing at all. The Princeton Review book *500 Ways for Teens to Spend the Summer* offers plenty of suggestions of ways for you to get involved in summer activities. It's full of advice and features a directory of 500 summer programs for college-bound teens. Our new book, *The Road to College*, also has great suggestions for summer projects. Here are a few ideas to get you started:

- **Go to College**: No, not for real. However, you can participate in summer programs at colleges and universities at home and abroad. Programs can focus on anything from academics (stretch your brain by taking an intensive science or language course) to sports to admissions guidance. This is also a great opportunity to explore college life firsthand, especially if you get to stay in a dorm.
- **Prep for the PSAT, SAT, or ACT:** So maybe it's not quite as adventurous as trekking around Patagonia for the summer or as cool as learning to slam dunk at basketball camp, but hey, there's nothing adventurous or cool about being rejected from your top-choice college because of unimpressive test scores. Plus, you'll be ahead of the game if you can return to school with much of your PSAT, SAT, and ACT preparation behind you.
- **Research Scholarships:** College is expensive. While you should never rule out a school based on cost, the more scholarship money you can secure beforehand, the more college options you will have. You'll find loads of info on financial aid and scholarships (including a scholarship search tool) on our site, PrincetonReview.com.

Junior Year

You'll start the year off by taking the PSAT in October. High PSAT scores in junior year qualify you for the National Merit Scholarship competition. To become a finalist, you also need great grades and a recommendation from your school.

Make sure your grades are high this year. When colleges look at your transcripts they put a heavy emphasis on junior year grades. Decisions are made before admissions officers see your second-semester senior-year grades, and possibly before they see your first-semester senior-year grades! It's critical that your junior-year grades are solid.

During your junior year, you'll probably take the SAT or ACT test for the first time. Most colleges require scores from one of these tests for admission and/or scholarship award decisions. Plan to spend 3–12 weeks preparing for the tests. The SAT is comprised of Math, Critical Reading, and Writing sections. Colleges will see your individual section scores and your composite score, but generally they'll be most concerned with your composite score.

More and more students are opting to take the ACT in addition to, or instead of, the SAT. Most colleges accept the ACT in lieu of the SAT. The ACT has an English, Reading, Math, and Science section, plus the optional Writing section. (Some schools require the essay, so be sure to ask before you take the test.) One great advantage of the ACT is that you can take the test several times and choose what scores to send. If you take the SAT several times, all your scores are sent to the colleges. If you're not sure which test to take, first make sure that all the schools to which you're applying accept both tests. If they do, then take the test on which you do better. Visit PrincetonReview.com to take a free assessment test that will help you identify whether the ACT or SAT is better for you.

Most highly selective colleges also require you to take three SAT Subject Tests in addition to the SAT or ACT. If you have SAT Subject Tests to take, plan now. You can't take the SAT and SAT Subject Tests on the same day. It's worth noting that The Princeton Review can help with all the standardized tests you will need to take throughout high school. Log on to PrincetonReview.com/college/testprep/.

Also take time during your junior year to research colleges, and, if possible, visit schools high on your "hopes" list. When researching colleges, you'll want to consider a variety of factors besides whether or not you can get in, including location, school size, majors or programs offered that interest you, and cost and availability of financial aid. It helps to visit schools because it's the best way to learn whether a school may be right for you. If you can schedule an interview with an admissions officer during your visit, it may help him or her discover how right *you may be* for the school. The Princeton Review book, *Guide to College Visits,* offers plenty of tips on how you can make the most of your college visits, plus it has profiles of more than 370 popular colleges with tips on how to get there, where to stay, and what to do on campus.

Senior Year

It's time to get serious about pulling everything together on your applications. Deadlines will vary from school to school and you will have a lot to keep track of, so make checklists of what's due when. If you're not happy with your previous SAT scores, you should take the October SAT. If you still need to take any SAT Subject Tests, now's the time.

If you have found the school of your dreams and you're happy with your grades and test scores, consider filing an Early Decision application. Many selective colleges commit more than half of their admissions spots to Early Decision applicants. To take this route, you must file your application in early November. By mid-December, you'll find out whether you got in—but there's a catch. If you're accepted Early Decision to a college, you must withdraw all applications to other colleges. This means that your financial aid offer might be hard to negotiate, so be prepared to take what you get.

Regardless of which route you decide to take, have a backup plan. Make sure you apply to at least one safety school—one that you feel confident you can get into and afford. Another option is to apply Early Decision at one school, but apply to other colleges during the regular decision period in the event that you are rejected from the early decision college.

Financial Aid 101

All students applying for financial aid (including federal, state, and institutional need-based aid), need to complete the FAFSA (Free Application for Federal Student Aid) form. The form is available in high schools in December, but you can't submit it until January. You may also need to complete the CSS/PROFILE form, state aid forms, and any additional forms provided by the colleges. The Princeton Review's *Paying for College Without Going Broke* is the only annually-updated guide that explains how the financial aid process works and how to maximize your eligibility for aid. It gives line-by-line strategies for completing the FAFSA, which is particularly complicated and crucial. The FASFA is the need analysis document used to determine your "EFC" (Expected Family Contribution)—the amount of money the family is expected to ante up towards the cost of college.

When you ask teachers to write recommendations for you, give them everything they need. Tell them your application deadline and include a stamped, addressed envelope, or directions on how to submit the recommendation online, and be sure to send them a thank-you note after you know the recommendation was turned in. Your essay, on the other hand, is the one part of your application you have total control over. Don't repeat information from other parts of your application. And by all means, proofread! You'll find tips from admissions officers on what they look for (and what peeves them the most) about college applicants' essays in our book, *College Essays That Made a Difference*.

In March/April, colleges will send you a decision from the admissions office regarding your admission or rejection. If you are admitted (and you applied for financial aid) you'll also receive a decision from the financial aid office detailing your aid award package. The decision from the financial aid office can sometimes be appealed. The decision from the admissions office is almost always final. If you are wait-listed, don't lose hope. Write a letter to the college expressing how much you'd still like to attend the school and include an update on your recent activities. When colleges admit students from wait lists, they almost always give preference to students who have made it clear that they really want to attend.

It's important to wait until you've heard from all of the colleges you've applied to before making your final choice. May 1 is when you'll need to commit to the lucky college that will have you in its freshman class. We know how exciting but stressful that decision can be. If you're having a difficult time choosing between two colleges, try to visit each of them one more time. Can you imagine yourself walking around that campus, building a life in that community, and establishing friendships with those people? Finally, decide and be happy. Don't forget to thank your recommenders and tell them where you'll be going to school. Some of the best times of your life await!

GREAT SCHOOLS FOR 15 OF THE MOST POPULAR UNDERGRADUATE MAJORS

CHECK IT OUT: Unsure about what you want to major in at college? Our *Guide to College Majors* profiles more than 375 undergraduate majors and covers what you can do in high school to prepare yourself, the courses you'll have to take, and your career options and salary prospects once you graduate. Pick it up at PrincetonReview.com/bookstore.

Worried about having to declare a major on your college application? Relax. Most colleges won't require you to declare a major until the end of your sophomore year, giving you plenty of time to explore some possibilities. However, problems may arise if you are thinking about majoring in a program that limits its enrollment—meaning that if you don't declare that major now, you might not get into that program later on. On the flip side, some students declare a major on their application because they believe it will boost their chances of gaining admission. This is a slippery slope to climb, however. If you're planning to switch majors at a later date, know that it can be tricky if it involves switching from one school within the college to another (from the school of arts and sciences to the school of business, for example). If you are concerned about this, talk to your college admissions officer. Remember, you'll have an academic advisor once on campus, too. Keeping him or her in the loop as you get your undergrad feet wet is universally the finest strategy.

Never choose a college based on the perceived prestige of a particular program, especially if you haven't experienced it in person. College will expose you to new and exciting thoughts and possibilities. To choose a school based on a major before you even know what else is out there would limit you in many ways. You may also want to investigate opportunities to design your own major.

Choosing a school based on program availability, however, is a different story. Each year we collect data from colleges on the subject of—among many other things—undergraduate academic offerings. We not only ask colleges to report which undergraduate majors they offer, but also to identify which of their majors have the highest academic enrollment. The list below represents fifteen of the forty "most popular" majors (in alphabetical order) reported by the schools responding to our survey. We also conducted our own independent research, looking at institutional data, talking to our in-house college admissions experts, and getting input from guidance counselors, college admissions counselors, and education experts across the country to identify schools that offer great programs in these majors. Of the roughly 3,500 schools across the United States, the relatively few that appear on the lists below represent only a snapshot of the many schools offering great programs in these majors. Use these lists as a starting point for further research. Some of the schools on these lists may not appear in the *Best 366 Colleges* (these schools are marked with an asterisk*), but you can find profiles of them in our *Complete Book of Colleges: 2008 Edition*.

We have scads of other lists of colleges covering everything from terrific schools for various majors to those with exceptional extracurriculars and more in our new book, *College Navigator: Find a School to Match Any Interest from Archery to Zoology*. It's designed to help you winnow your list of schools to the ones that are the best fit for your individual talents and interests.

We also have two college guides that identify great schools in special categories. Interested in a major to prepare you for a career in the entertainment or digital media field? Check out our *Television, Film, and Digital Media Programs* book. We teamed up with the Academy of Television Arts and Sciences Foundation on this guide which profiles more than 500 media arts programs at top colleges and universities. If you're looking for a college with exceptional programs in community involvement or service-learning opportunities, pick up a copy of *Colleges with a Conscience*. Developed in partnership with Campus Compact (www.Compact.org), a coalition of college presidents committed to supporting the public services purposes of higher education, the book profiles 81 great schools with outstanding citizenship track records and student programs.

You'll find these and all of our 200 college guidebooks at PrincetonReview.com/bookstore. Good luck with your search!

Great Schools for Accounting Majors

- Alfred University
- Auburn University
- Babson College
- Baylor University
- Birmingham—Southern College
- Boston College
- Boston University
- Brigham Young University
- Bucknell University
- Calvin College
- Claremont McKenna College
- Clemson University
- College of Charleston
- Cornell University
- DePaul University
- Drexel University
- Duquesne University
- Elon University
- Emory University
- Fordham University
- Georgetown University
- Indiana University—Bloomington
- Iowa State University
- James Madison University
- Lehigh University
- Michigan State University
- New York University
- Northeastern University
- Pepperdine University
- Rider University
- Rochester Institute of Technology
- Seton Hall University
- Suffolk University
- Temple University
- Texas A&M University—College Station
- University of Illinois at Urbana-Champaign
- University of Michigan—Ann Arbor
- University of Pennsylvania
- University of Southern California
- The University of Texas at Austin

Great Schools for Biology Majors

- Agnes Scott College
- Albion College
- Austin College
- Baylor University
- Brandeis University

Schools marked with an asterisk do not appear in the *Best 366 Colleges*. You can find those school profiles in *Complete Book of Colleges, 2008 Edition*.

- Colby College
- Cornell University
- Drexel University
- Guilford College
- Harvard College
- Haverford College
- Howard University
- Illinois Wesleyan University
- Indiana University—Bloomington
- Louisiana State University
- Loyola University—Chicago
- Massachusetts Institute of Technology
- Mount Holyoke College
- The Ohio State University—Columbus
- Pomona College
- Reed College
- Rice University
- Siena College
- Swarthmore College
- Temple University
- Texas A&M University—College Station
- University of California—Davis
- The University of Chicago
- University of Dallas
- University of Delaware
- University of Denver
- University of New Mexico
- University of the Pacific
- Wofford College
- Xavier University of Louisiana

Great Schools for Business/Finance Majors
- Babson College
- Bentley College
- Boston College
- Carnegie Mellon University
- Cornell University
- DePaul University
- Emory University
- Florida State University
- Indiana University—Bloomington

- Iowa State University
- Lehigh University
- Massachusetts Institute of Technology
- Miami University
- Michigan State University
- New York University
- Ohio University—Athens
- Rice University
- Seattle University
- University of California—Berkeley
- University of California—Los Angeles
- University of Florida
- University of Illinois at Urbana-Champaign
- University of Michigan
- University of Pennsylvania
- University of Southern California
- The University of Texas at Austin
- University of Virginia
- Washington University in St. Louis

Great Schools for Communications Majors
- Augsburg College*
- Baylor University
- Boise State University*
- Bradley University
- City University of New York—Hunter College
- Clemson University
- College of Charleston
- Cornell University
- Denison University
- DePaul University
- Duquesne University
- Eckerd College
- Emerson College
- Fairfield University
- Fordham University
- Gonzaga University
- Gustavus Adolphus College

Schools marked with an asterisk do not appear in the *Best 366 Colleges*. You can find those school profiles in *Complete Book of Colleges, 2008 Edition*.

- Hollins University
- Indiana University—Bloomington
- Iowa State University
- Ithaca College
- James Madison University
- Lake Forest College
- Loyola University—New Orleans
- Michigan State University
- Muhlenberg College
- New York University
- Northwestern University
- Pepperdine University
- Ripon College
- Salisbury University
- Seton Hall University
- St. John's University (NY)
- Suffolk University
- Syracuse University
- University of California—San Diego
- University of California—Santa Barbara
- University of Iowa
- University of Maryland—College Park
- The University of Texas at Austin
- University of Utah

Great Schools for Computer Science/ Computer Engineering Majors

- Auburn University
- Boston University
- Bradley University
- Brown University
- California Institute of Technology
- Carnegie Mellon University
- Clemson University
- Drexel University
- Florida State University
- George Mason University
- Georgia Institute of Technology
- Gonzaga University
- Hampton University

- Harvey Mudd College
- Iowa State University
- Johns Hopkins University
- Lehigh University
- Massachusetts Institute of Technology
- Michigan State University
- New Jersey Institute of Technology
- Northeastern University
- Northwestern University
- Princeton University
- Rice University
- Rochester Institute of Technology
- Rose-Hulman Institute of Technology
- Seattle University
- Stanford University
- State University of New York at Binghamton
- State University of New York—University at Buffalo
- Texas A&M University—College Station
- United States Air Force Academy
- University of Arizona
- University of California—Berkeley
- University of California—Los Angeles
- University of California—Riverside
- University of Illinois at Urbana-Champaign
- University of Massachusetts—Amherst
- University of Michigan—Ann Arbor
- University of Washington

Schools marked with an asterisk do not appear in the *Best 366 Colleges*.
You can find those school profiles in *Complete Book of Colleges, 2008 Edition*.

Great Schools for Criminology Majors

- American University
- Auburn University
- City University of New York—John Jay College of Criminal Justice*
- North Carolina State University
- The Ohio State University—Columbus
- Ohio University—Athens
- Quinnipiac University
- Suffolk University
- University of Delaware
- University of Denver
- University of Maryland—College Park
- University of Miami
- University of New Hampshire
- University of South Florida
- University of Utah
- Valparaiso University

Great Schools for Education Majors

- Adelphi University*
- Alma College*
- Arcadia University*
- Ashland University*
- Auburn University
- Augsburg College*
- Barnard College
- Bethany College (WV)*
- Bryn Athyn College of the New Church*
- Bucknell University
- California State University—Sacramento*
- Carthage College*
- City University of New York—Brooklyn College
- City University of New York—Hunter College
- Colgate University
- College of William & Mary
- Columbia College (MO)
- Columbia University
- Cornell College
- Cornell University
- Duquesne University
- Elon University
- Franklin Pierce College*
- Gonzaga University
- Goucher College
- Hardin-Simmons University*
- Hillsdale College
- Indiana University—Bloomington
- Jewish Theological Seminary—Albert A. List College*
- LaSalle University*
- Loyola Marymount University
- Marquette University
- McGill University
- Miami University
- Montana State University—Bozeman*
- Nazareth College of Rochester*
- New York Institute of Technology*
- New York University
- Northeastern University
- Northwestern University
- The Ohio State University—Columbus
- San Francisco State University*
- Simmons College
- Smith College
- State University of New York—New Paltz*
- Trinity University (Washington, DC)*
- Trinity University (San Antonio, TX)
- University of Maine
- The University of Montana
- University of St. Thomas (TX)
- University of Toledo*
- Villanova College
- Wagner College
- Wellesley College
- Xavier University (OH)

Schools marked with an asterisk do not appear in the *Best 366 Colleges*. You can find those school profiles in *Complete Book of Colleges, 2008 Edition*.

Great Schools for Engineering Majors
- California Institute of Technology
- Carnegie Mellon University
- Columbia University
- Cooper Union
- Cornell University
- Drexel University
- Duke University
- Franklin W. Olin College
  of Engineering
- Georgia Institute of Technology
- Harvard College
- Harvey Mudd College
- Illinois Institute of Technology
- Johns Hopkins University
- Massachusetts Institute
  of Technology
- Pennsylvania State University
- Princeton University
- Purdue University—
  West Lafayette
- Rose-Hulman Institute
  of Technology
- Stanford University
- Texas A&M University—
  College Station
- University of California—Berkeley
- University of California—
  Los Angeles
- The University of Texas at Austin
- University of Wisconsin—Madison

Great Schools for English Literature and Language Majors
- Amherst College
- Auburn University
- Bard College
- Barnard College
- Bennington College
- Boston College
- Brown University
- City University of New York—
  Hunter College
- Claremont McKenna College

- Clemson University
- Colby College
- Colgate University
- Columbia University
- Cornell University
- Dartmouth College
- Denison University
- Duke University
- Emory University
- Fordham University
- George Mason University
- Gettysburg College
- Harvard College
- Johns Hopkins University
- Kenyon College
- The New School University
- Pitzer College
- Princeton University
- Rice University
- Stanford University
- Syracuse University
- Tufts University
- University of California—Berkeley
- The University of Chicago
- University of Michigan—
  Ann Arbor
- University of Notre Dame
- University of Utah
- Vassar College
- Washington University
  in St. Louis
- Wellesley College
- Yale University

Great Schools for History Majors
- Bowdoin College
- Brown University
- Centre College
- Colgate University
- College of the Holy Cross
- Columbia University
- Furman University
- Grinnell College
- Hampden-Sydney College

Schools marked with an asterisk do not appear in the *Best 366 Colleges*.
You can find those school profiles in *Complete Book of Colleges, 2008 Edition*.

- Harvard College
- Haverford College
- Hillsdale College
- Kenyon College
- Oberlin College
- Princeton University
- Trinity College (CT)
- Tulane University
- Wabash College
- Washington and Lee University
- Yale University

Great Schools for Journalism Majors

- American University
- Boston University
- Carleton College
- Emerson College
- Hampton University
- Howard University
- Indiana University at Bloomington
- Loyola University—New Orleans
- Middle Tennessee State University
- Northwestern University
- Ohio University—Athens
- Pennsylvania State University
- Samford University
- St. Bonaventure University
- Syracuse University
- Temple University
- University of Florida
- University of Maryland— College Park
- University of Missouri—Columbia
- The University of North Carolina at Chapel Hill
- University of Oregon
- The University of Texas at Austin
- University of Wisconsin— Madison

Great Schools for Marketing and Sales Majors

- Babson College
- Baylor University
- Bentley College
- Duquesne University
- Fairfield University
- Hofstra University
- Indiana University—Bloomington
- Iowa State University
- James Madison University
- Miami University
- Providence College
- Seattle University
- Siena College
- Syracuse University
- University of Central Florida
- University of Michigan— Ann Arbor
- University of Mississippi
- University of Pennsylvania
- University of South Florida
- The University of Texas at Austin

Great Schools for Mechanical Engineering Majors

- Bradley University
- California Institute of Technology
- Clarkson University
- Colorado School of Mines*
- Drexel University
- Franklin W. Olin College of Engineering
- Georgia Institute of Technology
- Harvey Mudd College
- Iowa State University
- Lehigh University
- Massachusetts Institute of Technology
- New Jersey Institute of Technology
- North Carolina State University
- Purdue University— West Lafayette

Schools marked with an asterisk do not appear in the *Best 366 Colleges*. You can find those school profiles in *Complete Book of Colleges, 2008 Edition*.

- Rose-Hulman Institute of Technology
- Stanford University
- State University of New York— University at Buffalo
- Stevens Institute of Technology
- United States Military Academy
- University of California—Berkeley
- University of Illinois at Urbana-Champaign
- University of Michigan— Ann Arbor
- University of Missouri—Rolla
- Worcester Polytechnic Institute

Great Schools for Political Science/ Government Majors
- American University
- Amherst College
- Bard College
- Bates College
- Bowdoin College
- Brigham Young University
- Bryn Mawr College
- Carleton College
- Claremont McKenna College
- College of the Holy Cross
- Columbia University
- Davidson College
- Dickinson College
- Drew University
- Furman University
- George Mason University
- Georgetown University
- Gettysburg College
- Gonzaga University
- Harvard College
- Kenyon College
- Macalester College
- Princeton University
- Stanford University
- Swarthmore College
- Syracuse University
- University of Arizona
- University of California—Berkeley

- University of California— Los Angeles
- University of Washington
- Vassar College
- Yale University

Great Schools for Psychology Majors
- Albion College
- Bates College
- Carnegie Mellon University
- Colorado State University
- Columbia University
- Cornell University
- Dartmouth College
- Duke University
- George Mason University
- Gettysburg College
- Harvard College
- James Madison University
- Lewis & Clark College
- Loyola University—Chicago
- New York University
- Pitzer College
- Princeton University
- Smith College
- Stanford University
- University of California—Davis
- University of California— Los Angeles
- University of California— Riverside
- University of California— Santa Barbara
- University of California— Santa Cruz
- University of Michigan— Ann Arbor
- University of Southern California
- The University of Texas at Austin
- University of Utah
- Yale University

Schools marked with an asterisk do not appear in the *Best 366 Colleges*. You can find those school profiles in *Complete Book of Colleges, 2008 Edition*.

AMERICA'S BEST VALUE COLLEGES

No way around it: college is expensive. At some schools the sticker price for one year is—*yikes*—now $50,000. College costs overall have risen more than 35 percent in the past five years. As a result, many parents and students are understandably looking for great schools that are, well, education bargains. That's why, in 2004 we devoted an entire book to this subject: *America's Best Value Colleges.* Inspired by a ranking list that appeared in our annual *Best Colleges* guide (it named the "Top 20 Best Academic Bang for Your Buck" schools of the year), we dug deeper into our database of school information and student surveys to produce a guide with far more than 20 "best value" schools for applicants to consider.

Our goal each year since has been to identify the colleges with excellent academics, generous financial aid packages and/or relatively low costs of attendance. We select the schools based on data we collect from 650 institutions each academic year and our surveys of students attending the schools. To winnow our list of "best values," we consider more than 30 factors in four key areas: academics, tuition, financial aid, and student borrowing.

The 2008 edition of *America's Best Value Colleges* features our recommendations of 165 best value colleges—90 public and 75 private institutions—in 45 states. The book's profiles report facts and stats about the schools and, most importantly, information on what their admissions officers look for as well as their financial aid and scholarship programs, policies, and track records. Visit our website (www.PrincetonReview.com) to learn more about our criteria or to see the complete list of the 165 schools in *America's Best Value Colleges*—available at your local bookstore or at PrincetonReview.com/bookstore.

In the meantime, here's a sneak peek at the top ten best value public and top ten best value private colleges featured in *America's Best Value Colleges, 2008 edition:*

Top Ten Best Value—Public Colleges

1. New College of Florida (Sarasota, FL)
2. Truman State University (Kirksville, MO)
3. The University of North Carolina at Asheville (Asheville, NC)
4. University of Virginia (Charlottesville, Virginia)
5. University of California—Berkeley (Berkeley, CA)
6. University of California—San Diego (San Diego, CA)
7. University of California—Santa Cruz (Santa Cruz, CA)
8. University of Minnesota—Morris (Morris, MN)
9. University of Wisconsin—Madison (Madison, WI)
10. St. Mary's College of Maryland (St. Mary's City, MD)

Top Ten Best Value—Private Colleges

1. Rice University (Houston, TX)
2. Williams College (Williamstown, MA)
3. Grinnell College (Grinnell, IA)
4. Swarthmore College (Swarthmore, PA)
5. Thomas Aquinas College (Santa Paula, CA)
6. Wabash College (Crawfordsville, IN)
7. Whitman College (Walla Walla, WA)
8. Amherst College (Amherst, MA)
9. Scripps College (Claremont, CA)
10. Harvard College (Cambridge, MA)

HOW AND WHY WE PRODUCE THIS BOOK

When we published the first edition of this book in 1992, there was a void in the world of college guides (hard to believe, but true!). No publication provided college applicants with statistical data from colleges that covered academics, admissions, financial aid, and student demographics along with narrative descriptions of the schools *based on comprehensive surveys of students attending them.* Of course, academic rankings of colleges had been around for some time. They named the best schools on hierarchical lists, from 1 to 200 and upwards, some in tiers. Their criteria factored in such matters as faculty salaries, alumni giving, and peer reviews (i.e. what college administrators thought of the schools that, in many cases, they competed with for students). But no one was polling students at these terrific colleges about their experiences on campus—both inside and outside the classroom. We created our first *Best Colleges* guide to address that void. It was born out of one very obvious omission in college guide publishing and two very deep convictions we held then and hold even more strongly today:

- **One:** The key question for students and parents researching colleges shouldn't be *"What college is best, academically?"* The thing is, it's not hard to find academically great schools in this country. (There are hundreds of them.) The key question—and one that is truly tough to answer—is *"What is the best college for me?"*

- **Two:** We believe the best way for students and parents to know if a school is right—and ultimately best—for them is to visit it. Travel to the campus, get inside a dorm, audit a class, browse the town and—most importantly—talk to students attending the school. In the end it's the school's customers—its students—who are the real experts about the college. Only they can give you the most candid and informed feedback on what life is really like on the campus.

Fueled by these convictions, we worked to create a guide that would help people who couldn't always get to the campus nonetheless get in-depth campus feedback to find the schools best for them. We culled an initial list of 250 academically great schools, based on our own college knowledge and input we got from 50 independent college counselors. We gathered institutional data from those schools and we surveyed 30,000 students attending them (about 120 per campus on average). We wrote the school profiles featured in the book, incorporating extensive quotes from surveyed students, and we included in the book over 60 ranking lists of top 20 schools in various categories based on our surveys of students at the schools. In short, we designed a college guide that did something no other guide had done: It brought the opinions of a huge number of students at the nation's top colleges to readers' doorsteps.

In the 15 years since, our *Best Colleges* guide has grown considerably. We've added over 100 colleges to the guide (and deleted several along the way). For this edition, we feature 366 "best" colleges at which we surveyed 120,000 students (about 320 per campus on average). How we choose the schools for the book, and how we produced it, however, has not changed significantly over the years (with the exception of how we conduct our student survey—more on this follows).

To determine which schools will be included in each edition, we don't use mathematical calculations or formulas. Instead we rely on a wide range of quantitative and qualitative input. Every year we collect data from nearly 2,000 colleges for our *Complete Book of Colleges* and our web-based profiles of schools. We visit colleges and meet with scores of admissions officers and college presidents. We talk with hundreds of high school counselors, parents, and students. Colleges also submit information to us requesting consideration for inclusion in the book. As a result, we are able to maintain a constantly evolving list of colleges to consider adding to each new edition of the book. Any college we add to the guide, however, must agree to allow its students to complete our anonymous student survey. (Sometimes a college's administrative protocols will not allow it to participate in our student survey; this has caused some academically outstanding schools to be absent from the guide.) Finally, we work to ensure that our book features a wide representation of colleges by region, character, and type. It includes public and private schools, historically black colleges and universities, men's and women's colleges, science- and technology-focused institutions, nontraditional colleges, highly selective schools, and some with virtually open-door admissions policies. We added eight schools to the guide this year: California State University—Stanislaus, Florida Southern College, Sacred Heart University, Thomas Aquinas College, Tuskegee University, Washington College, Washington & Jefferson College, and University of Cincinnati.

Our student survey for the book is a mammoth undertaking. In the early years, our surveys were conducted on campuses and on paper, but the launch several years ago of our online survey (http://survey.review.com), has made it possible for students to complete a survey anytime and anywhere. In fact, 90 percent of our student surveys are now completed online. Some schools prefer the old-fashioned paper survey route; in those instances we work with the administration to hire a campus representative (usually a student) to set up shop in one or more highly-trafficked areas of the campus where students can stop and fill out the survey.

Early on we surveyed all of the colleges and universities in the book on an annual basis. By the time we'd gone through a few editions, we found that unless there's been some grand upheaval or administrative change on campus, there's little change in student opinion from one year to the next, but that shifts tended to emerge in a third or fourth year (as surveyed students leave or matriculate). With this in mind, we switched to a three-year cycle for resurveying each campus. Thus, each year we target about 100 campuses for resurveying. We resurvey colleges more often than that if colleges request it (and we can accommodate the request) or if we believe it is warranted for one reason or another. Online surveys submitted by students outside of a school's normal survey cycle and independent of any solicitation on our part are factored into the subsequent year's rankings and ratings calculations. In that respect, our surveying is a continuous process.

All colleges and universities whose students we plan to survey are notified about the survey through our administrative contacts at the schools. We depend upon them for assistance either in notifying the student body about the availability of the online survey via email or, if the school opts for a paper version of the survey, in identifying common, high-traffic areas on campus at which to survey. The survey has more than 80 questions divided into four sections: "About Yourself," "Your School's Academics/Administration," "Students," and "Life at Your School." We ask about all sorts of things, from "How many out-of-class hours do you spend studying each day?" to "How do you rate your campus food?" Most questions offer students a five-point grid on which to indicate their answer choices (headers may range from "Excellent" to "Awful"). Eight questions offer students the opportunity to expand on their answers with narrative comment. These essay-type responses are the sources of the student quotations that appear in the school profiles.

Once the surveys have been completed and responses stored in our database, every college is given a score (similar to a grade point average) for its students' answers to each question. This score enables us to compare students' responses to a particular question from one college to the next. We use these scores as an underlying data point in our calculation of the ratings in the profile sidebars and the ranking lists in the section of the book titled "Schools Ranked by Category." Once we have the student survey information in hand, we write the college profiles. Student quotations in each profile are chosen because they represent the sentiments expressed by the majority of survey respondents from the college; or, they illustrate one side or another of a mixed bag of student opinion, in which case there will also appear a counterpoint within the text. We do not select quotes for their extreme nature, humor, or unique perspective. (Instead, we dedicate a section of this book titled, "Cow Tipping Is Definitely Passé Here," to these kinds of quotes—flip to the back to check them out!)

Our survey is qualitative and anecdotal rather than quantitative. In order to guard against producing a write-up that's off the mark for any particular college, we send our administrative contact at each school a copy of the profile we intend to publish prior to its publication date, with ample opportunity to respond with corrections, comments, and/or outright objections. In every case in which we receive requests for changes, we take careful measures to review the school's suggestions against the student survey data we collected and make appropriate changes when warranted.

For this year's edition, on average, we surveyed 320 students per campus, though that number varies depending on the size of the student population. We've surveyed anywhere from 20-odd men at Deep Springs College (100 percent of the student body) to over 1,000 collegians at such colleges as Drexel University, Clemson University, and the United States Military Academy. Whether the number of students we survey at a particular school is 100 or 1,000, on the whole we have found their opinions to be remarkably consistent over the years. What is most compelling to us about how representative our survey findings are is this: We ask students who take the survey—after they have completed it—to review the information we published about their school in the previous edition of our book and grade us on its accuracy and validity. Year after year we've gotten high marks: This year, 81 percent of students said we were *right on.*

All of the institutions in this guide are academically terrific in our opinion. The 366 schools featured—our picks of the cream of the crop colleges and universities—comprise only the top 10 percent of all colleges in the nation. Not every college will appeal to every student but that is the beauty of it. These are all very different schools with many different and wonderful things to offer.

We hope you will use this book as a starting point (it will certainly give you a snapshot of what life is like at these schools) but not as the final word on any one school. Check out other resources. Visit as many colleges as you can. Talk to students at those colleges—ask what they love and what bothers them most about their schools. Finally, *form your own opinions* about the colleges you are considering. At the end of the day, it's what YOU think about the schools that matters most, and that will enable you to answer that all-important question: *"Which college is best for me?"*

How This Book Is Organized

Each of the colleges and universities in this book has its own two-page profile. To make it easier to find and compare information about the schools, we've used the same profile format for every school. Look at the sample pages below:

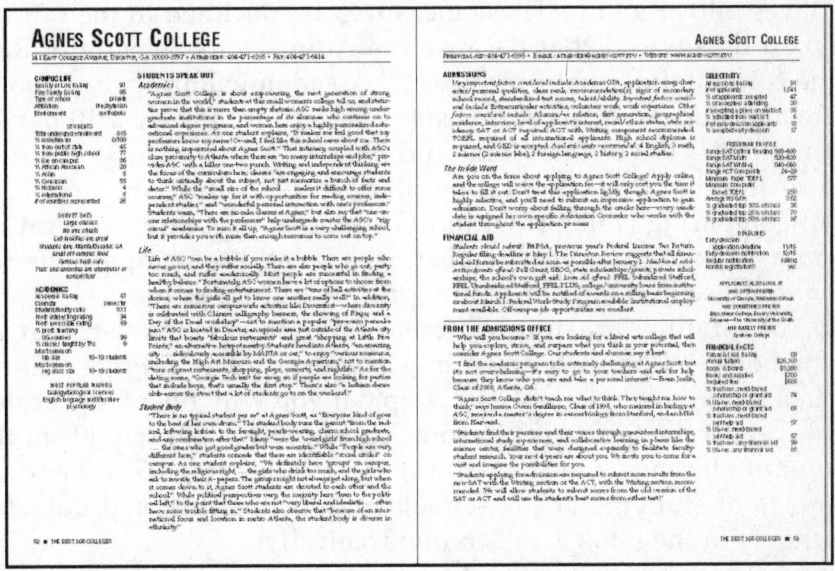

Each profile has nine major components. First, at the very top of the profile you will see the school's address, telephone, and fax numbers for the admissions office, the telephone number for the financial aid office, and the school's website and/or e-mail address. Second, there are two sidebars (the narrow columns on the outside of each page, which consist mainly of statistics) divided into the categories of Campus Life, Academics, Selectivity, and Financial Facts. Third, there are four headings in the narrative text: Students Say, Admissions, Financial Aid, and From the Admissions Office. Here's what you'll find in each part:

The Sidebars

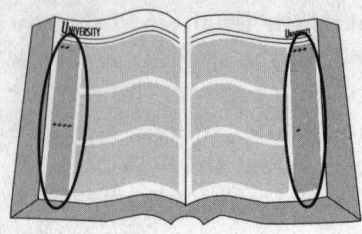

The sidebars contain various statistics culled from our surveys of students attending the school and from detailed questionnaires that school administrators complete at our request in the Fall of each year. Keep in mind that not every category will appear for every school—in some cases the information is not reported or not applicable.

We compile the seven ratings—Quality of Life, Fire Safety, Academic, Profs Interesting, Profs Accessible, Admissions Selectivity, and Financial Aid—listed in the sidebars based on the results from our student surveys and/or institutional data we collect from school administrators. These ratings are on a scale of 60–99 If a **60*** (60 with an asterisk) appears as any rating for any school, it means that the school reported so few of the rating's underlying data points by our deadline that we were unable to calculate an accurate rating for it. In such cases the reader is advised to follow up with the school about the specific measures the rating takes into account. (These measures are outlined in the ratings explanation below.) Be advised that because the Admissions Selectivity Rating is a factor in the computation that produces the Academic Rating, a school that has **60*** (60 with an asterisk) as its Admissions Selectivity Rating will have an Academic Rating that is lower than it should be.

Also bear in mind that each rating places each college on a continuum for purposes of comparing colleges within *this edition only*. Since our ratings computations may change from year to year, it is invalid to compare the ratings in this edition to those that appear in any prior or future edition.

Finally, these ratings are quite different from the ranking lists that appear in Part 2 of the book, "Schools Ranked by Category." The ratings are numerical measures that show how a school "sizes up," if you will, on a fixed scale. Our 62 ranking lists report the top 20 (or in some cases bottom 20) schools of the 366 in the book (not of all schools in the nation) in various categories. They are based on our surveys of students at the schools and/or institutional data. We don't rank the schools in the book 1 to 366 hierarchically.

Here is what each heading in the sidebar tells you, in order of their appearance:

Quality of Life Rating

On a scale of 60–99, this rating is a measure of how happy students are with their lives outside the classroom. To compile this rating, we weighed several factors, all based on students' answers to questions on our survey. They included the students' assessments of: their overall happiness; the beauty, safety, and location of the campus; comfort of dorms; quality of food; ease of getting around campus and dealing with administrators; friendliness of fellow students; and the interaction of different student types on campus and within the greater community.

Fire Safety Rating

On a scale of 60–99, this rating measures how well prepared a school is to prevent or respond to campus fires, specifically in residence halls.

We asked schools several questions about their efforts to ensure fire safety for campus residents. We developed the questions in consultation with the Center for

Campus Fire Safety (www.CampusFire.org). Each school's responses to nine questions were considered when calculating its Fire Safety Rating. They cover:

1. The percentage of student housing sleeping rooms protected by an automatic fire sprinkler system with a fire sprinkler head located in the individual sleeping rooms;
2. The percentage of student housing sleeping rooms equipped with a smoke detector connected to a supervised fire alarm system;
3. The number of malicious fire alarms that occur in student housing per year;
4. The number of unwanted fire alarms that occur in student housing per year;
5. The banning of certain hazardous items and activities in residence halls, like candles, smoking, halogen lamps, etc.;
6. The percentage of student housing building fire alarm systems that, if activated, result in a local alarm only;
7. The percentage of student housing fire alarm systems that, if activated, result in a signal being transmitted to a monitored location, where security investigates before notifying the fire department;
8. The percentage of student housing fire alarm systems that, if activated, result in a signal being transmitted immediately to a continuously monitored location which can then immediately notify the fire department to initiate a response;
9. How often fire safety rules-compliance inspections are conducted each year.

Schools that did not report answers to any of the questions receive a Fire Safety Rating of 60* (60 with an asterisk). The schools have an opportunity to update their fire safety data every year and will have their fire safety ratings recalculated and published annually. You can also find Fire Safety Ratings for the *Best 366 Colleges* (and several additional schools) in our *Complete Book of Colleges, 2008 Edition*.

Type of school

Whether the school is public or private.

Affiliation

Any religious order with which the school is affiliated.

Environment

Whether the campus is located in an urban, suburban, or rural setting.

Total undergrad enrollment

The total number of degree-seeking undergraduates who attend the school.

"% male/female" through "# countries represented"

Demographic information about the full-time undergraduate student body, including male to female ratio, ethnicity, and the number of countries represented by the student body. Also included are the percentages of the student body who are from out of state, attended a public high school, live on campus, and belong to Greek organizations.

Survey Says

A snapshot of the key results of our student survey. This list shows what the students we surveyed felt unusually strongly about, both positively and negatively, at their schools (see the end of this section for a detailed explanation of items on the list).

Academic Rating

On a scale of 60–99, this rating is a measure of how hard students work at the school and how much they get back for their efforts. The rating is based on results from our surveys of students and institutional data we collect from administrators. Factors weighed included how many hours students reported that they study each day outside of class, and the quality of students the school attracts as measured by admissions statistics. We also considered students' assessments of their professors' teaching abilities and of their accessibility outside the classroom.

Calendar

The school's schedule of academic terms. A "semester" schedule has two long terms, usually starting in September and January. A "trimester" schedule has three terms, one usually beginning before Christmas and two after. A "quarterly" schedule has four terms, which go by very quickly: the entire term, including exams, usually lasts only nine or ten weeks. A "4-1-4" schedule is like a semester schedule, but with a month-long term in between the fall and spring semesters. (Similarly, a 4-4-1 has a short term following two longer semesters.) When a school's academic calendar doesn't match any of these traditional schedules, we note that by saying "other." For schools that have "other" as their calendar, it is best to call the admissions office for details.

Student/faculty ratio

The ratio of full-time undergraduate instructional faculty members to all undergraduates.

Profs interesting rating

On a scale of 60–99, this rating is based on levels of surveyed students' agreement or disagreement with the statement: "Your instructors are good teachers."

Profs accessible rating

On a scale of 60–99, this rating is based on levels of surveyed students' agreement or disagreement with the statement: "Your instructors are accessible outside the classroom."

% profs teaching UG courses

This category reports the percentage of professors who teach undergraduates and distinguishes between faculty who teach and faculty who focus solely on research.

% classes taught by TAs

This category reports the percentage of classes that are taught by TAs (teaching assistants) instead of regular faculty. Many universities that offer graduate programs use graduate students as teaching assistants. They teach undergraduate courses, primarily at the introductory level.

Most common lab size; Most common regular class size

Institutionally-reported figures of the most commonly occurring class size for regular courses and for labs/discussion sections.

Most Popular Majors

The three majors with the highest enrollments at the school.

Admissions Selectivity Rating

On a scale of 60–99, this rating is a measure of how competitive admission is at the school. This rating is determined by several factors, including the class rank of entering freshmen, test scores, and percentage of applicants accepted. By incorporating these factors (and a few others), our admissions selectivity rating adjusts for "self-selecting" applicant pools. The University of Chicago, for example, has a very high admissions selectivity rating, even though it admits a surprisingly large proportion of its applicants. This is because Chicago's applicant pool is self-selecting; that is, nearly all the school's applicants are exceptional students.

% of applicants accepted

The percentage of applicants to whom the school offered admission.

% of acceptees attending

The percentage of those who were accepted who eventually enrolled.

accepting a place on wait list

The number of students who decided to take a place on the wait list when offered this option.

% admitted from wait list

The percentage of applicants who opted to take a place on the wait list and were subsequently offered admission. These figures will vary tremendously from college to college, and should be a consideration when deciding whether to accept a place on a college's wait list.

of early decision applicants

The number of students who applied under the college's early decision or early action plan.

% accepted early decision

The percentage of early decision or early action applicants who were admitted under this plan. By the nature of these plans, the vast majority who are admitted ultimately enroll. (See the early decision/action description that follows in the Glossary section for more detail.)

Range/Average SAT Verbal, Range/Average SAT Math, Range/Average SAT Writing

The average and the middle 50 percent range of test scores for entering freshmen. Don't be discouraged from applying to the school of your choice even if your combined SAT scores are 80 or even 120 points below the average, because you may still have a chance of getting in. Remember that many schools value other aspects of your application (e.g., your grades, how good a match you make with the school) more heavily than test scores.

Minimum TOEFL

The minimum test score necessary for entering freshmen who are required to take the TOEFL (Test of English as a Foreign Language). Most schools will require all international students or non-native English speakers to take the TOEFL in order to be considered for admission.

Average HS GPA

The average grade point average of entering freshman. We report this on a scale of 1.0–4.0 (occasionally colleges report averages on a 100 scale, in which case we report those figures). This is one of the key factors in college admissions.

% graduated top 10%, top 25%, top 50% of class

Of those students for whom class rank was reported, the percentage of entering freshmen who ranked in the top tenth, quarter, and half of their high school classes.

Early decision/action deadlines

The deadline for submission of application materials under the early decision or early action plan.

Early decision, early action, priority, and regular admission deadlines

The dates by which all materials must be postmarked (we'd suggest "received in the office") in order to be considered for admission under each particular admissions option/cycle for matriculation in the fall term.

Early decision, early action, priority, and regular admission notification

The dates by which you can expect a decision on your application under each admissions option/cycle.

Nonfall registration

Some schools will allow incoming students to matriculate at times other than the fall term, which is the traditional beginning of the academic calendar year. Other schools will allow you to register for classes only if you can begin in the fall term. A simple "yes" or "no" in this category indicates the school's policy on nonfall registration.

Applicants also look at

These lists are based on information we receive directly from the colleges. Admissions officers are annually given the opportunity to review and suggest alterations to these lists for their schools, as most schools track as closely as they can other schools to which applicants they accepted applied, and whether the applicants chose their school over the other schools, or vice versa.

Financial Aid Rating

On a scale of 60–99, this rating is a measure of the financial aid the school awards and how satisfied students are with the aid they receive. It is based on school-reported data on financial aid and students' responses to the survey question, "If you receive financial aid, how satisfied are you with your financial aid package?"

Annual in-state tuition

The tuition at the school, or for public colleges, the cost of tuition for a resident of the school's state. Usually much lower than out-of-state tuition for state-supported public schools.

Annual out-of-state tuition

For public colleges, the tuition for a nonresident of the school's state. This entry appears only for public colleges, since tuition at private colleges is generally the same regardless of state of residence.

Required fees

Any additional costs students must pay beyond tuition in order to attend the school. These often include fitness center fees and the like. A few state schools may not officially charge in-state students tuition, but those students are still responsible for hefty fees.

Tuition and fees

In cases when schools do not report separate figures for tuition and required fees, we offer this total of the two.

Comprehensive fee

A few schools report one overall fee that reflects the total cost of tuition, room and board, and required fees. If you'd like to see how this figure breaks down, we recommend contacting the school.

Room & board

Estimated annual room and board costs.

Books and supplies

Estimated annual cost of necessary textbooks and/or supplies.

% frosh receiving need-based aid

The percentage of all degree-seeking freshmen who applied for financial aid, were determined to have financial need, and received any sort of aid, need-based or otherwise.

% UG receiving need-based aid

The percentage of all degree-seeking undergrads who applied for financial aid, were determined to have financial need, and received any sort of aid, need-based or otherwise.

Avg frosh grant

The average grant or scholarship given to freshmen who receive either or both.

Avg frosh loan

The average amount of loans disbursed to freshmen.

Nota Bene: The statistical data reported in this book, unless otherwise noted, was collected from the profiled colleges from the fall of 2006 through the summer of 2007. In some cases, we were unable to publish the most recent data because schools did not report the necessary statistics to us in time, despite our repeated outreach efforts. Because the enrollment and financial statistics, as well as application and financial aid deadlines, fluctuate from one year to another, we recommend that you check with the schools to make sure you have the most current information before applying.

Students Say

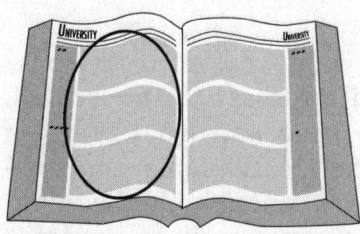

This section shares the straight-from-the-campus feedback we get from the school's most important customers: The students attending them. It summarizes the opinions of freshman through seniors we've surveyed and it includes direct quotes from scores of them. When appropriate, it also incorporates statistics provided by the schools. The Students Say section is divided into three subsections: Academics, Life, and Student Body. The Academics section describes how hard students work and how satisfied they are with the education they are getting. It also often tells you which programs or academic departments students rated most favorably and how professors interact with students. Student opinion regarding administrative departments also works its way into this section. The Life section describes life outside the classroom and addresses questions ranging from "How comfortable are the dorms?" to "How popular are fraternities and sororities?" In this section, students describe what they do for entertainment both on-campus and off, providing a clear picture of the social environment at their particular school. The Student Body section will give you the lowdown on the types of students the school attracts and how the students view the level of interaction among various groups, including those of different ethnic, socioeconomic, and religious backgrounds.

All quotations in these sections are from students' responses to open-ended questions on our survey. We select quotations based on the accuracy with which they reflect overall student opinion about the school as conveyed in the survey results. Entertaining but non-representative student responses about the Academics, Life, and Student Body at a school are featured in a special section in the back of this book titled "Cow Tipping Is Definitely Passé Here." Be sure to check it out for a good laugh.

Admissions

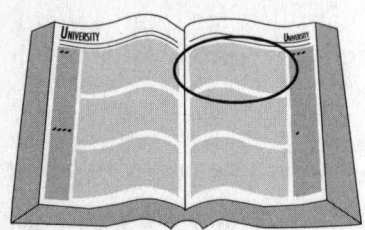

This section lets you know which aspects of your application are most important to the admissions officers at the school. It also lists the high school curricular prerequisites for applicants, which standardized tests (if any) are required, and special information about the school's admissions process (e.g., Do minority students and legacies, for example, receive special consideration? Are there any unusual application requirements for applicants to special programs?).

The Inside Word

This section gives you the inside scoop on what it takes to gain admission to the school. It reflects our own insights about each school's admissions process and acceptance trends. (We visit scores of colleges each year and talk with hundreds of admissions officers in order to glean this info.) It also incorporates information from institutional data we collect and our surveys over the years of students at the school.

Financial Aid

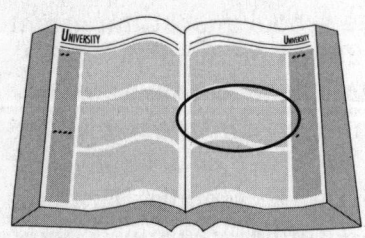

Here you'll found out what you need to know about the financial aid process at the school, namely what forms you need and what types of merit-based aid and loans are available. Information about need-based aid is contained in the financial aid sidebar. This section includes specific deadline dates for submission of materials as reported by the colleges. We strongly encourage students seeking financial aid to file all forms—federal, state, and institutional—carefully, fully, and on time. Check out our annually-updated book, *Paying for College Without Going Broke*, for advice on completing the forms and strategies for getting the most financial aid possible.

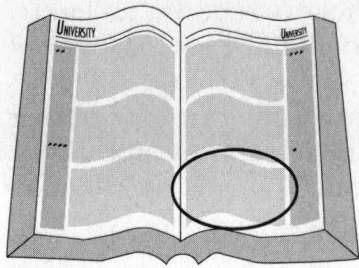

From the Admissions Office

This section is the school's chance to speak directly to you about the key things they would like you to know about their institution. For schools that did not respond to our invitation to supply text for this space, we excerpted an appropriate passage from the school's catalog, web site, or other admissions literature.

For this section, we also invited schools to submit a brief paragraph explaining their admissions policies regarding the SAT (especially the Writing portion of the exam) and the SAT Subject Tests. We are pleased that nearly every school took this opportunity to clarify its policies as we know there has been some student and parent confusion about how these scores are evaluated for admission.

Survey Says

Our Survey Says list, located in the Campus Life sidebar on each school's two-page spread, is based entirely on the results of our student survey. In other words, the items on this list are based on the opinions of the students we surveyed at those schools (*not* on any quantitative analysis of library size, endowment, etc.). These items reveal popular or unpopular trends on campus for the purpose of providing a snapshot of life on *that campus only*. The appearance of a Survey Says item in the sidebar for a particular school does *not* reflect the popularity of that item relative to its popularity amongst the student bodies at other schools. To ascertain the relative popularity of certain items/trends on campus, see the appropriate ranking (e.g., for the Survey Says item "Library needs improving," see the "This is a Library?" ranking). Some of the terms that appear on the Survey Says list are not entirely self-explanatory; these terms are defined below.

Different types of students interact: We asked students whether students from different class and ethnic backgrounds interacted frequently and easily. When students' collective response is "yes," the heading "Different types of students interact" appears on the list. When the collective student response indicates there are not many interactions between students from different class and ethnic backgrounds, the phrase "Students are cliquish" appears on the list.

No one cheats: We asked students how prevalent cheating is at their school. If students reported cheating to be rare, the term "No one cheats" shows up on the list.

Students are happy: This category reflects student responses to the question "Overall, how happy are you?"

Students are very religious *or* **Students aren't religious:** We asked students how religious students are at their school. Their responses are reflected in this category.

Diverse student types on campus: We asked students whether their student body is made up of a variety of ethnic groups. This category reflects their answers to this question. This heading shows up as "Diversity lacking on campus" or "Diverse student types on campus." It does not reflect any institutional data on this subject.

Students get along with local community: This category reflects student responses to a question concerning how well the student body gets along with residents of the college town or community.

Career services are great: New to the book this year, this category reflects student opinion on the quality of career/job placement services on campus. This heading shows up as "Career services are great."

GLOSSARY

ACT: Like the SAT but less tricky—the ACT tests stuff you actually learned in the classroom. Most schools accept either SAT or ACT scores; if you consistently get blown away by the SAT, consider taking the ACT instead of (or in addition to) the SAT.

APs: Advanced Placement courses are essentially college-level courses offered in various high schools that culminate in the Advanced Placement Examinations each May. Students who obtain a minimum score on their AP exams may be awarded college credit or placement out of intro-level courses in the subject area. Excellent deal, no matter how you cut it!

College-prep curriculum: 16 to 18 academic credits (each credit equals a full year of a high school course), usually including: 4 years of English, 3 to 4 years of social studies, and at least 2 years each of science, mathematics, and foreign language.

Common Application: A general application form (available online and in a paper version) used by nearly 300 colleges and universities. Students who complete the Common Application save on time and mental frenzy, but may be required to submit application supplements to schools.

Core curriculum: Students at schools with core curricula must take a number of required courses, usually in such subjects as world history, western civilization, writing skills, and fundamental math and science.

CSS/Financial Aid PROFILE: The College Scholarship Service PROFILE, an optional financial aid form required by some colleges in addition to the FAFSA.

Direct Lender: Direct Lending schools participate in the federal Direct Loan Program. See "Direct Loan Program."

Direct Loan Program: With this federal educational loan program, funds are lent directly by the U.S. Government through the school's financial aid office, with no need of a private lender such as a bank. If the college only participates in the (William D. Ford) Direct Loan Program, the borrower must obtain any Stafford, PLUS, or GradPLUS loan through this program, though one can use a private alternative loan program for any additional non-federal funding.

Distribution or general education requirements: Students at schools with distribution requirements must take a number of courses in various subject areas, such as foreign language, humanities, natural science, and social science. Distribution requirements do not specify which courses you must take, only which types of courses.

Early Decision/Early Action: Early decision is generally for students for whom the school is a first choice. The applicant commits to attending the school if admitted; in return, the school renders an early decision, usually in December or January. Early action is similar to early decision, but less binding; applicants need not commit to attending the school and in some cases may apply early action to more than one school. Early decision and early action policies of a few of the most selective colleges in the country have changed quite dramatically recently. It's a good idea to call the school and get full details if you plan to pursue one of these options.

FAFSA: Stands for the Free Application for Federal Student Aid. This is a financial aid need analysis form written by the U.S. Department of Education. This form is required for virtually all students applying to colleges for financial aid. Some colleges also require that applicants complete other aid application forms (such as the CSS/Financial Aid PROFILE or the college's own form) to be considered for financial aid.

Greek system, Greeks: Fraternities and sororities.

Humanities: The branches of knowledge concerned with human art and culture. These include such disciplines as art history, drama, English, foreign languages, music, philosophy, and religion.

Merit-based grant: A scholarship (not necessarily covering the full cost of tuition) given to students because of some special talent or attribute. Artists, athletes, community leaders, and academically outstanding applicants are typical recipients.

Natural sciences: The branches of knowledge concerned with the rational study of the universe using the rules or laws of natural order. These include such disciplines as astronomy, biology, chemistry, genetics, geology, mathematics, physics, and zoology.

Need-based grant: A scholarship (not necessarily covering the full cost of tuition) given to students because they would otherwise be unable to afford college. Student need is determined on the basis of the FAFSA. Some schools also require the CSS PROFILE and/or institutional applications to determine a student's need.

Priority deadline: Some schools will list a deadline for admission and/or financial aid as a "priority deadline," meaning that while they will accept applications after that date, all applications received prior to the deadline are assured of getting the most thorough, and potentially more generous, appraisal possible.

RA: Residence assistant (or residential advisor). Someone, usually an upperclassman or graduate student, who supervises a floor or section of a dorm, usually in return for free room and board. RAs are responsible for enforcing the drinking and noise rules.

SAT: A college entrance exam required by many schools; most schools will accept either the ACT or the SAT.

SAT Subject Tests: Subject-specific exams administered by the Educational Testing Service (the same folks who do the SAT). These tests are required by some, but not all, colleges.

Social sciences: The branches of knowledge which emphasize the use of the scientific method in the study of the human aspects of the world. These include such disciplines as anthropology, economics, geography, history, international studies, political science, psychology, and sociology.

Work-study: A federally-funded financial aid program that provides assistance to students by subsidizing their wages for on-campus and off-campus jobs. Eligibility is based on need.

ABOUT THOSE COLLEGE RANKINGS

We've shed some light on how we publish our *Best Colleges*, how we select the schools featured in it, how we compile our school profiles, and how we conduct the student survey which is the centerpiece of the book.

But the part of our *Best Colleges* guide that many people turn to first is the section titled "Schools Ranked By Category." Here you won't find the colleges in the book ranked hierarchically, 1 to 366. We think such lists—particularly those driven by and perpetuating a "best academics" mania—are not useful for the people they are supposed to serve (college applicants). More and more college administrators—including several at schools ranked high on these lists—agree.

In fact, the primary reason we developed this book was to give applicants and parents better and broader information that will help them winnow a list of colleges right for them. Finding a college that has terrific academics is the easy part. There are hundreds of academically great colleges in this country. Their campus cultures, student bodies, and school offerings, however, differ widely. Finding the academically great school that is right for you is the tough part. Hence, we compile not one ranking list but 62 unique lists, each one reporting the top 20 (or in some cases bottom 20) schools from our *Best Colleges* book in a specific category.

None of the lists are based on what we think of the schools (though members of the media, the public and school administrators mistakenly credit or blame us for the results, saying "According to The Princeton Review, X school is the best in the nation for..." or "The Princeton Review ranks Y school the 10th most...."). In fact, the only thing *we* say is that all of the 366 colleges in this book are outstanding (hence, the "Best" designation). It's what students think of their schools—how they rate various aspects of their colleges' offerings and what they report to us about their campus experiences—that results in a school's appearance on our ranking lists. About 85 percent of the schools in our book end up on one or more of the lists in each edition. The students are the raters—we are simply the folks who compile the ranking lists based on their opinions. To college officials happy about the lists their schools are on, we say don't thank us, we're just the messengers. To college officials unhappy about the lists their schools are on (and unsurprisingly, it is mainly they who say our student survey has no validity whatsoever), we say don't blame us, we're just the messengers.

Sixty-one of these ranking lists are based entirely on students' answers to questions on our surveys (e.g. our "Best Campus Food" list and inverse list, "Is it Food?" are each based on the single survey question, "How do you rate your campus food?") or students' answers to a combination of survey questions (e.g. our "Party Schools" list and our inverse list, "Stone-cold Sober Schools" are each based on students' answers to survey questions concerning the use of alcohol and drugs on their campuses, the popularity of the frat/sorority scene on their campuses, and the number of hours they say they study each day outside of class time). Only one of our 62 ranking lists factors in statistical data from the colleges: "Toughest to Get Into."

Each list, even those with somewhat irreverent titles (such as "Dorms Like Dungeons"), covers one of many aspects of a college's character that can be helpful in deciding if it's the right or wrong place for an individual student. They report on a wide range of issues that may be important, either singly or, more likely, in combination. Our ranking lists cover: financial aid, campus facilities and amenities, extracurriculars, town-gown relations, the student body's political leanings, social life, race/class relations, gay-friendly (or not so friendly) atmosphere, and more. New in this edition is a ranking list category inspired by a parent who urged us to report on schools most likely to help his son find a job—thus, our "Best Career Services" ranking was born. Also new is our "Best Classroom Experience" list, based on students' answers to five survey questions concerning their professors, classroom/lab facilities, the percentage of class time devoted to discussion, and the percentage of classes they attend.

The ranking list category that media covers the most (though it appears 57th among the lists in our "Schools Ranked by Category" section, and is only referenced briefly in our press materials) is the "Party Schools" list. It's even been the subject of a *Doonesbury* cartoon (which appears on the frontispiece of this book) as well as a *USA Today* editorial in which the paper commended us for reporting the list, calling it "a public service." Our "Party Schools" list draws a wide range of reaction every year. Some students complain that their college didn't make the list, while others are irate because their college did. One reporter from the *Washington Post* whose alma mater was #1 on the list several years back wrote a column in which he argued that the ranking was grossly undeserved: He had recently visited his campus and pronounced the then current student body lame as "partiers" compared to the revelers of *his day*.

Many incorrectly assume that an institution that shows up on the "Party Schools" list is not an advisable college to attend. We recommend all 366 schools in this book as outstanding institutions at which to earn one's college degree. But just as the schools on our "Alternative Lifestyle Not an Alternative" (gay-unfriendly) list may not be ideal campuses for gay students, the schools on our "Party Schools" list may not be ideal for students seeking a campus at which the use of alcohol and drugs and the frat/sorority scene is, well, less exuberant.

On the other hand, no one should make the mistake of assuming that the colleges and universities that don't show up on our "Party Schools" list are in any way insulated from the influences of alcohol and drugs on their campuses. An oft-quoted Harvard University School of Public Health study a few years back found that 44 percent of undergraduates, in general, binge drink (consume five or more alcoholic beverages in one sitting for men, four drinks or more for women).[1] These facts are alarming, as they should be. College administrators face tremendous challenges in creating and enforcing campus alcohol and drug use/abuse policies. Many struggle with problems resulting from the prevalence

1 Harvard University School of Public Health. "College Student Binge Drinking Rates Remain High Despite Efforts by School Administrations." www.hsph.harvard.edu/news/press-releases/2000-releases/press03142000.html.

of bars and liquor stores near their campuses; at some universities that have appeared on our "Party Schools" list there are more than 100 such establishments within a few miles from the campus. "Dry campus" policies often exacerbate the problem, driving drinking off-campus, making it even more dangerous for students.

Despite the claims of some administrators at colleges that have repeatedly made our "Party School" list that our reporting this list promotes drinking on campuses (a group of such administrators receiving funding through the American Medical Association to address their campus alcohol problems made the news several years back with this claim, after which *USA Today* published the editorial praising our ranking as a "public service"), we neither encourage nor discourage students who wish to drink. None of our lists promote behavior: They report on it, plain and simple. What we promote is information.

What we do say to college students—as we have said in this very section of this book for over 10 years—is this: If you're going to drink, do it safely, smartly, responsibly, and legally. If you're going off campus to drink, don't drive back drunk—get a designated driver. Don't let a peer situation (fraternity rush, etc.) put you in jeopardy—it's simply not worth it. Don't use alcohol or drugs as a badge of your coolness—there's not much of a fine line between someone who's socially engaging and someone who's totally disengaging because he or she has performed a chemical auto-lobotomy. Last, don't simply take responsibility for yourself; remember to keep an eye on your friends, and never leave them passed out and alone.

Finally, we'd like to thank all the college officials, college counselors, advisors, students, and parents, who have made this annual guide possible by supporting us these past fifteen years. Our ranking lists have, collectively, been based on surveys of more than 750,000 students whose input has been vital to our publication of this book. We know that it has helped students find great colleges perfect for them, and it has brought to the colleges in our book many outstanding students who otherwise may not have considered attending their institutions.

To all of our readers, we welcome your feedback on how we can continue to improve this guide. We hope you will share with us your comments, questions, and suggestions. Please contact us at Editorial Department, Princeton Review Books, 2315 Broadway, New York, NY 10024, or e-mail us at bookeditor@review.com. We welcome it.

To college applicants, we wish you all the best in your college search. And when you get to your campuses and settle in to your college life, come back to us online; participate in our survey for this book at http://survey.review.com. Let your honest comments about your schools guide prospective students who want your help answering the $64,000 question (goodness knows, the sticker price at some schools may be that high or even higher!): *Which is the best college for me?*

## PART 2

Schools
Ranked by
Category

One of the great things about a multiple-choice survey administered to more than 120,000 college students is that the results give you lots of numbers. We wanted to present those numbers to you in a fun and informative way; hence, the following rankings of schools in 62 categories. In the following lists, the top 20 schools in each category appear in descending order. Remember, of course, that our survey included only students at *The Best 366 Colleges*, and that all schools appearing on what you might consider to be negative lists have many assets that counterbalance their various potential deficiencies.

Simply put, our ranking lists are unique. They can be used to help you clarify some of the choices you have to make in picking the right college. College-bound students, their parents, and counselors searching for substantive, easy-to-understand information will benefit from these kinds of rankings because they are based on the opinions of tens of thousands of in-the-trenches college experts—students. As you read through them, focus on those categories that are important to you: Do you want to go to a school where discussion takes up most of class time? Would you prefer only to be lectured to? Do you care? Do you want to go to a school where students party nonstop? Or would you rather go somewhere with a subdued social scene? By looking through these lists, you should be able to get a good idea of what are and are not important considerations to you.

We've broken the rankings down into eight categories: Academics; Administration; Quality of Life; Politics; Demographics; Social Life; Extracurriculars; Parties; and Schools by Type. Under each list heading, we tell you the survey question or assessment that we used to tabulate the list. For the Schools by Type rankings, we combined student responses to several questions to determine whether a school was a "jock" school, a "party" school, and so on. These lists have changed considerably since the first edition of this book, as we have had time to rethink what truly defines a school's character. For instance, we now factor students' answers to the question "How many hours a day do you study?" into our party-school calibrations. After all, as some of our readers have pointed out, at some schools students drink and do drugs to relieve the stress of their demanding curricula. And, in some cases, statistical data reported by the colleges is also factored in.

Be aware that all of these lists are based on our survey results. Therefore, they do not reflect our opinions, nor do they perfectly reflect reality; that is to say, we can't tell you at which schools registration is actually the biggest hassle. What we can tell you is the schools at which students are most ticked off about registration hassles. Our feeling is that students' self-perceptions are quite valuable. After all, what better way is there to judge a school than by how its students feel about it?

ACADEMICS

The Toughest to Get Into
Based on The Princeton Review ADMISSIONS RATING (page 23)

1. Harvard College
2. Princeton University
3. Massachusetts Institute of Technology
4. Yale University
5. Stanford University
6. Brown University
7. Columbia University
8. University of Pennsylvania
9. Washington University in St. Louis
10. California Institute of Technology
11. Pomona College
12. Duke University
13. Amherst College
14. Williams College
15. Dartmouth College
16. Middlebury College
17. The Cooper Union for the Advancement of Science and Art
18. Georgetown University
19. Haverford College
20. Swarthmore College

Best Classroom Experience
Based on a combination of survey questions concerning teachers, classroom/lab facilities, classes attended, and amount of in-class discussion

1. Reed College
2. Wabash College
3. Thomas Aquinas College
4. Wellesley College
5. Mount Holyoke College
6. Middlebury College
7. Pomona College
8. United States Military Academy
9. Whitman College
10. Kenyon College
11. Hendrix College
12. Sarah Lawrence College
13. Williams College
14. Bowdoin College
15. Agnes Scott College
16. Pitzer College
17. Hanover College
18. Claremont McKenna College
19. Ursinus College
20. Colgate University

Their Students Never Stop Studying
How many out-of-class hours do you spend studying each day?

1. Reed College
2. Franklin W. Olin College of Engineering
3. California Institute of Technology

4. The University of Chicago
5. Harvey Mudd College
6. Bennington College
7. Wabash College
8. Massachusetts Institute of Technology
9. Swarthmore College
10. Middlebury College
11. Marlboro College
12. Grinnell College
13. College of the Holy Cross
14. Haverford College
15. Davidson College
16. United States Military Academy
17. Harvard College
18. Carleton College
19. Bryn Mawr College
20. Whitman College

Their Students (Almost) Never Study
How many out-of-class hours do you spend studying each day?

1. West Virginia University
2. University of Maryland—College Park
3. University of Georgia
4. University of Mississippi
5. University of Massachusetts—Amherst
6. Flagler College
7. Arizona State University
8. George Mason University
9. University of North Dakota
10. University of Rhode Island
11. Florida State University
12. University of Florida
13. University of Central Florida
14. The University of Alabama—Tuscaloosa
15. The University of Texas at Austin
16. The University of Tennessee at Knoxville
17. Ohio University—Athens
18. Indiana University—Bloomington
19. University of New Hampshire
20. Florida Southern College

Professors Get High Marks
Are your instructors good teachers?

1. Wellesley College
2. Harvey Mudd College
3. Middlebury College
4. Sarah Lawrence College
5. Simon's Rock College of Bard
6. Ripon College
7. St. John's College (NM)
8. Wabash College
9. Reed College
10. Sweet Briar College

11. Hendrix College
12. St. John's College (MD)
13. Kenyon College
14. Hampden-Sydney College
15. Marlboro College
16. Centre College
17. Bennington College
18. Hillsdale College
19. Thomas Aquinas College
20. Sewanee—The University of the South

Professors Get Low Marks
Are your instructors good teachers?

1. United States Merchant Marine Academy
2. Stevens Institute of Technology
3. California Institute of Technology
4. New Jersey Institute of Technology
5. University of Hawaii—Manoa
6. Rensselaer Polytechnic Institute
7. State University of New York—University at Albany
8. Georgia Institute of Technology
9. Illinois Institute of Technology
10. University of Rhode Island
11. City University of New York—Brooklyn College
12. State University of New York—Stony Brook University
13. University of California—Los Angeles
14. Arizona State University
15. Drexel University
16. Purdue University—West Lafayette
17. Rutgers, The State University of New Jersey—New Brunswick
18. University of New Mexico
19. Iowa State University
20. University of Arizona

Professors Make Themselves Accessible
Are your instructors accessible outside the classroom?

1. United States Air Force Academy
2. Harvey Mudd College
3. United States Naval Academy
4. Thomas Aquinas College
5. Webb Institute
6. Cornell College
7. Wabash College
8. Sweet Briar College
9. United States Military Academy
10. Washington and Lee University
11. St. John's College (NM)
12. College of the Atlantic
13. Ripon College
14. Wellesley College
15. Franklin W. Olin College of Engineering

16. Sewanee—The University of the South
17. Hampden-Sydney College
18. Centre College
19. Davidson College
20. Hillsdale College

17. Wells College
18. St. John's College (NM)
19. Hanover College
20. Oglethorpe University

Professors Make Themselves Scarce
Are your instructors accessible outside the classroom?

1. University of New Mexico
2. State University of New York—University at Albany
3. University of Toronto
4. Illinois Institute of Technology
5. New Jersey Institute of Technology
6. Tuskegee University
7. University of Hawaii—Manoa
8. Stevens Institute of Technology
9. Rutgers, The State University of New Jersey—New Brunswick
10. University of Rhode Island
11. University of Utah
12. Drexel University
13. City University of New York—Brooklyn College
14. New York University
15. University of California—Los Angeles
16. State University of New York at Binghamton
17. Purdue University—West Lafayette
18. Georgia Institute of Technology
19. St. John's University
20. State University of New York—Stony Brook University

Class Discussions Encouraged
How much of your overall class time is devoted to discussion as opposed to lectures?

1. Sarah Lawrence College
2. Bard College
3. Eugene Lang College—The New School for Liberal Arts
4. St. John's College (MD)
5. Bennington College
6. United States Military Academy
7. Marlboro College
8. Simon's Rock College of Bard
9. Hampshire College
10. Reed College
11. Wesleyan College
12. College of the Atlantic
13. Sweet Briar College
14. Thomas Aquinas College
15. Stephens College
16. Colorado College

Class Discussions Rare
How much of your overall class time is devoted to discussion as opposed to lectures?

1. New Mexico Institute of Mining & Technology
2. Georgia Institute of Technology
3. California Institute of Technology
4. McGill University
5. State University of New York—Stony Brook University
6. University of Toronto
7. North Carolina State University
8. Colorado State University
9. University of California—Davis
10. Louisiana State University
11. Grove City College
12. Illinois Institute of Technology
13. Stevens Institute of Technology
14. University of Missouri—Rolla
15. University of California—Santa Barbara
16. Clarkson University
17. Rose-Hulman Institute of Technology
18. Marquette University
19. Texas A&M University—College Station
20. State University of New York—University at Buffalo

Best Career/Job Placement Services
Based on students' rating of campus career/job placement services

1. The University of Texas at Austin
2. University of Notre Dame
3. Pennsylvania State University—University Park
4. Clemson University
5. Sweet Briar College
6. Rose-Hulman Institute of Technology
7. Southwestern University
8. Smith College
9. Bryant University
10. Cornell University
11. Bentley College
12. Franklin W. Olin College of Engineering
13. American University
14. Villanova University
15. University of Virginia
16. Stevens Institute of Technology
17. Grove City College
18. University of Miami
19. Connecticut College
20. University of Missouri—Rolla

Best College Library
Based on students' assessment of library facilities

1. Harvard College
2. Princeton University
3. Brigham Young University (UT)
4. Cornell University
5. West Virginia University
6. Loyola University—New Orleans
7. Whitman College
8. Columbia University
9. St. Olaf College
10. Wesleyan University
11. The University of Chicago
12. Dickinson College
13. Stanford University
14. Mount Holyoke College
15. Emory University
16. University of Virginia
17. The University of Texas at Austin
18. Valparaiso University
19. Furman University
20. University of Tennessee at Knoxville

This is a Library?
Based on students' assessment of library facilities

1. Clarkson University
2. United States Coast Guard Academy
3. Bennington College
4. Bradley University
5. Spelman College
6. Loyola College in Maryland
7. Saint Mary's College of California
8. University of Dallas
9. Bard College
10. Duquesne University
11. Wells College
12. Tuskegee University
13. American University
14. Wagner College
15. Washington College
16. State University of New York—Purchase College
17. Catawba College
18. Stevens Institute of Technology
19. Loyola Marymount University
20. The Catholic University of America

Students Happy with Financial Aid
Based on students' assessments of how satisfied they are with their financial aid package.

1. Princeton University
2. Stanford University
3. Thomas Aquinas College
4. Pomona College
5. Lake Forest College

6. Claremont McKenna College
7. Wabash College
8. Beloit College
9. Cornell College
10. College of the Atlantic
11. New College of Florida
12. Williams College
13. California Institute of Technology
14. Truman State University
15. Knox College
16. Grinnell College
17. Rice University
18. The University of North Carolina at Asheville
19. Randolph College
20. Amherst College

Students Dissatisfied with Financial Aid
Based on students' assessments of how satisfied they are with their financial aid package.

1. New York University
2. Pennsylvania State University—University Park
3. University of Mary Washington
4. Rutgers, The State University of New Jersey—New Brunswick
5. George Mason University
6. James Madison University
7. Hampton University
8. Drexel University
9. State University of New York at Geneseo
10. Emerson College
11. State University of New York—Purchase College
12. Spelman College
13. University of Oregon
14. Hofstra University
15. State University of New York at Binghamton
16. Quinnipiac University
17. College of the Holy Cross
18. Eugene Lang College—The New School for Liberal Arts
19. University of Delaware
20. Duquesne University

School Runs Like Butter
Overall, how smoothly is your school run?

1. Princeton University
2. Whitman College
3. Middlebury College
4. Wabash College
5. Claremont McKenna College
6. Pomona College
7. Bowdoin College

8. Davidson College
9. Rose-Hulman Institute of Technology
10. Williams College
11. Stanford University
12. Washington University in St. Louis
13. Carleton College
14. Washington and Lee University
15. Amherst College
16. Harvey Mudd College
17. Haverford College
18. University of Notre Dame
19. Elon University
20. Brigham Young University (UT)

Long Lines and Red Tape
Overall, how smoothly is your school run?

1. Tuskegee University
2. Eugene Lang College—
   The New School for Liberal Arts
3. University of Hawaii—Manoa
4. State University of New York—
   Purchase College
5. The Cooper Union for the
   Advancement of Science and Art
6. Hampton University
7. Drexel University
8. New York University
9. Bennington College
10. State University of New York—
    Stony Brook University
11. Wells College
12. Fisk University
13. State University of New York—
    University at Albany
14. Howard University
15. Illinois Institute of Technology
16. Hampshire College
17. University of Massachusetts—Amherst
18. City University of New York—
    Hunter College
19. University of New Orleans
20. The Catholic University of America

QUALITY OF LIFE

Happiest Students
Overall, how happy are you?

1. Whitman College
2. Brown University
3. Clemson University
4. Princeton University
5. Stanford University
6. The University of Tulsa

7. The College of New Jersey
8. Bowdoin College
9. Yale University
10. Thomas Aquinas College
11. St. Mary's College of Maryland
12. Claremont McKenna College
13. The University of North Carolina
    at Chapel Hill
14. Brigham Young University (UT)
15. William Jewell College
16. Indiana University—Bloomington
17. Wabash College
18. Loyola Marymount University
19. St. Olaf College
20. University of Notre Dame

Least Happy Students
Overall, how happy are you?

1. State University of New York—
   Stony Brook University
2. New Mexico Institute of Mining
   & Technology
3. United States Merchant Marine Academy
4. University of Hawaii—Manoa
5. New Jersey Institute of Technology
6. Fisk University
7. Illinois Institute of Technology
8. Clarkson University
9. Tuskegee University
10. Albion College
11. University of California—Riverside
12. State University of New York—
    University at Albany
13. Rensselaer Polytechnic Institute
14. Drexel University
15. Hofstra University
16. Hanover College
17. George Mason University
18. University of Toronto
19. Case Western Reserve University
20. University of Massachusetts—Amherst

Most Beautiful Campus
Based on students' rating of campus beauty

1. Sweet Briar College
2. Princeton University
3. Pepperdine University
4. Wellesley College
5. Mount Holyoke College
6. Wagner College
7. Loyola Marymount University
8. University of California—Santa Cruz
9. Elon University
10. Sewanee—The University of the South

11. Scripps College
12. Colgate University
13. Vassar College
14. Warren Wilson College
15. College of the Atlantic
16. College of the Holy Cross
17. Thomas Aquinas College
18. University of Miami
19. St. Mary's College of Maryland
20. The College of New Jersey

Campus is Tiny, Unsightly, or Both
Based on students' rating of campus beauty

1. State University of New York—University at Albany
2. Drexel University
3. State University of New York—Purchase College
4. City University of New York—Hunter College
5. New Jersey Institute of Technology
6. The Cooper Union for the Advancement of Science and Art
7. Illinois Institute of Technology
8. North Carolina State University
9. University of Dallas
10. State University of New York—University at Buffalo
11. The University of Tennessee at Knoxville
12. University of Massachusetts—Amherst
13. Massachusetts Institute of Technology
14. State University of New York at Binghamton
15. Harvey Mudd College
16. Clarkson University
17. Rider University
18. Rutgers, The State University of New Jersey—New Brunswick
19. State University of New York—Stony Brook University
20. Rochester Institute of Technology

Best Campus Food
Based on students' rating of campus food

1. Virginia Polytechnic Institute and State University (Virginia Tech)
2. Bowdoin College
3. Wheaton College (IL)
4. Bryn Mawr College
5. James Madison University
6. Colby College
7. Franklin W. Olin College of Engineering
8. St. Olaf College
9. Cornell University
10. Washington University in St. Louis

11. University of Notre Dame
12. Scripps College
13. Middlebury College
14. Miami University
15. University of Georgia
16. Claremont McKenna College
17. College of the Atlantic
18. Bates College
19. Macalester College
20. Gustavus Adolphus College

Is It Food?
Based on students' rating of campus food

1. United States Merchant Marine Academy
2. Catawba College
3. Fisk University
4. Guilford College
5. State University of New York—University at Albany
6. Hampton University
7. Wells College
8. Stevens Institute of Technology
9. University of Missouri—Rolla
10. Carnegie Mellon University
11. United States Air Force Academy
12. Flagler College
13. Grove City College
14. New College of Florida
15. Hiram College
16. Fordham University
17. The Evergreen State College
18. Bard College
19. Cornell College
20. Centenary College of Louisiana

Dorms Like Palaces
Based on students' rating of dorm comfort

1. Smith College
2. Loyola College in Maryland
3. The George Washington University
4. Scripps College
5. Bryn Mawr College
6. Franklin W. Olin College of Engineering
7. Pepperdine University
8. Pomona College
9. Bowdoin College
10. Claremont McKenna College
11. Wellesley College
12. Whitman College
13. Washington University in St. Louis
14. Bennington College
15. Williams College
16. Skidmore College
17. New College of Florida

18. Harvard College
19. Mount Holyoke College
20. Trinity University (TX)

Dorms Like Dungeons
Based on students' rating of dorm comfort

1. United States Coast Guard Academy
2. University of Hawaii—Manoa
3. United States Merchant Marine Academy
4. University of New Orleans
5. Tuskegee University
6. University of Louisiana at Lafayette
7. Hampton University
8. Indiana University of Pennsylvania
9. University of Rhode Island
10. State University of New York—
    University at Albany
11. Rider University
12. Georgia Institute of Technology
13. University of Florida
14. University of Idaho
15. Hanover College
16. University of Washington
17. The Evergreen State College
18. The University of South Dakota
19. University of Missouri—Rolla
20. United States Military Academy

Best Quality of Life
Based on The Princeton Review's QUALITY OF LIFE RATING (page 20)

1. Macalester College
2. Bowdoin College
3. Whitman College
4. Princeton University
5. St. Olaf College
6. Rice University
7. Washington University in St. Louis
8. Claremont McKenna College
9. The University of Tulsa
10. Franklin W. Olin College of Engineering
11. Clemson University
12. Webb Institute
13. Middlebury College
14. Thomas Aquinas College
15. Pomona College
16. Barnard College
17. Stanford University
18. Agnes Scott College
19. Brigham Young University (UT)
20. Villanova University

POLITICS

Students Most Nostalgic for Ronald Reagan
Based on students' assessment of their personal political views

1. Thomas Aquinas College
2. Hillsdale College
3. Grove City College
4. Brigham Young University (UT)
5. Hampden-Sydney College
6. United States Naval Academy
7. College of the Ozarks
8. Wheaton College (IL)
9. University of Dallas
10. United States Merchant Marine Academy
11. United States Air Force Academy
12. Baylor University
13. Samford University
14. Clemson University
15. The University of Alabama—Tuscaloosa
16. Texas A&M University—College Station
17. United States Military Academy
18. University of Mississippi
19. Washington and Lee University
20. United States Coast Guard Academy

Students Most Nostalgic for Bill Clinton
Based on students' assessment of their personal political views

1. Warren Wilson College
2. Eugene Lang College—The New School
   for Liberal Arts
3. Hampshire College
4. New College of Florida
5. Bennington College
6. Bard College
7. Sarah Lawrence College
8. Marlboro College
9. Reed College
10. Oberlin College
11. Pitzer College
12. The Evergreen State College
13. Macalester College
14. Wesleyan University
15. Lewis & Clark College
16. Vassar College
17. Mills College
18. Swarthmore College
19. Beloit College
20. Clark University

Most Politically Active Students
How popular are political/activist groups?

1. The George Washington University
2. New College of Florida
3. Macalester College
4. Lewis & Clark College
5. Princeton University
6. American University
7. Eugene Lang College—
   The New School for Liberal Arts
8. Pitzer College
9. Harvard College
10. Hampden-Sydney College
11. Wesleyan University
12. United States Naval Academy
13. Warren Wilson College
14. Claremont McKenna College
15. United States Military Academy
16. University of Oregon
17. Simon's Rock College of Bard
18. Georgetown University
19. Hampshire College
20. Marlboro College

Election? What Election?
How popular are political/activist groups?

1. Sacred Heart University
2. Quinnipiac University
3. Bradley University
4. Florida Southern College
5. Worcester Polytechnic Institute
6. Rose-Hulman Institute of Technology
7. Fisk University
8. University of Louisiana at Lafayette
9. University of Hawaii—Manoa
10. University of Connecticut
11. University of California—Riverside
12. Salisbury University
13. City University of New York—
    Queens College
14. Hobart and William Smith Colleges
15. Ripon College
16. Washington State University
17. St. Bonaventure University
18. Saint Mary's College of California
19. Stevens Institute of Technology
20. Bucknell University

Diverse Student Population
Is your student body made up of diverse social and ethnic types?

1. Temple University
2. Wesleyan College
3. Mount Holyoke College
4. George Mason University
5. University of Miami
6. Wellesley College
7. Stanford University
8. City University of New York—
   Hunter College
9. State University of New York—
   University at Buffalo
10. University of Maryland—
    Baltimore County
11. Manhattanville College
12. State University of New York—
    Stony Brook University
13. Macalester College
14. New Jersey Institute of Technology
15. St. John's University
16. University of Maryland—College Park
17. University of South Florida
18. University of San Francisco
19. Illinois Institute of Technology
20. DePaul University

Homogeneous Student Population
Is your student body made up of diverse social and ethnic types?

1. Providence College
2. Grove City College
3. Saint Anselm College
4. Washington and Lee University
5. Miami University
6. University of Mary Washington
7. Fairfield University
8. Muhlenberg College
9. University of New Hampshire
10. Samford University
11. Loyola College in Maryland
12. Ohio Northern University
13. Lehigh University
14. Bucknell University
15. Hampden-Sydney College
16. University of Richmond
17. Marlboro College
18. Wake Forest University
19. Quinnipiac University
20. Hillsdale College

Lots of Race/Class Interaction
Do different types of students (Black/White, rich/poor) interact frequently and easily?

1. Wesleyan College
2. Thomas Aquinas College
3. Franklin W. Olin College of Engineering
4. Webb Institute
5. Macalester College
6. Rice University
7. St. John's College (MD)
8. Pitzer College
9. Beloit College
10. Stanford University
11. The University of Tulsa
12. Whitman College
13. Mount Holyoke College
14. Randolph College
15. St. John's College (NM)
16. McGill University
17. University of Miami
18. Yale University
19. Eugene Lang College—
    The New School for Liberal Arts
20. Hendrix College

Little Race/Class Interaction
Do different types of students (Black/White, rich/poor) interact frequently and easily?

1. Trinity College (CT)
2. Washington and Lee University
3. Miami University
4. University of New Hampshire
5. Duke University
6. Wake Forest University
7. University of Richmond
8. Providence College
9. Samford University
10. Vanderbilt University
11. College of the Holy Cross
12. Texas Christian University
13. Rollins College
14. University of California—San Diego
15. Saint Anselm College
16. Lafayette College
17. Fairfield University
18. Union College (NY)
19. Southern Methodist University
20. State University of New York
    at Binghamton

Gay Community Accepted
Is there very little discrimination against homosexuals?

1. Macalester College
2. New College of Florida

3. New York University
4. Simon's Rock College of Bard
5. College of the Atlantic
6. Stanford University
7. Wellesley College
8. Mount Holyoke College
9. Bennington College
10. Emerson College
11. Sarah Lawrence College
12. Bryn Mawr College
13. Eugene Lang College—
    The New School for Liberal Arts
14. Beloit College
15. Hampshire College
16. Harvey Mudd College
17. Lawrence University
18. Grinnell College
19. Swarthmore College
20. Cornell College

Alternative Lifestyles Not an Alternative*
Is there very little discrimination against homosexuals?

1. Hampden-Sydney College
2. Baylor University
3. Wheaton College (IL)
4. University of Notre Dame
5. The University of Tennessee at Knoxville
6. Grove City College
7. Trinity College (CT)
8. Samford University
9. Washington and Lee University
10. Seton Hall University
11. Brigham Young University (UT)
12. Pepperdine University
13. Valparaiso University
14. Hanover College
15. Texas A&M University—College Station
16. University of Utah
17. William Jewell College
18. Calvin College
19. Miami University
20. Purdue University—West Lafayette

* Each of the five military academies was excluded from this list because of current, "Don't ask, don't tell" policies.

Students Pray on a Regular Basis
Are students very religious?

1. Brigham Young University (UT)
2. Thomas Aquinas College
3. Wheaton College (IL)
4. Grove City College
5. University of Dallas
6. University of Notre Dame

7. Samford University
8. Hillsdale College
9. Pepperdine University
10. College of the Ozarks
11. University of Utah
12. Baylor University
13. Furman University
14. William Jewell College
15. Calvin College
16. Texas A&M University—College Station
17. University of Mississippi
18. Valparaiso University
19. United States Air Force Academy
20. The Catholic University of America

Students Ignore God on a Regular Basis
Are students very religious?

1. Lewis & Clark College
2. Bennington College
3. Reed College
4. Bard College
5. Marlboro College
6. Eugene Lang College—
   The New School for Liberal Arts
7. Emerson College
8. Sarah Lawrence College
9. New College of Florida
10. Simon's Rock College of Bard
11. Hampshire College
12. Vassar College
13. Wesleyan University
14. Skidmore College
15. Macalester College
16. Beloit College
17. Grinnell College
18. Pomona College
19. Pitzer College
20. State University of New York—
    Purchase College

SOCIAL LIFE

Great College Towns
Based on students' assessment of the surrounding city or town

1. Eugene Lang College—The New School
   for Liberal Arts
2. Barnard College
3. The George Washington University
4. American University
5. DePaul University
6. Columbia University
7. Suffolk University

8. University of San Francisco
9. Macalester College
10. New York University
11. Lewis & Clark College
12. The University of Texas at Austin
13. Georgetown University
14. The Cooper Union for the Advancement
    of Science and Art
15. Northeastern University
16. Emerson College
17. College of Charleston
18. McGill University
19. Boston University
20. Tulane University

More to Do on Campus
Based on students' assessment of the surrounding city or town

1. Union College (NY)
2. Tuskegee University
3. United States Military Academy
4. New Jersey Institute of Technology
5. Rensselaer Polytechnic Institute
6. New Mexico Institute of Mining
   & Technology
7. Albion College
8. United States Coast Guard Academy
9. Hofstra University
10. Lehigh University
11. Duke University
12. Beloit College
13. Rose-Hulman Institute of Technology
14. Wheaton College (MA)
15. Vassar College
16. DePauw University
17. Trinity College (CT)
18. College of the Holy Cross
19. University of Notre Dame
20. University of the Pacific

Town-Gown Relations are Great
Do students get along well with members of the local community?

1. St. Olaf College
2. William Jewell College
3. Franklin W. Olin College of Engineering
4. Ripon College
5. The University of Tulsa
6. Clemson University
7. Wheaton College (IL)
8. Davidson College
9. Stephens College
10. College of the Ozarks
11. Eugene Lang College—The New School
    for Liberal Arts

12. Brigham Young University (UT)
13. Agnes Scott College
14. Millsaps College
15. Wesleyan College
16. Saint Michael's College
17. United States Naval Academy
18. University of Louisiana at Lafayette
19. Samford University
20. Loyola University—New Orleans

Town-Gown Relations are Strained
Do students get along well with members of the local community?

1. Trinity College (CT)
2. Union College (NY)
3. Duke University
4. Illinois Institute of Technology
5. Colorado College
6. University of New Hampshire
7. DePauw University
8. Howard University
9. University of Pennsylvania
10. Sarah Lawrence College
11. New Mexico Institute of Mining & Technology
12. New Jersey Institute of Technology
13. Rensselaer Polytechnic Institute
14. Vassar College
15. Northwestern University
16. Bennington College
17. State University of New York at Binghamton
18. Bates College
19. College of the Holy Cross
20. Hofstra University

EXTRACURRICULARS

Students Pack the Stadiums
How popular are intercollegiate sports?

1. University of Maryland—College Park
2. University of Notre Dame
3. University of Florida
4. West Virginia University
5. University of Georgia
6. Pennsylvania State University—University Park
7. University of Michigan—Ann Arbor
8. University of Southern California
9. Gonzaga University
10. The University of Tennessee at Knoxville
11. The University of Texas at Austin
12. Clemson University

13. The University of North Carolina at Chapel Hill
14. Boston College
15. The Ohio State University—Columbus
16. Virginia Polytechnic Institute and State University (Virginia Tech)
17. Texas A&M University—College Station
18. University of Wisconsin—Madison
19. United States Naval Academy
20. The University of Alabama—Tuscaloosa

Intercollegiate Sports Unpopular or Nonexistent
How popular are intercollegiate sports?

1. New College of Florida
2. Eugene Lang College—The New School for Liberal Arts
3. St. John's College (NM)
4. Bennington College
5. College of the Atlantic
6. Thomas Aquinas College
7. Marlboro College
8. Franklin W. Olin College of Engineering
9. St. John's College (MD)
10. Emerson College
11. New York University
12. Reed College
13. Hampshire College
14. Sarah Lawrence College
15. The University of Chicago
16. State University of New York—Purchase College
17. Simon's Rock College of Bard
18. The Cooper Union for the Advancement of Science and Art
19. Bard College
20. The Evergreen State College

Everyone Plays Intramural Sports
How popular are intramural sports?

1. University of Notre Dame
2. Whitman College
3. Wabash College
4. Ripon College
5. Pennsylvania State University—University Park
6. United States Naval Academy
7. Grove City College
8. Iowa State University
9. The University of Tennessee at Knoxville
10. Colorado College
11. University of Dayton
12. Clemson University
13. Carleton College
14. United States Air Force Academy

15. University of Florida
16. University of Nebraska—Lincoln
17. Brigham Young University (UT)
18. United States Coast Guard Academy
19. Providence College
20. Baylor University

Nobody Plays Intramural Sports
How popular are intramural sports?

1. Stephens College
2. Eugene Lang College—
   The New School for Liberal Arts
3. Emerson College
4. Marlboro College
5. New York University
6. College of the Atlantic
7. Sarah Lawrence College
8. New College of Florida
9. Hollins University
10. The Cooper Union for the Advancement
    of Science and Art
11. Suffolk University
12. Bennington College
13. Bryn Mawr College
14. Hampshire College
15. Simon's Rock College of Bard
16. Spelman College
17. The Evergreen State College
18. Barnard College
19. Randolph College
20. State University of New York—
    Purchase College

Best College Radio Station
How popular is the radio station?

1. St. Bonaventure University
2. Emerson College
3. DePauw University
4. Ithaca College
5. Brown University
6. Guilford College
7. Seton Hall University
8. Knox College
9. University of Puget Sound
10. Howard University
11. Carleton College
12. Whitman College
13. The Evergreen State College
14. Reed College
15. Alfred University
16. Skidmore College
17. Swarthmore College
18. Manhattanville College
19. Bates College
20. Denison University

Best College Newspaper
How popular is the newspaper?

1. The University of North Carolina
   at Chapel Hill
2. Yale University
3. University of Pennsylvania
4. Howard University
5. University of Georgia
6. University of Maryland—College Park
7. Harvard College
8. West Virginia University
9. University of Mississippi
10. Pennsylvania State University—
    University Park
11. Michigan State University
12. Louisiana State University
13. Indiana University—Bloomington
14. Northwestern University
15. Duke University
16. University of Wisconsin—Madison
17. The University of Texas at Austin
18. Syracuse University
19. University of Florida
20. Texas A&M University—College Station

Best College Theater
How popular are college theater productions?

1. Yale University
2. Wagner College
3. Emerson College
4. Catawba College
5. Bennington College
6. Drew University
7. Muhlenberg College
8. Stephens College
9. Whitman College
10. Vassar College
11. Ithaca College
12. College of the Ozarks
13. Brown University
14. Simon's Rock College of Bard
15. Knox College
16. Hendrix College
17. Lawrence University
18. Manhattanville College
19. Wesleyan College
20. Hampshire College

Lots of Beer
How widely used is beer?

1. University of Wisconsin—Madison
2. DePauw University
3. Pennsylvania State University—University Park
4. University of New Hampshire
5. The University of Texas at Austin
6. West Virginia University
7. Washington and Lee University
8. Randolph-Macon College
9. University of Florida
10. University of Mississippi
11. Sewanee—The University of the South
12. Ohio University—Athens
13. Colgate University
14. University of Illinois at Urbana-Champaign
15. Hamilton College
16. James Madison University
17. Union College (NY)
18. University of Iowa
19. Trinity College (CT)
20. Claremont McKenna College

Got Milk?
How widely used is beer?

1. Brigham Young University (UT)
2. Wheaton College (IL)
3. City University of New York—Queens College
4. College of the Ozarks
5. Grove City College
6. Wesleyan College
7. Spelman College
8. City University of New York—Brooklyn College
9. Thomas Aquinas College
10. Howard University
11. City University of New York—Hunter College
12. Fisk University
13. Wellesley College
14. Xavier University of Louisiana
15. Calvin College
16. Berea College
17. Hampton University
18. Samford University
19. Agnes Scott College
20. Mills College

Lots of Hard Liquor
How widely used is hard liquor?

1. Washington and Lee University
2. Louisiana State University
3. University of Mississippi
4. Providence College
5. University of Iowa
6. Indiana University—Bloomington
7. West Virginia University
8. The University of Texas at Austin
9. University of Florida
10. DePauw University
11. University of California—Santa Barbara
12. University of Georgia
13. Trinity College (CT)
14. Wake Forest University
15. Ohio University—Athens
16. Loyola College in Maryland
17. Pennsylvania State University—University Park
18. State University of New York—University at Albany
19. Centre College
20. Hampden-Sydney College

Scotch and Soda, Hold the Scotch
How widely used is hard liquor?

1. Brigham Young University (UT)
2. Wheaton College (IL)
3. City University of New York—Queens College
4. College of the Ozarks
5. Grove City College
6. Thomas Aquinas College
7. City University of New York—Brooklyn College
8. Wesleyan College
9. City University of New York—Hunter College
10. Calvin College
11. Wellesley College
12. Samford University
13. Spelman College
14. Webb Institute
15. Berea College
16. United States Air Force Academy
17. United States Coast Guard Academy
18. William Jewell College
19. United States Naval Academy
20. Mills College

Reefer Madness
How widely used is marijuana?

1. Warren Wilson College
2. Bard College
3. University of Vermont
4. University of California—Santa Cruz
5. Lewis & Clark College
6. Pitzer College
7. Hampshire College
8. New College of Florida
9. The University of Texas at Austin
10. Sarah Lawrence College
11. West Virginia University
12. Wesleyan University
13. Guilford College
14. Skidmore College
15. University of Colorado—Boulder
16. Ithaca College
17. University of California—Santa Barbara
18. Eckerd College
19. Vassar College
20. Oberlin College

Don't Inhale
How widely used is marijuana?

1. United States Air Force Academy
2. Brigham Young University (UT)
3. United States Coast Guard Academy
4. United States Naval Academy
5. United States Military Academy
6. Thomas Aquinas College
7. Webb Institute
8. United States Merchant Marine Academy
9. Wheaton College (IL)
10. Grove City College
11. College of the Ozarks
12. City University of New York— Queens College
13. University of Notre Dame
14. Samford University
15. William Jewell College
16. Calvin College
17. Wesleyan College
18. Franklin W. Olin College of Engineering
19. Hillsdale College
20. Wellesley College

Major Frat and Sorority Scene
How popular are fraternities/sororities?

1. DePauw University
2. Washington and Lee University
3. Birmingham-Southern College
4. Wofford College
5. Bucknell University
6. Dartmouth College
7. University of Tennessee at Knoxville
8. Wabash College
9. University of Mississippi
10. Texas Christian University
11. Transylvania University
12. Randolph-Macon College
13. University of Illinois at Urbana-Champaign
14. Vanderbilt University
15. University of Georgia
16. Wake Forest University
17. Pennsylvania State University— University Park
18. Gettysburg College
19. Miami University
20. Millsaps College

SCHOOL BY TYPE

Party Schools
Based on a combination of survey questions concerning the use of alcohol and drugs, hours of study each day, and the popularity of the Greek system

1. West Virginia University
2. University of Mississippi
3. The University of Texas at Austin
4. University of Florida
5. University of Georgia
6. Pennsylvania State University— University Park
7. University of New Hampshire
8. Indiana University—Bloomington
9. Ohio University—Athens
10. University of California—Santa Barbara
11. Randolph-Macon College
12. University of Iowa
13. Louisiana State University
14. University of Maryland—College Park
15. The University of Tennessee at Knoxville
16. University of Illinois at Urbana-Champaign
17. Arizona State University
18. Florida State University
19. The University of Alabama—Tuscaloosa
20. State University of New York— University at Albany

Stone-Cold Sober Schools

Based on a combination of survey questions concerning the use of alcohol and drugs, hours of study each day, and the popularity of the Greek system

1. Brigham Young University (UT)
2. Wheaton College (IL)
3. Thomas Aquinas College
4. College of the Ozarks
5. Grove City College
6. United States Coast Guard Academy
7. United States Air Force Academy
8. United States Naval Academy
9. City University of New York—
   Queens College
10. Webb Institute
11. Wellesley College
12. Calvin College
13. Wesleyan College
14. United States Military Academy
15. Franklin W. Olin College of Engineering
16. Berea College
17. St. Olaf College
18. Agnes Scott College
19. Bryn Mawr College
20. Spelman College

Jock Schools

Based on a combination of survey questions concerning intercollegiate and intramural sports, the popularity of the Greek system

1. Clemson University
2. Pennsylvania State University—
   University Park
3. University of Florida
4. University of Notre Dame
5. Wabash College
6. University of Nebraska—Lincoln
7. The University of Tennessee at Knoxville
8. Wake Forest University
9. University of Michigan—Ann Arbor
10. Florida State University
11. United States Naval Academy
12. Iowa State University
13. University of Georgia
14. The University of North Carolina
    at Chapel Hill
15. University of Virginia
16. University of Connecticut
17. Villanova University
18. Duke University
19. University of Southern California
20. Texas A&M University—College Station

Dodgeball Targets

Based on a combination of survey questions concerning intercollegiate and intramural sports, the popularity of the Greek system

1. Eugene Lang College—
   The New School for Liberal Arts
2. Marlboro College
3. Emerson College
4. Bennington College
5. New College of Florida
6. College of the Atlantic
7. New York University
8. Sarah Lawrence College
9. Stephens College
10. Hampshire College
11. St. John's College (NM)
12. Reed College
13. Simon's Rock College of Bard
14. Bard College
15. The Evergreen State College
16. State University of New York—
    Purchase College
17. Suffolk University
18. Hollins University
19. Lewis & Clark College
20. Oberlin College

Future Rotarians and Daughters of the American Revolution

Based on a combination of survey questions concerning political persuasion, the use of marijuana and hallucinogens, the prevalence of religion, the popularity of student government, and the students' level of acceptance of the gay community on campus

1. Brigham Young University (UT)
2. Grove City College
3. Wheaton College (IL)
4. Thomas Aquinas College
5. Hillsdale College
6. College of the Ozarks
7. Samford University
8. University of Dallas
9. United States Air Force Academy
10. United States Naval Academy
11. University of Notre Dame
12. William Jewell College
13. Baylor University
14. Texas A&M University—College Station
15. United States Military Academy
16. Calvin College
17. United States Coast Guard Academy
18. Furman University
19. United States Merchant Marine Academy
20. Pepperdine University

Birkenstock-Wearing, Tree-Hugging, Clove-Smoking Vegetarians

Based on a combination of survey questions concerning political persuasion, the use of marijuana and hallucinogens, the prevalence of religion, the popularity of student government, and the students' level of acceptance of the gay community on campus

1. Hampshire College
2. Bard College
3. Warren Wilson College
4. Bennington College
5. The Evergreen State College
6. New College of Florida
7. Sarah Lawrence College
8. Reed College
9. Lewis & Clark College
10. Eugene Lang College—
    The New School for Liberal Arts
11. Wesleyan University
12. Simon's Rock College of Bard
13. Marlboro College
14. Oberlin College
15. Vassar College
16. Pitzer College
17. University of California—Santa Cruz
18. Emerson College
19. Macalester College
20. State University of New York—
    Purchase College

Deep Springs Honor Roll

Since Deep Springs is a two-year college—the only one of its kind in The Best 366 Colleges—we've decided to remove it from the body of our individual rankings in order to avoid comparing "apples and oranges." Instead we've created this "honor roll," which includes all categories in which Deep Springs ranks high (or low, as it were) among the best colleges.

Best Overall Academic Experience for
    Undergraduates
The Toughest to Get Into
Professors Make Themselves Accessible
Their Students Never Stop Studying
Class Discussions Encouraged
This is a Library?
School Runs Like Butter
Most Beautiful Campus
Dorms Like Palaces
Best Quality of Life
Students Most Nostalgic for Bill Clinton
Lots of Race/Class Interaction
Gay Community Accepted
Students Ignore God on a Regular Basis
Great College Towns
Town-Gown Relations are Great
Intercollegiate Sports Unpopular or Nonexistent
Got Milk?
Scotch and Soda, Hold the Scotch
Don't Inhale
Stone-Cold Sober Schools
Dodgeball Targets

A Final Note

The following schools have been excluded from our ranking lists dealing with financial aid:

Berea College
College of the Ozarks
The Cooper Union for the Advancement
    of Science and Art
Franklin W. Olin College of Engineering
United States Air Force Academy
United States Coast Guard Academy
United States Merchant Marine Academy
United States Military Academy
United States Naval Academy
Webb Institute

The reason—they're free!
We would like to commend each of these schools on their ability to do the seemingly impossible—not charge tuition. However, we thought it less than fair to include each of these schools in our financial lists, since each would have an unfair advantage over schools that charged even a moderate tuition.

PART 3

THE BEST
366 COLLEGES

AGNES SCOTT COLLEGE

141 EAST COLLEGE AVENUE, DECATUR, GA 30030-3797 • ADMISSIONS: 404-471-6285 • FAX: 404-471-6414

STUDENTS SPEAK OUT
Academics

"Agnes Scott College is about empowering the next generation of strong women in the world," students at this small women's college tell us, and statistics prove that this is more than empty rhetoric. ASC ranks high among undergraduate institutions in the percentage of its alumnae who continue on to advanced degree programs, and women here enjoy a highly personalized educational experience. As one student explains, "It makes me feel good that my professors know my name! Overall, I feel like this school cares about me. There is nothing impersonal about Agnes Scott." That intimacy, coupled with ASC's close proximity to Atlanta where there are "so many internships and jobs," provides ASC with a killer one-two punch. Writing and independent thinking are the focus of the curriculum here; classes "are engaging and encourage students to think critically about the subject, not just memorize a bunch of facts and dates." While the "small size of the school . . . makes it difficult to offer some courses," ASC "makes up for it with opportunities for reading courses, independent studies," and "wonderful personal interaction with one's professors." Students warn, "There are no cake classes at Agnes," but also say that "one-on-one relationships with the professors" help undergrads master the ASC's "rigorous" academics. To sum it all up, "Agnes Scott is a very challenging school, but it provides you with more than enough resources to come out on top."

Life

Life at ASC "can be a bubble if you make it a bubble. There are people who never go out, and they suffer socially. There are also people who go out, party too much, and suffer academically. Most people are successful in finding a healthy balance." Fortunately, ASC women have a lot of options to choose from when it comes to finding entertainment. There are "tons of hall activities at the dorms, where the girls all get to know one another really well!" In addition, "There are numerous campus-wide activities like Diversifest—where diversity is celebrated with Chinese calligraphy banners, the showing of *Ringu*, and a Day of the Dead workshop"—not to mention a popular "pre-exam pancake jam." ASC is located in Decatur, an upscale area just outside of the Atlanta city limits that boasts "fabulous restaurants" and great "shopping at Little Five Points," an alternative hotspot nearby. Students head into Atlanta, "an amazing city . . . ridiculously accessible by MARTA or car," to enjoy "various museums, including the High Art Museum and the Georgia Aquarium," not to mention "tons of great restaurants, shopping, plays, concerts, and nightlife." As for the dating scene, "Georgia Tech isn't far away, so if people are looking for parties that include boys, that's usually the first stop." There's also "a lesbian dance club across the street that a lot of students go to on the weekend."

Student Body

"There is no typical student per se" at Agnes Scott, as "Everyone kind of goes to the beat of her own drum." The student body runs the gamut "from the radical, left-wing lesbian to the far-right, pearls-wearing, charm school graduate, and any combination after that." Many "were the 'weird girls' from high school . . . the ones who got good grades but were eccentric." While "People are very different here," students concede that there are identifiable "social circles" on campus. As one student explains, "We definitely have 'groups' on campus, including the religious right, . . . the girls who drink too much, and the girls who ask to rewrite their A- papers. The groups might not always get along, but when it comes down to it, Agnes Scott students are devoted to each other and the school." While political perspectives vary, the majority here "lean to the political left," to the point that those who are not "very liberal and idealistic . . . often have some trouble fitting in." Students also observe that "because of an international focus and location in metro Atlanta, the student body is diverse in ethnicity."

AGNES SCOTT COLLEGE

FINANCIAL AID: 404-471-6395 • E-MAIL: ADMISSION@AGNESSCOTT.EDU • WEBSITE: WWW.AGNESSCOTT.EDU

ADMISSIONS

Very important factors considered include: Academic GPA, application essay, character/personal qualities, class rank, recommendation(s), rigor of secondary school record, standardized test scores, talent/ability. *Important factors considered include:* Extracurricular activities, volunteer work, work experience. *Other factors considered include:* Alumni/ae relation, first generation, geographical residence, interview, level of applicant's interest, racial/ethnic status, state residency. SAT or ACT required; ACT with Writing component recommended. TOEFL required of all international applicants. High school diploma is required, and GED is accepted. *Academic units recommended:* 4 English, 3 math, 2 science (2 science labs), 2 foreign language, 2 history, 2 social studies.

The Inside Word

Are you on the fence about applying to Agnes Scott College? Apply online, and the college will waive the application fee—it will only cost you the time it takes to fill it out. Don't treat this application lightly, though; Agnes Scott is highly selective, and you'll need to submit an impressive application to gain admission. Don't worry about falling through the cracks here—every candidate is assigned her own specific Admission Counselor who works with the student throughout the application process.

FINANCIAL AID

Students should submit: FAFSA, previous year's Federal Income Tax Return. Regular filing deadline is May 1. The Princeton Review suggests that all financial aid forms be submitted as soon as possible after January 1. *Need-based scholarships/grants offered:* Pell Grant, SEOG, state scholarships/grants, private scholarships, the school's own gift aid. *Loan aid offered:* FFEL Subsidized Stafford, FFEL Unsubsidized Stafford, FFEL PLUS, college/university loans from institutional funds. Applicants will be notified of awards on a rolling basis beginning or about March 1. Federal Work-Study Program available. Institutional employment available. Off-campus job opportunities are excellent.

FROM THE ADMISSIONS OFFICE

"Who will you become? If you are looking for a liberal arts college that will help you explore, strive, and surpass what you think is your potential, then consider Agnes Scott College. Our students and alumnae say it best:

"'I find the academic program to be extremely challenging at Agnes Scott; but it's not overwhelming—it's easy to go to your teachers and ask for help because they know who you are and take a personal interest.'—Evan Joslin, Class of 2008, Atlanta, GA.

"'Agnes Scott College didn't teach me what to think. They taught me how to think,' says Jessica Owen Sanfilippo, Class of 1998, who majored in biology at ASC, received a master's degree in cancer biology from Stanford, and an MBA from Harvard.

"Students find their passions and their voices through guaranteed internships, international study experiences, and collaborative learning in places like the science center, facilities that were designed expressly to facilitate faculty-student research. Your next 4 years are about you. We invite you to come for a visit and imagine the possibilities for you.

"Students applying for admission are required to submit score results from the new SAT with the Writing section or the ACT, with the Writing section recommended. We will allow students to submit scores from the old version of the SAT or ACT and will use the student's best scores from either test."

SELECTIVITY

Admissions Rating	**91**
# of applicants	1,541
% of applicants accepted	47
% of acceptees attending	30
# accepting a place on wait list	35
% admitted from wait list	6
# of early decision applicants	18
% accepted early decision	17

FRESHMAN PROFILE

Range SAT Critical Reading	565–680
Range SAT Math	520–630
Range SAT Writing	540–660
Range ACT Composite	24–29
Minimum Paper TOEFL	577
Minimum Computer Based TOEFL	250
Average HS GPA	3.62
% graduated top 10% of class	36
% graduated top 25% of class	70
% graduated top 50% of class	97

DEADLINES

Early decision application deadline	11/15
Early decision notification	12/15
Regular notification	rolling
Nonfall registration?	yes

APPLICANTS ALSO LOOK AT
AND OFTEN PREFER
University of Georgia, Wellesley College
AND SOMETIMES PREFER
Bryn Mawr College, Emory University, Sewanee—The University of the South
AND RARELY PREFER
Spelman College

FINANCIAL FACTS

Financial Aid Rating	**89**
Annual tuition	$25,100
Room & Board	$8,990
Books and supplies	$700
Required fees	$685
% frosh rec. need-based scholarship or grant aid	74
% UG rec. need-based scholarship or grant aid	66
% frosh rec. need-based self-help aid	57
% UG rec. need-based self-help aid	57
% frosh rec. any financial aid	99
% UG rec. any financial aid	88

ALBERTSON COLLEGE

2112 CLEVELAND BOULEVARD, CALDWELL, ID 83605 • ADMISSIONS: 208-459-5305 • FAX: 208-459-5757

CAMPUS LIFE

Quality of Life Rating	80
Fire Safety Rating	81
Type of school	private
Environment	town

STUDENTS

Total undergrad enrollment	788
% male/female	42/58
% from out of state	28
% live on campus	52
% in (# of) fraternities	12 (3)
% in (# of) sororities	13 (4)
% African American	1
% Asian	3
% Caucasian	73
% Hispanic	5
% Native American	1
% international	2
# of countries represented	8

SURVEY SAYS . . .

Small classes
Students are friendly
Students are happy
Lots of beer drinking

ACADEMICS

Academic Rating	89
Calendar	semester
Student/faculty ratio	11:1
Profs interesting rating	92
Profs accessible rating	89
% profs teaching	
UG courses	100
% classes taught by TAs	0
Most common	
reg class size	10–19 students

MOST POPULAR MAJORS

biology/biological sciences
business administration/
management
psychology

STUDENTS SPEAK OUT

Academics

With only about 800 undergraduates, Albertson College of Idaho provides "a close, personal, friendly learning environment" to students seeking a "balanced liberal arts education." All students must complete the liberal arts core curriculum that "integrates disciplines to produce a better understanding of the world, how it works, and how people come together to make it work"; the graduates, as a result, are a well-rounded bunch. One undergrad explains, "A class from just about every major is required before you graduate; [this] gives you the opportunity to enjoy [things] you never knew you even liked." The core also "teaches you how to write," a facet of the curriculum that students appreciate, if sometimes grudgingly. Top offerings at ACI include a "really great premedical program," a "very good psychology department," science programs that "offer many research opportunities you can't find anywhere else," and music program that offers instruction from professionals: "With the Langroise Trio in residence at the college, you are guaranteed get great instruction and good small ensemble experience." The Gipson Honors Program here "allows students to choose concentrations rather than majors and work on a final thesis-like project," an excellent option for those who know exactly what they want from their bachelor's degree. Students overwhelmingly praise the school's small size and the individual attention they receive. In all areas, "The professors are absolutely amazing. They genuinely care about your progress and are willing to go out of their way to assist you in any way possible."

Life

ACI "is the type of school academics dream of and the type of community that party-goers and the quiet type can both enjoy." Schoolwork keeps students busy here—but not so busy that they can't take advantage of the "huge amount of opportunities for involvement in athletics, clubs, and other extracurricular activities." Undergrads "consistently obligate themselves to volunteer activities, student government, extracurriculars, sports, and so on. They really keep the atmosphere at Albertson dynamic and constantly on the move, so there's never a dull moment." Students especially love to take advantage of the school's location. While some note that hometown Caldwell "is not the best," Boise is "only about 20 minutes away, and it has good shopping and cultural events, so that's where a lot of students spend their time." Students who like the outdoors find great resources for "tour kayaking, backpacking, hiking, camping, rock climbing, canyoneering, road tripping, caving, scuba diving . . . and even skydiving." On weekends, "The party scene is very active, but there are always things to do if you don't want to drink. Most fraternities are very accepting of nondrinkers. Parties are a big part of campus life, but all activities have some place on the campus."

Student Body

"The stereotype is that ACI is mostly a bunch of White, affluent Republicans from around the state," but that reputation is changing: "As the population diversifies, political views are becoming less homogeneous." Political differences, students point out, tend to be less important than common interests: "How you orient yourself politically isn't really of any consequence on campus. For example, the debate team is extremely cohesive despite a wide array of varying political views. We all seem to get along." Above all, the students here immerse themselves in the things they do. This is particularly the case with school spirit. One remarks, "The student fans are becoming known as 'Coyote Crazies' because they are so loud at sporting events." Energetic ACI students "work hard at studies and at extracurricular activities. Due in part to the limited student population on campus, [students are] likely to be involved in many clubs and organizations outside of class."

FINANCIAL AID: 208-459-5308 • E-MAIL: ADMISSION@ALBERTSON.EDU • WEBSITE: WWW.ALBERTSON.EDU

ADMISSIONS

Very important factors considered include: Academic GPA, recommendation(s), rigor of secondary school record, standardized test scores. *Important factors considered include:* Application essay, character/personal qualities, extracurricular activities, interview, level of applicant's interest, talent/ability, volunteer work, work experience. *Other factors considered include:* Alumni/ae relation, class rank, first generation, geographical residence, racial/ethnic status. SAT or ACT required; ACT with Writing component required. TOEFL required of all international applicants. High school diploma is required, and GED is accepted. *Academic units required:* 4 English, 3 history, 3 math, 2 science, 3 academic electives. *Academic units recommended:* 3 science, 2 foreign language, 2 social studies.

The Inside Word

Despite its high acceptance rate, Albertson offers a quality academic program. Students who have thrived in the classroom and actively participated in extracurriculars will be the handed the keys to a unique college experience, one which stresses self-confidence and social responsibility.

FINANCIAL AID

Students should submit: FAFSA, institution's own financial aid form. The Princeton Review suggests that all financial aid forms be submitted as soon as possible after January 1. *Need-based scholarships/grants offered:* Pell Grant, SEOG, state scholarships/grants, private scholarships, the school's own gift aid. *Loan aid offered:* Direct Subsidized Stafford, Direct Unsubsidized Stafford, Direct PLUS, Federal Perkins Loan, alternative loans. Applicants will be notified of awards on a rolling basis beginning or about March 1. Federal Work-Study Program available. Institutional employment available. Off-campus job opportunities are fair.

FROM THE ADMISSIONS OFFICE

"While the mission of Albertson College is traditional in that it remains committed to the teaching of the liberal arts, many of the approaches to accomplishing this goal are unique. Within the campus community is the creativity to create classroom opportunities for students that span the globe—both technologically and geographically. Here, students are just as apt to attend a biology class on campus as they are to hike in the nearby Owyhee or Sawtooth Mountains to carry out field research. During the college's 6-week winter term, more than 30 percent of the students are emailing friends and family from such locales as Australia, Israel, France, Ireland, England, Peru, or Mexico while taking part in faculty-led, multidisciplinary trips. Students are invited to visit the campus and the Admissions Counselors, either in person or through the website at www.albertson.edu.

"ACI requires all admission candidates (who have not reached sophomore status in college) to submit either the new SAT or the ACT with the Writing component as of October 2005. ACI will consider all scores, including the old SAT without Writing. There is no SAT Subject Test requirement, but scores will be considered as part of a holistic evaluation."

SELECTIVITY

Admissions Rating	**91**
# of applicants	924
% of applicants accepted	84
% of acceptees attending	25

FRESHMAN PROFILE

Range SAT Critical Reading	520–643
Range SAT Math	530–640
Range ACT Composite	23–28
Minimum Paper TOEFL	550
Minimum Computer Based TOEFL	213
Average HS GPA	3.6
% graduated top 10% of class	34
% graduated top 25% of class	70
% graduated top 50% of class	92

DEADLINES

Regular application deadline	6/1
Regular notification	rolling
Nonfall registration?	yes

APPLICANTS ALSO LOOK AT

AND OFTEN PREFER
Gonzaga University, Linfield College, University of Puget Sound, Whitman College, Willamette University

AND SOMETIMES PREFER
Carroll College (MT), University of Idaho, Whitworth College

AND RARELY PREFER
Northwest Nazarene University

FINANCIAL FACTS

Financial Aid Rating	**89**
Annual tuition	$16,000
Room & Board	$6,191
Books and supplies	$900
Required fees	$625
% frosh rec. need-based scholarship or grant aid	45
% UG rec. need-based scholarship or grant aid	39
% frosh rec. need-based self-help aid	56
% UG rec. need-based self-help aid	53
% frosh rec. any financial aid	93
% UG rec. any financial aid	92

ALBION COLLEGE

611 East Porter, Albion, MI 49224 • Admissions: 517-629-0321 • Fax: 517-629-0569

CAMPUS LIFE

Quality of Life Rating	**65**
Fire Safety Rating	**72**
Type of school	private
Affiliation	Methodist
Environment	village

STUDENTS

Total undergrad enrollment	1,953
% male/female	44/56
% from out of state	10
% from public high school	75
% live on campus	88
% in (# of) fraternities	32 (6)
% in (# of) sororities	32 (7)
% African American	4
% Asian	2
% Caucasian	89
% Hispanic	1
% Native American	1
% international	1
# of countries represented	20

SURVEY SAYS . . .
Small classes
Lab facilities are great
Great computer facilities
Students are friendly
Frats and sororities
dominate social scene
Lots of beer drinking

ACADEMICS

Academic Rating	**84**
Calendar	semester
Student/faculty ratio	13:1
Profs interesting rating	84
Profs accessible rating	92
% profs teaching UG courses	100
% classes taught by TAs	0
Most common lab size	10–19 students
Most common reg class size	10–19 students

MOST POPULAR MAJORS
biology/biological sciences
economics
psychology

STUDENTS SPEAK OUT

Academics

A strong sense of community is among Albion College's strongest selling points, according to the students we surveyed. Many here mention "an immediate feeling of comfort when you come to this campus" that is reinforced over time by a school that "is truly dedicated to its students and their futures. The academics are excellent, the faculty top-notch, and the opportunities are amazing." Undergrads love the strong pre-professional programs, which include "awesome pre-med and pre-dental institutes with very high acceptance rates at medical/dental schools" and a "strong business program." There's less unanimity over the school's liberal arts core curriculum; its champions laud the "multidimensional academic experience in a variety of departments" the core provides, while naysayers tell us that "it doesn't work, because most students just don't care about learning anything other than their major." Professors earn high marks; students describe them as "very brilliant and having much to offer in regards to academia. They teach all of their courses as well as engage in research." They are also active in the campus community, "attending sporting, service, visual arts, Greek and other events hosted by different clubs and organizations on campus. They are an active faculty and involved with the campus." So, too, is the school's president, who "is rare in [the] sense that he is visible to students on a regular basis, dances with the dance team at half-time, sits in dunk tanks for philanthropic events, hosts dinner and dessert parties at his home, is always smiling, and knows the majority, if not all, of the students' names."

Life

Albion, Michigan, is a "small town that has nothing to offer a college student. The movie theater is really the only reason anyone from the school would walk to downtown. There's not even a Wal-Mart here!" How big a problem this poses depends on the student. Some here tell us that "There are so many things to get involved in that the town we are in isn't that big of a deal." They cite athletic teams—the small student population means a relatively large proportion of students participate in intercollegiate sports—"meetings for various organizations, which are easy to start," "working with the community," and, of course, Greek life, which is "huge" here. Others feel that the campus doesn't make up for the dearth of opportunities in town; they tell us that "there's not a whole lot to do on campus that doesn't involve fraternity life in some way, so parties are obviously popular. Unfortunately, the school really doesn't have much else to offer." One student adds, "Life is just like high school. There are your same basic drama, Greek, athletic, and 'alternative' groups. People usually have small parties or get-togethers, go to frat parties, or see movies at the movie theater. Otherwise, there's not much." As a result, "Leaving campus is popular on weekends. We are in close proximity to a lot of larger schools." Students generally "escape 20 minutes to a bigger town," such as Lansing, Ann Arbor, or Kalamazoo, "and a very high percentage goes home every weekend and/or every other weekend."

Student Body

Typical Albion undergrads "strive to do well in classes, study hard, are involved in extracurricular activities, and still finds time to relax and enjoy themselves." Students here usually "take on many extracurricular responsibilities: clubs, campus groups, community-service organizations, athletic teams, intramural sports, and Greek life, to name a few of the possibilities. Everyone is here for academics first, however." One student observes, "We have high goals for ourselves and others. We are hardworking and motivated." Students are also "outgoing and friendly, for the most part." The majority here "are White, suburban, upper-middle-class, and mostly conservative. Most are incredibly sheltered too. It sometimes seems that a good number of students here have never stepped foot outside of suburbia."

FINANCIAL AID: 517-629-0440 • E-MAIL: ADMISSIONS@ALBION.EDU • WEBSITE: WWW.ALBION.EDU

ADMISSIONS

Very important factors considered include: Academic GPA, character/personal qualities, interview, level of applicant's interest, recommendation(s), rigor of secondary school record. *Important factors considered include:* Application essay, extracurricular activities, standardized test scores, talent/ability, volunteer work. *Other factors considered include:* Alumni/ae relation, class rank, geographical residence, racial/ethnic status, work experience. ACT with Writing component recommended. TOEFL required of all international applicants. High school diploma is required, and GED is accepted. *Academic units required:* 4 English, 3 math, 3 science (1 science lab), 3 social studies, 1 history. *Academic units recommended:* 4 English, 3 foreign language, 3 history, 3 math, 3 science, 3 social studies.

The Inside Word

Albion prides itself on fostering community, and this idea extends to the Admissions Office—the school looks for students who want to engage in and enhance the Albion experience. To that end, Admissions Officers carefully assess personal character; extracurriculars and volunteer work; essays; and a candidate's willingness to challenge him or herself intellectually. Interviews and visits to the campus are highly encouraged.

FINANCIAL AID

Students should submit: FAFSA. The Princeton Review suggests that all financial aid forms be submitted as soon as possible after January 1. *Need-based scholarships/grants offered:* Pell Grant, SEOG, state scholarships/grants, private scholarships, the school's own gift aid. *Loan aid offered:* FFEL Subsidized Stafford, FFEL Unsubsidized Stafford, FFEL PLUS, Federal Perkins Loan, state loans. Applicants will be notified of awards on a rolling basis beginning or about March 15.

FROM THE ADMISSIONS OFFICE

"Albion offers a purposeful blend of a classical foundation in the liberal arts with a strong emphasis on professional development through highly selective institutes in environmental science, public policy and service, professional management, premedical and health care studies, honors and education, world-class internships, and study abroad opportunities. *Yahoo! Internet Life* ranks Albion the 'Seventh Most Wired College in America' for integrating technology into academic, professional, and cocurricular programs; and a recent study conducted by the Council on Undergraduate Research ranked Albion among the top four colleges in the nation for the percentage of students engaged in original, funded undergraduate research. Albion is among the top 85 private, liberal arts colleges for the number of alumni who are corporate executives, including top executives and CEOs of *Newsweek*, the Lahey Clinic (MA), the Wharton School (University of Pennsylvania), PricewaterhouseCoopers, Dow Corning, Avon, the NCAA, and the Federal Accounting Standards Board (FASB). Albion's places over 95 percent of graduates into law, dental, and medical schools including Harvard, Michigan, Columbia, Northwestern, Notre Dame, Vanderbilt, and Wisconsin. A full-service equestrian center opens August 2004 for all students, including the IHSA equestrian team. Campus organizations include Model United Nations, Fellowship of Christian Athletes, Canoe Club, Black Student Alliance, Equestrian Club, Ecological Awareness Club and Greek life. Of particular note are Albion's athletics (Britons), often dominating Division III football, women's basketball and soccer, and men's and women's golf and swimming. Five varsity teams have recently earned the highest grade point average in the MIAA conference, NCAA Division III, or any division nationwide.

"Submission of SAT or ACT test scores are optional. Students with weighted GPA above a 3.85 need not submit scores. Homeschooled students, learning disabled, and students with a GPA less than 3.85 should contact the Admission Office."

SELECTIVITY
Admissions Rating	84
# of applicants	1,946
% of applicants accepted	82
% of acceptees attending	36

FRESHMAN PROFILE
Range SAT Critical Reading	520–645
Range SAT Math	540–670
Range ACT Composite	22–27
Minimum Paper TOEFL	550
Minimum Computer Based TOEFL	270
Average HS GPA	3.55
% graduated top 10% of class	30
% graduated top 25% of class	64
% graduated top 50% of class	90

DEADLINES
Regular application deadline	3/1
Regular notification	rolling
Nonfall registration?	yes

APPLICANTS ALSO LOOK AT
AND OFTEN PREFER
Grinnell College, University of Michigan—Ann Arbor
AND SOMETIMES PREFER
DePauw University, Hope College, Kalamazoo College, Kenyon College, Michigan State University
AND RARELY PREFER
Adrian College, Alma College, Calvin College, Olivet College

FINANCIAL FACTS
Financial Aid Rating	90
Annual tuition	$25,668
Room & Board	$7,496
Books and supplies	$700
Required fees	$454
% frosh rec. need-based scholarship or grant aid	60
% UG rec. need-based scholarship or grant aid	60
% frosh rec. need-based self-help aid	43
% UG rec. need-based self-help aid	46
% frosh rec. any financial aid	95
% UG rec. any financial aid	94

ALFRED UNIVERSITY

ALUMNI HALL, ONE SAXON DRIVE, ALFRED, NY 14802-1205 • ADMISSIONS: 607-871-2115 • FAX: 607-871-2198

CAMPUS LIFE

Quality of Life Rating	**84**
Fire Safety Rating	**60***
Type of school	private
Environment	rural

STUDENTS

Total undergrad enrollment	1,971
% male/female	51/49
% from out of state	35
% African American	6
% Asian	2
% Caucasian	76
% Hispanic	4
% international	2

SURVEY SAYS . . .
Small classes
Career services are great
Students are friendly
Campus feels safe
Frats and sororities are unpopular or nonexistent

ACADEMICS

Academic Rating	**82**
Calendar	semester
Student/faculty ratio	12:1
Profs interesting rating	82
Profs accessible rating	84
% profs teaching UG courses	100
% classes taught by TAs	0
Most common lab size	10–19 students
Most common reg class size	10–19 students

MOST POPULAR MAJORS
business administration/ management
ceramic sciences and engineering
fine/studio arts

STUDENTS SAY

Academics

Alfred University is "a small school with a big heart." The School of Engineering and the School of Art and Design receive state funding, resulting in reduced tuition for both New Yorkers and out-of-state students (although state residents receive a larger discount for the art school). Not surprisingly, Alfred is "known" for its "great financial aid." The School of Engineering is famous for its "very strong" glass and ceramics program (in fact, Alfred's one of the few schools in the nation offering a degree in ceramic engineering). Students are also drawn to the business and English departments. Alfred provides a cozy community that students, professors, and administrators enjoy. One student says, "There is excellent interaction between students and professors; and with small classes, the faculty can devote more time to each individual student." Alfred is the kind of place where "about half our professors, maybe more, want to go by first name." All agree that "professors know very much about what they are teaching" and "reach out to students," making them "very approachable." Another student reports, "Within a few months of being here, I had met the President of the university and the Chairman of the Board of Trustees. I am now on a first-name basis with the President and the Dean of Students. I babysit the Dean of Students' kids." No wonder students tell us that "the level of personal connection here, all across the board, is exceptional."

Life

Small-town life can be a rough go for college students, especially in the wintry landscape of upstate New York, but fortunately "Alfred provides desperately needed entertainment. The school seems to realize that its position in the world (an hour away from civilization) requires some extra effort as far as keeping the students from going stir-crazy, and they really pull through." The school "is really good about bringing different performers and movies into town every weekend," while "art shows, visiting lecturers in every division," and "over 100 clubs and activities" help round out the schedule. That said, there are some who wish that "outside businesses" could be "brought in" to give students something "to do off campus." But why go off campus when all you need is snow? "Traying, or stealing dining hall trays and riding them down the dangerously steep hill between upper and lower campus, is a perennial favorite. I've seen [people do it in the] nude, in subzero weather too," a student says. Another adds that though "Alfred is a small town . . . if you're not a boring person you won't be bored on campus." Students with cars remind us that "within [a] 30 to 60 minute [drive] . . . are most of the major entertainments you could want—movies, a mall or two, bowling, places to volunteer if you're so inclined, restaurants, and places to cut loose and dance."

Student Body

At Alfred University, students tell us, "The typical student is atypical. A lot of students are artsy and into alternative things. But there are a lot [of] sporty types too." Art does get a lot of mentions around campus. As one student explains, "AU is artistic, or at least appreciative of the arts." "Minorities and LGBT kids are well-represented on campus and in campus leadership positions," and "There's even peaceful coexisting with (neighboring) Alfred State. We rib them, and they probably rib us, but we have Alfred State kids in some of our extracurricular groups, and until I was told they weren't Alfred University kids, I would never have known the difference." All in all, "Diversity works so well on this campus" thanks to a population of "friendly" and "hardworking" students.

FINANCIAL AID: 607-871-2159 • E-MAIL: ADMWWW@ALFRED.EDU • WEBSITE: WWW.ALFRED.EDU

ADMISSIONS

Very important factors considered include: Character/personal qualities, class rank, extracurricular activities, recommendation(s), rigor of secondary school record. *Important factors considered include:* Application essay, standardized test scores, volunteer work, work experience. *Other factors considered include:* Interview, racial/ethnic status, talent/ability. SAT or ACT required; ACT with Writing component required. TOEFL required of all international applicants. High school diploma is required, and GED is accepted. *Academic units required:* 4 English, 2 math, 2 science (2 science labs), 2 social studies. *Academic units recommended:* 4 math, 3 science (3 science labs), 3 social studies.

The Inside Word

Alfred is renowned for its high quality of academics and its focus on the arts— yet the university's general lack of name recognition and relatively isolated campus has always affected both the applicant pool and number of admitted students who enroll, meaning that selectivity was relatively low for a school of its caliber. Now, thanks to Marlin Miller's $35 million donation given to support the school's visual and performing arts programs—one of the largest endowments ever given for arts education—expect Alfred's stature in the national academic community to grow exponentially.

FINANCIAL AID

Students should submit: FAFSA, institution's own financial aid form, state aid form, Noncustodial PROFILE, Business/Farm Supplement. The Princeton Review suggests that all financial aid forms be submitted as soon as possible after January 1. *Need-based scholarships/grants offered:* Pell Grant, SEOG, state scholarships/grants, private scholarships, the school's own gift aid. *Loan aid offered:* FFEL Subsidized Stafford, FFEL Unsubsidized Stafford, FFEL PLUS, Federal Perkins Loan, college/university loans from institutional funds, private alternative loans. Applicants will be notified of awards on a rolling basis beginning or about February 15. Federal Work-Study Program available. Institutional employment available. Off-campus job opportunities are poor.

FROM THE ADMISSIONS OFFICE

"The admissions process at Alfred University is the foundation for the personal attention that a student can expect from this institution. Each applicant is evaluated individually and can expect genuine, personal attention at Alfred University.

"Alfred University requires that freshman applicants for Fall 2008 submit scores from either the new SAT or the ACT (with Writing component)."

SELECTIVITY

Admissions Rating	74
# of applicants	2,243
% of applicants accepted	73
% of acceptees attending	31
# of early decision applicants	61
% accepted early decision	74

FRESHMAN PROFILE

Range SAT Critical Reading	500–610
Range SAT Math	500–610
Range ACT Composite	20–26
Minimum Paper TOEFL	550
Minimum Computer Based TOEFL	213
% graduated top 10% of class	15
% graduated top 25% of class	47
% graduated top 50% of class	84

DEADLINES

Early decision application deadline	12/1
Early decision notification	12/15
Regular notification	rolling
Nonfall registration?	yes

APPLICANTS ALSO LOOK AT

AND OFTEN PREFER
State University of New York at Geneseo

AND SOMETIMES PREFER
State University of New York—University at Buffalo, Syracuse University

FINANCIAL FACTS

Financial Aid Rating	92
Annual tuition	$21,250
Room & Board	$9,780
Required fees	$850
% frosh rec. need-based scholarship or grant aid	80
% UG rec. need-based scholarship or grant aid	80
% frosh rec. need-based self-help aid	72
% UG rec. need-based self-help aid	74
% frosh rec. any financial aid	92
% UG rec. any financial aid	90

ALLEGHENY COLLEGE

OFFICE OF ADMISSIONS, ALLEGHENY COLLEGE, MEADVILLE, PA 16335 • ADMISSIONS: 814-332-4351 • FAX: 814-337-0431

CAMPUS LIFE

Quality of Life Rating	74
Fire Safety Rating	64
Type of school	private
Affiliation	United Methodist
Environment	town

STUDENTS

Total undergrad enrollment	2,095
% male/female	46/54
% from out of state	36
% from public high school	84
% live on campus	78
% in (# of) fraternities	21 (5)
% in (# of) sororities	28 (4)
% African American	2
% Asian	3
% Caucasian	93
% Hispanic	1
% international	1
# of countries represented	31

SURVEY SAYS . . .

Small classes
Lab facilities are great
Athletic facilities are great
Career services are great
Students are friendly
Students are happy
Lots of beer drinking

ACADEMICS

Academic Rating	89
Calendar	semester
Student/faculty ratio	14:1
Profs interesting rating	91
Profs accessible rating	89
% profs teaching	
UG courses	100
% classes taught by TAs	0
Most common	
reg class size	10–19 students

MOST POPULAR MAJORS

biology/biological sciences
English language and literature
psychology

STUDENTS SAY

Academics

For students ready to hit the books hard, Allegheny College offers great rewards; one undergrad explains, "We have a huge workload here, with a lot of reading and a ton of writing. It really prepares you for graduate school and taking many upper-level courses at one time." The experience also benefits those looking to move directly into the business world after graduation because of its "great opportunities in experiential learning." As one student puts it, "Allegheny's strengths are its ample amounts of opportunity to excel both in and out of the classroom. The college provides numerous internship opportunities in addition to solid career services." Before they can reap the rewards of their degrees, though, Allegheny undergrads must complete a rigorous curriculum, one they praise for its "openness to individuality. It gave me the option of self-designing a major." Professors at Allegheny "are personally interested not only in you as a student, but in your personal well-being as well. You can't skip a class without a professor noticing and worrying about you, and you can be sure that they will go out of their way to help you whether or not you fall behind in class or are having a personal problem." Students say a larger school could not provide this kind of "professor–student connection." Administrators also integrate themselves wholly into the school community. One undergrad notes, "Students will greet the dean or president from across campus, and there is a great deal of interaction between administrators and students. No one is too important to make personal connections with students."

Life

A heavy workload keeps Allegheny students very busy during the week, so much so that, come the weekend, most look for a way "to relieve the stress caused by the demands of the school." Sometimes that involves drinking, sometimes not. Students report that "provisions by the school to crack down on off-campus parties in the past year have made social life pretty dull," making it harder—though certainly not impossible—to blow off some steam with a brew or four. Because of the new policy enforcement, "The greater portion of the campus community is more secluded from one another, with smaller groups of friends forming." This is especially true in the winter months, "when many students seem to hibernate," or hole up in the coffeehouse, "a hotspot for concerts, open mic nights, and general chillin.' " "The school's newly renovated and expanded campus center has also increased late-night programming." The campus is considerably more active "in the early fall and late spring months, during which campus-wide activities from sports to college-run activities become much more common." Hometown Meadville—which some describe as "a bit backward"—is a quiet, low- to middle-income town, some of whose locals "resent the students who pay all this money to go to school and drive around in nice cars and wear nice clothes," according to Allegheny undergrads. As a result, students "band together to fight boredom" and "head up to Erie to go shopping or to Port Erie's Bayfront district for nightlife." Pittsburgh is an occasional destination, "but only for concerts or other big events."

Student Body

"Everyone is involved in a variety of activities" at Allegheny, students report. "No one is just involved in religious life or just involved in Greek life. Therefore, it's not hard to fit in somewhere." One undergrad agrees: "We have athletes, sorority and fraternity members, very religious people, very artsy dreadlocked students, students heavily involved with the radio station and music department, etc. There are so many things to get involved in that it's hard to classify students." A common thread is that on this "politically opinionated campus, people can get pretty heated. Political and philosophical debates randomly occur." When not involved in a hot-button conversation, just about everyone "is studious to the point that it nags them during the week."

FINANCIAL AID: 800-835-7780 • E-MAIL: ADMISSIONS@ALLEGHENY.EDU • WEBSITE: WWW.ALLEGHENY.EDU

ADMISSIONS

Very important factors considered include: Academic GPA, class rank, rigor of secondary school record. *Important factors considered include:* Character/personal qualities, extracurricular activities, interview, recommendation(s), standardized test scores. *Other factors considered include:* Alumni/ae relation, application essay, first generation, geographical residence, level of applicant's interest, racial/ethnic status, talent/ability, volunteer work, work experience. SAT or ACT required; TOEFL required of all international applicants. High school diploma is required, and GED is accepted. *Academic units required:* 4 English, 3 math, 3 science, 2 foreign language, 3 social studies, 1 academic elective.

The Inside Word

Academic promise plays a large role in the admissions process at Allegheny. The college looks for students who go beyond their high school's minimum requirements, particularly those who dabble in honors and Advanced Placement courses. Admissions Officers are known for their individualized approach—while standardized test scores and class rank factor significantly in their decisions, consideration is also given to personal character and extracurricular activities.

FINANCIAL AID

Students should submit: FAFSA. The Princeton Review suggests that all financial aid forms be submitted as soon as possible after January 1. *Need-based scholarships/grants offered:* Pell Grant, SEOG, Academic Competitiveness Grant, National SMART Grant, state scholarships/grants, private scholarships, the school's own gift aid, Veterans Educational Benefits. *Loan aid offered:* FFEL Subsidized Stafford, FFEL Unsubsidized Stafford, FFEL PLUS, Federal Perkins Loan, private loans from commercial lenders. Applicants will be notified of awards on a rolling basis beginning or about March 1.

FROM THE ADMISSIONS OFFICE

"We're proud of Allegheny's beautiful campus and cutting-edge technologies,. and we know that our professors are leading scholars who pride themselves even more on being among the best teachers in the United States. Yet it's our students who make Allegheny the unique and special place that it is.

"Allegheny attracts students with unusual combinations of interests, skills, and talents. How do we characterize them? Although it's impossible to label our students, they do share some common characteristics. You'll find an abiding passion for learning and life, a spirit of camaraderie, and shared inquiry that spans across individuals as well as areas of study. You'll see over and over again such a variety of interests and passions and skills that, after a while, those unusual combinations don't seem so unusual at all.

"Allegheny is not for everybody. If you find labels reassuring, if you're looking for a narrow technical training, if you're in search of the shortest distance between point A and point B, then perhaps another college will be better for you.

"But, if you recognize that everything you experience between points A and B will make you appreciate point B that much more; if you've noticed that when life gives you a choice between two things, you're tempted to answer both or simply yes; if you start to get excited because you sense there is a college willing to echo the resounding *yes*, then we look forward to meeting you.

"Applicants for Fall 2008 are required to take either the new SAT or ACT (the new ACT Writing section is recommended but not required). If both tests are taken, we will use the better score of the two. The Writing score of both the SAT and ACT will be reviewed but will not be a major factor in admission decisions."

SELECTIVITY

Admissions Rating	90
# of applicants	3,668
% of applicants accepted	63
% of acceptees attending	25
# accepting a place on wait list	292
% admitted from wait list	5
# of early decision applicants	93
% accepted early decision	80

FRESHMAN PROFILE

Range SAT Critical Reading	550–660
Range SAT Math	560–650
Range ACT Composite	23–28
Minimum Paper TOEFL	550
Minimum Computer Based TOEFL	213
Average HS GPA	3.76
% graduated top 10% of class	41
% graduated top 25% of class	75
% graduated top 50% of class	98

DEADLINES

Early decision application deadline	11/15
Early decision notification	12/15
Regular application deadline	2/15
Regular notification	4/1
Nonfall registration?	yes

APPLICANTS ALSO LOOK AT

AND OFTEN PREFER
Bucknell University, Carnegie Mellon University, Kenyon College, University of Rochester

AND SOMETIMES PREFER
Denison University, Dickinson College, Gettysburg College, State University of New York at Geneseo, The College of Wooster

AND RARELY PREFER
Duquesne University, Miami University, Pennsylvania State University—World Campus, University of Pittsburgh—Pittsburgh Campus, Washington & Jefferson College

FINANCIAL FACTS

Financial Aid Rating	86
Annual tuition	$29,680
Room & Board	$7,500
Required fees	$320
% frosh rec. need-based scholarship or grant aid	70
% UG rec. need-based scholarship or grant aid	67
% frosh rec. need-based self-help aid	61
% UG rec. need-based self-help aid	57
% frosh rec. any financial aid	98
% UG rec. any financial aid	98

AMERICAN UNIVERSITY

4400 MASSACHUSETTS AVENUE, NORTHWEST, WASHINGTON, DC 20016-8001 • ADMISSIONS: 202-885-6000 • FAX: 202-885-1025

STUDENTS SAY
Academics
American University in Washington, DC boasts a "rigorous" and "very challenging" academic experience that offers students all the benefits of its location close to the political center of the country. The School of Public Affairs is nationally renowned, and "The international studies program is one of the best in the world." There's a "strong business school" too. "Aside from its location," "The best thing about American University is its ability to offer the course catalog of a midsized university while maintaining the feel of a small liberal arts college." "Small classes" ensure that "discussion flows freely." "Extremely accessible" professors "love to teach" and "look forward to speaking with students and helping them in their academic careers." It's not uncommon for an AU faculty member to "have real-world experience with a major corporation, government agency, or international organization." The "amazing" Career Center helps students to find "good jobs" and brings big-time recruiters to campus. "Volunteering with a nonprofit organization" is also a common student activity. Though the AU campus is "completely wireless," "a few buildings are in need of repair," and many students think that the library could use some improvement. "The science facilities don't need any TLC," but only because "No one is using them," one student says.

Life
"The best thing about AU is if you want to do it, it's here for you; if not, it won't bother you." A club exists "for just about every type of person you can think of." Parties "are big on the weekends, but they don't dominate campus life," and "The nightlife on and off campus is always active." AU is located "a little ways outside of the downtown area," but virtually everything is "just a short Metro ride away." "There's so much to do for fun in DC, it's stunning," asserts a sophomore. "Midnight trips to the national monuments" are popular, as are "touring the Smithsonian Museums for free, sampling ethnic food in Adams Morgan, and visiting trendy coffee shops" near Dupont Circle. Attending "protests" is big, too, if that's your bag. Back on campus, AU provides a plethora of speakers. Recent invitees have included Bob Dole, John Kerry, and "former presidents of several countries." Of course, because of the school's location, politics "infect the campus": "Watching CNN" and "working on the Hill" are everyday activities for many students. "Social justice and community-service groups" are also "very popular." "This school lives, breathes, eats, and sleeps politics," explains one student. "When William Rehnquist died, I was at a fraternity party, and when we heard about it over half the party left to go watch the news."

Student Body
American is not really a place for the "college-y college experience," asserts one undergrad, though "It can be if that's what you want." "The atypical student is the norm": The "passionate" and highly "eclectic" student population here runs the gamut from "hippies to hard-core young Republicans." There are "pretty-boy frat guys looking for their next keg to conquer" and "political enthusiasts who love to debate the hottest issues." There are "bookish students" and "pseudo-serious intellectuals." You'll find students of every socioeconomic level and "a good number of minorities." One student says that "for every person who pops his collar, there is someone with blue hair." AU boasts a throng of international students, "a large gay population," and lots of women: "Our female/male ratio is 60/40. I would not complain if we had more guys on campus," laments a frustrated female. Not surprisingly, the biggest differences among students involve politics. "There is a huge amount of contention between the liberals and conservatives on campus," observes a sophomore. "The conservatives walk around like high and mighty warriors of truth, and the liberals walk around like they're saving the world from the conservatives."

FINANCIAL AID: 202-885-6100 • E-MAIL: AFA@AMERICAN.EDU • WEBSITE: WWW.AMERICAN.EDU

ADMISSIONS

Very important factors considered include: Rigor of secondary school record, standardized test scores. *Important factors considered include:* Academic GPA, application essay, class rank, extracurricular activities, recommendation(s), volunteer work. *Other factors considered include:* Alumni/ae relation, character/personal qualities, first generation, geographical residence, interview, level of applicant's interest, racial/ethnic status, talent/ability, work experience. SAT or ACT required; SAT Subject Tests recommended; ACT with Writing component required. TOEFL required of all international applicants. High school diploma is required, and GED is accepted. *Academic units required:* 4 English, 3 math, 2 science (2 science labs), 2 foreign language, 2 social studies, 3 academic electives. *Academic units recommended:* 4 English, 4 math, 4 science, 3 foreign language, 4 social studies, 4 academic electives.

The Inside Word

While DC is a popular locale for undergrads, it also has its fair share of top-notch universities. For that reason, American must compete for students with a number of area schools, so its admissions stats are relatively relaxed for applicants who have strong academic records. Nonetheless, American is a solid option, especially for those interested in government and international relations. Candidates with leadership experience are particularly appealing to Admissions Officers at AU.

FINANCIAL AID

Students should submit: FAFSA, institution's own financial aid form. Regular filing deadline is February 15. The Princeton Review suggests that all financial aid forms be submitted as soon as possible after January 1. *Need-based scholarships/grants offered:* Pell Grant, SEOG, state scholarships/grants, private scholarships, the school's own gift aid. Academic merit scholarships: Presidential Scholarships, Dean's Scholarships, Leadership Scholarships, Phi Theta Kappa Scholarships (transfers only), Tuition Exchange Scholarships, United Methodist Scholarships, and other private/restricted scholarships are awarded by the Undergraduate Admissions Office. Most scholarships do not require a separate application and are renewable for up to 3 years if certain criteria are met. *Loan aid offered:* Direct Subsidized Stafford, Direct Unsubsidized Stafford, Direct PLUS, FFEL PLUS, Federal Perkins Loan, college/university loans from institutional funds. Applicants will be notified of awards on or about April 1.

FROM THE ADMISSIONS OFFICE

"Ideas, action, and service—at AU, you interact regularly with decision makers and leaders in every profession and corner of the globe. You'll be academically challenged in a rich multicultural environment. Our expert teaching faculty provide a strong liberal arts education, characterized by small classes, the use of cutting-edge technology, and an interdisciplinary curriculum in the arts, education, humanities, social sciences, and sciences. Not just a political town, Washington, DC offers a variety of research, internship, and community-service opportunities in every field. Our AU Abroad Program, with over 80 international locations, lets you expand your studies into international settings. The Princeton Review selected AU for the 2005 edition of *America's Best Value Colleges*. AU was one of 77 schools, and the only one from DC, selected as a 'best value' for its combination of outstanding academics, moderate tuition, and financial aid packages.

"AU requires all applicants graduating from high school in, or after, 2006 to take the new SAT or the ACT with the Writing section. Fall 2008 applicants are allowed to submit scores from the old versions of both tests as their best scores will be used in making admissions decisions."

SELECTIVITY

Admissions Rating	92
# of applicants	13,583
% of applicants accepted	51
% of acceptees attending	18
# of early decision applicants	417
% accepted early decision	57

FRESHMAN PROFILE

Range SAT Critical Reading	600–690
Range SAT Math	580–670
Range ACT Composite	26–30
Minimum Paper TOEFL	590
Minimum Computer Based TOEFL	213
% graduated top 10% of class	47
% graduated top 25% of class	82
% graduated top 50% of class	98

DEADLINES

Early decision application deadline	11/15
Early decision notification	12/31
Regular application deadline	1/15
Regular notification	4/1
Nonfall registration?	yes

APPLICANTS ALSO LOOK AT

AND OFTEN PREFER
Boston College, Boston University, Georgetown University, New York University, Syracuse University, The George Washington University

AND SOMETIMES PREFER
University of California—Santa Barbara, University of Delaware, University of Southern California, University of Virginia, Villanova University

AND RARELY PREFER
Fordham University, George Mason University, Northeastern University, Rutgers, The State University of New Jersey—New Brunswick, The Catholic University of America, University of Massachusetts—Amherst

FINANCIAL FACTS

Financial Aid Rating	82
Annual tuition	$29,206
Room & Board	$11,570
Books and supplies	$600
Required fees	$467
% frosh rec. need-based scholarship or grant aid	39
% UG rec. need-based scholarship or grant aid	5
% frosh rec. need-based self-help aid	45
% UG rec. need-based self-help aid	6
% frosh rec. any financial aid	82
% UG rec. any financial aid	69

AMHERST COLLEGE

CAMPUS BOX 2231, PO BOX 5000, AMHERST, MA 01002 • ADMISSIONS: 413-542-2328 • FAX: 413-542-2040

CAMPUS LIFE

Quality of Life Rating	**97**
Fire Safety Rating	**60***
Type of school	private
Environment	town

STUDENTS

Total undergrad enrollment	1,612
% male/female	52/48
% from out of state	87
% from public high school	59
% live on campus	97
% African American	9
% Asian	13
% Caucasian	45
% Hispanic	6
% international	7
# of countries represented	39

SURVEY SAYS . . .

No one cheats
School is well run
Campus feels safe
Students are happy

ACADEMICS

Academic Rating	**97**
Calendar	semester
Student/faculty ratio	8:1
Profs interesting rating	98
Profs accessible rating	95
% profs teaching UG courses	100
% classes taught by TAs	0
Most common lab size	10–19 students
Most common reg class size	10–19 students

MOST POPULAR MAJORS
economics
English language and literature
political science and government

STUDENTS SAY

Academics

At Amherst College, a small, elite liberal arts school in western Massachusetts, "The academic experience is well balanced, comprehensive, and tailored to the desires and needs of each individual student." Students truly get exactly what they want because "There are no core requirements. Every person in every class . . . is enthusiastic about the subject and wants to learn." Students love this set-up, telling us that "the open curriculum guarantees that every student in every class really wants to be there, which makes a huge difference in the liveliness of discussion." Academics "are extremely challenging without being overly burdensome," in part because support networks are so strong. Students "really develop personal relationships with professors, which makes classes that much more enjoyable." Students also appreciate that they "get all the things [they] need and want (services, advice, etc.) when [they] need and want them." As one student puts it, "Amherst College is a small family. Everyone here wants you to succeed; however, it's up to you to reach out for that guidance. If you knock, Amherst shall respond." Professors "all have a great sense of humor" and "are engaging and eclectic." As one student writes, "Even in introductory courses, professors literally bounce off the walls with enthusiasm for the subject." The results tell the story: Nearly three-quarters of all Amherst alumni proceed to postgraduate study within 5 years of graduation.

Life

"Life is usually busy" at Amherst, where "People are generally pretty involved." Academics are demanding, but fortunately "Everyone is here for the same reason: to learn. We learn as much from each other as we do in the classroom because everyone is just so different and has a story to tell. I stay up till the wee hours of the morning with some of my dorm-mates sharing stories and ordering Antonio's Pizza." When they're not working, students "are often playing sports" or "engaging in some other activity." Undergrads "love the academic culture of the Five Colleges area. You can go to music performances, plays, or poetry readings any night of the week." As one student reports, "Events are happening all the time, and there is always something going on . . . concerts, talks about Brazilian economics, West African dance shows, etc. Life here is comfortable and exciting." A "free bus to get to other colleges and towns" makes it easy to access these events, even without a car. It's not only about personal enrichment here, though; while students "work hard throughout the week," they "party on Thursday and Saturday." Why not on Friday? "Because nearly one-third of the student body [are] athletes, parties are often thrown by various teams, but open to all. As a result, Friday nights are pretty dead, since all the athletes are resting up for their games."

Student Body

"It seems like there are many of your typical White, private school students from the New England area" at Amherst, but "Then there are [also] students from all over the United States and from other countries who are so diverse." Most of these "typically well-rounded and motivated" undergraduates "played some sort of sport in high school, and a very large percentage play club or varsity sports at college." These students are "witty, friendly, thoughtful, non-competitive, self-effacing, and know how to have a good time."

While some tell us, "You could call a lot of the kids preppy," others insist that the "conception of Amherst as preppy [is there], but it's wrong." Nearly everyone agrees that "Amherst is amazing because of its small size. It's a really close-knit community where everyone is extremely open-minded and considerate." According to another student, "I love that [Amherst's] students are politically aware and serious students but also willing to have a good time. The first thing that struck me about my school is how nice everyone is. The school has a reputation for being stuck-up, but I have not experienced that in the least."

FINANCIAL AID: 413-542-2296 • E-MAIL: ADMISSION@AMHERST.EDU • WEBSITE: WWW.AMHERST.EDU

ADMISSIONS

Very important factors considered include: Academic GPA, application essay, character/personal qualities, extracurricular activities, first generation, recommendation(s), rigor of secondary school record, standardized test scores, talent/ability. *Important factors considered include:* Alumni/ae relation, class rank, volunteer work. *Other factors considered include:* Geographical residence, state residency, work experience. SAT and SAT Subject Tests or ACT required; ACT with Writing component recommended. TOEFL required of all international applicants. High school diploma or equivalent is not required. *Academic units recommended:* 4 English, 4 math, 3 science (1 science lab), 4 foreign language, 2 social studies, 2 history.

The Inside Word

A $1 billion endowment allows Amherst to provide admitted students with generous financial aid packages. The school is deeply committed to economic diversity in the student body, increasing the number of working-class and low-income students in the Class of 2010 from 15 percent to 20 percent (*New York Times*, September 19, 2006). The school is also considering scaling back, or even doing away with, early decision admissions, which are believed to favor upper-income students.

FINANCIAL AID

Students should submit: FAFSA, CSS/Financial Aid PROFILE, Noncustodial PROFILE, Business/Farm Supplement, income documentation (Federal Income Tax Return, W-2s). The Princeton Review suggests that all financial aid forms be submitted as soon as possible after January 1. *Need-based scholarships/grants offered:* Pell Grant, SEOG, state scholarships/grants, private scholarships, the school's own gift aid. *Loan aid offered:* Direct Subsidized Stafford, Direct Unsubsidized Stafford, Direct PLUS, Federal Perkins Loan, college/university loans from institutional funds. Applicants will be notified of awards on or about April 1. Federal Work-Study Program available. Institutional employment available. Off-campus job opportunities are good.

FROM THE ADMISSIONS OFFICE

"Amherst College looks, above all, for men and women of intellectual promise who have demonstrated qualities of mind and character that will enable them to take full advantage of the college's curriculum. . . . Admission decisions aim to select from among the many qualified applicants those possessing the intellectual talent, mental discipline, and imagination that will allow them most fully to benefit from the curriculum and contribute to the life of the college and of society. Whatever the form of academic experience—lecture course, seminar, conference, studio, laboratory, independent study at various levels—intellectual competence and awareness of problems and methods are the goals of the Amherst program, rather than the direct preparation for a profession.

"Applicants must submit scores from the new SAT plus two SAT Subject Tests, or the old SAT plus three SAT Subject Tests. Students may substitute the ACT with the Writing component (as of Spring 2005) or without Writing if the test was taken prior to Spring 2005."

SELECTIVITY

Admissions Rating	99
# of applicants	6,284
% of applicants accepted	19
% of acceptees attending	37
# accepting a place on wait list	506
of early decision applicants	364
% accepted early decision	35

FRESHMAN PROFILE

Range SAT Critical Reading	670–780
Range SAT Math	680–780
Range ACT Composite	29–33
Minimum Paper TOEFL	600
Minimum Computer Based TOEFL	250
% graduated top 10% of class	80
% graduated top 25% of class	95
% graduated top 50% of class	100

DEADLINES

Early decision application deadline	11/15
Early decision notification	12/15
Regular application deadline	1/1
Regular notification	4/5
Nonfall registration?	no

APPLICANTS ALSO LOOK AT

AND OFTEN PREFER
Harvard College, Princeton University, Yale University

AND SOMETIMES PREFER
Brown University, Dartmouth College, Stanford University, Williams College

AND RARELY PREFER
Tufts University, University of Virginia, Vassar College

FINANCIAL FACTS

Financial Aid Rating	92
Annual tuition	$34,280
Room & Board	$9,080
Books and supplies	$1,000
Required fees	$636
% frosh rec. need-based scholarship or grant aid	46
% UG rec. need-based scholarship or grant aid	46
% frosh rec. need-based self-help aid	48
% UG rec. need-based self-help aid	45
% frosh rec. any financial aid	47
% UG rec. any financial aid	48

ARIZONA STATE UNIVERSITY

PO Box 870112, Tempe, AZ 85287-0112 • Admissions: 480-965-7788 • Fax: 480-965-3610

CAMPUS LIFE
Quality of Life Rating	71
Fire Safety Rating	83
Type of school	public
Environment	city

STUDENTS
Total undergrad enrollment	38,984
% male/female	51/49
% from out of state	25
% live on campus	17
% in (# of) fraternities	7 (31)
% in (# of) sororities	8 (20)
% African American	4
% Asian	5
% Caucasian	69
% Hispanic	13
% Native American	2
% international	3
# of countries represented	114

SURVEY SAYS . . .
Great computer facilities
Great library
Athletic facilities are great
Great off-campus food
Student publications are popular
Lots of beer drinking
Hard liquor is popular
(Almost) everyone smokes

ACADEMICS
Academic Rating	69
Calendar	semester
Student/faculty ratio	23:1
Profs interesting rating	62
Profs accessible rating	69
% profs teaching UG courses	70
Most common lab size	20–29 students
Most common reg class size	10–19 students

MOST POPULAR MAJORS
business administration/
management
journalism
psychology

STUDENTS SAY
Academics
"Perfect weather, cheaper tuition," and "a great academic environment," bring many students to Arizona State University. With over 38,000 undergraduates on campus, any description of ASU has to begin with its sheer size. As one student sums up, "Arizona State University is an enormous institution," and that means "Variety is inevitable." There are over 100 majors to choose from in more than 20 colleges and schools, so students have access to "tons of resources, and you can study whatever you want." Variety also comes in the form of teacher quality; "Some professors are fantastic, others are ridiculous—it's luck of the draw." That said, students generally agree that "professors are always available and willing to listen, as long as students make the effort to meet with them." Getting one-on-one time with professors isn't the only sphere where a little student initiative goes a long way. The secret to overall success at ASU seems to be "tak[ing] charge of your own education." Because of the school's size, administrators have to "run ASU like a business," which means "Some of the personal touch is lost." But if students "feel like just a number [when dealing with the bureaucracy] at the university level," at the college/school level, administrators "are very easy to meet." When it comes to gripes, many students list the fact that "academic advisors are not very helpful" at the very top.

Life
Students note that "the administration is doing [its] all to diminish the party school image ASU has been known for," although many are skeptical of the success of these efforts. One student echoes the feelings of many of his fellow undergraduates when he states, "Partying is a big part of the ASU experience." Intercollegiate sporting events are "very popular with students," and while only a small minority of students joins frats and sororities, the Greek scene on campus is very visible and "active." But parties aren't all ASU has to offer. There is also "excellent nightlife in the valley," including Mill Avenue, with its movie theaters and "easy access to bars, shopping, and eating places"; College Avenue, offering "many campus stores and more food options"; and Old Town Scottsdale, "which also has shopping, clubs, [and] fine dining." "Friendly, diverse, and inexpensive . . . Tempe is a great place to go to college," but it can be "difficult to go places off campus if you don't have a car." Perhaps one of the nicest benefits of ASU's Tempe location is that "most of the school year it is pool weather."

Student Body
It's "Barbie and Ken go to college" at ASU. Simply put, ASU is "a school overflowing with beautiful people." The campus' numerous "California types" are "concerned with material things," but are "normally very friendly" and "basically good-hearted." Students say they value "fashion and the virtue of exercising," and they "like to party." While many students are "not religious," there is a "mutual respect of individuals among everyone." Sprinkled amongst these bronzed gods and goddesses are a "lot of international students, and the usual mix of people who live like monks," as well as a few "students over the age of 30." Yet even if there's consensus on what the typical ASU student is like, it's worth stating the obvious: "This campus is so big [that] if you can't find someone to fit in with here, you're not going to anywhere." However you categorize them, most of ASU's students are "open-minded and polite." "Racial, ethnic, and sexual orientation [are] not taboo subject[s] here."

FINANCIAL AID: 480-965-3355 • E-MAIL: ASKASU@ASU.EDU • WEBSITE: WWW.ASU.EDU

ADMISSIONS

Very important factors considered include: Academic GPA, class rank, standardized test scores. *Important factors considered include:* State residency. SAT or ACT required; ACT with Writing component recommended. TOEFL required of all international applicants. High school diploma is required, and GED is accepted. *Academic units required:* 4 English, 4 math, 3 science (3 science labs), 2 foreign language, 1 social studies, 1 history, 1 fine arts.

The Inside Word

Numbers count for a lot at ASU. You have excellent odds of acceptance if you meet the minimum curriculum, GPA, and standardized test requirements. These minimums are slightly higher for out-of-state students. Additionally, three of the undergraduate colleges at ASU (business, engineering, and journalism and mass communications) have additional admission requirements; we suggest visiting ASU's website to find out what they are. ASU awards a great many merit-based scholarships. To be eligible for many of them, you must be an Arizona resident and apply for admission to the school by December 1.

FINANCIAL AID

Students should submit: FAFSA. The Princeton Review suggests that all financial aid forms be submitted as soon as possible after January 1. *Need-based scholarships/grants offered:* Pell Grant, SEOG, state scholarships/grants, private scholarships, the school's own gift aid, Federal Nursing Scholarship. *Loan aid offered:* Direct Subsidized Stafford, Direct Unsubsidized Stafford, Direct PLUS, FFEL PLUS, Federal Perkins Loan. Federal Work-Study Program available. Institutional employment available. Off-campus job opportunities are good.

FROM THE ADMISSIONS OFFICE

"ASU is a place where students from all 50 states and abroad come together to live and study in one of the nation's premier collegiate environments. Situated in metropolitan Phoenix, ASU boasts a physical setting and climate second to none. ASU offers more than 250 academic programs of study leading to the BS and BA in 19 undergraduate colleges and schools. Many of these programs have received national recognition for their quality of teaching, innovative curricula, and outstanding facilities. Barrett, the Honors College at Arizona State University, the only honors college in the Southwest that spans all academic disciplines, provides unique and challenging experiences for its students and was recently named as one of three honors colleges that offer "an Ivy League–style education minus the sticker shock" by Reader's Digest.

"In addition to ASU's Tempe campus, ASU offers comprehensive undergraduate and graduate programs at campuses throughout the metropolitan Phoenix area: the Polytechnic campus in the East Valley, the West campus in northwest Phoenix, and the Downtown Phoenix campus.

"ASU does not require the submission of either ACT of SAT scores in order to be reviewed for undergraduate admission, however, test scores are needed for merit scholarship consideration and class placement. Presently, the essay portions of either exam are not required in order to be admitted."

SELECTIVITY

Admissions Rating	**78**
# of applicants	20,702
% of applicants accepted	92
% of acceptees attending	41

FRESHMAN PROFILE

Range SAT Critical Reading	480–600
Range SAT Math	490–620
Range ACT Composite	20–26
Minimum Paper TOEFL	500
Minimum Computer Based TOEFL	173
Average HS GPA	3.3
% graduated top 10% of class	28
% graduated top 25% of class	55
% graduated top 50% of class	83

DEADLINES

Nonfall registration?	yes

FINANCIAL FACTS

Financial Aid Rating	**73**
Annual in-state tuition	$4,591
Annual out-of-state tuition	$15,750
Room & Board	$6,900
Books and supplies	$950
Required fees	$97
% frosh rec. need-based scholarship or grant aid	35
% UG rec. need-based scholarship or grant aid	34
% frosh rec. need-based self-help aid	20
% UG rec. need-based self-help aid	29
% frosh rec. any financial aid	73
% UG rec. any financial aid	65

AUBURN UNIVERSITY

202 MARY MARTIN HALL, AUBURN, AL 36849-5149 • ADMISSIONS: 334-844-4080 • FAX: 334-844-6179

STUDENTS SAY
Academics

Auburn University, a school that "is about family, traditions, and education," is the sort of place that inspires "a strong sense of pride in the past and future of [the school]." In fact, Auburn's "traditions and sense of family continue even after graduation." These traditions are numerous, beloved, and often involve football. The education isn't half bad here, either; Auburn numbers among its many academic assets "a good business school, one of the best vet schools, and one of the best architecture schools in the nation." The school also excels in engineering, education, and communications. Students enrolled in Auburn's honors program enjoy "priority registration [and] smaller classes" that are almost always taught by professors—not TAs. Speaking of Auburn's professors, students appreciate that they are "readily available," "super friendly," and "always willing to help no matter what size the class." They are "concerned with each student's progress," and "always willing to work with [students] to teach the curriculum and how it applies to [their] life." Academically, "As with any school, you get out of it what you put into it. You can put in the bare minimum and be happy with your C, or you can go to class every day, study hard, and make an A. No one here is going to baby you. You won't get reminders not to miss class, and teachers won't hunt you down for make-ups."

Life

Auburn is "an ideal college town" with "enough bars and such to keep one occupied but small enough to where there is a definite sense of community." The town also offers "movies, bowling, a park," and the attractions of Birmingham, which "isn't that far away." Auburn might not be a good fit for the sort of big-city types who "lament about how few options we have for entertainment, and how food consists [solely] of pizza, chicken tenders (on every corner), and subs," but everyone else seems to love it. They also love that the campus is "beautiful" and "life is slow paced—full of sweet tea and Southern food." Be warned, though: Auburn "is a drinking town with a football problem." "Football seems to dominate the Fall semester here. It's a huge deal, and it's when most big parties and events [take place]. If you hate football, this might not be the place for you." In the off-season, students take advantage of Auburn's "very popular" outdoor activities, and when they want to head off-campus, nearby Atlanta is a "great stop for city life and entertainment."

Student Body

Auburn students share "an incredible sense of pride" that "most who have never been here will never comprehend. Ask any Auburn student or alumn[us], and they'll generally tell you that Auburn ranks among God, country, family, and the South as things most beloved." Many students "love how Auburn is deeply Republican when most colleges are quite banal in their liberalism," and "prides itself in not being politically correct, and this is not due to ignorance." Not everyone at this large university fits this description—"At a school this large, there are people from all walks of life"—but a significant number of students do, and they set the tone for the campus. While "slightly conservative," Southern," "White, Protestant" students may dominate the student body here, there are also "Black, Asian, and also a lot of foreign exchange students [at Auburn]." Whatever their background, Auburn students across the board "are very open-minded, and accept everyone for who they are."

AUBURN UNIVERSITY

FINANCIAL AID: 334-844-4367 • E-MAIL: ADMISSIONS@AUBURN.EDU • WEBSITE: WWW.AUBURN.EDU

ADMISSIONS

Very important factors considered include: Academic GPA, rigor of secondary school record, standardized test scores. *Important factors considered include:* State residency. *Other factors considered include:* Alumni/ae relation, application essay, class rank, extracurricular activities, first generation, geographical residence, level of applicant's interest, racial/ethnic status, recommendation(s), talent/ability, volunteer work. SAT or ACT required; TOEFL required of all international applicants. High school diploma is required, and GED is accepted. *Academic units required:* 4 English, 3 math, 2 science, 3 social studies. *Academic units recommended:* 4 English, 3 math, 3 science, 1 foreign language, 4 social studies.

The Inside Word

Auburn Admissions Officers crunch the numbers, sorting students according to high school GPA and standardized test scores, then offering admission to all who qualify from the top of the list on down. The school also looks at "fit" and the student's potential to make contributions to the Auburn community, but with an 80 percent admit rate, it's safe to say that these factors only come into play for marginal candidates, and then only to mitigate poor grades or test scores.

FINANCIAL AID

Students should submit: FAFSA, institution's own financial aid form. The Princeton Review suggests that all financial aid forms be submitted as soon as possible after January 1. *Need-based scholarships/grants offered:* Pell Grant, SEOG, state scholarships/grants, private scholarships, the school's own gift aid. *Loan aid offered:* FFEL Subsidized Stafford, FFEL Unsubsidized Stafford, FFEL PLUS, Federal Perkins Loan, college/university loans from institutional funds. Off-campus job opportunities are good.

FROM THE ADMISSIONS OFFICE

"Auburn University is a comprehensive land-grant university serving Alabama and the nation. The university is especially charged with the responsibility of enhancing the economic, social, and cultural development of the state through its instruction, research, and extension programs. In all of these programs, the university is committed to the pursuit of excellence. The university assumes an obligation to provide an environment of learning in which the individual and society are enriched by the discovery, preservation, transmission, and application of knowledge; in which students grow intellectually as they study and do research under the guidance of competent faculty, and in which the faculty develop professionally and contribute fully to the intellectual life of the institution, community, and state. This obligation unites Auburn University's continuing commitment to its land-grant traditions and the institution's role as a dynamic and complex, comprehensive university.

"Applicants for Fall 2008 must submit scores from the SAT or ACT (with or without the Writing components from either test)."

SELECTIVITY
Admissions Rating	**86**
# of applicants	15,919
% of applicants accepted	72
% of acceptees attending	35

FRESHMAN PROFILE
Range SAT Critical Reading	500–600
Range SAT Math	520–630
Range ACT Composite	22–27
Minimum Paper TOEFL	550
Minimum Computer Based TOEFL	213
Average HS GPA	3.56
% graduated top 10% of class	36
% graduated top 25% of class	59
% graduated top 50% of class	87

DEADLINES
Regular application deadline	8/1
Regular notification	10/1
Nonfall registration?	yes

APPLICANTS ALSO LOOK AT AND SOMETIMES PREFER
Clemson University, Georgia Institute of Technology, Louisiana State University, The University of Alabama at Tuscaloosa, University of Florida, University of Georgia, University of Mississippi, The University of Tennessee at Knoxville

FINANCIAL FACTS
Financial Aid Rating	**61**
Annual in-state tuition	$5,240
Annual out-of-state tuition	$15,240
Room & Board	$7,564
Books and supplies	$1,100
Required fees	$256
% frosh rec. need-based scholarship or grant aid	20
% UG rec. need-based scholarship or grant aid	20
% frosh rec. need-based self-help aid	22
% UG rec. need-based self-help aid	28
% frosh rec. any financial aid	55
% UG rec. any financial aid	56

AUSTIN COLLEGE

900 NORTH GRAND AVENUE, SUITE 6N, SHERMAN, TX 75090-4400 • ADMISSIONS: 903-813-3000 • FAX: 903-813-3198

CAMPUS LIFE
Quality of Life Rating	78
Fire Safety Rating	68
Type of school	private
Affiliation	Presbyterian
Environment	town

STUDENTS
Total undergrad enrollment	1,313
% male/female	46/54
% from out of state	7
% from public high school	86
% live on campus	70
% in (# of) fraternities	24 (7)
% in (# of) sororities	29 (7)
% African American	3
% Asian	13
% Caucasian	74
% Hispanic	8
% Native American	1
% international	1
# of countries represented	25

SURVEY SAYS . . .
Small classes
Students are friendly
Campus feels safe
Students are happy
Lots of beer drinking

ACADEMICS
Academic Rating	84
Calendar	4-1-4
Student/faculty ratio	12:1
Profs interesting rating	87
Profs accessible rating	94
% profs teaching UG courses	100
% classes taught by TAs	0
Most common lab size	fewer than 10 students
Most common reg class size	10–19 students

MOST POPULAR MAJORS
biology/biological sciences
business administration/
management
psychology

STUDENTS SAY
Academics
Whether they are biochemists-in-training or budding musicians, "challenging" is the word most undergraduates use to describe the academics at Austin College. Among all of the demanding disciplines at this small liberal arts school in way-north Texas, the premed curriculum has a rep for being especially so. (Nearly 10 percent of this school's graduates attend medical school after graduation.) The work here may be tough, but "Class sizes are small, the teachers are extremely well qualified (no TAs), and people really care about you as a person." When push comes to shove in the academic arena, the "Academic Skills Center is an excellent resource, and other students will often volunteer their assistance on school matters." Alternatively, students can seek help from their professors, who "are more like really wise friends" than aloof academics. Students can stop by during office hours or wait until they're invited over for a meal, which, students tell us, happens from time to time. Other unique attributes of an AC education include an Academic Integrity Policy that students pledge to follow before classes begin. Fans like it because they "don't have to worry about other students cheating. As a matter of fact, my teachers sometimes leave the room after handing out quizzes with no reaction from the class." As far as the administration goes, "Oscar Page (the school's president, affectionately known as 'O Page') is the most down-to-earth guy ever; he's often in the cafeteria eating with students."

Life
"We go to Starbucks and Wal-Mart a lot because there's not much to do in Sherman." According to students, "Sherman is a boring city with little shopping, no fine dining, and no outdoor parks worth exploring." To make things worse, "There is no night life." This does not mean, however, that the resourceful students at AC do not find ways to divert themselves from their studies when they need a little R&R. They mainly line up for two kinds of fun: The kind offered by the Greeks, which usually means partying, and the kind offered by groups like Christian Intervarsity, which usually means something a little more wholesome. On the one hand, "Greek parties are fun and a popular weekend activity. Ninety-nine percent of them are open to the entire student body." On the other, activities sponsored by Intervarsity include "box-sledding [down a snow-covered hill], Ultimate Frisbee, video scavenger hunts, and community service projects." In addition, a "local dance hall, Calhoun's; local parties; free movies on campus; art exhibitions; choral and music recitals; guest musicians every Thursday; varsity athletic events to watch; or intramural games to compete in" round out the busy scene on campus. Fun further afield can be found in Dallas, an hour-and-a-half drive away, or at "the lake campus [recreational property owned by the college] out at Lake Texoma." Be mindful that "a car is required to get anywhere, because nothing useful is within walking distance of the school."

Student Body
The typical undergraduate at AC is often "one who started off premed but ended up doing something else." He or she is "open-minded, casual, cares about the community around them, works hard for [his or her] grades, and is overly involved in school organizations and committees." "Many are religious." Contrary to what such devoutness might suggest, AC undergrads mainly feel that "for a Texas school, it is very liberal." "There are not that many students who are from states other than Texas and Oklahoma," and while "Most students here are White and middle-class," minorities are in no way excluded. Indian students are well-represented, as "The Indian Cultural Association is the largest group on campus, made up of more than Indian students, followed by the Muslim Students Association, and then by Los Amigos and Black Expressions."

FINANCIAL AID: 903-813-2900 • E-MAIL: ADMISSION@AUSTINCOLLEGE.EDU • WEBSITE: WWW.AUSTINCOLLEGE.EDU

ADMISSIONS

Very important factors considered include: Academic GPA, rigor of secondary school record. *Important factors considered include:* Application essay, character/personal qualities, class rank, extracurricular activities, recommendation(s), standardized test scores, talent/ability. *Other factors considered include:* Alumni/ae relation, first generation, geographical residence, interview, racial/ethnic status, religious affiliation/commitment, state residency, volunteer work, work experience. SAT or ACT required; ACT with Writing component required. TOEFL required of all international applicants. High school diploma is required, and GED is accepted. *Academic units required:* 4 English, 3 math, 3 science (2 science labs), 2 foreign language, 2 social studies, 1 academic elective, 1 fine art. *Academic units recommended:* 4 English, 4 math, 4 science (3 science labs), 3 foreign language, 3 social studies, 2 fine art.

The Inside Word

Candidates hoping for an acceptance letter from Austin should keep a rigorous academic schedule. The college covets students who challenge themselves and Admissions Officers are prone to prefer students who have slightly lower GPAs but have proven themselves in difficult courses. Of course, applicants are more than just statistics and counselors are also looking for caring, committed students who want to contribute to the Austin community. An interview is strongly encouraged.

FINANCIAL AID

Students should submit: FAFSA, institution's own financial aid form. The Princeton Review suggests that all financial aid forms be submitted as soon as possible after January 1. *Need-based scholarships/grants offered:* Pell Grant, SEOG, state scholarships/grants, private scholarships, the school's own gift aid. *Loan aid offered:* FFEL Subsidized Stafford, FFEL Unsubsidized Stafford, FFEL PLUS, Federal Perkins Loan, state loans, college/university loans from institutional funds, alternative loans through various sources. Applicants will be notified of awards on a rolling basis beginning or about March 1. Federal Work-Study Program available. Institutional employment available. Off-campus job opportunities are good.

FROM THE ADMISSIONS OFFICE

"Students visiting Austin College immediately sense something different about the campus community. People look you in the eye. They call you by name. They want to see you succeed.

"That success comes from a strong academic foundation in the liberal arts and sciences, plus added opportunities like international study, January Term, and close involvement with committed faculty who become your partners in learning.

"The comments on these pages from students make it clear that there is no 'typical' student at Austin College. Students can retain their individuality and still fit in. Our students value and respect differences of background, style, and belief. Campus organizations offer activities for all interests.

"Austin College prepares you to do more than make a living. It prepares you to make a difference in the place you work, in the community you call home, in the friends you make, and in the way you live. Service to others is an important part of campus life.

"Visit and discover Austin College's legacy of learning, leadership, and lasting values for yourself.

"Applicants for Fall 2008 must submit Writing scores from the new SAT or ACT."

SELECTIVITY

Admissions Rating	86
# of applicants	1,385
% of applicants accepted	76
% of acceptees attending	32
# accepting a place on wait list	15
% admitted from wait list	67
# of early decision applicants	51
% accepted early decision	59

FRESHMAN PROFILE

Range SAT Critical Reading	560–670
Range SAT Math	580–670
Range ACT Composite	23–28
Minimum Paper TOEFL	550
Minimum Computer Based TOEFL	213
% graduated top 10% of class	48
% graduated top 25% of class	78
% graduated top 50% of class	97

DEADLINES

Early decision application deadline	12/1
Early decision notification	1/10
Regular application deadline	5/1
Regular notification	4/1; space-available basis thereafter
Nonfall registration?	yes

APPLICANTS ALSO LOOK AT

AND OFTEN PREFER
Southwestern University, Trinity University

AND SOMETIMES PREFER
Baylor University, Rice University, Southern Methodist University, Texas A&M University—College Station, Texas Christian University, The University of Texas at Austin

AND RARELY PREFER
Hendrix College, University of Dallas

FINANCIAL FACTS

Financial Aid Rating	97
Annual tuition	$24,760
Room & Board	$8,234
Books and supplies	$1,000
Required fees	$160
% frosh rec. need-based scholarship or grant aid	56
% UG rec. need-based scholarship or grant aid	57
% frosh rec. need-based self-help aid	44
% UG rec. need-based self-help aid	45
% frosh rec. any financial aid	95
% UG rec. any financial aid	96

BABSON COLLEGE

LUTHER UNDERGRADUATE ADMISSION CENTER, BABSON PARK, MA 02457 • ADMISSIONS: 781-239-5522 • FAX: 781-239-4135

CAMPUS LIFE

Quality of Life Rating	82
Fire Safety Rating	80
Type of school	private
Environment	village

STUDENTS

Total undergrad enrollment	1,776
% male/female	61/39
% from out of state	70
% live on campus	81
% in (# of) fraternities	10 (4)
% in (# of) sororities	12 (3)
% African American	3
% Asian	10
% Caucasian	43
% Hispanic	7
% international	17
# of countries represented	60

SURVEY SAYS . . .

Small classes
Great computer facilities
Great library
Career services are great
Diverse student types on campus
Campus feels safe
Lots of beer drinking
Hard liquor is popular

ACADEMICS

Academic Rating	90
Calendar	semester
Student/faculty ratio	14:1
Profs interesting rating	87
Profs accessible rating	87
% profs teaching	
UG courses	100
% classes taught by TAs	0
Most common	
reg class size	20–29 students

MOST POPULAR MAJORS

accounting
entrepreneurial and small business
operations
finance

STUDENTS SAY

Academics

If you already know anything about Babson, you probably know that at this small school in the suburbs of Boston, "everything is related to business. So if you don't like business, you should not even think about coming here." Indeed, Babson has one of the best known and most respected undergraduate business programs in the country. It begins with the Foundations of Management and Entrepreneurship (FME) freshman year, during which students work in groups to conceive and launch a (hopefully) profitable small business. This segues into the sophomore year in which students participate in an integrated experience that includes instruction in core business disciplines like accounting, marketing, and finance, among others. By nearly all accounts the curriculum is extremely challenging, and the severe grade curve based on an average of 2.7 comes as a shock to some. But most students feel that although "the homework tends to be a lot compared to most of my friends at other business schools . . . we receive a better education." In large part that's because "Many of the professors have started or still run very successful companies," and they share their invaluable "industry experience" in the classroom. At least business professors do. "The liberal arts teachers vary a lot more in quality." By and large, the administration receives average marks, but most students don't focus on any administrative shortcomings. "At the end of the day, if you want to be a successful entrepreneur or business person, Babson is the best place for you."

Life

The "business boot camp" that is Babson is not known for its social life. During the week, "People are consumed by work, and are constantly concentrating on their future. On the weekends people socialize a lot because they need a break from the stress of the week." The student body splinters into distinct factions when it's time to unwind: "American kids typically party on campus more often, the athletes will party together, frats do their thing, and the international rich kids go in town and are scarce on the weekends since they live at the clubs in Boston." Some undergrads cross-pollinate groups, of course, but these are generally where the lines are drawn. Students who choose to party on campus, however, are well aware that "the campus police [referred to locally as 'Babo'] and Office of Campus Life take a strong stance against parties and alcohol" and that Babo is quite adept at breaking up unauthorized get-togethers. School-sanctioned on-campus activities include "'Knight Parties' on one Saturday night during each month (a club-like atmosphere with a DJ, dancing, and lots of free food and drinks, and beer for 21-year-olds)." Additionally, "The on-campus pub is fun and a common hangout for upperclassmen." For those who feel the lure of Boston, a car definitely makes getting there easier, but "The school also offers a bus that runs into Boston on the weekends for students."

Student Body

At this small business school where "Professionalism is a part of your grade," a "typical student is pretty well off, dressed well no matter what their style is, and pretty intelligent on business and similar subjects." Given its business focus, some students speculate that "Babson is probably the only school in Massachusetts where Republicans are in the majority." Noticeable cliques include the BISOs (Babson International Students), the athletes, and the Greeks, but regardless of the groups students fall into, nearly all of them "constantly think about the next great business idea, internship, or great job at firms like Lehman Brothers, KPMG, Ernst & Young, etc." It should come as no surprise, then, that "we are short on hippies, punks, and extreme liberals. If you fall into those categories, people will still accept you, but eventually you'll probably want to strangle the rest of us and will transfer." No matter what you start out as, the consensus seems to be that 4 years of "Babson will transform you from a driven/motivated individual into a lethal business machine."

FINANCIAL AID: 781-239-4219 • E-MAIL: UGRADADMISSION@BABSON.EDU • WEBSITE: WWW.BABSON.EDU

ADMISSIONS

Very important factors considered include: Academic GPA, application essay, character/personal qualities, recommendation(s), rigor of secondary school record, standardized test scores. *Important factors considered include:* Class rank, extracurricular activities. *Other factors considered include:* Alumni/ae relation, first generation, geographical residence, interview, level of applicant's interest, racial/ethnic status, state residency, talent/ability, volunteer work, work experience. SAT or ACT required; SAT and SAT Subject Tests or ACT recommended; ACT with Writing component required. TOEFL required of all international applicants. High school diploma is required, and GED is accepted. *Academic units recommended:* 4 English, 4 math, 4 science (3 science labs), 4 foreign language, 2 social studies, 2 history, 1 precalculus.

The Inside Word

Though Babson offers a unique educational opportunity, their admissions practices are as traditional as they come. Personal qualities and extracurricular activities are taken into consideration, but the best way to impress a Babson Admissions Officer is through strong academic performance. Both scholastic rigor and the demonstration of intellectual curiosity are extremely important. Additionally, applicants will want to focus on their essay—writing ability is viewed as vital at Babson.

FINANCIAL AID

Students should submit: FAFSA, CSS/Financial Aid PROFILE, Noncustodial PROFILE, Business/Farm Supplement, Federal Income Tax Returns, W-2s, and Verification Worksheet. Regular filing deadline is February 15. The Princeton Review suggests that all financial aid forms be submitted as soon as possible after January 1. *Need-based scholarships/grants offered:* Pell Grant, SEOG, state scholarships/grants, the school's own gift aid. *Loan aid offered:* FFEL Subsidized Stafford, FFEL Unsubsidized Stafford, FFEL PLUS, Federal Perkins Loan, state loans. Applicants will be notified of awards on or about April 1.

FROM THE ADMISSIONS OFFICE

"In addition to theoretical knowledge, Babson College is dedicated to providing its students with hands-on business experience. The Foundations of Management and Entrepreneurship (FME) and Management Consulting Field Experience (MCFE) are two prime examples of this commitment. During the FME, all freshmen are placed into groups of 30 and actually create their own businesses that they operate until the end of the academic year. The profits of each FME business are then donated to the charity of each group's choice.

"MCFE offers upperclassmen the unique and exciting opportunity to work as actual consultants for private companies and/or nonprofit organizations in small groups of three to five. Students receive academic credit for their work as well as invaluable experience in the field of consulting. FME and MCFE are just two of the ways Babson strives to produce business leaders with both theoretical knowledge and practical experience.

"Babson College requires freshmen applicants to submit scores from either the new SAT or the ACT with Writing component. The school recommends that students also submit results from SAT Subject Tests."

SELECTIVITY

Admissions Rating	93
# of applicants	3,436
% of applicants accepted	37
% of acceptees attending	35
# accepting a place on wait list	190
% admitted from wait list	35
# of early decision applicants	236
% accepted early decision	51

FRESHMAN PROFILE

Range SAT Critical Reading	530–630
Range SAT Math	600–640
Range SAT Writing	560–640
Range ACT Composite	25–29
Minimum Paper TOEFL	600
Minimum Computer Based TOEFL	250
% graduated top 10% of class	47
% graduated top 25% of class	87
% graduated top 50% of class	99

DEADLINES

Early decision application deadline	11/15
Early decision notification	12/15
Regular application deadline	1/15
Regular notification	4/1
Nonfall registration?	no

FINANCIAL FACTS

Financial Aid Rating	87
Annual tuition	$34,112
Room & Board	$11,670
% frosh rec. need-based scholarship or grant aid	37
% UG rec. need-based scholarship or grant aid	40
% frosh rec. need-based self-help aid	31
% UG rec. need-based self-help aid	39
% frosh rec. any financial aid	40
% UG rec. any financial aid	44

BARD COLLEGE

OFFICE OF ADMISSIONS, ANNANDALE-ON-HUDSON, NY 12504 • ADMISSIONS: 845-758-7472 • FAX: 845-758-5208

STUDENTS SAY

Academics

Bard College, a small school that excels in the liberal and fine arts, takes a "progressive approach" to academics, allowing students "the opportunity to control your own education and learn more than you would at most other academic institutions." It doesn't make for a walk in the park, though; students claim that the workload can get heavy, "But if you're passionate about your classes, as most people here are, time often goes quickly as you study. This is not the place for anyone who is not intellectually motivated." A "relaxed, pressure-free environment" makes Bard "a great place to learn" and takes some of the stress out of the hard work, as do the "great professors, who are passionate about the subjects they teach and have often just written a book about the material in a class they are currently teaching." Bard doesn't do as much hand-holding as do comparable liberal arts schools; here "The academics rely heavily on the motivation of the individual student," although "Once you begin coming up with your own special projects and supplementing the required reading, professors bend over backward to help you." The relaxed atmosphere does have its downside, though; students claim that "things are extremely disorganized, and you can easily find yourself being told five different things from five different people."

Life

"People are really involved, both inside and outside of the classroom" at Bard, where "There is a really active club life. We have everything from the International Student Organization to the Surrealist Training Circus and the Children's Expressive Arts Project. There are always dance, theater, music, and art events every weekend," and "The shows are really popular, both those that are student-run and those put on by professionals." Bard undergrads also indulge in "a lot of after-hours discussion about what we're all doing in classes. My friends and I talk about experiments, theories, literature, and various artistic/scientific installations." The Bard campus "is gorgeous, so some people take advantage of amazing hiking and outdoor sports. Other people enjoy Blithewood, a hill that overlooks the Catskills, in a more passive fashion, sunbathing or lounging with friends." Students tell us that they "always feel safe here, even walking in the middle of the night." Bard's party scene is primarily confined to weekends; one student explains, "People party a lot on the weekends but during the week everyone seems to be working." The quaint towns that surround Bard appeal to some, but many prefer "the 2-hour train ride to New York City. It's convenient when you have nothing else to do on the weekend."

Student Body

"Hippies, hipsters, and geek chic" are common sights on the Bard campus, as are "people who have that 'I'm on the cutting edge of underground fashion' look." However, while Bard might appear to be "all about tight designer jeans, indie rock, and everything else NYC or LA," the reality is "There are really a lot of normal college kids here—people seem to think everyone here was a social outcast in high school, but most people here are friendly, social, and pretty normal (although certainly a bit cerebral)." Undergrads tend to be "politically conscious and left-wing-activist types." One student notes, "If you're uncreative or conservative you probably wouldn't fit in. Other than that, just about anything works." Another agrees, "A large percentage of people are extremely talented and creative and express themselves best through creative writing, music, art, dance, or theater." In short, Bard is about "a lot of kids being different together."

BARD COLLEGE

ADMISSIONS

Very important factors considered include: Academic GPA, application essay, character/personal qualities, extracurricular activities, recommendation(s), rigor of secondary school record, talent/ability. *Important factors considered include:* Volunteer work, work experience. *Other factors considered include:* Alumni/ae relation, class rank, first generation, geographical residence, interview, level of applicant's interest, racial/ethnic status, religious affiliation/commitment, standardized test scores, state residency. TOEFL required of all international applicants. High school diploma is required, and GED is accepted. *Academic units recommended:* 4 English, 4 math, 4 science (3 science labs), 4 foreign language, 4 social studies, 4 history.

The Inside Word

Because Bard boasts healthy application numbers, it is in a position to concentrate on matchmaking. To that end, Admissions Officers seek students with independent and inquisitive spirits. Applicants who exhibit academic ambition while extending their intellectual curiosity beyond the realm of the classroom are particularly appealing. Successful candidates typically have several honors and Advanced Placement courses on their transcripts, as well as strong letters of recommendation and well-written personal statements.

FINANCIAL AID

Students should submit: FAFSA, CSS/Financial Aid PROFILE, state aid form, Business/Farm Supplement. Regular filing deadline is February 15. The Princeton Review suggests that all financial aid forms be submitted as soon as possible after January 1. *Need-based scholarships/grants offered:* Pell Grant, SEOG, state scholarships/grants, private scholarships, the school's own gift aid. *Loan aid offered:* FFEL Subsidized Stafford, FFEL Unsubsidized Stafford, FFEL PLUS, Federal Perkins Loan, college loans from institutional funds (for international students only). Applicants will be notified of awards on or about April 1.

FROM THE ADMISSIONS OFFICE

"An alliance with Rockefeller University, the renowned graduate scientific research institution, gives Bardians access to Rockefeller's professors and laboratories and to places in Rockefeller's Summer Research Fellows Program. Almost all our math and science graduates pursue graduate or professional studies; 90 percent of our applicants to medical and health professional schools are accepted.

"The Globalization and International Affairs (BGIA) Program is a residential program in the heart of New York City that offers undergraduates a unique opportunity to undertake specialized study with leading practitioners and scholars in international affairs and to gain internship experience with international-affairs organizations. Topics in the curriculum include human rights, international economics, global environmental issues, international justice, managing international risk, and writing on international affairs, among others. Internships/tutorials are tailored to students' particular fields of study.

"Student dormitory and classroom facilities are in Bard Hall, 410 West Fifty-eighth Street, a newly renovated 11-story building near the Lincoln Center District in New York City.

"Bard College does not require SAT scores, new or old, to be submitted for admissions consideration. Students may choose to submit scores, and, if submitted, we will consider them in the context of the overall application."

SELECTIVITY

Admissions Rating	95
# of applicants	4,828
% of applicants accepted	29
% of acceptees attending	36
# accepting a place on wait list	263
% admitted from wait list	4

FRESHMAN PROFILE

Range SAT Math	640–690
Range SAT Writing	680–740
Minimum Paper TOEFL	600
Minimum Computer Based TOEFL	250
Average HS GPA	3.5
% graduated top 10% of class	59
% graduated top 25% of class	85
% graduated top 50% of class	99

DEADLINES

Regular application deadline	1/15
Regular notification	4/1
Nonfall registration?	no

APPLICANTS ALSO LOOK AT

AND OFTEN PREFER
Amherst College, Brown University, Harvard College, Yale University

AND SOMETIMES PREFER
Boston University, New York University, Oberlin College, Reed College, Vassar College

AND RARELY PREFER
Hampshire College, Ithaca College, Macalester College, Sarah Lawrence College, Skidmore College

FINANCIAL FACTS

Financial Aid Rating	87
Annual tuition	$34,080
Room & Board	$9,850
Books and supplies	$750
Required fees	$702
% frosh rec. need-based scholarship or grant aid	60
% UG rec. need-based scholarship or grant aid	57
% frosh rec. need-based self-help aid	54
% UG rec. need-based self-help aid	52
% frosh rec. any financial aid	70
% UG rec. any financial aid	67

BARNARD COLLEGE

3009 BROADWAY, NEW YORK, NY 10027 • ADMISSIONS: 212-854-2014 • FAX: 212-854-6220

STUDENTS SAY

Academics

Barnard College, the all-women liberal arts school associated with Columbia University, "offers students the best of both worlds: The seclusion and intimacy of a small liberal arts college within a tremendous research university and one of the greatest cities in the world." Women here explain that "because Barnard students have complete cross registration privileges at Columbia, full access to all of its resources and libraries, and upon graduation receive a degree from the university, we enjoy the full benefits of an Ivy League education, without the punishment of having to take Columbia's core curriculum, pass a swim test, or eat at the lousy Columbia dining room." Students here also get more of a small-college experience than do their Columbia peers; one student explains, "While the Columbia professors can be arrogant and pompous, most of the Barnard professors are really nice, down-to-earth people." Administrators are "unequivocally dedicated to finding rapid, individualized solutions to students' problems." Because the school is in New York City, "There are amazing opportunities here; the city really is our learning lab!" In short, "Barnard is really great as a small school to act as your home base. From here, you can explore the university and the city as much as you want. You have to take the initiative, but if you do, you can find a way to do anything you want. And Barnard is so supportive, you'll be able to find someone on campus who's willing to help."

Life

"Life at school is dominated by studies." Undergraduates agree that "most students here spend at least 60 percent of their week on schoolwork." Still, to the degree allowed by their academic workload, "Most undergraduates make a conscious effort to take advantage of NYC through internships, nightlife, museums, and exhibits. Many of us love to just spend an afternoon walking down Broadway and shopping." The campus is a magnet for high-powered speakers and prestigious events; one student reports, "There are always rallies or lectures going on that are highly attended. In the past year, Janeane Garofalo, John Edwards, Anna Quindlen, and Alice Walker have spoken on campus, to name a few." Barnard is located in Morningside Heights, "a neighborhood that thrives very much on the college community." Students here miss out a bit on the classic college experience, but they don't mind; one undergrad explains, "Barnard feels that, since we are in the city, they don't need to create a community for us. Therefore, occasionally I feel like I'm just living in the city and taking classes. It's definitely worth it, though, and my friends and I make our own college touch!" Women here also warn that "Barnard's facilities could use drastic remodeling. With the exception of a few recently renovated lecture spaces, the classrooms are in need of major technological and aesthetic updates. New resident halls need to be built because many of the existing buildings are too old."

Student Body

Barnard, like its hometown, is a magnet for the idiosyncratic. One student explains, "New York is a place that allows people to be anyone they want to be. You can wear a zebra-striped bikini in the middle of winter on a snow-covered street here and people would hardly look twice . . . because we go to school in such an eclectic place, I don't think it's possible to describe a 'typical' Barnard student." Some here try all the same; they tell us that Barnard students are "driven, intelligent, cosmopolitan young women who come from every corner of the country and throughout the world, from different socioeconomic backgrounds, and varying life experiences." Because of a dual degree program with the Jewish Theological Seminary, "there are many Orthodox Jews here" who "typically socialize only with other Orthodox Jews." There's also a large, less insular Asian population. There are "many feminists and lesbians, too, but fewer than one might expect."

FINANCIAL AID: 212-854-2154 • E-MAIL: ADMISSIONS@BARNARD.EDU • WEBSITE: WWW.BARNARD.EDU

ADMISSIONS

Very important factors considered include: Academic GPA, application essay, character/personal qualities, extracurricular activities, recommendation(s), rigor of secondary school record. *Important factors considered include:* Class rank, standardized test scores, talent/ability, volunteer work. *Other factors considered include:* Alumni/ae relation, first generation, geographical residence, interview, level of applicant's interest, racial/ethnic status, work experience. SAT and SAT Subject Tests or ACT required; ACT with Writing component required. TOEFL required of all international applicants. High school diploma or equivalent is not required. *Academic units recommended:* 4 English, 3 math, 3 science (2 science labs), 3 foreign language, 3 history.

The Inside Word

As at many top colleges, early decision applications have increased at Barnard—although the admissions standards are virtually the same as for their regular admissions cycle. The college's Admissions Staff is open and accessible, which is not always the case at highly selective colleges with as long and impressive a tradition of excellence. The Admissions Committee's expectations are high, but their attitude reflects a true interest in who you are and what's on your mind. Students have a much better experience throughout the admissions process when treated with sincerity and respect—perhaps this is why Barnard continues to attract and enroll some of the best students in the country.

FINANCIAL AID

Students should submit: FAFSA, CSS/Financial Aid PROFILE, Noncustodial PROFILE, institution's own financial aid form, state aid form, Business/Farm Supplement, parent's individual, corporate, and/or partnership federal income tax returns. Regular filing deadline is February 1. The Princeton Review suggests that all financial aid forms be submitted as soon as possible after January 1. *Need-based scholarships/grants offered:* Pell Grant, SEOG, state scholarships/grants, private scholarships, the school's own gift aid. *Loan aid offered:* FFEL Subsidized Stafford, FFEL Unsubsidized Stafford, FFEL PLUS, Federal Perkins Loan, state loans, college/university loans from institutional funds. Applicants will be notified of awards on or about March 31.

FROM THE ADMISSIONS OFFICE

"Barnard College is a small, distinguished liberal arts college for women that is affiliated with Columbia University and located in the heart of New York City. The college enrolls women from all over the United States, Puerto Rico, and the Caribbean. More than 30 countries, including France, England, Hong Kong, and Greece, are also represented in the student body. Students pursue their academic studies in over 40 majors and are able to cross register at Columbia University.

"Applicants for the Fall 2008 entering class must submit scores from the SAT Reasoning Test and two SAT Subject Tests of their choice, or the ACT with the Writing component."

SELECTIVITY

Admissions Rating	**98**
# of applicants	4,599
% of applicants accepted	26
% of acceptees attending	47
# accepting a place on wait list	547
% admitted from wait list	13
# of early decision applicants	456
% accepted early decision	38

FRESHMAN PROFILE

Range SAT Critical Reading	640–740
Range SAT Math	640–710
Range SAT Writing	640–740
Range ACT Composite	29–31
Minimum Paper TOEFL	600
Minimum Computer Based TOEFL	250
Average HS GPA	3.91
% graduated top 10% of class	84
% graduated top 25% of class	96
% graduated top 50% of class	100

DEADLINES

Early decision application deadline	11/15
Early decision notification	12/15
Regular application deadline	1/1
Regular notification	4/1
Nonfall registration?	no

APPLICANTS ALSO LOOK AT

AND OFTEN PREFER
Brown University, Columbia University, Harvard College, University of Pennsylvania, Yale University

AND SOMETIMES PREFER
Princeton, Stanford, The University of Chicago, Wellesley College, Wesleyan University

AND RARELY PREFER
University of California—Berkley, Bryn Mawr, Cornell, Vassar

FINANCIAL FACTS

Financial Aid Rating	**94**
Annual tuition	$31,714
Room & Board	$11,392
Books and supplies	$1,080
Required fees	$1,364
% frosh rec. need-based scholarship or grant aid	45
% UG rec. need-based scholarship or grant aid	41
% frosh rec. need-based self-help aid	47
% UG rec. need-based self-help aid	43
% frosh rec. any financial aid	47
% UG rec. any financial aid	43

BATES COLLEGE

23 CAMPUS AVENUE, LINDHOLM HOUSE, LEWISTON, ME 04240 • ADMISSIONS: 207-786-6000 • FAX: 207-786-6025

STUDENTS SAY

Academics

Those seeking "a high-paced rigorous academic college with a low-key, laid-back, and fun student body and campus life" should consider Maine's Bates College, a small liberal arts school that "focuses on students becoming critically and creatively thinking citizens of the world" through first-year seminars, mandatory senior theses, and a range of departmental, interdisciplinary, and student-designed majors. Undergrads report that departments in economics, biology, chemistry, religion, philosophy, and English are all "very good," with academics that "are challenging indeed, but not to the point where they interfere with all the other enjoyable aspects of life here." Professors are exemplars of exclusive, small-school pedagogy; they "are always willing to chat about classes, internship possibilities, future jobs, graduate school, further readings to be done and just about life." This is because "Teaching is their main priority, and as a result, they have an invested interest in their students that facilitates meaningful and personal relationships." Another student adds, "The feeling of community fostered at Bates is unparalleled. The students are truly welcoming, and the professors seem to really enjoy their jobs. The administration really gives the students a say in what happens at their college."

Life

"You can really develop into a complete person at Bates through involvement in athletics, community service, and supportive relationships with faculty and staff. At Bates you don't have to choose between activities; you can do it all if you decide that is what you want." Another undergrad adds, "I can't think of a single person who isn't busy 24 hours a day but by choice. People fill up their lives with things that are important to them, whether it be academics, sports, student government, political activism, outdoor activities, or clubs. Many people can't choose just one." "Student organizations are easy to become involved in here. For instance, anyone, regardless of experience or major, may try out for a play, and most likely will land a part." Students also love outdoor activities, especially "skiing at Sunday River in the winter," but also "varsity or club sports, which even those who aren't quite athletic enjoy. Bates really emphasizes an overall health of mind and body." Parties "are quite common on the weekends, especially in the wood-frame houses that serve as one housing option." While "There isn't much to do in the Lewiston-Auburn area," that hardly matters because "Bates does an excellent job of providing entertainment on the weekends for students." As one undergrad puts it, "Students rarely leave campus for the weekends; no one wants to leave because there is so much going on here!" When students feel they just have to get away, "Bates pays for buses to nearby cities like Freeport, Portland, and Boston."

Student Body

Far from big-city pressures, Bates students can afford the luxury of being "laid-back and willing to take time to chat with friends over coffee, read the newspaper, go to plays, become engaged in the community, and be active politically. Students value not only the academic experience they are offered at Bates, but take advantage of other [facets] of learning." The student body includes "a lot of pseudo-hippies who cruise around campus pedaling their junkyard bikes with their Birkenstocked feet while toting their Nalgenes, who then spend their holidays in palatial mansions," and also has its share of "New Englander Ralph Lauren–wearing preppies." One student explains, "Bates combines hippies with Cape Cod kids, athletes with intellectuals. Everyone is a dork in his or her own way, and everyone's passionate about something ridiculous, and totally unpredictable." Students speculate that "Bates has one of the more vocal gay/bisexual populations out there," and proudly report that "straight students (even those who might come in with some prejudices in this regard) interact with them freely and openly. This is one instance where one really sees Bates overcoming prejudice."

FINANCIAL AID: 207-786-6096 • E-MAIL: ADMISSIONS@BATES.EDU • WEBSITE: WWW.BATES.EDU

ADMISSIONS

Very important factors considered include: Academic GPA, application essay, character/personal qualities, class rank, extracurricular activities, interview, level of applicant's interest, recommendation(s), rigor of secondary school record, talent/ability. *Other factors considered include:* Alumni/ae relation, first generation, geographical residence, racial/ethnic status, standardized test scores, state residency, volunteer work, work experience. TOEFL required of all international applicants. High school diploma is required, and GED is not accepted. *Academic units required:* 4 English, 3 math, 3 science (2 science labs), 2 foreign language, 3 social studies. *Academic units recommended:* 4 English, 4 math, 4 science (3 science labs), 4 foreign language, 4 social studies.

The Inside Word

While holding its applicants to lofty standards, Bates strives to adopt a personal approach to the admissions process. Officers favor qualitative information and focus more on academic rigor, essays, and recommendations than GPA and test scores. They seek students who look for challenges and take advantage of opportunities in the classroom and beyond. Interviews are strongly encouraged—candidates who opt out may place themselves at a disadvantage.

FINANCIAL AID

Students should submit: FAFSA, CSS/Financial Aid PROFILE, Noncustodial PROFILE, Business/Farm Supplement. Regular filing deadline is February 1. The Princeton Review suggests that all financial aid forms be submitted as soon as possible after January 1. *Need-based scholarships/grants offered:* Pell Grant, SEOG, state scholarships/grants, private scholarships, the school's own gift aid. *Loan aid offered:* FFEL Subsidized Stafford, FFEL Unsubsidized Stafford, FFEL PLUS, Federal Perkins Loan, state loans. Applicants will be notified of awards on or about April 1. Federal Work-Study Program available. Institutional employment available. Off-campus job opportunities are good.

FROM THE ADMISSIONS OFFICE

"Bates College is widely recognized as one of the finest liberal arts colleges in the nation. The curriculum and faculty challenge students to develop the essential skills of critical assessment, analysis, expression, aesthetic sensibility, and independent thought. Founded by abolitionists in 1855, Bates graduates have always included men and women from diverse ethnic and religious backgrounds. Bates highly values its study abroad programs, unique calendar (4-4-1), and the many opportunities available for one-on-one collaboration with faculty through seminars, research, service-learning, and the capstone experience of senior thesis.

"Co-curricular life at Bates is rich; most students participate in club or varsity sports; many participate in performing arts; and almost all students participate in one of more than 100 student-run clubs and organizations. More than two-thirds of alumni enroll in graduate study within 10 years.

"The Bates College Admissions Staff reads applications very carefully; the high school record and the quality of writing are of particular importance. Applicants are strongly encouraged to have a personal interview, either on campus or with an alumni representative. Students who choose not to interview may place themselves at a disadvantage in the selection process. Bates offers tours, interviews and information sessions throughout the summer and fall. Drop-ins are welcome for tours and information sessions. Please call ahead to schedule an interview.

"At Bates, the submission of standardized testing (the SAT, SAT Subject Tests, and the ACT) is not required for admission. After two decades of optional testing, our research shows no differences in academic performance and graduation rates between submitters and nonsubmitters."

SELECTIVITY
Admissions Rating	96
# of applicants	4,305
% of applicants accepted	32
% of acceptees attending	36

FRESHMAN PROFILE
Range SAT Critical Reading	630–700
Range SAT Math	640–700
Minimum Paper TOEFL	200
% graduated top 10% of class	62
% graduated top 25% of class	92
% graduated top 50% of class	100

DEADLINES
Early decision application deadline	11/15
Early decision notification	12/20
Regular application deadline	1/1
Regular notification	3/31
Nonfall registration?	yes

APPLICANTS ALSO LOOK AT
AND OFTEN PREFER
Amherst College, Dartmouth College, Middlebury College
AND SOMETIMES PREFER
Bowdoin College, Brown University, Colby College
AND RARELY PREFER
Connecticut College, Hamilton College, Trinity College (CT)

FINANCIAL FACTS
Financial Aid Rating	94
Comprehensive fee	$44,350
Books and supplies	$1,150
% frosh rec. need-based scholarship or grant aid	33
% UG rec. need-based scholarship or grant aid	37
% frosh rec. need-based self-help aid	31
% UG rec. need-based self-help aid	36
% frosh rec. any financial aid	33
% UG rec. any financial aid	38

BAYLOR UNIVERSITY

ONE BEAR PLACE #97056, WACO, TX 76798-7056 • ADMISSIONS: 254-710-3435 • FAX: 254-710-3436

CAMPUS LIFE

Quality of Life Rating	72
Fire Safety Rating	60*
Type of school	private
Affiliation	Baptist
Environment	city

STUDENTS

Total undergrad enrollment	11,786
% male/female	41/59
% from out of state	17
% live on campus	32
% in (# of) fraternities	13 (18)
% in (# of) sororities	17 (15)
% African American	8
% Asian	7
% Caucasian	72
% Hispanic	10
% Native American	1
% international	2
# of countries represented	90

SURVEY SAYS . . .
Small classes
Lab facilities are great
Great computer facilities
Great library
Athletic facilities are great
Intramural sports are popular
Frats and sororities dominate social scene

ACADEMICS

Academic Rating	81
Calendar	semester
Student/faculty ratio	16:1
Profs interesting rating	80
Profs accessible rating	82
Most common lab size	10–19 students
Most common reg class size	20–29 students

MOST POPULAR MAJORS
biology/biological sciences
marketing/marketing management
psychology

STUDENTS SAY

Academics

"Even though we're in the Big Twelve, you don't feel like just a number because people really reach out and try to make you feel welcome," writes one of the 11,000-plus undergraduates at Baylor University, the nation's biggest and most prominent Baptist academic institution. "Personal attention" is one of the surprise perks of attending this large school; less surprising, but no less welcome is Baylor's emphasis on Christian values, which "are instilled in almost every class, but in a way that doesn't pressure kids to be religious. It's pretty effective, too, presenting one path to kids and letting them choose on their own without forcing anything on them." The resulting atmosphere is one in which "Most people on campus take spirituality seriously, whatever their beliefs or lack thereof. It creates an environment where people are much more free to explore their own beliefs than at many universities that lack a religious affiliation, because faith is something that is so openly and fully discussed." Undergrads also praise Baylor's "amazing facilities in the classrooms and labs," including "top-of-the-line technology and wireless connections." Those facilities are only bound to get better, as the school is in the midst of "an ambitious plan that will take it into the top tier of schools by 2012." Outstanding programs here include premedical and pre-dental offerings, nursing, engineering, business, pre-law, and the seminary.

Life

Usually by choice but always by school regulation, religion is central to life at Baylor University. "You have to attend chapel for two semesters twice a week, and freshmen have to go to chapel Fridays, which is a Bible study," students explain. The curriculum also includes two required religion courses. Many students seek more faith-related activity, participating in "ministry, community outreach and service, and involvement within and outside of the university." There are plenty of other things for students to do here besides explore their faith; in fact, "Students can find something to be involved in no matter what their interests. There is an organization for everyone, from those interested in sororities and fraternities to those interested in video games or anime." This being Texas, "Sports are huge," with the school boasting strong teams in tennis, women's basketball, and track. The football team, unfortunately, "is not highly skilled," to the great vexation of many. Also, "A lot of students like to party, whether or not school policy permits any drinking or use of drugs," and Baylor's popular Greek scene is happy to accommodate them. Students love Baylor's "terrific campus," with "its great overall layout and beautiful landscaping and architecture." The campus is so homey, in fact, that the academic community tends to get isolated here, resulting in an effect known as the "Baylor Bubble." One student explains, "We close ourselves off from the rest of Waco. A block in any direction from campus will take you to some of the poorest areas in town."

Student Body

"There are generally two types of students at Baylor," students here tell us, because "The fact that Baylor is a pricey private school attracts students that come from wealthy families; these students wear trendy clothes and drive expensive cars. However, Baylor is also a Christian university, and that attracts students who are interested in growing in the Lord while they are working toward earning a degree." While "There are not many other types of students," the student body does include "the occasional non-Christian student. We wonder why they chose Baylor. They fit in okay, but definitely stick out at a university that upholds Christianity in the classroom, in the dorms, and pretty much all other areas." Traditionally, "Baylor students tend to be conservative, socially conscious, and hardworking. They are also self-confident and friendly, with friendliness being one of Baylor's biggest strengths."

FINANCIAL AID: 254-710-2611 • E-MAIL: ADMISSIONS_SERV_OFFICE@BAYLOR.EDU • WEBSITE: WWW.BAYLOR.EDU

ADMISSIONS

Very important factors considered include: Class rank, rigor of secondary school record, standardized test scores. *Important factors considered include:* Academic GPA, recommendation(s). *Other factors considered include:* Alumni/ae relation, application essay, character/personal qualities, extracurricular activities, first generation, geographical residence, interview, level of applicant's interest, religious affiliation/commitment, talent/ability, volunteer work. SAT or ACT required; ACT with Writing component required. TOEFL required of all international applicants. High school diploma is required, and GED is accepted. *Academic units required:* 4 English, 3 math, 2 science (2 science labs), 2 foreign language, 1 social studies, 1 history, 3 academic electives.

The Inside Word

A largely self-selected applicant pool and the need for a fairly large freshman class each year makes for a high admit rate. If your values reflect those of the community at Baylor, chances are you will be offered admission.

FINANCIAL AID

Students should submit: FAFSA, State Residency Affirmation. The Princeton Review suggests that all financial aid forms be submitted as soon as possible after January 1. *Need-based scholarships/grants offered:* Pell Grant, SEOG, state scholarships/grants, the school's own gift aid. *Loan aid offered:* FFEL Subsidized Stafford, FFEL Unsubsidized Stafford, FFEL PLUS, Federal Perkins Loan, state loans. Applicants will be notified of awards on a rolling basis beginning or about March 5.

FROM THE ADMISSIONS OFFICE

"Baylor University is a Christian university in the Baptist tradition and is affiliated with the Baptist General Convention of Texas. As the oldest institution of higher learning in the state, Baylor's founders sought to establish a college dedicated to Christian principles, superior academics, and a shared sense of community. Students come from all 50 states and some 90 foreign countries. Baylor's nationally recognized academic divisions offer 141 undergraduate degree programs, 71 master's degree programs, and 20 doctoral degree programs. Baylor ranks in the top 15 percent of colleges and universities participating in the National Merit Scholarship program. Baylor is one of the select 11 percent of U.S. colleges and universities with a Phi Beta Kappa chapter. The Templeton Foundation repeatedly names Baylor as one of America's top character-building colleges. Baylor's undergraduate programs emphasize the central importance of vocation (calling) and service in students' lives, helping them explore their value and role in society. Baylor is a charter member of the Independent 529 Tuition Plan, a prepaid college tuition plan. Baylor's tuition is one of the lowest of any major private university in the Southwest and one of the least expensive in the nation. Approximately 75 percent of Baylor students receive student financial assistance. The 508-acre main campus adjoins the Brazos River near downtown Waco, a Central Texas city of 110,000 people. By 2012, Baylor intends to enter the top tier of American universities while reaffirming its distinctive Christian mission. This bold 10-year vision, Baylor 2012, is well underway, benefiting students entering Baylor now.

"Baylor University requires applicants for admission into the Fall 2008 freshman class to take the new version of the SAT or the ACT with the Writing section. Students may also choose to submit scores from the old version of the SAT or ACT (prior to March 2005) as their best scores (old/new) will be used when making admissions decisions."

SELECTIVITY

Admissions Rating	**88**
# of applicants	21,393
% of applicants accepted	43
% of acceptees attending	31

FRESHMAN PROFILE

Range SAT Critical Reading	540–650
Range SAT Math	560–660
Range SAT Writing	530–640
Range ACT Composite	23–28
Minimum Paper TOEFL	540
Minimum Computer Based TOEFL	207
% graduated top 10% of class	40
% graduated top 25% of class	70
% graduated top 50% of class	93

DEADLINES

Regular application deadline	2/1
Regular notification	12/01, 1/15, 3/15
Nonfall registration?	yes

APPLICANTS ALSO LOOK AT
AND OFTEN PREFER
Texas A&M University—College Station, Texas Christian University, The University of Texas at Austin

AND SOMETIMES PREFER
Southern Methodist University, Texas Tech University, Trinity University

AND RARELY PREFER
Pepperdine University, Tulane University, Vanderbilt University

FINANCIAL FACTS

Financial Aid Rating	**70**
Annual tuition	$22,220
Room & Board	$7,526
Books and supplies	$1,548
Required fees	$2,270
% frosh rec. need-based scholarship or grant aid	47
% UG rec. need-based scholarship or grant aid	46
% frosh rec. need-based self-help aid	38
% UG rec. need-based self-help aid	38

BELLARMINE UNIVERSITY

2001 NEWBURG ROAD, LOUISVILLE, KY 40205 • ADMISSIONS: 502-452-8131 • FAX: 502-452-8002

CAMPUS LIFE
Quality of Life Rating	**82**
Fire Safety Rating	**60***
Type of school	private
Affiliation	Roman Catholic
Environment	village

STUDENTS
% from out of state	17
% from public high school	50
% live on campus	36
% in (# of) fraternities	2 (1)
% in (# of) sororities	2 (1)

SURVEY SAYS . . .
Small classes
Lab facilities are great
Great computer facilities
Great library
Students love Louisville, KY
Great off-campus food
Student government is popular

ACADEMICS
Academic Rating	**79**
Calendar	semester
Student/faculty ratio	13:1
Profs interesting rating	87
Profs accessible rating	86
% profs teaching	
UG courses	100
% classes taught by TAs	0
Most common	
reg class size	20–29 students

STUDENTS SAY

Academics

Perched atop a hill in the storied city of Louisville, Bellarmine University's "beautiful campus" earns student praise for being a "sheltering creative community." Students also laud their "entertaining and passionate educators," who "bend over backward to help students." Professors here are like "big brothers and sisters: They harass you, but they're there when you need a helping hand." They are more than just buddies, though: "Each has a strong professional and academic background" and challenges students to strive for success, both inside the classroom and out. Particularly "popular professors," however, teach courses that are sometimes "hard to get into." It's not just the professors who are accessible at Bellarmine; the "administration has an open-door policy that actually means open door!" There "seems to be no administrative 'red tape'; administrators know what's going on and do their jobs very well." Students looking for support praise the "Academic Resource Center that aids students with tutoring, editing essays, and presentations," and appreciate the fact that the school helps them "find internships and co-op programs" for experiential learning outside the classroom.

Life

"Bellarmine is located in the center of the Highlands, Kentucky's cultural mecca. There's everything from sushi to Rasta stores, skate shops to thrift malls" to be found, as well as "many coffee shops in this area, most locally owned. There is a great music scene here, and many bars and venues offer live music." Louisville's "downtown is growing and flourishing. There are gallery hops twice a month, and trolley hops every Friday." Housing off-campus is "awesome and pretty cheap in this area for what you get." With such terrific off-campus amenities, it's no wonder that so few people opt to live on campus. Still, students report that they stay connected with on-campus life, especially during the week; one writes: "Our school provides a lot of activities throughout the week," such as guest lecturers and intercollegiate sporting events, "but lacks events during the weekend." "Greek life at Bellarmine is [also] almost nonexistent," though students claim that "they are working on that" problem. As a result of a tame Greek scene and relatively quiet weekend campus life, "A lot of people go home during the weekend or to parties off campus," including "the University of Louisville's frat/sorority parties."

Student Body

"The typical student at Bellarmine comes from a private Catholic high school in and around Louisville, and is therefore usually cut from the same political, moral, and educational mold." While the perception is that there are many "high-middle-class White people" at the school, students stress the fact that "our student body does have diversity"; as one student puts it, "The student body at Bellarmine definitely gets more and more diverse each year. The administration is working hard to emphasize the importance of diversity. The only area [in which] they do not seem to be focusing is religious background diversity. I do not know one student at Bellarmine who is not Christian, whether it be Catholic, Baptist, Methodist," or other Christian faiths. The small size of the school creates a close "community atmosphere": "Most of the campus knows who you are." This closeness can be a benefit or a drawback, depending on how you look at it; one respondent remarks: "If you do something stupid, the whole campus has heard about it by lunch."

FINANCIAL AID: 502-452-8124 • E-MAIL: ADMISSIONS@BELLARMINE.EDU • WEBSITE: WWW.BELLARMINE.EDU

ADMISSIONS

Very important factors considered include: Application essay, recommendation(s), rigor of secondary school record, standardized test scores. *Important factors considered include:* Character/personal qualities. *Other factors considered include:* Alumni/ae relation, class rank, extracurricular activities, interview, talent/ability, volunteer work, work experience. SAT or ACT required; TOEFL required of all international applicants. High school diploma is required, and GED is accepted. *Academic units required:* 4 English, 3 math, 2 science, 2 social studies. *Academic units recommended:* 4 math, 3 science, 2 foreign language.

The Inside Word

Bellarmine views applicants as more than the sum total of their GPA and test scores. Aspects of the application, such as recommendations and personal statements, which present a more complete picture of the students seeking admission, hold significant weight. Candidates with solid grades and diverse interests are likely to earn acceptance.

FINANCIAL AID

Students should submit: FAFSA. The Princeton Review suggests that all financial aid forms be submitted as soon as possible after January 1. *Need-based scholarships/grants offered:* Pell Grant, SEOG, state scholarships/grants, the school's own gift aid. *Loan aid offered:* FFEL Subsidized Stafford, FFEL Unsubsidized Stafford, FFEL PLUS, Federal Perkins Loan, college/university loans from institutional funds. Applicants will be notified of awards on or about April 1. Federal Work-Study Program available. Institutional employment available. Off-campus job opportunities are excellent.

FROM THE ADMISSIONS OFFICE

"Bellarmine University is known for providing students with outstanding personal attention in the classroom. For many out-of-town students, however, Bellarmine's location makes the difference. Just five miles from downtown Louisville, Bellarmine is at the heart of the cultural and recreational offerings of the nation's sixteenth-largest city. The 135-acre campus is set in a safe, historic neighborhood that features an executive golf course, indoor and outdoor tennis courts, a fitness center, sand volleyball court, and athletic fields.

"Recent additions to the campus reflect the university's academic emphasis on a liberal arts core curriculum surrounded by competitive graduate and professional schools. The state-of-the-art Norton Health Sciences Center and a Service Learning Clinic offer real-life, hands-on experience for nursing and physical therapy students, while the campus library houses the largest collection of works by and about internationally renowned author and Trappist monk Thomas Merton.

"With over 50 clubs and organizations on campus and 18 NCAA Division II athletic teams, Bellarmine offers a variety of recreational opportunities for all students. Countless internships and study abroad programs offer additional opportunities for students to expand their horizons outside the classroom.

"Students who live on campus will also find a Bellarmine difference, namely the living arrangements. From the traditional college residence hall layout to apartment-style and suite living arrangements, students have many housing options. All residence halls offer amenities such as laundry facilities, computer labs, study rooms, and air conditioning.

"As of this book's publication, Bellarmine University did not have information available about their policy regarding the new SAT."

SELECTIVITY

Admissions Rating	**78**
# of applicants	1,485
% of applicants accepted	82
% of acceptees attending	37

FRESHMAN PROFILE

Range SAT Critical Reading	480–620
Range SAT Math	480–610
Range ACT Composite	21–26
Minimum Paper TOEFL	550
Minimum Computer Based TOEFL	213
Average HS GPA	3.51
% graduated top 10% of class	18
% graduated top 25% of class	51
% graduated top 50% of class	81

DEADLINES

Regular application deadline	8/15
Regular notification	rolling
Nonfall registration?	yes

APPLICANTS ALSO LOOK AT
AND OFTEN PREFER
Butler University, Centre College, Transylvania University, University of Dayton, Xavier University (OH)
AND SOMETIMES PREFER
University of Kentucky, University of Louisville, Western Kentucky University
AND RARELY PREFER
Spalding University

FINANCIAL FACTS

Financial Aid Rating	**60***
Annual tuition	$17,820
Room & Board	$5,690
Books and supplies	$750
Required fees	$670

BELOIT COLLEGE

700 COLLEGE STREET, BELOIT, WI 53511 • ADMISSIONS: 608-363-2500 • FAX: 608-363-2075

STUDENTS SAY

Academics

"It feels like a big family here" at Beloit College. Professors "are on a first-name basis with students (you never hear someone say 'Professor _____')." "The Dean of Students will sit and eat with students," and at least one student has "e-mailed a comment to the president, and . . . received a reply e-mail the very next day." The professors here "love what they're doing, and it shows in how they manage their class." They each have a very distinctive teaching style that students either love or hate. It's important to do some research before signing up for any class," advises one sophomore. Even though professors have a range of teaching styles, "Classes are very interdisciplinary and often unintentionally work well in conjunction with other courses." When it comes to curricula, the college affords undergrads a generous dose of independence "with the freedom for students to explore what it is that they want to do . . . [including] the opportunity students have to create their own interdisciplinary major." Students tell us that the faculty and administration here recognize that not every student's interests fit neatly into a few categories, which is why the interdisciplinary major program is an excellent way for students to pursue multiple interests. If there is one complaint that some students have about such a self-directed academic experience, it's that the "Classes are not as challenging as I hoped they would be."

Life

Beloit is the kind of place where "Cultural relativism is very popular," and where special interest houses throw parties that serve as foils (or supplements, perhaps) to the Greek parties that go down nearly every weekend. Students generally praise "a liberal alcohol policy [that] is nice and does lower the overall abuse among the student body." Most of the drinking seems to happen on the weekends at Beloit; "During the week, there are all sorts of presentations, [and] lectures by guests, etc.," that capture the interest of many undergrads. In addition, there's the "[the] Coughy Haus Hause (a type of 'bar' run by the college) where they often have live bands." On the quiet side of the spectrum, some "People like to go to the Java Joint, the campus coffee shop, and play chess, board games, or do a puzzle." And "Almost everyone hangs out at 'The Wall' [a catch-all meeting place in the middle of campus] at some point in their time at Beloit." Also on campus, "movies [are] shown almost every weekend—sometimes very good ones." When they need a change of scenery, students find a friend with a car and road trip to Madison, Milwaukee, or Chicago to go out on the town. When they're not relaxing, "People are very politically active; they encourage voting and the signing of a ridiculous amount of petitions."

Student Body

"Atypical at other schools is typical here—being genderless, atheist/agnostic, liberal, and 'weird' is a 'normal' Beloit student." Since everyone at Beloit is at least partially weird, lines have to be drawn somewhere. On one end of the spectrum are the conservative kids (who are considered unusual at Beloit). On the other end, on the very outer limit of weirdness, are the folks who make up the "Beloit Science Fiction and Fantasy Association (BSFFA), who like Dungeons & Dragons, and who pretend to be wizards, etc." All other Beloiters exist somewhere between these two extremes. But no matter how they are weird, Beloiters are good at their weirdness: "A Beloit student is the kid in high school who played Ping-Pong even though it wasn't cool, and just because it wasn't considered cool, became state Ping-Pong champion to prove a point," explains one freshman. As far as diversity in its traditional sense is concerned, "There are lots of rich kids, but the school does a good job recruiting (and financing) students from lower socioeconomic classes." Students are eager, however, to see the fruits of the Office of Admissions' efforts to recruit more minority students.

FINANCIAL AID: 608-363-2500 • E-MAIL: ADMISS@BELOIT.EDU • WEBSITE: WWW.BELOIT.EDU

ADMISSIONS

Very important factors considered include: Application essay, recommendation(s), rigor of secondary school record. *Important factors considered include:* Class rank, interview, standardized test scores. *Other factors considered include:* Alumni/ae relation, character/personal qualities, extracurricular activities, talent/ability, volunteer work, work experience. SAT or ACT required; TOEFL required of all international applicants. High school diploma is required, and GED is accepted. *Academic units recommended:* 4 English, 4 math, 3 science, 2 foreign language, 4 social studies, 4 history.

The Inside Word

Beloit takes a well-rounded approach to the admissions game. Realizing that applicants are more than statistics on a page, the college works diligently to assess the total package. While most weight is given to a candidate's secondary school transcript, which is evaluated not only for grades but for academic rigor, significant attention is also paid to his or her essay and recommendations. Counselors strive to find students who not only demonstrate success in the classroom but also display strong character and leadership skills.

FINANCIAL AID

Students should submit: FAFSA, institution's own financial aid form, state aid form. Regular filing deadline is March 1. The Princeton Review suggests that all financial aid forms be submitted as soon as possible after January 1. *Need-based scholarships/grants offered:* Pell Grant, SEOG, state scholarships/grants, private scholarships, the school's own gift aid. *Loan aid offered:* FFEL Subsidized Stafford, FFEL Unsubsidized Stafford, FFEL PLUS, Federal Perkins Loan, college/university loans from institutional funds. Applicants will be notified of awards on a rolling basis beginning or about April 1.

FROM THE ADMISSIONS OFFICE

"While Beloit students clearly understand the connection between college and career, they are more apt to value learning for its own sake than for the competitive advantage that it will afford them in the workplace. As a result, Beloit students adhere strongly to the concept that an educational institution, in order to be true to its own nature, must imply and provide a context in which a free exchange of ideas can take place. This precept is embodied in the mentoring relationship that takes place between professor and student and the dynamic, participatory nature of the classroom experience.

"Beloit College requires that students applying for the Fall of 2008 submit scores from the ACT or SAT. The writing exam from either test is not evaluated for purposes of admission. Beloit offers a nonbinding early action plan with a December 1 deadline. The preferred deadline for regular decision applicants is January 15."

SELECTIVITY

Admissions Rating	**90**
# of applicants	2,048
% of applicants accepted	67
% of acceptees attending	25
# accepting a place on wait list	44
% admitted from wait list	0

FRESHMAN PROFILE

Range SAT Critical Reading	600–730
Range SAT Math	560–650
Range ACT Composite	25–29
Minimum Paper TOEFL	550
Minimum Computer Based TOEFL	213
Minimum Internet Based TOEFL	80
Average HS GPA	3.46
% graduated top 10% of class	35
% graduated top 25% of class	70
% graduated top 50% of class	97

DEADLINES

Regular notification	rolling
Nonfall registration?	yes

APPLICANTS ALSO LOOK AT
AND OFTEN PREFER
Carleton College, Colorado College, Oberlin College
AND SOMETIMES PREFER
Grinnell College, Lawrence University, Macalester College, St. Olaf College
AND RARELY PREFER
Gustavus Adolphus College, Lewis & Clark College, Ripon College, University of Illinois at Urbana-Champaign, University of Wisconsin—Madison

FINANCIAL FACTS

Financial Aid Rating	**99**
Annual tuition	$29,678
Room & Board	$6,408
% frosh rec. need-based scholarship or grant aid	57
% UG rec. need-based scholarship or grant aid	58
% frosh rec. need-based self-help aid	56
% UG rec. need-based self-help aid	58
% frosh rec. any financial aid	92
% UG rec. any financial aid	91

BENNINGTON COLLEGE

OFFICE OF ADMISSIONS, BENNINGTON, VT 05201 • ADMISSIONS: 800-833-6845 • FAX: 802-440-4320

CAMPUS LIFE

Quality of Life Rating	**77**
Fire Safety Rating	**80**
Type of school	private
Environment	town

STUDENTS

Total undergrad enrollment	523
% male/female	34/66
% from out of state	96
% live on campus	98
% African American	2
% Asian	2
% Caucasian	89
% Hispanic	2
% international	3
# of countries represented	13

SURVEY SAYS . . .

Class discussions encouraged
Small classes
No one cheats
Students aren't religious
Dorms are like palaces
Campus feels safe
Intercollegiate sports are unpopular
or nonexistent
Frats and sororities are unpopular or
nonexistent
Theater is popular

ACADEMICS

Academic Rating	**97**
Calendar	semester
Student/faculty ratio	7:1
Profs interesting rating	98
Profs accessible rating	96
% profs teaching UG courses	100
Most common lab size	10–19 students
Most common reg class size	10–19 students

MOST POPULAR MAJORS

English language and literature
music
visual and performing arts

STUDENTS SAY

Academics

"I chose Bennington because it was everything high school wasn't," one undergrad writes, neatly summing up what makes this small school with a no distribution-requirements curriculum so appealing to many. Bennington students don't declare majors; rather, they formulate an interdisciplinary academic plan in consultation with faculty advisors. The system makes Bennington a great place "for motivated self-starters who may not know exactly what they want from school but who will thrive if they have control of their education." Prospective students should be forewarned that "it is truly up to the student to decide whether they wish to make their education demanding. Although no one will be allowed to slip by through our plan process, motivation is a must to be extremely successful." Bennington is strongest in the arts; students love their work in writing, visual arts, and theater. In these and all disciplines, professors "are all active participants in their fields, so literature classes are taught by writers, painting classes by painters, dancing classes by dancers, and so on. This ensures that all faculty members are knowledgeable and have personal experiences that are of use to students. As an added bonus, it is not infrequent that a professor will ask for the help of students in big, exciting projects." Bennington is a small school, and that naturally creates some limitations. Several students in our survey wished for an Art History Department, for example.

Life

Undergraduates at Bennington "work really, really hard and play with the same intensity. In fact, if you were going to describe Bennington in one word, you would call it 'intense.'" Daily life consists of "a mix of independent work and cooperative work. Everyone is working on a project that they are excited about, stressed out about, etc." As one student explains, "A Bennington student reflects the passion that burns in their interests, and the way that they express these interests is by not creating boundaries between work and play. Our lives are our passions. You will be living, working, and playing with dedicated students, supportive and motivated faculty, and a diverse curriculum." When they take a work break, "People here like to hang out a lot, watch movies or just chill and talk, or attend on-campus activities, bands, sponsored parties, theater events, and art openings." The school organizes a lot of "extracurricular opportunities. The campus activities board tries really hard to have things going on all the time for students, and if there isn't something to your liking it isn't very hard to get away to New York or Boston for the weekend." The ease of visiting these cities is a good thing, because there's not much happening immediately off campus; Bennington "is so secluded" that "it's possible to be completely cut off from the world outside if you don't make an attempt to watch/read the news. The closest big city is Albany (a 40- to 50-minute drive), and that's not saying much."

Student Body

"Most of the students enjoy going against the grain" at Bennington. These "really interesting, crazy, creative, brilliant people . . . try to 'out-different' each other: Who can be the most eccentric? Everyone, no matter how nerdy, will not only be super cool here, but have a group of friends just like them." Although they insist that "there is no typical Bennington student," most students would concede that their peers "are usually creative, self-motivated, smart, and hilarious. The only students who don't feel like they fit in are those unwilling to work or take charge of their own college experience." Bennington "is racially very homogenous," but, one student says, "Racial diversity doesn't guarantee diversity of experience or ideals, anyway. Among students here, there is a wide variety of social backgrounds, religious upbringings, intended academic concentrations, and motivations. Politically, though, we are quite limited—the vast majority of students are very liberal."

FINANCIAL AID: 802-440-4325 • E-MAIL: ADMISSIONS@BENNINGTON.EDU • WEBSITE: WWW.BENNINGTON.EDU

ADMISSIONS

Very important factors considered include: Academic GPA, application essay, character/personal qualities, class rank, extracurricular activities, interview, recommendation(s), rigor of secondary school record, talent/ability. *Other factors considered include:* Alumni/ae relation, first generation, geographical residence, level of applicant's interest, racial/ethnic status, standardized test scores, state residency, volunteer work, work experience. SAT or ACT recommended; TOEFL required of all international applicants. High school diploma is required, and GED is accepted. *Academic units recommended:* 4 English, 3 math, 3 science, 2 foreign language, 3 social studies, 3 history.

The Inside Word

Given the freedom and flexibility inherent in a Bennington education, ideal prospective applicants tend to be motivated and independent students. The college hopes to learn as much about each applicant as possible in the admissions process and tries to have a conversation with each applicant in person or via telephone or email. Applicants may (and should!) use their personal statements and interviews to distinguish themselves.

FINANCIAL AID

Students should submit: FAFSA, institution's own financial aid form, CSS/Financial Aid PROFILE, Noncustodial PROFILE, student and parent Federal Income Tax Returns and W-2s. The Princeton Review suggests that all financial aid forms be submitted as soon as possible after January 1. *Need-based scholarships/grants offered:* Pell Grant, SEOG, state scholarships/grants, private scholarships, the school's own gift aid. *Loan aid offered:* FFEL Subsidized Stafford, FFEL Unsubsidized Stafford, FFEL PLUS, college/university loans from institutional funds (international students only). Applicants will be notified of awards on or about April 1.

FROM THE ADMISSIONS OFFICE

"The educational philosophy of Bennington is rooted in an abiding faith in the talent, imagination, and responsibility of the individual; thus, the principle of learning by practice underlies every major feature of a Bennington education. We believe that a college education should not merely provide preparation for graduate school or a career, but should be an experience valuable in itself and the model for lifelong learning. Faculty, staff, and students at Bennington work together in a collaborative environment based upon respect for each other and the power of ideas to make a difference in the world. We are looking for intellectually curious students who have a passion for learning, are willing to take risks, and are open to making connections.

"Submission of standardized test scores (the SAT, SAT Subject Tests, or the ACT) is recommended, but not required."

SELECTIVITY

Admissions Rating	89
# of applicants	798
% of applicants accepted	66
% of acceptees attending	24
# accepting a place on wait list	15
% admitted from wait list	73
# of early decision applicants	58
% accepted early decision	34

FRESHMAN PROFILE

Range SAT Critical Reading	570–700
Range SAT Math	520–620
Range SAT Writing	580–680
Range ACT Composite	23–28
Minimum Paper TOEFL	577
Minimum Computer Based TOEFL	233
Average HS GPA	3.45
% graduated top 10% of class	31
% graduated top 25% of class	62
% graduated top 50% of class	91

DEADLINES

Early decision application deadline	11/15
Early decision notification	12/15
Regular application deadline	1/3
Regular notification	4/1
Nonfall registration?	yes

APPLICANTS ALSO LOOK AT

AND OFTEN PREFER

Bard College, Hampshire College, Oberlin College, Reed College, Sarah Lawrence College, Smith College

AND SOMETIMES PREFER

Alfred University, Beloit College, Boston University, Connecticut College, Emerson College, Grinnell College, Middlebury College, Princeton University, Whitman College

AND RARELY PREFER

Allegheny College, Antioch University, Clark University, Eugene Lang College—The New School for Liberal Arts, Fordham University, Gordon College, Goucher College, Keene State College, Marlboro College, Mount Holyoke College

FINANCIAL FACTS

Financial Aid Rating	73
Annual tuition	$35,850
Room & Board	$9,380
Required fees	$950
% frosh rec. need-based scholarship or grant aid	62
% UG rec. need-based scholarship or grant aid	65
% frosh rec. need-based self-help aid	62
% UG rec. need-based self-help aid	63
% frosh rec. any financial aid	76
% UG rec. any financial aid	76

BENTLEY COLLEGE

175 FOREST STREET, WALTHAM, MA 02452-4705 • ADMISSIONS: 781-891-2244 • FAX: 781-891-3414

STUDENTS SAY

Academics

Bentley College, an institution dedicated to creating "business and business-technical leaders," combines a winning location with an intense focus on technology to produce "the business moguls of tomorrow." Students say that the "Resources here are second to none, if you need help scheduling classes, choosing a major, creating a resume . . . anything at all, then there is an entire office of people ready and willing to help you in any way possible." Some of Bentley's perks include "a state-of-the-art trading room that would be used in the case of an emergency on Wall Street," a "superbly wired campus," and a brand-new library that "has all the resources a student could need, with quite a few significant, (not so necessary) extras" (such as a "large flat-panel TV monitors in each of its 20-some odd study rooms"). Bentley doesn't just flash the hardware, though; it also teaches students how to "integrate the newest technological resources into the business environment" by "embedding them into [your] courses. This is important, because technology "is key to success in the business world, whatever profession you are interested in." Bentley's proximity to Boston "makes this a very special place," helping students find meaningful internships and, after graduation, meaningful jobs. Academics here "are challenging but not overwhelming," and most of the classes "weigh class participation in the overall grade, which motivates [you] to complete the readings and assignments in a timely manner." Professors typically have "previous real-life experience in the business world. They like to incorporate that in the classroom."

Life

Life is "very hectic" at Bentley, where "Students tend to crack down during the weekdays and really get their work done. By Thursday [we're] ready for the weekend to start." Bentley's "beautiful campus" has "tons to offer" when it comes to finding activities outside of class, including "Greek life, sports, other organizations" and "tons of bars, restaurants, sports events, and concerts" so that "it's hard to be bored." Intramural sports "are also very popular, as is exercising in general. Being fit and working out are definitely the 'in' things to do." There are also plenty of parties; "Registered parties are allowed (with regulations) where of-age students can have keg parties in their room," but "There is also substance-free housing available if that's not your fancy." Students across the board agree that "Boston is Bentley's main attraction." Fortunately the city "is easily accessible via the school's shuttle service." Students love to head for Cambridge, the North End, Quincy Market, and other city destinations on the weekend "just to see a show, eat at a restaurant, shop, or just walk around," although some prefer to hang out on campus because the city can be "pretty expensive."

Students

The typical Bentley undergrad is "rich, foreign, and smart." Check that, they're "usually two out of the three: rich and foreign, rich and smart, or smart and foreign." Internationals make up a conspicuous subpopulation, "which is interesting" because you get to "learn from other cultures." One student writes, "Venture through any apartment complex to be greeted to the smells of Indian, Creole, Chinese, South American, and European foods. Diversity is greatly appreciated, as is evidenced by the fact that one of the events with the largest attendance each year is the Festival of Colors, an international extravaganza." The exception to the rule, we're told, is that students from Europe "hail from very big money" and "very rarely interact with domestic students." Most here, unsurprisingly, "are typical business students, usually quite driven and business oriented. They are fairly fun loving as well," the sort who are "studious during the week, rowdy on weekends." Overall, students tend to be "preppy collar-poppin' kids" who can "talk the talk" and "take pride [in] attending Bentley."

FINANCIAL AID: 781-891-3441 • E-MAIL: UGADMISSION@BENTLEY.EDU • WEBSITE: WWW.BENTLEY.EDU

ADMISSIONS

Very important factors considered include: Rigor of secondary school record, standardized test scores. *Important factors considered include:* Academic GPA, application essay, character/personal qualities, class rank, extracurricular activities, recommendation(s), volunteer work, work experience. *Other factors considered include:* Alumni/ae relation, first generation, geographical residence, interview, level of applicant's interest, racial/ethnic status, state residency, talent/ability. SAT or ACT required; ACT with Writing component required. TOEFL required of all international applicants. High school diploma is required, and GED is accepted. *Academic units recommended:* 4 English, 4 math, 3 science (3 science labs), 3 foreign language, 3 history, 2 additional English, mathematics, social or lab science, foreign language, speech.

The Inside Word

If you've got a bunch of electives available to you senior year, you may think that choosing business classes is the best way to impress the Bentley Admissions Office. Not so; the school would prefer you take a broad range of challenging classes—preferably at the AP level—in English, history/social sciences, math, lab sciences, and foreign language. The school enjoys a sizable applicant pool, so you'll need solid grades and test scores to gain admission.

FINANCIAL AID

Students should submit: FAFSA, CSS/Financial Aid PROFILE, Noncustodial PROFILE, Business/Farm Supplement, Federal Income Tax Returns (including all schedules for parents and student). Regular filing deadline is February 1. The Princeton Review suggests that all financial aid forms be submitted as soon as possible after January 1. *Need-based scholarships/grants offered:* Pell Grant, SEOG, state scholarships/grants, private scholarships, the school's own gift aid. *Loan aid offered:* FFEL Subsidized Stafford, FFEL Unsubsidized Stafford, FFEL PLUS, Federal Perkins Loan, state loans. Applicants will be notified of awards on a rolling basis beginning or about March 25. Federal Work-Study Program available. Institutional employment available. Off-campus job opportunities are good.

FROM THE ADMISSIONS OFFICE

"Bentley is a national leader in business education. Centered on education and research in business and related professions, Bentley blends the breadth and technological strength of a university with the values and student focus of a small college. A Bentley education combines an unparalleled array of business courses with hands-on technology experience, and a strong foundation in liberal arts. Half of all required courses are in the arts and sciences. In addition, students have the opportunity to pursue a double major in business and liberal studies. The result is that students gain expertise for a competitive edge in today's economy and broad-based skills essential for success in all areas of life.

"An average class size of 25 students and a student/faculty ratio of 12:1 allow for personal attention and meaningful class discussion. Concepts and theories that students learn in the classroom come alive in several hands-on, high-tech learning laboratories like the Financial Trading Room, Center for Marketing Technology, and Media and Culture Labs and Studio. Outside the classroom, students choose from a number of athletic, social, and cultural opportunities."

"Ethics and social responsibility are woven throughout the school's curriculum; the Bentley Service-Learning Program is ranked among the top in the United States. Students also choose from 27 countries to study abroad. Students develop skills and build their resume thanks to internships with leading companies."

"State-of-the-art athletic and recreation facilities complement the 23 varsity teams in Division I and II, and the extensive intramural and recreational sports programs. Boston and Cambridge, just minutes from campus, are accessible via the school's free shuttle. Both cities are great resources for internships, job opportunities, cultural events, and social life."

"Students applying for freshman admission are required to take the SAT or the ACT with the Writing section. SAT Subject Tests are not required."

SELECTIVITY

Admissions Rating	91
# of applicants	6,156
% of applicants accepted	39
% of acceptees attending	37
# accepting a place on wait list	427
% admitted from wait list	1
# of early decision applicants	169
% accepted early decision	62

FRESHMAN PROFILE

Range SAT Critical Reading	530–620
Range SAT Math	590–680
Range SAT Writing	530–620
Range ACT Composite	23–27
Minimum Paper TOEFL	550
Minimum Computer Based TOEFL	213
% graduated top 10% of class	40
% graduated top 25% of class	76
% graduated top 50% of class	99

DEADLINES

Early decision application deadline	11/15
Early decision notification	12/15
Regular application deadline	1/15
Regular notification	4/1
Nonfall registration?	yes

APPLICANTS ALSO LOOK AT

AND OFTEN PREFER
Babson College, Boston College, Villanova University

AND SOMETIMES PREFER
Boston University, New York University

AND RARELY PREFER
Bryant University, Fairfield University, Northeastern University, Stonehill College, University of Massachusetts—Amherst

FINANCIAL FACTS

Financial Aid Rating	79
Annual tuition	$31,450
Room & Board	$10,940
Books and supplies	$1,000
Required fees	$246
% frosh rec. need-based scholarship or grant aid	48
% UG rec. need-based scholarship or grant aid	42
% frosh rec. need-based self-help aid	50
% UG rec. need-based self-help aid	46
% frosh rec. any financial aid	78
% UG rec. any financial aid	73

BEREA COLLEGE

CPO 2220, BEREA, KY 40404 • ADMISSIONS: 859-985-3500 • FAX: 859-985-3512

STUDENTS SAY

Academics

Among a handful of schools nationwide that allow students to earn the cost of their tuition by working on campus, Berea College lets undergrads "learn as much at work and in work training as [they] do in the classroom." But this is not to say that academics are a walk in the park; one junior reports, "You study, study, study." A sophomore adds, "The classes definitely are not easy. The professors expect you to show up for class and try your hardest." You're likely to find professors who are "down-to-earth, accessible, [and] willing to spend time outside of class with students." A sophomore tells us, "I have often enjoyed dinners at their houses or lunches with them around town." While there may be a few bad apples in the bunch, the professors overall encourage undergrads "to think in ways you never would have imagined." Be aware, though, that one of these ways is "liberal"—a term that tends to characterize the college's faculty, to the chagrin of some members of the largely conservative student body. Because Berea was founded in 1855 by abolitionists, students have little reason to be surprised that their ideas will be "challenged" here. The college's administration earns both cheers and jeers from the student body. Many hail the "free laptops" that all students receive and write that "the administration is agreeable and willing to help students"; yet others complain that "decisions are made on the basis of what is cheapest, what will look best, and what will make them look progressive." Overall, "Berea College students, faculty, and staff are committed to using their knowledge to leave the world a little better than they found it through learning, labor, and service."

Life

"We work at Berea," writes a sophomore, "either with our labor or school work." Between the "mandatory" work-study program and the "demanding" academics, students find plenty to keep them busy. And this is a good thing, because the "small, dry town" of Berea in central Kentucky offers few distractions, with the exception of—you guessed it—"Wal-Mart!" Though cars on campus are heavily restricted, "One can get on the school shuttle and go to the Richmond Mall on Fridays, or sign up for the Lexington Mall shuttle on Saturdays. But if you spend most of your time on campus, it can quickly get really boring," warns a sophomore. Not everyone feels this way: "During the academic year, there is lots of stuff on campus other than classes," writes a French-economics double major. Many praise the Campus Activities Board for keeping the campus "always buzzing with activities." In their free time, students like to "think about life, society, classes, work, the world, food, contra dance, swing dance, Bible study, partying, sex, drugs, and Christian rock. We also like to knit and hike." The college's 8,000-acre forest provides plenty of space for Berea's outdoor adventurers. Self-identified as a Christian school, Berea does put limits on the indoor "adventures" in which students are allowed to participate. While "campus policies are restrictive"—with a zero-tolerance alcohol regulations and prohibited overnighters by members of the opposite sex—some remark that they're also "inconsistently enforced."

Student Body

While the largest crop of students come "from the Appalachian area and low-income families," students are quick to remind us that the college's "diversity" includes "international, independent, nontraditional, married, and students of many colors, religions, and backgrounds." Berea also has a huge (almost 60 percent of the student body) out-of-state constituency. There are some students here who claim that groups "do not really mix very well"; but overall these undergrads give each other props for being "very tolerant and open-minded." Considering all these differences, what's the "typical" undergrad here like? A junior muses, "This creature is a sleep-deprived individual that spends most of its time studying."

FINANCIAL AID: 859-985-3310 • E-MAIL: ADMISSIONS@BEREA.EDU • WEBSITE: WWW.BEREA.EDU

ADMISSIONS

Very important factors considered include: Academic GPA, class rank, geographical residence, rigor of secondary school record, standardized test scores. *Important factors considered include:* Application essay, character/personal qualities, extracurricular activities, interview, racial/ethnic status, talent/ability, volunteer work. *Other factors considered include:* First generation, level of applicant's interest, recommendation(s), state residency, work experience. SAT or ACT required; TOEFL required of all international applicants. High school diploma is required, and GED is accepted. *Academic units recommended:* 4 English, 3 math, 2 science, 2 foreign language, 1 social studies, 1 history.

Inside Word

The full-tuition scholarship every entering student receives understandably entices lots of applicants, so competition among candidates is intense. To make matters worse, you may be too wealthy to get in here: Berea won't admit students whose parents can afford to send them to a school with comparable educational quality. In 2001, a family of four had to earn less than $51,000 to send a child here.

FINANCIAL AID

Students should submit: FAFSA. The Princeton Review suggests that all financial aid forms be submitted as soon as possible after January 1. *Need-based scholarships/grants offered:* Pell Grant, SEOG, state scholarships/grants, private scholarships, the school's own gift aid, United Negro College Fund. *Loan aid offered:* FFEL Subsidized Stafford, FFEL Unsubsidized Stafford, FFEL PLUS, Federal Perkins Loan, college/university loans from institutional funds. Applicants will be notified of awards on a rolling basis beginning or about May 1.

FROM THE ADMISSIONS OFFICE

"Founded in 1855 by ardent abolitionists, Berea College was the first racially integrated coeducational college in the South. Over the past 150 years, Berea's has evolved into one of the most distinctive colleges in the United States. Serving students primarily from the Appalachian region, Berea College seeks to serve students who possess great academic promise but have access to limited financial resources. Berea provides an inviting and personal educational experience, evidenced in part by an 11:1 student/faculty ratio and extensive, faculty-led advising and orientation programs.

"In support of students with limited financial resources, every enrolling student receives a full-tuition scholarship, a laptop computer, as well as a paid on-campus job. Students pay room, board, and fee charges to the extent that they are able as determined by their FAFSA results. Any remaining room, board, and fee charges are covered through scholarships and grant-based aid. Students may use earnings from their job to assist with their portion of room, board, and fee charges; books and supplies; and other personal expenses.

"As a result of this combination of academic reputation and generous financial assistance, Berea attracts many more applicants than are able to be accepted and thus admission is competitive. The best means of improving the chances for admission is to complete the application process as early as possible, preferably by November 30 of the senior year.

"Applicants for Fall 2008 must submit scores from the SAT or ACT (with or without the Writing components from either test)."

SELECTIVITY

Admissions Rating	91
# of applicants	1,818
% of applicants accepted	29
% of acceptees attending	73

FRESHMAN PROFILE

Range SAT Critical Reading	500–630
Range SAT Math	530–613
Range ACT Composite	21–25
Minimum Paper TOEFL	500
Minimum Computer Based TOEFL	173
Average HS GPA	3.51
% graduated top 10% of class	27
% graduated top 25% of class	67
% graduated top 50% of class	94

DEADLINES

Regular application deadline	4/30
Regular notification	rolling
Nonfall registration?	yes

FINANCIAL FACTS

Financial Aid Rating	81
Annual tuition	$0*
% frosh rec. need-based scholarship or grant aid	100
% UG rec. need-based scholarship or grant aid	100
% frosh rec. need-based self-help aid	100
% UG rec. need-based self-help aid	100
% frosh rec. any financial aid	100
% UG rec. any financial aid	100

*Tuition is covered by a full scholarship and mandatory work-study.

BIRMINGHAM-SOUTHERN COLLEGE

900 ARKADELPHIA ROAD, BIRMINGHAM, AL 35254 • ADMISSIONS: 205-226-4696 • FAX: 205-226-3074

STUDENTS SAY

Academics

"Birmingham-Southern college is the best school in Alabama" students at this small, academically intense college in the state's largest city insist. Undergrads praise how the school achieves a "happy medium between well-rounded education and focused concentration on one's major," reporting that "BSU does a great job of preparing students for graduate, law, and medical schools." It also has "a good education program . . . and an excellent dance department that offers a top-notch dance faculty with a focus on ballet." Students tell us that "the overall academic experience is challenging, yet very rewarding," and that "classroom discussion is not only encouraged, but is a necessity, since much of the grades are derived from participation." Experiential learning is paramount; one student reports, "I have not had a class yet that didn't provide some sort of hands-on experience. I have participated in everything from labs at the Cahaba River in my population ecosystem course to observations at a local Montessori school in my human growth and development class." The small classes mean "Teachers get to know you by name, and many are willing to spend countless hours working with you individually on school matters and helping you plan [your] future. They take an interest in you as a person, not just as a student." Some here point out that "while being small is a benefit, it is also sometimes a downfall. Most classes are available every year, but you must be careful to schedule courses that only occur every other year or once a year carefully in order to graduate on time."

Life

"Most people live on campus because BSC is a smaller college," students here tell us, and "This allows for an attractive community-like atmosphere." Campus life includes "many student organizations, a very strong Greek system, [and] many different shows throughout the year, from dance to theater to music to art, all produced by the performing arts departments." Youth groups and religious organizations "are also big at the school. Many people attend chapel services and UCF [University Christian Fellowship]." There's fun to be had off campus as well, as "Birmingham is a rockin' city. There is always a concert or something off campus." Exploring Birmingham "is very easy [because] the school is located downtown, although it doesn't feel that way. You can go out to the middle of the academic quad at 11:00 P.M. and feel safe." There's "plenty to do off campus, including shopping, visiting the zoo, or going to see a show at one of the many theaters in town." One student sums up, "Fun is either a night out in Birmingham—that's what you do if you have money: You go out to eat, then to the bars, a movie, or a small off-campus party at someone's apartment—or, if you're broke and you want to have fun, you usually end up on Fraternity Row. At least one of the fraternities is usually having a party, and there are always people down there."

Student Body

BSC undergrads "typically come from the Alabama, Mississippi, Tennessee, and Georgia areas," although "there are some students here from elsewhere." Many "are involved in Greek life, probably about 60 percent. Many more girls go Greek than guys, and the independents are still like their own Greek group," as they "find their own groups in which to socialize, such as the Ultimate Frisbee team or service clubs such as Triangle Club or Students Offering Support." Most here agree that "the school could do better at attracting minorities and people of color," but point out that "with the size of our school you can only expect so much."

FINANCIAL AID: 205-226-4688 • E-MAIL: ADMISSION@BSC.EDU • WEBSITE: WWW.BSC.EDU

ADMISSIONS

Very important factors considered include: Academic GPA, application essay, recommendation(s), rigor of secondary school record, standardized test scores. *Important factors considered include:* Character/personal qualities, level of applicant's interest. *Other factors considered include:* Extracurricular activities, interview, talent/ability, volunteer work, work experience. SAT or ACT required; ACT with Writing component recommended. TOEFL required of all international applicants. High school diploma is required, and GED is accepted. *Academic units required:* 4 English. *Academic units recommended:* 4 math, 4 science (2 science labs), 2 foreign language, 2 social studies, 2 history, 10 academic electives.

The Inside Word

Birmingham-Southern's lack of widespread national recognition by students and parents results in a small applicant pool, the majority of whom are admitted. Most of the admits are looking for a quality Southern college, recognize a good situation here, and decide to enroll. Our impression is that few regret their decision. In a reflection of the entire administration, the Admissions Staff is truly personal and very helpful to prospective students.

FINANCIAL AID

Students should submit: FAFSA, state aid form. The Princeton Review suggests that all financial aid forms be submitted as soon as possible after January 1. *Need-based scholarships/grants offered:* Pell Grant, SEOG, private scholarships, the school's own gift aid, United Negro College Fund. *Loan aid offered:* FFEL Subsidized Stafford, FFEL Unsubsidized Stafford, FFEL PLUS, Federal Perkins Loan. Applicants will be notified of awards on or about March 1.

FROM THE ADMISSIONS OFFICE

"Respected publishers continue to recognize Birmingham-Southern College as one of the top-ranked liberal arts colleges in the nation. One guide highlights our small classes and the fact that we still assign each student a 'faculty-cum-mentor,' to assure individualized attention to our students. One notable aspect of our academic calendar is our January interim term, a 4-week period in which students can participate in special projects in close collaboration with faculty members, either on or off campus. One dimension of Birmingham-Southern's civic focus is the commitment to volunteerism. In fact, former President George Bush visited the campus to present our conservancy group with one of his 'Points of Light' volunteer service awards. The Center for Leadership Studies assists students in realizing their leadership potential by combining the academic study of leadership with significant community service.

"Freshman applicants must present acceptable scores on the SAT or the ACT; they must also submit an original essay and a satisfactory recommendation from the high school."

SELECTIVITY

Admissions Rating	88
# of applicants	2,198
% of applicants accepted	57
% of acceptees attending	23

FRESHMAN PROFILE

Range SAT Critical Reading	530–660
Range SAT Math	520–630
Range SAT Writing	520–650
Range ACT Composite	23–28
Minimum Paper TOEFL	500
Minimum Computer Based TOEFL	173
Average HS GPA	3.34
% graduated top 10% of class	34
% graduated top 25% of class	64
% graduated top 50% of class	84

DEADLINES

Regular notification	rolling
Nonfall registration?	yes

APPLICANTS ALSO LOOK AT

AND OFTEN PREFER
Rhodes College, Vanderbilt University

AND SOMETIMES PREFER
Auburn University, Furman University, Samford University, Sewanee—The University of the South, The University of Alabama at Tuscaloosa

AND RARELY PREFER
Louisiana State University, Tulane University

FINANCIAL FACTS

Financial Aid Rating	86
Annual tuition	$22,260
Room & Board	$7,740
Books and supplies	$1,000
Required fees	$780
% frosh rec. need-based scholarship or grant aid	34
% UG rec. need-based scholarship or grant aid	26
% frosh rec. need-based self-help aid	34
% UG rec. need-based self-help aid	28
% frosh rec. any financial aid	95
% UG rec. any financial aid	95

BOSTON COLLEGE

140 COMMONWEALTH AVENUE, DEVLIN HALL 208, CHESTNUT HILL, MA 02467-3809 • ADMISSIONS: 617-552-3100

CAMPUS LIFE

Quality of Life Rating	**92**
Fire Safety Rating	**88**
Type of school	private
Affiliation	Roman Catholic
Environment	city

STUDENTS

Total undergrad enrollment	9,020
% male/female	48/52
% from out of state	71
% from public high school	60
% live on campus	82
% African American	6
% Asian	9
% Caucasian	72
% Hispanic	8
% international	2
# of countries represented	97

SURVEY SAYS . . .

Great library
Students love Chestnut Hill, MA
Campus feels safe
Everyone loves the Eagles
Frats and sororities are unpopular or
nonexistent
Lots of beer drinking

ACADEMICS

Academic Rating	**90**
Calendar	semester
Student/faculty ratio	13:1
Profs interesting rating	83
Profs accessible rating	82
% profs teaching	
UG courses	100
Most common	
reg class size	10–19 students

MOST POPULAR MAJORS

communications and media studies
English language and literature
finance

STUDENTS SAY

Academics

Students praise the strong academics, the competitive athletic teams, the lively social scene, and the premium location that all combine to create a remarkable all-around college experience at Boston College. For many, though, BC's greatest asset is the "strong spiritual presence [that] shows how positive an influence religion can have on one's life." Don't worry; "They don't try to make anybody be Catholic" here. Rather, the school "simply reflects the Jesuit ideals of community, spirituality, and social justice," and these ideals pervade both the curriculum and the academic community. True to the Jesuit ideal of "educating the entire person," BC requires a thorough core curriculum "including philosophy, theology, and language requirements," rounded out by "strong [but optional] programs, such as internships and studying abroad." Beyond the core curriculum, "BC offers something for everyone. If you go here, you are with business students, nursing students, education majors, and arts and science majors." Even though this is a fairly large school, students insist that "you never feel like a number here. Yes, you have to be independent and seek out your professors. But when you do seek them out, you get incredible individualized attention." One undergrad sums it up like this: "BC's strength is a mix of everything. It may not be an Ivy League school in academics or win national championships everywhere in NCAA athletics, but it is a 'jack of all trades' when it comes to academics, athletics, art, and social activity."

Life

There is a "real spirit of volunteerism and giving back to the community [that] is one of BC's greatest strengths," many students here tell us, reporting that "there are about a million volunteer groups on campus, as well as a bunch of immersion trips to different places, the most renowned of which is the Appalachia group trip." Students here "really care about the world outside of Chestnut Hill. In a way, even the notion of studying abroad has turned into a question of 'How can I help people while there?' BC's Jesuit mission is contagious." Not all extracurricular life at BC is so altruistic, however; students here love to have fun in "the greatest location of any college ever! We are on the T [train], so we can get into the city of Boston whenever we like, but we are in suburbia so we can relax without all of the gimmicks of city life." Undergrads love to explore Boston, a city with "tons of great museums, historical sights, restaurants, and a lot of great concerts," that also happens to be "such a big college town. It's easy to meet kids that go to BU, Harvard, Emerson, Northeastern, or any of the other universities in the area." Closer to campus, BC has "great sports. Our football team has won six bowl games in a row and basketball is, at this writing, playing Georgetown in the men's NCAA Tournament. The ice hockey team is consistently ranked high nationally," and students turn out to support their Eagles in both men's and women's athletics.

Student Body

Boston magazine once described the BC student body as "a J. Crew catalogue with a slight hangover," and while students protest that "there are a number of students who do not conform to such a vision of the student body," they also admit that "there are a lot of preppy people at our school. Girls usually wear skirts and Uggs (unless it's freezing out, but it has to be very, very cold), and boys usually wear jeans and t-shirts or collared cotton shirts." And yes, "the typical BC student is White, Catholic, usually from the Northeast, who probably had family who went to BC," but with 9,000 undergrads, "We have students from all sorts of backgrounds, religions, sexual orientations." BC students tend to be extremely ambitious; they are "those super-involved people in high school who were three-season team captains, class president, and straight-A students. [They] have carried over that focus and determination into college."

ADMISSIONS

Very important factors considered include: Academic GPA, rigor of secondary school record, standardized test scores. *Important factors considered include:* Alumni/ae relation, application essay, character/personal qualities, class rank, extracurricular activities, recommendation(s), religious affiliation/commitment, talent/ability, volunteer work. *Other factors considered include:* First generation, racial/ethnic status, work experience. SAT and SAT Subject Tests or ACT required; ACT with Writing component required. TOEFL required of all international applicants. High school diploma is required, and GED is accepted. *Academic units recommended:* 4 English, 4 math, 4 science (4 science labs), 4 foreign language, 4 social studies.

The Inside Word

BC is one of many selective schools that eschew set admissions formulae. While a challenging high school curriculum and strong test scores are essential for any serious candidate, the college seeks students who are passionate and make connections between academic pursuits and extracurricular activities. The application process should reveal a distinct, mature voice and a student whose interest in education goes beyond the simple desire to earn an A.

FINANCIAL AID

Students should submit: FAFSA, CSS/Financial Aid PROFILE, Noncustodial PROFILE, Business/Farm Supplement, parent and student Federal Income Tax Returns and W-2 statements. The Princeton Review suggests that all financial aid forms be submitted as soon as possible after January 1. *Need-based scholarships/grants offered:* Pell Grant, SEOG, state scholarships/grants, private scholarships, the school's own gift aid. *Loan aid offered:* FFEL Subsidized Stafford, FFEL Unsubsidized Stafford, FFEL PLUS, Federal Perkins Loan, Federal Nursing Loan, state loans. Applicants will be notified of awards on or about April 15. Federal Work-Study Program available. Institutional employment available. Off-campus job opportunities are excellent.

FROM THE ADMISSIONS OFFICE

"Boston College students achieve at the highest levels with honors including two Rhodes scholarship winners, nine Fulbrights, and one each for Marshall, Goldwater, Madison, and Truman Postgraduate Fellowship Programs. Junior Year Abroad and Scholar of the College Program offer students flexibility within the curriculum. Facilities opened in the past 10 years include: the Merkert Chemistry Center, Higgins Hall (housing the Biology and Physics departments), three new residence halls, the Yawkey Athletics Center, the Vanderslice Commons Dining Hall, the Hillside Cafe, and a state-of-the-art library. Students enjoy the vibrant location in Chestnut Hill with easy access to the cultural and historical richness of Boston.

"Boston College requires freshman applicants for Fall 2008 to take the new SAT with writing (or the ACT with the Writing exam required). Students may submit scores from the old SAT as their best scores from either test will be used in admissions decisions. Two SAT Subject Tests are required; students are encouraged to take Subject Tests in fields in which they excel. "

SELECTIVITY

Admissions Rating	97
# of applicants	26,584
% of applicants accepted	29
% of acceptees attending	30
# accepting a place on wait list	2,000
% admitted from wait list	6

FRESHMAN PROFILE

Range SAT Critical Reading	610–700
Range SAT Math	640–720
Range SAT Writing	610–700
Minimum Paper TOEFL	600
Minimum Computer Based TOEFL	250
% graduated top 10% of class	80
% graduated top 25% of class	95
% graduated top 50% of class	99

DEADLINES

Regular application deadline	1/1
Regular notification	4/15
Nonfall registration?	yes

APPLICANTS ALSO LOOK AT
AND OFTEN PREFER
Cornell University, Georgetown University, University of Notre Dame, University of Pennsylvania, University of Virginia
AND SOMETIMES PREFER
New York University, Tufts University, University of California—Los Angeles, University of Michigan—Ann Arbor, University of Southern California
AND RARELY PREFER
College of the Holy Cross, Fordham University, Northeastern University, University of Connecticut, University of Massachusetts—Amherst

FINANCIAL FACTS

Financial Aid Rating	92
Annual tuition	$33,000
Room & Board	$11,438
Books and supplies	$650
Required fees	$506
% frosh rec. need-based scholarship or grant aid	38
% UG rec. need-based scholarship or grant aid	36
% frosh rec. need-based self-help aid	39
% UG rec. need-based self-help aid	38
% frosh rec. any financial aid	70
% UG rec. any financial aid	70

BOSTON UNIVERSITY

121 BAY STATE ROAD, BOSTON, MA 02215 • ADMISSIONS: 617-353-2300 • FAX: 617-353-9695

STUDENTS SAY

Academics

Boston University's greatest strengths, students tell us, lie in "the choices students are granted. Do you want to be an alterna-teen or a jock? Do you want to drink or go to shows? Do you want to study ballet, bio, or film? Do you want a scenic riverside location or an energetic urban one? You can have all of the above at BU, which is both overwhelming and exciting." A "top-notch educational institution in the middle of one of the best college cities in the world," BU is the perfect place for independent students anxious to explore all options. As one student puts it, "BU not only allowed me access to over 65 majors in my school, the College of Arts and Sciences (I tried out astronomy, international relations, psychology, and anthropology before deciding on anthro/religion and French), but also majors in other schools (I took two drama classes in the College of Fine Arts)." Many are drawn here by the "top-notch pre-professional programs" that include "an excellent communications program," a "great management program," and "a great biology program." Students note that "BU fosters independence: Students can do whatever they want; they just have to have the motivation." Academics "are very, very rigorous," with more than a few students hypothesizing the existence of an unwritten "grade deflation" policy, which, understandably, they regard as unfair.

Life

BU "doesn't have a campus in a traditional sense, and that takes some getting used to. It also means that most of your social life isn't centered on the university," but more on the city itself. To many here, "Boston is the perfect city. Easy to walk around; not as big and crazy as NYC; and plenty to do on the weekends besides party," such as "walking all the way downtown, passing through all the big entertainment areas, or walking over to Cambridge and Central Square or down the river and over the footbridge to Harvard Square . . . A short T-ride puts you in the North End with its Italian food heaven. If you can't find what you're looking for within 20 minutes of campus, you just haven't looked hard enough." Parties typically occur off campus "since the university has a fairly strict alcohol and drug policy which RAs monitor closely. The off-campus parties are typically big (100-plus) and, of course, have beer and cheap liquor more than accessible. The bar and club scene is also big, with Lansdowne Street only a few blocks away, so going out to drink and dance on the weekends is also pretty common. . . . Because cabs are everywhere, getting around the city, even when [you are] drunk and [it is] late at night, is pretty simple." For those who prefer to stick with school activities, "The school makes a real effort to get students involved and to provide activities for us, albeit through our yearly undergraduate student fee. They have comedy clubs, student concerts, several interesting lectures for every interest imaginable, etc."

Student Body

The undergraduate student body at BU is 16,000 strong, so "there is no 'typical' BU student." Students here "tend to be liberal and politically aware, but other than that, one of the most desirable aspects of BU is that there are no 'types.' Because BU has strong athletics, as well as strong programs in the arts, there is a nice mix . . . and everyone seems to get along well enough. This diversity . . . adds an amazing dynamic to class discussions. This is one of the most valuable aspects of a BU education." That said, many here tell us that "a solid majority of people are very rich, well dressed, and reasonably snobby." New England prep-school grads are well represented, but so, too, are a broad array of states and nations.

FINANCIAL AID: 617-353-2965 • E-MAIL: ADMISSIONS@BU.EDU • WEBSITE: WWW.BU.EDU

ADMISSIONS

Very important factors considered include: Rigor of secondary school record. *Important factors considered include:* Academic GPA, application essay, class rank, recommendation(s), standardized test scores. *Other factors considered include:* Alumni/ae relation, character/personal qualities, extracurricular activities, first generation, geographical residence, level of applicant's interest, racial/ethnic status, state residency, volunteer work, work experience. SAT and SAT Subject Tests or ACT required; ACT with Writing component required. TOEFL required of all international applicants. High school diploma is required, and GED is accepted. *Academic units required:* 4 English, 3 math, 3 science (3 science labs), 2 foreign language, 3 social studies. *Academic units recommended:* 4 English, 4 math, 4 science (4 science labs), 2–3 foreign language, 4 social studies.

The Inside Word

BU has grown more selective over the years; the school added SAT subject exams to its admissions requirements in 2005, a solid indicator that the school is now looking for more ways to eliminate applicants from its pool. Requirements and admissions standards are somewhat more lenient for the College of General Studies, a 2-year program that takes students right up to the point at which they declare a major and enter one of the university's 10 other undergraduate schools. Those who choose this route must basically reapply during their sophomore years in order to gain admission to their schools of choice.

FINANCIAL AID

Students should submit: FAFSA, CSS/Financial Aid PROFILE, Noncustodial PROFILE, state aid form, Business/Farm Supplement. Regular filing deadline is February 15. The Princeton Review suggests that all financial aid forms be submitted as soon as possible after January 1. *Need-based scholarships/grants offered:* Pell Grant, SEOG, state scholarships/grants, private scholarships, the school's own gift aid. *Loan aid offered:* Direct Subsidized Stafford, Direct Unsubsidized Stafford, Direct PLUS, Federal Perkins Loan, state loans. Applicants will be notified of awards on a rolling basis beginning or about March 15.

FROM THE ADMISSIONS OFFICE

"Boston University (BU) is a private teaching and research institution with a strong emphasis on undergraduate education. We are committed to providing the highest level of teaching excellence, and fulfillment of this pledge is our highest priority. Boston University has 11 undergraduate schools and colleges offering more than 250 major and minor areas of concentration. Students may choose from programs of study in areas as diverse as biochemistry, theater, physical therapy, elementary education, broadcast journalism, international relations, business, and computer engineering. BU has an international student body, with students from every state and more than 100 countries. In addition, opportunities to study abroad exist through 66 semester-long programs, spanning 33 cities and 22 countries on six continents.

"BU requires freshman applicants for Fall 2007 to take the SAT, and two SAT Subject Tests. Students are encouraged to take subject tests in fields in which they excel. Students may submit the results of the ACT (with the Writing section) in lieu of the SAT and SAT Subject Tests."

SELECTIVITY

Admissions Rating	93
# of applicants	31,851
% of applicants accepted	58
% of acceptees attending	22
# accepting a place on wait list	1,464
% admitted from wait list	36
# of early decision applicants	1079
% accepted early decision	40

FRESHMAN PROFILE

Range SAT Critical Reading	580–680
Range SAT Math	600–690
Range SAT Writing	590–690
Range ACT Composite	25–29
Minimum Paper TOEFL	550
Minimum Computer Based TOEFL	215
Average HS GPA	3.46
% graduated top 10% of class	53
% graduated top 25% of class	87
% graduated top 50% of class	99

DEADLINES

Early decision application deadline	11/1
Early decision notification	12/15
Regular application deadline	1/1
Regular notification	late March–mid-April
Nonfall registration?	yes

APPLICANTS ALSO LOOK AT

AND OFTEN PREFER
New York University, The George Washington University, University of Southern California

AND SOMETIMES PREFER
Boston College, Cornell University, Syracuse University, Tufts University

AND RARELY PREFER
Brown University, Northeastern University, University of Massachusetts—Amherst

FINANCIAL FACTS

Financial Aid Rating	83
Annual tuition	$34,930
Room & Board	$10,950
Books and supplies	$840
Required fees	$488
% frosh rec. need-based scholarship or grant aid	41
% UG rec. need-based scholarship or grant aid	41
% frosh rec. need-based self-help aid	39
% UG rec. need-based self-help aid	39
% frosh rec. any financial aid	46
% UG rec. any financial aid	44

BOWDOIN COLLEGE

5000 COLLEGE STATION, BOWDOIN COLLEGE, BRUNSWICK, ME 04011-8441 • ADMISSIONS: 207-725-3100 • FAX: 207-725-3101

STUDENTS SAY
Academics

Highly selective Bowdoin College is all about providing an "excellent liberal arts education in a supportive, small community" in "a beautiful part of the country." Undergrads cite Bowdoin's "intelligent" and "diverse" student body, "absolutely top-notch" professors, and "challenging, fascinating academic program that allows you to explore all your areas of interest" as particularly deserving of praise. Students here reap the benefits of "a close-knit community of learners, teachers, and leaders pursuing academics, athletics, music, art, clubs, and fun with relentless positive enthusiasm" in "a very nurturing and safe environment, [where] you can develop without worrying about stuff you don't need to worry about, such as money, food, housing, etc." Standout programs include environmental studies, neuroscience, foreign language, and the English and education departments which students describe as "excellent, bar none." The workload at Bowdoin "is just a few steps shy from unmanageable, which is good" because it forces you to "not only do your work," but "to do it carefully." Students also appreciate a faculty that is "truly interested in learning everyone's name," and "will stay hours after review sessions" until the students grasp the concepts. "They challenge you, and push you to go beyond just the books." Great facilities include the Career Planning Center, Writing Center, Baldwin Teaching Center, Counseling Center, and administrative offices. The cherry on the sundae? "Excellent alumni networking."

Life

Students love how Bowdoin "embraces the intellectual experience in a balanced, healthy way, so that its students are generally very happy. There is an awareness that in college, learning comes from everywhere, so there is a real effort by the Bowdoin administration as well as Bowdoin students to bring speakers, events, and entertainment to the campus so that students can learn in every way possible." Extracurriculars are part of the constant learning; students here "are always doing at least one if not 10 things at a time." Physical activity is part of the mix; many students participate in Outing Club events, hiking, whitewater kayaking, and rafting at nearby parks, and "It seems like almost everyone is on a sports team, so during the week most people find a release there." Students tell us that "on the weekends, there is a lot of partying (and with that comes a lot of alcohol)," but "It's not excessive." Plus, the "Alcohol policies are also pretty sweet—as long as everyone can be responsible and things are not out of control, security does not want to get anyone in trouble," and "a safe ride system" provides free rides home to intoxicated students for free. Those who don't drink tell us "There is plenty of music at night" and "Brunswick is great for a concert, coffee shop, or bowling." Gourmands, take note: "Bowdoin food is the best!"

Student Body

While "a fair amount of preppy kids" congregate on Bowdoin's campus, "There are all types of people here, providing an interesting mix of personalities, backgrounds, and interactions." Personality types "range from typical straight-out-of-prep-school preppy individuals to crusty hippies to jocks to artsy kids." "Bowdoin students either wear Chacos or Polos with their collars popped. Some even alternate between these two personalities." They also tend to be "multifaceted and multilayered; they are great intellectuals, as well as athletes, political activists, dancers, and community leaders. No one here is involved in just academic activities." Students say everyone here is "down to earth and very passionate about something—the environment, politics, science, the welfare of goats in Chile, etc." Despite being "extremely intelligent" and "highly motivated," Bowdoin undergrads "are not fiercely competitive or grade-grubby," and "Everyone gets along well."

FINANCIAL AID: 207-725-3273 • E-MAIL: ADMISSIONS@BOWDOIN.EDU • WEBSITE: WWW.BOWDOIN.EDU

ADMISSIONS

Very important factors considered include: Academic GPA, application essay, character/personal qualities, class rank, extracurricular activities, recommendation(s), rigor of secondary school record, talent/ability. *Important factors considered include:* Alumni/ae relation, first generation, geographical residence, racial/ethnic status, volunteer work, work experience. *Other factors considered include:* Interview, level of applicant's interest, standardized test scores, state residency. TOEFL required of all international applicants. High school diploma is required, and GED is not accepted. *Academic units recommended:* 4 English, 4 math, 4 science (3 science labs), 4 foreign language, 4 social studies.

The Inside Word

Standardized test scores are optional at Bowdoin, but if you aced the SAT or ACT you should definitely report your scores. The school will almost certainly look at them; in the spring of 2006, the Dean of Admissions at Bowdoin said as much to the *New York Times*, explaining that he considers test scores helpful. He noted that high school transcripts are difficult to compare, especially in light of grade inflation at many schools, and that the provenance of student essays is often uncertain.

FINANCIAL AID

Students should submit: FAFSA, institution's own financial aid form, CSS/Financial Aid PROFILE, Noncustodial PROFILE, Business/Farm Supplement. Regular filing deadline is February 15. The Princeton Review suggests that all financial aid forms be submitted as soon as possible after January 1. *Need-based scholarships/grants offered:* Pell Grant, SEOG, state scholarships/grants, private scholarships, the school's own gift aid. *Loan aid offered:* FFEL Subsidized Stafford, FFEL Unsubsidized Stafford, FFEL PLUS, Federal Perkins Loan, state loans, college/university loans from institutional funds. Applicants will be notified of awards on or about April 5. Federal Work-Study Program available. Institutional employment available. Off-campus job opportunities are good.

FROM THE ADMISSIONS OFFICE

"Each year Bowdoin sponsors myriad events, including performances by bands, comedians, artists, and dancers as well as lectures and film series, community-service events, and the occasional scavenger hunt. Performers who have appeared at the college recently include Savion Glover, Dar Williams, Guster, Wynton Marsalis, and Mos Def. Speakers have included David Sedaris, Adrienne Rich, Robert Reich, Spike Lee, Nobel Laureate Thomas Cech, and playwright Tony Kushner. The college has more than 100 active student organizations. About 70 percent of students participate in community service during their time at Bowdoin, and the college's many volunteer programs allow students to interact with the Brunswick community. Club and intramural sports and the Outing Club enable students to get involved in physical fitness without having to be star athletes. Bowdoin is determined to be a place that brings together people from widely diverse ethnic and economic backgrounds, from different parts of the country and the world, and with divergent political beliefs, a full range of religious identities, and broad academic interests.

"Submission of the SAT or the ACT is optional for students applying to Bowdoin. Both the old and new versions of the SAT and ACT are acceptable. For candidates electing to submit them, the scores will be reviewed along with other indicators of academic achievement and potential. "

SELECTIVITY

Admissions Rating	98
# of applicants	5,401
% of applicants accepted	22
% of acceptees attending	41
# of early decision applicants	633
% accepted early decision	31

FRESHMAN PROFILE

Range SAT Critical Reading	650–750
Range SAT Math	650–730
Minimum Paper TOEFL	600
Minimum Computer Based TOEFL	250
% graduated top 10% of class	82
% graduated top 25% of class	96
% graduated top 50% of class	100

DEADLINES

Early decision application deadline	11/15
Early decision notification	12/31
Regular application deadline	1/1
Regular notification	4/5
Nonfall registration?	no

APPLICANTS ALSO LOOK AT

AND OFTEN PREFER
Harvard College, Princeton University, Yale University

AND SOMETIMES PREFER
Brown University, Dartmouth College, Williams College

AND RARELY PREFER
Amherst College, Bates College, Colby College, Middlebury College

FINANCIAL FACTS

Financial Aid Rating	98
Annual tuition	$34,280
Room & Board	$9,310
Books and supplies	$800
Required fees	$360
% frosh rec. need-based scholarship or grant aid	39
% UG rec. need-based scholarship or grant aid	44
% frosh rec. need-based self-help aid	33
% UG rec. need-based self-help aid	41
% frosh rec. any financial aid	48
% UG rec. any financial aid	43

BRADLEY UNIVERSITY

1501 WEST BRADLEY AVENUE, PEORIA, IL 61625 • ADMISSIONS: 309-677-1000 • FAX: 309-677-2797

STUDENTS SAY

Academics

Offering "the variety and opportunities of a large school with the personal interaction that only a small university can offer," Bradley University is "the perfect size," a place "large enough to provide students with a variety of choices but small enough that there is not much difficulty getting into the classes that you want to take." Small class sizes "allow the students to get to know the professors on a personal as well as professional level," creating a "family environment" reinforced by the fact that "the faculty is more focused on teaching and less focused on research," and that "all classes are taught by professors" and not by teaching assistants. The Bradley approach yields some impressive results: The school boasts excellent placement rates for its graduates in medical, dental, and natural science graduate programs. Students tell us that Bradley also has a "good graphic design program," "a great engineering school," and is "an excellent school for education majors." Bradley's "strong College of Communications" benefits from top-notch facilities at its Global Communications Center, which is "quite high-tech with good computers and even their own studio." Academic demands at Bradley "are pretty straightforward"; professors "are demanding and expect students to do a lot of work and work hard," in return for which students receive "lots of academic opportunities . . . as long as you take the time to discover them." Bradley's administration "is extremely open to student suggestions. Although not all suggestions are adopted, the administration will listen to any and all concerns."

Life

For many at Bradley, "Social life is focused on fraternities and sororities, but these groups are far more open here than at other places." Others find different social outlets; students report that "some split exists between the three major social groups on campus (Greeks, residence hall staff, and athletes) but each offers its own unique opportunities. Any student wanting to get involved on campus will not struggle for opportunities." The Bradley campus "always has things going on, as do our student organizations. We go to concerts (like Black Eyed Peas, Emerson Drive, etc.), listen to comedians, participate in all-school philanthropies (like Relay for Life, Dance Marathon, Habitat for Humanity,, etc.), on campus. Those are always well attended and usually really cheap." While "Drinking plays a big role in the campus social life . . . students can find sober social opportunities if they want them." Men's basketball is popular, although the games are off campus so "You'll have to be lucky enough to have a car/bus ride" to enjoy them. Overall, "People do a pretty good job balancing social life and school life" here. Students give hometown Peoria middling grades, warning that "if you go very far from the 'Bradley streets,' you'll find yourself in a tough neighborhood."

Student Body

The typical Bradley student "is from the Chicago/St. Louis suburbs or from a small town in Central Illinois. . . . Students tend to be upper-middle class, but there are many exceptions. Many students seem to identify as Catholics but don't practice, and there are also large numbers of Jewish and Protestant students. The campus is very White, although the university is taking steps to attempt to change that." Most "are very intelligent. They worked hard in high school and they have a drive and ambition to be here." Yet, despite that drive, they are generally "jeans and t-shirt-wearing people, very relaxed, and not super-stressed out." They tend to be "friendly, outgoing, and active in organizations or Greek life."

FINANCIAL AID: 309-677-3089 • E-MAIL: ADMISSIONS@BRADLEY.EDU • WEBSITE: WWW.BRADLEY.EDU

ADMISSIONS

Very important factors considered include: Rigor of secondary school record. *Important factors considered include:* Academic GPA, class rank, standardized test scores. *Other factors considered include:* Alumni/ae relation, application essay, character/personal qualities, extracurricular activities, geographical residence, interview, level of applicant's interest, racial/ethnic status, recommendation(s), talent/ability, volunteer work, work experience. SAT or ACT required; TOEFL required of all international applicants. High school diploma is required, and GED is accepted. *Academic units required:* 4 English, 3 math, 2 science (2 science labs), 2 social studies. *Academic units recommended:* 5 English, 4 math, 3 science (3 science labs), 2 foreign language, 3 social studies, 2 history.

The Inside Word

Bradley continues to be a regional school, with the vast majority of students originating from Illinois. It would undoubtedly love to broaden its geographic demographics, so the school presents an opportunity for out-of-staters seeking to attend an excellent university without having to endure a grueling admissions process. Above average students should find that gaining admission here is a relatively painless experience.

FINANCIAL AID

Students should submit: FAFSA. The Princeton Review suggests that all financial aid forms be submitted as soon as possible after January 1. *Need-based scholarships/grants offered:* Pell Grant, SEOG, state scholarships/grants, private scholarships, the school's own gift aid. *Loan aid offered:* Direct Subsidized Stafford, Direct Unsubsidized Stafford, Direct PLUS, FFEL PLUS, Federal Perkins Loan, Federal Nursing Loan.

FROM THE ADMISSIONS OFFICE

"Unlike many smaller private colleges, Bradley offers the academic variety of more than 100 undergraduate and 30 graduate programs of study. In addition to the traditional liberal arts and sciences, academic programs include business, communications, education, engineering, fine and performing arts, and health sciences. Unique programs include entrepreneurship, multimedia, and a doctorate program in physical therapy.

"While students have the academic choices of a larger university, they also have the guidance and mentoring of faculty. Unlike many larger institutions, the Bradley academic experience happens in faculty-taught classes that average just 23 students. One-on-one interaction with professionals is the expectation at Bradley.

"Beyond a great academic experience, what really makes Bradley exceptional is campus life. Bradley students are involved in more than 220 student organizations, including more than 50 dedicated to student leadership and community service.

"Integration of career development is central to the Bradley experience. One measurable outcome of this career development integration is that 95 percent of graduates begin work, graduate school, or other postgraduate experiences within 6 months of graduation.

"The Peoria area is the largest metropolitan region in Illinois south of Chicago and is home to more than 360,000 residents. The sizeable city provides ample opportunities for internships, practicums, cooperative education, and volunteer experiences.

"In summary, the Bradley experience is unlike most other universities. A Bradley student will experience a blend of quality academics, focused career preparation, extensive activities, and leadership opportunities.

"Bradley requires freshman applicants to submit scores from either the old or the new SAT. Students may also choose to submit scores from the ACT, with or without the Writing component, in lieu of the SAT."

SELECTIVITY

Admissions Rating	77
# of applicants	4,321
% of applicants accepted	83
% of acceptees attending	30
# accepting a place on wait list	13
% admitted from wait list	100

FRESHMAN PROFILE

Range SAT Critical Reading	520–620
Range SAT Math	550–650
Range ACT Composite	22–29
Minimum Paper TOEFL	525
Minimum Computer Based TOEFL	213
% graduated top 10% of class	28
% graduated top 25% of class	63
% graduated top 50% of class	92

DEADLINES

Regular application deadline	rolling
Regular notification	rolling
Nonfall registration?	yes

APPLICANTS ALSO LOOK AT

AND OFTEN PREFER
DePaul University, Illinois Wesleyan University, University of Illinois at Urbana-Champaign

AND SOMETIMES PREFER
Loyola University—Chicago, Marquette University, Purdue University—West Lafayette

AND RARELY PREFER
Illinois State University, Northern Illinois University, University of Illinois at Chicago

FINANCIAL FACTS

Financial Aid Rating	72
Annual tuition	$21,200
Room & Board	$7,050
Required fees	$178
Books and supplies	$500
% frosh rec. need-based scholarship or grant aid	64
% UG rec. need-based scholarship or grant aid	69
% frosh rec. need-based self-help aid	55
% UG rec. need-based self-help aid	52
% frosh rec. any financial aid	96
% UG rec. any financial aid	92

BRANDEIS UNIVERSITY

415 SOUTH STREET, MS003, WALTHAM, MA 02454 • ADMISSIONS: 781-736-3500 • FAX: 781-736-3536

STUDENTS SAY

Academics

Home to "lots of 'pre-somethings' trying to figure out if that 'something' is right for them," Brandeis University is "a good jumping-off point for those looking to go into medicine or law." Boasting "a very good liberal arts education," Brandeis also provides plenty of alternatives to those who start down the "pre-something" path only to find that it's not for them. Even those who stay the course appreciate the "large variety of options"; as one student explains, "Brandeis is very academically stimulating and has many interesting courses, professors who make themselves available outside of class, and teaching assistants who are very helpful." Aspiring doctors are drawn here by a "stellar" neuroscience department that gives undergraduates "the experience of graduate students as far as research is concerned," in addition to "a very high acceptance rate at medical schools." Other strong programs include psychology ("amazing, but very biology-based, making it difficult for students who aren't good at science and math to complete the major requirements"), music, economics, political science, and history. Students agree that most professors are "passionate about what they teach." Classes "are generally small, which puts pressure on you to come prepared," and there is "a fair amount of class discussion, which can be great or awful." Students are ready to be engaged in class, as they are typically "friendly and talkative. An intense philosophical discussion is more common at Brandeis than drunken boorishness."

Life

Brandeis boasts "plenty of performance-based clubs (theater, musical, improv comedy, sketch comedy, dance), community-service organizations, activist clubs, ethnic clubs, religious clubs, political clubs, independent sports clubs, and also clubs just for fun, like the hookah club. There are so many opportunities to be involved here," and students "take [their] extracurriculars just as seriously as [their] studies, and tend to excel in both." Students also love their access to Boston, noting that "a free shuttle runs us to and from the city Thursdays through Sundays." The proximity of Boston helps offset the fact that "there is really nothing to do in Waltham. There is a movie theater, and some restaurants, and bars, but that is about it. Proximity to [Boston College] and Bentley is nice, however." Students say the social scene at Brandeis "is somewhat lacking. If you are looking for big sporting events with lots of spirit or parties with lots of people, you won't like Brandeis." Parties "don't ever fall into your lap at Brandeis; you have to look for them." For some, this is a plus; as one student writes, "I like the school because if you want a quiet Friday night with board games and old movies, it's very easy to do. People won't judge you or pressure you into drinking. But on Saturday when you're ready for some fun, you have to do a little digging."

Student Body

Brandeis has long been a popular destination for Jewish students. About 40 percent of the student population (undergrad and grad) is Jewish, and undergrads tell us that "there are a lot of orthodox Jews here, more than at your average college. Yet, there are also a lot of non-religious students, observant Muslims, and Christians. So the school just teaches us to recognize each others' religions," and "You never feel like your fellow students are judging you." A "nice-sized international community" also "helps diversify the school." Many here tend to be "pretty socially awkward, and kind of an overachiever, but generally well-intentioned and sweet." One student told us that students tend to be "quirky, prone to traditionally nerdy pursuits, and very friendly. At Brandeis, weird is normal." Everyone works hard here "because they want to do well," and students "spend most of their time studying." Politically, "It's hard to be anything but a mainstream-to-radical liberal at Brandeis, because conservative or completely alternative viewpoints are viewed as either foolish or crazy."

FINANCIAL AID: 781-736-3700 • E-MAIL: SENDINFO@BRANDEIS.EDU • WEBSITE: WWW.BRANDEIS.EDU

ADMISSIONS

Very important factors considered include: Academic GPA, class rank, level of applicant's interest, rigor of secondary school record, standardized test scores. *Important factors considered include:* Application essay, character/personal qualities, extracurricular activities, first generation, recommendation(s), talent/ability, volunteer work, work experience. *Other factors considered include:* Alumni/ae relation, geographical residence, interview, racial/ethnic status. SAT and SAT Subject Tests or ACT required; ACT with Writing component required. TOEFL required of all international applicants. High school diploma is required, and GED is accepted. *Academic units recommended:* 4 English, 3 math, 1 science (1 science lab), 3 foreign language, 1 history, 4 academic electives.

The Inside Word

Brandeis requires one of two combinations of standardized test scores: the SAT plus two SAT Subject Tests or the ACT with Writing component. Most students choose the ACT with Writing option, but if you've already taken all your SATs and aced them, submit those scores instead. Brandeis is often looked at as a safety school for students applying to Ivies; as the Ivies now routinely reject many highly qualified applicants, admission to Brandeis is extremely competitive despite its safety school reputation.

FINANCIAL AID

Students should submit: FAFSA, CSS/Financial Aid PROFILE, Noncustodial PROFILE, Business/Farm Supplement. The Princeton Review suggests that all financial aid forms be submitted as soon as possible after January 1. *Need-based scholarships/grants offered:* Pell Grant, SEOG, state scholarships/grants, private scholarships, the school's own gift aid. *Loan aid offered:* Direct Subsidized Stafford, Direct Unsubsidized Stafford, Direct PLUS, Federal Perkins Loan, state loans, college/university loans from institutional funds. Federal Work-Study Program available. Off-campus job opportunities are fair.

FROM THE ADMISSIONS OFFICE

"Education at Brandeis is personal, combining the intimacy of a small liberal arts college and the intellectual power of a large research university. Classes are small and are taught by professors, 98 percent of whom hold the highest degree in their fields. They give students personal attention in state-of-the-art resources, giving them the tools to succeed in a variety of postgraduate endeavors.

"This vibrant, freethinking, intellectual university was founded in 1948. Brandeis University reflects the values of the first Jewish Supreme Court Justice Louis Brandeis, which are passion for learning, commitment to social justice, respect for creativity and diversity, and concern for the world.

"Brandeis has an ideal location on the commuter rail nine miles west of Boston; state-of-the-art sports facilities; and internships that complement interests in law, medicine, government, finance, business, and the arts. Brandeis offers generous university scholarships and need-based financial aid that can be renewed for 4 years.

"Brandeis requires that students send official scores for the new SAT and two SAT Subject Tests, or the ACT with Writing in place of all SATs. Students for whom English is not their first language should take the TOEFL (Test of English as a Foreign Language)."

SELECTIVITY

Admissions Rating	97
# of applicants	7,640
% of applicants accepted	36
% of acceptees attending	28
# accepting a place on wait list	469
% admitted from wait list	10
# of early decision applicants	259
% accepted early decision	68

FRESHMAN PROFILE

Range SAT Critical Reading	630–730
Range SAT Math	630–730
Range ACT Composite	27–32
Minimum Paper TOEFL	600
Minimum Computer Based TOEFL	250
Average HS GPA	3.83
% graduated top 10% of class	76
% graduated top 25% of class	96
% graduated top 50% of class	99

DEADLINES

Early decision application deadline	11/15
Early decision notification	12/15
Regular application deadline	1/15
Regular notification	4/1
Nonfall registration?	yes

APPLICANTS ALSO LOOK AT

AND OFTEN PREFER
Brown University, Cornell University, Dartmouth College, University of Pennsylvania

AND SOMETIMES PREFER
New York University, Tufts University, Washington University in St. Louis

AND RARELY PREFER
Boston College, Boston University, State University of New York at Binghamton

FINANCIAL FACTS

Financial Aid Rating	81
Annual tuition	$32,951
Room & Board	$9,463
Books and supplies	$700
% frosh rec. need-based scholarship or grant aid	52
% UG rec. need-based scholarship or grant aid	46
% frosh rec. need-based self-help aid	39
% UG rec. need-based self-help aid	41
% frosh rec. any financial aid	54
% UG rec. any financial aid	47

BRIGHAM YOUNG UNIVERSITY (UT)

A-153 ASB, PROVO, UT 84602-1110 • ADMISSIONS: 801-422-2507 • FAX: 801-422-0005

CAMPUS LIFE

Quality of Life Rating	97
Fire Safety Rating	62
Type of school	private
Affiliation	Church of Jesus Christ of Latter-day Saints
Environment	city

STUDENTS

Total undergrad enrollment	30,798
% male/female	51/49
% from out of state	72
% live on campus	20
% Asian	3
% Caucasian	76
% Hispanic	3
% Native American	1
% international	2
# of countries represented	121

SURVEY SAYS . . .

Students are very religious
Very little hard liquor
(Almost) no one smokes
Very little drug use

ACADEMICS

Academic Rating	82
Calendar	semester
Student/faculty ratio	21:1
Profs interesting rating	83
Profs accessible rating	77
Most common reg class size	20–29 students

MOST POPULAR MAJORS

English language and literature
political science and government
psychology

STUDENTS SAY

Academics

Students at Brigham Young University in Provo, the flagship campus of the BYU system, love the amenities their big school provides. They praise the "great research opportunities for undergraduates, [the] amazing library with its great resources," and the availability of "lots of classes and almost every major imaginable." The school is also committed to "keeping ahead technologically and keeping current on world events." What students love most about their school, however, is "the opportunity to receive a religious education at the same time as you receive your academic education, and the opportunity for those to mingle. In classes that are not religion-based, there are often discussions of how religion fits into the subject area of that course. It is nice to be able to discuss those things thoughtfully in a university atmosphere." Incoming students should prepare for a big-school experience; one undergrad explains, "It's initially overwhelming to pour into your classrooms with hundreds of other students," and freshmen are well advised to "take advantage of the Freshman Academy or honors programs." One student writes, "As you accrue credits, you will personally get to know some fabulous teachers . . . the key is that you have to take the initiative" in introducing yourself to them. Students praise the required curriculum, which they believe "helps [them] to be well-rounded individuals."

Life

"Religion defines what BYU is and why it is such a great school," students agree, frequently reminding us that "we don't have to worry about a lot of things that other schools worry about. At the holidays we don't have 'don't drink and drive' campaigns . . . we don't have to worry about the drug and alcohol abuse." BYU's honor code sets the tone; it "prohibits drinking, drugs, cheating, and dishonest actions. [BYU's dress and grooming standards] also require men to be clean shaven (no beards)." In short, "Students are expected to keep high standards at BYU, and this helps the students to be better people." Undergrads find plenty of ways to have fun without intoxicants, they assure us; one reports, "There is never a night when something isn't happening on campus, whether it's an athletic event, or a play, or a smaller social event planned by some section of the student council." There are "tons of events like movies, dance performances, museums, lots of student clubs and organizations, and good restaurants" to choose from on campus, and then, of course, there's also all that Provo has to offer. Students especially love the outdoors; many "enjoy skiing and snowboarding, and there are others that love to hike." Dating is also a major focal point of social life. One student explains, "BYU is a school where people come to get married. Due to the fact that BYU is sponsored by the Church of Jesus Christ of Latter-day Saints . . . people pretty much go to BYU to meet people with their same standards, and get married."

Student Body

The vast majority of BYU undergrads are members of the Church of Jesus Christ of Latter-day Saints, which results in a high comfort level for the majority; "It's nice to know that over 90 percent of the student body shares your morals and beliefs," explains one student. There are also "international students and ethnic minorities, and there is a fairly large Islamic community within BYU, and atypical students seem to fit in pretty well. Those who are not of our faith are still respected and encouraged to practice their own faith." One student writes, "The greatest strength of BYU lies in its unity—unity that comes through diversity, not homogeneity. BYU students come from all over the world but are mostly people who have very high religious standards and come to BYU for that reason. This is a great strength because in unity we can address concerns with greater strength than [in] places that are torn with strife."

BRIGHAM YOUNG UNIVERSITY (UT)

FINANCIAL AID: 801-378-4104 • E-MAIL: ADMISSIONS@BYU.EDU • WEBSITE: WWW.BYU.EDU

ADMISSIONS

Very important factors considered include: Academic GPA, character/personal qualities, interview, religious affiliation/commitment, rigor of secondary school record, standardized test scores. *Important factors considered include:* Application essay, extracurricular activities, racial/ethnic status, recommendation(s), volunteer work. *Other factors considered include:* Talent/ability, work experience. ACT required; TOEFL required of all international applicants. High school diploma is required, and GED is accepted. *Academic units required:* 4 English, 3 math, 2 science (2 science labs), 2 foreign language, 2 history, 2 literature or writing. *Academic units recommended:* 4 English, 4 math, 3 science (3 science labs), 4 foreign language.

The Inside Word

Despite the high acceptance rate, this is a rigorous application process that will quickly and efficiently eliminate candidates who make a poor match. Most eliminate themselves by not applying to begin with, as the matchmaking places exceptionally great weight on the ideological fit.

FINANCIAL AID

Students should submit: FAFSA. The Princeton Review suggests that all financial aid forms be submitted as soon as possible after January 1. *Need-based scholarships/grants offered:* Pell Grant, state scholarships/grants, private scholarships, the school's own gift aid. *Loan aid offered:* FFEL Subsidized Stafford, FFEL Unsubsidized Stafford, FFEL PLUS, college/university loans from institutional funds. Applicants will be notified of awards on or about April 20.

FROM THE ADMISSIONS OFFICE

"The mission of Brigham Young University—founded, supported, and guided by the Church of Jesus Christ of Latter-day Saints—is to assist individuals in their quest for perfection and eternal life. That assistance should provide a period of intensive learning in a stimulating setting where a commitment to excellence is expected and the full realization of human potential is pursued. All instruction, programs, and services at BYU, including a wide variety of extracurricular experiences, should make their own contribution toward the balanced development of the total person. Such a broadly prepared individual will not only be capable of meeting personal challenge and change but will also bring strength to others in the tasks of home and family life, social relationships, civic duty, and service to mankind.

"Freshman applicants for Fall 2008 classes are required to take either the new ACT (with or without the optional Writing section) or the new version of the SAT. Students may also submit scores from the old (prior to the March 2005) version of either test. Their highest composite score will be used in admissions decisions."

SELECTIVITY

Admissions Rating	87
# of applicants	8,696
% of applicants accepted	78
% of acceptees attending	79

FRESHMAN PROFILE

Range SAT Critical Reading	550–660
Range SAT Math	570–670
Range ACT Composite	25–29
Minimum Paper TOEFL	500
Minimum Computer Based TOEFL	173
Average HS GPA	3.73
% graduated top 10% of class	49
% graduated top 25% of class	35
% graduated top 50% of class	99

DEADLINES

Regular application deadline	2/1
Nonfall registration?	yes

APPLICANTS ALSO LOOK AT AND SOMETIMES PREFER

Brigham Young University—Idaho, University of Utah

FINANCIAL FACTS

Financial Aid Rating	80
Annual tuition	$3,620
Room & Board	$5,640
Books and supplies	$1,380
% frosh rec. need-based scholarship or grant aid	13
% UG rec. need-based scholarship or grant aid	29
% frosh rec. need-based self-help aid	6
% UG rec. need-based self-help aid	15
% frosh rec. any financial aid	20
% UG rec. any financial aid	36

BROWN UNIVERSITY

PO BOX 1876, 45 PROSPECT STREET, PROVIDENCE, RI 02912 • ADMISSIONS: 401-863-2378 • FAX: 401-863-9300

CAMPUS LIFE
Quality of Life Rating	96
Fire Safety Rating	60*
Type of school	private
Environment	city

STUDENTS
Total undergrad enrollment	5,927
% male/female	47/53
% from out of state	96
% from public high school	60
% live on campus	85
% in (# of) fraternities	12 (10)
% in (# of) sororities	2 (3)
% African American	7
% Asian	14
% Caucasian	51
% Hispanic	7
% Native American	1
% international	6
# of countries represented	72

SURVEY SAYS . . .
No one cheats
Students are friendly
Great off-campus food
Students are happy

ACADEMICS
Academic Rating	85
Calendar	semester
Student/faculty ratio	9:1
Profs interesting rating	88
Profs accessible rating	88
% profs teaching UG courses	100
% classes taught by TAs	13

MOST POPULAR MAJORS
history
international relations and affairs

STUDENTS SAY
Academics

"It's like the school has a motto," writes a typical Brown University undergrad, "and that motto is: 'It's your money. Why should we choose your classes?'" Thanks to the school's open curriculum, "Being at Brown means you will never again have to take a class if you don't want to." Students who flock here are the types who yearn for such academic freedom; they "love the open curriculum and the chance it gives us to really invest ourselves in what we're most interested in. Brown allows you to explore academically without punishing you for it." Brown also "allows students to choose how we are evaluated in our classes by choosing to take any class S/NC (Satisfactory/No Credit). This says a lot about the learning philosophy of the school, which is mainly focused on the process of learning rather than simply the results." Brown professors "are engaging, challenging us as students and as participants in the learning process," and are "very accessible, dedicated to undergraduate students and usually pretty funny outside the classroom." Students appreciate that "a lot of the introductory classes are taught by brilliant professors. The concentration is truly on the undergraduates." Administrators, "as strange as it seems, are also incredibly accessible." One student sums up, "Everything is at your fingertips, but you have to reach out for it. At Brown, very few things will simply come to you, but you can be sure that if you want it, it will be there."

Life

"The social scene is a lot like the academic scene" at Brown "in that there is a huge variety of options, and people tend to experience most of them. From hanging out to cocktail parties, from hippies partying in their co-ops to kids studying in the library, from fraternity parties to watching a movie, everything you can imagine doing for fun happens." Students agree that "Brown is a school that definitely parties, and Wednesday night through Sunday students here are partying," but not until they get their schoolwork done. Academics are demanding, and students here work hard, but "Aside from exams and major assignments, life is laid-back. That isn't to say the students lack passion or drive—quite the opposite—but there's a marked lack of nervous tension." Undergrads find plenty of time for extracurriculars, populating "over 150 extracurricular clubs and activities," including "great theater and music" opportunities. They also enjoy "free lectures by everyone from Spike Lee to Mikhail Gorbachev, free concerts, free comedy show[s], plays. We have anything and everything. There is almost too much going on." And then there's Providence, "a nice location with all sorts of cool night clubs and restaurants that don't make it easy to be bored on a Saturday night. There are hot spots like Fish Company, where people drink and dance, and there's Thayer Street, with anything a college student could ever need, from groceries, books, and clothes to videos, bikes, and clubs." Brown undergrads also take advantage of the fact that "Boston and New York City are relatively close by."

Student Body

Most Brown undergrads are "individual, freethinking, and eager to learn." They are "very smart, have a keen knowledge of current affairs, and can talk about Plato, FDR, or biology," but "They don't have swelled heads. They're generally pretty well grounded, open to new ideas, and fun." Like the New Englanders who surround them, "They tend to be very liberal and very politically active. It is a necessity to be up-to-date on current events, as discussions and debates take place from dorm rooms to the gym to the cafeteria." The "Typically small 'outsider' communities (e.g., GLBT students) here have a lot of support on campus and generally hang out together." While "Brown has a reputation as a hippie school, it really isn't: There are people who fit into every social niche, and although it's not always easy to find the right people right away, they're out there."

FINANCIAL AID: 401-863-2721 • E-MAIL: ADMISSION_UNDERGRADUATE@BROWN.EDU • WEBSITE: WWW.BROWN.EDU

ADMISSIONS

Very important factors considered include: Character/personal qualities, rigor of secondary school record, talent/ability. *Important factors considered include:* Academic GPA, application essay, class rank, extracurricular activities, recommendation(s), standardized test scores. *Other factors considered include:* Alumni/ae relation, geographical residence, interview, racial/ethnic status, state residency, volunteer work, work experience. SAT and SAT Subject Tests or ACT required; ACT with Writing component required. TOEFL required of all international applicants. High school diploma is required, and GED is not accepted. *Academic units required:* 4 English, 3 math, 3 science (2 science labs), 3 foreign language, 2 history, 1 academic elective. *Academic units recommended:* 4 English, 4 math, 4 science (3 science labs), 4 foreign language, 2 history, 1 academic elective.

The Inside Word

The cream of just about every crop applies to Brown. Gaining admission requires more than just a superior academic profile from high school. Some candidates, such as the sons and daughters of Brown graduates (who are admitted at virtually double the usual acceptance rate), have a better chance for admission than most others. Minority students benefit from some courtship, particularly once admitted. Ivies like to share the wealth and distribute offers of admission across a wide range of constituencies. Candidates from states that are overrepresented in the applicant pool, such as New York, have to be particularly distinguished in order to have the best chance at admission. So do those who attend high schools with many seniors applying to Brown, as it is rare for several students from any one school to be offered admission.

FINANCIAL AID

Students should submit: FAFSA, CSS/Financial Aid PROFILE, Noncustodial PROFILE, Business/Farm Supplement. Regular filing deadline is February 1. The Princeton Review suggests that all financial aid forms be submitted as soon as possible after January 1. *Need-based scholarships/grants offered:* Pell Grant, SEOG, state scholarships/grants, private scholarships, the school's own gift aid. *Loan aid offered:* Direct Subsidized Stafford, Direct Unsubsidized Stafford, Direct PLUS, Federal Perkins Loan, state loans, college/university loans from institutional funds. Applicants will be notified of awards on or about April 1. Federal Work-Study Program available. Institutional employment available. Off-campus job opportunities are excellent.

FROM THE ADMISSIONS OFFICE

"Founded in 1764, Brown is a private, coeducational, Ivy League university in which the intellectual development of undergraduate students is fostered by a dedicated faculty on a traditional New England campus.

"Applicants will be required to submit results of the SAT Reasoning Test and any two SAT Subject Tests (except for the SAT Subject Test Writing). Students may substitute any SAT tests with the ACT with the Writing component."

SELECTIVITY

Admissions Rating	99
# of applicants	16,911
% of applicants accepted	15
% of acceptees attending	57
# accepting a place on wait list	450
% admitted from wait list	22
# of early decision applicants	2046
% accepted early decision	28

FRESHMAN PROFILE

Range SAT Critical Reading	660–760
Range SAT Math	670–770
Range ACT Composite	27–33
Minimum Paper TOEFL	600
Minimum Computer Based TOEFL	250
% graduated top 10% of class	90
% graduated top 25% of class	99
% graduated top 50% of class	100

DEADLINES

Early decision application deadline	11/1
Early decision notification	12/15
Regular application deadline	1/1
Regular notification	4/1
Nonfall registration?	no

APPLICANTS ALSO LOOK AT

AND OFTEN PREFER
Harvard College, Princeton University, Stanford University, Yale University

AND SOMETIMES PREFER
Amherst College, Massachusetts Institute of Technology, Smith College, Williams College

AND RARELY PREFER
Bowdoin College, Georgetown University, Oberlin College, Tufts University

FINANCIAL FACTS

Financial Aid Rating	95
Annual tuition	$32,264
Room & Board	$8,796
Books and supplies	$2,515
Required fees	$955
% frosh rec. need-based scholarship or grant aid	40
% UG rec. need-based scholarship or grant aid	40
% frosh rec. need-based self-help aid	32
% UG rec. need-based self-help aid	39

BRYANT UNIVERSITY

1150 DOUGLAS PIKE, SMITHFIELD, RI 02917 • ADMISSIONS: 401-232-6100 • FAX: 401-232-6741

CAMPUS LIFE

Quality of Life Rating	84
Fire Safety Rating	83
Type of school	private
Environment	town

STUDENTS

Total undergrad enrollment	3,231
% male/female	58/42
% from out of state	84
% live on campus	81
# of fraternities	6
# of sororities	3
% African American	3
% Asian	3
% Caucasian	85
% Hispanic	4
% international	2
# of countries represented	31

SURVEY SAYS . . .
Small classes
Great computer facilities
Great library
Athletic facilities are great
Career services are great
Campus feels safe
Lots of beer drinking
Hard liquor is popular

ACADEMICS

Academic Rating	78
Calendar	semester
Student/faculty ratio	16:1
Profs interesting rating	78
Profs accessible rating	82
% profs teaching	
UG courses	100
% classes taught by TAs	0
Most common	
lab size	20–29 students
Most common	
reg class size	30–39 students

MOST POPULAR MAJORS
accounting
business administration/
management
marketing/marketing management

STUDENTS SAY

Academics

Bryant University offers some majors outside of business and management, but there's no doubt that these courses remain the school's bread and butter. Students report that "every class, including the liberal arts classes . . . will involve business in one way or another." Another trumpets, "All my sociology, psychology, even ecology classes somehow discussed the business world within them!" Technologically, the school goes all-out, with "an enormous amount of resources on campus, including a simulated trading floor of the NYSE. Also, the entire campus is now wireless, so students can connect to the Internet with their laptops anywhere." Studying in such technologically advanced facilities means that "students can relate classes to the real world. We really do live in a business environment." The school's "student-centered" approach distinguishes it as well; "Everything on campus is designed to help out the student body, from the student programming, to the facilities, to the faculty. It is a very nurturing environment," explains one undergrad. Students also appreciate the "strong alumni relations, which help with internships and job placement." Solid programs in accounting, finance, marketing, and management have earned Bryant "a strong academic reputation. The school challenges its students to think creatively, both alone and in group settings, to reach goals."

Life

Because many "Students at Bryant have—on top of a full course load—a job and/or internship, are members of a minimum of two organizations and/or sports, and hold some type of position of leadership," undergraduates "have little free time during the week." The campus is a very work-friendly environment, students tell us; "The abundance of technology on our campus—television monitors in almost every corner that you look, Voice Over IP phones in the dorm rooms, wireless Internet connectivity all over campus—creates an environment where students can work hard, relax a little, and work some more." The "very clean and well-landscaped [campus] is basically in the middle of the woods," providing "peace to study," but with the benefit "of a great city not far away." While weekdays are devoted to work and clubs, "Thursday through Sunday there are parties or people going out to Providence who you can catch a ride with, with more studying on the weekends at intermittent times."

Student Body

"Since it's a business school with all serious business students for the most part, it excludes a wide diversity of people and their quirks," Bryant students observe. "Every day, either you're dressing in a business suit or you're in your daily clothing (mainly Abercrombie & Fitch and North Face and other high-end brand names, such as Burberry, Gucci, Seven, etc)." In other words, "Idiosyncrasy is not encouraged; business etiquette and manners are a must at most times in this school." Most here are "preppy and financially stable. There are not many people who come from nonwealthy backgrounds." They can be cliquish; one student explains, "People rarely leave their own groups and the drama caused by much of it can get annoying by senior year." The school "has a sizeable population of international students, including students from China, India, Spain, South Africa, Turkey, and Italy. These students, many of whom belong to the Multicultural Student Union, are among the most active members of the Bryant community and take part in a number of events to educate Bryant students and faculty about different races and cultures."

BRYANT UNIVERSITY

FINANCIAL AID: 401-232-6020 • E-MAIL: ADMISSION@BRYANT.EDU • WEBSITE: ADMISSION.BRYANT.EDU

ADMISSIONS

Very important factors considered include: Academic GPA, rigor of secondary school record. *Important factors considered include:* Application essay, class rank, recommendation(s), standardized test scores. *Other factors considered include:* Alumni/ae relation, character/personal qualities, extracurricular activities, first generation, geographical residence, interview, level of applicant's interest, racial/ethnic status, state residency, talent/ability, volunteer work, work experience. SAT or ACT required; ACT with Writing component required. TOEFL required of all international applicants. High school diploma is required, and GED is accepted. *Academic units required:* 4 English, 4 math, 3 science (2 science labs), 2 foreign language, 2 history/social sciences. *Academic units recommended:* 4 history/social sciences.

The Inside Word

If you're a solid student you should meet little trouble getting into Bryant. The university's admissions effort has brought in qualified applicants from across the country, but the heaviest draw remains from New England. Students attending Bryant will receive a solid business education as well as precious connections in the corporate worlds of Providence and Boston.

FINANCIAL AID

Students should submit: FAFSA. Regular filing deadline is February 15. The Princeton Review suggests that all financial aid forms be submitted as soon as possible after January 1. *Need-based scholarships/grants offered:* Pell Grant, SEOG, state scholarships/grants, private scholarships, the school's own gift aid. *Loan aid offered:* Direct Subsidized Stafford, Direct Unsubsidized Stafford, FFEL PLUS, Federal Perkins Loan. Applicants will be notified of awards on or about March 24.

FROM THE ADMISSIONS OFFICE

"Bryant is a 4-year, private university in New England where students build knowledge, develop character, and achieve success—as they define it. In addition to a first-class faculty, state-of-the-art facilities, and advanced technology, Bryant offers stimulating classroom dynamics; internship opportunities at more than 350 companies; 70-plus student clubs and organizations; varsity, intramural, and club sports for men and women; and many opportunities for community service and leadership development.

"Bryant is the choice for individuals seeking the best integration of business and liberal arts, utilizing state-of-the-art technology. Bryant offers degrees in applied mathematics, applied economics, applied psychology, business administration, communication, global studies, history, information technology, international business, literary and cultural studies, and politics and law.

"A cross-disciplinary academic approach teaches students the creative problem-solving and communication skills they need to successfully compete in a complex, global environment. Students can also pursue one of 24 minors in business and liberal arts, and several additional areas of study. Bryant's rigorous academic standards have been recognized and accredited by NEASC and AACSB International.

"Technology is a fundamental component of the learning process at Bryant. Every entering freshman is provided with a Thinkpad laptop for personal use. Students exchange their laptop for a new one in their junior year, which they will own upon graduation.

"Bryant University is situated on a beautiful 420-acre campus in Smithfield, Rhode Island. The campus is only 15 minutes away from the state capital, Providence; 45 minutes from Boston; and 3 hours from New York City. Enjoy an array of activities on and off campus, excellent restaurants, and sports events.

"Bryant requires that students enrolling in Fall 2008 take the new SAT with the Writing component, or the ACT with the Writing section."

SELECTIVITY
Admissions Rating	89
# of applicants	5,829
% of applicants accepted	44
% of acceptees attending	32
# accepting a place on wait list	472
% admitted from wait list	26
# of early decision applicants	204
% accepted early decision	60

FRESHMAN PROFILE
Range SAT Critical Reading	500–580
Range SAT Math	540–620
Range SAT Writing	510–590
Range ACT Composite	21–25
Minimum Paper TOEFL	550
Minimum Computer Based TOEFL	213
Average HS GPA	3.42
% graduated top 10% of class	24
% graduated top 25% of class	63
% graduated top 50% of class	93

DEADLINES
Early decision application deadline	11/15
Early decision notification	12/15
Regular application deadline	2/1
Regular notification	3/15
Nonfall registration?	yes

APPLICANTS ALSO LOOK AT
AND OFTEN PREFER
Bentley College, Providence College, University of Massachusetts—Amherst
AND SOMETIMES PREFER
Quinnipiac University, Stonehill College, University of Connecticut, University of New Hampshire
AND RARELY PREFER
Assumption College, Merrimack College, University of Rhode Island

FINANCIAL FACTS
Financial Aid Rating	71
Annual tuition	$26,099
Room & Board	$10,909
Books and supplies	$1,200
% frosh rec. need-based scholarship or grant aid	57
% UG rec. need-based scholarship or grant aid	55
% frosh rec. need-based self-help aid	60
% UG rec. need-based self-help aid	60
% frosh rec. any financial aid	85
% UG rec. any financial aid	85

THE BEST 366 COLLEGES ■ 109

BRYN MAWR COLLEGE

101 NORTH MERION AVENUE, BRYN MAWR, PA 19010-2859 • ADMISSIONS: 610-526-5152 • FAX: 610-526-7471

STUDENTS SAY
Academics
"In order to excel at Bryn Mawr, you need to be willing to do more work than you've ever done in your life," undergrads at this small, prestigious women's college warn. Most are willing, in fact. They "challenge themselves, always doing their individual best" to meet the demands of the school's "insanely rigorous, but rewarding, academics." Why? One student writes, "I feel that the hours and hours of work are worthwhile. The students know that their work isn't just busy work and that there are high standards; that pushes us to improve and learn in a way that wouldn't otherwise be possible." Bryn Mawr's "great track record for sending students to medical school" attests to the success of the school's approach; students' devotion to the school does likewise. Undergrads here especially appreciate the important role they play in running the school. One student explains, "With the oldest self-governing association in the entire country, Bryn Mawr prides itself on the close communication between everyone in the community, from the president of the college to the incoming freshmen, each year." A student-administered honor code, one of the school's many treasured traditions, "makes taking final exams incredibly easy. Almost all exams are self-scheduled, so you can take them when you're ready, not when they're assigned." Additionally, "The Student Curriculum Committee is very active in fulfilling the students' needs and desires for the academic process." Academic partnerships with Haverford, Swarthmore, and Penn heavily supplement the "sometimes pitiful course selection" here.

Life
"Because Bryn Mawr is all women, the social life is different from the traditional college experience," students here explain. "When you're a freshman, traditions like Lantern Night, Hell Week, and Parade Night really make you feel like a part of 'the sisterhood' of Bryn Mawr." Undergrads also point out that except for the aforementioned traditions, "you really have to go off campus if you want to party. Fortunately there are so many colleges in such close proximity, including Villanova, Haverford, Swarthmore, and Penn, that you can always go out to a party if you want to, and you get to come home to a clean and quiet dorm." Many here report that "we spend most weekends in Philadelphia." For those who stick around campus on weekends, activities "usually include watching a movie and ordering out or going to some campus activity." The surrounding town, students agree, "is pretty boring." On a more positive note, "The campus is gorgeous. Imagine a Welsh castle," one undergrad suggests.

Student Body
"The only really common feature to Bryn Mawr women is an intense commitment to our studies. Other than that, everyone here really does her own thing," students agree. Even so, they see some dominant strains within their ranks; they detect, for example, a strong contingent of women who are "preppy, liberal, and open to homosexuality. Because it is an all-women school, there are a lot of gay students, and those who aren't gay are accepting of the gay community." There are also conspicuous minorities of "high school misfits who come here to fit in, as well as students who take Harry Potter a little too seriously. They wear capes every day." Women here agree that "the community is overwhelmingly liberal politically, and the more moderate or conservative approaches or viewpoints of an issue can get lost in the majority at times. It would be nice to see more diversity of political opinion at Bryn Mawr." Otherwise, Bryn Mawr students "run the gamut from the well-groomed New Jersey girl, to the vegan Girl Scout, to the hairy rugby player."

ADMISSIONS

Very important factors considered include: Recommendation(s), rigor of secondary school record. *Important factors considered include:* Academic GPA, application essay, character/personal qualities, extracurricular activities. *Other factors considered include:* Alumni/ae relation, class rank, first generation, geographical residence, interview, racial/ethnic status, standardized test scores, talent/ability, volunteer work, work experience. SAT and SAT Subject Tests or ACT required; TOEFL required of all international applicants. High school diploma is required, and GED is accepted. *Academic units required:* 2 academic electives. *Academic units recommended:* 4 English, 3 math, 2 science (1 science lab), 3 foreign language, 2 social studies, 2 history.

The Inside Word

Do not be deceived by Bryn Mawr's admission rate; its student body is among the academically best in the nation. Outstanding preparation for graduate study draws an applicant pool that is well prepared and intellectually curious. The Admissions Committee includes eight faculty members and four seniors. Each applicant is reviewed by four readers, including at least one faculty member and one student.

FINANCIAL AID

Students should submit: FAFSA, CSS/Financial Aid PROFILE, Business/Farm Supplement, statement of earnings from parent's employer. Regular filing deadline is March 1. The Princeton Review suggests that all financial aid forms be submitted as soon as possible after January 1. *Need-based scholarships/grants offered:* Pell Grant, SEOG, Academic Competitiveness Grant, National SMART Grant, state scholarships/grants, the school's own gift aid. *Loan aid offered:* FFEL Subsidized Stafford, FFEL Unsubsidized Stafford, FFEL PLUS, Federal Perkins Loan. Applicants will be notified of awards on or about March 23.

FROM THE ADMISSIONS OFFICE

"One wouldn't ordinarily assume that a small institution could offer as diverse a range of opportunities as many large universities, or that a campus that looks like the English countryside could exist within 20 minutes of downtown Philadelphia, but Bryn Mawr is far from ordinary. Prepare to be surprised. Innovative, creative, and purposeful, the students at Bryn Mawr inspire their peers as much and as often as any faculty member. Spirited intellectual inquiry, a commitment to academic excellence, and a desire to impact the world in a meaningful way are the hallmarks of this community of equals. Students at Bryn Mawr learn by doing and lead by example. They take full advantage of all that Bryn Mawr has to offer, including internship opportunities, an active alumnae association, a lively Community-Service Office and a consortium of schools that includes Haverford, Swarthmore, and the University of Pennsylvania. Bryn Mawr's Student Government Association is the oldest in the country, and students participate in every aspect of the college's decision-making process, serving as representatives to Admissions, the Honor Board, the Curriculum Committee, and even the Board of Trustees. Bryn Mawr is a demanding and caring place where both ideas and individuals matter.

"The new SAT and two SAT Subject Tests are required for admission. Students may choose SAT Subject Tests. Students may submit the ACT in lieu of the SAT and SAT Subject Tests. We recommend that students also take the optional ACT Writing Test."

SELECTIVITY

Admissions Rating	**95**
# of applicants	2,133
% of applicants accepted	44
% of acceptees attending	38
# accepting a place on wait list	194
% admitted from wait list	19
# of early decision applicants	180
% accepted early decision	49

FRESHMAN PROFILE

Range SAT Critical Reading	620–740
Range SAT Math	580–680
Range SAT Writing	590–710
Range ACT Composite	27–31
Minimum Paper TOEFL	600
Minimum Computer Based TOEFL	250
% graduated top 10% of class	62
% graduated top 25% of class	88
% graduated top 50% of class	100

DEADLINES

Early decision application deadline	11/15
Early decision notification	12/15
Regular application deadline	1/15
Regular notification	4/15
Nonfall registration?	no

APPLICANTS ALSO LOOK AT

AND OFTEN PREFER
Brown University, Harvard College, University of Pennsylvania,

AND SOMETIMES PREFER
Haverford College, Mount Holyoke College, Scripps College, Smith College, Swarthmore College, Wellesley College

AND RARELY PREFER
Oberlin College, Vassar College

FINANCIAL FACTS

Financial Aid Rating	**96**
Annual tuition	$32,230
Room & Board	$10,550
Books and supplies	$1,000
Required fees	$780
% frosh rec. need-based scholarship or grant aid	55
% UG rec. need-based scholarship or grant aid	56
% frosh rec. need-based self-help aid	46
% UG rec. need-based self-help aid	48
% frosh rec. any financial aid	73
% UG rec. any financial aid	68

BUCKNELL UNIVERSITY

FREAS HALL, BUCKNELL UNIVERSITY, LEWISBURG, PA 17837 • ADMISSIONS: 570-577-1101 • FAX: 570-577-3538

CAMPUS LIFE

Quality of Life Rating	82
Fire Safety Rating	83
Type of school	private
Environment	village

STUDENTS

Total undergrad enrollment	3,528
% male/female	49/51
% from out of state	73
% from public high school	69
% live on campus	88
% in (# of) fraternities	39 (13)
% in (# of) sororities	40 (6)
% African American	3
% Asian	7
% Caucasian	80
% Hispanic	4
% Native American	1
% international	3
# of countries represented	41

SURVEY SAYS . . .

Small classes
Great library
Athletic facilities are great
Campus feels safe
Frats and sororities
dominate social scene
Lots of beer drinking

ACADEMICS

Academic Rating	93
Calendar	semester
Student/faculty ratio	12:1
Profs interesting rating	87
Profs accessible rating	89
% profs teaching UG courses	100
% classes taught by TAs	0
Most common lab size	10–19 students
Most common reg class size	10–19 students

MOST POPULAR MAJORS

business administration/
management
economics
psychology

STUDENTS SAY

Academics

Bucknell University, "a liberal arts school with a top engineering program," is "a typical Patriot League school where students somehow find a way to balance studying and partying" while remaining "ambitious about their studies, extremely friendly and caring in nature, and bound to succeed." "Small class sizes, a beautiful campus, friendly students and faculty, and amazing facilities" all conspire to justify the premium price tag on a Bucknell education; $31 million in annual financial aid means about half the students don't have to foot the entire bill. "The courses are tough, and the workload is heavy" here, "but the academic experience is a wonderful one," with professors who "are passionate and energetic and convey their love for their field to their students. They give us their home phone numbers and e-mail addresses and tell us to come to their offices just to say hello. They want to teach us, but also want to be our friends." Bucknell offers more than 50 majors and 60 minors, an impressive array for a school of this size; business and engineering majors are most popular, while premeds benefit from numerous opportunities to get involved in research. It's the kind of school that inspires lifelong loyalty; as one undergrad sums up, "Bucknell boasts a tight-knit community where most people are friends with most other people and 99 percent of varsity athletes graduate in four years. Bucknell is a community of scholars as well as social [beings], with many students possessing both qualities. Few students regret their choice and remain involved in campus affairs for lifetimes."

Life

"Life at Bucknell is centered on a social structure," and "While students do work hard at their academics, they party equally as hard." Indeed, according to some, "On weekends, you have a few choices: dorms or downtown, beer or hard liquor, drugs or alcohol. Partying is it, though." This perception is reinforced by the fact that hometown Lewisburg is very small and very quiet. Greek organizations play a huge role on campus; one reluctant fraternity member writes, "I never thought I would join a fraternity, and the prevalence of Greek life was one of the downsides of coming here originally, but I found a group of guys where I fit in quite well, so I spend a lot of time on fraternity activities. But that's really my choice because I enjoy it." Many here will tell you that there are options "that do not revolve around the party scene, such as the outing club, the nationally known Conservatives Club," and a number of religious- and service-related organizations such as Catholic Campus Ministry and Student Emergency Response Volunteers. Bucknell competes in the Patriot League against the likes of Army, Navy, Lehigh, and Lafayette; "The basketball team has been very good lately, so they're a lot of fun."

Student Body

"A lot of people are preppy—super preppy" on the Bucknell campus, many students tell us, observing that "the sheer number of student-owned luxury cars on this campus is astounding." An adamant minority insists that "Bucknell has a reputation for being a preppy school, but in my experience that reputation is overblown." Most everyone agrees that 'preppy' doesn't have to mean boring; the student body includes "plenty of interesting and different people to hang out with if you look for them." Undergrads tend to be "energetic" and "involved in many things on campus. Students try their best at everything they do." Students typically "come from Pennsylvania, New Jersey, or New York. There are a lot from New England also, and Maryland's probably next."

FINANCIAL AID: 570-577-1331 • E-MAIL: ADMISSIONS@BUCKNELL.EDU • WEBSITE: WWW.BUCKNELL.EDU

ADMISSIONS

Very important factors considered include: Academic GPA, character/personal qualities, class rank, rigor of secondary school record, standardized test scores, talent/ability. *Important factors considered include:* Extracurricular activities, level of applicant's interest, racial/ethnic status, recommendation(s), volunteer work. *Other factors considered include:* Alumni/ae relation, application essay, first generation, geographical residence, interview, religious affiliation/commitment, work experience. SAT or ACT required; ACT with Writing component required. TOEFL required of all international applicants. High school diploma is required, and GED is accepted. *Academic units required:* 4 English, 3 math, 2 science, 2 foreign language, 2 social studies, 2 history, 1 academic elective. *Academic units recommended:* 4 English, 4 math, 3 science, 4 foreign language, 2 social studies, 2 history, 1 academic elective.

The Inside Word

Admissions rates vary by intended major at Bucknell. The school receives applications from more prospective business majors than the school can handle; as a result, only about 23 percent were admitted to the class of 2010. Admit rates are higher among populations that tend to be self-selecting, including science majors, computer science majors, and engineers. Those listing "undecided" as prospective major made up about 17 percent of admitted applicants; 33 percent of such applicants were admitted. You certainly don't hurt yourself by listing "undecided" as your intended major.

FINANCIAL AID

Students should submit: FAFSA, CSS/Financial Aid PROFILE, Noncustodial PROFILE. Regular filing deadline is January 1. The Princeton Review suggests that all financial aid forms be submitted as soon as possible after January 1. *Need-based scholarships/grants offered:* Pell Grant, SEOG, state scholarships/grants, private scholarships, the school's own gift aid. *Loan aid offered:* FFEL Subsidized Stafford, FFEL Unsubsidized Stafford, FFEL PLUS, Federal Perkins Loan. Applicants will be notified of awards on or about April 1.

FROM THE ADMISSIONS OFFICE

"Bucknell combines the personal experience of a small liberal arts college with the breadth and opportunity typically found at larger research universities. With a low student/faculty ratio, students gain exceptional hands-on experience, working closely with faculty in an environment enhanced by first-class academic, residential, and athletic facilities. Together, the College of Arts and Sciences and the College of Engineering offer 53 majors and 64 minors. Learning opportunities permeate campus life in and out of the classroom and across the disciplines. For example, engineering students participate in music ensembles, theater productions, and poetry readings, while arts and sciences students take engineering courses, conduct scientific research in the field, and produce distinctive creative works. Students also pursue their interests in more than 150 organizations and through athletic competition in the prestigious Division I Patriot League. These activities constitute a comprehensive approach to learning that teaches students how to think critically and develop their leadership skills so that they are prepared to make a difference locally, nationally, and globally.

"Applicants graduating from high school in—or after—2006 are required to take the new SAT or the ACT with the Writing section. Fall 2008 applicants are allowed to submit scores from the old versions of both tests as their best scores (old/new) will be used in making admissions decisions. "

SELECTIVITY

Admissions Rating	96
# of applicants	9,021
% of applicants accepted	33
% of acceptees attending	31
# accepting a place on wait list	724
% admitted from wait list	6
# of early decision applicants	761
% accepted early decision	52

FRESHMAN PROFILE

Range SAT Critical Reading	600–680
Range SAT Math	630–710
Range SAT Writing	590–680
Range ACT Composite	27–30
Minimum Paper TOEFL	550
Minimum Computer Based TOEFL	213
% graduated top 10% of class	71
% graduated top 25% of class	94
% graduated top 50% of class	100

DEADLINES

Early decision application deadline	11/15
Early decision notification	12/15
Regular application deadline	1/1
Regular notification	4/1
Nonfall registration?	no

APPLICANTS ALSO LOOK AT

AND OFTEN PREFER
Boston College, Cornell University, Georgetown University, Tufts University, University of Virginia

AND SOMETIMES PREFER
Carnegie Mellon University, Colgate University, The College of William & Mary, Lehigh University, Wake Forest University

AND RARELY PREFER
Dickinson College, Franklin & Marshall College, Hamilton College, Lafayette College, Skidmore College

FINANCIAL FACTS

Financial Aid Rating	96
Annual tuition	$37,934
Room & Board	$8,052
Books and supplies	$750
Required fees	$200
% frosh rec. need-based scholarship or grant aid	46
% UG rec. need-based scholarship or grant aid	46
% frosh rec. need-based self-help aid	46
% UG rec. need-based self-help aid	48
% frosh rec. any financial aid	60
% UG rec. any financial aid	62

CALIFORNIA INSTITUTE OF TECHNOLOGY

1200 EAST CALIFORNIA BOULEVARD, MAIL CODE 328-87, PASADENA, CA 91125 • ADMISSIONS: 626-395-6341 • FAX: 626-683-3026

CAMPUS LIFE
Quality of Life Rating	82
Fire Safety Rating	60*
Type of school	private
Environment	metropolis

STUDENTS
Total undergrad enrollment	864
% male/female	72/28
% from out of state	68
% from public high school	70
% live on campus	92
% African American	1
% Asian	37
% Caucasian	46
% Hispanic	6
% international	8
# of countries represented	30

SURVEY SAYS . . .
Small classes
No one cheats
Lab facilities are great
Great library
Students are friendly
Campus feels safe
Frats and sororities are unpopular or nonexistent

ACADEMICS
Academic Rating	78
Calendar	quarter
Student/faculty ratio	3:1
Profs interesting rating	61
Profs accessible rating	67

MOST POPULAR MAJORS
mathematics
mechanical engineering
physics

STUDENTS SAY
Academics
Nestled in sunny Pasadena, this world-renowned research university makes no concessions to students expecting to coast on natural ability alone. As one student explains, "Every day is a new challenge, and sometimes I find it miraculous that I'm able to keep up." Achieving success at this school is due in large part to "a tremendous amount of determination and will," as well as a collaborative atmosphere that encourages "students to learn to work together to solve problems." Chalk this kind of support up to a test-taking policy that "allows you to take your exams whenever you want, wherever you want" and a much-respected honor code that stipulates, "No member of the Caltech community shall take unfair advantage of any other member of the Caltech community." Many students are quick to admit, however, that "a lot of people have been unhappy with the administration recently," citing "budget decisions that were made with little or no input from students or faculty." Despite these recent concerns, students note they "have a closer relationship to [the administration] than [they might at] many other larger schools" and the administration "does appear to be taking steps to improve communication." Students love that they have the opportunity to "come into close contact with Nobel Laureates and other famed scientists, as they all teach courses and accept students into their labs for research." As one student sums up, "The amount of information each student is expected to digest in the course of the year is daunting, but once achieved makes a Caltech grad ready for anything."

Life
Despite the proximity of Los Angeles and all the forms of entertainment it provides, most students "work—a lot." As one student explains, "We live in our own little bubble of problem sets and lectures. The academics here are intense, probably the most intense you could hope to find. Not for the faint of heart." In this high-stakes environment the need to blow off steam is equally pressing, often involving "whatever crazy spontaneous stuff happens to pop up." "Athletics, movies, and video games" are also popular. Caltech students have a reputation for pranks, thanks to inventive minds and a housing system "which is very unique and a big part of the social life. The houses combine the feel and purpose of a dorm with the pride and spirit of a fraternity." "Each house plans social events" and "provides the main social community" for students who find it to be "Caltech's greatest feature." According to one student, the house system ensures that "everyone has a place in a tight-knit community with people who share their interests and personality." That said, if you ever want to get away from it all to hit the bar, club, stadium, or beach, "The key is to know someone with a car."

Student Body
As you might expect from such an academically rigorous university, at Caltech "Your worth is determined by your work ethic and your intelligence, not your appearance." As one student explains, most students "have an interest in what are conventionally considered nerdy topics." It is in this embrace of difference that Caltech students find themselves united, since "All together we form a very atypical, brainy, hardworking but fun group." Consider it a meeting of the minds as, "The typical student is smarter than you, no matter how smart you are." While the notion that "more than one person in your class will win the Nobel prize someday" may seem intimidating at first, being in such close proximity to brilliance is very useful "when you need help with problem sets." The student population is mostly male and not hugely diverse, but "The student body makes up for its lack of physical diversity with personality diversity." All in all, it's an "accepting" campus where "everyone finds a place."

CALIFORNIA INSTITUTE OF TECHNOLOGY

FINANCIAL AID: 626-395-6280 • E-MAIL: UGADMISSIONS@CALTECH.EDU • WEBSITE: ADMISSIONS.CALTECH.EDU

ADMISSIONS

Very important factors considered include: Rigor of secondary school record. *Important factors considered include:* Academic GPA, application essay, character/personal qualities, class rank, extracurricular activities, recommendation(s), standardized test scores. *Other factors considered include:* Alumni/ae relation, first generation, racial/ethnic status, talent/ability, volunteer work, work experience. SAT or ACT required; SAT Subject Tests required. High school diploma or equivalent is not required. *Academic units required:* 3 English, 4 math, 2 science (1 science lab), 1 social studies, 1 history. *Academic units recommended:* 4 English, 4 science.

The Inside Word

Each Caltech application receives three independent reads before it is presented to the Admissions Committee. This ensures that all candidates receive a thorough evaluation. The school values the unique drive and energy of its current students and desires applicants whom display a similar combination of creativity and intellect. Stellar academic credentials are a must, and prospective students must display an aptitude for math and science.

FINANCIAL AID

Students should submit: FAFSA, CSS/Financial Aid PROFILE, state aid form, Noncustodial PROFILE, Business/Farm Supplement; Noncustodial PROFILE and Business/Farm Supplement forms are required only when applicable. Regular filing deadline is January 15. The Princeton Review suggests that all financial aid forms be submitted as soon as possible after January 1. *Need-based scholarships/grants offered:* Pell Grant, SEOG, state scholarships/grants, private scholarships, the school's own gift aid. *Loan aid offered:* Direct Subsidized Stafford, Direct Unsubsidized Stafford, Direct PLUS, Federal Perkins Loan, college/university loans from institutional funds. Applicants will be notified of awards on or about April 15.

FROM THE ADMISSIONS OFFICE

"Admission to the freshman class is based on many factors—some quantifiable, some not. What you say in your application is important! Because we don't interview students for admission, your letters of recommendation are weighed heavily. High school academic performance is very important, as is a demonstrated interest in math, science, and/or engineering. We are also interested in your character, maturity, and motivation. We are very proud of the process we use to select each freshman class. It's very individual, it has great integrity, and we believe it serves all the students who apply. If you have any questions about the process or about Caltech in general, write us a letter or give us a call. We'd like to hear from you!

"Freshman applicants must submit scores from either the new or old SAT (or ACT, Writing section optional). In addition, students must submit the results of two SAT Subject Tests: Mathematics IIC and one of the following: Biology (Ecological or Molecular), Chemistry, or Physics."

SELECTIVITY

Admissions Rating	**99**
# of applicants	3,330
% of applicants accepted	17
% of acceptees attending	37
# accepting a place on wait list	240
% admitted from wait list	28

FRESHMAN PROFILE

Range SAT Critical Reading	690–770
Range SAT Math	780–800
Range SAT Writing	670–760
% graduated top 10% of class	88
% graduated top 25% of class	97
% graduated top 50% of class	100

DEADLINES

Regular application deadline	1/1
Regular notification	4/1
Nonfall registration?	no

APPLICANTS ALSO LOOK AT

AND OFTEN PREFER
Harvard College, Princeton University, Stanford University

AND SOMETIMES PREFER
Harvey Mudd College, Massachusetts Institute of Technology, University of California—Berkeley

AND RARELY PREFER
Rensselaer Polytechnic Institute, Virginia Tech

FINANCIAL FACTS

Financial Aid Rating	**99**
Annual tuition	$28,515
Room & Board	$9,102
Books and supplies	$1,077
Required fees	$1,080
% frosh rec. need-based scholarship or grant aid	53
% UG rec. need-based scholarship or grant aid	53
% frosh rec. need-based self-help aid	31
% UG rec. need-based self-help aid	38
% frosh rec. any financial aid	60
% UG rec. any financial aid	60

CALIFORNIA STATE UNIVERSITY—STANISLAUS

801 WEST MONTE VISTA AVENUE, TURLOCK, CA 95382 • ADMISSIONS: 209-667-3070 OR 800-300-7420 (CA ONLY) • FAX: 209-667-3394

CAMPUS LIFE

Quality of Life Rating	80
Fire Safety Rating	76
Type of school	public
Environment	town

STUDENTS

Total undergrad enrollment	6,576
% male/female	34/66
% from out of state	1
% from public high school	93
% live on campus	10
% in (# of) fraternities	3 (5)
% in (# of) sororities	3 (7)
% African American	4
% Asian	12
% Caucasian	40
% Hispanic	29
% Native American	1
% international	1
# of countries represented	35

SURVEY SAYS . . .

Small classes
Great computer facilities
Great library
Students are friendly
Diverse student types on campus
Great off-campus food
Campus feels safe
Students are happy

ACADEMICS

Academic Rating	62
Calendar	4-1-4
Student/faculty ratio	19:1
Profs interesting rating	75
Profs accessible rating	73
% profs teaching UG courses	94
Most common lab size	10–19 students
Most common reg class size	20–29 students

MOST POPULAR MAJORS

business administration/
management
liberal arts and sciences/liberal
studies
psychology

STUDENTS SAY

Academics

"California State University—Stanislaus is all about getting an education that's useful in the real world," students at this smallish state university in California's Central Valley tell us. CSUS boasts a "great nursing program" that "only has 40 students each year, so you get great personal attention," a College of Business that "is one of the strongest pieces to the CSUS puzzle," and solid programs in psychology, social work, criminal justice, and biology. That's not a bad selection for a school that is "small enough to make a true commitment to accommodate its students. It's also a school that does not forget its students once they graduate." One student quotes CSU Stanislaus president Hamid Shirvani who says, "We are small enough to foster the formation of lifelong relationships inside the classroom and out, yet big enough to offer a wide range of courses and activities to encourage you to stretch yourself and to make the most of some of the most precious years of your life: your college years." Students appreciate their school's dedication to "bringing every student the highest quality education in the Central Valley by providing up-to-speed technology in the classrooms, high diversity of classes, and most importantly, excellent professors who personally care for their students."

Campus Life

The CSUS campus is "a very tranquil place to study, very quiet, and with beautiful scenery." It's not a wild social hub, though, in large part because there are relatively few resident students on campus. As one commuter notes, "There aren't many fun organized activities on campus, especially not for commuters; this is because the activities that are fun are usually late at night after classes have ended." Those who stick around after class report that "we have Late Night Stanislaus every Friday night with a wide range of activities ranging from comedy to crafts, and there is always free food!" They also point out that "the RAs plan fun things for the students living on the campus to do, from camping to rock climbing to special events during the holidays." Recreational facilities include "two game rooms, one on campus and one on the villa, tennis courts, basketball courts, and a soccer field with access to equipment." Hometown Turlock "is a small town so there is not much to do," but fortunately "Modesto is close and San Francisco is not that far. Plays, dinner, movies, and sporting events are all within reach."

Student Body

With fewer than 1,000 students residing on campus, CSUS "can be best described as a 'commuter' school" with "different ages, ethnicities, and social groups on campus" though the school has been steadily losing its commuter population in recent years. Hispanic and Asian students constitute the largest minority groups at this "rural college in an agrarian area." The typical undergrad, we're told, "is from a middle-middle-class or upper-middle-class background, very Abercrombie & Fitch." There aren't "a lot of outcasts," and "atypical students seem to fit in just fine." Some students observe that "CSUS is divided into two sections: Serious students who enjoy the small school size, and casual students who are just there for the ride."

CALIFORNIA STATE UNIVERSITY—STANISLAUS

FINANCIAL AID: 209-667-3336 • E-MAIL: OUTREACH_HELP_DESK@CSUSTAN.EDU • WEBSITE: WWW.CSUSTAN.EDU

ADMISSIONS

Very important factors considered include: Academic GPA, rigor of secondary school record, standardized test scores, *Important factors considered include:* Class rank. TOEFL required of all international applicants. High school diploma is required, and GED is accepted. *Academic units required:* 4 English, 3 math, 2 science, (2 science labs), 2 foreign language, 1 social studies, 1 history, 1 academic elective, 1 visual and performing arts.

The Inside Word

Typical of most state schools, CSUS's admissions practices are fairly straightforward. The university adheres to the eligibility index as defined by the California state system. Therefore, applicants who meet GPA and standardized test score minimums are automatically granted admission. Out-of-state candidates do face more stringent requirements as do those applying for certain majors/programs such as the Pre-Licensure Nursing Program. If you are a student applying from out-of-state, make sure your GPA, test scores, and application package are in top form.

FINANCIAL AID

Students should submit: FAFSA, the institution's own financial aid form. The Princeton Review suggests that all financial aid forms be submitted as soon as possible after January 1. *Need-based scholarships/grants offered:* Pell, SEOG, state scholarships/grants, private scholarships, the school's own gift aid, Federal Nursing Scholarships. *Loan aid offered:* FFEL Subsidized Stafford, FFEL Unsubsidized Stafford, FFEL PLUS, Federal Perkins Loan, college/university loans from institutional funds. Applicants will be notified of awards on a rolling basis beginning or about March 15 Federal Work-Study Program available. Institutional employment available. Off-campus job opportunities are good.

FROM THE ADMISSIONS OFFICE

"CSUS was recognized by the American Association of State Colleges and Universities as one of 12 public universities nationwide that demonstrate exceptional performance in retention and graduation rates. Student success is facilitated by a dense network of on-campus resources including consistent advising, a strong first-year program, frequent and meaningful contact with professors, and supportive staff and administrators.

"CSUS has 10 nationally accredited programs widely recognized for its quality academics. A new state-of-the-art science building opened in 2007 along with a new bookstore and student recreation complex in 2008. The campus is widely known as the most beautiful and friendly of the CSU campuses, blending modern facilities with the pastoral charm of the countryside. The campus enjoys an ideal location in the heart of California's Central Valley, a short distance from the San Francisco Bay Area, Monterey, the Sierra Nevada mountains, and Yosemite National Park. The proximity allows for hiking, skiing, snowboarding, kayaking, surfing, and other outdoors sports and activities.

"CSUS awarded more than $16.9 million in merit- and need-based grants and scholarships for the 2006–2007 school year. Approximately 68 percent of freshmen received need-based aid and the average gift aid for the group was $6,116. Scholarships range from full tuition, board, and books through the President's Scholarship to hundreds of other scholarships ranging from $100 to $5,000 per school year. The CSUS experience can be summed up as providing a small private school atmosphere at a public school price.

"CSU—Stanislaus considers only the Critical Reading and Math portions of the new SAT for admission eligibility and accepts the Math, Verbal, and total of the old SAT."

SELECTIVITY

Admissions Rating	**60***
# of applicants	3,003
% of applicants accepted	93
% of acceptees attending	34

FRESHMAN PROFILE

Range SAT Critical Reading	410–530
Range SAT Math	430–540
Range ACT Composite	17–23
Minimum Paper TOEFL	500
Minimum Computer Based TOEFL	173
Average HS GPA	3.2
% graduated top 10% of class	
% graduated top 25% of class	
% graduated top 50% of class	

DEADLINES

Regular application deadline	7/1
Regular notification	rolling
Nonfall registration?	yes

FINANCIAL FACTS

Financial Aid Rating	**62**
Annual in-state tuition	$0
Annual out-of-state tuition	$10,170
Required fees	$3,307
Room & Board	$7,634
Books and supplies	$1,386
% frosh rec. need-based scholarship or grant aid	53
% UG rec. need-based scholarship or grant aid	45
% frosh rec. need-based self-help aid	28
% UG rec. need-based self-help aid	35
% frosh rec. any financial aid	68
% UG rec. any financial aid	57

CALVIN COLLEGE

3201 BURTON STREET SOUTHEAST, GRAND RAPIDS, MI 49546 • ADMISSIONS: 616-526-6106 • FAX: 616-526-6777

CAMPUS LIFE

Quality of Life Rating	**88**
Fire Safety Rating	**60***
Type of school	private
Affiliation	Christian Reformed
Environment	metropolis

STUDENTS

Total undergrad enrollment	4,040
% male/female	46/54
% from out of state	41
% from public high school	42
% live on campus	58
% African American	1
% Asian	3
% Caucasian	85
% Hispanic	1
% international	7
# of countries represented	62

SURVEY SAYS . . .
Small classes
Great computer facilities
Great library
Frats and sororities are unpopular or nonexistent

ACADEMICS

Academic Rating	**83**
Calendar	4-1-4
Student/faculty ratio	12:1
Profs interesting rating	89
Profs accessible rating	89
% profs teaching UG courses	100
% classes taught by TAs	0
Most common lab size	20–29 students
Most common reg class size	20–29 students

MOST POPULAR MAJORS
business administration/
management
elementary education and teaching
engineering

STUDENTS SAY
Academics
"The greatest strength of Calvin is the emphasis on becoming a better person," undergraduates at this Christian Reformed school tell us, observing that "every accredited college or university offers education, but not every school prepares students for the real world [in the way that] Calvin does." Calvin accomplishes this feat through "great study-abroad opportunities, chapel services, group discussions, community service, and an emphasis on 'taking ownership' of one's faith," which "encourages students to think about how their faith integrates with all other parts of their life, including academics." The goal is to "equip students to engage and serve the world from a compassionate and professional Christian viewpoint." Students are quick to point out, however, that religious education and indoctrination are not synonymous here; on the contrary, "Calvin puts an emphasis on making your own choices—'responsible freedom'" is a key phrase. They also warn that "this school is one tough cookie. But it's the kind of cookie you love. Academics here are rigorous, to say the least, but they're interesting and led by the most wonderful professors." Students appreciate Calvin's demanding core curriculum, which "forces students to get out of their comfort zone by requiring them to take classes they wouldn't choose to. This ensures that graduates are well rounded and well prepared for the real world." Best of all, perhaps, Calvin "provides a fantastic Christian education for little money, compared to other private schools."

Life
"There's a lot to do without really leaving campus, [including] sporting activities like hockey and basketball, movies shown on campus, and the Dance Guild, which produces a show every semester." The school does a great job of bringing in "state-of-the-art musicians," including (in the last 4 years) John Mayer, Jason Mraz, Indigo Girls, Jimmy Eat World, The Calling, Michelle Branch, Ladysmith Black Mambazo, and Emmylou Harris. With all these options, "Your time at Calvin can be whatever you decide. You can be on a national championship team, you can use lab equipment that many graduate students don't even have, you can be part of an awesome Christian community, or if you really want, you can hide in your room all day and only come out for midterms and finals." (Those who choose the last option benefit from "dorms that are really beautiful, with huge rooms and nice furniture.") While "you can get involved in religious activities if you want, if you don't want to, you don't have to. There's not a lot of pressure even though it is a Christian school." Calvin is officially a dry campus, "and pretty strict rules about getting caught under the influence of controlled substances are enforced." You can also head into downtown Grand Rapids, a town that "can hold its own" even though "It's not a big metropolitan city. There are great restaurants here, too, excellent movie complexes, malls, and extracurricular seasonal stuff, so you won't be bored unless you decide to be."

Student Body
Because of Calvin's affiliation with the Christian Reformed Church, "the Van, Vander and Sma last names are somewhat dominant in the directory. This can't really be helped because this school is in the middle of Dutch country. However, there are several students from other areas, states, and countries. There are a lot of African and Asian international students." Many here reckon that CRC members make up about half the student body and that "the typical student is tall and blond." Calvin undergrads tend to be conservative; one writes, "Bolt Hall (one of the residence halls) had about 70 Bush-Cheney posters in windows and one Kerry-Edwards poster in 2004." The school is home to "a smaller, but very active liberal group of students," as well.

FINANCIAL AID: 616-957-6134 • E-MAIL: ADMISSIONS@CALVIN.EDU • WEBSITE: WWW.CALVIN.EDU

ADMISSIONS

Very important factors considered include: Academic GPA, religious affiliation/commitment, rigor of secondary school record, standardized test scores. *Important factors considered include:* Application essay, character/personal qualities, extracurricular activities, recommendation(s). *Other factors considered include:* Class rank, level of applicant's interest, volunteer work, work experience. SAT or ACT required (writing optional); TOEFL, ELTS or other documentation of English language proficiency required of all international applicants. High school diploma is required, and GED is accepted. *Academic units required:* 3 English, 3 math, 2 science, 2 social studies, 3 academic electives. *Academic units recommended:* 4 English, 3 math, 2 science (1 science lab), 2 foreign language, 3 social studies, 3 academic electives.

The Inside Word

Calvin's applicant pool is highly self-selected and small. Nearly all candidates get in, and over half choose to enroll. The freshman academic profile is fairly solid, but making a good match with the college philosophically is much more important for gaining admission than anything else.

FINANCIAL AID

Students should submit: FAFSA, institution's own financial aid form. The Princeton Review suggests that all financial aid forms be submitted as soon as possible after January 1. *Need-based scholarships/grants offered:* Pell Grant, SEOG, state scholarships/grants, private scholarships, the school's own gift aid. *Loan aid offered:* Direct Subsidized Stafford, Direct Unsubsidized Stafford, Direct PLUS, Federal Perkins Loan, state loans, college/university loans from institutional funds, private alternative loans. Applicants will be notified of awards on a rolling basis beginning or about March 15. Federal Work-Study Program available. Institutional employment available. Off-campus job opportunities are excellent.

FROM THE ADMISSIONS OFFICE

"Calvin's well-respected faculty, innovative core curriculum, and inquiring student body come together in an environment that links intellectual freedom with a heart for service. Calvin's 400-acre campus is home to 4,200 students and 400 professors who chose Calvin because of its national reputation for academic excellence and faith-shaped thinking. Calvin encourages students to explore all things and offers over 100 academic options to choose from, including accredited professional programs.

"Quality teaching and accessibility to students are considered top priorities by faculty members. More than 80 percent of Calvin professors hold the highest degree in their field, the student/faculty ratio is 12:1, and the average class size is 22. The college's 4-1-4 calendar offers opportunities for off-campus and international study, while service-learning projects draw Calvin students into the local community. Internships allow students to try their individual gifts in the workplace while gaining professional experience. In a recent survey, 96 percent of Calvin graduates reported that they had either secured a job or begun graduate school within 6 months of graduation. Calvin is among the top 3 percent of 4-year private colleges in the number of graduates who go on to earn a PhD.

"Students applying for admission are required to submit scores from either the SAT or the ACT college entrance exam. Calvin does not require the Writing section of either test."

SELECTIVITY

Admissions Rating	80
# of applicants	2,156
% of applicants accepted	98
% of acceptees attending	48

FRESHMAN PROFILE

Range SAT Critical Reading	540–663
Range SAT Math	550–670
Range ACT Composite	23–28
Minimum Paper TOEFL	550
Minimum Computer Based TOEFL	213
Average HS GPA	3.57
% graduated top 10% of class	26
% graduated top 25% of class	54
% graduated top 50% of class	80

DEADLINES

Regular application deadline	8/15
Regular notification	rolling
Nonfall registration?	yes

APPLICANTS ALSO LOOK AT

AND OFTEN PREFER
Hope College

AND SOMETIMES PREFER
Grand Valley State University, University of Michigan—Ann Arbor, Wheaton College (IL)

AND RARELY PREFER
Michigan State University, Michigan Technological University

FINANCIAL FACTS

Financial Aid Rating	77
Annual tuition	$20,245
Room & Board	$7,040
Books and supplies	$760
Required fees	$225
% frosh rec. need-based scholarship or grant aid	62
% UG rec. need-based scholarship or grant aid	61
% frosh rec. need-based self-help aid	52
% UG rec. need-based self-help aid	51
% frosh rec. any financial aid	93
% UG rec. any financial aid	92

CARLETON COLLEGE

100 SOUTH COLLEGE STREET, NORTHFIELD, MN 55057 • ADMISSIONS: 507-646-4190 AND 800-995-2275 • FAX: 507-646-4526

CAMPUS LIFE

Quality of Life Rating	**92**
Fire Safety Rating	**60***
Type of school	private
Environment	village

STUDENTS

Total undergrad enrollment	1,958
% male/female	47/53
% from out of state	73
% from public high school	73
% live on campus	90
% African American	6
% Asian	10
% Caucasian	73
% Hispanic	5
% Native American	1
% international	5
# of countries represented	30

SURVEY SAYS . . .

Small classes
No one cheats
Frats and sororities are unpopular or nonexistent

ACADEMICS

Academic Rating	**98**
Calendar	trimester
Student/faculty ratio	9:1
Profs interesting rating	96
Profs accessible rating	95
% profs teaching UG courses	100
% classes taught by TAs	0
Most common lab size	10–19 students
Most common reg class size	10–19 students

MOST POPULAR MAJORS

biology/biological sciences
economics
political science and government

STUDENTS SAY

Academics

"There is a sense of community that's hard to find elsewhere" at Carleton College, a small, liberal arts school "well known for its all-around academic rigor." One undergraduate explains, "You'll find yourself striking up conversations with complete strangers at the post office, in town, and along sidewalks in the middle of a snowy night. New friends are found everywhere." This is true even among the faculty; "Carleton is not a research college, so while professors do some research, they are much more focused on students." One student adds, "Know those special teachers you had in high school, the ones you will actually remember after graduation? That's what Carleton professors are like." Carleton operates on a trimester calendar, which students endorse. "It's nice to be only taking three classes, though more intensely, rather than spreading yourself over four or five." Students also love the "great Study Abroad Office," which has provided students here with "opportunities to travel to Hong Kong, China, Thailand, Spain, and, soon, Africa." But most of all, they love this Midwestern school's "intellectually stimulating environment. People are not afraid to work hard and get engrossed in what they study. At the same time, no one takes themselves too seriously, and we're always ready for a good time."

Life

"Small and quaint" are two words Carleton students frequently use to describe their school's hometown. "Northfield is not that exciting," cedes a freshman, "but I'm not sure anyone wants to change that." Most students are content simply to find "nice restaurants" and "locals [who] are darn helpful in [just] about any situation" in town. This might be because things are much livelier on campus. "An evening doesn't go by without some kind of event, whether it be musical, artistic, theatrical, or political," a sophomore writes. The notoriously heavy workload can make students a little wacky, to the point that "eventually some people lose it. This comes more in the form of weird, creative outlets than it does self-destructive behavior, though. There are a lot of Naked Winter Olympics, pranks, tradition[s], and general goofing off." Students are proud of this "little bit of eccentricity [that] makes everything fun." Intramurals "are really hot at Carleton; the people who aren't playing them are much fewer and far between than the people who are." Ultimate Frisbee and broomball are the games of choice. "Don't know how to play broomball?" queries one student. "It's easy to pick up. And if you're really horrible at it, don't worry. That doesn't stop anyone from playing." There are also "plenty of parties," and while "a third of the student body will be drunk on a typical weekend," there is "absolutely no pressure to drink if you don't want to." One freshman told us that for fun she "makes a smoothie run to the Sayles-Hill Student Center," then later stops by "Dacie Moses House, a place where students gather to bake cookies."

Student Body

The "creative, warm, compassionate, and helpful" undergrads of Carleton are "super smart and nerdy, but fun-nerdy, not scary-nerdy." Notably, they "don't form cliques based on [conventional] criteria" such as "socioeconomic background, race, gender, [or] sexual orientation"—students report they're more "interested in each other's quirks." An upbeat studio art major writes, "We have a wonderful mix of people that reach[es] from nerds to jocks, people who dye their hair to [those] who swear by Abercrombie, people who are Republican to those who are Democrat to those who are Independent to those who don't care; we have vegetarians and we have people who would live on steak if you let them. We have a truly rich mix of all sorts of people and we all enjoy each other and end up with the most amazing groups of friends." Basically, you'll find the campus to be "a place where energy, creativity, and a good sense of humor get you really far."

FINANCIAL AID: 507-646-4138 • E-MAIL: ADMISSIONS@ACS.CARLETON.EDU • WEBSITE: WWW.CARLETON.EDU

ADMISSIONS

Very important factors considered include: Academic GPA, class rank, rigor of secondary school record. *Important factors considered include:* Application essay, character/personal qualities, extracurricular activities, racial/ethnic status, recommendation(s), standardized test scores, talent/ability, volunteer work, work experience. *Other factors considered include:* Alumni/ae relation, first generation, geographical residence, interview, state residency. SAT or ACT required; SAT Subject Tests recommended; ACT with Writing component required. TOEFL required of all international applicants. High school diploma is required, and GED is accepted. *Academic units recommended:* 4 English, 3 math, 3 science (1 science lab), 3 foreign language, 3 social studies and history.

The Inside Word

Admission to Carleton would be even more difficult if the college had more name recognition. Current applicants should be grateful for this because standards are already rigorous. Only intense competition with the best liberal arts colleges in the country prevents an even lower admit rate.

FINANCIAL AID

Students should submit: FAFSA, CSS/Financial Aid PROFILE, Noncustodial PROFILE, Business/Farm Supplement, prior year tax forms. Regular filing deadline is February 15. The Princeton Review suggests that all financial aid forms be submitted as soon as possible after January 1. *Need-based scholarships/grants offered:* Pell Grant, SEOG, state scholarships/grants, private scholarships, the school's own gift aid. *Loan aid offered:* FFEL Subsidized Stafford, FFEL Unsubsidized Stafford, FFEL PLUS, Federal Perkins Loan, state loans, college/university loans from institutional funds, Minnesota SELF Loan program. Applicants will be notified of awards on or about April 1.

FROM THE ADMISSIONS OFFICE

"In an annual college freshmen survey, Carleton students identify themselves as everything from conservatives to liberals, with a majority of them falling in the moderate to liberal range. Although individualistic and energetic Carls take their academics seriously, they don't take themselves seriously. Participation in athletics, theater, or music, religious events, or dining hall discussion over hearty fare marks the Carleton experience. Cool fact: More snow fell in the Northeast than did here in the past 5 years. Since the year 2000, Carleton has opened a new recreation center with indoor track and fitness center, a new language and dining center, and nine townhouse complexes, providing some apartment-style living for students.

"With nearly three-fifths of the student body receiving need-based grant aid, there is a broad socioeconomic representation across the student body. Five percent of all students are international, and nearly 20 percent come from traditionally underrepresented groups. A look at majors in the past decade shows that graduates cover all areas, with about one-third of them in each of the following: math/science, humanities and arts, and social sciences. Typically, over two-thirds of all students will spend time studying off campus; Carleton participates in programs worldwide from Asia to Africa. You can scuba dive off the Greater Barrier Reef or walk the Great Wall of China.

"Five years after graduating, between 65 percent and 75 percent of alumni pursue graduate or professional degrees. More Carleton graduates have pursued their doctorates in the sciences in the past 20 years than have graduates of other small, comparable liberal arts colleges.

"2008 high school graduates must take the new SAT or ACT with Writing component. Carleton will not accept results from the old SAT format for 2008 application. SAT Subject Tests are not required, though it is recommended that a student submit these if they have taken any."

SELECTIVITY

Admissions Rating	97
# of applicants	4,450
% of applicants accepted	32
% of acceptees attending	36
# accepting a place on wait list	361
% admitted from wait list	3
# of early decision applicants	392
% accepted early decision	49

FRESHMAN PROFILE

Range SAT Critical Reading	670–750
Range SAT Math	660–740
Range ACT Composite	28–32
Minimum Paper TOEFL	600
Minimum Computer Based TOEFL	250
% graduated top 10% of class	78
% graduated top 25% of class	97
% graduated top 50% of class	100

DEADLINES

Early decision application deadline	11/15
Early decision notification	12/15
Regular application deadline	1/15
Regular notification	4/15
Nonfall registration?	no

APPLICANTS ALSO LOOK AT

AND OFTEN PREFER
Williams College, Yale University

AND SOMETIMES PREFER
Bowdoin College, Grinnell College, Washington University in St. Louis, Wesleyan College

AND RARELY PREFER
Macalester College, Oberlin College

FINANCIAL FACTS

Financial Aid Rating	97
Comprehensive fee	$42,864
Books and supplies	$602
% frosh rec. need-based scholarship or grant aid	50
% UG rec. need-based scholarship or grant aid	56
% frosh rec. need-based self-help aid	48
% UG rec. need-based self-help aid	55

CARNEGIE MELLON UNIVERSITY

5000 FORBES AVENUE, PITTSBURGH, PA 15213 • ADMISSIONS: 412-268-2082 • FAX: 412-268-7838

STUDENTS SAY

Academics

Carnegie Mellon University is "all about technology. Whether it be engineering, music, theater, robotics, science, or psychology; it's about learning by breaking things down to find out how they work." With nearly half the students engaged in computer- and engineering-related disciplines, Carnegie Mellon can seem to be the domain of number-crunchers, but in fact the school also excels in music, theater, design, architecture, all the hard sciences, business, and economics; it is truly "a place where nerds of all kinds can thrive." One student observes, "Carnegie Mellon is strong in so many different fields. I wasn't sure what I wanted to do, but I wanted to be in a place where I could find out early in a hands-on way, and switch to an equally great program if I wanted." Those who choose Carnegie Mellon should prepare for academic demands that can "overwhelm you with work and stress in order to weed out the weak from the strong." To help students cope, the school offers "tons of academic resources to get extra help, from peer tutoring to office hours to student-led review sessions. Still, it's incredibly important to stay on top of assignments, or they really pile up." Hard work "prepares Carnegie Mellon students for post-undergraduate success," students agree, and when you reach that stage you'll be assisted by "a great career center" that draws "constant job recruiting on campus" and maintains "fantastic alumni connections," though this is somewhat dependent on a student's major.

Life

"Work hard, then work harder" might be the mantra of some Carnegie Mellon students; among them is the undergrad who tells us: "I go to class, I study in the library, and I work out. The day is so long that generally by the time I get home, I eat and am ready for bed because most of the time it's 11:00 or 12:00 at night already." Others tell us, however, that "if you are a social person, you can and will find other social people that you can have fun with." The weekend, or Friday night and Saturday—"Sunday will of course be spent doing work"—is the time to cut loose. Greek life and movies are the big on-campus draws: "Every Friday, Saturday, and Sunday night a just-released movie from the main theaters plays on campus; you can get a ticket, popcorn, and a drink for under three dollars." A good deal of students, though, prefer to have their fun in the city. Pittsburgh "offers a wide variety of things to do off-campus and the Port Authority bus system (free with a Carnegie Mellon ID) does a decent job of transporting students wherever they want to go." There's "always a gallery show to go see" in Pittsburgh, and professional sports, "great restaurants, shopping centers, and malls" are also a draw. The city "has a pretty big bar and club scene, but you must be 21." One student writes, "You can do virtually anything within a reasonable distance, including a trip to a ski mountain."

Student Body

The workload at Carnegie Mellon can be pretty daunting, so it's no surprise that the typical undergrad here "is extremely studious and serious about academics." In terms of priorities, "Extracurricular activities and a social life are far behind academics. Socially, people can be awkward." Even so, "For every recluse or extroverted musical theater major that you'd expect at Carnegie Mellon, there is a polar opposite. People here feel a need to define themselves some way, to defy established stereotypes." Carnegie Mellon draws "a very diverse student body where most people, regardless of race, ethnicity, or gender, tend to get along. Occasionally some cliques form on campus (for example, a certain set of international students, or students from a particular major), but most of the time everyone is friendly."

CARNEGIE MELLON UNIVERSITY

FINANCIAL AID: 412-268-2068 • E-MAIL: UNDERGRADUATE-ADMISSIONS@ANDREW.CMU.EDU • WEBSITE: WWW.CMU.EDU

ADMISSIONS

Very important factors considered include: Academic GPA, rigor of secondary school record. *Important factors considered include:* Application essay, class rank, recommendation(s), standardized test scores. *Other factors considered include:* Alumni/ae relation, character/personal qualities, extracurricular activities, first generation, geographical residence, interview, racial/ethnic status, talent/ability, volunteer work, work experience. SAT or ACT required; ACT with Writing component required. TOEFL required of all international applicants. High school diploma is required, and GED is accepted. *Academic units required:* 4 English, 4 math, 3 science (3 science labs), 2 foreign language, 3 academic electives. *Academic units recommended:* 4 English, 4 math, 3 science (3 science labs), 2 foreign language, 4 academic electives.

The Inside Word

Don't be misled by Carnegie Mellon's acceptance rate. Although relatively high for a university of this caliber, the applicant pool is fairly self-selecting. If you haven't loaded up on demanding courses in high school, you are not likely to be a serious contender. The Admissions Office explicitly states that it doesn't use formulas in making admissions decisions. That said, a record of strong academic performance in the area of your intended major is key.

FINANCIAL AID

Students should submit: FAFSA, institution's own financial aid form, parent and student Federal Income Tax Returns, parent W-2s. Regular filing deadline is May 1. The Princeton Review suggests that all financial aid forms be submitted as soon as possible after January 1. *Need-based scholarships/grants offered:* Pell Grant, SEOG, state scholarships/grants, private scholarships, the school's own gift aid. *Loan aid offered:* FFEL Subsidized Stafford, FFEL Unsubsidized Stafford, FFEL PLUS, Federal Perkins Loan, Gate Student Loan. Applicants will be notified of awards on or about March 15. Federal Work-Study Program available. Institutional employment available. Off-campus job opportunities are good.

FROM THE ADMISSIONS OFFICE

"Carnegie Mellon is a private, coeducational university with approximately 5,300 undergraduates; 4,400 graduate students; and 1,200 full-time faculty members. The university's 144-acre campus is located in the Oakland area of Pittsburgh, five miles from downtown. The university is composed of seven colleges: the Carnegie Institute of Technology (engineering), the College of Fine Arts, the College of Humanities and Social Sciences (combining liberal arts education with professional specializations), the Tepper School of Business (undergraduate business and industrial management), the Mellon College of Science, the School of Computer Science, and the H. John Heinz III School of Public Policy and Management.

"Freshman applicants for Fall 2008 must take the SAT plus two SAT Subject Tests, depending on their major interest. Students may take the ACT with Writing in lieu of the SAT. An applicant's best scores will be used in admissions decision-making.

"Carnegie Mellon has campuses in the Silicon Valley, California, and Qatar in the Arabian Gulf."

SELECTIVITY

Admissions Rating	97
# of applicants	18,864
% of applicants accepted	34
% of acceptees attending	22
# accepting a place on wait list	319
% admitted from wait list	18
# of early decision applicants	813
% accepted early decision	35

FRESHMAN PROFILE

Range SAT Critical Reading	610–710
Range SAT Math	690–780
Range SAT Writing	610–700
Range ACT Composite	28–32
Minimum Paper TOEFL	600
Minimum Computer Based TOEFL	250
Average HS GPA	3.61
% graduated top 10% of class	75
% graduated top 25% of class	95
% graduated top 50% of class	100

DEADLINES

Early decision application deadline	11/1
Early decision notification	12/15
Regular application deadline	1/1
Regular notification	4/15
Nonfall registration?	no

FINANCIAL FACTS

Financial Aid Rating	78
Annual tuition	$36,950
Room & Board	$9,660
Books and supplies	$966
% frosh rec. need-based scholarship or grant aid	49
% UG rec. need-based scholarship or grant aid	46
% frosh rec. need-based self-help aid	49
% UG rec. need-based self-help aid	47
% frosh rec. any financial aid	68
% UG rec. any financial aid	66

Case Western Reserve University

103 Tomlinson Hall, 10900 Euclid Avenue, Cleveland, OH 44106-7055 • Admissions: 216-368-4450 • Fax: 216-368-5111

CAMPUS LIFE
Quality of Life Rating	65
Fire Safety Rating	84
Type of school	private
Environment	metropolis

STUDENTS
Total undergrad enrollment	3,998
% male/female	59/41
% from out of state	45
% from public high school	70
% live on campus	79
% in (# of) fraternities	29 (16)
% in (# of) sororities	23 (6)
% African American	5
% Asian	17
% Caucasian	64
% Hispanic	2
% international	4
# of countries represented	28

SURVEY SAYS . . .
Lab facilities are great
Great computer facilities
Great library

ACADEMICS
Academic Rating	84
Calendar	semester
Student/faculty ratio	9:1
Profs interesting rating	71
Profs accessible rating	72
% profs teaching UG courses	72
% classes taught by TAs	5
Most common lab size	fewer than 10 students
Most common reg class size	10–19 students

MOST POPULAR MAJORS
biology/biological sciences
biomedical/medical engineering
business administration/
management

STUDENTS SAY
Academics

Case has long been perceived as a school that "is all about hard-core, technology-enhanced learning," and tech-related areas—particularly engineering and the sciences—certainly remain the school's greatest strengths, but Case has worked hard to broaden its offerings in recent years. One student reports, "The focus [has] come off of engineering a little, as the school has spent (or received in donations) large sums of money to both arts and sciences and especially the Weatherhead School of Management." As a result, the picture at Case has grown more complex. For tech-oriented students, the school remains a place where "A lot of what you learn you must teach yourself and you receive most of your help from TAs and fellow students." Students in other areas tell a different story; they report that "professors here generally show a genuine interest in their students. They have tons of office hours and have review sessions set up to help students get the most out of the material as possible." Students in all disciplines agree that "the administration is just that—administration. There are often a lot of hoops to jump through when dealing with paying tuition, financial aid, and similar paperwork issues. There is a definite need for more and better undergraduate advising. Class registration, however, is easy."

Life

"Day-to-day student life isn't the greatest" at Case. "It's an urban campus, [so] it doesn't have that tight-knit college feel," explains one student. The heavy workload—"Life here is very studious, and there is rarely free time available"—is another factor. A third is the lopsided male/female ratio, which "makes it impossible for guys to get dates." One student jokes, "This place is about remaining a virgin until you're 22." Greek life is one option students pursue in an effort to avoid "spending all your free time sitting in front of a computer bored out of your mind." Those who choose the latter at least benefit from the fact that "the campus is really wired and everyone pretty much relies on the Internet. Download speeds are amazing. A lot of classes post homework assignments, grades, and syllabi online, and most of my labs require you to download and read lab instructions online." There is a third way, however: Greater Cleveland offers lots of options, including "great clubbing downtown or in Lakewood; theater, movies, museums, the botanical gardens, and Severance Hall where the Cleveland Orchestra plays," and three other area schools, Cleveland State University, the Cleveland Institute of Music, and the Cleveland Institute of Art, with more lively social scenes.

Student Body

"Typical students at Case spend the majority of their time studying and engrossing themselves in their courses," explains one student. Or, as another puts it, "The typical Case student is a nerd who is obsessed with his computer. But there are lots of other types, too. They're only in love with their computers, not obsessed." Students are proud of who they are; one explains, "It's great to be at a school where everyone is like you and is as focused on academics as you are. I know that's why I chose to come here!" Some study too hard, we're told; one undergrad writes, "The typical student is hard to define because you rarely see him or her. Students become so focused on schoolwork that they lose track of the fact that there is more to college than simply studying." Case undergrads consider the student body diverse, in part because of the mix of "foreign students from all over Europe and especially Asia, even though a majority of them are graduate students."

CASE WESTERN RESERVE UNIVERSITY

FINANCIAL AID: 216-368-4530 • E-MAIL: ADMISSION@CASE.EDU • WEBSITE: WWW.CASE.EDU

ADMISSIONS

Very important factors considered include: Academic GPA, class rank, extracurricular activities, rigor of secondary school record, standardized test scores. *Important factors considered include:* Application essay, character/personal qualities, class rank, interview, recommendation(s), work experience. *Other factors considered include:* Alumni/ae relation, first generation, level of applicant's interest, racial/ethnic status. SAT or ACT required; ACT with Writing component required. TOEFL required of all international applicants. High school diploma is required, and GED is accepted. *Academic units required:* 4 English, 3 math, 3 science (2 science labs), 2 foreign language, 3 social studies. *Academic units recommended:* 4 math, 3 science lab, 3 foreign language, 4 social studies.

The Inside Word

Case faces tough competition, and they handle it very well. The university received a record number of applications last year, and as a result it's quite a bit tougher to get admitted. Even if you solidly meet the academic profile, don't be complacent—Case Western's freshman profile reflects well on the academic preparedness of its candidates, and due to their good fortune they've got an opportunity to be significantly more choosy about who gets an offer.

FINANCIAL AID

Students should submit: FAFSA, institution's own financial aid form, Business/Farm Supplement, parent and student Federal Income Tax Returns and W-2 forms. The Princeton Review suggests that all financial aid forms be submitted as soon as possible after January 1. *Need-based scholarships/grants offered:* Pell Grant, SEOG, state scholarships/grants, private scholarships, the school's own gift aid. *Loan aid offered:* FFEL Subsidized Stafford, FFEL Unsubsidized Stafford, FFEL PLUS, Federal Perkins Loan, Federal Nursing Loan, state loans, college/university loans from institutional funds. Applicants will be notified of awards on a rolling basis beginning or about February 15. Federal Work-Study Program available. Institutional employment available. Off-campus job opportunities are good.

FROM THE ADMISSIONS OFFICE

"Challenging and innovative academic programs, next-level technology, experiential learning, real-world environments, and faculty mentors are at the core of the Case Western Reserve University experience. Case's faculty challenges and supports motivated students, and its partnerships with world-class cultural, educational, and scientific institutions ensure that your education extends beyond the classroom.

"Case offers more than 75 majors and minors and a single-door admission policy; once admitted to Case, you can major in any of our programs, or double and even triple major in several of them. Our student/faculty ratio, among the best in the nation, allows students to have close interaction with professors. Co-ops, internships, study abroad and other opportunities bring theory to life in amazing settings, and 66 percent of students participate in research and independent study. SAGES, Case's 4-year undergraduate core curriculum, connects students with faculty, peers and the community through small seminars that explore effective communication and analytical skills, and culminates in a Senior Capstone project.

"With 85 percent of students living on campus, Case has a residential feel unique to urban universities. First-year students live together in one of three themed residential colleges that involve resources from across Northeast Ohio: Cedar (arts), Juniper (world culture) or Mistletoe (leadership through service).

"Admission Counselors consider all sections of the SAT, taking the best score for each section from multiple dates. The SAT (or ACT with writing) is used for evaluating applications for admission (and not used for course placement purposes)."

SELECTIVITY
Admissions Rating	93
# of applicants	7,508
% of applicants accepted	67
% of acceptees attending	20
# accepting a place on wait list	900
% admitted from wait list	21

FRESHMAN PROFILE
Range SAT Critical Reading	600–700
Range SAT Math	630–730
Range SAT Writing	590–680
Range ACT Composite	26–31
Minimum Paper TOEFL	550
Minimum Computer Based TOEFL	213
% graduated top 10% of class	68
% graduated top 25% of class	93
% graduated top 50% of class	99

DEADLINES
Regular application deadline	1/15
Regular notification	4/1
Nonfall registration?	yes

APPLICANTS ALSO LOOK AT
AND OFTEN PREFER
Cornell University, Johns Hopkins University, Northwestern University
AND SOMETIMES PREFER
Boston University, Carnegie Mellon University, The Ohio State University—Columbus, University of Pittsburgh—Pittsburgh Campus
AND RARELY PREFER
Pennsylvania State University—University Park, Purdue University—West Lafayette, University of Rochester

FINANCIAL FACTS
Financial Aid Rating	92
Annual tuition	$30,240
Room & Board	$9,280
Books and supplies	$1,040
Required fees	$298
% frosh rec. need-based scholarship or grant aid	65
% UG rec. need-based scholarship or grant aid	61
% frosh rec. need-based self-help aid	58
% UG rec. need-based self-help aid	56
% frosh rec. any financial aid	97
% UG rec. any financial aid	96

CATAWBA COLLEGE

2300 WEST INNES STREET, SALISBURY, NC 28144 • ADMISSIONS: 704-637-4402 • FAX: 704-637-4222

STUDENTS SAY

Academics

Catawba College is a small private school that offers "a strong, well-rounded education" bolstered by exceptional programs in theater, environmental science, and athletic training. Catawba's Theater Department "offers excellent training in a variety of areas," students tell us, reporting that "you can get fairly specialized degrees, including Bachelor's of Fine Arts in Performance, Musical Theater, Directing, or Technical Theater. The department is also very good about encouraging students to try areas outside their concentration so that they are well-rounded and have a better appreciation for what it takes to put on a theater production." Environmental science offerings benefit from "an entirely environmentally conscious building, plus an entire preserve protected and dedicated to studying and preserving wildlife." Athletic training reaps the benefits of the school's active intercollegiate sports programs. The business program here is also strong. Undergrads tell us that "the administration and professors at Catawba are awesome. They are there for you for any problem you have, whether it's school-related or personal." On the downside, "some of the facilities, like the theater labs and performance areas, have very out-of-date equipment," and the offline "registration process can get confusing."

Life

"Life at Catawba is generally enjoyable, although sometimes a little boring," due to the school's small-town location and the sometimes-strict rules enforced by the administration. Fortunately, "the Student Activity Board, Wigwam Productions, usually has some activity planned for the weekend such as Late Nights with food and games, casino nights, laser tag, carnival rides, and big screen movies, free for any student." Also, "There are many places for fun within 45 minutes' driving distance from the school, including malls, clubs, and the entirety of downtown Charlotte, North Carolina," so students have options. The school's active Theater Department mounts regular productions, and Catawba's 17 NCAA Division II intercollegiate athletic teams draw a lot of support. Hunting and fishing are popular with one subset of students, and most everyone enjoys being outdoors; one student reports, "In spring and fall it's really warm, so everyone will go outside and [lie] on blankets and do their homework. A lot of times students will toss around a Frisbee or get a pick-up game of football together." Because "There are no sororities or fraternities," there are "no big parties, but there are usually smaller room parties" that "never get out of hand." The food on campus, students agree, "is terrible, and the most frequently complained about aspect of campus life. Plan to spend at least $20 a week eating out, ordering pizza, or buying frozen dinners." Word to the wise: Lexington, the state barbecue mecca, is just 20 miles up the road. The tea is sweet, the slaw goes on the sandwich, and yes, hush puppies come with that.

Student Body

"I'd love to see more diversity on campus," writes one Catawba undergrad, observing that "we have a sizable African American presence on campus, but other than a handful of individuals of other minorities, it's somewhat monotone, ethnically and religiously speaking." The "two main groups on campus are the athletes and the theater majors," and "Although the theater kids are not all best friends with the jocks, there seems to be more camaraderie between the two groups than would stereotypically be expected." A "fairly large population of homosexuals [is] occasionally mistreated by athletes" but "otherwise very understood and accepted by the majority of the campus."

FINANCIAL AID: 704-637-4416 • E-MAIL: ADMISSION@CATAWBA.EDU • WEBSITE: WWW.CATAWBA.EDU

ADMISSIONS

Very important factors considered include: Academic GPA, application essay, class rank, recommendation(s), standardized test scores. *Important factors considered include:* Character/personal qualities, extracurricular activities, interview, level of applicant's interest, rigor of secondary school record, talent/ability. *Other factors considered include:* Volunteer work. SAT or ACT required; ACT with Writing component recommended. TOEFL required of all international applicants. High school diploma is required, and GED is accepted. *Academic units required:* 4 English, 2 math, 2 science, 2 social studies, 6 academic electives. *Academic units recommended:* 4 English, 3 math, 3 science (3 science labs), 2 foreign language, 3 social studies, 2 academic electives.

The Inside Word

Catawba's applicant pool is mainly from the Southeast, which tends to give candidates from far afield some extra appeal. There is serious competition for students among similar colleges in this neck of the woods, and the Admissions Staff here has to work hard to bring in the freshman class each year. They succeed because they are truly friendly and personal in their dealings with students and their families, and the college seems to have carved a worthwhile niche for itself amid the myriad choices available in the area.

FINANCIAL AID

Students should submit: FAFSA, state aid form. The Princeton Review suggests that all financial aid forms be submitted as soon as possible after January 1. *Need-based scholarships/grants offered:* Pell Grant, SEOG, state scholarships/grants, private scholarships, the school's own gift aid. *Loan aid offered:* FFEL Subsidized Stafford, FFEL Unsubsidized Stafford, FFEL PLUS, Federal Perkins Loan, college/university loans from institutional funds, TERI Loans, Nellie Mae Loans, Advantage Loans, alternative loans. Applicants will be notified of awards on a rolling basis beginning or about February 15.

FROM THE ADMISSIONS OFFICE

"Catawba College prepares students for rewarding lives and careers in the liberal arts tradition. This attractive campus is centrally located in Salisbury, North Carolina, a short drive away from the mountains and Atlantic beaches. The community possesses a rich past and commitment to preserving its cultural and historic charm. In contrast, just 45 minutes away is the much faster pace of Charlotte, North Carolina where shopping, transportation, and entertainment of all kinds are readily available.

"On campus, students study and socialize in a small college setting that offers strong traditions, excellent facilities, and beautiful surroundings. The high standards of quality set by Catawba's academic programs are matched by equally demanding sports and co-curricular programs. Students describe the community as caring and personable. They also exhibit a high rate of involvement in campus activities ranging form the performing arts to homecoming and travel abroad. Faculty and staff are described by students as being important mentors. Whether in a state-of-the-art environmental science facility, attractive music and theatrical performance center, classroom, or one of the college's first-class athletic facilities, students report they feel as if they are among family when on campus.

"Perhaps the most important testimony to the attractiveness of Catawba is found in the words of its graduates who report numerous successful careers and rich memories of their time at school.

"Students applying for admissions to Catawba College are required submit to scores from the SAT, including the Writing test. In lieu of SAT scores, Catawba will accept student scores on the ACT when they include scores on the ACT Writing test. Catawba will use the student's best scores from either test in making admissions decisions."

SELECTIVITY

Admissions Rating	76
# of applicants	792
% of applicants accepted	68
% of acceptees attending	45

FRESHMAN PROFILE

Range SAT Critical Reading	450–570
Range SAT Math	480–580
Range ACT Composite	19–26
Minimum Paper TOEFL	525
Minimum Computer Based TOEFL	197
Average HS GPA	3.31
% graduated top 10% of class	9
% graduated top 25% of class	34
% graduated top 50% of class	68

DEADLINES

Regular notification	rolling
Nonfall registration?	yes

APPLICANTS ALSO LOOK AT AND SOMETIMES PREFER

Appalachian State University, The University of North Carolina at Chapel Hill, The University of North Carolina at Charlotte

AND RARELY PREFER

North Carolina State University, The University of North Carolina at Greensboro, The University of North Carolina at Wilmington

FINANCIAL FACTS

Financial Aid Rating	83
Annual tuition	$20,835
Room & board	$7,190
Books and supplies	$800
% frosh rec. need-based scholarship or grant aid	50
% UG rec. need-based scholarship or grant aid	45
% frosh rec. need-based self-help aid	61
% UG rec. need-based self-help aid	51
% frosh rec. any financial aid	96
% UG rec. any financial aid	96

THE CATHOLIC UNIVERSITY OF AMERICA

OFFICE OF ENROLLMENT SERVICES, WASHINGTON, DC 20064 • ADMISSIONS: 202-319-5305 • FAX: 202-319-6533

STUDENTS SAY

Academics

You'll receive "an education heavy in philosophy and theology" at the Catholic University of America, "a beautiful college campus located in the heart of our nation's capital." That's because every student at CUA completes a core curriculum with an "emphasis on philosophy and religion. Students are required to take a series of both. Unless you are planning on making a career out of either, when else in life will you study these in depth, other than college?" For a school of just over 3,000 students, CUA has a remarkable number of strong disciplines. Undergrads laud the "incredibly strong" nursing program, a "wonderful music program" that's ideal for students who "don't want conservatory straight out of high school but still want a challenging program," "the best education in architecture in the DC area," and a "very strong" drama department. While liberal arts and science programs aren't as highly regarded, students appreciate that "Professors and staff are helpful and always available," and point out that political studies are greatly abetted by the school's location. Of DC, one student observes that the school's location in the nation's provides, "easy access to internships, government, and seemingly endless other political opportunities." The school also offers an honors program that "challenges students to push [to] the edge of their abilities."

Life

CUA's Washington, DC address "is absolutely one of the great strengths of the school. A student can get on the Metro and go basically wherever they want, and get whatever it is that they need." Indeed, students "have DC, a storied and cosmopolitan city," at their fingertips, "with plenty of concert venues, movie theaters, play houses, shopping districts, landmarks, and museums to visit on the weekends." Undergrads "go to Starbucks and have study sessions . . . on Sundays, or go and visit friends at George Washington or Georgetown on the weekends." "Chinatown, Dupont Circle, and Union Station" are also popular destinations for "fun times." As one student sums up, "We are in the nation's capital, we have plenty to do." Students tell us that "almost everyone on this campus likes to drink," and while "The school tries really hard to offer nonalcoholic alternatives on the weekends," their efforts "aren't quite enticing enough to lure us away from the neighborhood bars." Drinking generally takes place in the bars, as "House parties are almost nonexistent" on campus. However, students also tell us that "if you don't feel like drinking on the weekends, there is always some option for you" including campus ministry events which provide "students [with] a healthy environment and people to be around as an alternative to drinking."

Student Body

The typical student at CUA "is from the Mid-Atlantic states, White, and went to a Catholic high school"; "fairly conservative," and looks like a "page out of an Abercrombie & Fitch ad." "Everyone wears flip-flops, polo shirts, and khakis. People only wear jeans during the wintertime." Exceptions to the rule include "the very vocal minority groups" who work to make sure "Diversity is highlighted" on campus, "people of other religious backgrounds," and the many "musical theater students" including a large number of "gay men, which is pretty surprising at a Catholic university." Many students are devout and "very open about their faith," but "Very few people will force religion down your throat." Atypical students are "generally welcomed and accepted by these 'typical' students with little or no friction due to religion, sexual orientation, race, socioeconomic class."

THE CATHOLIC UNIVERSITY OF AMERICA

FINANCIAL AID: 202-319-5307 • E-MAIL: CUA-ADMISSIONS@CUA.EDU • WEBSITE: WWW.CUA.EDU

ADMISSIONS

Very important factors considered include: Academic GPA, character/personal qualities, recommendation(s), rigor of secondary school record, standardized test scores, volunteer work. *Important factors considered include:* Application essay, extracurricular activities, first generation, interview, talent/ability. *Other factors considered include:* Alumni/ae relation, class rank, racial/ethnic status, work experience. SAT or ACT required; SAT Subject Tests recommended; ACT with Writing component required. TOEFL required of all international applicants. High school diploma is required, and GED is accepted. *Academic units recommended:* 4 English, 3 math, 3 science (1 science lab), 2 foreign language, 4 social studies, 1 fine arts or humanities.

The Inside Word

The Catholic University of America is a conservative school that adopts a very traditional approach to higher education. Your application should demonstrate an appreciation for the school's unique qualities and educational philosophy. Present your strongest case by showing solid grades in a demanding curriculum, backed by above average test scores, and you should have little trouble gaining admission. CUA now accepts the Common Application.

FINANCIAL AID

Students should submit: FAFSA, Alumni and Parish Scholarship Applications if appropriate. The Princeton Review suggests that all financial aid forms be submitted as soon as possible after January 1. *Need-based scholarships/grants offered:* Pell Grant, SEOG, state scholarships/grants, private scholarships, the school's own gift aid, Federal Nursing Scholarship. *Loan aid offered:* FFEL Subsidized Stafford, FFEL Unsubsidized Stafford, FFEL PLUS, Federal Perkins Loan, Federal Nursing Loan, college/university loans from institutional funds, commercial loans. Applicants will be notified of awards on a rolling basis beginning or about April 1. Federal Work-Study Program available. Institutional employment available. Off-campus job opportunities are good.

FROM THE ADMISSIONS OFFICE

"The Catholic University of America's friendly atmosphere, rigorous academic programs, and emphasis on time-honored values attract students from all 50 states and more than 95 foreign countries. Its 193-acre, tree-lined campus is only 10 minutes from the nation's capital. Distinguished as the national university of the Catholic Church in the United States, CUA is the only institution of higher education established by the U.S. Catholic bishops; however, students from all religious traditions are welcome.

"CUA offers undergraduate degrees in more than 80 major areas in seven schools of study. Students enroll into the School of Arts and Sciences, Architecture, Nursing, Engineering, Metropolitan College, Music, or Philosophy. Additionally, CUA students can concentrate in areas of preprofessional study including law, dentistry, medicine, or veterinary studies.

"With Capitol Hill, the Smithsonian Institution, NASA, the Kennedy Center, and the National Institutes of Health among the places students obtain internships, firsthand experience is a valuable piece of the experience that CUA offers. Numerous students also take the opportunity in their junior year to study abroad at one of Catholic's 17 country program sites. Political science majors even have the opportunity to do a Parliamentary Internship in either England or Ireland. With the campus just minutes away from downtown via the Metrorail rapid transit system, students enjoy a residential campus in an exciting city of historical monuments, theaters, festivals, ethnic restaurants, and parks.

"Freshman applicants for Fall 2008 must take the new SAT or ACT. Additionally, students may submit scores from the old SAT, and the best scores from either test will be used. Matriculating students should submit the SAT Subject Test: Foreign Language exam if they plan to continue studying that language at CUA."

SELECTIVITY

Admissions Rating	**84**
# of applicants	3,492
% of applicants accepted	81
% of acceptees attending	30

FRESHMAN PROFILE

Range SAT Critical Reading	520–620
Range SAT Math	520–620
Range ACT Composite	22–27
Minimum Paper TOEFL	560
Minimum Computer Based TOEFL	220
Average HS GPA	3.32
% graduated top 10% of class	25
% graduated top 25% of class	53
% graduated top 50% of class	87

DEADLINES

Regular application deadline	2/15
Regular notification	3/15
Nonfall registration?	yes

APPLICANTS ALSO LOOK AT
AND OFTEN PREFER
Boston College, University of Maryland University College, University of Notre Dame
AND SOMETIMES PREFER
University of Virginia
AND RARELY PREFER
American University, Fordham University, Saint Joseph's University (PA), The George Washington University

FINANCIAL FACTS

Financial Aid Rating	**85**
Annual tuition	$27,700
Room & Board	$10,808
Books and supplies	$1,000
Required fees	$1,290
% frosh rec. need-based scholarship or grant aid	55
% UG rec. need-based scholarship or grant aid	51
% frosh rec. need-based self-help aid	52
% UG rec. need-based self-help aid	49
% frosh rec. any financial aid	99
% UG rec. any financial aid	92

CENTENARY COLLEGE OF LOUISIANA

2911 CENTENARY BOULEVARD, SHREVEPORT, LA 71104 • ADMISSIONS: 318-869-5131 • FAX: 318-869-5005

CAMPUS LIFE
Quality of Life Rating	**77**
Fire Safety Rating	**88**
Type of school	private
Affiliation	Methodist
Environment	metropolis

STUDENTS
Total undergrad enrollment	891
% male/female	40/60
% from out of state	43
% from public high school	80
% live on campus	66
# of fraternities	5
# of sororities	2
% African American	8
% Asian	2
% Caucasian	82
% Hispanic	4
% international	2
# of countries represented	12

SURVEY SAYS . . .
Small classes
Athletic facilities are great
Musical organizations are popular

ACADEMICS
Academic Rating	**84**
Calendar	semester
Student/faculty ratio	10:1
Profs interesting rating	87
Profs accessible rating	86
% profs teaching UG courses	100
% classes taught by TAs	0
Most common reg class size	10–19 students

MOST POPULAR MAJORS
biology/biological sciences
business administration/
management
communication

STUDENTS SAY
Academics
The old saying that dynamite comes in small packages holds true when it comes to Centenary College, at least according to its students. With an enrollment of 900 undergraduates, the academic experience here is nothing if not personal. "Just the other night, I had dinner with the president and provost," writes one typical senior. "They both know me by my first name. They, as well as the professors, are always available by appointment to meet with students." One fast-moving freshman brags that already "I have the cell phone numbers of my professors and have visited several of their homes." A small enrollment means small class sizes, which allow for learning to assume the form of a dialogue between teacher and student, rather than the former spitting out facts in a lecture hall and the latter parroting it back on tests. Students agree that professors "don't expect us to merely regurgitate onto paper later" what they say in classes. "In our First-Year Experience classes, we are taught to question everything," and this questioning, which should lead students to learn how to come to their own conclusions, is an integral part of the undergraduate experience and is continually developed through the subsequent 3 years. But the small size also has its drawbacks. For instance, students wish "there were more class options available." Major offerings are heavy on the liberal arts, though the few preprofessional programs draw a fair number of students.

Life
First thing's first: This is not Mardi Gras country. In fact, the drive from Centenary to New Orleans takes about twice as long as it takes to drive to Dallas, which itself is almost 200 miles away. But distance doesn't deter students from thinking about the attractions of these other big cities; despite the fact that hometown area Shreveport has a population of 400,000, students gripe that it's not the best college town. This sentiment seems tied to the strict door policies at most of the bars off-campus. "Shreveport is a great town for fun if you are 21. But most college students are not 21," and as a result many students turn to the Greeks to create opportunities to socialize. They visit "fraternity houses every weekend. There is some drinking going on, but no one pressures anyone." However, "once you are 21," you most likely spend quality time with friends in the local watering holes, and if you are feeling particularly adventurous, "The casinos are very fun (but expensive)." During the week, "Most people are involved in an activity on campus, whether it's the newspaper, choir, sorority, fraternity," intramural sports, or "working out in our wonderful fitness center." The school also plays host to many "plays, concerts, [and] sports" events. The food on campus is universally despised. One thing that students would absolutely hate to see change, however, is the choir, which is the pride of the campus.

Student Body
Despite the influence of the Greeks, "The students on campus are not your typical party-all-night, football-playing frat boys and girls." Instead, Centenary students form a community based primarily on strong ethics and sharp intellects. As one student puts it, this is a "friendly and academically driven" environment. While Centenary is not the most culturally or geographically diverse campus on earth, "There are students here with different belief systems and alternative lifestyles," and "They are accepted with open arms." That said, there are a few students who "thought there would be a good number of genuine Christians here—big mistake on that one." In general, there's a liberal breeze in the air in this little corner of Shreveport. "Although we are in a conservative, Southern area," writes a freshman, "campus (known as the "Centenary Bubble" in the community) is surprisingly liberal, both with students and faculty." Since the school is so small, "Everybody knows everybody, [so] rumors get around very quickly."

CENTENARY COLLEGE OF LOUISIANA

FINANCIAL AID: 318-869-5137 • E-MAIL: ADMISSIONS@CENTENARY.EDU • WEBSITE: WWW.CENTENARY.EDU

ADMISSIONS

Very important factors considered include: Academic GPA, rigor of secondary school record. *Important factors considered include:* Application essay, character/personal qualities, extracurricular activities, interview, level of applicant's interest, standardized test scores, talent/ability. *Other factors considered include:* Alumni/ae relation, class rank, geographical residence, racial/ethnic status, recommendation(s), religious affiliation/commitment, work experience. SAT or ACT required; TOEFL required of all international applicants. High school diploma is required, and GED is accepted. *Academic units recommended:* 4 English, 3 math, 3 science (2 science labs), 2 foreign language, 3 social studies.

The Inside Word

Centenary has historically had a small applicant pool, and thus has had to admit the majority to meet its freshman enrollment goals. Currently, the school has attracted a larger applicant pool and become noticeably more strict in its admission rate. Its reputation, though regional, is quite solid, and the college does a good job of enrolling its admits. A very friendly and efficient Admissions Office no doubt contributes to such success.

FINANCIAL AID

Students should submit: FAFSA. The Princeton Review suggests that all financial aid forms be submitted as soon as possible after January 1. *Need-based scholarships/grants offered:* Pell Grant, SEOG, state scholarships/grants, private scholarships, the school's own gift aid. *Loan aid offered:* FFEL Subsidized Stafford, FFEL Unsubsidized Stafford, FFEL PLUS, Federal Perkins Loan. Applicants will be notified of awards on or about March 15. Federal Work-Study Program available. Institutional employment available. Off-campus job opportunities are good.

FROM THE ADMISSIONS OFFICE

"Just as a student's 4-year experience at Centenary will be very personalized, so too is the application process. We pride ourselves on treating each applicant as an individual. We encourage all interested students to visit us—not only so they can see our campus and get a sense of the atmosphere, but also to provide us the opportunity to meet and get to know them.

"Consider Centenary for a life-changing experience. Our professors value your ideas and contributions and are passionate about teaching. We consider the Centenary Experience to be more than just a degree. You will live in a comprehensive learning environment that features connections to your academic, social, personal, and residential lives.

"Our students work and live within a strong community to create personalized, distinctive experiences. Our students enjoy a vibrant college life and graduate from Centenary prepared for their professional and personal lives.

"First-year applicants for Fall 2007 must submit either ACT or SAT examination scores. If either exam was taken before the recently revised version (February 2005 for ACT and March 2005 for the SAT), those scores can be submitted. We recommend, but do not require, the ACT Writing exam."

SELECTIVITY

Admissions Rating	**84**
# of applicants	1,069
% of applicants accepted	65
% of acceptees attending	34

FRESHMAN PROFILE

Range SAT Critical Reading	500–620
Range SAT Math	510–620
Range SAT Writing	500–620
Range ACT Composite	22–28
Minimum Paper TOEFL	550
Minimum Computer Based TOEFL	213
% graduated top 10% of class	37
% graduated top 25% of class	67
% graduated top 50% of class	91

DEADLINES

Early decision application deadline	12/1
Early decision notification	12/15
Regular application deadline	8/1
Regular notification	1/15
Nonfall registration?	yes

FINANCIAL FACTS

Financial Aid Rating	**84**
Annual tuition	$19,850
Room & Board	$7,280
% frosh rec. need-based scholarship or grant aid	60
% UG rec. need-based scholarship or grant aid	56
% frosh rec. need-based self-help aid	30
% UG rec. need-based self-help aid	34
% frosh rec. any financial aid	96
% UG rec. any financial aid	95.5

CENTRE COLLEGE

600 WEST WALNUT STREET, DANVILLE, KY 40422 • ADMISSIONS: 800-423-6236 • FAX: 859-238-5373

CAMPUS LIFE

Quality of Life Rating	86
Fire Safety Rating	60*
Type of school	private
Affiliation	Presbyterian
Environment	village

STUDENTS

Total undergrad enrollment	1,144
% male/female	47/53
% from out of state	35
% from public high school	79
% live on campus	92
% in (# of) fraternities	34 (4)
% in (# of) sororities	37 (4)
% African American	3
% Asian	2
% Caucasian	92
% Hispanic	1
% international	2
# of countries represented	12

SURVEY SAYS . . .

Small classes
No one cheats
Great library
Students are friendly
Students are happy
Frats and sororities dominate social
scene
Lots of beer drinking
Hard liquor is popular

ACADEMICS

Academic Rating	93
Calendar	4-1-4
Student/faculty ratio	10:1
Profs interesting rating	98
Profs accessible rating	97
% profs teaching	
UG courses	100
% classes taught by TAs	0
Most common	
lab size	10–19 students
Most common	
reg class size	10–19 students

MOST POPULAR MAJORS

economics
English language and literature
history

STUDENTS SAY

Academics

Many schools offer opportunities for major-related internships and study abroad. Few, however, guarantee both. Centre College, a small liberal arts school in Kentucky, does. Under "The Centre Commitment," Centre not only ensures an internship and international study, it also guarantees graduation in 4 years and offers up to an additional year of tuition-free study to those who cannot graduate on time. Undergrads here praise the "awesome study abroad programs," reporting that "a wide variety of CentreTerm (i.e., January term) and long-term programs promises that there is something to study abroad that everyone will enjoy. It's a great way to get a break from campus and to see the world (and it really isn't that expensive)." They are even more impressed, however, with the amount of personal attention lavished on each student by faculty and administration. "Centre's greatest strength is that no one can slip through the figurative cracks, since nearly every person at Centre seems genuinely concerned about the students," writes one student. "Even the president of the college tries to get to know each student by name." Not only that, but "Where else would your college president have you over for a BBQ, teach a class, and perform in a concert? Only at Centre." All this support helps students handle Centre's "strong academic program" that requires that "either you work hard or you flunk out." As one student puts it, "Classes, as a rule, are difficult, but we learn to push ourselves and achieve more." The entire experience leaves many here concluding that "Centre is just perfect. The small school environment lends itself so well to the liberal arts education platform, and Centre excels at everything it does."

Life

Centre "is academics-driven during the week, but on the weekend the school knows how to have fun," with a lively Greek scene occupying center (no pun intended) stage. One student writes, "The 'Centre Experience' is all about being a part of the Centre community. We all work hard but we all know how to party hard as well. Weekends are filled with frat parties, the 'running of the flame' (streaking from a dorm to the statue in front of the library and back to the dorm), and playing pool at the Warehouse (i.e., the Student Center)." Students must devote some extracurricular time to fulfilling Centre's convocation requirement, which mandates attendance at 30 convocation-designated events per year; such events typically include lectures and performances. Many fulfill their obligations at the Norton Center for the Arts, which "brings in many musicals, operas, ballets, plays, speakers, orchestras, etc., that would normally cost quite a bit to go see, but students get to go for free." Because "There isn't much to do in Danville," a lot of free time is spent "hanging out in each other's rooms, listening to music, or watching shows." Students have discovered that "although Danville is a small town, Centre is a revitalizing, dynamic force in this community." And "The occasional jaunt to Lexington or Louisville helps to throw in some variety."

Student Body

"Most Centre students are from upper-middle-class families in the South" and are "quite friendly and usually willing to go to great extents to help out other students." They tend to be "Christian, moderately conservative, and very enthusiastic about Greek life." One student writes, "The boys have that Southern gentleman quality about them, and the girls are pretty and outgoing." Beyond the mainstream crowd, "There is a fair amount of atypical students. For example, there are many active liberals on campus as well as conservatives, and Greek life is big but you can have fun without it. Since everyone is pretty well acquainted with everyone else on such a small campus, it's easy to fit in." Most everyone "works very hard but leaves room in their schedule to participate in sports and clubs and to just hang out with friends."

CENTRE COLLEGE

FINANCIAL AID: 859-238-5365 • E-MAIL: ADMISSION@CENTRE.EDU • WEBSITE: WWW.CENTRE.EDU

ADMISSIONS

Very important factors considered include: Academic GPA, rigor of secondary school record. *Important factors considered include:* Application essay, standardized test scores. *Other factors considered include:* Alumni/ae relation, character/personal qualities, class rank, extracurricular activities, first generation, geographical residence, interview, racial/ethnic status, recommendation(s), talent/ability. SAT or ACT required; TOEFL or SAT required of all international applicants. High school diploma or equivalent is not required. *Academic units required:* 4 English, 4 math, 2 science (2 science labs), 2 foreign language, 2 history. *Academic units recommended:* 3 science (3 science labs).

The Inside Word

Centre's small but very capable student body reflects solid academic preparation from high school, and it's no surprise that this is exactly what the Admissions Committee expects from applicants. If you're ranked in the top quarter of your graduating class and have taken challenging courses throughout your high school career, you should have smooth sailing through the admissions process. Those who rank below the top quarter or who have inconsistent academic backgrounds will find entrance here more difficult, and may benefit from an interview.

FINANCIAL AID

Students should submit: FAFSA, institution's own financial aid form. Regular filing deadline is March 1. The Princeton Review suggests that all financial aid forms be submitted as soon as possible after January 1. *Need-based scholarships/grants offered:* Pell Grant, SEOG, state scholarships/grants, private scholarships, the school's own gift aid, Academic Competitiveness Grant, National SMART Grant. *Loan aid offered:* FFEL Subsidized Stafford, FFEL Unsubsidized Stafford, FFEL PLUS, Federal Perkins Loan, college/university loans from institutional funds. Applicants will be notified of awards on or about March 25. Federal Work-Study Program available. Institutional employment available. Off-campus job opportunities are fair.

FROM THE ADMISSIONS OFFICE

"Centre provides its students with a personal education that enables them to achieve extraordinary success in advanced study and their careers. Centre Professors, virtually all of whom hold the highest degree available in their field, challenge their students and give them the individual attention and support they need to meet those challenges. The end result is highly capable graduates with a can-do attitude and the ability to accomplish their goals.

"Centre offers a multitude of advantages, such as a national top-50 academic reputation, 'majors' options, and exposure to the internationally known artists and scholars; benefits like these produce extraordinary success. For example, entrance to top graduate and professional schools; the most prestigious postgraduate scholarships (Rhodes, Fulbright, Goldwater); interesting, rewarding jobs (96 percent of graduates are either employed or engaged in advance study within nine months of graduation).

"How do alumni respond? They have expressed their customer satisfaction by leading the United States in their percentage of annual financial support over the last 20 years. How much does all this cost? Because of our nation-leading alumni support, Centre is the most affordable of America's top 50 national liberal arts colleges.

"Centre's admissions policies have not been affected by the new SAT, and we will not consider a student's scores from the new Writing section."

SELECTIVITY

Admissions Rating	**93**
# of applicants	2,092
% of applicants accepted	60
% of acceptees attending	26
# accepting a place on wait list	48
% admitted from wait list	8

FRESHMAN PROFILE

Range SAT Critical Reading	550–690
Range SAT Math	560–670
Range ACT Composite	25–29
Minimum Paper TOEFL	580
Average HS GPA	3.6
% graduated top 10% of class	63
% graduated top 25% of class	88
% graduated top 50% of class	99

DEADLINES

Regular application deadline	2/1
Regular notification	3/15
Nonfall registration?	no

APPLICANTS ALSO LOOK AT
AND OFTEN PREFER
Davidson College, Washington and Lee University
AND SOMETIMES PREFER
Furman University, Kenyon College, Rhodes College
AND RARELY PREFER
Transylvania University, University of Kentucky, University of Louisville

FINANCIAL FACTS

Financial Aid Rating	**85**
Comprehensive fee	$35,000
Books and supplies	$900
% frosh rec. need-based scholarship or grant aid	64
% UG rec. need-based scholarship or grant aid	58
% frosh rec. need-based self-help aid	43
% UG rec. need-based self-help aid	41

CHAPMAN UNIVERSITY

One University Drive, Orange, CA 92866 • Admissions: 714-997-6711 • Fax: 714-997-6713

CAMPUS LIFE

Quality of Life Rating	84
Fire Safety Rating	60*
Type of school	private
Affiliation	Disciples of Christ
Environment	metropolis

STUDENTS

Total undergrad enrollment	4,053
% male/female	42/58
% from out of state	23
% from public high school	70
% live on campus	42
% in (# of) fraternities	26 (6)
% in (# of) sororities	30 (5)
% African American	2
% Asian	8
% Caucasian	69
% Hispanic	10
% Native American	1
% international	2
# of countries represented	51

SURVEY SAYS . . .
Small classes
Great computer facilities
Great library

ACADEMICS

Academic Rating	84
Calendar	4-1-4
Student/faculty ratio	16:1
Profs interesting rating	80
Profs accessible rating	82
% profs teaching	
UG courses	84
% classes taught by TAs	0
Most common	
lab size	10–19 students
Most common	
reg class size	20–29 students

MOST POPULAR MAJORS
advertising
business administration/
management
cinematography and film/video
production

STUDENTS SAY

Academics

"A great small school dedicated to personalized education," Chapman University has lately been making a concerted effort to grow in size, particularly in its popular film production department. Most students see expansion as a good thing—"Our school is doing a good job at building up its reputation"—but growth does come at a cost. For some, the school isn't big enough: "Because the school is so small, there aren't enough classes offered," so students with "obscure majors" sometimes feel that they are forced to "take what they can get." Students praise professors who "are excellent scholars in their fields," but admit that "the growing enrollment and courses of studies" sometimes necessitates hiring "part-time professors" who are at times "not the greatest." Most students recognize that this problem is "a necessary evil in order to accommodate" the school's expansion. For the most part, however, "Professors are fastidious in keeping office hours, and great advising is easy to come across. On the whole, GE [general education] classes are challenging, interesting, and inspiring." Administrators also receive generally high marks: "The president of our school even takes the time to teach classes here, as well [as] get to know the students at his school. I even run with him once a month, and then we get breakfast together."

Life

Most social life at Chapman is an off-campus occurrence: "A great deal of students live off-campus at the La Veta Grand Apartments, which have pretty much become the off-campus dorms. La Veta is always the party place." Not far from campus, a popular student hangout is "the Block, which is an amazing outdoor shopping mall that has a bowling alley, laser tag, a 30-screen AMC theater, and a skate park." More "stores and restaurants" can be found at the nearby Orange Circle. Since Disneyland is "right down the street," many students "have Disneyland annual passes, and people go there a lot." Disneyland's theme park competition, Knotts Berry Farm, is also only "minutes away. Newport Beach is only about 15 minutes away. LA is only a half an hour away." Ambitious students who have the means "can even go to Vegas for a weekend." All these distances, however, are calculated in driving minutes; for many excursions from Chapman, "You will need a car, since Southern California public transportation is awful." Students who don't have cars can rest assured that there's also "a constant stream of things to do on campus."

Student Body

Life seems to imitate art at Chapman; the school is located in the real "OC" (Orange County), and "If you have ever seen *The OC* on Fox, then you have seen a sample of the students who attend Chapman University. The students in general are very wealthy, and personal appearance and designer clothes are pretty important to the average student," writes one typical respondent. Not everyone agrees, however: "If you want warm weather and friendly smiles along with a good education, Chapman is the place to come. Just please don't bring any obsessions with *The OC* or *Laguna Beach* with you—when you live in the OC, you find out that it is not really like that here." Another oft-stereotyped demographic at Chapman is "the film majors, who can tend to be moody and brooding" but also "artistic and fun." Politically, "Even though Chapman is located in the middle of conservative Orange County, there is an equal mix of liberal, conservative, and moderate students at the school." While ethnic diversity is described by some as "pretty thin," the school has a lot of "social diversity"; in particular, students praise the "very strong and welcoming GLBT community," who are "well accepted" by peers. This fact is not surprising; according to many students, "Chapman is all about community."

FINANCIAL AID: 714-997-6741 • E-MAIL: ADMIT@CHAPMAN.EDU • WEBSITE: WWW.CHAPMAN.EDU

ADMISSIONS

Very important factors considered include: Academic GPA, application essay, character/personal qualities, class rank, rigor of secondary school record, standardized test scores. *Important factors considered include:* Extracurricular activities, interview, talent/ability, volunteer work. *Other factors considered include:* Alumni/ae relation, racial/ethnic status, recommendation(s), work experience. SAT or ACT required; SAT Subject Tests recommended, ACT with Writing component required. TOEFL required of all international applicants. High school diploma is required, and GED is accepted. *Academic units required:* 2 English, 2 math, 2 science (1 science lab), 2 foreign language, 3 social studies.

Inside Word

Despite a plethora of California schools, Chapman continues to receive a steady stream of applications. Rather than work with formulas or cut-offs, Admissions Officers here prefer to take many factors into account. Well-rounded students are likely to make the most impact. Applicants who are service oriented are also apt to do well, particularly given Chapman's "global responsibility" program.

FINANCIAL AID

Students should submit: FAFSA, state aid form. The Princeton Review suggests that all financial aid forms be submitted as soon as possible after January 1. *Need-based scholarships/grants offered:* Pell Grant, SEOG, state scholarships/grants, private scholarships, the school's own gift aid. *Loan aid offered:* FFEL Subsidized Stafford, FFEL Unsubsidized Stafford, FFEL PLUS, Federal Perkins Loan, college/university loans from institutional funds. Applicants will be notified of awards on a rolling basis beginning or about March 15. Federal Work-Study Program available. Institutional employment available. Off-campus job opportunities are excellent.

FROM THE ADMISSIONS OFFICE

"During our 144-year history, Chapman has evolved from a small, church-related liberal arts college into a vibrant and comprehensive midsized liberal arts and sciences university distinguished for an eclectic group of nationally recognized programs including athletic training, film and television production, business and economics, dance, music, theater, writing, and teacher education. Our Orange County, California location was recently rated by *Places Rated Almanac* as "the number-one place to live in North America" citing superior climate, cultural, recreational, educational, and career entry opportunities.

"Chapman's environment is involving, and we seek students who are willing to enter an atmosphere of healthy competition where their talents will be nurtured and manifest to the fullest—whether in the classroom, on the stage, or the athletic field. We challenge prospective students to thoroughly investigate our fine balance of liberal and professional learning so they may make a fully informed decision about 'fit' with regard to their personalities and that of the university.

"Applicants for freshman admission to Chapman University will be required to submit scores from either the new SAT or the ACT including the ACT Writing section. Transfer applicants, if requested, will be allowed to submit scores from either the old or new SAT, or ACT with or without the Writing section."

SELECTIVITY
Admissions Rating	93
# of applicants	4,269
% of applicants accepted	53
% of acceptees attending	43
# accepting a place on wait list	387
% admitted from wait list	15

FRESHMAN PROFILE
Range SAT Critical Reading	547–660
Range SAT Math	551–666
Range SAT Writing	549–665
Range ACT Composite	24–29
Minimum Paper TOEFL	550
Minimum Computer Based TOEFL	213
Average HS GPA	3.65
% graduated top 10% of class	61
% graduated top 25% of class	96
% graduated top 50% of class	99

DEADLINES
Regular application deadline	1/31
Regular notification	rolling
Nonfall registration?	yes

APPLICANTS ALSO LOOK AT

AND OFTEN PREFER
Loyola Marymount University, New York University, University of California—Los Angeles, University of San Diego, University of Southern California

AND SOMETIMES PREFER
Ithaca College, Santa Clara University, University of California—Irvine, University of Redlands

FINANCIAL FACTS
Financial Aid Rating	97
Annual tuition	$31,700
Room & Board	$11,880
Books and supplies	$1,100
Required fees	$908
% frosh rec. need-based scholarship or grant aid	59
% UG rec. need-based scholarship or grant aid	59
% frosh rec. need-based self-help aid	47
% UG rec. need-based self-help aid	50
% frosh rec. any financial aid	74
% UG rec. any financial aid	75

CITY UNIVERSITY OF NEW YORK—BROOKLYN COLLEGE

2900 BEDFORD AVENUE, BROOKLYN, NY 11210-2889 • ADMISSIONS: 718-951-5001 • FAX: 718-951-4506

CAMPUS LIFE

Quality of Life Rating	65
Fire Safety Rating	60*
Type of school	public
Environment	metropolis

STUDENTS

Total undergrad enrollment	11,524
% male/female	40/60
% from out of state	2
% from public high school	60
% in (# of) fraternities	2 (6)
% in (# of) sororities	2 (6)
% African American	28
% Asian	13
% Caucasian	41
% Hispanic	12
% international	7
# of countries represented	90

SURVEY SAYS . . .

Small classes
Great computer facilities
Great library
Diverse student types on campus
Very little drug use

ACADEMICS

Academic Rating	64
Calendar	semester
Student/faculty ratio	16:1
Profs interesting rating	61
Profs accessible rating	61
% profs teaching	
UG courses	80
% classes taught by TAs	2
Most common	
reg class size	20–29 students

MOST POPULAR MAJORS

business administration/
management
education
psychology

STUDENTS SAY

Academics

It's "all about getting a quality, affordable education" at Brooklyn College, a New York City school that serves a large undergraduate population of both traditional and nontraditional students. About 16 percent of undergraduates here major in business. Computer and information sciences, boosted by "very up-to-date technology," attracts a sizable percentage of students, too. Psychology, education, and premedical studies are also popular programs. Undergrads report that it's rough going at first at BC; frequent griping by students has led to a change in the core requirements that have been deemed "too numerous," and "The professors who teach core courses are not the greatest." Things get much better once students find an area of specialization; one explains, "Until I found a program that I could tailor to my needs, I found BC to be a cold place lacking interest in its students. Now I realize that once students find their key supporting office or department, we actually have a chance to accomplish wonderful things." Professors here include "everything from a former truck driver to a top experienced CPA. . . . There are also professors from every background and religion." Although some teachers in the sciences and technology "don't really speak much English," students generally are impressed with the quality of the faculty, telling us that instructors "push us to do our best" and "foster a great environment for academic quality and success." Undergrads also appreciate the "great tutors" and "helpful writing center"; they complain, however, that "the school needs to do a better job helping students find jobs when they graduate"; the college has recently responded to these complaints with the creation of a Career Development Center. Those in the honors program tell us that "courses are compelling and challenging, fully preparing you to be at the top of your grad school class."

Life

Brooklyn College "does not have too much of a social life outside of fraternities and sororities," in large part because there is no residential life here. The school's location in Midwood, a quiet, unhip neighborhood, also stifles extracurricular life. Students tell us that "there are basketball games, parties, and fashion shows, but relative to the number of students here, they are not that well attended." Perhaps the most popular extracurricular outlets on campus are the many interest- and background-related clubs and organizations, which "get together frequently and are very accepting no matter what your race, gender, or ethnicity." Students also like the student center, which "has fun games, sports, and other activities." Otherwise, undergrads visit campus to attend classes and study, then typically head home or off to another part of New York City for diversion. Manhattan and other areas are, fortunately, easy to reach by subway. Undergrads note that the BC campus is "quite beautiful" and that "library facilities are great." Sports facilities have improved since the college opened the West Quad Building in 2007.

Student Body

The "busy, hurried" undergrads of Brooklyn College are "generally mature and look forward to earning their degrees." They are "very street smart" and typically "in a rush to graduate, so they focus more on receiving their credentials than on participating in student life." One student notes, "As a commuter college, BC is merely a brief stopping point for most of us." Students here "represent the plurality of ethnicities that make up Brooklyn," the most populous, and by some accounts, most diverse of the Big Apple's five boroughs. As one student puts it, "There are so many different types of students in terms of race, ethnicity, and religion. In addition, the day students differ from the night students who all tend to be working full-time jobs." Undergrads here are impressed that "Brooklyn College graduates go on to do great things," like Eugene Shenderov, a 2005 Rhodes Scholar, who is the second BC student to win the prestigious award. "Perhaps it's that tough Brooklyn attitude they help us build."

CITY UNIVERSITY OF NEW YORK—BROOKLYN COLLEGE

FINANCIAL AID: 718-951-5051 • E-MAIL: ADMINQRY@BROOKLYN.CUNY.EDU • WEBSITE: WWW.BROOKLYN.CUNY.EDU

ADMISSIONS

Very important factors considered include: Academic GPA, rigor of secondary school record, standardized test scores. *Other factors considered include:* Recommendation(s). SAT or ACT required; TOEFL required of all international applicants. High school diploma is required, and GED is accepted. *Academic units recommended:* 4 English, 3 math, 3 science, 3 foreign language, 4 social studies, 4 academic electives.

The Inside Word

Like other CUNY schools, Brooklyn College provides easy access to a college education for students who want one. Brooklyn raises the bar, however, with superior offerings in the arts and sciences. You don't have to have a spotless academic record to get into Brooklyn College, but once there you will receive a solid and respected education.

FINANCIAL AID

Students should submit: FAFSA, state aid form. The Princeton Review suggests that all financial aid forms be submitted as soon as possible after January 1. *Need-based scholarships/grants offered:* Pell Grant, SEOG, state scholarships/grants, private scholarships, the school's own gift aid. *Loan aid offered:* Direct Subsidized Stafford, Direct Unsubsidized Stafford, Direct PLUS, Federal Perkins Loan. Applicants will be notified of awards on or about May 1. Federal Work-Study Program available. Institutional employment available. Off-campus job opportunities are excellent.

FROM THE ADMISSIONS OFFICE

"Brooklyn College, a premier public liberal arts college founded in 1930, ranked sixth this year in The Princeton Review's *America's Best Value Colleges.* In the 2003 edition of The Princeton Review's *The Best 351 Colleges* the college ranked first in the country for its "Beautiful Campus" and fifth for providing the "Best Academic Bang for Your Buck" and for its friendly diversity on the "Students from Different Backgrounds Interact" list. It again placed among the top five in the guide's 2004 edition.

"Brooklyn College's 15,000 undergraduate and graduate students represent the ethnic and cultural diversity of the borough. And the college's accessibility by subway or bus allows students to further enrich their educational experience through New York City's many cultural events and institutions.

"The college continues on an ambitious program of expansion and renewal. The dazzling new library is the most technologically advanced educational and research facility in the CUNY system. A state-of-the-art student services and physical education building, currently under construction, is scheduled to be completed in 2009.

"Respected nationally for its rigorous academic standards, the college takes pride in such innovative programs as its award-winning Freshman Year College; the Honors Academy, which houses nine programs for high achievers; and the core curriculum. Brooklyn College's strong academic reputation has attracted an outstanding faculty of nationally renowned teachers and scholars. Among the awards they have won are Pulitzers, Guggenheims, Fulbrights, and National Institutes of Health grants. Brooklyn College students also receive such prestigious honors as Fulbright Scholarships, the Beinecke Memorial Scholarship, and the Paul and Daisy Soros Fellowships for New Americans.

"Brooklyn College only factors in the Critical Reading and Math components of the current SAT."

SELECTIVITY

Admissions Rating	80
# of applicants	13,615
% of applicants accepted	45
% of acceptees attending	23

FRESHMAN PROFILE

Range SAT Critical Reading	450–560
Range SAT Math	490–580
Minimum Paper TOEFL	500
Minimum Computer Based TOEFL	173
Average HS GPA	2.9
% graduated top 10% of class	14
% graduated top 25% of class	45
% graduated top 50% of class	74

DEADLINES

Regular notification	rolling
Nonfall registration?	yes

APPLICANTS ALSO LOOK AT

AND OFTEN PREFER
New York University, St. John's University, State University of New York at Binghamton

AND SOMETIMES PREFER
Columbia University, State University of New York—Stony Brook University, State University of New York—University at Albany

AND RARELY PREFER
Long Island University—Brooklyn, Saint Francis College (NY)

FINANCIAL FACTS

Financial Aid Rating	93
Annual in-state tuition	$4,000
Annual out-of-state tuition	$10,800
Books and supplies	$850
Required fees	$377
% frosh rec. need-based scholarship or grant aid	74
% UG rec. need-based scholarship or grant aid	66
% frosh rec. need-based self-help aid	69
% UG rec. need-based self-help aid	68
% frosh rec. any financial aid	78
% UG rec. any financial aid	71

CITY UNIVERSITY OF NEW YORK—HUNTER COLLEGE

695 PARK AVENUE, NEW YORK, NY 10021 • ADMISSIONS: 212-772-4490 • FAX: 212-650-3336

CAMPUS LIFE

Quality of Life Rating	**70**
Fire Safety Rating	**85**
Type of school	public
Environment	metropolis

STUDENTS

Total undergrad enrollment	14,434
% male/female	57/43
% from out of state	4
% from public high school	70
% live on campus	4
% in (# of) fraternities	1 (2)
% in (# of) sororities	1 (2)
% African American	14
% Asian	17
% Caucasian	39
% Hispanic	19
% international	10
# of countries represented	150

SURVEY SAYS . . .

Great library
Diverse student types on campus
Different types of students interact
Students love New York, NY
Very little drug use

ACADEMICS

Academic Rating	**63**
Calendar	semester
Student/faculty ratio	16:1
Profs interesting rating	69
Profs accessible rating	64
% profs teaching UG courses	96
Most common reg class size	20–29 students

MOST POPULAR MAJORS

accounting
English language and literature
psychology

STUDENTS SAY

Academics

Prospective students for looking for an academic "bang for the buck" in New York City should take a long look at Hunter College, the largest (in terms of enrollment) and most selective of the CUNY colleges. Physically, Hunter is a reflection of its hometown; with nearly 16,000 undergraduates attending classes in four buildings on three blocks of the Upper East Side, the "halls of Hunter College are extremely crowded." There are figurative similarities to the city, too. Like the Big Apple itself, Hunter has a ton to offer academically, but it's not just handed to you: "The academic experience can be inspiring or painfully dull, depending on one's interests, motivation, and desire to be challenged intellectually, as well as luck." Take professors, for example. "Many professors are accomplished and respected," are "often winners of the highest awards in their chosen profession[s], work as professionals in New York City, and are excellent contacts for further academic pursuits or for work after college." Others are "graduate students with limited experience or time" for students. Moreover, "Dealing with administrative matters at this school is not for the faint of heart," and "run of the mill transactions (processing of financial aid paperwork, registering for classes)" can "devour hours of your life." But students assure us that "if you are self-motivated you'll be fine." Registration is tough "because everyone is competing against each other for classes," but on the upside, "Hunter's class schedule is very accommodating to people who work either part- or full-time" and "Evening classes are abundant."

Life

As a commuter school, "There isn't as much campus life as you would find in other schools." Only about 600 of Hunter's 16,000 undergraduates live in the college's lone residence hall, and of the vast majority of students who are commuters, many simply "have too much going on outside of school to try to experience all that college life has to offer." But that's not to say that school unity is totally lacking. In lieu of residence life bonding experiences, "Clubs are very good at connecting people with similar interests." Plus, during the school day, "There's plenty of places [around campus] to just lounge with friends." Off campus—the question is, what *isn't* there? For those who like to unwind outside, "The school is close to Central Park." For the more urban-minded, "There are concerts, Broadway plays, and comedy shows." There are "movies," "great restaurants, bars, nightclubs, and shopping." And let's not forget that this is New York City; "just walking down the street can be a very entertaining experience."

Student Body

The typical Hunter student "is from one of the five boroughs and commutes to school every day." That's pretty much where generalizations of the student body end. Hunter College has made repeated appearances on this publication's "Diverse Student Population" top 20 ranking list, and for good reason. "In terms of socioeconomic status, immigrants, languages, cultures, religion, race, ethnicity, age . . . Hunter has it all." "Students range in age from newly graduated high schoolers to retirees." And "There really doesn't seem to be [a] dominant ethnic group." It's the kind of place where "nothing seems too out of the ordinary," "everyone fits in fine," and where it won't surprise you to see a "White punk rock girl having a friendly conversation with a Muslim girl in the full head-to-toe [garb]." If you must generalize, it's easier to say what most Hunter students are not. This list is short: "out-of-state students" who are "not liberal."

CITY UNIVERSITY OF NEW YORK—HUNTER COLLEGE

FINANCIAL AID: 212-772-4820 • E-MAIL: ADMISSIONS@HUNTER.CUNY.EDU • WEBSITE: WWW.HUNTER.CUNY.EDU

ADMISSIONS

Very important factors considered include: Academic GPA, rigor of secondary school record, standardized test scores. SAT or ACT required; TOEFL required of all international applicants. High school diploma is required, and GED is accepted. *Academic units required:* 2 English, 2 math, 1 science (1 science lab). *Academic units recommended:* 4 English, 3 math, 2 science (2 science labs), 2 foreign language, 4 social studies, 1 visual or performing arts.

The Inside Word

In terms of statistics, Hunter College is the most selective of the CUNY undergraduate colleges, but this doesn't mean that you have to be an academic superstar in high school to be admitted. Hunter is, after all, first and foremost a CUNY, dedicated to educating the citizens of New York City. But given an applicant pool comprised mainly of New York City residents, high school grades and test scores are the main factors separating those admitted from those who are not. If you are planning to apply to Hunter's Honors College, note that applications are due December 15, rather than on the regular application deadline of March 15.

FINANCIAL AID

Students should submit: FAFSA, state aid form, institutional direct loan request form from DL applicants. The Princeton Review suggests that all financial aid forms be submitted as soon as possible after January 1. *Need-based scholarships/grants offered:* Pell Grant, SEOG, state scholarships/grants, private scholarships, the school's own gift aid. *Loan aid offered:* Direct Subsidized Stafford, Direct Unsubsidized Stafford, Direct PLUS, Federal Perkins Loan, alternative loans. Applicants will be notified of awards on a rolling basis beginning or about May 15. Federal Work-Study Program available. Institutional employment available. Off-campus job opportunities are fair.

FROM THE ADMISSIONS OFFICE

"Located in the heart of Manhattan, Hunter offers students the stimulating learning environment and career-building opportunities you might expect from a college that's been a part of the world's most exciting city since 1870. The largest college in the City University of New York, Hunter pulses with energy. Hunter's vitality stems from a large, highly diverse faculty and student body. Its schools—Arts and Sciences, Education, the Health Professions, and Social Work—provide an affordable first-rate education. Undergraduates have extraordinary opportunities to conduct high-level research under renowned faculty, and many opt for credit-bearing internships in such exciting fields as media, the arts, and government. The college's high standards and special programs ensure a challenging education. The Block Program for first-year students keeps classmates together as they pursue courses in the liberal arts, pre-health science, pre-nursing, premed, or honors. A range of honors programs is available for students with strong academic records, including the highly competitive tuition-free Hunter CUNY Honors College for entering freshmen and the Thomas Hunter Honors Program, which emphasizes small classes with personalized mentoring by outstanding faculty. Qualified students also benefit from Hunter's participation in minority science research and training programs, the prestigious Andrew W. Mellon Minority Undergraduate Program, and many other passports to professional success.

"Applicants for the Fall 2008 entering class are required to take either the SAT or the ACT. We will accept scores from the new SAT and scores from the old (prior to March 2005) version of the SAT. We will use the student's best scores from any of these tests."

SELECTIVITY

Admissions Rating	86
# of applicants	21,830
% of applicants accepted	34
% of acceptees attending	25

FRESHMAN PROFILE

Range SAT Critical Reading	490–580
Range SAT Math	500–600
Minimum Paper TOEFL	500
Minimum Computer Based TOEFL	173
Average HS GPA	3.0
% graduated top 10% of class	21
% graduated top 25% of class	48
% graduated top 50% of class	78

DEADLINES

Regular application deadline	3/15
Regular notification	rolling
Nonfall registration?	yes

APPLICANTS ALSO LOOK AT

AND OFTEN PREFER
New York University

AND SOMETIMES PREFER
Fordham University, State University of New York at Binghamton, State University of New York—Stony Brook University

FINANCIAL FACTS

Financial Aid Rating	84
Annual in-state tuition	$4,000
Room & Board	$3,726
Books and supplies	$879
Required fees	$329
% frosh rec. need-based scholarship or grant aid	64
% UG rec. need-based scholarship or grant aid	53
% frosh rec. need-based self-help aid	4
% UG rec. need-based self-help aid	17
% frosh rec. any financial aid	90
% UG rec. any financial aid	90

CITY UNIVERSITY OF NEW YORK—QUEENS COLLEGE

65-30 KISSENA BOULEVARD, FLUSHING, NY 11367 • ADMISSIONS: 718-997-5000 • FAX: 718-997-5617

CAMPUS LIFE
Quality of Life Rating	**66**
Fire Safety Rating	**60***
Type of school	public
Environment	metropolis

STUDENTS
Total undergrad enrollment	12,991
% male/female	39/61
% from out of state	1
% from public high school	67
% in (# of) fraternities	1 (3)
% in (# of) sororities	1 (3)
% African American	9
% Asian	19
% Caucasian	47
% Hispanic	18
% international	8
# of countries represented	140

SURVEY SAYS . . .
Small classes
Great library
Diverse student types on campus
Very little beer drinking
Very little hard liquor
Very little drug use

ACADEMICS
Academic Rating	**61**
Calendar	semester
Student/faculty ratio	17:1
Profs interesting rating	66
Profs accessible rating	62
% profs teaching UG courses	90
% classes taught by TAs	1
Most common reg class size	20–29 students

MOST POPULAR MAJORS
accounting
psychology
sociology

STUDENTS SAY
Academics

New York state residents can get "a great education for a cheap price" at Queens College, one of the premier campuses of the City University of New York system. The school's affordable tuition "gives many students a chance to get a higher education." Some here go so far as to call QC "the Harvard of the CUNY system," although students at Baruch, Hunter, City College, and Brooklyn College would probably beg to differ. Regardless of its relative status in the CUNY system, QC undoubtedly provides "great and challenging programs" that are "unique and comprehensive, and are compatible [with one's objectives]." With no residence halls on or near the campus, QC serves a commuter population focused on "building career opportunities" by "getting an education in service of your future profession (and maybe having some fun)." Business and management, English, psychology, health sciences, and sociology are among the most popular majors here; QC is also home to a competitive school of music. Students at QC tell us that "the administration is okay—comparable to any other out there," and that teachers here are surprisingly "easy to talk to and very helpful, not at all intimidating. You're not afraid to express yourself in class." Students say "smaller classes" and "more students in campus involvement" would be nice, but overall they are satisfied with the college's "multicultural feast sprinkled with a quasi-intellectual environment."

Life

Queens College "is a commuter school, so campus life is not very lively." Its students "are primarily education- and career-oriented." Many "Students work part-time jobs so they really do not have much time left for other activities." Even so, "Queens has a strong community that is diverse and conducive to positive social interactions and communication." The campus is home to tons of "clubs and organizations," and those with the time to do so report that "joining a club helps make the experience at Queens College worthwhile." One student writes, "Political clubs are pretty popular. A lot of times there are club fairs on the grass. Also, anyone can play club sports. The girls could join the soccer club with the boys if they wanted to." While few students stick around campus once their final classes for the day are done, "Between classes students lounge around in the cafeterias or Student Union to talk with friends." Undergrads tell us that there are events to go to "almost every day of the week," in part because the school's New York City location allows it to attract some prominent speakers. The QC campus is surprisingly large and sports a surprisingly large expanse of green for an urban campus. Hometown Queens is a truly international borough and the area surrounding QC is no exception; right outside the campus gates students will find restaurants serving everything from kosher to Korean, from pizza to pita sandwiches.

Student Body

"There is no typical student at Queens College, and that's what's great about the student body," say the students who belong to this "diverse and dedicated community." "Every racial background imaginable is represented and has a group [on campus], and every religious background is apparent." QC is a place where "Everywhere you turn people are able to speak more than one language." There's also plenty of diversity in personality types, although all students tend to be "very focused." Expect "some very religious students" and some nonbelievers as well; "Most students are very different and that makes it easy for everybody to fit in." In short, "Everyone is unique" here, but students across the board "work hard, and are eager to learn," and "This is something that bonds people together."

FINANCIAL AID: 718-997-5101 • E-MAIL: ADMISSIONS@QC.EDU • WEBSITE: WWW.QC.EDU

ADMISSIONS

Very important factors considered include: Academic GPA, rigor of secondary school record, standardized test scores. SAT or ACT required; SAT Subject Tests recommended. TOEFL required of all international applicants. High school diploma is required, and GED is accepted. *Academic units required:* 4 English, 3 math, 2 science (2 science labs), 3 foreign language, 4 social studies. *Academic units recommended:* 4 English, 3 math, 3 science (3 science labs), 3 foreign language, 4 social studies.

The Inside Word

Minority enrollment has declined at CUNY in the past 7 years, partially as a result of changes to admissions criteria and stiffer competition for minority applicants. The school would love to boost its numbers, meaning that qualified minority students could be able to finagle a pretty sweet financial aid package here, making an already economical education even more affordable.

FINANCIAL AID

Students should submit: FAFSA, institution's own financial aid form, state aid form. The Princeton Review suggests that all financial aid forms be submitted as soon as possible after January 1. *Need-based scholarships/grants offered:* Pell Grant, SEOG, state scholarships/grants, private scholarships, the school's own gift aid. *Loan aid offered:* Direct Subsidized Stafford, Direct Unsubsidized Stafford, Direct PLUS, Federal Perkins Loan. Applicants will be notified of awards on a rolling basis beginning or about March 1. Federal Work-Study Program available. Institutional employment available. Off-campus job opportunities are good.

FROM THE ADMISSIONS OFFICE

"Often called "the jewel of the City University of New York," Queens College boasts an award-winning faculty committed to scholarship and teaching, as well as students from more than 140 nations. Combined with our fast-growing student-life program, this creates an exceptionally dynamic learning environment.

"A commuter college with a residential feel, Queens has a beautifully landscaped, 77-acre campus and a traditional quad facing the Manhattan skyline. Powdermaker Hall, our major classroom building, features state-of-the-art technology throughout. Queens College is also the only CUNY college to participate in Division II sports.

"Consistently included in the Princeton Review America's Best Value Colleges, Queens College offers nationally recognized programs in many fields, including the Aaron Copland School of Music. Recently added degrees include a Bachelor of Business Administration with majors in finance, international business, and actuarial studies, and a Bachelor of Science in Graphic Design. Queens College is the ideal choice for aspiring teachers, preparing more educators than any college in the tristate area through its innovative programs. Would-be teachers admitted to the University Teacher Academy receive free tuition while working towards a degree in math or science. The college also participates in the Macaulay Honors College and offers qualified students its own honors programs in the arts and humanities, sciences, and social sciences.

"Applicants for Fall 2008 should submit the SAT comprising Critical Reading, Writing, and Math. Pending further research on the merits of the Writing section, students will continue to be assessed based on their highest Math and Critical Reading scores."

SELECTIVITY
Admissions Rating	60*
# of applicants	12,911
% of applicants accepted	43
% of acceptees attending	30

FRESHMAN PROFILE
Range SAT Critical Reading	440–550
Range SAT Math	475–580
Minimum Paper TOEFL	500
Minimum Computer Based TOEFL	173
Average HS GPA	3.2

DEADLINES
Regular notification	rolling
Nonfall registration?	yes

FINANCIAL FACTS
Financial Aid Rating	68
Annual in-state tuition	$4,000
Annual out-of-state tuition	$10,800
Required fees	$377
% frosh rec. need-based scholarship or grant aid	35
% UG rec. need-based scholarship or grant aid	46
% frosh rec. need-based self-help aid	18
% UG rec. need-based self-help aid	26
% frosh rec. any financial aid	76
% UG rec. any financial aid	45

CLAREMONT MCKENNA COLLEGE

890 COLUMBIA AVENUE, CLAREMONT, CA 91711 • ADMISSIONS: 909-621-8088 • FAX: 909-621-8516

CAMPUS LIFE

Quality of Life Rating	98
Fire Safety Rating	60*
Type of school	private
Environment	village

STUDENTS

Total undergrad enrollment	1,153
% male/female	54/46
% from out of state	52
% from public high school	73
% live on campus	96
% African American	4
% Asian	15
% Caucasian	56
% Hispanic	12
% Native American	1
% international	4

SURVEY SAYS . . .

Career services are great
Small classes
Frats and sororities are unpopular or
nonexistent
Lots of beer drinking

ACADEMICS

Academic Rating	87
Calendar	semester
Student/faculty ratio	9:1
Profs interesting rating	95
Profs accessible rating	97
% profs teaching	
UG courses	100
% classes taught by TAs	0

MOST POPULAR MAJORS

economics
international relations and affairs
political science and government

STUDENTS SAY

Academics

"Determined, intellectual preprofessionals in government, business, law, and medicine" fill the classrooms of Claremont McKenna College, where students who pursue less pragmatic disciplines (e.g., philosophy, religious studies) should "be prepared for a lot of 'What are you going to do with that?' from fellow students." The "amazing economics and government programs" are top draws thanks to high-profile professors and an excellent DC internship program. All programs benefit from CMC's strong ties to the community; one student explains, "There are many CMC companies in downtown LA that start with one alumnus and slowly absorb more CMCers. Since all the Claremont Colleges intermingle, alumni from the other colleges are often as nice as CMC alumni. There are many five-college alumni groups that foster 5-C interaction after college." CMC's proximity to LA also helps feed the Athenaeum, "a Monday-through-Thursday speaker series that is amazing, attracting many well-known academics and celebrities, authors, musicians, and comedians!" Further enhancing the experience here are "13 research institutes that give undergraduates the ability to do graduate-level research." The only drawback is that "CMC is small, so some of the less popular majors are really small," but even that isn't too big a deal, since the Claremont Colleges Consortium allows CMC students to supplement their curricula with classes at the other four consortium schools.

Life

"Some say CMC should stand for Club Med College, because it's fun in the sun and a great place to learn," but the nickname probably puts too much emphasis on "Club Med" and too little on "College." Students here work hard; they "focus intently on schoolwork Monday through Thursday, plus they usually have jobs on-campus doing anything from research to tutoring to technology assistance. People also work diligently to find great internships and jobs during the summers." They also know how to kick back and relax, though, often with the help of the administration, which "is very lenient in its alcohol policy, as long as we're all responsible with what we do." The laid-back party atmosphere helps create a strong sense of campus community, as does the fact that "almost everyone at Claremont lives on campus. It's a very healthy scene, people carve out their niches for all 4 years on campus, and there's a stronger sense of tradition when different class years are always rubbing shoulders." Campus life also "provides awesome concerts two or three times a year" and "a bunch of different clubs on campus to get involved with." Still, "If there isn't anything going on at Claremont McKenna, chances are there is something going on at one of the other colleges, to which we have access," writes one student.

Student Body

Undergraduates are "very driven to succeed. We genuinely work hard and have large goals that we wish to achieve." The result is a friendly but competitive atmosphere "in which most people seem to thrive." Most here "are from middle-to upper-class families, which cause many to come to school with a sheltered perspective on the world, but through the Athenaeum and study abroad, undergrads develop informed views and diverse thoughts." The school's popular programs in political science, government, international relations, and economics mean that most undergrads are "very politically astute" and "willing to debate political issues frequently, but never to the point of anger. It is hardly a rarity to see a liberal and conservative sharing some beers over discussion, and it's a beautiful thing." Nearly everyone fits the CMC mold "because the Admissions Office does a good job of making sure that students are a good match for the college" and because the school is so small.

CLAREMONT MCKENNA COLLEGE

FINANCIAL AID: 909-621-8356 • E-MAIL: ADMISSION@CLAREMONTMCKENNA.EDU • WEBSITE: WWW.CLAREMONTMCKENNA.EDU

ADMISSIONS

Very important factors considered include: Application essay, character/personal qualities, extracurricular activities, rigor of secondary school record, standardized test scores. *Important factors considered include:* Recommendation(s), talent/ability. *Other factors considered include:* Alumni/ae relation, class rank, geographical residence, interview, racial/ethnic status, state residency, volunteer work, work experience. SAT or ACT required; SAT Subject Tests recommended, ACT with Writing component required. TOEFL required of all international applicants. High school diploma is required, and GED is accepted. *Academic units required:* 4 English, 3 math, 2 science, 3 foreign language, 2 social studies, 1 history. *Academic units recommended:* 4 English, 4 math, 3 science, 3 foreign language, 2 social studies, 2 history.

The Inside Word

Although applicants have to possess solid academic qualifications to gain admission to Claremont McKenna, the importance of making a good match should not be underestimated. Colleges of such small size and selectivity devote much more energy to determining whether the candidate as an individual fits than they do to whether a candidate has the appropriate test scores.

FINANCIAL AID

Students should submit: FAFSA, CSS/Financial Aid PROFILE, Noncustodial PROFILE, state aid form. Regular filing deadline is February 1. The Princeton Review suggests that all financial aid forms be submitted as soon as possible after January 1. *Need-based scholarships/grants offered:* Pell Grant, SEOG, state scholarships/grants, private scholarships, the school's own gift aid. *Loan aid offered:* Direct Subsidized Stafford, Direct Unsubsidized Stafford, Direct PLUS, FFEL Subsidized Stafford, FFEL Unsubsidized Stafford, Federal Perkins Loan, Federal Nursing Loan, college/university loans from institutional funds. Applicants will be notified of awards on or about April 1. Federal Work-Study Program available. Institutional employment available. Off-campus job opportunities are excellent.

FROM THE ADMISSIONS OFFICE

"CMC's mission is clear: To educate students for meaningful lives and responsible leadership in business, government, and the professions. While many other colleges champion either a traditional liberal arts education with emphasis on intellectual breadth or training that stresses acquisition of technical skills, CMC offers a clear alternative. Instead of dividing the liberal arts and working world into separate realms, education at CMC is rooted in the interplay between the world of ideas and the world of events. By combining the intellectual breadth of liberal arts with the more pragmatic concerns of public affairs, CMC students gain the vision, skills, and values necessary for leadership in all sectors of society.

"Applicants for Fall 2008 must take the new SAT Reasoning Test or ACT with Writing. Scores from the old SAT Reasoning Test (before March 2005) or ACT without the Writing section will not be accepted for application purposes. We will use the highest scores from the SAT or ACT. SAT Subject Tests are recommended, but not required."

SELECTIVITY

Admissions Rating	**97**
# of applicants	3,593
% of applicants accepted	22
% of acceptees attending	37
# accepting a place on wait list	279
# of early decision applicants	267
% accepted early decision	30

FRESHMAN PROFILE

Range SAT Critical Reading	630–730
Range SAT Math	640–740
Range ACT Composite	28–33
Minimum Paper TOEFL	600
Minimum Computer Based TOEFL	250
% graduated top 10% of class	83
% graduated top 25% of class	95
% graduated top 50% of class	100

DEADLINES

Early decision application deadline	11/15
Early decision notification	12/15
Regular application deadline	1/2
Regular notification	4/1
Nonfall registration?	yes

APPLICANTS ALSO LOOK AT

AND OFTEN PREFER
Harvard College, Stanford University

AND SOMETIMES PREFER
Georgetown University, Pomona College, Princeton University

AND RARELY PREFER
Occidental College, University of California—Berkeley, The University of Chicago

FINANCIAL FACTS

Financial Aid Rating	**99**
Annual tuition	$33,000
Room & Board	$10,740
Books and supplies	$1,850
Required fees	$210
% frosh rec. need-based scholarship or grant aid	45
% UG rec. need-based scholarship or grant aid	46
% frosh rec. need-based self-help aid	33
% UG rec. need-based self-help aid	34
% frosh rec. any financial aid	65
% UG rec. any financial aid	72

CLARK UNIVERSITY

950 Main Street, Worcester, MA 01610-1477 • Admissions: 508-793-7431 • Fax: 508-793-8821

CAMPUS LIFE

Quality of Life Rating	**70**
Fire Safety Rating	**84**
Type of school	private
Environment	city

STUDENTS

Total undergrad enrollment	2,175
% male/female	40/60
% from out of state	62
% from public high school	70
% live on campus	74
% African American	3
% Asian	4
% Caucasian	66
% Hispanic	2
% international	8
# of countries represented	58

SURVEY SAYS . . .

Small classes
Students are friendly
Frats and sororities are unpopular or nonexistent
Lots of beer drinking
Hard liquor is popular

ACADEMICS

Academic Rating	**81**
Calendar	semester
Student/faculty ratio	10:1
Profs interesting rating	75
Profs accessible rating	79
% profs teaching UG courses	100
% classes taught by TAs	0
Most common lab size	10–19 students
Most common reg class size	10–19 students

MOST POPULAR MAJORS

biology/biological sciences
political science and government
psychology

STUDENTS SAY

Academics

"Clark is geared toward providing every student with the opportunity for personal growth," students at this prestigious liberal arts school report. The school achieves this goal "by offering a wide and fascinating variety of courses, programs, travel opportunities, and events that inform and intrigue." The solid academic community on campus is key to the Clark experience; a "group of mentors (your professors, the administration, and your peers)" is "always willing to help" students deal with the "extremely challenging classes" that make up the Clark curriculum. A typical undergrad writes, "I know all my professors and all my professors know me (even in my larger classes)." Classes that are "usually small in size" are "intimate enough to give you a chance to connect with professors" who "really do want their students to actually understand the material, not just know it to succeed on tests. They also take a personal interest in the students; several friends have gone to their professors' houses for dinner (as first-year students)." This closeness between professors and students encourages "opportunities to get involved with research," a real boon to students' curricula vitae. Research is further promoted by Clark's constant efforts at self-improvement; students tell us that the school "keeps adding new facilities that are up-to-date so that learning can be more hands-on." Psychology and the hard sciences are standout offerings here; political science, government, and history are all also reportedly strong.

Life

"Clark is a small school with a very strong sense of community" where "you can sit down at a random table in the cafeteria and the odds are that you'll know at least one other person at the table." One undergrad writes, "I can count on one hand the number of meals I've eaten alone this semester." Students love how Clark "retains its community feel without feeling cramped. The opportunities for community service, studying abroad, and internships provide plenty of opportunities to broaden oneself socially, and there are other ways to get away from people if one wants to be alone or lose oneself." Otherwise, "If you leave your room at all, ever, you will have a social life here, and that doesn't have to mean drinking or drugs, since there's a lot more to life here. There's also very little pressure to drink if you don't." If you do drink, you'll find plenty of company, as "People party a good amount. Going to local bars after parties is very popular. Hard liquor and beer is always around and never cheap beer or hard liquor, always good stuff." Other diversions include "sports, movies, theater performances, comedy sketches, and lectures. Mostly indoor stuff, because Worcester gets really cold in the winter." Hometown Worcester has other problems; it "isn't the best city to go to school in, despite having eight colleges here. There's very little to do off campus on weekends unless you go to Boston."

Student Body

"We have a really unique combination of preppy, hippie, artsy, jock, and everything in between" at Clark, students tell us, and "Most people fit into more than one category." Asked which category is represented with the greatest frequency, most here will tell you that "it's the student who looks like he's just returning from Woodstock: Birkenstocks, bandannas, grubby-looking, loose clothing, reeking of weed." Everyone is welcome, we're told; one outlier writes, "I myself am a practicing Republican ROTC cadet who abstains from nearly every vice, and I have no trouble fitting in." Clark undergrads appreciate that "students are focused more on learning than on competition with one another, so there are very few cutthroats about grades." Students tend to be bright and curious, so "It's easy to get involved in a very long conversation about some class topic, which is how a recent study session was extended from 3 to 7 hours."

FINANCIAL AID: 508-793-7478 • E-MAIL: ADMISSIONS@CLARKU.EDU • WEBSITE: WWW.CLARKU.EDU

ADMISSIONS

Very important factors considered include: Academic GPA, character/personal qualities, recommendation(s), rigor of secondary school record, standardized test scores. *Important factors considered include:* Application essay, extracurricular activities, talent/ability, volunteer work. *Other factors considered include:* Alumni/ae relation, class rank, first generation, geographical residence, interview, level of applicant's interest, racial/ethnic status, work experience. SAT or ACT required; TOEFL required of all international applicants. High school diploma is required, and GED is accepted. *Academic units recommended:* 4 English, 3 math, 3 science (2 science labs), 2 foreign language, 2 social studies, 2 history.

The Inside Word

Clark is surrounded by formidable competitors, and its selectivity suffers because of it. Most B students will encounter little difficulty gaining admission. Given the university's solid academic environment and access to other member colleges in the Worcester Consortium, it can be a terrific choice for students who are not up to the ultra-competitive admission expectations of "top-tier" universities.

FINANCIAL AID

Students should submit: FAFSA, CSS/Financial Aid PROFILE. Regular filing deadline is February 1. The Princeton Review suggests that all financial aid forms be submitted as soon as possible after January 1. *Need-based scholarships/grants offered:* Pell Grant, SEOG, state scholarships/grants, the school's own gift aid. *Loan aid offered:* FFEL Subsidized Stafford, FFEL Unsubsidized Stafford, FFEL PLUS, Federal Perkins Loan, state loans. Applicants will be notified of awards on or about March 31.

FROM THE ADMISSIONS OFFICE

"Challenge Convention, Change Our World" isn't just a motto at Clark University. It's a long tradition that our students and faculty continue in their work—inside and outside the classroom—every day. At Clark, students and faculty are encouraged to follow their intellectual curiosity, seek innovative solutions to real-world problems and create positive change in the world.

"Clark's vibrant intellectual environment is built upon learning through inquiry, making a difference and experiencing diverse cultures. These key elements of a Clark education permeate campus life through courses, independent projects, internships, and other learning opportunities; through research and social action, both locally and globally; through the diverse, urban campus community; through interactions with members of the Clark community, and study-abroad experiences.

"Clark as an institution and its faculty and students have an obligation and a rare opportunity to make our world a better place. Whether in science and technology, international development or business, students who apply to Clark want to be in an environment that will challenge their assumptions and encourage them to understand the ways in which their work as adults will make a difference.

"Clark requires that students submit scores from the SAT. Students will be judged by their performance in Critical Reading and Math. Pending further analysis of the new Writing section, writing aptitude is evaluated as part of the application review process."

SELECTIVITY

Admissions Rating	89
# of applicants	4,726
% of applicants accepted	60
% of acceptees attending	20
# accepting a place on wait list	31
% admitted from wait list	26
# of early decision applicants	85
% accepted early decision	72

FRESHMAN PROFILE

Range SAT Critical Reading	550–670
Range SAT Math	540–640
Range ACT Composite	23–29
Minimum Paper TOEFL	550
Minimum Computer Based TOEFL	213
Average HS GPA	3.45
% graduated top 10% of class	31
% graduated top 25% of class	71
% graduated top 50% of class	96

DEADLINES

Early decision application deadline	11/15
Early decision notification	12/15
Regular application deadline	1/15
Regular notification	4/1
Nonfall registration?	yes

APPLICANTS ALSO LOOK AT

AND OFTEN PREFER
Boston College, Boston University, Brandeis University, Tufts University, Vassar College

AND SOMETIMES PREFER
Connecticut College, Ithaca College, Northeastern University, Skidmore College, Syracuse University, University of New Hampshire

AND RARELY PREFER
Goucher College, University of Connecticut, University of Massachusetts—Amherst, University of Vermont, Wheaton College (MA)

FINANCIAL FACTS

Financial Aid Rating	89
Annual tuition	$31,200
Room & Board	$5,900
Books and supplies	$800
Required fees	$265
% frosh rec. need-based scholarship or grant aid	53
% UG rec. need-based scholarship or grant aid	53
% frosh rec. need-based self-help aid	44
% UG rec. need-based self-help aid	44
% frosh rec. any financial aid	78
% UG rec. any financial aid	77

CLARKSON UNIVERSITY

PO BOX 5605, POTSDAM, NY 13699 • ADMISSIONS: 315-268-6479 • FAX: 315-268-7647

CAMPUS LIFE
Quality of Life Rating	61
Fire Safety Rating	75
Type of school	private
Environment	village

STUDENTS
Total undergrad enrollment	2,515
% male/female	74/26
% from out of state	26
% from public high school	85
% live on campus	83
% in (# of) fraternities	14 (10)
% in (# of) sororities	16 (3)
% African American	2
% Asian	2
% Caucasian	90
% Hispanic	2
% Native American	1
% international	3
# of countries represented	40

SURVEY SAYS . . .
Career services are great
Students are friendly
Low cost of living
Lots of beer drinking
Hard liquor is popular

ACADEMICS
Academic Rating	67
Calendar	semester
Student/faculty ratio	16:1
Profs interesting rating	65
Profs accessible rating	75
% profs teaching	
UG courses	88
Most common	
lab size	10–19 students
Most common	
reg class size	20–29 students

MOST POPULAR MAJORS
business, engineering, biology, chemistry, psychology, digital arts, communicartions

STUDENTS SAY
Academics
"Academics and hockey are the greatest strengths at Clarkson University," a tech-heavy school in upstate New York where it sometimes seems that "99 percent of us are here for business, engineering, or science." For many here, Clarkson's chief appeal is the way it opens doors for graduates; explains one student, "Clarkson has a very good name . . . alumni have gone on to become CEOs or own their own companies. Employers come here to recruit because they know the Clarkson student is likely to be successful." This is because Clarkson grads have conquered a curriculum that "is challenging even for people who are skilled in math, science, and engineering." It's so challenging, in fact, that "teamwork is essential here. It is the only way we can successfully learn all the material." Undergrads appreciate Clarkson's "interdisciplinary approach to all learning, as well as the emphasis on leadership" in the curriculum. They're less enamored of the liberal arts offerings, noting that the departments are small and classes are few. Professors get wildly mixed reviews, which actually puts them in the upper stratum of tech instructors, whose marks are usually quite low. Students warn that "the school often has new professors teaching classes in which they are unprepared to teach. Most of the time they are very well-qualified individuals but do not yet have the ability to properly teach a classroom full of students." Better teachers here "have a genuine interest in their students' succeeding, and enjoy their jobs."

Life
Located in Potsdam, New York, Clarkson "is in the middle of nowhere." Some see that as an asset; one such student explains, "It forces you to meet people and make friends to have fun. And since it is in the middle of nowhere, it is easier to get work done . . . there are fewer things to distract you from doing your work." Others see a downside; "Unless you are an avid hunter/fisherman, your options for not getting bored doing the same exact thing week after week are very poor. Remember the movie *Groundhog Day*? Life here is comparable." Compounding the challenges of extracurricular life here are the heavy workload and the fact that "it's freezing up there for about half of the school year," which drives many students "to bars, Canada, dinner, or hockey games. Or we stay in, playing video games or hanging out with friends." Some feel the school could do more to improve things; one undergrad observes, "There isn't enough money spent on bringing events to campus. Every year they bring the same comedians, the same small bands. The only event that seems to be any good is the spring concert, but that's about it." As a result, "Most of the students spend their free time hanging with friends and drinking." One student sums up, "When I'm not working . . . I drink. We are a technical school that certainly knows how to party. There isn't much else to do up here."

Student Body
"There are typically two groups at Clarkson," students tell us. There are "those focused on learning and interested in having a good time, and there are those solely focused on learning." Most Clarkson students share "a drive to succeed, an ability to learn in multidisciplinary environments, and a strong career/graduate study focus." This focus can be overwhelming at times; "Even in party atmospheres you will find numerous conversations regarding nothing but academic-related topics. Not enough separation between 'business and pleasure,' so to speak." Like many tech-oriented schools, "Clarkson needs more women. The ratio is so completely horrible that it is probably the top of every male student's list of what needs improving here." Scattered among the student population are "a number of athletes and quite a few outdoorsy people."

FINANCIAL AID: 315-268-7699 • E-MAIL: ADMISSION@CLARKSON.EDU • WEBSITE: WWW.CLARKSON.EDU

ADMISSIONS

Very important factors considered include: Academic GPA, interview, rigor of secondary school record. *Important factors considered include:* Class rank, extracurricular activities, recommendation(s), standardized test scores, volunteer work. *Other factors considered include:* Alumni/ae relation, application essay, character/personal qualities, first generation, level of applicant's interest, talent/ability, work experience. SAT or ACT required; SAT Subject Tests recommended. TOEFL required of all international applicants. High school diploma is required, and GED is accepted. *Academic units required:* 4 English, 3 math, 2 science. *Academic units recommended:* 4 math, 3 science.

The Inside Word

Clarkson's acceptance rate is too high for solid applicants to lose much sleep about gaining admission. Serious candidates should interview anyway. If you are particularly solid and really want to come here, it could help you get some scholarship money. Women and minorities will encounter an especially friendly Admissions Committee.

FINANCIAL AID

Students should submit: FAFSA, institution's own financial aid form, state aid form. The Princeton Review suggests that all financial aid forms be submitted as soon as possible after January 1. *Need-based scholarships/grants offered:* Pell Grant, SEOG, state scholarships/grants, private scholarships, the school's own gift aid, Higher Education Opportunity Program. *Loan aid offered:* Direct Subsidized Stafford, Direct Unsubsidized Stafford, Direct PLUS, Federal Perkins Loan, college/university loans from institutional funds, Nellie Mae, and Bank of America. Applicants will be notified of awards on or about March 16. Federal Work-Study Program available. Institutional employment available.

FROM THE ADMISSIONS OFFICE

"Clarkson University, a private, nationally ranked research university located in Potsdam, New York, is the institution of choice for 3,000 enterprising, high-ability scholars from diverse backgrounds who embrace challenge and thrive in a rigorous, highly collaborative learning environment.

"Clarkson's programs in engineering, business, the sciences, liberal arts, and health sciences emphasize team-based learning as well as creative problem solving and leadership skills. Clarkson is also on the leading edge of today's emerging technologies and fields of study offering innovative, boundary-spanning degree programs in engineering and management, digital arts and sciences, and environmental science and policy, among others.

"At Clarkson, students and faculty work closely together in a supportive, friendly environment. Students are encouraged to participate in faculty-mentored research projects from their first year, and to take advantage of co-ops and study abroad programs. Our collaborative approach to education translates into graduates in high demand; our placement rates are among the highest in the country. Alumni experience accelerated career growth. One in seven alumni is already a CEO, president, or vice president of a company.

"Recent awards and honors include: Among the Top 100 engineering schools (*U.S. News & World Report* 2007); ranked number 10 in the nation in 'Supply Chain Management' (*U.S. News & World Report* 2007); top 25 in the nation in Innovation and Entrepreneurship' (*The Princeton Review/Entrepreneur* magazine); and among the 'Top 20 Most Wired Colleges' (*The Princeton Review/PC* magazine 2007)."

"Applicants for Fall 2008 are required to take the ACT with Writing section optional, or the new version of the SAT. We will allow students to submit scores from the old (prior to March 2005) version of the SAT (or ACT) as well, and will use the student's best scores from either test. SAT Subject Tests are recommended but not required."

SELECTIVITY

Admissions Rating	85
# of applicants	2,428
% of applicants accepted	84
% of acceptees attending	32
# accepting a place on wait list	9
% admitted from wait list	56
# of early decision applicants	134
% accepted early decision	95

FRESHMAN PROFILE

Range SAT Critical Reading	520–620
Range SAT Math	560–660
Range ACT Composite	22–28
Minimum Paper TOEFL	550
Minimum Computer Based TOEFL	213
Average HS GPA	3.47
% graduated top 10% of class	31
% graduated top 25% of class	69
% graduated top 50% of class	95

DEADLINES

Early decision application deadline	12/1
Early decision notification	12/30
Regular application deadline	1/15
Regular notification	continuous
Nonfall registration?	yes

APPLICANTS ALSO LOOK AT

AND OFTEN PREFER

Pennsylvania State University—University Park, Rensselaer Polytechnic Institute, Rochester Institute of Technology, State University of New York—Buffalo, University of Vermont

AND SOMETIMES PREFER

Alfred University, Lehigh University, University of Connecticut, University of Rochester, Worcester Polytechnic Institute

AND RARELY PREFER

Syracuse University

FINANCIAL FACTS

Financial Aid Rating	61
Annual tuition	$26,650
Room & Board	$9,648
Required fees	$440
Books and supplies	$1,100
% frosh rec. need-based scholarship or grant aid	48
% UG rec. need-based scholarship or grant aid	62
% frosh rec. need-based self-help aid	59
% UG rec. need-based self-help aid	71
% frosh rec. any financial aid	90
% UG rec. any financial aid	88

CLEMSON UNIVERSITY

106 Sikes Hall, Box 345124, Clemson, SC 29634-5124 • Admissions: 864-656-2287 • Fax: 864-656-2464

CAMPUS LIFE

Quality of Life Rating	98
Fire Safety Rating	60*
Type of school	public
Environment	village

STUDENTS

Total undergrad enrollment	13,959
% male/female	54/46
% from out of state	32
% from public high school	89
% live on campus	44
% in (# of) fraternities	11 (26)
% in (# of) sororities	14 (17)
% African American	7
% Asian	2
% Caucasian	82
% Hispanic	1

SURVEY SAYS . . .

Career services are great
Great library
Athletic facilities are great
Students are friendly
Campus feels safe
Students are happy
Everyone loves the Tigers

ACADEMICS

Academic Rating	84
Calendar	semester
Student/faculty ratio	15:1
Profs interesting rating	80
Profs accessible rating	85
% profs teaching UG courses	95
% classes taught by TAs	7
Most common lab size	10–19 students
Most common reg class size	10–19 students

MOST POPULAR MAJORS

business administration/management
engineering
secondary education and teaching

STUDENTS SAY

Academics

Clemson University, a tradition-rich Southern school "that focuses on engineering, agriculture, science, and football," draws students who want to experience "a true community where everyone shares the same passion for education, friendship, kindness, and cheering on the Tigers." Students here speak lovingly of "the spirit of 'the Clemson family,'" and "bleeding orange" (if you don't understand what that means, perhaps Clemson isn't the right school for you). They're almost as enthusiastic about their school's academics, lauding their beloved president's efforts "to transform Clemson into a top 20 university." Clemson is already an engineering powerhouse, with "a great program for civil engineering" and "a well-organized and challenging industrial engineering program." The school's nursing program, education department, and hard sciences also earn raves from undergrads. The legendary family spirit here pervades student-faculty relations: professors "are very approachable and truly care about their students. If a faculty member is working on a research project and you stop by with a question from class, they will stop what they're doing and work with you as long as it takes until you understand the subject matter." Administrators are also "surprisingly helpful and available," and they make an effort to show that they are people, too: "Even the school president has been seen at the late night 'Cookie Break' sponsored by the dining hall, talking with students and getting their opinions on the school," says one undergrad. For those "who enjoy a cozy life in a rural area," Clemson offers "a big-university feel on a slightly smaller scale, and a solid education."

Life

"Clemson football and tailgating are the most amazing experiences of college," most Clemson undergrads agree, noting that "Saturdays in the fall there is no question where everyone is, and that's Death Valley [the nickname of the stadium, so dubbed because it's such a hostile environment for the opposing team]. We don't just show up, either; everyone is tailgating at least 3 to 4 hours before the game, and I mean everyone." The city of Clemson, "a town completely devoted to the school," "comes to a complete stop for games, which is great." Aside from their intensity for football, "Clemson students approach life 'Southern style': We're pretty laid-back, we like to have a good time, we work hard, and we have pride." The surrounding area offers plenty in the way of outdoor activity, as "Lake Hartwell borders the campus. We're about a half hour from great hiking and mountain biking, and the weather is great most of the time, so we spend a lot of time outdoors." Undergrads tell us that "Clemson is a typical college in that there is definitely a party scene" that often centers on Greek life, "which is very big." They also point out that "there are abundant activities for those who aren't into partying. There are movies, sporting events and intramural sports, and plenty of places to eat." Hometown Clemson is small, but "With Greenville, Anderson, and Atlanta reasonably close by, you can do all of the shopping you need within driving distance."

Student Body

While "the typical student is White, from South Carolina, somewhat religious, and preppy" at Clemson, "there are plenty of students who do not fit that profile" among the school's nearly 14,000 undergraduates. Students tell us that "Clemson has become more diverse as its reputation has grown. Even in the 2 years since I got here," says one, "I would say that there are more students of different cultures, ethnicities, and especially religions other than Christianity; many, many more students not from the South; and also plenty of students who are not conservative." Even so, the student body tends to be "very conservative." Of course, regardless of students' political views, football is a unifying force: Almost all undergrads here are "smart but laid-back, and huge football fans."

CLEMSON UNIVERSITY

FINANCIAL AID: 864-656-2280 • E-MAIL: CUADMISSIONS@CLEMSON.EDU • WEBSITE: WWW.CLEMSON.EDU

ADMISSIONS

Very important factors considered include: Academic GPA, class rank, rigor of secondary school record, standardized test scores, state residency. *Important factors considered include:* Alumni/ae relation. *Other factors considered include:* Application essay, extracurricular activities, recommendation(s), talent/ability. SAT or ACT required; ACT with Writing component required. TOEFL required of all international applicants. High school diploma is required, and GED is accepted. *Academic units required:* 4 English, 3 math, 3 science (3 science labs), 3 foreign language, 3 social studies, 1 history, 2 academic electives, 1 physical education or ROTC. *Academic units recommended:* 4 math, 4 science lab.

The Inside Word

Clemson's admissions decisions are based largely on academic credentials. As is typically the case at sizeable public institutions, if you fit the formula, you're in. A straightforward admissions philosophy doesn't come with any guarantees, though. The university has seen its popularity grow steadily, and as a result, it's become increasingly selective.

FINANCIAL AID

Students should submit: FAFSA. The Princeton Review suggests that all financial aid forms be submitted as soon as possible after January 1. *Need-based scholarships/grants offered:* Pell Grant, SEOG, state scholarships/grants, private scholarships, the school's own gift aid, Federal Nursing Scholarship. *Loan aid offered:* FFEL Subsidized Stafford, FFEL Unsubsidized Stafford, FFEL PLUS, Federal Perkins Loan, state loans, college/university loans from institutional funds. Applicants will be notified of awards on a rolling basis beginning or about April 1. Federal Work-Study Program available. Institutional employment available. Off-campus job opportunities are fair.

FROM THE ADMISSIONS OFFICE

"One of the country's most selective public research universities, Clemson University was founded with a mission to be a high seminary of learning dedicated to teaching, research, and service. Nearly 120 years later, these three concepts remain at the heart of this university and provide the framework for an exceptional educational experience for Clemson students.

"At Clemson, professors take the time to get to know students and to explore innovative ways of teaching. Exceptional teaching is one reason Clemson's retention and graduation rates rank among the highest in the country among public universities. Exceptional teaching is also why Clemson continues to attract an increasingly talented student body. The class rank and SAT scores of Clemson's incoming freshman are among the highest of the nation's public research universities.

"Clemson offers over 250 student clubs and organizations; the spirit that students show for this university is unparalleled.

"Midway between Charlotte, North Carolina, and Atlanta, Georgia, Clemson University is located on 1,400 acres of beautiful rolling hills within the foothills of the Blue Ridge Mountains and along the shores of Lake Hartwell.

"Applicants are required to take either the new version of the SAT or the ACT with the Writing section. Scores from the old version of the SAT (prior to March 2005) will be accepted as well, and the best combined scores from either SAT test will be used in the admission process. We do not however, combine sub scores from the ACT in order to create a new composite score."

SELECTIVITY

Admissions Rating	92
# of applicants	12,784
% of applicants accepted	55
% of acceptees attending	40
# accepting a place on wait list	163
% admitted from wait list	13

FRESHMAN PROFILE

Range SAT Critical Reading	540–640
Range SAT Math	590–680
Range ACT Composite	25–29
Minimum Paper TOEFL	550
Minimum Computer Based TOEFL	213
Average HS GPA	4.08
% graduated top 10% of class	45
% graduated top 25% of class	74
% graduated top 50% of class	93

DEADLINES

Regular application deadline	5/1
Regular notification	rolling
Nonfall registration?	yes

APPLICANTS ALSO LOOK AT

AND OFTEN PREFER
Duke University, University of Georgia, The University of North Carolina at Chapel Hill

AND SOMETIMES PREFER
Furman University, Georgia Institute of Technology, Wake Forest University

AND RARELY PREFER
Auburn University, North Carolina State University, University of South Carolina—Columbia

FINANCIAL FACTS

Financial Aid Rating	69
Annual in-state tuition	$9,868
Annual out-of-state tuition	$20,292
Room & Board	$5,874
Books and supplies	$820
Required fees	$122
% frosh rec. need-based scholarship or grant aid	15
% UG rec. need-based scholarship or grant aid	18
% frosh rec. need-based self-help aid	24
% UG rec. need-based self-help aid	28
% frosh rec. any financial aid	87
% UG rec. any financial aid	71

COE COLLEGE

1220 FIRST AVENUE NORTHEAST, CEDAR RAPIDS, IA 52402 • ADMISSIONS: 319-399-8500 • FAX: 319-399-8816

CAMPUS LIFE

Quality of Life Rating	85
Fire Safety Rating	60*
Type of school	private
Affiliation	Presbyterian
Environment	city

STUDENTS

Total undergrad enrollment	1,250
% male/female	45/55
% from out of state	31
% from public high school	90
% live on campus	84
% in (# of) fraternities	23 (5)
% in (# of) sororities	19 (3)
% African American	2
% Asian	1
% Caucasian	89
% Hispanic	2
% international	4
# of countries represented	15

SURVEY SAYS . . .

Small classes
Great library
Lots of beer drinking

ACADEMICS

Academic Rating	87
Calendar	semester
Student/faculty ratio	13:1
Profs interesting rating	86
Profs accessible rating	90
% profs teaching	
UG courses	100
% classes taught by TAs	0
Most common	
lab size	fewer than 10 students
Most common	
reg class size	10–19 students

MOST POPULAR MAJORS

biology/biological sciences
business administration/
management
psychology

STUDENTS SAY

Academics

Coe College, a small liberal arts school in Iowa, "encompasses everything someone would want out of a college: close relationships between students and faculty, a supportive surrounding community, and a curriculum that is flexible to fit each student." With just over 1,300 undergraduates, Coe is "small enough that if you have a real problem, they can work with you." One student notes, "The personal attention you get from your teachers makes you feel like they have an investment in your future." Central to the Coe educational experience is the Coe Plan, which requires community service of freshmen and a practicum—"an internship, study abroad experience, or research," among a few other possibilities—of upperclassmen. Many students use the Coe Plan to stretch themselves; one such undergrad writes, "Since coming to Coe, I've had three internships and completed research for my honors thesis." Coe is small, so "Don't come here if you're expecting a huge number of classes. Some of the departments are very limited as far as offered classes go." In its most popular departments, though, Coe "gives you the resources you need to develop your own critical-thinking abilities and effectively learn what you need to know." Students tell us that the math and science departments here are excellent; "We have one of the best physics programs in the country," one physics major brags. Across disciplines, undergraduates claim academics "are challenging, leaving students more prepared when they graduate than students from other schools."

Life

Coe "gives students of all interests opportunities to have fun on and off campus, whether it's through free movie nights at a local theater, concerts of any musical style, or pretty much anything else one could imagine," which is a good thing, because "Cedar Rapids is a boring town" that offers little in the way of diversion. Iowa City, only 20 minutes away by car, is much better, students assure us, with "plenty of clubs that students enjoy." When the weekend rolls around, "Coe students party a lot," but "If you don't like to party, there are always weekend activities that students can participate in, and sometimes these activities draw a bigger crowd than parties do!" The biggest party of the year is Flunk Day, a "day where people skip classes and drink all day," though there is "a canoe trip that day for nondrinkers, but space is limited." When the weather is nice, "Coe is almost parklike. During spring and fall, there are always games going and people gathered on the quads." When the weather turns cold, students generally stay indoors; "many students get involved with some type of activity, either intramurals or a club or group." They also pass the time with your standard small-group quiet activities, "watching movies, playing cards [or] just hanging out and talking."

Student Body

Undergraduates can be "somewhat cliquish" at Coe College, students tell us. One reports, "It seems as though students who do not fit into one of the 'categories' (categories: students with high socioeconomic status, students who are involved in the religious group on campus, homosexual/bisexual students, minority/exchange students, students in sports, etc.) seem to get lost and left behind." While "most students are from Iowa, [Coe] does try to mix it up and prides itself on having many foreign exchange students and people from different states, though most of them are still from the Midwest." Internationals here "are mostly from Japan." Many students play sports, and "Everyone here has something they are passionate about, whether it is athletics, academics, research, clubs, or community involvement."

FINANCIAL AID: 319-399-8540 • E-MAIL: ADMISSION@COE.EDU • WEBSITE: WWW.COE.EDU

ADMISSIONS

Very important factors considered include: Rigor of secondary school record, standardized test scores. *Important factors considered include:* Application essay, class rank, recommendation(s). *Other factors considered include:* Alumni/ae relation, character/personal qualities, extracurricular activities, interview, racial/ethnic status, talent/ability, volunteer work. SAT or ACT required; TOEFL required of all international applicants. High school diploma is required, and GED is accepted. *Academic units recommended:* 4 English, 3 math, 3 science (1 science lab), 2 foreign language, 3 social studies, 2 academic electives.

The Inside Word

Coe's admissions process places a very high level of importance on your numbers. Candidates who don't have at least a 2.75 high school GPA and at least a 22 on the ACT may find tough going with the Admissions Committee. As is true of nearly all small liberal arts colleges, Coe conducts a thorough application review that also considers your personal background and involvements, but an emerging national reputation enables them to keep their focus upon academic achievement as the primary gatekeeper.

FINANCIAL AID

Students should submit: FAFSA. The Princeton Review suggests that all financial aid forms be submitted as soon as possible after January 1. *Need-based scholarships/grants offered:* Pell Grant, SEOG, state scholarships/grants, private scholarships, the school's own gift aid. *Loan aid offered:* Direct Subsidized Stafford, Direct Unsubsidized Stafford, Direct PLUS, Federal Perkins Loan, college/university loans from institutional funds. Applicants will be notified of awards on a rolling basis beginning or about March 15. Federal Work-Study Program available. Institutional employment available. Off-campus job opportunities are excellent.

FROM THE ADMISSIONS OFFICE

"A Coe education begins to pay off right away. In fact, 98 percent of last year's graduating class was either working or in graduate school within 6 months of graduation. One reason our graduates do so well is the Coe Plan—a step-by-step sequence of activities designed to prepare our students for life after Coe. This required sequence stretches from the first-year seminar to community service, issue dinners, career planning seminars, and the required hands-on experience. The hands-on component may be satisfied through an internship, research, practicum, or study abroad. One student lived with a Costa Rican family while she studied the effects of selective logging on rain forest organisms. Others have interned at places like Warner Brothers in Los Angeles and the Chicago Board of Trade. Still others combine travel with an internship or student teaching for an unforgettable off-campus experience. Coe College is one of the few liberal arts institutions in the country to require hands-on learning for graduation.

"For Fall 2008, Coe will continue to focus on the Critical Reading/Verbal and Math subsections of the SAT. Coe Admission Counselors believe it is best to learn about the new Writing component at the same time as students and parents, and we want to know more before deciding to use them in our admission decision-making."

SELECTIVITY

Admissions Rating	86
# of applicants	1,647
% of applicants accepted	48
% of acceptees attending	25

FRESHMAN PROFILE

Range SAT Critical Reading	580–688
Range SAT Math	600–678
Range ACT Composite	22–28
Minimum Paper TOEFL	500
Minimum Computer Based TOEFL	173
Average HS GPA	3.68
% graduated top 10% of class	34
% graduated top 25% of class	67
% graduated top 50% of class	95

DEADLINES

Regular application deadline	3/1
Regular notification	3/15
Nonfall registration?	yes

APPLICANTS ALSO LOOK AT AND SOMETIMES PREFER

Beloit College, Cornell College, Grinnell College, Knox College, University of Iowa

FINANCIAL FACTS

Financial Aid Rating	82
Annual tuition	$26,100
Room & Board	$6,600
Books and supplies	$800
Required fees	$290
% frosh rec. need-based scholarship or grant aid	84
% UG rec. need-based scholarship or grant aid	80
% frosh rec. need-based self-help aid	69
% UG rec. need-based self-help aid	71
% frosh rec. any financial aid	98
% UG rec. any financial aid	96

COLBY COLLEGE

4000 MAYFLOWER HILL, WATERVILLE, ME 04901-8848 • ADMISSIONS: 207-872-3168 • FAX: 207-872-3474

STUDENTS SAY

Academics

This small, close-knit liberal arts college draws praise from students for its rigorous but caring approach to academics. It's a place where devoted professors "invite students to dinner" and learning happens "for learning's sake." Small classes are one of Colby's biggest draws. "Professors are always willing to go the extra mile," one student says. A senior adds, "Over the course of my time at Colby I've been to at least six different professors' houses for departmental events, class dinners, and group discussions." Professors get high grades for their teaching and accessibility, which together foster a "love for learning" in undergraduates. As one student dryly notes, "Waterville, Maine is not the country's academic capital, so the professors that choose to be at Colby are here to teach, not to use the facilities." This dedication to academics can make Colby an intense place to go to school, and students here aren't "afraid to work hard and study." In addition, students must not only complete their major requirements but also fulfill a hefty load of distribution requirements to graduate. The popular "Jan Plan" lets students take an extra month-long term of focused or independent study in January, sometimes accompanied by an internship. While the administration "works hard to keep students happy and entertained," some feel that their needs are "occasionally ignored in favor of the everlasting quest to turn Colby into a small Ivy."

Life

"Friends and a sense of community drive life at Colby," one senior writes. Students live together in coed, mixed-class dorms. Everything centers around the campus, which is "constructed on a gorgeous wooded hill near the Kennebec River in Central Maine." Since "There isn't a ridiculous amount to do" in these self-contained environs, "Colby works hard to fill the day with countless events, lectures, discussions, and concerts. People can study hard, party, take advantage of the beautiful outdoors, and most do all three." A student notes that "the size of the school is perfect: On any given day, I could see five friends or acquaintances (and countless familiar faces!) on my way to class." This makes for a friendly atmosphere as "it's easy to start up a conversation with pretty much anyone. When the great outdoors beckons, students answer the call by hiking in autumn and spring, skiing in winter, and participating in traditional outdoor sports like football. A senior explains, "People like to unwind after our incredibly stressful weeks with movies, skiing, and partying." Booze and drug use is not unheard of at Colby. The "alcohol-centered social scene" usually takes place at small dorm parties or at the few local pubs.

Student Body

While the prototypical Colby student may be "White and from 20 minutes outside of Boston," undergrads are quick to point out that their "campus is very open to diversity and ready to embrace it." Students single out the administration for "doing a great job of bringing in a more diverse student population." One student explains that "more and more international students and urban kids are coming through programs like the Posse Scholarship." A junior adds, "We have students here that dress in business suits and bow ties while others walk around in capes." Most students, however, settle for the more general description of "preppy students who enjoy the outdoors and enjoy having a good time." That said, students report that "there's pretty much a place for everyone somewhere at Colby; chances are you'll find people both very similar to you in interests, background, etc. and people who are completely the opposite." One student elaborates, explaining that despite all differences, "The one word I'd use to describe a Colby student is friendly."

FINANCIAL AID: 207-872-3168 • E-MAIL: ADMISSIONS@COLBY.EDU • WEBSITE: WWW.COLBY.EDU

ADMISSIONS

Very important factors considered include: Character/personal qualities, rigor of secondary school record. *Important factors considered include:* Academic GPA, application essay, class rank, extracurricular activities, interview, racial/ethnic status, recommendation(s), standardized test scores, talent/ability. *Other factors considered include:* Alumni/ae relation, first generation, geographical residence, level of applicant's interest, state residency, volunteer work, work experience. SAT or ACT required; TOEFL required of all international applicants. High school diploma or equivalent is not required. *Academic units recommended:* 4 English, 3 math, 2 science (2 science labs), 3 foreign language, 2 social studies, 2 academic electives.

The Inside Word

Colby continues to be both very selective and successful in converting admits to enrollees, which makes for a perpetually challenging admissions process. Currently, only 33 percent of applicants are accepted, so hit those books and ace those exams to stand a fighting chance. One thing that could set you apart from the pack? An interest in travel. Two-thirds of Colby students study abroad—in fact, for some degrees it's required.

FINANCIAL AID

Students should submit: FAFSA; either CSS Financial Aid PROFILE or institutional application. Regular filing deadline is February 1. The Princeton Review suggests that all financial aid forms be submitted as soon as possible after January 1. *Need-based scholarships/grants offered:* Pell Grant, SEOG, state scholarships/grants, private scholarships, the school's own gift aid. *Loan aid offered:* Direct Subsidized Stafford, Direct Unsubsidized Stafford, Direct PLUS, FFEL Subsidized Stafford, FFEL Unsubsidized Stafford, FFEL PLUS, Federal Perkins Loan, state loans, college/university loans from institutional funds, alternative loans. Applicants will be notified of awards on or about April 1. Federal Work-Study Program available. Institutional employment available. Off-campus job opportunities are fair.

FROM THE ADMISSIONS OFFICE

"Colby is one of only a handful of liberal arts colleges that offer world-class academic programs, recognized leadership in internationalism, an active community life, and rich opportunities after graduation.

"Set in Maine on one of the nation's most beautiful campuses, Colby provides students a growing array of opportunities for active engagement in Waterville or around the world. The Goldfarb Center for Public Affairs and Civic Engagement builds on Colby's strengths to connect teaching and research with current political, economic, and social issues at home and abroad.

"The college has won several awards for sustainable environmental practices. It also won the 2005 Senator Paul Simon Award for Internationalizing the Campus, which recognized the international content of the curriculum, Colby's emphasis on study abroad, and international diversity in the student body and faculty.

"Students' access to Colby's outstanding faculty is extraordinary, and the college is recognized as a national leader in undergraduate research and project-based learning. While the challenging academic experience is at the heart of Colby's programs, it is complemented by a vibrant community life and campus atmosphere, featuring more than 100 student-run organizations, more than 50 athletic and recreational choices, and numerous leadership and volunteer opportunities.

"Colby graduates succeed, finding their places at the finest medical and other graduate schools, top Wall Street firms, and in the arts, government service, social service, education, and nonprofit organizations.

"Students applying for admission must submit the new SAT or the ACT. The optional ACT Writing Test is recommended."

SELECTIVITY

Admissions Rating	96
# of applicants	4,242
% of applicants accepted	33
% of acceptees attending	34
# accepting a place on wait list	373
% admitted from wait list	11
# of early decision applicants	459
% accepted early decision	47

FRESHMAN PROFILE

Range SAT Critical Reading	630–720
Range SAT Math	640–720
Range SAT Writing	610–710
Range ACT Composite	27–31
Minimum Paper TOEFL	600
Minimum Computer Based TOEFL	240
% graduated top 10% of class	63
% graduated top 25% of class	88
% graduated top 50% of class	98

DEADLINES

Early decision application deadline	11/15
Early decision notification	12/15
Regular application deadline	1/1
Regular notification	4/1
Nonfall registration?	yes

APPLICANTS ALSO LOOK AT

AND OFTEN PREFER
Amherst College, Brown University, Dartmouth College, Middlebury College, Williams College

AND SOMETIMES PREFER
Bowdoin College, Colgate University, Tufts University

AND RARELY PREFER
Bates College, Connecticut College, Hamilton College, Trinity College (CT), Wellesley College

FINANCIAL FACTS

Financial Aid Rating	94
Comprehensive fee	$44,080
Books and supplies	$700
% frosh rec. need-based scholarship or grant aid	40
% UG rec. need-based scholarship or grant aid	35
% frosh rec. need-based self-help aid	34
% UG rec. need-based self-help aid	31
% frosh rec. any financial aid	41
% UG rec. any financial aid	37

COLGATE UNIVERSITY

13 OAK DRIVE, HAMILTON, NY 13346 • ADMISSIONS: 315-228-7401 • FAX: 315-228-7544

CAMPUS LIFE

Quality of Life Rating	82
Fire Safety Rating	89
Type of school	private
Environment	rural

STUDENTS

Total undergrad enrollment	2,756
% male/female	48/52
% from out of state	70
% from public high school	66
% live on campus	91
% in (# of) fraternities	33 (6)
% in (# of) sororities	29 (4)
% African American	5
% Asian	7
% Caucasian	75
% Hispanic	4
% Native American	1
% international	5
# of countries represented	36

SURVEY SAYS . . .

Career services are great
Small classes
Everyone loves the Raiders
Lots of beer drinking
Hard liquor is popular

ACADEMICS

Academic Rating	95
Calendar	semester
Student/faculty ratio	10:1
Profs interesting rating	90
Profs accessible rating	91
% profs teaching UG courses	100
% classes taught by TAs	0
Most common lab size	10–19 students
Most common reg class size	10–19 students

MOST POPULAR MAJORS
economics
English language and literature
history

STUDENTS SAY

Academics

Colgate University is the type of undergraduate institution that inspires fierce loyalty among students and alumni; as one undergrad puts it, "From the student athletes, professors, artists, political activists, to the maintenance people and administration, the majority of Colgate loves the school. People go into Colgate with numerous loves and passions and leave the university with Colgate as a newfound passion." A combination of factors spur this devotion: a beautiful campus, an accomplished and caring faculty, a bright and goal-oriented student body, and a strong sense of community forged at least in part by the school's geographic isolation. Students here report that "the academics are intense, but not overwhelming because the students are intelligent enough to handle the workload," and they praise the liberal arts core curriculum and distribution requirements that "serve as an excellent base for students to pursue other academic interests." They also love the "great study abroad opportunities; if you want to go anywhere in the world you generally can, and the trips are quite affordable." The Outdoor Education Program, through which "nearly 70 percent of students participate in physical education classes, Backyard Adventures or the Pre-Orientation trip, Wilderness Adventure," is popular, too. Most of all, students love how Colgate prepares them for success in the real world. "Colgate fosters the education of students outside the classroom as well as inside the classroom. Therefore, when students leave Colgate they have great interpersonal skills," explains one student. Another goes on to say, "The 'Colgate Connection' is probably one of the school's greatest benefits, as alumni are very helpful in finding and offering careers for graduates."

Life

Colgate's hometown of Hamilton is a "small town that, without Colgate students, has only around 3,000 people." The good news is that "administrators recognize that our location in a small rural community may be construed as a weakness, so they do a great job to make up for this with a profusion of programs on campus. There is always something to do, and if you leave Hamilton for even one day, you feel you've missed out on incredible things." Colgate's geographic isolation is also tempered by the school's "ridiculously beautiful campus, like a country club," its "awesome dorms," and its "clean and comfortable facilities." Intercollegiate sports are big here; "Good Division I athletics are also a rarity among liberal arts colleges, but unlike larger schools, the athletes here are also some of the best students," brags one undergrad. The school is well known for its lively party scene, but students point out that "Colgate has something for just about everyone, including special events, newly opened restaurants, dance halls, and the improved movie theater." And "Although people party, they know how to keep up with their schoolwork and do well academically." Overall, Colgate undergrads "work hard in school, but also look to have a good time outside the classroom. Whether that means joining groups, playing sports, or going out with their friends, Colgate students like to have fun."

Student Body

Colgate draws an accomplished student body; "The typical Colgate student was captain of a sports team, homecoming king or queen, president of the class, and an excellent student at his or her high school. At Colgate, this translates to a student body of incredibly bright, talented and congenial students," explains one student. Undergrads tell us that "while everyone is really smart, people aren't pretentious about it. You don't feel lower than anyone else, but rather challenged to expand your mind and develop your knowledge and talents." Undergrads tend to be on the preppy side and are typically athletic; it's no surprise, then, that "the gym is one of the hot spots on campus." Colgate "has a reputation as a conservative school, but in fact the bent of the campus is moderately liberal, if anything. While there is a very vocal, organized conservative element, most people seem to be either moderate or left-of-center."

FINANCIAL AID: 315-228-7431 • E-MAIL: ADMISSION@MAIL.COLGATE.EDU • WEBSITE: WWW.COLGATE.EDU

ADMISSIONS

Very important factors considered include: Academic GPA, class rank, rigor of secondary school record. *Important factors considered include:* Application essay, character/personal qualities, extracurricular activities, recommendation(s), standardized test scores, talent/ability. *Other factors considered include:* Alumni/ae relation, first generation, geographical residence, racial/ethnic status, volunteer work, work experience. SAT or ACT required; TOEFL required of all international applicants. High school diploma is required, and GED is accepted. *Academic units required:* 4 English, 3 math, 3 science (2 science labs), 3 foreign language, 2 social studies, 1 history. *Academic units recommended:* 4 English, 4 math, 4 science (3 science labs), 4 foreign language, 2 social studies, 3 history.

The Inside Word

Like many colleges, Colgate caters to some well-developed special interests. Athletes, minorities, and legacies (the children of alums) are among the most special of interests and benefit from more favorable consideration than applicants without particular distinction. Students without a solid, consistent academic record, beware—the university's wait list leans toward jumbo size.

FINANCIAL AID

Students should submit: FAFSA, CSS/Financial Aid PROFILE, Noncustodial PROFILE, Business/Farm Supplement. Regular filing deadline is January 15. The Princeton Review suggests that all financial aid forms be submitted as soon as possible after January 1. *Need-based scholarships/grants offered:* Pell Grant, SEOG, state scholarships/grants, the school's own gift aid. *Loan aid offered:* FFEL Subsidized Stafford, FFEL Unsubsidized Stafford, FFEL PLUS, Federal Perkins Loan. Applicants will be notified of awards on or about April 1. Federal Work-Study Program available. Institutional employment available. Off-campus job opportunities are fair.

FROM THE ADMISSIONS OFFICE

"Students and faculty alike are drawn to Colgate by the quality of its academic programs. Faculty initiative has given the university a rich mix of learning opportunities that includes a liberal arts core, 51 academic concentrations, and a wealth of Colgate faculty-led, off-campus study programs in the United States and abroad. But there is more to Colgate than academic life, including more than 100 student organizations, athletics and recreation at all levels, and a full complement of living options set within a campus described as one of the most beautiful in the country. A new center for community service builds upon the tradition of Colgate students interacting with the surrounding community in meaningful ways. Colgate students become extraordinarily devoted alumni, contributing significantly to career networking and exploration programs on and off campus. For students in search of a busy and varied campus life, Colgate is a place to learn and grow.

"All admission candidates must submit the results of standardized testing from one of two sources: the SAT Reasoning Test (Writing, Critical Reading, and Mathematics), or the American College Testing Program (ACT, optional Writing exam not required)."

SELECTIVITY

Admissions Rating	97
# of applicants	7,873
% of applicants accepted	28
% of acceptees attending	34
# accepting a place on wait list	579
% admitted from wait list	1
# of early decision applicants	640
% accepted early decision	51

FRESHMAN PROFILE

Range SAT Critical Reading	620–720
Range SAT Math	640–710
Range ACT Composite	28–32
Minimum Paper TOEFL	600
Minimum Computer Based TOEFL	250
Average HS GPA	3.6
% graduated top 10% of class	70
% graduated top 25% of class	92
% graduated top 50% of class	100

DEADLINES

Early decision application deadline	11/15
Early decision notification	12/15
Regular application deadline	1/15
Regular notification	4/1
Nonfall registration?	no

APPLICANTS ALSO LOOK AT

AND OFTEN PREFER
Cornell University, Dartmouth College, Georgetown University, Middlebury College, Tufts University

AND SOMETIMES PREFER
Boston College, Bowdoin College, Colby College, The College of William & Mary

AND RARELY PREFER
Boston University, Bucknell University, Hamilton College, Lafayette College, Trinity College (CT), University of Rochester

FINANCIAL FACTS

Financial Aid Rating	97
Annual tuition	$34,795
Room & Board	$8,530
Books and supplies	$1,840
Required fees	$235
% frosh rec. need-based scholarship or grant aid	34
% UG rec. need-based scholarship or grant aid	36
% frosh rec. need-based self-help aid	25
% UG rec. need-based self-help aid	29
% frosh rec. any financial aid	35
% UG rec. any financial aid	46

COLLEGE OF THE ATLANTIC

105 EDEN STREET, BAR HARBOR, ME 04609 • ADMISSIONS: 207-288-5015 • FAX: 207-288-4126

STUDENTS SAY

Academics

Every undergraduate at the tiny College of the Atlantic majors in human ecology. More than a course of study, human ecology is an approach to education that is interdisciplinary, in which all areas of study are seen in relationship to each other. In choosing an area of concentration, students can opt for one of the traditional sub-disciplines such as marine biology or public policy, or they can design their own concentration in another area as far-flung as painting or landscape and building design. This leaves students—bonded by a common major—stoked that they still "have the opportunity to shape their own educations. Students who are self-motivated and enthusiastic can have an awesome experience here." Whereas some schools offer a more prescribed program, COA calls on students to arrive inspired to take an active part in carving their own path to graduation. Also setting the school apart is the fact that it doesn't offer tenure to its teachers. Consequently, you'll find only the most dedicated professors at the head of these classrooms. "The professors at our school take a pay cut to work here. They truly love what it is they do, and their classes are incredible." With only 320 students total, it's no wonder that "by the end of your first year, most professors know you even if you haven't taken their classes." Concerning the "optional grades" policy, one sophomore warns prospective students that "just because we have optional grades doesn't mean that you can slack in a class. Evaluations are given at the end of each class. The evaluations give you a whole lot more feedback than a letter grade and make the academic experience a whole lot more personal."

Life

Bar Harbor, Maine, is "a small tourist town, [that's] beautiful in spring and summer, extremely cold and boring in winter." To fill the hole left by the closing of the seasonal Bar Harbor shops and restaurants, students take advantage of a variety of alternative activities. "There are coffeehouses, open mics, guest speakers, dance presentations, puppet shows, talent shows, bands, traveling drama performances, etc. It's wonderful! There will also be discussion groups that will get together. Professors will have their students over for meals. Students living off campus will always cook food together." In town, there's "a great movie theater" called Reel Pizza that serves pizza and beer. For outdoor enthusiasts, COA is a paradise, as it is located literally across the street from Acadia National Park. What's more, the college caters to activities that such a situation lends itself to, with "kayaks and canoes to take out. Many of us share the common passion for hiking. During the snow season, we throw a winter carnival and we also go skiing" and snowshoeing. Since only about a third of the student body resides on campus, "off-campus parties are popular, though there aren't many good ones." That's because "At COA, six people is a big party."

Student Body

"The typical COA student is very self-driven. (You have to be in a curriculum that is so open.) We are also very environmentally friendly. There is a lot of emphasis put on sustainability at the school. We take pride in our organic produce and our hippie ways." If you aren't a hippie when you come to COA, there is a pretty good chance that you'll start developing some of those tendencies before too long, just from pure exposure to the culture. Carnivores can take heart that "there are still meat eaters among our vegetarian population," though "it would be hard to find a right-wing Republican here." While leaning decidedly left on matters political, "People here tend to be accepting, curious, and open-minded, so I think it's hard to be an outcast." For such a small school, COA's student body includes a remarkably high percentage of international students; foreigners account for about one-fifth of the school's undergraduate population, "probably making it one the most diverse places in Maine."

FINANCIAL AID: 207-288-5015 • E-MAIL: INQUIRY@ECOLOGY.COA.EDU • WEBSITE: WWW.COA.EDU

ADMISSIONS

Very important factors considered include: Application essay, recommendation(s), rigor of secondary school record. *Important factors considered include:* Academic GPA, character/personal qualities, class rank, extracurricular activities, interview, talent/ability, volunteer work, work experience. *Other factors considered include:* Alumni/ae relation, first generation, geographical residence, level of applicant's interest, racial/ethnic status, standardized test scores, state residency. TOEFL required of all international applicants. High school diploma is required, and GED is accepted. *Academic units required:* 4 English, 3 math, 2 science (2 science labs), 2 social studies. *Academic units recommended:* 4 math, 3 science, 2 foreign language, 2 history, 1 academic elective.

The Inside Word

As applicants might expect, admissions standards at College of the Atlantic are somewhat atypical. The school covets students who carve their own intellectual course rather than follow a conventional academic path. Students at COA are expected to bring strong ideas and values to the classroom and applicants are assessed accordingly. Essays and interviews are where candidates make their mark. Of course, the college's integrated approach also means that applicants should have a well-rounded secondary school record. Candidates should also demonstrate a kinship with the philosophy of human ecology.

FINANCIAL AID

Students should submit: FAFSA, institution's own financial aid form, Noncustodial PROFILE, Business/Farm Supplement. Regular filing deadline is February 15. The Princeton Review suggests that all financial aid forms be submitted as soon as possible after January 1. *Need-based scholarships/grants offered:* Pell Grant, SEOG, state scholarships/grants, private scholarships, the school's own gift aid. *Loan aid offered:* FFEL Subsidized Stafford, FFEL Unsubsidized Stafford, FFEL PLUS, Federal Perkins Loan. Applicants will be notified of awards on or about April 1

FROM THE ADMISSIONS OFFICE

""College of the Atlantic is a small, intellectually challenging college on Mount Desert Island, Maine, that is different by design. We look for students seeing a rigorous academic experience but a different kind of education than that offered by traditional colleges and universities. Resolutely interdisciplinary—there are no departments and no majors—and value-centered, the college sees its mission as preparing people to become independent thinkers, to challenge conventional wisdom, to deal with pressing global change—both environmental and social—and to be passionately engaged in transforming the world around then into a better place.

"College of the Atlantic does not require standardized testing as part of the application process. Learning and intelligence can be gauged in many ways; standardized test scores are just one of many measures. If an applicant chooses to submit standardized test scores for consideration, the SAT (either version), SAT Subject Tests, or ACT scores are all acceptable."

SELECTIVITY

Admissions Rating	**89**
# of applicants	300
% of applicants accepted	66
% of acceptees attending	37
# accepting a place on wait list	1
% admitted from wait list	100
# of early decision applicants	31
% accepted early decision	90

FRESHMAN PROFILE

Range SAT Critical Reading	580–710
Range SAT Math	510–650
Range SAT Writing	540–690
Range ACT Composite	24–30
Minimum Paper TOEFL	567
Minimum Computer Based TOEFL	227
Average HS GPA	3.57
% graduated top 10% of class	41
% graduated top 25% of class	66
% graduated top 50% of class	90

DEADLINES

Early decision application deadline	12/1
Early decision notification	12/15
Regular application deadline	2/15
Regular notification	4/1
Nonfall registration?	yes

APPLICANTS ALSO LOOK AT

AND OFTEN PREFER
Bowdoin College, Colby College

AND SOMETIMES PREFER
Bard College, Hampshire College

AND RARELY PREFER
Oberlin College, University of Maine, Warren Wilson College

FINANCIAL FACTS

Financial Aid Rating	**83**
Annual tuition	$29,520
Room & Board	$8,190
Books and supplies	$600
Required fees	$465
% frosh rec. need-based scholarship or grant aid	85
% UG rec. need-based scholarship or grant aid	83
% frosh rec. need-based self-help aid	88
% UG rec. need-based self-help aid	87
% frosh rec. any financial aid	92
% UG rec. any financial aid	92

COLLEGE OF CHARLESTON

66 GEORGE STREET, CHARLESTON, SC 29424 • ADMISSIONS: 843-953-5670 • FAX: 843-953-6322

STUDENTS SAY

Academics

The College of Charleston, "a small school set in a charming Southern town," is a public school that creates "a private school atmosphere." The school offers "challenging academic programs," "small classes," and "highly qualified professors"—all "in a fun and innovative environment." Because there is only a small graduate student population, the "focus of the professors and the school is teaching undergraduates." About one in five students here majors in business and management. Premedical sciences are also popular, and students report that the science programs have a great reputation for preparing undergrads for medical school. Not all disciplines are as challenging; students concede that "academics are all what you make [of them] here. There are some dumb and unnecessary classes . . . but there are also some really challenging, interesting ones." Lower-level courses generate the majority of the complaints—most CofC students agree that "upper-level (major) classes" are "difficult" but "very good" in preparing undergrads for whatever their future holds. Professors here "love their jobs" and "are readily accessible by e-mail . . . . [T]hey encourage students to drop by their offices whenever to ask questions or just to talk. It is a very personable environment."

Life

Many students tell us that the College of Charleston provides "the perfect college experience." It's located "in the middle of downtown Charleston," but its "campus is very close-knit and easy to get around," "so you get the benefits of living in a city without the feeling of getting lost or overwhelmed." Undergrads enjoy "a lot of opportunities to go out: Bars, clubs, and restaurant[s] are right around the corner from the school." Charleston is also full of "beautiful parks, streets, and places to walk." Because "The weather is usually very nice," "outdoor activities dominate much of students' free time." The campus is only "15 minutes away" from the beach, and "In the spring and early fall you'll see students wearing their bathing suits to class to lay out in Marion Square afterwards." Exercise is also "an important aspect [of] the daily activities of many students. Hey, we like to look good!" Students tell us that CofC "is a big party school, but not as big as its reputation" would lead you to believe. There's a lot of diversity in the partying here, with a few frat parties a week and "house parties," "chill[ing] with your friends," and "the city bar scene downtown" as perennially popular options. Intercollegiate sports are not a big part of campus life; while some here pine for a football team, others feel the current extracurricular mix is just right.

Student Body

"Southern belles, hard-core Northerners, surfers, nerds, and party animals" are "all united by the beach" at the College of Charleston. While the "typical guy here wears a Polo with plaid shorts" and the "typical girl is a blonde with a set of pearls," there are "many, many others who do not fit the mold, and this makes our population interesting." Similarly, while students frequently describe the typical CofC student as "religious" and "Republican," they point out that there are also "a lot of liberals" and those who "practice a different religion." "Everybody can usually find a group they want to be part of," a biology and German double-major reports.

FINANCIAL AID: 843-953-5540 • E-MAIL: ADMISSIONS@COFC.EDU • WEBSITE: WWW.COFC.EDU

ADMISSIONS

Very important factors considered include: Academic GPA, rigor of secondary school record, standardized test scores, state residency. *Important factors considered include:* Character/personal qualities, class rank, first generation, talent/ability. *Other factors considered include:* Alumni/ae relation, application essay, extracurricular activities, geographical residence, racial/ethnic status, recommendation(s), volunteer work, work experience. SAT or ACT required; TOEFL required of all international applicants. High school diploma is required, and GED is accepted. *Academic units required:* 4 English, 3 math, 3 science (3 science labs), 3 foreign language, 3 social studies, 4 academic electives. *Academic units recommended:* 4 math, 4 science, 3 foreign language, 2 history.

The Inside Word

Prime location and relatively low tuition make admissions at College of Charleston quite competitive, and standards are a bit higher still for out-of-state applicants. High school grades and standardized test scores play a significant role in admissions decisions, but the school also takes the time to consider the "complete" student. Expect more personalized treatment here than you would receive from Clemson or the University of South Carolina.

FINANCIAL AID

Students should submit: FAFSA. The Princeton Review suggests that all financial aid forms be submitted as soon as possible after January 1. *Need-based scholarships/grants offered:* Pell Grant, SEOG, state scholarships/grants, private scholarships, the school's own gift aid. *Loan aid offered:* Direct Subsidized Stafford, Direct Unsubsidized Stafford, Direct PLUS, Federal Perkins Loan. Applicants will be notified of awards on a rolling basis beginning or about April 10. Federal Work-Study Program available. Institutional employment available. Off-campus job opportunities are excellent.

FROM THE ADMISSIONS OFFICE

"The College of Charleston is a highly respected student-centered public liberal arts and sciences university located in historic Charleston, South Carolina. Founded in 1770, the college prepares nearly 10,000 undergraduate students for a lifetime of change through an innovative and practical liberal arts and sciences experience combined with professional preparation in a wide variety of fields. Students are encouraged to study abroad, participate in independent research projects, and engage in experiential learning opportunities that typically would be available only at the graduate level. They can also take advantage of a beautifully preserved historic city with a vibrant arts community, a diverse natural environment, an innovative business climate, and a consortium of area schools.

"The college is first and foremost a teaching institution. Students work closely with nationally recognized faculty and are part of a close-knit community of scholars—experiences that are usually associated with small liberal arts colleges. They select from among 44 majors, 80 minors, and 39 concentrations, many of which take advantage of Charleston's distinctive location and history.

"Graduates of the college receive excellent preparation for further academic study or entry into the professional world through an education that combines a comprehensive general education program and intensive study within a major field with opportunities for faculty-student collaborative research and off-campus internships.

"The College of Charleston provides an education without equal—in a creative and intellectually stimulating environment where students are challenged by a committed and caring faculty, in an incomparable setting, and at an incredible value.

"Freshman applicants for Fall 2008 are required to submit scores of the Writing section of the SAT or the ACT. Applicants may also submit scores from the old versions of both tests, and their best scores (old/new) will be used in making admissions decisions."

SELECTIVITY
Admissions Rating	89
# of applicants	8,673
% of applicants accepted	61
% of acceptees attending	37
# accepting a place on wait list	216
% admitted from wait list	4

FRESHMAN PROFILE
Range SAT Critical Reading	560–650
Range SAT Math	570–650
Range ACT Composite	23–26
Minimum Paper TOEFL	550
Minimum Computer Based TOEFL	213
Average HS GPA	3.83
% graduated top 10% of class	30
% graduated top 25% of class	66
% graduated top 50% of class	95

DEADLINES
Regular application deadline	4/1
Regular notification	mid-Dec (early action)
Nonfall registration?	yes

APPLICANTS ALSO LOOK AT

AND OFTEN PREFER
University of Georgia, The University of North Carolina at Chapel Hill,

AND SOMETIMES PREFER
Clemson University, Furman University, James Madison University, University of South Carolina—Columbia

AND RARELY PREFER
Appalachian State University, Coastal Carolina University, Winthrop University, Wofford College

FINANCIAL FACTS
Financial Aid Rating	75
Annual in-state tuition	$7,234
Annual out-of-state tuition	$16,800
Room & Board	$7,106
% frosh rec. need-based scholarship or grant aid	24
% UG rec. need-based scholarship or grant aid	22
% frosh rec. need-based self-help aid	24
% UG rec. need-based self-help aid	30
% frosh rec. any financial aid	33
% UG rec. any financial aid	36

COLLEGE OF THE HOLY CROSS

ADMISSIONS OFFICE, ONE COLLEGE STREET, WORCESTER, MA 01610-2395 • ADMISSIONS: 508-793-2443 • FAX: 508-793-3888

STUDENTS SAY

Academics

Located in Worcester, the second-largest city in Massachusetts, Holy Cross offers an academic atmosphere that is "always challenging, never boring" thanks to professors who are "genuinely interested in getting their students to think critically about the world." Many students agree that "while it is hard to do well, the professors and overall state of mind here will push you to your maximum potential in every way." With an administration dedicated to making sure that "students are represented on virtually every administrative council at the college," and a system of departmental "student advisory councils which voice student opinion on professors who are up for tenure," it's no wonder the administration "is widely appreciated for its awesome accessibility." This accessibility carries over to the classroom where small class sizes allow for "a lot of faculty-student interaction." As one student explains, "There are no TAs at Holy Cross," which makes it easier for "students who are trying to form relationships" with their "accessible and interested professors." Be warned, however, that if you ever miss a class "Your professor will call to see where you were." Students here enjoy many opportunities for "independent research, study abroad, and intellectual enrichment," including "great internship programs" with "successful Holy Cross alumni" all designed to help them "learn and succeed."

Life

The mantra you might hear repeated often among students at Holy Cross is "work hard, party hard." As one student explains, "Based on all the partying that is done here, you can imagine how hard we work." The school's rigorous academic standards are offset by a lively social scene where the most popular relaxation activities come with a bar tab: "Beer is huge, particularly because our workload here is so intense." Students boast that they "have a bar for each day of the week" and "theme parties" each weekend. Everyone here is "always active," taking time off from studying to participate in "a varsity team, intramurals, student government, clubs, the newspaper, theater, or music." Holy Cross goes out of its way to "create many on-campus opportunities as well as encourage students to explore off-campus opportunities." "Countless restaurants and bars in Worcester" as well as in nearby Boston and Providence, create "a lively social scene off campus." Physically getting off campus, however, can prove difficult, as "Students cannot have cars until their third year."

Student Body

The typical Holy Cross student is "hardworking, and loves to have fun." With a "general atmosphere of friendliness and acceptance" on campus, most students find it hard to "feel lonely or bored." While the majority of Holy Cross students are "White, Irish Catholics" from "upper-middle-class families," the school's administration has "done a lot of work toward becoming a more diverse and inclusive place." As one student explains, "Most all faculty and administrators are exceptionally welcoming of diversity." Although a Jesuit university, "Religion is not a major issue" here. "Most students do not go to mass though they consider themselves Catholic," and non-Catholics can, if they wish, attend "nondenominational masses" offered on campus. Regardless of their beliefs, Holy Cross students are "very conscious about affairs outside of the college" and "involved in working to better the community." "Devoted to excellence in academics" first and foremost, the typical Holy Cross student "is not afraid to meet new people, go out on the weekends, and have a great time."

FINANCIAL AID: 508-793-2265 • E-MAIL: ADMISSIONS@HOLYCROSS.EDU • WEBSITE: WWW.HOLYCROSS.EDU

ADMISSIONS

Very important factors considered include: Academic GPA, class rank, rigor of secondary school record. *Important factors considered include:* Alumni/ae relation, application essay, character/personal qualities, extracurricular activities, interview, recommendation(s). *Other factors considered include:* First generation, geographical residence, level of applicant's interest, racial/ethnic status, standardized test scores, talent/ability, volunteer work, work experience. TOEFL required of all international applicants. High school diploma is required, and GED is accepted. *Academic units recommended:* 4 English, 4 math, 4 science, 3 foreign language, 2 social studies, 2 history, 1 academic elective.

The Inside Word

Admission to Holy Cross is competitive; therefore, a demanding high school course load is required to be a viable candidate. The college values effective communication skills—it thoroughly evaluates each applicant's personal statement and short essay responses. Interviews are important, especially for those applying early decision. Students who graduate from a Catholic high school might find themselves at a slight advantage.

FINANCIAL AID

Students should submit: FAFSA, CSS/Financial Aid PROFILE, Noncustodial PROFILE, Business/Farm Supplement, parent and student Federal Income Tax Returns. Regular filing deadline is February 1. The Princeton Review suggests that all financial aid forms be submitted as soon as possible after January 1. *Need-based scholarships/grants offered:* Pell Grant, SEOG, state scholarships/grants, private scholarships, the school's own gift aid. *Loan aid offered:* FFEL Subsidized Stafford, FFEL Unsubsidized Stafford, FFEL PLUS, Federal Perkins Loan, MDFA. Applicants will be notified of awards on or about March 30.

FROM THE ADMISSIONS OFFICE

"When applying to Holy Cross, two areas deserve particular attention. First, the essay should be developed thoughtfully, with correct language and syntax in mind. That essay reflects for the Board of Admissions how you think and how you can express yourself. Second, activity beyond the classroom should be clearly defined. Since Holy Cross [has only] 2,800 students, the chance for involvement/participation is exceptional. The board reviews many applications for academically qualified students. A key difference in being accepted is the extent to which a candidate participates in-depth beyond the classroom—don't be modest; define who you are.

"Standardized test scores (i.e., SAT, SAT Subject Tests, and ACT) are optional. Students may submit their scores if they believe the results paint a fuller picture of their achievements and potential, but those who don't submit scores will not be at a disadvantage in admissions decisions."

SELECTIVITY

Admissions Rating	**95**
# of applicants	6,706
% of applicants accepted	34
% of acceptees attending	33
# accepting a place on wait list	391
% admitted from wait list	4
# of early decision applicants	490
% accepted early decision	53

FRESHMAN PROFILE

Range SAT Critical Reading	590–680
Range SAT Math	600–690
Minimum Paper TOEFL	550
Minimum Computer Based TOEFL	213
% graduated top 10% of class	64
% graduated top 25% of class	93
% graduated top 50% of class	100

DEADLINES

Early decision application deadline	12/15
Early decision notification	1/15
Regular application deadline	1/15
Regular notification	4/1
Nonfall registration?	yes

APPLICANTS ALSO LOOK AT
AND OFTEN PREFER

Boston College, Georgetown University, Tufts University, University of Notre Dame

AND SOMETIMES PREFER

Boston University, Fairfield University, Fordham University, Loyola College in Maryland, Providence College, Villanova University

FINANCIAL FACTS

Financial Aid Rating	**92**
Annual tuition	$34,630
Room & Board	$9,960
Books and supplies	$700
Required fees	$512
% frosh rec. need-based scholarship or grant aid	47
% UG rec. need-based scholarship or grant aid	45
% frosh rec. need-based self-help aid	49
% UG rec. need-based self-help aid	51
% frosh rec. any financial aid	64
% UG rec. any financial aid	59

THE COLLEGE OF NEW JERSEY

PO Box 7718, Ewing, NJ 08628-0718 • Admissions: 609-771-2131 • Fax: 609-637-5174

STUDENTS SAY
Academics
Students at The College of New Jersey believe they've found "the best way to get private school education for public school cost." To hear them tell it, The College of New Jersey "is the total package," with "a beautiful campus, great location, top-notch faculty, the newest technology, an interested student body, and competitive sports teams." TCNJ students benefit from their small-school setting, which makes for lots of "interaction between students and professors. The classes are generally 15 to 20 students, enabling greater relationships between students and their professors." Those relationships yield substantial dividends "when it comes to getting recommendations, taking advantage of internship opportunities, and landing jobs in the 'real world,'" we're told. Of course, first they have to graduate, no small task given that "the classes aren't a joke. They're difficult and a lot of work, but at the end of your 4 years you'll be prepared because the professors know what they're talking about and want to make sure that you do well." Students appreciate that "professors and advisors will go out of their way to help you, whether it is with your schoolwork, your resume, or your career plans. Not only is the caliber of students high, but the professors are willing to work hard for you so you are willing to work hard for them, too!" What students appreciate most is "the affordable price" of a TCNJ education: "You get a great education and it will cost less than $20,000 a year for in-state residents and only a little over for out-of-state students."

Life
The TCNJ campus "is gorgeous, with tree-lined paths and brick buildings in the Georgian Colonial style," though some students wonder whether construction will ever end. Extracurricular options are varied here. Those involved in the Greek scene say it's "always available and fun"; the Greeks and the sports houses are the location of many off-campus parties, we're told. Tuesday, aka "Tuesday Booze Day," is one of the big party nights here, by the way—that's because "The school doesn't offer a lot of classes on Wednesday." There's "always something planned by the college that is announced in the newspaper (e.g., concerts, art exhibits, guest speakers)," and the school's proximity to New York and Philadelphia helps it draw some big names, including, recently, "John Leguizamo, Blessid Union of Souls, the cast of *Whose Line is it Anyway?*, and Wynton Marsalis." Of course, location also allows for "constant trips running to New York City and other off-campus destinations. Honestly, sometimes it's hard to say no to some of the stuff going on in order to get some work done." Students note that "on [any] given weekend, about half of the population empties out. Most of these students go home, to work, or to visit friends at other schools," but add that "people think everyone goes home on the weekends, and some people do, but for those of us who stay there are fun parties, bars, things to do."

Student Body
TCNJ draws primarily "from New Jersey middle-class suburbia," which "makes for fun 'arguments,' such as: Which is better, North or South Jersey? Is it 'jimmies' or 'sprinkles'? A 'hoagie' or a 'sub'?" A "decent number of students from other backgrounds, states, and countries" supplements the population and adds diversity. Students tend to be "hardworking, diligent, and very bright," and they are "able to balance their 18-credit workload and still have time to blow some steam off on the weekends. They're leaders, both in and out of the classrooms. Our 150-plus student organizations are a testament to that." The school attracts a reasonable cross-section of personality types; one student explains, "There are many different groups at TCNJ. There are athletes, artists, Greeks, and the few who are found playing with swords on Medieval Day out on the lawn. Everyone basically does their own thing, and it's generally just accepted."

FINANCIAL AID: 609-771-2211 • E-MAIL: ADMISS@VM.TCNJ.EDU • WEBSITE: WWW.TCNJ.EDU

ADMISSIONS

Very important factors considered include: Application essay, character/personal qualities, class rank, extracurricular activities, rigor of secondary school record, standardized test scores, talent/ability. *Important factors considered include:* Level of applicant's interest, recommendation(s), volunteer work. *Other factors considered include:* Academic GPA, alumni/ae relation, first generation, geographical residence, interview, racial/ethnic status, state residency, work experience. SAT or ACT required; TOEFL required of all international applicants. High school diploma is required, and GED is accepted. *Academic units required:* 4 English, 3 math, 3 science (2 science labs), 2 foreign language, 2 social studies. *Academic units recommended:* 4 English, 3 math, 3 science (3 science labs), 3 foreign language, 3 social studies.

The Inside Word

Don't be deceived by the relatively high acceptance rate at The College of New Jersey. The school boasts a number of rigorous and respected academic programs. Applicants cannot slack off in high school and expect to be handed an acceptance letter—or a favorable first-semester transcript. Those who have succeeded in demanding classes will have the opportunity to receive a stellar education at this lovely public institution and at bargain prices no less.

FINANCIAL AID

Students should submit: FAFSA. The Princeton Review suggests that all financial aid forms be submitted as soon as possible after January 1. *Need-based scholarships/grants offered:* Pell Grant, SEOG, state scholarships/grants, private scholarships, the school's own gift aid. *Loan aid offered:* FFEL Subsidized Stafford, FFEL Unsubsidized Stafford, FFEL PLUS, Federal Perkins Loan, Federal Nursing Loan. Applicants will be notified of awards on a rolling basis beginning or about June 1.

FROM THE ADMISSIONS OFFICE

"The College of New Jersey is one of the United States' great higher education success stories. With a long history as New Jersey's preeminent teacher of teachers, the college has grown into a new role as educator of the state's best students in a wide range of fields. The College of New Jersey has created a culture of constant questioning—a place where knowledge is not merely received but reconfigured. In small classes, students and faculty members collaborate in a rewarding process: As they seek to understand fundamental principles, apply key concepts, reveal new problems, and pursue new lines of inquiry, students gain a fluency of thought in their disciplines. The college's 289-acre tree-lined campus is a union of vision, engineering, beauty, and functionality. Neoclassical Georgian Colonial architecture, meticulous landscaping, and thoughtful design merge in a dynamic system, constantly evolving to meet the needs of TCNJ students. About 50 percent of TCNJ's 2004 entering class will be academic scholars, with large numbers of National Merit finalists and semifinalists. More than 400 students in the class received awards from New Jersey's Outstanding Student Recruitment Program. The College of New Jersey is bringing together the best ideas from around the nation and building a new model for public undergraduate education on one campus . . . in New Jersey!

"The College of New Jersey will accept both the new and old SAT (administered prior to March 2005 and without a Writing component), as well as the ACT with or without the Writing component."

SELECTIVITY

Admissions Rating	93
# of applicants	8,185
% of applicants accepted	44
% of acceptees attending	36
# accepting a place on wait list	497
% admitted from wait list	30
# of early decision applicants	617
% accepted early decision	41

FRESHMAN PROFILE

Range SAT Critical Reading	570–670
Range SAT Math	590–700
Range SAT Writing	560–670
Minimum Paper TOEFL	550
Minimum Computer Based TOEFL	215
% graduated top 10% of class	68
% graduated top 25% of class	93
% graduated top 50% of class	99

DEADLINES

Early decision application deadline	11/15
Early decision notification	12/15
Regular application deadline	2/15
Regular notification	rolling
Nonfall registration?	no

APPLICANTS ALSO LOOK AT
AND OFTEN PREFER

Lehigh University, New York University, Rowan University, Rutgers, The State University of New Jersey—New Brunswick, University of Delaware, Villanova University,

AND SOMETIMES PREFER

Boston College, Boston University, Drexel University, Pennsylvania State University—University Park, University of Maryland—College Park, University of Pennsylvania

AND RARELY PREFER

Bucknell University, Fordham University, Loyola College in Maryland, Montclair State University, Ramapo College of New Jersey, Stevens Institute of Technology

FINANCIAL FACTS

Financial Aid Rating	72
Annual in-state tuition	$7,615
Annual out-of-state tuition	$14,161
Room & Board	$8,843
Books and supplies	$1,000
Required fees	$2,938
% frosh rec. need-based scholarship or grant aid	16
% UG rec. need-based scholarship or grant aid	16
% frosh rec. need-based self-help aid	26
% UG rec. need-based self-help aid	29

COLLEGE OF THE OZARKS

OFFICE OF ADMISSIONS, POINT LOOKOUT, MO 65726 • ADMISSIONS: 417-334-6411 • FAX: 417-335-2618

CAMPUS LIFE
Quality of Life Rating	**87**
Fire Safety Rating	**78**
Type of school	private
Affiliation	Presbyterian
Environment	rural

STUDENTS
Total undergrad enrollment	1,345
% male/female	46/54
% from out of state	33
% from public high school	82
% live on campus	84
% African American	1
% Caucasian	95
% Hispanic	1
% Native American	1
% international	1
# of countries represented	13

SURVEY SAYS . . .
Small classes
Students are friendly
Frats and sororities are unpopular or nonexistent
Very little drug use

ACADEMICS
Academic Rating	**82**
Calendar	semester
Student/faculty ratio	14:1
Profs interesting rating	82
Profs accessible rating	82
% profs teaching UG courses	100
% classes taught by TAs	0
Most common lab size	10–19 students
Most common reg class size	10–19 students

MOST POPULAR MAJORS
business administration/ management
criminal justice/police science
elementary education and teaching

STUDENTS SAY
Academics
Offering a tuition-free education in exchange for weekly work-study hours, College of the Ozarks provides "an education for students who would not normally be able to afford it." A heavy emphasis on Christian values—both inside and outside of the academic halls—also makes this an ideal spot "for students who wish to earn their degree while growing closer to God." All of this adds up to a very personal education; "It's really like one big family," writes one undergraduate. Professors are praised for their willingness "to help the students in whatever way possible. They are very involved in the students' lives." In fact, at College of the Ozarks, the "administration and a few of the professors, live on campus, which allows us to go to them no matter what we may need," notes a freshman. Like the professors, the higher-ups in the administration are easily accessible. "They are not in their offices all day," a junior tells us. "They are out walking the campus and visiting with students." Even though they're talking to students, however, some undergrads wonder if they're listening. Responding to very strict campus regulations and having to live within a number of buildings (including dorms) that are in ill-repair, students complain that the "administration shows a complete lack of perspective on the students' needs, conditions, and desires."

Life
What did you expect? "Life is crazy busy at C of O." "We are required to work 15 hours a week on campus aside from our class hours," writes a sophomore. Students tell us that the work-for-tuition program "is a neat experience." They move up the job-rung hierarchy, starting in the cafeteria or bookstore, and progressively moving to sought-after positions in academic departments or computers. Because students still need to cover the costs of books, room and board, and other expenses, many find "off-campus work" to be a positive step toward a "debt-free" graduation. The campus offers a range of extracurricular activities, such as "bowling, movie night, dances, coffeehouses, and things of that nature." In addition, a variety of "different Bible studies" pepper the campus, each drawing "high attendance on average." Things you won't find in Point Lookout include "parties or big dorm functions." In fact, due to the list of campus rules, life at C of O is rather tame. What exactly are those rules? A "zero-tolerance policy for drugs and alcohol," restricted dorm visits by members of the opposite sex and "Freshman cars are locked up on weekdays to keep us working instead of partying," to name a few. Also, as a sophomore explains, appearance codes are rigidly enforced: "We aren't really allowed to dress or look outrageous in any way. Guys aren't allowed piercings and girls are only allowed a few in their ears. Guys are required to cut their hair if it reaches their collar. No funky colored hair or hairstyles, either." Some students feel these rules send the message: "Don't express yourself unless you are told how." But most students have no problem with the rules, which they say "help build character."

Student Body
Your average College of the Ozarks undergrad is "someone who is a strong Christian" and "certainly more conservative" than many college students nationwide. It's also true that many of these students come from a "lower socioeconomic background," drawn to the college by the affordable educational opportunity. In general, there's a sense of conformity at C of O, not only in terms of background and religion, but also in terms of looks. "Everyone dresses the same and looks basically the same because of the strict dress and behavioral codes," writes a senior. But on the whole, "It doesn't matter what you look like or what you wear, we'll look at you for who you truly are inside, as a Christian should." This is what defines a C of O undergrad: "Kind, happy, eager to help. Believe it or not, most of the campus is made up of just good people."

COLLEGE OF THE OZARKS

FINANCIAL AID: 417-334-6411 • E-MAIL: ADMISS4@COFO.EDU • WEBSITE: WWW.COFO.EDU

ADMISSIONS

Very important factors considered include: Character/personal qualities, class rank, interview, rigor of secondary school record. *Important factors considered include:* Academic GPA, recommendation(s), standardized test scores, volunteer work, work experience. *Other factors considered include:* Alumni/ae relation, extracurricular activities, first generation, geographical residence, level of applicant's interest, racial/ethnic status, religious affiliation/commitment, state residency, talent/ability. SAT or ACT required; ACT recommended. TOEFL required of all international applicants. High school diploma is required, and GED is accepted. *Academic units recommended:* 4 English, 3 math, 2 science (1 science lab), 2 foreign language, 3 social studies, 1 visual/performing arts/public speaking.

The Inside Word

The highly unusual nature of the College of the Ozarks translates directly into its admissions process. Because of the school's very purpose, providing educational opportunities to those with great financial need, one of the main qualifiers for admission is exactly that—demonstrated financial need. Despite not being a household name, Ozarks attracts enough interest to keep its admit rate consistently low from year to year. To be sure, the admissions process is competitive, but it's more important to be a good fit for the college philosophically and financially than it is to be an academic wizard. If you're a hard worker all around, you're just what they're looking for.

FINANCIAL AID

Students should submit: FAFSA. The Princeton Review suggests that all financial aid forms be submitted as soon as possible after January 1. *Need-based scholarships/grants offered:* Pell Grant, SEOG, state scholarships/grants, private scholarships, the school's own gift aid. Applicants will be notified of awards on or about February 1.

FROM THE ADMISSIONS OFFICE

"College of the Ozarks is unique because of its no-tuition, work-study program, but also because it strives to educate the head, the heart, and the hands. At C of O, there are high expectations of students—the college stresses character development as well as study and work. An education from 'Hard Work U.' offers many opportunities, not the least of which is the chance to graduate debt-free. Life at C of O isn't all hard work and no play, however. There are many opportunities for fun. The nearby resort town of Branson, Missouri, offers ample opportunities for recreation and summer employment, and Table Rock Lake, only a few miles away, is a terrific spot to swim, sun, and relax. Numerous on-campus activities such as Mudfest, Luau Night, dances, and holiday parties give students lots of chances for fun without leaving the college. At 'Hard Work U.,' we work hard, but we know how to have fun, too.

"Applicants for Fall 2008 are required to submit scores from the ACT or the new SAT. We will allow students to submit scores from the old (prior to March 2005) version of the SAT (or ACT) as well, and will use the student's best scores from either test. Writing scores are not required."

SELECTIVITY
Admissions Rating	89
# of applicants	2,654
% of applicants accepted	12
% of acceptees attending	83
# accepting a place on wait list	327
% admitted from wait list	3

FRESHMAN PROFILE
Range ACT Composite	21–26
Minimum Paper TOEFL	550
Minimum Computer Based TOEFL	213
Average HS GPA	3.34
% graduated top 10% of class	16
% graduated top 25% of class	48
% graduated top 50% of class	87

DEADLINES
Regular application deadline	3/15
Regular notification	rolling
Nonfall registration?	yes

**APPLICANTS ALSO LOOK AT
AND OFTEN PREFER**
Missouri State University

AND SOMETIMES PREFER
Southwest Baptist University

FINANCIAL FACTS
Financial Aid Rating	86
Annual tuition	$0*
Room & Board	$4,400
Books and supplies	$800
Required fees	$280
% frosh rec. need-based scholarship or grant aid	84
% UG rec. need-based scholarship or grant aid	90
% frosh rec. need-based self-help aid	76
% UG rec. need-based self-help aid	70
% frosh rec. any financial aid	100
% UG rec. any financial aid	100

*Tuition is covered by a full scholarship and mandatory work-study.

THE COLLEGE OF WILLIAM & MARY

PO BOX 8795, WILLIAMSBURG, VA 23187-8795 • ADMISSIONS: 757-221-4223 • FAX: 757-221-1242

CAMPUS LIFE

Quality of Life Rating	84
Fire Safety Rating	60*
Type of school	public
Environment	village

STUDENTS

Total undergrad enrollment	5,651
% male/female	46/54
% from out of state	32
% live on campus	76
% in (# of) fraternities	22 (16)
% in (# of) sororities	27 (11)
% African American	7
% Asian	7
% Caucasian	67
% Hispanic	5
% Native American	1
% international	1
# of countries represented	50

SURVEY SAYS . . .
No one cheats
Great library
Students are friendly
Campus feels safe
Students are happy

ACADEMICS

Academic Rating	87
Calendar	semester
Student/faculty ratio	11:1
Profs interesting rating	88
Profs accessible rating	85
% profs teaching	
UG courses	99
% classes taught by TAs	1
Most common	
reg class size	10–19 students

MOST POPULAR MAJORS
business administration/
management
multi/interdisciplinary studies
psychology

STUDENTS SAY
Academics
"Our history is an incredible strength," observes one William & Mary under-grad, pointing out that "it's pretty powerful to take classes in a building where Jefferson did, or to lounge on the Sunken Gardens where the British Army was once was encamped." More than 300 years after its founding, William & Mary is still "academically one of the best schools in the country, with an incredibly challenging curriculum and workload." Students see the challenge as a plus. "We're not just a degree factory," writes one. "The GPA you leave William & Mary with is one that you can really be proud of, because you earned it, and you had to work to earn it." This public institution "offers a wide selection of majors and courses in both the liberal and fine arts areas" and is "the ideal size. . . . It's big enough to provide students with plenty of opportunities both aca-demically and socially, but small enough to make you feel like you're part of a community." Students also love that "for a non-research institution, there are a good number of opportunities to conduct research along with professors." They are not so excited, however, about state-mandated budget cuts that "have made it difficult to keep pace with private institutions. Some of our programs are diminishing, and it has really hurt us." Fortunately the cuts haven't yet impacted the fact that "each student here enjoys personal attention in smaller classes, and easily accessible professors in larger classes."

Life
"Traditions and history are the best thing about William & Mary," according to students. "Yule Log, Convocation, King and Queen Dance, and seniors ringing the bell on the Wren Tower are things all students here look forward to." The campus "is yet another strength. It's incredibly beautiful year-round, green and lush, with lots of shady spots for those unable to weather the Billsburg heat and humidity, and plenty of open space for games and a relaxing sun-bathing/study session." Undergrads observe that "the Greek scene is huge" and that "the college is making strides to provide more late-night entertain-ment and activities for the crowd that does not go to frat parties." The "level of student involvement is very high, with student-run organizations for every-thing and anything." Intercollegiate athletics "are good for a school of our size," and "Musical groups are popular across campus. Even though the school isn't a conservatory, there is a great emphasis placed on a cappella groups and the choir." All these assets help offset the students' tumultuous relationship with their Williamsburg neighbors; one undergrad reports, "It seems as though the town really dislikes the student population." In fact, recently passed housing laws and noise-disturbance laws seem "aimed primarily at restricting students' ability to live off-campus, but the Student Assembly is working on getting those repealed." In an effort to appease the town, "a newly revised, extremely strict alcohol policy was put in place, which results in not much to do as far as parties on weekends."

Student Body
William & Mary undergrads "are all a little quirky and a little dorky in their own way, but because of that, we all fit in." Most students "were at the top of their high school class academically, athletically, and/or socially" and "are very involved in campus activities. There are over 380 clubs and organizations, so although students are involved in different types of clubs, they are all com-mitted to activities outside of the classroom." Many originate from Northern Virginia and the DC area, a wealthy enclave where they grew up "friendly, but sheltered." They arrive ready for work; one student explains, "They're com-mitted to their education: Half of them do it for grades, and the other half are motivated because they've got big plans."

THE COLLEGE OF WILLIAM & MARY

FINANCIAL AID: 757-221-2420 • E-MAIL: ADMISS@WM.EDU • WEBSITE: WWW.WM.EDU

ADMISSIONS

Very important factors considered include: Academic GPA, application essay, character/personal qualities, class rank, extracurricular activities, recommendation(s), rigor of secondary school record, standardized test scores, state residency, talent/ability. *Other factors considered include:* Alumni/ae relation, first generation, geographical residence, interview, racial/ethnic status, volunteer work, work experience. SAT or ACT required; TOEFL required of all international applicants. High school diploma is required, and GED is not accepted. *Academic units recommended:* 4 English, 4 math, 4 science (3 science labs), 4 foreign language, 4 social studies.

The Inside Word

The volume of applications at William & Mary is extremely high; thus admission is ultra-competitive. Only very strong students from out of state should apply. The large applicant pool necessitates a rapid-fire candidate evaluation process; each Admissions Officer reads roughly 100 application folders per day during the peak review season. But this is one Admissions Committee that moves fast without sacrificing a thorough review. There probably isn't a tougher public college Admissions Committee in the country.

FINANCIAL AID

Students should submit: FAFSA, CSS/Financial Aid PROFILE (CSS/Financial Aid PROFILE required of early decision applicants only). Regular filing deadline is February 15. The Princeton Review suggests that all financial aid forms be submitted as soon as possible after January 1. *Need-based scholarships/grants offered:* Pell Grant, SEOG, state scholarships/grants, private scholarships, the school's own gift aid. *Loan aid offered:* FFEL Subsidized Stafford, FFEL Unsubsidized Stafford, FFEL PLUS, Federal Perkins Loan, Applicants will be notified of awards on a rolling basis beginning or about March 10. Federal Work-Study Program available. Institutional employment available. Off-campus job opportunities are excellent.

FROM THE ADMISSIONS OFFICE

"William & Mary is the second-oldest institution of higher learning in the country. Yes, we have the lowest student/faculty ratio (11:1) of any public university. We're also know for what many have called the preeminent undergraduate business program in the United States, a model United Nations team that perennially vies for the world championship, and alumni who wrote everything from the revolutionary Declaration of Independence (Thomas Jefferson, Class of 1762) to the hilarious *Naked Pictures of Famous People* (Comedy Central's Jon Stewart, Class of 1984). In short, William & Mary offers a top-rated educational experience at a comparatively low cost and in the company of interesting people from a broad variety of backgrounds. If you are an academically strong, involved student looking for a challenge in a great campus community, William & Mary may well be the place for you.

"Applicants for Fall 2008 may submit old or new SAT scores, and William & Mary will combine the best scores from all submitted tests. Students may choose to submit ACT scores; the best composite scores will be used provided it is a better score than the highest combined SAT. "

SELECTIVITY

Admissions Rating	93
# of applicants	10,610
% of applicants accepted	31
% of acceptees attending	41
# accepting a place on wait list	589
% admitted from wait list	19
# of early decision applicants	915
% accepted early decision	50

FRESHMAN PROFILE

Range SAT Critical Reading	630–730
Range SAT Math	630–710
Range ACT Composite	28–32
Minimum Paper TOEFL	600
Minimum Computer Based TOEFL	250
% graduated top 10% of class	85
% graduated top 25% of class	97
% graduated top 50% of class	100

DEADLINES

Early decision application deadline	11/1
Early decision notification	12/1
Regular application deadline	1/1
Regular notification	4/1
Nonfall registration?	no

APPLICANTS ALSO LOOK AT AND OFTEN PREFER

Duke University, Georgetown University, University of Virginia

AND SOMETIMES PREFER

Brown University, Dartmouth College, Johns Hopkins University, Notre Dame de Namur University, The University of North Carolina at Chapel Hill, Vanderbilt University, Washington and Lee University, Yale University

FINANCIAL FACTS

Financial Aid Rating	81
Annual in-state tuition	$8,490
Annual out-of-state tuition	$25,048
Room & Board	$6,932
Books and supplies	$900
% frosh rec. need-based scholarship or grant aid	19
% UG rec. need-based scholarship or grant aid	22
% frosh rec. need-based self-help aid	22
% UG rec. need-based self-help aid	24

THE COLLEGE OF WOOSTER

847 COLLEGE AVENUE, WOOSTER, OH 44691 • ADMISSIONS: 330-263-2322 • FAX: 330-263-2621

STUDENTS SAY

Academics

Undergrads here maintain that The College of Wooster "is about developing the autonomy of its students in all areas" from "their academic achievement and extracurricular activities to their self-awareness and ability to help others." Nowhere is this more evident than in the curriculum's "nationally renowned senior Independent Study (IS) project," which is where, students say, the "gold of Wooster lies." One student explains, "The Independent Study allowed me to customize and focus my interests into a thoroughly challenging, yet enjoyable, year-long project. Being able to organize and approach my own selected topic was an invaluable experience that has prepared me for the prospect of graduate school." A junior states that she chose Wooster "because it seemed to me that if students were expected to create such an intensive project then the classes must also be at a high caliber. I have certainly found this to be the case." Physics, chemistry, business and management, music, and history are among the standout disciplines here. Like most top-notch liberal arts schools, Wooster features "a small, closely knit campus and accessible, genuinely interested professors, making it the ideal setting to branch out, both in and out of the classroom." Academics here involve "a lot of homework and reading," but students tell us that they get a good overall experience, one that "incorporat[es] relatively healthy doses of student activities, good dining halls, and a beautiful campus populated by (in general) great people."

Life

Wooster "is a tradition[s]-based school with awesome activities, from the kilt-wearing marching band to the many sports teams, varsity and intramural," and students embrace these traditions with gusto. "The school is good at providing activities on weekends," students say, which include "bands and outside entertainment" as well as showcases of "students' talents." This is a good thing given that the town of Wooster "is very small [and] has little to offer in terms of activities besides restaurants and movies." Big-city entertainment can be found in Cleveland and Columbus, but both are an hour's drive away, so they're only an option if you have a car or are chummy with someone who has wheels. The on-campus party scene is robust; on "Wooster Wednesday" "people drink like it's Friday" (on actual Fridays "Many students go to the college bar/club called the Underground") and the "fraternity and sorority houses" are known for their "themed parties (Beach Party, Funk Party, Heaven and Hell, Stop and Go)." For students in search of weekend options that don't involve alcohol, the school "sponsors events to substitute [for] partying for those of us who do not participate." Have we mentioned that Wooster also has "lots of student organizations"? Word on campus is that the average student "participates in a vast array" of them.

Student Body

"There are a lot of different types of students" at Wooster, including "people who seem to be at school just to have a good time," and many more people who "seem to be here to get as much as possible out of the[ir] education." Many are "from Ohio or the Midwest," but there are also "many international students on campus, and they fit in with the rest of the student population as much as anyone else." The typical undergrad is "liberal, but rather apathetic to politics and religion." Socially, the school "is divided into countless little social groups," many of which form "based on first-year experiences, athletic involvement, or extracurricular interests." Indeed, you'll find "a lot of athletes" among the student population, and many who "are involved in a wide array of extracurricular activities"; these activities prompt "students from different backgrounds and social groups [to] interact and work together."

FINANCIAL AID: 800-877-3688 • E-MAIL: ADMISSIONS@WOOSTER.EDU • WEBSITE: WWW.WOOSTER.EDU

ADMISSIONS

Very important factors considered include: Academic GPA, class rank, rigor of secondary school record. *Important factors considered include:* Application essay, character/personal qualities, recommendation(s), standardized test scores, talent/ability. *Other factors considered include:* Alumni/ae relation, extracurricular activities, geographical residence, interview, racial/ethnic status, state residency, volunteer work, work experience. SAT or ACT required; ACT with Writing component required. TOEFL required of all international applicants. High school diploma is required, and GED is accepted. *Academic units required:* 4 English, 3 math, 3 science, 2 foreign language, 3 social studies, 2 academic electives. *Academic units recommended:* 4 math, 4 science, 3 foreign language, 4 social studies.

The Inside Word

The College of Wooster is a small, selective liberal arts school. Stiff competition from similarly situated institutions means the school occasionally admits students who may not be up to the challenges of the curriculum, but, by and large, only solid students get past the gatekeepers here. Expect a thorough review of your entire application.

FINANCIAL AID

Students should submit: FAFSA, CSS/Financial Aid PROFILE. Regular filing deadline is September 1. The Princeton Review suggests that all financial aid forms be submitted as soon as possible after January 1. *Need-based scholarships/grants offered:* Pell Grant, SEOG, state scholarships/grants, private scholarships, the school's own gift aid. *Loan aid offered:* Direct Subsidized Stafford, Direct Unsubsidized Stafford, Direct PLUS, Federal Perkins Loan, college/university loans from institutional funds. Applicants will be notified of awards on or about April 1. Federal Work-Study Program available. Institutional employment available.

FROM THE ADMISSIONS OFFICE

"At The College of Wooster, our mission is to graduate educated, not merely trained, people; to produce responsible, independent thinkers, rather than specialists in any given field. Our commitment to independence is especially evident in IS, the college's distinctive program in which every senior works one-to-one with a faculty mentor to complete a project in the major. IS comes from 'independent study,' but, in reality, it is an intellectual collaboration of the highest order and permits every student the freedom to pursue something in which he or she is passionately interested. IS is the centerpiece of an innovative curriculum. More than just the project itself, the culture that sustains IS—and, in turn, is sustained by IS—is an extraordinary college culture. The same attitudes of student initiative, openness, flexibility, and individual support enrich every aspect of Wooster's vital residential college life.

"College of Wooster requires freshman applicants to submit scores from the old or new SAT. Students may also choose to submit scores from the ACT (with the Writing component) in lieu of the SAT."

SELECTIVITY

Admissions Rating	84
# of applicants	2,504
% of applicants accepted	80
% of acceptees attending	25
# accepting a place on wait list	25
% admitted from wait list	100
# of early decision applicants	66
% accepted early decision	91

FRESHMAN PROFILE

Range SAT Critical Reading	540–670
Range SAT Math	560–650
Range SAT Writing	550–650
Range ACT Composite	23–29
Minimum Paper TOEFL	550
Minimum Computer Based TOEFL	213
Average HS GPA	3.55
% graduated top 10% of class	27
% graduated top 25% of class	61
% graduated top 50% of class	92

DEADLINES

Early decision application deadline	12/1
Early decision notification	12/15
Regular application deadline	2/15
Regular notification	4/1
Nonfall registration?	yes

FINANCIAL FACTS

Financial Aid Rating	93
Comprehensive fee	$40,372
% frosh rec. need-based scholarship or grant aid	58
% UG rec. need-based scholarship or grant aid	55
% frosh rec. need-based self-help aid	59
% UG rec. need-based self-help aid	55
% frosh rec. any financial aid	100
% UG rec. any financial aid	100

COLORADO COLLEGE

14 EAST CACHE LA POUDRE STREET, COLORADO SPRINGS, CO 80903 • ADMISSIONS: 719-389-6344 • FAX: 719-389-6816

STUDENTS SAY
Academics

"Block Plan": These two words sum up a key aspect of the Colorado College experience for most students. The plan, which breaks the school year into eight 3.5 week chunks, allows students and professors to take and teach one class at a time. Students "either love or hate" the Block Plan; its supporters feel that "the block system provides a unique learning experience because we get to give our full attention to one class at a time." They love the way professors "make use of the block system to take field trips so that learning happens both inside and outside of the classroom." Inside the classroom, "the discussions rock." Students with complaints about the Block Plan gripe about visiting professors who "don't seem to understand how the system works and tend to either give way too much work or hardly any at all. They also have trouble making their classes last for the expected 3 hours each day." In addition, students report, the shortened time frame for each course means that students "can forget about getting sick, even for a day, because then they will most likely have to drop the class." Given all this pressure, undergrads appreciate the fact that professors "are available to students in and out of the classroom and care if the students succeed." For students seeking international experience, Colorado College is a great option, since "so many students study abroad." Some classes "even spend a whole block in another city or country." An "exceptionally accessible" administration gets the thumbs-up from students. The president in particular earns kudos; students report that he "is extremely open to suggestions and ideas. He has open office hours every week."

Life

The Block Plan gives life at Colorado College an unusual tempo. "Because of the Block Plan, studying is always in the forefront and intense," and "people joke that they can't plan beyond the increment of 3.5 weeks because they have no idea what the next block will be like." But at the end of each block comes a 4-day break, and students plan for that by "organizing outdoor trips or other road trips to see what Colorado has to offer." In the thick of any given block, "a lot of kids do intramural sports and party hard on the weekends. Hiking, camping, backpacking, and mountain biking are also huge activities." So are "the hockey games. People go crazy for Tiger hockey. Even the city of Colorado Springs is behind the team." Of course, "skiing is a big part of Colorado College life in the winter." Many students comment on the school's "hippie" culture, but respondents were quick to note that "almost all students are extremely accepting [of] cultural, sexual, racial, and class differences."

Student Body

One student characterizes the typical student thus: "The typical Colorado College student is White and from an upper-middle-class home in a metropolitan suburb, but wishes this weren't true and acts accordingly. He or she is relatively aware politically, socially, and environmentally, and cares enough to be motivated and take advantage of what Colorado College has to offer, but won't let this interfere with his or her skiing plans." Visitors to Colorado College, another writes, will probably find "three major demographics. First and largest: outdoor enthusiasts with a little bit of hippie in them. Second: classic frat type. The Greek scene is small, but there are plenty of folks sporting American Eagle clothes and hanging out in the gyms. Third: outright hippies. This is a smaller demographic than you'd think." Many students feel like "liberals in a conservative town." Students also admit that "there is not a whole lot of diversity at Colorado College in terms of race, sexual orientation, class, or background," but add that "there are numerous clubs and groups that support all types of minorities."

FINANCIAL AID: 719-389-6651 • E-MAIL: ADMISSION@COLORADOCOLLEGE.EDU • WEBSITE: WWW.COLORADOCOLLEGE.EDU

ADMISSIONS

Very important factors considered include: Rigor of secondary school record. *Important factors considered include:* Academic GPA, application essay, class rank, extracurricular activities, interview, recommendation(s), standardized test scores. *Other factors considered include:* Alumni/ae relation, character/personal qualities, first generation, level of applicant's interest, racial/ethnic status, religious affiliation/commitment, talent/ability, volunteer work, work experience. SAT or ACT required; TOEFL required of all international applicants. High school diploma or equivalent is not required. *Academic units required:* 4 English. *Academic units recommended:* 4 English.

The Inside Word

Colorado College works to identify those students who will most benefit from its distinct academic environment. Because the block program requires focus and demands that students become active participants in their education, Admissions Officers value applicants who take on a rigorous course load in high school and engage in activities that complement their intellectual achievements. All candidates should take the application essay seriously—strong writing skills are seen as critical to success at CC.

FINANCIAL AID

Students should submit: FAFSA, CSS/Financial Aid PROFILE, Noncustodial PROFILE, Federal 1040 parent and student tax returns and parent W-2 forms. Regular filing deadline is February 15. The Princeton Review suggests that all financial aid forms be submitted as soon as possible after January 1. *Need-based scholarships/grants offered:* Pell Grant, SEOG, state scholarships/grants, private scholarships, the school's own gift aid. *Loan aid offered:* FFEL Subsidized Stafford, FFEL Unsubsidized Stafford, FFEL PLUS, Federal Perkins Loan. Applicants will be notified of awards on or about March 20. Federal Work-Study Program available. Institutional employment available. Off-campus job opportunities are good.

FROM THE ADMISSIONS OFFICE

"Students enter Colorado College for the opportunity to study intensely in small learning communities. Groups of students work closely with one another and faculty in discussion-based classes and hands-on labs. CC encourages a well-rounded education, combining the academic rigor of an honors college with rich programs in athletics, community service, student government, the arts, and more. The college encourages students to push themselves academically, and many continue their studies at the best graduate and professional schools in the nation. CC is a great choice for field study and for international study (CC ranks fourth nationally in the number of students studying abroad). CC also takes advantage of its location, using its Baca campus in the San Luis Valley and the mountain cabin for a variety of classes. Its location at the base of the Rockies makes CC a great choice for students who enjoy backpacking, hiking, climbing, and skiing.

"Colorado College requires students to submit either the SAT or ACT. Scores are accepted for both with or without Writing component. CC uses the highest sub score on the SAT and the highest ACT composite. SAT Subject Tests are accepted for review, but are not required."

SELECTIVITY

Admissions Rating	96
# of applicants	4,386
% of applicants accepted	34
% of acceptees attending	33
# accepting a place on wait list	215
% admitted from wait list	43
# of early decision applicants	322
% accepted early decision	39

FRESHMAN PROFILE

Range SAT Critical Reading	620–700
Range SAT Math	620–700
Range SAT Writing	610–690
Range ACT Composite	27–30
Minimum Paper TOEFL	550
Minimum Computer Based TOEFL	213
% graduated top 10% of class	66
% graduated top 25% of class	92
% graduated top 50% of class	98

DEADLINES

Early decision application deadline	11/15
Early decision notification	12/20
Regular application deadline	1/15
Regular notification	4/1
Nonfall registration?	yes

APPLICANTS ALSO LOOK AT

AND OFTEN PREFER
Carleton College, Dartmouth College, Middlebury College, Pomona College, Stanford University

AND SOMETIMES PREFER
Colby College, Grinnell College, Macalester College

AND RARELY PREFER
Bates College, Kenyon College, Lewis & Clark College, University of Colorado—Boulder

FINANCIAL FACTS

Financial Aid Rating	88
Annual tuition	$32,124
Room & Board	$8,052
Books and supplies	$904
% frosh rec. need-based scholarship or grant aid	33
% UG rec. need-based scholarship or grant aid	38
% frosh rec. need-based self-help aid	30
% UG rec. need-based self-help aid	35

COLORADO STATE UNIVERSITY

SPRUCE HALL, FORT COLLINS, CO 80523 • ADMISSIONS: 970-491-6909 • FAX: 970-491-7799

CAMPUS LIFE

Quality of Life Rating	**84**
Fire Safety Rating	**66**
Type of school	public
Environment	city

STUDENTS

Total undergrad enrollment	20,385
% male/female	48/52
% from out of state	18
% live on campus	25
% in (# of) fraternities	5 (19)
% in (# of) sororities	5 (14)
% African American	2
% Asian	3
% Caucasian	82
% Hispanic	6
% Native American	2
% international	1
# of countries represented	86

SURVEY SAYS . . .

Great computer facilities
Great library
Athletic facilities are great
Students love Fort Collins, CO
Great off-campus food
Campus feels safe
Student publications are popular
Lots of beer drinking

ACADEMICS

Academic Rating	**70**
Calendar	semester
Student/faculty ratio	18:1
Profs interesting rating	76
Profs accessible rating	73
% profs teaching UG courses	100
% classes taught by TAs	9
Most common lab size	20–29 students
Most common reg class size	20–29 students

MOST POPULAR MAJORS

construction management
engineering
psychology
health and exercise science
biological science

STUDENTS SAY

Academics

With a variety of majors and strong science programs available to them, students at Colorado State University find a lot to get excited about: "I want to go to every single one of my classes, and I love looking at all the other ones I get to take later," says one junior. Regardless of the large size of the student body, students get a lot of individual attention. Professors are "very approachable and willing to help you anytime, and they love knowing the students in their classes by name." For those who are looking for an even more personalized experience, the honors program is a great option; participants claim that "it's a huge benefit to you for only a bit more effort" because "The classes are small," "The professors are approachable," and best of all, "Honors students register first." This last benefit is particularly important, since "A lot of interesting classes described in the General Catalog are rarely offered." While students enjoy classes as a whole, claiming that they "just keep getting better" as the years go on, many are discontent the larger size of the introductory classes: One undergrad was "shocked by how many TAs teach undergraduate classes."

Life

Let's just say that CSU students didn't come to Colorado to spend their days indoors. "The amount of outdoor activities is insane, and there is always something to do outside," one senior writes; local al fresco distractions include "biking, hiking, Horsetooth Reservoir, Poudre Canyon, camping, and skiing/snowboarding." "It's not unusual for students to skip class to head to the ski slopes (naturally!)," says one snow bunny. Indoor activities include "quite a bit of drinking and the typical party scene," but "The majority of students drink responsibly," and "Everyone seems to do a fairly good job of balancing school and work and other activities." Students speak highly of hometown Fort Collins, claiming that "the community feeling in the town is really great." One sophomore writes, "Town is an incredibly popular hangout for students on evenings and weekends, with its wide array of stores, restaurants, and bars." With "multiple extracurricular activities" on campus available to them, including "a lot of religious groups," CSU is "definitely not a 'suitcase campus.' People stay through the weekend because there are things to do on and off campus."

Student Body

CSU Rams are a generally harmonious bunch, typically composed of students who are "White, middle-class," "athletic," and "typically Coloradoan." "People here are pretty laid-back," says one student. "Atypical students are few and far between, but they find their own niche," probably because "A large student body provides a large pool of social groups or cliques to fit into." The 25,000-strong student body can prove a bit daunting for some freshmen, who could "feel overwhelmed with the size and amount of people." Students claim that diversity is "lacking in some areas," but the campus still appears to have "a student body that is representative of the population of Colorado," and "The minorities we do have on campus seem to fit in just fine." As one senior puts it, "It's hard not to make friends at CSU."

COLORADO STATE UNIVERSITY

FINANCIAL AID: 970-491-6321 • E-MAIL: ADMISSIONS@COLOSTATE.EDU • WEBSITE: WWW.COLOSTATE.EDU

ADMISSIONS

Very important factors considered include: Academic GPA, application essay, class rank, recommendation(s), rigor of secondary school record, standardized test scores. *Other factors considered include:* Character/personal qualities, extracurricular activities, first generation, geographical residence, level of applicant's interest, racial/ethnic status, state residency, talent/ability, volunteer work, work experience. SAT or ACT required; TOEFL required of all international applicants. High school diploma is required, and GED is accepted. *Academic units required:* 4 English, 3 math (Algebra I and higher), 3 science (1 science lab), 3 social studies, 2 academic electives. Engineering majors and individual colleges have additional requirements. *Academic units recommended:* 4 English, 4 math, 3 science (1 science lab), 2 foreign language, 3 social studies, 2 academic electives.

The Inside Word

Following the lead of other public schools, Colorado State uses GPA and standardized test scores as its chief admissions criteria. That said, the Admissions Team is interested in promoting and maintaining a campus of diverse student interests and backgrounds. Applicants interested in more competitive majors such as landscape architecture and engineering will face stricter requirements.

FINANCIAL AID

Students should submit: FAFSA. The Princeton Review suggests that all financial aid forms be submitted as soon as possible after January 1. *Need-based scholarships/grants offered:* Pell Grant, SEOG, state scholarships/grants, private scholarships, the school's own gift aid. *Loan aid offered:* Direct Subsidized Stafford, Direct Unsubsidized Stafford, Direct PLUS, Federal Perkins Loan, college/university loans from institutional funds, alternative loans. Applicants will be notified of awards on a rolling basis beginning or about March 1. Federal Work-Study Program available. Institutional employment available. Off-campus job opportunities are excellent.

FROM THE ADMISSIONS OFFICE

"Colorado State University is recognized throughout the world for its excellence in academic programs from the baccalaureate to the postgraduate level. A student-centered research university, Colorado State offers more than 150 undergraduate programs of study within the university's eight colleges. More students come to Colorado State to earn their degrees in science, math, engineering, and technology than to any other school in Colorado. The university emphasizes active learning and provides a variety of opportunities for field experience, laboratory research, professional internships, and study abroad. Students come to Colorado State from all over the United States and 86 countries. The student/faculty ratio is 18:1; 99 percent of regular tenure-track faculty hold doctorate, first professional, or other terminal degrees. A warm and welcoming place, the university values and promotes diversity and understands the importance of community in creating an excellent undergraduate learning experience.

"Freshman applicants for Fall 2008 can submit ACT or SAT results. Admission and scholarship consideration is based upon the highest composite/combined score from any one test date. The ACT/SAT Writing sections and SAT Subject Tests will not be used as part of the admission decision for Fall 2008."

SELECTIVITY

Admissions Rating	78
# of applicants	11,310
% of applicants accepted	86
% of acceptees attending	42

FRESHMAN PROFILE

Range SAT Critical Reading	500–600
Range SAT Math	500–620
Range ACT Composite	22–26
Minimum Paper TOEFL	525
Minimum Computer Based TOEFL	197
Average HS GPA	3.5
% graduated top 10% of class	19
% graduated top 25% of class	48
% graduated top 50% of class	86

DEADLINES

Priority application deadline	7/1
Regular notification	rolling
Nonfall registration?	yes

APPLICANTS ALSO LOOK AT AND OFTEN PREFER

Arizona State University at the Tempe Campus, Colorado College, Colorado School of Mines, Cornell University, University of Colorado—Boulder, University of Denver

FINANCIAL FACTS

Financial Aid Rating	80
Annual in-state tuition	$3,466
Annual out-of-state tuition	$14,994
Room & Board	$6,602
Books and supplies	$900
Required fees	$1,251
% frosh rec. need-based scholarship or grant aid	27
% UG rec. need-based scholarship or grant aid	26
% frosh rec. need-based self-help aid	25
% UG rec. need-based self-help aid	32
% frosh rec. any financial aid	64
% UG rec. any financial aid	64

COLUMBIA UNIVERSITY

212 HAMILTON HALL MC 2807, 1130 AMSTERDAM AVENUE, NY, NY 10027 • ADMISSIONS: 212-854-2522 • FAX: 212-894-1209

CAMPUS LIFE
Quality of Life Rating	**93**
Fire Safety Rating	**60***
Type of school	private
Environment	metropolis

STUDENTS
Total undergrad enrollment	5,593
% male/female	54/46
% from out of state	69
% from public high school	49
% live on campus	94
% in (# of) fraternities	15 (17)
% in (# of) sororities	10 (11)
% African American	8
% Asian	18
% Caucasian	43
% Hispanic	9
% Native American	1
% international	8
# of countries represented	87

SURVEY SAYS . . .
Great library
Diverse student types on campus
Students love New York, NY
Great off-campus food
Campus feels safe
Students are happy
Student publications are popular
Political activism is popular

ACADEMICS
Academic Rating	**96**
Calendar	semester
Student/faculty ratio	7:1
Profs interesting rating	80
Profs accessible rating	75
% profs teaching	
UG courses	100
% classes taught by TAs	0
Most common	
reg class size	10–19 students

MOST POPULAR MAJORS
biomedical/medical engineering
economics
English language and literature

STUDENTS SAY

Academics

Located on the upper west side of Manhattan, "Columbia University provides an exceptional education, fusing the chaos of New York City" with "the rigors of the Ivy League." The course work here "can be tremendously grueling." Expect to do a lot of studying and "thinking about the world in ways that are new and occasionally uncomfortable." Columbia's "inspiring" professors are "leaders in their fields" who are "brilliant (and don't hide the fact that they, too, think so)." They are "obsessed with what they study" and their "Enthusiasm is contagious." A few professors "have that certain scholarly air of arrogance" and can be tough graders. However, "The professors who are known to grade harshly and give hard tests are usually the ones who teach the best." Central to the academic experience here is the "eye-opening, thought-provoking" core curriculum, a sequence that immerses students in Western philosophy, literature, and fine arts. "Columbia's core prepares you to excel in any field," explains one first-year student. Taking core classes also helps "when you're first trying to make new friends" because "Everyone is dealing with the same classes." Most students feel that the administration here "listens to students" and "generally gets the job done," but can be "bureaucratic" at times. Be warned, however, that "advising is definitely not the strong point of Columbia." It's easy to feel "alone in the big city" on occasion. The resources are there, of course, but "People here don't treat you like a baby."

Life

Students on this "beautiful" campus "in the middle of Manhattan" say that they "study really hard during the week and party really hard on weekends." There's always something to do in the "chic, cultured city of opportunity" that is their home. "It's New York City," boasts one student, "the greatest city in the universe," where "Everything is only a subway ride away." As another student explains, "There is no one activity that dominates the social scene. Instead, everything is at our disposal." Options range from "a trip to the Met [and] shopping on Fifth Avenue" to "movies, clubs, theater, ice skating, and restaurants." Students can go to "art museums, comedy clubs, [and] jazz clubs." The bar scene is also popular. As one student explains, "[Lots of students get] a fake ID the first semester of their freshman year to give them access to New York City's nightlife." Students who plan on experiencing all the "glitzy things you hear about in NYC" should "make sure [they] have money to shell out," advises one cost-conscious student. "Even student tickets can add up and dining out is expensive." Students on a budget can do "plenty of other things around town that don't cost more than the subway fare." While Columbia students are "hardly bound by the campus gates," the university offers "as much of a campus life," including "frat parties or dorm parties," "various activity groups," and a popular "annual musical theater production" that "everyone goes to see."

Student Body

"Columbia is a microcosm of New York," sums up one student. The people here are a "mix of everything." Columbia's "very well-rounded" students "are very passionate about their interests." As one student explains, "You can find conversations about everything from the relationship between gods and mortals in Virgil's *Aeneid* to the latest hipster music group." On campus, you'll find "a great mix of ethnicities" as well as ample diversity of "religions, socioeconomic backgrounds, national heritage, sexual orientations, political beliefs, and geographic roots." These "smart, motivated, independent, and intellectually curious" students describe themselves as "hardworking, continuously busy," and "not very religious." One student warns, however, that "many students are book smart but not very worldly" and can be "very full of" themselves. Politically, left-liberalism is "raging" on campus, though Columbia is "not as crazy liberal as it used to be."

FINANCIAL AID: 212-854-3711 • WEBSITE: WWW.STUDENTAFFAIRS.COLUMBIA.EDU/ADMISSIONS

ADMISSIONS

Very important factors considered include: Academic GPA, application essay, character/personal qualities, class rank, recommendation(s), rigor of secondary school record, standardized test scores. *Important factors considered include:* Extracurricular activities, talent/ability. *Other factors considered include:* Alumni/ae relation, geographical residence, interview, racial/ethnic status, volunteer work. SAT or ACT required; SAT and SAT Subject Tests or ACT required; ACT with Writing component required. TOEFL required of all international applicants. High school diploma is required, and GED is accepted. *Academic units recommended:* 4 English, 4 math, 4 science (4 science labs), 4 foreign language, 4 history, 4 academic electives.

The Inside Word

Earning an acceptance letter from Columbia is no easy feat. Applications to the university continue to rise and many great candidates are rejected each year. Admissions officers take a holistic approach to evaluating applications; there's no magic formula or pattern to guide students seeking admission. One common denominator among applicants is stellar grades in rigorous classes and personal accomplishments in non-academic activities. Admissions Officers are looking to build a diverse class that will greatly contribute to the university.

FINANCIAL AID

Students should submit: FAFSA, institution's own financial aid form, CSS/Financial Aid PROFILE, Noncustodial PROFILE, Business/Farm Supplement, parent and student Federal Income Tax Returns. Regular filing deadline is February 10. The Princeton Review suggests that all financial aid forms be submitted as soon as possible after January 1. *Need-based scholarships/grants offered:* Pell Grant, SEOG, state scholarships/grants, private scholarships, the school's own gift aid. *Loan aid offered:* FFEL Subsidized Stafford, FFEL Unsubsidized Stafford, FFEL PLUS, Federal Perkins Loan, alternative loans. Applicants will be notified of awards on or about April 1. Federal Work-Study Program available. Institutional employment available. Off-campus job opportunities are excellent.

FROM THE ADMISSIONS OFFICE

"Columbia maintains an intimate college campus within one of the world's most vibrant cities. After a long day exploring the bustling streets of the Big Apple, you will come home to a traditional college campus within the Columbia gates. Nobel Prize–winning professors will challenge you in class discussions and sit down for a one-on-one afterward. The core curriculum attracts intensely free-minded scholars, eager to explore ideas. Science and engineering students pursue cutting-edge research in world-class laboratories with faculty members at the forefront of scientific discovery in every discipline. Classroom discussions are only the beginning of your education. Like the music that wafts from our concert halls, ideas spill out from the classrooms, electrifying the campus and Morningside Heights. Friendships you will form in the residence halls solidify during a game of Frisbee on the South Lawn or over bagels on the steps of Low Library, Columbia's urban beach. From your first day on campus, you will be part of our community.

"First-year applicants for Fall 2008 must take the SAT or the ACT with Writing. Two SAT Subject Tests are required; applicants to Columbia College may submit any Subject Test, while applicants to Columbia Engineering must submit one in math and one in either physics or chemistry."

SELECTIVITY

Admissions Rating	**99**
# of applicants	19,851
% of applicants accepted	12
% of acceptees attending	58
# accepting a place on wait list	1,254
% admitted from wait list	2
# of early decision applicants	2,236
% accepted early decision	26

FRESHMAN PROFILE

Range SAT Critical Reading	670–760
Range SAT Math	680–780
Range SAT Writing	660–760
Range ACT Composite	28–33
Minimum Paper TOEFL	600
Minimum Computer Based TOEFL	250

DEADLINES

Early decision application deadline	11/1
Early decision notification	12/15
Regular application deadline	1/2
Regular notification	4/1
Nonfall registration?	no

APPLICANTS ALSO LOOK AT

AND OFTEN PREFER
Harvard College, Massachusetts Institute of Technology, Stanford University, Yale University

AND SOMETIMES PREFER
Princeton University, University of Pennsylvania

AND RARELY PREFER
Brown University, Cornell University, Dartmouth College, New York University

FINANCIAL FACTS

Financial Aid Rating	**95**
Annual tuition	$33,664
Room & board	$8,640
% frosh rec. need-based scholarship or grant aid	48
% UG rec. need-based scholarship or grant aid	46
% frosh rec. need-based self-help aid	44
% UG rec. need-based self-help aid	44
% frosh rec. any financial aid	61
% UG rec. any financial aid	56

CONNECTICUT COLLEGE

270 MOHEGAN AVENUE, NEW LONDON, CT 06320 • ADMISSIONS: 860-439-2200 • FAX: 860-439-4301

CAMPUS LIFE

Quality of Life Rating	**81**
Fire Safety Rating	**60***
Type of school	private
Environment	town

STUDENTS

Total undergrad enrollment	1,773
% male/female	40/60
% from out of state	83
% from public high school	55
% live on campus	99
% African American	4
% Asian	4
% Caucasian	73
% Hispanic	5
% international	6
# of countries represented	41

SURVEY SAYS . . .

Small classes
Career services are great
Frats and sororities are unpopular or nonexistent
Lots of beer drinking

ACADEMICS

Academic Rating	**93**
Calendar	semester
Student/faculty ratio	10:1
Profs interesting rating	87
Profs accessible rating	92
% profs teaching UG courses	100
% classes taught by TAs	0
Most common lab size	10–19 students
Most common reg class size	10–19 students

MOST POPULAR MAJORS

English language and literature
political science and government
psychology

STUDENTS SAY

Academics

A "small liberal arts school with excellent academic standards" and an "interdisciplinary focus," Connecticut College provides its students with "a wide range of academic programs." The "enthusiastic," "approachable and involved" professors here are "great teachers" who regularly "meet with students outside of class to address any concerns." One student gushes, "I can honestly tell you that my professors have been some of the most inspiring, thought-provoking people I've ever met." Perhaps most important, "There are no teaching assistants, ever." The administration "can get a little exasperating," but most of the top brass is "readily available" and dedicated to "making the college run smoothly." Top programs include dance, chemistry, biological sciences, psychology, and international studies. Over half of all students study abroad during their 4 years here. The Career Center and internship programs receive solid praise as well: "A paid internship during the summer" after junior year is yours for the taking "if you complete all career services workshops," says one student. The "student-adjudicated" honor code "is also huge." "We wrote it; we enforce it," explains one student. "It applies to noise in the dorms, cheating on tests, self-scheduled exams, and tolerance of sexual orientations."

Life

Connecticut College's attractive and "very social" campus is its own little "close-knit" universe, complete with "a wide range of activities" and "a beautiful view of Long Island Sound and the ocean." Without question, students here "have a lot of fun." "Keg parties" are abundant, and "Small room parties are also popular." Dances "are quite popular" as well. "Thursday and Saturday nights are the big going-out nights," and there are "live bands every Friday." "If you aren't a party person, you can feel like an outsider," observes a first-year student. "But at the same time, academics are extremely important" to Connecticut College students. Because the school doesn't have Greek organizations, "It's important to make friends and be involved" in students organizations like "activism groups" and intramural and intercollegiate sports. Students tell us that athletics could use "more money," though, and "The fitness center and dorms need to be updated." As far as off-campus life goes, the surrounding town of New London is not particularly accessible. "It's hard or at least inconvenient to get off campus if you don't have a car," advises one student. If you do have a car—or if you take the train—"You can go to Boston or Providence or New York City for the weekend."

Student Body

Students here describe themselves as "open-minded, active, optimistic," and "not overly competitive." There is "a wide range of personalities" and "a good mix of hippies, jocks, book nerds, gamers, and conservatives." A notable international student population exists as well. "Conn says that it has a very diverse campus, but that's only if you've lived in a small New England town your whole life," asserts a jaded first-year student. "There is some diversity and the diversity that exists is fully embraced, but there isn't a huge variety of backgrounds." "A 'typical' student at Conn is involved in three to four extracurricular activities," including an intercollegiate athletic team. The typical student might also be "very rich," "preppy," and "from New England." Such students "look like they walked off the pages of a J. Crew catalog," comments one undergrad. Students are quick to emphasize, however, that stereotypes are often inaccurate: "We are not all trust-fund babies," a sophomore explains. "More students are on financial aid than it may seem." "There is a lot of wealth on this campus," another student asserts, "but one thing I like about this college is that people don't show their wealth off and everyone is able to get along with each other." "Atypical students" do "tend to stick together," though.

FINANCIAL AID: 860-439-2200 • E-MAIL: ADMISSION@CONNCOLL.EDU • WEBSITE: WWW.CONNCOLL.EDU

ADMISSIONS

TOEFL required of all international applicants. High school diploma is required, and GED is accepted. *Academic units recommended:* 4 English, 4 math, 4 science (3 science labs), 2 foreign language, 2 social studies, 3 history, 3 academic electives.

The Inside Word

Connecticut College is the archetypal selective New England college, and Admissions Officers are judicious in their decisions. Competitive applicants will have pursued a demanding course load in high school. Admissions Officers look for students who are curious and who thrive in challenging academic environments. Since Connecticut College has a close-knit community, personal qualities are also closely evaluated, and interviews are important.

FINANCIAL AID

Students should submit: FAFSA, CSS/Financial Aid PROFILE, Noncustodial PROFILE, Business/Farm Supplement, Federal Income Tax Returns; personal, partnership, W-2 statements. Regular filing deadline is February 1. The Princeton Review suggests that all financial aid forms be submitted as soon as possible after January 1. *Need-based scholarships/grants offered:* Pell Grant, SEOG, state scholarships/grants, the school's own gift aid. *Loan aid offered:* FFEL Subsidized Stafford, FFEL Unsubsidized Stafford, FFEL PLUS, Federal Perkins Loan, college/university loans from institutional funds. Federal Work-Study Program available. Institutional employment available. Off-campus job opportunities are good.

FROM THE ADMISSIONS OFFICE

"Distinguishing characteristics of the diverse student body at this small, highly selective college are honor and tolerance. Student leadership is pronounced in all aspects of the college's administration from exclusive jurisdiction of the honor code and dorm life to active representation on the president's academic and administrative cabinets. Differences of opinion are respected and celebrated as legitimate avenues to new understanding. Students come to Connecticut College seeking opportunities for independence and initiative and find them in abundance.

"Applicants must submit the results of either two SAT Subject Tests or the ACT. For candidates who choose to submit an ACT score, we will accept either the old or the new version, with or without the optional Writing component. Submission of SAT scores in addition to the required testing is optional."

SELECTIVITY

Admissions Rating	**95**
# of applicants	4,278
% of applicants accepted	38
% of acceptees attending	30
# accepting a place on wait list	379
% admitted from wait list	11
# of early decision applicants	333
% accepted early decision	61

FRESHMAN PROFILE

Range SAT Critical Reading	620–720
Range SAT Math	610–700
Range SAT Writing	615–710
Range ACT Composite	25–29
Minimum Paper TOEFL	600
Minimum Computer Based TOEFL	250
% graduated top 10% of class	52
% graduated top 25% of class	93
% graduated top 50% of class	100

DEADLINES

Early decision application deadline	11/15
Early decision notification	12/15
Regular application deadline	1/1
Regular notification	3/31
Nonfall registration?	yes

APPLICANTS ALSO LOOK AT

AND OFTEN PREFER
Bowdoin College, Brown University, Colby College, Middlebury College, Tufts University, Vassar College, Wesleyan University

AND SOMETIMES PREFER
Hamilton College, Trinity College (CT)

AND RARELY PREFER
Skidmore College

FINANCIAL FACTS

Financial Aid Rating	**94**
Comprehensive fee	$48,575
Books and supplies	$1,000
% frosh rec. need-based scholarship or grant aid	35
% UG rec. need-based scholarship or grant aid	39
% frosh rec. need-based self-help aid	34
% UG rec. need-based self-help aid	38
% frosh rec. any financial aid	41

THE COOPER UNION FOR THE ADVANCEMENT OF SCIENCE AND ART

30 COOPER SQUARE, NEW YORK, NY 10003 • ADMISSIONS: 212-353-4120 • FAX: 212-353-4342

STUDENTS SAY

Academics

You'll get a "free education" at Cooper Union—everyone receives a full-tuition scholarship for all 4 years—"but you have to pay it off with hard labor in the classroom." Cooper's "intense, engaging programs in engineering, art, and architecture" are the only options on the menu here; "while this seems narrow," explains one freshman, it "allows for more focus on those fields. As long as you're interested in one of the majors . . . you will receive one of the best educations in the country." The professors overall earn kudos for being "intelligent, accessible, [and] excellent," but a number of students complain that there are "too many adjunct professors," who are "underpaid" and teach "straight from the textbook." All professors expect a lot from students—"They can be quite sadistic toward the end of the semester, heaping more work on you than you could possibly handle," warns one electrical engineer—but "You never feel as if any of your effort is in vain." A number of students gripe about getting "mediocre grades" in exchange for "sweat" and "your immortal soul"—but just as many also point out that "you will leave knowing everything in your field about as well as it is possible to know it" and boast that Cooper students benefit from virtually "guaranteed job placement" after graduation. With "lots of work and little time," students learn to share the load: "We all work together to get projects done and to study for exams," explains one student. "I have spent the night before most of my major upper-level exams studying with about half, or more, of my classmates." The "physical registration" process has been described as nightmarish in the past and has students begging for an online alternative. However, the registration process has recently been reformed to allow students an assigned block of time to register, eliminating the long lines "the night before on Third Avenue to get the right classes." That said, time after time we read that Cooper's greatest incentive "is that it's free." In that regard, "Cooper's strength is also its drawback."

Life

"The overall school experience is pretty much academic" at Cooper Union, as "There is not much time to have any fun." That said, "The experience is about who surrounds you in your classes," notes a senior. When students can make free time, they usually like to get away from Cooper. As one puts it, "I associate school with hard work." "The school consists of five buildings in the middle of the East Village," and the surrounding neighborhood is famous for its funky shops, cheap eateries, theaters, bars, and live music venues; conveniently located subways can whisk students just about anywhere in the five boroughs at any time of day. On campus, "The school organizes several events that may seem kind of ridiculous but often prove to be lots of fun, such as ice cream and karaoke night, study break (a lunch party during finals), and Peter Cooper's birthday celebration." Whether on or off campus, "there is always something happening at school where people can eat and interact."

Student Body

"Everyone at Cooper fits into one of three distinct groups: engineers, artists, or architects," undergrads here tell us. "We are very divided by major. For the most part, no one is left out of their respective group, but the groups don't mix well." One student observes, "The engineering students tend to be the most strange and have all done very well in their high school careers and have very noticeable and unique talents. Art students tend to follow unique trends and are more creative and reclusive. Architecture students can be considered the link between engineering and art students." The average Cooper student is "a tad quirky with a nerdy sense of humor." "You'll find no cheerleader, jock, or regular, whimsical university students. Cooper students tend to all be extremely intelligent, ambitious, and studious individuals"—with an emphasis on individual.

THE COOPER UNION FOR THE ADVANCEMENT OF SCIENCE AND ART

FINANCIAL AID: 212-353-4130 • E-MAIL: ADMISSIONS@COOPER.EDU • WEBSITE: WWW.COOPER.EDU

ADMISSIONS

Very important factors considered include: Academic GPA, rigor of secondary school record, standardized test scores, talent/ability. *Important factors considered include:* Application essay, character/personal qualities, extracurricular activities, level of applicant's interest. *Other factors considered include:* Class rank, first generation, interview, racial/ethnic status, recommendation(s), volunteer work, work experience. SAT or ACT required; ACT with Writing component recommended. TOEFL required of all international applicants. High school diploma is required, and GED is accepted. *Academic units required:* 4 English, 1 math, 1 science, 1 social studies, 1 history, 8 academic electives. *Academic units recommended:* 4 English, 4 math, 4 science (3 science labs), 2 foreign language, 4 social studies.

The Inside Word

It is ultra-tough to gain admission to Cooper Union, and it will only get tougher. Loads of people apply here, and national publicity and the addition of dorms have brought even more candidates to the pool. Not only do students need to have top academic accomplishments, but also they need to be a good fit for Cooper's offbeat milieu.

FINANCIAL AID

Students should submit: FAFSA, CSS/Financial Aid PROFILE. Regular filing deadline is June 1. The Princeton Review suggests that all financial aid forms be submitted as soon as possible after January 1. *Need-based scholarships/grants offered:* Pell Grant, SEOG, state scholarships/grants, private scholarships, the school's own gift aid. *Loan aid offered:* FFEL Subsidized Stafford, FFEL Unsubsidized Stafford, FFEL PLUS, Federal Perkins Loan, college/university loans from institutional funds. Applicants will be notified of awards on or about June 1. Federal Work-Study Program available. Institutional employment available. Off-campus job opportunities are excellent.

FROM THE ADMISSIONS OFFICE

"Each of Cooper Union's three schools, architecture, art, and engineering, adheres strongly to preparation for its profession and is committed to a problem-solving philosophy of education in a unique, scholarly environment. A rigorous curriculum and group projects reinforce this unique atmosphere in higher education and contribute to a strong sense of community and identity in each school. With McSorley's Ale House and the Joseph Papp Public Theatre nearby, Cooper Union remains at the heart of the city's tradition of free speech, enlightenment, and entertainment. Cooper's Great Hall has hosted national leaders, from Abraham Lincoln to Booker T. Washington, from Mark Twain to Samuel Gompers, from Susan B. Anthony to Betty Friedan, and more recently, President Bill Clinton.

"In addition, we eagerly await the arrival of our new academic building slated to open in 2009. Designed by Pritzker Prize–winning architect, Thom Mayne, the new building is expected to enhance and encourage more interaction between students in all three schools.

"We're seeking students who have a passion to study our professional programs. Cooper Union students are independent thinkers, following the beat of their own drum. Many of our graduates become world-class leaders in the disciplines of architecture, fine arts, design, and engineering.

"For art and architecture applicants, SAT scores are considered after the home test and portfolio work. For engineering applicants, other than high school grades, the SAT and SAT Subject Test scores are the most important factors considered in admissions decisions. Currently, we do not use the Writing section of the SAT to assist in making admissions decisions. We expect to reconsider that policy as more data is available in the near future."

SELECTIVITY

Admissions Rating	**99**
# of applicants	2,600
% of applicants accepted	10
% of acceptees attending	78
# accepting a place on wait list	54
% admitted from wait list	11
# of early decision applicants	445
% accepted early decision	16

FRESHMAN PROFILE

Range SAT Critical Reading	600–700
Range SAT Math	640–770
Range ACT Composite	29–33
Minimum Paper TOEFL	600
Minimum Computer Based TOEFL	250
Average HS GPA	3.6
% graduated top 10% of class	90
% graduated top 25% of class	98
% graduated top 50% of class	99

DEADLINES

Early decision application deadline	12/1
Early decision notification	12/23
Regular application deadline	1/1
Regular notification	4/1
Nonfall registration?	no

APPLICANTS ALSO LOOK AT
AND OFTEN PREFER
Columbia University, Cornell University, Massachusetts Institute of Technology, University of Pennsylvania

AND SOMETIMES PREFER
Carnegie Mellon University, Franklin W. Olin College of Engineering, Georgia Institute of Technology, Harvey Mudd College

AND RARELY PREFER
Rochester Institute of Technology

FINANCIAL FACTS

Financial Aid Rating	**92**
Annual tuition	$0*
Room & Board	$13,360
Books and supplies	$1,800
Required fees	$1,500
% frosh rec. need-based scholarship or grant aid	34
% UG rec. need-based scholarship or grant aid	31
% frosh rec. need-based self-help aid	29
% UG rec. need-based self-help aid	21
% frosh rec. any financial aid	100
% UG rec. any financial aid	100

*Tuition covered by full scholarship.

CORNELL COLLEGE

600 FIRST STREET WEST, MOUNT VERNON, IA 52314-1098 • ADMISSIONS: 319-895-4477 • FAX: 319-895-4451

STUDENTS SAY

Academics

Cornell College employs a unique block plan academic calendar called One-Course-at-a-Time (OCAAT), under which "You take one class, and only one class, for 18 days." Students love it, telling us that "if you're in a class you don't like, you only have to tough it out for 18 days. If you're in a class you really enjoy, you can devote all your time and energy to that one class for 18 days." OCAAT also makes it easy "to develop personal relationships with your professors, because there are no more than 25 students in a class, and the professor of that class will only be teaching those 25 students during the 18 days of the course." and the intensive focus on a single subject provides for the close interaction with professors who "are more than willing to work individually with students on assignments and to answer questions. It is very obvious that all of the teachers care a lot about their students and genuinely want them to do well in their class. Therefore, they make themselves as available as possible." One student reports, "The professors make this school what it is. They come to teach, not to do research, although most of them are involved in exciting projects in which they often include students. Most don't hold scheduled office hours because they're there all the time, and they're always there for the students, whether it be to talk about last night's game or the upcoming test." Because Cornell "has been around so long, the college has good relations with the community, which means it's easy to find employment for after school or during the summer."

Life

Much of the fun on and around the Cornell campus is of the low-key variety, students tell us. Cornell's hometown of Mt. Vernon sets the pace; it's "an adorable little town, but without a lot of things to do for college students." There are a few choice destinations in town; one student writes, "The Lincoln Cafe is very popular, so it's sometimes hard to get a seat, but it's very good gourmet food. There is a place to grab an organic sandwich and coffee called Big Creek Market. They sell soups and sandwiches as well as organic groceries. There's also a nice little jewelry shop." On campus, "There are various different activities like sponsored movies, performances, and sledding." There are also "many organizations to support student interests." When students seek higher-energy entertainment, they get in their cars and travel to Iowa City or Cedar Rapids. One student reports, "Iowa City is great for bars and food. The best sushi I've had is in Iowa City. There are also places like Riverside Theatre and movie theaters, too. There's a huge mall there for shopping and indoor ice skating. Cedar Rapids is good 'cause it's pretty close, and you can always find a decent place to eat." Iowa City is home to the University of Iowa; Cedar Rapids is home to Coe College and Mount Mercy College.

Student Body

"Everybody here at Cornell is very friendly," students report. "Just walking to or from class people will say 'hi' to you or smile at you. Everyone is more than willing to help you out or point you in the right direction." The typical undergrad "is middle-class, White," and from the Midwest; the school is not very diverse." Some here disagree with this conclusion, asserting that "Cornell is diverse, just not culturally. We do have diverse groups, like the jocks, the preps, the frat boys, the sorority girls, the science nerds, and the boarders, and all different types of groups that seem to easily join together, especially in the classroom environment."

FINANCIAL AID: 319-895-4216 • E-MAIL: ADMISSIONS@CORNELLCOLLEGE.EDU • WEBSITE: WWW.CORNELLCOLLEGE.EDU

ADMISSIONS

Very important factors considered include: Academic GPA, application essay, recommendation(s), rigor of secondary school record. *Important factors considered include:* Character/personal qualities, class rank, extracurricular activities, first generation, level of applicant's interest, standardized test scores, talent/ability, volunteer work, work experience. *Other factors considered include:* Alumni/ae relation, geographical residence, interview, racial/ethnic status, state residency. SAT or ACT required; TOEFL required of all international applicants. High school diploma is required, and GED is accepted. *Academic units recommended:* 4 English, 3 math, 3 science, 2 foreign language, 3 social studies.

The Inside Word

Given Cornell's relatively unique approach to study, it's no surprise that the Admissions Committee here focuses attention on both academic and personal strengths. Cornell's small, highly self-selected applicant pool is chock-full of students with solid self-awareness, motivation, and discipline. Pay particular attention to offering evidence of challenging academic course work and solid achievement on your high school record. Strong writers can do much for themselves under admissions circumstances such as these.

FINANCIAL AID

Students should submit: FAFSA, institution's own financial aid form, Noncustodial PROFILE. Regular filing deadline is March 1. The Princeton Review suggests that all financial aid forms be submitted as soon as possible after January 1. *Need-based scholarships/grants offered:* Pell Grant, SEOG, state scholarships/grants, private scholarships, the school's own gift aid, Academic Competitiveness Grant, and National SMART Grant. *Loan aid offered:* FFEL Subsidized Stafford, FFEL Unsubsidized Stafford, FFEL PLUS, Federal Perkins Loan, McElroy Loan, Sherman Loan, United Methodist Loan. Applicants will be notified of awards on a rolling basis beginning or about March 1.

FROM THE ADMISSIONS OFFICE

"Very few colleges are truly distinctive like Cornell College. Founded in 1853, Cornell is recognized as one of the nation's finest colleges of the liberal arts and sciences. It is Cornell's combination of special features, however, that distinguishes it. An attractively diverse, caring residential college, Cornell places special emphasis on service and leadership. Foremost, it is a place where theory and practice are brought together in exciting ways through the college's One-Course-at-a-Time academic calendar. Here, students enjoy learning as they immerse themselves in a single subject for a 3.5-week term. They and their professor devote all of their efforts to that course in an engagingly interactive learning environment. This academic system also offers wonderful enrichment experiences through field-based-study, travel abroad, student research, and meaningful internship opportunities. Nine terms are offered each year; 32 course credits are required for graduation with each course equal to 4 credit hours. Since all classes are on a standard schedule, students are able to pursue their extracurricular interests, whether in the performing arts, athletics, or interest groups, with the same passion with which they pursue their course work. Typically, each year applicants from all 50 states and more than 40 countries apply for admission. Cornell graduates are in demand, with more than two-thirds eventually earning advanced degrees. The college's beautiful hilltop campus is one of only two campuses nationwide listed on the National Register of Historic Places. Located in the charming town of Mount Vernon, Cornell is also within commuting distance of Iowa City (home of the University of Iowa) and Cedar Rapids (the second largest city in the state).

"Freshman applicants for Fall 2008 are required to submit their SAT Reasoning or ACT results (the Writing component is optional for the ACT as students are required to submit an essay as part of the application for admission). In addition, for students submitting multiple score reports their best scores from either exam will be used in the application review process. SAT Subject tests are not required."

SELECTIVITY
Admissions Rating	**88**
# of applicants	1,718
% of applicants accepted	62
% of acceptees attending	23
# accepting a place on wait list	99
% admitted from wait list	30
# of early decision applicants	48
% accepted early decision	79

FRESHMAN PROFILE
Range SAT Critical Reading	560–670
Range SAT Math	540–670
Range SAT Writing	510–630
Range ACT Composite	24–29
Minimum Paper TOEFL	550
Minimum Computer Based TOEFL	213
Average HS GPA	3.51
% graduated top 10% of class	31
% graduated top 25% of class	58
% graduated top 50% of class	85

DEADLINES
Early decision application deadline	11/1
Early decision notification	1/15
Regular application deadline	3/1
Regular notification	4/1
Nonfall registration?	yes

APPLICANTS ALSO LOOK AT
AND OFTEN PREFER
Carleton College, Grinnell College, Macalester College
AND SOMETIMES PREFER
Beloit College, Colorado College, Knox College, Lawrence University
AND RARELY PREFER
Coe College, Lake Forest College, Ripon College

FINANCIAL FACTS
Financial Aid Rating	**89**
Annual tuition	$24,620
Room & Board	$6,660
Books and supplies	$720
Required fees	$180
% frosh rec. need-based scholarship or grant aid	73
% UG rec. need-based scholarship or grant aid	72
% frosh rec. need-based self-help aid	73
% UG rec. need-based self-help aid	72
% frosh rec. any financial aid	84
% UG rec. any financial aid	82

CORNELL UNIVERSITY

UNDERGRADUATE ADMISSIONS, 410 THURSTON AVENUE, ITHACA, NY 14850 • ADMISSIONS: 607-255-5241 • FAX: 607-255-0659

STUDENTS SAY

Academics

"A large, diverse university offering a huge variety of courses and majors," Cornell University seems intent on putting the "universe" in "university." Students tell us that "all the academic programs are strong, so no matter what you want to study, Cornell has the resources." But just in case Cornell's standout undergraduate departments in engineering, business, biology, industrial and labor relations, hotel administration, food science, animal science, and natural resources don't get you going, "You can [always] design your own major." Cornell offers "a mix of anything and everything, with more opportunities than you could ever want." Undergrads point out that "Cornell is a great place for people who know what they want to do in life and want to get things done sooner rather than later, because each major program is very focused and concentrated right from the beginning." Academics here "are hard, extremely tough." "We don't all have 4.0s, but we work harder than students at the other Ivy League schools. Cornell is the easiest Ivy to get into, and the hardest to graduate from. Grade inflation doesn't exist here." The school does its best to help students navigate the academic challenges, offering "enough help so that even the most lost student can find his/her way to a good, deserving grade." Professors "are available anytime you need them and are more than happy to lend you a helping hand," while both your "peer advisor and faculty advisor" are "easily accessible." The administration does a great job "running the school smoothly" and "makes the effort to keep lines of communication open." Students tell us that "undergraduates are offered unbelievable research opportunities and instruction from those who are at the top of their respective fields." And when it's time to find a job, "Cornell has a really good alumni network" and a "helpful Career Services" Office.

Life

Cornell is located in remote Ithaca, "on the top of a hill in the middle of a beautiful and cold nowhere." "Beautiful gorges" and "unrivaled" outdoor activities—"Everything from kayaking to pumpkin picking is just a small trip away either by foot or by bus." "There really isn't anything you can't do when it comes to nature at Cornell," but there is not much in the way of urban diversion. As a result, many "Students exist strictly within the Cornell bubble." They "have no escape from the stress of school and everything they do revolves around school." For many, weekend options consist of "bars in Collegetown and house parties," along with some on-campus "concerts, activities, and student-led initiatives." Lots of students "participate in intramural sports or one of the many clubs." One student observes, "Being in a small town like Ithaca means that most people do one thing for fun: drink. At the same time, some of the dorms—i.e. the ones with fewer drinkers—are still up on the weekends playing poker or GameCube or something like that. Nevertheless, the lack of a big city around you means that sometimes you can get pretty bored"—but then, there is always schoolwork to attend to.

Student Body

Cornell's student body "is diverse, and not just in the racial or ethnic sense. There are so many different courses of study at Cornell that a wide range of personalities and interests are represented. Every day, architects, engineers, hotel school students, and dairy farm majors sit down to lunch together." Furthermore, "Because Cornell is half private and half public, the students come from diverse economic backgrounds." Pressed to provide a general description of their peers, students tell us that "the student body is divided into about three groups: The well-off, stylish-if-conservatively dressed 'practical majors' (most frat members, premeds, pre-laws, sorority girls, hotelies, aggies); the study-a-holics (engineers, applied sciences, some of the premeds); and the Euro-acting, blazer-and-hoodie wearing, always-thin hipsters (English, comparative literature, philosophy, film, theater, etc.)."

FINANCIAL AID: 607-255-5145 • E-MAIL: ADMISSIONS@CORNELL.EDU • WEBSITE: WWW.CORNELL.EDU

ADMISSIONS

Very important factors considered include: Academic GPA, application essay, extracurricular activities, recommendation(s), rigor of secondary school record, standardized test scores, talent/ability. *Important factors considered include:* Class rank. *Other factors considered include:* Alumni/ae relation, character/personal qualities, first generation, geographical residence, interview, racial/ethnic status, state residency, volunteer work, work experience. SAT or ACT required; ACT with Writing component required. TOEFL required of all international applicants. High school diploma or equivalent is not required. *Academic units required:* 4 English, 3 math. *Academic units recommended:* 3 science (3 science labs), 3 foreign language, 3 social studies, 3 history.

The Inside Word

Gaining admission to Cornell is a tough coup regardless of your intended field of study, but some of the university's seven schools are more competitive than others. If you're thinking of trying to 'backdoor' your way into one of the most competitive schools—by gaining admission to one, then transferring after one year—be aware that you will have to resubmit the entire application and provide a statement outlining your academic plans. It's not impossible to accomplish, but Cornell works hard to discourage this sort of maneuvering.

FINANCIAL AID

Students should submit: FAFSA, institution's own financial aid form, CSS/Financial Aid PROFILE, Noncustodial PROFILE, Business/Farm Supplement, prior year Federal Income Tax Returns. Regular filing deadline is February 11. The Princeton Review suggests that all financial aid forms be submitted as soon as possible after January 1. *Need-based scholarships/grants offered:* Pell Grant, SEOG, state scholarships/grants, private scholarships, the school's own gift aid. *Loan aid offered:* Direct Subsidized Stafford, Direct Unsubsidized Stafford, Direct PLUS, FFEL Subsidized Stafford, FFEL Unsubsidized Stafford, FFEL PLUS, Federal Perkins Loan, college/university loans from institutional funds, Key Alternative Loan. Applicants will be notified of awards on or about April 1. Federal Work-Study Program available. Institutional employment available. Off-campus job opportunities are fair.

FROM THE ADMISSIONS OFFICE

"Cornell University, an Ivy League school and land-grant college located in the scenic Finger Lakes region of central New York, provides an outstanding education to students in seven small to midsize undergraduate colleges: Agriculture and Life Sciences; Architecture, Art, and Planning; Arts and Sciences; Engineering; Hotel Administration; Human Ecology; and Industrial and Labor Relations. Cornellians come from all 50 states and more than 100 countries, and they pursue their academic goals in more than 100 departments. The College of Arts and Sciences, one of the smallest liberal arts schools in the Ivy League, offers more than 40 majors, most of which rank near the top nationwide. Applied programs in the other six colleges also rank among the best in the world.

"Other special features of the university include a world-renowned faculty; 4,000 courses available to all students; an extensive undergraduate research program; superb research, teaching, and library facilities; a large, diverse study abroad program; and more than 700 student organizations and 36 varsity sports. Cornell's campus is one of the most beautiful in the country; students pass streams, rocky gorges, and waterfalls on their way to class. First-year students make their home on North Campus, a living-learning community that features a special advising center, faculty-in-residence, a fitness center, and traditional residence halls as well as theme-centered buildings such as Ecology House. Cornell University invites applications from all interested students and uses the Common Application exclusively with a short required Cornell Supplement.

"Students applying for admissions will submit scores from the SAT or ACT (with writing). We also require SAT Subject Tests. Subject test requirements are college-specific."

SELECTIVITY

Admissions Rating	**98**
# of applicants	28,098
% of applicants accepted	25
% of acceptees attending	47
# accepting a place on wait list	1,746
% admitted from wait list	1
# of early decision applicants	2,848
% accepted early decision	39

FRESHMAN PROFILE

Range SAT Critical Reading	620–730
Range SAT Math	660–760
Range ACT Composite	28–32
Minimum Paper TOEFL	550
Minimum Computer Based TOEFL	250
% graduated top 10% of class	84
% graduated top 25% of class	97
% graduated top 50% of class	100

DEADLINES

Early decision application deadline	11/1
Early decision notification	12/15
Regular application deadline	1/1
Regular notification	4/1
Nonfall registration?	no

FINANCIAL FACTS

Financial Aid Rating	**95**
Annual tuition	$32,800
Room & Board	$10,776
Books and supplies	$700
Required fees	$181
% frosh rec. need-based scholarship or grant aid	46
% UG rec. need-based scholarship or grant aid	44
% frosh rec. need-based self-help aid	43
% UG rec. need-based self-help aid	44
% frosh rec. any financial aid	49
% UG rec. any financial aid	47

CREIGHTON UNIVERSITY

2500 CALIFORNIA PLAZA, OMAHA, NE 68178 • ADMISSIONS: 402-280-2703 • FAX: 402-280-2685

STUDENTS SAY
Academics

Creighton University, a midsized Jesuit-led school with big-school resources, "is one of the premier premed factories of the Midwest," boasting "an outstanding science faculty that gears students up for the long road to and through medical school." With three undergraduate colleges and more than 50 available majors, Creighton offers a lot more than just great biology labs and killer organic chemistry classes; the school also excels in business, pre-law studies, nursing, and psychology. A core curriculum "allows students to take classes such as philosophy, religion, and foreign language" and ensures that "writing is a big part of the curriculum." Some here love the core, while others complain that it is "too time consuming and leaves little time for students to pursue electives outside their major." About 45 Jesuits teach classes or work with students in various areas of the university; "They live on campus and are solely interested in the students' understanding of the material as well as their overall progress." Classes are small, "allowing for a lot of one-on-one attention," and "with five (professional and) graduate schools attached—all of them giving preference to Creighton undergraduates—the opportunities for undergraduate research are wonderful." Students' wish lists include an engineering program (there is none) and increased support for students in the arts.

Life

"A lot of people think, 'Oh, CU is all academics, no fun,' but that's far from the truth," writes one student. "If you're into the party scene, you can almost always find one on the weekends, and there are bars within long walking distance to campus in the Old Market. However, if you're into the quieter weekends, there are plenty of people like that as well. The residence halls and other organizations on campus have events all the time for students to participate in if the party scene is not you. And every weekend, there's groups of friends who just hang out and watch movies all night." Creighton's intercollegiate teams provide a popular rallying point for the student body; undergrads "are huge supporters of our teams and going to the games is a huge part of social life here." One student observes, "We have awesome basketball and soccer teams, which is good because Omaha certainly isn't going to provide athletic team entertainment." What Omaha can provide—besides a good steak—is "a city that is surprisingly cultural and has a great musical and theatrical scene. Many students go to concerts on almost a weekly basis." Omaha also has "tons of fun things to do during the week and weekend. There are lots of restaurants and parks, bike trails, and camping, if you're the outdoors type," and if you're not, there's "enough of a nightlife for us. It's not a huge metropolis or anything, but it's a great city, and we live right in the heart of downtown."

Student Body

Creighton's "focused, ambitious" undergrads "are serious about getting a good education and spend quite a bit of time studying." They "usually had high high school GPAs and test scores," "are involved in three or more activities per semester while juggling hard courses," and "share many of the same values, which makes it easy to have a large number of friends." Faith is among those values; while not everyone is Catholic, nearly everyone has a deep interest in religion, and "It is a common topic of dinner conversation." Conservative social and political views are also among those shared values; students say that the bounty of Midwesterners "have conservative [frames of] mind," one undergrad writes. There are "a lot of athletic types, a good sign of both mental and physical health," and nearly everyone is friendly and fairly outgoing. One transplanted Yankee warns, "As a person from the East Coast, I have had to change the way I act and dress to fit in. Neither black clothing nor frowning will work here."

FINANCIAL AID: 402-280-2731 • E-MAIL: ADMISSIONS@CREIGHTON.EDU • WEBSITE: WWW.ADMISSION.CREIGHTON.EDU

ADMISSIONS

Very important factors considered include: Academic GPA, class rank, rigor of secondary school record. *Important factors considered include:* Application essay, standardized test scores. *Other factors considered include:* Character/personal qualities, extracurricular activities, first generation, level of applicant's interest, racial/ethnic status, recommendation(s), talent/ability, volunteer work. SAT or ACT required; TOEFL required of all international applicants. High school diploma is required, and GED is accepted. *Academic units recommended:* 4 English, 3 math, 2 science, 2 foreign language, 1 social studies, 1 history, 3 academic electives.

The Inside Word

In this world of literal translation, even colleges and universities with admission rates that are higher than Creighton's refer to themselves as selective. While it should not be particularly difficult to get in, some applicants don't.

FINANCIAL AID

Students should submit: FAFSA, institution's own financial aid form. The Princeton Review suggests that all financial aid forms be submitted as soon as possible after January 1. *Need-based scholarships/grants offered:* Pell Grant, SEOG, state scholarships/grants, private scholarships, the school's own gift aid. *Loan aid offered:* FFEL Subsidized Stafford, FFEL Unsubsidized Stafford, FFEL PLUS, Federal Perkins Loan, Federal Nursing Loan, college/university loans from institutional funds. Applicants will be notified of awards on a rolling basis beginning or about March 15. Federal Work-Study Program available. Institutional employment available. Off-campus job opportunities are excellent.

FROM THE ADMISSIONS OFFICE

"Students come to Creighton to become experts in their chosen fields . . . even if they haven't yet chosen a field of study! About 53 percent of our students go immediately into medical, dental, pharmacy, physical or occupational therapy, graduate or law school, or an MBA program after graduating or they leave Creighton for an early-entry professional program; this is one of the highest placement rates for any university in the United States. We also produce exceptional teachers, business professionals, scientists, journalists and writers, and community service advocates. Our size is ideal, with 6,981 students, 4,075 of which are undergraduates. Our students feel they have the best of both worlds—first-rate academic programs and facilities but also a more intimate relationship with our faculty that often lead to involvement in research projects and internships. Creighton students have a deeper focus on their careers and lifestyle choices. As a leading national Catholic/Jesuit liberal arts university, our students are encouraged to examine the moral as well as factual dimension of issues. Most students also get involved in our leadership training programs and community-service and/or campus ministry organizations. The campus has a garden setting with its own comfortable and safe sense of space. The downtown corporate headquarters, restaurants, and music spots are just a five minute walk.

"SAT or ACT is required but the Writing portion of the ACT is not required and the Writing portion of the SAT will not be used in the evaluation of the applicant."

SELECTIVITY

Admissions Rating	87
# of applicants	3,403
% of applicants accepted	89
% of acceptees attending	32
# accepting a place on wait list	77
% admitted from wait list	38

FRESHMAN PROFILE

Range SAT Critical Reading	520–630
Range SAT Math	540–650
Range ACT Composite	24–29
Minimum Paper TOEFL	550
Minimum Computer Based TOEFL	213
Average HS GPA	3.7
% graduated top 10% of class	44
% graduated top 25% of class	70
% graduated top 50% of class	92

DEADLINES

Regular application deadline	2/15
Nonfall registration?	yes

APPLICANTS ALSO LOOK AT
AND OFTEN PREFER
Boston College, University of Notre Dame
AND SOMETIMES PREFER
Marquette University, Saint Louis University, Santa Clara University, Washington University in St. Louis
AND RARELY PREFER
Loyola University—Chicago, Regis University, University of Iowa, University of Nebraska—Lincoln

FINANCIAL FACTS

Financial Aid Rating	82
Annual tuition	$24,166
Room & Board	$7,842
Required fees	$960
% frosh rec. need-based scholarship or grant aid	61
% UG rec. need-based scholarship or grant aid	50
% frosh rec. need-based self-help aid	47
% UG rec. need-based self-help aid	47
% frosh rec. any financial aid	96
% UG rec. any financial aid	91

DARTMOUTH COLLEGE

6016 McNutt Hall, Hanover, NH 03755 • Admissions: 603-646-2875 • Fax: 603-646-1216

CAMPUS LIFE

Quality of Life Rating	93
Fire Safety Rating	60*
Type of school	private
Environment	village

STUDENTS

Total undergrad enrollment	4,005
% male/female	49/51
% from out of state	96
% from public high school	61
% live on campus	85
% in (# of) fraternities	38 (14)
% in (# of) sororities	38 (6)
% African American	7
% Asian	14
% Caucasian	58
% Hispanic	6
% Native American	4
% international	5

SURVEY SAYS . . .

Great computer facilities
Great library
Campus feels safe
Frats and sororities dominate social scene
Lots of beer drinking

ACADEMICS

Academic Rating	96
Calendar	quarter
Student/faculty ratio	8:1
Profs interesting rating	81
Profs accessible rating	86
% profs teaching UG courses	100
% classes taught by TAs	0
Most common lab size	fewer than 10 students
Most common reg class size	10–19 students

MOST POPULAR MAJORS

economics
psychology
sociology

STUDENTS SAY

Academics

Dartmouth College "has a reputation of being like summer camp, and it's true: Students take their academic work very seriously, but they're also all extremely happy to be here, and they have a lot of fun, no matter what their idea of fun is." A school that is small "without being suffocating or lacking opportunities, challenging but not too competitive, has good academics and access to professors, and has its own ski hill" obviously has a lot to offer; how else could it entice "artists, athletes, musicians, and future leaders to all gather together in the middle of nowhere?" Students love that Dartmouth is "very undergraduate-focused, unlike the other Ivies that neglect their undergrads to only concentrate on research." They also love the D-Plan, which divides the academic year into four 10-week terms in order to provide maximum flexibility and study abroad opportunities ("Many students use the D-Plan to study abroad up to three times"). On the downside, it "makes being friends with members of other classes difficult," since "D-Plan means consistently being on campus . . . is tricky." Dartmouth professors "are some of the greatest minds in the country, and they're almost all willing to just sit and chat if you feel like it. I've had at least one professor each year who's invited the whole class to her/his house for dinner and discussion (sometimes with famous guests). It's a great way to learn information that is above and beyond what you're learning in the classroom." No wonder "everyone is happy here."

Life

Dartmouth's greatest strength, students tell us, "is its incredible sense of community and tradition," traditions that include "singing the Alma Mater, dancing the Salty Dog Rag, and running 100-plus laps around a 40-foot bonfire." One undergrad notes, "[Students] have a ton of school spirit," and "From the first day on campus, students are learning all about what it means to be a Dartmouth student." Situated in the Upper Connecticut River Valley, Dartmouth has "a great location for skiing and outdoor activities," and it's a place "where the student body is very active, both outdoors (i.e., hiking, biking, rock climbing, ice climbing, and skiing) as well as indoors partying. Whatever you want to do, you can find it here." That is, unless what you want is constant big-city entertainment; hometown Hanover is a "very small town," and "Boston and Montreal, though available, are rarely sought." Students are more likely to flock to the campus' popular Greek scene: "Most people like to go drink at frats on weekends and attend parties. I think like 20 percent of the student population abstains from drinking, but everyone else is pretty into it." Students are also "very involved in on campus organizations and sports teams." As one junior explains, "There's always more to do than can ever be done, and the hardest thing is making time for sleep along with classes, clubs, and friends."

Student Body

The typical Dartmouth student "is hard to define. If I mashed them all up into one person, it'd be a kid from Jersey driving a Lexus with a kayak on the top. His collar popped but his pants torn. In his bag there'd be the works of Marx next to those of Friedman. We're all so different, but at the same time, we're just all here to learn, to love, and to live." Dartmouth "strives to create a world of very different people," and its reputation allows it to cherry-pick top students from all around the globe. The school has a reputation for political conservatism that some argue is overblown: "There are very liberal students at Dartmouth, and there are very conservative student s. . ., but most tend to fall in between." Also, while the school "has a stereotype of being a big party school full of jocks," it's "not really that way" and "That should be more recognized." Across the board students tend to be "well-balanced" and "outgoing," and everyone from the "sweet frat dude to the library dweller all find a place to fit in."

FINANCIAL AID: 603-646-2451 • E-MAIL: ADMISSIONS.OFFICE@DARTMOUTH.EDU • WEBSITE: WWW.DARTMOUTH.EDU

ADMISSIONS

Very important factors considered include: Academic GPA, application essay, character/personal qualities, class rank, extracurricular activities, recommendation(s), rigor of secondary school record, standardized test scores. *Important factors considered include:* Talent/ability, volunteer work. *Other factors considered include:* Alumni/ae relation, first generation, geographical residence, interview, racial/ethnic status, work experience. SAT and SAT Subject Tests or ACT required; ACT with Writing component required. TOEFL required of all international applicants. High school diploma or equivalent is not required. *Academic units recommended:* 4 English, 4 math, 4 science, 3 social studies, 3 history.

The Inside Word

Like other elite schools, Dartmouth is swamped with more applications from qualified students than it can accommodate. According to *The Washington Post*, Dartmouth's 2006 admission rate of 15.4 percent was the lowest in the school's history. That wasn't because the applicant pool was less competitive; it's because more kids are applying to Dartmouth every year. Give this your best shot, and don't take it personally if you don't get in; unfortunately, many great candidates don't.

FINANCIAL AID

Students should submit: FAFSA, CSS/Financial Aid PROFILE, Noncustodial PROFILE, Business/Farm Supplement, current W-2 forms or Federal Income Tax Returns. Regular filing deadline is February 1. The Princeton Review suggests that all financial aid forms be submitted as soon as possible after January 1. *Need-based scholarships/grants offered:* Pell Grant, SEOG, the school's own gift aid. *Loan aid offered:* FFEL Subsidized Stafford, FFEL Unsubsidized Stafford, FFEL PLUS, Federal Perkins Loan, college/university loans from institutional funds. Applicants will be notified of awards on or about April 2. Federal Work-Study Program available. Institutional employment available. Off-campus job opportunities are excellent.

FROM THE ADMISSIONS OFFICE

"Dartmouth's mission is to endow students with the knowledge and wisdom needed to make creative and positive contributions to society. The college brings together a breadth of cultures, traditions, and ideas to create a campus that is alive with ongoing debate and exploration. The educational value of such discourse cannot be underestimated. From student-initiated round-table discussions that attempt to make sense of world events to the late-night philosophizing in a dormitory lounge, Dartmouth students take advantage of their opportunities to learn from each other. The unique benefits of sharing in this interchange are accompanied by a great sense of responsibility. Each individual's commitment to the principles of community ensures the vitality of this learning environment.

"All applicants, including those who apply from foreign countries, are required to take the SAT (or ACT) and any two SAT Subject Tests. All testing must be completed by January of the senior year in high school. If standardized testing is repeated, the Admissions Committee only considers highest scores."

SELECTIVITY
Admissions Rating	99
# of applicants	13,938
% of applicants accepted	16
% of acceptees attending	49
# accepting a place on wait list	669
% admitted from wait list	5
# of early decision applicants	1,316
% accepted early decision	30

FRESHMAN PROFILE
Range SAT Critical Reading	670–770
Range SAT Math	680–780
Range ACT Composite	28–34
Minimum Paper TOEFL	600
Minimum Computer Based TOEFL	250
Average HS GPA	3.75
% graduated top 10% of class	90
% graduated top 50% of class	100

DEADLINES
Early decision application deadline	11/1
Early decision notification	12/15
Regular application deadline	1/1
Regular notification	4/10
Nonfall registration?	no

APPLICANTS ALSO LOOK AT
AND OFTEN PREFER
Harvard College, Princeton University, Stanford University, Yale University
AND SOMETIMES PREFER
Amherst College, Brown University, Massachusetts Institute of Technology, Williams College
AND RARELY PREFER
Cornell University, Middlebury College, Northwestern University, University of Pennsylvania

FINANCIAL FACTS
Financial Aid Rating	93
Annual tuition	$33,297
Room & Board	$9,840
Books and supplies	$1,217
Required fees	$204
% frosh rec. need-based scholarship or grant aid	48
% UG rec. need-based scholarship or grant aid	50
% frosh rec. need-based self-help aid	44
% UG rec. need-based self-help aid	49
% frosh rec. any financial aid	48
% UG rec. any financial aid	50

DAVIDSON COLLEGE

PO BOX 7156, DAVIDSON, NC 28035-7156 • ADMISSIONS: 704-894-2230 • FAX: 704-894-2016

CAMPUS LIFE

Quality of Life Rating	95
Fire Safety Rating	60*
Type of school	private
Affiliation	Presbyterian
Environment	village

STUDENTS

Total undergrad enrollment	1,660
% male/female	50/50
% from out of state	81
% from public high school	48
% live on campus	91
% in (# of) fraternities	40 (8)
% African American	7
% Asian	3
% Caucasian	76
% Hispanic	5
% Native American	1
% international	3
# of countries represented	29

SURVEY SAYS . . .

Small classes
No one cheats
Lab facilities are great
School is well run
Students are friendly
Campus feels safe

ACADEMICS

Academic Rating	99
Calendar	semester
Student/faculty ratio	10:1
Profs interesting rating	97
Profs accessible rating	97
% profs teaching	
UG courses	100
% classes taught by TAs	0
Most common	
lab size	10–19 students
Most common	
reg class size	10–19 students

MOST POPULAR MAJORS

biology/biological sciences
English language and literature
history

STUDENTS SAY

Academics

Davidson College, which students insist is "the best liberal arts college in the South," is the ideal setting for students who are "not afraid to show their academic passions" and who seek "the incorporation of academics into all parts of life." One undergrad explains, "I feel like I am always learning, even when I am not in the classroom. The atmosphere provided by my fellow classmates provides almost as many new intellectual experiences as my time in class." A school "notorious for grade deflation" (according to one student, "This place is not a joke. And you won't be the smartest kid in your class . . . or any other class"), Davidson is a place where "You have to expect a fair bit of work. Classes are tiny and intense, and with the small size and high level of student participation, it is impossible to hide." The upshot is that "you will learn a lot, not just in terms of subject matter but also about your learning styles and how you learn the best." Davidson professors "are amazing. Not only are they renowned in their fields, but they are always available for extra help or even just to chat"—they are "rare combinations of teachers and researchers." Students tell us that "for such a small school, the amount of undergraduate research going on here is surprising," and that undergrads often contribute to faculty work. Davidson's honor code "is a huge part of life; for example, we have 100 community bikes that anyone can use at any time, and we trust them to not get stolen (and they don't!). Every quiz and test in my French class is take-home, and every exam at Davidson is self-scheduled unless that is logistically impossible."

Life

"Students do spend a lot of time studying at Davidson," claim undergrads, "but that doesn't mean they don't have fun." During the week "We study until our minds bleed," but "We find ways to relieve the pressure over the weekend." For those who drink, that often means "court parties at Patterson Court, home of our fraternity/eating house scene." These events, we're told, involve a lot of alcohol. The administration has sought to curtail drinking by "directing nonalcoholic events to the Student Union." Usually these events "are a viable alternative" to the party scene. Movies, free food, and various types of alcohol-free parties fill the Student Union calendar and are favored by the school's substantial religious population. Davidson basketball is popular; other sports aren't as well supported. Many students recommend frequent trips off campus to "nearby Birkdale for a movie or shopping," to the "small (but by no means boring) towns of Mooresville, Huntersville, and Cornelius," or to "downtown Charlotte for dinner and drinks."

Student Body

There are two noticeable populations at Davidson: "the driven, intelligent, likely wealthy White student who likes to party a lot," and "the driven, intelligent, likely wealthy White student who likes to read the Bible and go to church." One student observes, "To secular folks, this is the most religious place they've ever been, and to religious folks, it's the most secular place they've ever been." Money is rather visible on campus; one student claims, "Students drive much nicer cars than their professors." There are "not many African American students, and hardly any Asians here," and "There is not a lot of diversity in terms of economic status." There are lots of jocks, though, as "probably 25 percent of the student body is made up of Division I- or Division I AA-caliber athletes. They get no breaks in admissions or from professors, by the way, and they don't fit the stereotypes of being elitist or separatist. We all work hard." Regardless of differences in background, however, students assert that the school "is remarkably well integrated—while students certainly stick with their fraternity or sports team, often their best friends are from their freshman hall."

DAVIDSON COLLEGE

FINANCIAL AID: 704-894-2232 • E-MAIL: ADMISSION@DAVIDSON.EDU • WEBSITE: WWW.DAVIDSON.EDU

ADMISSIONS

Very important factors considered include: Character/personal qualities, recommendation(s), rigor of secondary school record, volunteer work. *Important factors considered include:* Application essay, extracurricular activities, talent/ability. *Other factors considered include:* Class rank, racial/ethnic status, standardized test scores, work experience. SAT or ACT required; SAT and SAT Subject Tests or ACT recommended; TOEFL required of all international applicants. High school diploma is required, and GED is not accepted. *Academic units required:* 4 English, 3 math, 2 science, 2 foreign language, 2 social studies and history. *Academic units recommended:* 4 math, 4 science, 4 foreign language, 4 social studies and history.

The Inside Word

The combination of Davidson's low acceptance rate and high yield really packs a punch. Prospective applicants beware: Securing admission at this prestigious school is no easy feat. Admitted students are typically at the top of their high school classes and have strong standardized test scores. Candidates with leadership experience generally garner the favor of Admissions Officers. The college takes its honor code seriously and, as a result, seeks out students of demonstrated reputable character.

FINANCIAL AID

Students should submit: FAFSA, CSS/Financial Aid PROFILE, Noncustodial PROFILE, Business/Farm Supplement, corporate and/or noncustodial parent tax return (if applicable); Federal Income Tax Returns and W-2 forms. Regular filing deadline is February 15. The Princeton Review suggests that all financial aid forms be submitted as soon as possible after January 1. *Need-based scholarships/grants offered:* Pell Grant, SEOG, state scholarships/grants, private scholarships, the school's own gift aid. *Loan aid offered:* FFEL Subsidized Stafford, FFEL Unsubsidized Stafford, FFEL PLUS, Federal Perkins Loan, alternative loans. Applicants will be notified of awards on or about April 1. Federal Work-Study Program available. Institutional employment available. Off-campus job opportunities are excellent.

FROM THE ADMISSIONS OFFICE

"Davidson College is one of the nation's premier academic institutions, a college of the liberal arts and sciences respected for its intellectual vigor, the high quality of its faculty and students, and the achievements of its alumni. It is distinguished by its strong honor system, close collaboration between professors and students, an environment that encourages both intellectual growth and community service, and a commitment to international education. Davidson places great value on student participation in extracurricular activities, intercollegiate athletics, and intramural sports. The college has a strong regional identity, grounded in traditions of civility and mutual respect, and has historic ties to the Presbyterian Church.

"Applicants for the Class of 2012 are required to complete the SAT or the ACT. SAT Subject Tests (Mathematics and one of your choices) and the ACT plus Writing are recommended. Students are permitted to submit scores from the SAT administered prior to March 2005. Davidson will utilize the scores that place the student in the greatest possible light."

SELECTIVITY
Admissions Rating	97
# of applicants	3,895
% of applicants accepted	30
% of acceptees attending	39
# of early decision applicants	357
% accepted early decision	57

FRESHMAN PROFILE
Range SAT Critical Reading	620–720
Range SAT Math	630–720
Range ACT Composite	27–31
Minimum Paper TOEFL	600
Minimum Computer Based TOEFL	250
% graduated top 10% of class	79
% graduated top 25% of class	97
% graduated top 50% of class	99

DEADLINES
Early decision application deadline	11/15
Early decision notification	12/15
Regular application deadline	1/2
Regular notification	4/1
Nonfall registration?	no

APPLICANTS ALSO LOOK AT
AND OFTEN PREFER
Dartmouth College, Duke University, Princeton University, Stanford University, Swarthmore College, Williams College
AND SOMETIMES PREFER
The University of North Carolina at Chapel Hill, University of Virginia, Vanderbilt University, Washington University in St. Louis
AND RARELY PREFER
Colgate University, Emory University, Furman University, University of Richmond, Wake Forest University

FINANCIAL FACTS
Financial Aid Rating	97
Annual tuition	$29,119
Room & Board	$8,590
Books and supplies	$1,000
Required fees	$1,075
% frosh rec. need-based scholarship or grant aid	31
% UG rec. need-based scholarship or grant aid	32
% frosh rec. need-based self-help aid	24
% UG rec. need-based self-help aid	27
% frosh rec. any financial aid	35
% UG rec. any financial aid	35

DEEP SPRINGS COLLEGE

HC 72 Box 45001, DEEP SPRINGS, CA VIA DYER, NV 89010-9803 • ADMISSIONS: 760-872-2000 • FAX: 760-872-4466

STUDENTS SAY

Academics

The "three pillars" of a Deep Springs education—"labor, academics, and self-governance"—combine to produce "the most intense experience you will ever have." That's what the 26 men who attend Deep Springs tell us, anyway. They basically run their own school, work the ranch where it is located, and complete a curriculum that "is the epitome of higher education," all of which sounds pretty intense to us too. The program "isn't merely vocational. It's about educating a whole human being, and it makes us more responsible, more sensitive people." Students best suited to this approach are those who "want to take as much control of their education as possible. I enjoy knowing that my actions seriously affect the day-to-day life as well as the future of Deep Springs." Because the school is "very small and governed by the students, the smoothness with which many programs run depends largely on the kind of responsibility students take. Sometimes students do a good job taking care of administrative tasks, sometimes a worse job. It's all part of the educational experience." The students "hire the professors and pretty much run the classes. As a result, when the students are motivated, the classes here are better than they can be anywhere else in the world." While the size of the school inevitably means that "lab and library facilities are not what they might be," students tell us that the quality of the students and professors more than makes up for these kinds of problems.

Life

"Deep Springs is totally unlike other colleges in terms of the everyday life of a student," because "No one drinks, everyone helps run the ranch in some way, and no one can be totally self-absorbed (unless they're out hiking in the desert)." Instead, students immerse themselves in the Deep Springs way. As one student explains, "The Deep Springs program is our whole life. The intellectual questions we're asking and the labor we're doing is all bound up with our identity." Students pass their free time by "having a lot of conversations: about life in general, about personal issues, and about intellectual questions." Occasionally "We have dance parties called 'boojies,'" and "We do some other strange things for fun, like sledding naked down 800-foot-tall sand dunes in neighboring Eureka Valley, for example, or watching every episode of *The Wonder Years*." Undergrads concede that Deep Springs "Life can be intense. Students usually are utterly exhausted. But most of the time we know that something good is coming out of this." That "something good" can take many forms; one student writes, "On Thanksgiving, four of my classmates and I took it upon ourselves to do all the cooking. We smoked and roasted seven turkeys, made several stuffings, and baked dozens of loaves of bread while the rest of our classmates played a game of football on one of the alfalfa fields. Afterward, the whole student body did the dishes while listening to upbeat techno and Led Zeppelin. The next day, over a third of the student body put on Shakespeare's *The Tempest*, moving from a reservoir to a dry wash and down to the center of campus as the play demanded. This sort of thing is typical of Deep Springs life."

Student Body

Given the many demands of a Deep Springs education, it should come as no surprise that "everyone is intelligent, motivated, and responsible" here. Students "must demonstrate depth of thought to be accepted" to the school, and most "are very intellectual and philosophically inclined, although there are some who would rather take a science class any day." As one undergrad puts it, Deep Spring students are "looking for a broader experience than can be found at the usual college. Most students are boys looking to become men. Most students are typical and fit in wonderfully because we're all pretty damn weird."

FINANCIAL AID: 760-872-2000 • E-MAIL: APCOM@DEEPSPRING.EDU • WEBSITE: WWW.DEEPSPRINGS.EDU

ADMISSIONS

Very important factors considered include: Application essay, character/personal qualities, interview, level of applicant's interest. *Important factors considered include:* Academic GPA, extracurricular activities, recommendation(s), rigor of secondary school record, volunteer work, work experience. *Other factors considered include:* Class rank, standardized test scores, talent/ability. SAT or ACT required. High school diploma or equivalent is not required.

The Inside Word

Students will be hard pressed to find a school that has a more personal or thorough application process than Deep Springs. Given the intimate and collegial atmosphere fostered at the college, matchmaking is the top priority. Candidates are evaluated by a body composed of students, faculty, and staff members. The application is rather writing intensive, and finalists are expected to spend several days on campus, during which time they will also have a lengthy interview.

FINANCIAL AID

All accepted students receive free tuition, room, and board.

FROM THE ADMISSIONS OFFICE

"Founded in 1917, Deep Springs College lies isolated in a high desert valley of eastern California, 30 miles from the nearest town. Its enrollment is limited to 26 students, each of whom receives a full scholarship that covers tuition, room and board and is valued at more than $50,000 per year. Students engage in rigorous academics, govern themselves, and participate in the operation of our cattle and alfalfa ranch. After 2 years, students generally transfer to other schools to complete their studies. Students regularly transfer to Harvard, The University of Chicago, and Brown, but also choose Cornell, Columbia, Stanford, Swarthmore, University of California—Berkeley, and Yale.

"In 2002, Deep Springs students garnered four major national scholarship awards: three Truman Scholarships for public service careers—more than any other school in the country—and one Udall scholarship for careers in environmental studies and ecology.

"As of this book's publication, Deep Springs College did not have information available about their policy regarding the new SAT."

SELECTIVITY
Admissions Rating	**99**
# of applicants	170
% of applicants accepted	7
% of acceptees attending	92
# accepting a place on wait list	3

FRESHMAN PROFILE
Range SAT Critical Reading	750–800
Range SAT Math	700–800
% graduated top 10% of class	86
% graduated top 25% of class	93
% graduated top 50% of class	100

DEADLINES
Regular application deadline	11/15
Regular notification	4/15
Nonfall registration?	no

APPLICANTS ALSO LOOK AT AND RARELY PREFER

Brown University, Cornell University, Harvard College, Stanford University, Swarthmore College, University of California—Berkeley, The University of Chicago, Yale University

FINANCIAL FACTS
Financial Aid Rating	**60***
Annual tuition	$0
Books and supplies	$1,200
% frosh rec. need-based scholarship or grant aid	0
% UG rec. need-based scholarship or grant aid	0
% frosh rec. need-based self-help aid	0
% UG rec. need-based self-help aid	0
% frosh rec. any financial aid	100
% UG rec. any financial aid	100

*Tuition covered by full scholarship.

DENISON UNIVERSITY

Box H, Granville, OH 43023 • Admissions: 740-587-6276 • Fax: 740-587-6306

CAMPUS LIFE

Quality of Life Rating	**82**
Fire Safety Rating	**85**
Type of school	private
Environment	village

STUDENTS

Total undergrad enrollment	2,235
% male/female	43/57
% from out of state	61
% from public high school	70
% live on campus	98
% in (# of) fraternities	25 (8)
% in (# of) sororities	30 (6)
% African American	5
% Asian	3
% Caucasian	84
% Hispanic	3
% international	4
# of countries represented	31

SURVEY SAYS . . .

Large classes
Lab facilities are great
Great computer facilities
Great library
Campus feels safe
Lots of beer drinking

ACADEMICS

Academic Rating	**92**
Calendar	semester
Student/faculty ratio	11:1
Profs interesting rating	86
Profs accessible rating	88
% profs teaching	
UG courses	100
% classes taught by TAs	0
Most common	
reg class size	20–29 students

MOST POPULAR MAJORS

communications and media studies
economics
English language and literature

STUDENTS SAY
Academics

Students describe Denison University as "a mecca of top-notch academics" located "in the seclusion of rural Ohio." By necessity Denison University may be "huge on community," but regardless of the impetus, students, faculty, and administrators here "become like a big family where everyone takes care of one another." Students agree that that's a good thing, as this environment provides "academically motivated students a chance to excel in their respective studies through a supportive student population and dedicated faculty, while also providing many social opportunities." Denison is "all about educating the whole student, whether it be through classes, speakers, sports, clubs, or even Greek life." Academically, Denison can be "challenging." "It is possible to spend an entire semester stressed out to the extreme with 20-plus academic credits and no time to do the readings for every class. But it is also very possible to manage your time well and get everything done in a mannerly fashion, without overexerting yourself, but still having a successful and productive semester." Students who find themselves in over their heads can count on "professors who are willing to go the extra mile with their students." Professors "have organized study groups before exams and extend their office hours so that you can meet with them about a paper or project." As one student observes, "It's your own fault if you do poorly, because there are so many ways for you to get help through teachers, study groups, tutoring, etc."

Life

"What is nice about Denison is that most people stay on campus during the weekends, so there is always something to do," students here report. The school and the Student Activities Committee "always sponsor concerts, speakers, and events around campus," and, of course, there is always a party or two available on the weekends. "There is so much to do all week, every week," which "is somewhat necessary, as the town of Granville is quite small and offers few diversions." A party scene "is available if that's what you want," and quite a few students do, telling us that "go-out-and-party nights" are Fridays and Saturdays and "Mondays and Wednesdays also, since most students have few classes on Tuesdays and Thursdays." There's a lot of partying on campus, either at the Greek houses ("Greek life encompasses about 40 percent of the student body") or in the student residences. Denison has "a number of sports teams that are nationally ranked," but students are just as likely to follow OSU as Denison. While hometown Granville is "small" and "very quiet," Columbus "is only 30 minutes away which allows [students] to visit other restaurants, bars, concerts, and, of course, big sister OSU." Easton "is just 25 minutes away and has a huge shopping center."

Student Body

While "There are not a lot of atypical students on the extreme ends of 'different'" at Denison, students hasten to point out that "Denison does not solely consist of popped collars and Uggs. Those students just like to make themselves known." True, "Most students here are WASPy" and "generally affluent," and there are "a lot of athletes on campus, and fraternities and sororities are pretty big," but most "Kids are hardworking and usually friendly." Also, Denison is not without its "internationals, artsy types, and [even] the socially awkward." There's "even a small counterculture made up of environmentalists and hippies who live at the homestead and hang out at Bandersnatch." These people "are the minority, but there's a niche for them." As one student explains, "It's pretty easy to find a core group of friends."

DENISON UNIVERSITY

FINANCIAL AID: 740-587-6279 • E-MAIL: ADMISSIONS@DENISON.EDU • WEBSITE: WWW.DENISON.EDU

ADMISSIONS

Very important factors considered include: Academic GPA, application essay, class rank, recommendation(s), rigor of secondary school record, standardized test scores. *Important factors considered include:* Extracurricular activities, interview, talent/ability. *Other factors considered include:* Alumni/ae relation, character/personal qualities, first generation, geographical residence, level of applicant's interest, racial/ethnic status, religious affiliation/commitment, state residency, volunteer work, work experience. SAT and SAT Subject Tests or ACT required; ACT with Writing component required. TOEFL required of all international applicants. High school diploma is required, and GED is accepted. *Academic units required:* 4 English, 4 math, 4 science, 3 foreign language, 2 social studies, 1 history, 1 academic elective.

The Inside Word

Admission to Denison is pretty straightforward. The school "suggests" an interview, meaning you should do one if at all possible. It's a great way to demonstrate your interest in the school, which improves your chances of admission, especially if your grades, test scores, and overall profile put you on the admit/reject borderline.

FINANCIAL AID

Students should submit: FAFSA, institution's own financial aid form. The Princeton Review suggests that all financial aid forms be submitted as soon as possible after January 1. *Need-based scholarships/grants offered:* Pell Grant, SEOG, state scholarships/grants, private scholarships, the school's own gift aid. *Loan aid offered:* Direct Subsidized Stafford, Direct Unsubsidized Stafford, Direct PLUS, Federal Perkins Loan, college/university loans from institutional funds. Applicants will be notified of awards on or about May 1. Federal Work-Study Program available. Institutional employment available. Off-campus job opportunities are fair.

FROM THE ADMISSIONS OFFICE

"Denison is a college that can point with pride to its success in enrolling and retaining intellectually motivated, diverse, and well-balanced students who are being taught to become effective leaders in the twenty-first century. This year, over 50 percent of our first-year students were in the top 10 percent of their high school graduating class; their average SAT scores have risen above 1240—an increase of some 80 points over the last 5 years; 18 percent of the class is multicultural; and 95 percent of our student body is receiving some type of financial assistance. Our First-Year Program focuses on helping students make a successful transition from high school to college, and the small classes and accessibility of faculty assure students the opportunity to interact closely with their professors and fellow students. We care about our students, and the loyalty of our 27,000 alumni proves that the Denison experience is one that lasts for a lifetime.

"Students applying for admission into the Fall 2008 freshman class are required to take the new version of the SAT (or the ACT with the Writing section), but we will allow students to submit scores from the old (prior to March 2005) version of the SAT (or ACT) as well."

SELECTIVITY

Admissions Rating	**91**
# of applicants	5,010
% of applicants accepted	39
% of acceptees attending	29
# accepting a place on wait list	281
% admitted from wait list	1
# of early decision applicants	153
% accepted early decision	67

FRESHMAN PROFILE

Range SAT Critical Reading	690–580
Range SAT Math	680–590
Range ACT Composite	30–26
Minimum Paper TOEFL	550
Minimum Computer Based TOEFL	213
Average HS GPA	3.6
% graduated top 10% of class	52
% graduated top 25% of class	34
% graduated top 50% of class	14

DEADLINES

Early decision application deadline	11/1
Regular application deadline	1/15
Regular notification	4/1
Nonfall registration?	no

APPLICANTS ALSO LOOK AT

AND OFTEN PREFER
Bucknell University, Butler University, Elon University, The Ohio State University—Columbus

AND SOMETIMES PREFER
DePauw University, Dickinson College, Franklin & Marshall College, Gettysburg College, Kenyon College

AND RARELY PREFER
Miami University, Oberlin College, Ohio Wesleyan University, The College of Wooster

FINANCIAL FACTS

Financial Aid Rating	**90**
Annual tuition	$29,860
Room & Board	$8,560
Books and supplies	$1,800
Required fees	$800
% frosh rec. need-based scholarship or grant aid	43
% UG rec. need-based scholarship or grant aid	46
% frosh rec. need-based self-help aid	28
% UG rec. need-based self-help aid	34
% frosh rec. any financial aid	95
% UG rec. any financial aid	95

DePaul University

ONE EAST JACKSON BOULEVARD, CHICAGO, IL 60604-2287 • ADMISSIONS: 312-362-8300 • FAX: 312-362-5749

CAMPUS LIFE

Quality of Life Rating	**91**
Fire Safety Rating	**75**
Type of school	private
Affiliation	Roman Catholic
Environment	metropolis

STUDENTS

Total undergrad enrollment	14,465
% male/female	44/56
% from out of state	16
% from public high school	74
% live on campus	19
% African American	8
% Asian	8
% Caucasian	50
% Hispanic	11
% international	1
# of countries represented	85

SURVEY SAYS . . .

Small classes
Athletic facilities are great
Diverse student types on campus
Students love Chicago, IL
Great off-campus food

ACADEMICS

Academic Rating	**77**
Calendar	quarter
Student/faculty ratio	16:1
Profs interesting rating	79
Profs accessible rating	80
% profs teaching UG courses	99
% classes taught by TAs	0
Most common lab size	fewer than 10 students
Most common reg class size	20–29 students

MOST POPULAR MAJORS

accounting
communications studies/speech
communication and rhetoric
finance

STUDENTS SAY

Academics

True to its "Vincentian ideals" of "community service, social justice, and critical thinking," DePaul University "is all about enriching the student not only academically but also socially, mentally, and physically," and "constantly challenging the student with new ideas, cultures, and thoughts to explore and understand." The school's urban setting plays a huge part in helping the school fulfill its mission by providing a diverse student body and endless service opportunities, as well as the widespread "availability of jobs and internships," which the school exploits through "'Discover Chicago' and 'Experiential Learning' requirements that get [students] involved in the city and with local communities." Standout programs include a strong business program and a top-notch theater conservatory; students tell us that the study abroad program is also excellent. DePaul operates on a quarterly academic calendar, which many enjoy: "We're able to learn about so much more than students at semester schools," an English major asserts. Others students feel that "sometimes it seems as though we do not spend enough time on subjects due to the quarter system." Professors earn solid grades as teachers and mentors; the administration, on the other hand, "is a huge bureaucracy, so it's often difficult dealing with issues [that are] non-classroom related." That being said, "Administrators are, for the most part, friendly, and issues always eventually get taken care of even if they require much more time and energy than they should."

Life

"Life at DePaul is just challenging enough so students are pressured to succeed in life but aren't too stressed out," which leaves them enough time to enjoy the benefits of living in one of America's great cities. It's "nearly impossible to be bored in Chicago," a junior writes, "but it's definitely possible to live up to the broke-college-student standard." "The tourist, theatrical, food, and bar scene[s are] amazing," a sophomore adds. "Getting around is easy thanks to the U-Pass students are provided with each quarter," which allows them "to use the CTA [Chicago Transit Authority] system as much as [they] like." DePaul's Lincoln Park location "is not a town based around the college"; rather, it is a well-heeled Chicago neighborhood with "multimillion-dollar homes, parks, boutiques, and families. The shopping is phenomenal, and the food is just as great. Plus, we're close to lots of other colleges." The Loop campus, home to business students, is "so close [to downtown Chicago] that you can do a variety of things based on your interests every weekend and even go shopping between classes." On campus, "DePaul Theater School performances are great and inexpensive for students," and "Student groups on campus hold fun events every weekend." Many undergrads drink at bars in the city, and "Most big drinkers have a fake ID if they're not 21." For the sober set, "There are always festivals, movies, shopping trips, bike rides, concerts, etc." either on campus or around Chicago.

Student Body

"DePaul is an extremely diverse school" with "people of all shapes, sizes, colors, etc.," students tell us. Classes encompass "a wide variety of religions, ethnicities, and orientations . . . I wouldn't have it any other way," beams a political science major. However, while diverse students interact in a friendly manner "on a daily basis," they largely remain segregated by class, major, background, and interests. Many students distinguish themselves through fashion: "There are a lot of very well-dressed students at DePaul"—"Many have the latest Coach, Ugg, and North Face attire." There are also "a lot of bohemian-style dressers" as well as "artists, bookish types, athletes, etc." Students "tend to be fairly liberal," but there's also an active and visible Conservative Club on campus. Many students are "socially conscious and relish the opportunity to work for causes in which they believe."

FINANCIAL AID: 312-362-8091 • E-MAIL: ADMITDPU@DEPAUL.EDU • WEBSITE: WWW.DEPAUL.EDU

ADMISSIONS

Very important factors considered include: Academic GPA, character/personal qualities, rigor of secondary school record. *Important factors considered include:* Application essay, class rank, extracurricular activities, recommendation(s), standardized test scores, talent/ability, volunteer work, work experience. *Other factors considered include:* Alumni/ae relation, first generation, geographical residence, interview, level of applicant's interest, racial/ethnic status, religious affiliation/commitment, state residency. SAT or ACT required; TOEFL required of all international applicants. High school diploma is required, and GED is accepted. *Academic units required:* 4 English, 2 math, 2 science (2 science labs), 2 social studies, 4 academic electives.

The Inside Word

DePaul has earned its reputation as one of the most diverse campuses in the United States. The school courts minority students not only as freshmen but also as transfers. It recognizes that its tuition is beyond the means of many (even with financial aid), so it works with area community colleges to allow students to fulfill requirements at a lower cost before completing their degrees at DePaul.

FINANCIAL AID

Students should submit: FAFSA. Regular filing deadline is May 1. The Princeton Review suggests that all financial aid forms be submitted as soon as possible after January 1. *Need-based scholarships/grants offered:* Pell Grant, SEOG, state scholarships/grants, private scholarships, the school's own gift aid. *Loan aid offered:* Direct Subsidized Stafford, Direct Unsubsidized Stafford, Direct PLUS, Federal Perkins Loan. Applicants will be notified of awards on a rolling basis beginning or about February 15. Off-campus job opportunities are excellent.

FROM THE ADMISSIONS OFFICE

"The nation's largest Catholic university, DePaul University is nationally recognized for its innovative academic programs that embrace a comprehensive 'learn by doing' approach. DePaul has two residential campuses and four commuter campuses in the suburbs. The Lincoln Park campus is located in one of Chicago's most exciting neighborhoods, filled with theaters, cafés, clubs, and shops. It is home to DePaul's College of Liberal Arts and Sciences, the School of Education, the Theater School, and the School of Music. New buildings on the 36-acre campus include residence halls, a science building, a student recreational facility, and the student center, which features a cybercafé where students can surf the Web or gather with friends. The Loop campus, located in Chicago's downtown—a world-class center for business, government, law, and culture—is home to DePaul's College of Commerce; College of Law; School of Computer Science, Telecommunications, and Information Systems; School for New Learning; and School of Accountancy and Management Information Systems.

"Applicants for the Fall 2008 freshman class are required to take either the ACT or the SAT. The Writing Test on the ACT and the Writing section on the SAT are not required for admission consideration; therefore, we will also accept results from tests taken prior to March 2005."

SELECTIVITY

Admissions Rating	80
# of applicants	10,414
% of applicants accepted	70
% of acceptees attending	35

FRESHMAN PROFILE

Range SAT Critical Reading	510–630
Range SAT Math	510–620
Range SAT Writing	520–610
Range ACT Composite	21–26
Minimum Paper TOEFL	550
Minimum Computer Based TOEFL	213
Average HS GPA	3.4
% graduated top 10% of class	19
% graduated top 25% of class	47
% graduated top 50% of class	79

DEADLINES

Regular notification	rolling
Nonfall registration?	yes

APPLICANTS ALSO LOOK AT AND OFTEN PREFER

Loyola University—Chicago, Northwestern University, The University of Chicago, University of Illinois at Urbana-Champaign, University of Notre Dame

AND SOMETIMES PREFER

Illinois State University, Indiana University—Bloomington, Marquette University, Northern Illinois University, University of Illinois at Chicago

FINANCIAL FACTS

Financial Aid Rating	68
Annual tuition	$22,365
Room & Board	$6,543
Required fees	$170
% frosh rec. need-based scholarship or grant aid	47
% UG rec. need-based scholarship or grant aid	47
% frosh rec. need-based self-help aid	48
% UG rec. need-based self-help aid	50
% frosh rec. any financial aid	66
% UG rec. any financial aid	66

DEPAUW UNIVERSITY

101 EAST SEMINARY, GREENCASTLE, IN 46135 • ADMISSIONS: 765-658-4006 • FAX: 765-658-4007

CAMPUS LIFE

Quality of Life Rating	**74**
Fire Safety Rating	**60***
Type of school	private
Affiliation	Methodist
Environment	village

STUDENTS

Total undergrad enrollment	2,276
% male/female	44/56
% from out of state	46
% from public high school	83
% live on campus	99
% in (# of) fraternities	75 (13)
% in (# of) sororities	70 (11)
% African American	6
% Asian	3
% Caucasian	84
% Hispanic	3
% international	2
# of countries represented	32

SURVEY SAYS . . .

Lab facilities are great
Great computer facilities
Students are friendly
Frats and sororities dominate social scene
College radio is popular
Lots of beer drinking
Hard liquor is popular

ACADEMICS

Academic Rating	**93**
Calendar	4-1-4
Student/faculty ratio	10:1
Profs interesting rating	88
Profs accessible rating	95
% profs teaching UG courses	100
% classes taught by TAs	0
Most common lab size	10–19 students
Most common reg class size	10–19 students

MOST POPULAR MAJORS

economics
English composition
mass communications/media studies

STUDENTS SAY

Academics

Serious-minded students are drawn to DePauw University for its "small classes," "encouraging" professors, and the "individual academic attention" they can expect to receive. Academically, DePauw is "demanding but rewarding," and "requires a lot of outside studying and discipline" in order to keep up. Professors' "expectations are very high," which means "You can't slack off and get good grades." Be prepared to pull your "fair share of all-nighters." Fortunately, DePauw professors are more than just stern taskmasters. Though they pile on the work, they "are always helpful and available" to students in need. When things get overwhelming, "They are very understanding and will cut you a break if you really deserve" it. As a result, students come to know their professors "on a personal level," making DePauw the kind of school where it is "common [for students] to have dinner at a professor's house." Beyond stellar professors, DePauw's other academic draws include "extraordinary" study abroad opportunities and a "wonderful" alumni network great for "connections and networking opportunities." Alums also "keep our endowment pretty high, making it easy for the school to give out merit scholarships," which undergraduates appreciate. Student opinion regarding the administration ranges from ambivalent to slightly negative. One especially thorny issue is class registration; you "rarely . . . get into all the classes you want."

Life

Few schools are as Greek as DePauw, but students are quick to point out that "it is by no means *Animal House*." The Greek system here is more holistic than that. It "promotes not only social activities but also philanthropic events." That's not to say there aren't lots of frat parties here. There are. But "The administration has cracked down big time" on the larger frat parties, and "Now there are just small parties in apartments and dorms." One recently issued rule is that freshmen "will not be allowed on Greek property until after Rush, which is the first week of second semester." In addition to administrative regulation, students exercise their own self-restraint; for the typical undergraduate, "[T]he week is mostly reserved for studying." Beyond the frats and sororities, "There is always a theater production, athletic event, or organization-sponsored event going on," and popular bands occasionally perform on campus. It's a good thing so much is happening at the school because off-campus entertainment options are scarce: "If there is really any fun to be had, it's not in Greencastle." The situation could be greatly improved if there were just a few "more restaurants and stores in the town or a nearby town." As things stand, however, students "have to go to Indianapolis (45 miles) to go shopping, watch a good movie, eat at a good restaurant, etc."

Student Body

The typical DePauw student is "upper-middle class," "a little preppy, a little athletic," and "hardworking"; "parties hard on weekends," and "usually becomes involved with the Greek system." Students describe their peers as "driven students" with "polos and pearls." They "have all had multiple internships, international experience, and [held] some type of leadership position." Though these folks may seem "overcommitted," they "always get their work done." For those who don't fit this mold, don't fret; most students seem to be "accepting of the different types" of people on campus. Diversity on campus is augmented through the school's partnership with the Posse Foundation, which brings in urban (though not necessarily minority) "students from Chicago and NYC every year." These students are described as "leaders on campus" and "take real initiative to hold their communities together."

FINANCIAL AID: 765-658-4030 • E-MAIL: ADMISSION@DEPAUW.EDU • WEBSITE: WWW.DEPAUW.EDU

ADMISSIONS

Very important factors considered include: Academic GPA, rigor of secondary school record, standardized test scores. *Important factors considered include:* Application essay, class rank, recommendation(s). *Other factors considered include:* Alumni/ae relation, character/personal qualities, extracurricular activities, first generation, geographical residence, interview, level of applicant's interest, state residency, talent/ability, volunteer work, work experience. SAT or ACT required; ACT with Writing component required. TOEFL required of all international applicants. GED is accepted. *Academic units recommended:* 4 English, 4 math, 4 science (2 science labs), 4 foreign language, 4 social studies.

The Inside Word

Prospective applicants should not be deceived by DePauw's high acceptance rate. The students who are accepted and choose to enroll here have the academic goods to justify their admission. Many of them are accepted by more "competitive" schools and still choose DePauw. DePauw's generous merit scholarships have a lot to do with students' choice to enroll.

FINANCIAL AID

Students should submit: FAFSA, institution's own financial aid form. Regular filing deadline is February 15. The Princeton Review suggests that all financial aid forms be submitted as soon as possible after January 1. *Need-based scholarships/grants offered:* Pell Grant, SEOG, state scholarships/grants, private scholarships, the school's own gift aid. *Loan aid offered:* FFEL Subsidized Stafford, FFEL Unsubsidized Stafford, FFEL PLUS, Federal Perkins Loan, college/university loans from institutional funds, alternative loans. Applicants will be notified of awards in mid-March. Federal Work-Study Program available. Institutional employment available. Off-campus job opportunities are fair.

FROM THE ADMISSIONS OFFICE

"DePauw University is nationally recognized for intellectual and experiential challenge that links liberal arts education with life's work, preparing graduates for uncommon professional success, service to others, and personal fulfillment. DePauw graduates count among their ranks a Nobel Laureate, a vice president and U.S. congressman, Pulitzer Prize and Newbery Award authors, and a number of CEOs and humanitarian leaders. Our students demonstrate a love for learning, a willingness to serve others, the reason and judgment to lead, an interest in engaging worlds and cultures unknown to them, the courage to question their assumptions, and a strong commitment to community. Preprofessional and career exploration are encouraged through winter term, when more than 700 students pursue their own off-campus internships. This represents more students in experiential learning opportunities than at any other liberal arts college in the nation. Other innovative programs include Honor Scholars, Information Technology Associates Program, Management Fellows, Media Fellows, and Science Research Fellows, affording selected students additional seminar and internship opportunities.

"Freshman applicants for Fall 2008 and thereafter are required to submit scores of the Writing section of the SAT or the ACT. Scores from previous SAT or ACT administrations will be considered, but a Writing score is required to complete an application for admission."

SELECTIVITY

Admissions Rating	90
# of applicants	4,074
% of applicants accepted	68
% of acceptees attending	22
# accepting a place on wait list	38
% admitted from wait list	68
# of early decision applicants	50
% accepted early decision	82

FRESHMAN PROFILE

Range SAT Critical Reading	560–660
Range SAT Math	570–660
Range SAT Writing	550–650
Range ACT Composite	25–29
Minimum Paper TOEFL	560
Minimum Computer Based TOEFL	225
Average HS GPA	3.6
% graduated top 10% of class	46
% graduated top 25% of class	81
% graduated top 50% of class	99

DEADLINES

Early decision application deadline	11/1
Early decision notification	1/1
Regular application deadline	2/1
Regular notification	4/1
Nonfall registration?	yes

APPLICANTS ALSO LOOK AT

AND OFTEN PREFER
Indiana University—Bloomington, Northwestern University, University of Notre Dame, Vanderbilt University

AND SOMETIMES PREFER
Denison University, Miami University, Purdue University—West Lafayette, University of Illinois at Urbana-Champaign, Washington University in St. Louis

AND RARELY PREFER
Hanover College

FINANCIAL FACTS

Financial Aid Rating	98
Annual tuition	$29,300
Room & Board	$8,100
Books and supplies	$700
Required fees	$480
% frosh rec. need-based scholarship or grant aid	50
% UG rec. need-based scholarship or grant aid	46
% frosh rec. need-based self-help aid	37
% UG rec. need-based self-help aid	35
% frosh rec. any financial aid	97
% UG rec. any financial aid	96

DICKINSON COLLEGE

PO BOX 1773, CARLISLE, PA 17013-2896 • ADMISSIONS: 717-245-1231 • FAX: 717-245-1442

CAMPUS LIFE

Quality of Life Rating	79
Fire Safety Rating	76
Type of school	private
Environment	city

STUDENTS

Total undergrad enrollment	2,369
% male/female	44/56
% from out of state	73
% from public high school	61
% live on campus	92
% in (# of) fraternities	18 (6)
% in (# of) sororities	24 (4)
% African American	5
% Asian	4
% Caucasian	80
% Hispanic	4
% international	6
# of countries represented	37

SURVEY SAYS . . .

Small classes
Great computer facilities
Great library
Lots of beer drinking

ACADEMICS

Academic Rating	91
Calendar	semester
Student/faculty ratio	12:1
Profs interesting rating	88
Profs accessible rating	93
% profs teaching	
UG courses	100
% classes taught by TAs	0
Most common	
lab size	fewer than 10 students
Most common	
reg class size	10–19 students

MOST POPULAR MAJORS
international business
political science and government
psychology

STUDENTS SAY

Academics

Offering "an intense and global curriculum" driven by a study abroad program "unsurpassed by most institutions," Dickinson College pursues a mission of "preparing future leaders to become important movers and shapers in America and abroad." A focus on international matters is just one way in which Dickinson is "constantly defining itself as a revolutionary institution." The school also has "a strong tradition of encouraging students to go beyond the things that are familiar and comfortable and to engage the world around them" through fieldwork and participation in faculty research. The workload here can be tough; one undergraduate warns, "Academically, Dickinson can be a bit overwhelming, as much is demanded from each student; however, all the work will be worth it in the long run." Help is always available: "The classes tend to be pretty small, which creates a good learning environment. The professors are great [and] would love nothing more than to meet with every student in every one of their classes." Reviews of administrators are mixed, but most appreciate the personal touches, like the fact that "the president of the college has open hours at a café where students can just come in and talk to him." Despite a few complaints about the brass being "much more concerned with image than with students, something is working [since] we've jumped a lot in the rankings" in recent years. Add up all the plusses here and you'll understand why "Dickinson is getting harder and harder to get into. Suddenly, when I go home people recognize where I go to school."

Life

How you react to life at Dickinson depends largely on how you react to Carlisle, Dickinson's hometown. There are those who "love small towns like this one, which has tons of good restaurants. The biggest thing in the town is the 24-hour Super Wal-Mart, which sits atop a hill on the edge of town. For fun, there are a few things to do in the town, including dining, movies, and a bowling alley." Undergrads "who are 21 go out to the couple of bars and mix it up with the townies." Then there are those who insist adamantly that Carlisle "is not a college town" and "Off campus there is virtually nothing to do." Most students fill their time by "getting involved in lots of different organizations, volunteer networks, and special housing activities," immersing themselves in Greek life and hitting the party scene. But "If students don't like to be around [partying], there are always numerous things happening on campus that do not involve alcohol on the weekends and weeknights. There are always two or three evening lectures per week as well as midnight movies, dry-dance parties, comedians, concerts—you name it, it has probably been done at Dickinson."

Student Body

Most students agree that at first glance, "Dickinson looks very preppy—the Louis Vuitton bags, popped collars, guys in pastels—but there is more to it than that. It took a bit of searching, but there are plenty of people here who run against the grain—and they all fit in fine. There may not be a ton of interaction between the sorority girls and the hippie kids, but there isn't any animosity." Since the late 1990s, Dickinson has aggressively recruited beyond its traditional core constituencies and has even created special interest housing: Arts Haüs, a residential community for "alternative punk kids," and Tree House, for environmentally conscious (i.e., hippie) students. Undergrads detect "a more politically active, alternative subculture 'within the limestone walls' that is rapidly emerging." The school is also home to "a large homosexual population, which is accepted by all students, [and] many international students coming from numerous foreign countries." As one junior declares, "The school is doing a great deal to make the campus more diverse. In my 3 years, I would say they have been successful in recruiting a more diverse student body, economically and ethnically."

FINANCIAL AID: 717-245-1308 • E-MAIL: ADMIT@DICKINSON.EDU • WEBSITE: WWW.DICKINSON.EDU

ADMISSIONS

Very important factors considered include: Academic GPA, extracurricular activities, rigor of secondary school record, talent/ability, volunteer work. *Important factors considered include:* Alumni/ae relation, class rank, recommendation(s), standardized test scores, work experience. *Other factors considered include:* Application essay, character/personal qualities, first generation, geographical residence, interview, level of applicant's interest, racial/ethnic status, state residency. SAT or ACT recommended; TOEFL required of all international applicants. High school diploma is required, and GED is accepted. *Academic units required:* 4 English, 3 math, 3 science (2 science labs), 2 foreign language, 2 social studies, 2 academic electives. *Academic units recommended:* 3 foreign language.

The Inside Word

Dickinson's admissions process is typical of most small liberal arts colleges. The best candidates for such a place are those with solid grades and broad extracurricular involvement—the stereotypical "well-rounded student." Admissions selectivity is kept in check by a strong group of competitor colleges that fight tooth and nail for their cross-applicants.

FINANCIAL AID

Students should submit: FAFSA, CSS/Financial Aid PROFILE, Noncustodial PROFILE, state aid form, Business/Farm Supplement. Regular filing deadline is February 1. The Princeton Review suggests that all financial aid forms be submitted as soon as possible after January 1. *Need-based scholarships/grants offered:* Pell Grant, SEOG, state scholarships/grants, private scholarships, the school's own gift aid. *Loan aid offered:* FFEL Subsidized Stafford, FFEL Unsubsidized Stafford, FFEL PLUS, Federal Perkins Loan, college/university loans from institutional funds. Applicants will be notified of awards on or about March 31.

FROM THE ADMISSIONS OFFICE

"College is more than a collection of courses. It is about crossing traditional boundaries, about seeing the interrelationships among different subjects, about learning a paradigm for solving problems, about developing critical thinking and communication skills, and about speaking out on issues that matter. Dickinson was intended as an alternative to the 15 colleges that existed in the U.S. at the time of its founding; its aim, then as now, was to provide a "useful" education whereby students would 'learn by doing' through hands-on experience and engagement with the community, the region, the nation, and the world. And this is truer today than ever, with workshop science courses replacing traditional lectures, fieldwork experiences in community studies in which students take oral histories, and 12 study centers abroad in nontourist cities where students, under the guidance of a Dickinson faculty director, experience a true international culture. Almost 58 percent of the student body study abroad and a total of 61 percent study off campus, preparing them to compete and succeed in a complex global world.

"Applicants wishing to be considered for academic scholarships are required to submit scores from either the SAT or ACT, but Dickinson does not require results from either test for admission into the 2008 entering class."

SELECTIVITY

Admissions Rating	**93**
# of applicants	5,298
% of applicants accepted	43
% of acceptees attending	27
# accepting a place on wait list	330
% admitted from wait list	10
# of early decision applicants	489
% accepted early decision	48

FRESHMAN PROFILE

Range SAT Critical Reading	600–690
Range SAT Math	600–680
Range ACT Composite	26–30
Minimum Paper TOEFL	600
Minimum Computer Based TOEFL	250
% graduated top 10% of class	53
% graduated top 25% of class	84
% graduated top 50% of class	97

DEADLINES

Early decision application deadline	11/15
Early decision notification	12/15
Regular application deadline	2/1
Regular notification	3/31
Nonfall registration?	no

APPLICANTS ALSO LOOK AT

AND OFTEN PREFER
Colby College, Georgetown University, Hamilton College

AND SOMETIMES PREFER
Bucknell University, Franklin & Marshall College, Gettysburg College, Lafayette College

AND RARELY PREFER
Kenyon College, Muhlenberg College, The George Washington University

FINANCIAL FACTS

Financial Aid Rating	**91**
Annual tuition	$35,450
Room & Board	$8,980
Books and supplies	$1,000
Required fees	$334
% frosh rec. need-based scholarship or grant aid	45
% UG rec. need-based scholarship or grant aid	46
% frosh rec. need-based self-help aid	41
% UG rec. need-based self-help aid	41
% frosh rec. any financial aid	50
% UG rec. any financial aid	55

DREW UNIVERSITY

OFFICE OF COLLEGE ADMISSIONS, MADISON, NJ 07940-1493 • ADMISSIONS: 973-408-3739 • FAX: 973-408-3068

STUDENTS SAY

Academics

Both as a small school with university resources and as a suburban school with easy access to big cities, Drew University successfully straddles divergent universes to fashion a unique undergraduate experience. With fewer than 2,000 undergrads, Drew can offer "perfect class sizes" that "really allow professors to teach their material well and students to get immediate feedback on questions they have." One student explains, "Because of Drew's small size, professors and administrators are highly accessible. They go out of their way to make sure that you understand what you're being taught, that you feel like you're going in the right direction. They even e-mail you with clarifications at midnight about that day's lecture because they couldn't sleep, worried you might be confused." Despite the small-school vibe, Drew offers some big-school amenities, including "wonderful opportunities to study abroad, [a] breadth [of] requirements that cause students to take classes they might not think about taking, which can often open up doors for them, [and] strong job-placement and internship programs." Some students warn, "Because Drew is so small, some upper-level classes are only offered every other year, which can make planning a major difficult. This is only true in the smaller departments, however, such as math and physics."

Life

"Drew has an extremely good balance between socializing and studying," students agree, pointing out that "we work hard during the week, but on any Thursday, Friday, or Saturday night, it is easy to find a party and drink, if that's what you want to do. It's just as easy, however, to stay in with friends and watch a movie or just hang out. The chill factor here is pretty high." Because "The alcohol policy is very lenient (it's basically 'If we don't see it, it's not happening'), alcohol is a popular pastime." Parties often occur in "the Suites," a residence for upperclassmen and are frequently hosted by male athletic teams. Some undergrads warn that these parties "are not always open to everyone," and "If you want to party and get drunk, it helps to be an athlete or friends with a large group of them." There is a lot more to life at Drew than drinking and working, though. The school boasts a very active Theater Department: "Theater is a very big part of Drew life. Students are more supportive of theatrical events than of most sporting events." Hometown Madison is "an art-oriented town, so there is a lot of opportunity for cultural activities," although be forewarned that "the town goes to sleep at 6:00 P.M." Fortunately, "New York City is close by, although it's harder to get there than the school would have you believe. Still, it's nice to be isolated in a safe suburb where you can be in NYC in an hour."

Student Body

"There are two main groups within the Drew student population," according to students: "the athletes and their friends" and the "artsy" crowd. The former congregate in such popular social science departments as political science, economics, and psychology; the latter dominate the Theater Department. Most students are active within the campus community, as "Drew is a predominantly student-run school. Students decide the activities, help work on policies, and generally run campus life. Drew is a campus of leaders, which is what makes it so exciting." Students are also active politically, with the balance tipped to the left; one student observes, "Drew can best be understood by viewing the movie *PCU*—minus the Republicans." Drew's relatively high price tag, coupled with its proximity to Northeastern wealth centers, means that "many students are loaded—sons and daughters of governors and ambassadors whose families have at least two houses somewhere around the world." The school "has a large gay population, and they tend to stick together but have no problems getting along with other students."

FINANCIAL AID: 973-408-3112 • E-MAIL: CADM@DREW.EDU • WEBSITE: WWW.DREW.EDU

ADMISSIONS

Very important factors considered include: Academic GPA, rigor of secondary school record, talent/ability. *Important factors considered include:* Application essay, extracurricular activities, interview, level of applicant's interest, recommendation(s). *Other factors considered include:* Alumni/ae relation, character/personal qualities, class rank, first generation, geographical residence, racial/ethnic status, standardized test scores, volunteer work, work experience. ACT with Writing component recommended. TOEFL required of all international applicants. High school diploma or equivalent is not required. *Academic units recommended:* 4 English, 3 math, 2 science, 2 foreign language, 2 social studies, 2 history, 3 academic electives.

The Inside Word

Drew University no longer requires standardized test scores for undergraduate admission consideration. Students applying to Drew for the 2006–2007 academic year may choose to submit SAT and ACT scores to Drew. Those who choose not to submit standardized test scores to Drew will be required to include with their admissions materials a high school paper graded by a teacher.

FINANCIAL AID

Students should submit: FAFSA, CSS/Financial Aid PROFILE. Regular filing deadline is February 15. The Princeton Review suggests that all financial aid forms be submitted as soon as possible after January 1. *Need-based scholarships/grants offered:* Pell Grant, SEOG, state scholarships/grants, private scholarships, the school's own gift aid. *Loan aid offered:* FFEL Subsidized Stafford, FFEL Unsubsidized Stafford, FFEL PLUS, Federal Perkins Loan, state loans. Applicants will be notified of awards on or about April 1. Federal Work-Study Program available. Institutional employment available. Off-campus job opportunities are excellent.

FROM THE ADMISSIONS OFFICE

"At Drew, great teachers are transforming the undergraduate learning experience. With a commitment to teaching, Drew professors have made educating undergraduates their top priority. With a spirit of innovation, they have brought the most advanced technology and distinctive modes of experiential learning into the Drew classroom. The result is a stimulating and challenging education that connects the traditional liberal arts and sciences to the workplace and to the world.

"Drew University will require applicants for the 2008–2009 academic year to take either the new SAT or the ACT. The Selection Committee will consider the highest Verbal, Math, and Writing scores individually in its evaluation of candidates for admission."

SELECTIVITY

Admissions Rating	88
# of applicants	4,532
% of applicants accepted	64
% of acceptees attending	17
# of early decision applicants	145
% accepted early decision	61

FRESHMAN PROFILE

Range SAT Critical Reading	530–650
Range SAT Math	530–630
Range ACT Composite	24–28
Minimum Paper TOEFL	550
Minimum Computer Based TOEFL	213
Average HS GPA	3.39
% graduated top 10% of class	37
% graduated top 25% of class	68
% graduated top 50% of class	94

DEADLINES

Early decision application deadline	12/1
Early decision notification	12/24
Regular application deadline	2/15
Regular notification	3/21
Nonfall registration?	yes

APPLICANTS ALSO LOOK AT AND SOMETIMES PREFER

Connecticut College, Dickinson College, Franklin & Marshall College, Muhlenberg College, New York University, Rutgers University—Rutgers College, Skidmore College, Trinity College (CT), Vassar College

FINANCIAL FACTS

Financial Aid Rating	79
Annual tuition	$32,508
Room & Board	$9,000
Books and supplies	$3,090
Required fees	$942
% frosh rec. need-based scholarship or grant aid	51
% UG rec. need-based scholarship or grant aid	48
% frosh rec. need-based self-help aid	42
% UG rec. need-based self-help aid	41
% frosh rec. any financial aid	90
% UG rec. any financial aid	82

DREXEL UNIVERSITY

3141 CHESTNUT STREET, PHILADELPHIA, PA 19104 • ADMISSIONS: 215-895-2400 • FAX: 215-895-5939

STUDENTS SAY
Academics
Drexel University "is a lot of work squarely aimed at integration into the professional world," whether that world involves the school's popular majors in engineering, technology, and business, or less-known offerings like the school's programs in the music industry or hospitality management. Drexel has a growing digital media program, making it "one of the only schools in the area with a developed program" in the field. Central to the Drexel experience is the "extremely beneficial" co-op program, which many agree is "the best thing about Drexel." Co-op provides 18 months of professional experience during the 5-year undergraduate program. One student writes, "You will learn as much in the first couple of months of working in the real world as you did in any college. Drexel gives you all of that knowledge before you're even out of school and gives you the preparation necessary to succeed in the real world." The school's location in Philadelphia, "a source of endless fun and opportunity," helps co-op considerably. "Engineering dominates" at Drexel, but the school "has a variety of programs fit for almost anyone," with "a lot of classes run with web-based resources. Lectures are posted online in WebCT, as well as course syllabi and assignments. This makes it easy to access information. Teachers are easy to get in touch with via e-mail and are very accessible to meet with as needed." Administrative tasks are not so convenient; students warn of "lots of red tape," adding that "most issues require visits to at least three different offices, sometimes on opposite ends of campus." Fortunately, the campus isn't that large.

Life
Campus life at Drexel must compete with the temptations offered by Philadelphia, one of the nation's largest cities. Philly provides "so many things to do (if you have the money) that it can be hard to know where to begin." Students tell us that "museums are great. Lots of kids go to concerts, and there are all sorts, all the time. First Fridays in Center City is also popular." The area immediately surrounding the school has plenty of "great bars, food, and dancing." Drexel is close to the UPenn campus, "and students often go into their parties, which are extraordinary." On campus, "There are numerous fraternities and societies you can join." Intercollegiate sports "aren't incredibly popular here," but "The basketball team is really taking off and is always sold out." Drexel's grounds, once an unbroken sea of brick and concrete, have been renovated; today "There are plenty of green grassy areas for students to hang out and relax," as well as "a new beautiful amphitheater and some nice tree-lined walkways with benches and tables."

Student Body
There "are no real typical students at Drexel. [It's] is a pretty diverse school, with students involved in different kinds of activities, dressing differently, and motivated differently." The school "is a melting pot" with "many, many international and minority students." One student notes, "Drexel's common factor seems to be not race or economic background, but a sense of personal drive. Drexel students work hard—it's a requirement to keep afloat—and that self-propulsion seems to be the tie that binds the student body together." If undergrads "seem to fit in well together," that may be because "Students here are very casual and easygoing." Some have quirky senses of humor; take the one who reports that "the students tend to be of the human variety, with genders varying from male to female. Everyone has their clique, and it takes quite a bit of effort to be excluded from them all."

DREXEL UNIVERSITY

FINANCIAL AID: 215-895-2535 • E-MAIL: ENROLL@DREXEL.EDU • WEBSITE: WWW.DREXEL.EDU

ADMISSIONS

Very important factors considered include: Academic GPA, application essay, class rank, rigor of secondary school record, standardized test scores. *Important factors considered include:* Character/personal qualities, extracurricular activities, interview, recommendation(s), talent/ability. *Other factors considered include:* Alumni/ae relation, first generation, level of applicant's interest, volunteer work, work experience. SAT or ACT required; TOEFL required of all international applicants. High school diploma is required, and GED is accepted. *Academic units required:* 3 math, 1 science (1 science lab). *Academic units recommended:* 1 foreign language.

The Inside Word

Drexel operates on a rolling admissions basis, meaning that admissions decisions are made relatively quickly after all application materials reach the school. Rolling admissions tend to favor those who apply early in the process, when schools are still worried about whether they will be able to fill their incoming classes. Regardless of when you apply, you shouldn't have too much trouble here if your application establishes you as firmly above average.

FINANCIAL AID

Students should submit: FAFSA. The Princeton Review suggests that all financial aid forms be submitted as soon as possible after January 1. *Need-based scholarships/grants offered:* Pell Grant, SEOG, state scholarships/grants, private scholarships, the school's own gift aid, United Negro College Fund. *Loan aid offered:* FFEL Subsidized Stafford, FFEL Unsubsidized Stafford, FFEL PLUS, Federal Perkins Loan, Federal Nursing Loan, college/university loans from institutional funds. Applicants will be notified of awards on a rolling basis beginning or about March 15. Federal Work-Study Program available.

FROM THE ADMISSIONS OFFICE

"Drexel has gained a reputation for academic excellence since its founding in 1891. In 2006, Drexel became the first top-ranked doctoral university in more than 25 years to open a law school. Its main campus is a 10-minute walk from Center City Philadelphia.

"Students prepare for successful careers through Drexel's prestigious experiential education program—The Drexel Co-op. Alternating periods of full-time professional employment with periods of classroom study, students can earn an average of $14,000 per 6-month co-op. At any one time, about 2,000 full-time undergraduates are on co-op assignments.

"Drexel integrates science and technology into all 70 undergraduate majors. Students looking for a special challenge can apply to one of 14 accelerated degree programs including the BS/MBA in business; BA/BS/MD in medicine; BA/BS/JD in law; BS/MS or BS/PhD in engineering; BS/MS in information technology; and BS/DPT in physical therapy.

"Pennoni Honors College offers high achievers unique opportunities. Students Tackling Advanced Research (STAR) allows qualified undergraduates to participate in a paid summer research project, and the Center for Civic Engagement matches students with community service opportunities. Students in any major can take dance, music, and theater classes offered through Drexel's performing arts programs.

"Drexel's study abroad program allows students to spend a term or more earning credits while gaining international experience. Adventurous students can also enjoy co-op abroad. Locations include London, Costa Rica, Prague, Rome, and Paris.

"The Admissions Office invites prospective students to schedule a campus visit for a first-hand look at all Drexel offers.

"Drexel University is currently exploring how to use the new Writing component in admission and placement decisions."

"Students who plan to enter in Fall 2008 will be one of the first classes to take the new SAT for college admissions. Drexel is exploring ways in which the additional Writing component can be used in admissions or placement decisions."

SELECTIVITY

Admissions Rating	85
# of applicants	14,301
% of applicants accepted	75.4
% of acceptees attending	27
# accepting a place on wait list	331
% admitted from wait list	N/A

FRESHMAN PROFILE

Range SAT Critical Reading	520–630
Range SAT Math	550–670
Minimum Paper TOEFL	550
Minimum Computer Based TOEFL	213
Average HS GPA	3.34
% graduated top 10% of class	30
% graduated top 25% of class	60
% graduated top 50% of class	90

DEADLINES

Regular application deadline	3/1
Regular notification	rolling basis
Nonfall registration?	yes

FINANCIAL FACTS

Financial Aid Rating	65
Annual tuition	$27,200
Room & Board	$11,610
Books and supplies	$1,580
% frosh rec. need-based scholarship or grant aid	31
% UG rec. need-based scholarship or grant aid	32
% frosh rec. need-based self-help aid	62
% UG rec. need-based self-help aid	60
% frosh rec. any financial aid	94
% UG rec. any financial aid	89

DUKE UNIVERSITY

2138 CAMPUS DRIVE, DURHAM, NC 27708 • ADMISSIONS: 919-684-3214 • FAX: 919-681-8941

STUDENTS SAY

Academics

Duke University, "the fun younger brother of the aging Ivies," offers a "well-rounded atmosphere" that allows students to enjoy "top 10 academics, a beautiful campus, a wonderful climate, a fun social scene, and the toughest place for opposing teams to play basketball in the country." Biomedical engineering and premedical sciences are all strong here, contributing to Duke's position as a leading national medical research institute. In fact, academics are excellent across disciplines, although a junior advises that "small departments—like Art History, History, Literature—are run better and tend to have better teachers, while the more popular departments—such as Political Science and Biology—are more bureaucratic and filled with tenured famous researchers who are not as interested in teaching." Duke expects a lot of work from students, and "Grading is very strict," but students "don't feel overly pressured." The school also operates under an honor code that "is taken very seriously. You see virtually no cheating." Students can single out particular strengths of their school when pressed, but they prefer to focus on the gestalt of the place; time and again they remind us that Duke is "a top-notch academic institution, unparalleled in the South, where emphasis is placed on both in-class academic experiences as well as cultivating sociable, friendly people who will be able to succeed in all future life situations."

Life

"Durham is far from a college town," Duke students agree, but fortunately "lots of activities occur at Duke," and Chapel Hill—a great college town—is only 15 minutes down the road. Raleigh, with nightlife considerably more active than Durham's, is less than a half-hour away by car. Duke's campus hosts "many theater productions, dance shows, music concerts, guest speakers, and artists" as well as lectures and movies, many of which are free or greatly discounted. Duke students also love to sit around and shoot the breeze—"The benches on campus definitely help the social scene"—and point out that "conversations can range from a biology lab one minute to the current health care debate the next, then eventually [move] on to the difference between Protestants and Catholics and [end] with a discussion of the next men's basketball game." Discussion often comes around to Duke basketball, which some claim "is what unites every single student at Duke. You can come to Duke not being a sports fan, but you will become a Blue Devils fan. We are not only a highly recognized tier-one academic institution, but we also have one of the top basketball teams in the country." Undergrads also love that their "campus is absolutely gorgeous" and that "the weather in the South is beautiful," accommodating year-round outdoor activity. Duke has a party scene, or rather, several (centered on the Greek houses, dorms, and off-campus apartments), although this may be changing, as "Strict alcohol policies are pushing a lot of weekend activity off campus."

Student Body

"A couple years ago, Duke may have been considered a school filled with rich White kids," students tell us, "but now there's such a high number of minorities that that stereotype no longer applies. I think we have one of the highest African American student populations of any top-ranked university. The Asian population is considerable too." The numbers bear out these reports. Vestiges of the 'old Duke' remain, especially in the "Southern fraternity types" who "account for about 30 percent of the students." Cost limits economic diversity here somewhat, since many of the students pay full fare; "It is amazing to me how many students here are able to pay full price to attend the university without financial aid, given that it costs close to $40,000 per year," marvels one aid recipient. Students may not always form one big happy family—"Self-segregation is evident everywhere"—but they all share a sincere love for the school. "I'd say 40 to 60 percent of the community is wearing some form of Duke gear at any given time," estimates one undergrad.

FINANCIAL AID: 919-684-6225 • E-MAIL: UNDERGRAD-ADMISSIONS@DUKE.EDU • WEBSITE: WWW.DUKE.EDU

ADMISSIONS

Very important factors considered include: Application essay, extracurricular activities, recommendation(s), rigor of secondary school record, standardized test scores, talent/ability. *Important factors considered include:* Character/personal qualities. *Other factors considered include:* Academic GPA, alumni/ae relation, class rank, geographical residence, interview, racial/ethnic status, state residency, volunteer work, work experience. SAT and SAT Subject Tests or ACT required. High school diploma is required, and GED is not accepted. *Academic units recommended:* 4 English, 4 math, 4 science, 4 foreign language, 4 social studies.

The Inside Word

The way in which Duke discusses its candidate review process should be a basic model for all schools to use in their literature. Just about all highly selective Admissions Committees use rating systems similar to the one described above, but few are willing to publicly discuss them.

FINANCIAL AID

Students should submit: FAFSA, CSS/Financial Aid PROFILE, Noncustodial PROFILE, Business/Farm Supplement, Federal Income Tax Returns. Regular filing deadline is March 1. The Princeton Review suggests that all financial aid forms be submitted as soon as possible after January 1. *Need-based scholarships/grants offered:* Pell Grant, SEOG, state scholarships/grants, private scholarships, the school's own gift aid, ROTC. *Loan aid offered:* FFEL Subsidized Stafford, FFEL Unsubsidized Stafford, FFEL PLUS, Federal Perkins Loan, college/university loans from institutional funds, private loans. Applicants will be notified of awards on or about April 1. Federal Work-Study Program available. Institutional employment available. Off-campus job opportunities are good.

FROM THE ADMISSIONS OFFICE

"Duke University offers an interesting mix of tradition and innovation, undergraduate college and major research university, Southern hospitality and international presence, and athletic prowess and academic excellence. Students come to Duke from all over the United States and the world and from a range of racial, ethnic, and socioeconomic backgrounds. They enjoy contact with a world-class faculty through small classes and independent study. More than 40 majors are available in the arts and sciences and engineering; arts and sciences students may also design their own curriculum through Program II. Certificate programs are available in a number of interdisciplinary areas. Special academic opportunities include the Focus Program and seminars for first-year students, study abroad, study at the Duke Marine Laboratory and Duke Primate Center, the Duke in New York and Duke in Los Angeles arts programs, and several international exchange programs. While admission to Duke is highly selective, applications of U.S. citizens and permanent residents are evaluated without regard to financial need and the university pledges to meet 100 percent of the demonstrated need of all admitted U.S. students and permanent residents. A limited amount of financial aid is also available for foreign citizens, and the university will meet the full demonstrated financial need for those admitted students as well.

"Applicants must take either the ACT with the Writing exam, or the three-part SAT plus two SAT Subject Tests (Mathematics Subject Test required for applicants to the Pratt School of Engineering)."

SELECTIVITY

Admissions Rating	99
# of applicants	18,090
% of applicants accepted	22
% of acceptees attending	43
# accepting a place on wait list	1,026
% admitted from wait list	10
# of early decision applicants	1,482
% accepted early decision	32

FRESHMAN PROFILE

Range SAT Critical Reading	690–770
Range SAT Math	690–800
Range ACT Composite	29–34
% graduated top 10% of class	90
% graduated top 25% of class	98
% graduated top 50% of class	100

DEADLINES

Early decision application deadline	11/1
Early decision notification	12/15
Regular application deadline	1/2
Regular notification	4/1
Nonfall registration?	no

APPLICANTS ALSO LOOK AT

AND OFTEN PREFER
Harvard College, Princeton University, Stanford University, Yale University

AND SOMETIMES PREFER
Brown University, Cornell University, Dartmouth College, University of Pennsylvania

AND RARELY PREFER
Georgetown University, Northwestern University, The University of North Carolina at Chapel Hill, University of Virginia

FINANCIAL FACTS

Financial Aid Rating	93
Annual tuition	$31,420
Room & Board	$8,950
Books and supplies	$970
Required fees	$1,180
% frosh rec. need-based scholarship or grant aid	38
% UG rec. need-based scholarship or grant aid	37
% frosh rec. need-based self-help aid	35
% UG rec. need-based self-help aid	35

DUQUESNE UNIVERSITY

600 FORBES AVENUE, PITTSBURGH, PA 15282 • ADMISSIONS: 412-396-2222 • FAX: 412-396-5644

STUDENTS SAY

Academics

Located in a great town for both career networking and college fun, Pittsburgh's Duquesne University offers a prestigious private school education to a "smart, ambitious, and very goal-oriented" student body that "prides itself on its 'Catholic' tradition." DU is perhaps best known for its health sciences programs; students laud the "rigorous pharmacy curriculum," the "wonderful" physical therapy program and "great" nursing, occupational, and athletic training programs, all of which benefit from "great access to all the hospitals in the area." The music program at Duquesne is "amazing," and students say "The employment rate of students that have graduated from the music education program is phenomenal. I'm almost positive every senior that graduated was placed at a job already." Students in many of these areas pursue DUs accelerated bachelor's/graduate degree programs. Regardless of what they study, all DU students must complete a core curriculum that stresses broad general knowledge; students have mixed feelings about the core, warning that these classes are "harder than other courses" and are especially labor intensive. Throughout the school, "Most classes are lecture-driven courses" with relatively large class sizes at the lower levels. The majority of professors are "excellent teachers and very knowledgeable of their respective fields," although, as anywhere, "There are a few awful ones." Nearly all "make themselves available to help you anytime you need. . . . If you are not good at a particular subject, they . . . have tutors available to help you."

Life

Student life at Duquesne "is lots of fun," although students say that has more to do with hometown Pittsburgh than with the DU campus. True, the campus offers numerous diversions, including "movies and crafts and sports and tons of organizations," in addition to weekend frat parties which are quite popular with the Greek crowd and underclassmen. However, most students find city life more tempting, reporting that they "like to go downtown to shop, or to the South Side, or to the Waterfront." Oakland is really close by, with "lots of bars, restaurants," and "other colleges." One student explains, "There's always something going on in Pittsburgh, whether it's free concerts, cultural events, or art exhibits, many of which you are admitted into for free or reduced price with a Duquesne ID." The only downside is the weather: "If you're looking for fun, be prepared to bundle up in the winter and to travel by bus or taxi," one student warns. The "beautiful" DU campus features "lots of fountains and grassy areas and stuff." Location is another plus, as the campus is in the middle of Pittsburgh but still has a very private feel. "We have the opportunities of the city but we are secluded on the bluff."

Student Body

The typical Duquesne undergrad is either "well put together" or "cares too much about the way they look"—it's all a matter of perspective. Since most here are the "dress for success" type, the former viewpoint is more popular than the latter, although the "wearing-sweats-and-being-comfortable crowd" make up "about a third" of the campus, so they're hardly a tiny minority. Because "many students at Duquesne went to high school together," the school tends to be quite clique-y. Undergrads also tend to self-segregate by major. As one music student writes, "The typical music major is completely different from the typical student. The majority of music majors have somewhat eclectic taste in fashion, clothing, hobbies . . . which reflects in our personalities. We also talk about stuff we're doing in class outside of school, which isn't very common among other majors." While most students here are Catholic, "There are also people of different religions," and the school "doesn't impose religion" on anyone.

DUQUESNE UNIVERSITY

FINANCIAL AID: 412-396-6607 • E-MAIL: ADMISSIONS@DUQ.EDU • WEBSITE: WWW.DUQ.EDU

ADMISSIONS

Very important factors considered include: Academic GPA, application essay, recommendation(s), rigor of secondary school record, standardized test scores. *Important factors considered include:* Character/personal qualities, class rank, extracurricular activities, interview, talent/ability, volunteer work. *Other factors considered include:* Alumni/ae relation, first generation, level of applicant's interest, racial/ethnic status, work experience. SAT or ACT required; ACT with Writing component required. High school diploma is required, and GED is accepted. *Academic units required:* 4 English, 2 math, 2 science, 2 foreign language, 2 social studies, 4 academic electives.

The Inside Word

Duquesne's overall high admit rate masks the competitiveness of its top programs. Applicants seeking admission to programs in pharmacy, physical therapy, physician's assistant, and forensic science should expect a rigorous review. Others should have little difficulty getting through the door provided they present a respectable complement of transcripts and test scores.

FINANCIAL AID

Students should submit: FAFSA, institution's own financial aid form. Regular filing deadline is May 1. The Princeton Review suggests that all financial aid forms be submitted as soon as possible after January 1. *Need-based scholarships/grants offered:* Pell Grant, SEOG, state scholarships/grants, private scholarships, the school's own gift aid, United Negro College Fund. *Loan aid offered:* FFEL Subsidized Stafford, FFEL Unsubsidized Stafford, FFEL PLUS, Federal Perkins Loan, Federal Nursing Loan, private alternative loans. Applicants will be notified of awards on a rolling basis beginning or about March 1. Federal Work-Study Program available. Institutional employment available. Off-campus job opportunities are good.

FROM THE ADMISSIONS OFFICE

"Duquesne University was founded in 1878 by the Holy Ghost Fathers. Although it is a private, Roman Catholic institution, Duquesne is proud of its ecumenical reputation. The total university enrollment is 10,110. Duquesne University's attractive and secluded campus is set on a 50-acre hilltop ('the bluff') overlooking the large corporate metropolis of Pittsburgh's Golden Triangle. It offers a wide variety of educational opportunities, from the liberal arts to modern professional training. Duquesne is a medium-sized university striving to offer personal attention to its students in addition to the versatility and opportunities of a true university. A deep sense of tradition is combined with innovation and flexibility to make the Duquesne experience both challenging and rewarding. The Palumbo Convocation/Recreation Complex features a 6,300-seat arena, home court to the university's Division I basketball teams; racquetball and handball courts, weight rooms, and saunas. Extracurricular activities are recognized as an essential part of college life, complementing academics in the process of total student development. Students are involved in nearly 100 university-sponsored activities, and Duquesne's location gives students the opportunity to enjoy sports and cultural events both on campus and in the city. There are six residence halls with the capacity to house 3,534 students.

"Although SAT Writing scores will not affect admissions decisions, all freshman applicants are required to take the new SAT (or the ACT with the Writing section). Applicants may choose to submit scores from the old (prior to March 2005) version of the SAT (or ACT) as well, and we will use the student's best scores from either test."

SELECTIVITY

Admissions Rating	84
# of applicants	5,252
% of applicants accepted	72
% of acceptees attending	35
# of early decision applicants	60
% accepted early decision	63

FRESHMAN PROFILE

Range SAT Critical Reading	510–600
Range SAT Math	520–620
Range SAT Writing	510–600
Range ACT Composite	21–26
Average HS GPA	3.65
% graduated top 10% of class	28
% graduated top 25% of class	57
% graduated top 50% of class	88

DEADLINES

Early decision application deadline	11/1
Early decision notification	12/15
Regular application deadline	7/1
Regular notification	rolling
Nonfall registration?	yes

APPLICANTS ALSO LOOK AT
AND OFTEN PREFER
Pennsylvania State University—University Park, University of Pittsburgh—Pittsburgh Campus, Washington & Jefferson College
AND SOMETIMES PREFER
Allegheny College, Gannon University, Saint Vincent College, West Virginia University
AND RARELY PREFER
Catholic University of Leuven, Marquette University, St. Bonaventure University

FINANCIAL FACTS

Financial Aid Rating	84
Annual tuition	$20,855
Room & Board	$8,296
Books and supplies	$600
Required fees	$1,810
% frosh rec. need-based scholarship or grant aid	73
% UG rec. need-based scholarship or grant aid	64
% frosh rec. need-based self-help aid	62
% UG rec. need-based self-help aid	56
% frosh rec. any financial aid	93
% UG rec. any financial aid	85

ECKERD COLLEGE

4200 FIFTY-FOURTH AVENUE SOUTH, ST. PETERSBURG, FL 33711 • ADMISSIONS: 727-864-8331 • FAX: 727-866-2304

CAMPUS LIFE
Quality of Life Rating	79
Fire Safety Rating	60*
Type of school	private
Affiliation	Presbyterian
Environment	city

STUDENTS
Total undergrad enrollment	1,826
% male/female	44/56
% from out of state	75
% live on campus	78
% African American	3
% Asian	2
% Caucasian	78
% Hispanic	4
% international	4
# of countries represented	33

SURVEY SAYS . . .
Great library
Frats and sororities are unpopular or nonexistent
Lots of beer drinking
Hard liquor is popular

ACADEMICS
Academic Rating	80
Calendar	4-1-4
Student/faculty ratio	13:1
Profs interesting rating	86
Profs accessible rating	90
% profs teaching UG courses	100
% classes taught by TAs	0
Most common lab size	20–29 students
Most common reg class size	20–29 students

MOST POPULAR MAJORS
business administration/ management
environmental studies
marine biology and biological oceanography

STUDENTS SAY

Academics
Florida's Eckerd College may be small, but it only seems small "where it matters, like class size[s] and relationships with professors." It also offers many "big-school opportunities that make it seem bigger than it is." Among the school's most distinguished offerings are an "amazing" marine science program—"If it's not your passion," students say, "it will eat you alive"—and a "great international relations program." The latter benefits from a school-wide commitment to undergraduate international travel. One student writes: "International education is great. I spent last January (winter term) in Vietnam, Thailand, Laos, and Cambodia, and next semester I'll be in Sweden on an exchange program." Students tell us that academic programs other than the sciences and international relations "aren't nearly as demanding, and professors don't seem to expect as much out of the students." As one student puts it, "There are two kinds of Eckerd students: Those with easy majors and those [who] watch everyone else party on Tuesdays and skip class to go the beach." Eckerd offers "much flexibility for designing your own concentration or for independent studies" as well as many opportunities "to do research with your professors and advance in ways you couldn't imagine at larger schools." How accessible are professors here? "Pitchers with Professors"—"where students and professors can discuss class lectures or [have] general conversation over a pitcher of beer or a soda"—"is a common occurrence each month."

Life
"It's Florida," explains one student. "Life at school is laid-back." The warm weather "definitely has an effect on the attitude of most people who live on campus." Eckerd's environs include various sports grounds, including beach volleyball courts and a private waterfront where students can take sailing and windsurfing classes. If that's not enough, two gorgeous beaches are less than 10 minutes away, downtown Tampa is only a half-hour away, and Busch Gardens and Disney World are 45 and 90 minutes away, respectively. One student sums up, "The location is amazing. Waking up on the Tampa Bay each morning energizes you." The only drawback is that "Eckerd is somewhat separated from St. Petersburg at large. It's [on] the southern tip of the city and you're really out of luck if you don't have a car or don't know someone who does, since mostly everything worth doing is far away." On campus "The most random of events happen. . . . We've got drum circles on the beach, Saturday Morning Market, Kappa Karnival, Pitchers with Professors, Saturday boat trips to Shell Island, Ybor City, and lots of other things to explore."

Student Body
The Eckerd student body includes "science majors (geeks, if you will)" along with "a small dosage of preppy students," "a lot of surfers, sailors, and tanners," "athletes," "church people," and "trustafarians." Athletes "stick together within their groups," and "The marine science majors sort of are a collective," but students report that "it's easy to make friends and know people in every group." "Overall my friends are a varied crowd," a junior declares. While Eckerd's student body is "mostly White and from a middle- to upper-class background" this "is not a typical college," especially by Florida standards: "Don't expect sorority girls and football players," students warn. It's worth noting that Eckerd "is a very liberal campus, with many Democrats, hippies, marijuana, parties, pets, environmental concern, and a basic openness to new things. If you're close-minded and don't want to see others' views, don't come here."

FINANCIAL AID: 727-864-8334 • E-MAIL: ADMISSIONS@ECKERD.EDU • WEBSITE: WWW.ECKERD.EDU

ADMISSIONS

Very important factors considered include: Academic GPA, rigor of secondary school record. *Important factors considered include:* Application essay, character/personal qualities, extracurricular activities, interview, recommendation(s), standardized test scores, talent/ability. *Other factors considered include:* Alumni/ae relation, class rank, first generation, level of applicant's interest, volunteer work, work experience. SAT or ACT required; TOEFL required of all international applicants. High school diploma is required, and GED is accepted. *Academic units required:* 4 English, 3 math, 3 science (2 science labs), 2 foreign language, 2 social studies, 1 history, 3 academic electives. *Academic units recommended:* 4 math, 4 science (3 science labs), 3 foreign language, 2 history, 3 academic electives.

The Inside Word

Eckerd is looking to upgrade its student body, but competition from other small liberal arts schools is stiff; the school is still a relatively easy admit for B-plus students with decent standardized test scores. The school practices rolling admissions, so apply early to improve your chances—Eckerd can afford to be more selective later in the admissions process, especially with candidates who appear to be headed for its most competitive programs (i.e., marine science and international relations).

FINANCIAL AID

Students should submit: FAFSA. The Princeton Review suggests that all financial aid forms be submitted as soon as possible after January 1. *Need-based scholarships/grants offered:* Pell Grant, SEOG, state scholarships/grants, private scholarships, the school's own gift aid. *Loan aid offered:* FFEL Subsidized Stafford, FFEL Unsubsidized Stafford, FFEL PLUS, Federal Perkins Loan, college/university loans from institutional funds. Applicants will be notified of awards on a rolling basis beginning or about February 1.

FROM THE ADMISSIONS OFFICE

"Eckerd's diverse student body comes from 49 states and 49 countries. In this international setting, the majors of international relations and international business are very popular. Close to 70 percent of our graduates spend at least one term studying abroad. The beautiful waterfront campus is a perfect location for the study of marine science and environmental studies. We characterize Eckerd students as competent givers because of their extensive involvement in the life of the campus and their many volunteer service contributions to the local environment and the St. Petersburg community. The Academy of Senior Professionals draws to campus distinguished persons who have retired from fields our students aspire to enter. Academy members, such as the late novelist James Michener, Nobel Prize–winner Elie Wiesel, and noted Black historian John Hope Franklin, enrich classes and offer valuable counsel for career and life planning.

"Students applying for admission into the Fall 2008 freshman class are allowed to submit old or new SAT or ACT examination results, and Eckerd will use the best scores from either test. The Writing portion will not be considered when determining a student's admission or scholarship."

SELECTIVITY

Admissions Rating	**85**
# of applicants	2,774
% of applicants accepted	72
% of acceptees attending	27
# accepting a place on wait list	26
% admitted from wait list	42

FRESHMAN PROFILE

Range SAT Critical Reading	500–610
Range SAT Math	500–620
Range ACT Composite	22–27
Minimum Paper TOEFL	550
Minimum Computer Based TOEFL	213
Average HS GPA	3.3

DEADLINES

Regular notification	rolling
Nonfall registration?	yes

APPLICANTS ALSO LOOK AT
AND OFTEN PREFER
College of Charleston, Rollins College, University of Central Florida
AND SOMETIMES PREFER
Stetson University, University of Miami, University of Tampa

FINANCIAL FACTS

Financial Aid Rating	**80**
Annual tuition	$27,352
Room & Board	$7,868
Books and supplies	$1,000
Required fees	$272
% frosh rec. any financial aid	96
% UG rec. any financial aid	96

ELON UNIVERSITY

2700 CAMPUS BOX, ELON, NC 27244-2010 • ADMISSIONS: 336-278-3566 • FAX: 336-278-7699

STUDENTS SAY
Academics
Elon University, a "small, preppy, somewhat conservative, highly academic private school" in central North Carolina, is "all about teaching you about your role as a global citizen and enabling you to do experiential learning, not only through discussion-based classes but also through opportunities to study abroad, undergrad research, internships, and involvement in a variety of student organizations." With about 4,850 undergraduates, Elon is "just the right size. It's not too small where everyone knows everyone, but small enough to still get the small-school attributes." At the same time, it's large enough to sustain excellence in a variety of disciplines, including business, communications, a "prestigious but extremely competitive music theater program," an "excellent Teaching Fellows program," and a premed program that's bolstered by an undergraduate cadaver lab—one of only five in the United States. Undergrads tell us that "you can choose how hard you want to work at Elon. One can get away with doing the bare minimum, but those who work hard will get more out of their experience as a whole." It's a plus that "teachers want to see students excel and are, for the most part, very supportive." Study abroad opportunities here are "phenomenal. They are easily arranged and add much to the college experience." One student notes, "I will have studied abroad three times (Peru, Namibia, and Australia) before graduating."

Life
The town of Elon is "a small town that has everything you need: a movie theater, bowling alley, and every food chain, as well as plenty of restaurants and pizza places." If you have no car, though, it can "feel like it's in the middle of nowhere." Access to an automobile opens many options, allowing students to "hit the highway and head to Greensboro, Raleigh, Durham, or Chapel Hill," all reasonably lively places. Even those who are campus bound still have plenty of options. One student explains, "Since Elon is not really a commuter school and there is not a great deal to do in the town itself, getting involved in organizations is really important. Many people commit themselves to a number of the over 150 campus organizations." Undergrads also enjoy a "gorgeous," meticulously maintained campus. "Elon's groundskeeping staff has to be among the best in the nation," offers one student. "If you go outside at 6:30 A.M., there is an army dedicated to lawn care!" Community is strong at this school, with Greek life being "a very big thing at Elon. [Many] of us are or have been in a sorority or fraternity." Another large part of Elon is "Elon Volunteers, the collection of Elon's service programs, organizations, and events." Intercollegiate athletics, in contrast, are neglected, since "Everyone knows our teams are most likely going to get beaten," although a winning men's basketball season has helped disprove that. Socially speaking, Elon has a hopping party scene, but though "most people party on the weekends, the library is packed on Sunday afternoons."

Student Body
"Attending Elon is a lot like attending a country club," students tell us, observing that "your typical Elon girl is clad in Vera Bradley and her Greek letters (don't forget the popped collar underneath [her] letter shirt!), and dresses to the max whether it's an 8:00 A.M. class or it's 2:00 A.M. in the library. For the typical Elon boy, it's a polo and shaggy hair. That says it all." There's more to students on this campus than surface appearances, though; as one explains, "The more time you spend here, the more you get to see how diverse the student population really is. Upon a deeper glance, one will find your atypical groups such as the Army ROTC cadets, the theater people, the musicians, and the socialites. The atypical students fit in pretty well but aren't that well advertised." Also, "There are so many students involved in so many cool things, and they're very passionate about what they're doing. Many people are involved in service work and are specifically passionate about eradicating AIDS."

FINANCIAL AID: 800-334-8448 • E-MAIL: ADMISSIONS@ELON.EDU • WEBSITE: WWW.ELON.EDU

ADMISSIONS

Very important factors considered include: Academic GPA, rigor of secondary school record, standardized test scores. *Important factors considered include:* Alumni/ae relation, application essay, extracurricular activities, recommendation(s), talent/ability. *Other factors considered include:* Character/personal qualities, class rank, first generation, level of applicant's interest, racial/ethnic status, state residency, volunteer work, work experience. SAT or ACT required; ACT with Writing component required. TOEFL required of all international applicants. High school diploma is required, and GED is accepted. *Academic units required:* 4 English, 3 math, 3 science (1 science lab), 2 foreign language, 3 social studies (including U.S. history). *Academic units recommended:* 4 math, 3 foreign language, 2 social studies.

The Inside Word

Admissions standards at Elon are fairly straightforward—solid grades and strong test scores make for a very competitive candidate. Leadership is a valued attribute and demonstrating an active role in extracurriculars augments one's application. Students who find themselves with an acceptance letter will discover a school with abundant internship and study abroad opportunities.

FINANCIAL AID

Students should submit: FAFSA, institution's own financial aid form, CSS/Financial Aid PROFILE. The Princeton Review suggests that all financial aid forms be submitted as soon as possible after January 1. *Need-based scholarships/grants offered:* Pell Grant, SEOG, state scholarships/grants, private scholarships, the school's own gift aid. *Loan aid offered:* FFEL Subsidized Stafford, FFEL Unsubsidized Stafford, FFEL PLUS, Federal Perkins Loan, state loans, college/university loans from institutional funds, privately funded alternative loans. Applicants will be notified of awards on a rolling basis beginning or about March 30. Federal Work-Study Program available. Institutional employment available. Off-campus job opportunities are good.

FROM THE ADMISSIONS OFFICE

"With an undergraduate enrollment of about 4,850, Elon is the ideal size, offering the comprehensive resources of a university in a close-knit community atmosphere. Academic offerings include 49 majors in the arts and sciences, business, communications, and education. Graduate programs are offered in business, education, physical therapy, and law. Elon is recognized by the National Survey of Student Engagement as one of the nation's most effective universities in actively engaging students in hands-on learning experiences. Academic and co-curricular activities are seamlessly blended, especially in flagship programs known as the Elon Experiences: study abroad, internships, service, leadership, and undergraduate research. Participation is among the highest in the nation. Sixty-four percent of graduating seniors have studied abroad, 78 percent have done internships, and 89 percent have volunteered in the community. As one of the few schools in the nation with a 4-1-4 academic calendar, Elon allows students to devote January to travel abroad or to immerse themselves in innovative on-campus courses. Elon's historic and picturesque campus has been recognized as one of the most beautiful in the country. New additions include the $10-million Ernest A. Koury Sr. Business Center, featuring a digital theater and finance trading room, and The Oaks, a 500-bed residence complex. Elon's Division I Phoenix athletics programs compete in the Southern Conference.

"Freshman applicants for Fall 2008 are required to take the SAT (or the ACT with the writing section). The student's best critical reading and math scores from either test will be used."

SELECTIVITY

Admissions Rating	92
# of applicants	9,204
% of applicants accepted	42
% of acceptees attending	33
# accepting a place on wait list	1,362
% admitted from wait list	3
# of early decision applicants	459
% accepted early decision	65

FRESHMAN PROFILE

Range SAT Critical Reading	560–650
Range SAT Math	570–660
Range ACT Composite	23–28
Minimum Paper TOEFL	550
Minimum Computer Based TOEFL	213
Average HS GPA	3.9
% graduated top 10% of class	30
% graduated top 25% of class	64
% graduated top 50% of class	92

DEADLINES

Early decision application deadline	11/1
Early decision notification	12/1
Regular application deadline	1/10
Regular notification	12/20
Nonfall registration?	no

APPLICANTS ALSO LOOK AT
AND OFTEN PREFER
James Madison University, The University of North Carolina at Chapel Hill

AND SOMETIMES PREFER
North Carolina State University, Wake Forest University

AND RARELY PREFER
College of Charleston, Furman University

FINANCIAL FACTS

Financial Aid Rating	83
Annual tuition	$20,171
Room & Board	$6,850
Books and supplies	$900
Required fees	$270
% frosh rec. need-based scholarship or grant aid	28
% UG rec. need-based scholarship or grant aid	29
% frosh rec. need-based self-help aid	28
% UG rec. need-based self-help aid	26
% frosh rec. any financial aid	69
% UG rec. any financial aid	70

EMERSON COLLEGE

120 BOYLSTON STREET, BOSTON, MA 02116-4624 • ADMISSIONS: 617-824-8600 • FAX: 617-824-8609

STUDENTS SAY

Academics

Students say that Emerson College "is great for passionate, talented people because not only will they be accepted for who they are but they will also be celebrated and will get the connections they need to survive in the real world." Because of the school's focus, "The majority of the learning time at Emerson is not spent in the classroom, but in rehearsal, at a film shoot, or going to press with their headline story." Due to this nontraditional learning environment, there is "a stigma towards Emerson that it is not as academically rigorous as it is at other less-artsy schools." Most students find this "untrue" since "There is a large population of students who are not film or theater majors and fully immerse themselves within the classroom and their academic work." "My professors are all practicing professionals in their respective fields and very dedicated to what they do and sharing it with people they expect to work with in the future," writes one undergraduate. Better still, "In many cases, they invite students to participate in their work outside of the college." You may not write as many term papers as you would at another school, but that doesn't mean you won't work hard. One student explains, "While at larger schools you may write 20-page term papers at the end of every course, at Emerson you're more likely to do a video. They take as long, trust me."

Life

"Life in Emerson is essentially life in Boston," claims one student. "The two are completely meshed. We go to a lot of concerts and see a lot of shows in the greater Boston area." That isn't to say students don't spend time on campus, as "Most people are usually working on a theater piece or a television show or some other kind of art that relates to their education but also counts as their fun activity." "There is always some student production or a comedy show to see [as well as] a giant movie theater on our campus grounds, which Emerson kids probably support solely." There are also "the campus television and radio stations, which run 24 hours a day, so students are always there." If you're looking for "something every weekend," then you can't go wrong heading into Boston with its "rich culture and history." Most students agree that "Boston is an amazing place to live" and it's "one of the best cities in the world for college students." The city offers "plenty to do, including concerts at the Hatch Shell, Red Sox games, a movie theater next door, and everything in Boston only a few subway stops away."

Student Body

"There is no typical student" at Emerson, undergraduates report. "The only commonality you can find is that they're all creative." One student explains that everyone is "very different, from quiet to noisy, outgoing to introverted, explorers to homebodies." But despite differences, "It's pretty easy to find a niche here." Many students confirm that Emerson's "rather large gay community is totally accepted" by the school's "population of creative people. People at Emerson are actors and actresses, advertising gurus, and entertainment reporters. I have met the coolest people who have exposed me to cultural scenes that I never knew existed." While they've garnered some fame for being sartorially expressive, students have more than just "the quirky sense of fashion" to make "them stand out." One freshman explains, "Emersonians are passionate, driven, and talented individuals preparing to take on the entertainment world." Emerson students also lean far left politically, "enough that a Texas Democrat could feel like Jesse Helms." A high tuition and limited endowment means that the student body is mostly upper-middle class . . . students whose parents can afford to pay for the school. Were Emerson a public college with half the tuition, it would be a very diverse, very politically correct institution."

FINANCIAL AID: 617-824-8655 • E-MAIL: ADMISSION@EMERSON.EDU • WEBSITE: WWW.EMERSON.EDU

ADMISSIONS

Very important factors considered include: Academic GPA, standardized test scores. *Important factors considered include:* Application essay, character/personal qualities, class rank, extracurricular activities, recommendation(s), rigor of secondary school record, talent/ability. *Other factors considered include:* Alumni/ae relation, first generation, geographical residence, racial/ethnic status, volunteer work, work experience. SAT or ACT required; ACT with Writing component required. TOEFL required of all international applicants. High school diploma is required, and GED is accepted. *Academic units required:* 4 English, 3 math, 3 science, 3 foreign language, 3 social studies, *Academic units recommended:* 4 English, 3 math, 3 science, 3 foreign language, 3 social studies, 4 academic electives.

The Inside Word

Expect your living situation to be made easier by recent developments on Emerson's campus. The Max Mutchnick Campus Center, named in recognition of the substantial gift made by the Emerson alumnus and co-creator/executive producer of *Will & Grace*, is an 185,000-square-foot building that features a gym, offices, and residence hall. This facility, combined with the recent acquisition of the Colonial Theatre (which will also feature dorm rooms), means nearly all students will be able to live on-campus and indulge in affordable rent.

FINANCIAL AID

Students should submit: FAFSA, CSS/Financial Aid PROFILE, Noncustodial PROFILE, Business/Farm Supplement, Federal Income Tax Return. The Princeton Review suggests that all financial aid forms be submitted as soon as possible after January 1. *Need-based scholarships/grants offered:* Pell Grant, SEOG, state scholarships/grants, private scholarships, the school's own gift aid. *Loan aid offered:* FFEL Subsidized Stafford, FFEL Unsubsidized Stafford, FFEL PLUS, Federal Perkins Loan, state loans. Applicants will be notified of awards on or about April 1. Off-campus job opportunities are excellent.

FROM THE ADMISSIONS OFFICE

"Founded in 1880, Emerson is one of the premier colleges in the United States for the study of communication and the arts. Students may choose from over more than two dozen undergraduate and graduate programs supported by state-of-the-art facilities and a nationally renowned faculty. The campus is home to WERS-FM, the oldest noncommercial radio station in Boston, the historic 1,200-seat Cutler Majestic Theatre, and *Ploughshares*, the award-winning literary journal for new writing.

"Located on Boston Common in the heart of the city's Theater District, the Emerson campus is walking distance from the Massachusetts State House, historic Freedom Trail, Public Garden, Chinatown, and numerous restaurants and museums. In addition to restoring the stunning Majestic Theater, the college has completed several major construction projects including an 11-story performance and production center, athletic field, and 13-story college center, gymnasium, and residence hall. Work begins on the nearby Paramount Center complex (to open in 2008).

"Emerson's 3,000 undergraduate and 900 graduate students come from over 50 countries and 45 states and territories. There are more than 60 student organizations and performance groups, 13 NCAA Division III teams, student publications, and honor societies. The college also sponsors programs in Los Angeles, Kasteel Well (the Netherlands), summer film study in Prague, and course cross registration with the six-member Boston ProArts Consortium.

"Students applying for admission into the Fall 2008 entering class are required to take the new version of the SAT (or ACT with Writing section), but we will allow students to submit scores from the old version of the SAT or ACT (prior to March 2005) as well. SAT Subject Tests are optional."

SELECTIVITY

Admissions Rating	92
# of applicants	4,849
% of applicants accepted	47
% of acceptees attending	32
# accepting a place on wait list	462
% admitted from wait list	2

FRESHMAN PROFILE

Range SAT Critical Reading	580–670
Range SAT Math	550–640
Range SAT Writing	580–660
Range ACT Composite	24–29
Minimum Paper TOEFL	550
Minimum Computer Based TOEFL	213
Average HS GPA	3.59
% graduated top 10% of class	36
% graduated top 25% of class	78
% graduated top 50% of class	98

DEADLINES

Regular application deadline	1/5
Regular notification	4/1
Nonfall registration?	yes

APPLICANTS ALSO LOOK AT

AND OFTEN PREFER
New York University

AND SOMETIMES PREFER
Ithaca College, University of Southern California

AND RARELY PREFER
Boston University, Syracuse University

FINANCIAL FACTS

Financial Aid Rating	85
Annual tuition	$25,248
Room & Board	$10,870
Books and supplies	$720
Required fees	$520
% frosh rec. need-based scholarship or grant aid	46
% UG rec. need-based scholarship or grant aid	41
% frosh rec. need-based self-help aid	54
% UG rec. need-based self-help aid	51
% frosh rec. any financial aid	84
% UG rec. any financial aid	71

EMORY UNIVERSITY

BOISFEUILLET JONES CENTER, ATLANTA, GA 30322 • ADMISSIONS: 404-727-6036 • FAX: 404-727-4303

STUDENTS SAY

Academics

Emory University, "a Northern school in the South," is a "school on the rise." It boasts "amazing academic resources" and tremendous "post-graduation employment opportunities," which makes it a strong choice for students who see their educations more as "a step on the way to a professional career" than the acquisition of knowledge for its own sake. Many career opportunities arrive via the school's "strong ties to the CDC [Centers for Disease Control and Prevention], the Carter Center, and Coca Cola, as well as its proximity to the American Cancer Society national headquarters." Emory's strong undergraduate business program and "great medical school" are big draws, and research-intensive disciplines benefit from "access to state-of-the-art equipment." While there is a sense that "some professors are here for only research," students generally agree that "professors are top-notch and approachable," noting in particular that "those in smaller departments are great! Those in larger departments have less time for students," and many "are less willing to go out of their way to make sure students understand material and are getting something out of the class." Emory's general education requirements earn some complaints, with students telling us that the requirements are "meant to give students a wide base of knowledge," but often "become more a chore than a learning experience." Even so, students here tell us: "On the whole, you leave classes thinking much more than you did when you entered, and class is almost always worthwhile to attend. Many professors place a great emphasis on theoretical application, making the material come alive."

Life

"Emory is interesting because there is a lack of school spirit," but "There is an abundance of support on campus for different activities. Almost everyone participates in some activity. Many people volunteer in some way or another or are extraordinarily active on campus." Greek life is huge at Emory; while "only one-third of the population" is involved, "It feels much stronger than it actually is in numbers. This is because students in Greek life tend to be community leaders." When it's party time, "People basically act like regular college kids: They drink, go out to bars or clubs, or [attend] Greek functions." Freshmen and sophomores are more likely to hang close to campus, while upperclassmen are more likely to explore Atlanta. Students tell us that "life at Emory is tricky, because Atlanta is one of the best and . . . worst college towns in the country. While there are a wealth of dining, culture, and sports opportunities, they must all be commuted to, which spells one thing: High taxi bills, unless you have a car." (Atlanta's mass transit system is considered "dangerous and unreliable" by most students here.) Popular destinations include Midtown, Virginia Highlands, Toco Hills, Buckhead, and Decatur.

Student Body

Though many people look at Emory as a predominately Jewish school, (about one-third of Emory undergraduates are Jewish) students point out that Jewish students "are definitely not the only type of student here, and everyone has their own niche. Emory is truly diverse." This diversity includes students from "every" "socioeconomic background" and "all over the world." A sophomore boasts that she has friends "from Chad, Senegal, and South Korea, in addition to friends from all over the country." The affluent are definitely well represented here, "giving everyone a slightly skewed world view that tends to overemphasize materialism," but within that context "Everyone is fairly cordial and approachable, and no one is looking to undercut you when you are competing over grades—in that respect, it is a very collegial environment." Some here detect "a split between the wealthier students and those who aren't."

FINANCIAL AID: 800-727-6039 • E-MAIL: ADMISS@EMORY.EDU • WEBSITE: WWW.EMORY.EDU

ADMISSIONS

Very important factors considered include: Academic GPA, application essay, extracurricular activities, recommendation(s), rigor of secondary school record, standardized test scores. *Important factors considered include:* Alumni/ae relation, character/personal qualities, talent/ability. *Other factors considered include:* Class rank, first generation, geographical residence, level of applicant's interest, racial/ethnic status, state residency, volunteer work, work experience. SAT or ACT required; SAT Subject Tests recommended, ACT with Writing component required. High school diploma is required, and GED is not accepted. *Academic units required:* 4 English, 3 math, 2 science (2 science labs), 2 foreign language, 2 social studies, 2 history, 2 academic electives. *Academic units recommended:* 4 math, 3 science, 3 foreign language.

The Inside Word

In 2006, early decision applications to Emory rose nearly 20 percent over the previous year, creating a quandary for aspiring Emory students: Do they join the growing crowd of early applicants and presumably increase the likelihood of admission, or do they take their chances with the regular admission date? Locking into one school early in the process can be a blessing or a curse; what if the aid package (which doesn't arrive until mid-April) isn't sufficient? Here's the good news: Emory financial aid has traditionally met 100 percent of applicants' demonstrated need.

FINANCIAL AID

Students should submit: FAFSA, CSS/Financial Aid PROFILE, Noncustodial PROFILE. Regular filing deadline is April 2. The Princeton Review suggests that all financial aid forms be submitted as soon as possible after January 1. *Need-based scholarships/grants offered:* Pell Grant, SEOG, state scholarships/grants, private scholarships, the school's own gift aid. *Loan aid offered:* FFEL Subsidized Stafford, FFEL Unsubsidized Stafford, FFEL PLUS, Federal Perkins Loan, Federal Nursing Loan, state loans, college/university loans from institutional funds. Applicants will be notified of awards on or about April 2.

FROM THE ADMISSIONS OFFICE

"As a destination for path-breaking researchers, renowned teachers, superb students, and dedicated staff, Emory University strives to help its community members fulfill their highest aspirations. Our vision is to discover truth, share it, and ignite in others a passion for its pursuit. The newly adopted Emory Strategic Plan provides a map to guide our growth and development over the next decade, focusing on strengthening faculty distinction, preparing engaged scholars, creating community, confronting the human condition and experience, and exploring new frontiers in science and technology. Similarly, our revised Campus Master Plan outlines a bold proposal for reshaping Emory's presence in Atlanta. Critical to that presence are programs in the arts, university-community partnerships, and the global reach of our initiatives through such Emory entities as the Carter Center.

"Emory remains more than the sum of its parts—a strong intellectual community that seeks excellence, not to compete with other institutions, but to contribute to the shaping of a better world.

"All applicants are required to submit scores from the SAT or the ACT. For those students applying for the 2008–2009 school year, Emory will require one of the following: the old SAT (without Writing), the ACT (without Writing), the new SAT (which includes a Writing section), or the ACT with Writing."

SELECTIVITY

Admissions Rating	98
# of applicants	14,222
% of applicants accepted	32
% of acceptees attending	30
# accepting a place on wait list	800
# of early decision applicants	1,434
% accepted early decision	34

FRESHMAN PROFILE

Range SAT Critical Reading	640–730
Range SAT Math	660–740
Range ACT Composite	29–33
Average HS GPA	3.72
% graduated top 10% of class	85
% graduated top 25% of class	95
% graduated top 50% of class	100

DEADLINES

Early decision application deadline	11/1
Early decision notification	12/15
Regular application deadline	1/15
Regular notification	4/1
Nonfall registration?	no

APPLICANTS ALSO LOOK AT

AND OFTEN PREFER
Duke University, Stanford University, University of Pennsylvania

AND SOMETIMES PREFER
Georgetown University, Northwestern University, Washington University in St. Louis

AND RARELY PREFER
The George Washington University, Tufts University, Vanderbilt University

FINANCIAL FACTS

Financial Aid Rating	92
Annual tuition	$33,900
Room & Board	$11,020
Books and supplies	$1,000
Required fees	$436
% frosh rec. need-based scholarship or grant aid	37
% UG rec. need-based scholarship or grant aid	37
% frosh rec. need-based self-help aid	36
% UG rec. need-based self-help aid	36
% frosh rec. any financial aid	61
% UG rec. any financial aid	60

EUGENE LANG COLLEGE—THE NEW SCHOOL FOR LIBERAL ARTS

65 WEST ELEVENTH STREET, OFFICE OF ADMISSION, NEW YORK, NY 10011 • ADMISSIONS: 212-229-5665 • FAX: 212-229-5166

CAMPUS LIFE

Quality of Life Rating	79
Fire Safety Rating	60*
Type of school	private
Environment	metropolis

STUDENTS

Total undergrad enrollment	1,147
% male/female	32/68
% from out of state	71
% from public high school	64
% live on campus	30
% African American	3
% Asian	5
% Caucasian	60
% Hispanic	6
% international	3
# of countries represented	15

SURVEY SAYS . . .

Class discussions encouraged
Small classes
Students love New York, NY
Great off-campus food
Intercollegiate sports are unpopular
or nonexistent
Frats and sororities are unpopular or
nonexistent
Political activism is popular
(Almost) everyone smokes

ACADEMICS

Academic Rating	88
Calendar	semester
Student/faculty ratio	22:1
Profs interesting rating	85
Profs accessible rating	82
% profs teaching	
UG courses	100
% classes taught by TAs	25
Most common	
lab size	10–19 students
Most common	
reg class size	10–19 students

MOST POPULAR MAJORS

area, ethnic, cultural, and gender
studies
creative writing
social sciences

STUDENTS SAY
Academics

The Eugene Lang College "offers a space for various kinds of interdisciplinary learning, critical thinking, and nontraditional study, often placing the responsibility for a fine education on its independent students." Those who thrive here are individuals who "want to push themselves and truly challenge themselves academically. Professors say they teach at Lang because of the students, and there is a true sense of students' wanting to explore and learn for education's sake rather than to simply 'get ahead' in life." As "one of very few schools in the nation that has seminar-style learning" where "You're not just crammed into a lecture hall with 300 other students and talked at," Lang promotes "the ability to freely express yourself in all levels, whether individually, intellectually, or politically." Classes here "tend to have really long, poetic titles, like 'Hearing Art, Seeing Music,' and the like," and "The material one learns at Lang is different from what would be core at another college, which is why the school attracts an interesting group of people and what makes for interesting conversations." Professors vary in teaching skills, but "The good professors who know a lot and know how to teach in 'the Lang style' (i.e., able to go off on tangents within the discussion and not lose focus of the bigger picture) are absolutely amazing." Because the school stresses independence, "You get out of Lang what you put into it. If you take advantage of what it has to offer, it can be one of the most rewarding and unique academic experiences in the country."

Life

"There is not much in the way of common space" in Eugene Lang's small facility, "so gatherings among students pretty much take to the streets." And they do take place: "We meet up with each other outside of the classroom and find that [we] have more in common than just a school. Often we are involved in the same music/art scene or political groups that exist outside of the school. The school just offers a starting point for relationships." Students spend most of their free time exploring New York City, where "There is always something to do that you've never done, or even heard of, before." The school is located on the northern end of Greenwich Village, the center of the city's youth social life. Public transportation makes the rest of Manhattan, and the other four boroughs of the city, easily accessible. One undergrad observes, "Life in the city is incredible. Every possible opportunity is open to you. Living in the city allows me to apply the concepts I'm learning in the classroom to the world immediately around me through internships in politics, law, communications, etc." New York also "offers much more real interaction than the forced 'You like X college sports team? I love X college sports team,' interaction that so many colleges pride themselves on," students insist.

Student Body

Lang undergrads are "independent, analytical, passionate" and "more urban, academic, and aware than your average college student." Although "the 'typical' Lang student is often characterized as a pierced and tattooed hipster," Lang also "has students who listen to Britney Spears, were very popular in high school, and played multiple varsity sports but know what they want in education, so they came to Lang." One undergrad adds, "You really can't be too weird or too normal for this place." Most Lang students "are extremely politically aware and very liberal." Lang boasts "an incredible amount of diversity in age, ethnicity, background, sexual identity, etc.," and students are cool with that.

EUGENE LANG COLLEGE—THE NEW SCHOOL FOR LIBERAL ARTS

FINANCIAL AID: 212-229-8930 • E-MAIL: LANG@NEWSCHOOL.EDU • WEBSITE: WWW.LANG.EDU

ADMISSIONS

Very important factors considered include: Academic GPA, application essay, recommendation(s), rigor of secondary school record. *Important factors considered include:* Character/personal qualities, interview, level of applicant's interest, standardized test scores, volunteer work. *Other factors considered include:* Alumni/ae relation, class rank, extracurricular activities, first generation, geographical residence, work experience. SAT or ACT required; TOEFL required of all international applicants. High school diploma is required, and GED is accepted. *Academic units required:* 4 English. *Academic units recommended:* 3 math, 2 foreign language, 3 social studies, 2 history.

The Inside Word

The college draws a very self-selected and intellectually curious pool, and applications are up. Those who demonstrate little self-motivation will find themselves denied.

FINANCIAL AID

Students should submit: FAFSA, state aid form. The Princeton Review suggests that all financial aid forms be submitted as soon as possible after January 1. *Need-based scholarships/grants offered:* Pell Grant, SEOG, state scholarships/grants, private scholarships, the school's own gift aid. *Loan aid offered:* FFEL Subsidized Stafford, FFEL Unsubsidized Stafford, Federal Perkins Loan, college/university loans from institutional funds. Applicants will be notified of awards on or about March 1.

FROM THE ADMISSIONS OFFICE

"Eugene Lang College offers students of diverse backgrounds an innovative and creative approach to a liberal arts education, combining stimulating classroom activity of a small, intimate college with rich resources of a dynamic, urban university—New School University. The curriculum at Lang College is challenging and flexible. Class size, limited to 18 students, promotes energetic and thoughtful discussions, and writing is an essential component of all classes. Students design their own program of study within one of 13 interdisciplinary concentrations in the social sciences and humanities. They also have the opportunity to pursue a 5-year BA/BFA, BA/MA, or BA/MST at one of the university's six other divisions. Our Greenwich Village location means that all the cultural treasures of the city—museums, libraries, music, theater—are literally at your doorstep.

"As of this book's publication, Eugene Lang College did not have information available about their policy regarding the new SAT."

SELECTIVITY

Admissions Rating	**85**
# of applicants	1,458
% of applicants accepted	66
% of acceptees attending	29
# accepting a place on wait list	35
% admitted from wait list	23

FRESHMAN PROFILE

Range SAT Critical Reading	560–670
Range SAT Math	500–620
Range SAT Writing	550–660
Range ACT Composite	22–28
Minimum Paper TOEFL	600
Minimum Computer Based TOEFL	250
Average HS GPA	3.22
% graduated top 10% of class	13
% graduated top 25% of class	58
% graduated top 50% of class	83

DEADLINES

Early decision application deadline	11/15
Early decision notification	12/15
Regular application deadline	2/1
Regular notification	rolling
Nonfall registration?	yes

APPLICANTS ALSO LOOK AT AND OFTEN PREFER
Bard College, New York University, Sarah Lawrence College

AND SOMETIMES PREFER
Hampshire College, Reed College

AND RARELY PREFER
Bennington College, St. John's College (MD)

FINANCIAL FACTS

Financial Aid Rating	**71**
Annual tuition	$28,600
Room & Board	$11,750
Books and supplies	$2,050
Required fees	$570

THE EVERGREEN STATE COLLEGE

2700 EVERGREEN PARKWAY, NORTHWEST, OFFICE OF ADMISSIONS, OLYMPIA, WA 98505 • ADMISSIONS: 360-867-6170 • FAX: 360-867-6576

CAMPUS LIFE
Quality of Life Rating	**75**
Fire Safety Rating	**60***
Type of school	public
Environment	town

STUDENTS
Total undergrad enrollment	3,931
% male/female	45/55
% from out of state	23
% live on campus	21
% African American	5
% Asian	5
% Caucasian	69
% Hispanic	5
% Native American	4

SURVEY SAYS . . .
Lots of liberal students
Small classes
Students are happy
Frats and sororities are unpopular or nonexistent
(Almost) everyone smokes

ACADEMICS
Academic Rating	**77**
Calendar	quarter
Student/faculty ratio	21:1
Profs interesting rating	86
Profs accessible rating	75
% profs teaching UG courses	100
% classes taught by TAs	0
Most common reg class size	10–19 students

STUDENTS SAY
Academics
The Evergreen State College "is about being in charge of your own education, and not being force-fed what others think you should know." That's because under TESC's "alternative education format" students enroll each quarter in a single program "with various areas of study emphasized rather than in a group of individual classes. You typically take one program for two quarters with the same students and faculty, exploring complexities of the issue of study and new ideas. Students always have a voice and decide on field trips, readings, and lecture topics." TESC undergrads are also encouraged to design their own independent or group studies, an option one student describes as "very rewarding, since you are given much choice and opportunity to make your mark." Another undergrad observes, "You can do almost anything for credit here if you're willing to wade through the red tape. If you have something unconventional or cross-disciplinary in mind for a career, this is the place to be. I want to design computers and digital aides for people with disabilities. There's really no place to do that undergrad but here, where there's the freedom to mix up the art and the computer stuff." Experiential learning—i.e., "learning through doing"—is well integrated into the TESC curriculum through "the many internships with local organizations" that students undertake. TESC undergrads don't receive grades. Rather, professors write narrative evaluations of each student's work (students' evaluations of their own work also becomes part of their academic records).

Life
"People spend a lot of time on homework" at TESC, although "Most may not say so because we don't really have worksheets, quizzes, or . . . reading (I say this as a transfer from a more traditionally 'prestigious' liberal arts college). The Evergreen life is a full-time experience." In their spare time, students like to "hang at local coffee shops, play Frisbee and soccer on the lawn, watch movies, go see live music, the usual stuff." The options for outdoor activity are myriad, with "rainforests, volcanoes, the ocean, dozens of rivers and lakes as well as two unique major cities (Portland and Seattle) within a 2-hour drive." Hometown Olympia "is a great place to live, with the culture of a town twice its size. There are great little shops downtown, and the city has a quaint atmosphere. Not only that, but the Olympia Transit Center links to nearly every bus you need to get through and out of Olympia. It's not hard to see why Greeners tend to settle here."

Student Body
"The hippie stereotype persists" at the Evergreen State College, but they are by far "fairly normal college students: studying, partying occasionally, and experimenting with different styles and points of view." True, "There seem to be more vegetarian, vegan, and health-conscious students at Evergreen" and the 'normal' TESC student "may be atypical elsewhere; when something offbeat or out of the norm happens, we just shrug our shoulders and say, 'Well, that's Evergreen!'" Still, the population runs the gamut from "neurotically brilliant grandmothers to Army veterans to 16-year-old geniuses to queer forestry students to mildly syndicated cartoonists." TESC also "has its fair share of opportunists. The school's reputation, decidedly unearned, is that of a slacker school. That means that some excellent fakers will come to school and dream of partying. They're not bad people. They just didn't realize what they were getting into. I really don't know what happens to these folks; I hope they quietly disappear and find a path that's better for them."

FINANCIAL AID: 360-867-6205 • E-MAIL: ADMISSIONS@EVERGREEN.EDU • WEBSITE: WWW.EVERGREEN.EDU

ADMISSIONS

Very important factors considered include: Academic GPA, application essay, rigor of secondary school record. *Important factors considered include:* First generation, level of applicant's interest, standardized test scores. *Other factors considered include:* Class rank, extracurricular activities, interview, recommendation(s), volunteer work, work experience. SAT or ACT required; TOEFL required of all international applicants. High school diploma is required, and GED is accepted. *Academic units required:* 4 English, 3 math, 2 science (1 science lab), 2 foreign language, 3 social studies, 1 academic elective; 1 fine, visual, or performing arts elective or other college-prep elective from the areas listed.

The Inside Word

Evergreen places a lot of credence in character and personal qualities when making admissions decisions. The school's atypical academic program calls for a curious and independent spirit, and Admissions Officers want to ensure that applicants will have the maturity to direct their own educational development.

FINANCIAL AID

Students should submit: FAFSA, institution's own financial aid form. The Princeton Review suggests that all financial aid forms be submitted as soon as possible after January 1. *Need-based scholarships/grants offered:* Pell Grant, SEOG, state scholarships/grants, private scholarships, the school's own gift aid. *Loan aid offered:* FFEL Subsidized Stafford, FFEL Unsubsidized Stafford, FFEL PLUS, Federal Perkins Loan. Applicants will be notified of awards on a rolling basis beginning or about April 15. Federal Work-Study Program available. Institutional employment available. Off-campus job opportunities are good.

FROM THE ADMISSIONS OFFICE

"Evergreen, a public college of arts and sciences, is a national leader in developing full-time interdisciplinary studies programs. Students work closely with faculty (there are no teaching assistants) to study an issue or theme from the perspective of several academic disciplines. They apply what's learned to real world issues, complete projects in groups, and discuss concepts in seminars that typically involve a faculty member and 22 students. The emphasis on seminars, interdisciplinary problem solving, and collaboration means students are well prepared for graduate school and the world of work. Our students tend to be politically active, environmentally savvy, and more concerned about social justice than competition and personal gain.

"All applicants are encouraged to complete a Free Application for Federal Student Aid (FAFSA). Evergreen's priority financial aid deadline is March 15, though applicants may submit the form later and may be awarded aid if funds are still available.

"Freshman applicants for Fall 2008 are required to submit test scores from either the SAT or ACT tests. Scores submitted from the old (prior to March 2005) SAT will be accepted. The student's best composite score will be used in the admission process."

SELECTIVITY

Admissions Rating	72
# of applicants	1,602
% of applicants accepted	95
% of acceptees attending	38

FRESHMAN PROFILE

Range SAT Critical Reading	520–650
Range SAT Math	470–590
Range ACT Composite	21–27
Minimum Paper TOEFL	550
Minimum Computer Based TOEFL	213
Average HS GPA	3.07
% graduated top 10% of class	10
% graduated top 25% of class	31
% graduated top 50% of class	63

DEADLINES

Regular notification	rolling
Nonfall registration?	yes

APPLICANTS ALSO LOOK AT

AND OFTEN PREFER
Central Washington University, Hampshire College, University of Washington, Washington State University, Western Washington University

AND SOMETIMES PREFER
Portland State University, Seattle University, University of California—Santa Cruz, University of Oregon, University of Puget Sound

AND RARELY PREFER
Earlham College, Eastern Washington University, Lewis & Clark College, Saint Martin's University, Southern Oregon University, University of Vermont, Warren Wilson College

FINANCIAL FACTS

Financial Aid Rating	72
Annual in-state tuition	$4,600
Annual out-of-state tuition	$15,000
Room & Board	$7,900
Books and supplies	$900
Required fees	$500
% frosh rec. need-based scholarship or grant aid	29
% UG rec. need-based scholarship or grant aid	45
% frosh rec. need-based self-help aid	30
% UG rec. need-based self-help aid	45
% frosh rec. any financial aid	45
% UG rec. any financial aid	56

FAIRFIELD UNIVERSITY

1073 NORTH BENSON ROAD, FAIRFIELD, CT 06824 • ADMISSIONS: 203-254-4100 • FAX: 203-254-4199

CAMPUS LIFE
Quality of Life Rating	80
Fire Safety Rating	84
Type of school	private
Affiliation	Roman Catholic/Jesuit
Environment	town

STUDENTS
Total undergrad enrollment	3,460
% male/female	42/58
% from out of state	78
% from public high school	54
% live on campus	80
% African American	2
% Asian	3
% Caucasian	89
% Hispanic	6
% international	1
# of countries represented	42

SURVEY SAYS . . .
Small classes
Great library
Frats and sororities are unpopular or nonexistent
Lots of beer drinking
Hard liquor is popular

ACADEMICS
Academic Rating	78
Calendar	semester
Student/faculty ratio	13:1
Profs interesting rating	83
Profs accessible rating	80
% profs teaching UG courses	100
% classes taught by TAs	0
Most common lab size	fewer than 10 students
Most common reg class size	20–29 students

MOST POPULAR MAJORS
biology
finance
marketing/marketing management
psychology

STUDENTS SAY

Academics

Fairfield University, a comprehensive Jesuit University that provides "so many opportunities because of its great resources and faculty," achieves the Jesuit ideal of "educating the whole person" through a "strong core curriculum" and extracurricular programs that "put the focus on finding balance in life." Through its four undergraduate divisions, Fairfield offers a wide range of choices to its moderately sized student body, further accommodating students with "small class sizes" and "lots of class discussions, which is awesome because we get to see stuff from a different perspective." Students explain that "since we are a liberal arts school, we get a taste of everything, which is so much fun" and report that "we have really good nursing, business, and arts and science programs." One biology major writes, "I chose this school because it had an excellent science program. Now I get to study with a professor who worked on the Human Genome Project." Course work here "is tough and certainly requires studying," as professors "are understanding people but, at the same time, take no crap. They are there to help us learn, and that is completely obvious. Overall, it is a challenging environment where a serious student can feel comfortable."

Life

Fairfield "is an extremely social school, both on and off campus. It's the antithesis of a suitcase school. Students tend to be very involved in a wide range of activities and the great social scene." Undergrads here enjoy a good party, whether it's at the beach or the townhouses on campus. One student writes, "There are parties on the beach every weekend, and you must be social in order to get the full experience at Fairfield." Many are apparently happy with only a partial experience; they skip the party scene, participating instead in "the many Fairfield University Student Association (FUSA)-sponsored events such as bowling, Broadway shows, Mega-Bingo, semiformals, concerts, and comedians." One student explains, "FUSA makes sure to plan things every single Thursday, Friday, and Saturday. There is always something to do." Campus ministry is also very active and very popular, as are such quiet diversions as "shopping in Westport or just hanging out with friends." The Stags, Fairfield's intercollegiate squads, compete in 19 men's and women's sports. Students here love that "it's easy enough to get to New York City," either by car or public transportation.

Student Body

The Fairfield stereotype is that "everyone falls into one of two basic categories: those who show up for class dressed like it's a Saturday night and they're going to a club, or those who get to class and look as though they need directions to the country club. If you don't fall into one of these categories in some sense, you are not Fairfield material." There is some debate here over the accuracy of Fairfield's nickname, "J. Crew U"—while there are those who insist "There are many different kinds of people that go here," they'll point out that "the majority of the people here are White, though." Many of our respondents suggest that Fairfield needs to improve its lack of diversity: "Most of the kids on campus are White [though] the minorities are usually the most popular kids around." One sophomore's advice to "freshmen who come to me complaining of the social homogeneity here: There are absolutely wonderful students who attend this school. Your challenge—and this is really not so hard—is to find them." Homogenous or not, Fairfield undergrads tend to be "smart, but not brainy" and often "have a strong interest in professional sports." Overall, "Everyone is very friendly and gets along well with one another."

FAIRFIELD UNIVERSITY

FINANCIAL AID: 203-254-4125 • E-MAIL: ADMIS@MAIL.FAIRFIELD.EDU • WEBSITE: WWW.FAIRFIELD.EDU

ADMISSIONS

Very important factors considered include: Academic GPA, application essay, recommendation(s), rigor of secondary school record, standardized test scores. *Important factors considered include:* Character/personal qualities, extracurricular activities, talent/ability, volunteer work. *Other factors considered include:* Class rank, alumni/ae relation, first generation, geographical residence, interview, racial/ethnic status, work experience. SAT or ACT required; TOEFL required of all international applicants. High school diploma is required, and GED is not accepted. *Academic units required:* 4 English, 3 math, 2 science (2 science labs), 2 foreign language, 2 social studies, 2 history, 1 academic elective. *Academic units recommended:* 4 English, 4 math, 3 science (2 science labs), 4 foreign language, 2 social studies, 2 history, 1 academic elective.

The Inside Word

Steady increases in the number of admission applications has nicely increased selectivity in recent years. Fairfield's campus and central location, combined with improvements to the library, campus center, classrooms, athletic facilities, and campus residences, make this a campus worth seeing.

FINANCIAL AID

Students should submit: FAFSA, CSS/Financial Aid PROFILE, Business/Farm Supplement. Regular filing deadline is February 15. The Princeton Review suggests that all financial aid forms be submitted as soon as possible after January 1. *Need-based scholarships/grants offered:* Pell Grant, SEOG, state scholarships/grants, private scholarships, the school's own gift aid, United Negro College Fund. *Loan aid offered:* FFEL Subsidized Stafford, FFEL Unsubsidized Stafford, FFEL PLUS, Federal Perkins Loan, Federal Nursing Loan, alternative loans. Applicants will be notified of awards on or about April 1.

FROM THE ADMISSIONS OFFICE

"Fairfield University's primary objectives are to develop the creative intellectual potential of its students and to foster in them ethical values and a sense of social responsibility. Towards this end, the application review process is holistic, including not just a student's academic credentials, but their extracurricular pursuits and outside interests. Our students are challenged to be creative and active members of a community in which diversity is not simply accepted, but encouraged and honored. Students learn in a supportive environment with faculty committed to individual development and personal enrichment. As a key to the lifelong process of learning, Fairfield has developed a core curriculum to introduce all students to the broad range of liberal learning. Students choose from 34 majors and 19 interdisciplinary minors. They also have outstanding internship opportunities in Fairfield County and New York City. Additionally, 35 percent of Fairfield's students take advantage of an extensive study abroad program. Fairfield graduates wishing to continue their education are highly successful in gaining graduate and professional school admission, while others pursue extensive job opportunities throughout the region. Thirty-nine Fairfield students have been tapped as Fulbright scholars since 1993.

"Applicants to Fairfield University for Fall 2008 may submit the results from either the SAT or the ACT. We will consider the student's best scores in the application process. Fairfield does not require any SAT Subject Tests."

SELECTIVITY

Admissions Rating	83
# of applicants	8,035
% of applicants accepted	61
% of acceptees attending	18
# accepting a place on wait list	844
% admitted from wait list	1

FRESHMAN PROFILE

Range SAT Critical Reading	540–630
Range SAT Math	550–640
Range SAT Writing	780–780
Range ACT Composite	25–27
Minimum Paper TOEFL	550
Minimum Computer Based TOEFL	213
Average HS GPA	3.47
% graduated top 10% of class	12
% graduated top 25% of class	26
% graduated top 50% of class	98

DEADLINES

Early action deadline	11/15
Regular application deadline	1/15
Regular notification	4/1
Nonfall registration?	no

APPLICANTS ALSO LOOK AT
AND OFTEN PREFER
Boston College, Georgetown University
AND SOMETIMES PREFER
College of the Holy Cross, Fordham University, Providence College, Villanova University
AND RARELY PREFER
Quinnipiac University, The University of Scranton, University of Connecticut

FINANCIAL FACTS

Financial Aid Rating	75
Annual tuition	$33,340
Room & Board	$10,430
Books and supplies	$900
Required fees	$565
% frosh rec. need-based scholarship or grant aid	49
% UG rec. need-based scholarship or grant aid	44
% frosh rec. need-based self-help aid	50
% UG rec. need-based self-help aid	50
% frosh rec. any financial aid	72
% UG rec. any financial aid	68

FISK UNIVERSITY

1000 SEVENTEENTH AVENUE NORTH, NASHVILLE, TN 37208-3051 • ADMISSIONS: 615-329-8665 • FAX: 615-329-8774

STUDENTS SAY

Academics

With its rich past and impressive list of alumni, Historically Black College/University Fisk University is "about history and continuing a legacy." But history and legacy alone wouldn't be enough to attract top students to this small Nashville school. To do that, Fisk has to deliver the goods, and it does: Fisk graduates over three-quarters of its enrollees, over 70 percent of whom go on to graduate and professional schools. Indeed, for every student who mentioned Fisk's illustrious history as a reason for choosing the school, at least two cite Fisk's reputation for "graduating African Americans to become wonderful professionals" as a reason to attend. As one student puts it, "Fisk University is all about nurturing young Black people with the goal of preparing them to thrive" in the world while remaining committed to "community involvement." With fewer than 1,000 undergraduates and limited finances, Fisk must focus its efforts on a few key disciplines. Departments that track to health care careers—biology, physics, chemistry, nursing, and psychology—fare well here, as do computer science and business administration. A core curriculum encompassing humanities, mathematics, and science ensures that everyone leaves with a well-rounded education. The school's size results in "wonderful" relationships with professors who "actually care about your matriculation through the school." The faculty and administration "are generally very approachable" and "take the time to work with you when you request help." Academics are "rigorous," and the mantra on campus is "Success is in the details (by which we mean diversity, excellence, teamwork, accountability, integrity, leadership, service)." Fisk also excels at procuring "internships and study abroad" opportunities.

Life

At a school as small as Fisk, "Campus life can be boring," and many students say they are "sheltered and separated from the real world." For some (especially freshmen, who are not yet fully integrated into campus life and often lack automobiles), free time consists of little more than "going out to the yard to throw the football around or hanging in the lounge playing spades, pool, or watching TV. Just enjoying one another's company is making our own fun." The campus sponsors a number of activities, including "step shows, organizational meetings, choir, sports, clubs, dances, yard gatherings, etc." Social life centers on Fisk's Greek organizations and the Jubilee Singers, the school's world-renowned singing group, famous for its repertoire of slave spirituals. On the weekends, "Students go to clubs or Greek-hosted parties," but are just as likely to head out to Nashville for fun. Nashville is a great music town, and as a tourist destination, boasts many attractions, including great restaurants, amusement parks, and plenty of shopping. Fisk fields 15 NCAA Division III athletic teams, seven for men (basketball, baseball, soccer, tennis, cross-country, track, and golf) and eight for women (basketball, softball, volleyball, cross-country, tennis, track, soccer, and golf).

Student Body

Fisk is a "small school" with a "family environment," even though "The only thing most students share in common is that we are all Black. There are, however, many different types of students," from those who "are first-generation college students to others who are fourth- and fifth-generation Fiskites." Undergraduates come from "various regions of the country" and all across the world, and range in personality types from "the really wild kids who are always partying to the students in really hard majors who no one ever sees to the different cliques of rich girls, international students, etc." With many students hailing from Tennessee and nearby states, "Southern hospitality" and "sociable" natures are the norm among students at Fisk.

FINANCIAL AID: 615-329-8735 • E-MAIL: ADMISSIONS@FISK.EDU • WEBSITE: WWW.FISK.EDU

ADMISSIONS

Very important factors considered include: Application essay, character/personal qualities, class rank, recommendation(s), rigor of secondary school record, standardized test scores, talent/ability. *Important factors considered include:* Alumni/ae relation, extracurricular activities, interview. *Other factors considered include:* Volunteer work. SAT or ACT required; TOEFL required of all international applicants. High school diploma is required, and GED is accepted. *Academic units required:* 4 English, 3 math, 2 science (2 science labs), 1 foreign language, 1 history, 4 academic electives. *Academic units recommended:* 4 English, 3 math, 3 science (2 science labs), 2 foreign language, 1 social studies, 1 history, 4 academic electives.

The Inside Word

Intangibles can play a big part in the admissions decision at Fisk, especially for borderline candidates. A marked improvement in high school grades during junior and senior years, a demonstrated high level of determination, and commitment to school, community, and/or church can all help create a successful application.

FINANCIAL AID

Students should submit: FAFSA. The Princeton Review suggests that all financial aid forms be submitted as soon as possible after January 1. *Need-based scholarships/grants offered:* Pell Grant, SEOG, state scholarships/grants, private scholarships, the school's own gift aid, United Negro College Fund. *Loan aid offered:* Direct Subsidized Stafford, Direct Unsubsidized Stafford, Direct PLUS, FFEL PLUS, Federal Perkins Loan. Applicants will be notified of awards on a rolling basis beginning or about April 1. Federal Work-Study Program available. Off-campus job opportunities are excellent.

FROM THE ADMISSIONS OFFICE

"Founded in 1866, the university is coeducational, private, and one of America's premier Historically Black Universities. The first Black college to be granted a chapter of Phi Beta Kappa Honor Society, Fisk serves a national student body, with an enrollment of 900 students. There are residence halls for men and women. The focal point of the 40-acre campus and architectural symbol of the university is Jubilee Hall, the first permanent building for the education of Blacks in the South, and named for the internationally renowned Fisk Jubilee Singers, who continue their tradition of singing the Negro spiritual. From its earliest days, Fisk has played a leadership role in the education of African Americans. Faculty and alumni have been among America's intellectual leaders. Among them include Fisk graduates Nikki Giovanni, poet/writer; John Hope Franklin, historian/scholar; David Lewis, professor/recipient of the prestigious Pulitzer Prize; Hazel O'Leary, U.S. Secretary of Energy; John Lewis, U.S. Representative—Georgia; and W. E. B. DuBois, the great social critic and cofounder of the NAACP. Former Fisk students whose distinguished careers bring color to American culture include Judith Jamison, director of the Alvin Ailey Dance Company, and Johnetta B. Cole, president of Spelman College. In proportion to its size, Fisk continues to contribute more alumni to the ranks of scholars pursuing doctoral degrees than any other institution in the United States.

"Fisk University does review all three aspects of the SAT exam. For regular admission, first-time freshman applicants must have a minimum combined (CR, Math, Writing) SAT score of 1410 or ACT composite of 20. Transfer applicants with at least 30 college credit hours at the time of application are not required to submit SAT scores. Transfer applicants with fewer than 30 college credit hours at the time of application must submit high school transcript and test scores. Submitted scores must meet minimum requirement (1410 SAT, 20 composite ACT). SAT Subject Tests are not required for admission or placement."

SELECTIVITY

Admissions Rating	83
# of applicants	1,146
% of applicants accepted	66
% of acceptees attending	29

FRESHMAN PROFILE

Range SAT Critical Reading	395–650
Range SAT Math	365–620
Range ACT Composite	17–29
Minimum Paper TOEFL	500
Minimum Computer Based TOEFL	250
Average HS GPA	3.0
% graduated top 10% of class	35
% graduated top 25% of class	48
% graduated top 50% of class	73

DEADLINES

Early decision application deadline	12/1
Regular application deadline	3/1
Regular notification	rolling
Nonfall registration?	yes

APPLICANTS ALSO LOOK AT AND SOMETIMES PREFER

Belmont University, Hampton University, Morehouse College, Spelman College

FINANCIAL FACTS

Financial Aid Rating	83
Annual tuition	$12,480
Room & Board	$6,730
Books and supplies	$1,500
Required fees	$700
% frosh rec. need-based scholarship or grant aid	58
% UG rec. need-based scholarship or grant aid	63
% frosh rec. need-based self-help aid	81
% UG rec. need-based self-help aid	85

FLAGLER COLLEGE

74 KING STREET, PO BOX 1027, ST. AUGUSTINE, FL 32085-1027 • ADMISSIONS: 800-304-4208 • FAX: 904-826-0094

CAMPUS LIFE
Quality of Life Rating	76
Fire Safety Rating	92
Type of school	private
Environment	town

STUDENTS
Total undergrad enrollment	2,253
% male/female	39/61
% from out of state	34
% from public high school	78
% live on campus	35
% African American	2
% Asian	1
% Caucasian	90
% Hispanic	4

SURVEY SAYS . . .
Small classes
Great computer facilities
Great library
Frats and sororities are unpopular or nonexistent

ACADEMICS
Academic Rating	77
Calendar	semester
Student/faculty ratio	20:1
Profs interesting rating	83
Profs accessible rating	80
% profs teaching UG courses	100
% classes taught by TAs	0
Most common lab size	fewer than 10 students
Most common reg class size	20–29 students

MOST POPULAR MAJORS
business administration/ management
communications, journalism, and related fields
elementary education and teaching

STUDENTS SAY

Academics
Undergrads at this small Florida liberal arts college love the "intimate campus experience" and the "personal attention" that the school provides. Professors "all have ample office hours and encourage us to use them. They are also accessible through e-mail and telephone. They genuinely care about their students, and this care even extends to non-academic issues." What's more, "The professors here are very understanding of students' personal lives and know that we have a life outside the classroom." The business and education programs are singled out for particular praise. Reviews of the administration, however, are more mixed. While some students assert that the "Members of the administration are some of the nicest people you will ever meet," others see them as the source of more than a little consternation. First on students' lists of complaints "is a stringent policy on attendance that forces the students to attend every class"; some argue that the policy is "why some students refer to Flagler College as 'Flagler High.'" Regardless of how "tightly wound" the administration may be, "They make things work pretty well"—and for a good value; finance-sensitive students appreciate the fact that "tuition is relatively inexpensive for a private school."

Life
"It's exhilarating to be able to wake up, walk downstairs, and step into an interesting little slice of history every day. Our school was once a very pricey and very elegant hotel. Everywhere you turn something has been hand-carved, gold-leafed, frescoed, marbled—you get the idea. It's just beautiful," enthuses one appreciative sophomore. Indeed, if there's one thing the majority of students appreciate about Flagler, it's the beauty of the school itself and of the "quaint, small tourist town" of St. Augustine in which it is located. Undergrads take advantage of "St. Augustine's awesome restaurants, many of which are located only a block away on St. George Street; many of the restaurants also have Flagler student discounts." In addition, "Surfing and the beach [about five miles away] are very, very popular at the school" when the weather is warm. Because Flagler has a "zero-tolerance [policy] for drugs and alcohol," many students "party with friends who have houses off campus." Some students also make the 45-minute drive to Jacksonville to go dancing. Two things about life at Flagler draw the ire of many respondents to our survey. First, the policy of "no interdormitory visits between males and females" can "drive students insane": "There's nowhere even to watch a movie with someone of the opposite sex." Second, the dining hall food is near-universally despised.

Students
Students agree that one can divide most of the Flagler student body into a few visible groups: The majority of students, respondents write, "are from the middle to upper-middle class, and have a car and a good amount of disposable income." They are "White," possibly "religious," and generally have "conservative views on politics." Then there are the surfers, who "all hang out together" and "often miss class when the waves are good." Finally (and somewhat surprisingly, given that the administration recently nixed the formation of a gay-straight alliance on campus), Flagler College has a relatively "large gay population." As far as ethnic diversity is concerned, "There are not many minorities on campus, but the Admissions Office tries to create a better balance each semester."

FINANCIAL AID: 904-819-6225 • E-MAIL: ADMISS@FLAGLER.EDU • WEBSITE: WWW.FLAGLER.EDU

ADMISSIONS

Very important factors considered include: Academic GPA, rigor of secondary school record, standardized test scores. *Important factors considered include:* Application essay, character/personal qualities, extracurricular activities, recommendation(s). *Other factors considered include:* Alumni/ae relation, class rank, first generation, interview, level of applicant's interest, talent/ability, volunteer work, work experience. SAT or ACT required; TOEFL required of all international applicants. High school diploma is required, and GED is accepted. *Academic units required:* 4 English, 3 math, 2 science (1 science lab), 2 social studies, 1 history, 1 academic elective. *Academic units recommended:* 4 English, 4 math, 3 science (2 science labs), 2 foreign language, 3 social studies, 2 history, 2 academic electives.

The Inside Word

Admission to Flagler is competitive, as evidenced by the low acceptance rate. Successful applicants must be well rounded, not only excelling in rigorous classes but also demonstrating strong writing skills and a willingness to devote significant time to extracurricular interests. Candidates should note that a few majors, such as education, require specific standardized test minimums. Students with a conservative bent will thrive best at Flagler.

FINANCIAL AID

Students should submit: FAFSA, institution's own financial aid form, state aid form. Regular filing deadline is April 1. The Princeton Review suggests that all financial aid forms be submitted as soon as possible after January 1. *Need-based scholarships/grants offered:* Pell Grant, SEOG, state scholarships/grants, private scholarships, the school's own gift aid. *Loan aid offered:* Direct Subsidized Stafford, Direct Unsubsidized Stafford, Direct PLUS, Federal Perkins Loan. Applicants will be notified of awards on a rolling basis beginning or about April 1. Federal Work-Study Program available. Institutional employment available. Off-campus job opportunities are excellent.

FROM THE ADMISSIONS OFFICE

"Flagler College is an independent, 4-year, coeducational, residential institution located in picturesque St. Augustine. A famous historic tourist center in northeast Florida, it is located to the south of Jacksonville and north of Daytona Beach. Flagler students have ample opportunity to explore the rich cultural heritage and international flavor of St. Augustine, and there's always time for a relaxing day at the beach, about four miles from campus. Flagler is one of the least expensive private colleges in the nation and is recognized in *MoneyGuide, U.S. News & World Report*, and *America's Best 100 Buys* as a top value in education at an affordable cost. The annual cost for tuition, room, and board at Flagler is about the same as state universities. The small student body helps to keep one from becoming 'just a number.' Flagler serves a predominately full-time student body and seeks to enroll students who can benefit from the type of educational experience the college offers. Because of the college's unique mission and distinctive characteristics, some students may benefit more from an educational experience at Flagler than others. The college's admission standards and procedures are designed to select from among the applicants those students most likely to succeed academically, to contribute significantly to the student life program at Flagler, and to become graduates of the college. Flagler College provides an exceptional opportunity for a private education at an extremely affordable cost.

"Freshman applicants for Fall 2008 must take the new SAT (or the ACT with the Writing component). In addition, students may submit scores from the old (before March 2005) SAT (or ACT), and we will use their best scores from either test."

SELECTIVITY

Admissions Rating	**88**
# of applicants	2,377
% of applicants accepted	26
% of acceptees attending	76
# accepting a place on wait list	181
% admitted from wait list	10
# of early decision applicants	634
% accepted early decision	59

FRESHMAN PROFILE

Range SAT Critical Reading	520–610
Range SAT Math	510–590
Range SAT Writing	520–600
Range ACT Composite	22–26
Minimum Paper TOEFL	550
Minimum Computer Based TOEFL	213
Average HS GPA	3.17
% graduated top 10% of class	18
% graduated top 25% of class	50
% graduated top 50% of class	84

DEADLINES

Early decision application deadline	12/1
Early decision notification	12/15
Regular application deadline	3/1
Regular notification	3/30
Nonfall registration?	yes

APPLICANTS ALSO LOOK AT

AND OFTEN PREFER
Florida State University, University of Central Florida, University of Florida, University of North Florida, University of South Florida

AND SOMETIMES PREFER
Florida Atlantic University, Stetson University, University of Miami, University of Tampa

AND RARELY PREFER
Eckerd College, Florida Gulf Coast University, Florida International University, Florida Southern College, Jacksonville State University, Rollins College

FINANCIAL FACTS

Financial Aid Rating	**73**
Annual tuition	$11,810
Room & Board	$6,310
Books and supplies	$900
% frosh rec. need-based scholarship or grant aid	16
% UG rec. need-based scholarship or grant aid	20
% frosh rec. need-based self-help aid	25
% UG rec. need-based self-help aid	33
% frosh rec. any financial aid	70
% UG rec. any financial aid	86

FLORIDA SOUTHERN COLLEGE

OFFICE OF ADMISSIONS, 111 LAKE HOLLINGSWORTH DRIVE, LAKELAND, FL 33801 • ADMISSIONS: 800-274-4131 • FAX: 863-680-4120

CAMPUS LIFE

Quality of Life Rating	**77**
Fire Safety Rating	**81**
Type of school	private
Affiliation	Methodist
Environment	town

STUDENTS

Total undergrad enrollment	1,753
% male/female	39/61
% from out of state	29
% from public high school	75
% live on campus	65
% in (# of) fraternities	30 (6)
% in (# of) sororities	36 (5)
% African American	6
% Asian	1
% Caucasian	79
% Hispanic	6
% international	4
# of countries represented	31

SURVEY SAYS . . .

Intramural sports are popular
Frats and sororities dominate social scene

ACADEMICS

Academic Rating	**81**
Calendar	semester
Student/faculty ratio	13:1
Profs interesting rating	77
Profs accessible rating	80
% profs teaching UG courses	100
% classes taught by TAs	0
Most common lab size	10–19 students
Most common reg class size	10–19 students

MOST POPULAR MAJORS

biological and biomedical sciences
elementary education and teaching
marketing/marketing management

STUDENTS SAY

Academics

Methodist-affiliated Florida Southern College offers "a fairly strong liberal arts core," "a total community atmosphere," and a throng of degrees and majors. Standout programs include business, music, and the sciences. There is "an incredible education program," too. "Extremely exciting" study-abroad programs will take you to England, Tahiti, Ghana, and many other places all across the globe. Classes are "small." FSC's "hands-on" administration "is very open to student ideas and easy to contact." The faculty is "a big mix." "Most of the professors are deeply committed to the students and will go to great lengths to help." "Teachers care when you miss class," says one happy student who appreciates the extra attention. "We don't have teaching assistants so the relationships are directly with the professors." "It is very uncommon" to have professors who don't "know you by name," "even if you only had them one time." Some professors "aren't so good," though. "A lot of professors are the only one teaching a particular subject, especially when you get to the upper-level classes in your major," one student told us. Also, the library here "needs more up-to-date resources."

Life

Florida Southern's lakefront campus is home to the largest single-site collection of Frank Lloyd Wright architecture on earth. As such, it's no wonder that students describe it as "very beautiful." "They just need to pressure-wash some of the Frank Lloyd Wright architecture," helpfully suggests one student. Life here is "interactive" and "comfortable." The Greek system is somewhat big. The Wellness Center, the campus pool, and activities on Lake Hollingsworth are popular hang-out spots for students. There are fairly strict rules regarding when males and females can be "in each others' dorms." Also, FSC is "supposed to be a dry campus" but "everybody drinks, anyway." While it's theoretically possible to "go out every night and party," "It's not your typical *Animal House* scene" here. "It's more laid-back." "There are going to be weekends when you'll end up just seeing a movie because nothing else is going on." The surrounding city of Lakeland "isn't too thrilling." A few "hole-in-the-wall bars" are the big draw on "Thursday nights" ("which makes Friday the most interesting class day"). For real off-campus fun, "Students often go to Tampa or Orlando," both just "short" rides away.

Students

"Everyone knows each other and gets along," notes one student. It's "one big community." "You can really be yourself here," says a sophomore, so just "being silly with [your] friends" isn't looked down on. "The majority of the campus is female," and from Florida, though about one-third of the students come from out of state. FSC students are "hardworking" and "energetic." Many are "rich" or, at least, "from a decently well-off family." Many others "act rich." Most students are "very friendly," though you will find a few "snotty" types. One student noted that "nearly the entire population is preppy." There is a smattering of minority students and international students but, by and large, ethnic diversity is minimal. There are many "very religious" people on campus. "A lot of students" are "involved in Christian ministries." Politically, you can find "both conservative and liberal extremes" on campus.

FINANCIAL AID: 800-205-1600 • E-MAIL: FSCADM@FLSOUTHERN.EDU • WEBSITE: WWW.FLSOUTHERN.EDU

ADMISSIONS

Very important factors considered include: Academic GPA, rigor of secondary school record. *Important factors considered include:* Application essay, character/personal qualities, extracurricular activities, recommendation(s), standardized test scores, talent/ability. *Other factors considered include:* Alumni/ae relation, class rank, first generation, interview, level of applicant's interest, racial/ethnic status, religious affiliation/commitment, volunteer work, work experience. SAT or ACT required; TOEFL required of all international applicants. High school diploma is required, and GED is accepted. *Academic units required:* 4 English, 3 math, 3 science (2 science labs), 3 social studies, 3 history, 2 academic electives. Academic units recomended: 2 foreign language.

The Inside Word

Individual attention is the cornerstone of a Florida Southern education and this sentiment extends to the admissions process. A close-knit community, officers seek out applicants who best embody FSC's spirit and are likely to contribute to the campus' vitality. Focus is therefore paid not only to grades and test scores, but personal attributes and experiences that reveal involvement beyond the classroom. Candidates are encouraged to employ creative measures throughout their application and are welcome to submit additional academic materials and portfolio samples.

FINANCIAL AID

Students should submit: FAFSA, institution's own financial aid form. Regular filing deadline is July 1. The Princeton Review suggests that all financial aid forms be submitted as soon as possible after January 1. *Need-based scholarships/grants offered:* Pell, SEOG, state scholarships/grants, private scholarships, the school's own gift aid. *Loan aid offered:* FFEL Subsidized Stafford, FFEL Unsubsidized Stafford, FFEL PLUS, Federal Perkins Loan. Applicants will be notified of awards on a rolling basis beginning or about March 1.

FROM THE ADMISSIONS OFFICE

"Florida Southern is intimate and nurturing, offering an extraordinary array of high quality student-faculty collaborative research, performance, study abroad, service-learning, and internship opportunities. For its size, the college offers an unusually wide choice of undergraduate degree majors—39—in such fields as art, business, communications, nursing, psychology, education, music performance, biochemistry and molecular biology, as well as pre-professional programs including premed and pre-law. Distinctive graduate degree programs are offered in business, nursing, and education. First-year students are introduced to an academic culture focused on engaged learning through a required "Examined Life" course and freshman reading program, which brought to campus noted authors Khaled Hosseini (*The Kite Runner*) and Tracey Kidder (*Mountains Beyond Mountains*) in 2006–2007. Students successfully compete nationally in diverse disciplines such as biology, advertising, psychology, and forensics. Nearly 40 percent of graduating seniors have studied abroad, and 40 percent have interned; each semester nearly 20 percent participate in service learning and 40 percent volunteer in the community. Florida Southern's collection of Frank Lloyd Wright architecture provides a stunning and modern setting for living and learning. New additions include a Residential Life Center (to open in Fall 2007), the Nina B. Hollis Wellness Center and adjacent Lakefront Program, a state-of-the-art cybercafé in the library, and an upcoming humanities building featuring a modern language lab and film studies center.

"Florida Southern requires the SAT or ACT; we recommend a combined score of 1,050 or better on the SAT or a composite score of 23 or better on the ACT, though other factors will be considered. The SAT and ACT Writing components are not currently used in making admissions decisions."

SELECTIVITY

Admissions Rating	**82**
# of applicants	2,351
% of applicants accepted	62
% of acceptees attending	29
# of early decision applicants	48
% accepted early decision	73

FRESHMAN PROFILE

Range SAT Critical Reading	480–570
Range SAT Math	480–550
Range SAT Writing	460–550
Range ACT Composite	20–26
Minimum Paper TOEFL	550
Minimum Computer Based TOEFL	213
Average HS GPA	3.51
% graduated top 10% of class	19
% graduated top 25% of class	51
% graduated top 50% of class	82

DEADLINES

Early decision application deadline	12/1
Early decision notification	12/15
Regular application deadline	3/1
Regular notification	rolling
Nonfall registration?	yes

FINANCIAL FACTS

Financial Aid Rating	**77**
Annual tuition	$20,690
Room & Board	$7,500
Books and supplies	$1,150
Required fees	$500
% frosh rec. need-based scholarship or grant aid	58
% UG rec. need-based scholarship or grant aid	58
% frosh rec. need-based self-help aid	56
% UG rec. need-based self-help aid	52
% frosh rec. any financial aid	98
% UG rec. any financial aid	96

FLORIDA STATE UNIVERSITY

2500 UNIVERSITY CENTER, TALLAHASSEE, FL 32306-2400 • ADMISSIONS: 850-644-6200 • FAX: 850-644-0197

CAMPUS LIFE

Quality of Life Rating	85
Fire Safety Rating	60*
Type of school	public
Environment	city

STUDENTS

Total undergrad enrollment	30,841
% male/female	44/56
% from out of state	12
% from public high school	84
% live on campus	15
% in (# of) fraternities	13 (28)
% in (# of) sororities	13 (23)
% African American	11
% Asian	3
% Caucasian	73
% Hispanic	11
% Native American	1

SURVEY SAYS . . .
Great library
Athletic facilities are great
Everyone loves the Seminoles
Frats and sororities dominate social
scene
Lots of beer drinking

ACADEMICS

Academic Rating	64
Calendar	semester
Student/faculty ratio	21:1
Profs interesting rating	73
Profs accessible rating	72
% profs teaching	
UG courses	100
% classes taught by TAs	32
Most common	
reg class size	20–29 students

MOST POPULAR MAJORS
criminal justice/safety studies
finance
psychology

STUDENTS SAY

Academics

You don't have to sell Florida State University to its prospective students; the school has established a clear and recognizable brand based on a tradition of "accomplishment in academics, athletics, and politics," and these are a source of "an enormous sense of school pride" for FSU's myriad devotees. Those traditions include a beloved football program, of course, but they're much more than that; they envelop a complete undergraduate experience that includes "a wonderful mix of both the academic and social spheres" and "an intimate social community," despite the fact that the "school is so large." Academics here "do an excellent job of preparing students for the real world," with standout programs that include an "amazing" international program that "encourages all majors to study abroad and bring many international students and teachers to campus," a college of business that "graduates some of the best businesspeople in the United States," an "extremely competitive" premed program, a "fantastic" music school, merchandising, education, criminology, and the only exercise science program in the state. Workloads in the research-intensive sciences are heavy; elsewhere, "It's just enough so that you have free time, but if you study and work hard you get a lot out of each class and a good grade." FSU's facilities are a mixed bag. Those that are good are fabulous; they include "one of the best career centers in the country, a state-of-the-art school of medicine, and magnet labs that are supposed to be among the most advanced in the country." However, as one student points out, while FSU's "incredible athletic facilities are great," other facilities "could be better taken care of."

Life

Life at FSU is "very social oriented," with "events always happening" either on campus or off. Weekdays, "Campus is always a-bustlin'," with tons of activities, presentations, organization meetings, and casual get-togethers. On weekends, the options are somewhat more limited; some here describe weekends as "calm, even tranquil, except of course on game weekends," but most report that the weekend is a time to blow off steam. One student explains, "A lot of people at FSU are big partiers. We love to drink and have a good time. We find many excuses to drink: holidays, sporting events, or a day at the pool." Home football games are the *ne plus ultra* of campus activity, as football "becomes a religion in the fall." The games attract "most students and many out-of-towners," and pre-game and post-game parties are both de rigueur. "Most students here seem to be very physically active and involved in the outdoor pursuits on our campus, such as hiking, running, fishing, skydiving, rock climbing, etc." Intramural sports "are also extremely popular . . . anyone can play and every sport is offered, from football to dodgeball." Greek life at FSU "is everywhere," as the Greeks "have established themselves within the university community portraying strong leadership, service, and scholarship." From "fraternity parties and tailgating to seminars on how to become an effective leader, Greek life at FSU is very interesting."

Student Body

While the typical FSU student is a "sweatpants-wearing, Starbucks-drinking, Dave Matthews Band listener," undergrads point out that "there are so many students of so many different types here that the 'typical student' is a very poor representation of the school as a whole." While that 'typical student' hails "from a middle- to upper-class family in Florida," for example, many students here receive substantial aid packages, and about one in seven undergrads is from out of state. Students tell us that almost everyone is "highly involved in extracurricular activities," whether it's a "fraternity/sorority, sports, the arts, or one of the many school organizations out there." FSU students also tend to be people who "strive for success, but also know how to enjoy the social experiences college has to offer." "Each and every student has their own place at FSU, and all students share a common identity of garnet and gold."

FLORIDA STATE UNIVERSITY

FINANCIAL AID: 850-644-5871 • E-MAIL: ADMISSIONS@ADMIN.FSU.EDU • WEBSITE: WWW.FSU.EDU

ADMISSIONS

Very important factors considered include: Academic GPA, rigor of secondary school record. *Important factors considered include:* Class rank, standardized test scores, state residency, talent/ability. *Other factors considered include:* Alumni/ae relation, application essay, character/personal qualities, extracurricular activities, first generation, geographical residence, recommendation(s), volunteer work, work experience. SAT or ACT required; ACT with Writing component required. TOEFL required of all international applicants. High school diploma is required, and GED is accepted. *Academic units required:* 4 English, 3 math, 3 science (2 science labs), 2 foreign language, 1 social studies, 2 history, 3 academic electives, *Academic units recommended:* 4 English, 4 math, 4 science (2 science labs), 4 foreign language, 1 social studies, 2 history, 3 academic electives.

The Inside Word

With 22,000 applications to process each year, FSU must rely on a formula-driven approach to triage its applicant pool. With the exception of those applying to special programs, only the applications of those on the borderline will receive a truly thorough review. Those hoping to study fine arts, creative arts, or the performing arts at FSU must undergo a more rigorous application process that includes a portfolio/audition.

FINANCIAL AID

Students should submit: FAFSA. The Princeton Review suggests that all financial aid forms be submitted as soon as possible after January 1. *Need-based scholarships/grants offered:* Pell Grant, SEOG, state scholarships/grants, private scholarships, the school's own gift aid. *Loan aid offered:* FFEL Subsidized Stafford, FFEL Unsubsidized Stafford, FFEL PLUS, Federal Perkins Loan. Applicants will be notified of awards on a rolling basis beginning or about March 15. Off-campus job opportunities are excellent.

FROM THE ADMISSIONS OFFICE

"Established in 1851, Florida State University is one of the nation's premier research universities, known for attracting leading scholars from all over the world and providing students with some of the best academic mentors of any university in the U.S. Sixteen colleges and schools offer nearly 200 undergraduate majors, 214 graduate degrees, and professional degrees in law and medicine. Florida State enjoys an excellent reputation for groundbreaking academic achievements, including establishing the first new medical college in the nation in 20 years. Technologically enhanced classrooms and wireless networking allow state-of-the-art teaching techniques in every discipline. Through the University Honors Program, faculty and undergraduate students who share academic interests can work on-on-one to design and conduct original research projects. Our innovative student services include an internationally renowned career center, a comprehensive campus-wide leadership learning program, and a center for community-based learning through service. World-class cultural events, championship athletics, extensive recreation facilities, and a friendly, close-knit university community enrich student life and extend learning well beyond the classroom. Our diverse student body hails from all 50 states and over 130 countries, and our many international programs throughout the world include year-round programs in Florence, Italy; London, England; Panama City, Panama; and Valencia, Spain.

"Students applying to the university are required to submit the Writing section of the new SAT or take the optional Writing test of the ACT. We will continue to use the highest subscores on the ACT and SAT for admission purposes."

SELECTIVITY

Admissions Rating	87
# of applicants	23,687
% of applicants accepted	59
% of acceptees attending	44

FRESHMAN PROFILE

Range SAT Critical Reading	530–620
Range SAT Math	540–630
Range SAT Writing	510–600
Range ACT Composite	23–27
Minimum Paper TOEFL	550
Minimum Computer Based TOEFL	213
Average HS GPA	3.62
% graduated top 10% of class	26
% graduated top 25% of class	63
% graduated top 50% of class	94

DEADLINES

Regular application deadline	2/14
Regular notification	11/1, 12/13, 2/14, 3/28
Nonfall registration?	yes

FINANCIAL FACTS

Financial Aid Rating	88
Annual in-state tuition	$2,465
Annual out-of-state tuition	$15,596
Room & Board	$6,778
Books and supplies	$856
Required fees	$842
% frosh rec. need-based scholarship or grant aid	18
% UG rec. need-based scholarship or grant aid	17
% frosh rec. need-based self-help aid	22
% UG rec. need-based self-help aid	23
% frosh rec. any financial aid	35
% UG rec. any financial aid	32

FORDHAM UNIVERSITY

441 EAST FORDHAM ROAD, THEBAUD HALL, NEW YORK, NY 10458 • ADMISSIONS: 718-817-4000 • FAX: 718-367-9404

STUDENTS SAY
Academics

Like Certs breath mints, Fordham University is two schools in one. First, there's the school's long-established campus in the Rose Hill section of the Bronx, which might best be regarded as Fordham's 'conventional' undergraduate site. Then there's the newer campus at Manhattan's Lincoln Center, which is "very small and geared toward theater and dance students (though the school says they're finally in the early stages of expanding the campus)." Students are adamant that "they are two different schools going in different directions with different student bodies and different academic focuses." The campuses do share a number of common traits, however. Each is a Jesuit school "with really big core requirements" that provide undergrads with "a strong background in a broad area of academics before actually specializing in one area, thereby educating the whole mind." The Jesuit influence is also seen in the way each school "promotes social awareness, caring for others, and expanding one's knowledge of the world and helping find one's contribution to it." Each school, of course, benefits from a city location that provides near limitless opportunities for networking, internships, and enriching extracurricular experiences. Rose Hill's students praise Fordham's College of Business ("the school for business professionals"), its pre-law and premedical programs, and its psychology program; undergrads at Lincoln Center boast of "one of the best Theater Departments in the country" and "a great dance program."

Life

Fordham's Rose Hill Campus "is truly beautiful, and the location is pretty much the best of both worlds—the city as well as plenty of green." Here, "Life centers around the weekends. Most people go out to local bars, leaving no one on campus on a Tuesday, Friday, or Saturday night. . . . There are numerous events going on on campus all the time, although many of these events are based in religion or politics." Students are also "very involved . . . in intramural sports teams as well as performing arts groups." There's also the city, of course; you can reach it in 15 minutes by Metro North train, or you can save a few bucks and ride the subway. Expect the trip downtown to take about 45 minutes. Closer by is Arthur Avenue, the Bronx's own (and, many say, much better) version of Manhattan's Little Italy. Life at Lincoln Center is understandably less campus-centric; no campus can compete with all that downtown New York City has to offer. One student explains, "The bar and restaurant scene at Lincoln Center is very popular because of the variety of places to go in Manhattan. Dorm parties are not as usual as I would imagine them to be at other colleges. Students from all . . . of Fordham come to Lincoln Center to set out for their various night activities because of the campus's proximity to everything . . . I try to take advantage of the incredible amount of things to do here that one isn't able to do in most other places, but things are very expensive." Lincoln Center dorms "are like apartments, which I know is a definite attraction for many students."

Student Body

Students on the Rose Hill campus tend to be "from an upper-class home in New Jersey, Connecticut, or Long Island . . . [and] wear sandals and jeans and polos, with some popped collars sprinkled in. . . . Off campus (in the Bronx) they stick out like a sore thumb." Many are business and communications majors who favor conservative politics and a businesslike approach to academics. Students at Lincoln Center are more diverse; one writes, "There is no such thing as a typical student at Lincoln Center. Most students who choose to go here are liberal and artsy (writers, dancers, actors). Students tend to be very creative in their clothing choices." The majority of students here are women, and "Most of the boys are gay."

FINANCIAL AID: 718-817-3800 • E-MAIL: ENROLL@FORDHAM.EDU • WEBSITE: WWW.FORDHAM.EDU

ADMISSIONS

Very important factors considered include: Class rank, rigor of secondary school record, standardized test scores. *Important factors considered include:* Application essay, character/personal qualities, extracurricular activities, recommendation(s), talent/ability. *Other factors considered include:* Alumni/ae relation, first generation, geographical residence, racial/ethnic status, volunteer work, work experience. SAT or ACT required; SAT Subject Tests recommended, ACT with Writing component recommended. TOEFL required of all international applicants. High school diploma is required, and GED is accepted. *Academic units required:* 4 English, 3 math, 3 science, 2 foreign language, 2 social studies, 2 history, 6 academic electives. *Academic units recommended:* 4 English, 4 math, 4 science, 3 foreign language, 2 social studies, 2 history, 6 academic electives.

The Inside Word

Applicants to Fordham are required to indicate whether they are applying to Fordham College—Rose Hill, Fordham College—Lincoln Center, or the College of Business Administration. Admissions criteria vary by school, but all are very competitive. Graduation from one of the area's many prestigious Catholic high schools is certainly a plus.

FINANCIAL AID

Students should submit: FAFSA, CSS/Financial Aid PROFILE, Noncustodial PROFILE, Business/Farm Supplement. Regular filing deadline is February 1. The Princeton Review suggests that all financial aid forms be submitted as soon as possible after January 1. *Need-based scholarships/grants offered:* Pell Grant, SEOG, state scholarships/grants, private scholarships, the school's own gift aid. *Loan aid offered:* FFEL Subsidized Stafford, FFEL Unsubsidized Stafford, FFEL PLUS, Federal Perkins Loan. Applicants will be notified of awards on or about April 1.

FROM THE ADMISSIONS OFFICE

"Fordham University offers a distinctive, values-centered educational experience that is rooted in the Jesuit tradition of intellectual rigor and personal attention. Located in New York City, Fordham offers to students the unparalleled educational, cultural, and recreational advantages of one of the world's greatest cities. Fordham has three residential campuses in New York—the tree-lined, 85-acre Rose Hill in the Bronx, the cosmopolitan Lincoln Center campus in the heart of Manhattan's performing arts center, and the scenic Marymount campus located on the banks of the Hudson River in Tarrytown, New York. The university's state-of-the-art facilities and buildings include one of the most technologically advanced libraries in the country. Fordham offers to its students a variety of majors, concentrations, and programs that can be combined with an extensive career planning and placement program. More than 2,600 organizations in the New York metropolitan area offer students internships that provide hands-on experience and valuable networking opportunities in fields such as business, communications, medicine, law, and education.

"Students applicants are required to take the new version of the SAT (or the ACT with or without the Writing section), but we will allow students to submit scores from the old (prior to March 2005) version of the SAT (or ACT) as well. We recommend that students provide scores from only two SAT Subject Tests."

SELECTIVITY

Admissions Rating	92
# of applicants	18,161
% of applicants accepted	47
% of acceptees attending	20
# accepting a place on wait list	1,189
% admitted from wait list	10

FRESHMAN PROFILE

Range SAT Critical Reading	550–650
Range SAT Math	550–640
Range SAT Writing	540–590
Range ACT Composite	24–24
Minimum Paper TOEFL	575
Minimum Computer Based TOEFL	231
Average HS GPA	3.7
% graduated top 10% of class	41
% graduated top 25% of class	73
% graduated top 50% of class	96

DEADLINES

Regular application deadline	1/15
Regular notification	4/1
Nonfall registration?	yes

APPLICANTS ALSO LOOK AT

AND OFTEN PREFER
Boston College, Columbia University, Georgetown University, New York University, University of Notre Dame

AND SOMETIMES PREFER
Boston University, College of the Holy Cross, Loyola College in Maryland, Northeastern University, Providence College, The George Washington University, Villanova University

AND RARELY PREFER
American University, Fairfield University, Hofstra University, Marist College, St. John's University

FINANCIAL FACTS

Financial Aid Rating	73
Annual tuition	$30,000
Room & Board	$11,780
Books and supplies	$800
Required fees	$730
% frosh rec. need-based scholarship or grant aid	66
% UG rec. need-based scholarship or grant aid	62
% frosh rec. need-based self-help aid	51
% UG rec. need-based self-help aid	52
% frosh rec. any financial aid	67
% UG rec. any financial aid	62

FRANKLIN & MARSHALL COLLEGE

PO Box 3003, Lancaster, PA 17604-3003 • Admissions: 717-291-3953 • Fax: 717-291-4381

STUDENTS SAY

Academics

"The workload is tremendous" at Franklin & Marshall College, a small private college that produces "great acceptance rates into graduate and professional schools." The school's "great reputation for its premed program" as well as "its success in placing graduates in top law schools" are among the reasons students endure the "make-you-or-break-you academics" here; the fact that "the school is dedicated to helping students get interesting opportunities, such as internships, study abroad programs, and independent research programs" is another attraction. And then there are the professors, identified by many as "the bright spot of the school. They are all very kind and helpful and enjoy teaching." One student writes, "The professors enliven the classroom and their accessibility outside of the classroom makes the academic experience at F&M that much better." Good grades are hard to come by at F&M. One undergrad writes, "F&M is known for its grade deflation. Professors do not inflate grades here. Students understand this and work hard." As one student puts it, "My parents must think I goof off sometimes when I come out with B's, yet I work more than I ever have. Getting an A-minus here for me is like finding the Holy Grail." But after they've put in their long hours of study, "Students realize how much they have truly learned, and how it was all worth it in the end. The results of the strong liberal arts education can be seen in F&M's extremely high number of acceptances to graduate, medical, and law schools."

Life

F&M has a long history of active Greek life on campus, despite the fact that the school "de-recognized" Greek organizations in 1988. In 2004, F&M brought the Greeks back into the fold, which should mean the popular system should grow even more popular in coming years. Even before the re-recognition, "frat parties were a huge part of campus life," in part due to a perceived lack of alternatives; many here feel that hometown Lancaster, Pennsylvania, "is a pretty small city with not too much for a college student to do." Of course, F&M's famous academic workload keeps students occupied weekdays. "Most students have no time for anything but work during the week, but party hardy when they get the chance on the weekend," undergrads agree. Come Friday afternoon, students "hang out and party at the off-campus frat houses or apartments," or they "enjoy events such as concerts, movies, comedy shows, lectures, and debates, which the college does a great job of setting up." A few adventurous undergrads venture into Lancaster, which we're told "has a few alternative venues, including Chameleon Club and Tally-Ho (a local gay club)." Lancaster also has "some excellent restaurants for when parents come up with the money to buy those kinds of dinners" and "great local shopping with a couple of big outlet malls." Many here "do volunteer work around the community," often in conjunction with their Greek organizations.

Student Body

"There are a significant number of your stereotypical Abercrombie frat boys and sorority girls" at F&M, "but there are also representatives of just about every other sociodemographic group you could think of," including "a very strong international population representing about 60 different countries." One student notes, "My four best friends here are a Shia Muslim from Tanzania, a New York Catholic, a minister's daughter, and an extremely rural Baha'i." The sameness of much of the school's "conservative, preppy, middle-class majority" is further counterbalanced by "a lot of atypical students: gays, nerds, a few potheads, people with different religious beliefs. Most of them are considered very interesting to talk to, and some of them are very popular on campus." Many who attend here "are not only capable academically, but also extremely talented in other areas such as sports, theater, and music."

FRANKLIN & MARSHALL COLLEGE

FINANCIAL AID: 717-291-3991 • E-MAIL: ADMISSION@FANDM.EDU • WEBSITE: WWW.FANDM.EDU

ADMISSIONS

Very important factors considered include: Academic GPA, character/personal qualities, class rank, rigor of secondary school record. *Important factors considered include:* Application essay, extracurricular activities, interview, recommendation(s), standardized test scores, talent/ability, volunteer work. *Other factors considered include:* Alumni/ae relation, geographical residence, level of applicant's interest, racial/ethnic status, work experience. TOEFL required of all international applicants. High school diploma is required, and GED is accepted. *Academic units required:* 4 English, 3 math, 2 science (2 science labs), 2 foreign language, 1 social studies, 2 history, 1 arts/music/theater. *Academic units recommended:* 4 math, 3 science (3 science labs), 4 foreign language, 3 social studies, 3 history.

The Inside Word

Applicants who are serious about attending the college should definitely interview; it will also help to make it known that F&M is one of your top choices. The college loses a lot of its admits to competitor colleges and will take notice of a candidate who is likely to enroll.

FINANCIAL AID

Students should submit: FAFSA, institution's own financial aid form, CSS/Financial Aid PROFILE, Noncustodial PROFILE, Business/Farm Supplement. Regular filing deadline is March 1. The Princeton Review suggests that all financial aid forms be submitted as soon as possible after January 1. *Need-based scholarships/grants offered:* Pell Grant, SEOG, state scholarships/grants, private scholarships, the school's own gift aid. *Loan aid offered:* FFEL Subsidized Stafford, FFEL Unsubsidized Stafford, FFEL PLUS, Federal Perkins Loan, college/university loans from institutional funds. Applicants will be notified of awards on or about March 15. Federal Work-Study Program available.

FROM THE ADMISSIONS OFFICE

"Franklin & Marshall students choose from a variety of fields of study, traditional and interdisciplinary, that typify liberal learning. Professors in all of these fields are committed to a common purpose, which is to teach students to think, speak, and write with clarity and confidence. Whether the course is in theater or in physics, the class will be small, engagement will be high, and discussion will dominate over lecture. Thus, throughout their 4 years, beginning with the First-Year Seminar, students at Franklin & Marshall are repeatedly invited to active participation in intellectual play at high levels. Our graduates consistently testify to the high quality of an F&M education as a mental preparation for life.

"Beginning with the Fall 2007 incoming class, the school offers an SAT option policy to all students."

SELECTIVITY

Admissions Rating	94
# of applicants	4,059
% of applicants accepted	46
% of acceptees attending	28
# accepting a place on wait list	392
% admitted from wait list	19
# of early decision applicants	412
% accepted early decision	65

FRESHMAN PROFILE

Range SAT Critical Reading	580–670
Range SAT Math	600–690
Minimum Paper TOEFL	600
Minimum Computer Based TOEFL	250
Average HS GPA	3.51
% graduated top 10% of class	57
% graduated top 25% of class	84
% graduated top 50% of class	98

DEADLINES

Early decision application deadline	11/15
Early decision notification	12/15
Regular application deadline	2/1
Regular notification	4/1
Nonfall registration?	yes

APPLICANTS ALSO LOOK AT AND OFTEN PREFER

Cornell University, Hamilton College, Haverford College, University of Pennsylvania

AND SOMETIMES PREFER

Bucknell University, Colgate University, Dickinson College, Lafayette College, Lehigh University

FINANCIAL FACTS

Financial Aid Rating	85
Annual tuition	$34,400
Room & Board	$8,540
Books and supplies	$650
Required fees	$50
% frosh rec. need-based scholarship or grant aid	56
% UG rec. need-based scholarship or grant aid	42
% frosh rec. need-based self-help aid	57
% UG rec. need-based self-help aid	43
% frosh rec. any financial aid	59
% UG rec. any financial aid	70

FRANKLIN W. OLIN COLLEGE OF ENGINEERING

OLIN WAY, NEEDHAM, MA 02492-1200 • ADMISSIONS: 781-292-2222 • FAX: 781-292-2210

STUDENTS SAY

Academics

An "innovative," "exceptional" "project-based" curriculum attracts the country's math and science whiz kids to Franklin W. Olin College of Engineering. The school's "small size" and "open atmosphere that's supportive of everyone" are very appealing to the approximately 300 undergraduates on campus. But the piece de resistance—the thing that has students choosing this place over schools like MIT and Cal Tech—has got to be the "free tuition." "Academics-wise, the school kicks people's [butts] right and left. It takes the best and the brightest and breaks them, pushing them when they likely have never had to work hard before. Around here, everyone is smart, and professors assume that, so the classes are taken to that level; there is no such thing as an easy class." One might describe professors here as "grown up Olin kids" insofar as they "are geniuses," but also "young" and just "generally awesome people." "They love teaching," and are "mostly on [a] first-name basis" with undergrads, professors bend over backwards to make themselves accessible, either in person or over e-mail, which means "that they always seem to be available." In terms of how smoothly things run, keep in mind that Olin is "an experiment, so you never really know what's going to happen," which "tends to lead to some chaos." That doesn't mean that the administration isn't trying—it's actually trying all the time. There is a "constant dialogue of feedback between the students, staff, and faculty" and the administration "always has open doors to everyone." "You can sit down and eat lunch [in the dining hall] with the president if you want to." Feedback drives a "continual reassessment" of the institution with the aim of constant "improvement in all departments."

Life

A popular saying used to describe student life at Olin goes like this: "Choose two: work, sleep, fun." The majority of students choose the first and the last because "An Oliner at rest is an unhappy Oliner." The "Entrepreneurial spirit is strong" here, leading many people to choose to spend what little free time they have "working on cool projects" like "hacking the thermostat in their room" and "playing with lasers and circuits." Not everyone engages in genius science "geek" endeavors in their free time. Instead many do plain-Jane, run-of-the-mill, vanilla geek activities like "playing DDR" and "video gaming." Still, normal college student stuff happens here, too. "There are definitely typical college parties with drinking games," and "Clubs and student organizations put on a lot of activities." Plenty of students also get heavily involved "with local service groups (FIRST Robotics and Habitat for Humanity are particularly active)." And as it is at every one of the gazillion colleges in the greater Beantown area, "going into Boston for events" is a popular pastime here too. Concerning the more mundane details of day-to-day life on campus, students are pleased. The dorms are "nice and warm," and "The food is amazing."

Student Body

Picture this: "Engineers with social skills." Yes, they really do exist, and about 300 of them live and learn happily together at this small college on the outskirts of Boston. These folks "are all extremely intelligent and very high-achieving." "There are students here that have held patents since high school, [and others] who have worked for NASA." Perhaps because people like this—people who have "already made incredible, insane contributions to the world"—are not in short supply, "The majority [of students] don't seem to feel like they're especially smart." So there's little threat of being smothered by peers' egos if one enrolls here. "Olin has a very diverse student body with regard to everything except race." "The full-tuition scholarship allows for students from less wealthy backgrounds" to attend, and a "strong group of very religious students" coexists peacefully with a "decent number of people who express alternative sexualities." In sum, a live-and-let-live philosophy is pervasive. "People are allowed to have their own passions and opinions so long as they have passions and opinions."

FINANCIAL AID: 781-292-2222 • E-MAIL: INFO@OLIN.EDU • WEBSITE: WWW.OLIN.EDU

ADMISSIONS

Very important factors considered include: Academic GPA, application essay, character/personal qualities, extracurricular activities, level of applicant's interest, recommendation(s), rigor of secondary school record, talent/ability. *Important factors considered include:* Class rank, interview, standardized test scores, volunteer work. *Other factors considered include:* First generation, geographical residence, racial/ethnic status, state residency, work experience. SAT or ACT required; SAT Subject Tests required; ACT with Writing component required. High school diploma is required, and GED is accepted. *Academic units required:* 4 English, 4 math including calculus, 3 science including physics (3 science labs), 2 foreign language, 2 social studie. *Academic units recommended:* 2 computing, engineering design.

The Inside Word

Not many colleges can boast that they are filled with students who turned down offers from the likes of MIT, Cal Tech, and Carnegie Mellon, but Olin can. Olin is unique among engineering schools in that the Admissions Office really looks for more than just brains. Things like social skills and eloquence are taken extremely seriously here, so reclusive geniuses seeking 4 years of technical monasticism will be at a disadvantage in the application process.

FINANCIAL AID

Students should submit: FAFSA. Regular filing deadline is March 15. The Princeton Review suggests that all financial aid forms be submitted as soon as possible after January 1. *Need-based scholarships/grants offered:* State scholarships/grants, private scholarships, the school's own gift aid. Applicants will be notified of awards on a rolling basis beginning or about April 1.

FROM THE ADMISSIONS OFFICE

"Every admitted student at Olin College receives a $130,000 4-year full-tuition scholarship. The endowment to support these scholarships, as well as the funds to build a brand new state-of-the-art campus, was provided by the F. W. Olin Foundation. This commitment, in excess of $460 million, is among the largest grants in the history of U.S. higher education. It is the intention of the founders that this scholarship will be offered in perpetuity.

"The selection process at Olin College is unique to college admission. Each year a highly self-selecting pool of approximately 800 applications is reviewed on traditional selection criteria. Approximately 180 finalists are invited to one of two Candidates' Weekends in February and March. These candidates are grouped into five-person teams for a weekend of design-and-build exercises, group discussions, and interviews with Olin students, faculty, and alumni. Written evaluations and recommendations for each candidate are prepared by all Olin participants and submitted to the faculty Admission Committee. The committee admits about 100 candidates to yield a freshman class of 75. The result is that the freshman class is ultimately chosen on the strength of personal attributes such as leadership, cooperation, creativity, communication, and their enthusiasm for Olin College.

"A waiting list of approximately 20 is also established. Some wait list candidates who are not offered a spot in the class may defer enrollment for 1 year—with the guarantee of the Olin Scholarship. Wait list students are strongly encouraged do something unusual, exciting, and productive during their sabbatical year.

"Students applying for admission in the Fall of 2007 are required to take the SAT (or the ACT with the writing section). Olin College also requires scores from two SAT Subject Tests: Math (level 1 or 2), and a Science of the student's choice."

SELECTIVITY

Admissions Rating	**99**
# of applicants	784
% of applicants accepted	17
% of acceptees attending	65
# accepting a place on wait list	16

FRESHMAN PROFILE

Range SAT Critical Reading	690–780
Range SAT Math	710–800
Range ACT Composite	33–35

DEADLINES

Regular application deadline	1/7
Regular notification	3/21
Nonfall registration?	no

APPLICANTS ALSO LOOK AT

AND OFTEN PREFER
Cornell University, Harvard College, Massachusetts Institute of Technology, Stanford University, University of California—Berkeley

AND SOMETIMES PREFER
California Institute of Technology, Carnegie Mellon University, Princeton University, Rensselaer Polytechnic Institute, Yale University

AND RARELY PREFER
Brown University, Northwestern University, Rice University, Washington University in St. Louis, Worcester Polytechnic Institute

FINANCIAL FACTS

Financial Aid Rating	**99**
Annual tuition	$32,100
	Covered by full scholarship.
Room & Board	$11,600
Books and supplies	$750
Required fees	$150
% frosh rec. need-based scholarship or grant aid	11
% UG rec. need-based scholarship or grant aid	3
% frosh rec. need-based self-help aid	0
% UG rec. need-based self-help aid	0
% frosh rec. any financial aid	100
% UG rec. any financial aid	100

FURMAN UNIVERSITY

3300 POINSETT HIGHWAY, GREENVILLE, SC 29613 • ADMISSIONS: 864-294-2034 • FAX: 864-294-3127

CAMPUS LIFE
Quality of Life Rating	**95**
Fire Safety Rating	**88**
Type of school	private
Environment	city

STUDENTS
Total undergrad enrollment	2,625
% male/female	44/56
% from out of state	71
% from public high school	63
% live on campus	90
% in (# of) fraternities	35 (8)
% in (# of) sororities	40 (8)
% African American	6
% Asian	2
% Caucasian	85
% Hispanic	1
% international	2
# of countries represented	41

SURVEY SAYS . . .
Great computer facilities
Great library

ACADEMICS
Academic Rating	**94**
Calendar	3-2-3
Student/faculty ratio	11:1
Profs interesting rating	90
Profs accessible rating	95
% profs teaching UG courses	100
% classes taught by TAs	0
Most common lab size	fewer than 10 students
Most common reg class size	10–19 students

MOST POPULAR MAJORS
business administration
history
political science

STUDENTS SAY

Academics

Furman University, "a small, private, liberal arts school with a gorgeous campus," has "a great reputation, especially in the Southeast." These are just some of the reasons that students choose the school. Undergraduates also love the "great collegiate atmosphere," "generous scholarships, plenty of undergraduate research opportunities, and personal attention from professors," and the "sweet downtown scene" in hometown Greenville. In short, they come because they feel that "Furman offers a great overall experience." Students warn that "Furman is hard. There are no 'gimmes' here. You work for what you get and oftentimes the result shocks freshmen who grew accustomed to cruising in high school." As one student writes, "Furman places a great deal of emphasis on class discussion and active participation. This is often quite fun, but it usually is a pretty effective test of whether you read the deconstruction article last night or whether you truly have the Greek aorist passive down." Students' efforts to keep up are abetted by "small class sizes and good faculty" that provide "the feeling that your professors not only know you as a person, but care about you. Even when classes are kicking your butt, Furman still provides a very enjoyable academic experience, and you're left thinking of the good over the bad."

Life

Furman University "is about students who have truly come to get an education but also find an abundance of other activities that they love." Even walking to class offers a pleasant diversion "because of how picturesque the campus is." For some, "Life at Furman is definitely centered around Furman itself. Students call it 'the bubble.' People are generally very active in at least one activity on campus other than their academic responsibilities." Major events include homecoming which is "one of the most fun weeks all year, with competitions and . . . gathering on the mall Friday night for float building, carnival rides, funnel cakes, and for many students, alcohol intake." Others leave campus fairly frequently to take advantage of downtown Greenville ("one of the coolest places") and the many "outdoor opportunities in the surrounding area." Students occasionally venture further a-field: "We're only 2 hours from Atlanta, Charlotte, and Columbia, so we go to concerts there. We're right in the mountains, so we go hiking and camping, and sometimes we make the 4-hour drive to the beach." Just about everyone enjoys the frequent and popular Greek parties; although "only about one-third of the student body is involved in Greek organizations, at least two-thirds go to the parties and other Greek events." A large jock population drives an active athletic scene; music groups and religious organizations are also "very popular."

Student Body

"Furman kids are often viewed as being rich, White, and preppy (sororadorable and frat-tastic are two common terms)," and "While the majority may fit into those categories," there are also "plenty that are outside that spectrum." True, the typical student is still "a Southern (probably from Tennessee, Georgia, or South Carolina), Protestant Christian of a conservative denomination, athletic, snappily dressed, and hard-studying, but not possessing deep intellectual interest in more than a couple of subjects," but the university is working hard to overcome its reputation as a "a school only for conservative, rich, White kids" by "opening up its doors to many different types of people. Last year, for example, the student body president was a Muslim of Pakistani descent." Most here "are religious to some degree," and many "can quote any and every line of the Bible, making those who are less religious feel a little out of place." Rich or not, religious or agnostic, Southern or otherwise, "The one unifying factor here is the desire for Furman to retain a spirit of Southern hospitality no matter the diversity of its student body."

FINANCIAL AID: 864-294-2204 • E-MAIL: ADMISSIONS@FURMAN.EDU • WEBSITE: WWW.FURMAN.EDU

ADMISSIONS

Very important factors considered include: Rigor of secondary school record. *Important factors considered include:* Academic GPA, application essay, character/personal qualities, class rank, extracurricular activities, standardized test scores. *Other factors considered include:* Alumni/ae relation, first generation, racial/ethnic status, recommendation(s), talent/ability, volunteer work, work experience. SAT or ACT required; ACT with Writing component required. TOEFL required of all international applicants. High school diploma is required, and GED is accepted. *Academic units required:* 4 English, 3 math, 2 science (2 science labs), 2 foreign language, 3 social studies. *Academic units recommended:* 4 English, 4 math, 3 science (3 science labs), 3 foreign language, 4 social studies.

The Inside Word

Furman's high acceptance rate is deceptive; the applicant pool here is highly self-selected, meaning that most who apply have pretty strong credentials. The following stats are more telling: The average applicant has completed five AP courses, earned an unweighted high school GPA of 3.68, and scored pretty well on standardized tests. In the absence of similarly strong credentials, you'll need to find some way to sell yourself to the Admissions Committee. A demonstrated ability to contribute to the school community—perhaps through athletics, the arts, or community service—will help.

FINANCIAL AID

Students should submit: FAFSA, institution's own financial aid form, state aid form; South Carolina residents must complete required state forms for South Carolina. Regular filing deadline is January 15. The Princeton Review suggests that all financial aid forms be submitted as soon as possible after January 1. *Need-based scholarships/grants offered:* Pell Grant, SEOG, state scholarships/grants, private scholarships, the school's own gift aid, National SMART Grant, and Academic Competitiveness Grant grants. *Loan aid offered:* FFEL Subsidized Stafford, FFEL Unsubsidized Stafford, FFEL PLUS, Federal Perkins Loan, state loans, donor-sponsored loans for study abroad. Applicants will be notified of awards on or about March 15.

FROM THE ADMISSIONS OFFICE

"From its position as a nationally ranked independent, coeducational liberal arts college of 2,600 students, Furman takes great pride in its beautiful campus, its gifted student body, its distinguished and active faculty, and the many notable accomplishments of its alumni. Furman emphasizes engaged learning, a hands-on, problem-solving, and collaborative educational philosophy that encourages students to put into practice the theories and methods learned from texts and lectures. Using the latest in wired and wireless technology, students have multiple opportunities to become engaged in their academic pursuits through an array of internships, service-learning programs, faculty/student creative projects and significant undergraduate research. Furman offers an unusual combination of a top-tier liberal arts college, 17 Division I men's and women's athletic teams, and a nationally competitive music program that features 26 performing ensembles. Students are involved in hundreds of organizations and clubs on campus ranging from professional organizations to fraternities and sororities. In sum, Furman is a diverse learning community that celebrates its differences and is committed to the development of the whole student.

"Students applying for admission for Fall 2008 must submit scores from the new version of the SAT (or the ACT with the writing section). Math or Verbal scores submitted from the old SAT (before March 2005) or ACT will be used, if they are better than those from the new test."

SELECTIVITY

Admissions Rating	94
# of applicants	3,887
% of applicants accepted	56
% of acceptees attending	32
# accepting a place on wait list	141
% admitted from wait list	10
# of early decision applicants	669
% accepted early decision	58

FRESHMAN PROFILE

Range SAT Critical Reading	590–690
Range SAT Math	590–690
Range ACT Composite	25–31
Minimum Paper TOEFL	570
Minimum Computer Based TOEFL	230
Average HS GPA	3.7
% graduated top 10% of class	64
% graduated top 25% of class	87
% graduated top 50% of class	98

DEADLINES

Early decision application deadline	11/15
Early decision notification	12/15
Regular application deadline	1/15
Regular notification	3/15
Nonfall registration?	no

APPLICANTS ALSO LOOK AT

AND OFTEN PREFER
Duke University, The University of North Carolina at Chapel Hill, Vanderbilt University, Wake Forest University, Washington and Lee University

AND SOMETIMES PREFER
Davidson College, Emory University, Georgia Institute of Technology, University of South Carolina—Columbia, Wofford College

AND RARELY PREFER
Auburn University, Clemson University

FINANCIAL FACTS

Financial Aid Rating	85
Annual tuition	$28,352
Room & Board	$7,552
Books and supplies	$775
Required fees	$488
% frosh rec. need-based scholarship or grant aid	42
% UG rec. need-based scholarship or grant aid	40
% frosh rec. need-based self-help aid	26
% UG rec. need-based self-help aid	25
% frosh rec. any financial aid	85
% UG rec. any financial aid	86

GEORGE MASON UNIVERSITY

4400 UNIVERSITY DRIVE MSN 3A4, FAIRFAX, VA 22030-4444 • ADMISSIONS: 703-993-2400 • FAX: 703-993-2392

STUDENTS SAY

Academics

George Mason University, a large public school with "an award-winning faculty," offers several options to students seeking a small-school environment. First is the honors program in general education, which allows students to replace large, required intro classes with smaller, "more enlightening classes with names like 'Reading Cultural Signs'." Students love that the program "allows for more one-on-one interaction with professors and is a bit more challenging"; the most practical-minded undergrads here, however, question the applicability of honors courses to real life. The second option, New Century College, is even further afield from traditional undergraduate academics; it offers three integrative/self-designed degrees in a "seminar-style environment with collaborative faculty involvement." More conventional options are offered through seven of Mason's divisions; students report that the School of Management and the School of Public Policy are both excellent, benefiting from the fact that "the area attracts heaps of over-qualified people who wind up teaching here." Mason boasts "two Nobel Prize winners in its economics department and Washington, DC insiders" in all government- and policy-related areas. Access to the DC area also allows for "a wonderful partnership with other DC universities, providing library links and also classes at Georgetown, Catholic, American, Marymount, Gallaudet, Maryland—College Park, and UDC (University of the District of Columbia)," as well as "great connections with potential employers in the northern Virginia/DC area."

Life

Life at GMU is tempered by the fact that only around one in four students lives on campus, and a considerable number of them "seem to leave for the weekends." As a result, "The campus is deserted by Friday afternoon." Those who remain tell us either that "there is nothing to do," or more frequently, "There are things to do, but you really have to look for them. We've got some campus activities like free movies at a movie theater in our student center, but they are often underpromoted, and many students don't know what's going on." Weekends are generally spent "hanging out in the dorms on the weekends and watching movies" or, for those who are more adventurous and well heeled, "taking the metro into DC to go to the museums, clubs, and restaurants. The only problem with that is it can be a bit expensive." There's more happening on campus during the week; the "college newspaper is top-notch," the basketball team "is fun to watch and highly supported because we don't have a football team," and "The athletic facilities are fantastic. We have a nice-sized weight room, a good quality training room, an indoor track, an outdoor track, plus many different various athletic fields. The coaching staff, trainers, and other personnel are very knowledgeable and helpful." Students belonging to fraternities and sororities assure us that "if you are in a Greek organization, there are always tons of things to do at GMU."

Student Body

"George Mason University is number one in the nation for the most diversity," students claim. One student reports, "On my freshman floor there were kids from seven nations other than America, which is quite diverse for a group of about 30. We also have a huge population of returning students, so depending on which door you wait near, you're just as likely to see a stream of twenty-somethings as you are a line of people who could be your parents." Student types run the gamut from "the frat types to the athletes, to sorority girls to the slackers, nerds, rich, poor, and average Joes. Everyone seems to interact pretty well." The predominant look on campus is "preppy lite"; as one student explains, "We don't flip up our collars like one expects from a Georgetown undergrad, but cashmere socks in the winter and Armani Exchange t-shirts in the summer aren't rare."

FINANCIAL AID: 703-993-2353 • E-MAIL: ADMISSIONS@GMU.EDU • WEBSITE: WWW.GMU.EDU

ADMISSIONS

Very important factors considered include: Academic GPA, rigor of secondary school record. *Important factors considered include:* Alumni/ae relation, application essay, character/personal qualities, class rank, recommendation(s), talent/ability. *Other factors considered include:* Extracurricular activities, first generation, level of applicant's interest, standardized test scores, volunteer work, work experience. SAT and SAT Subject Tests or ACT recommended; TOEFL required of all international applicants. High school diploma is required, and GED is accepted. *Academic units required:* 4 English, 4 math, 4 science (4 science labs), 3 foreign language, 4 social studies, 5 academic electives. *Academic units recommended:* 4 English, 3 math, 3 science (3 science labs), 2 foreign language, 3 social studies, 3 academic electives.

The Inside Word

George Mason is a popular destination for college for two key reasons: Its proximity to Washington, DC and the fact that it is not nearly as difficult to gain admission at Mason as it is at University of Virginia or William & Mary, the two flagships of the Virginia state system. The university's quality faculty and impressive facilities make it worth taking a look if low-cost, solid programs in the DC area are high on your list.

FINANCIAL AID

Students should submit: FAFSA. The Princeton Review suggests that all financial aid forms be submitted as soon as possible after January 1. *Need-based scholarships/grants offered:* Pell Grant, SEOG, state scholarships/grants, private scholarships, the school's own gift aid. *Loan aid offered:* FFEL Subsidized Stafford, FFEL Unsubsidized Stafford, FFEL PLUS, Federal Perkins Loan, Federal Nursing Loan. Applicants will be notified of awards on or about April 1. Federal Work-Study Program available. Institutional employment available. Off-campus job opportunities are good.

FROM THE ADMISSIONS OFFICE

"George Mason University enjoys the best location in the world. Our connections to the DC area result in faculty members who are engaged in the top research in their fields. We have professors who are regular contributors on all of the major news networks, and you can hardly listen to a program on National Public Radio without hearing from one of our scholars. This connectivity extends to our students, who take internships and get jobs at some of the best organizations and companies in the world. We have students at AOL/Time Warner, the National Institutes of Health, the Kennedy Center, the World Bank, the White House, and the National Zoo. We have all the advantages of the excitement of our Nation's Capital combined with the comfort and security of this beautiful suburban campus.

"At Mason, we pride ourselves on being among the most innovative universities in the world. Many of our degree programs are the first of their kind, including the first PhD program in biodefense, the first DC-based undergraduate program in conflict resolution, the first integrated school of information technology and engineering based on computer related programs, and one of the most innovative performing arts management programs in the United States. As a result, George Mason University is at the forefront of the emerging field of biotechnology, is a natural leader in the performing arts, and holds a preeminent position in the fields of economics, electronic journalism, and history, just to name a few.

"George Mason University will accept the ACT, with or without the written portion, and either the old or new version of the SAT. Scores from the Writing section will not be considered in our admission decisions, as our faculty does not feel the Writing section reflects quality or methodology of our award-winning writing across the curriculum program."

SELECTIVITY

Admissions Rating	**81**
# of applicants	11,015
% of applicants accepted	61
% of acceptees attending	37
# accepting a place on wait list	213

FRESHMAN PROFILE

Range SAT Critical Reading	500–600
Range SAT Math	510–610
Range SAT Writing	490–590
Range ACT Composite	20–25
Minimum Paper TOEFL	570
Minimum Computer Based TOEFL	230
Average HS GPA	3.36
% graduated top 10% of class	15
% graduated top 25% of class	48
% graduated top 50% of class	94

DEADLINES

Regular application deadline	1/15
Regular notification	4/1
Nonfall registration?	yes

APPLICANTS ALSO LOOK AT AND OFTEN PREFER

James Madison University, University of Virginia, Virginia Tech

AND SOMETIMES PREFER

The George Washington University

FINANCIAL FACTS

Financial Aid Rating	**66**
Annual in-state tuition	$4,752
Annual out-of-state tuition	$16,896
Room & Board	$6,750
Books and supplies	$810
Required fees	$1,656
% frosh rec. need-based scholarship or grant aid	27
% UG rec. need-based scholarship or grant aid	26
% frosh rec. need-based self-help aid	27
% UG rec. need-based self-help aid	27
% frosh rec. any financial aid	56
% UG rec. any financial aid	42

THE GEORGE WASHINGTON UNIVERSITY

2121 I STREET NORTHWEST, SUITE 201, WASHINGTON, DC 20052 • ADMISSIONS: 202-994-6040 • FAX: 202-994-0325

CAMPUS LIFE
Quality of Life Rating	**90**
Fire Safety Rating	**60***
Type of school	private
Environment	metropolis

STUDENTS
Total undergrad enrollment	10,563
% male/female	44/56
% from out of state	98
% from public high school	70
% live on campus	67
% in (# of) fraternities	16 (12)
% in (# of) sororities	13 (9)
% African American	6
% Asian	10
% Caucasian	66
% Hispanic	5
% international	4
# of countries represented	101

SURVEY SAYS . . .
Athletic facilities are great
Students love Washington, DC
Great off-campus food
Dorms are like palaces
Campus feels safe
Students are happy
Student publications are popular
Student government is popular
Political activism is popular

ACADEMICS
Academic Rating	**87**
Calendar	semester
Student/faculty ratio	13:1
Profs interesting rating	74
Profs accessible rating	74
% profs teaching	
UG courses	67
% classes taught by TAs	3
Most common	
lab size	20–29 students
Most common	
reg class size	10–19 students

STUDENTS SAY

Academics

At George Washington University, it's all about "being in the center of the most powerful city in the world and deciding where to make your mark," where students can tap "the nation's capital, whether [for] sports, science and medicine, politics, or psychology." Politics are the primary drawing card; the stellar Elliot School of International Affairs trains tomorrow's diplomats, while solid programs in political science and political communication benefit from heavyweight guest speakers (one student writes, "DeeDee Myers came to my Washington Reporters class, and I got to go interview Bob Siegel of NPR—it's experiences like that that make GW special"), and access to incredible internships; as one student puts it, "GW is government's largest source of slave labor. It isn't uncommon . . . [to] see people from your different classes in the halls of Capital Hill." GW doesn't begin and end with government though; the school also has "a wonderful business program with an abundance of internship opportunities," a "computer security and information assurance" program "that's one of the best in the world and is actually one of only a handful accredited by the National Security Agency," and numerous other strengths. GW's administration seems geared toward training future government workers; students describe it as very "bureaucratic." The school maintains a large adjunct faculty; while some love that the adjuncts "have other projects or jobs on the side that can give students firsthand experience with real issues," others complain that "we lose many great adjunct professors every year" and that the large turnover "would be avoided if we just shelled out a little more money [to take on more full-time faculty]."

Life

"Whether it's going to the Kennedy Center, [to] the 9:30 Club, or [for] a midnight monument tour . . . DC is at the center of a GW student's experience." Undergrads boast that "of all DC universities, GW is the best situated. Where else can you party, get drunk, stumble your way to the steps of the Lincoln [Memorial], and attempt to hurry back to get enough sleep to function at your internship on the Hill?" Being in DC "makes it easy to always have something to do, from the monuments to the museums . . . from just hanging out on campus [to] going to sporting events." Speaking of sports, GW basketball "is huge. However, other than that, we're not much of a sports school. Students are much more interested in joining the College Democrats or the College Republicans." Many are also interested in partying, but a junior stresses that she'd "never call GW a party school. It's definitely there if you want it, but it's not pressured on you at all. Same thing with frats and sororities: Those who want to be in Greek life can be, and those who don't, don't have to [be] in order to have a fulfilling college experience."

Student Body

GW attracts "a lot of wealthy students" (its tuition is among the nation's highest), but there is also "a sense of diversity on campus." Jewish students make up about one-quarter of the undergraduate population; there are also "a lot of international students," "students from each of the 50 states," and, sprinkled among the wealthy, "plenty of middle-class students." At GW, undergrads say, you'll find "people that have disabilities, and people from every race, religion, sexual orientation, and ideology." (While all ideologies are represented, it should be noted that "most students characterize themselves as Democrats.") Students tell us that GW isn't as much "a melting pot as a tossed salad, where people from different backgrounds, frats, and student org[anizations] all blend together and taste pretty darn good." Undergrads here tend to be "very driven, constantly thinking about what their next internship is going to be, and how they're going to get out into Washington more and things like that."

THE GEORGE WASHINGTON UNIVERSITY

FINANCIAL AID: 202-994-6620 • E-MAIL: GWADM@GWU.EDU • WEBSITE: WWW.GWU.EDU

ADMISSIONS

Very important factors considered include: Rigor of secondary school record. *Important factors considered include:* Application essay, class rank, extracurricular activities, interview, recommendation(s), standardized test scores, talent/ability, volunteer work. *Other factors considered include:* Alumni/ae relation, character/personal qualities, geographical residence, racial/ethnic status, work experience. SAT or ACT required; TOEFL required of all international applicants. High school diploma is required, and GED is not accepted. *Academic units required:* 4 English, 2 math, 2 science (1 science lab), 2 foreign language, 2 social studies. *Academic units recommended:* 4 English, 4 math, 4 science, 4 foreign language, 4 social studies.

The Inside Word

With over 20,000 applications to process annually, GW would be forgiven if it gave student essays only a perfunctory glance. However, the school considers essays carefully; a school Admissions Officer recently told the *Washington Times* that student essays represent "the student's voice in the application," adding that the school's low admit rate means that "everything (in the application) takes on significance."

FINANCIAL AID

Students should submit: FAFSA, CSS/Financial Aid PROFILE. Regular filing deadline is February 1. The Princeton Review suggests that all financial aid forms be submitted as soon as possible after January 1. *Need-based scholarships/grants offered:* Pell Grant, SEOG, state scholarships/grants, the school's own gift aid. *Loan aid offered:* FFEL Subsidized Stafford, FFEL Unsubsidized Stafford, FFEL PLUS, Federal Perkins Loan. Applicants will be notified of awards on a rolling basis beginning or about March 24. Federal Work-Study Program available. Institutional employment available. Off-campus job opportunities are excellent.

FROM THE ADMISSIONS OFFICE

"At GW, we welcome students who show a measure of impatience with the limitations of traditional education. At many universities, the edge of campus is the real world, but not at GW, where our campus and Washington, DC are seamless. We look for bold, bright students who are ambitious, energetic, and self-motivated. Here, where we are so close to the centers of thought and action in every field we offer, we easily integrate our outstanding academic tradition and faculty connections with the best internship and job opportunities of Washington, DC. A generous scholarship and financial assistance program attracts top students from all parts of the country and the world.

"Students applying for Fall 2008 may send either an old or revised SAT score. Regardless of the version of the SAT submitted, we will use those scores that best work to the student's advantage. Applicants to the BA/MD, IEMP, and BA/JD programs are required to submit SAT Subject Tests. "

SELECTIVITY

Admissions Rating	95
# of applicants	20,159
% of applicants accepted	38
% of acceptees attending	35
# accepting a place on wait list	788
% admitted from wait list	23
# of early decision applicants	1881
% accepted early decision	63

FRESHMAN PROFILE

Range SAT Critical Reading	590–690
Range SAT Math	590–680
Range ACT Composite	25–30
Minimum Paper TOEFL	550
Minimum Computer Based TOEFL	300
% graduated top 10% of class	59
% graduated top 25% of class	80
% graduated top 50% of class	99

DEADLINES

Early decision application deadline	12/1
Early decision notification	12/15
Regular application deadline	1/15
Regular notification	3/15
Nonfall registration?	yes

APPLICANTS ALSO LOOK AT

AND OFTEN PREFER
Boston University, Emory University, Georgetown University, New York University, University of Virginia

AND SOMETIMES PREFER
American University, The Catholic University of America, Tufts University, University of Maryland—College Park, University of Vermont

FINANCIAL FACTS

Financial Aid Rating	88
Annual tuition	$34,000
Room & Board	$10,470
Books and supplies	$850
Required fees	$30
% frosh rec. need-based scholarship or grant aid	40
% UG rec. need-based scholarship or grant aid	38
% frosh rec. need-based self-help aid	34
% UG rec. need-based self-help aid	35

GEORGETOWN UNIVERSITY

THIRTY-SEVENTH AND P STREETS, NORTHWEST, WASHINGTON, DC 20057 • ADMISSIONS: 202-687-3600 • FAX: 202-687-5084

STUDENTS SAY

Academics

It's impossible to separate the virtues of a Georgetown education with the opportunities afforded by the school's Washington, DC location. The "out-of-this-world" internship opportunities include positions at "all kinds of businesses and law firms"; one seasoned senior reports, a considerable number of students "have a congressional internship during their time at Georgetown." Washington also provides a never-ending source of amazing faculty; another senior boasts, "I've had a 25-person class with Donna Brazile, a 50-person class with Madeleine Albright, and a 10-person class with Ron Faucheaux (editor of *Campaigns and Elections* magazine)." In the words of a first-year, "It is not uncommon after class to go back to your room, turn on CNN or MSNBC, and see your professor." With so many power brokers floating about, "Georgetown is easily the best school for finding a mentor: There are genius Jesuits, serving diplomats, authors, and other luminaries walking about campus every day, not only waiting to be approached but approaching you." One international political economy major assures us, "Even though they are busy, they are always available if you need help." Students point out that "Georgetown is also a great place to come if you want to study anything international or go abroad. Half of the junior class goes abroad, and the school offers or is affiliated with a lot of programs that support direct matriculation into a local university." While best known for its programs in the liberal arts, foreign affairs, language, and nursing, Georgetown, in the words of a senior, "embodies a unique combination of true academic commitment, social and political awareness, rich tradition, a diverse student body, and all the crazy fun of college."

Life

"Georgetown has a great social life," undergrads here agree; the school offers "tons of on- and off-campus parties as well as bars within walking distance." Extracurricular options include numerous "a cappella and theater groups on campus," and students can choose to attend any of the frequent on-campus lectures and readings. And, of course, there's always Hoyas basketball, which enjoys a fanatical following among the student body. Students like to spend free time in Washington, DC, which they hail as "an amazing place to live." The District "has a ton of free museums, exhibits, plays, and concerts." One student reports, "I have been dancing for free at the Kennedy Center, seen concerts just a few minutes into Pennsylvania Avenue, visited museums (also free), eaten great food throughout DC, volunteered in afterschool programs, and gone running along the canal and through the monuments at night. The public transportation in DC makes it easy to go anywhere without a car." Georgetown takes the edge off urban living with a campus that's "isolated by walls and gates . . . we've got all the fun of the city in a homier atmosphere." Prospective students should take note that "the cost of living in Georgetown as a whole is high, so you're definitely better off either having a job or learning to manage your money fast!"

Student Body

"You hear a lot about 'Joe and Jane Hoya,' the typical preppy types" at Georgetown—and while "There is definitely a strong presence of the rich boarding school students," there are "way more students from public schools of every stripe, from countries ranging from Romania to India to Spain, from all kinds of socioeconomic backgrounds, and with all kinds of interests." Although Georgetown is religiously affiliated, "This is not your typical Catholic university"; there is "lots of diversity across cultural, ethnic, and religious categories." A common thread among students is that they are all "very ambitious and driven. Also, most people tend to have either lived in another country, know more than two languages, or have traveled a lot. In general there's a big interest in learning about diverse cultures." Not surprisingly, most here "are highly political" and "conscious of international affairs." While students' views may differ, a sophomore promises, "There is a place for everyone on campus."

ADMISSIONS

Very important factors considered include: Academic GPA, application essay, character/personal qualities, class rank, recommendation(s), rigor of secondary school record, standardized test scores, talent/ability. *Important factors considered include:* Extracurricular activities, interview, volunteer work. *Other factors considered include:* Alumni/ae relation, geographical residence, racial/ethnic status, state residency, work experience. SAT or ACT required; SAT Subject Tests recommended; TOEFL required of all international applicants. High school diploma is required, and GED is accepted. *Academic units recommended:* 4 English, 2 math, 1 science, 2 foreign language, 2 social studies, 2 history.

The Inside Word

It was always tough to get admitted to Georgetown, but in the early 1980s Patrick Ewing and the Hoyas created a basketball sensation that catapulted the place into position as one of the most selective universities in the nation. There has been no turning back since. GU gets almost 10 applications for every space in the entering class, and the academic strength of the pool is impressive. Virtually 50 percent of the entire student body took AP courses in high school. Candidates who are wait listed should hold little hope for an offer of admission; over the past several years Georgetown has taken very few off their lists.

FINANCIAL AID

Students should submit: FAFSA, CSS/Financial Aid PROFILE, Noncustodial PROFILE, Business/Farm Supplement, Federal Income Tax Returns. Regular filing deadline is February 1. The Princeton Review suggests that all financial aid forms be submitted as soon as possible after January 1. *Need-based scholarships/grants offered:* Pell Grant, SEOG, state scholarships/grants, private scholarships, the school's own gift aid. *Loan aid offered:* FFEL Subsidized Stafford, FFEL Unsubsidized Stafford, FFEL PLUS, Federal Perkins Loan, Federal Nursing Loan, alternative loans. Applicants will be notified of awards on or about April 1. Federal Work-Study Program available. Institutional employment available. Off-campus job opportunities are excellent.

FROM THE ADMISSIONS OFFICE

"Georgetown was founded in 1789 by John Carroll, who concurred with his contemporaries Benjamin Franklin and Thomas Jefferson in believing that the success of the young democracy depended upon an educated and virtuous citizenry. Carroll founded the school with the dynamic Jesuit tradition of education, characterized by humanism and committed to the assumption of responsibility and action. Georgetown is a national and international university, enrolling students from all 50 states and over 100 foreign countries. Undergraduate students are enrolled in one of four undergraduate schools: the College of Arts and Sciences, School of Foreign Service, Georgetown School of Business, and Georgetown School of Nursing and Health Studies. All students share a common liberal arts core and have access to the entire university curriculum.

"Applicants who graduate from high school in 2008 have the option of submitting scores from either the new or existing version of the SAT. Only the Verbal and Math portions of the new SAT will be considered. The student's best composite score will be used in the admission process."

SELECTIVITY

Admissions Rating	99
# of applicants	15,070
% of applicants accepted	22
% of acceptees attending	47
# accepting a place on wait list	1,190
% admitted from wait list	1

FRESHMAN PROFILE

Range SAT Critical Reading	640–750
Range SAT Math	650–740
Minimum Paper TOEFL	200
% graduated top 10% of class	84
% graduated top 25% of class	96
% graduated top 50% of class	99

DEADLINES

Regular application deadline	1/10
Regular notification	4/1
Nonfall registration?	no

APPLICANTS ALSO LOOK AT

AND OFTEN PREFER
Duke University, University of Pennsylvania

AND SOMETIMES PREFER
Cornell University, Northwestern University, University of Notre Dame, University of Virginia

AND RARELY PREFER
Boston College, New York University, The George Washington University, Tufts University

FINANCIAL FACTS

Financial Aid Rating	93
Annual tuition	$33,552
Room & Board	$11,567
Books and supplies	$1,000
Required fees	$382
% frosh rec. need-based scholarship or grant aid	38
% UG rec. need-based scholarship or grant aid	36
% frosh rec. need-based self-help aid	33
% UG rec. need-based self-help aid	35
% frosh rec. any financial aid	39
% UG rec. any financial aid	40

GEORGIA INSTITUTE OF TECHNOLOGY

219 UNCLE HEINE WAY, ATLANTA, GA 30332-0320 • ADMISSIONS: 404-894-4154 • FAX: 404-894-9511

CAMPUS LIFE

Quality of Life Rating	**80**
Fire Safety Rating	**84**
Type of school	public
Environment	metropolis

STUDENTS

Total undergrad enrollment	12,103
% male/female	72/28
% from out of state	29
% live on campus	51
% in (# of) fraternities	22 (34)
% in (# of) sororities	27 (14)
% African American	7
% Asian	16
% Caucasian	68
% Hispanic	4
% international	4
# of countries represented	72

SURVEY SAYS . . .
Great computer facilities
Athletic facilities are great
Diverse student types on campus
Students love Atlanta, GA
Great off-campus food
Everyone loves the Yellow Jackets

ACADEMICS

Academic Rating	**73**
Calendar	semester
Student/faculty ratio	14:1
Profs interesting rating	61
Profs accessible rating	62
% profs teaching UG courses	100
% classes taught by TAs	3
Most common lab size	10–19 students
Most common reg class size	20–29 students

MOST POPULAR MAJORS
business administration/
management
industrial engineering
mechanical engineering

STUDENTS SAY

Academics

Students coming to Georgia Tech should be prepared to be "challenged in many new ways." Here, "Professors are very demanding. They're the most brilliant people I've ever met," and they "don't spoon-feed you"; if you want to succeed at Tech, students advise that "you have to learn how to suck it up and study." There's one big upside to the rigors of Tech's academics. As one student puts it, after being here, "The rest of the world seems easy." Students interested in hands-on learning appreciate the fact that "a lot of the professors are doing major research, so it's [a] great [school] for research opportunities." "Because the professors are deep in their research," however, they sometimes "don't do that great a job teaching." Luckily, "The professors are required to have office hours," and students suggest taking advantage of them: "Professors are mostly great one-on-one. They really want you to talk to them and for you to learn."

Life

As one undergrad puts it, "Basically people bust their asses during the week, and when the weekends arrive they're prepared to let loose a bit." Options for letting loose include "a 'good enough' NCAA Division I sports program, a good social scene," a welcoming Greek community, "and for everyone else, there's the city of Atlanta right at your doorstep. You're just a short ride away from movies, shopping, the Fox Theatre, the High Museum of Art, Piedmont Park, and one of the best club and bar scenes in the South," centered mainly in the neighborhoods of Buckhead and Midtown. For those without cars in this driving city, transportation comes in the form of "a 'Tech Trolley' that takes a route around midtown, and a 'Stinger Shuttle' that goes to the grocery store on the weekends. The trolley also goes to the MARTA [Atlanta's subway] station, giving students access to the airport, downtown (although that is walkable), and Lenox Mall." With "over 300 organizations already on campus," students seeking leadership experience can most likely find it, as too they can find other students with like-minded interests.

Student Body

Students claim that "Tech is broken down into two different types of college students. First you have the 'typical' college students, who take their academics seriously, but who enjoy being social, going out on weekends, and interacting with the rest of the student population. Then there's the group of 'Techies' who are sometimes socially awkward and who like to stay in their rooms a lot and only interact with others like them." The guys here bemoan a "70:30 male/female ratio, but" optimistically declare that "The ratio is getting better." "A large international student population" also gives the "student body as a whole something extra." And those who have found their talents to be liabilities in the past will be pleased to learn that at GT, "Unlike at high school, no one looks down upon you if you know the entire periodic table, if you can do differential equations, or you can speak three languages; rather, you are respected."

FINANCIAL AID: 404-894-4160 • E-MAIL: ADMISSION@GATECH.EDU • WEBSITE: WWW.GATECH.EDU

ADMISSIONS

Very important factors considered include: Academic GPA. *Important factors considered include:* Application essay, extracurricular activities, geographical residence, rigor of secondary school record, standardized test scores, state residency, talent/ability, volunteer work, work experience. SAT or ACT required; ACT with Writing component required. TOEFL required of all international applicants. High school diploma is required, and GED is accepted. *Academic units required:* 4 English, 4 math, 3 science (2 science labs), 2 foreign language, 3 social studies.

The Inside Word

Students considering Georgia Tech should not be deceived by the relatively high acceptance rate. GT is a demanding school, and its applicant pool is largely self-selecting. While Admissions Counselors have begun to implement a more well-rounded approach to the admissions process, grades and test scores are still where candidates make their mark. Requirements vary depending on the school one applies to at GT—applicants are advised to inquire in advance.

FINANCIAL AID

Students should submit: FAFSA, institution's own financial aid form. Regular filing deadline is March 1. The Princeton Review suggests that all financial aid forms be submitted as soon as possible after January 1. *Need-based scholarships/grants offered:* Pell Grant, SEOG, state scholarships/grants, private scholarships, the school's own gift aid. *Loan aid offered:* FFEL Subsidized Stafford, FFEL Unsubsidized Stafford, FFEL PLUS, Federal Perkins Loan, college/university loans from institutional funds. Applicants will be notified of awards on a rolling basis beginning or about April 1. Federal Work-Study Program available. Institutional employment available. Off-campus job opportunities are excellent.

FROM THE ADMISSIONS OFFICE

"Georgia Tech consistently ranks among the nation's leaders in engineering, computing, management, architecture, and the sciences while remaining one of the best college buys in the country. The 330-acre campus of red brick buildings and green rolling hills is nestled in the heart of the fun, dynamic, and progressive city of Atlanta in the shadows of a majestic skyline dominated by the work of Georgia Tech–trained architects and designers. During the past decade, over $400 million invested in campus improvements has yielded new state-of-the-art academic and research buildings, apartment-style housing, enhanced social and recreational facilities, and the most extensive fiber-optic cable system on any college campus. Georgia Tech's combined commitment to technologically focused, hands-on educational experiences, teamwork, great teaching, innovation, leadership development, and community service make it unique. Great things are happening at Georgia Tech. We hope you will join us, become a part of our community, and help us create the future.

"Freshman applicants for Fall 2008 are required to submit scores from the Writing assessment portion of the SAT or ACT. Students may also submit scores from the old (prior to March 2005) SAT or ACT. Tech will use the highest combined scores regardless of test date."

SELECTIVITY

Admissions Rating	92
# of applicants	9,389
% of applicants accepted	69
% of acceptees attending	44
# accepting a place on wait list	293
% admitted from wait list	53

FRESHMAN PROFILE

Range SAT Critical Reading	590–680
Range SAT Math	640–720
Range SAT Writing	570–660
Range ACT Composite	26–30
Minimum Paper TOEFL	600
Minimum Computer Based TOEFL	250
Average HS GPA	3.7
% graduated top 10% of class	54
% graduated top 25% of class	83
% graduated top 50% of class	98

DEADLINES

Regular application deadline	1/15
Regular notification	3/15
Nonfall registration?	yes

APPLICANTS ALSO LOOK AT

AND OFTEN PREFER
Duke University, Massachusetts Institute of Technology, Princeton University, Stanford University, The University of North Carolina at Chapel Hill

AND SOMETIMES PREFER
Clemson University, Emory University, University of Florida, University of Georgia, University of Virginia

AND RARELY PREFER
Auburn University, North Carolina State University, Vanderbilt University, Virginia Tech

FINANCIAL FACTS

Financial Aid Rating	75
Annual in-state tuition	$4,164
Annual out-of-state tuition	$20,584
Room & Board	$7,100
Books and supplies	$1,000
Required fees	$1,106
% frosh rec. need-based scholarship or grant aid	18
% UG rec. need-based scholarship or grant aid	18
% frosh rec. need-based self-help aid	20
% UG rec. need-based self-help aid	22
% frosh rec. any financial aid	85
% UG rec. any financial aid	74

GETTYSBURG COLLEGE

ADMISSIONS OFFICE, EISENHOWER HOUSE, GETTYSBURG, PA 17325-1484 • ADMISSIONS: 717-337-6100 • FAX: 717-337-6145

CAMPUS LIFE

Quality of Life Rating	87
Fire Safety Rating	79
Type of school	private
Affiliation	Lutheran
Environment	village

STUDENTS

Total undergrad enrollment	2,511
% male/female	47/53
% from out of state	73
% from public high school	70
% live on campus	94
% in (# of) fraternities	40 (10)
% in (# of) sororities	26 (6)
% African American	4
% Asian	1
% Caucasian	73
% Hispanic	2
% international	1
# of countries represented	27

SURVEY SAYS . . .

Lab facilities are great
Great computer facilities
Great library
Campus feels safe
Frats and sororities dominate social scene
Lots of beer drinking

ACADEMICS

Academic Rating	93
Calendar	semester
Student/faculty ratio	11:1
Profs interesting rating	86
Profs accessible rating	88
% profs teaching UG courses	100
% classes taught by TAs	0
Most common reg class size	10–19 students

MOST POPULAR MAJORS

business administration/
management
political science and government
psychology

STUDENTS SAY

Academics

Gettysburg College is a quintessential small liberal arts college, a place where "You can be challenged academically in an intimate environment of smaller class sizes and a smaller student-to-faculty ratio," enabling "students to develop a close rapport with peers and professors." Students here speak glowingly of the "welcoming community with limitless opportunities" to get involved and "grow in and out of the classroom." Those opportunities include "strong study abroad programs, community service activities, internships, and externships." Academically, "Gettysburg isn't a walk in the park. Your professors have expectations of you whether you are a first-year in a 101 class or a senior looking into a research proposal." Help is available to those in danger of falling behind; one student writes, "The offices are there to help you from Calc-Aid [tutors], biology [reviews], and the Writing Center . . . There is so much available; you just need to go take advantage of it." The school's strongest disciplines include political science, music, biology, environmental studies, and (unsurprisingly) Civil War–era studies. Gettysburg also "has a great management department for a small liberal arts school."

Life

"Greek life is where the majority of social life is centered" at Gettysburg, with nearly half of all male students joining a fraternity, "But that's not to say that there are not options beyond that." True, "Greek life is huge at Gettysburg, and for a male who chooses not to 'go Greek' life can be hard socially." It's not as big a deal for females, because "Gettysburg does not have sorority houses." The Greek scene as a whole is "not exclusive"—everyone "goes to the frats." Moreover, "The college doesn't allow rush to take place until second year, so hopefully students have made friends before making the choice to branch out into other social groups such as the frats." "Most everyone makes a conscious effort to get involved on campus in lots of different activities," so the Greeks, while big, aren't the only game in town. The school "does a lot of extras for the students, such as themed dinners, concerts, and special events," and "The Activity Board also brings bands and movies on weekends so there are other things to do." College sports teams "are very strong, both men's and women's," and "lots of students play intramurals or work out." Hometown Gettysburg, with its battlefield and 'ghost tours,' is great for history buffs and has a lot of "small town charm"; others may prefer to "take day trips" to DC and Baltimore for fun, although each requires a 90-minute drive.

Student Body

Gettysburg students tend to be "smart, outgoing, preppy, and determined," the kind of folks who "work real hard during the week and then have fun on the weekend," but also find time to "volunteer and [get] involved in extracurriculars, clubs, and athletics." Students admit that "there is very little diversity on campus, but the majority of the students come from high schools with the same situation," so many "don't notice the lack of diversity, though this can make you stand out if you're different." Students who don't fit the mold tell us they are comfortable here; one writes, "Gettysburg students tend to come from families who are mid- to upper-class, [and] there is a high percentage of legacy students on campus." Quite frequently students show their wealth "in the form of clothing or cars," but "Money isn't the only thing that matters here." While it may be plentiful, "Even if you don't wear Lily Pulitzer or Burberry you will be just fine as long as flip-flops are your favorite footwear!" Students tend to be politically conservative, although the "The Frisbee team is one niche of politically liberal people" on campus.

FINANCIAL AID: 717-337-6611 • E-MAIL: ADMISS@GETTYSBURG.EDU • WEBSITE: WWW.GETTYSBURG.EDU

ADMISSIONS

Very important factors considered include: Academic GPA, class rank, recommendation(s), rigor of secondary school record. *Important factors considered include:* Application essay, character/personal qualities, extracurricular activities, interview, standardized test scores, talent/ability, volunteer work. *Other factors considered include:* Alumni/ae relation, first generation, geographical residence, level of applicant's interest, racial/ethnic status, work experience. SAT or ACT recommended; TOEFL required of all international applicants. High school diploma is required, and GED is accepted. *Academic units required:* 4 English, 3 math, 3 science (3 science labs), 3 foreign language, 3 social studies, 3 history. *Academic units recommended:* 4 English, 4 math, 4 science (4 science labs), 4 foreign language, 4 social studies, 4 history.

The Inside Word

Expect a thorough and highly personalized review of your application at Gettysburg College. Excellent students with relatively weak standardized test scores, take note: Gettysburg no longer requires test scores as part of its application package. The goal of this new policy is to "enrich the classroom environment by encouraging students with a high secondary school grade point average (GPA) and other creative talents who do not perform well on standardized tests to apply for admission." The effect should be to open Gettysburg's doors to capable students who might otherwise not have been previously admitted.

FINANCIAL AID

Students should submit: FAFSA, CSS/Financial Aid PROFILE, business/farm supplement. Regular filing deadline is February 15. The Princeton Review suggests that all financial aid forms be submitted as soon as possible after January 1. *Need-based scholarships/grants offered:* Pell Grant, SEOG, state scholarships/grants, private scholarships, the school's own gift aid. *Loan aid offered:* FFEL Subsidized Stafford, FFEL Unsubsidized Stafford, FFEL PLUS, Federal Perkins Loan, college/university loans from institutional funds. Applicants will be notified of awards on or about March 26. Federal Work-Study Program available. Institutional employment available.

FROM THE ADMISSIONS OFFICE

"Four major goals of Gettysburg College to best prepare students to enter the twenty-first century, include: first, to accelerate the intellectual development of our first-year students by integrating them more quickly into the intellectual life of the campus; second, to use interdisciplinary courses combining the intellectual approaches of various fields; third, to encourage students to develop an international perspective through course work, study abroad, association with international faculty, and a variety of extracurricular activities; and fourth, to encourage students to develop (1) a capacity for independent study by ensuring that all students work closely with individual faculty members on an extensive project during their undergraduate years and (2) the ability to work with their peers by making the small group a central feature in college life.

"Gettysburg College requires that freshman applicants submit scores from the old or new SAT. Students may also choose to submit scores from the ACT (with or without the Writing component) in lieu of the SAT."

SELECTIVITY

Admissions Rating	**95**
# of applicants	5,310
% of applicants accepted	41
% of acceptees attending	33
# accepting a place on wait list	605
# of early decision applicants	427
% accepted early decision	70

FRESHMAN PROFILE

Range SAT Critical Reading	620–690
Range SAT Math	600–670
Minimum Paper TOEFL	570
Minimum Computer Based TOEFL	230
% graduated top 10% of class	66
% graduated top 25% of class	89
% graduated top 50% of class	100

DEADLINES

Early decision application deadline	11/15
Early decision notification	12/15
Regular application deadline	2/15
Regular notification	4/1
Nonfall registration?	yes

APPLICANTS ALSO LOOK AT

AND OFTEN PREFER
Colgate University
AND SOMETIMES PREFER
Bucknell University
AND RARELY PREFER
Muhlenberg College

FINANCIAL FACTS

Financial Aid Rating	**98**
Annual tuition	$33,700
Room & Board	$8,260
Books and supplies	$500
Required fees	$250
% frosh rec. need-based scholarship or grant aid	54
% UG rec. need-based scholarship or grant aid	56
% frosh rec. need-based self-help aid	44
% UG rec. need-based self-help aid	49
% frosh rec. any financial aid	70
% UG rec. any financial aid	70

GONZAGA UNIVERSITY

502 EAST BOONE AVENUE, SPOKANE, WA 99258 • ADMISSIONS: 509-323-6572 • FAX: 509-323-5780

CAMPUS LIFE

Quality of Life Rating	79
Fire Safety Rating	60*
Type of school	private
Affiliation	Roman Catholic
Environment	city

STUDENTS

Total undergrad enrollment	4,186
% male/female	46/54
% from out of state	50
% from public high school	65
% live on campus	49
% African American	1
% Asian	6
% Caucasian	78
% Hispanic	4
% Native American	1
% international	1
# of countries represented	36

SURVEY SAYS . . .

Small classes
Athletic facilities are great
Everyone loves the Bulldogs
Frats and sororities are unpopular or nonexistent

ACADEMICS

Academic Rating	84
Calendar	semester
Student/faculty ratio	12:1
Profs interesting rating	84
Profs accessible rating	85
% profs teaching UG courses	94
% classes taught by TAs	0
Most common lab size	10–19 students
Most common reg class size	20–29 students

MOST POPULAR MAJORS

business/commerce
political science and government
psychology

STUDENTS SAY

Academics

"From the professors to the groundskeepers, the people make Gonzaga what it is," students at this Jesuit university agree, citing "the very positive vibe to the whole university" as the school's greatest asset. Students credit the Jesuit approach to education, which focuses on "educating the whole person" as leading "the school to sponsor a lot of interesting lectures and classes," as well as "popular study abroad programs (especially junior year in Florence)," and a "broad and far-reaching liberal arts core curriculum [that] ensures that all students leave GU with a broader appreciation of the world." Of the core, undergrads observe that "many people arrive resenting the core requirements in philosophy and religion, but then they grow to love them." Throughout the curriculum, "Gonzaga has a wonderful reputation for holding academic ethics in high regard. The faculty makes it a priority to weave some discussion of ethics into every class offered at the university." The university's areas of strength include engineering, business, nursing, education, the sciences and "subjects loved dearly by Jesuits, such as history and philosophy. Gonzaga is a good 'thinking students' school." With so many assets, it's no wonder Gonzaga is quickly building its national stature (its upstart basketball team has helped a little in this area, too). The accompanying increase in enrollment has not been trouble-free; one undergrad reports, "Gonzaga is starting to outgrow itself. More buildings are going to be built, but for now we have more students than our campus is used to accommodating."

Life

"School spirit is very high at Gonzaga due to the success of the basketball team," which has put up an impressive run of NCAA tournament appearances in recent years. "The spirit of the crowd at a home game is incredible" and has not been dampened at all by the team's move from its beloved old home (affectionately nicknamed 'the Kennel') to new, swankier digs. Otherwise, extracurricular life at GU is a mixed bag. Many students feel they "need more things to do on the weekend. Gonzaga's effort to provide events to go to and sponsoring of on-campus bands is commendable, but there are still many weekends where not much is going on." On the other hand, "Gonzaga's community-service program is very good. The Knights (the closest thing Gonzaga has to a fraternity) is a group of male students who put on many community-service events. The Knights' female counterpart, the Setons, do similar activities." The campus "strikes a good balance between beauty and utility. It's easily navigable and plush with vegetation nearly year-round, yet within walking distance of college are essentials like a grocery store, a Laundromat, a video store, and plenty of fast food." Some complain that "the surrounding area is a bit sketchy; there've been too many vehicle break-ins and theft this year," but even they feel that "Spokane, on the whole, is a great town. It's fairly large, but people are friendly, and it often feels like a small town." Just about everyone agrees that the meal plan is "very bad," even by institutional standards.

Student Body

The student body "is a different breed. We don't have many of the tough, frat, 'I'm gonna beat up the next guy who looks at me' guys. Everything is more laid-back. You can go up to anyone and talk to them and you at least won't get completely blown off, which is a refreshing change." Gonzaga is "a fairly conservative school, and compared to most colleges, most people are open-minded," although "Students who are gay, while not ridiculed, won't find this environment especially nurturing" (although the school offers GLBT support and education). That's in part because GU is a Catholic school, with "a small but vocal contingent of very devout students" and many more that practice, but are only "somewhat religious." About half the students here are Catholic.

GONZAGA UNIVERSITY

FINANCIAL AID: 800-793-1716 • E-MAIL: ADMISSIONS@GONZAGA.EDU • WEBSITE: WWW.GONZAGA.EDU

ADMISSIONS

Very important factors considered include: Academic GPA, character/personal qualities, first generation, rigor of secondary school record. *Important factors considered include:* Application essay, class rank, extracurricular activities, recommendation(s), standardized test scores, talent/ability. *Other factors considered include:* Alumni/ae relation, interview, level of applicant's interest, racial/ethnic status, volunteer work, work experience. SAT or ACT required; TOEFL required of all international applicants. High school diploma is required, and GED is not accepted. *Academic units required:* 4 English, 3 math, 3 science (3 science labs), 3 foreign language, 2 social studies, 2 history, 2 academic electives. *Academic units recommended:* 4 English, 4 math, 4 science (4 science labs), 4 foreign language, 3 social studies, 3 history, 3 academic electives.

The Inside Word

As with many religiously affiliated universities, getting into Gonzaga is largely a matter of making a good match philosophically. However, keep an eye on the steadily rising SAT/ACT requirements. As always, an above-average academic record is a given for admission.

FINANCIAL AID

Students should submit: FAFSA. The Princeton Review suggests that all financial aid forms be submitted as soon as possible after January 1. *Need-based scholarships/grants offered:* Pell Grant, SEOG, state scholarships/grants, private scholarships, the school's own gift aid, United Negro College Fund, Federal Nursing Scholarship. *Loan aid offered:* FFEL Subsidized Stafford, FFEL Unsubsidized Stafford, FFEL PLUS, Federal Perkins Loan, Federal Nursing Loan, state loans, college/university loans from institutional funds. Applicants will be notified of awards on a rolling basis beginning or about March 1. Federal Work-Study Program available. Institutional employment available. Off-campus job opportunities are excellent.

FROM THE ADMISSIONS OFFICE

"Education at Gonzaga is not comparable to an academic 'assembly line'; rather, it is person to person and face to face. This personal quality is also true of our admission and financial aid processes. Therefore, allow us to know you beyond the boundaries of your college application. Visit campus, phone us, e-mail us—let us see the person behind the data. Good luck with your college search and your applications. Go Zags!

"All sections of the new SAT will be accepted, but the new Written portion will not receive universal consideration until further studies are done which examine the success of underrepresented college-bound groups. The Written score will be considered in cases where more information specific to writing ability would be helpful in decision making."

SELECTIVITY

Admissions Rating	90
# of applicants	4,965
% of applicants accepted	67
% of acceptees attending	29
# accepting a place on wait list	240
% admitted from wait list	87

FRESHMAN PROFILE

Range SAT Critical Reading	530–650
Range SAT Math	550–650
Range ACT Composite	23–29
Minimum Paper TOEFL	550
Minimum Computer Based TOEFL	213
Average HS GPA	3.72
% graduated top 10% of class	44
% graduated top 25% of class	79
% graduated top 50% of class	97

DEADLINES

Regular application deadline	2/1
Regular notification	3/15
Nonfall registration?	yes

APPLICANTS ALSO LOOK AT

AND OFTEN PREFER
University of Notre Dame
AND SOMETIMES PREFER
Loyola Marymount University, Santa Clara University, University of Washington
AND RARELY PREFER
University of San Francisco, Washington State University

FINANCIAL FACTS

Financial Aid Rating	82
Annual tuition	$24,590
Room & Board	$7,220
Books and supplies	$900
Required fees	$422
% frosh rec. need-based scholarship or grant aid	57
% UG rec. need-based scholarship or grant aid	59
% frosh rec. need-based self-help aid	37
% UG rec. need-based self-help aid	46
% frosh rec. any financial aid	96
% UG rec. any financial aid	97

GOUCHER COLLEGE

1021 DULANEY VALLEY ROAD, BALTIMORE, MD 21204-2794 • ADMISSIONS: 410-337-6100 • FAX: 410-337-6354

STUDENTS SAY

Academics

Goucher College, a "delightfully odd" school at which "Everybody is quirky in some way," offers a surprising number of first-rate programs for a school of its size. The performing and creative arts are big here, and students tout the dance program as "the best non-conservatory program in the country." Goucher's broad "liberal arts education" ensures that all students get to experience "a little bit of everything" academically. Students praise a "great science/premed program," "good writing and theater programs," and a riding program bolstered by "stables right on campus." Goucher's growing international relations program reflects the school's "education without boundaries" philosophy, and includes an "innovative and exciting" study abroad requirement. Most students love this requirement, citing it as a primary reason for choosing Goucher; a few naysayers complain that the program "can add up financially" (despite the $1,200 voucher students receive to help offset costs) and that "there are not many options." There's no disagreement about Goucher's professors, however, whom students describe as "amazing people and great mentors." They expect a lot from you, "but in the end [you] accomplish more than [you] ever thought possible, and they are willing to help you every step of the way." Goucher also offers "very good academic support services for students with learning disabilities."

Life

"Goucher students spend lots of time in class and studying hard," but when it's time to take a break, there is always something to do on campus. "A lot of students are very involved in stereotypically feminine activities like painting, horseback riding, and dancing," while others participate in "various clubs and organizations" on campus. Students "often travel into downtown Baltimore on the weekends, and like to hang out at the local cafes and farmer's markets, and see shows." Inner Harbor is "also a frequent destination for fun." Goucher runs "a free college shuttle that picks students up and drops them off at other area universities (Johns Hopkins, Loyola, College of Notre Dame, Towson University) as well as at Penn Station," from which students can easily access downtown Washington, DC, and the Inner Harbor. Hometown Towson, a satellite of Baltimore, provides "cute restaurants and stores," but little in the way of collegiate nightlife. On campus, undergrads can choose from "100 student clubs and activities, and "Anyone can start a new club (it is really easy)." Many here feel that "the lack of Greek societies [on campus] limits a lot of social life," which "isn't to say that drinking doesn't go on here. It does, but it happens quietly and [is] low-key in dorms." Dating "is pretty difficult" due to the lopsided male-female ratio. "The few straight boys are usually taken or they are extremely awkward. It's not uncommon to walk into any boys' dorm and find Magic cards and posters of *Lord of the Rings* all over."

Student Body

Goucher has "many of the staple groups, such as jocks," but also "a lot of atypical students" including "pirates [there is a Goucher Pirate Alliance], people who play zombies [regular combatants in Humans vs. Zombies, a game played with Nerf guns]," and "lots of aspiring artists and writers who think they are the cream of the crop." In fact, many here tell us that the atypical student in high school is the typical Goucher undergrad, the kid "who was not very popular in high school but rather the creative type, often existing on the periphery." The "only thing that makes Goucher students similar is their acceptance of other students' weirdness." Students also tend to be "laid-back people who enjoy getting an education rather than competing for one." Undergrads report that "there is a strong Jewish community here, but Christian groups are also present." Although "The student body is very friendly as a whole," conservatives warn that "someone with less-than-liberal views is not exactly welcome [on campus]."

FINANCIAL AID: 410-337-6141 • E-MAIL: ADMISSION@GOUCHER.EDU • WEBSITE: WWW.GOUCHER.EDU

ADMISSIONS

Very important factors considered include: Academic GPA, rigor of secondary school record. *Important factors considered include:* Application essay, recommendation(s), standardized test scores, talent/ability. *Other factors considered include:* Alumni/ae relation, character/personal qualities, class rank, extracurricular activities, first generation, interview, level of applicant's interest, racial/ethnic status, volunteer work, work experience. SAT or ACT required; ACT with Writing component required. TOEFL required of all international applicants. High school diploma is required, and GED is accepted. *Academic units required:* 4 English, 3 math, 2 science, 2 foreign language, 3 social studies, 2 academic electives. *Academic units recommended:* 4 English, 4 math, 3 science, 4 foreign language, 3 social studies, 2 academic electives.

The Inside Word

Goucher accepts the ACT with Writing in lieu of the new SAT and SAT Subject Tests; for most students, the ACT is the better option. Goucher's high admit rate masks a self-selecting applicant pool; you cannot gain acceptance here without a solid high school transcript and test scores.

FINANCIAL AID

Students should submit: FAFSA, CSS/Financial Aid PROFILE, Noncustodial PROFILE, Business/Farm Supplement. Regular filing deadline is February 15. The Princeton Review suggests that all financial aid forms be submitted as soon as possible after January 1. *Need-based scholarships/grants offered:* Pell Grant, SEOG, state scholarships/grants, private scholarships, the school's own gift aid. *Loan aid offered:* FFEL Subsidized Stafford, FFEL Unsubsidized Stafford, FFEL PLUS, Federal Perkins Loan, college/university loans from institutional funds. Applicants will be notified of awards on or about April 1. Federal Work-Study Program available. Institutional employment available. Off-campus job opportunities are excellent.

FROM THE ADMISSIONS OFFICE

"Through a broad-based arts and sciences curriculum and a groundbreaking approach to study abroad, Goucher College gives students a sweeping view of the world. Goucher is an independent, coeducational institution dedicated to both the interdisciplinary traditions of the liberal arts and a truly international perspective on education.

"The first college in the nation to pair required study abroad with a special travel stipend of $1,200 for every undergraduate, Goucher believes in complementing its strong majors and rigorous curriculum with abundant opportunities for hands-on experience. In addition to participating in the college's many study abroad programs (including innovative 3-week intensive courses abroad alongside traditional semester and academic year offerings), many students also complete internships and service-learning projects that further enhance their learning.

"The college's 1,350 undergraduate students live and learn on a tree-lined campus of 287 acres just north of Baltimore, Maryland. Goucher boasts a student/faculty ratio of just 10:1, and professors routinely collaborate with students on major research projects—often for publication, and sometimes as early as students' first or second years. The curriculum emphasizes international and intercultural awareness throughout, and students are encouraged to explore their academic interests from a variety of perspectives beyond their major disciplines.

"A Goucher College education encompasses a multitude of experiences that ultimately converge into one cohesive academic program that can truly change lives. Students grow in dramatic and surprising ways here. They graduate with a strong sense of direction and self-confidence, ready to engage the world—and succeed—as true global citizens.

"Freshman applicants to Goucher College are required to submit scores from either the new SAT or ACT (with the Writing component)."

SELECTIVITY

Admissions Rating	87
# of applicants	3,171
% of applicants accepted	70
% of acceptees attending	20
# accepting a place on wait list	75
% admitted from wait list	12

FRESHMAN PROFILE

Range SAT Critical Reading	560–670
Range SAT Math	530–630
Range ACT Composite	23–27
Minimum Paper TOEFL	550
Minimum Computer Based TOEFL	230
Average HS GPA	3.18
% graduated top 10% of class	28
% graduated top 25% of class	60
% graduated top 50% of class	93

DEADLINES

Regular application deadline	2/1
Regular notification	4/1
Nonfall registration?	yes

APPLICANTS ALSO LOOK AT
AND OFTEN PREFER
Boston University, Mount Holyoke College, Skidmore College
AND SOMETIMES PREFER
American University, Franklin & Marshall College, Loyola College in Maryland, The George Washington University

FINANCIAL FACTS

Financial Aid Rating	77
Annual tuition	$31,082
Room & Board	$9,478
Books and supplies	$800
Required fees	$425
% frosh rec. need-based scholarship or grant aid	47
% UG rec. need-based scholarship or grant aid	52
% frosh rec. need-based self-help aid	41
% UG rec. need-based self-help aid	47
% frosh rec. any financial aid	81
% UG rec. any financial aid	86

GRINNELL COLLEGE

OFFICE OF ADMISSION, 1103 PARK STREET, 2ND FLOOR, GRINNELL, IA 50112-1690 • ADMISSIONS: 641-269-3600 • FAX: 641-269-4800

CAMPUS LIFE

Quality of Life Rating	**80**
Fire Safety Rating	**60***
Type of school	private
Environment	village

STUDENTS

Total undergrad enrollment	1,555
% male/female	46/54
% from out of state	87
% from public high school	30
% live on campus	88
% African American	5
% Asian	6
% Caucasian	67
% Hispanic	5
% Native American	1
% international	10
# of countries represented	46

SURVEY SAYS . . .
Small classes
No one cheats
Frats and sororities are unpopular or
nonexistent
Lots of beer drinking

ACADEMICS

Academic Rating	**99**
Calendar	semester
Student/faculty ratio	8:1
Profs interesting rating	91
Profs accessible rating	94
% profs teaching UG courses	100
% classes taught by TAs	0
Most common lab size	10–19 students
Most common reg class size	10–19 students

MOST POPULAR MAJORS
biological and physical sciences
economics
history

STUDENTS SAY

Academics

"Hard work, critical thinking, and social consciousness" define the Grinnell experience. Students at this "haven of a big-city liberal arts college set in the cornfields" know that "professors expect a lot from us. I had one professor tell our class that professors at Grinnell assign their students graduate-level amounts of work and expect graduate-level results. Professors keep expecting that because Grinnell students deliver it." As a result, "Academics here are hard. We live in a culture of stress and constant studying, but we revel in it. You can't go a single day here without having your mind stimulated, your ideas questioned, and your brain flooded with knowledge." Grinnell imposes "no requirements other than freshman tutorial" on its students, granting undergrads incredible "power in the direction of their education." Thanks to a "huge endowment," students have tremendous latitude in plotting their studies. One undergrad observes, "Money never really seems to be an issue here. If you can dream it, Grinnell can pay for it." The school is "full of resources! Students needing to do research in museums, archives, and libraries for thesis-level research projects can easily get funding from the college. Also, the arts and science facilities are top of the line." For students who may stagger under the weight of academic demands, "Grinnell offers a great deal of academic assistance for those in need. There is a writing lab, a math lab, a reading lab; [and] Grinnell also offers tutors free of charge."

Life

The academic rigors at Grinnell are substantial. You "won't have to worry about surviving the Midwest winter" here, because "Being buried in books and papers and paper revisions and articles and essays and book reviews and to-do lists keeps you surprisingly warm." Even so, students still find time for jam-packed extracurricular schedules; undergrads here "are very well rounded. Forty percent are varsity athletes, and almost all participate in some extracurricular activity." The school "brings in a lot of activities and cultural events," such as "concerts by Grammy Award–winning a cappella groups, ambassadors delivering lectures, movies, concerts, [and] even therapy dogs during mid-semester exams." Best of all, "All events on campus are free." When it comes time to kick back and relax, "The school's fairly loose policy of 'self-governance' means that drinking isn't a huge hassle and can be casual and fun, not covert and antagonistic with the security guards and college administration." Hometown Grinnell is "isolated," but not without its charms. One student explains, "I love the town of Grinnell and think Midwest-nice is a great asset, but that's my personal taste. I like recognizing the lady who walks her dog by our house every day and the kid who bags our groceries. And I love going to the farmer's market and things like the 4-H tractor show that took place this summer."

Student Body

Grinnell undergrads describe themselves and their classmates as "liberal students interested in social justice and having a good time." Intellect seems to stand out most; as one student explains, "Most Grinnellians are the kids who were labeled as being a little weird in high school, but then they can come here and find other people just like them." Another adds, "Although the average Grinnell student may be a bit geeky, there is a wide variety of passions that drive each student. When you sit in a class with a diverse group of students who are all passionate about different things, it leads to some of the most interesting and intense discussions possible. Because I am surrounded by a group of highly intelligent, motivated, and inquisitive peers, I am constantly challenged to examine topics from different perspectives. This constant thinking outside of the box is a primary aspect of a true liberal arts education."

FINANCIAL AID: 641-269-3250 • E-MAIL: ASKGRIN@GRINNELL.EDU • WEBSITE: WWW.GRINNELL.EDU

ADMISSIONS

Very important factors considered include: Academic GPA, class rank, extracurricular activities, recommendation(s), rigor of secondary school record, standardized test scores, talent/ability. *Important factors considered include:* Application essay, interview, racial/ethnic status. *Other factors considered include:* Alumni/ae relation, character/personal qualities, first generation, geographical residence, state residency, volunteer work, work experience. SAT or ACT required; TOEFL required of all international applicants. High school diploma is required, and GED is accepted. *Academic units recommended:* 4 English, 4 math, 4 science (3 science labs), 4 foreign language, 4 social studies.

The Inside Word

Grinnell provides a first-rate academic experience and garners a talented applicant pool. You'll need a rigorous course load and top standardized test scores to be a contender. Matchmaking is also an important element of the admissions process; an interview is highly recommended. Admissions Officers will be glad for the opportunity to relay information about Grinnell, and you're likely to leave with a positive impression.

FINANCIAL AID

Students should submit: FAFSA, institution's own financial aid form, Noncustodial PROFILE. Regular filing deadline is February 1. The Princeton Review suggests that all financial aid forms be submitted as soon as possible after January 1. *Need-based scholarships/grants offered:* Pell Grant, SEOG, state scholarships/grants, private scholarships, the school's own gift aid. *Loan aid offered:* FFEL Subsidized Stafford, FFEL Unsubsidized Stafford, FFEL PLUS, Federal Perkins Loan, college/university loans from institutional funds. Applicants will be notified of awards on or about April 1.

FROM THE ADMISSIONS OFFICE

"Grinnell College is a place where independence of thought and social conscience are instilled. It is a wide-open space of resources, professors, and students in search of truth, understanding, and shared endeavors. Grinnell is a college with the resources of a school 10 times its size, a faculty that reads like a Who's Who of Teaching, and a learning environment where debate does not end in the classroom and often begins in the Campus Center.

"Grinnellians are committed to learning, respect for themselves and others, contributing to global social good, willing collaboration, and the courage to try. Grinnell College is a place of endless possibilities, a place where there are no limits.

"We require that applicants submit either the new SAT (taken prior to January of their senior year) or ACT scores. If students take both the new SAT and ACT, we will consider the higher of the two scores. Unlike our SAT policy, we do not create a best composite score from multiple sittings of the ACT."

SELECTIVITY

Admissions Rating	95
# of applicants	3,104
% of applicants accepted	45
% of acceptees attending	29
# accepting a place on wait list	349
% admitted from wait list	7
# of early decision applicants	161
% accepted early decision	80

FRESHMAN PROFILE

Range SAT Critical Reading	630–740
Range SAT Math	620–720
Range ACT Composite	29–32
Minimum Paper TOEFL	550
Minimum Computer Based TOEFL	220
% graduated top 10% of class	64
% graduated top 25% of class	90
% graduated top 50% of class	100

DEADLINES

Early decision application deadline	11/20
Early decision notification	12/20
Regular application deadline	1/20
Regular notification	4/1
Nonfall registration?	no

APPLICANTS ALSO LOOK AT AND SOMETIMES PREFER
Carleton College
AND RARELY PREFER
Kenyon College, Macalester College

FINANCIAL FACTS

Financial Aid Rating	98
Annual tuition	$28,566
Room & Board	$7,700
Books and supplies	$600
Required fees	$464
% frosh rec. need-based scholarship or grant aid	57
% UG rec. need-based scholarship or grant aid	55
% frosh rec. need-based self-help aid	45
% UG rec. need-based self-help aid	44
% frosh rec. any financial aid	85
% UG rec. any financial aid	88

GROVE CITY COLLEGE

100 Campus Drive, Grove City, PA 16127-2104 • Admissions: 724-458-2100 • Fax: 724-458-3395

CAMPUS LIFE
Quality of Life Rating	**78**
Fire Safety Rating	**80**
Type of school	private
Affiliation	Presbyterian
Environment	rural

STUDENTS
Total undergrad enrollment	2,473
% male/female	51/49
% from out of state	52
% from public high school	80
% live on campus	93
% in (# of) fraternities	18 (8)
% in (# of) sororities	20 (8)
% Asian	2
% Caucasian	94
% Hispanic	1
% international	1
# of countries represented	8

SURVEY SAYS . . .
Career services are great
Small classes
No one cheats
Students are very religious
Low cost of living
Intramural sports are popular
Very little drug use

ACADEMICS
Academic Rating	**85**
Calendar	semester
Student/faculty ratio	17:1
Profs interesting rating	78
Profs accessible rating	87
% profs teaching UG courses	100
% classes taught by TAs	0
Most common lab size	10–19 students
Most common reg class size	20–29 students

MOST POPULAR MAJORS
business administration/
management
elementary education and teaching
English language and literature

STUDENTS SAY
Academics
A small, private liberal arts school dedicated to "cohesive Christian education through academic rigor and integrity," Grove City College provides its students with "a challenging education in a thoroughly Christian environment." In fact, the word *challenge* is frequently used by respondents; says one, "Students here work their butts off." With a course load that many students describe as "insane," "There is a lot of work to be done and not much time to do it. Most of the work, however, is very beneficial." Students credit the school's "high academic standards" as one of the main reasons GCC enjoys "a fantastic job placement rate and reputation in the professional world." And although the professors assign plenty of homework, they are also "friendly and accessible. Professors give you their home phone numbers so that you can call them if you don't understand something after office hours." What's more, they "are interested mainly in teaching students, not publishing books or conducting research." Finally, undergrads appreciate the fact that professors "are also excellent Christian role models" who give their students a "sound moral foundation." All this is available at bargain-basement prices; the tuition at GCC is "incredibly reasonable," at less than half that of many other private colleges.

Life
At GCC, "people are very focused on God. Many are involved in campus ministry groups, and almost everyone attends church on Sundays." As one might suspect at such a place, the kind of fun most students go in for here is of the "good, clean" variety. Since "off-campus life is virtually nonexistent," students looking for fun "go to on-campus events, like coffeehouses, dances, plays, and movies," or play intramural sports. However, funding for these activities and clubs can be limited, students complain, because the school's low tuition necessitates a tight activities budget. The dorms at GCC are single sex, but "Intervis (Dorm Intervisitation) is pretty popular." Intervisitation rules are pretty strict; in the words of one student, "Members of the opposite sex can only come to our rooms to hang out during allotted hours on weekends, provided the door is propped open and the lights are on." Alcohol is forbidden on campus, and for those students who want to party off campus, "You have to be careful. Grove City is technically a dry town, and there are not many places that sell alcohol." Students caught drinking on campus, "whether they're 18 or 35," face strict penalties; the school administration "doesn't take that stuff lightly." Undergrads advise prospective students that at GCC, "There is pressure to find a mate by your senior year, so the opposite sex is often on one's mind." As one student puts it, the school's mission is "to provide a thorough education in a Christian environment (and hopefully get you married in the process)."

Student Body
Students at GCC are the first to point out that "Our school is pretty homogenous." The typical student is "an intelligent, studious, straight-edge Protestant" who "got straight A's in high school and has been pretty much a model person for most of his or her life." Ethnically and economically, undergrads are mainly "White and from middle- to upper-class families." One undergrad notes, "There are not too many atypical students, and everyone knows who those students are." Such atypical "Grovers" include "liberal students" who "face much opposition to their political views, but don't suffer discrimination," and the "very few minorities" on campus. While some students wish that the school would "reach out to minorities and people of different backgrounds more," others feel that the fact that GCC does "not try to be like other colleges is what makes it so unique."

FINANCIAL AID: 724-458-2163 • E-MAIL: ADMISSIONS@GCC.EDU • WEBSITE: WWW.GCC.EDU

ADMISSIONS

Very important factors considered include: Application essay, character/personal qualities, extracurricular activities, interview, religious affiliation/commitment, rigor of secondary school record, standardized test scores. *Important factors considered include:* Recommendation(s), talent/ability. *Other factors considered include:* Alumni/ae relation, class rank, geographical residence, racial/ethnic status, state residency, volunteer work, work experience. SAT or ACT required; ACT with Writing component recommended. TOEFL required of all international applicants. High school diploma is required, and GED is accepted. *Academic units recommended:* 4 English, 3 math, 3 science (2 science labs), 3 foreign language, 2 social studies, 2 history.

The Inside Word

Admission to Grove City has become very competitive, and any serious contender will need to hit the books. While a rigorous class schedule is a given, Admissions Officers also closely assess character and personal qualities. GCC is steeped in Christian values, and the school seeks students who will be comfortable in such an environment. As such, interviews and recommendations hold significant weight.

FINANCIAL AID

Students should submit: Institution's own financial aid form. Regular filing deadline is April 15. The Princeton Review suggests that all financial aid forms be submitted as soon as possible after January 1. *Need-based scholarships/grants offered:* State scholarships/grants, private scholarships, the school's own gift aid. *Loan aid offered:* Private alternative loans. Applicants will be notified of awards on a rolling basis beginning or about March 20. Institutional employment available. Off-campus job opportunities are good.

FROM THE ADMISSIONS OFFICE

"A good college education doesn't have to cost a fortune. For decades, Grove City College has offered a quality education at costs among the lowest nationally. Since the 1990s, increased national academic acclaim has come to Grove City College. Grove City College is a place where professors teach. You will not see graduate assistants or teacher's aides in the classroom. Our professors are also active in the total life of the campus. More than 100 student organizations on campus afford opportunity for a wide variety of cocurricular activities. Outstanding scholars and leaders in education, science, and international affairs visit the campus each year. The environment at GCC is friendly, secure, and dedicated to high standards. Character-building is emphasized and traditional Christian values are supported.

"Applicants are asked to submit scores from the new SAT. Pending the results of further study into the virtues of the new Writing assessment section, GCC will use the combined Critical Reading and Math scores for admissions decisions. Students may also submit scores from the old SAT for consideration."

SELECTIVITY

Admissions Rating	**94**
# of applicants	1,918
% of applicants accepted	57
% of acceptees attending	62
# accepting a place on wait list	170
% admitted from wait list	16
# of early decision applicants	640
% accepted early decision	51

FRESHMAN PROFILE

Range SAT Critical Reading	576–691
Range SAT Math	589–697
Range ACT Composite	26–30
Minimum Paper TOEFL	550
Minimum Computer Based TOEFL	213
Average HS GPA	3.75
% graduated top 10% of class	59
% graduated top 25% of class	86
% graduated top 50% of class	97

DEADLINES

Early decision application deadline	11/15
Early decision notification	12/15
Regular application deadline	2/1
Regular notification	3/15
Nonfall registration?	yes

APPLICANTS ALSO LOOK AT AND OFTEN PREFER

Hillsdale College, Pennsylvania State University—University Park, Wheaton College (IL)

AND RARELY PREFER

Slippery Rock University of Pennsylvania, Thiel College

FINANCIAL FACTS

Financial Aid Rating	**63**
Annual tuition	$11,500
Room & Board	$6,134
Books and supplies	$900
% frosh rec. need-based scholarship or grant aid	42
% UG rec. need-based scholarship or grant aid	33
% frosh rec. need-based self-help aid	22
% UG rec. need-based self-help aid	22
% frosh rec. any financial aid	42
% UG rec. any financial aid	35

GUILFORD COLLEGE

5800 West Friendly Avenue, Greensboro, NC 27410 • Admissions: 336-316-2100 • Fax: 336-316-2954

STUDENTS SAY

Academics

Guilford College, "promotes academic excellence, social and cultural awareness, critical analysis, and community involvement" while "incorporating Quaker ideals and traditions." Undergrads here warn that this small liberal arts school requires "a lot of work," and that the program "is very reading and writing intensive." As one student explains, "I've had to write papers for every class except chemistry, and in one class I've written around 10 papers." Support for students is strong, both from "incredible" professors who "are where they say they are going to be when they say they are going to be there, which makes it incredibly easy to get help." Guilford also offers "many resources" to help students handle the workload, such as "the Academic Skills Center." The school promotes autonomy, providing undergrads "the ability to design their own programs," without sacrificing "personal and positive relationships with most teachers and many members of the administration. They are always open to hear from students on any issue." Especially strong areas of study at Guilford include the Criminal Justice Program (it "rocks"), as well as "great programs for theater and adult studies."

Life

As at most small, rigorous, liberal arts schools, "Classes take up a good deal of time" at Guilford, and students keep themselves busy during their few off hours with "extracurricular activities, hanging out with friends, and going off campus." One student writes, "Considering the relatively small size of the campus, there is a constant list of social, political, and spiritual activities going on for seemingly every preference or belief one might have." Another student concurs: "Whether for class or socially, the campus is always active." The "great Quaker heritage here makes for an open and personal environment" in which "people leave their doors open all the time." Students are "very social . . . I've never heard of someone just sitting alone in their room if that wasn't what they wanted." Guilford's Quaker heritage also attracts a lot of politically active students, who share an "environmental concern." There are also "lots of sports and club activities," although intercollegiate athletics "are not held in as high regard" as they are at other area schools (which, to be fair, include UNC and Duke). Hometown Greensboro is a small city but big enough to support a decent club scene. Students say Guilford "is unique because it is within a fairly cosmopolitan area yet has many natural alcoves and secrets to explore. The lake, the woods, and the meadows on campus are beautiful and fun treasures for students to enjoy. Guilford is also beautifully landscaped and decorated with student-created art, but it isn't pretentious."

Student Body

Guilford is "definitely a counterculture school" where "The majority of students are atypical." The population includes "a lot of hippies and wanna-be hippies, and students who do anything except conform to the norm," although some here notice a trend toward greater diversity on campus. Recently the school has increased diversity in "ethnic backgrounds and spiritual, political, and sociocultural beliefs," and has also added to its continuing education population, meaning students here "range from 17 to 60-plus years old." As one student observes, "Because Guilford College promotes a global view of the world, the diverse student body is simply an extension of this academic principle and is nurtured as such." Some students feel the school's diversity is over-hyped, opining that "There are three types of students at Guilford: athletes, nonathletes, and hippies." These same critics note that "almost everyone who bridges these gaps bonds over a case or keg."

FINANCIAL AID: 336-316-2354 • E-MAIL: ADMISSION@GUILFORD.EDU • WEBSITE: WWW.GUILFORD.EDU

ADMISSIONS

Very important factors considered include: Rigor of secondary school record. *Important factors considered include:* Academic GPA, application essay, character/personal qualities, extracurricular activities, level of applicant's interest, standardized test scores, talent/ability. *Other factors considered include:* Alumni/ae relation, class rank, first generation, geographical residence, interview, racial/ethnic status, recommendation(s), religious affiliation/commitment, state residency, volunteer work, work experience. SAT or ACT recommended; TOEFL required of all international applicants. High school diploma is required, and GED is accepted. *Academic units recommended:* 4 English, 3 math, 3 science, 2 foreign language.

The Inside Word

Guilford has traditionally drawn its students primarily from the Mid-Atlantic and Southern states; the school has recently begun to recruit more aggressively outside these areas, and now employs a full-time regional recruiter based in Boston. Additional recruiting should yield additional applications, increasing competition for classroom seats. The upside in terms of admissions is that this effort to build a more national student body creates opportunities for students from outside the school's traditional target zones. If you're willing to travel a long way to attend Guilford, you may find yourself handsomely rewarded.

FINANCIAL AID

Students should submit: FAFSA. Regular filing deadline is March 1. The Princeton Review suggests that all financial aid forms be submitted as soon as possible after January 1. *Need-based scholarships/grants offered:* Pell Grant, SEOG, state scholarships/grants, private scholarships, the school's own gift aid. *Loan aid offered:* FFEL Subsidized Stafford, FFEL Unsubsidized Stafford, FFEL PLUS, Federal Perkins Loan, college/university loans from institutional funds. Applicants will be notified of awards on a rolling basis beginning or about February 1. Federal Work-Study Program available. Institutional employment available. Off-campus job opportunities are good.

FROM THE ADMISSIONS OFFICE

"We want you to know the following about Guilford:

- Guilford College has a challenging academic program that fosters critical and creative thinking through the development of essential skills: analysis, inquiry, communication, consensus-building, principled problem-solving, and leadership.
- Guilford College offers a values-rich affordable education that explores the ethical dimension of knowledge and promotes honesty, compassion, integrity, courage, and respect for the individual.
- Guilford College offers student-centered instruction that nurtures each individual amid an intentionally diverse community.
- Guilford College offers access to volunteer and service opportunities that forge a connection between action and thought.
- For more information on Guilford, create your individualized online brochure at: www.vip-page.net/guilford.

Guilford College is a selective college founded in 1837 by the Religious Society of Friends (Quakers). As one of the oldest coeducational institutions in the nation, we take our commitment to academics and the liberal arts seriously. To that end, we use a holistic method of application evaluation. Students are encouraged to challenge themselves within their high school environment, both in and out of the classroom. While the majority of our applicants submit some form of standardized test scores (ACT or SAT), students have the option of submitting a portfolio of written work in lieu of standardized test scores. We do not require SAT Subject Tests for admission or placement. Our campus community is full of active and involved citizens, and our evaluation process seeks to continue to admit students that bring a variety of backgrounds and interests to the college."

SELECTIVITY

Admissions Rating	**82**
# of applicants	2,603
% of applicants accepted	73
% of acceptees attending	22
# accepting a place on wait list	80
% admitted from wait list	81

FRESHMAN PROFILE

Range SAT Critical Reading	520–630
Range SAT Math	500–610
Range ACT Composite	20–26
Minimum Paper TOEFL	550
Minimum Computer Based TOEFL	213
Average HS GPA	3.14
% graduated top 10% of class	20
% graduated top 25% of class	51
% graduated top 50% of class	83

DEADLINES

Regular application deadline	2/15
Regular notification	rolling
Nonfall registration?	yes

APPLICANTS ALSO LOOK AT

AND OFTEN PREFER
Oberlin College

AND SOMETIMES PREFER
Earlham College, Elon University, Goucher College, The University of North Carolina at Chapel Hill

FINANCIAL FACTS

Financial Aid Rating	**90**
Annual tuition	$22,690
Books and supplies	$800
Required fees	$330
% frosh rec. need-based scholarship or grant aid	70
% UG rec. need-based scholarship or grant aid	60
% frosh rec. need-based self-help aid	61
% UG rec. need-based self-help aid	60
% frosh rec. any financial aid	88
% UG rec. any financial aid	92

GUSTAVUS ADOLPHUS COLLEGE

800 WEST COLLEGE AVENUE, SAINT PETER, MN 56082 • ADMISSIONS: 507-933-7676 • FAX: 507-933-7474

STUDENTS SAY

Academics

Named for a Swedish king and home to the yearly Nobel Conference, Gustavus Adolphus College gets high marks from students for its "demanding, yet encouraging" professors who are "there to help you learn, not just to give you a grade." As one student explains, "The professors are amazing, they will let you call them at home and work with your schedule for everything, whether you need extra help in a class or just want to talk." Although professors have "high expectations," the "extra guidance" that is offered helps students achieve "far beyond graduation." Expect to be challenged by "classes [that] are rigorous and discussion based." Small class sizes allow for "great interaction with professors" but will leave your "empty chair sticking out like a neon sign" if you are absent. According to one student, the administration is "nothing less than competent, articulate, and perceptive" and "is generally very easy to access." Students feel that they are "the number-one priority in everything" and enjoy a "great sense of community" on campus.

Life

In the words of one student, "Life at Gustavus is fun . . . maybe a little too fun." Although "School comes first," on the weekends students "attend a lot of sporting events, parties, and social events on campus and off." "Shows, concerts, and basketball games" are "especially popular," as are the "free movies on Fridays and Saturdays" and the "on-campus student dance club 'The Dive.'" Most students choose to unwind with "a good amount of partying and drinking." As one student explains, "Gusties drink a lot, and the administration doesn't like that reputation, so they are really cracking down on fun." While alcohol and parties are easy to find on campus, abstaining students "never feel any pressure to do either." Being located in a small town is no problem for students who claim that "there are always things going on at school." Students who get cabin fever can head to nearby Mankato with its "excellent mall and restaurants" for entertainment. Finding company for these activities is never a problem since Gustavus "is a small school" and "You get to know people easily." Although the Minnesotan winter may be long, things heat up in January during "J-term" when a light course load gives students a "chance to take a class outside their major" or just "hang out with friends." When students really want a thrill, they'll "borrow a tray from the cafeteria and sled down the many hills behind the dorms" in a Gustavus tradition called "traying."

Student Body

Students at Gustavus describe themselves as "White, suburban, middle-class" and "often of Swedish Lutheran descent." Although the students who "do not fit into this description" may find themselves sticking out "like sore thumbs" in a "land of Abercrombie," any discrimination "is met with the highest degree of denunciation from the administration/faculty/staff and much of the student body." In the words of one student, "Gustavus is a fairly liberal college" that "prides itself on focusing on nonracial diversity." While "most of the students are White, the mix of personalities and lifestyles is amazing," and the university is working to "recruit students of more diverse backgrounds." Despite any surface differences, "The typical student at Gustavus is very studious and cares very much about getting the most out of their education."

FINANCIAL AID: 507-933-7527 • E-MAIL: ADMISSION@GUSTAVUS.EDU • WEBSITE: WWW.GUSTAVUS.EDU

ADMISSIONS

Very important factors considered include: Application essay, rigor of secondary school record. *Important factors considered include:* Character/personal qualities, class rank, extracurricular activities, interview, recommendation(s), religious affiliation/commitment, talent/ability. *Other factors considered include:* Alumni/ae relation, geographical residence, racial/ethnic status, volunteer work, work experience. TOEFL required of all international applicants. High school diploma is required, and GED is accepted. *Academic units recommended:* 4 English, 4 math, 3 science (3 science labs).

The Inside Word

Gustavus Adolphus considers a variety of factors when making admissions decisions. Students should display motivation for tackling challenging courses and a desire to be active participants in their community. The majority of applicants are from local areas—those who can provide some geographic diversity are welcome. The school has a rolling admissions policy, so interested students should think about sending in their applications early. All available slots are usually filled by early spring.

FINANCIAL AID

Students should submit: FAFSA, institution's own financial aid form. Students who want to receive an award by March 1 must file the CSS/Financial Aid PROFILE. Regular filing deadline is April 15. The Princeton Review suggests that all financial aid forms be submitted as soon as possible after January 1. *Need-based scholarships/grants offered:* Pell Grant, SEOG, state scholarships/grants, private scholarships, the school's own gift aid. *Loan aid offered:* Direct Subsidized Stafford, Direct Unsubsidized Stafford, Direct PLUS, Federal Perkins Loan, state loans, college/university loans from institutional funds, alternative loans from private lenders. Applicants will be notified of awards on a rolling basis beginning or about March 1.

FROM THE ADMISSIONS OFFICE

"To better serve students and their families, there is no application fee.
"Applications completed by November 1 will be notified of an admission decision by November 20. Applications completed after November 1 will be reviewed on a competitive rolling basis beginning December 20.
"Early financial aid awards will be available to admitted students who submit the CSS/Financial Aid PROFILE prior to February 15. Students who submit the FAFSA will continue to receive a financial aid award in a timely fashion.
"The college is committed to excellence, community, justice, service, and faith. These values are pervasive in the college community and can be seen throughout campus activities and events like the 'Our Story' workshop on African American culture, Nobel Conference, Building Bridges Diversity Conference, MAYDAY! Peace Conference, and NYSP summer sports camp. Campus facilities support student life and development. Recent projects include a 200-bed apartment and suite configuration residence hall (also houses an additional 200-bed youth hostel), cardiovascular exercise area, Nobel Hall of Science equipment additions of a DNA sequencer, mass spectrometer microscope, cell growth culture labs, Old Main classroom renovation, International Center for residential living and international education, and, the Jackson Campus Center, which houses student services such as Diversity Center, Market Place cafeteria and Courtyard Café, Ticket Center, student activities offices and work space, Hillstrom Museum, bookstore, and much more.
"Gustavus Adolphus College requires freshman applicants to submit scores from the old or new SAT. Students may also choose to submit scores from the ACT (with or without the Writing component) in lieu of the SAT."

SELECTIVITY

Admissions Rating	87
# of applicants	2,663
% of applicants accepted	78
% of acceptees attending	33

FRESHMAN PROFILE

Range SAT Critical Reading	520–670
Range SAT Math	540–670
Range ACT Composite	23–28
Minimum Paper TOEFL	550
Minimum Computer Based TOEFL	213
Average HS GPA	3.66
% graduated top 10% of class	35
% graduated top 25% of class	70
% graduated top 50% of class	94

DEADLINES

Regular notification	rolling
Nonfall registration?	yes

APPLICANTS ALSO LOOK AT

AND OFTEN PREFER
Carleton College, University of Wisconsin—Madison

AND SOMETIMES PREFER
St. Olaf College, University of Minnesota—Twin Cities

FINANCIAL FACTS

Financial Aid Rating	84
Annual tuition	$28,125
Room & Board	$6,775
Required fees	$410
% frosh rec. need-based scholarship or grant aid	67
% UG rec. need-based scholarship or grant aid	62
% frosh rec. need-based self-help aid	58
% UG rec. need-based self-help aid	53
% frosh rec. any financial aid	98
% UG rec. any financial aid	92

HAMILTON COLLEGE

198 COLLEGE HILL ROAD, CLINTON, NY 13323 • ADMISSIONS: 315-859-4421 • FAX: 315-859-4457

CAMPUS LIFE
Quality of Life Rating	**80**
Fire Safety Rating	**92**
Type of school	private
Environment	town

STUDENTS
Total undergrad enrollment	1,801
% male/female	50/50
% from out of state	65
% from public high school	60
% live on campus	98
% in (# of) fraternities	29 (7)
% in (# of) sororities	19 (3)
% African American	4
% Asian	7
% Caucasian	71
% Hispanic	4
% Native American	1
% international	5
# of countries represented	40

SURVEY SAYS . . .
Small classes
Lab facilities are great
Great computer facilities
Great library
Lots of beer drinking

ACADEMICS
Academic Rating	**98**
Calendar	semester
Student/faculty ratio	10:1
Profs interesting rating	95
Profs accessible rating	95
% profs teaching UG courses	100
% classes taught by TAs	0
Most common lab size	10–19 students
Most common reg class size	10–19 students

MOST POPULAR MAJORS
economics
government
mathematics
psychology

STUDENTS SAY

Academics

"Cold winters, close friends, and great professors who care" are what make Hamilton "the true liberal arts experience." Indeed, "Its small student population, intelligent and accessible professors, and campus size make Hamilton the ideal small liberal arts college." Students praise the dedication and intellectual caliber of professors, who are more "interested in their students' success" than in "the next research grant." Small class sizes bring personal attention and increased responsibility for one's own learning; one student notes, "It is rarely the case for a professor to lecture for the entire class without engaging the students in the discussion. This way, students interact not only with the professor but [also] with each other, listening to each other and building off other students' ideas." Even "In 'big' lectures (50 students is huge for Hamilton), discussion is strongly encouraged." "Extremely knowledgeable" professors demand a lot of their students, and Hamilton's culture of "grade deflation" means that there are no easy A's at this school; one student observes, "Sometimes you're fighting for a B. The classes are that difficult." "I feel very challenged," says another, adding, "but I am learning so much!" Students who feel too challenged, however, can easily get help; the school offers "free tutoring at the Writing Center and the Quantitative Literacy Center," and the "Career Center is always asking you to come visit, even as a freshman." Those looking for international experience also appreciate the fact that the "school makes it so easy to go abroad."

Life

"Work hard, play hard" is the motto among Hamilton students. "Every weekend, without fail, there is at least one party (often three or four) held in one of the social spaces provided by the campus, generally funded by one of Hamilton's many Greek organizations." Off-campus parties are also popular. To wet your whistle closer to home, the college has its own pub, where professors and students (those over 21, that is) are often seen sharing a pint together. While some students complain that drinking draws too great a focus, there are plenty of options for the straight-edge crowd, including substance-free dorms. Those looking for nonalcoholic fun gather at "Cafe Opus, our own little coffee place, and sit and talk for a while." For the "intellectual population," "all kinds of student-run discussion groups" address "topics ranging from politics to religion to psychology," and "We get great name speakers, ranging from B. B. King to Clinton or Nader." Intrepid Hamiltonians brave upstate New York weather to make the most of their bucolic surroundings: "The glen behind campus is great for running, skiing, or other escapades, and cheering on the perpetually bad football team and the much better soccer and hockey teams is a must." Hometown Clinton's "outdoorsy environment, including extensive acres of hiking/cross-country skiing trails and a ropes course make the college often seem more like camp than school when there is no snow." In the words of one student, "It's small, it's isolated, but Hamilton rock 'n' rolls like nowhere else on earth!"

Student Body

"There is a general impression that many students come from places like Fairfield County [Connecticut]," claims one student, but "While there is certainly a healthy representation, their pink polo shirts and yellow shorts probably just make them more conspicuous. We have students from most states, many countries, and just about every ethnic background. There are all kinds of people here, and they generally associate with everyone else." Another states, "Everyone here is different. That's what makes Hamilton so wonderful." Politically, "The student body seems more moderate than most selective Eastern schools and certainly more tolerant of conservatives than most. Still, many seem nostalgic for Clinton." Whatever their political or social differences, Hamilton students unequivocally characterize themselves as friendly and accepting: "Incredible warmth emanates from all people, regardless of age or status, and despite the snow."

FINANCIAL AID: 800-859-4413 • E-MAIL: ADMISSION@HAMILTON.EDU • WEBSITE: WWW.HAMILTON.EDU

ADMISSIONS

Very important factors considered include: Academic GPA, class rank, rigor of secondary school record. *Important factors considered include:* Application essay, character/personal qualities, extracurricular activities, interview, recommendation(s), standardized test scores. *Other factors considered include:* Alumni/ae relation, first generation, geographical residence, level of applicant's interest, racial/ethnic status, talent/ability, volunteer work, work experience. TOEFL required of all international applicants. High school diploma or equivalent is not required. *Academic units recommended:* 4 English, 3 math, 3 science, 3 foreign language, 3 social studies.

The Inside Word

Similar to many prestigious liberal arts schools, Hamilton takes a well-rounded, personal approach to admissions. Academic achievement and intellectual promise are of first importance, but Admissions Officers also put great weight on leadership and diversity. The college strives to attain a complete, accurate profile of each applicant and relies heavily upon interviews either on or off campus with alumni volunteers. Students who decline to interview put themselves at a competitive disadvantage.

FINANCIAL AID

Students should submit: FAFSA, institution's own financial aid form, CSS/Financial Aid PROFILE, Noncustodial PROFILE, Business/Farm Supplement. Regular filing deadline is February 1. *Need-based scholarships/grants offered:* Pell Grant, SEOG, state scholarships/grants, private scholarships, the school's own gift aid. *Loan aid offered:* FFEL Subsidized Stafford, FFEL Unsubsidized Stafford, FFEL PLUS, Federal Perkins Loan. Applicants will be notified of awards on or about April 1. Federal Work-Study Program available. Institutional employment available.

FROM THE ADMISSIONS OFFICE

"As a national leader for teaching students to write effectively, learn from one another, and think for themselves, Hamilton produces graduates who have the knowledge, skills, and confidence to make their own voices heard on issues of importance to them and their communities.

"A key component of the Hamilton experience is the college's open, yet rigorous, liberal arts curriculum. In place of distribution requirements that are common at most colleges, Hamilton gives its students freedom to choose the courses that reflect their unique interests and plans. Faculty advisors assist students in planning a coherent and highly individualized academic program. In fact, close student-faculty relationships at Hamilton are a distinguishing characteristic of the college, but ultimately students at Hamilton take responsibility for their own future. Part of that future includes a lifelong relationship with the college. Hamilton alumni are exceptionally loyal and passionate supporters of their alma mater. That support manifests itself through internships, speaking engagements, job-shadowing opportunities, and financial donations.

"The intellectual maturity that distinguishes a Hamilton education extends to the application process. Students are free to choose which standardized tests to submit, based on a specific set of options, so that those who do not test well on the SAT or ACT may decided to submit the results of their AP or SAT Subject Tests. This approach allows students the freedom to decide how to present themselves best to the Committee on Admission."

"The intellectual maturity that distinguishes a Hamilton education extends to the application process. Students are free to choose which standardized tests to submit, based on a specified set of options, so that those who do not test well on the SAT or ACT may decide to submit the results of their AP or SAT Subject Tests. The approach allows students the freedom to decide how to present themselves best to the Committee on Admission."

SELECTIVITY

Admissions Rating	96
# of applicants	4,266
% of applicants accepted	33
% of acceptees attending	35
# accepting a place on wait list	183
# of early decision applicants	515
% accepted early decision	48

FRESHMAN PROFILE

Range SAT Critical Reading	630–740
Range SAT Math	630–720
Minimum Paper TOEFL	600
Minimum Computer Based TOEFL	250
% graduated top 10% of class	74
% graduated top 25% of class	92
% graduated top 50% of class	99

DEADLINES

Early decision application deadline	11/15
Early decision notification	12/15
Regular application deadline	1/1
Regular notification	4/1
Nonfall registration?	yes

APPLICANTS ALSO LOOK AT

AND OFTEN PREFER
Amherst College, Williams College

AND SOMETIMES PREFER
Bowdoin College, Colgate University, Middlebury College

AND RARELY PREFER
Dickinson College, Skidmore College, Union College (NY), Colby College

FINANCIAL FACTS

Financial Aid Rating	98
Annual tuition	$36,500
Room & Board	$9,350
Books and supplies	$500
Required fees	$360

HAMPDEN-SYDNEY COLLEGE

PO Box 667, HAMPDEN-SYDNEY, VA 23943 • ADMISSIONS: 434-223-6120 • FAX: 434-223-6346

CAMPUS LIFE
Quality of Life Rating	81
Fire Safety Rating	65
Type of school	private
Affiliation	Presbyterian
Environment	rural

STUDENTS
Total undergrad enrollment	1,106
% male/female	100/0
% from out of state	33
% from public high school	58
% live on campus	95
% in (# of) fraternities	22 (11)
% African American	6
% Caucasian	89
% Hispanic	1
% international	1
# of countries represented	17

SURVEY SAYS . . .
Small classes
No one cheats
Lots of beer drinking
Hard liquor is popular

ACADEMICS
Academic Rating	85
Calendar	semester
Student/faculty ratio	11:1
Profs interesting rating	98
Profs accessible rating	97
% profs teaching	
UG courses	100
% classes taught by TAs	0
Most common	
reg class size	10–19 students

MOST POPULAR MAJORS
economics
history
political science and government

STUDENTS SAY

Academics

"Hampden-Sydney is not for everybody," students at this traditional all-male college advise. "But if it is for you, one look will make your decision." What will that one look reveal? "The last true refuge for men who are looking to study hard and party hard with other true gentlemen who both dress and act with the highest level of class, and do not accept anything other than 100 percent manners, 100 percent class, 100 percent preppy, and 100 percent conservative all the time," students tell us. You'll also see a place where tradition is paramount; one undergrad explains, "Coming on 'the Hill' is like stepping back in time. Like those who have been here before us, we are not hesitant to walk around in madras and pink bow-ties." Other age-old traditions at this colonial-era institution include "the strongest honor code in the nation, one that tolerates no lying, cheating, or stealing," a mandatory Rhetoric Program that "has made H-SC students famous for their writing," a solid core that creates "liberal arts Renaissance men who dabble in Plato's *Republic*, supply-side economics, *The Federalist Papers*, and Chaucer all in one day," and "a great network of graduates who work hard with Career Services to find other Hampden-Sydney graduates internships and future jobs." Students love that "opportunities are abundant for out-of-the-classroom experience (study abroad, May term abroad, internships)," and that "small class sizes allow you to know your teachers personally, and also hold you more accountable than a class with 200 kids."

Life

Hampden-Sydney's hometown of Farmville lives up to its name; it's "a very rural area, so there isn't much more than a Wal-Mart and a few fast food restaurants nearby." "If you are not comfortable just hanging out with a bunch of dudes, you will occasionally be bored," undergrads tell us, "but if you are pretty used to being in the middle of nowhere, this place can be a lot of fun." "Old traditions and strong Southern values are important" at Hampden-Sydney, and students expect their peers to embrace both. Tailgating, hunting, fishing, and, perhaps most of all, the Greek system are more than just diversions from schoolwork; they are a major source of its *esprit de corps*. Fraternities "drive the entire social scene of this school, and H-SC would be disastrously dull without them," most here agree, noting that the school's all-male status doesn't kill on-campus parties because "Girls from Longwood and Sweet Briar come often, and others come on big weekends. Hollins University, Randolph College, Mary Baldwin College, University of Virginia, James Madison University, and Virginia Tech are all within a reasonable distance." This well-unified campus grows even more united and spirited on game day; one undergrad reports, "Our teams (football, basketball, lacrosse) kick ass in the ODAC and usually finish the season in the NCAA tournaments."

Student Body

"There are a few atypical students" among the majority "White, heterosexual, Republican, middle- to upper-middle-class students from the South, who tend to enjoy the outdoors more than most [and] who know the difference between casual, semiformal, and formal dress." Other things a Hampden-Sydney gentleman knows that you may not? "We know how to treat women and alcohol. We party hard and work hard as well." Those who don't fit the mold "keep to themselves, and most people don't like them and want them to leave." One student sums up the vibe here neatly: "We say grace, and we say 'ma'am,' and if you ain't into that, we don't give a damn." North Face and Polo "are a must in this haven from the average Joe," as is camouflage (during hunting season, anyway). Many here warn that Hampden-Sydney is not a hospitable environment for gay students.

FINANCIAL AID: 804-223-6119 • E-MAIL: ADMISSIONS@HSC.EDU • WEBSITE: WWW.HSC.EDU

ADMISSIONS

Very important factors considered include: Character/personal qualities, recommendation(s), rigor of secondary school record, standardized test scores. *Important factors considered include:* Academic GPA, class rank, extracurricular activities. *Other factors considered include:* Alumni/ae relation, application essay, first generation, interview, level of applicant's interest, racial/ethnic status, talent/ability, volunteer work, work experience. SAT or ACT required; ACT with Writing component recommended. TOEFL required of all international applicants. High school diploma is required, and GED is accepted. *Academic units required:* 4 English, 3 math, 2 science (1 science lab), 2 foreign language, 1 social studies, 1 history, 3 academic electives. *Academic units recommended:* 4 math, 3 science, 3 foreign language.

The Inside Word

Hampden-Sydney is one of the last of its kind. Understandably, the applicant pool is heavily self-selected, and a fairly significant percentage of those who are admitted choose to enroll. This enables the Admissions Committee to be more selective, which in turn requires candidates to take the process more seriously than might otherwise be necessary. Students with consistently sound academic records should have little to worry about nonetheless.

FINANCIAL AID

Students should submit: FAFSA, CSS/Financial Aid PROFILE, state aid form. Regular filing deadline is May 1. The Princeton Review suggests that all financial aid forms be submitted as soon as possible after January 1. *Need-based scholarships/grants offered:* Pell Grant, SEOG, state scholarships/grants, private scholarships, the school's own gift aid. *Loan aid offered:* FFEL Subsidized Stafford, FFEL Unsubsidized Stafford, FFEL PLUS, Federal Perkins Loan, college/university loans from institutional funds, private loans. Applicants will be notified of awards on a rolling basis beginning or about December 15. Federal Work-Study Program available. Institutional employment available. Off-campus job opportunities are fair.

FROM THE ADMISSIONS OFFICE

"The spirit of Hampden-Sydney is its sense of community. As one of only 1,026 students, you will be in small classes and find it easy to get extra help or inspiration from professors when you want it. Many of our professors live on campus and enjoy being with students in the snack bar as well as in the classroom. They give you the best, most personal education as possible. A big bonus of small-college life is that everybody is invited to go out for everything, and you can be as much of a leader as you want to be. From athletics to debating to publications to fraternity life, this is part of the process that produces a well-rounded Hampden-Sydney graduate.

"Hampden-Sydney College requires either the SAT or ACT standardized test with essay."

SELECTIVITY

Admissions Rating	**75**
# of applicants	1,509
% of applicants accepted	69
% of acceptees attending	33
# of early decision applicants	102
% accepted early decision	80

FRESHMAN PROFILE

Range SAT Critical Reading	500–600
Range SAT Math	510–620
Range ACT Composite	20–25
Minimum Paper TOEFL	570
Minimum Computer Based TOEFL	230
Average HS GPA	3.22
% graduated top 10% of class	9
% graduated top 25% of class	20
% graduated top 50% of class	50

DEADLINES

Early decision application deadline	11/15
Early decision notification	12/15
Regular application deadline	3/1
Regular notification	4/15
Nonfall registration?	yes

APPLICANTS ALSO LOOK AT

AND OFTEN PREFER
University of Virginia, Virginia Tech

AND SOMETIMES PREFER
James Madison University, Sewanee—The University of the South, University of Georgia, University of Mississippi, The University of North Carolina at Chapel Hill

AND RARELY PREFER
Randolph-Macon College

FINANCIAL FACTS

Financial Aid Rating	**82**
Annual tuition	$26,676
Room & Board	$8,671
Books and supplies	$1,000
Required fees	$1,056
% frosh rec. need-based scholarship or grant aid	48
% UG rec. need-based scholarship or grant aid	48
% frosh rec. need-based self-help aid	35
% UG rec. need-based self-help aid	38
% frosh rec. any financial aid	98
% UG rec. any financial aid	97

HAMPSHIRE COLLEGE

ADMISSIONS OFFICE, 893 WEST STREET, AMHERST, MA 01002 • ADMISSIONS: 413-559-5471 • FAX: 413-559-5631

CAMPUS LIFE

Quality of Life Rating	84
Fire Safety Rating	60*
Type of school	private
Environment	town

STUDENTS

Total undergrad enrollment	1,434
% male/female	41/59
% from out of state	83
% from public high school	49
% live on campus	91
% African American	4
% Asian	3
% Caucasian	71
% Hispanic	5
% Native American	1
% international	3
# of countries represented	28

SURVEY SAYS . . .

Lots of liberal students
Small classes
No one cheats
Great off-campus food
Frats and sororities are unpopular or nonexistent
(Almost) everyone smokes

ACADEMICS

Academic Rating	91
Calendar	4-1-4
Student/faculty ratio	12:1
Profs interesting rating	86
Profs accessible rating	82
% profs teaching UG courses	100
% classes taught by TAs	0
Most common reg class size	10–19 students

MOST POPULAR MAJORS

English language and literature
social sciences
visual and performing arts

STUDENTS SAY

Academics

Hampshire College presents a "do-it-yourself, do-it-as-yourself" approach to education, offering students "a self-designed curriculum" facilitated by "close relationships with professors, small classes, and the great combination of communal living and individualism that a true Hampshire student embodies." Here's how it works: "In class, students learn as a group in discussions or hands-on activities (few lectures, no tests), while outside of class one focuses on independent projects (research, reading, writing, art-making)." The experience culminates in a 'Division III,' an all-consuming year-long senior thesis project "that allows students to become excited and completely invested" while "producing a unique product at the end of the year." Students "receive evaluations instead of grades, which we feel is a much more productive system." The goal is a "hands-on, interdisciplinary education, with the option to incorporate internships and experience abroad," and many here say that's exactly what they accomplish. Undergrads see Hampshire as the "embodiment of academic freedom, personal vision, and self-motivation," a place for students "who can handle the huge responsibility that comes with great opportunities" and "great freedom." Hampshire "is very small," which might limit students' choices; fortunately, "It belongs to the Five College[s] consortium," a group that includes the massive University of Massachusetts—Amherst. With the course offerings of five colleges available to them, Hampshire students can "take any course we could dream of."

Life

Hampshire students enjoy domestic pleasures: At this "very community-based school," undergrads "live together in mods, on-campus, apartment-style housing where they can cook together and share a living space while having their own room." "Potlucks are abundant since most people cook for themselves." Students tell us, "We take our class discussions to our dinner tables. We have a lot of passionate people who infect everybody else with their passion." Hampshire students also enjoy "playing music together" and "chilling out and watching a movie or just having some coffee together." Every weekend students can find plenty of parties, which "generally consist of 50 people or fewer—never the roaring, dangerously wild parties that are often found at other colleges." Overall, undergrads describe it as "a very chill campus. There is no Greek life, and the Frisbee team is the closest thing we have to jocks." The surrounding area provides opportunities "for water sports, biking, hikes," or "bonfires in the woods," and "the nearby towns of Amherst and Northampton aren't too bad," offering "lots of art galleries and live music." Of course, the school's proximity to numerous other colleges provides ample opportunities for those who grow bored with the Hampshire campus.

Student Body

As befits their school's curriculum, "Hampshire students tend to be very self-motivated people who would rather invent their own approach to knowledge than follow a pre-established track." This independent bent means that "we were maybe the 'black sheep' of our high schools, the outcasts, the ones looking for more of a challenge, more say in what they were learning or what they were expected to do with their lives." Students here are "usually good at improvising and, because of the emphasis on class discussion and writing papers, very verbal." They also tend to be "socially conscious, left-wing, and artistic. We are fond of do-it-yourself philosophies, from 'zines to music and film production to designing ecologically sustainable communities. We like a wide variety of music, and like to have parties in cramped mods at which we play this music at high volume. We are comfortable with smoking, drinking, and drug use, in a laissez-faire sort of way. We may be vegetarian, vegan, or meat eaters, but we like to cook, and we love to complain about the dining hall."

FINANCIAL AID: 413-559-5484 • E-MAIL: ADMISSIONS@HAMPSHIRE.EDU • WEBSITE: WWW.HAMPSHIRE.EDU

ADMISSIONS

Very important factors considered include: Application essay, character/personal qualities. *Important factors considered include:* Extracurricular activities, level of applicant's interest, recommendation(s), rigor of secondary school record, talent/ability. *Other factors considered include:* Academic GPA, alumni/ae relation, class rank, interview, racial/ethnic status, standardized test scores, volunteer work, work experience. TOEFL required of all international applicants. High school diploma is required, and GED is accepted. *Academic units required:* 4 English, 4 math, 4 science (2 science labs), 3 foreign language, 2 social studies, 2 history.

The Inside Word

As some prospective students have probably deduced, Hampshire's admissions policies are the antithesis of formula-based practices. Officers want to know the individual behind the transcript, and so personal characteristics hold substantial weight. Demonstrating discipline and an independent and inquisitive spirit may just carry more weight than a perfect 4.0. Writing is seen as pivotal to a Hampshire education, and applicants must put considerable thought into their personal statements.

FINANCIAL AID

Students should submit: FAFSA, CSS/Financial Aid PROFILE, Noncustodial PROFILE. The Princeton Review suggests that all financial aid forms be submitted as soon as possible after January 1. *Need-based scholarships/grants offered:* Pell Grant, SEOG, state scholarships/grants, private scholarships, the school's own gift aid. *Loan aid offered:* Direct Subsidized Stafford, Direct Unsubsidized Stafford, FFEL PLUS, Federal Perkins Loan. Applicants will be notified of awards on or about April 1. Federal Work-Study Program available.

FROM THE ADMISSIONS OFFICE

"Students tell us they like our application. It is less derivative and more open-ended than most. Rather than assigning an essay topic, we ask to learn more about you as an individual and invite your ideas. Instead of just asking for lists of activities, we ask you how those activities (and academic or other endeavors) have shown some of the traits that lead to success at Hampshire (initiative, independence, persistence, for example). This approach parallels the work you will do at Hampshire, defining the questions you will ask and the courses and experiences that will help you to answer them, and integrating your interests.

"Hampshire College requires freshman applicants to submit scores from the old or new SAT. Students may also choose to submit scores from the ACT (with or without the Writing component) in lieu of the SAT."

SELECTIVITY

Admissions Rating	**89**
# of applicants	2,454
% of applicants accepted	56
% of acceptees attending	29
# accepting a place on wait list	223
% admitted from wait list	10
# of early decision applicants	75
% accepted early decision	69

FRESHMAN PROFILE

Range SAT Critical Reading	610–700
Range SAT Math	540–660
Range SAT Writing	600–690
Range ACT Composite	26–29
Minimum Paper TOEFL	577
Minimum Computer Based TOEFL	233
Average HS GPA	3.42
% graduated top 10% of class	25
% graduated top 25% of class	59
% graduated top 50% of class	88

DEADLINES

Early decision application deadline	11/15
Early decision notification	12/15
Regular application deadline	1/15
Regular notification	4/1
Nonfall registration?	yes

APPLICANTS ALSO LOOK AT

AND OFTEN PREFER
Bard College

AND SOMETIMES PREFER
Sarah Lawrence College

AND RARELY PREFER
Bennington College

FINANCIAL FACTS

Financial Aid Rating	**91**
Annual tuition	$33,855
Room & Board	$9,030
Books and supplies	$500
Required fees	$750
% frosh rec. need-based scholarship or grant aid	56
% UG rec. need-based scholarship or grant aid	57
% frosh rec. need-based self-help aid	56
% UG rec. need-based self-help aid	57
% frosh rec. any financial aid	72
% UG rec. any financial aid	70

HAMPTON UNIVERSITY

OFFICE OF ADMISSIONS, HAMPTON UNIVERSITY, HAMPTON, VA 23668 • ADMISSIONS: 757-727-5328 • FAX: 757-727-5095

CAMPUS LIFE

Quality of Life Rating	**64**
Fire Safety Rating	**60***
Type of school	private
Environment	city

STUDENTS

Total undergrad enrollment	5,056
% male/female	36/64
% from out of state	69
% from public high school	90
% live on campus	59
% in (# of) fraternities	5 (6)
% in (# of) sororities	4 (3)
% African American	96
% Asian	1
% Caucasian	12
% Hispanic	1

SURVEY SAYS . . .

Small classes
Great library
Campus feels safe
Everyone loves the Pirates
Frats and sororities dominate social scene
Student government is popular

ACADEMICS

Academic Rating	**75**
Calendar	semester
Student/faculty ratio	16:1
Profs interesting rating	68
Profs accessible rating	67
% profs teaching UG courses	98
% classes taught by TAs	0
Most common lab size	10–19 students
Most common reg class size	20–29 students

MOST POPULAR MAJORS

business administration/
management
journalism
psychology

STUDENTS SAY

Academics

Hampton University, "one of the premier Historically Black Colleges and Universities in the country," is "perfect for students who desire to be around other intelligent and focused Black students who have a future and are making plans to achieve their goals. Our students are making changes in this world and will always continue to." With popular programs in business and management, psychology, pharmacy, nursing, sociology, the hard sciences, and communications, Hampton "is about producing successful, bright, and talented professionals." The school has made a special commitment to journalism and communications, opening a state-of-the-art facility in 2002 that includes a full working studio with editing facilities, a student-run radio station, and five computer labs. Throughout its many departments, Hampton stresses the importance of experiential learning, "presenting a host of opportunities for students to get internships and jobs." One student reports, "I have had three internships and have been on the campus radio station for my entire career at HU." Professors here earn good marks for dedication and teaching skills; the administration, on the other hand, is notorious for 'The Hampton Run-Around,' in which "A student spends their day running around campus trying to get a simple form signed or for a person to help them in whatever way, and in the end find out that the initial person they met with could have dealt with the problem." Most agree the inconvenience is worth it for "the connections and networking" Hampton provides. As one student notes, "Everyone here is important, related to, or knows someone important, and everyone will become successful and important."

Life

"Hampton is not the typical party school," students agree. One student writes, "Life at Hampton is pretty boring compared to where I'm from. There, the parties are wack. But, looking on the bright side, I'm not here to party and have fun; I'm here for school and to get my degree." Undergrads report that "most events take place off campus, so you really have to find your own fun." Fortunately the area provides some diversion, including "malls, fine dining, and parties … Also, Hampton is surrounded by cities that are no more than 15 to 20 minutes away," including Norfolk, Newport News, and Virginia Beach. "Nearby amusement parks are also great attractions for the spring and summer." On campus, "There is a really nice student center that turns into a virtual party every day from noon to 2:00 P.M. The student center is tri-level and has everything from a theater to [a] bowling ally and a fitness center." Hampton's Greek system is very popular; the most popular ones "are highly competitive and selective, and the whole process is crazy and oh-so-hard to get into." Some here complain that restrictive regulations dampen campus life. One student writes, "Rules and regulations prevent us from body painting at sporting events. Students are not allowed to have refrigerators apparently due to outdated wiring in the dorms. . . . Administration, faculty, and staff do not respect students as adults."

Student Body

Hampton "is a Historically Black [College and] University, but the range of Black students here is amazing. There is a niche for everyone, and I mean everyone, and most are universally accepted." Many are "very outgoing and professional," and "are well off and come from a nice home." Some "tend to be very materialistic and . . . care a lot about social matters. They all dress well, spend plenty of money on clothes, and drive very nice cars (even better cars than teachers)," but "There are many different types of students" here, not just the well heeled. Atypical students here "mesh well with the others" because Hampton students are a part of a family. "We are called Hamptonians, symbolizing our unity. Here we have a bond that is very strong—we all fit in—and it is not to be broken."

266 ■ THE BEST 366 COLLEGES

FINANCIAL AID: 800-624-3341 • E-MAIL: ADMIT@HAMPTONU.EDU • WEBSITE: WWW.HAMPTONU.EDU

ADMISSIONS

Very important factors considered include: Application essay, character/personal qualities, rigor of secondary school record, standardized test scores. *Important factors considered include:* Class rank, recommendation(s). *Other factors considered include:* Alumni/ae relation, extracurricular activities, talent/ability, volunteer work. SAT or ACT required; TOEFL required of all international applicants. High school diploma is required, and GED is accepted. *Academic units required:* 4 English, 3 math, 2 science (2 science labs), 2 social studies, 6 academic electives. *Academic units recommended:* 2 foreign language.

The Inside Word

Hampton University allows for early action admissions, meaning that students can receive an early decision without having to commit to attending the school. Well more than half of HU's applicant pool pursues this option. You would be wise to follow suit; the school is bound to be more lenient early in the process than later, when it has already admitted many qualified students. Don't be fooled by the fact that the number of applicants to HU has dropped in recent years; that is the result of more stringent admission standards, not a drop in the school's cachet.

FINANCIAL AID

Students should submit: FAFSA. The Princeton Review suggests that all financial aid forms be submitted as soon as possible after January 1. *Need-based scholarships/grants offered:* Pell Grant, SEOG, state scholarships/grants, private scholarships, the school's own gift aid, Federal Nursing Scholarship. *Loan aid offered:* Direct Subsidized Stafford, Direct Unsubsidized Stafford, Direct PLUS, FFEL Subsidized Stafford, FFEL Unsubsidized Stafford, FFEL PLUS, Federal Perkins Loan, alternative loans. Applicants will be notified of awards on a rolling basis beginning or about April 15. Federal Work-Study Program available. Off-campus job opportunities are excellent.

FROM THE ADMISSIONS OFFICE

"Hampton attempts to provide the environment and structures most conducive to the intellectual, emotional, and aesthetic enlargement of the lives of its members. The university gives priority to effective teaching and scholarly research while placing the student at the center of its planning. Hampton will ask you to look inwardly at your own history and culture and examine your relationship to the aspirations and development of the world.

"As of this book's publication, Hampton University did not have information available about their policy regarding the new SAT."

SELECTIVITY
Admissions Rating	87
# of applicants	7,120
% of applicants accepted	37
% of acceptees attending	43

FRESHMAN PROFILE
Range SAT Critical Reading	481–552
Range SAT Math	464–606
Range ACT Composite	17–26
Minimum Paper TOEFL	550
Minimum Computer Based TOEFL	214
Average HS GPA	3.2
% graduated top 10% of class	20
% graduated top 25% of class	45
% graduated top 50% of class	90

DEADLINES
Regular notification	rolling,
Nonfall registration?	yes

APPLICANTS ALSO LOOK AT AND OFTEN PREFER
Florida A&M University, Morehouse College, Spelman College

AND SOMETIMES PREFER
Howard University, University of Maryland—College Park, Virginia Tech

FINANCIAL FACTS
Financial Aid Rating	61
Annual tuition	$13,358
Room & Board	$6,746
Books and supplies	$750
Required fees	$1,460
% frosh rec. need-based scholarship or grant aid	96
% UG rec. need-based scholarship or grant aid	44
% frosh rec. need-based self-help aid	79
% UG rec. need-based self-help aid	44
% frosh rec. any financial aid	44
% UG rec. any financial aid	100

HANOVER COLLEGE

PO Box 108, Hanover, IN 47243-0108 • Admissions: 812-866-7021 • Fax: 812-866-7098

STUDENTS SAY

Academics

"Demanding course work" and a "small-school atmosphere" pervade the "picturesque" Georgian-style campus of Hanover College, an "excellent" bastion of the liberal arts and sciences in southeastern Indiana. Hanover operates on a fairly unique 4-4-1 calendar, in which there are two traditional semesters followed by a spring term during which students concentrate on a single class, participate in an array of off-campus internships, or study abroad. Classes are very small, and there is a strong focus on "teaching students to think and write critically." Students must complete a wide range of distribution requirements and agree that the curriculum is "intense." Sometimes "The workload is barely manageable." While the "amazing" and "very intelligent" professors at Hanover may "require a lot from the students," they are "very attentive." "Personal attention from professors" is commonplace and they "spend a lot of time out of class with the students." "Teachers are tough" but in the end, "You really learn." "The professors here are some of the best teachers, mentors, and friends that one could hope to find anywhere," beams a classical studies major. Over 90 percent of all students receive at least some financial assistance and more than a few say they chose Hanover because they got "a lot of scholarship money." Students say the Career Services staff is "really good," although registration can be "a hassle." Also, the "distant," "unpredictable," "unorganized," and "indecisive" administration is almost uniformly unpopular.

Life

"Hanover's campus is one of the most beautiful places I have ever been," swears a junior. "This place is beautiful the whole year round," "even in the soggy dreariness of late March." A "family-like" environment "allows people to really get to know each other and have connections." "Academics are very important" but "There are also many opportunities to get involved in extracurricular activities." Greek life is an exceptionally big deal here ("most students on campus are strongly Greek affiliated") and fraternities and sororities dominate the social scene. During the week, "Most students are doing homework and studying" and "just hang out casually"—except for Wednesday. "Wednesday nights and the weekends are when people party." Students say most people on campus "at least talk about partying a lot" and that "parties are pretty much just at the fraternities." "Though the rules about alcohol are rather strict, they are not necessarily heavily enforced (in the fraternities anyway). It is much harder to drink in residence halls." Some students complain that there is little to do "outside of fraternity parties or bars." To be sure, "the surrounding towns of Hanover and Madison" are "not very exciting" and may be a little "too rural" for some tastes. "This is the worst place a college town could be," laments one junior. Students with cars can avail themselves of more urban pursuits available in nearby "Cincinnati, Louisville, and Indianapolis."

Student Body

There are just over 1,000 students here from over 35 states and 18 countries, though "Most tend to be from Indiana, Kentucky, or Ohio." "The typical student is an upper-middle-class White athlete" and very likely "Christian." A lot of students come from "suburbia," while others come from small Midwestern towns. "There are a few Blacks, a few gays, and a lot of Nepalese and Hawaiian students." "The little ethnic diversity here is from the international students, not diverse Americans," though. "There are not a lot of atypical students" and those that are "tend to stick together." The generally homogenous nature of the student population creates a good deal of cohesion. "We pretty much all get along," reports one first-year student. Students describe themselves as "friendly," "easygoing," and "pretty casual." "There's a little bit of everything as far as goals, interests, and ambitions." There are "quite a few [students who] like to party frequently;" "However, most study and work hard." Over 60 percent of Hanover's newly minted graduates eventually go on to graduate and professional schools.

FINANCIAL AID: 812-866-7030 • E-MAIL: ADMISSION@HANOVER.EDU • WEBSITE: WWW.HANOVER.EDU

ADMISSIONS

Very important factors considered include: Academic GPA, class rank, rigor of secondary school record. *Important factors considered include:* Recommendation(s), standardized test scores, talent/ability. *Other factors considered include:* Alumni/ae relation, application essay, character/personal qualities, extracurricular activities, first generation, geographical residence, interview, level of applicant's interest, racial/ethnic status, state residency, volunteer work, work experience. SAT or ACT required; ACT with Writing component required. TOEFL required of all international applicants. High school diploma is required, and GED is not accepted. *Academic units required:* 4 English, 3 math, 3 science (2 science labs), 2 foreign language, 2 social studies, 2 history, 2 academic electives. *Academic units recommended:* 4 English, 4 math, 4 science (3 science labs), 4 foreign language, 3 social studies, 3 history, 3 academic electives.

The Inside Word

Admission is competitive, but the applicant pool is not huge, and Hanover accepts a relatively high percentage of its applicants. High school grades (especially during your junior and senior years) and class rank are the most important determining factors for the Admissions Committee. If you are vying for an academic scholarship—and many, many applicants will be—it pays to invest some serious thought and time into Hanover's application process.

FINANCIAL AID

Students should submit: FAFSA. The Princeton Review suggests that all financial aid forms be submitted as soon as possible after January 1. *Need-based scholarships/grants offered:* Pell Grant, state scholarships/grants, private scholarships, the school's own gift aid. *Loan aid offered:* FFEL Subsidized Stafford, FFEL Unsubsidized Stafford, FFEL PLUS. Applicants will be notified of awards on or about March 1. Off-campus job opportunities are fair.

FROM THE ADMISSIONS OFFICE

"Since our founding in 1827, we have been committed to providing students with a personal, rigorous, and well-rounded liberal arts education. Part of the college search process is finding that school that proves to be a good match. For those who see the value in an education that demands engagement and who see college as a time for exploration and involvement, they will find that Hanover is all they could hope for and more.

"The admission process serves as an introduction to the personal education that students receive at Hanover College. Every application is considered individually with emphasis being placed on a student's high school curriculum and the student's academic performance in that curriculum. While we realize that not every high school has the same course offerings, we expect students to have selected a college preparatory curriculum as challenging as possible within his or her particular high school or academic setting.

"Hanover College accepts both the SAT and ACT. Students taking the ACT are required to take the optional writing section. For students who have taken one or both of the tests multiple times, we will use the highest sub scores when calculating a student's score on either test for admission and scholarship purposes."

SELECTIVITY
Admissions Rating	85
# of applicants	1,556
% of applicants accepted	64
% of acceptees attending	23

FRESHMAN PROFILE
Range SAT Critical Reading	520–640
Range SAT Math	510–640
Range ACT Composite	23–28
Minimum Paper TOEFL	550
Minimum Computer Based TOEFL	213
% graduated top 10% of class	34
% graduated top 25% of class	75
% graduated top 50% of class	97

DEADLINES
Regular application deadline	3/1
Regular notification	rolling
Nonfall registration?	yes

APPLICANTS ALSO LOOK AT
AND OFTEN PREFER
Butler University, DePauw University
AND SOMETIMES PREFER
Centre College, Indiana University—Bloomington, Miami University, University of Evansville, Wabash College, Wittenberg University
AND RARELY PREFER
Earlham College, Kenyon College

FINANCIAL FACTS
Financial Aid Rating	79
Annual tuition	$23,700
Room & Board	$7,150
Books and supplies	$900
Required fees	$520
% frosh rec. need-based scholarship or grant aid	43
% UG rec. need-based scholarship or grant aid	39
% frosh rec. need-based self-help aid	41
% UG rec. need-based self-help aid	38
% frosh rec. any financial aid	98
% UG rec. any financial aid	98

HARVARD COLLEGE

BYERLY HALL, EIGHT GARDEN STREET, CAMBRIDGE, MA 02138 • ADMISSIONS: 617-495-1551 • FAX: 617-495-8821

CAMPUS LIFE
Quality of Life Rating	91
Fire Safety Rating	60*
Type of school	private
Environment	metropolis

STUDENTS
Total undergrad enrollment	6,715
% male/female	51/49
% from out of state	84
% from public high school	65
% live on campus	98
% African American	8
% Asian	14
% Caucasian	47
% Hispanic	7
% Native American	1
% international	9

SURVEY SAYS . . .
Registration is a breeze
Great library
Students love Cambridge, MA
Student publications are popular
Political activism is popular
Dorms are like palaces

ACADEMICS
Academic Rating	99
Calendar	semester
Student/faculty ratio	7:1
Profs interesting rating	81
Profs accessible rating	74
% profs teaching	
UG courses	100
% classes taught by TAs	0

MOST POPULAR MAJORS
economics
political science and government
psychology

STUDENTS SAY
Academics

"Harvard has distinguished faculty, an extremely accomplished and diverse student body, a million-and-one extracurriculars, and very generous alumni," a student at this *ne plus ultra* of American academia explains, adding "What more could you ask for from a school?" What more, indeed? With "unparalleled academics" and "a huge endowment that really allows Harvard to give its students every available resource," Harvard has it all for the aspiring intellectual. By throwing in Cambridge and Boston, have we discovered academic nirvana? Close, but not quite. Students complain that "Harvard would benefit from a more active advising system, because a substantial number of courses, including many options for fulfilling requirements under the core program, are offered only once every 2 years, and many students don't realize this." Even so, the pros far outweigh the cons here. Students especially love the "high number of tutorials and seminars, which are always taught by a professor to a small group of students. They are a great chance to find a mentor." They're also pretty psyched about "interacting with and learning from world experts in almost every subject" and their access to "the best university library in America." Four in five students admitted here attend; that figure pretty much says it all.

Life

"In terms of life in general, there is a lot of studying" at Harvard, "but letting it rule your life means you miss out on so many experiences. The happiest Harvard students are probably those who do their schoolwork but make sure that they have a life outside of it. Otherwise, you never meet people and you stress yourself out." Cambridge and Boston offer plenty of opportunities to get out, but "Unfortunately, it's too easy to just get stuck on campus, especially since there's always something going on." Students report that "there is always a cultural show, musical concert, movie showing, information session, graduate-school talk, or colloquium to attend, and the hardest part is balancing all of the work with all the other interesting options on campus." Student clubs and organizations pull double duty, "serving a strong social function; for example, the board of the Gilbert and Sullivan Players has lots of meetings and produces shows, but then we throw about six parties a semester." Undergrads here tell us that "most people do one or two extracurriculars, often pretty intensely. There's not that frantic volunteering for everything that distinguishes the future Harvard student in high school. Once we get in, we skip the resume padders and only do the stuff we're actually into doing." Just about everyone here "lives on campus in the huge suites," and "Since we are allowed to have parties with alcohol in our suites, that is a popular social activity."

Student Body

Harvard can handpick top candidates to create the degree of student diversity it wants, so it should come as no surprise that "there is no 'typical' student here. You get someone from West Philly who is the first person in his family to go to college; you have the daughter of a Saudi prince who will be married to a 60-year-old oil baron after graduation; you get 'development cases' and legacies with surnames like Kilroy and Lynch; and you get a range of students from blue- to white-collar backgrounds." One student explains, "The admissions process goes to great lengths to find students that they feel will add to the community at Harvard. As a result, even a simple meal in the dining hall is always an entertaining part of the day, just laughing and goofing off with friends, or even debating about political issues." Undergrads here tend to be "multitalented, overextended, articulate," and "secure in their own fabulousness, so they really don't brag, and they'll totally be happy for you if you do something cool."

FINANCIAL AID: 617-495-1581 • E-MAIL: COLLEGE@FAS.HARVARD.EDU • WEBSITE: WWW.FAS.HARVARD.EDU

ADMISSIONS

Very important factors considered include: Character/personal qualities, extracurricular activities, recommendation(s), rigor of secondary school record, talent/ability. *Important factors considered include:* Application essay, class rank, interview, standardized test scores. *Other factors considered include:* Alumni/ae relation, first generation, geographical residence, racial/ethnic status, volunteer work, work experience. SAT or ACT required; SAT Subject Tests required. High school diploma or equivalent is not required. *Academic units recommended:* 4 English, 4 math, 4 science, 4 foreign language, 3 social studies, 2 history.

The Inside Word

It just doesn't get any tougher than this. Candidates to Harvard face dual obstacles—an awe-inspiring applicant pool and, as a result, admissions standards that defy explanation in quantifiable terms. Harvard denies admission to the vast majority, and virtually all of them are top students. It all boils down to splitting hairs, which is quite hard to explain and even harder for candidates to understand. Rather than being as detailed and direct as possible about the selection process and criteria, Harvard keeps things close to the vest—before, during, and after. They even refuse to admit that being from South Dakota is an advantage. Thus the admissions process does more to intimidate candidates than to empower them. Moving to a common application seemed to be a small step in the right direction, but with the current explosion of early decision applicants and a super-high yield of enrollees, things are not likely to change dramatically.

FINANCIAL AID

Students should submit: FAFSA, CSS/Financial Aid PROFILE, Noncustodial PROFILE, Business/Farm Supplement, Federal Income Tax Returns through IDOC. Regular filing deadline is February 1. The Princeton Review suggests that all financial aid forms be submitted as soon as possible after January 1. *Need-based scholarships/grants offered:* Pell Grant, SEOG, state scholarships/grants, private scholarships, the school's own gift aid. *Loan aid offered:* Direct Subsidized Stafford, Direct Unsubsidized Stafford, Direct PLUS, Federal Perkins Loan, state loans, college/university loans from institutional funds. Applicants will be notified of awards on or about April 1. Federal Work-Study Program available. Institutional employment available. Off-campus job opportunities are excellent.

FROM THE ADMISSIONS OFFICE

"The Admissions Committee looks for energy, ambition, and the capacity to make the most of opportunities. Academic ability and preparation are important, and so is intellectual curiosity—but many of the strongest applicants have significant non-academic interests and accomplishments as well. There is no formula for admission, and applicants are considered carefully, with attention to future promise.

"Freshman applicants for Fall 2008 may submit either the old SAT taken before March 2005, or the new SAT. The ACT with Writing component is also accepted. All students must also submit three SAT Subject Tests of their choosing."

SELECTIVITY

Admissions Rating	**99**
# of applicants	22,754
% of applicants accepted	9
% of acceptees attending	79

FRESHMAN PROFILE

Range SAT Critical Reading	690–800
Range SAT Math	700–790
Range SAT Writing	690–780
Range ACT Composite	31–34
% graduated top 10% of class	95
% graduated top 25% of class	100
% graduated top 50% of class	100

DEADLINES

Regular application deadline	1/1
Regular notification	4/1
Nonfall registration?	no

APPLICANTS ALSO LOOK AT AND SOMETIMES PREFER

Princeton University, Stanford University, University of Pennsylvania, Yale University

AND RARELY PREFER

Amherst College, Georgetown University, Northwestern University, Williams College

FINANCIAL FACTS

Financial Aid Rating	**95**
Annual tuition	$30,275
Room & Board	$9,946
Books and supplies	$1,000
Required fees	$3,434
% frosh rec. need-based scholarship or grant aid	53
% UG rec. need-based scholarship or grant aid	49
% frosh rec. need-based self-help aid	30
% UG rec. need-based self-help aid	42

HARVEY MUDD COLLEGE

301 EAST TWELFTH STREET, CLAREMONT, CA 91711-5990 • ADMISSIONS: 909-621-8011 • FAX: 909-621-8360

CAMPUS LIFE
Quality of Life Rating	87
Fire Safety Rating	63
Type of school	private
Environment	town

STUDENTS
Total undergrad enrollment	729
% male/female	71/29
% from out of state	51
% from public high school	75
% live on campus	99
% African American	1
% Asian	19
% Caucasian	48
% Hispanic	8
% Native American	1
% international	4
# of countries represented	20

SURVEY SAYS . . .
Career services are great
No one cheats
Lab facilities are great
Great computer facilities
Students are friendly
Low cost of living
Frats and sororities are unpopular or nonexistent

ACADEMICS
Academic Rating	99
Calendar	semester
Student/faculty ratio	8:1
Profs interesting rating	99
Profs accessible rating	99
% profs teaching UG courses	100
% classes taught by TAs	0
Most common lab size	10–19 students
Most common reg class size	fewer than 10 students

MOST POPULAR MAJORS
computer and information sciences
engineering
physics

STUDENTS SAY
Academics
"Incredible math, science, and engineering programs," delivered in "a small school atmosphere, but with four other undergraduate schools [Claremont McKenna, Pomona, Pitzer, and Scripps Colleges] in walking distance," distinguish Harvey Mudd College, a tiny "powerhouse [where] every department is fantastic." Students love the "world-renowned" Physics Department and remind us that "every year we do extraordinarily well in math competitions." They also insist that "we have the best undergraduate chemistry department in the world and our engineering department is likewise top-notch." But what students love most is the professors who "choose to teach here because they want to focus on teaching, not on research; as a result, everything is organized around making the classes as good as possible, not around getting that next grant dollar." Whatever research is done here "provides opportunities for undergraduates to conduct original research with professors, usually over the summers (but sometimes during the semester)." The workload is massive and the grading system is brutal; "They really take their anti-grade inflation stance a bit too seriously," complains one student. Students shoulder their load in a "cooperative, accepting environment. At times it definitely feels like everyone sticks together because we're all going through a trial by fire." An "awesome honor code" sets the tone for the campus; there's "complete trust among all students and faculty. Most tests are self-administered take-home tests." A "broad range of requirements in both other sciences and humanities . . . ensure that students learn their field starting from a very strong and expansive background."

Life
"There is a lot of work to be done, and a lot of time is spent either doing homework or reading for class," Mudd students report, adding that "other than that, there are a great number of things people do for fun: sports, video/computer games, parties, movies," and "random acts of weirdness." One student explains, "Every dorm has unusual traditions and pastimes. Mine has 'dorm togetherness activities,' which usually involve isopropanol and matches, and then food. Another dorm has competitions to see who can go to the most doughnut shops the fastest. Another has pick-up games of unicycle hockey." "Pranking" is "a staple of campus culture, and one that the administration encourages." Pranks are "usually harmless, and everyone enjoys them. For example: Once people from Atwood, one of the dorms, snuck into another dorm, Sontag, to 'steal' the sofas and put them on Atwood's roof as a display of superiority." Students also entertain themselves by "leaving campus to see plays, visit museums, go to theme parks (Disneyland is only 30 minutes away), go to the beach, or explore Los Angeles." There are also four other Claremont campuses to enjoy. Mudd students brag that their campus "has the best parties of all the five C's," but not the nicest campus; "Campus beauty is certainly lacking. The local decor is made up of squares of concrete we call 'warts': interesting, but not exactly inspiring."

Student Body
HMC students form "an incredible community" in which "Everyone looks out for each other." Community is built into HMC's curriculum; one student explains, "Everyone takes Mudd's massive core that for the most part completely dictates the classes you will take as a freshman. As a result, the freshmen get to know each other really fast and quickly form many friendships. This sense of community is strengthened by the fact that dorms are not segregated by class year. By the end of the semester, there are countless friendships and relationships that extend across the class lines, which are close to nonexistent." Students grant that "a typical student at Mudd is probably a little more on the dorky side than your average American college student" because "Mudders all have an affinity for math and science, and some of us can get pretty obsessed with those subjects, [but] on the whole, Mudders aren't just a bunch of nerds. Almost everyone is friendly, most of us are pretty sociable and fun-loving, and some people are just plain partiers."

FINANCIAL AID: 909-621-8055 • E-MAIL: ADMISSION@HMC.EDU • WEBSITE: WWW.HMC.EDU

ADMISSIONS

Very important factors considered include: Application essay, character/personal qualities, class rank, recommendation(s), rigor of secondary school record, standardized test scores. *Important factors considered include:* Alumni/ae relation, interview. *Other factors considered include:* Extracurricular activities, geographical residence, racial/ethnic status, talent/ability, volunteer work, work experience. SAT or ACT required; SAT and SAT Subject Tests or ACT required; ACT with Writing component required. TOEFL required of all international applicants. High school diploma is required, and GED is accepted. *Academic units required:* 4 English, 4 math, 3 science (3 science labs). *Academic units recommended:* 2 foreign language, 1 social studies, 1 history.

The Inside Word

Harvey Mudd is a place for serious students, and its admissions process expects excellence from all candidates. This is not to say that they don't have a sense of humor out there in Claremont. The college attracted national attention in the past by mailing recruitment literature that poked fun at the overly serious world of college admissions while at the same time showcasing the school's academic quality. Any Admissions Staff that contributes to the lessening of student stress in the college search and admissions process is to be commended.

FINANCIAL AID

Students should submit: FAFSA, CSS/Financial Aid PROFILE, state aid form, Noncustodial PROFILE, Business/Farm Supplement. Regular filing deadline is February 1. The Princeton Review suggests that all financial aid forms be submitted as soon as possible after January 1. *Need-based scholarships/grants offered:* Pell Grant, SEOG, state scholarships/grants, private scholarships, the school's own gift aid. *Loan aid offered:* FFEL Subsidized Stafford, FFEL Unsubsidized Stafford, FFEL PLUS, Federal Perkins Loan, college/university loans from institutional funds, alternative loans. Applicants will be notified of awards on or about April 1.

FROM THE ADMISSIONS OFFICE

"Students interested in HMC must have a talent and passion for science and mathematics. The college offers majors in mathematics, physics, engineering, chemistry, biology, and computer science. 'Mudders' have very diverse interests. Because nearly one-third of the course work at HMC is in the humanities and social sciences, HMC students also enjoy studying economics, psychology, philosophy, history, the fine arts, and literature.

"Freshman applicants for Fall 2008 are required to submit test scores from the new SAT test. Scores submitted from the old (prior to March 2005) SAT will be accepted. The student's best composite score will be used in the admission process. SAT Subject Tests are required: Math Level II and one examination of choice. In addition, students submitting old SAT scores must also submit SAT Subject Test in Writing."

SELECTIVITY

Admissions Rating	97
# of applicants	2,119
% of applicants accepted	30
% of acceptees attending	28
# accepting a place on wait list	115
% admitted from wait list	26
# of early decision applicants	118
% accepted early decision	37

FRESHMAN PROFILE

Range SAT Critical Reading	680–760
Range SAT Math	740–790
Range SAT Writing	670–740
Minimum Paper TOEFL	600
Minimum Computer Based TOEFL	250
Average HS GPA	3.8
% graduated top 10% of class	89
% graduated top 50% of class	100

DEADLINES

Early decision application deadline	11/15
Early decision notification	12/15
Regular application deadline	1/15
Regular notification	4/1
Nonfall registration?	no

APPLICANTS ALSO LOOK AT

AND OFTEN PREFER
Massachusetts Institute of Technology, Stanford University

AND SOMETIMES PREFER
Carnegie Mellon University, Cornell University, Rice University

AND RARELY PREFER
Virginia Tech, Worcester Polytechnic Institute

FINANCIAL FACTS

Financial Aid Rating	96
Annual tuition	$33,113
Room & Board	$10,933
Books and supplies	$800
Required fees	$212
% frosh rec. need-based scholarship or grant aid	60
% UG rec. need-based scholarship or grant aid	51
% frosh rec. need-based self-help aid	48
% UG rec. need-based self-help aid	45
% frosh rec. any financial aid	84
% UG rec. any financial aid	81

HAVERFORD COLLEGE

370 WEST LANCASTER AVENUE, HAVERFORD, PA 19041 • ADMISSIONS: 610-896-1350 • FAX: 610-896-1338

STUDENTS SAY

Academics

Any fitting description of academic life at Haverford College should start with "two words: honor code!" Here "Students are allowed a great deal of freedom and self-governance," and the "honor code holds the students responsible for their learning, and trusts them to have both concern and respect for their fellow students. That is why our school has both unscheduled and unproctored final exams." As one student puts it, "The success of the institution is dependent upon a body of students who are actively concerned and engaged." Equally concerned and engaged are members of the faculty: "Despite the fact that professors here do incredible research and publish regularly, it is evident that they have come to Haverford to teach. Students are their first priority, and they absolutely make themselves available to discuss anything." In the classroom, professors "are funny and interesting, and lead very good discussions. Class discussions even run overtime every so often, and the students voluntarily stay late to continue the discussions." "If you take one small step toward a Haverford professor," attests one student, "that professor will take a giant leap toward you. Our professors like teaching students and developing personal relationships with us." Like professors here, the administration also draws almost exclusively rave reviews: "Only at a school like Haverford would we have something called 'First Thursdays,' where the entire student community is invited to have an open-forum discussion with the president. Even he makes time for student opinions." Proximity to other great colleges means that Haverford students also have the "opportunity to take classes at Bryn Mawr, Swarthmore, or Penn."

Life

Haverford is "a place where people like to study hard and play hard. During the week students are very hardworking, but on the weekends we like to let our hair down and enjoy ourselves, [by] going into Philly, watching an a cappella group perform, or hanging out with friends. We know how to keep ourselves happy. Since we do not have any Greek life, everyone is part of the social life on campus." Another notes, "The lack of Greek life (which goes against the inclusive nature of Haverford's Quaker roots) on campus is a really strong point." Indeed, "Clubs and organizations are always sponsoring events, like dinners, dances, and parties. The hardest thing to do on weekends is to decide what your plans are for the night." Parties on campus "are open to everyone, and "While many students drink," undergrads say, "it is not necessary to do so to have a good time." If you want to stay in, that's okay, too; Haverford's small size means that "everyone knows everyone else by sophomore year, so it's not like you'll really meet anyone new by going out."

Student Body

Undergrads frequently use the term "closet nerd" to describe their peers. One student defines the term as "someone who is very smart and works very hard but also pursues other interests and has fun." Someone who is "a bit awkward," but "often athletic in some way." Another student sums up Haverfordians in this way: "The typical Haverford student is friendly but not bubbly, self-motivated but not obsessive, smart but not obnoxious, slightly eccentric but not truly weird, nerdy but not socially hopeless. We mill around the edges of the liberal arts stereotypes without quite embodying them." In his or her interactions with others, the Haverfordian is "academically honest and socially respectful, and hopes to make a real difference in the world. There's a variety of personalities, but we're all basically geeks"—"idealist geeks who want to change the world."

HAVERFORD COLLEGE

FINANCIAL AID: 610-896-1350 • E-MAIL: ADMITME@HAVERFORD.EDU • WEBSITE: WWW.HAVERFORD.EDU

ADMISSIONS

Very important factors considered include: Academic GPA, application essay, character/personal qualities, rigor of secondary school record, standardized test scores. *Important factors considered include:* Class rank, extracurricular activities, recommendation(s), talent/ability, volunteer work, work experience. *Other factors considered include:* Alumni/ae relation, first generation, geographical residence, interview, level of applicant's interest, racial/ethnic status. ACT with Writing component required. TOEFL required of all international applicants. High school diploma or equivalent is not required. *Academic units required:* 4 English, 3 math, 1 science (1 science lab), 3 foreign language, 2 social studies. *Academic units recommended:* 4 math, 2 science.

The Inside Word

Haverford's applicant pool is an impressive and competitive lot. Intellectual curiosity is paramount, and applicants are expected to keep a demanding academic schedule in high school. Additionally, the college places a high value on ethics, as evidenced by its honor code. The Admissions Office seeks students who will reflect and promote Haverford's ideals.

FINANCIAL AID

Students should submit: FAFSA, CSS/Financial Aid PROFILE, Business/Farm Supplement; Noncustodial PROFILE is required—not the Noncustodial supplement. Regular filing deadline is January 31. The Princeton Review suggests that all financial aid forms be submitted as soon as possible after January 1. *Need-based scholarships/grants offered:* Pell Grant, SEOG, state scholarships/grants, the school's own gift aid. *Loan aid offered:* FFEL Subsidized Stafford, FFEL Unsubsidized Stafford, FFEL PLUS, Federal Perkins Loan. Applicants will be notified of awards on or about April 1. Federal Work-Study Program available. Institutional employment available. Off-campus job opportunities are good.

FROM THE ADMISSIONS OFFICE

"Haverford strives to be a college in which integrity, honesty, and concern for others are dominant forces. The college does not have many formal rules; rather, it offers an opportunity for students to govern their affairs and conduct themselves with respect and concern for others. Each student is expected to adhere to the honor code as it is adopted each year by the Students' Association. Haverford's Quaker roots show most clearly in the relationship of faculty and students, in the emphasis on integrity, in the interaction of the individual and the community, and through the college's concern for the uses to which its students put their expanding knowledge. Haverford's 1,100 students represent a wide diversity of interests, backgrounds, and talents. They come from public, parochial, and independent schools across the United States, Puerto Rico, and 28 foreign countries. Students of color are an important part of the Haverford community.

"Haverford College requires that all applicants submit the results of the new three-part SAT exam or the ACT with the optional writing test. Two SAT Subject Tests are required."

SELECTIVITY

Admissions Rating	**98**
# of applicants	3,351
% of applicants accepted	26
% of acceptees attending	36
# accepting a place on wait list	312
% admitted from wait list	17
# of early decision applicants	235
% accepted early decision	42

FRESHMAN PROFILE

Range SAT Critical Reading	640–760
Range SAT Math	650–740
Minimum Paper TOEFL	600
Minimum Computer Based TOEFL	250
% graduated top 10% of class	88
% graduated top 25% of class	97
% graduated top 50% of class	100

DEADLINES

Early decision application deadline	11/15
Early decision notification	12/15
Regular application deadline	1/15
Regular notification	4/15
Nonfall registration?	no

FINANCIAL FACTS

Financial Aid Rating	**96**
Annual tuition	$33,394
Room & Board	$10,390
Books and supplies	$1,194
Required fees	$316
% frosh rec. need-based scholarship or grant aid	39
% UG rec. need-based scholarship or grant aid	40
% frosh rec. need-based self-help aid	37
% UG rec. need-based self-help aid	38
% frosh rec. any financial aid	41
% UG rec. any financial aid	42

HENDRIX COLLEGE

1600 WASHINGTON AVENUE, CONWAY, AR 72032 • ADMISSIONS: 501-450-1362 • FAX: 501-450-3843

STUDENTS SAY

Academics

"The opportunities available are amazing" at Hendrix College, a small liberal arts school near Little Rock where students here benefit from "more than enough available money for research and special projects," especially in the school's well-respected science programs. For students in the sciences as well as the humanities, Hendrix offers a wide range of choices: "It doesn't matter what you're interested in academically, you will find faculty that will amaze you and that will open your mind to things you've never imagined," explains one junior. In all areas, "The academic environment feels collaborative." Hendrix is a place "where you are challenged daily in a rigorous academic setting"; as a result, students feel prepared to undertake "serious graduate work." Students describe professors as "truly exceptional," writing that they "are extremely accessible and go out of their way to help students." "This is not a school for people to fall into the cracks," notes a sophomore. The solid alumni network is hailed as "phenomenal." One junior writes: "People who attend Hendrix really do stay connected for life." Students also praise the "very strong and plentiful financial aid packages." They worry, however, about course administrators who are plotting for the future. In the words of one international relations major, "There is a widely shared perception among students that the higher-ups have an agenda for Hendrix: to attract a wealthier, cleaner-cut brand of student to a pricier, cleaner-cut school. . . . For high school graduates in a state with shocking rates of poverty and the most financially strapped public schools in the nation, the increasing elitism of the state's premier liberal arts school cannot be a good thing."

Life

Most students agree that Hendrix is a largely self-contained community; undergrads don't spend a lot of time mixing in with either the residents of Conway or students at the town's two other schools, University of Central Arkansas and Central Baptist College. "It is not unusual not to leave campus for two or three days at a time," explains one student, and "This can lead to some serious cabin fever." Fortunately, Hendrix "always has something to offer pretty much every day of the week, from study break-type events to lectures and concerts, drive-in movie nights, etc." There are "strong focuses in the campus on music and art," as well. "You name it, we've pretty much done it." "There is no Greek system," notes a junior; but students here still keep busy. Hendrix "even has Friday Afternoon Discussions on the most interesting topics, such as 'What do your dreams really mean?' or 'Women in Modern Religious Movements.' Students are always engaged in conversations." "When the weather is nice, people often sit outside to study, chat, or toss around a Frisbee." To get "good food" (and alcohol; Hendrix is in a "dry" county), "you have to make the 30-minute drive into Little Rock." Overall, one sophomore writes, "Daily life is pretty laid-back, and we like it that way."

Student Body

A number of students write that "at Hendrix, typical is atypical." Nevertheless, a few students supplied generalizations like the following: "Most students are vegetarian, politically leftist, middle-class, interested in social justice issues, attentive, and incredibly involved. . . . It doesn't feel too homogenous though. Some students are really rich or really poor; a few (a very few) vote Republican . . . and some of us are slackers. A few of us even eat meat." Undergrads pride themselves on their tolerance; one explains, "This is the most accepting and supportive crowd I've ever been around. Here, Bush-lovers (though they are a minority) and Bush-haters respectfully debate, devout Christians and atheists room together, and heterosexuals and homosexuals are best friends." Some here see a trend developing with each incoming class: "It does seem like the student body is tending more and more towards the athletic, ballcap-wearing, woo-hoo-Spring-Break-in-Cancun, business major folks," observes one undergrad. Although a number of students write that Hendrix "could definitely be more ethnically diverse," many still characterize the atmosphere as "accepting."

ADMISSIONS

Very important factors considered include: Academic GPA, application essay, rigor of secondary school record, standardized test scores. *Important factors considered include:* Character/personal qualities, class rank, extracurricular activities, interview, recommendation(s). *Other factors considered include:* Racial/ethnic status, talent/ability, volunteer work. SAT or ACT required; TOEFL required of all international applicants. High school diploma is required, and GED is accepted. *Academic units recommended:* 4 English, 3 math, 2 science, 2 foreign language, 3 social studies.

The Inside Word

Hendrix has a small but well-qualified applicant pool. The college is a sleeper, and is an especially good bet for students with strong grades who lack the test scores usually necessary for admission to colleges on a higher level of selectivity. Look for Hendrix to get tougher as they continue to garner attention from national publications. This place has been making the lists, and it is solid.

FINANCIAL AID

Students should submit: FAFSA, state aid form. The Princeton Review suggests that all financial aid forms be submitted as soon as possible after January 1. *Need-based scholarships/grants offered:* Pell Grant, SEOG, state scholarships/grants, private scholarships, the school's own gift aid. *Loan aid offered:* FFEL Subsidized Stafford, FFEL Unsubsidized Stafford, FFEL PLUS, Federal Perkins Loan, Methodist Loan. Applicants will be notified of awards on a rolling basis beginning or about March 1. Federal Work-Study Program available. Institutional employment available. Off-campus job opportunities are good.

FROM THE ADMISSIONS OFFICE

"Hendrix students are participants, not spectators. They like to be involved, and they like to know that what they do makes a difference. Hendrix students are voting members of almost every campus committee, which gives them an important voice in college governance. They are very hands-on about their education as well. Internships, study abroad, research projects, service projects, expressive arts projects, and leadership development—these are all areas that Hendrix students find attractive. In Fall 2005, Hendrix introduced a new program that guarantees every Hendrix student will have at least three hands-on experiences selected from six categories. The program is called *Your Hendrix Odyssey: Engaging in Active Learning*. Students receive transcript credit for their Odyssey projects. The benefits of this hands-on approach to learning are so obvious that we believe every Hendrix student should have the opportunity to participate. The college is raising money to provide grants and fellowships that will help remove the economic barriers to participation in out-of-class experiences. It is an exciting time to be a Hendrix student! The Hendrix curriculum is demanding, but the environment is one of support and cooperation—not competition. Hendrix students form a close-knit, inclusive community. They build lifetime connections and close friendships, the kind of relationships that grow in a residential college where learning is a 24/7 kind of thing. It doesn't hurt that the campus is beautifully maintained and that Hendrix graduates are admitted to top graduate schools and recruited for good jobs around the world.

"Hendrix College has no preference on which test (SAT/ACT) or version (old/new) is taken, but we strongly encourage all applicants to take one of the tests during their senior year. While the Writing scores will be considered, at this point weight will be given to the Critical Reading and Math of the SAT and the required sections of the ACT."

SELECTIVITY

Admissions Rating	88
# of applicants	1,263
% of applicants accepted	85
% of acceptees attending	37
# accepting a place on wait list	23
% admitted from wait list	13

FRESHMAN PROFILE

Range SAT Critical Reading	560–690
Range SAT Math	560–660
Range ACT Composite	25–31
Minimum Paper TOEFL	550
Minimum Computer Based TOEFL	215
Average HS GPA	3.7
% graduated top 10% of class	46
% graduated top 25% of class	74
% graduated top 50% of class	95

DEADLINES

Regular application deadline	8/1
Regular notification	rolling
Nonfall registration?	yes

APPLICANTS ALSO LOOK AT AND OFTEN PREFER
Rhodes College, University of Arkansas—Fayetteville, University of Central Arkansas

AND SOMETIMES PREFER
Arkansas State University, Millsaps College, Trinity University

AND RARELY PREFER
Lambuth University, Monmouth University (NJ)

FINANCIAL FACTS

Financial Aid Rating	83
Annual tuition	$22,616
Room & Board	$6,738
Books and supplies	$900
Required fees	$300
% frosh rec. need-based scholarship or grant aid	57
% UG rec. need-based scholarship or grant aid	56
% frosh rec. need-based self-help aid	41
% UG rec. need-based self-help aid	46
% frosh rec. any financial aid	100
% UG rec. any financial aid	99

HILLSDALE COLLEGE

33 EAST COLLEGE STREET, HILLSDALE, MI 49242 • ADMISSIONS: 517-607-2327 • FAX: 517-607-2223

STUDENTS SAY

Academics

"Hillsdale is built on a vision," students at this small school "steeped in the wisdom from classical Western history" tell us. That vision involves "imparting the wisdom of the past ages" through immersion in "Greco-Roman and Judeo-Christian classics" in order to "wrestle with the difficult questions facing the contemporary world." Everyone here agrees the school is conservative, although not everyone agrees on the term's exact meaning; some see the school exclusively as "a defender of free markets, limited government, and other conservative values," while others have a more nuanced view, telling us that "we're conservative in that we reach to the past to expand the number of interlocutors in class discussion, one incarnation of the 'Great Conversation.' That, I believe, defines Hillsdale and its true academic character." Course work here is "challenging, with a strong emphasis on reading and writing." Required classes guarantee that "each student takes a class on the Constitution, Western Heritage, American Heritage, and the Great Books (*The Odyssey*, Dante's *Inferno*, *Confessions of St. Augustine*, etc.)." History, classics, sciences, and business are all considered strong majors here; "If you want to go into politics or business, this is the place for you; there is a huge network of alums and donors waiting to give you jobs," writes one student. Sums up one student, "Hillsdale caters to students dissatisfied with 'modern' education and hungry for learning steeped in the wisdom from classical Western history. The emphasis is definitely on what is old and traditional, not what is new and trendy. Hillsdale is about grasping with the ideas, ideas that are fundamental to the human experience in history."

Life

"At Hillsdale, you have to be able to create your own fun," because the school is located in "a typical, small Midwestern town surrounded by cornfields, and it's not considered the most exciting place in the world." The student body, like the town, "is very small, and therefore no one is presenting you with 50 entertainment options every night." Campus life does offer some options; Greek life is very popular, and there's also "swing dancing on Friday nights; lessons and a band are available on campus and many people attend." Undergrads also "attend theatrical or musical performances, and the arts are well supported here." There are parties, but a well-enforced dry campus policy means they must be found in off-campus houses. Hillsdale's sports program draws less interest, as it "is a significant weakness. We should not be a Division II school—we are far too small." As one student puts it, "May God have mercy on our football team, for our opponents have none." Popular road-trip destinations include Jackson, Lansing, and Ann Arbor, the last of which "is only 50 minutes away. There countless coffeehouses, book stores, restaurants, and night clubs can be found."

Student Body

"Typical students are smart and religious" at Hillsdale; they "go to church every Sunday, and his or her religious beliefs come out in how he or she speaks and acts." Students guess that "about 11 percent are homeschoolers," with many others arriving from religious prep schools. Although unified in their religious conservatism, students split on the issue of their right to party. An undergrad explains, "One group consists of overly religious, holier-than-thou people who condemn the slightest bit of socialization. The second group are the ones standing on the speakers at a frat party with a beer in their hand. There is no middle ground, and everyone is a conservative White Christian." Just about everyone here has a passion for the world of ideas; as one student puts it, "Hillsdale is only really attractive to people who enjoy learning; people who want a degree that is more than just career preparation." Another adds, "Get ready for rich conversation, where invocations or allusions to Homer, Virgil, Augustine, Aquinas, Dante, Shakespeare, Descartes, Kant, Dickens, and T. S. Eliot are frequent, and the best students become part of a rich intellectual tradition."

FINANCIAL AID: 517-437-7341 • E-MAIL: ADMISSIONS@HILLSDALE.EDU/ADMISSIONS • WEBSITE: WWW.HILLSDALE.EDU

ADMISSIONS

Very important factors considered include: Academic GPA, character/personal qualities, rigor of secondary school record, standardized test scores. *Important factors considered include:* Application essay, class rank, extracurricular activities, interview, recommendation(s), volunteer work, work experience. *Other factors considered include:* Alumni/ae relation, level of applicant's interest, talent/ability. SAT or ACT required; TOEFL required of all international applicants. High school diploma is required, and GED is accepted. *Academic units recommended:* 4 English, 4 math, 3 science (1 science lab), 2 foreign language, 1 social studies, 2 history.

Inside Word

Don't let Hillsdale's high acceptance rate fool you: at this point, the only folks who apply to this school are serious, solid candidates. As the school's national reputation grows, expect the number of applications to tick upward. While you don't have to be a political conservative to get in, a passionate and well-reasoned personal essay defending conservative values certainly can't hurt you.

FINANCIAL AID

Students should submit: FAFSA, Institution's own financial aid form, Noncustodial PROFILE, Business/Farm Supplement. The Princeton Review suggests that all financial aid forms be submitted as soon as possible after January 1. *Need-based scholarships/grants offered:* State scholarships/grants, private scholarships, the school's own gift aid. *Loan aid offered:* College/university loans from institutional funds. Applicants will be notified of awards on or about April 1. Institutional employment available. Off-campus job opportunities are good.

FROM THE ADMISSIONS OFFICE

"Personal attention is a hallmark at Hillsdale. Small classes are combined with teaching professors who make their students a priority. The academic environment at Hillsdale will actively engage you as a student. Extracurricular activities abound at Hillsdale with the over 50 clubs and organizations that offer excellent leadership opportunities. From athletics and the fine arts, to Greek life and community volunteer programs, you will find it difficult not to be involved in our thriving campus community. In addition, numerous study abroad programs, a conservation research venture in South Africa, a professional sales internship program with national placements and the Washington-Hillsdale Internship Program (WHIP) are just a few of the unique off-campus opportunities available to you at Hillsdale.

"Our strength as a college is found in our mission and in our curriculum. The core curriculum at Hillsdale contains the essence of the classical liberal arts education. Through it you are introduced to the history, the philosophical and theological ideas, the works of literature, and the scientific discoveries that set Western Civilization apart. As explained in our mission statement, 'The college considers itself a trustee of modern man's intellectual and spiritual inheritance from the Judeo-Christian faith and Greco-Roman culture, a heritage finding its clearest expression in the American experiment of self-government under law.'

"We seek students who are ambitious, intellectually curious and who are ready to become leaders worthy of this heritage in their personal as well as professional lives.

"Applicants for Fall of 2008 can meet admissions requirements by submitting the results of one of three tests: the new SAT, the old SAT (taken prior to March 2005), or the ACT (Writing section optional). We will use the student's best composite/combined score in the evaluation process. The SAT Subject Tests in Literature and U.S. History are recommended."

SELECTIVITY

Admissions Rating	90
# of applicants	1,240
% of applicants accepted	75
% of acceptees attending	44
# accepting a place on wait list	25
% admitted from wait list	8
# of early decision applicants	40
% accepted early decision	88

FRESHMAN PROFILE

Range SAT Critical Reading	640–710
Range SAT Math	580–660
Range ACT Composite	24–30
Minimum Paper TOEFL	570
Minimum Computer Based TOEFL	210
Average HS GPA	3.66
% graduated top 10% of class	43
% graduated top 25% of class	73
% graduated top 50% of class	97

DEADLINES

Early decision application deadline	11/15
Early decision notification	12/1
Regular application deadline	2/15
Regular notification	12/1, 1/20, 4/1
Nonfall registration?	yes

FINANCIAL FACTS

Financial Aid Rating	85
Annual tuition	$17,850
Room & Board	$7,030
Books and supplies	$850
Required fees	$410
% frosh rec. need-based scholarship or grant aid	51
% UG rec. need-based scholarship or grant aid	40
% frosh rec. need-based self-help aid	51
% UG rec. need-based self-help aid	40
% frosh rec. any financial aid	83
% UG rec. any financial aid	86

HIRAM COLLEGE

PO BOX 67, HIRAM, OH 44234 • ADMISSIONS: 800-362-5280 • FAX: 330-569-5944

CAMPUS LIFE

Quality of Life Rating	**73**
Fire Safety Rating	**60***
Type of school	private
Affiliation	Disciples of Christ
Environment	rural

STUDENTS

Total undergrad enrollment	1,060
% male/female	44/56
% from out of state	17
% from public high school	86
% live on campus	86
# of fraternities	3
# of sororities	3
% African American	8
% Asian	1
% Caucasian	64
% Hispanic	1
% international	3
# of countries represented	17

SURVEY SAYS . . .

Small classes
Athletic facilities are great
Students are friendly
Low cost of living
Lots of beer drinking

ACADEMICS

Academic Rating	**84**
Calendar	12-3-12-3 Hiram plan
Student/faculty ratio	12:1
Profs interesting rating	84
Profs accessible rating	84
% profs teaching	
UG courses	100
% classes taught by TAs	0
Most common	
lab size	10–19 students
Most common	
reg class size	fewer than 10 students

MOST POPULAR MAJORS

business/commerce
education

STUDENTS SAY

Academics

Students at Hiram don't shy away from discussing what most feel to be the best part of the academic experience at their school: the professors. "They genuinely care about their students—I've even had a home-cooked meal at a professor's house," gushes one. According to another, Hiram is a "loving community where students and faculty are encouraged to talk to each other." With a great student/faculty ratio, the average class size is small, which allows professors to "push you to your full potential while guiding you carefully along the way" and "speak to you as equals." Readily available professors "will stop whatever they're doing to help you out" and students find plenty of opportunities to conduct personalized research projects. Most complaints can be traced back to the administration's recent belt-tightening: "Just because we are a small school does not justify the cutting of our tennis and track teams and other programs," asserts a sophomore. A more upbeat undergrad counters that the school "want[s] to have a personal touch with every student, and may sometimes sacrifice other things for that, but it's mostly a good thing." Most students swear that the school as a whole lives by its motto of "intimate learning and global reach," citing strong science programs, a great study-abroad program, and the opportunity to "grow academically inside the classroom and socially outside of it."

Life

Located in small-town Ohio, Hiram strikes more than a few students as being "in the middle of nowhere." Some, however, cite the "quaint" and remote location as a plus, allowing them to make closer friends. Social life at Hiram largely revolves around "improvised activities" and a typical roster of events includes "intramural sports, playing music, intercollegiate sports, hanging out, watching movies, and going to bars." A student-run coffee shop and a swanky new $12.3 million fitness center are also popular on-campus draws. In addition, "Campus groups do a pretty good job of bringing fun things to campus"; student organizations are also big: "You can get involved in as many things as you want, and most people do." Students are "constantly going from one thing to another—this is a Hiram trademark." As far as off-campus life goes, "Having a car gives one a huge advantage, as there are plenty of cities and towns in reasonable driving distance." It also extends one's culinary options beyond on-campus fare.

Student Body

"There is no "typical" Hiram student," says one junior, speaking for most undergraduates. "This is because of the small student body and the many varieties that make [that] body up. Different types of people interact with each other everyday." Nearly all are "outgoing and love to have fun, but able to balance a social life with all of their academic rigors. All students seem to fit in on campus; there is something for everyone here." The "diverse" student body seems to exist in enviable harmony, with "easygoing" and "open-minded" being common descriptors. Of course, "Like on any campus you have those kids who party a lot and do not care about school," but undergrads are quick to point out that many students at Hiram "study all the time." Regardless of what side of the spectrum they fall on, everyone here is friendly: "Our campus is like a little community, everybody knows everybody and they are always willing to help."

HIRAM COLLEGE

Financial Aid: 330-569-5107 • E-mail: admission@hiram.edu • Website: www.hiram.edu

ADMISSIONS

Very important factors considered include: Academic GPA, rigor of secondary school record. *Important factors considered include:* Character/personal qualities, extracurricular activities, standardized test scores, talent/ability. *Other factors considered include:* Alumni/ae relation, application essay, class rank, interview, racial/ethnic status, recommendation(s), volunteer work, work experience. SAT or ACT required; TOEFL required of all international applicants. High school diploma is required, and GED is accepted. *Academic units required:* 4 English, 3 math, 3 science (2 science labs), 2 foreign language, 3 social studies, 1 history, 2 academic electives. *Academic units recommended:* 4 math, 3 lab science, 3 foreign language.

The Inside Word

Applicants to Hiram can breathe easy. As the high admission rate indicates, students who enroll in a challenging, college-prep curriculum and produce satisfactory grades should not find it too difficult to gain acceptance. Admission is rolling, and students are admitted on a space-available basis. Therefore, it is in each candidate's best interest to apply early.

FINANCIAL AID

The Princeton Review suggests that all financial aid forms be submitted as soon as possible after January 1.

FROM THE ADMISSIONS OFFICE

"Hiram College offers several distinctive programs that set us apart from other small, private liberal arts colleges. Over half of Hiram's students participate in our nationally recognized study abroad program at some point during their four years here. In 2001–2002, Hiram faculty lead trips to England, France, Costa Rica, Pakistan, Greece, and Turkey; in 2002–2003, we visited Australia, Germany, Denmark, Zimbabwe, Israel, Guatemala, and Mexico. Because Hiram students receive credits for the courses taught by faculty on these trips, studying abroad will not impede progress in their majors or delay graduation. Another unique aspect of a Hiram education is our academic calendar, known as the Hiram Plan. Our semesters are divided into 12-week and 3-week periods. Students usually enroll in three courses during each 12-week period, and one intensive course during the 3-week periods. Many students spend the 3-week periods on study abroad trips or taking unusual courses not typically offered during the 12-week periods. In addition to numerous study abroad options and the Hiram Plan, our small classes (the average class size is 15) encourage interaction between students and their professors, both in and out of the classroom. Students can work with professors on original research projects and often participate in musical groups and intramural sports teams alongside faculty members.

"For Fall 2008 admission, Hiram College will accept either the new SAT or the old SAT administered prior to March 2005 without a Writing component. The school will also accept the ACT with or without the Writing component."

SELECTIVITY
Admissions Rating	77
# of applicants	832
% of applicants accepted	85
% of acceptees attending	30

FRESHMAN PROFILE
Range SAT Critical Reading	480–630
Range SAT Math	490–620
Range ACT Composite	20–26
Minimum Paper TOEFL	550
Average HS GPA	3.4
% graduated top 10% of class	24
% graduated top 25% of class	52
% graduated top 50% of class	83

DEADLINES
Regular application deadline	4/15
Regular notification	rolling
Nonfall registration?	yes

APPLICANTS ALSO LOOK AT
AND OFTEN PREFER
Denison University, Kenyon College
AND SOMETIMES PREFER
The College of Wooster, Ohio Wesleyan University
AND RARELY PREFER
Mount Union College, The University of Akron

FINANCIAL FACTS
Financial Aid Rating	60*
Annual tuition	$23,510
Room & Board	$7,580
Books and supplies	$700
Required fees	$670

HOBART AND WILLIAM SMITH COLLEGES

629 SOUTH MAIN STREET, GENEVA, NY 14456 • ADMISSIONS: 315-781-3472 • FAX: 315-781-3471

CAMPUS LIFE

Quality of Life Rating	73
Fire Safety Rating	60*
Type of school	private
Environment	village

STUDENTS

Total undergrad enrollment	1,855
% male/female	46/54
% from out of state	55
% from public high school	65
% live on campus	90
% in (# of) fraternities	15 (5)
% African American	4
% Asian	2
% Caucasian	88
% Hispanic	4
% international	2
# of countries represented	18

SURVEY SAYS . . .

Small classes
Great computer facilities
Great library
Everyone loves the Statesmen
Lots of beer drinking
Hard liquor is popular
Athletic facilities are great

ACADEMICS

Academic Rating	88
Calendar	semester
Student/faculty ratio	11:1
Profs interesting rating	86
Profs accessible rating	83
% profs teaching	
UG courses	100
% classes taught by TAs	0
Most common	
reg class size	10–19 students

MOST POPULAR MAJORS

economics
English language and literature
history

STUDENTS SAY

Academics

The Hobart and William Smith Colleges (HWS), a pair of associated single-sex colleges that share a campus, faculty, and administration, is known primarily for its "top-notch" study abroad program, "great internships," and "an emphasis on interdisciplinary courses, majors, and minors." Students appreciate that the school is "about growing intellectually and emotionally" thanks to the "small, personal classes" that "require student involvement." This intimate setting offers "great professors and a great community for learning." One student explains, "The professors and administrators stand out so much here because of two things: Easy access and looking out for student interests." Accordingly, instructors who "provide both liberal and conservative viewpoints and encourage you to think outside of the box"——receive high grades from their students. Undergraduates especially praise their accessibility; one student says, "Teachers have met with me outside their office hours and been at school for extra help sessions as late as 10:00 P.M. because students still had questions." As is sometimes the case when a number of schools are housed under one roof, "bureaucratic organization among the administrations of separate offices on campus" can be "frustrating." However, most students accept this in light of the close, caring instruction. One science student explains, "HWS is very supportive of work done off campus. I personally have done research at a different, larger university."

Life

Students report that while classes at HWS "are challenging, there are plenty of opportunities to give you a breather" since "for the most part life at HWS is a lot of fun." There's plenty to do as "Weekends run the gamut from frat parties to house parties, to going downtown, or just taking it easy, hanging with friends." Because "Athletic programs are top-notch," one scene revolves around sports; at least a few students say they're too busy studying and practicing to do much else. Another scene focuses on the "many organizations here that are easy to get involved with, and every organization is eager to have help." There's also the orbit of the "Student Life Office that coordinates many events on campus" such as "Day of Service and the speakers at the Fisher Center of President's Forum." The largest scene of all, however, is the party scene. HWS kids "have parties in their rooms or they go out together to the frats, which always have parties. The downtown bars are very popular too." However, there has been a gradual "crackdown" on these more raucous times. Some students mention that "the frats rarely have parties now, there are much stricter policies." The campus "is absolutely beautiful, especially in the warm weather." Hometown Geneva is "a small town with very few good restaurants and places to hang out. Many of us like to take weekend trips to Ithaca, Rochester, and Syracuse."

Student Body

The Hobart and William Smith student has a reputation as "a preppy, popped collar type kid," however, most insist that "once you see past that you realize that there really isn't a typical student, and while the stereotype has some basis in truth, it doesn't tell the whole story." One student explains, "There are so many different people with unique personalities, and once you take your concentration away from the negative and become open to people, you realize that the majority of students are really nice." Many note that "the typical student is interested in engaging in the world around them" and "those students who don't fit the 'normal' mold are accepted pretty openly since we all as a whole tend to be open to, and excited by, new or different ideas." One student describes the various ways everyone spends free time: "There are students here that go to class and do their work and chill at night. Then there are those students that get involved, set up new clubs, compete in athletics, and organize study groups. All students on this campus [can] find a group/club for them to get involved with and easily fit in."

FINANCIAL AID: 315-781-3315 • E-MAIL: ADMISSIONS@HWS.EDU • WEBSITE: WWW.HWS.EDU

ADMISSIONS

Very important factors considered include: Rigor of secondary school record. *Important factors considered include:* Academic GPA, application essay, character/personal qualities, class rank, extracurricular activities, recommendation(s), standardized test scores, volunteer work, work experience. *Other factors considered include:* Alumni/ae relation, first generation, geographical residence, interview, level of applicant's interest, racial/ethnic status, talent/ability. SAT or ACT required; ACT with Writing component required. TOEFL required of all international applicants. High school diploma is required, and GED is accepted. *Academic units required:* 4 English, 3 math, 3 science (2 science labs), 2 foreign language, 2 social studies, 2 history, 2 academic electives. *Academic units recommended:* 3 foreign language, 3 social studies, 4 academic electives.

The Inside Word

Applicants to the academic side of Seneca Lake's scenic shore should know that HSW likes to see a student who embraces a challenge. They recommend that hopefuls prepare themselves for a rigorous college curriculum by taking at least two years of a foreign language and a couple of AP courses for good measure. Some good news for people who don't like tests: HSW doesn't require standardized test scores.

FINANCIAL AID

Students should submit: FAFSA, CSS/Financial Aid PROFILE, state aid form, Noncustodial PROFILE, parent's and student's Federal Income Tax Returns. Regular filing deadline is February 1. The Princeton Review suggests that all financial aid forms be submitted as soon as possible after January 1. *Need-based scholarships/grants offered:* Pell Grant, SEOG, state scholarships/grants, private scholarships, the school's own gift aid. *Loan aid offered:* FFEL Subsidized Stafford, FFEL Unsubsidized Stafford, FFEL PLUS, Federal Perkins Loan. Applicants will be notified of awards on or about April 1. Federal Work-Study Program available. Institutional employment available. Off-campus job opportunities are good.

FROM THE ADMISSIONS OFFICE

"Hobart and William Smith Colleges seek students with a sense of adventure and a commitment to the life of the mind. Inside the classroom, students find the academic climate to be rigorous, with a faculty that is deeply involved in teaching and working with them. Outside, they discover a supportive community that helps to cultivate a balance and hopes to foster an integration among academics, extracurricular activities, and social life. Hobart and William Smith, as coordinate colleges, have an awareness of gender differences and equality and are committed to respect and a celebration of diversity.

"Freshman applicants for Fall 2008 class are required to take either the ACT (old or new, with or without the optional Writing portion) or either version of the SAT. Their highest composite score will be used in admissions decisions. Students are encouraged to submit results of any SAT Subject Test they have taken."

SELECTIVITY

Admissions Rating	88
# of applicants	3,410
% of applicants accepted	65
% of acceptees attending	25
# accepting a place on wait list	194
% admitted from wait list	16

FRESHMAN PROFILE

Range SAT Critical Reading	530–640
Range SAT Math	540–630
Range ACT Composite	24–27
Minimum Paper TOEFL	550
Minimum Computer Based TOEFL	220
Average HS GPA	3.22
% graduated top 10% of class	33
% graduated top 25% of class	67
% graduated top 50% of class	95

DEADLINES

Early decision application deadline	11/15
Early decision notification	12/15
Regular application deadline	2/1
Regular notification	4/1
Nonfall registration?	no

APPLICANTS ALSO LOOK AT

AND OFTEN PREFER
Colgate University, Connecticut College, Trinity College (CT)

AND SOMETIMES PREFER
Dickinson College, Gettysburg College, Kenyon College, Skidmore College, St. Lawrence University

AND RARELY PREFER
Ithaca College, State University of New York at Geneseo, University of Rochester, University of Vermont

FINANCIAL FACTS

Financial Aid Rating	91
Annual tuition	$31,850
Room & Board	$8,386
Books and supplies	$850
Required fees	$887
% frosh rec. need-based scholarship or grant aid	58
% UG rec. need-based scholarship or grant aid	60
% frosh rec. need-based self-help aid	48
% UG rec. need-based self-help aid	53
% frosh rec. any financial aid	74
% UG rec. any financial aid	64

HOFSTRA UNIVERSITY

ADMISSIONS CENTER, BERNON HALL, HEMPSTEAD, NY 11549 • ADMISSIONS: 516-463-6700 • FAX: 516-463-5100

CAMPUS LIFE
Quality of Life Rating	**62**
Fire Safety Rating	**98**
Type of school	private
Environment	city

STUDENTS
Total undergrad enrollment	8,383
% male/female	47/53
% from out of state	32
% live on campus	47
% in (# of) fraternities	6 (18)
% in (# of) sororities	7 (14)
% African American	10
% Asian	5
% Caucasian	61
% Hispanic	8
% international	2
# of countries represented	67

SURVEY SAYS . . .
Small classes
Great computer facilities
Great library
Frats and sororities dominate
social scene
Lots of beer drinking
Hard liquor is popular
(Almost) everyone smokes

ACADEMICS
Academic Rating	**77**
Calendar	4-1-4
Student/faculty ratio	14:1
Profs interesting rating	73
Profs accessible rating	70
% profs teaching UG courses	84
% classes taught by TAs	0
Most common lab size	10–19 students
Most common reg class size	10–19 students

MOST POPULAR MAJORS
accounting
marketing/marketing management
psychology

STUDENTS SAY

Academics

To experience "Long Island in a nutshell," consider Hofstra University, a school that "is dedicated to preparing its students for successful careers." Nearly one-third of the student body are business majors; Hofstra's "great finance program" benefits from "the number-one college Financial Trading Room in the country," while the marketing program supports the Hofstra American Marketing Cub, "which won 'Business Club of the Year.'" Hofstra is also "a great place for accounting majors." Students tell us that the Communications Department is "amazing," with "a state-of-the art radio station" that "offers a large variety of ways to get involved, whether it's having a show or being behind the scenes." It also plays "a large variety of music," from "rap to rock to Irish." Hofstra's education program is also highly regarded, boasting "one of the best music education programs in the country." In all areas, students laud "real-world experience on real-world equipment" and great opportunities for internships. In fact, "There are more internships available than there are people, so we are always informed of new opportunities in our majors as they emerge. Our location [relative] to the city presents many summer and winter internships in Manhattan, especially for communications and business majors." Hofstra is a big university, meaning students can't wait for someone to tell them what to do; one student writes, "If you want to get something done, you definitely can't wait for it to happen. You have to put yourself out there and meet with teachers and join clubs."

Life

Those who live on or near campus tell us that "there is plenty to do here, but you have to have a car to really do it, [because] walking in the area isn't that safe." There are a "ton of malls, movie theaters, and restaurants right around campus." Hofstra "is known as a bar school," and students have many venues to choose from in Hempstead and "cute little surrounding towns" like Mineola and Garden City. On campus, "Interest in [intercollegiate] athletics has grown dramatically"; even so, "It sometimes gets a little dead here on the weekends because a lot of people go home" (the phrase "commuter campus" is often brought up). But enthusiasts say this just forces students "to be more creative" when it comes to finding fun. "With Manhattan only 45 minutes away via the Long Island Railroad," lots of "people also go into New York City for fun, whether it is to shop, see shows, or go to nightclubs." Hofstra makes it easy for students to take regular trips into the city, offering a "free bus from campus that takes students to the train station."

Student Body

Long Island is a pretty diverse place, and Hofstra University reflects that diversity reasonably well. One student writes, "My first roommate was a White Orthodox Jew, very serious about school; my second set of roommates were White Greek and Italian Christians, loud partiers who played beer pong every night," and "my third roommate is White, Catholic, and gay," and "is the nicest person I know." Undergrads tell us that "there are two types of students at Hofstra University: The kind that work hard, study and succeed, and the other kind who carelessly roll into class 25 minutes late (if they even go at all) with their Chanel sunglasses and Ugg boots, talking on their cell phones to their friends about their fabulous night out." The latter group is sometimes referred to derisively as "the Long Island kids," and some students describe them as "materialistic" and "apathetic" about school. While there might be lot of "stereotypical Long Island kids" on campus, the school also has "a large minority population," and "It's not hard to find someone here who is interested in the same things you are."

HOFSTRA UNIVERSITY

FINANCIAL AID: 516-463-6680 • E-MAIL: ADMITME@HOFSTRA.EDU • WEBSITE: WWW.HOFSTRA.EDU

ADMISSIONS

Very important factors considered include: Academic GPA, application essay, class rank, recommendation(s), rigor of secondary school record, standardized test scores. *Important factors considered include:* Character/personal qualities, extracurricular activities, interview, talent/ability. *Other factors considered include:* Alumni/ae relation, geographical residence, level of applicant's interest, racial/ethnic status, volunteer work, work experience. SAT Subject Tests recommended, ACT with Writing component required. TOEFL required of all international applicants. High school diploma is required, and GED is accepted. *Academic units required:* 4 English, 3 math, 3 science (1 science lab), 2 foreign language, 3 social studies. *Academic units recommended:* 4 math, 4 science (2 science lab), 3 foreign language, 4 social studies.

The Inside Word

This is not your father's Hofstra; the school reports that admission requirements have grown tougher over the years. Average GPAs and standardized test scores of admitted students have gone up, and this has been accompanied by a rise in rejection rates among applicants. Expect an especially thorough review if you indicate communications as your intended field of study.

FINANCIAL AID

Students should submit: FAFSA, state aid form. The Princeton Review suggests that all financial aid forms be submitted as soon as possible after January 1. *Need-based scholarships/grants offered:* Pell Grant, SEOG, state scholarships/grants, private scholarships, the school's own gift aid. *Loan aid offered:* FFEL Subsidized Stafford, FFEL Unsubsidized Stafford, FFEL PLUS, Federal Perkins Loan. Applicants will be notified of awards on a rolling basis beginning or about March 15. Federal Work-Study Program available. Institutional employment available. Off-campus job opportunities are excellent.

FROM THE ADMISSIONS OFFICE

"Hofstra University is a nationally recognized university, that offers all the benefits of a traditional college experience, including challenging academic programs with small classes, faculty devoted to teaching, and a vibrant campus life. Hofstra enrolls students from almost every state and 67 foreign countries. Our students have the opportunity to choose from about 140 undergraduate and 150 graduate programs in arts and sciences, business, communications, education and allied human services, and honors studies. A distinctive aspect of the Hofstra experience is our focus on teaching. All of our classes are taught by faculty who are devoted to working with undergraduate students. On our faculty are recipients of top academic honors including Emmy Award winners, National Endowment for the Humanities fellows, Guggenheim fellows, a Pulitzer Prize winner, and major grant recipients. Thanks to a student/faculty ratio of 14:1 and average class size of 25, students work closely with their professors.

"Complementing the classroom experience is the incomparable resource of New York City, just 25 miles from our beautiful campus. Our students make full use of the city for internships and as a social and cultural outlet.

"Students applying for admission for Fall 2008 may submit either the new SAT or the ACT for consideration. Students submitting the ACT will be required to complete the Writing component. Hofstra University will require a writing sample as part of its admission requirements for freshmen in 2007."

SELECTIVITY

Admissions Rating	84
# of applicants	13,493
% of applicants accepted	62
% of acceptees attending	21
# accepting a place on wait list	111

FRESHMAN PROFILE

Range SAT Critical Reading	530–620
Range SAT Math	550–630
Range ACT Composite	22–26
Minimum Paper TOEFL	550
Minimum Computer Based TOEFL	213
Average HS GPA	3.26
% graduated top 10% of class	23
% graduated top 25% of class	46
% graduated top 50% of class	80

DEADLINES

Regular notification	rolling
Nonfall registration?	yes

APPLICANTS ALSO LOOK AT

AND OFTEN PREFER
Boston University, Fordham University, New York University, Syracuse University

AND SOMETIMES PREFER
Ithaca College, St. John's University, State University of New York—Stony Brook University, Temple University

AND RARELY PREFER
Adelphi University, Long Island University—C.W. Post, University of Hartford

FINANCIAL FACTS

Financial Aid Rating	64
Annual tuition	$23,800
Room & Board	$9,800
Books and supplies	$1,000
Required fees	$1,030
% frosh rec. need-based scholarship or grant aid	54
% UG rec. need-based scholarship or grant aid	49
% frosh rec. need-based self-help aid	51
% UG rec. need-based self-help aid	48
% frosh rec. any financial aid	90
% UG rec. any financial aid	83

HOLLINS UNIVERSITY

PO Box 9707, Roanoke, VA 24020-1707 • Admissions: 540-362-6401 • Fax: 540-362-6218

STUDENTS SAY

Academics

According to its students, the two greatest strengths of Hollins University are its small size and its all-women demographic. "The combination allows for a much more comfortable atmosphere because [you] don't have to impress guys, and it is much more intimate, so you know everyone and are comfortable talking to people and speaking up in class." This small western Virginia school boasts plenty of other assets as well, including "a strong and well-known internship program" used by over 80 percent of the student body. During the school's January term, the program places students in plum positions with the likes of the London *Times*, the Bronx Zoo, Amnesty International, the Centers for Disease Control, and the Metropolitan Museum of Art. The study abroad program, enjoyed by nearly 50 percent of all undergrads, is another winner; the school sponsors programs in Paris and London and accommodates student requests for learning opportunities in such varied locales as Seville; Kyoto, Japan; Legon, Ghana; Cork, Ireland; and Athens. Hollins "is mainly known for the arts," with strong departments in English, writing, dance, psychology, and communication studies. The sciences are reportedly excellent too; one premed writes, "Small class sizes, small labs, and one-on-one instruction from professors are an advantage in the sciences, and we learn how to incorporate other aspects of life into medicine, psychology, chemistry, and biology. The resources are wonderful, and the department works to give each science major the resources she needs for research and learning."

Life

Hollins is justly famous for its equestrian team, which has placed among the nation's top 10 11 times since 1993. The school competes in six other varsity sports, with nearly one-quarter of the student body participating; many other students take advantage of the Hollins Outdoor Program, which organizes whitewater rafting, hiking, caving, and rock climbing excursions. The school is also famous for its many traditions, including a truly odd event known as Tinker Day, "some unknown day in October after the first frost. Before the actual day, seniors go through the residence hall banging on pots and pans (called 'Tinker Scares'). On the actual day, classes are canceled, we eat Krispy Kremes, and then we dress up in wacky costumes and hike Tinker Mountain. Up there we sing songs to our fellow classes and perform skits before having a yummy meal of fried chicken and chocolate Tinker Cake!" The Student Activities Board "offers a lot of fun things throughout each month, such as music groups, speakers, game nights, karaoke night, comedians," but otherwise "The campus is generally pretty quiet, although we have some good parties every now and then." Some tell us that "Hollins is generally considered a suitcase school," but others report that "while some underclassmen leave on weekends, many upperclassmen stay. There is a special bond between girls at Hollins that many students choose to embrace, and we enjoy spending time with one another." Many students travel to other schools, such as Virginia Tech, for weekend parties.

Student Body

"The majority of students are classified as either pearl girls or riders," Hollins women tell us. "Pearl girls are the girls who wear a strand of pearls and pearl earrings every day to class, even if they are wearing their pj's. Riders are girls who horseback ride almost every day, and many have their own horse on campus." But they're far from the only two groups on campus, students are quick to add. "The next most common stereotype would be the writers, those who want to write for a living. Then there are the NEFA (Near East Fine Arts) girls that are your bards and artists. And then there's everybody else, who just find their own little niche somewhere in between, or carve out their own place." Hollins hosts "a strong lesbian minority, and they are treated with respect." The typical student "is politically moderate to liberal, although there are a growing number of conservatives speaking out."

FINANCIAL AID: 540-362-6332 • E-MAIL: HUADM@HOLLINS.EDU • WEBSITE: WWW.HOLLINS.EDU

ADMISSIONS

Very important factors considered include: Academic GPA, level of applicant's interest, standardized test scores. *Important factors considered include:* Application essay, recommendation(s), talent/ability. *Other factors considered include:* Alumni/ae relation, character/personal qualities, class rank, extracurricular activities, first generation, interview, racial/ethnic status, rigor of secondary school record, volunteer work, work experience. SAT or ACT required; TOEFL required of all international applicants. High school diploma is required, and GED is accepted. *Academic units required:* 4 English, 3 math, 3 science, 3 foreign language, 3 social studies.

The Inside Word

Only candidates who overtly display their lack of compatibility with the Hollins milieu are likely to encounter difficulty in gaining admission. A high level of self-selection and its weak-but-improving freshman profile allow most candidates to relax.

FINANCIAL AID

Students should submit: FAFSA, state aid form. The Princeton Review suggests that all financial aid forms be submitted as soon as possible after January 1. *Need-based scholarships/grants offered:* Pell Grant, SEOG, state scholarships/grants, private scholarships, the school's own gift aid. *Loan aid offered:* Direct Subsidized Stafford, Direct Unsubsidized Stafford, Direct PLUS, Federal Perkins Loan, Campus Door, CitiAssist, Nelnet, PLATO, Sallie Mae, college/university loans from institutional funds. Applicants will be notified of awards on or about March 1.

FROM THE ADMISSIONS OFFICE

"Hollins University's slogan, 'Women who are going places start at Hollins,' endures because it captures what this independent liberal arts institution means to its students. Hollins has been a motivating force for women to go places creatively, intellectually, and geographically since it was founded over 160 years ago. As Hollins graduate and Pulitzer Prize–winner Annie Dillard said, Hollins is a place 'where friendships thrive, minds catch fire, careers begin, and hearts open to a world of possibility.' "

"Hollins offers majors in 29 fields. While perhaps best known for its creative writing discipline, the university features strong programs in the visual and performing arts (especially dance) and the social and physical sciences. Hollins also has an innovative general education program called Education Through Skills and Perspectives (ESP). In ESP, students acquire knowledge across the curriculum. One of the most sought-after programs at Hollins is the Batten Leadership Institute, a comprehensive curricular program designed to maximize each student's leadership style and potential and teach her skills she will use both now and in the future. It is the only program of its kind in the nation.

"Hollins was among the first colleges in the nation to offer an international study abroad program. Today, almost half of Hollins' students—many times the national average—study abroad. Internship opportunities are another of Hollins' distinctions. Thanks to an active, dedicated network of alumnae and friends of the university, more than 80 percent of Hollins students put their education to work with a diverse group of organizations.

"Hollins' slogan underscores the most important question each student is asked from the moment she arrives until the day she leaves, and it is asked by her professors, her peers, and especially by herself: 'Where do you want to go?'

"Currently, students applying for admission can submit scores from either the old or new version of the SAT, and Hollins will use the best scores from either test."

SELECTIVITY

Admissions Rating	**82**
# of applicants	651
% of applicants accepted	84
% of acceptees attending	35
# accepting a place on wait list	12
% admitted from wait list	50
# of early decision applicants	38
% accepted early decision	76

FRESHMAN PROFILE

Range SAT Critical Reading	500–670
Range SAT Math	470–600
Range SAT Writing	490–620
Range ACT Composite	21–28
Minimum Paper TOEFL	550
Minimum Computer Based TOEFL	213
Average HS GPA	3.5
% graduated top 10% of class	28
% graduated top 25% of class	56
% graduated top 50% of class	86

DEADLINES

Early decision application deadline	12/1
Early decision notification	12/15
Regular notification	rolling
Nonfall registration?	yes

FINANCIAL FACTS

Financial Aid Rating	**77**
Annual tuition	$25,110
Room & Board	$9,140
Books and supplies	$800
Required fees	$535
% frosh rec. need-based scholarship or grant aid	71
% UG rec. need-based scholarship or grant aid	79
% frosh rec. need-based self-help aid	58
% UG rec. need-based self-help aid	62
% frosh rec. any financial aid	97
% UG rec. any financial aid	93

HOWARD UNIVERSITY

2400 SIXTH STREET NORTHWEST, WASHINGTON, DC 20059 • ADMISSIONS: 202-806-2700 • FAX: 202-806-4462

CAMPUS LIFE
Quality of Life Rating	**66**
Fire Safety Rating	**60***
Type of school	private
Environment	metropolis

STUDENTS
Total undergrad enrollment	7,309
% male/female	33/67
% from out of state	77
% from public high school	80
% live on campus	58
% in (# of) fraternities	2 (10)
% in (# of) sororities	1 (8)
% African American	84
% Asian	1
% Hispanic	1
% international	7
# of countries represented	88

SURVEY SAYS . . .
Small classes
Students are happy
Frats and sororities dominate social scene
Musical organizations are popular
Student publications are popular
Student government is popular

ACADEMICS
Academic Rating	**82**
Calendar	semester
Student/faculty ratio	8:1
Profs interesting rating	65
Profs accessible rating	64
% profs teaching UG courses	64
Most common lab size	10–19 students
Most common reg class size	fewer than 10 students

MOST POPULAR MAJORS
biology/biological sciences
journalism
radio and television

STUDENTS SAY

Academics

A school with "a rich legacy" that "continues to produce successful leaders," Howard produces more on-campus PhDs than any other university in the world. Howard University is truly "one of the nation's most prestigious Historically Black Universities." The history is worth noting; the parade of impressive Howard graduates includes Nobel Prize–winning author Toni Morrison and former UN ambassador and civil rights activist Andrew Young. So, too, is the present; Howard is well-regarded for its "excellent biology program" and other premed majors, as well as for communications and business. With its outstanding reputation, Howard "attracts big companies that come looking for strong Black students to employ, which makes it slightly easier for us as Blacks to find jobs in today's market." One undergrad observes, "We profit from an incredible amount of networking with large and prominent companies." Students also benefit from the school's location in DC, "a city where there are an unlimited number of resources open to students." Undergrads report that "academics at Howard are unparalleled; professors are masters of their skills, and the students are not here to play around but to actually learn and earn their education." The school's famously bureaucratic administration remains true to its reputation; "Anything dealing with administration and Student Services tends to be long and unnecessarily tedious," students warn. They also caution that "the facilities definitely need upgrading."

Life

"During the week, most people's main priority is their classes" at Howard, "but weekends are a time to [take a] break." "There is always something to do in Washington, DC," including "going to eat in exotic restaurants, watching movies, going to museums, and visiting other colleges and universities in the area." The school is "located literally in the middle of Washington, DC. It sits on top of a large hill (a rarity in the area), giving us a view of the city's landmarks." The surrounding neighborhood "was once considered the Black Georgetown, the side of town for wealthy Black intellectuals who were affiliated with Howard. They built large, fashionable row houses. . . . The area turned into a ghetto, though, when people began to move into the newer suburbs out of the city. Within the last few years, the neighborhood has been revitalized, and people are buying and fixing the abandoned mansions and row houses. It's still somewhat dangerous, especially at night, but it is coming around. It's wonderful to witness the growth of this neighborhood (with my school's help)." On campus there is "a wide array of student organizations available. There is something for everybody, and we have people from all types of cultural and socioeconomic backgrounds." Many involve community service, as "The students are aware of the struggles faced by minorities, and many study to make a difference in the lives of the disadvantaged. Many students take part in volunteer programs such as elementary tutoring." There's also "Greek life, parties, choirs, the arts, our great school newspaper, mock trials, student government, you name it." Homecoming, we're assured, "is a very big event every year, with lots of celebrities."

Student Body

The "outgoing, fashionable, confident" undergrads of Howard are "predominantly Black," but "This doesn't mean we are all African American. Besides coming from all over the United States, we come from Africa, Trinidad, Jamaica, Haiti, and everywhere else." Americans contribute mightily to the geographic diversity, since "Black people are not all the same, in case you didn't know. Black students from New Orleans act completely differently from Black students from New York, etc. Howard is one big melting pot of Black culture, and I love that!" Most here "came from a high school where they were probably popular, were class presidents or held some sort of leadership role in some student activity, and think they can take over the world." One student adds, "We are definitely leaders by nature. As different as we are, we all think that we can and will be the best at something. We all have a drive that cannot be taught, just developed."

FINANCIAL AID: 202-806-2800 • E-MAIL: ADMISSION@HOWARD.EDU • WEBSITE: WWW.HOWARD.EDU

ADMISSIONS

Very important factors considered include: Class rank, rigor of secondary school record, standardized test scores. *Important factors considered include:* Character/personal qualities, recommendation(s). *Other factors considered include:* Alumni/ae relation, application essay, extracurricular activities, talent/ability, volunteer work, work experience. SAT or ACT required; TOEFL required of all international applicants. High school diploma is required, and GED is accepted. *Academic units required:* 4 English, 2 math, 2 science, 2 foreign language, 2 social studies, 2 history. *Academic units recommended:* 4 English, 3 math, 4 science (2 science labs), 2 foreign language, 2 social studies, 2 history, 4 academic electives.

The Inside Word

A large applicant pool and solid yield of acceptees who enroll is a combination that adds up to selectivity for Howard. Pay strict attention to the formula.

FINANCIAL AID

Students should submit: FAFSA. Regular filing deadline is August 15. The Princeton Review suggests that all financial aid forms be submitted as soon as possible after January 1. *Need-based scholarships/grants offered:* Pell Grant, SEOG, state scholarships/grants, private scholarships, the school's own gift aid, Federal Nursing Scholarship. *Loan aid offered:* Direct Subsidized Stafford, Direct PLUS, FFEL Subsidized Stafford, FFEL Unsubsidized Stafford, FFEL PLUS, Federal Perkins Loan, Federal Nursing Loan, state loans, college/university loans from institutional funds. Applicants will be notified of awards on or about April 1.

FROM THE ADMISSIONS OFFICE

"Since its founding, Howard has stood among the few institutions of higher learning where African Americans and other minorities have participated freely in a truly comprehensive university experience. Thus, Howard has assumed a special responsibility to prepare its students to exercise leadership wherever their interest and commitments take them. Howard has issued approximately 99,318 degrees, diplomas, and certificates to men and women in the professions, the arts and sciences, and the humanities. The university has produced and continues to produce a high percentage of the nation's African American professionals in the fields of medicine, dentistry, pharmacy, engineering, nursing, architecture, religion, law, music, social work, education, and business. There are more than 8,906 students from across the nation and approximately 85 countries and territories attending the university. Their varied customs, cultures, ideas, and interests contribute to Howard's international character and vitality. More than 1,598 faculty members represent the largest concentration of African American scholars in any single institution of higher education.

"Beginning with the entering class of Fall 2008 all applicants who have never been to college will be required to submit scores from either the new SAT or the ACT (with the Writing component)."

SELECTIVITY

Admissions Rating	88
# of applicants	8,661
% of applicants accepted	48
% of acceptees attending	37

FRESHMAN PROFILE

Range SAT Critical Reading	460–690
Range SAT Math	460–680
Range ACT Composite	20–29
Minimum Paper TOEFL	550
Minimum Computer Based TOEFL	213
Average HS GPA	3.2
% graduated top 10% of class	24
% graduated top 25% of class	53
% graduated top 50% of class	84

DEADLINES

Regular application deadline	2/15
Regular notification	rolling
Nonfall registration?	yes

APPLICANTS ALSO LOOK AT

AND OFTEN PREFER
Hampton University, Morehouse College, Spelman College

AND SOMETIMES PREFER
Florida A&M University, The George Washington University, University of Maryland—College Park

AND RARELY PREFER
Morgan State University

FINANCIAL FACTS

Financial Aid Rating	66
Annual tuition	$12,180
Room & Board	$6,522
Books and supplies	$1,300
Required fees	$805
% frosh rec. need-based scholarship or grant aid	64
% UG rec. need-based scholarship or grant aid	32
% frosh rec. need-based self-help aid	17
% UG rec. need-based self-help aid	28
% frosh rec. any financial aid	82
% UG rec. any financial aid	74

ILLINOIS INSTITUTE OF TECHNOLOGY

10 WEST THIRTY-THIRD STREET, CHICAGO, IL 60616 • ADMISSIONS: 312-567-3025 • FAX: 312-567-6939

STUDENTS SAY
Academics
Illinois Institute of Technology "is all about the demanding work and promised payoffs" students report, warning that "the IIT experience is focused on the career afterwards. There is very little pizzazz about the atmosphere (it was designed by Mies van der Rohe, after all) and virtually no social life, unless you can relate to all of the other geeks who either stare at their computers in their rooms or just sit and chat about academics." Not that you'd have time for much of a social life here anyway, since "Classes are difficult and lots of studying is required. If you got straight A's in high school, expect to work hard to get B's and C's." The various Engineering Departments are, of course, a major strength here; civil engineering "is definitely one of the best departments in the school," while the biomedical, electrical, and mechanical engineering programs also earn students' accolades, with "an emphasis on practicality" across the board. The computer science program "is run like a well-oiled machine." IIT is also renowned for its architecture program, which students tell us is "incredible, and quite influential on the Chicago scene." Students in all disciplines benefit from "a small-school environment" that promotes "personal attention" and allows the professors to "get to know you." "For instance, I can walk into my department chair office or my professor's office whenever and they know me personally." Professors "are really accommodating" and explain the material to you "when you have a problem," although whether you'll understand them is another question entirely. "Professors in certain classes may barely speak English, or may be awesome teachers, it varies greatly,"—and sometimes, they're both.

Life
In the past, IIT has earned a reputation for having a dreary extracurricular life; the situation has improved somewhat, as "The school has put forth a great effort and a vast amount of money to create a school-sponsored program every single weekend. This practice started last year, and the school has kept up with it. Whether it's a movie night, a dance, or a comedy act we have at least one thing every weekend, [and] this has improved IIT." Of course, some students "would rather sit in their room and play computer games than socialize" in their free time, but at least the options are expanding, and more students are taking advantage of them. IIT's frat scene "offers numerous chances for social activities from sports to parties and community service," we're told; for many, joining "makes life a lot more enjoyable." Others leave campus whenever they can spare the time away; ITT is only "five miles south of downtown Chicago," a city that "provides a good playground" with "a lot of things to do." For good cheap eats, "Chinatown is just one stop down" on the El.

Student Body
IIT has "plenty of typical math and science students," meaning "many nerds" and more than a few "students who like their computers more than seems humanly possible and whose only human contact occurs when they make a weekly trip to the cafeteria or their biweekly trip to the shower." There are also "many atypical students, enough so that they can form or join a club or group that fits their own personality," and their numbers appear to be growing as a result of "significant outreach by students groups and more social incoming classes." The international population is substantial, with many students from "India, China, and Korea." While "Not everyone talks to each other," "When they do talk, they learn a lot about [each] other's culture." Undergrads tend to be stressed out, "the kind of people who feel guilty when they have no work to do for a day." A lopsided male/female ratio means there are "barely any women on campus."

FINANCIAL AID: 312-567-7219 • E-MAIL: ADMISSION@IIT.EDU • WEBSITE: WWW.IIT.EDU

ADMISSIONS

Very important factors considered include: Academic GPA, standardized test scores. *Important factors considered include:* Application essay, recommendation(s). *Other factors considered include:* Alumni/ae relation, character/personal qualities, class rank, extracurricular activities, interview, rigor of secondary school record, talent/ability, volunteer work, work experience. SAT or ACT required; TOEFL required of all international applicants. High school diploma is required, and GED is not accepted. *Academic units required:* 4 English, 4 math, 3 science (2 science labs), 2 social studies, 2 history. *Academic units recommended:* 4 English, 4 math, 3 science (2 science labs), 2 social studies, 2 history.

The Inside Word

Students at IIT say it's "easy to get in, tough to get out," but the term "easy" is relative in this case; easy in comparison to MIT or CalTech, perhaps, but not in comparison to the vast majority of undergraduate institutions. IIT's high acceptance rate is deceptive; few bother to apply here unless they suspect they can handle the demanding curriculum, meaning only the extremely bright and/or extremely ambitious actually do.

FINANCIAL AID

Students should submit: FAFSA. The Princeton Review suggests that all financial aid forms be submitted as soon as possible after January 1. *Need-based scholarships/grants offered:* Pell Grant, SEOG, state scholarships/grants, private scholarships, the school's own gift aid. *Loan aid offered:* FFEL Subsidized Stafford, FFEL Unsubsidized Stafford, FFEL PLUS, Federal Perkins Loan, college/university loans from institutional funds. Applicants will be notified of awards on a rolling basis beginning or about March 1.

FROM THE ADMISSIONS OFFICE

"IIT is committed to providing students with the highest-caliber education through dedicated teachers, small class sizes, and undergraduate research opportunities. Classes are taught by senior faculty—not teaching assistants—who bring firsthand research experience into daily class discussion. The university's diverse student population mirrors the global work environment faced by all graduates. IIT promotes a unique interdisciplinary approach to learning. Students experience team-based, creative problem solving through two required Interprofessional Projects (IPROs). Our entrepreneurship program challenges students to develop start-up technology companies. The Leadership Academy teaches leadership skills that advance students in their personal and professional development. IIT's location in one of the nation's great cities affords many opportunities for internships and employment. The new, visually enticing McCormick Tribune Campus Center and ultra-modern State Street Village residence halls provide exciting living and campus opportunities that are sure to create a positive student experience for years to come.

"Students applying for admission into the Fall 2008 entering class are required to submit an SAT or ACT score (old and new test versions accepted). We will use the student's best scores from either test. Subject tests are accepted, but not required."

SELECTIVITY

Admissions Rating	91
# of applicants	4,966
% of applicants accepted	54
% of acceptees attending	18

FRESHMAN PROFILE

Range SAT Critical Reading	550–660
Range SAT Math	640–710
Range ACT Composite	25–30
Minimum Paper TOEFL	550
Minimum Computer Based TOEFL	213
Average HS GPA	3.89
% graduated top 10% of class	36
% graduated top 25% of class	71
% graduated top 50% of class	96

DEADLINES

Regular notification	rolling
Nonfall registration?	yes

APPLICANTS ALSO LOOK AT
AND OFTEN PREFER
Case Western Reserve University, Northwestern University, University of Illinois at Urbana-Champaign, University of Michigan—Ann Arbor, Washington University in St. Louis
AND SOMETIMES PREFER
DePaul University, Iowa State University, Marquette University, Milwaukee School of Engineering, University of Wisconsin—Madison
AND RARELY PREFER
Loyola University—Chicago, Northern Illinois University, Purdue University—West Lafayette, Rose-Hulman Institute of Technology, University of Minnesota—Twin Cities

FINANCIAL FACTS

Financial Aid Rating	77
Annual tuition	$24,962
Room & Board	$8,618
Books and supplies	$1,000
% frosh rec. need-based scholarship or grant aid	72
% UG rec. need-based scholarship or grant aid	58
% frosh rec. need-based self-help aid	52
% UG rec. need-based self-help aid	46
% frosh rec. any financial aid	100
% UG rec. any financial aid	92

ILLINOIS WESLEYAN UNIVERSITY

PO Box 2900, BLOOMINGTON, IL 61702-2900 • ADMISSIONS: 309-556-3031 • FAX: 309-556-3820

STUDENTS SAY

Academics

Illinois Wesleyan University, "a small liberal arts school that will give you lots of personal attention," is "the right size, small enough that you feel comfortable walking around because you always see familiar faces wherever you go, but also big enough where you don't know everybody and you can find your own niche." The school strives to "create a personal educational experience with professors, classmates, and staff"; it's the kind of place where professors "make themselves available to read essay drafts, offer career advice, and write letters of recommendation on top of giving great lectures." IWU excels in such diverse areas as biology (the school "has a great reputation in the sciences"), nursing, English, psychology, theater, and music ("extremely competitive," but much more liberal arts–oriented than "conservatory-like"). "The school encourages exploring multiple interests, and double majors and dual degrees are pursued by many students." One student writes, "Right now, I'm a business major with a philosophy minor, and I'm making up my own minor between the Music and Physics Department in electroacoustic music, and I'm still going to graduate in 4 years." You can really "make your degree yours" here. Students on track for graduate study love "the high acceptance rates into grad school" IWU enjoys in many programs, and everyone appreciates the school's May Term, which "gives you a really great option to take inventive, unique classes or travel abroad."

Life

IWU is located in Bloomington-Normal, which "certainly isn't Chicago" but is still a "great place to live with so much to do." While some kids from the Chicago area complain about the location, telling us that "it's not very exciting," those from elsewhere are more generous in their assessments, observing that "it's better than a suburb. Both Bloomington and Normal have downtown areas with quaint boutiques next to new bars and eateries, and the recent boom in the Latino and East Asian populations have provided excellent cuisine options!" With well over one-quarter of the student body involved in Greek life, "Frats and sororities play a large part in social activities" of the campus. Illinois State University is "just down the street," offering another party alternative "to those who want to escape the IWU bubble." The Student Activities Office "brings awesome entertainment to our campus on the weekends like concerts, movies, [and] comedians," and since they are covered by the student activity fee, there is "no charge to the student," though they are usually "over pretty early." IWU has numerous intercollegiate teams, but "Basketball is the only main sports attraction. Very few students actually attend football games or other sporting events." Wesleyan dormitories "are amazing. The majority of students live on campus all 4 years because of all the great living options."

Student Body

IWU draws heavily from the affluent suburbs of Chicago, attracting a student body that "is White," and "somewhat wealthy" although "There are many who do not fit this mold." Most "have very diverse interests, sometimes even majors that you never thought would be possible: music and science, foreign language and pre-professional science, and so on. Furthermore, they are usually involved in a diverse number of extracurricular activities: sports, clubs, organizations, etc." Students tell us that everyone here is "pretty easy-going, though if one is a bio or chem major, studying is constantly on the mind due to the amount needed to be memorized," though for many, "a long week of paper-writing and test taking is rewarded with a few long nights of debauchery." IWU also has a fair number of international students; one woman writes, "My floor alone has girls from Nigeria, Germany, and Bangladesh and there are other girls of Asian, Indian, and African descent as well."

ILLINOIS WESLEYAN UNIVERSITY

FINANCIAL AID: 309-556-3096 • E-MAIL: IWUADMIT@TITAN.IWU.EDU • WEBSITE: WWW.IWU.EDU

ADMISSIONS

Very important factors considered include: Academic GPA, interview, rigor of secondary school record. *Important factors considered include:* Application essay, character/personal qualities, class rank, extracurricular activities, standardized test scores, talent/ability. *Other factors considered include:* Alumni/ae relation, first generation, geographical residence, level of applicant's interest, racial/ethnic status, recommendation(s), state residency, volunteer work, work experience. SAT or ACT required; TOEFL required of all international applicants. High school diploma is required, and GED is accepted. *Academic units recommended:* 4 English, 3 math, 3 science (2 science labs), 3 foreign language, 2 social studies.

The Inside Word

There's no application fee at IWU and the school accepts the Common Application (with the IWU Common Application Supplement, which asks for your intended major and an essay explaining your reasons for wanting to attend IWU), so there are few reasons not to apply to IWU if you're at all interested in the school. Don't expect to breeze through, though; you won't get in here without a solid academic profile or a compelling story.

FINANCIAL AID

Students should submit: Institution's own financial aid form or CSS/Financial Aid PROFILE (either is accepted). Regular filing deadline is March 1. The Princeton Review suggests that all financial aid forms be submitted as soon as possible after January 1. *Need-based scholarships/grants offered:* Pell Grant, SEOG, state scholarships/grants, private scholarships, the school's own gift aid. *Loan aid offered:* FFEL Subsidized Stafford, FFEL Unsubsidized Stafford, FFEL PLUS, Federal Perkins Loan, Federal Nursing Loan, college/university loans from institutional funds. Applicants will be notified of awards on a rolling basis beginning or about February 15. Federal Work-Study Program available. Institutional employment available. Off-campus job opportunities are good.

FROM THE ADMISSIONS OFFICE

"Illinois Wesleyan University attracts a wide variety of students who are interested in pursuing diverse fields such as vocal performance, biology, psychology, German, physics, or business administration. At IWU, students are not forced into either/or choices. Rather, they are encouraged to pursue multiple interests simultaneously—a philosophy that is in keeping with the spirit and value of a liberal arts education. The distinctive 4-4-1 calendar allows students to follow their interests each school year in two semesters followed by an optional month-long class in May. May term opportunities include classes on campus; research collaboration with faculty; travel and study in such places as Australia, China, South Africa, and Europe; as well as local, national, and international internships.

"The IWU mission statement reads in part: 'A liberal education at Illinois Wesleyan fosters creativity, critical thinking, effective communication, strength of character, and a spirit of inquiry; it deepens the specialized knowledge of a discipline with a comprehensive world view. It affords the greatest possibilities for realizing individual potential while preparing students for democratic citizenship and life in a global society.... The university, through its policies, programs, and practices, is committed to diversity, social justice, and environmental sustainability. A tightly knit, supportive university community, together with a variety of opportunities for close interaction with excellent faculty, both challenges and supports students in their personal and intellectual development.

"Freshman applicants for Fall 2008 may submit scores from either the old or new SAT exams. For the ACT, students may submit scores with or without the Writing section."

SELECTIVITY

Admissions Rating	89
# of applicants	3,156
% of applicants accepted	52
% of acceptees attending	34
# accepting a place on wait list	83
% admitted from wait list	43

FRESHMAN PROFILE

Range SAT Critical Reading	580–680
Range SAT Math	580–680
Range ACT Composite	26–30
Minimum Paper TOEFL	550
Minimum Computer Based TOEFL	213
% graduated top 10% of class	46
% graduated top 25% of class	82
% graduated top 50% of class	98

DEADLINES

Regular notification	rolling
Nonfall registration?	yes

APPLICANTS ALSO LOOK AT
AND OFTEN PREFER
Northwestern University, University of Notre Dame
AND SOMETIMES PREFER
University of Illinois at Urbana-Champaign, Washington University in St. Louis
AND RARELY PREFER
Augustana College (IL), Marquette University

FINANCIAL FACTS

Financial Aid Rating	84
Annual tuition	$30,580
Room & Board	$7,030
Books and supplies	$780
Required fees	$170
% frosh rec. need-based scholarship or grant aid	61
% UG rec. need-based scholarship or grant aid	56
% frosh rec. need-based self-help aid	50
% UG rec. need-based self-help aid	46
% frosh rec. any financial aid	90
% UG rec. any financial aid	88

INDIANA UNIVERSITY—BLOOMINGTON

300 NORTH JORDAN AVENUE, BLOOMINGTON, IN 47405-1106 • ADMISSIONS: 812-855-0661 • FAX: 812-855-5102

CAMPUS LIFE
Quality of Life Rating	**90**
Fire Safety Rating	**60***
Type of school	public
Environment	town

STUDENTS
Total undergrad enrollment	29,258
% male/female	48/52
% from out of state	30
% live on campus	36
% African American	5
% Asian	4
% Caucasian	84
% Hispanic	2
% international	4
# of countries represented	132

SURVEY SAYS . . .
Student publications are popular
Students are happy
Hard liquor is popular
Everyone loves the Hoosiers
Great computer facilities

ACADEMICS
Academic Rating	**76**
Calendar	semester
Student/faculty ratio	18:1
Profs interesting rating	76
Profs accessible rating	79
% profs teaching	
UG courses	46
Most common	
lab size	20–29 students
Most common	
reg class size	10–19 students

MOST POPULAR MAJORS
accounting and finance
biology/biological sciences
marketing/marketing management

STUDENTS SAY
Academics
"Perhaps our greatest strength, which some people tend to see as a weakness, is our size," writes an observant IU undergraduate who points to "the sheer magnitude of available majors and minors, organizations to join, and annual activities. It's mind-boggling. The benefit of a big school is that it can accommodate so many different interests, and can even accommodate changes in personal interest." Students caution that "since IU is such a big school, it's up to you to get as good or as bad an education as you would like. You can load up on BS classes like human sexuality (which everyone seems to take eventually) or take really hard classes that challenge you to think." A great education can certainly be found here, especially in the school's nationally renowned business and music programs; education, journalism, and the hard sciences are also reportedly strong, with the latter benefiting from "great opportunities to research with some world-famous scientists." Undergrads across disciplines praise "smaller class sizes than you would expect," professors who "are easy to get along with and accessible," and an "extraordinary honors college." As is the case at many large universities, the administration gets mixed reviews. Some more forgiving students attribute bureaucratic headaches to the growing pains associated with the school recently going onto the PeopleSoft system, while other more splenetic types say simply that "logic has no place in the IU administration."

Life
"Bloomington is a perfect college town, and it is absolutely beautiful," students agree, pointing out also that "the school interacts with the town as well as any campus in the country. Bloomington has to be one of the best college towns, and the town is based around the university, not the other way around like the big city schools (i.e., NYU, BU, BC, UCLA)." Add the "sheer beauty of the campus" and you begin to understand why students feel so at home in Bloomington. Then consider the other perks of life at IU: for instance, the "famed Hoosier basketball team," whose popularity "makes Indiana tickets the hardest to get in the country. They cannot keep up with the alumni and student season ticket requests and, therefore, are unable to sell single-game tickets." Students want you to know that "support is also strong for soccer, swimming, volleyball, football, and baseball." Consider also the "wild party scene," which students generally love; one explains, "With 30-something-thousand students going to IU, at least half of them are out partying on the weekend, so you can always find something wild, crazy, and drunken to do!" Best of all is the Little 500—"the greatest college weekend in the world," students claim—a bike race that "requires standing-room-only viewing from the thousands of students, faculty, and fans who come to watch the 30-plus teams compete. They train year-round to win the event, riding thousands of miles just for the chance to win." The town of Bloomington itself offers "different types of entertainment in music, theater, and the arts," as well as a number of student-oriented eateries.

Student Body
"The thing about going to a big school is that there is a wide variety of kinds of people here," IU students enthusiastically explain. "We have frat and sorority snobs, pot-smoking hippies, library nerds, D-1 athletes, gays and lesbians, musicians, and so on. Basically, you will find a group to fit in with at IU." Undergrads arrive "from different states, different countries, and different social and economic backgrounds. Everyone seems to get along pretty well, despite their differences." Many here "are athletic and involved—working out is like a second major for some people—and extracurriculars are huge." While a lot of students "are very grade-focused and only want to learn enough to pass the test," there are also "a lot of serious students, too. They just don't stick out as much, or they look like the other kids and party as much as [they do], but take their work seriously as well."

FINANCIAL AID: 812-855-0321 • E-MAIL: IUADMIT@INDIANA.EDU • WEBSITE: WWW.IUB.EDU

ADMISSIONS

Very important factors considered include: Academic GPA, class rank, rigor of secondary school record. *Important factors considered include:* Standardized test scores. *Other factors considered include:* Alumni/ae relation, application essay, character/personal qualities, extracurricular activities, first generation, geographical residence, interview, level of applicant's interest, racial/ethnic status, recommendation(s), state residency, talent/ability. SAT or ACT required; SAT Subject Tests recommended, ACT with Writing component required. High school diploma is required, and GED is accepted. *Academic units required:* 4 English, 3 math, 1 science (1 science lab), 2 social studies, 4 academic electives, *Academic units recommended:* 4 math, 3 science, 3 foreign language, 3 social studies.

The Inside Word

A high volume of applicants makes Indiana's individual admissions review process relatively selective for a university of its size. Candidates to the School of Music face a highly selective audition process.

FINANCIAL AID

Students should submit: FAFSA. The Princeton Review suggests that all financial aid forms be submitted as soon as possible after January 1. *Need-based scholarships/grants offered:* Pell Grant, SEOG, state scholarships/grants, private scholarships, the school's own gift aid. *Loan aid offered:* FFELP Subsidized Stafford, FFELP Unsubsidized Stafford, FFELP PLUS, Federal Perkins Loan, Federal Nursing Loan, college/university loans from institutional funds. Applicants will be notified of awards on or about March 10. Off-campus job opportunities are good.

FROM THE ADMISSIONS OFFICE

"Indiana University—Bloomington, one of America's great teaching and research universities, extends learning and teaching beyond the walls of the traditional classroom. When visiting campus, students and parents typically describe IU as 'what a college should look and feel like.' Students bring their diverse experiences, beliefs, and backgrounds from all 50 states and 132 countries, which adds a richness and diversity to life at IU—a campus often cited as one of the most beautiful in the nation. Indiana University—Bloomington truly offers a quintessential college town, campus, and overall experience. Students enjoy all of the advantages, opportunities, and resources that a larger school can offer, while still receiving personal attention and support. For the third year in a row, *U.S. News & World Report* has recognized IU—Bloomington for the range of programs offered to help freshmen succeed. Because of the variety of outstanding academic and cultural resources, students at IU have the best of both worlds.

"Indiana offers more than 5,000 courses and more than 100 undergraduate programs, of which many are known nationally and internationally. IU—Bloomington is known worldwide for outstanding programs in the arts, sciences, humanities, and social sciences as well as for highly rated Schools of Business, Music, Education, Journalism, Optometry; Public and Environmental Affairs; and Health, Physical Education, and Recreation. Students can customize academic programs with double and individualized majors, internships, and research opportunities, while utilizing state-of-the-art technology. Representatives from more than 1,000 businesses, government agencies, and not-for-profit organizations come to campus each year to recruit IU students.

"IUB requires the new version of the SAT with writing and/or the ACT with writing. The university will use the writing sections to determine possible credit, placement or exemption from writing requirements. We encourage, but do not require, SAT Subject Tests."

SELECTIVITY

Admissions Rating	83
# of applicants	24,169
% of applicants accepted	80
% of acceptees attending	38

FRESHMAN PROFILE

Range SAT Critical Reading	490–610
Range SAT Math	510–630
Range ACT Composite	22–27
Average HS GPA	3.5
% graduated top 10% of class	27
% graduated top 25% of class	61
% graduated top 50% of class	95

DEADLINES

Nonfall registration?	yes

APPLICANTS ALSO LOOK AT

AND OFTEN PREFER
University of Illinois at Urbana-Champaign, University of Michigan—Ann Arbor

AND SOMETIMES PREFER
Miami University, Purdue University—West Lafayette, University of Wisconsin—Madison

FINANCIAL FACTS

Financial Aid Rating	65
Annual in-state tuition	$5,507
Annual out-of-state tuition	$18,498
Room & Board	$6,352
Books and supplies	$740
Required fees	$803
% frosh rec. need-based scholarship or grant aid	19
% UG rec. need-based scholarship or grant aid	19
% frosh rec. need-based self-help aid	31
% UG rec. need-based self-help aid	31

INDIANA UNIVERSITY OF PENNSYLVANIA

216 PRATT HALL, INDIANA, PA 15705 • ADMISSIONS: 724-357-2230 • FAX: 724-357-6281

CAMPUS LIFE

Quality of Life Rating	67
Fire Safety Rating	88
Type of school	public
Environment	village

STUDENTS

Total undergrad enrollment	11,976
% male/female	45/55
% from out of state	4
% from public high school	95
% live on campus	31
# of fraternities	18
# of sororities	14
% African American	9
% Asian	1
% Caucasian	79
% Hispanic	1
% international	1
# of countries represented	73

SURVEY SAYS . . .

Small classes
Frats and sororities dominate social scene
Student publications are popular
Lots of beer drinking
Hard liquor is popular
(Almost) everyone smokes

ACADEMICS

Academic Rating	65
Calendar	semester
Student/faculty ratio	16:1
Profs interesting rating	76
Profs accessible rating	76
% profs teaching UG courses	100
% classes taught by TAs	0
Most common lab size	fewer than 10 students
Most common reg class size	20–29 students

MOST POPULAR MAJORS

communications studies/speech communication and rhetoric
criminology
elementary education and teaching

STUDENTS SAY

Academics

Named not for the state, but for the actual town in which the school is located, Indiana University of Pennsylvania (IUP) is "academically challenging but not impossible if you make an honest effort." Students enjoy "awesome professors" who are "concerned with their welfare and academic growth," and find their teachers "ridiculously easy to get into contact with—no need to make an appointment." Thanks to "strong educators" and "small class sizes" students are "pushed to think critically," and those who want even more of a challenge can take part in "excellent honors classes and programs." In recent years, the administration has gone through several changes, leaving some students feeling that it is "often out of touch with the real world." That said, students enjoy an "equal say in the policies that form the foundation of their education" through the Student Senate, and "can always access [the administration] when in need." While some students have experienced "scheduling problems" in certain departments, students feel, overall, that they get more for less at IUP: "Anyone attending can achieve the same education as another student at an Ivy League school" as long as "They are truly interested in learning and willing to put forth the effort."

Life

Indiana, Pennsylvania, is the kind of town John Mellencamp would sing about—small, working-class, but not without its charms or bars. As one student explains, "socializing is a large part of IUP life." Since the school is located "in a backwoods kind of area," most students "go to parties for fun," and most but "not all parties involve a keg." While many students "go to fraternities and house parties and drink" there are options available for students "who want no alcohol/drugs involved in their college life whatsoever." For non-partiers, "Life usually consists of movies and games" and "outdoor activities when the weather is nice." The school also boasts a "good selection of clubs" that provides a quick way "to meet people." While "Going to a grocery store or a mall would be much easier" if you "get a car," most students take advantage of the "free bus system" to get to town. There, students enjoy "a pool hall, two bowling alleys, a local theater that shows current, old, and foreign films," as well as "tons of restaurants and bars" and some "great coffeehouses." If you need a taste of city life, "Pittsburgh is an hour and a half away."

Student Body

According to one student, IUP is "more diverse" than the local "predominantly White area," but "less diverse than U.S. Census percentage numbers." As a "public university" the "student body is very mixed," and students have "the opportunity to interact with more people" than they would at "many other colleges," from the "very conservative" to the "extremely unique." As one student explains, "No matter what your interest is, it wouldn't be too hard to find someone that you can share this interest with." While fraternities and sororities are "popular," there is "a place for everyone" on campus. In other words, "No matter who you are, if you go to this college you are going to have a damn good time." Students view themselves as "down to earth" and adept at "balancing academics" with "social outlets." The dorms help instill "a strong feeling of community" as do the honors courses, which provide "a bonding experience without the drinking" for students.

Financial Aid: 724-357-2218 • E-mail: ADMISSIONS-INQUIRY@IUP.EDU • Website: WWW.IUP.EDU

ADMISSIONS

Very important factors considered include: Academic GPA. *Important factors considered include:* Class rank, rigor of secondary school record, standardized test scores. *Other factors considered include:* Application essay, character/personal qualities, extracurricular activities, interview, level of applicant's interest, recommendation(s), talent/ability, volunteer work, work experience. SAT or ACT required; TOEFL required of all international applicants. High school diploma is required, and GED is accepted. *Academic units recommended:* 4 English, 3 math, 3 science, 2 foreign language, 3 social studies.

The Inside Word

Indiana University of Pennsylvania offers an academic environment unique among most public universities: undergraduate classes taught solely by professors. Pennsylvania residents will find it especially worthwhile to investigate this school as it offers a solid education at an affordable price to state residents. The admissions process should not give much trouble to students with an above-average secondary school record.

FINANCIAL AID

Students should submit: FAFSA. The Princeton Review suggests that all financial aid forms be submitted as soon as possible after January 1. *Need-based scholarships/grants offered:* Pell Grant, SEOG, state scholarships/grants, private scholarships, the school's own gift aid, United Negro College Fund. *Loan aid offered:* FFEL Subsidized Stafford, FFEL Unsubsidized Stafford, FFEL PLUS, Federal Perkins Loan, private alternative loans. Applicants will be notified of awards on a rolling basis beginning or about March 15. Federal Work-Study Program available. Off-campus job opportunities are good.

FROM THE ADMISSIONS OFFICE

"At IUP, we look at each applicant as an individual, not as a number. That means we'll review your application materials very carefully. When reviewing applications, the Admissions Committee's primary focus is on the student's high school record and SAT scores. In addition, the committee often reviews the optional personal essay and letters of recommendations submitted by the student to help aid in the decision-making process. We're always happy to speak with prospective students. Call us toll-free at 800-422-6830 or 724-357-2230 or e-mail us at admissions-inquiry@iup.edu.

"Students applying for admission into the Fall 2008 entering class are required to take the new version of the SAT. Students will be allowed to submit scores from the old (prior to March 2005) version of the SAT (or ACT) as well, and we will use the student's best scores from either test."

SELECTIVITY

Admissions Rating	**75**
# of applicants	8,349
% of applicants accepted	71
% of acceptees attending	43

FRESHMAN PROFILE

Range SAT Critical Reading	430–530
Range SAT Math	430–530
Minimum Paper TOEFL	500
Minimum Computer Based TOEFL	300
% graduated top 10% of class	7
% graduated top 25% of class	22
% graduated top 50% of class	56

DEADLINES

Regular notification	rolling
Nonfall registration?	yes

APPLICANTS ALSO LOOK AT AND OFTEN PREFER

Clarion University of PA, Duquesne University, Millersville University of Pennsylvania, Pennsylvania State University—University Park, Shippensburg University of Pennsylvania, Westminster College

AND SOMETIMES PREFER

James Madison University, Kutztown University of Pennsylvania, Slippery Rock University of Pennsylvania, University of Delaware, West Virginia University

AND RARELY PREFER

Bloomsburg University of Pennsylvania, Lock Haven University of Pennsylvania, Mansfield University of Pennsylvania, Ohio University—Athens

FINANCIAL FACTS

Financial Aid Rating	**73**
Annual in-state tuition	$5,038
Annual out-of-state tuition	$12,598
Room & Board	$5,162
Books and supplies	$1,000
Required fees	$1,352
% frosh rec. need-based scholarship or grant aid	52
% UG rec. need-based scholarship or grant aid	47
% frosh rec. need-based self-help aid	62
% UG rec. need-based self-help aid	58
% frosh rec. any financial aid	81
% UG rec. any financial aid	77

IOWA STATE UNIVERSITY

100 ALUMNI HALL, AMES, IA 50011-2011 • ADMISSIONS: 515-294-5836 • FAX: 515-294-2592

STUDENTS SAY

Academics

Students tell us the academic experience is "tough but fulfilling" at Iowa State University, where "science, engineering, and technology" are all the rage. "Iowa State is a massive engineering school, and that's probably its biggest asset," explains one first-year student. ISU also boasts "one of the top agricultural universities in the nation," "a great program for landscape architecture," and a notable School of Journalism and Communication. Iowa State is also a "great school for internships," bringing big-time recruiters to career fairs. Students do say that "more classes in liberal arts" would be nice. ISU "should offer more opportunities in the humanities since they are still offered as majors at the university," gripes a junior. Like a lot of schools containing the word *state* in their names, Iowa State is really big. Professors "don't hold your hand," especially in lower-level courses that often enroll upwards of "500 people." ISU's faculty gets mixed reviews: "Sixty percent of the professors are good," estimates one student. "The rest are average." "Professors are usually very dedicated, knowledgeable, and fair," counters another. Overall, students tell us that their professors are "approachable and available for help outside class"—"You just have to ask." However, some are "very typical of the stereotypical state school": These professors are "fantastic researchers, which is why they're hired, but sometimes can't teach for their lives." The administration is seen by some students as a little bureaucratic. Otherwise, "The university seems to be running pretty smoothly."

Life

"It is easy to get involved" at ISU. "Hundreds of clubs and organizations" are "available in everything from medieval recreation, to chemistry club (ice cream and explosions), to service organizations, to major-specific professional organizations." Fraternities and sororities don't overwhelm campus life, but "There are a lot of parties," and "Drinking has to be one of the more popular activities," reports a senior. Students here usually start off the weekend by hitting the bars Thursday nights, although students contend that there are activities on campus for nondrinkers, too. Sports play a dominant role in campus life—"Getting involved in intramurals" is very common, and students are "die-hard" fans of their beloved Cyclones. Iowa State's "gorgeous" campus is full of "lots of trees and green space," though "During the winter it's a bit of a bummer to have to walk all over campus." "Most of the buildings are pretty modern"—perhaps too modern. "The campus could use a little more color," as opposed to "all the gray," says one student. The "very quaint" and "safe" surrounding town of Ames is a "typical college town" with "decent amenities and activities." When students need a change of pace, the city of Des Moines is "close enough."

Student Body

Iowa State is home to many students "from different countries and backgrounds"—including a noticeable contingent of students from Asia—who "enrich the environment" and "fit in surprisingly well." And you can find "every type of personality," "from your basic frat boy/sorority girl to goth kids to nerds" to "hick-ish" students who "grew up in very rural communities." Overall, you won't find a great deal of ethnic variation on this campus. "The typical student" here is "White, conservative," and "comes from a middle-class Midwestern family." These "basically good students" describe themselves as "very polite," "pretty well-rounded," and often religious. "There is a great sense of community here." One thing you won't see at ISU is too many high-falutin' snobs: "There are a lot of students who are paying for their education themselves and are very motivated to succeed," observes a first-year student.

IOWA STATE UNIVERSITY

FINANCIAL AID: 515-294-2223 • E-MAIL: ADMISSIONS@IASTATE.EDU • WEBSITE: WWW.IASTATE.EDU

ADMISSIONS

Very important factors considered include: Academic GPA, class rank, rigor of secondary school record, standardized test scores. *Other factors considered include:* Application essay, character/personal qualities, extracurricular activities, geographical residence, interview, recommendation(s), state residency, talent/ability, volunteer work, work experience. SAT or ACT required; TOEFL required of all international applicants. High school diploma is required, and GED is accepted. *Academic units required:* 4 English, 3 math, 3 science (2 science labs), 2 foreign language, 2 social studies. *Academic units recommended:* 4 English, 4 math, 4 science (3 science labs), 4 foreign language, 4 social studies.

The Inside Word

As is the case at many public institutions, Iowa State is fairly straightforward about its requirements. It's undeniably a numbers game, so prospective students will want to focus on grades and standardized test scores. Candidates to the College of Arts and Sciences will need an extra year of social science course work and 2 years of a single foreign language to remain competitive. Applicants who do not meet these standards need not panic: They will have an opportunity to gain acceptance after an individual review.

FINANCIAL AID

Students should submit: FAFSA. The Princeton Review suggests that all financial aid forms be submitted as soon as possible after January 1. *Need-based scholarships/grants offered:* Pell Grant, SEOG, state scholarships/grants, the school's own gift aid. *Loan aid offered:* Direct Subsidized Stafford, Direct Unsubsidized Stafford, Direct PLUS, Federal Perkins Loan, state loans, college/university loans from institutional funds, private alternative loans. Applicants will be notified of awards on a rolling basis beginning or about April 1. Off-campus job opportunities are excellent.

FROM THE ADMISSIONS OFFICE

"Iowa State University offers all the advantages of a major university along with the friendliness and warmth of a residential campus. There are more than 100 undergraduate programs of study in the Colleges of Agriculture, Business, Design, Education, Engineering, Family and Consumer Sciences, Liberal Arts and Sciences, and Veterinary Medicine. Our 1,700 faculty members include Rhodes Scholars, Fulbright Scholars, and National Academy of Sciences and National Academy of Engineering members. Recognized for its high quality of life, Iowa State has taken practical steps to make the university a place where students feel like they belong. Iowa State has been recognized for the high quality of campus life and the exemplary out-of-class experiences offered to its students. Along with a strong academic experience, students also have opportunities for further developing their leadership skills and interpersonal relationships through any of the more than 500 student organizations, 60 intramural sports, and a multitude of arts and recreational activities. All residence hall rooms are wired for Internet connections, and all students have the opportunity to create their own World Wide Web pages.

"Iowa State University will accept either the new SAT or the old SAT (administered prior to March 2005 and without a Writing component). The school will also accept the ACT with or without the Writing component."

SELECTIVITY

Admissions Rating	81
# of applicants	9,634
% of applicants accepted	90
% of acceptees attending	46

FRESHMAN PROFILE

Range SAT Critical Reading	510–640
Range SAT Math	540–690
Range ACT Composite	22–27
Minimum Paper TOEFL	500
Minimum Computer Based TOEFL	173
Average HS GPA	3.49
% graduated top 10% of class	24
% graduated top 25% of class	52
% graduated top 50% of class	92

DEADLINES

Regular application deadline	7/1
Regular notification	rolling
Nonfall registration?	yes

APPLICANTS ALSO LOOK AT

AND OFTEN PREFER
Purdue University—West Lafayette, University of Illinois at Urbana-Champaign, University of Minnesota—Twin Cities, University of Wisconsin—Madison

AND SOMETIMES PREFER
Drake University, Kansas State University, University of Nebraska—Lincoln, University of Northern Iowa

AND RARELY PREFER
Baylor University, Western Michigan University

FINANCIAL FACTS

Financial Aid Rating	80
Annual in-state tuition	$5,086
Annual out-of-state tuition	$15,580
Room & Board	$6,445
Books and supplies	$892
Required fees	$774
% frosh rec. need-based scholarship or grant aid	53
% UG rec. need-based scholarship or grant aid	53
% frosh rec. need-based self-help aid	42
% UG rec. need-based self-help aid	46
% frosh rec. any financial aid	88
% UG rec. any financial aid	79

ITHACA COLLEGE

100 JOB HALL, ITHACA, NY 14850-7020 • ADMISSIONS: 607-274-3124 • FAX: 607-274-1900

STUDENTS SAY

Academics

With a "world-recognized music school," a stellar "Communications department with amazing facilities," and "extremely strong programs in theater and physical therapy," Ithaca College stakes out a lot of high ground for a school of its size. Perhaps the school strives to achieve so much because of its formidable cross-town competition: Ithaca shares its namesake hometown with Cornell University. IC "offers a wide variety of majors [that] do a good job of opening your eyes to new ideas and the world." Business programs are popular, and many come for the "great programs in the entertainment industry. In the music school, the a cappella groups are so cool to go watch." The "fabulous" Theater Department "has a program in London for theater students and nontheater majors in theater. It's an amazing experience." The equally distinguished communications program is home to an active radio station and award-winning TV station. "Newswatch16, Ithaca College's own locally broadcasted news program won a College Emmy in the Fall of 2003 for a spectacular broadcast." In all areas, professors "are very accessible, and, because the class sizes are small, they actually know you." Teachers "love class discussions more than just lecturing, and there is always time for questions. Those who exert the extra effort to participate will generally excel more than those who sit in the shadows." At IC "You won't get lost in a sea of people, but it's large enough to offer diverse classes and lots of extracurriculars" as well as "a study abroad program that totally rocks!"

Life

"Everyone has fun on the weekends" at Ithaca College, "either through the college or through someone who is having a party. If not, you can travel 2 minutes to Cornell frats and party there, or go downtown and have tons of fun listening to music or eating out." There's "a lot of culture on and off campus—tons of music, theater, hippie stuff, political happenings." Variety reigns: "One day there's a sold-out football game; the next there's a gay pride rally or a drum circle on the quad." The weather dictates extracurricular life to some extent. "The first month or two of the fall semester, the weather is breathtaking and you get to experience all the beauty the Ithaca area has to offer. You can go hiking, cliff-jumping, camping, swimming, fishing, explore the head shops in the Commons, or just lay outside on one of the many grassy quads and relax in the sun—then the first snowstorm hits and everything changes. Your list of possible activities shortens drastically; unless you're a ski enthusiast, you're basically forced into hibernation until the last month or so of school, when the weather finally gets nice again." Intercollegiate athletics are "a big thing at IC. Even though we're only Division III, students get psyched for football games and such. Intramural and club sports are also big." But "even more people are into our musical and non-sporty exploits. If there was an NCAA thing for band and choir, we would be at the top of Division I."

Student Body

"Ithaca has several different types of 'typical' students," undergrads here tell us. "As far as groups go, there seem to be the jocks, the preps, and the hippies. But even if you don't fit into these groups, you will fit in someplace else." Besides, at IC "jocks and hippies interact much more than they would at another school." While the "majority are White, come from privilege, don't have strong religious backgrounds, and are liberal and well-informed in politics," there are also plenty "who come from very religious backgrounds and those who are conservative and/or Republican, those who are politically apathetic, a mixture of ethnic/minority students and foreign students (all of whom get along with the majority students), [and] a large gay community that seems to be generally accepted by the population. There is very little discrimination on this campus." Students see "an even spread of Protestant, Catholic, and Jewish faith students. There is even a strict 'Kosher Kitchen' in one of the campus dining halls."

FINANCIAL AID: 607-274-3131 • E-MAIL: ADMISSION@ITHACA.EDU • WEBSITE: WWW.ITHACA.EDU

ADMISSIONS

Very important factors considered include: Academic GPA, rigor of secondary school record, standardized test scores. *Important factors considered include:* Application essay, character/personal qualities, class rank, extracurricular activities, recommendation(s), talent/ability. *Other factors considered include:* Alumni/ae relation, first generation, interview, level of applicant's interest, volunteer work, work experience. SAT or ACT required; ACT with Writing component required. TOEFL required of all international applicants. High school diploma is required, and GED is accepted. *Academic units required:* 4 English, 3 math, 3 science, 2 foreign language, 3 social studies, 1 academic elective.

The Inside Word

Ithaca has enjoyed a renaissance of interest from prospective students of late, and its moderately competitive admissions profile has been bolstered as a result. In addition to a thorough review of academic accomplishments, candidates' personal background, talents, and achievements are given close consideration. Programs requiring an audition or portfolio review are among the college's most demanding for admission; the arts have always been particularly strong.

FINANCIAL AID

Students should submit: FAFSA. The Princeton Review suggests that all financial aid forms be submitted as soon as possible after January 1. *Need-based scholarships/grants offered:* Pell Grant, SEOG, state scholarships/grants, private scholarships, the school's own gift aid. *Loan aid offered:* FFEL Subsidized Stafford, FFEL Unsubsidized Stafford, FFEL PLUS, Federal Perkins Loan, alternative loans. Applicants will be notified of awards on a rolling basis beginning or about February 15.

FROM THE ADMISSIONS OFFICE

"Ithaca College was founded in 1892 as a music conservatory, and it continues that commitment to performance and excellence. Its modern, residential 750-acre campus, equipped with state-of-the-art facilities, is home to the Schools of Business, Communications, Health Sciences and Human Performance, Humanities and Sciences, and Music and our new Division of Interdisciplinary and International Studies. With more than 100 majors—from biochemistry to business administration, journalism to jazz, philosophy to physical therapy, and special programs in Washington, DC, Los Angeles, London, and Australia—students enjoy the curricular choices of a large campus in a personalized, smaller school environment. And Ithaca's students benefit from an education that emphasizes active learning, small classes, collaborative student-faculty research, and development of the whole student. Located in central New York's spectacular Finger Lakes region in what many consider the classic college town, the college has 25 highly competitive varsity teams, more than 130 campus clubs, two radio stations and a television station, as well as hundreds of concerts, recitals, and theater performances annually.

"Students applying for admission must have official scores from either the SAT or the ACT with the Writing section sent to Ithaca College by the testing agency. The college will also consider results of SAT Subject Tests, if submitted."

SELECTIVITY

Admissions Rating	**85**
# of applicants	11,312
% of applicants accepted	69
% of acceptees attending	20

FRESHMAN PROFILE

Range SAT Critical Reading	530–640
Range SAT Math	540–640
Minimum Paper TOEFL	550
Minimum Computer Based TOEFL	213
% graduated top 10% of class	32
% graduated top 25% of class	70
% graduated top 50% of class	95

DEADLINES

Regular application deadline	2/1
Regular notification	rolling
Nonfall registration?	yes

APPLICANTS ALSO LOOK AT

AND OFTEN PREFER

Boston University, Cornell University, New York University

AND SOMETIMES PREFER

Pennsylvania State University—University Park, Skidmore College, Syracuse University, Union College (NY), University of Rochester, University of Vermont

AND RARELY PREFER

State University of New York at Binghamton, State University of New York at Geneseo, University of Delaware, University of Massachusetts—Amherst

FINANCIAL FACTS

Financial Aid Rating	**81**
Annual tuition	$26,832
Room & Board	$10,314
Books and supplies	$1,005
% frosh rec. need-based scholarship or grant aid	65
% UG rec. need-based scholarship or grant aid	64
% frosh rec. need-based self-help aid	67
% UG rec. need-based self-help aid	64
% frosh rec. any financial aid	85
% UG rec. any financial aid	84

James Madison University

Sonner Hall, MSC 0101, Harrisonburg, VA 22807 • Admissions: 540-568-5681 • Fax: 540-568-3332

CAMPUS LIFE

Quality of Life Rating	**88**
Fire Safety Rating	**84**
Type of school	public
Environment	town

STUDENTS

Total undergrad enrollment	15,653
% male/female	39/61
% from out of state	30
% live on campus	37
% in (# of) fraternities	8 (12)
% in (# of) sororities	10 (8)
% African American	4
% Asian	5
% Caucasian	83
% Hispanic	2
% international	1
# of countries represented	55

SURVEY SAYS . . .

Athletic facilities are great
Students are friendly
Great food on campus
Lots of beer drinking

ACADEMICS

Academic Rating	**79**
Calendar	semester
Student/faculty ratio	16:1
Profs interesting rating	86
Profs accessible rating	85
% profs teaching UG courses	89
% classes taught by TAs	1
Most common lab size	20–29 students
Most common reg class size	20–29 students

MOST POPULAR MAJORS

liberal arts and sciences/
liberal studies
marketing/marketing management
psychology

STUDENTS SAY

Academics

Students at James Madison University, a state institution whose strengths include "a good business school" and solid health services programs, love their school's "welcoming environment, in which you feel comfortable within your surroundings, whether it is in class, one-on-one with a professor, out at a party, or sitting in your dorm room." "Almost all the students you meet are in love with this school," both for its "well-ranked academics" and for its capacity to deliver "more fun than you can have anywhere else." Undergrads here tout the school's technology-related disciplines, singling out the "unique integrated science and technology major" as an example of their school's eagerness to innovate. The Physics Department is also "exceptional," students report, "with professors who are friendly and willing to get to know you on a personal level" and a "small, research-oriented environment." In many other areas, students praise the faculty's "willingness to extend learning outside of the classroom if students have ideas for projects [and] research," and their "realistic method of teaching to prepare students for real-world job applications." Class sizes here vary widely by department; classes in disciplines with high enrollments are often overcrowded, especially at the introductory level, while students in less popular programs report that they "have very few classes with over 50 people in them."

Life

"Extracurricular activities are a definite strength" of JMU, where "There is something for everyone to get involved in. I don't know one person who is not involved with at least something or another on campus. This is not limited to fraternities or sororities, though Greek life is inviting and generally respected." Partying is big here; "We have made the top 25 party school list in *Playboy*," students brag, explaining that "it's not like we have those gigantic theme parties where half the school attends. Instead, there are just so many apartment parties and each weekend. I'd say, at least 50 on any Friday or Saturday. Thursday is also a big 'go out' day." Most here agree that "everyone is pretty balanced when it comes to work and play" and that "the attendance [at games] and strength of the athletic teams at JMU could stand to improve. No one is really interested in athletic events, nor do people really attend them, including the football games. Let's be serious: sports are a big part of the collegiate experience, and quite frankly, we have one of the most pathetic sports programs of any school with 15,000 students." Undergrads here love to work out in their spare time; the University Recreation Center (UREC) "is always packed. It is an amazing facility with tons of options for an individual or group workout. UREC also hosts many of the intramural sports that JMU students are involved in."

Student Body

The "friendly and outgoing" student body of James Madison University evinces Southern courtesy; one Yankee transplant writes, "Everyone holds the door open for you; guys are nice and girls are too. Everyone is very trusting." "Republicans dominate" this Red State campus "and will aggressively defend their values." The school "has a fairly homogeneous population." One student writes, "It isn't that people don't accept differences; it's that there just aren't any. I think people are even friendlier to those students who don't fit the mold as a way of saying, 'Hey, thank you for being different.' There is a kid in my dorm with blue hair. He is everyone's friend because they all want to be friends with the kid who has blue hair." Some point out that "each entering class appears to be more diverse." While "Most students are from middle-class Virginia suburbs," the school attracts many others from "Washington, DC, New York City, and Philadelphia."

FINANCIAL AID: 540-568-7820 • E-MAIL: GOTOJMU@JMU.EDU • WEBSITE: WWW.JMU.EDU

ADMISSIONS

Very important factors considered include: Academic GPA, rigor of secondary school record. *Important factors considered include:* Standardized test scores. *Other factors considered include:* Alumni/ae relation, application essay, character/personal qualities, class rank, extracurricular activities, geographical residence, recommendation(s), state residency, talent/ability, volunteer work, work experience. SAT or ACT required; TOEFL required of all international applicants. High school diploma is required, and GED is accepted. *Academic units required:* 4 English, 4 math, 4 science (3 science labs), 3 foreign language, 3 social studies. *Academic units recommended:* 4 English, 5 math, 4 science (4 science labs), 4 foreign language, 4 social studies.

The Inside Word

James Madison has prospered from the applications of students faced with severe competition for admission to University of Virginia and William & Mary. Third place on the Virginia public university totem pole is not a bad spot to be, as JMU's Admissions Committee will attest. Pay attention when they stress that your high school schedule should be chock-full of challenging academic courses.

FINANCIAL AID

Students should submit: FAFSA. The Princeton Review suggests that all financial aid forms be submitted as soon as possible after January 1. *Need-based scholarships/grants offered:* Pell Grant, SEOG, state scholarships/grants, private scholarships, the school's own gift aid. *Loan aid offered:* FFEL Subsidized Stafford, FFEL Unsubsidized Stafford, FFEL PLUS, Federal Perkins Loan. Applicants will be notified of awards on a rolling basis beginning or about April 1.

FROM THE ADMISSIONS OFFICE

"James Madison University's philosophy of inclusiveness—known as 'all together one'—means that students become a part of a real community that nurtures its own to learn, grow, and succeed. Our professors, many of whom have a wealth of real-world experience, pride themselves on making teaching their top priority. We take seriously the responsibility to maintain an environment that fosters learning and encourages students to excel in and out of the classroom. Our rich variety of educational, social, and extracurricular activities include more than 100 innovative and traditional undergraduate majors and programs, a well-established study abroad program, a cutting-edge information security program, more than 280 student clubs and organizations, and a 147,000-square-foot, state-of-the-art recreation center. The university's picturesque, self-contained campus is located in the heart of the Shenandoah Valley, a four-season area that's easy to call home. Great food, fun times, exciting intercollegiate athletics, and rigorous academics all combine to create the unique James Madison experience. From the library to the residence halls and from our outstanding honors program to our highly successful career placement program, the university is committed to equipping our students with the tools they need to achieve their dreams.

"The new SAT will be used starting with the freshman applicants for Fall 2008. High school students graduating in 2006 or 2007 will have the option of submitting scores from either the new or old versions of the SAT. The highest composite score will be used in admissions decisions."

SELECTIVITY

Admissions Rating	89
# of applicants	17,765
% of applicants accepted	63
% of acceptees attending	34
# accepting a place on wait list	600
% admitted from wait list	25

FRESHMAN PROFILE

Range SAT Critical Reading	520–610
Range SAT Math	530–620
Range SAT Writing	520–610
Range ACT Composite	21–26
Minimum Paper TOEFL	570
Minimum Computer Based TOEFL	230
Average HS GPA	3.69
% graduated top 10% of class	31
% graduated top 25% of class	78
% graduated top 50% of class	98

DEADLINES

Regular application deadline	1/15
Regular notification	4/1
Nonfall registration?	no

APPLICANTS ALSO LOOK AT AND OFTEN PREFER

The College of William & Mary, University of Virginia

AND SOMETIMES PREFER

George Mason University, Pennsylvania State University—University Park, Rutgers, The State University of New Jersey—New Brunswick, University of Delaware, University of Maryland—College Park, Villanova University, Virginia Tech

FINANCIAL FACTS

Financial Aid Rating	62
Annual in-state tuition	$6,666
Annual out-of-state tuition	$17,386
Room & Board	$6,836
Required fees	$140
% frosh rec. need-based scholarship or grant aid	16
% UG rec. need-based scholarship or grant aid	12
% frosh rec. need-based self-help aid	29
% UG rec. need-based self-help aid	23
% frosh rec. any financial aid	53
% UG rec. any financial aid	51

JOHNS HOPKINS UNIVERSITY

3400 NORTH CHARLES STREET/140 GARLAND, BALTIMORE, MD 21218 • ADMISSIONS: 410-516-8171 • FAX: 410-516-6025

CAMPUS LIFE

Quality of Life Rating	**68**
Fire Safety Rating	**85**
Type of school	private
Environment	metropolis

STUDENTS

Total undergrad enrollment	4,429
% male/female	53/47
% from out of state	86
% from public high school	69
% live on campus	61
% in (# of) fraternities	21 (11)
% in (# of) sororities	22 (7)
% African American	6
% Asian	22
% Caucasian	61
% Hispanic	6
% Native American	1
% international	5
# of countries represented	71

SURVEY SAYS . . .

Lab facilities are great
Great computer facilities
Great library
Athletic facilities are great
Diverse student types on campus
Lots of beer drinking

ACADEMICS

Academic Rating	**88**
Calendar	4-1-4
Student/faculty ratio	9:1
Profs interesting rating	62
Profs accessible rating	69
% profs teaching	
UG courses	96
Most common	
lab size	10–19 students
Most common	
reg class size	10–19 students

MOST POPULAR MAJORS

biomedical/medical engineering
economics
international relations and affairs

STUDENTS SAY

Academics

Johns Hopkins University is a premed powerhouse and one of the nation's great producers of tomorrow's prominent doctors and medical researchers. Boasting one of the "top research [hospitals] in the country," the country's "number-one undergraduate biomedical engineering program," and "the number-one school for public health studies," it's no wonder JHU draws so many aspiring doctors that students sometimes think "Almost everyone is premed." That misconception is one of the reasons JHU's many other strengths are often overlooked. Those strengths are many, including "a fantastic international studies program," a highly respected Writing Seminar that "is paving the way for liberal arts on this science-dominated campus," a School of Engineering that offers students "amazing research experience," and "a wonderful relationship with the Peabody Conservatory for those seriously interested in music." No matter what they study, students at JHU inhabit "an intense academic environment that works hard to make us the best applicants we can be for grad school while teaching us how to be a part of a global community." Research is "a big highlight here"; as one student explains, "JHU was the first research university in the U.S.A.," and you'll find "a lot of [research] opportunities" from freshman year on. What you won't find is a lot of hand-holding, since "Hopkins is an institution where students are given a wide range of freedom with their classes and with their social life, but more importantly, it teaches students to be responsible for their own actions and decisions, both academically and socially."

Life

"Johns Hopkins has a reputation for being a living hell; however, it is actually quite nice," students assure us. One explains, "It is true that we have a very rigorous academic program, but that does not prevent us from having fun and enjoying the many activities and enjoyments that are offered by the school and the neighborhood. The frats and sororities are quite active but not ridiculous; there are many trendy areas in Baltimore with good bars, restaurants, and clubs; and there are many events on campus ranging from a cappella concerts to lectures from prominent political figures to concerts by artists like Guster and Talib Kweli." Hometown Baltimore "gets a bad rep" (if you watch HBO's *The Wire*, you know what that rep is) "but there is a lot to do in and around campus. There is tons of shopping, and lots of really good restaurants to eat at in the city." There's also "a good band scene, as well as really cheap baseball tickets." All in all, "It's a very fun city." For fun on campus, "Students normally go to frat parties." JHU has some "great Division I sports teams"—men's lacrosse and soccer are always highly ranked—and the student body regularly rallies to their support. The "beautiful" campus is a short walk from the Baltimore Museum of Art, a great place to blow off steam when the pressures of school start to build, and "is free for students."

Student Body

JHU students aren't sure "whether there is such a thing as one typical student here, because there is a strong division between engineering and arts and science students." That said, "Most students work hard and play hard." There are "lots of complaints about the workload, but people are secretly proud of the work they do." Many here "are intensely competitive," which is a "reflection of the pressure they feel on campus," but "It is a myth that Hopkins is filled with cutthroat nerds." Though "it is a stressful atmosphere at times because students want to get ahead, most of the students are very helpful and nice." Demographically speaking, "There are all kinds of people here, which means that everyone can fit in. No matter what kind of person someone may appear to be on the outside, you know that if they're at Hopkins they must be pretty nerdy on the inside, so there's a kind of camaraderie there." Most students "are a little of everything, and it seems like everyone here is exceptional at something."

FINANCIAL AID: 410-516-8028 • E-MAIL: GOTOJHU@JHU.EDU • WEBSITE: WWW.JHU.EDU

ADMISSIONS

Very important factors considered include: Academic GPA, character/personal qualities, recommendation(s), rigor of secondary school record. *Important factors considered include:* Application essay, class rank, extracurricular activities, standardized test scores, talent/ability, volunteer work, work experience. *Other factors considered include:* Alumni/ae relation, first generation, geographical residence, interview, racial/ethnic status, state residency. SAT or ACT required; SAT and SAT Subject Tests or ACT recommended; ACT with Writing component required. TOEFL required of all international applicants. High school diploma or equivalent is not required. *Academic units recommended:* 4 English, 4 math, 4 science, 4 foreign language (2 foreign language for engineering majors), 2 social studies, 2 history.

The Inside Word

Top schools like Hopkins receive more and more applications every year and, as a result, grow harder and harder to get into. With nearly 14,000 applicants for the class of 2010, Hopkins had to reject numerous applicants who were thoroughly qualified. Give your application everything you've got, and don't take it personally if you don't get a fat envelope in the mail.

FINANCIAL AID

Students should submit: FAFSA, CSS/Financial Aid PROFILE, Noncustodial PROFILE, Business/Farm Supplement, prior and current year Federal Income Tax Returns. Regular filing deadline is February 15. The Princeton Review suggests that all financial aid forms be submitted as soon as possible after January 1. *Need-based scholarships/grants offered:* Pell Grant, SEOG, state scholarships/grants, private scholarships, the school's own gift aid. *Loan aid offered:* Direct Subsidized Stafford, Direct Unsubsidized Stafford, FFEL PLUS, Federal Perkins Loan, college/university loans from institutional funds. Applicants will be notified of awards on or about April 1. Federal Work-Study Program available. Institutional employment available.

FROM THE ADMISSIONS OFFICE

"The Hopkins tradition of preeminent academic excellence naturally attracts the very best students in the nation and from around the world. The Admissions Committee carefully examines each application for evidence of compelling intellectual interest and academic performance as well as strong personal recommendations and meaningful extracurricular contributions. Every applicant who matriculates to Johns Hopkins University was found qualified by the Admissions Committee through a 'whole person' assessment, and every applicant accepted for admission is fully expected to graduate. The Admissions Committee determines whom they believe will take full advantage of the exceptional opportunities offered at Hopkins, contribute the most to the educational process of the institution, and be the most successful in using what they have learned and experienced for the benefit of society.

"Freshman applicants for Fall 2008 may take either the old SAT and three SAT Subject Tests (one must be Writing) or the ACT. Alternatively, students may take either the new SAT or the ACT with Writing component. For those submitting SAT scores, submitting scores from three SAT Subject Tests is recommended."

SELECTIVITY

Admissions Rating	98
# of applicants	13,900
% of applicants accepted	27
% of acceptees attending	32
# accepting a place on wait list	1,258
# of early decision applicants	935
% accepted early decision	51

FRESHMAN PROFILE

Range SAT Critical Reading	630–730
Range SAT Math	660–760
Range SAT Writing	630–720
Range ACT Composite	28–32
Minimum Paper TOEFL	600
Minimum Computer Based TOEFL	250
Average HS GPA	3.69
% graduated top 10% of class	80
% graduated top 25% of class	95
% graduated top 50% of class	100

DEADLINES

Early decision application deadline	11/15
Early decision notification	12/15
Regular application deadline	1/1
Regular notification	4/1
Nonfall registration?	no

APPLICANTS ALSO LOOK AT

AND OFTEN PREFER

Harvard College, Massachusetts Institute of Technology, Princeton University, University of Pennsylvania, Yale University

AND SOMETIMES PREFER

Brown University, Cornell University, Duke University, Georgetown University,

AND RARELY PREFER

Boston University, Carnegie Mellon University, Tufts University, University of California—Berkeley, Washington University in St. Louis

FINANCIAL FACTS

Financial Aid Rating	93
Annual tuition	$33,900
Room & Board	$10,622
Books and supplies	$1,000
Required fees	$500
% frosh rec. need-based scholarship or grant aid	42
% UG rec. need-based scholarship or grant aid	40
% frosh rec. need-based self-help aid	47
% UG rec. need-based self-help aid	42
% frosh rec. any financial aid	47
% UG rec. any financial aid	45

JUNIATA COLLEGE

1700 MOORE STREET, HUNTINGDON, PA 16652 • ADMISSIONS: 814-641-3420 • FAX: 814-641-3100

STUDENTS SAY

Academics

"Science is definitely big" at Juniata College, a small, rural liberal arts college in central Pennsylvania, and the school clearly plans to keep it that way. Juniata recently opened a new science center with "state-of-the-art lab facilities and high tech gadgets [that] give students hands-on opportunities to really dive into research. There are great opportunities to prepare for graduate school." But "Science isn't the only thing that we offer," students insist; many want you to know that "Juniata also has a much-overlooked yet highly competent education program" and that "you can't go wrong with English, communication, history, foreign languages, or philosophy," although a few warn that "certain departments are really small, and don't receive the support that the sciences have." Through a unique Program of Emphasis (POE) option, Juniata undergrads "can personalize their own program to get a better educational experience." One student writes, "Juniata's Program of Emphasis is a major strength. Students are able to have their major and involve other classes that they may be interested in. For an example, we have students who are computer science majors and also have an emphasis on acting. By allowing students to combine classes that may not be required, they can experience many different things." No matter what undergrads choose to study, "This school is about challenging yourself and your view on the world in preparation for becoming part of it."

Life

Because Juniata "is located in beautiful Huntingdon, Pennsylvania," "There are a lot of things to do outdoors, such as hiking, camping, and biking, [but] the town is predominantly residential, so with the exception of the bowling alley and movie theater, there is not much to do here." The college fills the void by "offering wonderful extracurricular activities, from the academic groups such as the Null Set (the mathematics club) and the Barristers Club (for pre-law students), to AWOL (our gay-straight alliance), to the Japanese Club and dozens of others." There's also "a very active campus ministry," as well as "concerts, speakers, shows, and screenings on campus all the time. It is impossible to do everything." Juniata's athletic teams "are another strength. Our men's and women's volleyball teams have both recently won NCAA championships . . . and our field hockey team is becoming one of the strongest in the nation." Furthermore, the JC calendar is peppered with "several unique traditions, such as Mountain Day, Mr. Juniata, Storming of the Arch, and Madrigal Tenting. These allow the entire Juniata community to get out and have fun with each other." When students seek larger crowds, they travel to Altoona or State College, each about a half-hour's drive away.

Student Body

The "self-driven" undergrads of Juniata "really love what they're studying, and it becomes their life. Once you've accepted that, the school really opens up to you. Everyone is equally interested in their own POE, so you find yourself in really interesting conversations about anything from science to politics to religion. It's great." A large proportion of "The kids who attend here play a varsity or club sport," so a "typical student at Juniata is an athlete." He or she is also "liberal and proud of it. If you walked around here the day before Election Day 2004 and thought that this campus was a reflection of the rest of the country, you would think that there is no way in hell that George Bush would win the election." Most undergrads "are from Pennsylvania or the surrounding Mid-Atlantic states," with a split of "half 'hicks,' half city kids." Although "this is mostly a middle- to upper-class, White, Christian campus . . . the new Office of Diversity has begun bringing in a promising increase in people of different ethnic and religious backgrounds, as well as different sexual orientations."

FINANCIAL AID: 814-641-3142 • E-MAIL: INFO@JUNIATA.EDU • WEBSITE: WWW.JUNIATA.EDU

ADMISSIONS

Very important factors considered include: Academic GPA, application essay, character/personal qualities, recommendation(s), rigor of secondary school record, standardized test scores. *Important factors considered include:* Extracurricular activities, first generation, interview, talent/ability, volunteer work. *Other factors considered include:* Alumni/ae relation, geographical residence, level of applicant's interest, state residency. SAT or ACT recommended; TOEFL required of all international applicants. High school diploma is required, and GED is accepted. *Academic units required:* 4 English, 3 math, 3 science (2 science labs), 2 foreign language, 1 social studies, 3 history. *Academic units recommended:* 4 English, 4 math, 4 science, 2 foreign language, 1 social studies, 3 history.

The Inside Word

Like at many traditional liberal arts schools, the admissions process at Juniata is a personal one. The school wants students who will decide to attend Juniata and stay for the next 4 years. Among Juniata's bragging rights are that a staggering 40 percent of students graduate with a degree in science, 60 percent of undergrads design their own major, and 78 percent participate in internships.

FINANCIAL AID

Students should submit: FAFSA. Regular filing deadline is March 1. The Princeton Review suggests that all financial aid forms be submitted as soon as possible after January 1. *Need-based scholarships/grants offered:* Pell Grant, SEOG, state scholarships/grants, private scholarships, the school's own gift aid. *Loan aid offered:* FFEL Subsidized Stafford, FFEL Unsubsidized Stafford, FFEL PLUS, Federal Perkins Loan, college/university loans from institutional funds. Applicants will be notified of awards on a rolling basis beginning or about February 1.

FROM THE ADMISSIONS OFFICE

"Juniata's unique approach to learning has a flexible, student-centered focus. With the help of two advisors, over half of Juniata's students design their own majors (called the "Program of Emphasis" or "POE"). Those who choose a more traditional academic journey still benefit from the assistance of two faculty advisors and interdisciplinary collaboration between multiple academic departments.

"In addition, all students benefit from the recent, significant investments in academic facilities that help students actively learn by doing. For example, the new Halbritter Performing Arts Center houses an innovative theater program where theater professionals work side by side with students; the Sill Business Incubator provides $5,000 in seed capital to students with a desire to start their own business; the LEEDS-certified Shuster Environmental Studies Field Station, located on nearby Raystown Lake, gives unparalleled hands-on study opportunities to students; and the von Liebig Center for Science provides opportunities for student/faculty research surpassing those available at even large universities.

"As the 2003 Middle States Accreditation Team noted, 'Juniata is truly a student-centered college. There is a remarkable cohesiveness in this commitment—faculty, students, trustees, staff, and alumni, each from their own vantage point, describe a community in which the growth of the student is central.' This cohesiveness creates a dynamic learning environment that enables students to think and grow intellectually, to evolve in their academic careers, and to graduate as active, successful participants in the global community.

"Freshman applicants for Fall 2008 may submit either the new SAT (or the ACT with the Writing component) or the old (before March 2005) SAT (or ACT); we will use their best scores from either test. "

SELECTIVITY

Admissions Rating	**89**
# of applicants	1,785
% of applicants accepted	65
% of acceptees attending	31
# accepting a place on wait list	85
% admitted from wait list	2
# of early decision applicants	50
% accepted early decision	86

FRESHMAN PROFILE

Range SAT Critical Reading	540–630
Range SAT Math	550–640
Minimum Paper TOEFL	550
Minimum Computer Based TOEFL	213
Average HS GPA	3.82
% graduated top 10% of class	36
% graduated top 25% of class	77
% graduated top 50% of class	95

DEADLINES

Early decision application deadline	11/1
Early decision notification	12/30
Regular application deadline	3/1
Regular notification	rolling
Nonfall registration?	yes

APPLICANTS ALSO LOOK AT

AND OFTEN PREFER
Bucknell University,

AND SOMETIMES PREFER
Dickinson College, Gettysburg College, Muhlenberg College, Ursinus College

AND RARELY PREFER
Allegheny College, Elizabethtown College, Lebanon Valley College, Susquehanna University, Washington & Jefferson College

FINANCIAL FACTS

Financial Aid Rating	**80**
Annual tuition	$28,250
Room & Board	$8,040
Books and supplies	$600
Required fees	$670
% frosh rec. need-based scholarship or grant aid	65
% UG rec. need-based scholarship or grant aid	71
% frosh rec. need-based self-help aid	68
% UG rec. need-based self-help aid	71
% frosh rec. any financial aid	99
% UG rec. any financial aid	99

KALAMAZOO COLLEGE

1200 ACADEMY STREET, KALAMAZOO, MI 49006 • ADMISSIONS: 616-337-7166 • FAX: 269-337-7390

STUDENTS SAY

Academics

Kalamazoo College "is all about the K-Plan and giving students the best liberal arts education possible." The K-Plan consists of two mandatory components (a core liberal arts curriculum and a Senior Individualized Project) and two voluntary components (externships/internships and study abroad) that the majority of students pursue. Students say the K-Plan makes Kalamazoo "the epitome of experiential education," starting with the Land/Sea first-year orientation experience, a team-building exercise that involves hiking, canoeing, climbing, and rappelling, and continuing with an "off-campus internship sophomore year, study abroad junior year, and a senior project before you graduate!" From beginning to end, it's a "very hands-on education." As at many selective small schools, rigorous academics are delivered by "a faculty who shares in the interests of the student" amid "an awesome collection of competitive but supportive peers." The intensity is ratcheted up somewhat by Kalamazoo's accelerated academic calendar; operating on a quarter system means that "courses last only 10 weeks" and "Everything moves extremely quickly. There's a lot of work involved." In other words, this place "is not a playground." Some feel the workload is a bit too much and feel a reduction would mean "less reading but more thinking," and even those who appreciate the challenge concede that "B's at K are like A's at other schools."

Life

Life at Kalamazoo is, "at the most basic level, heavily focused around academics. Everything else is just gravy." That's not to say that there aren't "a great many opportunities in which to take part," but rather that "before [you do any of that], you have to finish your homework" which is usually substantial. When the books are finally closed, "There are always events going on either here or at Western Michigan University [also in Kalamazoo], and nearly everyone at K is part of some club or organization. Political organizations like Campus Republicans and Campus Democrats are very popular, as is our Gay and Lesbian group, Kaleidoscope." Students say, "Choir and sports like tennis are also popular here. Our Theater Department is small but dedicated." And let's not forget the CGC, "the Childish Games Commission, where students play red rover, dodgeball, zombie tag, and jump in leaf piles. It gives us an excuse to goof around for an hour or two and a break from school work." Many here tell us that "Kalamazoo is a great town to live in. We are lucky to be a part of a real, thriving community, with which we can interact through service-learning, jobs, or even shopping and entertainment. There are theater productions, concerts, and festivals year-round." When students want a more conventional undergrad party scene, they head to the "keggers" happening "any day of the week" over at WMU.

Student Body

Kalamazoo students tend to be extremely bright and a little high strung, to the point that many are at least one standard deviation from the norm. As one undergrad puts it, "My friend has this theory: There is a secret question on the application that no one remembers answering. The question is 'On a scale of 1 to 10, 10 being the oddest, how odd are you?' If you don't score at least a 5, you don't get in." Mostly, "Students here are very smart and nice, but a little on the awkward anti-social side." Other, smaller demographics on campus include "the rich, party types who take blow-off classes and get all C's," the "people who can balance work and play but tend to be the type of people who enjoy a game of 'zombie tag'," the fervent feminists, and "the gay community, [which is] very strong, active, and supportive."

FINANCIAL AID: 269-337-7192 • E-MAIL: ADMISSION@KZOO.EDU • WEBSITE: WWW.KZOO.EDU

ADMISSIONS

Very important factors considered include: Academic GPA, extracurricular activities, rigor of secondary school record, standardized test scores, talent/ability. *Important factors considered include:* Application essay, character/personal qualities, class rank, recommendation(s), volunteer work, work experience. *Other factors considered include:* Alumni/ae relation, first generation, geographical residence, interview, level of applicant's interest, racial/ethnic status, state residency. SAT or ACT required; ACT with Writing component required. TOEFL required of all international applicants. High school diploma is required, and GED is accepted. *Academic units recommended:* 4 English, 3 math, 3 science, 3 foreign language, 2 social studies, 2 history.

The Inside Word

Kalamazoo offers early decision and two rounds of early action, indicating that the school works aggressively to fill its incoming class as early in the admissions process as possible. If you are dead certain you want to attend Kalamazoo, apply early decision. If the school is among your top choices, consider applying early action; your application will probably receive a slightly more generous review than will those that arrive later in the admissions process.

FINANCIAL AID

Students should submit: FAFSA, institution's own financial aid form. The Princeton Review suggests that all financial aid forms be submitted as soon as possible after January 1. *Need-based scholarships/grants offered:* Pell Grant, SEOG, state scholarships/grants, private scholarships, the school's own gift aid. *Loan aid offered:* Direct Subsidized Stafford, Direct Unsubsidized Stafford, Direct PLUS, Federal Perkins Loan, state loans. Applicants will be notified of awards on or about March 17.

FROM THE ADMISSIONS OFFICE

"Anyone can pursue any component of the K-Plan at any college, but it is rare to see the purposeful integration and high participation rate found at Kalamazoo. Over the last 40 years, 85 percent of our graduates have formally studied in another country while 80 percent have completed an internship or externship, and 100 percent complete a senior project. Our students often pursue international internships and senior project experiences, in addition to their planned study abroad terms. Also, Kalamazoo is one of the few selective liberal arts colleges to be found in a city—the Kalamazoo metro area has a population of approximately 225,000 with the advantage of being near a university of nearly 30,000 students. It is a diverse and vibrant community with wonderful access to the arts, athletics, service-learning, and community-service opportunities. We are a small and personal college with bigger opportunities.

"Kalamazoo College is one of 40 colleges selected to be in Loren Pope's popular book, *Colleges That Change Lives.* Loren selected Kalamazoo and the other 39 colleges based on reasonable cost, unique programs and curricula, and cocurricular activities that all contribute to dramatically changing the lives of those students who find us.

"An SAT or ACT score is required for admission; SAT Subject Tests are not. Because the writing portions of the SAT and ACT are new and still being evaluated, we have not yet determined what weight writing will hold in our decisions. Students taking only the ACT must take the writing portion."

SELECTIVITY
Admissions Rating	89
# of applicants	1,800
% of applicants accepted	69
% of acceptees attending	31
# accepting a place on wait list	65
% admitted from wait list	18
# of early decision applicants	13
% accepted early decision	100

FRESHMAN PROFILE
Range SAT Critical Reading	600–725
Range SAT Math	598–690
Range ACT Composite	26–30
Minimum Paper TOEFL	550
Minimum Computer Based TOEFL	213
Average HS GPA	3.58
% graduated top 10% of class	43
% graduated top 25% of class	72
% graduated top 50% of class	96

DEADLINES
Early decision application deadline	11/15
Early decision notification	12/1
Regular application deadline	2/15
Regular notification	4/1
Nonfall registration?	no

APPLICANTS ALSO LOOK AT
AND OFTEN PREFER
The College of Wooster, Dartmouth College, Georgetown University, Northwestern University, University of Michigan—Ann Arbor
AND SOMETIMES PREFER
Denison University, Earlham College, Macalester College, Oberlin College, University of Notre Dame
AND RARELY PREFER
Albion College, Alma College, DePauw University, Hope College

FINANCIAL FACTS
Financial Aid Rating	69
Annual tuition	$27,054
Room & Board	$6,915
% frosh rec. need-based scholarship or grant aid	51
% UG rec. need-based scholarship or grant aid	51
% frosh rec. need-based self-help aid	35
% UG rec. need-based self-help aid	47

KANSAS STATE UNIVERSITY

119 ANDERSON HALL, MANHATTAN, KS 66506 • ADMISSIONS: 800-432-8270 OR 785-532-6250 • FAX: 785-532-6393

CAMPUS LIFE
Quality of Life Rating	**86**
Fire Safety Rating	**64**
Type of school	public
Environment	village

STUDENTS
Total undergrad enrollment	18,761
% male/female	51/49
% from out of state	14
% from public high school	81
% live on campus	27
% in (# of) fraternities	20 (28)
% in (# of) sororities	20 (16)
% African American	3
% Asian	1
% Caucasian	84
% Hispanic	3
% Native American	1
% international	5
# of countries represented	111

SURVEY SAYS . . .
Great library
Athletic facilities are great
Students are friendly
Everyone loves the Wildcats
Student publications are popular
Lots of beer drinking

ACADEMICS
Academic Rating	**70**
Calendar	semester
Student/faculty ratio	19:1
Profs interesting rating	70
Profs accessible rating	74
% profs teaching	
UG courses	72
% classes taught by TAs	17
Most common	
reg class size	10–19 students

MOST POPULAR MAJORS
animal sciences
journalism
mechanical engineering

STUDENTS SAY

Academics

Kansas State University was founded under the Morrill Act, the nineteenth-century federal legislation designed to promote progress in agricultural science, engineering, and military science. Nearly 150 years after its founding, K-State still fulfills its original mission admirably; students here praise the school's offerings in pre-veterinary medicine, ecology, agronomy, biology, economics, engineering, and agriculture. "This is an ag school in the middle of farmland and the Bible Belt," students agree, noting that the liberal arts, while taught, definitely take a backseat to the more popular programs. Research opportunities abound here for ambitious undergrads, as "Students turn out papers and projects and often are required to meet people in industry to practice solving industry problems." Experiential learning options are popular, too: "K-State does a great job helping students to get the experience they need while they are still taking classes," undergrads tell us. With nearly 20,000 fellow students, undergrads must be assertive to get the most of their educations here; one student points out, "All professors and administrators here are accessible, as long as the effort is made by the student." For those who seek it, support is available in many forms; "Success in the classroom is possible for anyone and the school makes sure to let you know what resources are available to do well, such as the library, tutoring, and assistance for the learning challenged." Still on the fence about K-State? Consider this: "We have the best ice cream on earth from our own cows. We sell meat from our own Meat Science Department."

Life

Kansas State's hometown of Manhattan may not be the bustling metropolis that its name suggests, but it's big enough to suit most undergraduates. This "wonderful little town with tons of personality and good people" is home to Aggieville, "a mini-downtown across the street from the campus that has lots of bars as well as restaurants, bookstores, novelty shops, a laundromat, a pet shop, etc." Aggieville's bars are the center of social life for those older than 21; younger students congregate at house parties. Everyone, regardless of age, tailgates on game day, then "crams into the student section" to root on the Wildcats. "Student interaction at tailgating and sporting events is always a good time," undergrads agree, adding that there's "a lot of school spirit for the football team!" Women's basketball and track and field are other outstanding athletics programs; students tell us that "athletics at K-State are a major strength of the school. They are always a highlight of the week or month." There is smaller-scale diversion available here too: "Every weekend, there are free activities and a movie at the student union, so there's always something to do if you don't have any money," and "During the week the Union is a great place to spend extra time. Usually, there are speakers in the plaza, booths lining the main corridor, and always people around." One student observes, "The number of activities in which to become involved is an important ingredient in the recipe for success here because it gives students an opportunity to meet people."

Student Body

"The highly friendly nature of the student body" is one of K-State's biggest assets, students tell us. "The friendliness makes incoming freshman feel welcome and safe. It's easy to make friends in your classes and in the dorms." Most undergrads here "come from small-town backgrounds and they don't know a stranger." One student writes, "The flair is definitely Midwestern. Walking to class, you'll pass your jocks in their workout attire, the cowboys in their wranglers, and the occasional prep." Most are "religious conservatives and they're going to stay that way." One student explains, "Just about everyone is White, Republican, Christian, and from a smaller town with little experience with diversity. This doesn't mean they aren't nice or good people, they're just inexperienced."

FINANCIAL AID: 877-817-2287 OR 785-532-6420 • E-MAIL: K-STATE@K-STATE.EDU • WEBSITE: CONSIDER.K-STATE.EDU

ADMISSIONS

Very important factors considered include: Academic GPA, class rank, rigor of secondary school record, standardized test scores. SAT or ACT recommended; ACT preferred; High school diploma is required, and GED is accepted. *Academic units recommended:* 4 English, 3 math, 3 natural science, 3 social science, 1 history, 1 computer technology.

The Inside Word

As at most public universities, the admissions process is about as straightforward as it can get. Kansas high school grads are admitted with little trouble; out-of-state students are expected to be in the top third of their graduating class and to show evidence of academic potential via ACT scores. ACT is preferred, but SAT is acceptable. Don't be deceived by the seeming lack of rigor in admissions standards—K-State is chock full of strong students. Heightened national visibility for its athletic teams over the past few years will no doubt attract more applicants.

FINANCIAL AID

Students should submit: FAFSA. The Princeton Review suggests that all financial aid forms be submitted as soon as possible after January 1. *Need-based scholarships/grants offered:* Pell Grant, SEOG, state scholarships/grants, private scholarships, the school's own gift aid. *Loan aid offered:* FFEL Subsidized Stafford, FFEL Unsubsidized Stafford, FFEL PLUS, Federal Perkins Loan, college/university loans from institutional funds, alternative student loans. Applicants will be notified of awards on a rolling basis beginning or about March 15.

FROM THE ADMISSIONS OFFICE

"Kansas State University offers strong academic programs, a lively intellectual atmosphere, a friendly campus community, and an environment where students achieve: K-State's total of Rhodes, Marshall, Truman, Goldwater, and Udall scholars since 1986 ranks first in the nation among state universities. In the Goldwater competition, only Princeton, Harvard, and Duke have produced more winners. K-State's student government was named best in the nation in 1997 and 1995. The forensics squad finished seventh in the 2005 national tournament. A K-State team finished in the top eight at the national debate tournament in 2003. Research facilities include the Konza Prairie, the world's largest tall grass prairie preserve, and the Macdonald Lab, the only university accelerator devoted primarily to atomic physics. Open House, held each spring, is a great way to explore K-State's more than 250 majors and options and 400 student organizations.

"Kansas State University requires ACT or SAT scores to complete a freshman applicant file. The SAT or ACT Writing score is not considered for admission to the university. Students may submit scores from any or all test dates. The best score from any one test date is used."

SELECTIVITY
Admissions Rating	72
# of applicants	7,479
% of applicants accepted	83
% of acceptees attending	50

FRESHMAN PROFILE
Range ACT Composite	21–27
% graduated top 10% of class	23
% graduated top 25% of class	49
% graduated top 50% of class	78

DEADLINES
Regular notification	rolling
Nonfall registration?	yes

FINANCIAL FACTS
Financial Aid Rating	73
Annual in-state tuition	$4,830
Annual out-of-state tuition	$13,916
Room & Board	$5,912
Books and supplies	$1,093
Required fees	$604
% frosh rec. need-based scholarship or grant aid	41
% UG rec. need-based scholarship or grant aid	36
% frosh rec. need-based self-help aid	40
% UG rec. need-based self-help aid	46
% UG rec. any financial aid	53

KENYON COLLEGE

ADMISSIONS OFFICE, RANSOM HALL, GAMBIER, OH 43022-9623 • ADMISSIONS: 740-427-5776 • FAX: 740-427-5770

CAMPUS LIFE

Quality of Life Rating	85
Fire Safety Rating	62
Type of school	private
Affiliation	Episcopal; non-denominational in practice
Environment	rural

STUDENTS

Total undergrad enrollment	1,629
% male/female	48/52
% from out of state	78
% from public high school	51
% live on campus	98
% in (# of) fraternities	27 (8)
% in (# of) sororities	19 (4)
% African American	3
% Asian	5
% Caucasian	83
% Hispanic	3
% Native American	1
% international	3
# of countries represented	28

SURVEY SAYS . . .

Small classes
No one cheats
Lab facilities are great
Athletic facilities are great
Students are friendly
Campus feels safe
Students are happy
Lots of beer drinking

ACADEMICS

Academic Rating	96
Calendar	semester
Student/faculty ratio	10:1
Profs interesting rating	98
Profs accessible rating	96
% profs teaching UG courses	100
% classes taught by TAs	0
Most common reg class size	10–19 students

MOST POPULAR MAJORS

English language and literature
political science and government
psychology

STUDENTS SAY

Academics

At Kenyon College, an "entrancingly pretty" campus and "personal, small, and intimate" classes combine to create "a low-stress setting" for a "liberal arts experience that allows you to make profound changes in your approach to life." Kenyon is primarily "known as a writers' college." It seems fitting, then, that the English Department draws the lion's share of students' praise. The school's rep, however, seems to derive more from the fact that written communication skills are valued and emphasized "in all departments, ranging from history to math," rather than from a course catalogue only filled with fascinating fiction and poetry courses. In terms of academic workload, it "is large but manageable and students in general never seem overly worried about it." They seem to know that they can count on their "brilliant," "incredible" professors who "know their stuff" and "are capable of making it accessible and interesting." Professors give students "as much individual time as [they] need" to digest the material. Administratively the school has experienced "a lot of turn-over in the last year," leading many students to feel that administrators are "still getting their bearings." While they don't "always follow the student body's opinion," they are at least aware of it and "willing to listen" to students' input. Both "Professors and administrators love to take an active experience in the lives of Kenyon students outside of the classroom" by doing things like attending student "art shows, sporting events, [and] musical performances." Such beyond-the-books interaction leads many students to feel that "the school is more of a family than a business."

Life

Student life at Kenyon is a unique riff on the typical college social experience. For example, "There are a lot of parties in apartments and fraternity lodges and lounges." Yet though "Frats throw most of the parties," they are "almost always open to anyone," and Greeks are "incorporated into the same housing as everyone else," so it "doesn't feel exclusive." What's more, "People have academic conversations even while out at parties," which is certainly not the case at your typical college bash. Basically, Kenyon undergrads "know how to let go and have a good time, but there's always a slightly intellectual edge to it." Parties aren't the only social options on campus. Considering its small size, Kenyon may "have too much programming rather than too little." "There are movies shown at the KAC [Kenyon Athletic Center]," and regularly scheduled "concerts, theatrical and dance productions, and lectures." For "casual fun," students "go to Middle Ground Cafe or the Gambier Grill for coffee or food." Also, "People go to the bar on campus if [they're] of legal age." "In nice weather, Kenyon students are very outdoorsy." Students enjoy "[going] out to the nature preserve (the BFEC) and play[ing] Frisbee or go[ing] for walks." Off-campus entertainment options are pretty scarce, as hometown Gambier is "in the middle of nowhere." Luckily, "Columbus is under an hour away," so "When people need to go somewhere a little more exciting, they drive [there]."

Student Body

A stereotypical Kenyonian is "generally very smart but not pretentious." Most students are "rich, White, and Democratic," which might explain why they "spend lots of money trying to look like they don't have that much money." Kenyon students "love to party, and [are] generally involved in music, sports, or theater." On this "liberal," "laid-back" campus, students are "not competitive" and describe each other as "seriously friendly." People here "take academics very seriously, but also enjoy social lives." They also have a "wide variety of interests. It's not unusual to see a neuroscience major paired with a dance minor." As one student sums up, "The 'Kenyon Quirk' is something you hear of often—in that way, everyone is atypical, as it is typical to be different. Hippies, collar-poppers, girlie-girls, goths, nerds, and introverts all find their place at Kenyon."

FINANCIAL AID: 740-427-5430 • E-MAIL: ADMISSIONS@KENYON.EDU • WEBSITE: WWW.KENYON.EDU

ADMISSIONS

Very important factors considered include: Academic GPA, application essay, character/personal qualities, recommendation(s), rigor of secondary school record. *Important factors considered include:* Class rank, extracurricular activities, first generation, interview, level of applicant's interest, racial/ethnic status, standardized test scores, talent/ability. *Other factors considered include:* Alumni/ae relation, geographical residence, state residency, volunteer work, work experience. SAT or ACT required; TOEFL required of all international applicants. High school diploma is required, and GED is accepted. *Academic units required:* 4 English, 3 math, 3 science (3 science labs), 3 foreign language, 1 social studies, 1 history, 3 academic electives. *Academic units recommended:* 4 English, 4 math, 4 science (3 science labs), 4 foreign language, 2 social studies, 1 history, 4 academic electives, 1 fine arts.

The Inside Word

In terms of admissions selectivity, Kenyon is of the first order of selective, small Midwestern, liberal arts schools. Kenyon shares a lot of application and admit overlap with other schools in this niche, and the choice for many students comes down to "best fit." As Kenyon is a writing-intensive institution, applicants should expect that all written material submitted to the school in the admissions process will be scrutinized. Revise and proofread accordingly.

FINANCIAL AID

Students should submit: FAFSA, CSS/Financial Aid PROFILE, Noncustodial PROFILE. Regular filing deadline is February 15. The Princeton Review suggests that all financial aid forms be submitted as soon as possible after January 1. *Need-based scholarships/grants offered:* Pell Grant, SEOG, state scholarships/grants, private scholarships, the school's own gift aid. *Loan aid offered:* FFEL Subsidized Stafford, FFEL Unsubsidized Stafford, FFEL PLUS, Federal Perkins Loan, college/university loans from institutional funds. Applicants will be notified of awards on or about April 1. Federal Work-Study Program available. Institutional employment available. Off-campus job opportunities are fair.

FROM THE ADMISSIONS OFFICE

"Students and alumni alike think of Kenyon as a place that fosters 'learning in the company of friends.' While faculty expectations are rigorous and the work challenging, the academic atmosphere is cooperative, not competitive. Indications of intellectual curiosity and passion for learning, more than just high grades and test scores, are what we look for in applications. Important as well are demonstrated interests in non-academic pursuits, whether in athletics, the arts, writing, or another passion. Life in this small college community is fueled by the talents and enthusiasm of our students, so the Admission Staff seeks students who have a range of talents and interests.

"The high school transcript, recommendations, the personal statement, and answers on the supplement are of primary importance in reviewing preparedness and fit. Standardized tests (SAT or ACT) are of secondary importance."

SELECTIVITY

Admissions Rating	**96**
# of applicants	4,251
% of applicants accepted	32
% of acceptees attending	32
# accepting a place on wait list	362
% admitted from wait list	4
# of early decision applicants	342
% accepted early decision	40

FRESHMAN PROFILE

Range SAT Critical Reading	620–730
Range SAT Math	610–690
Range SAT Writing	620–710
Range ACT Composite	27–32
Minimum Paper TOEFL	600
Minimum Computer Based TOEFL	250
Average HS GPA	3.82
% graduated top 10% of class	58
% graduated top 25% of class	87
% graduated top 50% of class	99

DEADLINES

Early decision application deadline	11/15, 1/15
Early decision notification	12/15, 2/1
Regular application deadline	1/15
Regular notification	4/1
Nonfall registration?	no

APPLICANTS ALSO LOOK AT

AND OFTEN PREFER
Bowdoin College, Carleton College, Davidson College, Middlebury College, Vassar College, Washington University in St. Louis, Wesleyan College

AND SOMETIMES PREFER
Bates College, Colby College, Colorado College, Grinnell College, Hamilton College, Macalester College, Oberlin College

AND RARELY PREFER
Case Western Reserve University, Connecticut College, The College of Wooster, Dickinson College, Earlham College, Miami University, Skidmore College

FINANCIAL FACTS

Financial Aid Rating	**88**
Annual comprehensive tuition	$44,390
% frosh rec. need-based scholarship or grant aid	38
% UG rec. need-based scholarship or grant aid	41
% frosh rec. need-based self-help aid	32
% UG rec. need-based self-help aid	37
% frosh rec. any financial aid	65
% UG rec. any financial aid	69

KNOX COLLEGE

Box K-148, Galesburg, IL 61401 • Admissions: 309-341-7100 • Fax: 309-341-7070

CAMPUS LIFE

Quality of Life Rating	**74**
Fire Safety Rating	**72**
Type of school	private
Environment	town

STUDENTS

Total undergrad enrollment	1,351
% male/female	44/56
% from out of state	49
% from public high school	81
% live on campus	89
% in (# of) fraternities	21 (5)
% in (# of) sororities	13 (3)
% African American	4
% Asian	6
% Caucasian	74
% Hispanic	4
% Native American	1
% international	7
# of countries represented	44

SURVEY SAYS . . .

Small classes
No one cheats
Great library
Lots of beer drinking

ACADEMICS

Academic Rating	**89**
Calendar	3–3
Student/faculty ratio	12:1
Profs interesting rating	93
Profs accessible rating	89
% profs teaching UG courses	100
% classes taught by TAs	0
Most common lab size	10–19 students
Most common reg class size	10–19 students

MOST POPULAR MAJORS
anthropology
economics
political science and government

STUDENTS SAY

Academics

Knox College, a small liberal arts school with "a very strong creative writing program," offers its students the "freedom to flourish" (it's "the school's tagline, and it's actually very accurate") through the opportunity "to create their paths and discover their goals" and "provides a serious foundation for freethinking individuals." A combination of factors makes this degree of freedom possible: One is a relatively small amount of academic "requirements, both in general and within majors, which means that you can honestly take whatever classes interest you." Another is "the ease . . . you can do independent studies or design your own major or minor with a faculty sponsor. You can personalize your education plan to a great degree at Knox." Strengths include the aforementioned writing program, political science, education, and a premed program that offers early acceptance (no later than sophomore year) to Rush Medical School or George Washington University. All this freedom does have its price: One undergrad warns, "The school allows students to do what they want, but expects rigorous academic performance as well as maturity in return." Academics can be grueling in some students' opinion, because of the school's three-term calendar. One student writes, "Though you're only taking three classes at a time, you still have an amazing workload. Getting A's at Knox is no easy business." Undergrads here appreciate "the wide variety of activities and the opportunities students are given. My freshman year I was able to go to Hawaii with Habitat for Humanity, then Florida the following year. There are many opportunities for research and internships, and since there are fewer students competing for these opportunities than at a big school, the odds are better."

Life

Hometown Galesburg "is small and quaint," with "a few things to do if you're looking for something, like the Rootabaga Jazz Festival in the [winter], Carl Sandburg's home, and the railroad museum." Even so, many feel that "there's nothing to do in Galesburg. The reality of it is that we have a great school in the middle of a cornfield." Fortunately, "There is never a lack of things to do on campus, from clubs and Greek life and sports to Casino Nights and musical and theatrical performances." Student organizations present "a lot of programming to keep students busy: speakers, readings, comedians, trips, bands, etc. These events are publicized everywhere, so you can't miss them." Sporting events "are also fun to attend, especially when Knox is playing its rival, Monmouth." Some diversions are improvised, such as "sledding in the Bowl (the bowl-shaped football field) or hanging at a friend's suite and watching movies." There are also "a lot of parties at Knox. But they are not as one might expect. A lot of people even stay away from the official party places for the evening. Alcohol does factor a lot into campus life here but only if you choose to drink. Like many other schools, it is available if desired but easy enough to sidestep if not."

Student Body

It may seem like "The majority of students are middle-class liberal Whites from Midwestern suburbs" at Knox College, but "The school also draws students from both coasts and around the world. Although classes may be largely homogeneous, they nearly always include some students from other countries or more diverse backgrounds." There is also a diversity of personality types here; one student explains, "a Knox student's hair might be magenta and blue, or it might look like it was styled at a salon. Preppie, hippie, and punk styles all mesh together, and friends mix evenly through all crowds. Being weird doesn't make you an outcast, but neither does being average. At Knox you can find someone totally like you or totally opposite you. All at a school that only has 1,200 students."

FINANCIAL AID: 309-341-7149 • E-MAIL: ADMISSION@KNOX.EDU • WEBSITE: WWW.KNOX.EDU

ADMISSIONS

Very important factors considered include: Academic GPA, rigor of secondary school record. *Important factors considered include:* Application essay, class rank, recommendation(s). *Other factors considered include:* Alumni/ae relation, character/personal qualities, extracurricular activities, first generation, interview, level of applicant's interest, racial/ethnic status, standardized test scores, talent/ability, volunteer work. TOEFL required of all international applicants. High school diploma is required, and GED is accepted. *Academic units recommended:* 4 English, 4 math, 3 science (2 science labs), 3 foreign language, 2 social studies, 2 history.

The Inside Word

Knox prides itself on maintaining a diverse student body. Its Admissions Office truly focuses on the individual, closely assessing applicants in an attempt to predict how each will contribute to the campus. Prospective students who succeed in intellectually challenging classes in high school will set themselves apart.

FINANCIAL AID

Students should submit: FAFSA, institution's own financial aid form. The Princeton Review suggests that all financial aid forms be submitted as soon as possible after January 1. *Need-based scholarships/grants offered:* Pell Grant, SEOG, state scholarships/grants, private scholarships, the school's own gift aid. *Loan aid offered:* Direct Subsidized Stafford, Direct Unsubsidized Stafford, Direct PLUS, Federal Perkins Loan, state loans, college/university loans from institutional funds. Applicants will be notified of awards on a rolling basis beginning March 15. Federal Work-Study Program available. Institutional employment available. Off-campus job opportunities are good.

FROM THE ADMISSIONS OFFICE

"Knox was founded on the idea that education has the power to confer a kind of freedom—what we've come to call 'freedom to flourish.' On the surface, 'freedom to flourish' is a simple and powerful concept—it is the knowledge and skills one needs to live a rewarding personal, professional, and civic life. But 'freedom to flourish' also has more subtle meaning that touches on how education happens at Knox.

"Most schools ask what you want to study and give you a checklist of courses needed for that degree. Knox asks, 'What do you want to know, and what do you want to do with that knowledge?' Within the context of the goals and milestones of one of our many majors, you and your advisor will develop a personalized educational plan of classes, internships, off-campus study, and independent research projects that meet the agenda you set for yourself. In this sense, a Knox education is an act of imagination, an act of entrepreneurship, an act of freedom.'

"That self-direction doesn't end in advising sessions and course selection. You'll be encouraged to bring your own interests and perspective to every class you take, and you'll be challenged to apply what you learn to the world around you. In the end you will learn how to set goals, how to figure out what you need to know to achieve those goals, and how to identify and collaborate with mentors who can help you along the way. That is 'freedom to flourish.'

"At Knox, you'll never be a number. Knox reviews each application holistically, fully considering a student's academic record, course selection, and performance (grades), as well as essays, recommendations, interviews, and other accomplishments. As a result, the submission of SAT or ACT scores is optional for most applicants."

SELECTIVITY

Admissions Rating	**85**
# of applicants	2,085
% of applicants accepted	74
% of acceptees attending	27
# accepting a place on wait list	29
% admitted from wait list	3

FRESHMAN PROFILE

Range SAT Critical Reading	580–690
Range SAT Math	540–670
Range SAT Writing	560–690
Range ACT Composite	25–30
Minimum Paper TOEFL	550
Minimum Computer Based TOEFL	213
% graduated top 10% of class	34
% graduated top 25% of class	68
% graduated top 50% of class	94

DEADLINES

Regular application deadline	2/1
Regular notification	3/31
Nonfall registration?	yes

FINANCIAL FACTS

Financial Aid Rating	**88**
Annual tuition	$27,606
Room & Board	$5,925
Books and supplies	$900
Required fees	$294
% frosh rec. need-based scholarship or grant aid	69
% UG rec. need-based scholarship or grant aid	66
% frosh rec. need-based self-help aid	62
% UG rec. need-based self-help aid	58
% frosh rec. any financial aid	96
% UG rec. any financial aid	95

LAFAYETTE COLLEGE

118 MARKLE HALL, EASTON, PA 18042 • ADMISSIONS: 610-330-5100 • FAX: 610-330-5355

CAMPUS LIFE

Quality of Life Rating	70
Fire Safety Rating	60*
Type of school	private
Affiliation	Presbyterian
Environment	village

STUDENTS

Total undergrad enrollment	2,381
% male/female	52/48
% from out of state	70
% from public high school	68
% live on campus	96
% in (# of) fraternities	26 (7)
% in (# of) sororities	45 (6)
% African American	5
% Asian	3
% Caucasian	80
% Hispanic	5
% international	6
# of countries represented	46

SURVEY SAYS . . .
Small classes
Lab facilities are great
Great computer facilities
Great library
Athletic facilities are great
Lots of beer drinking

ACADEMICS

Academic Rating	91
Calendar	semester
Student/faculty ratio	11:1
Profs interesting rating	79
Profs accessible rating	86
% profs teaching	
UG courses	100
% classes taught by TAs	0
Most common	
lab size	10–19 students
Most common	
reg class size	10–19 students

STUDENTS SAY

Academics

"Lafayette's small size and exclusively undergraduate population create tight bonds between professors and students and open the door for research opportunities," students at this small-but-mighty liberal arts school tell us. That's true at many small schools; few others of this size can claim that "the small size does not prevent students from enjoying Division I sports, a nationally recognized engineering program, and great resources and facilities." Lafayette students can and do; they justifiably boast a "great Math Department, excellent programs in the sciences and engineering, [and] very good classes in the humanities and social sciences, which are under-noticed and underappreciated because of the well-known engineering programs." Students here benefit from a "strong emphasis on class discussion, individual attention from professors, [and] widely available internships and research opportunities with professors." Internships and externships are plentiful thanks in part to "a ton of alumni connections, people who have really stayed involved in the school after they graduated. They can provide resources, connections, ideas, opportunities and more. The sheer number of active alumni is amazing, and their willingness to interact with us is great." Lafayette also offers a number of "popular, widely used study-abroad programs," including six full-semester faculty-led opportunities (in Belgium, Greece, France, Germany, Spain, and Ghana).

Life

Lafayette "is located on a hill above downtown Easton, isolating most students on campus, or at least those without cars." Some here tell us that "there is not much to do on top of the hill except drink," which is why "Weekends are spent partying." Not everyone feels that way, though. Some are glad to be secluded from Easton, which they describe as "a tad sketchy at night," and they're perfectly happy to remain on their "beautiful campus, with its amazing attention paid to planting and replanting color-coordinated flowers." Others tout the many alcohol-free options available; one student writes, "There is always something to do at Lafayette. There are movies, speakers, comedians, and singing groups available for students. Community service and sporting events are also popular." Because the school is so small, "There are endless opportunities to get involved. If there is an association you want to start, start it! If there is a play you want to write and/or produce, do it! If you have a great new business idea, go for it. Lafayette professors and administrators are very supportive of students' creativity." The campus and the region do a good job of pulling in top-flight entertainment; one undergrad reports, "The amount of performing arts we get at both the Williams Center for the Arts (which is the art and music and theater building) and at the State Theater for the Arts is immense. At Williams, you get a ton of great classical and jazz music. At the State Theater, you get comedians such as Jon Stewart, Jeff Foxworthy, Bill Engvall, Larry 'The Cable Guy', Ron White, Drew Carey, as well as plays such as *The Full Monty* and *The Graduate*."

Student Body

"The typical student at Lafayette is very concerned with academics"—you can't last here very long if you're not—"but able to go out and have fun at the same time." He or she also makes time for extracurriculars; one student observes, "The typical Lafayette student has a full plate. Not only is he or she a serious academic student but at the same time is involved in some sort of club or organization on campus, whether it be sports, volunteering, music, or academic-related." Students tell us that "Lafayette is not very diverse, but minorities do have organizations that hold events for the whole campus. The typical student is middle- to upper-class, White, and has generally not had to work for much in their lives, but the student body as a whole is very friendly and accepting." Undergrads tend to be "politically conservative and most are religiously affiliated."

FINANCIAL AID: 610-330-5055 • E-MAIL: ADMISSIONS@LAFAYETTE.EDU • WEBSITE: WWW.LAFAYETTE.EDU

ADMISSIONS

Very important factors considered include: Rigor of secondary school record. *Important factors considered include:* Alumni/ae relation, application essay, character/personal qualities, class rank, extracurricular activities, racial/ethnic status, recommendation(s), standardized test scores, talent/ability, volunteer work. *Other factors considered include:* Geographical residence, interview, work experience. SAT or ACT required; ACT with Writing component required. TOEFL required of all international applicants. High school diploma or equivalent is not required. *Academic units recommended:* 4 English, 3 math, 2 science (2 science labs), 2 foreign language, 5 academic electives.

The Inside Word

Applications are reviewed three to five times and evaluated by as many as nine different committee members. In all cases, students who continually seek challenges and are willing to take risks academically win out over those who play it safe to maintain a high GPA.

FINANCIAL AID

Students should submit: FAFSA, CSS/Financial Aid PROFILE, Noncustodial PROFILE, Business/Farm Supplement. Regular filing deadline is February 1. The Princeton Review suggests that all financial aid forms be submitted as soon as possible after January 1. *Need-based scholarships/grants offered:* Pell Grant, SEOG, state scholarships/grants, private scholarships. *Loan aid offered:* FFEL Subsidized Stafford, FFEL Unsubsidized Stafford, FFEL PLUS, Federal Perkins Loan, state loans, college/university loans from institutional funds, HELP loans to parents. Applicants will be notified of awards on or about April 1. Federal Work-Study Program available. Institutional employment available. Off-campus job opportunities are good.

FROM THE ADMISSIONS OFFICE

"We choose students individually, one by one, and we hope that the ones we choose will approach their education the same way, as a highly individual enterprise. Our first-year seminars have enrollments limited to 15 or 16 students each in order to introduce the concept of learning not as passive receipt of information but as an active, participatory process. Our low average class size and 11:1 student/teacher ratio reflect that same philosophy. We also devote substantial resources to our Marquis Scholars Program, to one-on-one faculty-student mentoring relationships, and to other programs in engineering within a liberal arts context, giving Lafayette its distinctive character, articulated in our second-year seminars exploring values in science and technology. Lafayette provides an environment in which its students can discover their own personal capacity for learning, personal growth, and leadership.

"Submission of scores from either the SAT Reasoning Test or American College Testing Program (ACT) is required. If taking the ACT, the optional Writing Section is required. SAT Subject Test results are recommended, but not required. Scores must be submitted directly from the testing agency or via your college counselor on an 'official' high school transcript or testing summary sheet."

SELECTIVITY

Admissions Rating	96
# of applicants	5,875
% of applicants accepted	37
% of acceptees attending	29
# accepting a place on wait list	636
% admitted from wait list	9
# of early decision applicants	395
% accepted early decision	68

FRESHMAN PROFILE

Range SAT Critical Reading	580–670
Range SAT Math	620–710
Range SAT Writing	580–670
Range ACT Composite	24–29
Minimum Paper TOEFL	550
Average HS GPA	3.78
% graduated top 10% of class	62
% graduated top 25% of class	92
% graduated top 50% of class	100

DEADLINES

Early decision application deadline	2/15
Early decision notification	12/1
Regular application deadline	1/1
Regular notification	4/1
Nonfall registration?	yes

APPLICANTS ALSO LOOK AT

AND OFTEN PREFER
Boston College, Cornell University, Johns Hopkins University, Princeton University, Tufts University

AND SOMETIMES PREFER
Bucknell University, Colgate University, Lehigh University, Villanova University

AND RARELY PREFER
Franklin & Marshall College, Pennsylvania State University—University Park, Rensselaer Polytechnic Institute, Trinity College (CT)

FINANCIAL FACTS

Financial Aid Rating	95
Annual tuition	$33,634
Room & Board	$10,377
Books and supplies	$600
Required fees	$177
% frosh rec. need-based scholarship or grant aid	48
% UG rec. need-based scholarship or grant aid	48
% frosh rec. need-based self-help aid	32
% UG rec. need-based self-help aid	38

LAKE FOREST COLLEGE

555 NORTH SHERIDAN ROAD, LAKE FOREST, IL 60045 • ADMISSIONS: 847-735-5000 • FAX: 847-735-6291

STUDENTS SAY

Academics

Lake Forest College is a small liberal arts school north of Chicago where "a whole lot of personal attention, a study abroad program that is cheap because of the great financial aid, [and] professors who really care about students and how they are doing both inside and outside the classroom," help make satisfied students. Strengths here include business, English, performing arts, communications, education, and psychology; students may sample courses in all these areas easily since "requirements are very loose, allowing you to take pretty much whatever courses you want." Undergrads love the fact that "class sizes are so small that it's really hard to slack off. It feels really bad when your favorite professor writes 'I know you can do better' on the back of your paper." The small size of the school also means "you can have a great experience here, provided you make an effort to get to know your professors and administrators and get involved in the classroom." Outside the classroom there are "great leadership opportunities" available to go-getters. Other strengths include "great computer and science labs" and "a library that was just (massively) renovated."

Life

"Life at Lake Forest is generally laid-back," with a pace set by the quiet, high-end suburb in which the school is located. Students complain that "the town is not very friendly and is very elitist and boring. Every place seems to close at 6:00 P.M." Fortunately, Chicago is only a commuter train ride away, a "great asset to the school, both for academics and entertainment. Many students travel into the city to go to shows, sporting events, or just to walk around." A few undergrads, however, complain that "it is not as easy to get into the city as they make it sound in the school brochure. It's an hour by train and it's tough to get off campus without a car. A lot of people get frustrated and start to feel claustrophobic with the campus and its location." Undergrads prefer to hold small parties in their residences or find their way over to parties at Northwestern (about half as far away as downtown Chicago). The campus is more active during the week, when "student involvement in organizations and student government is high. Also, there is great support for the athletic teams," as well as a high level of participation in sports; with 17 intercollegiate teams and fewer than 1,400 undergrads, there are "a lot of jocks here."

Student Body

Lake Forest has long had a reputation as a preppy haven, a reputation that still holds true; students tell us that a good number of students "are private-school kids from the suburbs. Lots of khaki and North Face jackets." While "There are some rich annoying people" here, "on the whole everyone is pretty nice and friendly, although cliques are created quickly and held onto quite tightly by much of the student body." Athletes are one of the biggest cliques; others include "the musical people who only hang with other musical people, the actors who only hang with other actors, etc. However, many students broaden their range of friends by participating in multiple activities." Undergrads report "a good amount of diversity for such a small school, although most of it comes from international kids" who, like most other groups, "hang out with each other most of the time."

FINANCIAL AID: 847-735-5103 • E-MAIL: ADMISSIONS@LAKEFOREST.EDU • WEBSITE: WWW.LAKEFOREST.EDU

ADMISSIONS

Very important factors considered include: Academic GPA, interview, rigor of secondary school record. *Important factors considered include:* Application essay, character/personal qualities, extracurricular activities, level of applicant's interest, recommendation(s), talent/ability. *Other factors considered include:* Alumni/ae relation, class rank, first generation, geographical residence, standardized test scores, volunteer work, work experience. TOEFL required of all international applicants. High school diploma is required, and GED is accepted. *Academic units required:* 4 English, 3 math, 2 science (2 science labs), 2 social studies, 2 history, 2 academic electives. *Academic units recommended:* 4 English, 4 math, 3 science (3 science labs), 2 foreign language, 3 social studies, 3 history, 3 academic electives, 1 honors or AP course.

The Inside Word

Candidates with a solid academic record will meet with little resistance on the road to acceptance. But remember that Lake Forest definitely has a prep-school-at-the-college-level feel. It pays to keep in mind the Admissions Committee's eagerness to assess the whole person when completing the application.

FINANCIAL AID

Students should submit: FAFSA, institution's own financial aid form, Federal Income Tax Return. Regular filing deadline is January 31. The Princeton Review suggests that all financial aid forms be submitted as soon as possible after January 1. *Need-based scholarships/grants offered:* Pell Grant, SEOG, state scholarships/grants, private scholarships, the school's own gift aid. *Loan aid offered:* FFEL Subsidized Stafford, FFEL Unsubsidized Stafford, FFEL PLUS, Federal Perkins Loan, college/university loans from institutional funds, private loans. Applicants will be notified of awards on a rolling basis beginning or about March 1.

FROM THE ADMISSIONS OFFICE

"Lake Forest College is Chicago's national liberal arts college. Located 30 miles north of downtown Chicago, the college's proximity to the city provides Lake Forest students and faculty with unique academic, cultural, and employment resources. Through partnerships with a variety of cultural, educational, financial, research, and scientific institutions in Chicago and its environs, students are engaged in an active learning process that takes them beyond the traditional boundaries of the classroom, integrating the theoretical and the practical.

"The 1,400 students represent 54 countries and 47 states. Lake Forest College fosters interaction among a diverse community of students and faculty with a significant international and minority population. The faculty consists of dedicated teachers and accomplished scholars, and they do all the teaching; you will not find teaching assistants at Lake Forest.

"The college's Career Advancement Center (CAC) works with students during their first year on campus, and later provides mentoring opportunities with alumni from around the globe as well as internship assistance and job placement.

"With more than 80 student-run organizations and clubs, 17 varsity NCAA Division III teams, and a variety of intramural and club sports, students find many opportunities outside the classroom.

"Lake Forest has a test-optional admission process permitting students to choose whether or not to have their ACT or SAT scores considered for admission. International students and students applying for certain academic scholarships will still be required to submit scores. During the admission process, Lake Forest evaluates each student based on qualities that determine success in college: strong academic performance in a challenging high school curriculum, leadership experience and commitment to community, and extracurricular involvement and individual talent.

"Lake Forest College does not require the Writing component of the new SAT or ACT. We accept either the ACT or SAT scores and will use the student's best scores, as well as either the new or old (prior to March 2005) version."

SELECTIVITY

Admissions Rating	88
# of applicants	2,197
% of applicants accepted	63
% of acceptees attending	28
# accepting a place on wait list	34
# of early decision applicants	46
% accepted early decision	78

FRESHMAN PROFILE

Range SAT Critical Reading	530–630
Range SAT Math	520–630
Range SAT Writing	520–620
Range ACT Composite	24–28
Minimum Paper TOEFL	550
Minimum Computer Based TOEFL	220
Average HS GPA	3.5
% graduated top 10% of class	32
% graduated top 25% of class	59
% graduated top 50% of class	88

DEADLINES

Early decision application deadline	12/1
Early decision notification	12/20
Regular notification	3/15
Nonfall registration?	yes

APPLICANTS ALSO LOOK AT

AND OFTEN PREFER
Connecticut College, Kenyon College, Northwestern University

AND SOMETIMES PREFER
American University, The University of Chicago, University of Denver

AND RARELY PREFER
DePaul University, Loyola University—Chicago

FINANCIAL FACTS

Financial Aid Rating	99
Annual tuition	$28,700
Room & Board	$6,960
Books and supplies	$700
Required fees	$464
% frosh rec. need-based scholarship or grant aid	78
% UG rec. need-based scholarship or grant aid	76
% frosh rec. need-based self-help aid	50
% UG rec. need-based self-help aid	50
% frosh rec. any financial aid	78
% UG rec. any financial aid	76

LAWRENCE UNIVERSITY

PO BOX 599, APPLETON, WI 54912-0599 • ADMISSIONS: 920-832-6500 • FAX: 920-832-6782

STUDENTS SAY
Academics

"The conservatory is amazing, and so is the Biology Department" at Lawrence University, a small private Midwestern school between Oshkosh and Green Bay. But these high-profile programs aren't the only standouts here; on the contrary, "No major is a 'junk major' that one can fulfill without doing any work." "Lawrence is a very tough school academically. It is extremely rigorous when it comes to course work. There is time for athletics and fun, but know that you are coming here to study." Students warn that "there is no grade inflation. To do well here you cannot rest on your laurels. But by forcing you to work, Lawrence teaches you the skills to communicate effectively with the world." A trimester academic calendar further ratchets up the intensity; one student explains, "Everything moves very rapidly and you are stuck with major exams every 3 to 5 weeks for the most part." Lawrence professors "are amazing, and that's an understatement. Each is excited about his or her field in a way that inspires you to go above and beyond the class assignments. I took a physics class and wanted to be a physics major, then I took an intro-level religious studies course and wanted to take more religious studies courses." Students appreciate how "professors accept student input on textbooks, and some actively inquire as to the effectiveness of these texts. There's a sense at Lawrence that professors are constantly trying to improve the classroom experience." Premeds also love that "the percentage of Lawrentians who get into medical school is much higher than the national average."

Life

Hometown Appleton "isn't exactly a mecca of culture," but Lawrence's "large music program and active theater community help compensate for what the town lacks." A few intrepid souls who aggressively explore Appleton report that it offers some surprise diversions; most here, however, never discover them. Rather, they stick near their "strictly residential campus, which keeps the student body really close-knit and aware of each other," but also "means we don't leave campus much, except to visit the bars and coffee shops on College Avenue." Many social events "take place in the frat quad," including "Jell-O Wrestling, the Foam Party, and Heaven and Hell Party." Students also have access to "casual fun, such as movies and guest speakers. National acts come to campus occasionally; we recently had Ben Folds here and also Lewis Black." Even so, many here feel that "the school needs to find better ways for students to relieve stress. The pressure here drives many students to intense stress levels. They need to find a way to balance the academic workload." Lawrence's campus is "beautiful, but tiny and hard pressed for space, so it gets more and more crowded with each new building."

Student Body

Lawrence attracts "bright, motivated, overachievers who are also creative and innovative." They are enthusiastic about learning, often self-admittedly to the point of geekiness. One student writes, "The typical student at Lawrence was that dorky kid in your high school class who was reading *Henry V* for fun and writing grants to build energy gardens—and getting them." Another adds, "We are the band geeks, the drama nerds, the kids who went to French camp, the kids painting murals on the gym wall." While many here "are White and middle-class, we have a large number of international students from all over the world to accent our learning experience. Moreover, financial aid allows students from many demographic backgrounds to attend." Students agree that "discrimination here is almost a sin, with active campus groups for all races, sexual orientations, religious groups—you name it."

FINANCIAL AID: 920-832-6583 • E-MAIL: EXCEL@LAWRENCE.EDU • WEBSITE: WWW.LAWRENCE.EDU

ADMISSIONS

Very important factors considered include: Academic GPA, class rank, rigor of secondary school record. *Important factors considered include:* Application essay, character/personal qualities, extracurricular activities, recommendation(s), talent/ability. *Other factors considered include:* Alumni/ae relation, first generation, interview, racial/ethnic status, standardized test scores, volunteer work, work experience. TOEFL required of all international applicants. High school diploma is required, and GED is not accepted. *Academic units recommended:* 4 English, 3 math, 3 science, 2 foreign language, 2 social studies, 2 history.

The Inside Word

Although the admit rate is fairly high, getting into Lawrence demands an above-average academic record. Students who are serious about getting into the university should stick with a very challenging high school course load straight through senior year, put significant energy into their application essays, and definitely interview.

FINANCIAL AID

Students should submit: FAFSA, institution's own financial aid form, parent Federal Income Tax Returns and W-2s, student Federal Income Tax Returns. The Princeton Review suggests that all financial aid forms be submitted as soon as possible after January 1. *Need-based scholarships/grants offered:* Pell Grant, SEOG, state scholarships/grants, private scholarships, the school's own gift aid. *Loan aid offered:* Direct Subsidized Stafford, Direct Unsubsidized Stafford, Direct PLUS, FFEL PLUS, Federal Perkins Loan. Applicants will be notified of awards on a rolling basis beginning or about March 15.

FROM THE ADMISSIONS OFFICE

"Lawrence students are characterized by their energy, commitment to community service, respect for each other, and desire to achieve their full potential. Campus activities are abundant, off-campus study programs are popular (more than half of the students take advantage of them), small classes are the norm (65 percent of the classes have 10 or fewer students in them), and, yes, winters can be 'character-building.' But the diversity of interests and experiences, the drive to excel, the wealth of cultural opportunities presented by the Art, Theater, and Music Departments, the quality of research students undertake alongside PhD faculty, and the general friendly attitude of everyone at the university contribute to a uniquely engaging living and learning environment.

"We seek students who are intellectual, imaginative, and innovative: qualities best quantified from a thorough review of each applicant's curriculum, academic performance, essay, activities, and recommendations. Accordingly, Lawrence considers—but does not require—the ACT and the SAT in its review of applications for admission and scholarship."

SELECTIVITY

Admissions Rating	90
# of applicants	2,315
% of applicants accepted	56
% of acceptees attending	29
# accepting a place on wait list	116
% admitted from wait list	27
# of early decision applicants	28
% accepted early decision	86

FRESHMAN PROFILE

Range SAT Critical Reading	600–720
Range SAT Math	600–690
Range SAT Writing	600–690
Range ACT Composite	26–31
Minimum Paper TOEFL	575
Minimum Computer Based TOEFL	233
Average HS GPA	3.45
% graduated top 10% of class	34
% graduated top 25% of class	66
% graduated top 50% of class	96

DEADLINES

Early decision application deadline	11/15
Early decision notification	12/1
Regular application deadline	1/15
Regular notification	4/1
Nonfall registration?	no

APPLICANTS ALSO LOOK AT AND OFTEN PREFER

Beloit College, Carleton University, Macalester College, St. Olaf College, University of Wisconsin—Madison

AND SOMETIMES PREFER

Grinnell College, Illinois Wesleyan University, Knox College, Northwestern University, Oberlin College

FINANCIAL FACTS

Financial Aid Rating	95
Annual tuition	$29,376
Room & Board	$6,822
Books and supplies	$1,800
Required fees	$222
% frosh rec. need-based scholarship or grant aid	68
% UG rec. need-based scholarship or grant aid	66
% frosh rec. need-based self-help aid	58
% UG rec. need-based self-help aid	58
% frosh rec. any financial aid	94
% UG rec. any financial aid	95

LEHIGH UNIVERSITY

27 MEMORIAL DRIVE WEST, BETHLEHEM, PA 18015 • ADMISSIONS: 610-758-3100 • FAX: 610-758-4361

STUDENTS SAY

Academics

Nearly half the students at prestigious Lehigh University study either engineering or business; a select few even combine the two through the "excellent and very selective integrated business and engineering honors program." These disciplines are undoubtedly the marquee attractions at this demanding midsize school, but other programs certainly stand out. Lehigh is "strong in architecture" and "has very competitive science programs," students tell us. The humanities, on the other hand, "could be expanded a bit more," although the school hopes to improve this with the new Arts Lehigh initiative. In the most popular disciplines, "the work is extremely tough and you need to constantly keep on top of it all," with "some classes being mostly project-based, while others are mostly test-based." Grading can be a source of stress, as "your entire grade is based on a huge curve, especially in the science, math, and engineering classes, so you never know how well you are doing until your grades are posted at the end of the semester." Fortunately, "The faculty here are generally extremely helpful, and any of the professors are more than willing to set up meeting times with students to discuss problems or to provide you with extra help." Undergrads also love that "Lehigh has amazing research facilities and brilliant professors with tons of real-world experience. As an example, one chemistry professor created a method to remove arsenic from wells in India and Bangladesh, and then helped incorporate that into the freshman engineering class." Such assets play well with area businesses, translating into "great opportunities for internships and great job placement rates for graduates."

Life

Lehigh, with its "heavy workload and active social life . . . embodies the 'work hard, play hard' mantra. We party here like there is no tomorrow," students tell us. Partying on 'the Hill,' "where all frat and sorority houses are situated, is the main attraction when we aren't studying, which is rare," but parties in non-Greek off-campus housing are also common, and "The two social groups don't really mix or interact." There are activities for nondrinkers—"There's swing dancing Saturday nights, and guest singers and poetry readings at Lamberton Hall," as well as "some good concerts and comedians on weekends"—but "Even these events are mostly attended by people who drink (before they) go to them, then go out and party afterward." During the week "There is so much for the students to get involved with, which creates a lot of opportunities to partake in leadership roles and develop in many ways as a human being." College athletics are big, with the annual football square-off against nearby Lafayette as the highlight of each season. Although hometown Bethlehem "has some wonderful places for students to go and is very affordable," many here prefer either to hang near campus or "take the bus to Philly for some real city entertainment. It's really convenient."

Student Body

Lehigh's "typically athletic" students "want to do well in class but also love to party." They shop at the same places, procuring uniforms consisting of some combination of "khakis, polos with popped collars, North Face fleece, Gucci, Prada, Coach, Dooney & Bourke, pointy boots, Ugg boots, and rainbow sandals. We are prepped out and name-branded to the max; this is Lehigh." Some here observe that "the school is trying to diversify" and that "the freshman were more diverse in 2004–2005. Lots of freshmen have 'fros, and you notice. You can identify the punk kids and the handful of goth kids; everyone knows who you are if you look different." Students tend to be apolitical; one undergrad explains, "Politics is not a big topic, and current events tend to not be known. You end up in the 'Lehigh Bubble' here." An added benefit of attending Lehigh is that the campus landscape guarantees a daily workout; most undergrads "have great legs from climbing our mountain day in and day out!"

FINANCIAL AID: 610-758-3181 • E-MAIL: ADMISSIONS@LEHIGH.EDU • WEBSITE: WWW.LEHIGH.EDU

ADMISSIONS

Very important factors considered include: Recommendation(s), rigor of secondary school record. *Important factors considered include:* Application essay, character/personal qualities, extracurricular activities, standardized test scores, talent/ability, volunteer work,. *Other factors considered include:* Academic GPA, alumni/ae relation, class rank, first generation, geographical residence, level of applicant's interest, racial/ethnic status, work experience. SAT or ACT required; ACT with Writing component required. TOEFL required of all international applicants. High school diploma or equivalent is not required. *Academic units required:* 4 English, 3 math, 2 science (2 science labs), 2 foreign language, 2 social studies, 3 academic electives.

The Inside Word

Lots of work at bolstering Lehigh's public recognition for overall academic quality has paid off—liberal arts candidates will now find the admissions process to be highly selective. Students without solidly impressive academic credentials will have a rough time getting in regardless of their choice of programs, as will unenthusiastic, but academically strong candidates who have clearly chosen Lehigh as a safety.

FINANCIAL AID

Students should submit: FAFSA, CSS/Financial Aid PROFILE, Noncustodial PROFILE, Business/Farm Supplement. Regular filing deadline is February 15. The Princeton Review suggests that all financial aid forms be submitted as soon as possible after January 1. *Need-based scholarships/grants offered:* Pell Grant, SEOG, state scholarships/grants, private scholarships, the school's own gift aid, United Negro College Fund. *Loan aid offered:* FFEL Subsidized Stafford, FFEL Unsubsidized Stafford, FFEL PLUS, Federal Perkins Loan, college/university loans from institutional funds, private educational alternative loans. Applicants will be notified of awards on or about March 30. Federal Work-Study Program available. Institutional employment available. Off-campus job opportunities are good.

FROM THE ADMISSIONS OFFICE

"Lehigh University is located 50 miles north of Philadelphia and 75 miles southwest of New York City in Bethlehem, Pennsylvania, where a cultural renaissance has taken place with the opening of more than a dozen ethnic restaurants, the addition of several boutiques and galleries, and Lehigh's Campus Square residential/retail complex. Lehigh combines learning opportunities of a large research university with the personal attention of a small, private college, by offering an education that integrates courses from four colleges and dozens of fields of study. Students customize their experience to their interests by tailoring majors and academic programs from more than 2,000 courses, changing majors, carrying a double major, or taking courses outside their college or major field of study. Lehigh offers unique learning opportunities through interdisciplinary programs such as music and engineering and computer science and business (www.lehigh.edu/distinctive programs). The arts are essential to the learning experience and are integrated throughout the curriculum. Students develop their imagination and creativity while acquiring skills that will complement their professional development. Students have access to world-class faculty who offer their time and personal attention to help students learn and succeed. Students gain hands-on, real-world experience and take part in activities that build confidence and help them develop as leaders. Lehigh's vibrant campus life offers many social and extracurricular activities. Choose from 150 and 40 intramural and club sports, in which over 60 percent of undergraduates participate.

"Lehigh requires students to submit scores from the new SAT with the Writing component. Students may also take the ACT with the Writing portion in lieu of the SAT. SAT Subject Tests are recommended but not required."

SELECTIVITY

Admissions Rating	97
# of applicants	10,689
% of applicants accepted	39
% of acceptees attending	29
# accepting a place on wait list	807
# of early decision applicants	734
% accepted early decision	59

FRESHMAN PROFILE

Range SAT Critical Reading	580–670
Range SAT Math	640–720
Minimum Paper TOEFL	570
Minimum Computer Based TOEFL	230
% graduated top 10% of class	90
% graduated top 25% of class	99
% graduated top 50% of class	100

DEADLINES

Early decision application deadline	11/15
Early decision notification	12/15
Regular application deadline	1/1
Nonfall registration?	yes

APPLICANTS ALSO LOOK AT

AND OFTEN PREFER
Cornell University, Johns Hopkins University, University of Pennsylvania

AND SOMETIMES PREFER
Boston College, Bucknell University, Carnegie Mellon University, Tufts University

AND RARELY PREFER
Case Western Reserve University, Lafayette College, Pennsylvania State University—University Park, Villanova University

FINANCIAL FACTS

Financial Aid Rating	88
Annual tuition	$35,310
Room & board	$9,340
% frosh rec. need-based scholarship or grant aid	45
% UG rec. need-based scholarship or grant aid	43
% frosh rec. need-based self-help aid	46
% UG rec. need-based self-help aid	43
% frosh rec. any financial aid	65
% UG rec. any financial aid	60

LEWIS & CLARK COLLEGE

0615 SOUTHWEST PALATINE HILL ROAD, PORTLAND, OR 97219-7899 • ADMISSIONS: 503-768-7040 • FAX: 503-768-7055

CAMPUS LIFE
Quality of Life Rating	**89**
Fire Safety Rating	**72**
Type of school	private
Environment	city

STUDENTS
Total undergrad enrollment	1,926
% male/female	39/61
% from out of state	77
% from public high school	80
% live on campus	65
% African American	2
% Asian	6
% Caucasian	65
% Hispanic	4
% Native American	1
% international	4
# of countries represented	41

SURVEY SAYS . . .
Small classes
Great library
Students aren't religious
Students love Portland, OR
Great off-campus food
Frats and sororities are unpopular or nonexistent
Political activism is popular

ACADEMICS
Academic Rating	**88**
Calendar	semester
Student/faculty ratio	13:1
Profs interesting rating	90
Profs accessible rating	90
% profs teaching UG courses	100
% classes taught by TAs	0
Most common lab size	20–29 students
Most common reg class size	10–19 students

MOST POPULAR MAJORS
international relations and affairs
psychology
sociology

STUDENTS SAY
Academics
"The greatest strength of Lewis & Clark College is the strength of the community," students tell us, pointing out that "the majority of students and faculty are extremely personable. You become friends with everyone quickly." This "community, centered on academics, the outdoors, and a commitment to improving the world," boasts especially strong programs in psychology, premedical sciences, and international affairs; the last is bolstered by "very popular study abroad programs." One student writes, "Lewis & Clark's international perspective is especially appealing. There's an emphasis on a global world view with an effort to promote and influence change for the better in every situation. I know that attending this school will encourage me to grow and reach my full potential." Professors are "amazing people who really care about their students and how they are doing inside and outside of the classroom." They are "definitely available whenever you are having trouble or need to go over something from class. With a school like this, what you pay for is accessibility." One student sums up, "The best thing about this school is that it is such a well-rounded package. It is in a wonderful area, has amazing professors, a beautiful campus, a great surrounding city, a healthy endowment, and motivated students."

Life
Lewis & Clark is in "an incredible location," abutting "a very pretty state park with a view of Mount Hood, right in the city of Portland." The setting is bucolic; "Even though it is 10 minutes away from downtown Portland, you wouldn't even know you are in a city," students tell us. The campus is so alluring that some rarely venture off; one student writes, "You can go 3 weeks or so without leaving campus, and Lewis & Clark has often been described as a bubble campus." For such homebodies, student organizations and the school "do a good job of creating things to do on campus. There are many concerts by local artists, open mic nights, poetry slams, lectures, forums, and free university classes." "There are always plenty of things to do on campus," reports one undergrad. Students anxious to explore the city happily note that "getting off campus is easy with the free shuttle the school provides. It drops you off right downtown in the heart of things." The city offers "excellent restaurants, music venues and coffee shops [but] seems to close down early, even on weekends." For those "not into the urban scene" or campus extracurriculars, "There are many outdoor activities available if you have a car to get to them or are able to take advantage of the transportation provided by the college. "Rock climbing, camping, and backpacking are common activities."

Student Body
"There are many different types of Lewis & Clark students," including "academically minded individuals who attend the lectures and join clubs; athletes, who all seem to live and party together in one dorm; outdoorsy kids, who never seem to spend any time indoors; and students who do not fall neatly into any of these groups, such as international students or theater kids." The college has a reputation as a "pseudo-hippie" school, and there are certainly some students here who fit the bill; they "wear Birkenstocks and assorted clothing fitting the hippie stereotype, are usually unkempt, and smoke weed at least a few times during their college career." Republicans "are few and far between," among the "mainly liberal student body where everyone is doing their own thing."

FINANCIAL AID: 503-768-7090 • E-MAIL: ADMISSIONS@LCLARK.EDU • WEBSITE: WWW.LCLARK.EDU

ADMISSIONS

Very important factors considered include: Academic GPA, racial/ethnic status, rigor of secondary school record. *Important factors considered include:* Alumni/ae relation, application essay, character/personal qualities, class rank, extracurricular activities, first generation, recommendation(s), standardized test scores, talent/ability, volunteer work. *Other factors considered include:* Geographical residence, interview, level of applicant's interest, state residency, work experience. TOEFL required of all international applicants. High school diploma is required, and GED is accepted. *Academic units recommended:* 4 English, 3 math, 3 science (2 science labs), 3 foreign language, 3 social studies.

The Inside Word

Admissions evaluations are thorough, and the Portfolio Path is an intriguing option that guarantees a purely personal evaluation. Few colleges of Lewis & Clark's quality are as accommodating to students.

FINANCIAL AID

Students should submit: FAFSA. The Princeton Review suggests that all financial aid forms be submitted as soon as possible after January 1. *Need-based scholarships/grants offered:* Pell Grant, SEOG, state scholarships/grants, private scholarships, the school's own gift aid. *Loan aid offered:* FFEL Subsidized Stafford, FFEL Unsubsidized Stafford, FFEL PLUS, Federal Perkins Loan. Applicants will be notified of awards on a rolling basis beginning or about March 1. Federal Work-Study Program available. Institutional employment available. Off-campus job opportunities are fair.

FROM THE ADMISSIONS OFFICE

"The record number of applicants in recent years cited a variety of reasons they were drawn to Lewis & Clark. Many had to do with the multiple environments experienced by our students, including a small arts and sciences college with a 13:1 student/faculty ratio; a location only six miles from downtown Portland (metropolitan population 1.9 million); a setting in the heart of the Pacific Northwest, making more than 80 trips per year possible for our College Outdoors Program; and the rest of the world—almost 60 percent of our graduates included an overseas program in their curriculum. Since 1962, more than 9,337 students and 212 faculty members have participated in 578 programs in 66 countries on 6 continents. Our international curriculum has undergone a total review to better prepare graduates going into the twenty-first century.

"At Lewis & Clark College, SAT Subject Test scores are not required."

SELECTIVITY

Admissions Rating	90
# of applicants	4,698
% of applicants accepted	58
% of acceptees attending	19
# accepting a place on wait list	264
% admitted from wait list	9

FRESHMAN PROFILE

Range SAT Critical Reading	620–700
Range SAT Math	590–680
Range SAT Writing	590–680
Range ACT Composite	26–30
Minimum Paper TOEFL	550
Minimum Computer Based TOEFL	213
Average HS GPA	3.7
% graduated top 10% of class	42
% graduated top 25% of class	78
% graduated top 50% of class	98

DEADLINES

Regular application deadline	2/1
Regular notification	4/1
Nonfall registration?	yes

APPLICANTS ALSO LOOK AT

AND OFTEN PREFER
Occidental College, Stanford University, University of California—Santa Cruz

AND SOMETIMES PREFER
Colorado College, Reed College, University of Puget Sound, Whitman College, Willamette University

AND RARELY PREFER
Pitzer College, University of Colorado—Boulder, University of Oregon

FINANCIAL FACTS

Financial Aid Rating	88
Annual tuition	$31,408
Room & Board	$8,164
Books and supplies	$1,000
Required fees	$216
% frosh rec. need-based scholarship or grant aid	60
% UG rec. need-based scholarship or grant aid	61
% frosh rec. need-based self-help aid	38
% UG rec. need-based self-help aid	44
% frosh rec. any financial aid	78
% UG rec. any financial aid	80

LOUISIANA STATE UNIVERSITY

110 THOMAS BOYD HALL, BATON ROUGE, LA 70803 • ADMISSIONS: 225-578-1175 • FAX: 225-575-4433

STUDENTS SAY

Academics

At Louisiana State University's flagship campus, you'll find "outstanding academics combined with a great college life." Some students here opt for only the latter; for many, "LSU is about football and partying." "Those who wish to apply themselves," however, "have ample opportunity and resources," and they can learn almost anything, since "The greatest strength of LSU by far is its diversity. [You] can come to LSU for sports, music. . . science, economics, or nearly any sort of humanities discipline you are interested in." Areas of strength include programs in premedical science, engineering, agriculture, and mass communications. The school is huge, which means that "somewhere within that huge number is someone that you can get along with," but also that it is easy to "get lost in the crowd"; "You are just a number to the administration and a good amount of your professors," especially in intro-level classes. However, "Once you get into classes that are smaller and more geared toward your chosen major, you are able to develop more of a one-on-one relationship with your professors." Fortunately "many administrative tasks" (such as "bills and registration") "can be completed online, and computers are available all over campus for students who don't have personal computers," making the bureaucracy somewhat easier to navigate. The school also offers academic lifelines such as "free tutoring all day long. The tutors are students who have already taken [the] courses."

Life

LSU is a big enough school to offer something for everyone, and undergrads here enjoy countless activities within a variety subcultures. Most divisions, however, dissolve on game day, when tailgating is raised to the level of "an art form." A freshman reports, "On Saturdays during football season everyone is on campus before the game with friends, beer, and barbeque." Fans "come from all over and stay out all day. It's the one day when it doesn't matter who you are, as long as you're wearing purple and gold." Other LSU traditions include Thursday nights at the bars of Tigerland, "a street with three popular college bars right next to each other," and parties wherever and whenever possible. The Greek system here is "highly influential," but, students note, "This isn't the kind of school where a student doesn't have a social life if he/she isn't Greek." For the more aesthetically inclined, "LSU has an amazing art center—The Shaw Center—complete with a theater and fancy sushi bar on the top floor, which looks over the Mississippi River." Undergrads report that "the beauty of our campus is amazing. The 100-plus-year-old oaks and the Italian Renaissance architecture wow any visitor to LSU's campus."

Student Body

The typical student at LSU "studies moderately—enough to get the grade he/she desires in a class"—and "frequently spends time with friends, possibly going to parties or places that serve alcohol." Mixed in is "a good number of atypical students who study more and do not go partying over the weekends. These students find fulfillment in their own interests regardless of what others think." While "conservative frat boys and sorority girls dominate the campus," the school is home to a diverse population including "many from foreign countries and other ethnic group[s]" and "a huge subculture of indie-rock nerds, skateboarders, hippies, and liberals." There are even a few who "don't give a damn about LSU football"—hey, at a school this big, anything's possible. The student body also includes a substantial population of legacies.

LOUISIANA STATE UNIVERSITY

FINANCIAL AID: 225-578-3103 • E-MAIL: ADMISSIONS@LSU.EDU • WEBSITE: WWW.LSU.EDU

ADMISSIONS

Very important factors considered include: Academic GPA, rigor of secondary school record, standardized test scores. *Important factors considered include:* Class rank. *Other factors considered include:* Extracurricular activities, talent/ability. SAT or ACT required; ACT with Writing component required. TOEFL required of all international applicants. High school diploma is required, and GED is accepted. *Academic units required:* 4 English, 3 math, 3 science, 2 foreign language, 3 social studies, 3 academic electives. *Academic units recommended:* 4 math.

The Inside Word

Good students and great athletes are welcome at LSU, where the annual avalanche of applications necessitates a formula-driven approach to admissions. Check LSU's website to see which combinations of GPA, class rank, and test scores qualify students for admission.

FINANCIAL AID

Students should submit: FAFSA, institution's own financial aid form. The Princeton Review suggests that all financial aid forms be submitted as soon as possible after January 1. *Need-based scholarships/grants offered:* Pell Grant, SEOG, state scholarships/grants, private scholarships, the school's own gift aid. *Loan aid offered:* FFEL Subsidized Stafford, FFEL Unsubsidized Stafford, FFEL PLUS. Applicants will be notified of awards on or about March 1. Federal Work-Study Program available. Institutional employment available. Off-campus job opportunities are excellent.

FROM THE ADMISSIONS OFFICE

"LSU holds a prominent position in U.S. higher education and is committed to meeting the challenge of pursuing intellectual development for its students, expanding the bounds of knowledge through research, and creating economic opportunities for Louisiana. LSU, one of only 25 universities nationwide designated as both a land-grant and sea-grant institution, also holds the Carnegie Foundation's doctoral research, extensive designation.

"LSU's instructional programs include 198 undergraduate and graduate/professional degrees. Outside of the classroom, residential colleges, service-learning opportunites, and over 350 registered student organizations contribute to an exciting and meaningful college experience.

"Louisiana State University offers the Southern hospitality of a small community while providing the benefits of a large, technologically advanced institution.

"Freshman applicants for Fall 2008 are required to submit writing scores by taking the new version of the SAT (or the ACT with the Writing component). LSU will use the best scores from either SAT or ACT, including scores from the old (prior to March 2005) versions of the tests, in making admission decisions."

SELECTIVITY

Admissions Rating	**83**
# of applicants	10,135
% of applicants accepted	74
% of acceptees attending	60

FRESHMAN PROFILE

Range SAT Critical Reading	520–630
Range SAT Math	540–660
Range ACT Composite	22–27
Minimum Paper TOEFL	550
Minimum Computer Based TOEFL	213
Average HS GPA	3.47
% graduated top 10% of class	25
% graduated top 25% of class	53
% graduated top 50% of class	83

DEADLINES

Regular application deadline	4/15
Nonfall registration?	yes

FINANCIAL FACTS

Financial Aid Rating	**70**
Annual in-state tuition	$2,981
Annual out-of-state tuition	$11,281
Room & Board	$6,498
Books and supplies	$1,500
Required fees	$1,468
% frosh rec. need-based scholarship or grant aid	45
% UG rec. need-based scholarship or grant aid	37
% frosh rec. need-based self-help aid	26
% UG rec. need-based self-help aid	30
% frosh rec. any financial aid	94
% UG rec. any financial aid	78

LOYOLA COLLEGE IN MARYLAND

4501 NORTH CHARLES STREET, BALTIMORE, MD 21210 • ADMISSIONS: 410-617-5012 • FAX: 410-617-2176

CAMPUS LIFE
Quality of Life Rating	89
Fire Safety Rating	88
Type of school	private
Affiliation	Roman Catholic
Environment	village

STUDENTS
Total undergrad enrollment	3,483
% male/female	40/60
% from out of state	82
% from public high school	50
% live on campus	78
% African American	5
% Asian	3
% Caucasian	86
% Hispanic	3
% international	1
# of countries represented	31

SURVEY SAYS . . .
Small classes
Athletic facilities are great
Dorms are like palaces
Frats and sororities are unpopular or nonexistent
Lots of beer drinking
Hard liquor is popular

ACADEMICS
Academic Rating	83
Calendar	semester
Student/faculty ratio	12:1
Profs interesting rating	88
Profs accessible rating	88
% profs teaching UG courses	72
% classes taught by TAs	0
Most common lab size	10–19 students
Most common reg class size	20–29 students

MOST POPULAR MAJORS
business administration/ management
communications studies/speech communication and rhetoric
psychology

STUDENTS SAY

Academics

"Loyola is about the community experience, which can be seen in the way faculty and students are truly involved in the community," students at this small Jesuit liberal arts college in Baltimore report. Community service is just one of many ways in which a Loyola education embodies Jesuit ideals. The school also pursues the Jesuit *raison d'être* of educating the "whole person" through a thorough core curriculum that "pushes students to their full potential, requiring us to take classes that we would not necessarily choose to take" in such disciplines as writing, social science, philosophy, and theology. Professors here strive to create "an excellent environment for learning and discussion" in which "there is a general sense that everyone wants you to succeed. They let you know that they are willing to help you in whatever way they can, and they really mean it." This sense of community extends beyond the classroom; one undergraduate notes, "Professors do not just go home at the end of the day. They are present at school sporting events, concerts, plays, and much more. They really make an effort to get to know all students." Students also appreciate the "unbeatable study abroad program" and the way "professors try to incorporate cultural aspects of Baltimore into their classes. There are often trips to see plays, museum visits, and community service events incorporated into the class." The school's location offers not only numerous cultural outlets, but also "many opportunities to network with high business executives and land great internships."

Life

Loyola students enjoy an "amazingly beautiful campus for such a great location. We're right in Baltimore, but away from the hustle and bustle of downtown in a suburban atmosphere." The campus hosts a wide range of activities, including "great annual events with huge turnouts, such as Loyolapalooza, the Fall Football Classic, and Crabfests," as well as "midnight breakfasts, basketball games, and other weekend activities [like] excellent school concerts with great bands and comedians," all of which help to fill up students' extracurricular calendars. Many undergraduates also cite Baltimore's "many museums, coffee shops, restaurants, the Inner Harbor, and sporting events," as well as easy access to DC and Annapolis when joking that "there is almost too much to do here." Then there are those who love the area bars. Those who favor the bar scene—and there are quite a few of them—insist that "Loyola is a bar school. Everybody loves the Baltimore bars and everyone loves going to them. You can always be sure to find fellow Loyola students at any bar in Baltimore on any day of the week." Others temper their assessment, telling us, "a good amount of us do take advantage of the bar scene, but we are not out of control. There are plenty of activities to do aside from drinking." What students don't do is party in their "awesome dorms, [since] the college is looking to bust anyone and everyone for the slightest infringement on the rules."

Student Body

"Popped collars, Ugg boots, J. Crew, Abercrombie, American Eagle, flip-flops, and a North Face jacket" are all acceptable components of the unofficial Loyola uniform. Students also point out that "although everyone may look the same, they really are different people. You can tell based on the variety of groups and clubs the campus offers." While many students here are admittedly materialistic—"There is the unspoken desire to outdo each other: Who has the most expensive car, who wears the better clothes, who has the best sunglasses"— they are "friendly and outgoing" and also have an altruistic side; "volunteering is huge," many tell us. Although "The racial and social diversity at Loyola has increased greatly over the last few years," the student body remains "very homogeneous."

FINANCIAL AID: 410-617-2576 • WEBSITE: WWW.LOYOLA.EDU

ADMISSIONS

Very important factors considered include: Academic GPA, rigor of secondary school record. *Important factors considered include:* Standardized test scores. *Other factors considered include:* Alumni/ae relation, application essay, character/personal qualities, class rank, extracurricular activities, racial/ethnic status, recommendation(s), talent/ability, volunteer work, work experience. SAT or ACT required; TOEFL required of all international applicants. High school diploma is required, and GED is accepted. *Academic units required:* 4 English, 3 math, 3 science, 2 history. *Academic units recommended:* 4 English, 4 math, 4 science, 3 history.

The Inside Word

Loyola is to be commended for notifying outstanding candidates of acceptance early in the applicant review cycle without demanding an early commitment in return. Traditional early decision plans are confusing, archaic, and unreasonable to students. A binding commitment is a huge price to pay to get a decision four months sooner. This is obviously one place that cares.

FINANCIAL AID

Students should submit: FAFSA, CSS/Financial Aid PROFILE, Noncustodial PROFILE, Business/Farm Supplement. Regular filing deadline is February 15. The Princeton Review suggests that all financial aid forms be submitted as soon as possible after January 1. *Need-based scholarships/grants offered:* Pell Grant, SEOG, state scholarships/grants, private scholarships, the school's own gift aid. *Loan aid offered:* Direct Subsidized Stafford, Direct Unsubsidized Stafford, FFEL PLUS, Federal Perkins Loan, college/university loans from institutional funds. Applicants will be notified of awards on or about April 1. Federal Work-Study Program available. Institutional employment available. Off-campus job opportunities are good.

FROM THE ADMISSIONS OFFICE

"To make a wise choice about your college plans, you will need to find out more. We extend to you these invitations. Question-and-answer periods with an Admissions Counselor are helpful to prospective students. An appointment should be made in advance. Admissions office hours are 9:00 A.M. to 5:00 P.M., Monday through Friday. College day programs and Saturday information programs are scheduled during the academic year. These programs include a video about Loyola, a general information session, a discussion of various majors, a campus tour, and lunch. Summer information programs can help high school juniors to get a head start on investigating colleges. These programs feature an introductory presentation about the college and a campus tour.

"Loyola College will continue to accept results of both the former SAT and ACT. In addition, Loyola will continue to combine the highest sub scores from multiple test administrations from both the old and new tests (SAT: Reading/Math scores). Loyola will not explicitly require submission of results from the new SAT."

SELECTIVITY

Admissions Rating	89
# of applicants	7,909
% of applicants accepted	64
% of acceptees attending	19

FRESHMAN PROFILE

Range SAT Critical Reading	540–640
Range SAT Math	560–650
Minimum Paper TOEFL	550
Minimum Computer Based TOEFL	213
Average HS GPA	3.5
% graduated top 10% of class	40
% graduated top 25% of class	77

DEADLINES

Regular application deadline	1/15
Regular notification	4/1
Nonfall registration?	yes

APPLICANTS ALSO LOOK AT

AND OFTEN PREFER
Boston College, Georgetown University, University of Notre Dame

AND SOMETIMES PREFER
College of the Holy Cross, University of Richmond, Villanova University

AND RARELY PREFER
Fairfield University, Fordham University, Providence College

FINANCIAL FACTS

Financial Aid Rating	93
Annual tuition	$31,270
Room & board	$9,290
Required fees	$1,265
% frosh rec. need-based scholarship or grant aid	44
% UG rec. need-based scholarship or grant aid	39
% frosh rec. need-based self-help aid	42
% UG rec. need-based self-help aid	39

LOYOLA MARYMOUNT UNIVERSITY

ONE LMU DRIVE, SUITE 100, LOS ANGELES, CA 90045 • ADMISSIONS: 310-338-2750 • FAX: 310-338-2797

STUDENTS SAY

Academics

Jesuit Loyola Marymount University houses five undergraduate colleges, "each of which is very strong. We have business, communications and fine arts, film and television, science and engineering, and liberal arts. You really can't go wrong with a major," students assure us. All undergrads here must complete a thorough core curriculum "that ensures a great overall education," in which the core courses address "ethics, art, literature, social sciences, science, math, theology, philosophy, communication, and more. It is a strong education that makes us better people." Students also love the school's "philosophies of 'educating the whole person' and promoting social justice, which give us an attitude less focused on what we can do for ourselves and more focused on the greater good." With small classes (so small that attendance is taken and counted toward every grade), professors "are more like mentors: They all know your name, and they want to help students learn as much as possible. They come to teach at LMU knowing how personal the classroom environment is—no one is ever a number—and they do their best to help each student on a one-on-one basis." One student explains, "All classes include discussion, participation, and projects that apply to the field being studied."

Life

LMU boasts "one of the most beautiful campuses ever, right on a bluff overlooking LA. With palm trees abounding, you definitely feel like you're in Southern California." Students also love that "the surrounding area is very safe, and many people, even females, say they feel safe walking around campus at night. Our school maintains strong security on campus." Undergrads here enjoy "a great sense of community" reinforced by "convo hour, which occurs every Tuesday and Thursday. It's an hour and a half when no one has classes, and a lot of the school socializes and participates in various activities and charity drives." A whopping "90-odd percent of students do some type of community service before graduating, whether it be a service organization, service trips to Mexico to build schools, giving campus tours, or Special Games—our version of the Special Olympics." In fact, "It seems everyone at LMU is involved in at least one organization, if not three or four." "All it takes is the motivation to use what LMU offers." The campus after-hours scene, however, faces "tough competition from LA," and "While the school is working on it, the social scene could still be better." It doesn't help that "a lot of people go home on weekends." Those who stick around bide their time by "going to parties and shopping" or "playing beer pong, clubbing, cruising down Sunset, or just hanging out and watching movies." Nothing is more popular than "going to the beach for fun to watch the sunset, have a bonfire, or just go for an early dive and hit the surf. It's great having it so close."

Student Body

"There is quite a bit of money at LMU," enough that "two students brought 49-inch plasma TVs to their freshman dorm this year." Perhaps they are friends with the "skinny, rich-beyond-belief blonde girls whose version of 'scrubbing it' is wearing their Juicy Couture sweatshirts with their Manolo Blahniks." But "Not everyone is rich. The school isn't overly snobby, and there is a niche for everyone." The "most visible" LMU archetype is "the vaguely wholesome, *Saved By the Bell: The College Years* jocky frat/sorority type," but there are also plenty of "serious student types who are always in the library and no one else ever really gets to know them," as well as "the artsy, theater/coffee-shop types who wear whatever expresses their feelings" as part of the "chill underground." Many in this last group "participate in the film department and the radio station and form their own close community." While "some students here are very LA, others are more focused politically and spiritually and are committed to social justice, service, and participation in student life." At LMU, it may be "easy to feel like you belong" but some say there still "needs to be a stronger sense of the differences in people, races, sexual orientations, and cultures."

LOYOLA MARYMOUNT UNIVERSITY

FINANCIAL AID: 310-338-2753 • E-MAIL: ADMISSIONS@LMU.EDU • WEBSITE: WWW.LMU.EDU

ADMISSIONS

Very important factors considered include: Academic GPA, rigor of secondary school record. *Important factors considered include:* Application essay, character/personal qualities, class rank, standardized test scores, talent/ability. *Other factors considered include:* Alumni/ae relation, extracurricular activities, first generation, geographical residence, interview, recommendation(s), volunteer work, work experience. SAT or ACT required; TOEFL required of all international applicants. High school diploma is required, and GED is accepted. *Academic units recommended:* 4 English, 3 math, 2 science (2 science labs), 3 foreign language, 3 social studies, 1 academic elective.

The Inside Word

Loyola Marymount's Admissions Committee is particular about candidate evaluation, but a large applicant pool has more to do with the university's moderate acceptance rate than does academic selectivity. Even so, underachievers will have difficulty getting in.

FINANCIAL AID

Students should submit: FAFSA, CSS/Financial Aid PROFILE, Business/Farm Supplement. Regular filing deadline is April 1. The Princeton Review suggests that all financial aid forms be submitted as soon as possible after January 1. *Need-based scholarships/grants offered:* Pell Grant, SEOG, state scholarships/grants, private scholarships, the school's own gift aid. *Loan aid offered:* FFEL Subsidized Stafford, FFEL Unsubsidized Stafford, FFEL PLUS, Federal Perkins Loan, college/university loans from institutional funds. Applicants will be notified of awards on or about May 1. Federal Work-Study Program available. Institutional employment available. Off-campus job opportunities are excellent.

FROM THE ADMISSIONS OFFICE

"Loyola Marymount University is a dynamic, student-centered university. We are medium sized (5,000 undergraduates), and we are the only Jesuit university in the Southwestern United States.

"Our campus is located in Westchester, a friendly, residential neighborhood that is removed from the hustle and bustle of Los Angeles, yet offers easy access to all the richnesss of our most cosmopolitan environment. One mile from the ocean, our students enjoy ocean and mountain vistas as well as the moderate climate and crisp breezes characteristic of a coastal location.

"Loyola Marymount is committed to the ideals of Jesuit and Marymount education. We are a student-centered university, dedicated to the education of the whole person and to the preparation of our students for lives of service to their families, communities, and professions. Breadth and rigor are the hallmarks of the curriculum.

"Taken together, our academic program, our Jesuit and Marymount heritage, and our terrific campus environment afford our students unparalleled opportunity to prepare for life and leadership in the twenty-first century.

"Applicants to the Fall 2008 entering class must submit results from either the SAT or ACT. We expect most students will submit scores from the new version of the SAT (or the ACT with the Writing section). We will use the student's best scores from either test."

SELECTIVITY

Admissions Rating	**88**
# of applicants	7,730
% of applicants accepted	56
% of acceptees attending	31

FRESHMAN PROFILE

Range SAT Critical Reading	530–630
Range SAT Math	540–640
Minimum Paper TOEFL	550
Minimum Computer Based TOEFL	213
Average HS GPA	3.6
% graduated top 10% of class	30
% graduated top 25% of class	66
% graduated top 50% of class	99

DEADLINES

Regular notification	rolling
Nonfall registration?	yes

APPLICANTS ALSO LOOK AT

AND OFTEN PREFER
Stanford University, University of California—Los Angeles

AND SOMETIMES PREFER
University of California—Irvine, University of California—San Diego, University of California—Santa Barbara, University of Southern California

AND RARELY PREFER
Pepperdine University, Santa Clara University, University of California—Riverside

FINANCIAL FACTS

Financial Aid Rating	**76**
Annual tuition	$27,710
Room & Board	$8,709
Books and supplies	$820
Required fees	$430
% frosh rec. need-based scholarship or grant aid	46
% UG rec. need-based scholarship or grant aid	47
% frosh rec. need-based self-help aid	42
% UG rec. need-based self-help aid	44

LOYOLA UNIVERSITY—CHICAGO

820 NORTH MICHIGAN AVENUE, CHICAGO, IL 60611 • ADMISSIONS: 312-915-6500 • FAX: 312-915-7216

CAMPUS LIFE

Quality of Life Rating	**77**
Fire Safety Rating	**72**
Type of school	private
Affiliation	Roman Catholic/Jesuit
Environment	metropolis

STUDENTS

Total undergrad enrollment	9,076
% male/female	35/65
% from out of state	32
% from public high school	65
% live on campus	36
% in (# of) fraternities	5 (6)
% in (# of) sororities	5 (6)
% African American	6
% Asian	12
% Caucasian	61
% Hispanic	10
% international	1
# of countries represented	77

SURVEY SAYS . . .
Small classes
Lab facilities are great
Students love Chicago, IL
Great off-campus food
Lots of beer drinking
(Almost) everyone smokes

ACADEMICS

Academic Rating	**77**
Calendar	semester
Student/faculty ratio	13:1
Profs interesting rating	75
Profs accessible rating	76
% profs teaching UG courses	97
% classes taught by TAs	0
Most common lab size	20–29 students
Most common reg class size	10–19 students

MOST POPULAR MAJORS
biology/biological sciences
nursing/registered nurse training
(ASN, BSN, MSN, RN)
psychology

STUDENTS SAY
Academics
Standing tall alongside the shore of Lake Michigan, eight miles north of Chicago, many students are quick to affirm that Loyola's greatest asset is "the school's location." Proud of its "strong Jesuit tradition," Loyola University—Chicago "encourages creative thinking and allows students to explore the complexities of the world in and out of the classroom." The professors here are "very knowledgeable" and distinguished in their respective fields, and are always "willing to help students as much as they can." "Small class sizes" help students "feel comfortable asking questions," and professors' "expertise" and "passion" make it "much easier to learn." Many students, however, express disappointment with the administration citing "red tape" and "layers of bureaucracy," which make many offices "a bit inaccessible." Recently, efforts to "streamline university services" have been made, resulting in the creation of "a central location for the Dean's, Bursar, [and] Cash Office" with "easier accessibility" to students. The President's Office also holds regular town meetings and informal gatherings to encourage an ongoing dialogue between students, staff, and administration, and a service excellence initiative also continues to evaluate and enhance student services. While the administration can be "daunting," the "Professors are always in reach, and the academic experience is uplifting." As for the Loyola experience, in the words of one student, "I love this school and I love the city it is located in."

Life
It's all about location, location, location. As one student explains, "I've learned some lessons in the classroom, but more on the streets around campus." Living in Chicago, "Students tend to have plenty of options in terms of what to do for fun." There's an active "local bar scene," as well as "concerts, museums, plays, and almost anything else one can think of doing." Getting around town is really easy: "There is a [CTA] station dedicated to the campus which makes it extremely easy to travel anywhere within the city. Each student is also given a U-pass which provides unlimited rides on any Chicago public transportation." Students who prefer to stay on campus will find "plenty of other activities" to capture their attention, including "intramural sports, clubs, and Division I basketball games." Serious sports fans should be warned, however, as "Sports teams do not rule this school." Students don't let life in the big city deter their need for the great outdoors either. They enjoy "being right on Lake Michigan" where there are plenty of "parks close by with good running trails." The school itself is located in one of "the most diverse neighborhoods" in Chicago. There are "African, Thai, Chinese, Italian, and Puerto Rican restaurants next to Mexican grocery stores, Middle Eastern bakeries, and vegetarian stores." The entertainment options are so expansive that, as one student claims, "If you get bored in Chicago, it's your own fault."

Student Body
Loyola has a "very diverse mix of students." While many are "White and from the Chicago suburbs," many others are "of all different races, ethnicities, religions, and sexual orientations." One student was surprised to discover that a "large portion of students aren't Catholic." The university supports diversity through its on-campus "ethnic and cultural groups" so that students "rarely feel alone or ostracized." As one student explains, Loyola is a "good place to be surrounded by such a diverse student body" as "There's definitely room for different people." Students here "take academics seriously" and have a "good work ethic." Most are "politically active," "generally liberal," and "social justice oriented." Others caution that most students are "traditional-age, 4-year students who have been there since they were freshmen, making it hard for new transfer students and commuters to fit in."

LOYOLA UNIVERSITY—CHICAGO

FINANCIAL AID: 773-508-3155 • E-MAIL: ADMISSION@LUC.EDU • WEBSITE: WWW.LUC.EDU

ADMISSIONS

Very important factors considered include: Academic GPA, rigor of secondary school record, standardized test scores. *Important factors considered include:* Application essay, character/personal qualities, extracurricular activities, level of applicant's interest, recommendation(s), volunteer work. *Other factors considered include:* Alumni/ae relation, class rank, first generation, geographical residence, interview, state residency, talent/ability, work experience. SAT or ACT required; TOEFL required of all international applicants. High school diploma is required, and GED is accepted. *Academic units required:* 4 English, 2 math, 2 science, 2 social studies, 1 history, 1 academic elective. *Academic units recommended:* 4 English, 4 math, 3 science, 2 foreign language, 3 social studies, 2 history, 3 academic electives.

The Inside Word

Loyola is fairly conventional when it comes to admissions policies. Successful candidates usually have a combination of strong grades, success in a tough college preparatory curriculum, and solid extracurricular activities. The school adheres to Jesuit teachings, so applicants with significant volunteer work should impress Admissions Officers.

FINANCIAL AID

Students should submit: FAFSA. The Princeton Review suggests that all financial aid forms be submitted as soon as possible after January 1. *Need-based scholarships/grants offered:* Pell Grant, SEOG, state scholarships/grants, private scholarships, the school's own gift aid. *Loan aid offered:* FFEL Subsidized Stafford, FFEL Unsubsidized Stafford, FFEL PLUS, Federal Perkins Loan, Federal Nursing Loan. Applicants will be notified of awards on a rolling basis beginning or about February 15. Federal Work-Study Program available. Institutional employment available. Off-campus job opportunities are good.

FROM THE ADMISSIONS OFFICE

"To accommodate recent record-breaking freshman classes, Loyola University—Chicago continues to open new facilities and renovate existing buildings, including the state-of-the-art Quinlan Life Sciences Education and Research Center, new residence halls at both the Lake Shore and Water Tower Campuses, and the Sullivan Center for Student Services, a new one-stop center that consolidates more than a dozen campus offices. Loyola frequently enhances its undergraduate academic programs and adds new majors in emerging fields. A new core curriculum enhances student credentials, because it emphasizes lifelong skills and values, and it gives students the opportunity to more easily complete a second major or additional minor. Nationally recognized researchers and scholars continue to teach freshman-level as well as advanced courses. These new developments build on Loyola's rich Jesuit tradition, which fosters academic excellence, instills service to others, and educates the whole person.

"Loyola's Lake Shore and Water Tower Campuses enable students to experience both traditional residential campus life and a vibrant urban environment. With more than 125 campus organizations offering numerous activities and events, as well as cultural, recreational, and internship opportunities throughout the world-class city of Chicago, undergraduate student education at Loyola extends well beyond the classroom. For more information about undergraduate academics, housing, student life, financial assistance, and more, please visit: www.luc.edu/undergrad.

"Pending further examination into the validity of the new Writing portions offered by the SAT and ACT, LUC will not require applicants to submit Writing scores from either test. All applicants are required to submit a writing sample with their application materials."

SELECTIVITY

Admissions Rating	86
# of applicants	15,178
% of applicants accepted	77
% of acceptees attending	18

FRESHMAN PROFILE

Range SAT Critical Reading	530–640
Range SAT Math	520–640
Range SAT Writing	520–620
Range ACT Composite	23–28
Minimum Paper TOEFL	550
Minimum Computer Based TOEFL	213
Average HS GPA	3.53
% graduated top 10% of class	32
% graduated top 25% of class	67
% graduated top 50% of class	95

DEADLINES

Regular notification	rolling
Nonfall registration?	yes

APPLICANTS ALSO LOOK AT AND OFTEN PREFER

DePaul University, Marquette University, Northwestern University, University of Illinois at Chicago, University of Illinois at Urbana-Champaign

AND SOMETIMES PREFER

Michigan State University, University of Michigan—Ann Arbor, University of Wisconsin—Madison, Washington University in St. Louis

AND RARELY PREFER

Illinois State University

FINANCIAL FACTS

Financial Aid Rating	73
Annual tuition	$27,200
Room & Board	$9,930
Books and supplies	$1,200
Required fees	$766
% frosh rec. need-based scholarship or grant aid	71
% UG rec. need-based scholarship or grant aid	67
% frosh rec. need-based self-help aid	64
% UG rec. need-based self-help aid	61
% frosh rec. any financial aid	97
% UG rec. any financial aid	97

LOYOLA UNIVERSITY—NEW ORLEANS

6363 ST. CHARLES AVENUE, BOX 18, NEW ORLEANS, LA 70118 • ADMISSIONS: 504-865-3240 • FAX: 504-865-3383

STUDENTS SAY

Academics

Loyola University—New Orleans provides students with "an excellent Jesuit education," that emphasizes a "commitment to the community" in "an intimate college setting," all capped with life in New Orleans, "a great place to go to school." Small by university standards, Loyola has a wonderful "community feeling." "You feel it when you first walk on campus." Professors "know you by name and it's not uncommon to stop by their office hours just to chat. They truly care about their students and how we are doing academically and otherwise." Among Loyola's top offerings is its music industry studies program, "the second-best in the nation," right up there with Berklee College of Music in Boston (but with much better weather!). The communications program is "great," as is the "awesome" College of Business (nearly one in four students here pursues a business major). Loyola also boasts a "strong program in criminal justice, with great internship opportunities in New Orleans," and an "outstanding" music program that "produces many successful musicians." One music student notes, "The greatest thing about the music school here is you are never second to a graduate student. Undergraduates are the priority." All undergraduates must complete a common curriculum covering English, math, natural science, history, philosophy, and religious studies; the common curriculum consumes most of freshman year. Hurricane Katrina robbed Loyola of much-needed tuition funds; cost-cutting measures to deal with subsequent budget shortfalls "have resulted in entire fields of study being cut from the curriculum." While that's been the source of some "discontent" on campus, many feel that under the circumstances, "The university is doing the very best that it can to function under the same ideals that it represented pre-Katrina."

Life

New Orleans, in case you hadn't heard, was hit by a pretty big hurricane in 2005. The city is still rebuilding and will be for some time; Loyola's campus, fortunately, was spared the substantial damage so much of the city endured. Students are undaunted, reporting that "going to school in New Orleans is so much fun, even after Hurricane Katrina. There's salsa dancing on Friday nights at Cafe Brazil, live music every night of the week at Snug Harbor, D.B.A., Maple Leaf, or the Howlin' Wolf (just to name a few!). There's great food everywhere in the city: Cajun, Creole, or ethnic." Audubon Park is right "up the street," and is "a great place to hang out, feed the ducks, relax, and maybe even do homework." Another distinguishing characteristic of the town is that "drinking is a way of life in New Orleans, and it's a way of life for kids on campus. You only have to be 18 to get into the bars." Most Loyola students get involved in service, and, "Post-Katrina, there's a ridiculous amount of community service that's easily accessible through the university." Loyola's frats provide plenty of on-campus diversion, as do "a wide variety of campus organizations."

Student Body

Loyola undergrads "want a real college life, not just an education. They want to have experiences and take advantage of the city and truly care about impacting their community." All students "go out and do service." "So many people mentor kids at area schools. Social justice is a theme you can't escape at Loyola." Post-Katrina, "People are very keenly aware of what's going on in the world at large," and students report feeling "more camaraderie and oneness since the hurricane." The school is home to "a wide range of different ethnicities, interests, and so forth. People mostly tend to stick to their own circles, even though people are almost always nice to each other." Prominent subpopulations include the many "sorority and frat people," sometimes "annoying," but "nice people in the end," and the "bohemians and free spirits" drawn here by the music school. "They don't really clash with the more preppy students here." It's New Orleans, so it should come as no surprise that "most students like to drink." "So-called 'straight-edge' students are a minority, but exist."

FINANCIAL AID: 504-865-3231 • E-MAIL: ADMIT@LOYNO.EDU • WEBSITE: WWW.LOYNO.EDU

ADMISSIONS

Very important factors considered include: Rigor of secondary school record, standardized test scores. *Important factors considered include:* Academic GPA, application essay, character/personal qualities, extracurricular activities, first generation, interview, recommendation(s), talent/ability. *Other factors considered include:* Alumni/ae relation, class rank, level of applicant's interest, volunteer work, work experience. ACT with Writing component required. TOEFL required of all international applicants. High school diploma is required, and GED is accepted. *Academic units required:* 4 English, 2 math, 2 science, 2 social studies. *Academic units recommended:* 4 English, 3 math, 3 science, 3 social studies.

The Inside Word

Volunteer work and community service will serve your application to any school well, but they're especially helpful at this Jesuit institution. Post-Katrina New Orleans has spooked some prospective applicants, causing Loyola to have to dig deeper into its applicant pool to fill its classes. Leverage others' squeamishness to your benefit.

FINANCIAL AID

Students should submit: FAFSA. Regular filing deadline is June 1. The Princeton Review suggests that all financial aid forms be submitted as soon as possible after January 1. *Need-based scholarships/grants offered:* Pell Grant, SEOG, private scholarships, the school's own gift aid. *Loan aid offered:* FFEL Subsidized Stafford, FFEL Unsubsidized Stafford, FFEL PLUS, Federal Perkins Loan. Applicants will be notified of awards on a rolling basis beginning or about March 1. Federal Work-Study Program available. Institutional employment available. Off-campus job opportunities are excellent.

FROM THE ADMISSIONS OFFICE

"Founded by the Jesuits in 1912, Loyola University—New Orleans has had more than 35,000 graduates who have excelled in innumerable professions for more than 80 years. Loyola's rich Jesuit tradition, its commitment to academic excellence, and its ideal size set it apart from other academic institutions. The total enrollment is approximately 5,900 students; 3,800 of whom are undergraduates. Loyola welcomed back 91 percent of its student body after Hurricane Katrina and experienced only minor damage to its campus.

"Loyola has a student/faculty ratio of 13:1. Ninety-one percent of our faculty hold the highest degrees in their fields. Loyola offers more than 60 majors, the largest of which are communications, business, psychology, music, and premed. Our undergraduate students enjoy individual attention in a university that strives to educate the whole person, not only intellectually, but also spiritually, socially, and athletically. Students hail from all 50 states, Puerto Rico, the District of Columbia, and 56 foreign countries.

"Students applying for admission for the Fall of 2008 are required to take the new version of the SAT (or the ACT with the writing section), but students may also submit scores from the old (prior to March 2005) version of the SAT (or ACT). The highest composite scores will be used in admissions decisions."

SELECTIVITY

Admissions Rating	88
# of applicants	3,021
% of applicants accepted	58
% of acceptees attending	30

FRESHMAN PROFILE

Range SAT Critical Reading	560–690
Range SAT Math	540–650
Range ACT Composite	23–28
Minimum Paper TOEFL	550
Minimum Computer Based TOEFL	213
Average HS GPA	3.65
% graduated top 10% of class	26
% graduated top 25% of class	51
% graduated top 50% of class	85

DEADLINES

Regular notification	rolling
Nonfall registration?	yes

APPLICANTS ALSO LOOK AT

AND OFTEN PREFER
Louisiana State University, Saint Louis University, Southern Methodist University, Tulane University, University of Miami

AND SOMETIMES PREFER
Boston University, College of Charleston, Florida State University, Fordham University, Loyola University—Chicago, Xavier University of Louisiana

AND RARELY PREFER
Boston College, Texas Christian University, University of Georgia

FINANCIAL FACTS

Financial Aid Rating	85
Annual tuition	$24,410
Room & Board	$9,150
Books and supplies	$1,000
Required fees	$876
% frosh rec. need-based scholarship or grant aid	56
% UG rec. need-based scholarship or grant aid	45
% frosh rec. need-based self-help aid	48
% UG rec. need-based self-help aid	41
% frosh rec. any financial aid	84
% UG rec. any financial aid	87

LYNCHBURG COLLEGE

1501 LAKESIDE DRIVE, LYNCHBURG, VA 24501 • ADMISSIONS: 434-544-8300 • FAX: 434-544-8653

Academics

On this "beautiful campus" in Lynchburg, Virginia, "a small, personable environment" gives rise to a "tight knit community" in which students partake in a "well-balanced liberal arts education." Academic highlights include a "good psychology program," a "fabulous nursing program" that draws many students, an "excellent biomedical sciences program," and a "phenomenal" Connections Leader Program that helps freshman "transition into college" life. "Classes at LC are challenging and interesting" and are taught by "intelligent" professors who are "helpful and available at most times for extra help or to answer questions." Professors want their students to "succeed and all of them care about every student and know them all by name." Not surprisingly, then, they are "willing to work around things to help you out" if the academic demands become too overwhelming. Professors aren't the only sources of academic support. "There are so many resources available for extra help, especially the Writing Center to help with papers." In sum, "There is just so much academic assistance available that if someone fails at LC they simply don't want to be in college." The "administration at Lynchburg does a fine job of communicating with its student body and working to meet the needs of the students. They are constantly asking questions and working on improving the school" in order to "make [students] happy and provide [them] with the best experience possible." Students appreciate the "friendly" and "supportive" deans on campus, and love the fact that if they need help with something, all they "have to do is e-mail them and they are ready and willing [to help] at any time"—and that extends all the way up to the college president. "No one has to go through red tape to talk with the administration."

Life

Student life at Lynchburg "consists of three things: school work, parties, and sports." The first category is pretty self-explanatory. The second ranges in size from "small groups" just hanging out to "bigger parties at the Southside houses." Concerning the third category, "Students are very interested in sports. Just about everyone plays intramurals." Not surprisingly, "The gym is somewhat popular as well," even though students pine for "a better fitness center." For the student looking for a little more variety in terms of entertainment, "LC offers a lot of lectures and cultural events." Student opinion is split about the off-campus opportunities for letting off steam. Some feel that "on weekends there is nothing to do around town because it is a small Southern town. There are no clubs or anything." Others believe that "the town of Lynchburg has a lot to offer as far as shopping, dining out, [and] activities." The "dollar theater" is a hit with cost-conscious students.

Student Body

Temperamentally, typical Lynchburg students "wants to have fun, but also succeed in school." That's why they "[go] to class, [do] their work, and [study] hard," but they also tend to "party mostly on weekends." Besides academics, "many LC students are very active in multiple student associations, athletics, volunteerism, and so forth." Because sports are such a popular pastime, there are "a lot of athletes on campus." In terms of geographic and socioeconomic variety, there doesn't seem to be much. Students describe their peers as "preppy White kids from rich families in fairly close areas." "There are not a lot of atypical students," but the few that are there have no problem finding "a niche on campus where they can fit in. There is no huge problem with hazing, bullying, or racism." To sum up, "It doesn't matter if you are different, you're not judged," and almost everyone is "easy to get along with."

FINANCIAL AID: 434-544-8228 • E-MAIL: ADMISSIONS@LYNCHBURG.EDU • WEBSITE: WWW.LYNCHBURG.EDU

ADMISSIONS

Very important factors considered include: Academic GPA, rigor of secondary school record, standardized test scores. *Important factors considered include:* Class rank, interview. *Other factors considered include:* Application essay, extracurricular activities, level of applicant's interest, recommendation(s), talent/ability, volunteer work. SAT or ACT required; TOEFL required of all international applicants. High school diploma is required, and GED is accepted. *Academic units required:* 4 English, 3 math, 3 science (2 science labs), 2 foreign language, 2 social studies, 2 history. *Academic units recommended:* 4 English, 4 math, 4 science (2 science labs), 3 foreign language, 2 social studies, 2 history, 1 academic elective.

Inside Word

The admissions process at Lynchburg is about as typical as they come. The school expects that you will have completed a college preparatory curriculum in high school with a B average and have scored near the national mean on the SAT and/or ACT. Two somewhat unique attributes of the process is that letters of recommendation are not required and applications are reviewed on a rolling basis. For those who know that Lynchburg is their first choice, the school has an early decision option.

FINANCIAL AID

Students should submit: FAFSA, state aid form. The Princeton Review suggests that all financial aid forms be submitted as soon as possible after January 1. *Need-based scholarships/grants offered:* Pell Grant, SEOG, state scholarships/grants, private scholarships, the school's own gift aid. *Loan aid offered:* FFEL Subsidized Stafford, FFEL Unsubsidized Stafford, FFEL PLUS, Federal Perkins Loan. Applicants will be notified of awards on or about March 5. Federal Work-Study Program available. Institutional employment available. Off-campus job opportunities are good.

FROM THE ADMISSIONS OFFICE

"Lynchburg College is Virginia's most comprehensive private college, nationally recognized for going above and beyond in its commitment to student success. From the moment that prospective students step onto the spectacular campus, they are aware that LC is a place where they will have opportunities to grow intellectually, morally, and spiritually, and that there are faculty, staff, and peer mentors waiting to support them in their quest to achieve their personal goals.

"The emphasis at Lynchburg College is on the development of the whole person, as evidenced by the low student/faculty ratio and an abundance of student organizations, athletic teams, intramural and club sports, and experiential learning opportunities, including service learning, internships, study abroad, and faculty-student collaborative research.

"Lynchburg College seeks to enroll students who wish to take advantage of all that the school has to offer and who want to be part of a caring community. LC welcomes and encourages interested high school students to visit the campus to see for themselves why the college has received record numbers of applications and multiple national honors in recent years. The Admissions Office sponsors open houses and other events for prospective students throughout the year. For more information visit www.lynchburg.edu.

"We allow students to submit scores from either version of the SAT or the ACT, and will use the student's best score from these tests. In regard to the current SAT, and pending further evaluation of Writing scores, the Critical Reading and Math scores will be the primary SAT scores used for admission decisions."

SELECTIVITY

Admissions Rating	76
# of applicants	4,277
% of applicants accepted	69
% of acceptees attending	19
# of early decision applicants	70
% accepted early decision	76

FRESHMAN PROFILE

Range SAT Critical Reading	460–560
Range SAT Math	460–570
Range ACT Composite	18–22
Minimum Paper TOEFL	525
Minimum Computer Based TOEFL	197
Average HS GPA	3.11
% graduated top 10% of class	12
% graduated top 25% of class	35
% graduated top 50% of class	73

DEADLINES

Early decision application deadline	11/15
Early decision notification	12/15
Regular notification	rolling
Nonfall registration?	yes

FINANCIAL FACTS

Financial Aid Rating	84
Annual tuition	$26,360
Room & Board	$7,370
Books and supplies	$750
Required fees	$405
% frosh rec. need-based scholarship or grant aid	66
% UG rec. need-based scholarship or grant aid	63
% frosh rec. need-based self-help aid	60
% UG rec. need-based self-help aid	59
% frosh rec. any financial aid	98
% UG rec. any financial aid	95

MACALESTER COLLEGE

1600 GRAND AVENUE, ST. PAUL, MN 55105 • ADMISSIONS: 651-696-6357 • FAX: 651-696-6724

STUDENTS SAY

Academics

Macalester College is "a small, personalized liberal arts college in the midst of a larger urban environment, which offers many resources and an extremely liberal environment." There's a "community feel" to Mac, where "Students take academics seriously but without any cutthroat competition. There is an honest and genuine thirst for knowledge that doesn't turn vicious." The "fantastic working relationships between students and professors" further enhance the homey atmosphere, which undergrads love. They also appreciate Mac's "focus on internationalism," pointing out that "there are very few schools of our size . . . [who] have an alum who is the secretary general of the UN (and Nobel Peace Prize winner), a huge international student population," and "forums, talks, and international roundtables that focus on pressing, intellectual, international matters." Mac is "academically demanding, sometimes to the point of insanity, but balancing it all is possible, [and] the professors are always there to help and support the students." In addition, "There is also a fantastic tutoring program called the MAX (Macalester Academic eXcellence), which all students go to for help in classes or to have papers peer edited." Administrators are described as generally helpful but can be "a little confused at times."

Life

Mac students often cite the Twin Cities as one of their main reasons for choosing the college. The area, they agree, is "very cool, with lots of opportunities for culture." Mac is located in St. Paul, in "a great neighborhood for the bored college student, with lots of neat shops and restaurants, and when we get tired of Grand Avenue, we can explore the rest of the Twin Cities with their stellar music scene and great sporting events." Some here find that they explore the city less often than they had expected when they chose Mac, both because "Typically, Mac students don't have a lot of funds at their disposal" to pay for urban amenities and also because "Between October and April it's winter here, and it's hard to motivate yourself to leave your nice, warm dorm room." For the snowbound, there's "always something to do on campus, whether it's a movie, a conference, an *American Idol* spoof, or a political protest," but "Organized activities on campus tend to be underattended, unfortunately." During the winter, "a lot of activity is centered on just chilling out in the dorms, partying a little and talking about life, and listening to music," which "is fun but can get old." Community service is popular—"The Community Service Office has won numerous awards"—as is "studying abroad or getting off campus with internships and employment opportunities." Student organizations are also big, as "There seems to be a minority organization for every possible minority: political organizations, an active queer union, dance groups, international groups, [and] issue groups."

Student Body

"Walking from one end of campus to the other, it would not be uncommon to hear four or five different languages being spoken" at Macalester, where students representing more than 90 different countries attended in 2005–2006. Mac undergrads tend to be very liberal; their visits to the Mall of America are as likely precipitated by an anti-sweatshop protest as by their desire to shop. The 'PC' atmosphere can be a bit stifling at times, students admit; "You end up debating whether 'white lie' is a racist term for hours on end. The costs of being overtly respectful sometimes borders on overwhelming PC-ness," explains one student. Mac students are typically quirky, nerdy, "intelligent, friendly, and grounded thrift-store junkies [who] are likely to study abroad somewhere, probably in a third-world country."

MACALESTER COLLEGE

FINANCIAL AID: 651-696-6214 • E-MAIL: ADMISSIONS@MACALESTER.EDU • WEBSITE: WWW.MACALESTER.EDU

ADMISSIONS

Very important factors considered include: Academic GPA, rigor of secondary school record. *Important factors considered include:* Application essay, character/personal qualities, extracurricular activities, recommendation(s), standardized test scores. *Other factors considered include:* Alumni/ae relation, class rank, first generation, interview, racial/ethnic status, talent/ability, volunteer work, work experience. SAT or ACT required; TOEFL required of all international applicants. High school diploma or equivalent is not required. *Academic units recommended:* 4 English, 3 math, 3 science (3 science labs), 3 foreign language, 3 social studies.

The Inside Word

Macalester is just a breath away from moving into the highest echelon of U.S. colleges; a gift of *Reader's Digest* stock several years ago has recently translated into over $500 million in endowment. As the college has reaped the benefits of this generous gift, the applicant pool has grown dramatically. Macalester is already among the 25 or so most selective colleges in the country. An interview is a good idea. Although interviews are offered across the country, we also encourage you to visit the campus.

FINANCIAL AID

Students should submit: FAFSA, CSS/Financial Aid PROFILE, Noncustodial PROFILE, parent and student Federal Income Tax Returns. Regular filing deadline is March 1. The Princeton Review suggests that all financial aid forms be submitted as soon as possible after January 1. *Need-based scholarships/grants offered:* Pell Grant, SEOG, state scholarships/grants, private scholarships, the school's own gift aid. *Loan aid offered:* FFEL Subsidized Stafford, FFEL Unsubsidized Stafford, FFEL PLUS, Federal Perkins Loan, state loans. Applicants will be notified of awards on or about April 1. Federal Work-Study Program available. Institutional employment available. Off-campus job opportunities are excellent.

FROM THE ADMISSIONS OFFICE

"Macalester students come from all 50 states and 90 other countries. The campus is an international community; the curriculum is replete with global perspectives; and the classroom is abuzz with world views. Even the dining commons offers international options, earning the college high marks for food quality and variety. Most students study abroad for a semester or more, visiting more than 50 countries in any given year. Internships relevant to academic and career goals are abundant and easily accessible. For over 30 years, Macalester's debate program has been ranked among the top 10 in the nation. A Macalester team has qualified for the International Collegiate Programming Contest in 4 of the past 7 years, and recently tied with Stanford, Columbia, Carnegie Mellon, and Harvard. The women's soccer team earned the highest cumulative GPA in the nation in 2003–2004 and has advanced to the national competition in 8 of the past 10 years. Each year Macalester students win an impressive number of postgraduate awards and fellowships. Recent graduates fare well in the job market and graduate programs. One reports that she was accepted into top med school choices: Mayo, Stanford, UCLA, and Minnesota, and another that he had a 'striking advantage over many other candidates,' is now enrolled in a PhD program in economics at Princeton University. Macalester continues to meet the full financial need for all admitted students, as determined by standard methodology.

"Freshman applicants for Fall 2008 may submit the results from either the old or the new version of the SAT, or the results of the ACT with or without the Writing component. The Admissions Committee does not have a preference for one test over the other."

SELECTIVITY

Admissions Rating	95
# of applicants	4,826
% of applicants accepted	39
% of acceptees attending	27
# accepting a place on wait list	211
% admitted from wait list	30
# of early decision applicants	277
% accepted early decision	49

FRESHMAN PROFILE

Range SAT Critical Reading	630–740
Range SAT Math	630–710
Range ACT Composite	27–32
Minimum Paper TOEFL	573
Minimum Computer Based TOEFL	230
% graduated top 10% of class	66
% graduated top 25% of class	91
% graduated top 50% of class	99

DEADLINES

Early decision application deadline	11/15
Early decision notification	12/15
Regular application deadline	1/15
Regular notification	3/30
Nonfall registration?	no

APPLICANTS ALSO LOOK AT

AND OFTEN PREFER
Brown University, The University of Chicago, Washington University in St. Louis

AND SOMETIMES PREFER
Grinnell College, Pomona College, Wesleyan College

AND RARELY PREFER
Colorado College, Kenyon College, University of Wisconsin—Madison

FINANCIAL FACTS

Financial Aid Rating	97
Annual tuition	$30,870
Room & Board	$7,982
Books and supplies	$820
Required fees	$168
% frosh rec. need-based scholarship or grant aid	66
% UG rec. need-based scholarship or grant aid	67
% frosh rec. need-based self-help aid	67
% UG rec. need-based self-help aid	67
% frosh rec. any financial aid	70
% UG rec. any financial aid	73

MANHATTANVILLE COLLEGE

2900 PURCHASE STREET, ADMISSIONS OFFICE, PURCHASE, NY 10577 • ADMISSIONS: 914-323-5124 • FAX: 914-694-1732

STUDENTS SAY

Academics

"Qualified and committed" professors, "very involved" administrators, and an "excellent location" near New York City (one still far enough from its "pollution and distractions") all contribute to the "close and supportive community" that is Manhattanville College. Students here have the "unbelievable" opportunity to "exchange ideas" with professors who have "studied in the best universities in the world. There are so many distinguished professors here, ranging from experts in world religions, to former ambassadors in the UN. Almost all of them are well known in their areas of study." Yet regardless of the faculty's impressive credentials, "Each one of them makes you feel comfortable enough to go and see him or her if you need help, and is more than willing to use his or her own time to help you." Getting such help is made easier by the fact that "one-third of professors live on campus." Mville (as it is affectionately called by its students) places a lot of emphasis on experiential learning, and the school's location is an asset in that regard. Not only is Mville close to the myriad internship opportunities of the megalopolis next door, but "We [also] have tons of corporations literally in our neighborhood, like MasterCard, IBM, MBIA, JPMorgan—[these bring] plenty of internships." In addition to internships, the school reportedly "is very successful in finding students interesting jobs in their fields after they graduate." Students praise a "very helpful" administration, and the president is such a hit with students that one goes so far as to say that he "is probably more popular than the star of the basketball team."

Life

Manhattanville's campus "is a quiet place." Students here "generally focus on their academics first and on partying and having fun second." While "There are parties on campus every 2 weeks or so [at which] alcohol is served," the residential directors and RAs "are so strict, the party scene is not so big." Parties are typically "small get-togethers," and "People are usually nervous that they are going to get caught [if they drink]." Such a tame on-campus party scene means that the drinkers here make it a "very big bar school." They take "the Valiant Express [a campus shuttle] to downtown White Plains," where "dozens of bars" can be found. Students can also find "other stuff to do [in White Plains]," such as visiting its "malls, movie theaters, restaurants, and clubs." The "college bus also takes students [to New York City] every Saturday"; people go there to "see Broadway shows or [attend] professional athletic events." For those students seeking more wholesome fun on campus, There are "lots of interest groups and activities that one can join," and "there is also a game room with different things like billiards and Ping-Pong." Finally, "The students here have a lot of school spirit, so there is always a great turnout for games."

Student Body

"The community at Manhattanville is very diverse," with a community that includes students "from 59 different countries around the world." A typical student might even have "lived in more than three countries." Despite the diversity (or perhaps as a natural consequence of it), sometimes "People tend to hang out with the group they feel most comfortable with (i.e., international students hanging out with fellow international students, sport students with fellow sport students, etc.)." Regardless of any cliques, "All of the students at the school are extremely cordial. Since it is such a small school, you get to know everyone's face." "The typical student works hard about half the time," one claims. "There are atypical students who care a lot about their work and do a lot of studying. Some of them stick out, and others fit in fine."

FINANCIAL AID: 914-323-5357 • E-MAIL: ADMISSIONS@MVILLE.EDU • WEBSITE: WWW.MVILLE.EDU

ADMISSIONS

Very important factors considered include: Rigor of secondary school record, standardized test scores. *Important factors considered include:* Application essay, extracurricular activities, interview, recommendation(s). *Other factors considered include:* Alumni/ae relation, character/personal qualities, geographical residence, talent/ability, volunteer work, work experience. SAT or ACT required; TOEFL required of all international applicants. High school diploma is required, and GED is accepted. *Academic units required:* 4 English, 3 math, 2 science, 2 social studies, 5 academic electives.

The Inside Word

Applicants evincing middle-of-the-road academic achievement will most likely find themselves with an acceptance letter from Manhattanville. The college still seeks to achieve greater gender balance, so male candidates enjoy a slightly higher admission rate than female candidates. In addition to meeting regular admissions requirements, students who wish to pursue a degree in fine arts or performing arts must present a portfolio or audition, respectively.

FINANCIAL AID

Students should submit: FAFSA, state aid form. The Princeton Review suggests that all financial aid forms be submitted as soon as possible after January 1. *Need-based scholarships/grants offered:* Pell Grant, SEOG, state scholarships/grants, private scholarships, the school's own gift aid. *Loan aid offered:* FFEL Subsidized Stafford, FFEL Unsubsidized Stafford, FFEL PLUS, Federal Perkins Loan. Applicants will be notified of awards on a rolling basis beginning or about March 1. Federal Work-Study Program available. Institutional employment available. Off-campus job opportunities are excellent.

FROM THE ADMISSIONS OFFICE

"Manhattanville's mission—to educate ethically and socially responsible leaders for the global community—is evident throughout the college, from academics to athletics to social and extracurricular activities. With 1,600 undergraduates from 59 nations and 39 states, our diversity spans geographic, cultural, ethnic, religious, socioeconomic, and academic backgrounds. Students are free to express their views in this tight-knit community, where we value the personal as well as the global. Any six students with similar interest can start a club, and most participate in a variety of campus wide programs. Last year, students engaged in more than 23,380 hours of community service and social justice activity. Study abroad opportunities include not only the most desirable international locations, but also a semester-long immersion for living, studying, and working in New York City. In the true liberal arts tradition, students are encouraged to think for themselves and develop new skills—in music, the studio arts, on stage, in the sciences, or on the playing field. With more than 50 areas of study and a popular self-designed major, there is no limit to our academic scope. Our Westchester County location, just 35 miles north of New York City, gives students an edge for jobs and internships. Over the past few years, Manhattanville has been rated among the '100 Most Wired,' the '100 Most Undeservedly Underappreciated,' the '320 Hottest,' and in *U.S. News & World Report*'s first tier. Last year, the men's and women's ice hockey teams were ranked #1 in the nation for Division III.

"As of this book's publication, Manhattanville College did not have information available about their policy regarding the new SAT."

SELECTIVITY

Admissions Rating	79
# of applicants	3,464
% of applicants accepted	53
% of acceptees attending	28
# of early decision applicants	100
% accepted early decision	50

FRESHMAN PROFILE

Range SAT Critical Reading	500–620
Range SAT Math	500–610
Range ACT Composite	20–25
Minimum Paper TOEFL	550
Minimum Computer Based TOEFL	217
% graduated top 10% of class	21
% graduated top 25% of class	47
% graduated top 50% of class	80

DEADLINES

Early decision application deadline	12/1
Early decision notification	12/31
Regular application deadline	3/1
Regular notification	rolling
Nonfall registration?	yes

APPLICANTS ALSO LOOK AT

AND OFTEN PREFER
New York University

AND SOMETIMES PREFER
Fordham University

AND RARELY PREFER
Pace University, White Plains

FINANCIAL FACTS

Financial Aid Rating	78
Annual tuition	$28,540
Room & Board	$12,240
Books and supplies	$800
Required fees	$1,140
% frosh rec. need-based scholarship or grant aid	62
% UG rec. need-based scholarship or grant aid	57
% frosh rec. need-based self-help aid	58
% UG rec. need-based self-help aid	54

MARIST COLLEGE

3399 NORTH ROAD, POUGHKEEPSIE, NY 12601-1387 • ADMISSIONS: 845-575-3226 • FAX: 845-575-3215

STUDENTS SAY

Academics

Marist College, a "midsized institute that proudly offers competitive academics, career placement, and a well-rounded college experience," is "the perfect size." Students tell us that it's "small enough that professors remember your name and address you as a person, not a number, but large enough that you are not constantly seeing the same people every day." Pre-professional and career-track programs are most popular here; students laud the "great communications program" with its "unique digital media major" and "strong internship connections," the "very good education program," the popular business programs, and the "excellent Chemistry Department, where personal attention is unmatched." Students here keep their eyes on the prize: They sing the praises of the Center for Career Services, noting that "Our career services and internship opportunities are amazing. By the end of your senior year you will most likely complete an internship with a big-name company, either in the local area or in New York City, which we are in close proximity to." They also love the Study Abroad Office, which "has connected students with many countries around the world, allowing students to study abroad for a semester, year, or short-term period." Further sweetening the deal are the school's "strong connections to IBM" and "an amazing library that is ranked among the top 20 in the country." The arts, on the other hand, are a weak spot; students report that Marist "could try to emphasize a stronger interest in fine arts: music, orchestra, choirs, and independent groups."

Life

"Classes keep you busy" at Marist College, but not so busy that you can't also enjoy a variety of extracurricular activities. These include "social organizations, religious organizations, academic organizations, to name simply a few" as well as "campus events such as sports, plays, lectures, seminars, and concerts. Marist is not a suitcase campus, as students who live on campus stay on campus over the weekends." The bar scene is big; some here see Marist as "very much a bar school. Kids go out Tuesday, Thursday, Friday, and Saturday. House parties happen, but they aren't as popular as the bars. There's tons of nonalcoholic fun, too." While "The city of Poughkeepsie is generally not safe outside of the venues Marist students flock to," the "diverse" area surrounding Poughkeepsie "allows outdoor experiences like hiking, kayaking, and swimming." Undergrads appreciate the fact that "the Marist campus is beautiful, with the most amazing views ever"—"The Hudson River can be seen from almost every dorm."

Student Body

Marist seems to draw "lots of kids from Long Island, New Jersey, and Connecticut, many of them White, upper-middle-class, immigrant-descended Catholics." (One student adds, "They shop at Abercrombie.") Another undergrad notes, "While walking through campus, one may notice that Marist is filled with very similar people." The student body includes "many athletes [Marist fields 10 men's and 11 women's intercollegiate teams] and preppy students. Many are involved in clubs." Students here "are going to school to gain experience, get their degree, and dive into the competitive workforce. They focus on attaining good grades while also being involved in on-campus activities and having a diverse social life. They are fun-loving people." Undergrads are also "extremely friendly and will go out of their way to hold a door for you." All students "fit in well and get along," we're told.

MARIST COLLEGE

FINANCIAL AID: 845-575-3230 • E-MAIL: ADMISSIONS@MARIST.EDU • WEBSITE: WWW.MARIST.EDU

ADMISSIONS

Very important factors considered include: Academic GPA, rigor of secondary school record, standardized test scores. *Important factors considered include:* Application essay, character/personal qualities, extracurricular activities, geographical residence, recommendation(s), state residency, talent/ability, volunteer work, work experience. *Other factors considered include:* Alumni/ae relation, class rank, level of applicant's interest, racial/ethnic status. SAT or ACT required; ACT with Writing component required. TOEFL required of all international applicants. High school diploma is required, and GED is accepted. *Academic units required:* 4 English, 3 math, 3 science (2 science labs), 2 foreign language, 2 social studies, 1 history, 2 academic electives. *Academic units recommended:* 4 math, 4 science (3 science labs), 3 foreign language.

The Inside Word

Marist attracts some solid students, and viable candidates are usually in the top quarter of their class. Additionally, Admissions Counselors tend to favor applicants who have attained leadership roles and contributed to their communities. State residency is also taken into consideration, as Marist aims to maintain a diverse campus.

FINANCIAL AID

Students should submit: FAFSA, institution's own financial aid form. Regular filing deadline is May 1. The Princeton Review suggests that all financial aid forms be submitted as soon as possible after January 1. *Need-based scholarships/grants offered:* Pell Grant, SEOG, state scholarships/grants, private scholarships, the school's own gift aid. *Loan aid offered:* FFEL Subsidized Stafford, FFEL Unsubsidized Stafford, FFEL PLUS, Federal Perkins Loan, alternative loans. Applicants will be notified of awards on or about March 15.

FROM THE ADMISSIONS OFFICE

"Marist is a 'hot school' among prospective students. We are seeing a record number of applications each year. But the number of seats available for the freshman class remains the same, about 950. Therefore, becoming an accepted applicant is an increasingly competitive process. Our recommendations: keep your grades up, score well on the SAT, participate in community service both in and out of school, and exercise leadership in the classroom, athletics, extracurricular activities, and your place of worship. We encourage a campus visit. When prospective students see Marist—our beautiful location on a scenic stretch of the Hudson River, the quality of our facilities, the interaction between students and faculty, and the fact that everyone really enjoys their time here— they want to become a part of the Marist College community. We'll help you in the transition from high school to college through an innovative first-year program that provides mentors for every student. You'll also learn how to use technology in whatever field you choose. We emphasize three aspects of a true Marist experience: excellence in education, community, and service to others. At Marist, you'll get a premium education, develop your skills, have fun and make lifelong friends, be given the opportunity to gain valuable experience through our great internship and study abroad programs, and be ahead of the competition for graduate school or work.

"Marist requires the SAT with the Writing component. We recommend all students take the test at least twice and the ACT once. Marist will use the best Verbal, Math, and Writing scores from the SAT or the highest composite ACT score."

SELECTIVITY
Admissions Rating	89
# of applicants	7,296
% of applicants accepted	49
% of acceptees attending	29
# accepting a place on wait list	352
# of early decision applicants	92
% accepted early decision	64

FRESHMAN PROFILE
Range SAT Critical Reading	530–610
Range SAT Math	540–630
Range SAT Writing	530–620
Range ACT Composite	20–26
Minimum Paper TOEFL	550
Minimum Computer Based TOEFL	213
Average HS GPA	3.3
% graduated top 10% of class	26
% graduated top 25% of class	78
% graduated top 50% of class	95

DEADLINES
Early decision application deadline	11/15
Early decision notification	12/15
Regular application deadline	2/15
Regular notification	3/15
Nonfall registration?	yes

APPLICANTS ALSO LOOK AT
AND OFTEN PREFER
Boston College, College of the Holy Cross, State University of New York at Binghamton, Villanova University
AND SOMETIMES PREFER
Fordham University, Loyola College in Maryland, Providence College, State University of New York at Geneseo
AND RARELY PREFER
Hofstra University, Iona College, Quinnipiac University, Rider University, State University of New York—College at Oneonta

FINANCIAL FACTS
Financial Aid Rating	65
Annual tuition	$22,066
Room & Board	$9,790
Required fees	$695
% frosh rec. need-based scholarship or grant aid	58
% UG rec. need-based scholarship or grant aid	58
% frosh rec. need-based self-help aid	45
% UG rec. need-based self-help aid	50
% frosh rec. any financial aid	90
% UG rec. any financial aid	86

MARLBORO COLLEGE

PO Box A, South Road, Marlboro, VT 05344-0300 • Admissions: 802-258-9236 • Fax: 802-451-7555

STUDENTS SAY

Academics

Finally, a school that offers, "a great undergrad program for students who would rather be in grad school." Tiny, remote Marlboro College "seeks to nurture critical thinking, effective writing, and engaged citizens" through a program that emphasizes closely supervised independent study and the ideal of self-government. The apex of Marlboro's nontraditional education is "the Plan," which requires students to design their own junior- and senior-year curricula, culminating in a senior research paper. Under the Plan, students "attend one-on-one tutorials with professors in which we spend the entire class asking all of the questions we want to ask and exploring the subjects we want to learn about." One undergrad writes, "The encouragement of critical thinking on both an academic and a social level is incredible here." Freshman and sophomore years are dedicated to more traditional classroom study; classes are "engaging and interesting, everyone is encouraged to speak, and every class is a lively discussion." Professors and administrators are not only mentors and facilitators of learning, but also serve as peers and friends, students tell us. Classes are small—the school has a student/faculty ratio of 8:1—a benefit that outweighs some of the drawbacks of the school's size, which "requires Marlboro to be very economical. While there are ways to make up for what the bigger universities have to offer, we must think realistically and be cost-conscious."

Life

Located "on a tiny hill in Vermont at least 20 minutes from the nearest town," Marlboro "really is in the middle of nowhere." Students learn to adapt to the low excitement level here. As one student explains, "I didn't realize that there was nothing to do here until my friend came to visit me. He was saying, 'Okay! Let's go do something!' and I realized that showing him the library and playing a round of Ping-Pong had already exhausted all of our options." One student warns, "It's a little boring. You are responsible for making your own entertainment. People try, but how many times can you go to see different mutations of the same band and that annoying kid from next door reading his erotic beat poetry at the open mic?" Schoolwork keeps students busy a good part of the time, and many even appreciate how the lack of distraction facilitates academics. When it's time to unwind, "People hang out, watch movies, and play video games. Some people get completely plastered." An appreciation for the outdoors helps. Anyone who's willing can "take advantage of rock climbing, white-water paddling, snowboarding, hiking, caving, mountain biking, cross-country skiing, and snowshoeing. None of it is more than 45 minutes away, and we have a great outdoor program (that loans equipment to students at no cost), which makes it easy for people to learn these things."

Students

"Atypical is typical, but not in an obnoxious way," Marlboro students report, pointing out that "we bathe; some girls even shave!" One student notes, "Sometimes our nonconformity is manifest in our clothes, be it flashy hipness, dirty hippieness, caps with hoods, or just the standard drag-queen apparel." Students are fond of saying that everyone here "is really bright in some way or another." They "often come from alternative educational institutions—Waldorf schools, home schools, and special high schools of different kinds—so they sort of have that 'I'm not doing it the mainstream way' attitude about them." Most "are quite liberal in their thinking and are encouraged to share their views." Among their ranks are "many bisexual and gay students, but anyone can talk to anyone else. It's very open." Diversity here "is less focused on race than it is on sexuality and socioeconomics, where it truly is diverse. The geography and current demographic seems to be unappealing to some minority groups, which drives the administrators nuts." As one undergrad puts it, "The only segment of student demographics less represented than students of color are students of conformity."

MARLBORO COLLEGE

FINANCIAL AID: 800-343-0049 • E-MAIL: ADMISSIONS@MARLBORO.EDU • WEBSITE: WWW.MARLBORO.EDU

ADMISSIONS

Very important factors considered include: Academic GPA, application essay, character/personal qualities, rigor of secondary school record. *Important factors considered include:* Extracurricular activities, interview, talent/ability. *Other factors considered include:* Alumni/ae relation, class rank, first generation, geographical residence, level of applicant's interest, recommendation(s), standardized test scores, state residency, volunteer work, work experience. SAT or ACT required; TOEFL required of all international applicants. High school diploma is required, and GED is accepted. *Academic units recommended:* 4 English, 3 math, 3 science (1 science lab), 3 foreign language, 3 social studies, 3 history, 3 academic electives.

The Inside Word

Don't be misled by Marlboro's high acceptance rate; the college's applicant pool consists mainly of candidates who are sincerely interested in a nontraditional path to their BA or BS. They also possess sincere intellectual curiosity, and students who don't should not bother applying. The admissions process here is driven by matchmaking and a search for those who truly want to learn. For the right kind of person, Marlboro can be a terrific college choice.

FINANCIAL AID

Students should submit: FAFSA. Regular filing deadline is March 1. The Princeton Review suggests that all financial aid forms be submitted as soon as possible after January 1. *Need-based scholarships/grants offered:* Pell Grant, SEOG, state scholarships/grants, private scholarships, the school's own gift aid. *Loan aid offered:* FFEL Subsidized Stafford, FFEL Unsubsidized Stafford, FFEL PLUS, state loans. Applicants will be notified of awards on or about April 1. Federal Work-Study Program available. Institutional employment available. Off-campus job opportunities are fair.

FROM THE ADMISSIONS OFFICE

"Marlboro College is distinguished by its curriculum, praised in higher education circles as unique; it is known for its self-governing philosophy, in which each student, faculty, and staff has an equal vote on many issues affecting the community; and it is recognized for its 60-year history of offering a rigorous, exciting, self-designed course of study taught in very small classes and individualized study with faculty. Marlboro's size also distinguishes it from most other schools. With 300 students and a student/faculty ratio of 8:1, it is one of the nation's smallest liberal arts colleges. Few other schools offer a program where students have such close interaction with faculty, and where community life is inseparable from academic life. The result, the self-designed, self-directed Plan of Concentration, allows students to develop their own unique academic work by defining a problem, setting clear limits on an area of inquiry, and analyzing, evaluating, and reporting on the outcome of a significant project. A Marlboro education teaches you to think for yourself, articulate your thoughts, express your ideas, believe in yourself, and do it all with the clarity, confidence, and self-reliance necessary for later success, no matter what postgraduate path you take.

"Marlboro College requires all applicants for admission to submit results of either the ACT and ACT Writing Test or SAT Reasoning Test. Students who have previously taken older versions of the ACT or SAT may submit those test results and are not required to retake the 'new' ACT or SAT. We do not require SAT Subject Tests."

SELECTIVITY

Admissions Rating	89
# of applicants	459
% of applicants accepted	68
% of acceptees attending	30
# of early decision applicants	21
% accepted early decision	67

FRESHMAN PROFILE

Range SAT Critical Reading	590–690
Range SAT Math	510–650
Range SAT Writing	640–720
Range ACT Composite	24–32
Minimum Paper TOEFL	550
Minimum Computer Based TOEFL	220
Average HS GPA	3.2
% graduated top 10% of class	40
% graduated top 25% of class	60
% graduated top 50% of class	95

DEADLINES

Early decision application deadline	11/15
Early decision notification	12/15
Regular application deadline	2/15
Regular notification	rolling
Nonfall registration?	yes

APPLICANTS ALSO LOOK AT

AND OFTEN PREFER
Reed College

AND SOMETIMES PREFER
Bard College, College of the Atlantic, The Evergreen State College

AND RARELY PREFER
Bennington College, Green Mountain College, Hampshire College, University of Vermont

FINANCIAL FACTS

Financial Aid Rating	89
Annual tuition	$29,700
Room & Board	$8,860
Books and supplies	$800
Required fees	$980
% frosh rec. need-based scholarship or grant aid	70
% UG rec. need-based scholarship or grant aid	77
% frosh rec. need-based self-help aid	75
% UG rec. need-based self-help aid	76
% frosh rec. any financial aid	75
% UG rec. any financial aid	84

MARQUETTE UNIVERSITY

PO Box 1881, Milwaukee, WI 53201-1881 • Admissions: 414-288-7302 • Fax: 414-288-3764

STUDENTS SAY

Academics

Marquette University, "a small campus in a big city with a big heart and a comfortable atmosphere," serves up "a great Jesuit education" to those "seeking a happy medium between working hard academically, making great friends while having a good social life, and getting prepared for life after college." Marquette is also a great choice for those "really interested in community service and exploring their Catholic faith. Marquette has a lot of opportunities in these areas." Popular majors include business, nursing, engineering, and education; these programs are so popular, in fact, that "as a junior it is really difficult to transfer into them and still graduate in 4 years." Premedical programs in physical therapy and dentistry are also strong. In most areas, Marquette's faculty is "truly top-notch and cares about both teaching and research. Marquette is highly underrated for what we receive. Most professors personally care about the learning experiences of their students and make every effort to offer help or insight inside and outside of class." That help can be important, since "Classes are challenging." Students also appreciate the school's "state-of-the-art computer facilities" and the "amazing new Raynor Memorial Library." The "very generous financial aid packages" also earn praise. The few students with leftist political leanings warn that "the professors and the students are incredibly conservative, which can be difficult because the university requires a ton of theology and philosophy credits."

Life

"It seems as if much of the student body leads two separate lives" at Marquette. "During the week we are very studious, because this is a very demanding school. But on weekends we know how to have a great time. We work hard, but we play hard, too." For many, "having a good time" involves drinking, either at a campus party or in one of Milwaukee's many bars. Students who don't drink tell us they still find plenty to do. Marquette "has many active organizations, especially the student government and the newspaper. These organizations are very involved in campus life and do well at making their presence known." College athletics are also a big draw; men's basketball is especially popular. Other options include the on-campus Varsity Theater, "which has good two-dollar movies every weekend"; an on-campus art museum; events such as "Late Night Marquette, which includes games and other fun stuff"; and strolling along Lake Michigan. Milwaukee brings a lot to the mix, including "professional sports and lots of concerts," but beware of winters here, which "can get pretty cold," to put it mildly.

Student Body

The majority of Marquette undergrads "are White and come either from rural areas in Wisconsin or from Chicago suburbs." Many come from economically comfortable families and "went to private Catholic high schools. Marquette students could be considered preppy and snobby." Dig below the surface, though, and you'll find "a large range of people, at least from an economic standpoint. There are some very rich kids and at the same time there are those who are less fortunate." The same diversity is absent from the school's racial makeup—there are "very few minority students," which, according to one Latina student, "can make it very difficult to feel a part of campus life." Students tend to be "very conservative," but apparently not dogmatically so, since "Despite the Catholic environment, no one is ashamed of being homosexual. There is even a Gay/Straight Alliance club."

FINANCIAL AID: 414-288-7390 • E-MAIL: ADMISSIONS@MARQUETTE.EDU • WEBSITE: WWW.MARQUETTE.EDU

ADMISSIONS

Very important factors considered include: Academic GPA, rigor of secondary school record. *Important factors considered include:* Application essay, class rank, recommendation(s), standardized test scores. *Other factors considered include:* Alumni/ae relation, character/personal qualities, extracurricular activities, first generation, geographical residence, racial/ethnic status, religious affiliation/commitment, state residency, talent/ability. SAT or ACT required; ACT with Writing component recommended. High school diploma is required, and GED is accepted. *Academic units required:* 4 English, 2 math, 2 science (2 science labs), 2 foreign language, 2 social studies, 2 academic electives. *Academic units recommended:* 4 English, 4 math, 3 science (3 science labs), 2 foreign language, 3 social studies, 5 academic electives.

The Inside Word

Marquette does not take admissions decisions lightly: Each application is evaluated by at least two committee members. Qualified applicants are academically competitive with their peers and maintain consistent grades. Essays are also highly valued, as Admissions Officers seek students with strong writing skills.

FINANCIAL AID

Students should submit: FAFSA, MU Admissions Application. The Princeton Review suggests that all financial aid forms be submitted as soon as possible after January 1. *Need-based scholarships/grants offered:* Pell Grant, SEOG, state scholarships/grants, private scholarships, the school's own gift aid. *Loan aid offered:* Direct Subsidized Stafford, Direct Unsubsidized Stafford, Direct PLUS, Federal Perkins Loan, Federal Nursing Loan, state loans, college/university loans from institutional funds, private educational/alternative loans. Applicants will be notified of awards on a rolling basis beginning or about March 20.

FROM THE ADMISSIONS OFFICE

"Since 1881, Marquette has been noted for its commitment to educational excellence in the 450-year-old Catholic/Jesuit tradition. Marquette embraces the philosophy that true education should be more than an acquisition of knowledge; it should develop your intellect as well as your moral and spiritual character. This all-encompassing education will challenge you to develop the goals and values that will shape the rest of your life. Each of Marquette's 7,500 undergraduates are admitted as freshman to one of six colleges: Arts and Sciences, Business Administration, Communication, Engineering, Health Sciences, or Nursing. Many co-enroll in the School of Education. The faculty within these colleges are prolific writers and researchers, but more importantly, they all teach and advise students.

"Marquette is nestled in the financial center of Milwaukee, the nation's eighteenth-largest city, allowing you to take full advantage of the city's cultural, professional, and governmental opportunities. Marquette's urban experience is unique; an 80-acre campus, an outdoor athletic complex, and an internationally diverse student body (90 percent of which live on or near campus) all make Marquette a close-knit community in which you can learn and live.

"Marquette applicants must submit scores from either the new version of the SAT or the ACT with Writing component. The highest composite score will be used in admissions decisions for students that submit scores from multiple administrations of these tests."

SELECTIVITY

Admissions Rating	85
# of applicants	11,514
% of applicants accepted	70
% of acceptees attending	23
# accepting a place on wait list	448
% admitted from wait list	17

FRESHMAN PROFILE

Range SAT Critical Reading	540–640
Range SAT Math	550–660
Range SAT Writing	530–630
Range ACT Composite	24–29
Minimum Paper TOEFL	520
Minimum Computer Based TOEFL	190
% graduated top 10% of class	35
% graduated top 25% of class	67
% graduated top 50% of class	92

DEADLINES

Regular application deadline	12/1
Regular notification	1/31
Nonfall registration?	yes

APPLICANTS ALSO LOOK AT

AND OFTEN PREFER
Boston College, Case Western Reserve University, University of Michigan—Ann Arbor, University of Notre Dame

AND SOMETIMES PREFER
Augustana College (IL), Loyola University—Chicago, Michigan State University, University of Wisconsin—Madison

AND RARELY PREFER
Carroll College (WI), Milwaukee School of Engineering, St. Norbert College, University of Wisconsin—Milwaukee

FINANCIAL FACTS

Financial Aid Rating	76
Annual tuition	$24,670
Room & Board	$8,120
Books and supplies	$900
Required fees	$404
% frosh rec. need-based scholarship or grant aid	54
% UG rec. need-based scholarship or grant aid	52
% frosh rec. need-based self-help aid	51
% UG rec. need-based self-help aid	50
% frosh rec. any financial aid	88
% UG rec. any financial aid	85

MASSACHUSETTS INSTITUTE OF TECHNOLOGY

MIT ADMISSIONS OFFICE, ROOM 3-108, 77 MASSACHUSETTS AVENUE, CAMBRIDGE, MA 02139 • ADMISSIONS: 617-253-4791

CAMPUS LIFE

Quality of Life Rating	87
Fire Safety Rating	88
Type of school	private
Environment	city

STUDENTS

Total undergrad enrollment	4,114
% male/female	56/44
% from out of state	90
% from public high school	71
% live on campus	91
% in (# of) fraternities	55 (27)
% in (# of) sororities	26 (5)
% African American	6
% Asian	26
% Caucasian	37
% Hispanic	12
% Native American	1
% international	8
# of countries represented	86

SURVEY SAYS . . .

Registration is a breeze
Lab facilities are great
Great computer facilities
Great library
Athletic facilities are great
Diverse student types on campus
Students love Cambridge, MA

ACADEMICS

Academic Rating	99
Calendar	4-1-4
Student/faculty ratio	7:1
Profs interesting rating	71
Profs accessible rating	77
% profs teaching UG courses	100
Most common lab size	10–19 students
Most common reg class size	fewer than 10 students

MOST POPULAR MAJORS

chemical engineering
computer science
mechanical engineering

STUDENTS SAY

Academics

Massachusetts Institute of Technology, the East Coast mecca of engineering, science, and mathematics, "is the ultimate place for information overload, endless possibilities, and expanding your horizons." The "amazing collection of creative minds" includes enough Nobel laureates to fill a jury box as well as brilliant students who are given substantial control of their educations; one explains, "The administration's attitude towards students is one of respect. As soon as you come on campus, you are bombarded with choices." Students need to be able to manage a workload that "definitely push[es you] beyond your comfort level." A chemical engineering major elaborates: "MIT is different from many schools in that its goal is not to teach you specific facts in each subject. MIT teaches you how to think. Not about opinions, but about problem solving. Facts and memorization are useless unless you know how to approach a tough problem." Professors here range from "excellent teachers who make lectures fun and exciting" to "dull and soporific" ones, but most "make a serious effort to make the material they teach interesting by throwing in jokes and cool demonstrations." "Access to an amazing number of resources, both academic and recreational," "research opportunities for undergrads with some of the nation's leading professors," and a rock-solid alumni network complete the picture. If you ask "MIT alumni where they went to college, most will immediately stick out their hand and show you their 'brass rat' (the MIT ring, the second most recognized ring in the world)."

Life

At MIT "It may seem . . . like there's no life outside problem sets and studying for exams," but "There's always time for extracurricular activities or just relaxing" for those "with good time-management skills" or the "ability to survive on [a] lack of sleep." Options range from "building rides" (recent projects have included a motorized couch and a human-sized hamster wheel) "to partying at fraternities to enjoying the largest collection of science fiction novels in the U.S. at the MIT Science Fiction Library." Students occasionally find time to "pull a hack," which is an ethical prank "like the life-size Wright brothers' plane that appeared on top of the Great Dome for the one-hundredth anniversary of flight." Undergrads tell us that "MIT has great parties—a lot of Wellesley, Harvard, and BU students come to them," but also that "There are tons of things to do other than party" here. "Movies, shopping, museums, and plays are all possible with our location near Boston. There are great restaurants only [blocks] away from campus, too . . . From what I can tell, MIT students have way more fun on the weekends then their Cambridge counterpart[s at] Harvard."

Student Body

"There actually isn't one typical student at MIT," students here assure us, explaining that "Hobbies range from building robots and hacking to getting wasted and partying every weekend. The one thing students all have in common is that they are insanely smart and love to learn. Pretty much anyone can find the perfect group of friends to hang out with at MIT." While "Most students do have some form of 'nerdiness'" (like telling nerdy jokes, being an avid fan of *Star Wars*, etc.), "Contrary to MIT's stereotype, most MIT students are not geeks who study all the time and have no social skills. The majority of the students here are actually quite 'normal.'" The "stereotypical student [who] looks techy and unkempt . . . only represents about 25 percent of the school." The rest include "multiple-sport standouts, political activists, fraternity and sorority members, hippies, clean-cut business types, LARPers, hackers, musicians, and artisans. There are people who look like they stepped out of an Abercrombie & Fitch catalog and people who dress in all black and carry flashlights and multitools. Not everyone relates to everyone else, but most people get along, and it's almost a guarantee that you'll fit in somewhere."

FINANCIAL AID: 617-253-4971 • WEBSITE: WEB.MIT.EDU

ADMISSIONS

Very important factors considered include: Character/personal qualities. *Important factors considered include:* Academic GPA, class rank, extracurricular activities, interview, recommendation(s), rigor of secondary school record, standardized test scores, talent/ability. *Other factors considered include:* Alumni/ae relation, application essay, first generation, geographical residence, level of applicant's interest, racial/ethnic status, volunteer work, work experience. ACT with Writing component required. High school diploma or equivalent is not required. *Academic units recommended:* 4 English, 4 math, 4 science, 2 foreign language, 2 social studies.

The Inside Word

MIT has one of the nation's most competitive admissions processes. The school's applicant pool is so rich it turns away numerous qualified candidates each year. Put your best foot forward and take consolation in the fact that rejection doesn't necessarily mean that you don't belong at MIT, but only that there wasn't enough room for you the year you applied. Your best chance to get an edge: Find ways to stress your creativity, a quality that MIT's admissions director told *USA Today* is lacking in many prospective college students.

FINANCIAL AID

Students should submit: FAFSA, CSS/Financial Aid PROFILE, Business/Farm Supplement, parent's complete Federal Income Tax Returns from prior year and W-2s. Regular filing deadline is February 15. The Princeton Review suggests that all financial aid forms be submitted as soon as possible after January 1. *Need-based scholarships/grants offered:* Pell Grant, SEOG, state scholarships/grants, private scholarships, the school's own gift aid. *Loan aid offered:* Direct Subsidized Stafford, Direct Unsubsidized Stafford, Direct PLUS, Federal Perkins Loan, college/university loans from institutional funds. Applicants will be notified of awards on or about March 15. Federal Work-Study Program available. Institutional employment available. Off-campus job opportunities are excellent.

FROM THE ADMISSIONS OFFICE

"The students who come to the Massachusetts Institute of Technology are some of America's—and the world's—best and most creative. As graduates, they leave here to make real contributions—in science, technology, business, education, politics, architecture, and the arts. From any class, many will go on to do work that is historically significant. These young men and women are leaders, achievers, and producers. Helping such students make the most of their talents and dreams would challenge any educational institution. MIT gives them its best advantages: a world-class faculty, unparalleled facilities, and remarkable opportunities. In turn, these students help to make the institute the vital place it is. They bring fresh viewpoints to faculty research: More than three-quarters participate in the Undergraduate Research Opportunities Program. They play on MIT's 41 intercollegiate teams as well as in its 15 musical ensembles. To their classes and to their out-of-class activities, they bring enthusiasm, energy, and individual style.

"For freshman admission in the Fall 2008, MIT requires scores from either the SAT (old/new) or the ACT (with or without the optional Writing test). In addition, we require three SAT Subject Tests: one in Math (Level IC or IIC), one in science (Physics, Chemistry, or Biology), and the third in any area of your choosing."

SELECTIVITY

Admissions Rating	99
# of applicants	11,374
% of applicants accepted	13
% of acceptees attending	66
# accepting a place on wait list	319
% admitted from wait list	13

FRESHMAN PROFILE

Range SAT Critical Reading	660–760
Range SAT Math	720–800
Range ACT Composite	30–34
% graduated top 10% of class	97
% graduated top 25% of class	100
% graduated top 50% of class	100

DEADLINES

Regular application deadline	1/1
Regular notification	3/25
Nonfall registration?	no

APPLICANTS ALSO LOOK AT
AND OFTEN PREFER
Harvard College
AND SOMETIMES PREFER
Princeton University, Stanford University, Yale University
AND RARELY PREFER
California Institute of Technology, Columbia University, Cornell University, Duke University, University of Pennsylvania

FINANCIAL FACTS

Financial Aid Rating	95
Annual tuition	$33,400
Room & Board	$9,950
Books and supplies	$1,100
Required fees	$200
% frosh rec. need-based scholarship or grant aid	61
% UG rec. need-based scholarship or grant aid	60
% frosh rec. need-based self-help aid	53
% UG rec. need-based self-help aid	56
% frosh rec. any financial aid	76
% UG rec. any financial aid	70

McGill University

845 Sherbrooke Street West, Montreal, QC H3A 2T5, Canada • Admissions: 514-398-3910 • Fax: 514-398-3683

CAMPUS LIFE
Quality of Life Rating	**87**
Fire Safety Rating	**73**
Type of school	public
Environment	metropolis

STUDENTS
Total undergrad enrollment	22,074
% male/female	40/60
% from out of state	36
% live on campus	10
% international	18
# of countries represented	153

SURVEY SAYS . . .
Diverse student types on campus
Students love Montreal, QC
Great off-campus food
Student publications are popular
Lots of beer drinking

ACADEMICS
Academic Rating	**62**
Calendar	semester
Student/faculty ratio	16:1
Profs interesting rating	65
Profs accessible rating	63
% profs teaching UG courses	100
Most common lab size	20–29 students
Most common reg class size	10–19 students

MOST POPULAR MAJORS
business commerce
political science and government
psychology

STUDENTS SAY

Academics

McGill University has "an excellent reputation that is looked on favorably by graduate schools and employers." That reputation is built on "universally high academic standards, so there is no question that everyone here gets a good education" and also means that "an A at McGill means a lot, because it is very hard to get." Students tell us that "science and medicine, as well as music, are the noted strengths of McGill," and that any departments involved in research benefit from "the presence of groundbreaking work by teachers who are all masters of the material" as well as "a lot of funding, meaning that there are a lot of opportunities for students to get experiences that look great on your curriculum vitae." Success at McGill requires undergrads to be "very independent"—"Sometimes it is impossible to navigate the bureaucracy," students warn, and "There is virtually no guidance; everything, even your class schedule is done completely on your own, and if you mess up, it's your fault." Some undergrads see benefits in this; one points out, "This school churns out people with excellent time-management skills and pressure-coping mechanisms." First-year class sizes can be quite a shock—"All of my classes first year are prerequisites, and the class size is almost 600 in all my lectures," writes one science major—but "Once you get to upper-level classes, you forget the lack of personality in the big lectures and fall into a more familiar pattern of small classes like in high school." Another positive: "Many of the larger science lectures are available online, so you can watch them again (slides and voice recording) to make sure your notes are complete."

Life

"Montreal is a perfect place to spend your university life," McGill students agree, and with "a beautiful campus where you can lie back on the lawn and take a nap in nice weather and forget you're in the middle of a huge metropolis," it's no wonder they feel that way. Montreal offers "great restaurants, fabulous arts, and plenty of things to do." "McGill's lucky to be located in such a great city," writes one undergrad. "There's less dependence on the school to keep students entertained. At the same time, I think it allows students to experience a wider variety of activities and cultures, and thus learn more about themselves." McGill's housing situation, which forces most students into off-campus housing after their first year, further integrates undergrads into the life of the city; "Living in your own apartment in a big city where the official language is French and where the university is smack-dab in the middle of downtown, you learn some real life lessons here," explains one student. While some here report a "lack of campus life due to the fact that most students live off-campus," others tout the school's "clubs and services—we have so many of them and so many varieties!" One student advises, "It is important at a large university like McGill to join some clubs and organizations. If you don't, you end up feeling lost and alone."

Student Body

"The diversity of the student community at McGill never ceases to impress," as the university boasts a "multilingual student body and faculty. Working and studying with many kinds of people from all over the world makes studying here a great experience." Undergrads tell us that "it's hard to pinpoint the typical student. There are a number of 'types': well-dressed Americans and Torontonians with cell phones and Ugg boots, wealthy internationals, typical hippie/stoner/hacky-sacking folk, and, last but not least, the 'egghead,' who is rarely seen outside of the library." What they all have in common is that they are all bright; one undergrad writes, "It's humbling when you get here, because you are going to classes with really intelligent people. These are people who were also top students in their schools, people who also did lots of extracurricular activities and are overachievers; however, nobody seems to be bragging about these things."

FINANCIAL AID: 514-398-6013 • E-MAIL: ADMISSIONS@MCGILL.CA • WEBSITE: WWW.MCGILL.CA

ADMISSIONS

Very important factors considered include: Academic GPA, rigor of secondary school record, standardized test scores. *Important factors considered include:* Class rank. *Other factors considered include:* Recommendation(s). Proof of English proficiency is required of most international applicants. High school diploma is required, and GED is not accepted.

The Inside Word

McGill is as tough as it comes in Canadian higher education. The university is provincially funded. As there are no geographic quotas, competition from applicants around the world is intense. The admissions process is thorough and demanding, and high SAT and SAT Subject Test scores just don't guarantee admission across the board. While English is the language of instruction, French is the language of Montreal, and those who speak it fare much better in everyday life than those who do not.

FINANCIAL AID

The Princeton Review suggests that all financial aid forms be submitted as soon as possible after January 1. Institutional employment available. Off-campus job opportunities are fair.

FROM THE ADMISSIONS OFFICE

"McGill processes over 30,000 online applications a year. Very few programs are available to non-Quebec students for January admission; consult the website for details.

"Applicants for Fall 2008 may submit results from either version (old/new) of the SAT (plus at least two appropriate SAT Subject Tests). The ACT is accepted in lieu of the SAT and SAT Subject Test combination. Please note that certain programs can require specific SAT Subject Tests."

SELECTIVITY

Admissions Rating	60*
# of applicants	19,406
% of applicants accepted	56
% of acceptees attending	45

FRESHMAN PROFILE

Minimum Paper TOEFL	577
Minimum Computer Based TOEFL	233
Average HS GPA	3.71

DEADLINES

Regular application deadline	1/15
Regular notification	rolling
Nonfall registration?	yes

APPLICANTS ALSO LOOK AT

AND OFTEN PREFER
Brown University, Cornell University, New York University, Queen's University, Tufts University, University of Toronto

AND SOMETIMES PREFER
Harvard College, Massachusetts Institute of Technology, The University of Chicago, University of Michigan—Ann Arbor, University of Pennsylvania

FINANCIAL FACTS

Financial Aid Rating	60*
In-province tuition	$1,668
Out-of-province tuition	$4,914
International tuition	$12,930–$15,000
Room & Board	$11,104
Books and supplies	$1,000
Required fees	$1,597

MERCER UNIVERSITY—MACON

ADMISSIONS OFFICE, 1400 COLEMAN AVENUE, MACON, GA 31207-0001 • ADMISSIONS: 478-301-2650 • FAX: 478-301-2828

CAMPUS LIFE

Quality of Life Rating	**78**
Fire Safety Rating	**69**
Type of school	private
Affiliation	Baptist
Environment	city

STUDENTS

Total undergrad enrollment	2,293
% male/female	46/54
% from out of state	24
% live on campus	67
% in (# of) fraternities	23 (10)
% in (# of) sororities	26 (6)
% African American	17
% Asian	6
% Caucasian	69
% Hispanic	2
% international	2
# of countries represented	19

SURVEY SAYS . . .
Small classes
Great computer facilities
Great library
Athletic facilities are great
Frats and sororities dominate social scene

ACADEMICS

Academic Rating	**85**
Calendar	semester
Student/faculty ratio	12:1
Profs interesting rating	85
Profs accessible rating	85
% classes taught by TAs	0
Most common lab size	10–19 students
Most common reg class size	10–19 students

MOST POPULAR MAJORS
biology/biological sciences
business administration/
management
engineering

STUDENTS SAY

Academics

"Good scholarships," "challenging courses," an appealing "professor-to-student ratio, small class sizes," and "a great campus" initially convince many students to attend Mercer University in Macon—but it's the "very good professors who actually care about the students" who keep them here. The "professors are very friendly and love to interact with the students," and what's more, professors "can devote more time and energy to students' education" because they "are not required to do research." And that devotion starts on day one: "Even the introductory courses in the School of Engineering are taught only by professors with PhDs. I've never been taught by a TA." Outside of class, professors are "easily accessible, and they're very likely to actually know who you are." As at any college, there may be "some dud teachers, but overall," most students are very "pleased with the level of instruction here." Students have a lot of praise for the administration, as well: "Our administration is focused on what's best for the students and the university, not on money. For example, we are breaking ties with the GA Baptist Convention because it had issues with a student organization [a GBLT group], how trustees were elected, and, in general, how liberal the university was becoming. [The administration] stood up for the students in the face of the convention's removing its financial support."

Life

Technically, Mercer is a dry campus with a curfew: Men have to leave the women's dorms by a certain hour. But students stress that in reality, the school "is more of a 'moist' campus," and "The curfew rules [are] not [strictly] enforced." As is the case on many campuses, Greek life provides a lot of the party scene, but "The Greeks on campus are cut from a different cloth from most Greeks on other campuses. At Mercer they are more dedicated to philanthropy and community service than to hazing or binge drinking." Greeks "also have higher GPAs and are more active in campus life." To offer alternatives to frat parties, Mercer "has a group called 'Quadworks' that tries to make sure that students aren't stuck on campus with nothing to do. They host bands and sponsor drive-in movies and other events." Off campus "There are lots of great restaurants," and students "frequent bars and clubs in downtown Macon." "Mercer rents a trolley service Thursday–Saturday nights that runs from campus to downtown where all of the bars and clubs are." This makes socializing a little easier for those without wheels. Some "People jet away to Atlanta" for fun and big-city cultural events on weekends. Intercollegiate athletics are not particularly well-supported at Mercer; one student remarks, "No one goes to sporting events. People will [only] go if there is a free t-shirt or cup" giveaway.

Students

Mercer students describe the majority of their peers as "Georgia residents with Judeo-Christian heritages" who are "conservative, from a wealthy family, [and] generally well bred." As one student puts it, a typical Mercer undergrad "is a Friday/Saturday night partier with a knack for Sunday-morning churchgoing." The numbers reveal a high percentage of minority students in the student body, especially African Americans, "but ethnic/racial groups tend to remain separated." Students emphasize, however, that this separation is "not because of any explicit racism or intolerance—it's mostly self-imposed and self-perpetuating." "A good number of students" are "involved in religious organizations" and Greek life here, but "Nearly everyone is involved in some club or another; everyone can find some niche to fit into." No matter what their niche, though, Mercer undergraduates remain true to their Southern roots by being "welcoming" as well as "friendly and courteous" to all. Though the student body has been reputed to be politically apathetic, the school's recent confrontation with the Georgia Baptist Convention and the debates it stirred up got some students to thinking that "The campus is becoming a little more politically active."

Financial Aid: 478-301-2670 • E-mail: admissions@mercer.edu • Website: www.mercer.edu

ADMISSIONS

Very important factors considered include: Academic GPA, level of applicant's interest, rigor of secondary school record, standardized test scores. *Important factors considered include:* Character/personal qualities, extracurricular activities, talent/ability, volunteer work. *Other factors considered include:* Alumni/ae relation, class rank, interview, recommendation(s), work experience. SAT or ACT required; ACT with Writing component recommended. TOEFL required of all international applicants. High school diploma is required, and GED is accepted. *Academic units required:* 4 English, 4 math, 3 science (2 science labs), 2 foreign language, 1 social studies, 2 history.

The Inside Word

Mercer University's approach to the admissions process is fairly conventional—academics are where applicants distinguish themselves. Candidates with solid test scores and moderately challenging college preparatory curricula should be able to secure admittance. Students with a Christian background who want higher education with a religious foundation will thrive best at Mercer.

FINANCIAL AID

Students should submit: FAFSA, institution's own financial aid form, state aid form. The Princeton Review suggests that all financial aid forms be submitted as soon as possible after January 1. *Need-based scholarships/grants offered:* Pell Grant, SEOG, state scholarships/grants, the school's own gift aid, Federal Nursing Scholarship. *Loan aid offered:* Direct Subsidized Stafford, Direct Unsubsidized Stafford, Direct PLUS, Federal Perkins Loan, Federal Nursing Loan, college/university loans from institutional funds. Applicants will be notified of awards on a rolling basis beginning or about March 15. Federal Work-Study Program available. Institutional employment available. Off-campus job opportunities are good.

FROM THE ADMISSIONS OFFICE

"The mission of the Mercer University Office of Admissions is to attract, admit, and enroll qualified and talented students who will ultimately become happy, successful alumni. We do this by becoming personally involved with each admitted student and family during the admissions process. Mercer Admissions Staff (98 percent of whom are Mercer graduates) takes time to know each admitted applicant on a personal level and are concerned about the family's questions regarding financial assistance, campus life, and academic affairs. High school and campus visits, regional receptions, and programs are all conducted by Admissions Staff who are knowledgeable about the high schools and 2-year colleges in a particular region. This makes for a truly enjoyable and productive admissions experience for all involved.

"Freshman applicants for Fall 2008 must take the new SAT, which includes a written essay, or the ACT with Writing component."

SELECTIVITY

Admissions Rating	87
# of applicants	2,857
% of applicants accepted	79
% of acceptees attending	25

FRESHMAN PROFILE

Range SAT Critical Reading	530–630
Range SAT Math	550–640
Range SAT Writing	520–620
Range ACT Composite	22–27
Minimum Paper TOEFL	550
Minimum Computer Based TOEFL	213
Average HS GPA	3.6
% graduated top 10% of class	42
% graduated top 25% of class	72
% graduated top 50% of class	80

DEADLINES

Regular application deadline	7/1
Regular notification	rolling
Nonfall registration?	no

APPLICANTS ALSO LOOK AT

AND OFTEN PREFER
Emory University, Georgia Institute of Technology, Samford University, University of Georgia

AND SOMETIMES PREFER
Auburn University, Florida State University, Furman University, Stetson University, Vanderbilt University

AND RARELY PREFER
Clemson University, Georgia Southern University

FINANCIAL FACTS

Financial Aid Rating	88
Annual tuition	$25,056
Room & Board	$7,710
Books and supplies	$900
Required fees	$200
% frosh rec. need-based scholarship or grant aid	68
% UG rec. need-based scholarship or grant aid	64
% frosh rec. need-based self-help aid	40
% UG rec. need-based self-help aid	41
% frosh rec. any financial aid	99
% UG rec. any financial aid	97

MIAMI UNIVERSITY

301 SOUTH CAMPUS AVENUE, OXFORD, OH 45056 • ADMISSIONS: 513-529-2531 • FAX: 513-529-1550

CAMPUS LIFE

Quality of Life Rating	75
Fire Safety Rating	60*
Type of school	public
Environment	village

STUDENTS

Total undergrad enrollment	14,471
% male/female	46/54
% from out of state	29
% live on campus	48
% in (# of) fraternities	21 (28)
% in (# of) sororities	24 (20)
% African American	3
% Asian	3
% Caucasian	86
% Hispanic	2
% Native American	1
% international	1
# of countries represented	50

SURVEY SAYS . . .
Great library
Athletic facilities are great
Great food on campus
Frats and sororities dominate social scene
Lots of beer drinking
Hard liquor is popular

ACADEMICS

Academic Rating	78
Calendar	semester
Student/faculty ratio	16:1
Profs interesting rating	77
Profs accessible rating	74
% profs teaching UG courses	100
% classes taught by TAs	10
Most common lab size	20–29 students
Most common reg class size	20–29 students

MOST POPULAR MAJORS
finance
marketing/marketing management
zoology/animal biology

STUDENTS SAY

Academics

The "beautiful" "wooded campus" of Miami University is just one of the reasons "This is a public school that feels like a private school." Another reason is the school's "commitment to the liberal arts via the Miami Plan." The Miami Plan refers to the university's core curriculum of 48 semester hours. Students also appreciate having the option of the Western College Program, which allows them to design their own interdisciplinary majors. Unlike tiny private schools, however, MU offers students scads of prescribed majors. The number of students enrolled decides which departments get the most funding, and favored majors are those in the business school, though the architecture program receives healthy funding as well. With such a focus on the business school, it makes sense that "Miami is very well organized in getting students into internships and onto management fast-tracks." The vast study abroad opportunities and summer program activities draw widespread student praise too. But some students claim that "professors are hit or miss. Some are amazingly available, very dedicated teachers, and some couldn't care less what happens to their students." The "administration seems the same way: Some have actual office hours; [others] the students couldn't identify in a lineup." This aloofness reportedly has something to do with the university's strategic plan, called "First in 2009." This initiative seeks to make Miami an even better university. Toward this end, the school is raising $350 million to hire more professors, create scholarships, build a new business school, and an ice arena, a new engineering school, and new parking garages." Consequently, the administration may at times seem preoccupied, some students gripe, "unless you have a check to write."

Life

Miami University is a "work hard, play hard" school. "During a generally tough week throughout campus, most people are studying, and the library is packed. But at the beginning of any semester, a lot of people go out on a Wednesday or Thursday night." Miami's "small rural classic college town" of Oxford "is very college-oriented. The street is lined with bars and restaurants" where lots of students "drink and party." Since "All of the bars pretty much have dance floors" and "People under 21 can go to bars here," under- and upperclassmen alike may take advantage of the nightlife. Greek life is also "strong here, so there are Greek functions to go to as well." There are also "university concerts, plays, and musicals, which are usually pretty well attended. As for athletics, Miami has lots of fair-weather fans," one student contends. "When we are doing well, everyone is at the game; when we aren't doing so well, lots of people are doing something else." As far as opportunities for entertainment outside of town are concerned, "There isn't any public transportation to leave Oxford," but "If you have a car, you can travel to Cincinnati or other neighboring cities for a night on the town."

Student Body

Old stereotypes die hard. Just ask the undergrads here, and they will tell you that, yes, "Miami is 'J. Crew U.'": "The typical student is White, relatively wealthy, equipped with their parents' credit card, good-looking, and only seen in the hottest fashions." (We're serious about the fashions: "Students dress up for their 8:00 A.M. classes," one student claims.). But students are adamant that there are two "sides of the J. Crew U. stereotype. To be sure, if you look at Miami U. from the Goodyear Blimp, it is J. Crew U. If you looked at Miami U. under a microscope and saw students interacting in everyday situations, you would see another school entirely." One undergrad observes that "Minorities seem to be in short supply." Another calls "this student body composition . . . self-perpetuating."

FINANCIAL AID: 513-529-8734 • E-MAIL: ADMISSION@MUOHIO.EDU • WEBSITE: WWW.MUOHIO.EDU

ADMISSIONS

Very important factors considered include: Academic GPA, application essay, character/personal qualities, class rank, recommendation(s), rigor of secondary school record, standardized test scores, talent/ability. *Other factors considered include:* Alumni/ae relation, extracurricular activities, first generation, geographical residence, state residency, volunteer work, work experience. SAT or ACT required; ACT with Writing component required. TOEFL required of all international applicants. High school diploma is required, and GED is accepted. *Academic units recommended:* 4 English, 3 math, 3 science, 2 foreign language, 3 social studies, 1 fine arts.

The Inside Word

Miami's Admissions Officers employ a practice that certainly distinguishes the Miami admissions process from that of other large, public universities. While most peer institutions typically adopt a numbers-driven process, this school is concerned about the total package. Counselors closely examine every facet of each application and consider applicants' achievements in the context of their experiences.

FINANCIAL AID

Students should submit: FAFSA. The Princeton Review suggests that all financial aid forms be submitted as soon as possible after January 1. *Need-based scholarships/grants offered:* Pell Grant, SEOG, state scholarships/grants, private scholarships, the school's own gift aid. *Loan aid offered:* Direct Subsidized Stafford, Direct Unsubsidized Stafford, Direct PLUS, Federal Perkins Loan, Federal Nursing Loan, college/university loans from institutional funds, bank alternative loans. Applicants will be notified of awards on or about March 20. Federal Work-Study Program available. Institutional employment available. Off-campus job opportunities are good.

FROM THE ADMISSIONS OFFICE

"At Miami, you'll find a level of involvement—in your classes, in your research, in your extracurricular activities—that you won't find at other schools. What sets Miami apart and makes it a 'Public Ivy' and a 'Hidden Treasure' is the ability to give students a small-college experience within the excitement and opportunities of a large university, all at a public school cost. With more than 100 majors to choose from, and a liberal arts foundation that allows students to explore different areas of interest, finding the right career path is at the heart of what the MU experience is all about. Miami's reputation for producing outstanding graduates makes us a target school for top national firms. In fact, our Office of Career Services sponsors one of the largest career fairs in the country. For getting into the best possible graduate school, *The Wall Street Journal* ranks Miami at No. 22 among undergraduate colleges that feed into elite graduate programs. And our graduates' acceptance rate into law and medical school are far above the national average.

"Freshman applicants for Fall 2007 must take the new SAT, which includes a written essay, or the ACT with Writing component. The Writing component of these tests, however, will not play a role in our decisions for Fall 2008 admission. These scores will simply help us collect important data that will be useful for future admission decisions."

SELECTIVITY

Admissions Rating	88
# of applicants	15,468
% of applicants accepted	78
% of acceptees attending	30
# accepting a place on wait list	274
# of early decision applicants	704
% accepted early decision	75

FRESHMAN PROFILE

Range SAT Critical Reading	540–640
Range SAT Math	570–660
Range ACT Composite	24–29
Minimum Paper TOEFL	533
Minimum Computer Based TOEFL	200
Average HS GPA	3.66
% graduated top 10% of class	38
% graduated top 25% of class	74
% graduated top 50% of class	98

DEADLINES

Early decision application deadline	11/1
Early decision notification	12/15
Regular application deadline	1/31
Regular notification	3/15
Nonfall registration?	yes

APPLICANTS ALSO LOOK AT

AND OFTEN PREFER
Northwestern University, University of Notre Dame, Vanderbilt University

AND SOMETIMES PREFER
Boston College, Pennsylvania State University—University Park, University of Illinois at Urbana-Champaign, University of Michigan—Ann Arbor, University of Wisconsin—Madison, Washington University in St. Louis

AND RARELY PREFER
Denison University, Ohio University—Athens, Purdue University—West Lafayette, The Ohio State University—Columbus, University of Dayton, Xavier University (OH)

FINANCIAL FACTS

Financial Aid Rating	74
Annual in-state tuition	$20,991
Annual out-of-state tuition	$21,011
Room & Board	$8,140
Books and supplies	$1,140
Required fees	$2,006
% frosh rec. need-based scholarship or grant aid	16
% UG rec. need-based scholarship or grant aid	17
% frosh rec. need-based self-help aid	28
% UG rec. need-based self-help aid	29
% frosh rec. any financial aid	87
% UG rec. any financial aid	85
Independent 529 member?	TK

MICHIGAN STATE UNIVERSITY

250 ADMINISTRATION BUILDING, EAST LANSING, MI 48824-1046 • ADMISSIONS: 517-355-8332 • FAX: 517-353-1647

CAMPUS LIFE
Quality of Life Rating	85
Fire Safety Rating	60*
Type of school	public
Environment	town

STUDENTS
Total undergrad enrollment	35,521
% male/female	46/54
% from out of state	8
% live on campus	41
# of fraternities	27
# of sororities	13
% African American	8
% Asian	5
% Caucasian	78
% Hispanic	3
% Native American	1
% international	3
# of countries represented	129

SURVEY SAYS . . .
Great library
Students are friendly
Everyone loves the Spartans
Student publications are popular
Lots of beer drinking

ACADEMICS
Academic Rating	73
Calendar	semester
Student/faculty ratio	17:1
Profs interesting rating	71
Profs accessible rating	74
Most common	
lab size	20–29 students
Most common	
reg class size	20–29 students

MOST POPULAR MAJORS
biology/biological sciences
business administration/
management
communications studies/speech
communication and rhetoric

STUDENTS SAY

Academics

Michigan State University's large size is both its greatest asset and its greatest potential downside. The benefits of size include near-unlimited choice: "MSU is extremely varied, and there are opportunities for anyone who wishes to take advantage of them," including "over 200 majors to choose from." Those majors include "good engineering and science programs," an "amazing communications program," "the best political science program in Michigan," "the only agriculture school in the state," and "an absolutely amazing School of Hospitality Business." Economies of scale also allow MSU to offer "great study abroad programs," "a lot of helpful free tutoring in math and other subjects," and "great web programs that make it very easy to download class materials and view assignments. You can also e-mail the whole class questions or just your professor, through our Angel system." As far as possible downsides to the school's size, MSU students find that they have to "fend for [themselves]." One student noted, "Initially I came from a smaller college where there was more guidance and interaction with professors. At MSU, this is just not the case, although MSU's residential colleges do make the university seem smaller for students in related majors." That means potential peril for students who aren't self-motivated. One undergrad explains, "There are two roads you can follow when at MSU. You can study hard and earn a degree in a reputable, challenging setting; or you can soak your brain cells with alcohol instead of academia."

Life

Life on the MSU campus "generally revolves around the weekend and the basketball or football team. You get through the week looking forward to one of the two." Indeed, "Sports are huge here, and nothing beats football Saturdays or basketball nights. Tailgating is a religion." The school has a well-known party scene; one undergrad concedes, "We're known as somewhat of a party school, and MSU lives up to the title. Although during the winter there is less to do around campus, being here in the fall more than makes up for it! If you attend MSU, you're bound to have a great time." Even teetotalers can have fun here, since "Between free on-campus movies and club meetings and concerts, there is never a dull moment on campus." East Lansing has its own allures: a student explains, "Walking downtown on Grand River is awesome when it gets warmer out"; there are "decent stores and restaurants. Also, in the warm weather you are bound to see people sitting out on their porches. Many of them are having parties or just hanging out, and a lot of times they'll invite you to come on up!" Or you can just enjoy the "breathtaking beauty of the campus," with its "old buildings and beautiful trees and plants that make every walk to class a great one."

Student Body

MSU's size ensures that "This is a fairly diverse campus, especially considering that it is located in the northern Midwest." Because "Study abroad is emphasized at MSU," there are "a lot of foreign students, and they seem to fit right into the general population." One undergrad observes, "For the most part, everyone seems to do their own thing, and no one seems to have problems with that." The predominant attitude seems to be "live and let live," as "A lot of people tend to associate mostly with members from the same racial or ethnic background, although that's not always the case." What unites students—besides their love of MSU sports—is that most "are extremely friendly. Random people in classes ask you if you need a ride home, and, even better, random people offer you a seat on the bus. It's comforting to know that these are the people soon entering the workforce and 'the real world.'"

MICHIGAN STATE UNIVERSITY

FINANCIAL AID: 517-353-5940 • E-MAIL: ADMIS@MSU.EDU • WEBSITE: WWW.MSU.EDU

ADMISSIONS

Very important factors considered include: Academic GPA, rigor of secondary school record, standardized test scores. *Important factors considered include:* Extracurricular activities, first generation. *Other factors considered include:* Alumni/ae relation, application essay, character/personal qualities, class rank, geographical residence, recommendation(s), talent/ability, volunteer work, work experience. SAT or ACT required; ACT with Writing component required. TOEFL required of all international applicants. High school diploma is required, and GED is accepted. *Academic units required:* 4 English, 3 math, 2 science, 2 foreign language, 2 social studies, 1 history.

The Inside Word

Given the extraordinary volume of applications the Admissions Office receives, it's no wonder that Michigan State relies primarily on numbers. Decisions typically come down to grades, class rank, and test scores. Applicants who have proven to be capable students in college prep courses are relatively likely to find themselves the proud addressees of fat admissions envelopes.

FINANCIAL AID

Students should submit: FAFSA. The Princeton Review suggests that all financial aid forms be submitted as soon as possible after January 1. *Need-based scholarships/grants offered:* Pell Grant, SEOG, state scholarships/grants, private scholarships, the school's own gift aid, United Negro College Fund, Federal Nursing Scholarship. *Loan aid offered:* FFEL Subsidized Stafford, FFEL Unsubsidized Stafford, FFEL PLUS, Federal Perkins Loan, Federal Nursing Loan, state loans, college/university loans from institutional funds. Applicants will be notified of awards on a rolling basis beginning or about March 15. Off-campus job opportunities are excellent.

FROM THE ADMISSIONS OFFICE

"Although Michigan State University is a graduate and research institution of international stature and acclaim, your undergraduate education is a high priority. More than 2,600 instructional faculty members (90 percent of whom hold a terminal degree) are dedicated to providing academic instruction, guidance, and assistance to our undergraduate students. Our 35,000 undergraduate students are a select group of academically motivated men and women. The diversity of ethnic, racial, religious, and socioeconomic heritage makes the student body a microcosm of the state, national, and international community.

"Students applying for Fall 2008 admission to Michigan State University are required to take the new version of the SAT or the ACT exam with the Writing section. The Writing assessment will be considered in the holistic review of the application for admission. SAT Subject Tests are not required."

SELECTIVITY

Admissions Rating	**85**
# of applicants	23,247
% of applicants accepted	73
% of acceptees attending	44
# accepting a place on wait list	770
% admitted from wait list	34

FRESHMAN PROFILE

Range SAT Critical Reading	500–630
Range SAT Math	530–600
Range SAT Writing	490–610
Range ACT Composite	22–27
Minimum Paper TOEFL	550
Minimum Computer Based TOEFL	213
Average HS GPA	3.61
% graduated top 10% of class	29
% graduated top 25% of class	69
% graduated top 50% of class	95

DEADLINES

Regular notification	rolling
Nonfall registration?	yes

APPLICANTS ALSO LOOK AT AND OFTEN PREFER

Central Michigan University, Eastern Michigan University, Kalamazoo College, University of Michigan—Ann Arbor, Western Michigan University

AND SOMETIMES PREFER

Indiana University—Bloomington, Oakland University, University of Illinois at Urbana-Champaign, University of Wisconsin—Madison

AND RARELY PREFER

Wayne State University

FINANCIAL FACTS

Financial Aid Rating	**74**
Annual in-state tuition	$7,665
Annual out-of-state tuition	$20,310
Room & Board	$6,044
Books and supplies	$884
Required fees	$1,228
% frosh rec. need-based scholarship or grant aid	23
% UG rec. need-based scholarship or grant aid	24
% frosh rec. need-based self-help aid	35
% UG rec. need-based self-help aid	35
% frosh rec. any financial aid	42
% UG rec. any financial aid	40

MICHIGAN TECHNOLOGICAL UNIVERSITY

1400 TOWNSEND DRIVE, HOUGHTON, MI 49931 • ADMISSIONS: 906-487-2335 • FAX: 906-487-2125

CAMPUS LIFE

Quality of Life Rating	80
Fire Safety Rating	83
Type of school	public
Environment	village

STUDENTS

Total undergrad enrollment	5,534
% male/female	78/22
% from out of state	26
% live on campus	41
% in (# of) fraternities	7 (15)
% in (# of) sororities	11 (8)
% African American	2
% Asian	1
% Caucasian	87
% Hispanic	1
% Native American	1
% international	4
# of countries represented	72

SURVEY SAYS . . .

Great computer facilities
Athletic facilities are great
Students are friendly
Campus feels safe
Frats and sororities dominate social scene
Lots of beer drinking

ACADEMICS

Academic Rating	74
Calendar	semester
Student/faculty ratio	12:1
Profs interesting rating	64
Profs accessible rating	75
% profs teaching UG courses	100
% classes taught by TAs	4
Most common lab size	10–19 students
Most common reg class size	10–19 students

MOST POPULAR MAJORS

civil engineering
electrical, electronics, and
communications engineering
mechanical engineering

STUDENTS SAY

Academics

"Michigan Tech will definitely prepare you for your future," engineers at this small, tech powerhouse tell us, promising that "you will get a great education, and employers, especially in the Midwest, recognize Michigan Tech as a premier engineering school." More than half of MTU's undergraduates are enrolled in the College of Engineering. Among the other divisions, students tell us that "the School of Business and Economics is gaining a lot of ground" as the school attempts to diversify its appeal. Those efforts have produced mixed results, students report; while improvements to business and biology offerings are welcome, some here feel efforts to upgrade liberal arts offerings dilute MTU's strengths. "We're trying to be like the University of Michigan with great engineering and hundreds of other major programs, but we just don't have the money to do it all," writes one student. Like most tech schools, MTU "expects a lot of students," but, as a result, "You will graduate being very proficient in your field, and you'll have a competitive advantage over graduates from other universities." You may not even have to wait for graduation to benefit from that advantage, since "Michigan Tech has a great program for getting internships and co-ops." Professors "are involved in research and have professional commitments outside the classroom, but most are still there for the students. Have a problem? Schedule a time to meet with your professor and talk about it. Most will even find a time outside their scheduled office hours that works with [your] schedule to meet with you."

Life

Michigan Tech "is separated from the rest of the country. It's located in a small town in the very northern part of the UP (upper peninsula). Most students have an 8-plus-hour drive home. This makes the community rather tight knit," which "helps when you get to the killer classes." The university combats its isolation by "providing entertainment for the students by way of comedians, musical acts, and plays." Students also enjoy "lots of Greek parties (the Greek scene is not exclusive, which is cool) [and] sporting events, like the very successful football and basketball programs. We also have an important ice hockey program." Do you like snow? We hope so, because at MTU "It snows from October through April," which naturally has a huge impact on campus life. For fans of winter sports, MTU is a virtual paradise, with "several ski hills in close proximity to the campus. Snowmobiling, cross-country and downhill skiing, as well as ice skating, are popular activities." Students also point out that hometown "Houghton is also beautiful in the summer, and is strategically located by large bodies of fresh water. When it's warm, we fish, hike, bike, rock-climb, and play the school golf course."

Student Body

One MTU student writes, "There doesn't seem to be a single typical student at Michigan Tech. There is a bipolar distribution with a lot of smart engineers that party little and study hard. There are also a lot of students that drink heavily and just barely get by in their classes. As with any school, there are many outliers that find their own niche here." Students tell us there are also quite a few "Indian, Chinese, and Middle Eastern" students; most other undergraduates are "White, Midwestern, from middle-class families [and] lean to the conservative side." Men far outnumber women here, which, one woman tells us, "you [would] think would be great for women, but it's not. Once you take away the guys who won't even approach a girl, the ratio is more like two guys to every girl, and then out of all the guys who are single it is more like 0.5 guys to every girl. People think it is so easy to be a girl at Tech, but after a while you are just viewed as one of the guys, and then it is hard to get a date."

MICHIGAN TECHNOLOGICAL UNIVERSITY

FINANCIAL AID: 906-487-2622 • E-MAIL: MTU4U@MTU.EDU • WEBSITE: WWW.MTU.EDU

ADMISSIONS

Very important factors considered include: Academic GPA, class rank, rigor of secondary school record, standardized test scores. *Other factors considered include:* Alumni/ae relation, application essay, character/personal qualities, extracurricular activities, interview, recommendation(s), talent/ability, volunteer work, work experience. SAT or ACT required; TOEFL required of all international applicants. High school diploma is required, and GED is accepted. *Academic units required:* 3 English, 3 math, 2 science. *Academic units recommended:* 4 English, 4 math, 3 science, 2 foreign language, 3 social studies, 1 history, 1 academic elective.

The Inside Word

Michigan Tech has a pretty good reputation and a highly self-selected applicant pool. In light of this, students who are interested should not be deceived by the high admit rate and should spend a little time on self-assessment of their ability to handle an engineering curriculum. There's nothing gained by getting yourself into a program that you can't get through successfully.

FINANCIAL AID

Students should submit: FAFSA. The Princeton Review suggests that all financial aid forms be submitted as soon as possible after January 1. *Need-based scholarships/grants offered:* Pell Grant, SEOG, state scholarships/grants, private scholarships, the school's own gift aid. *Loan aid offered:* Direct Subsidized Stafford, Direct Unsubsidized Stafford, Direct PLUS, Federal Perkins Loan, state loans, college/university loans from institutional funds, external private loans. Applicants will be notified of awards on or about May 1. Federal Work-Study Program available. Institutional employment available. Off-campus job opportunities are good.

FROM THE ADMISSIONS OFFICE

"At Michigan Tech, our students create the future. Our unique Enterprise Program lets students work on real industry problems involving homeland security, wireless technology, communication, environmental sustainability, and nanotechnology. Through student groups like Engineers without Borders and the campus-wide Make A Difference Day, our students impact lives in our community and around the world. Students can choose from 120 degree programs in arts and human sciences, business, computing, engineering, environmental studies, sciences, and technology as they begin their careers here. We offer exciting degree programs in growing fields including biomedical engineering, applied ecology and environmental science, and pre-health studies.

"Outside of the classrooms and labs, students enjoy our golf course, ski hill, trails and recreational forest, and friendly, small-town atmosphere in beautiful Upper Michigan. Located on Portage Waterway, the campus is only minutes from Lake Superior.

"We recommend that students applying for admission take the new SAT (or the ACT with the writing section).

"Apply online for free at www.mtu.edu."

SELECTIVITY
Admissions Rating	**84**
# of applicants	3,802
% of applicants accepted	82
% of acceptees attending	38

FRESHMAN PROFILE
Range SAT Critical Reading	500–623
Range SAT Math	560–670
Range SAT Writing	480–590
Range ACT Composite	23–28
Minimum Paper TOEFL	500
Minimum Computer Based TOEFL	173
Average HS GPA	3.5
% graduated top 10% of class	29
% graduated top 25% of class	57
% graduated top 50% of class	86

DEADLINES
Regular notification	rolling
Nonfall registration?	yes

APPLICANTS ALSO LOOK AT AND SOMETIMES PREFER
Kettering University, Michigan State University, Milwaukee School of Engineering, University of Michigan—Ann Arbor, University of Minnesota—Twin Cities, University of Wisconsin—Madison, Western Michigan University

AND RARELY PREFER
Grand Valley State University, Lawrence Technological University, Northern Michigan University

FINANCIAL FACTS
Financial Aid Rating	**78**
Annual in-state tuition	$8,271
Annual out-of-state tuition	$20,040
Room & Board	$6,840
% frosh rec. need-based scholarship or grant aid	52
% UG rec. need-based scholarship or grant aid	50
% frosh rec. need-based self-help aid	49
% UG rec. need-based self-help aid	53
% frosh rec. any financial aid	86
% UG rec. any financial aid	94

MIDDLEBURY COLLEGE

THE EMMA WILLARD HOUSE, MIDDLEBURY, VT 05753-6002 • ADMISSIONS: 802-443-3000 • FAX: 802-443-2056

CAMPUS LIFE

Quality of Life Rating	**98**
Fire Safety Rating	**81**
Type of school	private
Environment	village

STUDENTS

Total undergrad enrollment	2,376
% male/female	48/52
% from out of state	93
% from public high school	52
% live on campus	97
% African American	3
% Asian	9
% Caucasian	65
% Hispanic	6
% Native American	1
% international	10
# of countries represented	70

SURVEY SAYS . . .

Great food on campus
Small classes
Lab facilities are great
Athletic facilities are great
School is well run

ACADEMICS

Academic Rating	**98**
Calendar	4-1-4
Student/faculty ratio	9:1
Profs interesting rating	99
Profs accessible rating	96
% profs teaching	
UG courses	100
% classes taught by TAs	0
Most common	
reg class size	10–19 students

MOST POPULAR MAJORS

economics
English language and literature
psychology

STUDENTS SAY

Academics

Home to "smart people who enjoy Aristotelian ethics and quantum physics, but aren't too stuck up to go sledding in front of Mead Chapel at midnight," Middlebury College is a small, exclusive liberal arts school with "excellent foreign language programs" as well as standout offerings in environmental studies, the sciences, theater, and writing. Distribution requirements and other general requirements ensure that a Middlebury education "is all about providing students with a complete college experience including excellent teaching, exposure to many other cultures, endless opportunities for growth and success, and a challenging (yet relaxed) environment." Its "small class size and friendly yet competitive atmosphere make for the perfect college experience," as do "the best facilities of a small liberal arts college in the country. The new library, science center, athletic complex, arts center, and a number of the dining halls and dorms have been built in the past 10 years." Expect to work hard here; "It's tough, but this is a mini-Ivy, so what should one expect? There is plenty of time to socialize, and due to the collaborative atmosphere here, studying and socializing can often come hand in hand. The goal of many students here is not to get high grades" but rather "learning in its purest form, and that is perhaps this college's most brightly shining aspect." The collaborative atmosphere is abetted by the fact that "Admissions doesn't just bring in geniuses, they bring in people who are leaders and community servants. Think of the guy or girl in your high school whom everybody describes as 'so nice' . . . that's your typical Middlebury student."

Life

"This high level of involvement in everything translates into an amazing campus atmosphere" at Middlebury, where "Most people are very involved. There is a club for just about everything you can imagine, and if you can imagine one that hasn't yet been created, you go ahead and create it yourself." With great skiing and outdoor activity close by, "Almost everyone is athletic in some way. This can translate into anything from varsity sports to intramural hockey (an extremely popular winter pastime!). People are enthusiastic about being active and having fun." Because the school "is set in a very small town, there aren't too many (if any) problems with violence, drugs, [or] crime. It's the ideal college town because of its rural setting, in that there are no real distractions other than those that are provided within the college campus." Of course, the small-town setting also means that "the only real off-campus activity is going out to eat at the town's quaint restaurants or going to the one bar in town," but fortunately "When it comes to on-campus activities, Middlebury provides the student population with tons of great events. Everything from classy music concerts to late-night movies and dance parties can be found as a Midd-supported activity. The student activity board does a fabulous job with entertaining the students virtually every day."

Student Body

"The typical [Middlebury] student is athletic, outdoorsy, and very intelligent." The two most prominent demographics are "very preppy students (popped collars)" and "extreme hippies." One undergrad explains: "The typical students are one of two types: either 'Polo, Nantucket red, pearls, and summers on the Cape,' or 'Birks, wool socks, granola, and suspicious smells about them.' A lot of people break these two molds, but they often fall somewhere on the spectrum between them." There's also "a huge international student population, which is awesome," but some international students, "tend to separate out and end up living in language houses." There's also "a really strong theater/artsy community" here. One student notes, "Other than a few groups, everyone mingles pretty well. We're all too damn friendly and cheerful for our own good."

FINANCIAL AID: 802-443-5158 • E-MAIL: ADMISSIONS@MIDDLEBURY.EDU • WEBSITE: WWW.MIDDLEBURY.EDU

ADMISSIONS

Very important factors considered include: Academic GPA, character/personal qualities, class rank, extracurricular activities, rigor of secondary school record, talent/ability. *Important factors considered include:* Application essay, racial/ethnic status, recommendation(s), standardized test scores. *Other factors considered include:* Alumni/ae relation, first generation, geographical residence, level of applicant's interest, volunteer work, work experience. SAT and SAT Subject Tests or ACT required. High school diploma or equivalent is not required. *Academic units recommended:* 4 English, 4 math, 3 science (3 science labs), 4 foreign language, 3 social studies, 2 history, 1 academic elective, 1 fine arts, music, or drama course.

The Inside Word

Middlebury gives you options in standardized testing. The school will accept either the SAT or the ACT or three SAT Subject Tests, AP, or International Baccalaureate exams, or any combination of three SAT Subject Tests, AP, and International Baccalaureate exams (the three must be in different subject areas, however). Middlebury is extremely competitive; improve your chances of admission by crafting a standardized test profile that shows you in the best possible light.

FINANCIAL AID

Students should submit: FAFSA, CSS/Financial Aid PROFILE, state aid form, Noncustodial PROFILE, Business/Farm Supplement. Regular filing deadline is January 1. The Princeton Review suggests that all financial aid forms be submitted as soon as possible after January 1. *Need-based scholarships/grants offered:* Pell Grant, SEOG, state scholarships/grants, private scholarships, the school's own gift aid. *Loan aid offered:* Direct Subsidized Stafford, Direct Unsubsidized Stafford, Direct PLUS, Federal Perkins Loan, college/university loans from institutional funds. Applicants will be notified of awards on or about April 1.

FROM THE ADMISSIONS OFFICE

"The successful Middlebury candidate excels in a variety of areas including academics, athletics, the arts, leadership, and service to others. These strengths and interests permit students to grow beyond their traditional 'comfort zones' and conventional limits. Our classrooms are as varied as the Green Mountains, the Metropolitan Museum of Art, or the great cities of Russia and Japan. Outside the classroom, students informally interact with professors in activities such as intramural basketball games and community service. At Middlebury, students develop critical-thinking skills, enduring bonds of friendship, and the ability to challenge themselves.

"Applicants must submit standardized test results in at least three different areas of study. This requirement may be met by any one of the following three options: the ACT (optional Writing Test recommended, but not required), the new SAT, or three tests in different subject areas from the SAT Subject Tests, Advanced Placement, or International Baccalaureate exams."

SELECTIVITY

Admissions Rating	99
# of applicants	6,205
% of applicants accepted	22
% of acceptees attending	42
# accepting a place on wait list	646
% admitted from wait list	8
# of early decision applicants	905
% accepted early decision	24

FRESHMAN PROFILE

Range SAT Critical Reading	630–740
Range SAT Math	640–740
Range SAT Writing	630–740
Range ACT Composite	29–32
Average HS GPA	4.0
% graduated top 10% of class	82
% graduated top 25% of class	96
% graduated top 50% of class	99

DEADLINES

Early decision application deadline	11/1
Early decision notification	12/15
Regular application deadline	1/1
Regular notification	4/1
Nonfall registration?	yes

APPLICANTS ALSO LOOK AT

AND OFTEN PREFER
Amherst College, Dartmouth College, Harvard College, Williams College

AND SOMETIMES PREFER
Brown University, Duke University, Pomona College, Stanford University, Yale University

AND RARELY PREFER
Bowdoin College, Colby College, Colgate University, Hamilton College

FINANCIAL FACTS

Financial Aid Rating	94
Comprehensive fee	$44,330
Books and supplies	$750
% frosh rec. need-based scholarship or grant aid	45
% UG rec. need-based scholarship or grant aid	43
% frosh rec. need-based self-help aid	45
% UG rec. need-based self-help aid	43

MILLS COLLEGE

5000 MacArthur Boulevard, Oakland, CA 94613 • Admissions: 510-430-2135 • Fax: 510-430-3314

STUDENTS SAY

Academics

Mills College, a Bay Area all-women's liberal arts school "so small that most freshwomen even know the president of the college personally," is "all about the empowerment of women, innovative thought, independence, and activism." The "creative, unique, leftist women" who attend Mills may sometimes be "skeptical of the world in general" and love the "many opportunities to get involved and make a difference" that their academic community encourages. Of course, Mills also has a "rigorous and challenging" curriculum that consumes substantial proportions of each undergrad's time. The workload is considerable here; fortunately, however, undergrads enjoy "plenty of support and guidance from the faculty to aid in each student's individual success." This help may take the form of "workshops and tutoring if you are struggling." Professors "are nurturing in their teaching methods, and they are [also] experts in their fields. The teachers are here to help the students learn, and, therefore, they take the time to give individualized attention." Students lavish praise on the nursing program, computer sciences and mathematics, the "strong Psychology Department," the "amazing Child Development Department," an English Department that "accommodates and often encourages experimentation," and an ethnic studies program "that will challenge and push you." As is the case at many small schools, course availability is sometimes a problem; one undergrad writes, "Incoming students should simply be aware that many classes are only offered every 2 years (and the very rare ones, every 3), so they need to plan carefully if they are expecting to take some of Mills' more unique classes." All told, however, students tend to agree that "the benefits of attending Mills far outweigh these compromises."

Life

"Mills is not for everyone," students concede, pointing out that "If you're looking for a party school, Mills is not for you." One student puts it more bluntly: "Life at Mills is usually pretty dull. Social activities, whether endorsed by the school or not, are scarce. We generally go to UC—Berkeley if we want to interact with other students, either at a party or just a coffee shop. So many things are closed at Mills on the weekends that it doesn't really provide a great atmosphere for socializing once classes are done for the week." Activities are a little more lively during the week, when undergrads "have social lives, but parties do not consume them. We have many free activities such as dances, movie screenings, guest speakers, art shows, outdoor outings such as water rafting and horseback riding, and many sporting events." Many here relish the fact that "campus life is usually quiet and peaceful," and they praise the beautiful campus, which they liken to "a park in the middle of the city" that provides "lots of quiet space to study." At the same time, the urban setting provides the hustle and bustle missing from campus: "The rest of the Bay Area . . . is a great asset. The opportunities for entertainment in Berkeley, San Francisco, etc. are endless."

Student Body

Mills students "tend to differ from socially imposed expectations about what a young woman ought to be in at least one major way. "A typical student at Mills is usually either gay, transgender, minority, impoverished, vegetarian, or anarchist." The student body is thus, to some degree, "reverse mainstream." With students of color representing one-third of the population, a significant lesbian population, and lots of nontraditional undergrads—that is, "a relatively high percentage of older, resuming, and transferring students"—Mills achieves the diversity that its community members enthusiastically champion. One student notes, "The only thing that is 'typical' about the women at Mills is that all of them are smart, independent-thinking, strong women who want to make their lives the best that they can be."

FINANCIAL AID: 510-430-2000 • E-MAIL: ADMISSION@MILLS.EDU • WEBSITE: WWW.MILLS.EDU

ADMISSIONS

Very important factors considered include: Rigor of secondary school record. *Important factors considered include:* Academic GPA, application essay, character/personal qualities, class rank, extracurricular activities, recommendation(s), standardized test scores. *Other factors considered include:* Alumni/ae relation, first generation, geographical residence, interview, level of applicant's interest, racial/ethnic status, state residency, talent/ability, volunteer work, work experience. SAT or ACT required; SAT Subject Tests recommended. TOEFL required of all international applicants. High school diploma is required, and GED is accepted. *Academic units required:* 3 math, 2 science (2 science labs), 2 foreign language, 2 social studies, 2 history. *Academic units recommended:* 4 English, 4 math, 4 science, 4 foreign language, 4 social studies, 4 history.

Inside Word

Mills recognizes that no individual factor fully encompasses an applicant. The Admissions Office endeavors to give equal attention and weight to all facets of the application, from the secondary school record and standardized test scores to the extracurricular interests and recommendations. While this means that candidates need to concentrate on a variety of areas, it also ensures they won't be discounted due to any one weakness.

FINANCIAL AID

Students should submit: FAFSA, institution's own financial aid form, state aid form, Noncustodial PROFILE. Regular filing deadline is February 15. The Princeton Review suggests that all financial aid forms be submitted as soon as possible after January 1. *Need-based scholarships/grants offered:* Pell Grant, SEOG, state scholarships/grants, private scholarships, the school's own gift aid. *Loan aid offered:* FFEL Subsidized Stafford, FFEL Unsubsidized Stafford, FFEL PLUS, Federal Perkins Loan, college/university loans from institutional funds. Applicants will be notified of awards on a rolling basis beginning or about March 1. Federal Work-Study Program available. Off-campus job opportunities are excellent.

FROM THE ADMISSIONS OFFICE

"For more than 150 years, Mills College has shaped women's lives. Offering a progressive liberal arts and sciences curriculum taught by nationally renowned faculty, Mills gives students the personal attention that leads to extraordinary learning. Through intensive, collaborative study in a community of forward-thinking individuals, students gain the ability to make their voices heard, the strength to risk bold visions, an eagerness to experiment, and a desire to change the world.

"Nestled on 135 lush acres in the heart of the San Francisco Bay Area, Mills draws energy from the college's location. Mills students connect with centers of learning, business, and technology; pursue research and internship opportunities; and explore the Bay Area's many sources of cultural, social, and recreational enrichment.

"Consistently ranked one of the top liberal arts colleges in the nation, as well as one of the most diverse, Mills offers a renowned education for students who are seeking an intimate, collaborative college experience. You'll learn from distinguished professors who are truly dedicated to teaching. You'll interact with dynamic women of different backgrounds, ethnicities, cultures, ages, and mindsets, making your learning rich and inspiring.

"With more than 40 different majors to choose from—including a self-designed program—you'll have lots of educational options. The classroom debate will be your intellectual catalyst, but you'll find plenty of opportunities to express yourself, both in and out of the classroom.

"First-year applicants should submit either the SAT or the ACT. A student's overall candidacy may be enhanced by the submission of SAT Subject Tests."

SELECTIVITY

Admissions Rating	**87**
# of applicants	1,122
% of applicants accepted	65
% of acceptees attending	28

FRESHMAN PROFILE

Range SAT Critical Reading	500–640
Range SAT Math	470–590
Minimum Paper TOEFL	550
Minimum Computer Based TOEFL	213
Average HS GPA	3.57
% graduated top 10% of class	34
% graduated top 25% of class	66
% graduated top 50% of class	95

DEADLINES

Regular application deadline	3/1
Regular notification	rolling
Nonfall registration?	yes

APPLICANTS ALSO LOOK AT
AND OFTEN PREFER
Mount Holyoke College, Smith College, University of California—Berkeley
AND SOMETIMES PREFER
Oberlin College, Occidental College, Scripps College, Wellesley College
AND RARELY PREFER
Pitzer College, Sarah Lawrence College, University of Southern California

FINANCIAL FACTS

Financial Aid Rating	**79**
Annual tuition	$32,542
Room & Board	$10,820
Books and supplies	$1,200
Required fees	$968
% frosh rec. need-based scholarship or grant aid	86
% UG rec. need-based scholarship or grant aid	83
% frosh rec. need-based self-help aid	86
% UG rec. need-based self-help aid	75
% frosh rec. any financial aid	98
% UG rec. any financial aid	93

MILLSAPS COLLEGE

1701 NORTH STATE STREET, JACKSON, MS 39210-0001 • ADMISSIONS: 601-974-1050 • FAX: 601-974-1059

CAMPUS LIFE
Quality of Life Rating	84
Fire Safety Rating	78
Type of school	private
Affiliation	Methodist
Environment	metropolis

STUDENTS
Total undergrad enrollment	1,065
% male/female	51/49
% from out of state	50
% from public high school	67
% live on campus	81
% in (# of) fraternities	54 (6)
% in (# of) sororities	52 (6)
% African American	12
% Asian	3
% Caucasian	82
% Hispanic	1
% international	1
# of countries represented	15

SURVEY SAYS . . .
Small classes
Students are friendly
Frats and sororities dominate social
scene
Lots of beer drinking

ACADEMICS
Academic Rating	88
Calendar	semester
Student/faculty ratio	12:1
Profs interesting rating	95
Profs accessible rating	95
% profs teaching UG courses	100
% classes taught by TAs	0
Most common lab size	20–29 students
Most common reg class size	10–19 students

MOST POPULAR MAJORS
biology/biological sciences
business administration/
management
psychology

STUDENTS SAY
Academics

At last, a college where "The brochures are true! The classes are not too big, the instructors love what they do (and do it well), upperclassmen are helpful, and the out-of-class experience is fun." It's hard to find an undergraduate dissatisfied with the academic experience at this small gem of a school in Jackson. Foremost, there are the professors, who "are simply top of the line. They are intellectually stimulating, approachable, and respectable in their fields." And if there's one thing they're not, it's pushovers; one student says, "Professors here have very high standards as a whole, and grade inflation is quite low. Many teachers have reputations for being hard-core graders." But while grading may be "tough," students also agree that it is "fair." Writing is "stressed" in Millsaps classes, so prospective students should "Be prepared to write all the time, in anything and everything." "You have to write a paper for every class, including math classes." Most in-class time "is composed of classroom discussion." The result of all this class discussion and writing, of course, is that "professors teach you how to think, not what to think."

Life

"A little more than half of the girls at Millsaps are in sororities," and nearly the same percentage of guys are in fraternities. Needless to say, "Greek life is very big at Millsaps, and almost all on-campus entertainment options are centered around places like the frat houses." "During the week, class is the focus," but "We have frat parties on Fridays and Saturdays and occasionally on Thursdays. Anyone can come to these parties," including "guys from other fraternities." "During football and basketball season students and faculty turn out to cheer on our team. This is probably when there is the most unity on campus." Beyond campus, "Our city, Jackson, also introduces [us to] many cultural opportunities, such as musicals (sometimes with sponsored tickets for students), gallery and museum exhibits, and more." Jackson also "has plenty of bars, clubs, both 21-plus and 18-plus, parks, and good bands playing somewhere just about every weekend." Students can also find "good concerts" at the Mississippi State Fairgrounds. The civic-minded will appreciate that "community service is huge" at Millsaps, with numerous "philanthropic activities off campus" sponsored by the Greek organizations and even "a Habitat for Humanity chapter" based on the campus. One downside to campus? Due to Millsaps' small size, "People gossip like crazy, so if you hook up with somebody, everybody is going to know."

Student Body

"The typical Millsaps student was that cool nerd in high school." You know, "the A student from high school who was involved in every club offered." In other words, Millsaps students are "friendly and eager to engage in conversation about anything! Economically, many students are middle- to upper-middle-class, but almost everyone is on some type of scholarship. Politically, Millsaps students are on both sides of the spectrum, and most people are aware of politics." Students estimate that the "majority of students are religious or spiritual, and typically Millsaps students are interested in social justice issues and service to the community at large." These "friendly, studious, driven" undergraduates "like to party as hard as they work." But even if you don't fit this mold, don't fret: "We're too small to have outcasts."

FINANCIAL AID: 601-974-1220 • E-MAIL: ADMISSIONS@MILLSAPS.EDU • WEBSITE: WWW.GO.MILLSAPS.EDU

ADMISSIONS

Very important factors considered include: Academic GPA, character/personal qualities, rigor of secondary school record, standardized test scores. *Important factors considered include:* Application essay, class rank, extracurricular activities, interview, recommendation(s), talent/ability, volunteer work. *Other factors considered include:* Work experience. SAT or ACT required; TOEFL required of all international applicants. High school diploma is required, and GED is accepted. *Academic units required:* 4 English, 3 math, 3 science (1 science lab), 2 social studies, 2 history. *Academic units recommended:* 4 English, 4 math, 4 science (1 science lab), 2 foreign language, 2 social studies, 2 history, 2 academic electives.

The Inside Word

High school seniors looking for a quality liberal arts college with Southern charm should look no further than Millsaps. While the applicant pool is somewhat self-selecting, the high admit rate is indicative of a relatively painless application process. Candidates with solid transcripts and a variety of extracurriculars should make the cut.

FINANCIAL AID

Students should submit: FAFSA, institution's own financial aid form. The Princeton Review suggests that all financial aid forms be submitted as soon as possible after January 1. *Need-based scholarships/grants offered:* Pell Grant, SEOG, state scholarships/grants, private scholarships, the school's own gift aid. *Loan aid offered:* FFEL Subsidized Stafford, FFEL Unsubsidized Stafford, FFEL PLUS, Federal Perkins Loan, college/university loans from institutional funds. Applicants will be notified of awards on a rolling basis beginning or about March 15. Federal Work-Study Program available. Institutional employment available. Off-campus job opportunities are good.

FROM THE ADMISSIONS OFFICE

"Millsaps offers outstanding value in nationally ranked liberal arts education. Your academic journey begins with Introduction to Liberal Arts Studies, a comprehensive freshman experience that develops reasoning, communication, quantitative thinking, historical consciousness, aesthetic judgment, global, and multicultural awareness, and valuing and decision-making. Throughout your Millsaps years you'll be encouraged to think differently; learn critical, analytical skills; embrace independence of thought; and prepare for study in your chosen major. We offer unique opportunities such as study abroad and in the field at our Yucatán Program; an exploration of your personal and professional future in relation to issues of ethics, values, faith, and the common good through our Faith and Work Initiative; highly respected pre-professional programs in law, medicine, and social work; and a 5-year business track leading to an MBA or master's in accountancy with a liberal arts perspective that is accredited by the Association to Advance Collegiate Schools of Business. Our student body included Mississippi's 2003–2004 Rhodes scholar, and the faculty included the Carnegie Foundation's 2003 Mississippi Professor of the Year. Our courses are taught without graduate assistants and our intimate student-faculty-community relationship is a hallmark of a Millsaps education. The emerging cultural climate in Jackson, Mississippi's capital city, provides unique artistic, athletic, and social opportunities in the modern South. We encourage you to look at Millsaps College. You'll appreciate the quality of our educational experience in comparison to the costs you'll discover at other national liberal arts institutions. Millsaps College: where minds matter.

"Although it is not required, Millsaps College highly recommends that students take the ACT Writing test for Fall 2008 admission."

SELECTIVITY

Admissions Rating	86
# of applicants	910
% of applicants accepted	86
% of acceptees attending	29

FRESHMAN PROFILE

Range SAT Critical Reading	510–670
Range SAT Math	530–630
Range ACT Composite	23–29
Minimum Paper TOEFL	550
Minimum Computer Based TOEFL	220
Average HS GPA	3.5
% graduated top 10% of class	40
% graduated top 25% of class	65
% graduated top 50% of class	87

DEADLINES

Regular application deadline	6/1
Regular notification	rolling
Nonfall registration?	yes

APPLICANTS ALSO LOOK AT

AND OFTEN PREFER
Baylor University, Hendrix College, Rhodes College, Sewanee—The University of the South, Washington University in St. Louis

AND SOMETIMES PREFER
Birmingham-Southern College, Centenary College of Louisiana, Loyola University—New Orleans, Trinity University, Tulane University, Vanderbilt University

AND RARELY PREFER
Furman University, Samford University, Spring Hill College, Texas Christian University

FINANCIAL FACTS

Financial Aid Rating	80
Annual tuition	$20,660
Room & Board	$7,956
Books and supplies	$1,000
Required fees	$1,372
% frosh rec. need-based scholarship or grant aid	55
% UG rec. need-based scholarship or grant aid	55
% frosh rec. need-based self-help aid	37
% UG rec. need-based self-help aid	42
% frosh rec. any financial aid	97
% UG rec. any financial aid	94

MONMOUTH UNIVERSITY (NJ)

400 CEDAR AVENUE, WEST LONG BRANCH, NJ 07764-1898 • ADMISSIONS: 732-571-3456 • FAX: 732-263-5166

CAMPUS LIFE
Quality of Life Rating	**73**
Fire Safety Rating	**99**
Type of school	private
Environment	village

STUDENTS
Total undergrad enrollment	4,577
% male/female	42/58
% from out of state	9
% from public high school	83
% live on campus	44
% in (# of) fraternities	8 (7)
% in (# of) sororities	9 (6)
% African American	4
% Asian	2
% Caucasian	75
% Hispanic	5

SURVEY SAYS . . .
Small classes
Campus feels safe
Lots of beer drinking
Hard liquor is popular
(Almost) everyone smokes

ACADEMICS
Academic Rating	**72**
Calendar	semester
Student/faculty ratio	15:1
Profs interesting rating	75
Profs accessible rating	78
% profs teaching UG courses	90
% classes taught by TAs	0
Most common reg class size	20–29 students

MOST POPULAR MAJORS
business administration/
management
communications and media studies
education

STUDENTS SAY

Academics

New Jersey's Monmouth University "is a comfortably-sized school (not too big, not too small) with helpful faculty and staff members and many opportunities for real-world experience." Most students find professors to be "fair, knowledgeable, and most importantly, willing to compromise," though some note that "the quality of professors varies from class to class." Overall, students agree that "the quality of instruction at Monmouth is good." The school's new president, Paul Gaffney, "is very interested in student affairs and can be seen regularly at campus events. He has even helped incoming freshmen move into their dorms," says one student, adding, "The lower-level administrators aren't as impressive, but do treat students as human beings, which is always nice." Communications is a popular major at Monmouth; many students were lured to the school by its impressive $13-million Jules L. Plangere Jr. Center for Communication and Instructional Technology, a "state-of-the-art facility" that features a "brand-new $5-million television and radio production studio." MU students have wrestled with in-person class registration hassles in the past, but students report that "we have online registration now (thank God!), so no more waiting in line, although sometimes the servers are slow during the initial days of registration." Fortunately, the school changed the registration process starting in Spring 2005 and now activates smaller groups of students every 30 minutes to minimize the load on the system.

Life

"Monmouth is in perfect proximity to the beach or the city," undergrads tell us. "A person can hop on the train and be in New York City in 45 minutes, or drive 2 minutes up the road and be at the beach." Students seeking other means of entertainment "go to bars, clubs, an athletic event, Greek house, or hang out in their room or apartment." There are "great local clubs like the Stone Pony and the Groove Lounge, and there are also coffeehouses like Starbucks and the Ink Well." Students also frequent the local mall, which is 10 minutes away. In addition, the university sponsors "a lot of events on campus, from concerts to guest speakers." Monmouth is somewhat of a suitcase school; "A lot of people go home on the weekend because they live so close." Students feel confident in the campus security at Monmouth. One writes, "Security is always around. I can walk from my car at 1:00 A.M. and feel safe. I also feel safe when walking from my night classes."

Students

Monmouth undergrads are split down the middle when it comes to describing the student body. On one side, the words "rich, preppy, cliquey, Gucci, [and] Armani" routinely pop up in descriptions. On the flipside, undergrads describe their fellow students as "friendly, involved, outgoing, [and] fun." Students of both opinions, however, agree that most MU undergrads hail from a "White, upper-middle-class" background. As one student explains, "There are a lot of upper-class students who come from wealth. The people I've met are generally all nice and friendly. But I've heard stories that say otherwise. I think it depends on who you meet. There are intelligent, hardworking students, and [there are] others who aren't. It's a mix of many different people." Another student adds that "Monmouth is a lot like high school" in that "there are lots of different groups of kids on campus and all types of people fit in. You just have to find your group."

MONMOUTH UNIVERSITY (NJ)

FINANCIAL AID: 732-571-3463 • E-MAIL: ADMISSION@MONMOUTH.EDU • WEBSITE: WWW.MONMOUTH.EDU

ADMISSIONS

Very important factors considered include: Academic GPA, extracurricular activities, rigor of secondary school record, standardized test scores, volunteer work, work experience. *Other factors considered include:* Alumni/ae relation, application essay, class rank, interview, recommendation(s). SAT or ACT required; ACT with Writing component required. TOEFL required of all international applicants. High school diploma is required, and GED is accepted. *Academic units required:* 4 English, 3 math, 2 science (1 science lab), 2 history, 5 academic electives. *Academic units recommended:* 2 foreign language, 2 social studies.

Inside Word

B students with average standardized test scores should have little trouble getting into Monmouth University, whose admissions standards are fairly generous. However, a rapidly decreasing acceptance rate following the elimination of a popular admissions program means that entry is by no means a sure thing.

FINANCIAL AID

Students should submit: FAFSA. Regular filing deadline is June 30. The Princeton Review suggests that all financial aid forms be submitted as soon as possible after January 1. *Need-based scholarships/grants offered:* Pell Grant, SEOG, state scholarships/grants, private scholarships, the school's own gift aid, Federal Nursing Scholarship. *Loan aid offered:* Direct Subsidized Stafford, Direct Unsubsidized Stafford, Direct PLUS, FFEL PLUS, Federal Perkins Loan, state loans, college/university loans from institutional funds, alternative loans. Applicants will be notified of awards on a rolling basis beginning or about February 1.

FROM THE ADMISSIONS OFFICE

"Monmouth University offers a well-rounded but bold academic environment with plenty of opportunities—personal, professional, and social. Monmouth graduates are poised for success and prepared to assume leadership roles in their chosen professions, because the university invests in students beyond the classroom.

"Monmouth emphasizes hands-on learning, while providing exceptional undergraduate and graduate degree programs. There are programs for medical scholars, honors students, marine scientists, software engineers, teachers, musicians, broadcast producers, and more. Faculty members are lively participants in the education of their students. These teacher/scholars, dedicated to excellence, are often recognized experts in their fields. Students may be in a class with no more than 35 students (half of Monmouth's classes have fewer than 21 students) learning from qualified professors who know each student by name.

"Monmouth recognizes its students are the energy of its campus. The Monmouth community celebrates student life with cultural events, festivals, active student clubs, and organizations that reflect its school spirit. Athletics play a big part in campus life. A well-established member of the NCAA Division I, Monmouth athletics is a rising tide supported by some of the best fans in the Northeast.

"The president of Monmouth University, Paul G. Gaffney II, believes the reputation of the university starts with the achievements and successes of its students. At Monmouth, students find the support and guidance needed to make their mark in the world.

"Students applying for admission for Fall 2008 are encouraged to take the new SAT (or the ACT with the Writing section), but we will allow students to submit scores from the old (prior to March 2005) version of the SAT (or ACT) as well, and will use the student's best scores from either test. "

SELECTIVITY

Admissions Rating	**76**
# of applicants	5,952
% of applicants accepted	61
% of acceptees attending	27
# of early decision applicants	349
% accepted early decision	38

FRESHMAN PROFILE

Range SAT Critical Reading	490–570
Range SAT Math	500–580
Range SAT Writing	480–570
Range ACT Composite	20–25
Minimum Paper TOEFL	550
Minimum Computer Based TOEFL	213
Average HS GPA	3.17
% graduated top 10% of class	9
% graduated top 25% of class	32
% graduated top 50% of class	72

DEADLINES

Early decision application deadline	12/1
Early decision notification	1/1
Regular application deadline	3/1
Regular notification	prior to 4/1
Nonfall registration?	yes

FINANCIAL FACTS

Financial Aid Rating	**74**
Annual tuition	$21,248
Room & Board	$8,472
Books and supplies	$900
Required fees	$620
% frosh rec. need-based scholarship or grant aid	21
% UG rec. need-based scholarship or grant aid	34
% frosh rec. need-based self-help aid	48
% UG rec. need-based self-help aid	51
% frosh rec. any financial aid	65
% UG rec. any financial aid	92

MONTANA TECH OF THE UNIVERSITY OF MONTANA

1300 WEST PARK STREET, BUTTE, MT 59701 • ADMISSIONS: 406-496-4178 • FAX: 406-496-4710

CAMPUS LIFE
Quality of Life Rating	**73**
Fire Safety Rating	**60***
Type of school	public
Environment	town

STUDENTS
Total undergrad enrollment	1,913
% male/female	56/44
% from out of state	10
% live on campus	17
% Asian	1
% Caucasian	85
% Hispanic	1
% Native American	2
% international	3
# of countries represented	16

SURVEY SAYS . . .
Small classes
Great computer facilities
Career services are great
Frats and sororities are unpopular or nonexistent
Lots of beer drinking

ACADEMICS
Academic Rating	**76**
Calendar	semester
Student/faculty ratio	16:1
Profs interesting rating	76
Profs accessible rating	79
% profs teaching UG courses	100
% classes taught by TAs	0
Most common lab size	fewer than 10 students
Most common reg class size	fewer than 10 students

MOST POPULAR MAJORS
business administration/
management
engineering
petroleum engineering

STUDENTS SAY

Academics

Montana Tech students know exactly what they want from their college: a reputable degree that translates quickly into a plum job. According to the students here, that's exactly what the school delivers. As a surprising number of students in our survey remind us, Tech has a fantastic job placement rate in its areas of strength, which include petroleum, environmental, metallurgical, geological, geophysical, and mining engineering ("anything that deals with the oil and gas industries" is how one helpful engineer summarizes it), nursing, mathematics, and computer science. One student explains, "We have a great reputation with employers as very good students [who are] willing to work." Like most tech schools, "Tech is very difficult. The first couple of years are spent by professors trying to weed out the slackers, but once you get through all that and get to know your professors, they are actually really friendly and very helpful." Professors also "have industry experience, which is vital to producing good professionals." Small classes promote "a feeling of community. At Tech it is strange for a professor not to know what your name and major are if you are in his class." Students also appreciate that "Tech gives aid to tons of students in every field. Even if you don't qualify for much need-based aid, you can still get scholarships in your field of study."

Life

"Most people are academically focused, but still like to have fun" at Tech. Unfortunately, however, "Life here isn't all that exciting. Since it is so small, it's hard to get anything going on campus." The main outlets for extracurricular activity are sporting events—football and men's basketball "both get a lot of support from the students"—parties and the bar scene, quiet fun (hanging out with friends, going to movies, bowling, playing billiards), and outdoor activities. Many students here "take part in the excellent hiking, camping, fishing, kayaking, and rock climbing" spots nearby. And there's plenty of excellent skiing within driving distance of the campus. Be forewarned: "The weather puts a damper on what there is to do for fun. It's already snowed at least three times," reported one student in October, adding that "the weather is in the low 40s to high 30s most of the time," at least during academic semesters. As one undergrad advises, "If you don't like winter, don't come here." Hometown Butte is "a rough and rowdy mining town" with "not much to offer, so a lot of people end up drinking for fun." Although the town has a few champions among the student body, most prefer Missoula, "for the shopping and nightlife." Bear in mind that Missoula is 120 miles away, but in Montana terms, that's spitting distance.

Student Body

"Most Tech students are from rural Montana and are familiar with an agricultural lifestyle," students tell us, noting that the occasional city kid who finds his way here usually finds the experience a little disorienting. It's the kind of place where "The dorms have gun racks in them for the hunters," and few would have it any other way. Like the population of their home state, Montana Tech students are "typically Caucasian and conservative." Those from outside the state generally come from Canada or overseas; "There is a large contingency of well-to-do Arab students from oil-producing countries in the Middle East, and they have a good relationship with the rest of the student body."

FINANCIAL AID: 406-496-4212 • E-MAIL: ADMISSIONS@MTECH.EDU • WEBSITE: WWW.MTECH.EDU

ADMISSIONS

Other factors considered include: Class rank, standardized test scores. SAT or ACT required; TOEFL required of all international applicants. High school diploma is required, and GED is accepted. *Academic units required:* 4 English, 3 math, 2 science (2 science labs), 3 social studies, 2 combined, 2 years of foreign language, visual and performing arts, computer science, or vocational education units. *Academic units recommended:* 4 English, 4 math, 4 science (2 science labs), 2 foreign language.

The Inside Word

Underrecognized schools like Montana Tech can be a godsend for students who are strong academically but not likely to be offered admission to nationally renowned technical institutes. In fact, because of its small size and relatively remote location, Montana Tech is a good choice for anyone leaning toward a technical career. You'd be hard-pressed to find many other places that are as low-key and personal in this realm of academia.

FINANCIAL AID

Students should submit: FAFSA. The Princeton Review suggests that all financial aid forms be submitted as soon as possible after January 1. *Need-based scholarships/grants offered:* Pell Grant, SEOG, state scholarships/grants, private scholarships, the school's own gift aid. *Loan aid offered:* FFEL Subsidized Stafford, FFEL Unsubsidized Stafford, FFEL PLUS, Federal Perkins Loan, college/university loans from institutional funds. Applicants will be notified of awards on or about April 1. Federal Work-Study Program available. Institutional employment available. Off-campus job opportunities are good.

FROM THE ADMISSIONS OFFICE

"Characterize Montana Tech by listening to what employers say. They tell us Tech graduates stand out with an incredible work ethic and top-notch technical skills. Last year, 130 employers came to our small campus competing for our students and graduates. The beneficiaries: the students! Montana Tech has had a 10-year placement rate of over 95 percent. Learning takes place in a personalized environment, in first-class academic facilities, and in the heart of the Rocky Mountains. Student at Tech work hard and play hard. Outdoor recreation provides a great balance to the rigors of the course work at Montana Tech. It's not a large, multifaceted university with lots of frills, but our students get a terrific education, and in the end, great jobs!

"The new version of the SAT (or the ACT with the Writing section) is recommended for all students applying for admission. Students who do not take the tests with the Writing component may be required to take an additional English Placement test from the college before they enroll."

SELECTIVITY

Admissions Rating	72
# of applicants	414
% of applicants accepted	98
% of acceptees attending	98

FRESHMAN PROFILE

Range SAT Critical Reading	470–600
Range SAT Math	490–630
Range ACT Composite	21–27
Minimum Paper TOEFL	525
Minimum Computer Based TOEFL	195
Average HS GPA	3.2
% graduated top 10% of class	13
% graduated top 25% of class	35
% graduated top 50% of class	66

DEADLINES

Regular notification	rolling
Nonfall registration?	yes

APPLICANTS ALSO LOOK AT

AND OFTEN PREFER
Michigan Technological University

AND SOMETIMES PREFER
Colorado School of Mines, Montana State University—Bozeman, The University of Montana, University of Washington, Western Montana College

AND RARELY PREFER
Carroll College (MT)

FINANCIAL FACTS

Financial Aid Rating	71
Annual in-state tuition	$5,606
Annual out-of-state tuition	$14,766
Room & Board	$5,594
Books and supplies	$800
% frosh rec. need-based scholarship or grant aid	58
% UG rec. need-based scholarship or grant aid	62
% frosh rec. need-based self-help aid	57
% UG rec. need-based self-help aid	50
% frosh rec. any financial aid	80
% UG rec. any financial aid	68

MORAVIAN COLLEGE

1200 MAIN STREET, BETHLEHEM, PA 18018 • ADMISSIONS: 610-861-1320 • FAX: 610-625-7930

CAMPUS LIFE
Quality of Life Rating	**86**
Fire Safety Rating	**93**
Type of school	private
Affiliation	Moravian
Environment	city

STUDENTS
Total undergrad enrollment	1,625
% male/female	40/60
% from out of state	44
% from public high school	82
% live on campus	70
% in (# of) fraternities	15 (3)
% in (# of) sororities	22 (4)
% African American	2
% Asian	2
% Caucasian	90
% Hispanic	3
% international	1
# of countries represented	9

SURVEY SAYS . . .
Small classes
Great computer facilities
Great library
Students are friendly
Low cost of living

ACADEMICS
Academic Rating	**84**
Calendar	semester
Student/faculty ratio	11:1
Profs interesting rating	84
Profs accessible rating	86
% profs teaching	
UG courses	100
% classes taught by TAs	0
Most common	
lab size	10–19 students
Most common	
reg class size	10–19 students

MOST POPULAR MAJORS
business administration/
management
psychology
sociology

STUDENTS SAY

Academics

The sixth-oldest undergraduate institution in the United States (founded in 1742), there's no arguing that Moravian College is "a historic institution." But this small eastern Pennsylvanian liberal arts school also knows how to keep up with the times; through its Learning in Common general education curriculum, Moravian exposes all undergraduates to a broad range of skills taught within a multidisciplinary framework, preparing them, in theory, to adapt to rapid and dramatic changes in the world, no matter what fields they choose to pursue. Undergraduates appreciate the approach, telling us that there are "few, if any, colleges that rival our curriculum." Students also give high marks to the business, education, nursing, art, and music departments (the last two of which are housed separately, on the school's Priscilla Payne Hard Campus). Professors here "are mostly all amazing. These teachers get to know their students and make sure that they are available to the students, and our classes are small, allowing engaging, open, free discussion." While the school is small— "If you went to a small high school, Moravian isn't going to be a big shift for you"—academic options are unusually broad thanks to the school's participation in the Lehigh Valley Association of Independent Colleges, which allows students to take classes and use the libraries at Lafayette College, Lehigh University, Muhlenberg College, DeSales University, and Cedar Crest College. The school works hard to offer "an infinite number of opportunities for students, such as on-campus jobs, internships, [and] study abroad programs."

Life

"The greatest strength of Moravian is combining the emphasis on academics with enjoying college life," undergraduates tell us, observing that "everyone here realizes that students don't want to study 100 percent of the time, so the workload is reasonable, sports are very important, and there are many on-campus activities." Those activities include "plenty of concerts, plays, and speakers, as well as movies and athletic events." Student clubs and organizations are popular, with a number of students involved in numerous extracurricular endeavors. Fraternities and sororities figure into the mix. While "There's always a party" somewhere, "There's always another option, too, [so] there's no excuse for anyone being bored and not making friends" here. Those on a budget appreciate that "most of the activities are free of charge, or there's a student discount" and that "a lot of the fun around here comes from just hanging out with friends whenever you can, and there is almost always time for that." All these activities dovetail into a renewed sense of campus vitality. "While Moravian was once considered to be a 'suitcase' college, these days more and more students stay on campus. They feel they miss out on too much leaving for the weekend." Students are also fond of Bethlehem, describing its downtown as "a lovely, scenic area that is good for light shopping and browsing. Our school provides trips to the mall and grocery store, which are always fun breaks to take with friends."

Student Body

Many Moravian students see themselves in the context of their closest neighbors; one undergrad writes, "Moravian is surrounded by Lehigh, Lafayette, and Muhlenberg, which are known as more prissy schools, where the students are a lot more stuck-up. There isn't a lot of priss at Moravian." Here, "The typical student comes from the Mid-Atlantic region, grew up in suburbia, and is often of a middle-class background." Most are "very friendly; they smile and say hi to one another." Observers detect a clear difference between students on the Main Campus and their counterparts on the Priscilla Payne Hard Campus, who are relatively "more artsy, more open-minded, dress different, and are more city-smart."

FINANCIAL AID: 610-861-1330 • E-MAIL: ADMISSIONS@MORAVIAN.EDU • WEBSITE: WWW.MORAVIAN.EDU

ADMISSIONS

Very important factors considered include: Academic GPA, character/personal qualities, class rank, rigor of secondary school record. *Important factors considered include:* Alumni/ae relation, application essay, extracurricular activities, level of applicant's interest, racial/ethnic status, recommendation(s), standardized test scores, talent/ability, volunteer work. *Other factors considered include:* First generation, geographical residence, interview, work experience. SAT or ACT required; ACT with Writing component required. TOEFL required of all international applicants. High school diploma is required, and GED is accepted. *Academic units required:* 4 English, 3 math, 3 science (2 science labs), 2 foreign language, 4 social studies. *Academic units recommended:* 4 math, 3 foreign language.

The Inside Word

Moravian is a small liberal arts school with all the bells and whistles. Applicants will find a pretty straightforward admissions process—solid grades and test scores are required. Counselors will look closely to find the extras—community service, extracurricular activities—that make students stand out from the crowd. Moravian has many programs that should not be overlooked, including music, education, and the sciences.

FINANCIAL AID

Students should submit: FAFSA, CSS/Financial Aid PROFILE, Noncustodial PROFILE, Business/Farm Supplement, parent and student W-2s and 1040s. Regular filing deadline is March 15. The Princeton Review suggests that all financial aid forms be submitted as soon as possible after January 1. *Need-based scholarships/grants offered:* Pell Grant, SEOG, state scholarships/grants, the school's own gift aid. *Loan aid offered:* FFEL Subsidized Stafford, FFEL Unsubsidized Stafford, FFEL PLUS, Federal Perkins Loan. Applicants will be notified of awards on a rolling basis beginning or about April 1.

FROM THE ADMISSIONS OFFICE

"Founded in 1742, Moravian is proud of its history as one of America's oldest and most respected liberal arts colleges. The low student/faculty ratio allows for an immediate and unusually close bond. The Moravian family, comprising current students and faculty, as well as alumni and emeritus professors, praises the college as a supportive environment for learning, personal exploration, and character development. The overarching emphasis of our curriculum is on scholarship enriched by self-discovery. In the last 5 years, Moravian has produced four Fulbright scholars, a Goldwater scholar, a Rhodes finalist, a Truman Scholar finalist, and three NCAA Postgraduate Scholars. Its robust varsity athletic program has produced All-American student athletes, Academic All-Americans, national champions, a national Player of the Year, and several Olympic hopefuls. In the Fall of 2005, the college will dedicate Rocco Calvo Field, a state-of-the-art synthetic multi-sport field and the eight-lane Timothy Breidegam Olympic track. At the heart of the campus is a new $20-million academic building. It houses 15 new classrooms, four faculty departments, laboratories, research facilities, and "smart" classrooms for easy technological interface. In 2004, the college established a unique Leadership Center, the goal of which is to engage the campus community in discussion, discovery, and dialogue about the many aspects of leadership as applied to the academic disciplines, professions, the community, and campus organizations. The college welcomes inquiries from students eager to participate in an environment of self-directed, lifelong learning.

"Fall 2008 applicants must submit scores from either the new SAT or the ACT with Writing. Writing scores will establish a baseline for later years and will generally not be used for admission or scholarship consideration. Scores from previously administered SAT's will also be considered if submitted by Fall 2008 applicants."

SELECTIVITY

Admissions Rating	80
# of applicants	1,871
% of applicants accepted	65
% of acceptees attending	31
# accepting a place on wait list	117
% admitted from wait list	33
# of early decision applicants	191
% accepted early decision	82

FRESHMAN PROFILE

Range SAT Critical Reading	510–600
Range SAT Math	510–610
Range SAT Writing	500–590
Minimum Paper TOEFL	550
Minimum Computer Based TOEFL	213
% graduated top 10% of class	24
% graduated top 25% of class	61
% graduated top 50% of class	91

DEADLINES

Early decision application deadline	2/1
Early decision notification	12/15
Regular application deadline	3/1
Regular notification	3/15
Nonfall registration?	yes

APPLICANTS ALSO LOOK AT

AND OFTEN PREFER
Bucknell University, Lafayette College, Muhlenberg College

AND SOMETIMES PREFER
Gettysburg College, Susquehanna University, Ursinus College

AND RARELY PREFER
DeSales University, Fairleigh Dickinson University, College at Florham, Kutztown University of Pennsylvania

FINANCIAL FACTS

Financial Aid Rating	76
Annual tuition	$26,300
Room & Board	$7,760
Books and supplies	$850
Required fees	$475
% frosh rec. need-based scholarship or grant aid	74
% UG rec. need-based scholarship or grant aid	73
% frosh rec. need-based self-help aid	67
% UG rec. need-based self-help aid	67
% frosh rec. any financial aid	94
% UG rec. any financial aid	96

MOUNT HOLYOKE COLLEGE

OFFICE OF ADMISSIONS, NEWHALL CENTER, SOUTH HADLEY, MA 01075 • ADMISSIONS: 413-538-2023 • FAX: 413-538-2409

CAMPUS LIFE

Quality of Life Rating	**90**
Fire Safety Rating	**89**
Type of school	private
Environment	village

STUDENTS

Total undergrad enrollment	2,149
% male/female	0/100
% from out of state	75
% from public high school	62
% live on campus	93
% African American	4
% Asian	11
% Caucasian	51
% Hispanic	5
% Native American	1
% international	16
# of countries represented	71

SURVEY SAYS . . .

Dorms are like palaces
Very little beer drinking
Great library
Diverse student types on campus
Campus feels safe

ACADEMICS

Academic Rating	**97**
Calendar	semester
Student/faculty ratio	10:1
Profs interesting rating	96
Profs accessible rating	92
% profs teaching UG courses	100
% classes taught by TAs	0
Most common lab size	10–19 students
Most common reg class size	10–19 students

MOST POPULAR MAJORS

biology/biological sciences
English language and literature
international relations and affairs

STUDENTS SAY

Academics

"Empowering" is a word the women of Mount Holyoke often use when describing the school. Mount Holyoke "provides an environment in which women can be challenged and encouraged to meet their goals and dreams without societal pressure telling them otherwise because they're women." The school is nurturing, but not mollycoddling; students warn that "academically, Mount Holyoke College is challenging. You cannot get behind and expect to catch up." Not that students mind; they tell us that "Mount Holyoke's academic reputation, and the fact that it lives up to that reputation, is commendable," and that its trial by fire makes its students "stronger writers, thinkers, friends, students, daughters, sisters, but most of all, better people." Mount Holyoke's offerings are augmented by its participation in the Five College Consortium, "which opens a lot of opportunities to take other courses that aren't offered at Mount Holyoke." Another education-broadening experience is to study abroad, "which the school encourages and enthusiastically facilitates." Still other opportunities present themselves in the many independent study options available. One student reports, "Professors are sincerely interested in developing student research projects and helping students find and partake in projects that sincerely interest them."

Life

The Mount Holyoke campus is quiet—not dead, mind you, just quiet—a situation most students appreciate. As one undergraduate puts it, "One of the greatest strengths of this school is that you are able to study without any distraction, but if you choose to party you are able to." On campus, "People are active in clubs and sports and hanging out in the common areas or on the green with friends." While the campus isn't bustling, it is beautiful. Students lovingly describe "greens surrounded only by classic brick buildings covered in ivy." One vibrant undergraduate writes, "In the fall, the colors welcome students. In the winter, the skating rink is within walking distance of many sledding hills and cross-country skiing trails. In the spring, the lakes are home to baby geese and the campus is covered in flowers." Mount Holyoke is also home to the "best golf course and equestrian center ever, dorms like palaces, [which have] dining rooms right downstairs [serving] food that's better than any other school I've been to, with a wide variety of choices and special attention paid to vegetarians and vegans," writes one enthusiastic student. Beyond campus, hometown South Hadley "is admittedly not the most happening town ever (to put it mildly), but the slightly more active towns of Amherst and Northampton are only a free bus ride away," and they offer "plenty of shopping and other things of interest." There's also "plenty to do in the Pioneer Valley: hiking, climbing, and camping, and Boston is only an hour and a half away."

Student Body

Mount Holyoke women are "extremely diverse, from ethnicity to race to religion to sexual orientation to individual interests. However, the community works as a whole because of the common interest in academics and openness of the students who attend." Students feel that a "large international population also provides for a very diverse atmosphere". If there is common ground among all students, it is that they are "open-minded, smart, [and] socially aware with at least one issue they are passionate about." Undergraduates "are generally serious about their work, interested in their world, and politically left." Students pride themselves on their tolerance, although campus conservatives complain that it's selective. One undergraduate tells us, "A word to the wise, unless you agree with the vast majority on campus—or at least the vocal majority—keep your mouth shut or wear flame-retardant clothing."

MOUNT HOLYOKE COLLEGE

FINANCIAL AID: 413-538-2291 • E-MAIL: ADMISSION@MTHOLYOKE.EDU • WEBSITE: WWW.MTHOLYOKE.EDU

ADMISSIONS

Very important factors considered include: Academic GPA, application essay, class rank, recommendation(s), rigor of secondary school record. *Important factors considered include:* Character/personal qualities, extracurricular activities, first generation, interview, talent/ability, volunteer work, work experience. *Other factors considered include:* Alumni/ae relation, geographical residence, level of applicant's interest, racial/ethnic status, standardized test scores. TOEFL required of all international applicants. High school diploma is required, and GED is accepted. *Academic units recommended:* 4 English, 3 math, 3 science (3 science labs), 3 foreign language, 3 history, 1 academic elective.

The Inside Word

Mount Holyoke has benefited well from the renaissance of interest in women's colleges; selectivity and academic quality are on the rise. Considering that the college was already fairly selective, candidates are well advised to take the admissions process seriously. Matchmaking is a significant factor here; strong academic performance, well-written essays, and an understanding of and appreciation for "the Mount Holyoke experience" will usually carry the day.

FINANCIAL AID

Students should submit: FAFSA, CSS/Financial Aid PROFILE, Noncustodial PROFILE, Business/Farm Supplement, Federal Income Tax Returns. Regular filing deadline is March 1. The Princeton Review suggests that all financial aid forms be submitted as soon as possible after January 1. *Need-based scholarships/grants offered:* Pell Grant, SEOG, state scholarships/grants, private scholarships, the school's own gift aid. *Loan aid offered:* Direct Subsidized Stafford, Direct Unsubsidized Stafford, Direct PLUS, Federal Perkins Loan, college/university loans from institutional funds. Applicants will be notified of awards on or about April 1. Federal Work-Study Program available. Institutional employment available. Off-campus job opportunities are fair.

FROM THE ADMISSIONS OFFICE

"The majority of students who choose Mount Holyoke do so simply because it is an outstanding liberal arts college. After a semester or two, they start to appreciate the fact that Mount Holyoke is a women's college, even though most Mount Holyoke students never thought they'd go to a women's college when they started their college search. Students talk of having 'space' to really figure out who they are. They speak about feeling empowered to excel in traditionally male subjects such as science and technology. They talk about the remarkable array of opportunities—for academic achievement, career exploration, and leadership—and the impressive, creative accomplishments of their peers. If you're looking for a college that will challenge you to be your best, most powerful self and to fulfill potential, Mount Holyoke should be at the top of your list.

"Submission of standardized test scores is optional for most applicants to Mount Holyoke College. However, the TOEFL is required of students for whom English is not their primary language, and the SAT Subject Tests are required for homeschooled students."

SELECTIVITY

Admissions Rating	94
# of applicants	3,065
% of applicants accepted	53
% of acceptees attending	35
# accepting a place on wait list	203
% admitted from wait list	2
# of early decision applicants	269
% accepted early decision	68

FRESHMAN PROFILE

Range SAT Critical Reading	620–710
Range SAT Math	590–680
Range SAT Writing	620–700
Range ACT Composite	27–30
Minimum Paper TOEFL	600
Minimum Computer Based TOEFL	250
Average HS GPA	3.66
% graduated top 10% of class	54
% graduated top 25% of class	82
% graduated top 50% of class	99

DEADLINES

Early decision application deadline	11/15
Early decision notification	1/1
Regular application deadline	1/15
Regular notification	4/1
Nonfall registration?	yes

APPLICANTS ALSO LOOK AT
AND OFTEN PREFER
Barnard College, Wellesley College
AND SOMETIMES PREFER
Bryn Mawr College, Smith College
AND RARELY PREFER
Boston University

FINANCIAL FACTS

Financial Aid Rating	97
Annual tuition	$35,760
Room & Board	$10,520
Books and supplies	$1,900
Required fees	$180
% frosh rec. need-based scholarship or grant aid	51
% UG rec. need-based scholarship or grant aid	57
% frosh rec. need-based self-help aid	51
% UG rec. need-based self-help aid	58
% frosh rec. any financial aid	59
% UG rec. any financial aid	66

MUHLENBERG COLLEGE

2400 WEST CHEW STREET, ALLENTOWN, PA 18104-5596 • ADMISSIONS: 484-664-3200 • FAX: 484-664-3234

STUDENTS SAY
Academics
Muhlenberg bills itself as "the college that cares," and for many students, it more than lives up to that designation. "The small community and small, personal class sizes" allow "professors [to] become friends, mentors, and role models" to students. "They love what they do, they love students, and they love interacting with the students." In addition, professors are "always very approachable. I've become close with many professors and frequently chat with them outside of class. Professors are often on campus with their families, and some hold parties at their houses at the end of the year." But professors aren't just friendly faces; "They are [also] very knowledgeable in their fields" and "challenge students to achieve more than they thought they were capable of." In addition to excellent professors, the school's size also provides students with numerous "research opportunities." Muhlenberg students "write a lot" because of the individual attention made possible in the "small, discussion-based classes." Among many quality majors, the Premedical, Pre-Law, Education, and Political Science Departments get rave reviews, and students note that "the theater and dance programs are extremely well regarded," as well.

Life
Some students claim that hometown Allentown "is not a vibrant place, and prospective students should be aware of this," while others point to the "two bars, an excellent deli, a famous movie and art theater, as well as restaurants and all the normal everyday places that a student needs" within walking distance of the campus. As far as partying goes, "If you are looking for a school with 15 parties to choose from every night of the week, then stop reading about Muhlenberg right now." The "school does have Greek life, but the administration is cracking down on [fraternities and sororities] more and more," largely through "a very strict alcohol and drug policy." As a result, "People go to house parties [off-campus] or the bars." Besides parties, "There is a pretty decent mall nearby and good restaurants." On campus "There are always school-sponsored events going on: bands, movies, magicians, comedians, the works," although many claim that "students don't generally participate in the on-campus activities." Particularly popular are the school's "community-service programs," which "work very well with Allentown," challenging students to carry the school's reputation for "caring" to their fellow citizens beyond the campus gates. To get away from the Muhlenberg scene altogether for some fresh experiences, "It's not too long a drive to Philadelphia." "Also, there are several other colleges in the area." Students do caution, however, that a "parking problem" makes owning a car on campus a little difficult.

Student Body
Although "'preppy' would be the word to describe most students on this campus, there are others who do not fit this category at all." And many students emphasize that the student body is not cliquey: "Students have groups of friends, but that can be very fluid." Such intermixing is a function of how "amazingly nice" the students here are, regardless of the fact that "most of the students come from fairly wealthy homes." Politically, students have liberal leanings, and students report that most of their classmates seem to "come from the surrounding areas of New Jersey, Pennsylvania, and New York." "Muhlenberg is extremely gay-friendly," but in terms of ethnicity, "There is little diversity," a fact "that the college is interested in changing." On the bright side, "The little bit of ethnic and racial diversity that we have here is celebrated." According to one student, however, regardless of social groups or differences, "The majority of people that I have come into contact with are their own selves, and they pride themselves on that. After all, college is about finding out who you are as a person, not conforming to the majority."

FINANCIAL AID: 484-664-3175 • E-MAIL: ADMISSION@MUHLENBERG.EDU • WEBSITE: WWW.MUHLENBERG.EDU

ADMISSIONS

Very important factors considered include: Academic GPA, rigor of secondary school record. *Important factors considered include:* Application essay, character/personal qualities, class rank, extracurricular activities, interview, recommendation(s), standardized test scores, talent/ability. *Other factors considered include:* Alumni/ae relation, first generation, geographical residence, level of applicant's interest, racial/ethnic status, volunteer work, work experience. ACT with Writing component required. TOEFL required of all international applicants. High school diploma is required, and GED is accepted. *Academic units required:* 4 English, 3 math, 2 science (2 science labs), 2 foreign language, 2 history, 3 academic electives. *Academic units recommended:* 4 math, 3 science (3 science labs), 4 foreign language.

The Inside Word

Akin to many liberal arts colleges, Muhlenberg doesn't adhere to a set admissions formula. With application numbers on the rise, however, and the school's selectivity increasing, a strong secondary school transcript is necessary. Standardized tests, on the other hand, are optional at Muhlenberg. Those who don't submit scores can provide a graded paper and sit for an interview instead. Prospective students who have determined Muhlenberg to be their top choice will find it advantageous to apply early decision.

FINANCIAL AID

Students should submit: FAFSA, institution's own financial aid form, CSS/Financial Aid PROFILE, Noncustodial PROFILE. Regular filing deadline is February 15. The Princeton Review suggests that all financial aid forms be submitted as soon as possible after January 1. *Need-based scholarships/grants offered:* Pell Grant, SEOG, state scholarships/grants, private scholarships, the school's own gift aid. *Loan aid offered:* FFEL Subsidized Stafford, FFEL Unsubsidized Stafford, FFEL PLUS, Federal Perkins Loan, private loans. Applicants will be notified of awards on or about April 1.

FROM THE ADMISSIONS OFFICE

"Listening to our own students, we've learned that most picked Muhlenberg mainly because it has a long-standing reputation for being academically demanding on one hand but personally supportive on the other. We expect a lot from our students, but we also expect a lot from ourselves in providing the challenge and support they need to stretch, grow, and succeed. It's not unusual for professors to put their home phone numbers on the course syllabus and encourage students to call them at home with questions. Upperclassmen are helpful to underclassmen. 'We really know about collegiality here,' says an alumna who now works at Muhlenberg. 'It's that kind of place.' The supportive atmosphere and strong work ethic produce lots of successes. The premed and pre-law programs are very strong, as are programs in theater arts, English, psychology, the sciences, business, and accounting. 'When I was a student here,' recalls Dr. Walter Loy, now a professor emeritus of physics, 'we were encouraged to live life to its fullest, to do our best, to be honest, to deal openly with others, and to treat everyone as an individual. Those are important things, and they haven't changed at Muhlenberg.'

"Students have the option of submitting SAT or ACT scores (including the Writing sections on each), or submitting a graded paper with teacher's comments and grade on it from junior or senior year and interviewing with a member of the Admissions Staff. Muhlenberg will accept old or new SAT scores and will use the student's best scores from either test."

SELECTIVITY

Admissions Rating	93
# of applicants	4,347
% of applicants accepted	44
% of acceptees attending	32
# accepting a place on wait list	477
% admitted from wait list	1
# of early decision applicants	460
% accepted early decision	67

FRESHMAN PROFILE

Range SAT Critical Reading	560–660
Range SAT Math	560–660
Range ACT Composite	26–29
Minimum Paper TOEFL	550
Minimum Computer Based TOEFL	213
Average HS GPA	3.44
% graduated top 10% of class	45
% graduated top 25% of class	81
% graduated top 50% of class	98

DEADLINES

Early decision application deadline	2/1
Early decision notification	12/1
Regular application deadline	2/15
Regular notification	3/15
Nonfall registration?	yes

APPLICANTS ALSO LOOK AT
AND OFTEN PREFER
Bucknell University, Lafayette College, Lehigh University, Villanova University
AND SOMETIMES PREFER
Dickinson College, Franklin & Marshall College, Gettysburg College, University of Delaware
AND RARELY PREFER
Drew University, Pennsylvania State University—University Park, Rutgers, The State University of New Jersey—New Brunswick/Piscataway, Susquehanna University

FINANCIAL FACTS

Financial Aid Rating	92
Annual tuition	$30,490
Room & Board	$225
Books and supplies	$750
% frosh rec. need-based scholarship or grant aid	44
% UG rec. need-based scholarship or grant aid	42
% frosh rec. need-based self-help aid	31
% UG rec. need-based self-help aid	31
% frosh rec. any financial aid	75
% UG rec. any financial aid	78

NEW COLLEGE OF FLORIDA

5800 BAY SHORE ROAD, SARASOTA, FL 34243-2109 • ADMISSIONS: 941-487-5000 • FAX: 941-487-5010

STUDENTS SAY

Academics

Students enjoy "the freedom to study whatever you're interested in to make things happen and take action" at New College of Florida, an innovative state school where "taking responsibility for yourself academically and socially and learning how to function in a community that truly cares about each person" define the undergraduate experience. In consultation with a faculty advisor, students design their own curricula and meet at the beginning of each semester to plot out a course of study (which includes classes, tutorials, research projects, and study abroad), define academic objectives, and sign a contract outlining the semester's goals. Instead of grades, students receive written narrative evaluations of their work. All students must complete three independent study projects (completed during January interterm) and a senior thesis, which must be defended before a committee of three faculty members. It takes a special student to flourish here; one who has explains, "If you are self-motivated, New College provides a great opportunity to work closely with professors to provide an intellectually stimulating and challenging educational experience. Self-motivation, however, is the key; without it you will receive a second-rate education and probably not be any better for it in the end." Undergraduates warn that "you can't take the lack of grades as [a] joke—you still need to focus and do your work [because] your professors expect a lot from you, as if they were your parents. Because they trust the students to do their work—and they do—students are able to have the freedom of designing their own education." For those with the self-discipline and academic drive required by this unique program, "The academic experience is unparalleled because you are given so many opportunities to advance in your area of interest."

Life

"There is always something social happening on campus" at New College, although it's "not so much planned, organized events as it is hangouts with welcoming groups of students watching a movie, cooking dinner, playing music or just sitting around talking." There are also regular school-sponsored parties, which many students take advantage of, and "tons of free food all the time." One student sums up weekend life here thusly: "Scene: A Friday night. If you're in a square court filled with palm trees and there aren't 20 people drunk and discussing Hegel, planning a bike ride to a local beach for a nude swim, or dancing to OutKast and Violent Femmes, then you aren't at New College." (Oh, and just so you'll be in the know, parties aren't called "parties" at this school where students are proud of their independence. They're called "walls.") Other benefits of a New College education include "amazing dorms" that "not only provide a good place for study and relaxation but also somehow facilitate the need for privacy (private entrances) and social interaction (courtyard design)." And then there are the school's environs, which include "St. Armand's Circle and Lido Beach, less than 10 minutes from campus." Sarasota "is a beautiful, artsy community, but not much of a college town," although "The downtown isn't too bad. We usually get discounts for shows at Van Wezel, Performing Arts Center, which is halfway to the beach. Dinner out is always a treat; there are lots of tasty places to go around here. And the dollar theater is awesome!"

Student Body

Reports one New College undergrad, "Whenever I pass somebody on campus, they're always talking about French politics or particle physics or weird linguistic connections from the Indus Valley . . . I love it." Another agrees, "You will never want for intellectual conversation during your undergraduate experience if New College is your undergraduate choice. Everyone can learn something from everyone here." The typical student here is "outspoken, intellectual, warm, open, curious, driven [and] would be atypical anywhere else." Above all, they are "interested in nothing besides the demolition of boredom on all fronts."

ADMISSIONS

Very important factors considered include: Academic GPA, application essay, rigor of secondary school record, standardized test scores. *Important factors considered include:* Character/personal qualities, level of applicant's interest, recommendation(s). *Other factors considered include:* Alumni/ae relation, class rank, extracurricular activities, geographical residence, interview, state residency, talent/ability, volunteer work, work experience. SAT or ACT required; TOEFL required of all international applicants. High school diploma is required, and GED is accepted. *Academic units required:* 4 English, 3 math, 3 science (2 science labs), 2 foreign language, 3 social studies, 3 academic electives. *Academic units recommended:* 4 English, 3 math, 3 science (2 science labs), 2 foreign language, 3 social studies, 5 academic electives.

The Inside Word

Applications keep rolling in to New College like the evening tide on Sarasota Bay. Increases in the academic quality of entering students are virtually perpetual, as is recognition by the media. Perhaps the biggest drawback is a high attrition rate for a college of this caliber—just as the Admissions Committee strives to choose wisely, so should prospective students. Don't apply simply because it's a great buy; make sure that it's what you're seeking. In order to be successful, candidates must demonstrate a high level of intellectual curiosity, self-awareness, and maturity. It also helps to be a strong writer, given that the application has an optional process that requires candidates to submit a graded paper from school. Did we forget to mention high grades and test scores? They'll help, too, but if you're someone with lots of "potential" as opposed to "credentials," the Admissions Committee might still vote you in provided you've put together some very convincing evidence that you make a match and deserve a shot.

FINANCIAL AID

Students should submit: FAFSA. The Princeton Review suggests that all financial aid forms be submitted as soon as possible after January 1. *Need-based scholarships/grants offered:* Pell Grant, SEOG, Academic Competitiveness Grant, state scholarships/grants, private scholarships, the school's own gift aid. *Loan aid offered:* FFEL Subsidized Stafford, FFEL Unsubsidized Stafford, FFEL PLUS, alternative loans. Applicants will be notified of awards on or about March 15. Federal Work-Study Program available. Institutional employment available. Off-campus job opportunities are good.

FROM THE ADMISSIONS OFFICE

"Inspired individualism, with a dash of quirkiness, best describes New College of Florida and its students. At New College, you participate directly in your education by collaborating with faculty to develop an individualized program of classes, seminars, independent research projects, and off-campus experiences designed to meet your personal academic interests and needs. As a result, you receive the high-quality, personalized education of a top-tier private college yet at the affordable cost of a public university. If you are independent, open-minded, and welcome the challenge of a rigorous academic program matched with a relaxed social environment, then New College may be the perfect fit for you.

"Students applying for Fall 2008 must submit scores from the SAT (or ACT). It is not required that they take the new version of the SAT (or the ACT with the Writing section). We will allow students to submit scores from either version of the SAT (or ACT) and will use the student's best scores from either test."

SELECTIVITY	
Admissions Rating	**94**
# of applicants	1,065
% of applicants accepted	49
% of acceptees attending	33
# accepting a place on wait list	112
% admitted from wait list	88

FRESHMAN PROFILE	
Range SAT Critical Reading	650–740
Range SAT Math	600–690
Range SAT Writing	610–690
Range ACT Composite	26–30
Minimum Paper TOEFL	560
Minimum Computer Based TOEFL	220
Average HS GPA	3.94
% graduated top 10% of class	49
% graduated top 25% of class	82
% graduated top 50% of class	96

DEADLINES	
Regular application deadline	4/15
Regular notification	4/25
Nonfall registration?	yes

APPLICANTS ALSO LOOK AT
AND OFTEN PREFER
Brown University, University of Florida
AND SOMETIMES PREFER
Florida State University, University of Miami
AND RARELY PREFER
Eckerd College, Stetson University

FINANCIAL FACTS	
Financial Aid Rating	**92**
Annual in-state tuition	$3,850
Annual out-of-state tuition	$20,575
Room & Board	$7,080
Books and supplies	$800
% frosh rec. need-based scholarship or grant aid	42
% UG rec. need-based scholarship or grant aid	37
% frosh rec. need-based self-help aid	31
% UG rec. need-based self-help aid	30
% frosh rec. any financial aid	100
% UG rec. any financial aid	88

NEW JERSEY INSTITUTE OF TECHNOLOGY

UNIVERSITY HEIGHTS, NEWARK, NJ 07102 • ADMISSIONS: 973-596-3300 • FAX: 973-596-3461

CAMPUS LIFE
Quality of Life Rating	61
Fire Safety Rating	85
Type of school	public
Environment	metropolis

STUDENTS
Total undergrad enrollment	5,380
% male/female	80/20
% from out of state	7
% from public high school	80
% live on campus	27
% in (# of) fraternities	7 (17)
% in (# of) sororities	5 (8)
% African American	11
% Asian	21
% Caucasian	37
% Hispanic	16
% international	6
# of countries represented	98

SURVEY SAYS . . .
Small classes
Registration is a breeze
Great computer facilities
Great library
Diverse student types on campus
Campus feels safe

ACADEMICS
Academic Rating	68
Calendar	semester
Student/faculty ratio	12:1
Profs interesting rating	61
Profs accessible rating	61
% profs teaching	
UG courses	70
% classes taught by TAs	0
Most common	
reg class size	20–29 students

MOST POPULAR MAJORS
architecture (BArch, BA/BS, MArch,
MA/MS, PhD)
information technology
mechanical engineering

STUDENTS SAY

Academics

Mathematics, science, technology, and architecture offerings all shine at New Jersey Institute of Technology, a "leader in the field of technology in the Tri-State Area" whose public school pricing allows students to "graduate without the bank owning our first-borns, which is a definite plus." As is the case at many prestigious tech-oriented schools, "The professors are generally hired for research rather than teaching ability, [so] there are some who cannot teach, and they aren't that great at grading assignments or handing back papers either." The demanding undergraduate curriculum means "You have to be serious about studies if you are choosing NJIT. There is no time for fun and games." Students groan about the demands made on them but also recognize the benefits; "NJIT is an intense academic university that allows students to be prepared for the working world," explains one architect. Another plus of studying at NJIT is "how well the students interact, especially during exam time. Seniors help juniors, who help sophomores, who help freshman. It's helpful when someone who has taken the courses you're taking at the moment can put things into perspective, and give you hints about what may be on the test."

Life

NJIT is "not the best school socially, but few engineering schools are," students here concede. Since "a lot of classes give amazing amounts of homework, it is hard to have a normal social life. Most nights are spent doing homework late, then getting a few hours of fun before passing out." Extracurricular life has improved recently with the addition of new recreation facilities; one student notes, "The game room has been improved, with pool tables, bowling, and arcades, and a much-needed pub on campus." The institute also boasts "a pretty good gym to work out in, and a brand-new soccer field." Undergrads note optimistically that "our team sports are all performing better, and the students are starting to feel a sense of competition building. There are plenty of parties on Thursday nights on campus, organized by frats or clubs." And, of course, "Possibilities are endless because New York City is minutes away" by affordable public transportation, opening the door to "major league sports, world-class museums, and theater." Hometown Newark, although much maligned by students and locals, offers "great food and restaurants less than half a mile away from campus, in the Ironbound section." Students do appreciate how the "small classes and campus make a 'small-town' atmosphere during the semester," even though they also acknowledge the school's urban environs.

Student Body

"There are two types of students at NJIT," writes one undergrad, elaborating: "The first are the ones who are involved with athletics, clubs, organizations, and other things. The others are the antisocial ones. These people stay in their dorms and play computer games all day." How many of each category populate this campus? One student offers some pertinent data: "Class attendance dropped 32 percent the day Halo 2 came out." Like the region surrounding it, "NJIT is a total melting pot; the mix of ethnic backgrounds of students is diverse." While many say the various groups interact well, just as many others describe the student body as "clusters of ethnic groups isolated from each other." Because of curricular demands, "Everyone is pretty smart. But you also have the very smart people." When asked in what ways his school could stand to improve, one succinct information technologist wrote "girls!" reflecting a sentiment running through much of the student body. The male/female ratio is about 4:1.

NEW JERSEY INSTITUTE OF TECHNOLOGY

FINANCIAL AID: 973-596-3480 • E-MAIL: ADMISSIONS@NJIT.EDU • WEBSITE: WWW.NJIT.EDU

ADMISSIONS

Very important factors considered include: Class rank, rigor of secondary school record, standardized test scores. *Important factors considered include:* Academic GPA. *Other factors considered include:* Alumni/ae relation, application essay, character/personal qualities, extracurricular activities, geographical residence, interview, level of applicant's interest, racial/ethnic status, recommendation(s), religious affiliation/commitment, state residency. SAT or ACT required; TOEFL required of all international applicants. High school diploma is required, and GED is accepted. *Academic units required:* 4 English, 4 math, 2 science (2 science labs). *Academic units recommended:* 2 foreign language, 1 social studies, 1 history, 2 academic electives.

The Inside Word

NJIT is a great choice for students who aspire to technical careers but don't meet the requirements for better-known and more selective universities. To top it off, it's a pretty good buy.

FINANCIAL AID

Students should submit: FAFSA. Regular filing deadline is May 15. The Princeton Review suggests that all financial aid forms be submitted as soon as possible after January 1. *Need-based scholarships/grants offered:* Pell Grant, SEOG, state scholarships/grants, private scholarships, the school's own gift aid. *Loan aid offered:* Direct Subsidized Stafford, Direct Unsubsidized Stafford, Direct PLUS, Federal Perkins Loan, state loans, college/university loans from institutional funds. Applicants will be notified of awards on a rolling basis beginning or about March 1. Federal Work-Study Program available. Institutional employment available. Off-campus job opportunities are good.

FROM THE ADMISSIONS OFFICE

"Talented high school graduates from across the nation come to NJIT to prepare for leadership roles in architecture, business, engineering, medical, legal, science, and technological fields. Students experience a public research university conducting more than $75 million in research that maintains a small-college atmosphere at a modest cost. Our attractive 45-acre campus is just minutes from New York City and less than an hour from the Jersey shore. Students find an outstanding faculty and a safe, diverse, caring learning and residential community. All dormitory rooms have sprinklers. NJIT's academic environment challenges and prepares students for rewarding careers and full-time advanced study after graduation. The campus is computing-intunsive. For 5 consecutive years, *Yahoo! Internet Life* ranked NJIT among America's 'Most Wired Universities.'

"Students applying for admission to NJIT for Fall 2008 may provide scores from either version of the SAT, or the ACT. Writing sample scores will be collected but will not be used for admission purposes for 2008. SAT Subject Test scores are not required for any major."

SELECTIVITY

Admissions Rating	**78**
# of applicants	2,891
% of applicants accepted	53
% of acceptees attending	55

FRESHMAN PROFILE

Range SAT Critical Reading	470–570
Range SAT Math	540–640
Minimum Paper TOEFL	550
Minimum Computer Based TOEFL	213
% graduated top 10% of class	12
% graduated top 25% of class	60
% graduated top 50% of class	89

DEADLINES

Regular application deadline	4/1
Regular notification	rolling
Nonfall registration?	yes

APPLICANTS ALSO LOOK AT

AND OFTEN PREFER

Drexel University, Rensselaer Polytechnic Institute, Rutgers, The State University of New Jersey—New Brunswick, The College of New Jersey

AND SOMETIMES PREFER

Pennsylvania State University—University Park, Virginia Tech, Worcester Polytechnic Institute

FINANCIAL FACTS

Financial Aid Rating	**77**
Annual in-state tuition	$9,066
Annual out-of-state tuition	$15,850
Room & Board	$8,980
Books and supplies	$1,200
Required fees	$1,440
% frosh rec. need-based scholarship or grant aid	51
% UG rec. need-based scholarship or grant aid	42
% frosh rec. need-based self-help aid	38
% UG rec. need-based self-help aid	34
% frosh rec. any financial aid	70
% UG rec. any financial aid	70

New Mexico Institute of Mining & Technology

Campus Station, 801 Leroy Place, Socorro, NM 87801 • Admissions: 505-835-5424 • Fax: 505-835-5989

CAMPUS LIFE

Quality of Life Rating	**63**
Fire Safety Rating	**60***
Type of school	public
Environment	village

STUDENTS

Total undergrad enrollment	1,170
% male/female	72/28
% from out of state	13
% from public high school	80
% live on campus	59
% African American	1
% Asian	3
% Caucasian	69
% Hispanic	23
% Native American	3
% international	2
# of countries represented	30

SURVEY SAYS . . .

Class discussions are rare
Small classes
Frats and sororities are unpopular or nonexistent
(Almost) everyone smokes

ACADEMICS

Academic Rating	**78**
Calendar	semester
Student/faculty ratio	12:1
Profs interesting rating	73
Profs accessible rating	65
% profs teaching UG courses	85
Most common lab size	10–19 students
Most common reg class size	10–19 students

MOST POPULAR MAJORS

computer and information sciences
electrical, electronics and communications engineering
mechanical engineering

STUDENTS SAY

Academics

New Mexico Institute of Mining and Technology—known simply as "Tech" to insiders—is a school geared toward students interested in geological science, engineering, or computers. Like most such "science-oriented" schools, students at Tech ("Techies") are no strangers to hard work. "At Tech, you must be prepared to be a serious student because professors expect a lot from their students." Tech's atmosphere doesn't suffer, perhaps because "It's a small school where you can get to know personally the people in the Financial Aid Office, Student Accounts, the Registrar, etc." A few praise the financial aid packages, and many commend the professors for being researchers as well as teachers: "It is an incredible feeling to listen to a lecture by someone who actually does research in that field and enjoys teaching." And to top it all off, "The research opportunities are incredible. We have an explosives field for the Materials Engineering Department, and our Computer Science Department does Department of Defense cryptography. The Physics Department has done experiments on NASA's Vomit Comet (which simulates zero gravity)." While students sometimes grumble that "Tech is very difficult," they appreciate how "Most departments have help sessions almost every day for most of the day; just drop by with a problem and you'll have an upper-level student or grad student helping you understand." And they also realize that the hard work "means that you are going to learn the material and be an expert by the time you graduate."

Life

Given its rural location, Tech doesn't offer much in the way of urban fun. Outdoor activities such as rock climbing and mountain biking are popular. In addition, "There are events like movies, barbeques, dancing, or theatrical events every week. You can also use the athletic facilities or play with dry ice for fun." Otherwise, though, Tech's surroundings don't offer a whole lot; Socorro, according to its harshest critics, is "a depressed town that flaunts the failure of the American Dream." Tech's distance from an urban center is particularly appreciable for the handful of students who grumble about the food. Culinary discontentment aside, there is fun to be had at Tech— even for those who don't enjoy outdoor activities. Popular indoor activities include "dances, movies, and computer games." Students tell us that "large, crazy parties are fairly infrequent, but they exist. Small social gatherings are more common and often involve something nerdy, whether it be video games or mixing volatile chemicals." Once each semester "There are weekend school-wide celebrations, known as 'Forty-niners' and 'Spring Fling,' which have plenty of alcohol." One sophomore writes: "Techies have to make their own fun, and we do— after we finish our homework."

Student Body

The "friendly oddballs" of Tech "are mostly nerds . . . no, actually, we're all nerds." It's the kind of place where "Half the students on campus built their own computers" and, in the words of one junior, some students seem "surgically attached to their computers." While Techies assert that they know how to party, they "also take pride in knowing the chemical formula of the substances they consume." Students characterize their peers by major, writing that "the science people tend to spend a lot of time outside; the engineers tend to be in the library; and the computer science people tend to be in their rooms." A physics major writes that "all the students are incredibly interested in their fields." There aren't many women at Tech (a member of this minority notes that "the guy-to-girl ratio at Tech is rather ridiculous"); one male student observes, "To find an attractive girl who has no boyfriend is like finding Brigadoon." That said, a good portion of the student body consists of "people with senses of humor who make the best out of the town and life on campus."

New Mexico Institute of Mining & Technology

Financial Aid: 505-835-5333 • E-mail: admission@admin.nmt.edu • Website: www.nmt.edu

ADMISSIONS

Very important factors considered include: Academic GPA, rigor of secondary school record, standardized test scores. *Other factors considered include:* Class rank, extracurricular activities, talent/ability. ACT recommended; SAT or ACT required; TOEFL required of all international applicants. High school diploma is required, and GED is accepted. *Academic units required:* 4 English, 3 math, 2 science (2 science labs), 2 social studies, 1 history, 3 academic electives. *Academic units recommended:* 4 English, 4 math, 4 science (3 science labs), 2 foreign language, 3 social studies, 1 history.

The Inside Word

A 2.5 GPA and a 21 ACT score is far from stringent. This is one of those situations that call for serious self-examination. Are you really ready to take on the demands of a fairly solid technical institute? If you aren't sure, you should probably pass, even if you're admissible.

FINANCIAL AID

Students should submit: FAFSA, institution's own financial aid form. Regular filing deadline is March 1. The Princeton Review suggests that all financial aid forms be submitted as soon as possible after January 1. *Need-based scholarships/grants offered:* Pell Grant, SEOG, state scholarships/grants, private scholarships, the school's own gift aid. *Loan aid offered:* FFEL Subsidized Stafford, FFEL Unsubsidized Stafford, FFEL PLUS, Federal Perkins Loan, state loans. Applicants will be notified of awards on a rolling basis beginning or about April 1. Federal Work-Study Program available. Institutional employment available. Off-campus job opportunities are fair.

FROM THE ADMISSIONS OFFICE

"More than a century old, New Mexico Tech has research programs at the cutting edge of today's technology. This is exciting for students because many of them get jobs working for professors or for one of our many research divisions, learning skills they will use in graduate schools or high-tech careers. Pulsars, thunderstorms, volcanoes, lightning, quasars, earthquakes, energetic materials, and caves are just a few of the areas we study. We also teach and work in areas of computer and information security, business management, and several fields of engineering. Many of our research divisions are known worldwide in their fields, including Magdalena Ridge Observatory, the Energetic Materials Research and Testing Center, and Langmuir Laboratory for Atmospheric Research. Recent graduates with engineering degrees received starting salaries averaging $51,755, those with computer science degrees averaged $55,583; and those with degrees in both computer science and electrical engineering started at $63,333.

"From Fall 2008 on, students are required to submit scores from either the SAT or ACT. New Mexico Institute of Mining and Technology will continue to use the composite score from the ACT and/or the combined score of the Critical Reading and Math components *only* from the new SAT for both admission decisions and merit scholarships. The newly introduced Writing component will not be used for admission decisions and/or merit scholarships. We will continue to allow students to submit scores from the old (prior to March 2005) version of the SAT (or ACT) as well, and will use the student's best scores from either test. New Mexico Tech does not require the SAT Subject Test for consideration for admission or merit scholarships."

SELECTIVITY

Admissions Rating	88
# of applicants	834
% of applicants accepted	61
% of acceptees attending	56

FRESHMAN PROFILE

Range SAT Critical Reading	550–670
Range SAT Math	570–670
Range ACT Composite	23–29
Minimum Paper TOEFL	540
Minimum Computer Based TOEFL	207
Average HS GPA	3.6
% graduated top 10% of class	32
% graduated top 25% of class	67
% graduated top 50% of class	91

DEADLINES

Regular application deadline	8/1
Regular notification	rolling
Nonfall registration?	yes

APPLICANTS ALSO LOOK AT

AND OFTEN PREFER
California Institute of Technology, Massachusetts Institute of Technology

AND SOMETIMES PREFER
Colorado School of Mines, University of New Mexico

AND RARELY PREFER
Arizona State University at the Tempe Campus, New Mexico State University

FINANCIAL FACTS

Financial Aid Rating	88
Annual in-state tuition	$3,439
Annual out-of-state tuition	$10,873
Room & Board	$5,090
Books and supplies	$1,000
Required fees	$532
% frosh rec. need-based scholarship or grant aid	19
% UG rec. need-based scholarship or grant aid	25
% frosh rec. need-based self-help aid	16
% UG rec. need-based self-help aid	25
% frosh rec. any financial aid	34
% UG rec. any financial aid	39

NEW YORK UNIVERSITY

22 WASHINGTON SQUARE NORTH, NEW YORK, NY 10011 • ADMISSIONS: 212-998-4500 • FAX: 212-995-4902

STUDENTS SAY

Academics

Located in the heart of Manhattan's Greenwich Village, New York University feeds off its great home city. The school's layout reinforces this relationship; academic buildings and dormitories are scattered around Washington Square Park and are virtually indistinguishable from the private residences, hotels, and restaurants that are its neighbors. Asked to identify the school's greatest asset, so many students respond "location, location, location" that one could be forgiven for thinking that NYU is a training school for real-estate agents. Nonetheless, the school's location "attracts superb professors and well-known researchers and lecturers" and "It's pretty much guaranteed that you'll have a couple good connections in your field when you leave NYU." While at school, you'll find opportunities for "amazing internship possibilities and real-life experiences," and you'll learn the "independence, maturity, and time-management skills" that come with living in an "expensive place where space is limited but you have access to the best of everything." Students note that NYU "offers a great program for nearly anything you want to major in," including a world-renowned arts school, and excellent programs in business, the humanities, and education. The school's weak spot, undergrads agree, is the administration, where "too much red tape" creates an experience reminiscent of "a daily trip to the Department of Motor Vehicles." A relatively small price to pay, most here agree, for the "endless cultural, culinary, musical, artistic, and academic opportunities" that NYU offers.

Life

NYU isn't merely located in "the city that never sleeps." It is, in fact, located in one of the city's hottest social and cultural areas, an agora of restaurants, clubs, concert venues, movie theaters, retail shops, and galleries. Village life ain't cheap, however, and students warn that "money is always an issue. Kids are either worried about getting more money out of their parents or managing what money they have. But money seems to be considerably less of an issue when we're all going out on a Friday night. There is any number of ways to entertain yourself—it's New York City!" Inexpensive diversions include many of the city's famous museums, cheap ethnic eats, and the ever-popular pastime of people-watching. There are also "many free/discounted events put on by the university (like concerts, plays, forums, etc)." Don't expect a typical college party scene here, however, as "There are no frat parties at NYU, as Greek life is virtually nonexistent, even frowned upon by many students. Instead, students prefer to go out to bars and clubs on weekends." Dorm and apartment parties also "aren't too abundant, though pre-gaming is very popular." In fact, "NYU doesn't really provide much of an emphasis on campus activities, especially during the weekend. You're basically left to find your own entertainment which, thankfully, is always possible."

Student Body

Students agree that "NYU is just a diverse as the city it is surrounded by," noting that the campus "is a conglomeration of the atypical. If you are looking for a student body wearing J. Crew and discussing the next frat party, this isn't the school for you." Each college has a specific archetype—"The somewhat eccentric theater student in Tisch, the mostly international Stern business students, the Steinhardt musicians reminiscent of the band groups in high school"—but "The vast majority of students are really pretty average, just doing their own thing like everybody else." The community "is known for its acceptance of students of any ethnicity, religion, sexual orientation, gender, or race. We live in New York, so absolutely nothing shocks us, and virtually everything is accepted." The lack of a traditional campus attracts students of an "independent" bent and, on occasion, drives away those who discover they crave a more conventional college experience.

FINANCIAL AID: 212-998-4444 • E-MAIL: ADMISSIONS@NYU.EDU • WEBSITE: WWW.NYU.EDU

ADMISSIONS

Very important factors considered include: Academic GPA, recommendation(s), rigor of secondary school record, standardized test scores. *Important factors considered include:* Application essay, character/personal qualities, class rank, extracurricular activities, talent/ability. *Other factors considered include:* Alumni/ae relation, first generation, level of applicant's interest, racial/ethnic status, volunteer work, work experience. SAT or ACT required; ACT with Writing component required. TOEFL required of all international applicants. High school diploma is required, and GED is accepted. *Academic units required:* 4 English, 3 math, 3 science (2 science labs), 2 foreign language, 4 history. *Academic units recommended:* 4 math, 3 foreign language.

The Inside Word

NYU consists of eight schools and colleges; undergraduate applicants may apply only to one. Students applying to the Steinhardt School of Education, the Tisch School of the Arts, or the School of Continuing and Professional Studies must indicate an intended major (those applying to the College of Arts and Sciences or the Stern School of Business may indicate that they are undecided on their majors). This is different from the application process at most schools and obviously requires some forethought. Remember that this is a highly competitive school; if your application does not reflect a serious interest in your intended area of study, your chances of getting in will be diminished.

FINANCIAL AID

Students should submit: FAFSA, state aid form. Early decision applicants may submit an institutuional form for an estimated award. Regular filing deadline is February 15. The Princeton Review suggests that all financial aid forms be submitted as soon as possible after January 1. *Need-based scholarships/grants offered:* Pell Grant, SEOG, state scholarships/grants, private scholarships, the school's own gift aid. *Loan aid offered:* FFEL Subsidized Stafford, FFEL Unsubsidized Stafford, FFEL PLUS, Federal Perkins Loan, Federal Nursing Loan. Applicants will be notified of awards on a rolling basis beginning or about April 1. Federal Work-Study Program available. Institutional employment available. Off-campus job opportunities are excellent.

FROM THE ADMISSIONS OFFICE

"NYU is distinctive both in the quality of education we provide and in the exhilarating atmosphere in which our students study and learn. As an undergraduate in one of our eight small- to medium-sized colleges, you will enjoy a small faculty/student ratio and a dynamic, challenging learning environment that encourages lively interaction between students and professors. At the same time, you will have available to you all the resources of a distinguished university dedicated to research and scholarship at the highest levels, including a curriculum that offers over 2,500 courses and 160 programs of study and a faculty that includes some of the most highly regarded scholars, scientists, and artists in the country. New York University is a vital, vibrant community. There is an aura of energy and excitement here, a sense that possibilities and opportunities are limited only by the number of hours in a day. The educational experience at NYU is intense, but varied and richly satisfying. You will be actively engaged in your own education, both in the classroom and beyond.

"All freshman applicants must submit scores from the two SAT Subject Tests, except for applicants to the Tisch School of the Arts or to the art and music programs in the Steinhardt School of Education."

SELECTIVITY

Admissions Rating	96
# of applicants	35,448
% of applicants accepted	36
% of acceptees attending	37
# of early decision applicants	3397
% accepted early decision	33

FRESHMAN PROFILE

Range SAT Critical Reading	600–700
Range SAT Math	610–710
Range SAT Writing	600–700
Range ACT Composite	27–31
Minimum Paper TOEFL	600
Minimum Computer Based TOEFL	250
Average HS GPA	3.6
% graduated top 10% of class	67
% graduated top 25% of class	95
% graduated top 50% of class	100

DEADLINES

Early decision application deadline	11/1
Early decision notification	12/15
Regular application deadline	1/15
Regular notification	4/1
Nonfall registration?	yes

FINANCIAL FACTS

Financial Aid Rating	74
Annual tuition	$33,740
Room & Board	$11,730
% frosh rec. need-based scholarship or grant aid	48
% UG rec. need-based scholarship or grant aid	48
% frosh rec. need-based self-help aid	49
% UG rec. need-based self-help aid	48
% frosh rec. any financial aid	60
% UG rec. any financial aid	59

NORTH CAROLINA STATE UNIVERSITY

Box 7103, Raleigh, NC 27695 • Admissions: 919-515-2434 • Fax: 919-515-5039

CAMPUS LIFE
Quality of Life Rating	76
Fire Safety Rating	97
Type of school	public
Environment	metropolis

STUDENTS
Total undergrad enrollment	21,438
% male/female	58/42
% from out of state	7
% from public high school	90
% live on campus	34
% in (# of) fraternities	8 (29)
% in (# of) sororities	10 (14)
% African American	9
% Asian	5
% Caucasian	80
% Hispanic	2
% Native American	1
% international	1
# of countries represented	96

SURVEY SAYS . . .
Lab facilities are great
Great computer facilities
Great library
Everyone loves the Wolfpack
Student publications are popular
Lots of beer drinking

ACADEMICS
Academic Rating	76
Calendar	semester
Student/faculty ratio	16:1
Profs interesting rating	75
Profs accessible rating	74
% profs teaching UG courses	100
% classes taught by TAs	6
Most common lab size	20–29 students
Most common reg class size	20–29 students

MOST POPULAR MAJORS
biology/biological sciences
business administration/
management
mechanical engineering

STUDENTS SAY
Academics

North Carolina State University provides its student body with a combination of practical experience and theoretical knowledge in a curriculum with a technological bent. It offers strong programs in business, textiles and design, engineering, premedical sciences, and a host of agricultural and wildlife sciences. While some here feel that the school "offers no liberal arts program," others point out that its College of Humanities and Social Science is "underrated" and "becoming just as important as [the] engineering and agriculture" colleges. There is no doubt, however, that the school "emphasiz[es] out-of-classroom experiences." A senior boasts, "All I had to do was ask my professors about opportunities in my field and they heaped internships and research studies so high on me I had to reject six of them." A junior adds, "NCSU really cares about students and provid[es] them with great facilities, community resources, and professors—something you can't really say for many schools of this size." Students report that the faculty are "very knowledgeable." "Many people tell you in high school that professors do not care about you [or] your academic success, but from what I have seen here at NCSU, most professors do care as long as you are willing to put forth the effort to ask," a freshman reports. The administration, on the other hand, "is very difficult to get a hold of, unless it's something they themselves care about." Fortunately, many administrative tasks can be handled easily online.

Life

NC State benefits from a great location; "There is always something fun going on" in hometown Raleigh, with "lots of universities within a 30-mile radius, including Duke, UNC, Peace, Meredith, Shaw, and others. . . . There are many people in their early 20s to meet and hang out with." There are also "lots of golf courses, tennis courts, basketball courts, etc. for sports enthusiasts. You will not get bored in Raleigh, [but] if somehow you do . . . drive to Chapel Hill or Greenville." A slightly longer car trip—approximately 2 hours—puts you on the beach (east) or the mountains (west). ACC athletics dominate the thoughts of many in the area; NCSU's rivalries with nearby UNC and Duke are long-standing and legendary, especially in basketball, where all three schools typically field competitive teams; "Wolfpack pride is definitely evident throughout campus and even many portions of Raleigh." The school is home to "plenty of on-campus clubs and activities that many people participate in during the day. No matter what you are interested in, there is normally a club for it, and NCSU students are very active within their campus organizations and with the community." While "Most people stay focused during the week . . . when the weekend comes they leave that behind for the party scene," which centers on Greek houses and student housing until students hit the age of 21, when "Bars become the hang-out spot." Students point out, however, that "this doesn't mean that there aren't other things to do or that you won't have any friends" if "you aren't into drinking."

Student Body

At a school of 20,000, you'll find a little of everything, and NCSU is no exception to that rule; "athletes, computer geeks, frat dogs, sorority girls, skaters, intellects, grad students, goths, exchange students, etc." are peppered among the more populous "agriculture majors who wear overalls and talk with a thick Southern accent" and "engineering majors who are kind of geeky." In the same vein, NCSU "is a very conservative campus," but it is not without its "politically liberal students" and homosexual and minority advocacy groups. Atypical students "fit in really well in certain degree programs, especially textiles," but the campus isn't strife-free in this regard; one student reports, "There is lots of controversy over a new LGBT Center being built on campus."

NORTH CAROLINA STATE UNIVERSITY

FINANCIAL AID: 919-515-2421 • E-MAIL: UNDERGRAD_ADMISSIONS@NCSU.EDU • WEBSITE: WWW.NCSU.EDU

ADMISSIONS

Very important factors considered include: Academic GPA, class rank, rigor of secondary school record, standardized test scores. *Other factors considered include:* Alumni/ae relation, application essay, character/personal qualities, extracurricular activities, first generation, geographical residence, racial/ethnic status, recommendation(s), state residency, talent/ability, volunteer work, work experience. SAT or ACT required; ACT with Writing component required. TOEFL required of all international applicants. High school diploma is required, and GED is not accepted. *Academic units required:* 4 English, 4 math, 3 science (1 science lab), 2 foreign language, 1 social studies, 1 history, 1 academic elective. *Academic units recommended:* 4 English, 4 math, 4 science (2 science labs), 2 foreign language, 1 social studies, 1 history, 4 academic electives.

The Inside Word

Back in the mid 1990s, strong applicants could apply to NCSU as a safety school, but things have really changed in the last decade. Soaring tuition rates at private schools and the school's growing reputation in a wide variety of fields have expanded the applicant pool. Freshman applicants must apply to a specific program, and some are more selective than others. Agricultural programs, the College of Textiles, and the College of Natural Resources are not as selective as programs in engineering, mathematics, the sciences, business, and the humanities and social sciences.

FINANCIAL AID

Students should submit: FAFSA, institution's own financial aid form. The Princeton Review suggests that all financial aid forms be submitted as soon as possible after January 1. *Need-based scholarships/grants offered:* Pell Grant, SEOG, state scholarships/grants, private scholarships, the school's own gift aid, United Negro College Fund. *Loan aid offered:* FFEL Subsidized Stafford, FFEL Unsubsidized Stafford, FFEL PLUS, Federal Perkins Loan, state loans, college/university loans from institutional funds. Applicants will be notified of awards on a rolling basis beginning or about March 15.

FROM THE ADMISSIONS OFFICE

"NC State is arguably the most popular university in the state, with more NC students seeking admission than at any other college or university. Over 12,000 students from across the nation seek one of the 3,600 available freshman spaces. Students choose NC State for its strong and varied academic programs (approximately 90), national reputation for excellence, low cost, location in Raleigh and the Research Triangle Park area, and very friendly atmosphere. Our students like the excitement of a large campus and the many opportunities it offers, such as Cooperative Education, Study Abroad, extensive honors programming, and theme residence halls. Each year, hundreds of NC State graduates are accepted into medical or law schools or other areas of advanced professional study. More corporate and government entities recruit graduates from NC State than from any other university in the United States. In 1999, IBM hired more graduates from NC State than from any other university in the United States.

"Freshman applicants for Fall 2008 must take either the new SAT, which includes a written essay, or the ACT with the Writing component. Students may also submit scores from either the old SAT (taken before March 2005) or the ACT, but the new Writing score is still required."

SELECTIVITY

Admissions Rating	**89**
# of applicants	15,500
% of applicants accepted	61
% of acceptees attending	48

FRESHMAN PROFILE

Range SAT Critical Reading	520–620
Range SAT Math	560–660
Range SAT Writing	510–600
Range ACT Composite	21–26
Minimum Paper TOEFL	550
Minimum Computer Based TOEFL	213
Average HS GPA	4.11
% graduated top 10% of class	37
% graduated top 25% of class	79
% graduated top 50% of class	98

DEADLINES

Regular application deadline	2/1
Regular notification	rolling
Nonfall registration?	yes

APPLICANTS ALSO LOOK AT
AND OFTEN PREFER
The University of North Carolina at Chapel Hill
AND SOMETIMES PREFER
The University of North Carolina at Charlotte, Wake Forest University
AND RARELY PREFER
Auburn University, Clemson University, Georgia Institute of Technology, University of South Carolina—Columbia, Virginia Tech

FINANCIAL FACTS

Financial Aid Rating	**79**
Annual in-state tuition	$3,760
Annual out-of-state tuition	$15,958
Room & Board	$7,373
Books and supplies	$930
Required fees	$1,357
% frosh rec. need-based scholarship or grant aid	39
% UG rec. need-based scholarship or grant aid	36
% frosh rec. need-based self-help aid	29
% UG rec. need-based self-help aid	30
% frosh rec. any financial aid	68
% UG rec. any financial aid	61

NORTHEASTERN UNIVERSITY

360 HUNTINGTON AVENUE, 150 RICHARDS HALL, BOSTON, MA 02115 • ADMISSIONS: 617-373-2200 • FAX: 617-373-8780

STUDENTS SAY

Academics

For "incorporating classroom learning with real-world application in the middle of a great city," Northeastern University is hard to beat. That's because of the school's celebrated cooperative education (co-op) program, which "gives students a chance to try out jobs in the 'real world' and adjust their career paths accordingly. Co-op gives you the chance to meet new friends, both students and professionals, make some money, and build your resume." "Co-op is the reason many people are at this school," students agree, pointing out that "through the co-op program students are able to bring more to the table than the average college student. Many of the upperclassman have had experience working within their major beyond serving coffee and copying files for the higher-ups." They warn, however, that "co-ops are not just handed to you, and you must not assume that you will be guaranteed a co-op just by being a NU student. Many friends of mine have suffered through a semester working at the mall on 'no-op.'" A large school, NU excels in a number of areas; students report that health science, business, engineering, and criminal justice are all solid here. As at many large schools, the bureaucracy can be overwhelming; many students reference "the NU shuffle," explaining that "no one is ever willing to help you with a problem. All they're trained to do is send you to someone else." Advisors are in unfortunately short supply, as "Each advisor has hundreds of students. Getting a meeting with them is like pulling teeth. Once you get closer to graduation, and advisors become more important to you, you get little help, if any."

Life

"Campus life is very small at NU," students tell us, explaining, "We have a city to play in. Why waste time on campus where there's not much to do?" NU, located in the heart of Boston, is "in a great area in terms of proximity to places to eat and places to have fun. We are just a few minutes' walk away from Fenway Park and the surrounding bars, as well as Newberry Street, the Prudential Center, and Copley Square." The city is "a lot of fun during the day, with shopping and museums and other tourist attractions," and it's just as fun at night, especially if you're over 21. "Life at Northeastern is all about bars," confides one student. When the weekend rolls around, "Many students go out to parties, which can be found ongoing every night," or they "go to basketball and hockey games." They also "take weekend road trips to Cape Cod or just bike and Rollerblade around the city, weather permitting, see a lot of movies, [or] just explore the city and goof around." Although "The majority of the school parties," students who are "not into drinking" will "definitely find a niche, and it won't be hard."

Student Body

Undergraduates report that "the vast majority of the school is comprised of people very concerned with their appearance and club life." At a school this size though, those outside the "vast majority" constitute a sizable population, so "You can hang out with a bunch of different people from different groups, and you all get along well." There are students from all socioeconomic, ethnic, and racial backgrounds contentedly "all mixed together." Atypical students "have many resources and clubs available that cater to their ethnicity, sexual orientation, etc."

NORTHEASTERN UNIVERSITY

FINANCIAL AID: 617-373-3190 • E-MAIL: ADMISSIONS@NEU.EDU • WEBSITE: WWW.NORTHEASTERN.EDU

ADMISSIONS

Very important factors considered include: Academic GPA, rigor of secondary school record. *Important factors considered include:* Application essay, character/personal qualities, class rank, extracurricular activities, first generation, recommendation(s), standardized test scores, talent/ability. *Other factors considered include:* Alumni/ae relation, geographical residence, racial/ethnic status, state residency, volunteer work, work experience. SAT or ACT required; ACT with Writing component required. TOEFL required of all international applicants. High school diploma is required, and GED is accepted. *Academic units required:* 4 English, 3 math, 3 science (2 science labs), 2 foreign language, 2 social studies, 2 history. *Academic units recommended:* 4 math, 4 science (4 science labs), 4 foreign language.

The Inside Word

Northeastern is one of the Boston area's most selective schools; this makes it a desirable school for students who want a college experience in an urban environment. Northeastern has a large applicant pool and a low acceptance rate. Northeastern's admissions process relies on a comprehensive review process where personal qualities and interests are as important as academic achievement.

FINANCIAL AID

Students should submit: FAFSA, CSS/Financial Aid PROFILE. The Princeton Review suggests that all financial aid forms be submitted as soon as possible after January 1. *Need-based scholarships/grants offered:* Pell Grant, SEOG, state scholarships/grants, private scholarships, the school's own gift aid, Federal Nursing Scholarship. *Loan aid offered:* FFEL Subsidized Stafford, FFEL Unsubsidized Stafford, FFEL PLUS, Federal Perkins Loan, Federal Nursing Loan, state loans, MEFA, TERI, Signature, Massachusetts No Interest Loan (NIL), CitiAssist. Applicants will be notified of awards on a rolling basis beginning or about February 15. Federal Work-Study Program available. Institutional employment available. Off-campus job opportunities are excellent.

FROM THE ADMISSIONS OFFICE

"Northeastern students take charge of their education in a way you'll find nowhere else, because a Northeastern education is like no other. We integrate challenging liberal arts and professional studies with the world's largest cooperative education program, where undergraduates alternate semesters of full-time study with semesters of paid work in fields relevant to their professional interests and major, giving them nearly 2 years of professional experience upon graduation. Northeastern's dynamic of academic excellence and workplace experience means that our students are better prepared to succeed in the lives they choose. On top of that, they experience all of this on a beautifully landscaped, 67-acre campus in the heart of Boston, where culture, commerce, civic pride, and college students from around the globe are all a part of the mix.

"Freshman applicants must take the SAT or the ACT with Writing component."

SELECTIVITY

Admissions Rating	**90**
# of applicants	27,168
% of applicants accepted	45
% of acceptees attending	24
# accepting a place on wait list	1,326
% admitted from wait list	19

FRESHMAN PROFILE

Range SAT Critical Reading	560–650
Range SAT Math	590–680
Range ACT Composite	24–28
Minimum Paper TOEFL	550
Minimum Computer Based TOEFL	213
% graduated top 10% of class	38
% graduated top 25% of class	76
% graduated top 50% of class	95

DEADLINES

Regular application deadline	1/15
Regular notification	3/15–4/1
Nonfall registration?	yes

APPLICANTS ALSO LOOK AT
AND OFTEN PREFER
Boston College, New York University, The George Washington University
AND SOMETIMES PREFER
American University, Boston University, Syracuse University
AND RARELY PREFER
University of Connecticut, University of Massachusetts—Amherst, University of Vermont

FINANCIAL FACTS

Financial Aid Rating	**68**
Annual tuition	$29,910
Room & Board	$10,970
Books and supplies	$900
Required fees	$399
% frosh rec. need-based scholarship or grant aid	60
% UG rec. need-based scholarship or grant aid	55
% frosh rec. need-based self-help aid	53
% UG rec. need-based self-help aid	50
% frosh rec. any financial aid	90
% UG rec. any financial aid	83

NORTHWESTERN UNIVERSITY

PO Box 3060, 1801 HINMAN AVENUE, EVANSTON, IL 60208-3060 • ADMISSIONS: 847-491-7271

CAMPUS LIFE

Quality of Life Rating	77
Fire Safety Rating	98
Type of school	private
Environment	town

STUDENTS

Total undergrad enrollment	8,060
% male/female	47/53
% from out of state	65
% from public high school	73
% live on campus	65
% in (# of) fraternities	32 (23)
% in (# of) sororities	38 (19)
% African American	6
% Asian	16
% Caucasian	61
% Hispanic	6
% international	5
# of countries represented	95

SURVEY SAYS . . .

Great library
Athletic facilities are great
Great off-campus food
Frats and sororities dominate social scene
Student publications are popular

ACADEMICS

Academic Rating	91
Calendar	quarter
Student/faculty ratio	7:1
Profs interesting rating	74
Profs accessible rating	75
% profs teaching UG courses	100
% classes taught by TAs	2
Most common lab size	10–19 students
Most common reg class size	fewer than 10 students

MOST POPULAR MAJORS

economics
engineering
journalism

STUDENTS SAY

Academics

"The strength of the school is its range," Northwestern students agree, arguing that their school "has everything": "Intelligent but laid-back students," "excel[lence] in so many academic fields," "great extracurriculars and good parties," "strong [Big Ten] sports spirit," and "so many connections and opportunities during and after graduation." Undergrads here brag of "nationally acclaimed programs for almost anything anyone could be interested in, from engineering to theater to journalism to music," and report that "everything is given fairly equal weight. Northwestern students and faculty do not show a considerable bias" towards specific fields. The school accomplishes all this while maintaining a manageable scale. While its relatively small size allows for good student-professor interaction, it has "all the perks" of a big school, including "many opportunities" for research and internships. Be aware, however, that "Northwestern is not an easy school; it takes hard work to be average here." If you "learn from your failures quickly and love to learn for the sake of learning rather than the grade," students say it is quite possible to stay afloat and even to excel. Helping matters are numerous resources established by administrators and professors, including tutoring programs such as Northwestern's Gateway Science Workshop. Those who take advantage of these opportunities find the going much easier than those who don't.

Life

There are two distinct sections of the Northwestern campus. The North Campus is where "You can find a party every night of the week" and "The Greek scene is strong." The South Campus, about a one-mile trek from the action to the north, is "more artsy and has minimal partying on weeknights," but is closer to town so "it is easy" to "buy dinner, see a show at the movies, and go shopping. People who live on North Campus have a harder time getting motivated to go into Evanston and tap into all that is offered." As one South Campus resident puts it, "South Campus is nice and quiet in its own way. I enjoy reading and watching movies here, and the quietude is appreciated when study time rolls around. But for more exciting fun, a trip north is a must." Regardless of where students live, extracurriculars are "incredible here. There is a group for every interest, and they are amazingly well-managed by students alone. This goes hand-in-hand with how passionate students at Northwestern are about what they love." Many students "are involved in plays, a cappella groups, comedy troupes, and other organizations geared toward the performing arts. Activism is also very popular, with many involved in political groups, human rights activism, and volunteering." In addition, Northwestern's membership in the Big Ten means students "attend some of the best sporting events in the country." Chicago, of course, "is a wonderful resource. People go into the city for a wide variety of things—daily excursions, jobs, internships, nights out, parties, etc."

Student Body

The typical Northwestern student "was high school class president with a 4.0, swim team captain, and on the chess team." So it makes sense that everyone here "is an excellent student who works hard" and "has a leadership position in at least two clubs, plus an on-campus job." Students also tell us that "there's [a] great separation between North Campus (think: fraternities, engineering, state school mentality) and South Campus (think: closer to Chicago and its culture, arts and letters, liberal arts school mentality). Students segregate themselves depending on background and interests and it's rare for these two groups to interact beyond a superficial level." The student body here includes sizeable Jewish, Indian, and East Asian populations.

NORTHWESTERN UNIVERSITY

FINANCIAL AID: 847-491-7400 • E-MAIL: UG-ADMISSION@NORTHWESTERN.EDU • WEBSITE: WWW.NORTHWESTERN.EDU

ADMISSIONS

Very important factors considered include: Academic GPA, application essay, class rank, rigor of secondary school record, standardized test scores. *Important factors considered include:* Character/personal qualities, extracurricular activities, recommendation(s), talent/ability. *Other factors considered include:* Alumni/ae relation, first generation, interview, level of applicant's interest, racial/ethnic status, volunteer work, work experience. SAT or ACT required; ACT with Writing component required. TOEFL required of all international applicants. High school diploma or equivalent is not required. *Academic units recommended:* 4 English, 3 math, 2 science (2 science labs), 2 foreign language, 2 social studies, 1 academic elective.

The Inside Word

Northwestern is among the nation's most expensive undergraduate institutions, a fact that dissuades some qualified students from applying. The school is working to attract more low-income applicants by increasing the number of full scholarships available for students whose family income is less than $45,000. Low-income students who score well on the ACT may receive a letter from the school encouraging them to apply; even if you don't receive this letter, you should consider applying if you've got the goods—you may be pleasantly surprised by the offer you receive from the Financial Aid Office.

FINANCIAL AID

Students should submit: FAFSA, CSS/Financial Aid PROFILE, Noncustodial PROFILE, Business/Farm Supplement, parent and student Federal Income Tax Returns. Regular filing deadline is February 1. The Princeton Review suggests that all financial aid forms be submitted as soon as possible after January 1. *Need-based scholarships/grants offered:* Pell Grant, SEOG, state scholarships/grants, private scholarships, the school's own gift aid, United Negro College Fund. *Loan aid offered:* FFEL Subsidized Stafford, FFEL Unsubsidized Stafford, FFEL PLUS, Federal Perkins Loan, college/university loans from institutional funds. Applicants will be notified of awards on or about April 15. Federal Work-Study Program available. Institutional employment available.

FROM THE ADMISSIONS OFFICE

"Consistent with its dedication to excellence, Northwestern provides both an educational and an extracurricular environment that enables its undergraduate students to become accomplished individuals and informed and responsible citizens. To the students in all its undergraduate schools, Northwestern offers liberal learning and professional education to help them gain the depth of knowledge that will empower them to become leaders in their professions and communities. Furthermore, Northwestern fosters in its students a broad understanding of the world in which we live as well as excellence in the competencies that transcend any particular field of study: writing and oral communication, analytical and creative thinking and expression, quantitative and qualitative methods of thinking.

"Applicants for Fall 2008 are required to take the SAT or the ACT with the Writing section. Northwestern will allow students to submit scores from the old (prior to March 2005) SAT (or ACT) as well, and will use the student's best scores from either test. However, Writing scores will be required."

SELECTIVITY

Admissions Rating	98
# of applicants	18,385
% of applicants accepted	30
% of acceptees attending	38
# accepting a place on wait list	915
% admitted from wait list	24
# of early decision applicants	1,208
% accepted early decision	44

FRESHMAN PROFILE

Range SAT Critical Reading	650–740
Range SAT Math	670–760
Range SAT Writing	650–740
Range ACT Composite	29–33
Minimum Paper TOEFL	600
Minimum Computer Based TOEFL	250
% graduated top 10% of class	83
% graduated top 25% of class	97
% graduated top 50% of class	100

DEADLINES

Early decision application deadline	11/1
Early decision notification	12/15
Regular application deadline	1/1
Regular notification	4/15
Nonfall registration?	yes

APPLICANTS ALSO LOOK AT

AND OFTEN PREFER
Harvard College, Yale University

AND SOMETIMES PREFER
Columbia University, Princeton University, Stanford University, The University of Chicago

AND RARELY PREFER
DePaul University, Marquette University, Purdue University—West Lafayette

FINANCIAL FACTS

Financial Aid Rating	94
Annual tuition	$33,408
Room & Board	$10,266
Books and supplies	$1,488
Required fees	$151
% frosh rec. need-based scholarship or grant aid	40
% UG rec. need-based scholarship or grant aid	40
% frosh rec. need-based self-help aid	37
% UG rec. need-based self-help aid	37
% frosh rec. any financial aid	60
% UG rec. any financial aid	60

OBERLIN COLLEGE

101 NORTH PROFESSOR STREET, OBERLIN, OH 44074 • ADMISSIONS: 440-775-8411 • FAX: 440-775-6905

STUDENTS SAY

Academics

Oberlin College, a school "for laid-back people who enjoy learning and expanding social norms," "allows each and every student to have the undergrad experience for which he or she is looking, all the while challenging the students to change themselves and the world for the better." Oberlin is a place where students "focus on learning for learning's sake rather than making money in a career." As one student explains, "I didn't plan on becoming a scholar when I entered Oberlin. . . . As fate would have it, I ended up loving my college classes and professors. Now I hope to be a professor of religion." At Oberlin, "Academics are very highly valued, but balanced with a strong interest in the arts and a commitment to society." Wags might suggest that Oberlin puts the "liberal" in "liberal arts"; the school's staunchest supporters agree, stressing the school's emphasis on open-mindedness and the belief that "one person can change the world." Among the school's offerings, "the sciences, English, politics, religion, music, environmental studies, and East Asian studies are particularly noteworthy." The presence of a prestigious music school imbues the entire campus community; one undergrad writes, "Oberlin's greatest strength is the combination of the college and the conservatory. They are not separated, so students mix with each other all the time." Professors here—the "heart and soul of the school"—are dedicated teachers who "treat you more like collaborators and realize that even with their PhDs, they can learn and grow from you, as well as you from them." They are "excellent instructors and fantastic people" who are "focused on learning instead of deadlines." Undergrads also appreciate "a cooperative learning environment" in which "Students bond over studying together for difficult exams."

Life

Life during the week at Oberlin can be "pretty bland," as "Almost everyone has to crack the books and study it up." It's not always bland, though; some here manage to find time for the many "events [going on] each weekend—operas, plays, organ pumps, etc.," or "rally to stage to help the oppressed." Thursday afternoons at Oberlin means "Classical Thursdays," an event during which "You get free beer from the college if you bring a professor to the on-campus pub." Another feature of campus life is "the musical scene, which has its heart in the conservatory. All of the other arts—performing, studio, whatever—are intertwined with the talent in the conservatory." On weekends, "People let loose, rip out the bong (no pun intended), and drink beer. Not everyone does this every weekend. Some don't do it at all," and "There is absolutely no pressure on those who don't." There are also "tons of student-produced social events: parties, fundraisers, concerts, dances, etc.," keeping students "very connected to each other and to what's going on in the community." Hometown Oberlin "is a small town, and about all there is to do there is go out for pizza or Chinese, see a movie for $2 or $3 at the Apollo, or go to the Feve, the bar in town."

Student Body

"If you're a liberal, artsy, indie loner who likes to throw around the phrase 'heteronormative White privilege,'" then Oberlin might be the place for you. "We're like the Island of Misfit Toys, but together we make a great toy chest." "We're all different and unusual, which creates a common bond between students." "Musicians, jocks, science geeks, creative writing majors, straight, bi, questioning, queer, and trans [students]," all have their place here, alongside "straight-edge, international, local, and joker students." Oberlin has a reputation for a left-leaning and active student body; one undergrad observes, "They are less active politically than they would like to think, but still more active than most people elsewhere." Another adds, "Most students are very liberal, but the moderates and (few) Republicans have a fine time of it. Every student has different interests and isn't afraid to talk about them." Some here worry that "Oberlin's student body is becoming more and more mainstream each year."

FINANCIAL AID: 440-775-8142 • E-MAIL: COLLEGE.ADMISSIONS@OBERLIN.EDU • WEBSITE: WWW.OBERLIN.EDU

ADMISSIONS

Very important factors considered include: Academic GPA, class rank, rigor of secondary school record, standardized test scores. *Important factors considered include:* Application essay, audition, character/personal qualities, extracurricular activities, recommendation(s), talent/ability. *Other factors considered include:* Alumni/ae relation, first generation, interview, level of applicant's interest, racial/ethnic status, volunteer work, work experience. SAT or ACT required; ACT with Writing component required. TOEFL required of all international applicants. High school diploma is required, and GED is accepted. *Academic units recommended:* 4 English, 4 math, 3 science, 3 foreign language, 3 social studies.

The Inside Word

Oberlin's music conservatory is one of the most elite programs in the nation; aspiring music students should expect stiff competition for one of the 600 available slots. Other applicants won't have a much easier time of it; Oberlin is a highly selective institution that attracts a highly competitive applicant pool. Your personal statement could be the make-or-break factor here.

FINANCIAL AID

Students should submit: FAFSA, institution's noncustodial parent statement (if applicable), CSS/Financial Aid PROFILE, Federal Income Tax Return. Regular filing deadline is February 15. The Princeton Review suggests that all financial aid forms be submitted as soon as possible after January 1. *Need-based scholarships/grants offered:* Pell Grant, SEOG, state scholarships/grants, private scholarships, the school's own gift aid. *Loan aid offered:* FFEL Subsidized Stafford, FFEL Unsubsidized Stafford, FFEL PLUS, Federal Perkins Loan, college/university loans from institutional funds. Applicants will be notified of awards on or about April 1.

FROM THE ADMISSIONS OFFICE

"Oberlin College is an independent, coeducational, liberal arts college. It comprises two divisions, the College of Arts and Sciences, with roughly 2,200 students enrolled, and the Conservatory of Music, with about 600 students. Students in both divisions share one campus; they also share residence and dining halls as part of one academic community. Many students take courses in both divisions. Oberlin awards the Bachelor of Arts and the Bachelor of Music degrees; a 5-year program leads to both degrees. Selected master's degrees are offered in the conservatory. Oberlin is located 35 miles southwest of Cleveland. Founded in 1833, Oberlin College is highly selective and dedicated to recruiting students from diverse backgrounds. Oberlin was the first coeducational college in the United States, as well as a historic leader in educating African Americans. Oberlin's 440-acre campus provides outstanding facilities, modern scientific laboratories, a large computing center, a library unexcelled by other college libraries for the depth and range of its resources, and one of the top-five college- or university-based art museums in the country.

"Freshman applicants for Fall 2008 must take the new SAT (which includes a written essay), or the ACT with Writing component."

SELECTIVITY

Admissions Rating	97
# of applicants	6,686
% of applicants accepted	34
% of acceptees attending	32
# accepting a place on wait list	600
% admitted from wait list	6
# of early decision applicants	339
% accepted early decision	60

FRESHMAN PROFILE

Range SAT Critical Reading	650–750
Range SAT Math	620–710
Range ACT Composite	27–31
Minimum Paper TOEFL	600
Minimum Computer Based TOEFL	200
Average HS GPA	3.58
% graduated top 10% of class	68
% graduated top 25% of class	90
% graduated top 50% of class	97

DEADLINES

Early decision application deadline	11/15, 1/2
Early decision notification	12/20, 2/1
Regular application deadline	1/15
Regular notification	4/1
Nonfall registration?	no

APPLICANTS ALSO LOOK AT

AND OFTEN PREFER
Brown University, Stanford University, Swarthmore College, Wesleyan University, Yale University

AND SOMETIMES PREFER
Carleton College, Grinnell College, Macalester College, Northwestern University, Vassar College, Williams College

AND RARELY PREFER
Connecticut College

FINANCIAL FACTS

Financial Aid Rating	94
Annual tuition	$34,216
Room & Board	$8,720
Required fees	$210
% frosh rec. need-based scholarship or grant aid	45
% UG rec. need-based scholarship or grant aid	51
% frosh rec. need-based self-help aid	45
% UG rec. need-based self-help aid	48
% frosh rec. any financial aid	61
% UG rec. any financial aid	60

OCCIDENTAL COLLEGE

1600 CAMPUS ROAD, OFFICE OF ADMISSION, LOS ANGELES, CA 90041 • ADMISSIONS: 800-825-5262 • FAX: 323-341-4875

CAMPUS LIFE

Quality of Life Rating	87
Fire Safety Rating	60*
Type of school	private
Environment	metropolis

STUDENTS

Total undergrad enrollment	1,825
% male/female	44/56
% from out of state	53
% from public high school	60
% live on campus	70
% in (# of) fraternities	10 (4)
% in (# of) sororities	16 (4)
% African American	7
% Asian	15
% Caucasian	56
% Hispanic	15
% Native American	1
% international	3
# of countries represented	21

SURVEY SAYS . . .

Small classes
No one cheats
Students are friendly
Diverse student types on campus
Lots of beer drinking

ACADEMICS

Academic Rating	90
Calendar	semester
Student/faculty ratio	10:1
Profs interesting rating	82
Profs accessible rating	84
% profs teaching UG courses	100
% classes taught by TAs	0
Most common lab size	10–19 students
Most common reg class size	10–19 students

MOST POPULAR MAJORS

diplomacy and world affairs
economics
psychology

STUDENTS SAY

Academics

Located in sunny California, Occidental College has a "rising star" quality to it. Often in the "shadows" of other "heavyweight liberal arts colleges on the West Coast," Oxy is "stepping up its game" and this "striving to become something better embodies the ethos of Oxy." The professors at Oxy are "top quality" and "passionate" about what they teach and all seem to "care about their students." They don't exist to "publish or perish"; "They actually are at Oxy to teach—and not to teach so they can research." That said, Oxy is no slacker when it comes to research either. Students say it is "really easy" to get "independent study, internships, and grants" that would "not be offered anywhere else to undergraduates." At Oxy, there are "no slackers" and the "students are really intelligent and motivated." For students who need it, help is never far out of reach due to "incredible" services like the "Center for Academic Excellence, where student teachers are available for writing and study help." In recent years, the administration has undergone "a lot of changes," leaving some students feeling that "it is unable to help students due to overall bureaucracy." However, the restoration of "student government" after being "dissolved for about a year" has helped smooth out relations. One thing students agree on, however, is that "registration is awful."

Life

As one student quips, "Los Angeles, though the air is not spectacular, is a wonderful place to go to college." Students cite "great resources for academic pursuits," a "beach [that] is accessible practically all year," and "myriad events occurring" in the city. Bear in mind, however, that "a car is essential here" and "Everyone who doesn't have a car wishes they did and hangs out with people who do." Students with cars enjoy free parking on campus and the ability to be "in Chinatown, at Dodger Stadium, or in Hollywood" in less than a "15-minute drive." Other popular destinations include "Pasadena or Glendale where students go "to shop, eat, see movies, or just walk around." Neither is there a dearth of entertainment options on campus. Oxy students "have a great student service called Programming Board, which puts on tons of social events for the students which are really popular" including "a movie series every Wednesday, huge themed dances, debates, and poker tournaments." While most students are "fairly social," Oxy is "not what I would call a party school." Most of the parties "are all just off campus," and "Drinks are easy to obtain but also easy to refuse." Oxy's "smart and opinionated" students often forgo the party scene for "lively conversations about politics or topics from class" with their friends.

Student Body

Most students agree that "the one thing most everyone has in common" at Oxy is their "left-leaning political views." Republicans on campus "seem to somewhat not fit in" and "make it very known that they feel oppressed by faculty and other students." Everyone else seems to be treated "equally, regardless of ethnicity, sexual orientation, socioeconomic status, [or] religious affiliation." These self-described "Californian/Seattleite Ugg-wearing hipsters" are "very intellectually bright and interesting." Many are quite idealistic and "genuinely" want to "change the world." Although the students are very driven, "There is very little competition" and "very little cliquing." Most students on campus are "pretty laid-back and know how to have fun, but still work pretty hard."

FINANCIAL AID: 323-259-2548 • E-MAIL: ADMISSION@OXY.EDU • WEBSITE: WWW.OXY.EDU

ADMISSIONS

Very important factors considered include: Extracurricular activities, rigor of secondary school record, volunteer work, work experience. *Important factors considered include:* Application essay, character/personal qualities, class rank, recommendation(s), standardized test scores. *Other factors considered include:* Alumni/ae relation, geographical residence, interview, level of applicant's interest, racial/ethnic status, talent/ability. SAT or ACT required; SAT Subject Tests recommended, TOEFL required of all international applicants. High school diploma is required, and GED is accepted. *Academic units recommended:* 4 English, 4 math, 3 science (2 science labs), 3 foreign language, 2 social studies, 2 history, 2 academic electives.

The Inside Word

The Admissions Team at Occidental is adamant about not adhering to formulas. They rely heavily on essays and recommendations in their mission to create a talented and diverse incoming class. The college attracts some excellent students, so a demanding course load in high school is essential for the most competitive candidates. Successful applicants tend to be creative and academically motivated.

FINANCIAL AID

Students should submit: FAFSA, CSS/Financial Aid PROFILE, Noncustodial PROFILE, state aid form, Business/Farm Supplement. Regular filing deadline is February 1. The Princeton Review suggests that all financial aid forms be submitted as soon as possible after January 1. *Need-based scholarships/grants offered:* Pell Grant, SEOG, state scholarships/grants, private scholarships, the school's own gift aid. *Loan aid offered:* FFEL Subsidized Stafford, FFEL Unsubsidized Stafford, FFEL PLUS, Federal Perkins Loan, college/university loans from institutional funds. Applicants will be notified of awards on or about March 24. Federal Work-Study Program available. Institutional employment available. Off-campus job opportunities are good.

FROM THE ADMISSIONS OFFICE

"Here's what our students tell us:

"Tycho Bergquist '05: 'The professors have all been just amazing. Every person's needs are different, and they're all very willing to coordinate times to meet and discuss how you feel about a class and what you want to get out of it.'

"Molly Franz '05: 'I realize the caliber of discussion that occurs at Oxy is not easily matched. It's very uncommon. I've developed very strong relationships with many professors, and that's something I believe is unique to Oxy.'

"Zach Chinn '05: 'The program has been awesome. Whether you want to go to med school or grad school, it's a great experience. The professors really want you to succeed.'

"Stanley Burgos '06: "I've been working with postdoctoral researchers as an undergraduate. It's very rewarding. Oxy challenges me both inside and outside the classroom."

"Candace Ryan '05: 'Occidental opened my eyes to different beliefs, values, and ideas. The range of ideas and beliefs at Occidental is incredible. Discussions in class are much more interesting, because you consider things you might not have thought about before.'

"Sam Phang '06: 'Oxy's close-knit community and its size make me feel this is a place I can call home.'

"Devin Miller '06: 'Oxy instills curiosity and makes students want to go out and learn a subject on their own. I've gotten a broader sense of self and have been able to fulfill my learning goals.'

"Occidental requires all applicants (including international students) to take either the SAT or ACT with the new Writing component. SAT subject tests are recommended, but not required."

SELECTIVITY

Admissions Rating	94
# of applicants	5,309
% of applicants accepted	42
% of acceptees attending	21
# accepting a place on wait list	189
% admitted from wait list	13
# of early decision applicants	95
% accepted early decision	42

FRESHMAN PROFILE

Range SAT Critical Reading	590–690
Range SAT Math	600–690
Minimum Paper TOEFL	600
Minimum Computer Based TOEFL	250
% graduated top 10% of class	60
% graduated top 25% of class	86
% graduated top 50% of class	100

DEADLINES

Early decision application deadline	11/15
Early decision notification	12/15
Regular application deadline	1/10
Regular notification	4/1
Nonfall registration?	no

APPLICANTS ALSO LOOK AT

AND OFTEN PREFER
Pomona College, Stanford University, University of California—Berkeley, University of California—Los Angeles, University of Southern California,

AND SOMETIMES PREFER
Claremont McKenna College, Macalester College

FINANCIAL FACTS

Financial Aid Rating	96
Annual tuition	$34,400
Room & Board	$9,500
Books and supplies	$935
Required fees	$933
% frosh rec. need-based scholarship or grant aid	43
% UG rec. need-based scholarship or grant aid	53
% frosh rec. need-based self-help aid	40
% UG rec. need-based self-help aid	50
% frosh rec. any financial aid	75
% UG rec. any financial aid	78

OGLETHORPE UNIVERSITY

4484 PEACHTREE ROAD, NORTHEAST, ATLANTA, GA 30319 • ADMISSIONS: 404-364-8307 • FAX: 404-364-8491

STUDENTS SAY

Academics

How well students fit into the Oglethorpe approach to education depends on how enthusiastically they embrace the school's core curriculum, a set of nine interdisciplinary courses focusing on such themes as "Narratives of the Self" and "Human Nature and the Social Order." Nearly all student respondents to our survey love the core because it "allows students to learn about the thinkers that have shaped Western civilization, which reduces cultural illiteracy." Students appreciate the interdisciplinary approach; one writes, "Classes at Oglethorpe challenge us to think and introduce us to new concepts. Thanks to our core program, these concepts often build upon one another, so that I feel like my education is really coming together." What makes the core so effective are "the small class sizes and the availability of professors to easily voice concerns." As one student puts it, "The size [of the student body] allows students more opportunities to fine-tune their education by working with professors on a personal level. Instead of getting lost in the shuffle of huge classes and being just another name on a list of advisees, most students develop personal relationships with their advisors, professors, and staff of the school." Best of all, Oglethorpe "is set in a big city. Not only do you get an intimate education, but you also have endless resources in a city like Atlanta." Oglethorpe's professors, students agree, "are our greatest strength. It is hard to find a full-time professor who has not completed their doctorate degree or not been published. And you never find a professor on this campus that relies on an assistant to teach his or her classes. Every teacher takes pride in teaching their subject to every class."

Life

"Social life is pretty low-key" at Oglethorpe, due in equal measure to the small student body and the heavy workload for most majors. Greek parties "are generally open to all students, and on weekends that's where a lot of people end up for lack of anything else better to do, but there's no pressure to be involved in that scene." There's an active Theater Department that mounts frequent productions, but otherwise "Life here is sometimes boring, with little activity on campus." Fortunately, "With the city at your fingertips, there are a lot of things one can do, like shopping, coffee shops, museums, and concerts." Atlanta also has "lots of clubs, both your typical ones and the indie ones, and there are lots of other things to do (provided you have the money)." Oglethorpe is located well to the north of Atlanta's bustling downtown, meaning "The bothersome noises of traffic and the like don't reach the students' ears." The school isn't too secluded, though; it's "only 5 minutes from grocery stores, restaurants, movie theaters, malls, and pretty much everything you need." Undergraduates love the "gorgeous campus" that "looks like a castle." One student writes, "The neo-Gothic architecture of the buildings has more character than [that of] most collegiate buildings."

Student Body

Oglethorpe's core curriculum presupposes a value to learning beyond its immediate professional applications, so it should come as no surprise that "most students here are intelligent and want to learn. Their objective is often not 'career prep,' but more of becoming a learned person." They're the kind of kids "who were oddballs at their high schools. Of course, there are lots of different kinds of oddballs, so we have a strange blend of people that all match because they're all so different. While the typical student is smart and creative, there's lots of variety, from anime nerds to soccer-playing sorority girls." The school is home to "a lot of 'alternative people,' but also a large number of the typical everyday type. Also, there are a significant number of gay students who are quite outspoken." "The gender ratio is heavily skewed towards females, though this has been improving." Politically, there "are about as many liberals as conservatives."

FINANCIAL AID: 404-364-8356 • E-MAIL: ADMISSION@OGLETHORPE.EDU • WEBSITE: WWW.OGLETHORPE.EDU

ADMISSIONS

Very important factors considered include: Academic GPA, rigor of secondary school record, standardized test scores. *Important factors considered include:* Application essay, class rank, extracurricular activities, interview, level of applicant's interest, recommendation(s), volunteer work. *Other factors considered include:* Alumni/ae relation, character/personal qualities, first generation, talent/ability, work experience. SAT or ACT required; ACT with Writing component recommended. TOEFL required of all international applicants. High school diploma is required, and GED is accepted. *Academic units required:* 4 English, 3 math, 2 science, 3 social studies. *Academic units recommended:* 2 foreign language.

The Inside Word

With rising national interest in the South, it won't be long before the academic strength found at Oglethorpe attracts wider attention and more applicants. At present, it's much easier to gain admission here than at many universities of similar quality. Go to Atlanta for a campus interview—you'll leave impressed.

FINANCIAL AID

Students should submit: FAFSA, institution's own financial aid form, state aid form. The Princeton Review suggests that all financial aid forms be submitted as soon as possible after January 1. *Need-based scholarships/grants offered:* Pell Grant, SEOG, state scholarships/grants, private scholarships, the school's own gift aid, United Negro College Fund. *Loan aid offered:* Direct Subsidized Stafford, Direct Unsubsidized Stafford, Direct PLUS, FFEL Subsidized Stafford, FFEL Unsubsidized Stafford, FFEL PLUS, Federal Perkins Loan. Applicants will be notified of awards on a rolling basis beginning or about April 1. Federal Work-Study Program available. Institutional employment available. Off-campus job opportunities are excellent.

FROM THE ADMISSIONS OFFICE

"Promising students and outstanding teachers come together at Oglethorpe University in an acclaimed program of liberal arts and sciences. Here you'll find an active intellectual community on a beautiful English Gothic campus just 10 miles from the center of Atlanta, capital of the Southeast, site of the 1996 Summer Olympics, and home to 4 million people. If you want challenging academics, the opportunity to work closely with your professors, and the stimulation of a great metropolitan area, consider Oglethorpe, a national liberal arts college in a world-class city.

"Applicants for Fall 2008 are required to take the new SAT (or the ACT with the Writing section). Students may also submit scores from the old (prior to March 2005) SAT (or ACT), and we will use the student's best scores from either test. It is recommended that students submit scores from two SAT Subject Tests. "

SELECTIVITY

Admissions Rating	84
# of applicants	1,206
% of applicants accepted	80
% of acceptees attending	20

FRESHMAN PROFILE

Range SAT Critical Reading	520–630
Range SAT Math	500–600
Range SAT Writing	500–600
Range ACT Composite	22–27
Minimum Paper TOEFL	550
Minimum Computer Based TOEFL	200
Average HS GPA	3.6
% graduated top 10% of class	35
% graduated top 25% of class	60
% graduated top 50% of class	84

DEADLINES

Regular notification	rolling
Nonfall registration?	yes

FINANCIAL FACTS

Financial Aid Rating	76
Annual tuition	$23,310
Room & Board	$8,870
Books and supplies	$600
Required fees	$100
% frosh rec. need-based scholarship or grant aid	72
% UG rec. need-based scholarship or grant aid	60
% frosh rec. need-based self-help aid	62
% UG rec. need-based self-help aid	51
% frosh rec. any financial aid	95
% UG rec. any financial aid	95

OHIO NORTHERN UNIVERSITY

525 SOUTH MAIN STREET, ADA, OH 45810 • ADMISSIONS: 419-772-2260 • FAX: 419-772-2313

CAMPUS LIFE

Quality of Life Rating	76
Fire Safety Rating	60*
Type of school	private
Affiliation	Methodist
Environment	village

STUDENTS

Total undergrad enrollment	2,543
% male/female	53/47
% from out of state	14
% live on campus	53
% in (# of) fraternities	13 (7)
% in (# of) sororities	16 (4)
% African American	3
% Asian	1
% Caucasian	94
% Hispanic	1
% international	1
# of countries represented	15

SURVEY SAYS . . .

Small classes
Great library
Students are friendly
Campus feels safe
Low cost of living

ACADEMICS

Academic Rating	81
Calendar	quarter
Student/faculty ratio	13:1
Profs interesting rating	78
Profs accessible rating	83
% profs teaching UG courses	100
% classes taught by TAs	0
Most common reg class size	10–19 students

MOST POPULAR MAJORS

business, management, marketing, and related support services
education
engineering

STUDENTS SAY

Academics

"Many students are in some sort of science" at Ohio Northern University, "whether it is engineering, pharmacy, biology, chemistry, math, or physics," and most agree that "the science programs are amazing" here. The College of Pharmacy is the star of the show at ONU, students concur. One writes, "Within the state, I feel this school boasts the best-known and respected 6-year program. I feel very confident that upon leaving here I will know more information than will be necessary to do well on my boards and on rotations." Students in all science and tech majors report that "we have so many research opportunities, publications, and presentations as a result of being at this university." One undergrad elaborates, "I have been on trips with my professors and been given the option to present my research findings at major conferences. A bigger school would not have allowed me to accomplish so much." ONU's small-school setting "provides a challenging but nurturing environment" with "professors who are very student oriented and educated in their fields. This place is perfect for fostering growth and development in each of its students." Business administration is among ONU's other strong suits; the program provides "lots of chances for internships and practical experiences," students tell us.

Life

Ohio Northern is located in Ada, a town that "has more corn than people." One student asks, "Ever heard of Ada? Neither has anyone else. I interviewed students for scholarships, and they asked, 'So what do you do for fun?' and—no joke—I had to mention Wal-Mart. There is so little to do here that going to Wal-Mart is as exciting as a road trip." The town does have a modest offering of bars and restaurants. Fortunately, "The school does its very best to lay out an array of cool activities that keep students happy. For example, there are free athletic classes available in the evenings (yoga, Pilates, kickboxing), a small bowling alley on campus, movies shown regularly on campus, and numerous active extracurricular groups with which to associate." The Greek system "is responsible for much of the students' social life," with "parties to be found every Tuesday, Friday, and Saturday, if you look hard enough." Students also find creative ways to amuse themselves, "holding a Mud Volleyball tournament at the beginning of the year, and around Halloween, there are many haunted cornfields. In the winter, we go ice skating, and the popular Polar Bowl is a large football tournament in the snow." As at many small, remote schools, "A lot of people enjoy drinking because there is not much else to do. But there's not pressure that you have to drink." Students warn that there's not much time for fun here anyway, at least for those in demanding majors. "We are on the quarter system, and I almost never have any real relaxation time," explains one pharmacy major.

Student Body

"There are a lot of bookworms and a lot of partiers, and not much in between" at ONU, say students, reckoning about "a 60/40 split" between the two groups. High admissions standards means "The typical student is very smart," while the school's religious affiliation means there are "many ultraconservative Christians, with faith permeating many aspects of life, even organizations that have no apparent connection to religion." There are also those who feel that "Sometimes the religious kids can be a bit much for the rest of the student population." Diversity is not the school's strong suit; one undergrad explains, "Ohio Northern is trying its darndest to get a collection of different students to come to this university. I think I could count on my hands the number of African American students here, although they are welcomed with open arms and not treated differently. If anything, we're glad to see different people come because they are different." A majority of the students are noted as being "White, WASP, and Republican, and many are from small Ohio towns."

FINANCIAL AID: 419-772-2272 • E-MAIL: ADMISSIONS-UG@ONU.EDU • WEBSITE: WWW.ONU.EDU

ADMISSIONS

Very important factors considered include: Academic GPA, rigor of secondary school record, standardized test scores. *Important factors considered include:* Class rank, extracurricular activities, interview. *Other factors considered include:* Alumni/ae relation, application essay, character/personal qualities, first generation, level of applicant's interest, recommendation(s), talent/ability, volunteer work. SAT or ACT required; TOEFL required of all international applicants. High school diploma is required, and GED is accepted. *Academic units required:* 4 English, 2 math, 2 science (2 science labs), 2 social studies, 2 history, 4 academic electives. *Academic units recommended:* 4 English, 4 math, 3 science (2 science labs), 2 foreign language, 3 social studies, 2 history, 4 academic electives.

The Inside Word

Solid grades from high school are a pretty sure ticket for admission to Ohio Northern. Students who are above average academically are in good positions to take advantage of a very large number of no-need scholarships.

FINANCIAL AID

Students should submit: FAFSA, institution's own financial aid form. Regular filing deadline is June 1. The Princeton Review suggests that all financial aid forms be submitted as soon as possible after January 1. *Need-based scholarships/grants offered:* Pell Grant, SEOG, state scholarships/grants, private scholarships, the school's own gift aid, external scholarships. *Loan aid offered:* FFEL Subsidized Stafford, FFEL Unsubsidized Stafford, FFEL PLUS, Federal Perkins Loan, college/university loans from institutional funds, alternative loans, Federal Health Professions Loan. Applicants will be notified of awards on a rolling basis beginning or about February 15.

FROM THE ADMISSIONS OFFICE

"Ohio Northern's purpose is to help students develop into self-reliant, mature men and women capable of clear and logical thinking and sensitive to the higher values of truth, beauty, and goodness. ONU selects its student body from among those students possessing characteristics congruent with the institution's objectives. Generally, a student must be prepared to use the resources of the institution to achieve personal and educational goals.

"Students applying for admission for Fall 2008 are urged to take the new SAT (or the ACT with the Writing section), but we will allow students to submit scores from the old (prior to March 2005) SAT (or ACT) as well. The student's best composite scores will be used for scholarship purposes."

SELECTIVITY

Admissions Rating	85
# of applicants	3,190
% of applicants accepted	87
% of acceptees attending	27

FRESHMAN PROFILE

Range SAT Critical Reading	520–630
Range SAT Math	550–650
Range ACT Composite	23–29
Minimum Paper TOEFL	550
Minimum Computer Based TOEFL	213
Average HS GPA	3.63
% graduated top 10% of class	38
% graduated top 25% of class	66
% graduated top 50% of class	90

DEADLINES

Regular application deadline	8/15
Regular notification	rolling
Nonfall registration?	yes

APPLICANTS ALSO LOOK AT AND SOMETIMES PREFER

Bowling Green State University, Miami University, The Ohio State University—Columbus, University of Toledo, Wittenberg University

FINANCIAL FACTS

Financial Aid Rating	84
Annual tuition	$29,310
Room & Board	$7,470
Books and supplies	$1,800
Required fees	$210
% frosh rec. need-based scholarship or grant aid	86
% UG rec. need-based scholarship or grant aid	83
% frosh rec. need-based self-help aid	86
% UG rec. need-based self-help aid	83
% frosh rec. any financial aid	86
% UG rec. any financial aid	83

THE OHIO STATE UNIVERSITY—COLUMBUS

110 ENARSON HALL, 54 WEST TWELFTH AVENUE, COLUMBUS, OH 43210 • ADMISSIONS: 614-292-3980 • FAX: 614-292-4818

STUDENTS SAY

Academics

"In terms of resources, Ohio State University is a wonderful school," a place where you can access "just about any class you want, tons of knowledgeable professors, a huge library, and thousands of opportunities for research, study abroad, cultural events, etc." Undergraduates here appreciate that "the school is a huge research facility, which is a big plus because it means the education in the research areas is premium." One student points out, "The research opportunities mean that we can attract some of the best professors and students. This makes Ohio State a well-known institution in the job market worldwide. It also means that there's always someone around to help if you just can't seem to get something." Business studies are popular, as are engineering and the social sciences, but no matter what your interest, you're likely to find it here, as "OSU offers over 170 majors as well as the opportunity to create your own program of study. Academic diversity is a major strong point." Students tell us that "there are a lot of professors who are here just for research, and teaching is something that they have to do," but that "there are also teachers who love what they do and really connect with students." Course availability is also a problem; "Our scheduling system makes it difficult for non-honors students to get into every class they need in a given quarter," warns one undergrad. Students in the honors program have no such difficulties; they enjoy "priority scheduling" and "classes taught by professors, not TAs." One student concludes, "The Honors College is the way to go. Priority scheduling is a godsend."

Life

"With one of the largest schools in the country and the fifteenth-largest city in the country, you will find something to do every single day" at OSU, and "Whether that is studying or partying, you will have fun doing it." Favored activities change with the seasons: "Autumn quarter brings football Saturdays and is always pretty rowdy. Winter quarter is cold and fairly quiet. Come spring quarter the weather gets nice, and parties are happening everywhere." There are parties for anyone who wants one, but "There are also so many other alternatives to parties on campus. Every mall, theater, store, etc., is within walking distance or on a bus route with easy access." Because "OSU is kind of like a miniature city where most of the population is in the same walk of life, and in some cases, it's actually bigger than the towns its students are from," the school can draw big-name entertainment "like Chris Rock, Ludacris, and 311, as well as movie sneak previews, carnivals, and lectures, and the student activities board budget is big enough so that these events are often free." The school's relationship with hometown Columbus yields "discounted tickets to soccer games, symphony concerts, and other fun activities. And in Columbus there is always something going on. Hockey games, arena football, concerts, etc." In short, "You basically are nuts if you are bored on this campus."

Student Body

"You'd be hard pressed to find a student body with more school spirit and a genuine desire to get involved, including community-service activities," than the students at OSU, at least by their own reckoning. These "friendly, down-to-earth, and focused" undergrads "have typically loved the Buckeyes since they were young," and "evidence of Buckeye pride is apparent everywhere on campus." That's the common link here; otherwise, "There is no typical student at OSU. There are lots of African Americans, Asians, Indians, etc. We're probably about 50/50 Democrat/Republican. There are a lot of gay/lesbian people, also. Everyone seems pretty open to people of different ethnicities/lifestyles." As at most large schools, "The population is divided along program lines. For example, all of the art and art ed students hang out together, while the business students are all going to business dinners constantly, and the engineering students are the ones partying together every Thursday night."

THE OHIO STATE UNIVERSITY—COLUMBUS

FINANCIAL AID: 614-292-0300 • E-MAIL: ASKABUCKEYE@OSU.EDU (FRESHMEN AND TRANSFER)• WEBSITE: WWW.OSU.EDU

ADMISSIONS

Very important factors considered include: Academic GPA, class rank, rigor of secondary school record, standardized test scores. *Important factors considered include:* Application essay, extracurricular activities, first generation, talent/ability, volunteer work, work experience. *Other factors considered include:* Character/personal qualities, geographical residence, racial/ethnic status, recommendation(s), state residency. SAT or ACT required; ACT with Writing component required. TOEFL required of all international applicants. High school diploma is required, and GED is accepted. *Academic units required:* 4 English, 3 math, 2 science (2 science labs), 2 foreign language, 2 social studies, 1 academic elective, 1 visual and performing arts. *Academic units recommended:* 4 English, 4 math, 4 science (3 science labs), 3 foreign language, 3 social studies, 1 academic elective, 1 visual and performing arts.

The Inside Word

Although Admissions Officers consider extracurriculars and other personal characteristics of candidates, there is a heavy emphasis on numbers—grades, rank, and test scores. Admissions standards have become increasingly competitive in recent years, but OSU is still worth a shot for the average student. The university's great reputation and affordable cost make it a good choice for anyone looking at large schools.

FINANCIAL AID

Students should submit: FAFSA. The Princeton Review suggests that all financial aid forms be submitted as soon as possible after January 1. *Need-based scholarships/grants offered:* Pell Grant, SEOG, state scholarships/grants, private scholarships, the school's own gift aid. *Loan aid offered:* Direct Subsidized Stafford, Direct Unsubsidized Stafford, Direct PLUS, Federal Perkins Loan, Federal Nursing Loan, college/university loans from institutional funds. Applicants will be notified of awards on or about April 5.

FROM THE ADMISSIONS OFFICE

"Few universities have changed as much as the Ohio State University has in the last decade. Ohio State has undergone a physical transformation, attracted undergraduates of exceptional scholarly talent, and seen its reputation for academic excellence thrive.

"Despite remarkable rankings in most academic programs, the true strength of Ohio State's academic experience is the dialogue between faculty and students that is rarely found among large, research universities.

"With each incoming class, a new academic standard is set as the quality of its students reaches new heights. One of the nation's richest First-Year Experience programs helps students transition from talented freshmen to distinguished graduates.

"Ohio State is undergoing unprecedented physical change. The Fisher College of Business complex has been joined by a unique World Media and Culture Center, the $30 million Knowlton School of Architecture, two state-of-the-art recreation centers, and even a university-dedicated highway exit. The university's commitment to both tradition and technology make Ohio State an historic and modern atmosphere in which to learn.

"Although Ohio State is a university of change, it still has phenomenal faculty, incredible programs, competitive tuition, supportive environments, and distinctive tradition. Students never lack for something to do or fail to find a unique place. Whether participating in one of 650 student organizations, attending a lecture by a renowned author or politician, or simply sitting on the Oval, students find their niche at Ohio State, and become part of its living history.

"Students applying for admission are required to submit one writing score (SAT or the ACT with Writing) in order for their applications to be considered complete. The Writing score will not be used to determine admissibility for students entering in 2008. It will be used for research purposes only. "

SELECTIVITY

Admissions Rating	86
# of applicants	18,286
% of applicants accepted	68
% of acceptees attending	51
# accepting a place on wait list	149
% admitted from wait list	2

FRESHMAN PROFILE

Range SAT Critical Reading	530–640
Range SAT Math	560–670
Range SAT Writing	520–630
Range ACT Composite	24–29
Minimum Paper TOEFL	527
Minimum Computer Based TOEFL	197
% graduated top 10% of class	43
% graduated top 25% of class	80
% graduated top 50% of class	98

DEADLINES

Regular application deadline	2/1
Regular notification	rolling
Nonfall registration?	yes

APPLICANTS ALSO LOOK AT AND OFTEN PREFER

Bowling Green State University, Case Western Reserve University, Miami University, Ohio University—Athens, Purdue University—West Lafayette, University of Cincinnati

FINANCIAL FACTS

Financial Aid Rating	72
Annual in-state tuition	$8,298
Annual out-of-state tuition	$20,193
Room & Board	$6,720
Books and supplies	$1,080
Required fees	$261
% frosh rec. need-based scholarship or grant aid	52
% UG rec. need-based scholarship or grant aid	46
% frosh rec. need-based self-help aid	46
% UG rec. need-based self-help aid	48
% frosh rec. any financial aid	54
% UG rec. any financial aid	49

OHIO UNIVERSITY—ATHENS

120 CHUBB HALL, ATHENS, OH 45701 • ADMISSIONS: 740-593-4100 • FAX: 740-593-0560

CAMPUS LIFE

Quality of Life Rating	85
Fire Safety Rating	80
Type of school	public
Environment	rural

STUDENTS

Total undergrad enrollment	16,872
% male/female	48/52
% from out of state	13
% from public high school	92
% live on campus	45
% in (# of) fraternities	11 (19)
% in (# of) sororities	13 (13)
% African American	4
% Asian	1
% Caucasian	92
% Hispanic	2
% international	1
# of countries represented	111

SURVEY SAYS . . .

Great computer facilities
Great library
Athletic facilities are great
Students are friendly
Students are happy
Lots of beer drinking
Hard liquor is popular
(Almost) everyone smokes

ACADEMICS

Academic Rating	72
Calendar	quarter
Student/faculty ratio	19:1
Profs interesting rating	75
Profs accessible rating	77
% profs teaching	
UG courses	100
% classes taught by TAs	14
Most common	
lab size	10–19 students
Most common	
reg class size	10–19 students

MOST POPULAR MAJORS

clinical psychology
journalism
kinesiology and exercise science

STUDENTS SAY

Academics

Ohio University caters to the career-minded Ohioan looking for the greatest "bang for the buck" in education. Undergraduates "always look forward to" attending their "small classes" that feature "approachable" professors who "encourage students to attend their office hours." One student notes that "Ohio University makes it very difficult for someone to fail." Another explains, "Ohio University has only one 400-person classroom on campus, and although that can be a very scary experience to take a class there, they are always excellent, and the professors are the best in their fields. I had three classes in this room through my 3 years here at OU, and they rank up there as three of my favorite overall." On the other hand, the university's administration "has been under tough review lately" and "definitely needs more student input". However, students recently formed a group "to combat the lack of communication with the administration" and it is hoped this will help out. Also, Ohio University runs on a quarterly academic schedule, which "makes things move quickly." One student explains, "If I don't keep up with my readings for class, pretty soon I'm in a deep hole. It's not long after you begin a class that you are taking midterms again. Then a few more weeks and it's finals time! It's definitely stressful." Whereas another takes a brighter view: "If you don't like a class, it only lasts for 10 weeks."

Life

"Ohio University is the perfect mixture of business with pleasure," students tell us, adding, "We get the work done on the weekdays so we can party hard on the weekends." Many agree that OU has "an amazing party scene" with "a laid-back social life." Much of OU social life revolves around the downtown bar scene where students can kick back and enjoy the, "rock, punk, and folk bands that flourish in the many bars and cafes." That said, students appreciate the balance OU provides—"The people at this school teach you about awareness, confidence, and how to throw a really good party." Homecoming and Halloween events are both well-loved celebrations. For those who take soda over scotch, exaggerations like the following make their point: "There are 1,892,753,098 student organizations so it's easy to get involved and meet people," says a student. "I am personally very physically active on campus through intramurals and our rec facility . . . [and] the programming council does a lot to put on events during the weekends." Students also love their campus, which "is beautiful year-round." Their recreation center, called the Ping, features "a cardio room that overlooks the foothills of the Appalachian Mountains and makes workouts fun." Even freshman dorms are "great, almost like apartments." Students' wish lists include hopes for "a better sports program."

Student Body

The university's "very laid-back and friendly" undergrads "can be found wearing some sort of OU apparel (t-shirts don't cost much here!) and sweatpants, going to meetings because they are so involved in everything, and relaxing with friends when all is said and done." "We have a very casual atmosphere," says one student. But this doesn't keep "quite a few students" from "dressing up for class, so don't worry about looking overdressed." The typical student is described as "fun, socially intelligent, high-achieving, and involved." While there is "a majority of White, middle- to upper-class students," "There are many international students" and "Minority student admissions are increasing." In addition, there are groups that "are always open for anyone to join whether you are from a similar background or not" and "events that celebrate people of different sexual orientations, ethnic backgrounds, religious beliefs, and so on." "I think almost anybody can find their place here at OU," reports one student. Ultimately, there are "many different groups of people here—musicians, athletes, hippies, frat boys, quiet people—but we all get along."

FINANCIAL AID: 740-593-4141 • E-MAIL: ADMISSIONS.FRESHMEN@OHIOU.EDU • WEBSITE: WWW.OHIOU.EDU

ADMISSIONS

Very important factors considered include: Academic GPA, rigor of secondary school record. *Important factors considered include:* Class rank, standardized test scores. *Other factors considered include:* Alumni/ae relation, application essay, character/personal qualities, extracurricular activities, racial/ethnic status, recommendation(s), talent/ability, volunteer work, work experience. SAT or ACT required; ACT with Writing component recommended. High school diploma is required, and GED is accepted. *Academic units required:* 4 English, 3 math, 3 science, 2 foreign language, 3 social studies, 1 visual or performing arts.

The Inside Word

If you're looking to attend the first college in the Northwest Territory (or, in modern parlance, what became Ohio when the Indiana Territory was created) you'd best be doing your homework. Nearly half of all current admitted freshmen were in the top 15 percent of their high school class with an average GPA of 3.4. A word to the wise—OU admissions pay particular attention to a student's junior year performance, a traditional time of academic upheaval, so stay focused and you'll do just fine.

FINANCIAL AID

Students should submit: FAFSA. Regular filing deadline is March 15. The Princeton Review suggests that all financial aid forms be submitted as soon as possible after January 1. *Need-based scholarships/grants offered:* Pell Grant, SEOG, state scholarships/grants, private scholarships, the school's own gift aid. *Loan aid offered:* Direct Subsidized Stafford, Direct Unsubsidized Stafford, Direct PLUS, Federal Perkins Loan; institutional short-term loans are repaid in 30—60 days. Applicants will be notified of awards on or about April 1.

FROM THE ADMISSIONS OFFICE

"Pursuing your academic studies at Ohio University means immersing yourself in the quintessential college experience. The tree-lined streets and rolling hills of Athens provide a picture-perfect backdrop for this historic campus beloved for its brick paths and stately Georgian architecture. Live and learn in this classic, residential college town and you join a tight-knit academic community of faculty and student scholars who are welcoming, intellectually challenging, and civic-minded.

"Ohio is highly regarded for the strength of it undergraduate and graduate programs. As the oldest college in Ohio and the entire Northwest Territory, Ohio University offers an irrefutable history of academic excellence and prominence. Our students' success in winning many of the nation's most prestigious and competitive academic awards is at a record high. Our total number of Fulbright winners, for example, currently ranks us first in the state for the fourth straight year and ties us with the likes of Boston College, Princeton, and UCLA. The Honors Tutorial College is the only degree-granting college of its kind in the country and mirrors the same one-on-one tutorial system practiced for centuries Cambridge and Oxford. Close faculty mentoring and personal involvement is a university value that benefits all Ohio students.

"Visit our campus and you'll discover why students' first and lasting impression of Ohio University is 'It's what I always dreamed college would be.'"

SELECTIVITY

Admissions Rating	75
# of applicants	12,684
% of applicants accepted	85
% of acceptees attending	38

FRESHMAN PROFILE

Range SAT Critical Reading	490–600
Range SAT Math	490–600
Range SAT Writing	480–590
Range ACT Composite	21–26
Average HS GPA	3.35
% graduated top 10% of class	15
% graduated top 25% of class	42
% graduated top 50% of class	81

DEADLINES

Regular application deadline	2/1
Regular notification	rolling
Nonfall registration?	yes

APPLICANTS ALSO LOOK AT
AND OFTEN PREFER

Bowling Green State University, Kent State University—Kent Campus, Miami University, The Ohio State University—Columbus

AND SOMETIMES PREFER

Oberlin College, University of Cincinnati, University of Dayton, Wittenberg University

FINANCIAL FACTS

Financial Aid Rating	64
Annual in-state tuition	$8,316
Annual out-of-state tuition	$16,308
Room & Board	$7,839
Books and supplies	$870
% frosh rec. need-based scholarship or grant aid	20
% UG rec. need-based scholarship or grant aid	21
% frosh rec. need-based self-help aid	36
% UG rec. need-based self-help aid	38
% frosh rec. any financial aid	50
% UG rec. any financial aid	47

Ohio Wesleyan University

ADMISSIONS OFFICE, 61 SOUTH SANDUSKY STREET, DELAWARE, OH 43015 • ADMISSIONS: 740-368-3020 • FAX: 740-368-3314

CAMPUS LIFE

Quality of Life Rating	**72**
Fire Safety Rating	**60***
Type of school	private
Affiliation	Methodist
Environment	town

STUDENTS

Total undergrad enrollment	1,923
% male/female	48/52
% from out of state	42
% from public high school	72
% live on campus	84
% in (# of) fraternities	36 (11)
% in (# of) sororities	24 (6)
% African American	5
% Asian	2
% Caucasian	82
% Hispanic	1
% international	8
# of countries represented	37

SURVEY SAYS . . .
Small classes
Lab facilities are great
Great library
Lots of beer drinking

ACADEMICS

Academic Rating	**86**
Calendar	semester
Student/faculty ratio	13:1
Profs interesting rating	87
Profs accessible rating	86
% profs teaching UG courses	100
% classes taught by TAs	0
Most common lab size	10–19 students
Most common reg class size	10–19 students

MOST POPULAR MAJORS
economics/business management
psychology
zoology/animal biology

STUDENTS SAY

Academics

Students at Ohio Wesleyan University describe it as "a combination of all the things one might look for in a school. It isn't too small, but it isn't too big; it isn't too rural, but it also isn't too urban; it has a big focus on academics, but there is plenty of partying to be done, too. It seems to, and does, have the best of all worlds." An "excellent Science Department" is the star of the show here, with "professors who are amazing, very friendly and approachable, and always willing to help you and share their own knowledge, research, and insights." But the school also boasts a "reputable psychology program," strong Music and Foreign Language Departments, and "a great education program that sets you up for a job after 4 years." OWU undergrads warn that "classes are small, but the workload and intellectual participation required from students are rigorous. Making good grades here is really an achievement, and it won't happen without a lot of work." The environment at the school is "supportive but not coddling; students are expected to manage most of their own affairs. That said, professors and administrators are more than willing to provide whatever help they can." Dedicated professors will even spend free time "advising students on independent studies, even when they have no obligation to do so. They are interested in teaching and talking about what they know."

Life

OWU "is in a very small town, so don't expect packed dance clubs or huge theater productions." There are "two downtown bars that are popular hangout spots, and there are a few pretty good restaurants that are frequented by students," but students claim that this is about it for hometown Delaware. The small-town location makes life here "highly residential, with lots of activities centered [on] campus life." That life can include "a lot of drinking" for some, "But if you're not into it, there are other things you can do," including "different lectures and speakers to go to during the week," "the Strand, which is the university-owned movie theater in town," and "lots of shows, bands, and comedians." Those who find their way into the Small Living Units (SLU), nine "themed houses" based on specific areas of study or extracurricular interests, usually become deeply involved in their residential communities. One such student writes, "We at the House of Peace and Justice focus on promoting social justice activism on campus and educating students about world events." Columbus is less than a half-hour drive from the school, so "If you have a car, there is more to do than if you don't." But even for those who can't get off campus, "There is always some event happening."

Student Body

"The high percentage of international students" is one factor that causes OWU students to describe the school as "very diverse," although they also acknowledge the presence of "your usual preps with popped-up collars." As one student puts it, this "snobby, preppy image" is in fact "a stereotype that belies the camaraderie that really pervades the campus." The school's "Numerous student organizations facilitate cross-cultural discourse. OWU is also very GBLT friendly, with sexual identity courses and discussion forums a regular aspect of OWU's social and cultural scene." One student observes, "It is not unusual to see people walking around with mohawks, or to see people walking around in seersuckers." In other words, "There's a place here for everyone."

FINANCIAL AID: 740-368-3050 • E-MAIL: OWUADMIT@OWU.EDU • WEBSITE: WWW.OWU.EDU

ADMISSIONS

Very important factors considered include: Academic GPA, application essay, character/personal qualities, interview, recommendation(s), rigor of secondary school record. *Important factors considered include:* Class rank, extracurricular activities, standardized test scores, talent/ability. *Other factors considered include:* Alumni/ae relation, first generation, geographical residence, level of applicant's interest, racial/ethnic status, volunteer work, work experience. SAT or ACT required; TOEFL required of all international applicants. High school diploma is required, and GED is accepted. *Academic units required:* 4 English, 3 math, 3 science, 3 foreign language, 3 social studies. *Academic units recommended:* 4 math, 4 science, 4 foreign language, 4 social studies.

The Inside Word

Ohio Wesleyan takes a multitude of factors into consideration when examining applicants, and prospective students are expected to put a great deal of thought into every facet of the application. Notably, all candidates are automatically considered for merit-based scholarships.

FINANCIAL AID

Students should submit: FAFSA, institution's own financial aid form. Regular filing deadline is March 1. The Princeton Review suggests that all financial aid forms be submitted as soon as possible after January 1. *Need-based scholarships/grants offered:* Pell Grant, SEOG, state scholarships/grants, private scholarships, the school's own gift aid. *Loan aid offered:* FFEL Subsidized Stafford, FFEL Unsubsidized Stafford, FFEL PLUS, Federal Perkins Loan, college/university loans from institutional funds. Applicants will be notified of awards on a rolling basis beginning or about February 15. Federal Work-Study Program available. Institutional employment available. Off-campus job opportunities are excellent.

FROM THE ADMISSIONS OFFICE

"Balance and opportunity describe Ohio Wesleyan. Males make up 48 percent of the student body. There are 35 percent of all students who are members of Greek life. Eight percent of all students are international and 8 percent of them are U.S. minorities. Exceptional teaching and academics are hallmarks of an OWU education, and features such as the Woltemade Center for Economics, Business and Entrepreneurship, and the Arneson Institute for Practical Politics set us apart from other institutions of our kind. OWU houses a newly renovated $34-million science center and newly renovated fine art facilities. Our mission places a premium on community service-learning and interactive learning with more than 85 percent of students participating in community-service activities before graduation. Our annual Sagan National Colloquium is a semester-long program that brings leaders in academics, business, science, and the arts to campus for lectures, panel discussions, readings, exhibits, and performances related to a selected topic of importance to the community and the world. Ohio Wesleyan University is a competitive member of NCAA Division III and the North Coast Athletic Conference, with three National Championships in soccer in the last 6 years.

"Ohio Wesleyan is located in a small-town setting and is near Columbus, the state capital and the sixteenth-largest city in the United States.

"Applicants for Fall 2008 may submit the old SAT (taken before March 2005), the new SAT, or both. Best scores from either test will be considered in the application review. Additionally, students may submit the ACT in lieu of the SAT."

SELECTIVITY

Admissions Rating	88
# of applicants	3,579
% of applicants accepted	63
% of acceptees attending	25
# accepting a place on wait list	26
% admitted from wait list	38
# of early decision applicants	55
% accepted early decision	58

FRESHMAN PROFILE

Range SAT Critical Reading	540–660
Range SAT Math	540–660
Range ACT Composite	24–28
Minimum Paper TOEFL	550
Minimum Computer Based TOEFL	213
Average HS GPA	3.36
% graduated top 10% of class	36
% graduated top 25% of class	59
% graduated top 50% of class	84

DEADLINES

Early decision application deadline	12/1
Early decision notification	12/15
Regular notification	rolling
Nonfall registration?	yes

APPLICANTS ALSO LOOK AT
AND OFTEN PREFER
Bucknell University, Dickinson College, Gettysburg College, Trinity University
AND SOMETIMES PREFER
Allegheny College, Capital University, Case Western Reserve University, Centre College, Lake Forest College, Rhodes College, University of Delaware

FINANCIAL FACTS

Financial Aid Rating	81
Annual tuition	$29,870
Room & Board	$7,790
Books and supplies	$2,050
Required fees	$420
% frosh rec. need-based scholarship or grant aid	56
% UG rec. need-based scholarship or grant aid	54
% frosh rec. need-based self-help aid	45
% UG rec. need-based self-help aid	45
% frosh rec. any financial aid	99
% UG rec. any financial aid	98

PENNSYLVANIA STATE UNIVERSITY—UNIVERSITY PARK

201 SHIELDS BUILDING, BOX 3000, UNIVERSITY PARK, PA 16802-3000 • ADMISSIONS: 814-865-5471 • FAX: 814-863-7590

CAMPUS LIFE
Quality of Life Rating	84
Fire Safety Rating	88
Type of school	public
Environment	town

STUDENTS
Total undergrad enrollment	35,711
% male/female	55/45
% from out of state	23
% live on campus	38
% in (# of) fraternities	12 (54)
% in (# of) sororities	11 (31)
% African American	4
% Asian	6
% Caucasian	85
% Hispanic	3
% international	2
# of countries represented	121

SURVEY SAYS . . .
Career services are great
Everyone loves the Nittany Lions
Great library
Lots of beer drinking
Student publications are popular
Intramural sports are popular

ACADEMICS
Academic Rating	73
Calendar	semester
Student/faculty ratio	17:1
Profs interesting rating	66
Profs accessible rating	66
Most common lab size	20–29 students
Most common reg class size	20–29 students

STUDENTS SAY

Academics

At Penn State "You can do anything you want" academically because with "over 160 majors" to choose from, "There are unlimited opportunities" for every undergraduate. Such vast resources are typical of a sprawling public flagship university, but it's the personal touches that leave students "pretty impressed with how such a large school can run like a small one." For example, "Professors do a lot to facilitate personal interactions." They are "really easy to talk to both in and out of class, and they're always accessible." Unfortunately, it's not always a professor students end up with: "They do use a lot of teaching assistants, which can get frustrating." Still, professors are "thought-provoking" and "You can tell that a lot of them really do want to be teaching." If you can manage to get into it, the Schreyer Honors College's "rigorous" curriculum presents "tremendous opportunities." In addition to more challenging courses, it "offers incredible amounts of money for study abroad, internships, and faculty co-ops," and its students get perks like "priority registration for classes." Administratively, "Penn State is a huge machine . . . run with amazing efficiency." Credit is given to President Graham Spanier, who is praised for not only "holding office hours" and "responding personally to e-mails," but also for being "very involved in student life." Despite having "created Late-Night Penn State and the News Readership Program," he also finds time to be the "advisor to the magician's club" and "play the washboard in a bar downtown." Perhaps the greatest long-term benefit of a Penn State education is "the social networking." With an alumni association of over 159,000 members and growing, opportunities for success through networking are "well in your favor" at Penn State.

Life

At a university this size, "you can do anything and everything" in your free time. There are, however, a couple of common threads. First, "PSU football is a religion." During the fall, "Everyone goes to the football games and tailgates on Saturdays." Second, is the partying. "People party as hard on the weekends as they study during the week." "Popular choices" for freshmen and sophomores are "frat or apartment parties," while "For those over 21, Penn State's College Avenue has a great range of over 20 bars for students to choose from." However, "If someone is not a partier, there are plenty of activities and organizations" he or she can devote her time to. For example, "substance-free activities that occur during the weekends at the Student Union (such as movies, video game tournaments, concerts)" are alternatives for those that decline to imbibe. In terms of extracurriculars, the options are practically endless. According to several students, "with over 700 student clubs and organizations, there's something for everyone" at Penn State, offering "virtually limitless possibilities to carve out your own corner" and "help students get involved, build a resume, and network."

Student Body

"There is a bit of everything" on this huge campus in the center of the Keystone State. That's why some students find it so difficult to describe their peers succinctly. Rather than a "typical" student at Penn State, for some survey respondents it makes more sense to describe the school's "multitude of groups of 'atypical' students: frat boys . . . jocks, internationals, loners, skaters . . . 'jokers, smokers, midnight tokers' . . . city kids, rednecks, country bumpkins, and so on." In this way, "It's like a large high school, where everyone is in their own group." So "if you come to Penn State, don't worry about finding friends because there is someone up here for everyone." Yet even "Though there are a lot of differences, everyone wears blue and white on their sleeve." Ultimately, "All Penn State students . . . love this college."

PENNSYLVANIA STATE UNIVERSITY—UNIVERSITY PARK

FINANCIAL AID: 814-865-6301 • E-MAIL: ADMISSIONS@PSU.EDU • WEBSITE: WWW.PSU.EDU

ADMISSIONS

Very important factors considered include: Academic GPA, standardized test scores. *Important factors considered include:* Rigor of secondary school record. *Other factors considered include:* Alumni/ae relation, application essay, character/personal qualities, class rank, extracurricular activities, recommendation(s), talent/ability, volunteer work, work experience. SAT or ACT required; TOEFL required of all international applicants. High school diploma is required, and GED is accepted. *Academic units required:* 4 English, 3 math, 3 science, 2 foreign language, 3 social studies.

The Inside Word

Penn State evaluates applications on a rolling basis. As it is the first choice of a lot of students, the Admissions Office's recommended filing date for applications is about the same time as many other schools' early application deadlines—keep this in mind to avoid the cut-off date. In terms of what factors weigh heavily in terms of admissions decisions, Penn State is quite open, though high school GPA is paramount to securing your blue and white bid.

FINANCIAL AID

Students should submit: FAFSA. The Princeton Review suggests that all financial aid forms be submitted as soon as possible after January 1. *Need-based scholarships/grants offered:* Pell Grant, SEOG, state scholarships/grants, private scholarships, the school's own gift aid. *Loan aid offered:* FFEL Subsidized Stafford, FFEL Unsubsidized Stafford, FFEL PLUS, Federal Perkins Loan, college/university loans from institutional funds, private loans. Federal Work-Study Program available. Institutional employment available. Off-campus job opportunities are good.

FROM THE ADMISSIONS OFFICE

"Unique among large public universities, Penn State combines the over-35,000-student setting of its University Park campus with 20 academically and administratively integrated undergraduate locations—small-college settings ranging in size from 600 to 3,400 students. Each year, more than 60 percent of incoming freshmen begin their studies at these residential and commuter campuses, while nearly 40 percent begin at the University Park campus. The smaller locations focus on the needs of new students by offering the first 2 years of most Penn State baccalaureate degrees in settings that stress close interaction with faculty. Depending on the major selected, students may choose to complete their degree at University Park or one of the smaller locations. Your application to Penn State qualifies you for review for any of our campuses. Your two choices of location are reviewed in the order given. Entrance difficulty is based, in part, on the demand. Due to its popularity, the University Park campus is the most competitive for admission.

"Freshman applicants for Fall 2008 may submit the results from the current version of the SAT, the current ACT, the new version of the SAT, or the results of the new ACT with Writing test. The Writing portions of these tests will not necessarily be factored into admission decisions."

SELECTIVITY

Admissions Rating	89
# of applicants	34,813
% of applicants accepted	58
% of acceptees attending	40

FRESHMAN PROFILE

Range SAT Critical Reading	520–620
Range SAT Math	560–660
Minimum Paper TOEFL	550
Minimum Computer Based TOEFL	213
Average HS GPA	3.53
% graduated top 10% of class	37
% graduated top 25% of class	77
% graduated top 50% of class	98

DEADLINES

Regular notification	rolling
Nonfall registration?	yes

APPLICANTS ALSO LOOK AT
AND OFTEN PREFER
Carnegie Mellon University, Cornell University, Lehigh University, University of Maryland—College Park, University of Michigan—Ann Arbor

AND SOMETIMES PREFER
Emory University, Georgetown University, Harvard College, Johns Hopkins University, University of Virginia

FINANCIAL FACTS

Financial Aid Rating	65
Annual in-state tuition	$11,646
Annual out-of-state tuition	$22,194
Room & Board	$6,850
Books and supplies	$1,088
Required fees	$518
% frosh rec. need-based scholarship or grant aid	26
% UG rec. need-based scholarship or grant aid	29
% frosh rec. need-based self-help aid	41
% UG rec. need-based self-help aid	43
% frosh rec. any financial aid	77
% UG rec. any financial aid	73

PEPPERDINE UNIVERSITY

24255 PACIFIC COAST HIGHWAY, MALIBU, CA 90263-4392 • ADMISSIONS: 310-456-4861 • FAX: 310-506-4861

CAMPUS LIFE

Quality of Life Rating	96
Fire Safety Rating	60*
Type of school	private
Affiliation	Church of Christ
Environment	city

STUDENTS

Total undergrad enrollment	3,281
% male/female	43/57
% from out of state	50
% live on campus	62
% in (# of) fraternities	25 (5)
% in (# of) sororities	25 (7)
% African American	8
% Asian	10
% Caucasian	58
% Hispanic	11
% Native American	2
% international	6

SURVEY SAYS . . .

Students are friendly
Dorms are like palaces
Campus feels safe
Students are happy
Frats and sororities dominate social
scene

ACADEMICS

Academic Rating	90
Calendar	semester
Student/faculty ratio	12:1
Profs interesting rating	89
Profs accessible rating	90
% profs teaching UG courses	100
% classes taught by TAs	0
Most common lab size	fewer than 10 students
Most common reg class size	10–19 students

MOST POPULAR MAJORS

advertising
business administration/
management
psychology

STUDENTS SAY

Academics

"Combining great academic integrity and a sublime location with Christian morals and school spirit," Pepperdine University "integrates faith and learning and develops leaders with high goals and high regard for humanity," students at this Church of Christ school tell us. With its posh Malibu setting and its reputation for wealthy students, Pepp is regarded as "Club Med with church and professors" by a number of its students. The school differs from Club Med, though, in at least one significant way; everyone who comes here is expected to work, and work hard, throughout his or her 4-year tenure. Pepp's "challenging curriculum" includes required classes in the classics; one student reports, "No class has influenced my life as much as the Great Books classes. They consistently challenged my beliefs and made me intellectually sounder. It's a lot of work, but for an even bigger payoff." Undergrads love the study abroad program, which "the school has perfected. If you are on the fence about coming to Pepperdine, talk to any student who has been overseas." One student writes, "My two semesters in Buenos Aires was a great learning, as well as life, experience." Students here happily report that "an overwhelming majority of professors are wonderful in every way; they are not only amazingly smart but also good, nice people," and that "The school's administration is deeply concerned for the students, and their dedication is evident through their attitudes and willingness to help students."

Life

Pepperdine is located in Malibu, "a wonderful place to take a vacation, or to live if you're really rich." It's not such a great college setting, although it's not without its assets. One student writes, "Even though it's a pain to drive into LA all the time, it's nice to retreat back to Pepperdine. When visiting UCLA or USC, there is so much noise and so many people. It's refreshing to call serene Pepperdine home." Also, "It is fun seeing celebrities at Blockbuster or in their pajamas at the drugstore, and you couldn't ask for a more beautiful place to have a university," especially given the ocean view from many dorm rooms. Still, "There is nothing to do in Malibu except eat at expensive restaurants and go to the beach, and the town virtually shuts down at 10:00 P.M.," so "You have to head into LA to do anything that would be considered nightlife." On campus, "The quality of life is unmatched. There are spacious dorms with private bathrooms and working gas fireplaces. The sprinklers keep the grass green. People unfamiliar with campus often mistake it for a country club." Religious students happily report that "worship and religion opportunities are offered daily. Also, campus ministries provide a lot of opportunities for spiritual growth and fellowship with God, but the spiritual atmosphere isn't suffocating. It's there, but it isn't forced upon the students." Aesthetes add that "There's also a lot going on with fine arts, whether it's the museum or the theater."

Student Body

Conspicuous displays of wealth are not uncommon at Pepperdine, where "The latest must-have item is always in abundance and often precedes the national trend. There are plenty of Louis Vuitton purses, Ugg boots and Chanel sunglasses. Even the guys here wear Seven jeans." One undergrad explains, many of the students "come from wealthy families and arrive on campus in Mercedes and are wearing the latest clothes they picked up on Rodeo Drive," Rich or poor, most students here are "very much Republicans and not afraid to defend their political stances." Some here tell us that "the biggest dividing line on campus is probably religion. Pepperdine draws many conservative Christians, but also attracts those without faith, and often these students feel out of place [during] required convocations, where prayer and worship songs are included."

FINANCIAL AID: 310-506-4301 • E-MAIL: ADMISSION-SEAVER@PEPPERDINE.EDU • WEBSITE: WWW.PEPPERDINE.EDU

ADMISSIONS

Very important factors considered include: Academic GPA, application essay, character/personal qualities, extracurricular activities, recommendation(s), rigor of secondary school record, standardized test scores, talent/ability. *Important factors considered include:* Religious affiliation/commitment, volunteer work. *Other factors considered include:* Alumni/ae relation, first generation, racial/ethnic status, work experience. SAT or ACT required; ACT with Writing component required. TOEFL required of all international applicants. High school diploma is required, and GED is accepted. *Academic units recommended:* 4 English, 4 math, 4 science (3 science labs), 3 foreign language, 3 social studies, 3 history, 3 academic electives, 1 speech.

The Inside Word

A stunning physical location enables the Admissions Office to produce beautiful catalogs and viewbooks, which, when combined with the university's reputation for academic quality, help to attract a large applicant pool. In addition to solid grades and test scores, successful applicants typically have well-rounded extracurricular backgrounds. Involvement in school, church, and community is an overused cliché in the world of college admissions, but at Pepperdine it's definitely one of the ingredients in successful applications.

FINANCIAL AID

Students should submit: FAFSA, institution's own financial aid form. Regular filing deadline is February 15. The Princeton Review suggests that all financial aid forms be submitted as soon as possible after January 1. *Need-based scholarships/grants offered:* Pell Grant, SEOG, state scholarships/grants, private scholarships, the school's own gift aid. *Loan aid offered:* FFEL Subsidized Stafford, FFEL Unsubsidized Stafford, FFEL PLUS, Federal Perkins Loan, college/university loans from institutional funds. Applicants will be notified of awards on or about April 15.

FROM THE ADMISSIONS OFFICE

"As a selective university, Pepperdine seeks students who show promise of academic achievement at the collegiate level. However, we also seek students who are committed to serving the university community, as well as others with whom they come into contact. We look for community-service activities, volunteer efforts, and strong leadership qualities, as well as a demonstrated commitment to academic studies and an interest in the liberal arts.

"Seaver College of Pepperdine University requires freshman applicants to submit scores from either the Scholastic Aptitude Test (SAT Reasoning Test including the Writing portion) or the American College Test (ACT) (including the Writing test). The scores are evaluated in conjunction with the grade point average in specific courses completed."

SELECTIVITY

Admissions Rating	94
# of applicants	7,483
% of applicants accepted	28
% of acceptees attending	34

FRESHMAN PROFILE

Range SAT Critical Reading	560–670
Range SAT Math	570–680
Range ACT Composite	24–29
Minimum Paper TOEFL	550
Minimum Computer Based TOEFL	220
Average HS GPA	3.7

DEADLINES

Regular application deadline	1/15
Regular notification	4/1
Nonfall registration?	yes

APPLICANTS ALSO LOOK AT

AND OFTEN PREFER
Stanford University, University of California—Santa Barbara, University of California—Los Angeles, University of Pennsylvania, University of San Diego, University of Southern California

AND SOMETIMES PREFER
New York University, Santa Clara University, University of California—Berkeley, University of California—Irvine, University of California—San Diego, Vanderbilt University

AND RARELY PREFER
Biola University, Chapman University, Gonzaga University, Loyola Marymount University, Occidental College

FINANCIAL FACTS

Financial Aid Rating	87
Annual tuition	$32,620
Room & Board	$9,500
Book and supplies	$800
Required fees	$120
% frosh rec. need-based scholarship or grant aid	35
% UG rec. need-based scholarship or grant aid	45
% frosh rec. need-based self-help aid	36
% UG rec. need-based self-help aid	47

PITZER COLLEGE

1050 NORTH MILLS AVENUE, CLAREMONT, CA 91711-6101 • ADMISSIONS: 909-621-8129 • FAX: 909-621-8770

STUDENTS SAY

Academics

Pitzer College is the lovably quirky member of the Claremont College system, a repository of individualism and unconventional education in this otherwise traditional consortium. One satisfied undergrad notes, "No one tells you what to do or how much to read; everyone just does it because they want to, because they enjoy the material, and because they want to learn." Those who adapt to the system love how "It is very easy to design your own course work, curriculum, and major. You have to take the initiative to control your education here, and that is one of the aspects of Pitzer that truly enables students to grow and mature as individuals." You won't be going it totally alone, though. Pitzer's professors "make it a point to be available for students by keeping regular office hours, making appointments outside of those hours if necessary [and] inviting students to their homes for end-of-the-semester gatherings." This inclusive spirit extends to the school's administration as well; undergrads are "involved with decisions made by the Board of Trustees! The President invites students to sit on committees to make important decisions like facilitating the college's master plan, building new dorms, redesigning the dining halls, or reviewing professors." One undergrad sums up, "Pitzer is about constantly questioning the status quo and the mainstream, constantly thinking about better alternatives or creative solutions, and constantly reevaluating the way you see yourself, your community, and the world around you."

Life

Between the Five C's (i.e., the Claremont College Consortium) and Los Angeles, Pitzer students enjoy a wealth of entertainment and enrichment options. Partiers report that "you can count on a major party on one of the campuses every night except Sunday. Nights generally start with friends just hanging out or 'pregaming' in dorms and then heading out to one of the on campus parties. Since there is no frat scene, the parties are open to all students. Room parties are also popular." Those looking for something a little more intellectually stimulating "watch movies, take in a guest lecture, hang at the coffee shop, or sit around and play board games." Los Angeles is a popular destination "for music and sporting events, and the LA beaches (Laguna Beach is closest) are only 45 minutes away. They're popular for surfing and sunbathing all year long." Students generally don't hang around the surrounding community of Claremont, "a cute town, but one that's not there to quench your rebellion, so you can't rely on it for dancing or partying. If you'd like to look at antiques or shop for the newest herbal teas, Claremont Village is the place to be." Students caution that "Our dorms are getting old and look even older than they really are. But they're comfortable, fairly spacious, and economical for the school."

Student Body

The typical Pitzer undergrad tends to be "passionate, creative, dynamic, and socially involved. Even the so-called 'jock' subgroup volunteers to mentor young people in the surrounding area and are capable of passionately debating some issue of importance." Almost everyone here "is aware of what's going on in the world and in politics, and is likely to be left-wing politically." Pitzer has long had the reputation of a "hippie" school, and while "There are still remnants of hippies around—walking around with no shoes, no shaving (for guys or girls), caring about the environment—these days there are more preppy people wearing Abercrombie and sipping chai tea." No matter what demographic they fit, "Pitzer students tend to be really laid-back (not judgmental or snobby). You don't have to spend ridiculous amounts of money buying 'fashionable' clothing if you don't want to, because stuff like that doesn't impress people here. It's nice to leave all the horrible things about high school in high school and just relax for a few years."

FINANCIAL AID: 909-621-8208 • E-MAIL: ADMISSION@PITZER.EDU • WEBSITE: WWW.PITZER.EDU

ADMISSIONS

Very important factors considered include: Academic GPA, application essay, character/personal qualities, class rank, extracurricular activities, recommendation(s), rigor of secondary school record, talent/ability. *Important factors considered include:* Alumni/ae relation, first generation, geographical residence, interview, level of applicant's interest, racial/ethnic status, volunteer work, work experience. *Other factors considered include:* Standardized test scores, state residency. ACT with Writing component recommended. TOEFL required of all international applicants. High school diploma is required, and GED is accepted. *Academic units required:* 4 English, 3 math, 3 science (3 science labs), 3 foreign language, 3 social studies.

The Inside Word

This is a place where applicants can feel confident in letting their thoughts flow freely on admissions essays. Not only does the committee read them (a circumstance more rare in college admissions than one is led to believe) but also they've set up the process to emphasize them! Thus, what you have to say for yourself will go much further than numbers in determining your suitability for Pitzer. Paying greater attention to essays also helps Pitzer create a dynamic and engaging freshman class each year.

FINANCIAL AID

Students should submit: FAFSA, CSS/Financial Aid PROFILE, state aid form, Noncustodial PROFILE, Business/Farm Supplement. Regular filing deadline is February 1. The Princeton Review suggests that all financial aid forms be submitted as soon as possible after January 1. *Need-based scholarships/grants offered:* Pell Grant, SEOG, Academic Competitiveness Grant, National SMART Grant, state scholarships/grants, private scholarships, the school's own gift aid. *Loan aid offered:* FFEL Subsidized Stafford, FFEL Unsubsidized Stafford, FFEL PLUS, Federal Perkins Loan, college/university loans from institutional funds. Applicants will be notified of awards on or about April 1. Federal Work-Study Program available. Institutional employment available. Off-campus job opportunities are fair.

FROM THE ADMISSIONS OFFICE

"Pitzer is about opportunities. It's about possibilities. The students who come here are looking for something different from the usual 'take two courses from column A, two courses from column B, and two courses from column C.' That kind of arbitrary selection doesn't make a satisfying education at Pitzer. So we look for students who want to have an impact on their own education, who want the chief responsibility—with help from their faculty advisors—in designing their own futures.

"Pitzer's admission policy uses a test-optional policy. Students in the top 10 percent of their class or those who have an unweighted academic GPA of 3.5 or higher are not required to submit test scores. Others are allowed to choose from a variety of choices, including standardized tests (i.e., the new SAT and ACT with the Writing component).

SELECTIVITY

Admissions Rating	**93**
# of applicants	3,437
% of applicants accepted	37
% of acceptees attending	18
# accepting a place on wait list	19

FRESHMAN PROFILE

Range SAT Critical Reading	570–680
Range SAT Math	560–650
Minimum Paper TOEFL	587
Minimum Computer Based TOEFL	240
Average HS GPA	3.65
% graduated top 10% of class	38
% graduated top 25% of class	73
% graduated top 50% of class	96

DEADLINES

Early decision application deadline	11/15
Early decision notification	1/1
Regular application deadline	1/1
Regular notification	4/1
Nonfall registration?	no

APPLICANTS ALSO LOOK AT

AND OFTEN PREFER

Claremont McKenna College, Occidental College, Pomona College, Scripps College, University of California—Berkeley, University of California—Los Angeles, University of Southern California

AND SOMETIMES PREFER

Boston University, Colorado College, Lewis & Clark College, New York University, Whitman College

FINANCIAL FACTS

Financial Aid Rating	**96**
Annual tuition	$31,000
Room & Board	$9,670
Books and supplies	$900
Required fees	$3,038
% frosh rec. need-based scholarship or grant aid	34
% UG rec. need-based scholarship or grant aid	36
% frosh rec. need-based self-help aid	34
% UG rec. need-based self-help aid	35
% frosh rec. any financial aid	48
% UG rec. any financial aid	46

POMONA COLLEGE

333 NORTH COLLEGE WAY, CLAREMONT, CA 91711-6312 • ADMISSIONS: 909-621-8134 • FAX: 909-621-8952

STUDENTS SAY
Academics
In the words of its students, Pomona offers "the best atmosphere available to college students in the United States." This pint-size school has that "small college atmosphere"—but because it's part of a five-college consortium and allows cross registration at all the other colleges (Claremont McKenna, Harvey Mudd, Pitzer, Scripps), students benefit from the "perfect combination" of a "small liberal arts education with the resources of a larger university." Students happily report that professors "devote their time almost exclusively to undergraduate education" and get to know their students on a personal level—"even outside of office hours." "I routinely get a page or two of feedback on my essays," reports a content student. This kind of attention seems to be the rule, not the exception. One double major tells us, "I know eight deans and associate deans on a first-name basis, and my experience is by no means unusual for PC students." How tightly are administrators involved in students' lives? Pretty tightly: "Some even live in the dorms!" "When I hear about my friends' experiences at large universities, I sometimes wonder how they can live the way they do," writes one senior. While a friendly, discussion-based atmosphere is the norm in most classrooms, students assure us that the academics are rigorous; simply put, "Pomona makes you think way too hard." Keep in mind, however, that a lot of that hard thinking "is done in bathing suits in the courtyards." There may be some sweating before exams, but the college strives to maintain "a collaborative environment rather than a competitive one"—and this keeps students productive and content.

Life
"Life is very chill" at Pomona College, where the average student "wears flip-flops year-round" and boasts impressive Frisbee skills. Social bonding begins in the first year through the popular "sponsor groups"—10 to 18 freshmen "sponsored" by two sophomores who help the newbies adjust to college life—a program which, students believe, is "one of our great strengths." The party scene is "focused around the five colleges, which provide a sufficient social scene for students most nights of the week. The college funds parties on weekends, so organizations can easily sponsor parties and get a hold of kegs. For fun, people will socialize at such parties, hang out with friends, and sometimes go explore the bigger LA scene." But while "Alcohol is definitely a factor at Pomona . . . we have the option of substance-free housing, which is very popular, as well as substance-free events." "The mountains, the beach," and other "natural locales" are also equally accessible. No matter what students choose to do with their downtime, however, they all have their priorities straight; one typical student writes, "People here seem to almost always be very responsible in terms of work before play."

Student Body
"That Southern California vibe" is alive and well at Pomona College. Students proudly report that Pomona undergrads "are all really friendly, helpful, polite, and take a liking to making new friends." But not everyone thinks Pomona students are as chill as they claim to be. "Don't believe the BS about students being laid-back at Pomona," writes a senior. "They are definitely intense and competitive." Whether edgy or easygoing, almost every student at Pomona has one thing in common: politically liberal leanings. "Lots of liberal superheroes out to change the world" is how one sophomore describes her schoolmates. The widespread liberalism makes it tough for "those who differ in political views," because they "can sometimes be made to feel uncomfortable." Liberal, conservative, or somewhere in between, however, Pomona undergraduates rate themselves as among "the happiest students in the country"—mostly because they know how to strike a healthy balance between work and play. Among all the things they love about their school, undergrads agree that "the students are the single best thing about Pomona College."

FINANCIAL AID: 909-621-8205 • E-MAIL: ADMISSIONS@POMONA.EDU • WEBSITE: WWW.POMONA.EDU

ADMISSIONS

Very important factors considered include: Academic GPA, application essay, character/personal qualities, class rank, extracurricular activities, recommendation(s), rigor of secondary school record, standardized test scores, talent/ability. *Important factors considered include:* Interview. *Other factors considered include:* Alumni/ae relation, first generation, geographical residence, racial/ethnic status, volunteer work, work experience. SAT and SAT Subject Tests or ACT required; ACT with Writing component recommended. TOEFL required of all international applicants. High school diploma or equivalent is not required. *Academic units required:* 4 English, 3 math, 3 science (2 science labs), 2 foreign language, 2 social studies, 3 history. *Academic units recommended:* 4 math, 3 science (3 science labs), 3 foreign language, 2 social studies, 3 history.

The Inside Word

Even though it is tough to get admitted to Pomona, students will find the Admissions Staff to be accessible and engaging. An applicant pool full of such well-qualified students as those who typically apply, in combination with the college's small size, necessitates that candidates undergo as personal an admissions evaluation as possible. This is how solid matches are made and how Pomona does a commendable job of keeping an edge on the competition.

FINANCIAL AID

Students should submit: FAFSA, CSS/Financial Aid PROFILE, state aid form, Noncustodial PROFILE, Business/Farm Supplement, parent and student Federal Income Tax Returns. Regular filing deadline is February 1. The Princeton Review suggests that all financial aid forms be submitted as soon as possible after January 1. *Need-based scholarships/grants offered:* Pell Grant, SEOG, state scholarships/grants, the school's own gift aid. *Loan aid offered:* FFEL Subsidized Stafford, FFEL Unsubsidized Stafford, FFEL PLUS, Federal Perkins Loan, college/university loans from institutional funds. Applicants will be notified of awards on or about April 1. Federal Work-Study Program available. Institutional employment available. Off-campus job opportunities are good.

FROM THE ADMISSIONS OFFICE

"Perhaps the most important thing to know about Pomona College is that we are what we say we are. There is enormous integrity between the statements of mission and philosophy governing the college and the reality that students, faculty, and administrators experience. The balance in the curriculum is unusual. Sciences, social sciences, humanities, and the arts receive equal attention, support, and emphasis. Most importantly, the commitment to undergraduate education is absolute. Teaching awards remain the highest honor the trustees can bestow upon faculty. The typical method of instruction is the seminar and the average class size of 14 offers students the opportunity to become full partners in the learning process. Our location in the Los Angeles basin and in Claremont, with five other colleges, provides a remarkable community.

"Pomona College requires either the new SAT plus two SAT Subject Tests (in different fields) or the ACT. Scores from the old SAT (pre-March 2005) and the ACT are acceptable. For the old SAT, scores must be submitted with the results of three SAT Subject Tests, one of which must be the Writing test."

SELECTIVITY

Admissions Rating	**99**
# of applicants	5,440
% of applicants accepted	18
% of acceptees attending	39

FRESHMAN PROFILE

Range SAT Critical Reading	690–760
Range SAT Math	680–760
Range SAT Writing	680–760
Range ACT Composite	29–34
Minimum Paper TOEFL	600
Minimum Computer Based TOEFL	250
Average HS GPA	3.9
% graduated top 10% of class	87
% graduated top 25% of class	98
% graduated top 50% of class	100

DEADLINES

Early decision application deadline	11/15
Early decision notification	12/15
Regular application deadline	1/2
Regular notification	4/10
Nonfall registration?	no

APPLICANTS ALSO LOOK AT

AND OFTEN PREFER

Harvard College, Princeton University, Stanford University, University of California—Berkeley, Yale University

AND SOMETIMES PREFER

Claremont McKenna College, Dartmouth College, University of California—Los Angeles, Wesleyan University, Williams College

AND RARELY PREFER

Pitzer College, University of California—Davis

FINANCIAL FACTS

Financial Aid Rating	**99**
Annual tuition	$29,650
Room & Board	$10,851
Books and supplies	$850
Required fees	$273
% frosh rec. need-based scholarship or grant aid	54
% UG rec. need-based scholarship or grant aid	53
% frosh rec. need-based self-help aid	54
% UG rec. need-based self-help aid	53
% frosh rec. any financial aid	53
% UG rec. any financial aid	50

PRINCETON UNIVERSITY

PO Box 430, Admission Office, Princeton, NJ 08544-0430 • Admissions: 609-258-3060 • Fax: 609-258-6743

CAMPUS LIFE
Quality of Life Rating	99
Fire Safety Rating	60*
Type of school	private
Environment	village

STUDENTS
Total undergrad enrollment	4,775
% male/female	54/46
% from out of state	85
% from public high school	58
% live on campus	98
% African American	9
% Asian	14
% Caucasian	58
% Hispanic	7
% Native American	1
% international	9

SURVEY SAYS . . .
No one cheats
Lab facilities are great
Great computer facilities
Great library
School is well run
Campus feels safe
Students are happy

ACADEMICS
Academic Rating	99
Calendar	semester
Student/faculty ratio	5:1
Profs interesting rating	87
Profs accessible rating	95
Most common lab size	10–19 students
Most common reg class size	10–19 students

STUDENTS SAY

Academics

Princeton undergrads are adamant that their school is the "best place to get an undergraduate education," as it boasts "a combination of comprehensive resources, exceptional faculty, and brilliant students." Unlike many other prestigious universities, "The focus is all on undergraduate education" at Princeton, which has no business, law, or medical schools. There are fewer than 2,000 graduate students, enabling Princeton to ensure undergraduates access to "Nobel laureates who teach you and give you appointments" as well as "a wealth of academic, monetary, and social resources that students benefit from during and after their studies on campus." With fewer grads to elbow them out of the way, undergrads tell us that "the professors treat us like colleagues. They make themselves available and are intensely interested in the ideas of undergraduates." There is "an emphasis on independent undergraduate research, and funding is ample," as are resources at the library, which "has an amazing number and variety of books and other resources." The administration "truly runs like butter. From the application process to enrolling to being enrolled . . . If you made an error in one of these processes, to my experience, it's sometimes corrected for you!" No wonder one Princeton undergrad sums up the experience here this way: "They spoil you with amazing resources, world-class professors, beautiful architecture, great people, fun social life, and the inability of the school to say no to anything that you want."

Life

Eating clubs, a phenomenon unique to Princeton, "are the center of social life" at this "country-club-like school." One student explains how they work: "During daytime, the clubhouses serve as a place for upperclassmen to dine. (You don't have to join one because they are a bit costly.) Clubs range from those permanently soaked in beer and alcohol to some that are the most pretentious things one may lay an eye on, with gold-lined and embossed plates, cutlery and serviettes, and waiters to serve food to the students." All 10 eating clubs are located on Prospect Avenue, known to students simply as "the Street," and they function not only as dining halls but also as bars and party sites. Many hail the clubs "as great places to party because there is always somewhere to fit in. Because everyone parties on one street it is impossible to go out and not see someone you know." Others dismiss the clubs as "pretentious and pompous," especially the selective "bicker" clubs "in which current members choose new members," much as a Greek house screens pledges. Campus life tends to stay contained within the campus, as the surrounding town "closes up at 10:00 P.M.," but students are content with the situation. "Since everyone lives on campus and 'the Street' is so close, there is virtually no reason to need a car," explains one student. Another adds, "The best part is that even though Princeton is a small town, there is a train station on campus that takes you to Philly or New York in 45 minutes. Students use the 'dinky,' as the train's called, all the time."

Student Body

"Sure, Princeton's a bit East Coast preppy," undergrads here admit, "but everyone is unique and has her own style, which is totally welcomed and accepted. Princeton is a very kind, low-key, and charming place." It's also a place full of extremely accomplished people. One student writes, "I have friends who are Presidential Scholars, stayed with the UN Secretary General in Paris over fall break, produced hip-hop CDs, or represented different countries at the Olympics. Back home, I would have thought it amazing if I could meet just one of these people. If I stopped thinking of my friends as friends and thought of what they have accomplished, it's mind-boggling and a little humbling." Thanks to "a generous financial aid system," "Not everyone is a spoiled-rotten, BMW-driving, snooty rich kid. We have students from very diverse backgrounds."

FINANCIAL AID: 609-258-3330 • UAOFFICE@PRINCETON.EDU • WEBSITE: WWW.PRINCETON.EDU

ADMISSIONS

Very important factors considered include: Academic GPA, application essay, character/personal qualities, class rank, extracurricular activities, recommendation(s), rigor of secondary school record, standardized test scores, talent/ability. *Important factors considered include:* Volunteer work, work experience. *Other factors considered include:* Alumni/ae relation, geographical residence, interview, racial/ethnic status. SAT or ACT required; SAT Subject Tests required, ACT with Writing component required. TOEFL required of all international applicants. High school diploma is required, and GED is accepted. *Academic units recommended:* 4 English, 4 math, 3 science, 4 foreign language, 2 social studies, 2 history.

The Inside Word

Princeton is much more open about the admissions process than the rest of their Ivy compatriots. The Admissions Staff evaluates candidates' credentials using a 1–5 rating scale, common among highly selective colleges. Princeton's recommendation to interview should be considered a requirement, given the ultracompetitive nature of the applicant pool. In addition, three SAT Subject Tests are required.

FINANCIAL AID

Students should submit: FAFSA, institution's own financial aid form, College Noncustodial Form. The Princeton Review suggests that all financial aid forms be submitted as soon as possible after January 1. *Need-based scholarships/grants offered:* Pell Grant, SEOG, state scholarships/grants, private scholarships, the school's own gift aid. *Loan aid offered:* FFEL Subsidized Stafford, FFEL Unsubsidized Stafford, FFEL PLUS, Federal Perkins Loan, college/university loans from institutional funds. Applicants will be notified of awards on or about April 1.

FROM THE ADMISSIONS OFFICE

"Methods of instruction [at Princeton] vary widely, but common to all areas is a strong emphasis on individual responsibility and the free interchange of ideas. This is displayed most notably in the wide use of preceptorials and seminars, in the provision of independent study for all upperclass students and qualified underclass students, and in the availability of a series of special programs to meet a range of individual interests. The undergraduate college encourages the student to be an independent seeker of information and to assume responsibility for gaining both knowledge and judgment that will strengthen later contributions to society.

Princeton offers a distinctive financial aid program that provides grants, which do not have to be repaid, rather than loans. Princeton meets the full demonstrated financial need of all students—domestic and international—offered admission. More than half of Princeton's undergraduates receive financial aid.

"All applicants must submit results of either the new or old SAT, as well as SAT Subject Tests in three different subject areas. Students applying for the Class of 2010 and beyond will be required to submit results from the new version of the SAT."

SELECTIVITY

Admissions Rating	99
# of applicants	17,564
% of applicants accepted	10
% of acceptees attending	69
# accepting a place on wait list	789

FRESHMAN PROFILE

Range SAT Critical Reading	680–800
Range SAT Math	690–790
Range ACT Composite	30–34
Minimum Paper TOEFL	600
Minimum Computer Based TOEFL	250
Average HS GPA	3.85
% graduated top 10% of class	94
% graduated top 25% of class	99
% graduated top 50% of class	100

DEADLINES

Regular application deadline	1/1
Regular notification	4/10
Nonfall registration?	no

APPLICANTS ALSO LOOK AT AND SOMETIMES PREFER

Harvard College, Massachusetts Institute of Technology, Stanford University, Yale University

AND RARELY PREFER

Brown University, Columbia University, University of Pennsylvania

FINANCIAL FACTS

Financial Aid Rating	99
Annual tuition	$33,000
Room & Board	$10,980
% frosh rec. need-based scholarship or grant aid	55
% UG rec. need-based scholarship or grant aid	51
% frosh rec. need-based self-help aid	55
% UG rec. need-based self-help aid	51
% frosh rec. any financial aid	55
% UG rec. any financial aid	52

PROVIDENCE COLLEGE

RIVER AVENUE AND EATON STREET, PROVIDENCE, RI 02918 • ADMISSIONS: 401-865-2535 • FAX: 401-865-2826

STUDENTS SAY

Academics

Providence College, "a solid, respectable school with a reputation for having fun," appeals both to those who seek an "intense curriculum" ("especially the Development of Western Civilization course" that can be "stressful and time-consuming" though "It offers a great liberal arts background") and to those who simply want "challenging classes" in an atmosphere that balances "academic and personal growth with an incredibly fun social scene." The centerpiece of the PC experience is "the four-semester Civ program, through which the school truly molds the mind with classical training and gives us a basic understanding of how our civilization came to be where it is today." While some students dismiss the sequence as "unnecessary to our success in the future," others appreciate the forced immersion in philosophy, history, art, and theology, noting "I am happy that I am forced to take Civ because I would not have enrolled into any other courses that deal with the topics introduced in Civ." PC academics are "demanding," but "The school has great support systems for academics" "even outside the classroom stuff. The library has lots of different resources and there's always someone around to help." Undergrads also appreciate how "Being in a smaller school, there are more opportunities to excel in one's chosen field, whether it's getting an internship in a biology lab, writing for the newspaper, or starring in a theatrical production."

Life

Social life at Providence College "revolves around the off-campus bars and the off-campus houses. While there are other activities to participate in, the main focus is drinking." One undergrad reports, "Kids work hard from Sunday night to Thursday afternoon; then the weekend starts, and everyone hits the bars." However, it would be remiss to assume students here do nothing but study and drink—on the contrary, there is "a huge focus on extracurriculars," so much so that students always try to "balance and manage" their time between "schoolwork and a social life." Intercollegiate athletics "are extremely popular (all the hockey games are packed) and bring a great atmosphere to the campus," and intramurals "are lots of fun. There's even a noncompetitive division for students who only want to have fun." Community service "is also really popular. Students are always busy donating their time to different groups." Downtown Providence has a lot more to offer than bars; it has "a great music scene, theater, and lots of art venues. The restaurants are good too." Students can access the city easily as "public transportation is free for us. It's only 5 minutes to downtown, and the bus runs right through campus."

Student Body

Though Providence students "are not the most diverse group," "The administration is really emphasizing our need for people who are different" from what some perceive to be the usual "cookie-cutter" student. That said, students report, by and large, that they are "all comfortable with one another and it is easy to fit in," noting a "strong sense of community." The typical student here "is a White, upper-middle class kid who went to a private/Catholic prep school in New England" and "looks as though he stepped of the pages of the Hollister/Abercrombie catalogue." Students who do not fit the mold "seem to form their own peer groups for the most part. Interaction between atypical and typical students is not a problem." One student says that "Everyone is working together to try to come up with ways to make our student population more diverse, both ethnically and economically." Most here are "friendly and hardworking and are very involved in various organizations, from Student Government to intramural sports to the Board of Multicultural Student Affairs . . . we are proud of our school."

PROVIDENCE COLLEGE

FINANCIAL AID: 401-865-2286 • E-MAIL: PCADMISS@PROVIDENCE.EDU • WEBSITE: WWW.PROVIDENCE.EDU

ADMISSIONS

Very important factors considered include: Academic GPA, rigor of secondary school record. *Important factors considered include:* Application essay, character/personal qualities, extracurricular activities, recommendation(s). *Other factors considered include:* Alumni/ae relation, class rank, first generation, geographical residence, level of applicant's interest, racial/ethnic status, talent/ability, volunteer work, work experience. TOEFL required of all international applicants. High school diploma is required, and GED is not accepted. *Academic units required:* 4 English, 4 math, 3 science (2 science labs), 3 foreign language, 2 social studies, 2 history. *Academic units recommended:* 4 English, 4 math, 4 science (2 science labs), 3 foreign language, 2 social studies, 2 history.

The Inside Word

Few schools can claim a more transparent admissions process than Providence College. The admissions section of the school's website includes a voluminous blog authored by the school's senior Admissions Counselor. Surf on over to http://blogs.targetx.com/providence/ScottSeseske and learn everything you could possibly want to know about the how, what, when, and why of admissions decisions at Providence.

FINANCIAL AID

Students should submit: FAFSA, CSS/Financial Aid PROFILE, Business/Farm Supplement. Regular filing deadline is February 1. The Princeton Review suggests that all financial aid forms be submitted as soon as possible after January 1. *Need-based scholarships/grants offered:* Pell Grant, SEOG, state scholarships/grants, private scholarships, the school's own gift aid, National Academic Competitive Grant/SMART Grant. *Loan aid offered:* Direct Subsidized Stafford, Direct Unsubsidized Stafford, Direct PLUS, FFEL Subsidized Stafford, FFEL Unsubsidized Stafford, FFEL PLUS, Federal Perkins Loan. Applicants will be notified of awards on or about April 1. Federal Work-Study Program available. Institutional employment available. Off-campus job opportunities are good.

FROM THE ADMISSIONS OFFICE

"Infused with the history, tradition, and learning of a 700-year-old Catholic teaching order, the Dominican Friars, Providence College offers a value-affirming environment where students are enriched through spiritual, social, physical, and cultural growth as well as through intellectual development. Providence College offers over 51 programs of study leading to baccalaureate degrees in business, education, the sciences, arts, and humanities. Our faculty is noted for a strong commitment to teaching. A close student/faculty relationship allows for in-depth classwork, independent research projects, and detailed career exploration. While noted for the physical facilities and academic opportunities associated with larger universities, Providence also fosters personal growth through a small, spirited, family-like atmosphere that encourages involvement in student activities and athletics.

"Submission of standardized test scores is optional for students applying for admission. This policy change allows each student to decide whether they wish to have their standardized test results considered as part of their application for admission. Students who choose not to submit SAT or ACT test scores will not be penalized in the review for admission. Additional details about the test-optional policy can be found on our website at Providence.edu/testoptionalpolicy."

SELECTIVITY
Admissions Rating	93
# of applicants	8,799
% of applicants accepted	48
% of acceptees attending	25
# accepting a place on wait list	857
% admitted from wait list	2

FRESHMAN PROFILE
Range SAT Critical Reading	540–640
Range SAT Math	560–650
Range SAT Writing	560–650
Range ACT Composite	23–28
Minimum Paper TOEFL	550
Minimum Computer Based TOEFL	213
Average HS GPA	3.46
% graduated top 10% of class	45
% graduated top 25% of class	83
% graduated top 50% of class	97

DEADLINES
Regular application deadline	1/15
Regular notification	4/1
Nonfall registration?	yes

APPLICANTS ALSO LOOK AT
AND OFTEN PREFER
Boston College, College of the Holy Cross, Georgetown University, Tufts University, University of Notre Dame, University of Richmond
AND SOMETIMES PREFER
Boston University, Loyola College in Maryland, Northeastern University, Villanova University
AND RARELY PREFER
Fairfield University, Fordham University, Saint Anselm College, Stonehill College, The University of Scranton, University of Connecticut, University of Massachusetts—Amherst

FINANCIAL FACTS
Financial Aid Rating	74
Annual tuition	$28,920
Room & Board	$10,335
Books and supplies	$779
Required fees	$565
% frosh rec. need-based scholarship or grant aid	52
% UG rec. need-based scholarship or grant aid	56
% frosh rec. need-based self-help aid	55
% UG rec. need-based self-help aid	46
% frosh rec. any financial aid	82
% UG rec. any financial aid	80

PURDUE UNIVERSITY—WEST LAFAYETTE

1080 SCHLEMAN HALL, WEST LAFAYETTE, IN 47907 • ADMISSIONS: 765-494-1776 • FAX: 765-494-0544

CAMPUS LIFE

Quality of Life Rating	72
Fire Safety Rating	81
Type of school	public
Environment	town

STUDENTS

Total undergrad enrollment	31,290
% male/female	59/41
% from out of state	33
% live on campus	34
% in (# of) fraternities	15 (45)
% in (# of) sororities	16 (26)
% African American	4
% Asian	6
% Caucasian	82
% Hispanic	3
% international	6
# of countries represented	123

SURVEY SAYS . . .

Great computer facilities
Everyone loves the Boilermakers
Frats and sororities dominate social scene
Lots of beer drinking
Hard liquor is popular

ACADEMICS

Academic Rating	65
Calendar	semester
Student/faculty ratio	14:1
Profs interesting rating	62
Profs accessible rating	62
% profs teaching UG courses	76
% classes taught by TAs	24
Most common lab size	10–19 students
Most common reg class size	20–29 students

MOST POPULAR MAJORS

business
engineering
psychology

STUDENTS SAY

Academics

There is a perception, both on campus and off, that Purdue's main campus in West Lafayette is "mostly an engineer's college with a bunch of science-type majors and a few liberal arts degrees thrown in together," and with one in four students here pursuing an engineering degree, it's easy to understand why. But Purdue has a lot more to offer than a well-regarded engineering degree; the university's programs in pharmacy, nursing, business, hotel management, agriculture, and veterinary science all enjoy solid, well-earned reputations. Students in these competitive programs warn that "just about all of the classes you take in the first couple of years are 'weed-out' classes" and that "far too many courses are taught by TAs and grad students," a disconcerting number of whom "don't speak English very well." Engineers point out that "while all the classes are hard, there are always places to go to get assistance. There are always extra-help sessions, study groups, tutors available, etc., if I ever need help." Upper-level classes "are smaller in size and are very much hands-on. The professors and class sizes make learning information easier." Many here cite "the limited opportunity to take liberal arts electives" as a drawback. One film major gripes, "The film program is a joke. If you want to be an engineer, Purdue is great. If you want to study art or film, go somewhere else."

Life

With more than 30,000 undergraduates, Purdue can offer "something for everyone. If you want to join a church group, there are plenty of them. If you want to be in a fraternity, there are a lot of them. Ski club, psychology club, people who like The Princeton Review club . . . we've probably got it." One undergrad agrees, "There are so many opportunities to get involved. No matter what you are interested in, you are bound to find others that are interested in the same area." Students here "love Big Ten football" and especially enjoy Breakfast Club, a home-game-day tradition in which students dress in costumes and pre-game in local bars, which open at 7:00 A.M. for the occasion. "It's like Halloween every home football game," explains one student. Students like to party even when they're dressed in civvies, the sun is down, and the football team is nowhere in sight; they tell us that "during the week most people hit the books hard, but on thirsty Thursday and during the weekends, fun here is getting drunk at parties or, if you're 21, in the bars." Purdue's Greek scene "is incredible, and you don't get a lot of the Greeks versus non-Greeks like at other schools. Everyone parties together and has a good time!" Students here love the fact that "there are tons of kids around all the time. A few people go home on the weekends, but I'd say that 95 percent stay at school on the weekends." Indianapolis and Chicago are both within easy road-trip distance when urban life beckons.

Student Body

"Purdue is very representative of a typical small, rural Midwestern town," as "Most of the non-engineers are local Hoosiers. The engineers are a far more diverse group and are generally more academic." The engineering program draws a lot of international students; one engineer reports, "I have friends from at least 20 countries and most of the 50 states. Everyone mixes together and works together to get through these crazy engineering classes!" A "decent number of the students here are members of the Greek system," and "are generally preppy types who wear a lot of Abercrombie." Like their home state, Purdue students "are pretty conservative, and liberal activism is very low. What there is usually is countered by the College Republicans."

FINANCIAL AID: 765-494-5050 • E-MAIL: ADMISSIONS@PURDUE.EDU • WEBSITE: WWW.PURDUE.EDU

ADMISSIONS

Very important factors considered include: Academic GPA, class rank, rigor of secondary school record, standardized test scores. *Other factors considered include:* Alumni/ae relation, character/personal qualities, extracurricular activities, first generation, geographical residence, high school profile, level of applicant's interest, racial/ethnic status, recommendation(s), state residency, volunteer work, work experience. SAT or ACT required; ACT with Writing component required. TOEFL required of all international applicants. High school diploma is required, and GED is accepted. *Academic units required:* 4 English, 3 math, 2 science (2 science labs), 2 foreign language. *Academic units recommended:* 4 English, 3 math, 3 science (3 science labs), 2 foreign language.

The Inside Word

The fact that Purdue holds class rank as one of its most important considerations in the admission of candidates is troublesome. There are far too many inconsistencies in ranking policies and class size among the 25,000-plus high schools in the United States to place so much weight on an essentially incomparable number. The university's high admit rate thankfully renders the issue relatively moot, even though applications have increased.

FINANCIAL AID

Students should submit: FAFSA. The Princeton Review suggests that all financial aid forms be submitted as soon as possible after January 1. *Need-based scholarships/grants offered:* Pell Grant, SEOG, state scholarships/grants, private scholarships, the school's own gift aid. *Loan aid offered:* FFEL Subsidized Stafford, FFEL Unsubsidized Stafford, FFEL PLUS, Federal Perkins Loan, college/university loans from institutional funds. Applicants will be notified of awards on or about April 15.

FROM THE ADMISSIONS OFFICE

"Although it is one of America's largest universities, Purdue does not 'feel' big to its students. The campus is very compact when compared to universities with similar enrollment. Purdue is a comprehensive university with an international reputation in a wide range of academic fields. A strong work ethic prevails at Purdue. As a member of the Big Ten, Purdue has a strong and diverse athletic program. Purdue offers over 750 clubs and organizations. The residence halls and Greek community offer many participatory activities for students. Numerous convocations and lectures are presented each year. Purdue is all about people, and allowing students to grow academically as well as socially, preparing them for the real world.

"Applicants seeking admission are required to submit scores from the new Writing component of the SAT (or ACT)."

SELECTIVITY

Admissions Rating	81
# of applicants	24,883
% of applicants accepted	85
% of acceptees attending	36

FRESHMAN PROFILE

Range SAT Critical Reading	490–600
Range SAT Math	530–650
Range ACT Composite	22–28
Minimum Paper TOEFL	550
Minimum Computer Based TOEFL	213
Average HS GPA	3.5
% graduated top 10% of class	27
% graduated top 25% of class	61
% graduated top 50% of class	91

DEADLINES

Regular notification	rolling
Nonfall registration?	yes

APPLICANTS ALSO LOOK AT AND SOMETIMES PREFER

Indiana University—Bloomington, Rose-Hulman Institute of Technology, University of Illinois at Urbana-Champaign, Valparaiso University

FINANCIAL FACTS

Financial Aid Rating	79
Annual in-state tuition	$7,096
Annual out-of-state tuition	$21,266
Room & Board	$7,140
Books and supplies	$990
Required fees	$396
% frosh rec. need-based scholarship or grant aid	15
% UG rec. need-based scholarship or grant aid	13
% frosh rec. need-based self-help aid	36
% UG rec. need-based self-help aid	36
% frosh rec. any financial aid	80
% UG rec. any financial aid	76

QUINNIPIAC UNIVERSITY

275 MOUNT CARMEL AVENUE, HAMDEN, CT 06518 • ADMISSIONS: 203-582-8600 • FAX: 203-582-8906

STUDENTS SAY

Academics

The physical beauty of Quinnipiac University is a particularly appealing attribute. The "beautiful campus with Sleeping Giant Mountain in the background" boasts many a picturesque vista, both natural and man-made. As far as the latter is concerned, the library "is gorgeous, with huge three-story windows and leather armchairs everywhere!" Quinnipiac's "great" academics manage to draw students away from the windows and into the classrooms. Undergraduate academics at Quinnipiac are divided into five schools (and one new Division of Education), with the School of Health Sciences offering especially outstanding majors. Among these is a 6.5-year physical therapy program that leads to a Doctor of Physical Therapy degree. Students appreciate the fact that "classes here at Quinnipiac are small, with generally less than 30 students," that "not one class in the university is taught by a teacher's assistant" and that professors "have so much experience in the 'real world' with the subject they teach." They warn, however, that "sometimes you can have a little bit of trouble with the adjuncts." Regardless of how good they are as teachers and lecturers, professors "all seem to be willing to help outside of the class time and communicate rapidly through e-mail."

Life

According to students, life at Quinnipiac outside of class follows a regular schedule to it. "Thursday night everyone goes to the clubs in New Haven. Friday night everyone parties on campus. Saturday night most people go to Toad's (a popular New Haven nightclub)." And if you have "no transportation, no problem. Quinnipiac shuttles will take you into New Haven to the clubs." "However, if partying is not your thing, don't worry because Quinnipiac sends out e-mails every week with the [school-sponsored] weekend events. These events include comedians, movies, game room nights, and much more." For outdoorsy types, miles of hiking trails lie right across the street, and "climbing the Sleeping Giant" is a popular pastime here, weather permitting. When it's "nice out," students take full advantage of their gorgeous surroundings: "You will always see kids with their towels lying on the Quad doing work. Others also enjoy playing Frisbee on the beautiful grass." "Support for the athletic teams," however, "is so-so. Men's ice hockey draws the best. Students also support the men's basketball team pretty well."

Student Body

To get a picture of what students here look like, just grab the nearest name-brand clothing catalog: "J. Crew, Ralph Lauren, and the North Face could do a magazine shoot here. [There are lots of] very preppy-looking, clean-cut kids." If their clothes aren't enough to give you a sense of the socioeconomic background from which most QU students come, take a stroll through "the student parking lot, [which] is full of Mercedes, Lexus, BMW, and Acura cars." Intellectually, "Most students don't seem to be their high school class president or their high school overachiever," but respondents emphasize that QU students are "hard workers." Given QU's location, it's not completely shocking to learn that "Many of the students come from surrounding New England states as well as New York and New Jersey." Many respondents lament the female/male ratio (about 3:2), and the fact that there are "very, very, very few minorities"—"but with each entering freshman class the diversity does grow slightly." And regardless of their backgrounds, friendly students make Quinnipiac "a comfortable, enjoyable place to live. The students are understanding of one another."

FINANCIAL AID: 203-582-8750 • E-MAIL: ADMISSIONS@QUINNIPIAC.EDU • WEBSITE: WWW.QUINNIPIAC.EDU

ADMISSIONS

Very important factors considered include: Rigor of secondary school record. *Important factors considered include:* Academic GPA, application essay, class rank, recommendation(s), standardized test scores. *Other factors considered include:* Alumni/ae relation, character/personal qualities, extracurricular activities, interview, level of applicant's interest, racial/ethnic status, talent/ability, volunteer work, work experience. SAT or ACT required; TOEFL required of all international applicants. High school diploma is required, and GED is accepted. *Academic units required:* 4 English, 3 math, 3 science (2 science labs), 2 foreign language, 2 social studies, 4 years of science and math required for the nursing, occupational therapy, physical therapy, and physician assistant programs. *Academic units recommended:* 4 English, 4 math, 4 science (3 science labs), 2 foreign language, 3 social studies.

The Inside Word

Applicants with solid grades and test scores won't have much trouble gaining admission to Quinnipiac as long as they apply early in their senior year. Competition grows fiercer, however, as D-Day approaches. With the recent spike in applications, Admissions Officers have established the wait list in January. Students interested in either physical therapy or physician assistant should be aware that they face more stringent requirements.

FINANCIAL AID

Students should submit: FAFSA. The Princeton Review suggests that all financial aid forms be submitted as soon as possible after January 1. *Need-based scholarships/grants offered:* Pell Grant, SEOG, state scholarships/grants, private scholarships, the school's own gift aid, Federal Nursing Scholarship. *Loan aid offered:* FFEL Subsidized Stafford, FFEL Unsubsidized Stafford, FFEL PLUS, Federal Perkins Loan, Federal Nursing Loan, state loans. Applicants will be notified of awards on a rolling basis beginning or about February 15. Federal Work-Study Program available. Institutional employment available. Off-campus job opportunities are excellent.

FROM THE ADMISSIONS OFFICE

"The appeal of Quinnipiac University continues to grow each year. Our students come from a variety of states and backgrounds. Seventy-five percent of the freshman class is from out of state. Students come from 25 states and 18 countries. Nearly 30 percent of current undergraduates plan to stay at Quinnipiac to complete their graduate degrees. As admission becomes more competitive and our enrollment remains stable, the university continues to focus on its mission: to provide outstanding academic programs in a student-oriented environment on a campus with a strong sense of community. The development of an honors program, a highly regarded emerging leaders student-life program, and a 'writing across the curriculum' initiative in academic affairs, form the foundation for excellence in business, communications, health sciences, education, liberal arts, and law. The university has a fully digital high-definition production studio in the School of Communications; the Terry Goodwin '67 Financial Technology Center which provides a high-tech simulated trading floor in the School of Business; and a critical care lab for our nursing and physician assistant majors. All incoming students purchase a university-recommended laptop with wireless capabilities supported by a campus wide network. More than 70 student organizations, 21 Division I teams, recreation and intramurals, community service, student publications, and a strong student government offer a variety of outside-of-class experiences. There are many clubs that get students involved in campus life. Multicultural awareness is supported through the Black Student Union, Asian/Pacific Islander Association, Latino Cultural Society, and GLASS. An active alumni association reflects the strong connection Quinnipiac has with its graduates, and they give the faculty high marks for career preparation. Students are encouraged to apply early in the fall of their senior year and can access our online application or the Common Application easily from our website. We use the best individual scores on the SAT Reasoning Test (no Subject Tests required), or the ACT composite. We begin notifying students of our decisions in early January."

SELECTIVITY

Admissions Rating	88
# of applicants	10,313
% of applicants accepted	58
% of acceptees attending	24
# accepting a place on wait list	650
% admitted from wait list	2

FRESHMAN PROFILE

Range SAT Critical Reading	540–610
Range SAT Math	560–630
Range ACT Composite	23–27
Minimum Paper TOEFL	550
Minimum Computer Based TOEFL	213
Average HS GPA	3.5
% graduated top 10% of class	22
% graduated top 25% of class	60
% graduated top 50% of class	95

DEADLINES

Regular notification	rolling
Nonfall registration?	yes

APPLICANTS ALSO LOOK AT

AND OFTEN PREFER
Boston University, University of Connecticut, Villanova University

AND SOMETIMES PREFER
Fairfield University, Fordham University, Providence College, Syracuse University

AND RARELY PREFER
Assumption College, Hofstra University, Sacred Heart University

FINANCIAL FACTS

Financial Aid Rating	67
Annual tuition	$27,600
Room & Board	$11,200
Books and supplies	$800
Required fees	$1,120
% frosh rec. need-based scholarship or grant aid	59
% UG rec. need-based scholarship or grant aid	56
% frosh rec. need-based self-help aid	49
% UG rec. need-based self-help aid	51
% frosh rec. any financial aid	70
% UG rec. any financial aid	68

RANDOLPH COLLEGE

2500 RIVERMONT AVENUE, LYNCHBURG, VA 24503-1526 • ADMISSIONS: 434-947-8100 • FAX: 434-947-8996

CAMPUS LIFE
Quality of Life Rating	88
Fire Safety Rating	86
Type of school	private
Affiliation	Methodist
Environment	city

STUDENTS
Total undergrad enrollment	706
% male/female	0/100
% from out of state	61
% from public high school	78
% live on campus	88
% African American	9
% Asian	4
% Caucasian	69
% Hispanic	5
% Native American	1
% international	11
# of countries represented	46

SURVEY SAYS . . .
Small classes
No one cheats
Diverse student types on campus
Campus feels safe
Frats and sororities are unpopular or nonexistent

ACADEMICS
Academic Rating	93
Calendar	semester
Student/faculty ratio	8:1
Profs interesting rating	95
Profs accessible rating	88
% profs teaching UG courses	100
% classes taught by TAs	0
Most common lab size	10–19 students
Most common reg class size	10–19 students

MOST POPULAR MAJORS
biology/biological sciences
political science and government
psychology

STUDENTS SAY
Academics

Randolph College "is all about traditions: of learning, of excellence, of experiences, and of fun." Learning comes first in the "very academically oriented atmosphere" of this small, recently coed college with a "writing-intensive curriculum." Students here warn that "this school is difficult. It is really worth it, though, when, at the end of the day, you see that you were successful and made the grade. There is no feeling like it! My favorite saying from the professors here is: 'That C would have been an A at any other college.'" To help them handle the workload, students receive "a lot of personal time with teachers, and the teachers are very willing to work with you. They have lots of office hours and will have more if you want them to. There is a lot of class discussion, which I like because the classes are small." Also, while "You have to learn and you feel pressed to excel," "It's not like being pushed out onto a ship deck in a hurricane; they do give a lot of tutoring resources." Randolph's strong areas include a "great dance program," "solid foreign language departments," science programs "that have equipment my dad didn't even get to use until grad school," an "amazing riding program" with "a wonderful riding center," and "a good nursing program." Because the school is located "in the middle of nowhere," students tell us that it's easy to focus on academics and "not get yourself into too much trouble" at Randolph.

Life

Traditions "are what truly make Randolph so unique, and also so much fun to be at." And there are lots of them: There's Ring Week, when "First-years select a junior and spend a week decorating that junior's door and giving them (anonymous) presents; at the end of the week, the first-years present the juniors with their class ring." Then there's Even-Odd rivalry, a competition between classes teamed on the basis of their graduation year. There's also Pumpkin Parade, an October event in which sophomores gift seniors with lighted pumpkins. The traditions are fun, but more importantly, they "further strengthen the family bond" enjoyed by the Randolph community. Otherwise, life on the Randolph campus is "laid-back," with students "very focused on their studies during the week. Friday and Saturday are the nights that most students go out or have parties in their rooms. We seem to watch a lot of movies on campus and off (we have a dollar theater in Lynchburg) and there are a lot of fairly active clubs on campus." Many students "go to Hampden-Sydney College, University of Virginia, or Virginia Tech to party or meet people on weekends."

Student Body

Randolph students "study a lot and do a lot of work for classes. We also are all involved in a zillion different clubs and extracurricular activities at the same time. We're all always very busy, but we make time for hanging out with friends and having fun too." Students tend to be "very strong willed in their opinions and get done what they need to get done." One student elaborates: "The typical student at Randolph is a self-proclaimed hard worker. She is, in some way, a feminist. [Students have] a strong sense of self and are seeking a career in which [they] may exercise [their] talents; [they] feel the world is open to [them], and [they] would like to prove [themselves] in it. [Their] goals are endless, and [their] studies will bring [them] into the realm of accomplishment. Above all, [they are] forward thinkers, asking questions to which there may be no answers, and questioning answers which do not address the questions." While "Most students are Caucasian," Randolph also has "a surprising number of students from abroad—thriving Jamaican and Nepalese communities, as well as students from Saudi Arabia, India, and Argentina."

ADMISSIONS

Very important factors considered include: Academic GPA, character/personal qualities, rigor of secondary school record. *Important factors considered include:* Application essay, extracurricular activities, recommendation(s), standardized test scores, talent/ability, volunteer work. *Other factors considered include:* Alumni/ae relation, class rank, first generation, interview, level of applicant's interest, work experience. SAT or ACT required; TOEFL required of all international applicants. High school diploma is required, and GED is accepted. *Academic units required:* 4 English, 3 math, 2 science (2 science labs), 3 foreign language, 2 history, 2 academic electives.

The Inside Word

Finding well-matched students is a top priority at Randolph, and applicants can rest assured that their applications will be given due consideration. While there are no minimum GPA or standardized test score requirements, most candidates have proven successful in the classroom. Character also plays an important role in admissions decisions; officers especially value independent, confident women and men who are proactive about their educations.

FINANCIAL AID

Students should submit: FAFSA, state aid form. The Princeton Review suggests that all financial aid forms be submitted as soon as possible after January 1. *Need-based scholarships/grants offered:* Pell Grant, SEOG, state scholarships/grants, private scholarships, the school's own gift aid. *Loan aid offered:* FFEL Subsidized Stafford, FFEL Unsubsidized Stafford, FFEL PLUS, Federal Perkins Loan, college/university loans from institutional funds, private loans. Applicants will be notified of awards on a rolling basis beginning or about March 1.

FROM THE ADMISSIONS OFFICE

"Randolph College gives a liberal arts education new relevance. The college's global honors emphasis offers the best features of an honors education with a global outlook. All students are encouraged to travel, to take on real problems, to pursue and achieve a goal with personal meaning. Embedded within a student's education are opportunities to study abroad, national and international internships, career guidance, leadership development, and one-on-one faculty advising.

"A graduate of Randolph understands the intellectual foundations of the arts, sciences, and humanities and can pursue an idea with the goal of creating new knowledge. The college's strong emphasis on writing enables students to communicate clearly and persuasively, and our diverse student population and study abroad emphasis enable students to 'see through the eyes of another culture.' The honor system is a vital part of life at Randolph and all students are expected to behave ethically and honorably in all circumstances, to care for others less fortunate, and to act on their behalf.

"If you want to live in a world in which your intelligence, energy, and purpose make a difference, this is the education you need.

"At this time, first-year applicants for Fall 2008 must submit either the SAT or ACT; the Writing component scores for the new SAT and the new ACT are not required. Randolph College will accept the scores from either the new or old versions of both tests."

SELECTIVITY

Admissions Rating	**86**
# of applicants	745
% of applicants accepted	89
% of acceptees attending	28
# of early decision applicants	27
% accepted early decision	67

FRESHMAN PROFILE

Range SAT Critical Reading	520–650
Range SAT Math	490–630
Range ACT Composite	23–27
Minimum Paper TOEFL	550
Minimum Computer Based TOEFL	213
Average HS GPA	3.4
% graduated top 10% of class	38
% graduated top 25% of class	70
% graduated top 50% of class	90

DEADLINES

Early decision application deadline	11/15
Early decision notification	12/15
Regular application deadline	3/1
Regular notification	rolling
Nonfall registration?	yes

APPLICANTS ALSO LOOK AT AND OFTEN PREFER

Duke University, Smith College, Wellesley College

AND SOMETIMES PREFER

The College of William & Mary, Mount Holyoke College, Sweet Briar College, University of Virginia

AND RARELY PREFER

Hollins University, James Madison University, Virginia Tech

FINANCIAL FACTS

Financial Aid Rating	**86**
Annual tuition	$23,900
Room & Board	$8,800
Required fees	$510
% frosh rec. need-based scholarship or grant aid	68
% UG rec. need-based scholarship or grant aid	65
% frosh rec. need-based self-help aid	57
% UG rec. need-based self-help aid	57
% frosh rec. any financial aid	99
% UG rec. any financial aid	96

RANDOLPH-MACON COLLEGE

PO Box 5005, Ashland, VA 23005 • Admissions: 804-752-7305 • Fax: 804-752-4707

STUDENTS SAY

Academics

An "intimate and community-based campus" is what students find at Randolph-Macon College, a Virginia liberal arts school just north of Richmond, Virginia. Students rave that "the professors are the best part of Randolph-Macon"; professors are almost universally praised as "amazing, very social and easy to talk to and approach with problems." Often they won't just wait for you to come to them, but rather "will let you know when you [are] messing up, either by pulling you aside or arranging a meeting." Professors are not just caring people, however; they're also "very intelligent" and "extremely qualified" professionals "who have achieved amazing things during their careers." In at least one student's "opinion, the professors need to be given raises" for the hard work they do. Rather than singling out particular programs as standouts, students praise the overall "great liberal arts education" that RMC offers. Student opinion of the administration is somewhat negative, but many undergraduates are finding hope in the new president, whom R-MC students have dubbed the "Student's President."

Life

"Greek life is key" at R-MC. "When people say there is nothing going on, it is usually because no fraternity is having any parties for the students to go to." Whether at frat parties on campus or at bars in Richmond (which is just 10 miles away), drinking is a popular activity, many students claim. Even if you're not the type of person who likes to drink, "There are plenty of other things to do. There are places around to rent movies, places to go out to eat, or if you want to stay on campus, the school has a college movie channel [on which] they show specific movies each night." "Sporting events" are "also a large part of the social life": "We go to the football games in the fall, and grill out on the lawn in the spring while watching the lacrosse and softball games. Basketball games are always a big deal because we have a really good program here and usually do pretty well in the conference, or in the girls' [case], the nation." Intramural sports "are also very popular on campus," and competition for the "plaques and t-shirts" that are awarded to the best teams in each sport can be fierce. Regardless of the activities they engage in, however, R-MC students "aren't easygoing about academic commitments. They mean a lot to us!" "We are able to go out and party while still accomplishing our work," but "We take academics seriously."

Student Body

At RMC, "The typical student is White, wealthy, has a nice car, is a member of Greek life, dresses like a prep, drinks like a fish, parties like an animal, wears flip-flops all year round, and occasionally goes to the library to study," writes one student. Others claim that typical students are "conservative, Southern, polite, friendly" and "involved in sports." A lot of people seem to be "from Virginia, Maryland, Pennsylvania, New Jersey, or Connecticut" and exude certain "boarding school" manners, even though the majority of students come from public high schools. Many respondents lament the noticeable lack of diversity on campus, but also insist that "minorities do not seem to have a problem fitting in." Finally, at a school this small, "Everyone knows everyone," "so of course, the rumor mill" is a "strong" social force.

FINANCIAL AID: 804-752-7259 • E-MAIL: ADMISSIONS@RMC.EDU • WEBSITE: WWW.RMC.EDU

ADMISSIONS

Very important factors considered include: Academic GPA, rigor of secondary school record. *Important factors considered include:* Application essay, class rank, recommendation(s), standardized test scores. *Other factors considered include:* Alumni/ae relation, character/personal qualities, extracurricular activities, first generation, interview, racial/ethnic status, talent/ability, volunteer work, work experience. SAT or ACT required; ACT with Writing component recommended. TOEFL required of all international applicants. High school diploma is required, and GED is accepted. *Academic units required:* 4 English, 3 math, 3 science (2 science labs), 2 foreign language, 1 social studies, 2 history, 1 academic elective. *Academic units recommended:* 4 English, 4 math, 4 science (4 science labs), 4 foreign language, 4 social studies, 2 history.

The Inside Word

Randolph-Macon is a solid liberal arts college, but it must contend with a wealth of Virginia schools for applicants. Students who are academically competitive should easily gain acceptance. Admissions Officers ascribe the most weight to objective data, primarily grades and test scores.

FINANCIAL AID

Students should submit: FAFSA, state aid form, R-MC Entitlement Eligibility Form, College Prepaid Education Program Form. Regular filing deadline is March 1. The Princeton Review suggests that all financial aid forms be submitted as soon as possible after January 1. *Need-based scholarships/grants offered:* Pell Grant, SEOG, state scholarships/grants, private scholarships, the school's own gift aid. *Loan aid offered:* FFEL Subsidized Stafford, FFEL Unsubsidized Stafford, FFEL PLUS, Federal Perkins Loan, college/university loans from institutional funds. Applicants will be notified of awards on or about March 15. Federal Work-Study Program available. Institutional employment available. Off-campus job opportunities are excellent.

FROM THE ADMISSIONS OFFICE

"Randolph-Macon College, located in historic Ashland, just north of Richmond, is a coeducational, liberal arts and sciences college with a mission fulfilled through a combination of personal interaction and academic rigor. The student/faculty ratio is 11:1 and the average class size is 16 students. Enrollment is kept at approximately 1,150 to maintain this intimate atmosphere. Randolph-Macon College has an outstanding national reputation for its internships, study abroad, and undergraduate research. Founded in 1830, Randolph-Macon College is the oldest United Methodist Church–affiliated college in the nation, is a Phi Beta Kappa college, and is ranked as a Baccalaureate I college by the Carnegie Foundation. It offers the broadest liberal arts core curriculum of any college in Virginia.

"The college prepares students for any future, including success in securing a job or in gaining acceptance to graduate or professional school. The college offers a wide variety of social and recreational opportunities through more than 100 campus organizations. Forty percent of the students participate in one or more community-service activities; 70 percent play intramural sports; 40 percent join a fraternity or sorority; and everyone has a voice in student government. A $9.5 million sports and recreation center is very popular with students, and a new performing arts center offers a wealth of cultural arts programs. In addition, freshmen residence halls were recently renovated. 'Peaks of Excellence' center is now open to assist students with internships, study abroad, and undergraduate research.

"Freshman applicants for Fall 2008 must take the new SAT, which includes a written essay, or the ACT with Writing component."

SELECTIVITY

Admissions Rating	82
# of applicants	2,878
% of applicants accepted	58
% of acceptees attending	24
# accepting a place on wait list	50
% admitted from wait list	62
# of early decision applicants	33
% accepted early decision	73

FRESHMAN PROFILE

Range SAT Critical Reading	490–590
Range SAT Math	490–590
Range SAT Writing	480–580
Minimum Paper TOEFL	550
Minimum Computer Based TOEFL	213
Average HS GPA	3.3
% graduated top 10% of class	18
% graduated top 25% of class	44
% graduated top 50% of class	79

DEADLINES

Early decision application deadline	11/15
Early decision notification	12/1
Regular application deadline	3/1
Regular notification	4/1
Nonfall registration?	yes

APPLICANTS ALSO LOOK AT

AND OFTEN PREFER
University of Virginia

AND SOMETIMES PREFER
James Madison University, Roanoke College, University of Mary Washington, Virginia Tech

AND RARELY PREFER
Christopher Newport University, Longwood University, Lynchburg College

FINANCIAL FACTS

Financial Aid Rating	80
Annual tuition	$24,710
Room & Board	$7,695
Books and supplies	$1,000
Required fees	$635
% frosh rec. need-based scholarship or grant aid	58
% UG rec. need-based scholarship or grant aid	58
% frosh rec. need-based self-help aid	46
% UG rec. need-based self-help aid	49
% frosh rec. any financial aid	100
% UG rec. any financial aid	95

REED COLLEGE

3203 SOUTHEAST WOODSTOCK BOULEVARD, PORTLAND, OR 97202-8199 • ADMISSIONS: 503-777-7511 • FAX: 503-777-7553

STUDENTS SAY

Academics

"Quirky and intellectual," Reed College is an elite liberal arts school where students "can embrace academia without being ridiculed and can love to learn without fear of being ostracized." It's the type of place where students brag about the classics department and proudly report that "Preparation for professional disciplines is somewhat light." With "superior faculty and facilities" that include "an amazing library, lots of computers, a huge amount of free tutoring, [and] a computer help desk where assistance is free," Reed "very much cares what the students think, and is there to serve" students with whatever they might need. Except the work itself, of course; students here "work hard constantly." Most relish the challenge; one undergrad explains, "We take a great deal of pleasure in complaining about the amount of work we have on a daily basis, but never feel as though we are doing something that does not contribute to our ultimate academic project. I had never before understood the intrinsic value of learning. . . . Reed's academic experience is a catalyst for this kind of attitude." Students take a substantial role in running the school, as the administration "keeps a hands-off approach to management of student and faculty affairs, which is well appreciated by both groups. This also allows them to focus on funding the school and maintaining its facilities."

Life

"People spend a lot of time studying, frequently late into the night and on weekends" at Reed. As one undergrad puts it, "Reed allows only three of the following: sleep, a serious relationship, friends, academic success, extracurriculars, a job." Still, once they finish their work, most students find time to "take full advantage of every part of the world outside the library, be it the fantastic Portland restaurants, the huge outdoor sports scene in the Pacific Northwest, or other cultural events around the city, like the art walks that happen twice a month in Portland." On campus, "The Reed social environment is student generated, as all students decide what clubs get funding each semester. I like how this ensures all kinds of opportunities from the outdoors to dance parties to music shows to building crazy 10-foot bikes." Parties and recreational drugs are readily available, but "Overall, people here tend to smaller get-togethers rather than ragers; they tend to prefer doing unique and crazy things rather than the same old beer-drinkin' frat-goin' crapola; and they tend to do cultural activities if those are available to them rather than just go out and get smashed."

Student Body

Reed students "are characterized by a love of learning for its own sake as well as an inability to dance like normal people. Skilled dancers can be integrated into the community with little difficulty, but academic slackers are quickly weeded out." Most "are the kind of 'closet geeks' that you'd never have known about in high school—that is, the ones who looked really cool on the outside but on the inside were all about physics or classics or what-have-you—or 'closet cool kids,' the geeks who were actually really awesome if only you'd bothered to get to know them." There's "one type of student you won't find much of: neo-conservatives. There's a good minority of conservatives on the campus—Libertarians and Republicans who are pissed off by Bush." Mostly "students are left wing in political persuasion and are proud of it."

ADMISSIONS

Very important factors considered include: Academic GPA, application essay, rigor of secondary school record. *Important factors considered include:* Class rank, interview, level of applicant's interest, recommendation(s), standardized test scores. *Other factors considered include:* Alumni/ae relation, character/personal qualities, extracurricular activities, first generation, racial/ethnic status, talent/ability, volunteer work, work experience. SAT or ACT required; SAT Subject Tests optional. TOEFL required of all international applicants. High school diploma is required, and GED is accepted. *Academic units recommended:* 4 English, 4 math, 3 science, 3 foreign language, 1 social studies, 3 history.

The Inside Word

The prototypical Reed undergraduate is one who is more concerned with academic pursuits for their own sake than with the potential return on investment of their educations. Think The University of Chicago without the preponderance of math and science majors. You'll need solid credentials and positive indicators of genuine intellectual curiosity to get in the door here—just being smart isn't enough.

FINANCIAL AID

Students should submit: FAFSA, institution's own financial aid form, CSS/Financial Aid PROFILE, Noncustodial PROFILE. Regular filing deadline is January 15. The Princeton Review suggests that all financial aid forms be submitted as soon as possible after January 1. *Need-based scholarships/grants offered:* Pell Grant, SEOG, state scholarships/grants, private scholarships, the school's own gift aid. *Loan aid offered:* FFEL Subsidized Stafford, FFEL Unsubsidized Stafford, FFEL PLUS, Federal Perkins Loan. Applicants will be notified of awards on or about April 1. Federal Work-Study Program available. Institutional employment available.

FROM THE ADMISSIONS OFFICE

"Reed is animated and energized by its seemingly paradoxical features. Reed has, for example: 1) a traditional, classical, highly structured curriculum—yet, at the same time, a progressive, free-thinking, decidedly unstructured community culture; 2) a powerful emphasis on intellectuality, serious study, and the very highest standards of academic achievement—yet, at the same time, a rich and rewarding program of recreational and extracurricular activity, including a physical education requirement; 3) a refusal to overemphasize grades—yet, third in the nation in the production of future PhDs; 4) a faculty culture absolutely dedicated to superb undergraduate teaching—yet, at the same time, a faculty culture that supports and celebrates high-level research and scholarship at the cutting edge of each academic discipline.

"Reed is not a simple place. It's a complex amalgam of diverse elements. But those elements have been chosen and developed over the years with great care. The result is an intricate—even ornate—but utterly coherent and clearly articulated architecture that has been called by at least one outside observer 'exquisite' and by another 'the most intellectual college in the country.' Reed is not for everyone. But for students who are interested both in exploring great ideas and in developing personal autonomy, it makes very good sense indeed.

"Reed accepts either the ACT or SAT and does not require SAT Subject Tests or the ACT Writing exam. Until we are convinced that the new SAT and ACT Writing exams offer us significant information that we do not already factor into the admission matrix, Reed will not change its approach to standardized tests. Writing sections are recommended, though not required. With the SAT, we will continue to look most closely at the Critical Reading and Math sections and think of test scores on a 1,600-point, as opposed to a 2,400-point scale."

SELECTIVITY

Admissions Rating	**96**
# of applicants	3,361
% of applicants accepted	35
% of acceptees attending	31
# accepting a place on wait list	300
% admitted from wait list	14
# of early decision applicants	224
% accepted early decision	54

FRESHMAN PROFILE

Range SAT Critical Reading	660–750
Range SAT Math	620–710
Range SAT Writing	640–730
Range ACT Composite	28–32
Minimum Paper TOEFL	600
Minimum Computer Based TOEFL	259
Average HS GPA	3.9
% graduated top 10% of class	67
% graduated top 25% of class	89
% graduated top 50% of class	98

DEADLINES

Early decision application deadline	11/15
Early decision notification	12/15
Regular application deadline	1/15
Regular notification	4/1
Nonfall registration?	no

APPLICANTS ALSO LOOK AT

AND OFTEN PREFER
Brown University, Stanford University

AND SOMETIMES PREFER
Oberlin College, University of California—Berkeley, The University of Chicago

AND RARELY PREFER
Carleton College, Colorado College, Grinnell College, Haverford College, Whitman College

FINANCIAL FACTS

Financial Aid Rating	**96**
Annual tuition	$36,190
Room & Board	$9,540
Books and supplies	$1,050
Required fees	$230
% frosh rec. need-based scholarship or grant aid	45
% UG rec. need-based scholarship or grant aid	50
% frosh rec. need-based self-help aid	45
% UG rec. need-based self-help aid	45
% frosh rec. any financial aid	45
% UG rec. any financial aid	50

RENSSELAER POLYTECHNIC INSTITUTE

110 EIGHTH STREET, TROY, NY 12180-3590 • ADMISSIONS: 518-276-6216 • FAX: 518-276-4072

STUDENTS SAY

Academics

In recent years Rensselaer Polytechnic Institute, the venerable math/science/engineering heavyweight of the Hudson Valley, has made "strong efforts to diversify the school into a university, rather than [being satisfied with its stature as] a technical institute. Arts programs, both electronic and conventional, are now receiving funding, along with new biotechnology and nanotechnology programs." The goal—to "transform RPI to Rensselaer, a one-word synonym for an Ivy League-quality school"—has both champions and critics among the student body, who either praise "new programs that will help us provide the world with graduates very driven to do great things" or assert that "RPI is not and never could or should be a more liberal school. RPI is engineering and it should stay that way." While attempting to broaden the curriculum, Rensselaer remains "a very technology-oriented school that deals with cutting-edge innovations in science and engineering" and "emphasizes diversity, integrity, and above all, leadership in the context of a world-class research university." The workload here is tremendous and the concepts taught difficult to master, but students are protected by an institutional safety net; one engineer explains, "The Learning Assistance Center has an early-detection system that warns students who are below average and offers assistance. If they notice the slightest drop in performance, they will contact you in regards to what's up." For many here, "RPI's greatest strengths are its variety of options for students to gain experience in their field. We have an excellent Career Development Center, a study abroad program, undergraduate research programs, internships and co-ops, which are very popular." Placement services are excellent thanks to "many corporate connections; alumni are always coming back and recruiting, and many large and small companies love to recruit here."

Life

"Fraternity life is huge on campus," report RPI students, who note that the school is home to more than 30 Greek organizations. "If you're a girl you're associated with at least one. If you're a guy who isn't associated with one, you don't have much of a social life." One student explains, "Everyone either goes to frat parties on the weekend or stays in and plays video games." Not that there aren't other options; as one undergraduate points out, "If you want to do something on campus and be involved, it's incredibly easy to do so. The people who say otherwise are just apathetic. Between movie nights on campus, union-sponsored events, fraternity and sorority events, and downtown, there are tons of things to do." Everyone agrees that "hockey is king here; everyone goes, and it is amazing to watch." The men's and women's ice hockey teams compete in NCAA Division I; RPI's 21 other varsity teams play in Division III. When regarding hometown Troy, students are mixed. While some claim that "the city is devoid of all life and fun," others assert that "downtown Troy, although not the best place to hang out at night, is pretty cool. There are some beautiful buildings and some neat shops and small eateries." An even-handed student avers, "While the city of Troy is improving, it has a long way to go before it becomes a suitable location for Rensselaer."

Student Body

"The former stereotype for RPI, as everyone knows, was that we tend to be kind of nerdy bookworms, and that we are not very involved in campus activities." Students also tell us, "That is no longer true. Students are now much more involved in things all over campus, from our excellent football and hockey teams to our 150-plus clubs and activities, to new programs popping up all over campus." The school hasn't switched over entirely, of course; as one student explains, "Fifty percent of us are computer nerds who play video games and have their own social networks. The other 50 percent are normal college students who like to party and have a fun time." While the male/female ratio is quite unbalanced here, "It's not as big of a problem as it is made out to be, due to the closeness of other colleges, especially Russell Sage, an all-girls school."

RENSSELAER POLYTECHNIC INSTITUTE

FINANCIAL AID: 518-276-6813 • E-MAIL: ADMISSIONS@RPI.EDU • WEBSITE: WWW.RPI.EDU

ADMISSIONS

Very important factors considered include: Academic GPA, class rank, rigor of secondary school record, standardized test scores. *Important factors considered include:* Application essay, character/personal qualities, extracurricular activities, recommendation(s). *Other factors considered include:* Alumni/ae relation, geographical residence, level of applicant's interest, racial/ethnic status, talent/ability, volunteer work, work experience. SAT or ACT required; ACT with Writing component required. TOEFL required of all international applicants. High school diploma is required, and GED is accepted. *Academic units required:* 4 English, 4 math, 3 science, 2 social studies. *Academic units recommended:* 4 science, 3 social studies.

The Inside Word

Although scores and numbers may not be the only consideration of the Admissions Committee at RPI, it is important to remember that you have to have high ones in order to stay in the running for admission. Here at RPI and at many other highly selective colleges and universities, the first review weeds out those who are academically weak and without any special considerations. Underrepresented minorities and women are high on the list of desirables in the applicant pool here and go through the admissions process without any hitches if reasonably well qualified.

FINANCIAL AID

Students should submit: FAFSA, state aid form. The Princeton Review suggests that all financial aid forms be submitted as soon as possible after January 1. *Need-based scholarships/grants offered:* Pell Grant, SEOG, state scholarships/grants, private scholarships, the school's own gift aid, Gates Millennium Scholarship. *Loan aid offered:* FFEL Subsidized Stafford, FFEL Unsubsidized Stafford, FFEL PLUS, Federal Perkins Loan, college/university loans from institutional funds. Applicants will be notified of awards on or about March 25.

FROM THE ADMISSIONS OFFICE

"The oldest degree-granting technological research university in North America, Rensselaer was founded in 1824 to instruct students to apply 'science to the common purposes of life.' Rensselaer offers more than 100 programs and 1,000 courses leading to bachelor's, master's, and doctoral degrees. Undergraduates pursue studies in architecture, engineering, humanities and social sciences, management and technology, science, and information technology (IT). A pioneer in interactive learning, Rensselaer provides real-world, hands-on educational opportunities that cut across academic disciplines. Students have ready access to laboratories and attend classes involving lively discussion, problem solving, and faculty mentoring.

"New programs and facilities are enriching the student experience. The Office of First-Year Experience provides programs for students and their primary support persons that begin even before students arrive on campus. The new $80-million Biotechnology and Interdisciplinary Studies Center offers space for scientific research and discovery, while newly renovated residence halls, wireless computing network, and studio classrooms create a fertile environment for study and learning. The Experimental Media and Performing Arts Center opening in 2008 will encourage students to explore and create at the intersection of engineering and the arts.

"Rensselaer offers recreational and fitness facilities plus numerous student-run organizations and activities, including fraternities and sororities, a newspaper, a radio station, drama and musical groups, and more than 160 clubs. In addition to intramural sports, NCAA varsity sports include Division I men's and women's ice hockey teams and 21 Division III men's and women's teams in 13 sports.

"Applicants may submit scores from either SAT (Critical Reading, Math, and Writing) or ACT (which must include optional Writing component). Applicants to the accelerated program must either take the ACT or submit Math and Science scores from SAT Subject Tests."

SELECTIVITY

Admissions Rating	92
# of applicants	6,875
% of applicants accepted	67
% of acceptees attending	28
# accepting a place on wait list	359
% admitted from wait list	7
# of early decision applicants	162
% accepted early decision	77

FRESHMAN PROFILE

Range SAT Critical Reading	580–680
Range SAT Math	640–740
Range SAT Writing	560–660
Range ACT Composite	25–29
Minimum Paper TOEFL	570
Minimum Computer Based TOEFL	230
% graduated top 10% of class	62
% graduated top 25% of class	95
% graduated top 50% of class	100

DEADLINES

Early decision application deadline	11/1
Early decision notification	12/15
Regular application deadline	1/15
Regular notification	3/15
Nonfall registration?	yes

APPLICANTS ALSO LOOK AT

AND OFTEN PREFER
Cornell University, Massachusetts Institute of Technology

AND SOMETIMES PREFER
Boston University, Carnegie Mellon University, University of Rochester

AND RARELY PREFER
Clarkson University, Rochester Institute of Technology, State University of New York at Binghamton, Syracuse University, Worcester Polytechnic Institute

FINANCIAL FACTS

Financial Aid Rating	86
Annual tuition	$34,900
Room & Board	$10,420
Book and supplies	$1,802
Required fees	$978
% frosh rec. need-based scholarship or grant aid	66
% UG rec. need-based scholarship or grant aid	67
% frosh rec. need-based self-help aid	42
% UG rec. need-based self-help aid	42
% frosh rec. any financial aid	99
% UG rec. any financial aid	92

RHODES COLLEGE

OFFICE OF ADMISSIONS, 2000 NORTH PARKWAY, MEMPHIS, TN 38112 • ADMISSIONS: 901-843-3700 • FAX: 901-843-3631

CAMPUS LIFE
Quality of Life Rating	76
Fire Safety Rating	60*
Type of school	private
Affiliation	Presbyterian
Environment	metropolis

STUDENTS
Total undergrad enrollment	1,672
% male/female	41/59
% from out of state	73
% from public high school	52
% live on campus	74
% in (# of) fraternities	48 (7)
% in (# of) sororities	52 (6)
% African American	6
% Asian	4
% Caucasian	84
% Hispanic	2

SURVEY SAYS . . .
No one cheats
Great computer facilities
Great library
Students are friendly
Great off-campus food
Frats and sororities dominate social
scene
Lots of beer drinking
Hard liquor is popular

ACADEMICS
Academic Rating	93
Calendar	semester
Student/faculty ratio	11:1
Profs interesting rating	85
Profs accessible rating	86
% profs teaching	
UG courses	100
% classes taught by TAs	0
Most common	
lab size	20–29 students
Most common	
reg class size	10–19 students

MOST POPULAR MAJORS
biology/biological sciences
business administration/
management
English language and literature

STUDENTS SAY

Academics

As "an academically intense liberal arts college with outstanding opportunities for community service and study abroad," Rhodes College lures top area undergrads with "fabulous grad school acceptance ratings, great professor-student interactions and research, and great opportunities in Memphis" of both the career-building and leisure-time variety. Undergrads here praise the "exceptionally high quality of the academics, defined primarily by the small seminar-style classes and the highly approachable and knowledgeable professors," noting that "a distinct majority of professors genuinely love to teach and are just as passionate about their fields and research as they are with the progress [of] their students." As at similar small elite schools, "Academics are tough and the professors demand that you think for yourself. Academic life is characterized by writing papers all the time." Students see the rigors of their curriculum as "preparation and training to effectively translate academic ideas into leadership skills, with the ultimate goal of building stronger, more stable communities."

Life

Rhodes undergrads shoulder a "high commitment to schoolwork" and "often seem overwhelmed by the amount to do," but that doesn't keep them from being able "to balance work and play." "Most are involved either with some sort of on-campus job, internship, student organization or community service effort in the Memphis area." Campus life offers "something to do any night of the week," with "many students very involved in Greek life" and "lots of creative activities provided by the administration." Parties "are the norm on weekends, usually at the frat houses, although recently more parties have been off campus due to an administration crackdown." However, "If you are not into partying, then downtown Memphis is only a few minutes down the road, and there are tons of things to do there. Memphis seems like a little town, but it's really not. If you like music, Memphis is the capital of all music from blues to rock. I came from a city that was about three times larger than Memphis, and I will tell you that Memphis has more unique things…to do than anywhere I have ever been. It really is amazing." While some students worry about crime in Memphis ("It is often in the back of our minds but has never been a problem on campus"), most don't let it deter them from enjoying "one of the most fun cities to live in." As an added bonus, "Rhodes is across the street from the zoo, and Tuesdays are free, so it's a lot of fun to go see the pandas and polar bears."

Student Body

There is "a definite stereotype for the typical Rhodes student, but like all stereotypes, it does not accurately describe and assess the student body as a whole." It "is often tempting to describe the typical Rhodes student as a wealthy, White, Protestant Southerner," but as one student points out, "the fact that I am a liberal Jew from California shows that many students defy the stereotype. There are many atypical students, but students of different races, financial backgrounds, and religions upbringings still manage to interact with each other and with the Memphis community." Even so, a casual observer could be forgiven for drawing overly general conclusions based on the students' appearance, for there is definitely "a Rhodes look" consisting of "pastel polo shirts and pressed khaki pants." Undergrads tend to be "goal-oriented overachievers" who "work extremely hard" to "realize a future at a good law school, med school, or other graduate program." Many students are seen as being "very religious," and while it can be "a bit difficult" to find your "own niche," "You make a lot of good connections and friends here."

FINANCIAL AID: 901-843-3810 • E-MAIL: ADMINFO@RHODES.EDU • WEBSITE: WWW.RHODES.EDU

ADMISSIONS

Very important factors considered include: Academic GPA, class rank, rigor of secondary school record. *Important factors considered include:* Alumni/ae relation, application essay, character/personal qualities, racial/ethnic status, recommendation(s), standardized test scores. *Other factors considered include:* Campus visit, extracurricular activities, first generation, geographical residence, level of applicant's interest, state residency, talent/ability, volunteer work, work experience. SAT or ACT required; TOEFL required of all non-native, English-speaking international applicants. High school diploma is required, and GED is accepted. *Academic units required:* 4 English, 3 math, 2 science (2 science labs), 2 foreign language, 2 social studies, 3 academic electives. *Academic units recommended:* 4 math.

The Inside Word

Rhodes' profile is rising, and as it does, so do both the number of applications it receives and its rejection rate. You can improve your chances of acceptance by showing an active interest in attending—visit the school, meet with an Admissions Counselor, and maintain contact with the Admissions Office to remind administrators that Rhodes is high on your wish list, and hopefully, in return you'll be high on theirs.

FINANCIAL AID

Students should submit: FAFSA, CSS/Financial Aid PROFILE, Noncustodial PROFILE. Regular filing deadline is March 1. The Princeton Review suggests that all financial aid forms be submitted as soon as possible after January 1. *Need-based scholarships/grants offered:* Pell Grant, SEOG, state scholarships/grants, private scholarships, the school's own gift aid. *Loan aid offered:* FFEL Subsidized Stafford, FFEL Unsubsidized Stafford, FFEL PLUS, Federal Perkins Loan. Federal Work-Study Program available. Institutional employment available. Off-campus job opportunities are good.

FROM THE ADMISSIONS OFFICE

"It's not just one characteristic that makes Rhodes different from other colleges; it's a special blend of features that sets us apart. We are a selective liberal arts college yet without a cutthroat atmosphere; we are a small community yet located in a major city; we are in a metropolitan area yet offer one of the most beautiful and serene campuses in the nation. Our students are serious about learning and yet know how to have fun in an atmosphere of trust and respect brought about by adherence to the honor code. And they know that learning at Rhodes doesn't mean sitting in a lecture hall and memorizing the professor's lecture. It means interaction, discussion, and a process of teacher and student discovering knowledge together. Community service is an integral part of the culture at Rhodes. Our students are keenly aware of their social responsibility, and over 80 percent are involved as volunteers throughout their college years. Rhodes is a place that welcomes new people and new ideas. It's a place of energy and enlightenment, not of apathy and complacency. Everyone who is a part of the Rhodes community is striving to be the best at what she/he does.

"Applicants for Fall 2008 are required to take the SAT or the ACT. The ACT Writing section is optional. Homeschool students must submit two SAT Subject Tests from areas other than English and Mathematics."

SELECTIVITY

Admissions Rating	**94**
# of applicants	3,786
% of applicants accepted	49
% of acceptees attending	24
# accepting a place on wait list	250
% admitted from wait list	18
# of early decision applicants	154
% accepted early decision	53

FRESHMAN PROFILE

Range SAT Critical Reading	590–690
Range SAT Math	590–680
Range ACT Composite	26–30
Minimum Paper TOEFL	550
Minimum Computer Based TOEFL	213
Average HS GPA	3.85
% graduated top 10% of class	52
% graduated top 25% of class	78
% graduated top 50% of class	95

DEADLINES

Early decision application deadline	11/1, 1/1
Early decision notification	12/1, 2/1
Regular notification	
	4/1 regular decision
	12/1 spring semester
Nonfall registration?	yes

APPLICANTS ALSO LOOK AT

AND OFTEN PREFER

Davidson College, The University of Texas at Austin, Washington and Lee University, Washington University in St. Louis

AND SOMETIMES PREFER

Furman University, Sewanee—The University of the South, Trinity University, University of Richmond, Vanderbilt University

AND RARELY PREFER

Birmingham-Southern College, Centre College, Southern Methodist University, The University of Memphis, The University of Tennessee at Knoxville

FINANCIAL FACTS

Financial Aid Rating	**83**
Annual tuition	$30,342
Room & Board	$7,468
Books and supplies	$904
Required fees	$310
% frosh rec. need-based scholarship or grant aid	46
% UG rec. need-based scholarship or grant aid	39
% frosh rec. need-based self-help aid	29
% UG rec. need-based self-help aid	25

RICE UNIVERSITY

OFFICE OF ADMISSION MS 17, PO BOX 1892, HOUSTON, TX 77251-1892 • ADMISSIONS: 713-348-7423 • FAX: 713-348-5952

CAMPUS LIFE

Quality of Life Rating	99
Fire Safety Rating	78
Type of school	private
Environment	metropolis

STUDENTS

Total undergrad enrollment	2,988
% male/female	52/48
% from out of state	47
% from public high school	71
% live on campus	69
% African American	7
% Asian	16
% Caucasian	54
% Hispanic	12
% Native American	1
% international	3
# of countries represented	32

SURVEY SAYS . . .

No one cheats
Great off-campus food
Frats and sororities are unpopular
or nonexistent
Dorms are like palaces

ACADEMICS

Academic Rating	96
Calendar	semester
Student/faculty ratio	5:1
Profs interesting rating	87
Profs accessible rating	88
% profs teaching	
UG courses	91
% classes taught by TAs	8
Most common	
reg class size	10–19 students

MOST POPULAR MAJORS

biology/biological sciences
economics
political science and government

STUDENTS SAY

Academics

Rice University is "a small school with the scientific research capacities of a large university" whose "reputation is strong in a diverse number of areas: our Jones School of Business, our School of Architecture, our Engineering and Music schools are all huge strengths." The humanities, although less heralded, are also solid at this top-tier institution. The school's greatest strength, though, may be its ability to draw an extremely bright and intellectually curious student body. As one student explains, "If you were made in high school to feel ashamed of your true enjoyment of reading and learning, apply here. You won't be alone, as most Rice students are, first and foremost, budding scholars." Students and professors form a strong academic community at Rice. One student writes: "Professors become intellectual bridge-builders, and they take a real interest in the development of individual minds." This air of mutual respect is exemplified and reinforced by the school's honor code, which "is taken very seriously, and no one cheats because that would be dismissing what the school stands for and decreasing the integrity of the degree earned. Take-home tests are common; cheating is unheard of." Course work here is extremely demanding—"If you take a science or engineering class at Rice and you get an A, you will have learned. There are no easy A's, and actually, there aren't many easy B's, either"—but, as a result, "Students get a great education, which is what we came here for."

Life

"Hands down, the residential colleges system and lack of Greek life make Rice an incomparably tight-knit, unique, spirited school," students here report. The colleges "dominate the social scene, holding parties almost weekly, usually with various themes such as its two largest: Night of Decadence (NOD) (synonymous with 'campus-wide undergarment party') and Bacchanalia, complete with togas. Other parties include 80s or Pimps and Hos. Each week a different college sponsors 'Pub Night' with free drinks and pizza. Parties are well attended, and dancing is very popular." The residential college system's proponents, who are many, tell us that "it unites a variety of people who might not otherwise spend any time together, and provides the same spirit of unity and crazy enthusiasm that a frat would." Students here want you to know that "despite the amount of work we always have to do, we have a great time. Rice is a really fun place." The campus is active: "The Shepherd School puts on fabulous concerts, there are always plays going on, and there are loads of clubs to join. If that's not enough, there's usually a sporting event of some sort and those are all free." Then there's Houston; one student reports, "The location of the campus couldn't be better. We're in one of the truly well-heeled areas of Houston, graced by long-boughed oaks—'a tree for every student,' boasts the Admissions rhetoric—and home to many cultural institutions, such as the better museums, restaurants, and pubs of the greater Houston area."

Student Body

"No matter who you are or what you're into, you will find friends who are intelligent, approachable, and often wickedly funny" at Rice. Undergrads here "are passionate about what they are learning and can converse wildly on a number of subjects. People complain sometimes about how hard Rice is, but they are happy to be here." They're also happy that their classmates "are not pretentious. No one cares what car you drive or even if you have a car. No one will exclude you if you are on financial aid." While "Everyone is so different that you couldn't even begin to generalize," a few generalizations do in fact hold true. One is that "there are tons of engineering majors here, and they're always building things or writing code." The other is that science and engineering students are convinced they work harder than anyone else on campus, and humanities students "get sick and tired of hearing about it."

FINANCIAL AID: 713-348-4958 • E-MAIL: ADMISSION@RICE.EDU • WEBSITE: WWW.RICE.EDU

ADMISSIONS

Very important factors considered include: Academic GPA, application essay, character/personal qualities, class rank, extracurricular activities, recommendation(s), rigor of secondary school record, standardized test scores, talent/ability. *Other factors considered include:* Alumni/ae relation, first generation, geographical residence, interview, level of applicant's interest, racial/ethnic status, state residency, volunteer work, work experience. SAT or ACT required; SAT Subject Tests required, ACT with Writing component required. TOEFL required of all international applicants. High school diploma or equivalent is not required. *Academic units required:* 4 English, 3 math, 2 science (2 science labs), 2 foreign language, 2 social studies, 3 academic electives. *Academic units recommended:* 4 English, 4 math, 4 science (3 science labs), 4 foreign language, 2 social studies, 2 academic electives.

The Inside Word

Rice has gotten loads of positive publicity over the past few years. As a result, what was already an extremely selective university is even more so. Candidates with less than the most impressive applications are not likely to last long in the admissions process.

FINANCIAL AID

Students should submit: FAFSA, CSS/Financial Aid PROFILE, Noncustodial PROFILE, Business/Farm Supplement. The Princeton Review suggests that all financial aid forms be submitted as soon as possible after January 1. *Need-based scholarships/grants offered:* Pell Grant, SEOG, state scholarships/grants, private scholarships, the school's own gift aid. *Loan aid offered:* FFEL Subsidized Stafford, FFEL Unsubsidized Stafford, FFEL PLUS, Federal Perkins Loan, college/university loans from institutional funds. Applicants will be notified of awards on or about April 15.

FROM THE ADMISSIONS OFFICE

"We seek students of keen intellect and diverse backgrounds who show potential to succeed at Rice and will also contribute to the educational environment of those around them.

"Student applications are reviewed within the context of the division to which they apply. Admission Committee decisions are based not only on high school grades and test scores but also on such qualities as leadership, participation in extracurricular activities, and personal creativity. Admission is extremely competitive; Rice attempts to seek out and identify those students who have demonstrated exceptional ability and the potential for personal and intellectual growth.

"Our individualized, holistic evaluation process employs many different means to identify these qualities in applicants.

"Required admission testing includes the SAT or ACT with Writing. In addition, Rice requires all freshman applicants to take two SAT Subject Tests. All test scores must be sent to Rice directly from the official testing agency."

SELECTIVITY

Admissions Rating	**98**
# of applicants	7,890
% of applicants accepted	25
% of acceptees attending	37
# accepting a place on wait list	457
% admitted from wait list	10
# of early decision applicants	504
% accepted early decision	32

FRESHMAN PROFILE

Range SAT Critical Reading	660–760
Range SAT Math	670–780
Range ACT Composite	30–34
Minimum Paper TOEFL	600
Minimum Computer Based TOEFL	250
% graduated top 10% of class	88
% graduated top 25% of class	96
% graduated top 50% of class	99

DEADLINES

Early decision application deadline	11/1
Early decision notification	12/15
Regular application deadline	1/10
Regular notification	4/1
Nonfall registration?	no

APPLICANTS ALSO LOOK AT

AND OFTEN PREFER
Harvard College, Stanford University, Yale University

AND SOMETIMES PREFER
Cornell University, Duke University, University of Pennsylvania

AND RARELY PREFER
The University of Texas at Austin, Vanderbilt University, Washington University in St. Louis

FINANCIAL FACTS

Financial Aid Rating	**98**
Annual tuition	$23,782
Room & Board	$9,590
Books and supplies	$800
Required fees	$474
% frosh rec. need-based scholarship or grant aid	40
% UG rec. need-based scholarship or grant aid	34
% frosh rec. need-based self-help aid	23
% UG rec. need-based self-help aid	26
% frosh rec. any financial aid	65
% UG rec. any financial aid	63

RIDER UNIVERSITY

2083 LAWRENCEVILLE ROAD, LAWRENCEVILLE, NJ 08648 • ADMISSIONS: 609-896-5042 • FAX: 609-895-6645

STUDENTS SAY

Academics

Rider University, its undergrads tell us, "is about teaching you the necessary knowledge for your intended major while really focusing on making and sharpening the skills that make you stand out as a leader." For one in three students here, that major is business related, an area in which Rider excels. Students praise the College of Business Administration, singling out DAARSTOC—"an executive skill-building organization that has prepared me more for the business world than any other organization possibly could have"—for its unique contribution to their education. Business undergrads also appreciate "the opportunities to get involved" through internships and volunteer work, telling us that they "foster your leadership development and prepare you for the real world by teaching you and allowing you to practice the 'soft skills' that are essential to success in any career." The School of Education, part of the College of Liberal Arts, Education, and Sciences, offers an excellent program in elementary education, while the science departments, which "provide so many opportunities to do work-study lab work" are also among the most popular with students. Throughout the university, Rider emphasizes a cross-curricular approach to instruction. Students recognize the benefits; one writes, "Every class basically coexists with [all of the] others, and when you're a senior, you see how all your courses come full circle to give you a better understanding of your major." Professors here "truly care and will do anything to help you succeed, whether it's helping you outside of the classroom with certain material, or helping you to get an internship or full-time job."

Life

Rider is "centrally located between NYC and Philly," giving students plenty of reasons to flee campus in search of fun, and when the weekends arrive many—although certainly not all—do just that. A number of students return home on weekends, giving Rider its "suitcase college" reputation. An increasing number are sticking around, though, and that number is bound to increase further in coming years when new residence halls "with apartment- and suite-style rooms [and the] multimillion-dollar student recreation center currently under construction" open. On and around campus, "Our student entertainment council is allocated a lot of money and uses it wisely. Between movies, concerts, comedians, and themed Bronc Buffets, there is so much to do, you can't possibly make all the events." Parties are frequent and well attended; one undergrad notes, "Fraternities have parties on the weekend, but Rider does its best to offer the student body options on the weekends. Don't you worry, we do our fair share of partying, but that's just not all we're about." Hometown Lawrenceville "is not much of a town; everything is a drive away. There is nowhere to walk to."

Student Body

Rider undergrads tend to be "rich kids from New Jersey with nice cars," although "great financial aid packages" bring in talented students from other economic strata. Most here take a pragmatic approach to education; they will put in exactly the amount of work required to get good grades, but rarely more. "Not too many are particularly studious, except when midterms and finals roll around; then everyone is a Rhodes Scholar," explains one undergrad. Without an impending academic deadline, the majority here would "prefer to party, hang out with friends, and have a good time 4 or 5 nights a week." A substantial minority bucks the trend, though; one from among their ranks writes, "The typical student at Rider unfortunately overshadows how amazing the top 30 percent of Rider students are. The majority are uninformed and really don't take ownership in their university. But the top 30 percent are so amazing that I feel they could beat the top 30 percent in leadership ability and performance in jobs anywhere, because they are all so driven, passionate, and prepared."

FINANCIAL AID: 609-896-5360 • E-MAIL: ADMISSIONS@RIDER.EDU • WEBSITE: WWW.RIDER.EDU

ADMISSIONS

Very important factors considered include: Academic GPA, application essay, recommendation(s), rigor of secondary school record, standardized test scores. *Important factors considered include:* Level of applicant's interest. *Other factors considered include:* Alumni/ae relation, character/personal qualities, class rank, extracurricular activities, geographical residence, interview, state residency, talent/ability, volunteer work, work experience. SAT or ACT required; TOEFL required of all international applicants. High school diploma is required, and GED is accepted. *Academic units required:* 4 English, 3 math. *Academic units recommended:* 4 math, 4 science (2 science labs), 2 foreign language, 2 social studies, 2 history.

The Inside Word

In the admissions world there are two all-important mandates: recruit the college's home state, and recruit *Jersey*! As a school in the Garden State, Rider deserves some special attention for the diverse group of students it brings in each year. Students who wish to attend need to have a solid academic record and good test scores. A few bumps in your academic past, however, shouldn't pose too much of a threat.

FINANCIAL AID

Students should submit: FAFSA. The Princeton Review suggests that all financial aid forms be submitted as soon as possible after January 1. *Need-based scholarships/grants offered:* Pell Grant, SEOG, state scholarships/grants, private scholarships, the school's own gift aid. *Loan aid offered:* FFEL Subsidized Stafford, FFEL Unsubsidized Stafford, FFEL PLUS, Federal Perkins Loan, state loans, college/university loans from institutional funds, alternative loans. Applicants will be notified of awards on a rolling basis beginning or about March 15.

FROM THE ADMISSIONS OFFICE

"Freshman applicants for Fall 2008 are required to take either the SAT or ACT exams. Writing components from either exam are recommended optional but not required. Students may submit scores from the old (prior to March 2005) SAT or ACT, and we will use the highest scores from either test."

SELECTIVITY

Admissions Rating	**75**
# of applicants	5,006
% of applicants accepted	79
% of acceptees attending	26
# accepting a place on wait list	32
% admitted from wait list	88

FRESHMAN PROFILE

Range SAT Critical Reading	470–570
Range SAT Math	480–570
Range ACT Composite	18–21
Minimum Paper TOEFL	563
Minimum Computer Based TOEFL	202
Average HS GPA	3.24
% graduated top 10% of class	13
% graduated top 25% of class	40
% graduated top 50% of class	75

DEADLINES

Regular notification	rolling
Nonfall registration?	yes

FINANCIAL FACTS

Financial Aid Rating	**72**
Annual tuition	$24,220
Room & Board	$9,280
Books and supplies	$1,400
Required fees	$570
% frosh rec. need-based scholarship or grant aid	67
% UG rec. need-based scholarship or grant aid	64
% frosh rec. need-based self-help aid	54
% UG rec. need-based self-help aid	50
% frosh rec. any financial aid	85
% UG rec. any financial aid	66

RIPON COLLEGE

300 SEWARD STREET, PO BOX 248, RIPON, WI 54971 • ADMISSIONS: 920-748-8337 • FAX: 920-748-8335

STUDENTS SAY

Academics

"A small liberal arts college that prides itself on promoting close relationships between its students and faculty," Ripon College attracts bright students seeking a "personalized education in a unique learning environment." A "great atmosphere" energizes the "small but friendly campus" of this school; the professors here "get to know you by name as a person, not just as a face in a crowd." Students praise Ripon's "emphasis on written and oral communication" and the liberal arts curriculum that gives students "very personalized opportunities for broad-based learning, both inside and outside of the classroom." As one student puts it, "As clichéd as it sounds, the community is what makes Ripon worthwhile. Going to a professor's house for dinner or having class in the local coffee shop is common. A friend of mine slept through an exam, and her professor noticed her absence. The professor called the Dean of Students, who then called her hall director. Her hall director went to her room to check on her, waking her up in enough time to take the exam, albeit a little late. Stories like that might be unheard of at large universities, but they are really characteristic of Ripon."

Life

At many small rural schools, students complain about the tedium of campus life, but no such complaints are heard at Ripon, where undergrads insist that "there's tons to do for fun." Popular activities include seeing "comedians, movies, or speakers. There are always athletic events, musical concerts, or plays to watch. There are also many intramural sports to participate in. And if you want to get away, there are a campus theater and a bowling alley in town, not to mention the cute downtown [area], which is just a block away." Ripon's robust Greek scene keeps things hopping with "lounge parties and festivals," while other student organizations offer "every type of group you could possibly want to participate in. And if you don't want to join, you can still participate in their events." In addition to clubs, "Collegiate sports are another one of our strengths. Everyone has the opportunity to participate, play, and even be a superstar." Undergrads here really love "the friendliness on campus. Doors are unlocked, and people leave their backpacks in the foyer before going up to eat lunch. The fact that things are not stolen really shows just how much we respect each other."

Student Body

The majority of Ripon undergrads are Wisconsin natives, with many "coming from middle-class families from small rural Wisconsin towns. Most are outgoing and very friendly, and are quick to say hello even if they don't know your name." The school's size fosters this gregarious nature; as one student explains, "You don't go to a small liberal arts school if you don't enjoy participating in class discussions. That's why most students here are outgoing." The size and Midwestern setting can breed homogeneity as well as friendliness: In the past, "The stereotypical Ripon student has been White, likely from a small town or rural area, and conservative." But "The image is changing as each class becomes more diverse. Because of this increasing diversity, I don't think there is really an atypical student at Ripon." What is typical of Ripon students is their energetic involvement in all aspects of school life; students at Ripon are "smart and enjoy school, but also like to have fun. There are many students involved with sports, student organizations, student government, and Greek life. Students on campus are very involved in the activities that they do."

FINANCIAL AID: 920-748-8101 • E-MAIL: ADMINFO@RIPON.EDU • WEBSITE: WWW.RIPON.EDU

ADMISSIONS

Very important factors considered include: Interview, rigor of secondary school record. *Important factors considered include:* Academic GPA, character/personal qualities, class rank, extracurricular activities, recommendation(s), standardized test scores. *Other factors considered include:* Application essay, talent/ability, volunteer work. SAT or ACT required; TOEFL required of all international applicants. High school diploma is required, and GED is accepted. *Academic units required:* 4 English, 2 math, 2 science, 2 social studies. *Academic units recommended:* 4 math, 4 science, 2 foreign language, 4 social studies.

The Inside Word

The admissions process at Ripon College reflects the school's familial atmosphere. Matchmaking is a top priority and Admissions Officers are thorough in their assessments. They closely evaluate qualitative components such as interviews and extracurricular activities, searching for eager and committed applicants.

FINANCIAL AID

Students should submit: FAFSA. The Princeton Review suggests that all financial aid forms be submitted as soon as possible after January 1. *Need-based scholarships/grants offered:* Pell Grant, SEOG, state scholarships/grants, private scholarships, the school's own gift aid. *Loan aid offered:* FFEL Subsidized Stafford, FFEL Unsubsidized Stafford, FFEL PLUS, Federal Perkins Loan. Applicants will be notified of awards on a rolling basis beginning or about March 1. Federal Work-Study Program available. Institutional employment available. Off-campus job opportunities are good.

FROM THE ADMISSIONS OFFICE

"Since its founding in 1851, Ripon College has adhered to the philosophy that the liberal arts offer the richest foundation for intellectual, cultural, social, and spiritual growth. Academic strength is a 150-year tradition at Ripon. We attract excellent professors who are dedicated to their disciplines; they in turn attract bright, committed students. Together with the other members of our tightly knit learning community, students at Ripon learn more deeply, live more fully, and achieve more success. Students are surprised to discover that here there are more opportunities—to be involved, to lead, to speak out, to make a difference, to explore new interests—than at a college 10 times our size. Through collaborative learning, group living, teamwork, and networking, students tap into the power of a community where we all work together to ensure success—at Ripon and beyond.

"All of the best residential liberal arts colleges strive to be true learning communities like Ripon. We succeed better than most because our enrollment of about 1,000 students is perfect for fostering connections inside and outside the classroom. Our students flourish in this environment of mutual respect, where shared values are elevated and diverse ideas are valued. If you are seeking academic challenge and want to benefit from an environment of personal attention and support—then you should take a closer look at Ripon.

"Applicants to Ripon College must submit scores from either the ACT (Writing section not required) or the SAT. We will allow students to submit scores from the old (prior to March 2005) version of either test and will use their best scores for admission decisions."

SELECTIVITY

Admissions Rating	**81**
# of applicants	979
% of applicants accepted	78
% of acceptees attending	35

FRESHMAN PROFILE

Range SAT Critical Reading	490–620
Range SAT Math	480–610
Range ACT Composite	21–27
Minimum Paper TOEFL	550
Minimum Computer Based TOEFL	220
Average HS GPA	3.47
% graduated top 10% of class	26
% graduated top 25% of class	56
% graduated top 50% of class	86

DEADLINES

Regular notification	rolling
Nonfall registration?	yes

APPLICANTS ALSO LOOK AT

AND OFTEN PREFER
Marquette University, University of Wisconsin—Madison, University of Wisconsin—Oshkosh

AND SOMETIMES PREFER
Grinnell College, Illinois Wesleyan University, St. Norbert College

AND RARELY PREFER
Beloit College, Cornell College, Lake Forest College, St. Olaf College

FINANCIAL FACTS

Financial Aid Rating	**87**
Annual tuition	$22,162
Room & Board	$6,060
Books and supplies	$750
Required fees	$275
% frosh rec. need-based scholarship or grant aid	84
% UG rec. need-based scholarship or grant aid	78
% frosh rec. need-based self-help aid	64
% UG rec. need-based self-help aid	65
% frosh rec. any financial aid	100
% UG rec. any financial aid	98

ROCHESTER INSTITUTE OF TECHNOLOGY

60 LOMB MEMORIAL DRIVE, ROCHESTER, NY 14623-5604 • ADMISSIONS: 585-475-6631 • FAX: 585-475-7424

STUDENTS SAY

Academics

Rochester Institute of Technology is a "serious, no-nonsense school" "with amazing facilities" and a "unique" cooperative education program which is "very good" at "preparing you to work in the real world." The "great technical education" is a main draw for students. Other "high-quality programs" include animation, design, and the "renowned" College of Business. The National Technical Institute for the Deaf "makes for a diverse population." "Hard work" and a "fast pace" define academic life. Courses "go by fast" on RIT's "hard-core" 10-week quarter system. "Classes require a lot of outside work," says a junior. One bonus of attending RIT is that "the best employers in the country hold on-campus interviews frequently." Upon graduation, "Job placement is really high" thanks to RIT's co-op program that "is required for many majors and encouraged for all." Co-op students graduate with "hands-on" experience at firms across the country. The "very passionate" professors here "come to teach, not to do research." "Academic support" is ubiquitous. "Even the worst professors I've had in lecture have been helpful after class," says an engineering major. "If you don't do well, it's your own fault." The "visible" administration is "fairly helpful." Some students wish administrators would "listen to their students a little bit more," but "The dean of your college is just an e-mail and appointment away."

Life

"Everything is made of brick" here and the "freezing" winters can be "very hard to walk through every day." "They should put us in a dome," helpfully suggests a first-year student. The weather notwithstanding, "RIT is a place where you come to work hard and make a lot of money when you graduate," explains a senior. The "competitive academic environment" "makes a lot of the students stress out," and students really "have to study." "On weekends, people tend to relax." "If you're looking for a party school," look elsewhere. "Big parties" are sometimes held "off-campus," but "not like the ones that happen at other schools." "Very intense alcohol-free policies" also stifle the party scene, and Greek organizations "are kept on an annoyingly tight leash." "School spirit" is not the highest, but "There are many different types of activities on campus." "Almost anyone who is looking for something to do can find a place to fit in." Engineering clubs "give students hands-on experience and knowledge that they can apply to both their schoolwork and the career world." The campus "is a great venue for influential speakers" and "The College Activities Board does a great job of getting big acts to come perform." There is also "an amazing gym," and "downtown Rochester is close and has a lot" to offer, including "amazing Indian and sushi restaurants."

Student Body

RIT students are "very hardworking" and "career-motivated." "Grades are taken very seriously." Students say "super-smart" engineering majors and "crazy science students" are typical, as are "ragtag art students, preppy business students, jocks, [and] hippies." Many students "like to fool around with computers." Some students assert that "RIT is a nerd haven." Others complain that RIT has a "reputation of being a dork school when it really isn't." "There is a stereotype that students here are unsocial and like to sit in their room playing video games," complains a senior. Without question, there are "kids who don't come out of their rooms," but those that do leave their confines "are awesome." "The variety of programs offered draws a very diverse group of students that can in no way fit under one general description," explains a junior. "The interaction of these extremely different groups of students is part of what makes life on campus so interesting." That said, RIT is "predominantly male" and many would like to see the male/female ratio improved.

ROCHESTER INSTITUTE OF TECHNOLOGY

FINANCIAL AID: 585-475-2186 • E-MAIL: ADMISSIONS@RIT.EDU • WEBSITE: WWW.RIT.EDU

ADMISSIONS

Very important factors considered include: Academic GPA, rigor of secondary school record. *Important factors considered include:* Class rank, standardized test scores. *Other factors considered include:* Alumni/ae relation, application essay, character/personal qualities, extracurricular activities, first generation, geographical residence, interview, level of applicant's interest, racial/ethnic status, recommendation(s), talent/ability, volunteer work. SAT or ACT required; TOEFL required of all international applicants. High school diploma is required, and GED is accepted. *Academic units required:* 4 English, 2 math, 2 science (1 science lab), 4 social studies, 10 academic electives. *Academic units recommended:* 4 English, 3 math, 3 science (2 science labs), 3 foreign language, 4 social studies, 5 academic electives.

The Inside Word

Admission here is nowhere near as cutthroat as it is at other top-tier technical schools on the East Coast. But that doesn't mean admission isn't competitive, since RIT's co-op programs and its tremendous record of job placement with prestigious employers all over the country make it an attractive choice for many academically-talented applicants. The relatively high acceptance rate is somewhat deceiving because the applicant pool is largely self-selecting. The applicant pool is also small enough that RIT can go over your application with the finest-toothed of combs, for better or worse.

FINANCIAL AID

Students should submit: FAFSA, state aid form. The Princeton Review suggests that all financial aid forms be submitted as soon as possible after January 1. *Need-based scholarships/grants offered:* Pell Grant, SEOG, state scholarships/grants, private scholarships, the school's own gift aid, NACME. *Loan aid offered:* Direct Subsidized Stafford, Direct Unsubsidized Stafford, Direct PLUS, Federal Perkins Loan, RIT Loan program, alternative loans. Applicants will be notified of awards on a rolling basis beginning or about March 15. Federal Work-Study Program available. Institutional employment available. Off-campus job opportunities are excellent.

FROM THE ADMISSIONS OFFICE

"Ambitious, creative, diverse, and career-oriented students from every state and more than 95 foreign countries find a home in RIT's innovative, vibrant living-learning community. Distinguished globally as a leader in professional, technical, and career-focused education, few universities offer RIT's variety of specialized studies. The university's eight colleges offer more than 170 undergraduate and 70 graduate programs in business, engineering, art and design, science and mathematics, liberal arts, photography, computing, and hospitality management. Distinctive academic offerings include microelectronic and software engineering, imaging science, film and animation, biotechnology, physician assistant, new media, international business, telecommunications, and the programs in the School for American Crafts. As home of the National Technical Institute for the Deaf (NTID), RIT is a leader in providing educational opportunities and access services for deaf and hard-of-hearing students.

"Experiential learning has been a hallmark of an RIT education since 1912. Every academic program at RIT offers some form of experiential education opportunity which may include cooperative education, internships, study abroad, and undergraduate research. Experiential education is designed to enrich the learning experience by providing students the opportunity to apply what they are learning in the lab and classroom to real-world problems, projects, and settings. Students work hard, but learning is complemented with plenty of organized and spontaneous events and an emerging school spirit. RIT is a unique blend of rigor and fun, creativity and specialization, intellect and practice that prepares alumni for long-term career success.

"Students applying for freshman admission to RIT for Fall 2008 must submit test scores from either the new SAT (with Writing section) or the ACT. Students who complete the ACT may submit scores with or without the optional Writing section, but the Writing section is recommended."

SELECTIVITY

Admissions Rating	84
# of applicants	10,219
% of applicants accepted	65
% of acceptees attending	36
# accepting a place on wait list	147
% admitted from wait list	31
# of early decision applicants	1,065
% accepted early decision	74

FRESHMAN PROFILE

Range SAT Critical Reading	530–630
Range SAT Math	570–670
Range ACT Composite	23–28
Minimum Paper TOEFL	550
Minimum Computer Based TOEFL	215
% graduated top 10% of class	30
% graduated top 25% of class	62
% graduated top 50% of class	89

DEADLINES

Early decision application deadline	12/1
Early decision notification	1/15
Regular application deadline	2/1
Regular notification	rolling
Nonfall registration?	yes

APPLICANTS ALSO LOOK AT

AND OFTEN PREFER
Carnegie Mellon University, Case Western Reserve University, Cornell University

AND SOMETIMES PREFER
Rensselaer Polytechnic Institute, Syracuse University, University of Rochester, Worcester Polytechnic Institute

AND RARELY PREFER
Clarkson College, Drexel University, State University of New York—University at Buffalo

FINANCIAL FACTS

Financial Aid Rating	90
Annual tuition	$26,085
Room & Board	$9,054
Books and supplies	$900
Required fees	$396
% frosh rec. need-based scholarship or grant aid	68
% UG rec. need-based scholarship or grant aid	62
% frosh rec. need-based self-help aid	63
% UG rec. need-based self-help aid	59
% frosh rec. any financial aid	81
% UG rec. any financial aid	75

ROLLINS COLLEGE

CAMPUS BOX 2720, WINTER PARK, FL 32789-4499 • ADMISSIONS: 407-646-2161 • FAX: 407-646-1502

CAMPUS LIFE

Quality of Life Rating	**81**
Fire Safety Rating	**81**
Type of school	private
Environment	town

STUDENTS

Total undergrad enrollment	1,720
% male/female	40/60
% from out of state	47
% from public high school	53
% live on campus	67
% in (# of) fraternities	20 (6)
% in (# of) sororities	23 (7)
% African American	5
% Asian	4
% Caucasian	71
% Hispanic	10
% Native American	1
% international	3
# of countries represented	33

SURVEY SAYS . . .

Small classes
Great computer facilities
Students love Winter Park, FL
Great off-campus food
Frats and sororities dominate social
scene
Lots of beer drinking
Hard liquor is popular

ACADEMICS

Academic Rating	**89**
Calendar	semester
Student/faculty ratio	10:1
Profs interesting rating	88
Profs accessible rating	88
% profs teaching UG courses	100
% classes taught by TAs	0
Most common reg class size	10–19 students

MOST POPULAR MAJORS

economics
international business
psychology

STUDENTS SAY

Academics

Students seeking "strong academics in a country-club setting" should consider Rollins College. Undergrads proudly describe it as "one of the best liberal arts schools in the South." Students here form "a community of learners seeking an education experience that advances responsible citizenship in a lively, comfortable, and intimate liberal arts setting." They pursue their goals through a "solid interdisciplinary education" that "draws connections across the curriculum to engage the student in the learning process, putting them in the driver's seat of their education instead of making them passengers." Rollins' "extremely challenging academics" include "a writing-intensive curriculum" that "helps you become a critical thinker and a better writer and communicator." Areas of strength include "an impressive Physics Department, [a] great theater program with professors who are working professionals, [a] strong pre-law program, [and] a good Education Department." In all areas "There are small classes, which gives students the opportunity to build strong relationships with professors and other students in the same field." While the Rollins experience "is whatever a student makes it, because it is a great place to grow academically for those interested in academic experiences or it is a party for those looking for social life," the school "is becoming more serious each year, with better teachers, a wider variety of classes/majors, and better support from the alumni, so the endowment is only getting bigger. Better students are coming to Rollins, making it a better school."

Life

Rollins College is "in a perfect location in Winter Park. We're close to movies, shopping, parks, museums, and nightlife in downtown Orlando. The beach is only 45 minutes away, Disney World and Universal Studios are only 25 minutes away, and there are golf courses all over the place." "Close" is a relative term, of course; the campus is close to all these destinations for students who have cars, but "If you don't have a car, don't plan on going anywhere. Nothing's in walking distance except a couple of great bars that are loaded with Rollins students 24/7." On campus and close by, "There's not much to do other than party. Fraternity and sorority parties are big, and everyone goes. Greek life is huge," with more than one-third of the student body actively involved and many others peripherally involved (attending parties "thrown throughout the year that are open to the whole campus"). Intercollegiate athletics "are not as popular here for some reason. No one knows when games are or who's playing." Students are big fans, however, of Rollins' "absolutely gorgeous campus," which is "located on a lake where students love to sail or wakeboard." Its "structures and landscaping are very pretty and well kept."

Student Body

The typical Rollins student "is blond, very attractive, and wealthy"—and well-dressed. One undergrad elaborates, "The typical female student is one who carries a very expensive purse, wears huge dark sunglasses, has long hair, wears polo shirts, and dresses up to go to afternoon classes but will always be seen in the morning wearing glasses and sweatpants. A typical male student is cocky but, once you get through that, generally sweet. Guys are always sporting collared polo shirts in bright colors and extravagantly colored pants." Undergrads here report that "the student body seems to be changing in makeup in recent years. Still, the majority is wealthy and flaunts it." The growing diversity includes "some kids on scholarship, some smart kids, some minority students, etc." One student observes, "There are enough atypical students that there is some variety and everyone has a place to fit in."

FINANCIAL AID: 407-646-2395 • E-MAIL: ADMISSION@ROLLINS.EDU • WEBSITE: WWW.ROLLINS.EDU

ADMISSIONS

Very important factors considered include: Academic GPA, rigor of secondary school record. *Important factors considered include:* Application essay, extracurricular activities, recommendation(s), standardized test scores, talent/ability. *Other factors considered include:* Alumni/ae relation, character/personal qualities, class rank, first generation, interview, level of applicant's interest, racial/ethnic status, volunteer work, work experience. TOEFL required of all international applicants. High school diploma is required, and GED is accepted. *Academic units required:* 4 English, 3 math, 2 science, 2 foreign language, 2 social studies, 2 history, 2 academic electives. *Academic units recommended:* 4 English, 4 math, 4 science, 3 foreign language, 3 social studies, 3 history, 3 academic electives.

The Inside Word

The personalized nature and nurturing environment that Rollins College fosters even extends to its treatment of prospective students. Each applicant is assigned an Admissions Officer who acts as his or her liaison. The college gives equal weight to most admissions factors and favors well-rounded candidates. Students who have enrolled in challenging courses will also find themselves well positioned for admission. Early decision applicants are given priority in admissions as well as in considerations for merit-based scholarships and need-based financial aid.

FINANCIAL AID

Students should submit: FAFSA, institution's own financial aid form. Regular filing deadline is March 1. The Princeton Review suggests that all financial aid forms be submitted as soon as possible after January 1. *Need-based scholarships/grants offered:* Pell Grant, SEOG, state scholarships/grants, private scholarships, the school's own gift aid. *Loan aid offered:* Direct Subsidized Stafford, Direct Unsubsidized Stafford, Direct PLUS, Federal Perkins Loan, college/university loans from institutional funds. Applicants will be notified of awards on or about March 1.

FROM THE ADMISSIONS OFFICE

"As you begin the college selection process, remember that you are in control of your destiny. Your academic record—course load, grades earned, test scores—are the most important part of your application credentials. But Rollins also pays close attention to your personal dimension—interests, strengths, values, and potential to contribute to college life. Don't sell yourself short in the application process. Be proud of what you've accomplished and who you are, and be honest when you describe yourself. Finally, the Admission Committee always likes to see candidates who express interest in the college. If we're your first choice, apply early decision. Each year we admit approximately one-third of the entering class through the early decision process. Are you unsure about your choice? If you can, schedule some visits, meet with an Admission Counselor, tour campus, and spend time in a class so you can see for yourself what Rollins and other colleges are all about. Take control of your destiny, and enjoy the process along the way.

"First-year applicants for Fall 2008 may submit either SAT or ACT scores for admission consideration. Candidates are strongly encouraged to complete the new Writing components, but results without Writing will be considered. Each candidate's best score combination will be used in the selection process; we strongly recommend that candidates consider taking both the SAT and the ACT."

SELECTIVITY

Admissions Rating	**89**
# of applicants	2,998
% of applicants accepted	55
% of acceptees attending	30
# accepting a place on wait list	49
% admitted from wait list	100
# of early decision applicants	319
% accepted early decision	65

FRESHMAN PROFILE

Range SAT Critical Reading	545–630
Range SAT Math	545–630
Range ACT Composite	23–27
Minimum Paper TOEFL	550
Minimum Computer Based TOEFL	213
Average HS GPA	3.4
% graduated top 10% of class	35
% graduated top 25% of class	65
% graduated top 50% of class	90

DEADLINES

Early decision application deadline	11/15
Early decision notification	12/15
Regular application deadline	2/15
Regular notification	4/1
Nonfall registration?	yes

APPLICANTS ALSO LOOK AT

AND OFTEN PREFER
University of Richmond, Vanderbilt University

AND SOMETIMES PREFER
Southern Methodist University, University of Florida, University of Miami

AND RARELY PREFER
Elon University, Florida State University, Stetson University

FINANCIAL FACTS

Financial Aid Rating	**87**
Annual tuition	$32,640
Room & Board	$10,200
Books and supplies	$700
Required fees	$60
% frosh rec. need-based scholarship or grant aid	40
% UG rec. need-based scholarship or grant aid	41
% frosh rec. need-based self-help aid	38
% UG rec. need-based self-help aid	38
% frosh rec. any financial aid	70
% UG rec. any financial aid	70

ROSE-HULMAN INSTITUTE OF TECHNOLOGY

5500 WABASH AVENUE-CM 1, TERRE HAUTE, IN 47803-3999 • ADMISSIONS: 812-877-8213 • FAX: 812-877-8941

CAMPUS LIFE
Quality of Life Rating	**82**
Fire Safety Rating	**82**
Type of school	private
Environment	town

STUDENTS
Total undergrad enrollment	1,851
% male/female	81/19
% from out of state	57
% from public high school	84
% live on campus	61
% in (# of) fraternities	37 (8)
% in (# of) sororities	50 (3)
% African American	2
% Asian	4
% Caucasian	91
% Hispanic	1
% international	2
# of countries represented	20

SURVEY SAYS . . .
Small classes
Lab facilities are great
Great computer facilities
Athletic facilities are great
Career services are great
School is well run
Campus feels safe

ACADEMICS
Academic Rating	**86**
Calendar	quarter
Student/faculty ratio	12:1
Profs interesting rating	85
Profs accessible rating	95
% profs teaching UG courses	100
% classes taught by TAs	0
Most common lab size	20–29 students
Most common reg class size	20–29 students

MOST POPULAR MAJORS
chemical engineering
electrical, electronics, and
communications engineering
mechanical engineering

STUDENTS SAY
Academics
"It's all about the family" at the Rose-Hulman Institute of Technology, that rare engineering school "where everyone either knows you or smiles at you anyway" and "The classes are really small, so the professors know you and remember things that you are involved in and ask about them." Tech schools are not typically known for their nurturing environments, but then again most tech schools don't have "faculty who love teaching and staff who are outgoing and friendly." Rose's small size is one of the keys to its success; here "You will never have a class of more than 30 students—even as a freshman in something like Calculus I—so professors always have time to help students who are struggling or who are just really interested in something mentioned in class." Undergrads can also seek help at the Learning Center, "which provides upperclassmen as tutors to help the freshmen and sophomores on homework and such." Students can use the help, since "The typical policy at Rose is to give students 3 hours of homework per credit hour per week. Most students take 18 credit hours per quarter, so this means 54 hours of homework per week, and that does not include lab write-ups, pre-labs, etc. . . . The courses are very difficult and require a lot of work." The reward for this hard work is opportunity, especially for those looking to stay in the Midwest. One senior observes, "There are 31 seniors in my major looking for jobs, and there were over 40 companies on campus looking for seniors in my major at the career fair."

Life
"There are lots of activities provided to the student body" at Rose and "The school works really hard to make campus life as wonderful as possible, with things like free photocopying and printing, free comedians, hypnotists, music performances, 3-D virtual Pac-Man on a random Friday, free movie rentals . . . the list goes on." The Student Activities Board "has bimonthly to monthly activities which students can attend for free! These include recent movies, concerts, motivational speakers, etc. It's very cool." In a way, entertainment has to come to Rose students, because they're usually too busy to go find it on their own. Not that they'd have much success in Terre Haute, where options seem to be somewhat limited: "You can go to one of the two movie theaters (three if you count the really old one) or to one of the 20-plus bars in the area. Most people choose the bars." On campus, "Many social activities revolve around the Greek community." Intramurals are also a big part of life, as "Many students come to Rose first for the academics but still enjoying getting down to the intramural fields for a little stress relief."

Student Body
"Rose-Hulman caters to a somewhat nerdy student," writes one engineer, "but we love it because we are all way past the too-cool-to-care attitude that seems so prominent in high school. Rose students are here to learn and to try new things, and everyone puts a lot of time and effort into their projects, their presentations, their homework, and their studying." White males "probably make up 80 percent of the student body," with students divided among "those who play computers and stay in their rooms and those who do sports and get out." "The great thing is, none of this matters to the student body, as everyone is treated with equal respect." Students at Rose-Hulman seem to agree, adding that "no matter what" type of student you are, "You are definitely going to be doing a lot of homework." Some here do feel that the school "could stand to use more variation in political views. The extreme conservative Republican viewpoint of most of the students gets a little old after 4 years."

ROSE-HULMAN INSTITUTE OF TECHNOLOGY

FINANCIAL AID: 812-877-8259 • E-MAIL: ADMIS.OFC@ROSE-HULMAN.EDU • WEBSITE: WWW.ROSE-HULMAN.EDU

ADMISSIONS

Very important factors considered include: Class rank, rigor of secondary school record, standardized test scores. *Important factors considered include:* Character/personal qualities, racial/ethnic status, recommendation(s). *Other factors considered include:* Alumni/ae relation, extracurricular activities, interview, talent/ability, volunteer work, work experience. SAT or ACT required; TOEFL required of all international applicants. High school diploma is required, and GED is not accepted. *Academic units required:* 4 English, 4 math, 2 science (2 science labs), 2 social studies, 4 academic electives. *Academic units recommended:* 5 math, 3 science.

The Inside Word

Embracing the school's engineering roots, Admissions Counselors at Rose-Hulman really rely on numbers and statistics. Class rank and test scores are obvious areas in which applicants may distinguish themselves. Don't be misled by the straightforward process, though; academic standards here are high, and students must prove they are capable of success during what promises to be a rigorous 4 years. Women would do well to apply here, as the college continues to seek out additional female applicants.

FINANCIAL AID

Students should submit: FAFSA. The Princeton Review suggests that all financial aid forms be submitted as soon as possible after January 1. *Need-based scholarships/grants offered:* Pell Grant, SEOG, state scholarships/grants, the school's own gift aid. *Loan aid offered:* Direct Subsidized Stafford, Direct Unsubsidized Stafford, Direct PLUS, Federal Perkins Loan. Applicants will be notified of awards on or about March 10.

FROM THE ADMISSIONS OFFICE

"Rose-Hulman is generally considered one of the premier undergraduate colleges of engineering and science. We are nationally known as an institution that puts teaching above research and graduate programs. At Rose-Hulman, professors (not graduate students) teach the courses and conduct their own labs. Department chairmen teach freshmen. To enhance the teaching at Rose-Hulman, computers have become a prominent addition to not only our labs but also in our classrooms and residence halls. Additionally, all students are now required to purchase laptop computers. Ninety million dollars in new facilities have been added in the last 6 years.

"Students applying for admission into the Fall 2008 class may submit either the SAT or ACT, and the student's best scores from either test will be considered. Both new and old SAT test scores are acceptable. The Writing portion of either test will not be required for admission to the freshman class of 2008."

SELECTIVITY

Admissions Rating	92
# of applicants	3,059
% of applicants accepted	72
% of acceptees attending	24

FRESHMAN PROFILE

Range SAT Critical Reading	570–670
Range SAT Math	640–720
Range ACT Composite	27–31
Minimum Paper TOEFL	550
Minimum Computer Based TOEFL	210
% graduated top 10% of class	63
% graduated top 25% of class	93
% graduated top 50% of class	100

DEADLINES

Regular application deadline	3/1
Regular notification	rolling
Nonfall registration?	no

APPLICANTS ALSO LOOK AT
AND OFTEN PREFER
Case Western Reserve University, Purdue University—West Lafayette, University of Illinois at Urbana-Champaign

AND SOMETIMES PREFER
Georgia Institute of Technology, Rensselaer Polytechnic Institute, Worcester Polytechnic Institute

AND RARELY PREFER
Kettering University, Rochester Institute of Technology

FINANCIAL FACTS

Financial Aid Rating	73
Annual tuition	$28,530
Room & Board	$7,869
Books and supplies	$1,500
Required fees	$465
% frosh rec. need-based scholarship or grant aid	73
% UG rec. need-based scholarship or grant aid	67
% frosh rec. need-based self-help aid	65
% UG rec. need-based self-help aid	59
% frosh rec. any financial aid	100
% UG rec. any financial aid	99

RUTGERS, THE STATE UNIVERSITY OF NEW JERSEY—NEW BRUNSWICK

65 DAVIDSON ROAD, PISCATAWAY, NJ 08854-8097 • ADMISSIONS: 732-932-4636 • FAX: 732-445-0237

CAMPUS LIFE
Quality of Life Rating	63
Fire Safety Rating	87
Type of school	public
Environment	town

STUDENTS
Total undergrad enrollment	26,286
% male/female	50/50
% from out of state	7
% live on campus	49
# of fraternities	29
# of sororities	15
% African American	9
% Asian	24
% Caucasian	53
% Hispanic	8
% international	2
# of countries represented	112

SURVEY SAYS . . .
Great computer facilities
Great library
Athletic facilities are great
Diverse student types on campus
Student publications are popular
Lots of beer drinking
Hard liquor is popular

ACADEMICS
Academic Rating	70
Calendar	semester
Student/faculty ratio	16:1
Profs interesting rating	62
Profs accessible rating	61
% profs teaching UG courses	70
% classes taught by TAs	20
Most common lab size	30–39 students
Most common reg class size	10–19 students

MOST POPULAR MAJORS
biology/biological sciences
business/commerce
engineering

STUDENTS SAY
Academics
Rutgers, The State University of New Jersey—New Brunswick, "is the kind of university [at which], if you make the effort to create your niche and find opportunities to succeed, you will have one of the best experiences of your life." With "a great study abroad program, solid academic departments and professors, the vast resources of a large research . . . and lots of scholarship money for honors students," Rutgers "offers boundless opportunity, both educational and professional, but you have to be willing to go out and seek it." Rutgers' immenseness is made more manageable by its subdivision into 13 colleges, "each with its own unique community and environment, all unified under one entity that can afford all the opportunities of a large university." Even so, the university's bureaucracy is legendary; one student writes, "The school seems to take pride in its web of red tape. The famous 'RU Screw' has become so notorious that the university president had to publicly denounce it." It's a good sign that Rutgers "is progressively changing its administrative policies under the administration of its relatively new president. There is a renewed focus on student service, and the changes are evident." As at many state schools, "Good things will not happen at Rutgers by sitting in the corner and waiting for opportunity to knock. It is a big school, so the more you put yourself out and make yourself known, the more likely you'll be able to find help in academics and administration." For self-starters, the rewards can be great; one writes, "I've had the opportunity to [conduct] my own research in the Rutgers facilities." Indeed, "There is a lot of research going on at Rutgers. The topics are numerous, and there are plenty of spots to fill if you look around well enough."

Life
"Weekdays are busy, and you can find places crowded at any time of the day" on the Rutgers campus, as "There's always something going on: concerts, free movies, talks. It's all about diversity and going out to find what you want to do." Student government "is huge, as is Rock the Vote. . . . There's always voter registration drives, and we even have Tent State University in the spring, during which a bunch of political student groups set up tents on the main courtyard and camp out for a week handing out literature, having fun stuff (concerts, etc.), and talking to people about what they do and how they can get involved." For some, "drinking is a big thing." One student writes, "If there was no such thing as getting inebriated, there would be nothing to do here." Many refute that position, noting that "there are other things you can do as well besides. There are lots of places to eat and drink coffee, . . . stuff like Jazz 'n' Java put on by the Douglass Black Students Caucus, . . . or going to a small discussion group with Jhumpa Lahiri, the Pulitzer Prize–winning writer," to name a few. While weekdays are lively, weekends are another story. One student comments, "Life at Rutgers would feel more college-y if people didn't leave on weekends and it [didn't feel] so deserted."

Student Body
Rutgers "is huge, so there is just about every type of person you could think of here." One undergrad observes, "With so many students, it's hard not to find others with whom you fit in. But the drawback to such a large student body is that you need to go out and make friends; you can't expect them to come to you." Another student adds, "To be fair, sometimes it feels a bit like high school (there are 'skaters' and 'preps' and 'thugs' and all that), but once you're an upperclassmen you kind of learn to ignore it."

RUTGERS, THE STATE UNIVERSITY OF NEW JERSEY—NEW BRUNSWICK

FINANCIAL AID: 732-932-7057 • WEBSITE: WWW.RUTGERS.EDU

ADMISSIONS

Very important factors considered include: Academic GPA, class rank, rigor of secondary school record, standardized test scores. *Other factors considered include:* Application essay, character/personal qualities, extracurricular activities, geographical residence, interview, racial/ethnic status, recommendation(s), state residency, talent/ability, volunteer work, work experience. SAT or ACT required; TOEFL required of all international applicants whose secondary schooling has been outside of the U.S. in a country where English is not the principal language. High school diploma is required, and GED is accepted. *Academic units required:* 4 English, 3 math, 2 science, 2 foreign language, 5 academic electives. *Academic units recommended:* 4 math, 2 foreign language.

The Inside Word

With a literal mountain of applications to process each admissions season, Rutgers does not have the luxury of time. The school looks at your grades, the quality of your high school curriculum, your standardized test scores, and your essay to decide whether you can make the grade at Rutgers. Although the school grows more competitive each year, solid students should still find little difficulty getting in.

FINANCIAL AID

Students should submit: FAFSA. The Princeton Review suggests that all financial aid forms be submitted as soon as possible after January 1. *Need-based scholarships/grants offered:* Pell Grant, SEOG, state scholarships/grants, private scholarships, the school's own gift aid, outside scholarships. *Loan aid offered:* Direct Subsidized Stafford, Direct Unsubsidized Stafford, Direct PLUS, Federal Perkins Loan, state loans, college/university loans from institutional funds, educational loans. Applicants will be notified of awards on a rolling basis beginning or about February 1. Federal Work-Study Program available.

FROM THE ADMISSIONS OFFICE

"Rutgers, The State University of New Jersey, one of only 62 members of the Association of American Universities, is a research university that attracts students from across the nation and around the world. What does it take to be accepted for admission to Rutgers University? Our primary emphasis is on your past academic performance as indicated by your high school grades (particularly in required academic subjects), your class rank or cumulative average, the strength of your academic program, your standardized test scores on the SAT or ACT, any special talents you may have, and your participation in school and community activities. We seek students with a broad diversity of talents, interests, and backgrounds. Above all else, we're looking for students who will get the most out of a Rutgers education—students with the intellect, initiative, and motivation to make full use of the opportunities we have to offer.

"Fall 2008 first-year applicants should take the SAT Reasoning Test or the ACT (with Writing component) no later than November 2007 in order to meet our December 1 priority application date. SAT scores from the March 2007 test administration and later are acceptable. Test scores are not required for students who graduated high school more than 2 years ago or have completed more than 12 college credits since graduating."

SELECTIVITY

Admissions Rating	87
# of applicants	27,560
% of applicants accepted	58
% of acceptees attending	33

FRESHMAN PROFILE

Range SAT Critical Reading	530–640
Range SAT Math	570–680
Range SAT Writing	530–640
Minimum Paper TOEFL	550
Minimum Computer Based TOEFL	213
% graduated top 10% of class	41
% graduated top 25% of class	81
% graduated top 50% of class	99

DEADLINES

Regular notification	2/28
Nonfall registration?	yes

APPLICANTS ALSO LOOK AT

AND OFTEN PREFER
Cornell University, University of Pennsylvania, University of Virginia

AND SOMETIMES PREFER
Boston College, Montclair State University, New Jersey Institute of Technology, Pennsylvania State University—University Park

AND RARELY PREFER
Seton Hall University, The George Washington University

FINANCIAL FACTS

Financial Aid Rating	73
Annual in-state tuition	$8,085
Annual out-of-state tuition	$16,755
Room & Board	$9,042
Required fees	$2,035
% frosh rec. need-based scholarship or grant aid	32
% UG rec. need-based scholarship or grant aid	33
% frosh rec. need-based self-help aid	44
% UG rec. need-based self-help aid	44
% frosh rec. any financial aid	51
% UG rec. any financial aid	50

SACRED HEART UNIVERSITY

5151 PARK AVENUE, FAIRFIELD, CT 06825 • ADMISSIONS: 203-371-7880 • FAX: 203-365-7607

CAMPUS LIFE

Quality of Life Rating	**79**
Fire Safety Rating	**81**
Type of school	private
Affiliation	Roman Catholic
Environment	town

STUDENTS

Total undergrad enrollment	4,136
% male/female	38/62
% from out of state	68
% from public high school	70
% live on campus	68
% in (# of) fraternities	5 (4)
% in (# of) sororities	5 (6)
% African American	5
% Asian	2
% Caucasian	85
% Hispanic	6
% international	1
# of countries represented	41

SURVEY SAYS . . .

Small classes
Great computer facilities
Athletic facilities are great
Career services are great
Campus feels safe
Everyone loves the Pioneers

ACADEMICS

Academic Rating	**78**
Calendar	semester
Student/faculty ratio	13:1
Profs interesting rating	79
Profs accessible rating	81
% profs teaching UG courses	96
% classes taught by TAs	0
Most common	
reg class size	10–19 students

MOST POPULAR MAJORS

business administration/
management
kinesiology and exercise science
psychology

STUDENTS SAY

Academics

Looking for an "excellent education" in Southern New England? Then Sacred Heart University may be the place for you. As one undergrad says, "I feel as though Sacred Heart offers some of the most brilliant professors available in the academic world." High praise, though as another explains, "At SHU, you can really connect with your professors. It is the kind of school where professors know the names of all of their students and remember them after the semester ends." The net result is an academic atmosphere that is "both stimulating and intellectually fulfilling." Learning is enhanced by SHU's "advanced" technology, which means that "the whole campus is wireless and most professors use this to their advantage by putting notes and assignments online, which saves paper and students from arthritis." Some students do complain that some upper-level administrators "seem disconnected." Others note that they would like to see the "registration process improve." But, all in all, if you're willing to suffer a few administrative headaches, you just might discover that "the academic experience is great!"

Life

"If you don't get involved then you don't get the most of the life on campus"—and yes, there's plenty to pick from at SHU. According to one freshman, "There's pretty much a club for anyone, making it easy to become involved. There are also community service projects happening all the time." A classmate adds, "Every day they e-mail us with the 'Events of the Day,' and there's always something going on . . . midnight volleyball, acoustic shows at the Outpost, concerts, sports games, and even Ping-Pong tournaments." Athletics are also a "big part" of student life. "I'm usually at almost every athletic event with my face painted red and a crazy wig on," says an enthusiastic supporter. Though SHU is officially a "dry campus," there are many wet appetites here. "It is a big bar school," explains one student. "There are some parties that go on, but the bars are where people go." To get to the bars in nearby Fairfield or Bridgeport, most students take cabs—"and the cabs are very expensive." There's also "a shuttle that takes everyone to the mall and runs on the hour." Other popular weekend destinations include New Haven, only "20 minutes away," and New York is "an hour" from campus.

Student Body

Your typical SHU student "is either a Yankee or Red Sox fan." In other words, most undergrads hail from the Northeast—"from Massachusetts, New York, and Connecticut," in particular. But if you call some far-off land home, don't worry: "Everyone seems to fit in, even if you're not from these states." A freshman describes her fellow Pioneers as "easily approachable, kind, courteous, respectful, and outgoing." But another first-year says that the four words that best describe your average SHU undergrad are "White, rich, preppy, and Catholic." Look beyond the "average" undergrad and you'll see that "the students at Sacred Heart come in all different shapes and colors, and come from different backgrounds and come from all over the world."

E-MAIL: ENROLL@SACREDHEART.EDU • WEBSITE: WWW.SACREDHEART.EDU

ADMISSIONS

Very important factors considered include: Academic GPA, rigor of secondary school record. *Important factors considered include:* Character/personal qualities, class rank, extracurricular activities, geographical residence, interview, recommendation(s), standardized test scores, state residency, volunteer work. *Other factors considered include:* Alumni/ae relation, application essay, first generation, level of applicant's interest, racial/ethnic status, religious affiliation/commitment, talent/ability, work experience. SAT or ACT required; ACT with Writing component required. TOEFL required of all international applicants. High school diploma is required, and GED is accepted. *Academic units required:* 4 English, 3 math, 3 science (1 science lab), 2 foreign language, 3 social studies, 3 history, 3 academic electives. *Academic units recommended:* 4 English, 4 math, 4 science (2 science labs), 4 foreign language, 4 social studies, 4 history, 4 academic electives.

The Inside Word

Who's the person behind the application? This is what the Admissions Officers at student-friendly Sacred Heart University want to know. While they place heavy emphasis on traditional academic indicators like high-school curriculum and GPA, they also spend time reading each applicant's admissions essay. If you really want to make an impact, why not head to Fairfield for a campus visit? A strong interview can turn many tides to your favor.

FINANCIAL AID

Students should submit: FAFSA, CSS/Financial Aid PROFILE, Noncustodial PROFILE. The Princeton Review suggests that all financial aid forms be submitted as soon as possible after January 1. *Need-based scholarships/grants offered:* Pell Grant, SEOG, state scholarships/grants, private scholarships, the school's own gift aid, Federal Nursing Scholarships. *Loan aid offered:* FFEL Subsidized Stafford, FFEL Unsubsidized Stafford, FFEL PLUS, Federal Perkins Loans, state loans, alternative loans. Applicants will be notified of awards on a rolling basis beginning or about March 1. Federal Work-Study Program available. Institutional employment available. Off-campus job opportunities are excellent.

FROM THE ADMISSIONS OFFICE

"Sacred Heart University, distinguished by the personal attention it provides its students, is a thriving, dynamic university known for its commitment to academic excellence, cutting-edge technology, and community service. The second-largest Catholic university in New England, Sacred Heart continues to be innovative in its offerings to students; recently launched programs include Connecticut's first doctoral program in physical therapy, an MBA program for liberal arts undergraduates at the newly AACSB-accredited John F. Welch College of Business, and a campus in County Kerry, Ireland.

"The university's commitment to experiential learning incorporates concrete, real-life study for students in all majors. Drawing on the rich resources in New England and New York City, students are connected with research and internship opportunities ranging from co-ops at international advertising agencies to research with faculty on marine life in the Long Island Sound. These experiential learning opportunities are complemented by a rich student life program offering over 80 student organizations including strong music programs, media clubs, and academic honor societies. To help students transition to college life and navigate the many opportunities available, all freshmen are assigned mentors, who work one-on-one to facilitate students' personal development and enhance the learning process both in and out of the classroom.

"Students applying to Sacred Heart University benefit from a comprehensive, holistic admissions process which takes into account not only applicants' grade point averages and standardized test scores, but also their overall student profiles including strength of college preparatory curricula, leadership and community service experience, character, and extraordinary talents.

"Either the SAT or the ACT (with Writing component) is required for admission. For students taking the SAT more than once, the highest Math score and the highest Critical Reading score will be evaluated by the Admissions Committee. No current policy exists for the use of the SAT Writing component. SAT Subject Tests are not required. For students taking the ACT more than once, the highest composite score will be evaluated by the Admissions Committee."

SELECTIVITY

Admissions Rating	82
# of applicants	6,219
% of applicants accepted	62
% of acceptees attending	24
# of early decision applicants	139
% accepted early decision	56

FRESHMAN PROFILE

Range SAT Critical Reading	480–560
Range SAT Math	500–590
Minimum Paper TOEFL	500
Minimum Computer Based TOEFL	270
Average HS GPA	3.3
% graduated top 10% of class	14
% graduated top 25% of class	43
% graduated top 50% of class	80

DEADLINES

Early decision application deadline	11/15
Regular notification	rolling
Nonfall registration?	yes

APPLICANTS ALSO LOOK AT

AND OFTEN PREFER
University of Connecticut

AND SOMETIMES PREFER
Fairfield University, Fordham University, Marist College, Providence College, Quinnipiac University, The University of Scranton

AND RARELY PREFER
Hofstra University, Iona College, Seton Hall University

FINANCIAL FACTS

Financial Aid Rating	74
Annual tuition	$25,300
Room & Board	$10,266
Books and supplies	$700
Required fees	$100
% frosh rec. need-based scholarship or grant aid	65
% UG rec. need-based scholarship or grant aid	64
% frosh rec. need-based self-help aid	59
% UG rec. need-based self-help aid	58
% frosh rec. any financial aid	83
% UG rec. any financial aid	88

SAINT ANSELM COLLEGE

100 SAINT ANSELM DRIVE, MANCHESTER, NH 03102-1310 • ADMISSIONS: 603-641-7500 • FAX: 603-641-7550

STUDENTS SAY

Academics

"There is a really strong sense of community among students, faculty, and the monastic community" at Saint Anselm College, a small, Benedictine, liberal arts school in frosty New England. Students love "the one-on-one support of professors and the mentorship they provide," telling us, "If you are looking toward graduate study, you will stand out among other candidates due to the freedom you have to get involved with professors' work here." One undergrad notes, "When people here say their doors are always open, they really mean it. Countless times I have been able to walk right into the offices of the dean, the Dean of Students, any professor, and even the president. Their commitment to the students is absolutely unquestionable." Most here love "the very strong humanities program," a required 2-year sequence that "teaches you to think about what is important in life. The overarching theme of the program is 'portraits of human greatness.' It provides discussion on things many normally would not think about." Required philosophy and theology classes as well as an intermediate-level language requirement all "help you become a more well-rounded person." Saint A's is notoriously tough academically; "I have never had to work so hard in my life for a good grade, but I have also never enjoyed learning as much as I am enjoying it here," writes one student. Another observes, "Saint A's is nicknamed 'Saint C's.' It is extremely difficult to receive an A here, which makes the students work harder to be the few who do receive them."

Life

Saint Anselm "is a beautiful, small, and homey school" where "You are truly welcomed when you get here." After that, it's time to get to work. "You cannot have too much of a social life here at St. Anselm because the course requirements are so challenging," students warn, but "That's not to say you can't have fun." Students report that "from Monday to Thursday there isn't a whole lot that goes on unless you join a club or sport." Weekends are more active, as there's "always something entertaining to do, from open mic nights to trips into Boston/NYC, to gingerbread-house-building contests. These are always student run and student funded." You'll also "find a party if you're on a mission to find one, but it will most likely be off-campus [because] the rules on campus are so strict that it feels like you're in ninth grade again." Students often make the trip into Manchester, which "has a lot going on, from our semi-pro hockey team, the Manchester Monarchs (only $11 a ticket), to bars and clubs that hold college nights specifically targeting Saint A's students," as well as "a mall, places to eat, go bowling, and see movies." There's a lot of good skiing in the area, too, and Boston isn't too far down the road. Community service is big; in fact, "about 80 percent of students and faculty are involved to some degree." One student sums up life this way: "Our school is infamous for strict intervisitation hours, an arduous humanities program, hours of reading, severe grade deflation, and monks around the campus."

Student Body

The "mostly White, Irish Catholic" undergrads of Saint Anselm "are more than likely to talk with a Boston accent," as "most kids are from Boston or from small towns in New England." Prep-school grads are strongly represented, but so are public-school students. One undergrad explains, "There are mainly two groups of students: The ones who received excellent aid packages and the ones whose parents are very well-off. The wealth of some students can be a put-off to others," and there are a few reports of rudeness between the two groups. Most here "are hardworking, friendly, and love being involved. By involved, I do not just mean in volunteer work (though we have a large amount of that on campus), but involved in intramural sports, clubs, and other activities." While "there aren't many atypical students . . . those who are here are welcomed."

FINANCIAL AID: 603-641-7110 • E-MAIL: ADMISSION@ANSELM.EDU • WEBSITE: WWW.ANSELM.EDU

ADMISSIONS

Very important factors considered include: Academic GPA, character/personal qualities, rigor of secondary school record. *Important factors considered include:* Application essay, class rank, recommendation(s), standardized test scores, talent/ability. *Other factors considered include:* Alumni/ae relation, extracurricular activities, geographical residence, level of applicant's interest, racial/ethnic status, volunteer work, work experience. SAT or ACT required; TOEFL required of all international applicants. High school diploma is required, and GED is accepted. *Academic units required:* 4 English, 3 math, 3 science (3 science labs), 2 foreign language, 2 social studies, 1 history, 3 academic electives. *Academic units recommended:* 4 math, 4 science, 4 foreign language, 2 history.

The Inside Word

St. Anselm gets a predominately regional applicant pool, and Massachusetts is one of its biggest suppliers of students. An above-average academic record should be more than adequate to gain admission.

FINANCIAL AID

Students should submit: FAFSA, CSS/Financial Aid PROFILE. Regular filing deadline is March 15. The Princeton Review suggests that all financial aid forms be submitted as soon as possible after January 1. *Need-based scholarships/grants offered:* Pell Grant, SEOG, state scholarships/grants, private scholarships, the school's own gift aid. *Loan aid offered:* FFEL Subsidized Stafford, FFEL Unsubsidized Stafford, FFEL PLUS, Federal Perkins Loan, GATE student loans. Applicants will be notified of awards on or about March 15. Federal Work-Study Program available. Institutional employment available.

FROM THE ADMISSIONS OFFICE

"Why Saint Anselm? The answer lies with our graduates. Not only do our alumni go on to successful careers in medicine, law, human services, and other areas, but they also make connections on campus that last a lifetime. With small classes, professors are accessible and approachable. The Benedictine monks serve not only as founders of the college but as teachers, mentors, and spiritual leaders.

"Saint Anselm is rich in history, but certainly not stuck in a bygone era. In fact, the college has launched a $50-million fund-raising campaign, which will significantly increase funding for financial aid, academic programs, and technology. New initiatives include the New Hampshire Institute of Politics, where the guest list includes every major candidate from the 2000 presidential race, as well as other political movers and shakers. Not a political junkie? No problem. The NHIOP is a diverse undertaking that also involves elements of psychology, history, theology, ethics, and statistics.

"Saint Anselm encourages students to challenge themselves academically and to lead lives that are both creative and generous. On that note, more than 40 percent of our students participate in community service locally and globally. Each year, about 150 students take part in Spring Break Alternative to help those less fortunate across the United States and Latin America. High expectations and lofty goals are hallmarks of a Saint Anselm College education, and each student is encouraged to achieve his/her full potential here. Why Saint Anselm? Accept the challenge and soon you will discover your own answers.

"Freshman applicants for Fall 2008 must take the SAT or the ACT. Students may submit scores from the old or new SAT. The best scores from either test will be used in admissions decisions."

SELECTIVITY

Admissions Rating	84
# of applicants	3,163
% of applicants accepted	71
% of acceptees attending	25
# accepting a place on wait list	264
# of early decision applicants	106
% accepted early decision	77

FRESHMAN PROFILE

Range SAT Critical Reading	500–600
Range SAT Math	500–600
Range ACT Composite	20–25
Minimum Paper TOEFL	550
Minimum Computer Based TOEFL	213
Average HS GPA	3.15
% graduated top 10% of class	23
% graduated top 25% of class	56
% graduated top 50% of class	91

DEADLINES

Early decision application deadline	11/15
Early decision notification	12/1
Regular notification	rolling
Nonfall registration?	yes

APPLICANTS ALSO LOOK AT

AND OFTEN PREFER
Boston College, College of the Holy Cross, Fairfield University, Providence College, Stonehill College

AND SOMETIMES PREFER
University of Massachusetts—Amherst, University of New Hampshire

AND RARELY PREFER
Merrimack College

FINANCIAL FACTS

Financial Aid Rating	78
Annual tuition	$25,430
Room & Board	$9,620
Books and supplies	$750
Required fees	$750
% frosh rec. need-based scholarship or grant aid	71
% UG rec. need-based scholarship or grant aid	70
% frosh rec. need-based self-help aid	62
% UG rec. need-based self-help aid	63

SAINT LOUIS UNIVERSITY

221 NORTH GRAND BOULEVARD, SAINT LOUIS, MO 63103 • ADMISSIONS: 314-977-2500 • FAX: 314-977-7136

CAMPUS LIFE

Quality of Life Rating	**71**
Fire Safety Rating	**83**
Type of school	private
Affiliation	Roman Catholic
Environment	metropolis

STUDENTS

Total undergrad enrollment	7,279
% male/female	42/58
% from out of state	53
% live on campus	53
% in (# of) fraternities	16 (13)
% in (# of) sororities	24 (6)
% African American	8
% Asian	6
% Caucasian	71
% Hispanic	3
% international	2
# of countries represented	80

SURVEY SAYS . . .
Great library
Students are friendly
Lots of beer drinking
Hard liquor is popular
Very little drug use

ACADEMICS

Academic Rating	**78**
Calendar	semester
Student/faculty ratio	12:1
Profs interesting rating	70
Profs accessible rating	73
% profs teaching UG courses	78
% classes taught by TAs	9
Most common lab size	20–29 students
Most common reg class size	10–19 students

MOST POPULAR MAJORS
biology/biological sciences
business administration/
management
nursing/registered nurse training
(ASN, BSN, MSN, RN)

STUDENTS SAY

Academics

"A medium-sized Jesuit school with solid academic programs and a campus that feels close-knit," Saint Louis University is best known for its "great premedical programs," which include "a great direct-entry physical therapy program" and "a well-respected accelerated nursing program" as well as the school's pre-MD tracks. Students also speak highly of SLU's offerings in business and pre-law, as well as its unique programs in aviation and "the one-of-a-kind nutrition program with a culinary emphasis." Since SLU is a Catholic school, nearly all programs here require a solid core curriculum that emphasizes religion and ethics; students praise the way this curriculum "forces you to examine your worldview from the moment you step on campus and helps you discover what your beliefs really are." One student writes, "The Jesuit tradition means that SLU really strives to instill the values of service, leadership, and diversity in the students." Academics, especially in the high-profile departments, can be rigorous. In this regard, SLU is "perfect for high achievers and scholars who strive for the best. The professors are nice and professional but are very stern about assignments being turned in on time." One student says, "When it comes to natural sciences, particularly chemistry, biology, etc., I think SLU can be very hard. I guess it works, though. A nursing degree or physical therapy degree from SLU is very highly respected in the health care profession."

Life

St. Louis is a major city that "offers a lot of things to do off campus, with great attractions such as national sports teams, the zoo, Moolah Temple, malls, and other places downtown." The city also boasts "a very good variety of concerts at many different venues," while the presence of major league sports teams such as the Cardinals, Rams, and Blues helps make up for the fact that "SLU doesn't have genuine sports programs." A student observes, "The great thing about our campus is its location in the heart of downtown St. Louis. It is very easy to get around to the city." For those who prefer to stick closer to campus, "SLU has much to offer for just about every interest. There are so many clubs and organizations to get involved with. Plus, the Busch Student Center provides many opportunities for fun, with dining options, places to study and have meetings, and large auditoriums for special guests and movies." Service is a big part of many students' lives, and "SLU's Jesuit influence encourages the student body to become active in the community. SLU's efforts to encourage community service give many students their first taste of the real world and better prepare them to venture out into it after graduation."

Student Body

Naturally, "a large Catholic population attends Saint Louis University," and "many students here are from the Midwest." The student population includes "a lot of middle- to upper-class kids" who "have been through the Catholic school system their entire lives." There are also "quite a few kids who went to public school and kids who are lower-middle-class," but still the predominant vibe, students say, is "preppy, with pearls, polos, pink, Birkenstocks, etc." No matter what his or her background, though, "The typical SLU student is involved in various organizations and enjoys college life while staying focused and studying hard."

FINANCIAL AID: 314-977-2350 • E-MAIL: ADMITME@SLU.EDU • WEBSITE: WWW.SLU.EDU

ADMISSIONS

Very important factors considered include: Academic GPA, standardized test scores. *Important factors considered include:* Application essay, extracurricular activities, rigor of secondary school record. *Other factors considered include:* Alumni/ae relation, character/personal qualities, first generation, interview, level of applicant's interest, recommendation(s), talent/ability, volunteer work. SAT or ACT required; TOEFL required of all international applicants. High school diploma is required, and GED is accepted. *Academic units required:* 4 English, 4 math, 3 science, 2 foreign language, 3 social studies, 3 academic electives. *Academic units recommended:* 4 English, 4 math, 3 science, 2 foreign language, 3 social studies, 3 academic electives.

The Inside Word

Saint Louis University has become more competitive in recent years. Admissions officers look for students who display a commitment to both scholarship and Jesuit principles. Applicants must demonstrate success in college preparatory classes and a desire to be active participants in the community.

FINANCIAL AID

Students should submit: FAFSA. The Princeton Review suggests that all financial aid forms be submitted as soon as possible after January 1. *Need-based scholarships/grants offered:* Pell Grant, SEOG, state scholarships/grants, private scholarships, the school's own gift aid, Federal Nursing Scholarship. *Loan aid offered:* FFEL Subsidized Stafford, FFEL Unsubsidized Stafford, FFEL PLUS, Federal Perkins Loan, Federal Nursing Loan. Applicants will be notified of awards on or about March 1.

FROM THE ADMISSIONS OFFICE

"A hot Midwestern university with a growing national and international reputation, Saint Louis University gives students the knowledge, skills, and values to build a successful career and make a difference in the lives of those around them.

"Students live and learn in a safe and attractive campus environment. The beautiful urban, residential campus offers loads of internship, outreach, and recreational opportunities. Ranked as one of the best educational values in the country, the university welcomes students from all 50 states and 80 foreign countries who pursue rigorous majors that invite individualization. Accessible faculty, study abroad opportunities, and many small, interactive classes make SLU a great place to learn.

"A leading Jesuit, Catholic university, SLU's goal is to graduate men and women of competence and conscience—individuals who are not only capable of making wise decisions but who also understand why they made them. Since 1818, Saint Louis University has been dedicated to academic excellence, service to others, and preparing students to be leaders in society. Saint Louis University truly is the place *where knowledge touches lives.*

"For Fall 2008 admission, Saint Louis University will accept either the new SAT or the old SAT (administered prior to March 2005 and without a Writing component). The school will also accept the ACT with or without the Writing component."

SELECTIVITY

Admissions Rating	**88**
# of applicants	12,120
% of applicants accepted	67
% of acceptees attending	19

FRESHMAN PROFILE

Range SAT Critical Reading	530–640
Range SAT Math	550–660
Range ACT Composite	24–29
Minimum Paper TOEFL	525
Minimum Computer Based TOEFL	194
Average HS GPA	3.68
% graduated top 10% of class	34
% graduated top 25% of class	62
% graduated top 50% of class	88

DEADLINES

Regular application deadline	8/1
Regular notification	rolling
Nonfall registration?	yes

APPLICANTS ALSO LOOK AT

AND OFTEN PREFER
University of Notre Dame, Washington University in St. Louis

AND SOMETIMES PREFER
Loyola University—Chicago, Marquette University, Truman State University, University of Missouri—Columbia

AND RARELY PREFER
Rockhurst University, University of Missouri—St. Louis

FINANCIAL FACTS

Financial Aid Rating	**70**
Annual tuition	$26,250
Room & Board	$8,230
Books and supplies	$1,040
Required fees	$398
% frosh rec. need-based scholarship or grant aid	61
% UG rec. need-based scholarship or grant aid	57
% frosh rec. need-based self-help aid	49
% UG rec. need-based self-help aid	47
% frosh rec. any financial aid	99
% UG rec. any financial aid	86

SAINT MARY'S COLLEGE OF CALIFORNIA

PO BOX 4800, MORAGA, CA 94575-4800 • ADMISSIONS: 925-631-4224 • FAX: 925-376-7193

CAMPUS LIFE

Quality of Life Rating	72
Fire Safety Rating	84
Type of school	private
Affiliation	Roman Catholic
Environment	village

STUDENTS

Total undergrad enrollment	2,489
% male/female	39/61
% from out of state	11
% from public high school	56
% live on campus	61
% African American	6
% Asian	11
% Caucasian	53
% Hispanic	21
% Native American	1
% international	2
# of countries represented	31

SURVEY SAYS . . .

Small classes
Frats and sororities are unpopular or nonexistent
Lots of beer drinking
Hard liquor is popular

ACADEMICS

Academic Rating	60*
Calendar	4-1-4
Student/faculty ratio	11:1
Profs interesting rating	82
Profs accessible rating	84
% profs teaching	
UG courses	100
% classes taught by TAs	0
Most common	
reg class size	10–19 students

MOST POPULAR MAJORS

business administration/
management
communications studies/speech
communication and rhetoric
liberal arts and sciences/
liberal studies

STUDENTS SAY

Academics

The "Lasallian tradition" on which Saint Mary's College of California is based "is about quality education, faith, concern for the poor and social justice, respect for all persons, and inclusive community." A junior explains, "It is about learning about all aspects of life, and growth through that learning." SMC students tell us time and again that their school truly embodies these ideals, living up to its motto, "Enter to learn, leave to serve," through its emphasis on "learning and service." The former is embodied by the school's Seminar Program, which focuses on classics of Western literature ("You'll like at least 25 percent of the books," promises one student, adding, "as for the rest, you'll have to accept that you're going to be a little confused"); wide-ranging Area Requirements that ensure "You learn a little bit about everything"; and "seminar-style classes" that "teach critical thinking." Students "enjoy the small class sizes" and appreciate that they "are able to actually go to teachers for help rather than seek the help of some random teacher's aide." Also, "If you're still having trouble in classes, you can seek out the help of a free tutor." Undergrads note that "the facilities could be better, but it is the people, the professors, and the administration that makes academics here so enjoyable."

Life

"Life at Saint Mary's is pretty easygoing." The pace is set by the low (some say "nonexistent") level of activity in hometown Moraga, a "mountain town where everything closes early, even the Jack in the Box." Students report that "due to the small size of the school, there is little to do on campus. This year, though, the main focus is to create more campus activities. The Program Board has organized many events, but most people don't take the time to check them out." The Lasallian tradition means that students are always "putting on community-service events." Intercollegiate sports are also popular, particularly basketball, which "is really big here." Some students "leave campus for the weekend," while those who "stay usually party." One benefit of the school's location is that students are "very close to Berkeley, San Francisco, and the little up-and-coming Walnut Creek." Many students appreciate that SMC is "close enough to San Francisco to have fun, but far enough that you don't have to deal with the issues of city life."

Student Body

SMC offers a "tight-knit community," though as many note, "The typical Saint Mary's student is White and comes from money" and "probably attended a Catholic high school in the Bay Area." However, "There are many other types of people on campus," and one undergrad explains, "The great thing about this school is that everyone is treated the same among teachers and students no matter what their background." Saint Mary's has "a healthy population of international students, many of whom are athletes, and there are a great number of ethnic clubs on campus that host different events throughout the year for anybody to attend." What you won't find here is "many goth types or hippies or anything that's not mainstream. However, that doesn't mean that they wouldn't be accepted into our communities." Some note that "the school is pretty clique-y," though the average student is "athletic and academically oriented," looking to "further themselves."

SAINT MARY'S COLLEGE OF CALIFORNIA

FINANCIAL AID: 925-631-4370 • E-MAIL: SMCADMIT@STMARYS-CA.EDU • WEBSITE: WWW.STMARYS-CA.EDU

ADMISSIONS

Very important factors considered include: Academic GPA, rigor of secondary school record, standardized test scores. *Important factors considered include:* Application essay, first generation, recommendation(s). *Other factors considered include:* Alumni/ae relation, character/personal qualities, class rank, extracurricular activities, geographical residence, interview, level of applicant's interest, racial/ethnic status, religious affiliation/commitment, talent/ability, volunteer work, work experience. SAT or ACT required; TOEFL required of all international applicants. High school diploma is required, and GED is accepted. *Academic units required:* 4 English, 3 math, 2 science (1 science lab), 2 foreign language, 1 social studies, 1 history. *Academic units recommended:* 4 English, 4 math, 3 science (1 science lab), 3 foreign language, 1 social studies, 1 history, 2 academic electives.

The Inside Word

The Lasallian tradition that Saint Mary's adheres to is an awareness of social and economic injustice. In line with this, Saint Mary's reserves one quarter of its undergraduate population for students from the lowest economic strata. In spring 2006, the school announced that it would boost its own funding of financial aid by 13.5 percent in order to help such students attend the school. Saint Mary's commitment to serving the underprivileged provides a great opportunity for low-income students with strong academic potential.

FINANCIAL AID

Students should submit: FAFSA, state aid form. The Princeton Review suggests that all financial aid forms be submitted as soon as possible after January 1. *Need-based scholarships/grants offered:* Pell Grant, SEOG, state scholarships/grants, private scholarships, the school's own gift aid. *Loan aid offered:* FFEL Subsidized Stafford, FFEL Unsubsidized Stafford, FFEL PLUS, Federal Perkins Loan, state loans, college/university loans from institutional funds. Applicants will be notified of awards on or about April 15. Federal Work-Study Program available. Institutional employment available. Off-campus job opportunities are good.

FROM THE ADMISSIONS OFFICE

"Today, Saint Mary's College continues to offer a value-oriented education by providing a classical liberal arts background second to none. The emphasis is on teaching an individual how to think independently and responsibly, how to analyze information in all situations, and how to make choices based on logical thinking and rational examination. Such a program develops students' ability to ask the right questions and to formulate meaningful answers, not only within their professional careers but also for the rest of their lives. Saint Mary's College is committed to preparing young men and women for the challenge of an ever-changing world, while remaining faithful to an enduring academic and spiritual heritage. We believe the purpose of a college experience is to prepare men and women for an unlimited number of opportunities, and that this is best accomplished by educating the whole person, both intellectually and ethically. We strive to recruit, admit, enroll, and graduate students who are generous, faith-filled, and human, and we believe this is reaffirmed in our community of brothers, in our faculty, and in our personal concern for each student.

"For freshman applicants Fall 2008, we will accept either version of the SAT. The ACT is also accepted. The ACT Writing assessment is optional. The highest critical reading and the highest Math scores attained on the SAT will be used. SAT Subject Tests are not required."

SELECTIVITY

Admissions Rating	**60**
# of applicants	4,991
% of applicants accepted	70
% of acceptees attending	17
# accepting a place on wait list	143
% admitted from wait list	81

FRESHMAN PROFILE

Range SAT Critical Reading	480–590
Range SAT Math	480–600
Minimum Paper TOEFL	525
Minimum Computer Based TOEFL	197
Average HS GPA	3.33

DEADLINES

Regular application deadline	1/15
Regular notification	3/15
Nonfall registration?	yes

APPLICANTS ALSO LOOK AT

AND OFTEN PREFER
Stanford University, University of California—Berkeley, University of Notre Dame

AND SOMETIMES PREFER
Loyola Marymount University, Santa Clara University, University of California—Davis, University of California—San Diego

AND RARELY PREFER
Gonzaga University, University of California—Santa Barbara, University of California—Santa Cruz, University of the Pacific

FINANCIAL FACTS

Financial Aid Rating	**72**
Annual tuition	$25,020
% frosh rec. need-based scholarship or grant aid	66
% UG rec. need-based scholarship or grant aid	52
% frosh rec. need-based self-help aid	72
% UG rec. need-based self-help aid	55
% frosh rec. any financial aid	75
% UG rec. any financial aid	73

SAINT MICHAEL'S COLLEGE

ONE WINOOSKI PARK, COLCHESTER, VT 05439 • ADMISSIONS: 802-654-3000 • FAX: 802-654-2906

Academics

The inclusive atmosphere at Saint Michael's College is "all about creating a comfortable, caring place for students, professors, visitors, and neighboring people." First-year students quickly find themselves in seminars, and "lecture-based classes always leave room for questions." An English major appreciates that professors "aren't afraid to teach passionately." They keep in touch, says a junior in sociology, "even while I was abroad or home in the summer. They would e-mail me articles I might enjoy or just say hello." Students expected conservative teachers at a Catholic school but found "90 percent liberals" instead. The broad-minded approach encourages students "to challenge yourself, your peers, professors, and leaders around the world." The faculty spans "geniuses who deserve to be at a better school and charlatans who somehow got tenure." SMC isn't considered a school for science majors—its emphasis is on study abroad and international programming—subsequently, a physics major finds him/herself in "classes of one and four people"; however, program numbers are climbing. The college's main strength lies in the mandated religion courses, which "are more like ethical discussions than anything else." Students report that they can easily find help from their classmates. "The student-staffed tutoring program and Writing Center are both well run and provide a comfortable environment for improving one's academics." As an institution "devoted to social justice and community service," much of the learning "happens outside of the classroom." The college prioritizes "a high level of awareness regarding world events" among its students.

Life

Nearby Burlington, Vermont, considered "the best location imaginable," wins Saint Mike's students over with its charming waterfront and blooming music scene. "Church Street is so interesting and quaint with tons of cool stores and interesting side shops." When May finals roll around, "Everyone loves to go down to North Beach and sunbathe. Some daring ones even go in Lake Champlain." Students survive the winters by employing a two-pronged attack of winter sports and drinking. The school-subsidized $25 season passes to Smugglers' Notch ski resort helps students save money for the bars. The under-21 crowd gets drunk before and after the alcohol-free dances or makes the trek to Montreal. Of the "40 groups with substantial budgets on campus," MOVE attracts the most students, putting more than 85 percent to work in community service at some point during their SMC career. Many students sign up for "correctional volleyball," where they play with local inmates. The popular Wilderness Program leads hiking and climbing outings, even a kayaking trip to Maine. An upperclassman asserts, "There is no way you could ever be bored on this campus."

Student Body

Students find that their school "lives up to all the hype about having a friendly and supportive community." For example, "Everyone hugs at Saint Mike's. Whenever you see anyone you know, you are greeted by a big hug." SUV-driving, Lacoste-sporting "hockey jocks," and Birkenstock-wearing, jam-band-listening hippies can be found embracing each other. Even a Republican Yankees fan from Vermont claims to get along with the majority of "Democrat Red Sox fans from Massachusetts." Among the 2,000 students, we find common ground in a shared enthusiasm for winter sports, marijuana, and (mostly left-wing) political action. A senior offers the general template: "Most students do volunteer work, enjoy low-key partying, and care about grades but more about experiences."

FINANCIAL AID: 802-654-3243 • E-MAIL: ADMISSION@SMCVT.EDU • WEBSITE: WWW.SMCVT.EDU

ADMISSIONS

Very important factors considered include: Academic GPA, class rank, rigor of secondary school record. *Important factors considered include:* Application essay, character/personal qualities, extracurricular activities, recommendation(s), standardized test scores, talent/ability. *Other factors considered include:* Alumni/ae relation, first generation, geographical residence, interview, level of applicant's interest, racial/ethnic status, volunteer work, work experience. SAT or ACT required; ACT with Writing component required. TOEFL required of all international applicants. High school diploma is required, and GED is accepted. *Academic units required:* 4 English, 3 math, 3 science (2 science labs), 3 foreign language, 3 social studies. *Academic units recommended:* 4 English, 4 math, 4 science (3 science labs), 4 foreign language, 4 social studies.

Inside Word

The school is as selective because it trusts students to live up to its Catholic and academic standards without a lot of hand-holding after admittance. The non-interventionist attitude on campus spills over into nearby Burlington, but keep in mind that Vermont as a whole is strict about underage drinking.

FINANCIAL AID

Students should submit: FAFSA, parent and student Federal Income Tax Returns and W-2s. Regular filing deadline is March 15. The Princeton Review suggests that all financial aid forms be submitted as soon as possible after January 1. *Need-based scholarships/grants offered:* Pell Grant, SEOG, state scholarships/grants, private scholarships, the school's own gift aid. *Loan aid offered:* FFEL Subsidized Stafford, FFEL Unsubsidized Stafford, FFEL PLUS, Federal Perkins Loan. Applicants will be notified of awards on or about April 1. Federal Work-Study Program available. Institutional employment available. Off-campus job opportunities are excellent.

FROM THE ADMISSIONS OFFICE

"Saint Michael's is a residential, Catholic, liberal arts college for students who want to make the world a better place. As one of only 20 Catholic colleges nationwide allowed to host a prestigious Phi Beta Kappa chapter on campus, it is clear why Student Horizons identified Saint Michael's College as a 'College of Distinction.'

"A Saint Michael's education will prepare you for life, as each of our 29 majors is grounded in our liberal studies core. Our superb faculty are committed first and foremost to teaching, and are known for really caring about their students while simultaneously challenging them to reach higher than they ever thought possible. Because of our holistic approach, Saint Michael's graduates are prepared for their entire careers, not just their first jobs out of college.

"With nearly 100 percent of students living on campus, our '24/7' living and learning environment means exceptional teaching goes beyond the classroom. The remarkable sense of community encourages students to get involved, take risks, and think differently. A unique passion for social justice issues on campus reflects the heritage of the Edmundite priests who founded Saint Michael's in 1904.

"Saint Michael's is situated just outside of Burlington—Vermont's largest city and a true college town. Students take advantage of some of the best skiing in the East through an agreement with Smugglers' Notch ski resort—an all-access season pass is provided to any Saint Michael's student in good academic standing.

"We require applicants to submit the SAT or the ACT taken with Writing component."

SELECTIVITY

Admissions Rating	84
# of applicants	3,073
% of applicants accepted	73
% of acceptees attending	26
# accepting a place on wait list	166
% admitted from wait list	32

FRESHMAN PROFILE

Range SAT Critical Reading	500–600
Range SAT Math	510–610
Range SAT Writing	510–600
Range ACT Composite	21–26
Minimum Paper TOEFL	550
Minimum Computer Based TOEFL	213
Average HS GPA	3.43
% graduated top 10% of class	22
% graduated top 25% of class	53
% graduated top 50% of class	86

DEADLINES

Regular application deadline	2/1
Regular notification	4/1
Nonfall registration?	yes

APPLICANTS ALSO LOOK AT

AND OFTEN PREFER
Boston College, College of the Holy Cross

AND SOMETIMES PREFER
Fairfield University, Stonehill College, University of Vermont

AND RARELY PREFER
Quinnipiac University, Saint Anselm College, University of Massachusetts—Amherst, University of New Hampshire

FINANCIAL FACTS

Financial Aid Rating	77
Annual tuition	$29,695
Room & Board	$7,460
Books and supplies	$1,200
Required fees	$250
% frosh rec. need-based scholarship or grant aid	66
% UG rec. need-based scholarship or grant aid	63
% frosh rec. need-based self-help aid	59
% UG rec. need-based self-help aid	58
% frosh rec. any financial aid	94
% UG rec. any financial aid	85

SALISBURY UNIVERSITY

ADMISSIONS OFFICE, 1101 CAMDEN AVENUE, SALISBURY, MD 21801 • ADMISSIONS: 410-543-6161 • FAX: 410-546-6016

CAMPUS LIFE

Quality of Life Rating	80
Fire Safety Rating	73
Type of school	public
Environment	town

STUDENTS

Total undergrad enrollment	6,519
% male/female	45/55
% from out of state	14
% from public high school	85
% live on campus	40
% in (# of) fraternities	5 (6)
% in (# of) sororities	6 (5)
% African American	10
% Asian	3
% Caucasian	80
% Hispanic	3
% international	1
# of countries represented	47

SURVEY SAYS . . .

Small classes
Lab facilities are great
Great computer facilities
Students are friendly
Students are happy
Lots of beer drinking

ACADEMICS

Academic Rating	**75**
Calendar	4-1-4
Student/faculty ratio	16:1
Profs interesting rating	76
Profs accessible rating	78
% profs teaching	
UG courses	100
% classes taught by TAs	2
Most common	
lab size	20–29 students
Most common	
reg class size	20–29 students

MOST POPULAR MAJORS

business administration/
management
communications studies/speech
communication and rhetoric
elementary education and teaching

STUDENTS SAY

Academics

"Small, personable, and beautiful" Salisbury University, a state school on Maryland's Eastern Shore, is "large enough to be diverse, yet small enough to walk anywhere you need to go." Students here love that "teachers get to know you as students rather than a number, and they are able to help you at a more [personal] level." Salisbury is probably best known for its Perdue School of Business, the most popular program among undergraduates. Students report that "the school is about teaching students how to become more professional and giving them the skills to be successful in the real world of business." Also noteworthy is the Henson School of Science, which recently received a boost via a new facility "with incredible resources and great technology that provide a flood of information." Don't forget education, Salisbury's longest-running program; "Salisbury was originally a teacher's school before it opened its doors to other majors," undergrads remind us. Students across programs laud the "great internship opportunities, excellent study-abroad programs, and professors who are dedicated and open-minded." As at all smaller schools and nearly all state-funded schools, not all aspects of academic life are first-rate. Arts and music students complain that "the school constantly underfunds us," and everyone agrees that "the library is ancient and small, only two floors with mostly old reference books no one uses." An honors program offers top students "small, almost entirely discussion-based classes."

Life

"Salisbury is a big party school," many students tell us, and apparently locals agree: The "farmer's town" of Salisbury recently passed restrictions on off-campus housing intended to curtail the party scene. As you might guess, town-gown relations aren't the best. One student reports, "The locals hate us; we do not get along whatsoever. They are not willing to accept the fact that we are here and we are not leaving." The school and students are trying to address the problem by scheduling more appealing on-campus events and providing services such as SafeRide, a "student-run drunk bus that gets the kids home safe, for free, and without getting written up." But there's more going on at Salisbury besides the parties. Students can dabble in "over 100 active student organizations" including "a student-run program called SOAP that schedules movies, comedians, and other interesting stuff" as well as "school-sponsored trips, activities, and on-campus festivals." Athletics are solid, as "Salisbury is among the top teams in Division III in almost every sport." When the weather is nice, students frequently take the half-hour drive to Ocean City and other beach resort areas. Annapolis, Baltimore, and DC are the nearest large cities, but most here agree that "They are a bit far" for regular visits.

Student Body

Students tell us that at Salisbury, "Everyone fits in somewhere." That includes "those who want to party and drink all the time, those who like to study all the time, those who study all week and party and drink on the weekends, and those who just like to chill out and have fun." One junior tells us her motto is: "Study hard so you can party harder." Most students are "very laid-back and dress comfortably," like those who enjoy coming to "class in his or her pajamas, yet who still manages to finish the work that is supposed to be done." Salisbury's students, generally speaking, are "active in either a social group, fraternity, or club . . . study for about 2 hours a day outside of class," and "come from Maryland, Delaware, or New Jersey." While there are "a lot of White, middle-class preppy types" here, they mix in with "students from all over the world, so it's very diverse and interesting." Out of all of this come "a lot of unique or atypical students, especially in the Art, Anthropology, Biology, Philosophy, and Music Departments." Some students detect a divide between the minority (on-campus residents) and the majority (commuters), pointing out that "people who live on campus have a lot more time to interact with one another."

SALISBURY UNIVERSITY

FINANCIAL AID: 410-543-6165 • E-MAIL: ADMISSIONS@SALISBURY.EDU • WEBSITE: WWW.SALISBURY.EDU

ADMISSIONS

Very important factors considered include: Academic GPA, extracurricular activities, rigor of secondary school record, talent/ability. *Important factors considered include:* Alumni/ae relation, class rank, geographical residence, standardized test scores, volunteer work. *Other factors considered include:* Application essay, character/personal qualities, racial/ethnic status, recommendation(s), work experience. TOEFL required of all international applicants. High school diploma is required, and GED is accepted. *Academic units required:* 4 English, 3 math, 3 science (2 science labs), 2 foreign language, 3 social studies. *Academic units recommended:* 4 English, 4 math, 4 science (3 science labs), 3 foreign language, 3 social studies, 3 academic electives.

The Inside Word

As a part of the new wave of public institutions of higher learning focusing their energies on undergraduate research, Salisbury has seen its admissions standards and the quality of its freshman class steadily improve over the past few years. As a result, candidate review is also more personalized than the formula-driven approaches of most public colleges. The Admissions Committee will pay close attention to the match you make with the university, evaluating your entire background instead of simply your numbers—though most students are academically strong to begin with.

FINANCIAL AID

Students should submit: FAFSA. Regular filing deadline is December 31. The Princeton Review suggests that all financial aid forms be submitted as soon as possible after January 1. *Need-based scholarships/grants offered:* Pell Grant, SEOG, state scholarships/grants, private scholarships, the school's own gift aid. *Loan aid offered:* Direct Subsidized Stafford, Direct Unsubsidized Stafford, Direct PLUS, Federal Perkins Loan. Applicants will be notified of awards on or about March 15.

FROM THE ADMISSIONS OFFICE

"Friendly, convenient, safe, and beautiful are just a few of the words used to describe the campus of Salisbury University. The campus is a compact, self-contained community that offers the full range of student services. Beautiful, traditional-style architecture and impeccably landscaped grounds combine to create an atmosphere that inspires learning and fosters student pride. Located just 30 minutes from the beaches of Ocean City, Maryland, SU students enjoy a year-round resort social life as well as an inside track on summer jobs. Situated less than 2 hours from the urban excitement of Baltimore and Washington, DC, greater Salisbury makes up for its lack of size—its population is about 80,000—by being strategically located. Within easy driving distance of a number of other major cities, including New York City, Philadelphia, and Norfolk, Salisbury is the hub of the Delmarva Peninsula, a mostly rural region flavored by the salty air of the Chesapeake Bay and Atlantic Ocean.

"Applicants for Fall 2008 are required to take the new SAT or the ACT with the Writing section, but we will allow students to submit scores from the old version of the SAT (prior to March 2005) as well. The highest composite score will be used in admissions decisions."

SELECTIVITY

Admissions Rating	86
# of applicants	5,910
% of applicants accepted	55
% of acceptees attending	32

FRESHMAN PROFILE

Range SAT Critical Reading	510–590
Range SAT Math	510–600
Range SAT Writing	500–580
Range ACT Composite	20–25
Minimum Paper TOEFL	550
Minimum Computer Based TOEFL	213
Average HS GPA	3.43
% graduated top 10% of class	26
% graduated top 25% of class	58
% graduated top 50% of class	90

DEADLINES

Regular notification	3/15
Nonfall registration?	yes

APPLICANTS ALSO LOOK AT AND SOMETIMES PREFER

St. Mary's College of Maryland, Towson University, University of Maryland—Baltimore County

AND RARELY PREFER

University of Maryland—College Park

FINANCIAL FACTS

Financial Aid Rating	70
Annual in-state tuition	$4,814
Annual out-of-state tuition	$12,708
Room & Board	$7,246
Required fees	$1,598
% frosh rec. need-based scholarship or grant aid	32
% UG rec. need-based scholarship or grant aid	28
% frosh rec. need-based self-help aid	30
% UG rec. need-based self-help aid	33
% frosh rec. any financial aid	65
% UG rec. any financial aid	66

SAMFORD UNIVERSITY

800 LAKESHORE DRIVE, BIRMINGHAM, AL 35229 • ADMISSIONS: 205-726-3673 • FAX: 205-726-2171

CAMPUS LIFE

Quality of Life Rating	92
Fire Safety Rating	60*
Type of school	private
Affiliation	Baptist
Environment	town

STUDENTS

Total undergrad enrollment	2,846
% male/female	37/63
% from out of state	57
% from public high school	56
% live on campus	64
% in (# of) fraternities	27 (7)
% in (# of) sororities	39 (7)
% African American	7
% Asian	1
% Caucasian	89
% Hispanic	1

SURVEY SAYS . . .
Small classes
Lab facilities are great
Students love Birmingham, AL
Great off-campus food

ACADEMICS

Academic Rating	85
Calendar	4-1-4
Student/faculty ratio	12:1
Profs interesting rating	91
Profs accessible rating	87
% classes taught by TAs	0
Most common lab size	fewer than 10 students
Most common reg class size	10–19 students

MOST POPULAR MAJORS
law (LLB, JD)
nursing/registered nurse training
(ASN, BSN, MSN, RN)
pharmacy (PharmD, BS/BPharm)

STUDENTS SAY

Academics
"Samford University is definitely not your average college stereotype," students tell us, pointing out that "you either love it or you hate it. However, if it is your type of school, it's heaven on earth." Those who fit in best are conservative, Southern, and either Baptist or very comfortable with Baptist values. The "focus on Christian heritage" is strong here, as is the imperative to "use the knowledge obtained to bring glory and honor to God." Some students temper this assertion somewhat, pointing out that "although SU is a Southern Baptist college with a very strong religious background, no one is bombarded with Christianity. Everyone has the right to choose what they believe in here." During class, efforts are made in getting "to know each and every one of the students. Classes are small, which encourages a climate of discussion and deliberation." Professors are "excellent teachers/facilitators who are more than willing to collaborate with students, be confronted, entertain varying opinions, maintain an open mind, and help willing students to succeed both academically and in other aspects of their field of study, such as internships, conferences, graduate school recommendations, etc." A "very good pharmacy program," solid nursing and business programs, diverse offerings in journalism and communication, and the visual and performing arts are among the most popular programs. One student sums up, "The overall academic experience here is a very challenging and rewarding one."

Life
Samford's hometown of Birmingham is "a great medium-size city with tons of activities and things to do," students here tell us. The city "is starting to develop as a creative core. It's got amazing parks. It is slowly becoming the culinary capital of the South, with an amazing variety of ethnic restaurants. There are plenty of coffee shops, theaters, and art galleries to attend. Birmingham may not have several of everything, but it has one of everything, which, for its size, is enough." The city has a decent club scene, too—some here indulge, but many do not. On campus, "There is a huge variety of events offered" including "concerts, games, theatrical performances, and bonfires." There's also "an abundance of root-beer keggers and dance parties at frat houses, as well as late-night coffee and pancake runs." (One student divulges that while "fraternities and sororities do not encourage drinking, a lot of them do it. Call them 'closet drinkers' if you will.") Despite the campus activity and the city's many attractions, "Everyone who lives close by leaves on the weekend. It's maddening to stay on campus—unless you have a car, because there's lots to do in Birmingham." Campus rules are predictably strict at this conservative Christian school. "The dorms are all single sex, which is fine, but all the university buildings close down by 10:00 P.M. (on weekends). That means there is no on-campus place for mixed-gender groups of larger-than-clique size to meet or socialize." Welcome to "life in a calm, quiet, Christian bubble."

Student Body
"You have well-mannered, educated, tactful, Southern gentlemen and belles" at Samford, and, according to some, not much else. "Life is great!" says one senior. "Everyone dresses nice, is polite, and is constantly smiling." But another student laments: "I think we need improvement in diversity, and not just in ethnic diversity. Students need exposure to others in order to realize that you aren't going to hell if you aren't Southern Baptist, if you drink, or if you skip church. The school seems to nurture this type of student a lot." One sophomore explains, "If you're gay, you're literally breaking a school policy." "More students from the Northeast and West Coast" would help, some here believe. For now, the Samford archetype is "a very conservative, cookie-cutter sorority girl" (there are "more women than men" here) who, according to a stereotype accepted by many is "here to get her MRS [degree]." Some say Samford is where "tomorrow's businessmen, right-wing pastors, and housewives" come to "learn, fall in love, and prepare to live in the suburbs." Undergrads are "very conservative," "very preppy, and always dress up for class. You will get condescending looks if you wear a t-shirt and jeans."

FINANCIAL AID: 800-888-7245 • E-MAIL: ADMISS@SAMFORD.EDU • WEBSITE: WWW.SAMFORD.EDU

ADMISSIONS

Very important factors considered include: Academic GPA, application essay, character/personal qualities, recommendation(s), religious affiliation/commitment, rigor of secondary school record, standardized test scores. *Important factors considered include:* Alumni/ae relation, class rank, extracurricular activities, interview. *Other factors considered include:* Geographical residence, level of applicant's interest, racial/ethnic status, state residency, talent/ability, volunteer work, work experience. SAT or ACT required; ACT with Writing component recommended. TOEFL required of all international applicants. High school diploma is required, and GED is accepted. *Academic units required:* 4 English, 3 math, 3 science (2 science labs), 2 social studies, 2 history. *Academic units recommended:* 2 foreign language.

The Inside Word

Samford's use of admission credentials in scholarship considerations is something that is quite common at colleges across the country. Students should always complete their applications as if such is the case. Even for universities where you are clearly admissible academically, giving some additional attention to essays and visiting for an interview can make the difference between being a scholarship winner and taking on an additional summer job.

FINANCIAL AID

Students should submit: FAFSA. The Princeton Review suggests that all financial aid forms be submitted as soon as possible after January 1. *Need-based scholarships/grants offered:* Pell Grant, SEOG, state scholarships/grants, private scholarships, the school's own gift aid. *Loan aid offered:* FFEL Subsidized Stafford, FFEL Unsubsidized Stafford, FFEL PLUS, Federal Perkins Loan, college/university loans from institutional funds. Applicants will be notified of awards on or about April 1.

FROM THE ADMISSION OFFICE

"Students who are drawn to Samford are well-rounded individuals who not only expect to be challenged but are excited by the prospect. It is the critical and creative way you think, it is the articulate way you write and speak, it is the joy of learning that stays with you throughout your life, and it is the clarity of decision making guided by Christian principles."

"As of this book's publication, Samford University did not have information available about their policy regarding the new SAT."

SELECTIVITY

Admissions Rating	86
# of applicants	1,837
% of applicants accepted	86
% of acceptees attending	41

FRESHMAN PROFILE

Range SAT Critical Reading	510–630
Range SAT Math	520–630
Range ACT Composite	22–27
Minimum Paper TOEFL	550
Minimum Computer Based TOEFL	213
Average HS GPA	3.63
% graduated top 10% of class	40
% graduated top 25% of class	65
% graduated top 50% of class	90

DEADLINES

Regular notification	rolling
Nonfall registration?	yes

APPLICANTS ALSO LOOK AT AND SOMETIMES PREFER

Auburn University, Baylor University, Florida State University, University of Georgia

FINANCIAL FACTS

Financial Aid Rating	75
Annual tuition	$17,920
% frosh rec. need-based scholarship or grant aid	35
% UG rec. need-based scholarship or grant aid	34
% frosh rec. need-based self-help aid	31
% UG rec. need-based self-help aid	34
% frosh rec. any financial aid	35
% UG rec. any financial aid	34

SANTA CLARA UNIVERSITY

500 EL CAMINO REAL, SANTA CLARA, CA 95053 • ADMISSIONS: 408-554-4700 • FAX: 408-554-5255

STUDENTS SAY

Academics

Students at Santa Clara University consider it the "best Catholic school in the West." The "excessive and insane" workload stands as a hallmark of the SCU education. A sophomore warns, "It is a hard school, I won't lie." Some students even believe they do more than their counterparts up the highway at Stanford, without the recognition. The Civil Engineering, Physics, and Business Departments score big points with students, and "the Math Department is too awesome for words." Communications draws many undergraduates, too, thanks to exciting concentrations like video production. Even core classes manage to "provoke curiosity in the subject." Several students talk about instructors who transcend typical class expectations to create meaningful experiences. According to a junior, SCU "Professors are brilliant, fascinating, humane people who have been nothing short of an inspiration to my friends and me." A physics major found his philosophy professor to be "one of the most passionate people I've known, and his class helped to change my outlook on the world." The faculty also strives to make students feel comfortable. "There is a program where gay-friendly professors have a sticker on their door saying 'Safe space,' and I have never seen an office without a sticker." The Jesuit factor stresses "the importance of social justice and activism" within the academic environment. A senior biology major writes, "I like the balance they create by trying to cultivate you morally and spiritually without infringing on your own beliefs." Among faculty, administrators, and classmates, "There is always someone to give advice and always so many resources to build you up."

Life

Though Santa Clarans may be working harder than other students, they're not partying harder. "If you find a party at Santa Clara, it's guaranteed that by 10:00 P.M. either the police will try to shut it down or the beer will run out." Cops dwell in their station across the street from campus, which routinely encourages students to head to "San Jose State or Stanford for a livelier party scene." A sophomore explains, "The once-flourishing Greek system of the 1980s and 1990s is still here," just autonomous from the university. Some students maintain their "Party like it's your job" attitude even in the face of these obstacles and declare Wednesday an official party night. For casual fun, people hang out on campus at The Bronco for pool and big-screen TVs. With no football team, sports fans transfer their fervor to soccer. The "very active Music, Dance, Visual, and Theater Arts Departments" keep the campus cultured. "There are a lot of performances and galleries and opportunities to be seen by the community." Students love the local climate and routinely hop the Cal train up to San Francisco; those with cars or connections can hit the beach or the slopes. Even at the start of a busy week in Silicon Valley, "We have a great turnout for Mass on Sunday nights at 10:00 P.M."

Student Body

Santa Clara lies closer to Santa Barbara than Santa Cruz on the spectrum of California style. Californians will likely get this, but for out-of-state students, this means that students are more LA trendy than San Francisco bohemian— more elective surgery, fewer body piercings. The country-club surroundings and well-manicured students "look like they came out of Beverly Hills." Though women outnumber men, one out-of-state student has "noticed a lot of California surfer dudes." Channeling the university's recruiting material, a sophomore writes, "There technically is diversity, and that is one of the things the school is trying to stress." Interaction between groups lags behind these efforts. "Most students won't go to the Boat Dance because it is sponsored by the multicultural club. If you aren't 'multicultural' then you just don't do it." What sets these students apart from any old popular kids from private Catholic high schools is their "faith-based motivation to work for social justice and human rights." Several respondents note an "emphasis on being very ethical, doing the right thing, and helping out in the community."

FINANCIAL AID: 408-554-4505 • WEBSITE: WWW.SCU.EDU

ADMISSIONS

Very important factors considered include: Academic GPA, application essay, recommendation(s), rigor of secondary school record. *Important factors considered include:* Extracurricular activities, racial/ethnic status, standardized test scores, talent/ability, volunteer work. *Other factors considered include:* Alumni/ae relation, character/personal qualities, class rank, first generation, geographical residence, level of applicant's interest, religious affiliation/commitment, state residency, work experience. SAT or ACT required; TOEFL required of all international applicants. High school diploma is required, and GED is not accepted. *Academic units required:* 4 English, 3 math, 2 science, 2 foreign language, 3 social studies, 1 academic elective. *Academic units recommended:* 4 English, 4 math, 3 science, 3 foreign language, 3 social studies, 1 academic elective.

The Inside Word

Santa Clara deserves recognition as a rising star that still manages to be highly personal and accessible. It's always better when an Admissions Staff regards you as a person, not an enrollment target. Unfortunately, such is not always the case. It would be hard to find a place that is more receptive to minority students. There is a very significant minority presence here because Santa Clara works hard and earnestly to make everyone feel at home. The university's popularity is increasing across the board, which proves that nice guys sometimes finish first.

FINANCIAL AID

Students should submit: FAFSA, CSS/Financial Aid PROFILE. The Princeton Review suggests that all financial aid forms be submitted as soon as possible after January 1. *Need-based scholarships/grants offered:* Pell Grant, SEOG, state scholarships/grants, private scholarships, the school's own gift aid. *Loan aid offered:* Direct Subsidized Stafford, Direct Unsubsidized Stafford, Direct PLUS, Federal Perkins Loan, private alternative loans. Applicants will be notified of awards on a rolling basis beginning or about November 6.

FROM THE ADMISSIONS OFFICE

"Santa Clara University, located one hour south of San Francisco, offers its undergraduates an opportunity to be educated within a challenging, dynamic, and caring community. The university blends a sense of tradition and history (as the oldest college in California) with a vision that values innovation and a deep commitment to social justice. Santa Clara's faculty members are talented scholars who are demanding, supportive, and accessible. The students are serious about academics, are ethnically diverse, and enjoy a full range of athletic, social, community-service, religious, and cultural activities—both on campus and through the many options presented by our northern California location. The undergraduate program includes three divisions: the College of Arts and Sciences, the School of Business, and the School of Engineering.

"For Fall 2008, Santa Clara University will accept either the new SAT or the old SAT. The ACT may be taken in lieu of, or in addition to, the SAT. The ACT Writing component is optional. The highest verbal and the highest math scores attained on the SAT will be used."

SELECTIVITY

Admissions Rating	89
# of applicants	8,670
% of applicants accepted	66
% of acceptees attending	23
# accepting a place on wait list	48
% admitted from wait list	88

FRESHMAN PROFILE

Range SAT Critical Reading	
Range SAT Math	560–670
Range SAT Writing	550–650
Range ACT Composite	24–29
Minimum Paper TOEFL	550
Minimum Computer Based TOEFL	213
Average HS GPA	3.52

DEADLINES

Regular application deadline	1/15
Regular notification	rolling
Nonfall registration?	no

APPLICANTS ALSO LOOK AT
AND OFTEN PREFER
Loyola Marymount University, University of California—Berkeley, University of California—Davis, University of California—Los Angeles, University of Southern California
AND SOMETIMES PREFER
Boston College, Pepperdine University, University of California—Santa Barbara, University of Notre Dame, University of San Diego
AND RARELY PREFER
Creighton University, Gonzaga University, Saint Mary's College of California, University of California—Santa Cruz, University of San Francisco

FINANCIAL FACTS

Financial Aid Rating	78
Annual tuition	$30,900
Room & Board	$10,380
Books and supplies	$1,314
% frosh rec. need-based scholarship or grant aid	28
% UG rec. need-based scholarship or grant aid	33
% frosh rec. need-based self-help aid	23
% UG rec. need-based self-help aid	25
% frosh rec. any financial aid	83
% UG rec. any financial aid	69

SARAH LAWRENCE COLLEGE

One Mead Way, Bronxville, NY 10708-5999 • Admissions: 914-395-2510 • Fax: 914-395-2676

STUDENTS SAY

Academics

"Independently minded" students will love Sarah Lawrence because it provides students "an opportunity to pursue their interests in one of the most rigorous and engaging academic communities in the country." Those who require constant guidance and a structured curriculum should probably look elsewhere. By committing to "a radical and highly effective dismissal of cumbersome, outmoded, traditional undergraduate educational ideals," SLC offers undergrads "the flexibility to study anything [they] might want to." A senior adds, "There are very few requirements." Most SLC classes are year-long seminars, taught in groups that rarely exceed 15 students. Seminars are supplemented with regular individual meetings with professors, called conferences, during which students review their work and plan research projects. Do not mistake the personal guidance for handholding, though; SLC professors "challenge you to be independent and decisive in your studies. Teachers and administrators are there to help you, but in the end it's up to you." Undergrads also warn that "this place is pretty academic, so you really have to make sure that you want to take the classes that you sign up for." Students receive not only letter grades, but also thorough written evaluations of their work; some opt to see only the latter. Despite its small size, SLC excels in a wide variety of disciplines: Writing, psychology, film, computer science, and dance are all reportedly strong.

Life

SLC's proximity to New York City (a commuter train delivers students to midtown Manhattan in 40 minutes) "is a double-edged sword. On the one hand, there are millions of fun things to do just a train ride away. But the result of these enticing opportunities is that the campus really empties out on weekends." While Thursday and Friday nights tend to be somewhat "campus-centric," on Saturday and Sunday "Most students go find something fun to do off campus with their close group of friends." One student warns, "Do not come here if you are looking for a fun party scene!" SLC undergrads, however, seem to enjoy themselves without one. Clubs and organizations are active during the week, as "Everyone who attends SLC is passionate about one thing or another, which manifests [itself] in the plethora of activities, clubs, and organizations. Granted, there usually are no more than five people in a club" as "the student/club ratio is 1:1 (or so it seems)." True to the school's "learning for the sake of learning" spirit, students also "spend a lot of time talking about our work for our classes."

Student Body

"The NYC, bohemian-life-loving hipster definitely dominates the scene" at Sarah Lawrence, "but there are also major computer and science geeks, spiritual types, hippies/vegetarian types, and even the simple girls from the Midwest who seem like cheerleaders . . . are perfect here. Our range of clubs show[s] varying interests: SLC Christian Union, Queer Variety Coalition, Harambe (African Americans), Hillel (Jewish Faith), FLUX (Feminism), and many more." Given the school's curriculum, it should come as no surprise that undergrads here "focus on individuality." A broad range of academic strengths attracts a diverse range of interests and personality types, so, says one student, "there is someone for everyone, and I've never found a person who didn't find a great group of people. Even the unfortunate kids that look like dodgeball targets . . . are sitting at a huge table of kids." Most SLC students are "left-wing, non-religious, and 'White' in culture if not in ethnicity." Just about everyone "is slightly egocentric, but it comes from being so brilliant and passionate about their particular interests."

FINANCIAL AID: 914-395-2570 • E-MAIL: SLCADMIT@SLC.EDU • WEBSITE: WWW.SARAHLAWRENCE.EDU

ADMISSIONS

Very important factors considered include: Application essay, recommendation(s), rigor of secondary school record. *Important factors considered include:* Academic GPA, character/personal qualities, extracurricular activities, talent/ability. *Other factors considered include:* Alumni/ae relation, class rank, first generation, geographical residence, interview, level of applicant's interest, racial/ethnic status, volunteer work, work experience. TOEFL required of all international applicants. High school diploma is required, and GED is accepted. *Academic units required:* 4 English, 2 math, 2 science, 2 foreign language, 2 history. *Academic units recommended:* 4 math, 4 science, 4 foreign language, 4 history.

The Inside Word

Admissions Officers at Sarah Lawrence give each applicant a very thorough, highly personalized review. This is nothing new here; even before the school dropped its SAT requirement in 2003 (explaining to the *New York Times* that the SAT Writing Test was "well-intentioned" but "would not be helpful in assessing candidates"), standardized tests only comprised about 5 percent of each admissions decision. Expect your writing to be carefully scrutinized; the application requires at least one graded example of your writing and several essays.

FINANCIAL AID

Students should submit: FAFSA, CSS/Financial Aid PROFILE, Noncustodial PRO-FILE, state aid form. Regular filing deadline is February 1. The Princeton Review suggests that all financial aid forms be submitted as soon as possible after January 1. *Need-based scholarships/grants offered:* Pell Grant, SEOG, state scholarships/grants, private scholarships, the school's own gift aid. *Loan aid offered:* FFEL Subsidized Stafford, FFEL Unsubsidized Stafford, FFEL PLUS, Federal Perkins Loan. Applicants will be notified of awards on or about April 1.

FROM THE ADMISSIONS OFFICE

"Students who come to Sarah Lawrence are curious about the world, and they have an ardent desire to satisfy that curiosity. Sarah Lawrence offers such students two innovative academic structures: the seminar/conference system and the arts components. Courses in the humanities, social sciences, natural sciences, and mathematics are taught in the seminar/conference style. The seminars enroll an average of 11 students and consist of lecture, discussion, readings, and assigned papers. For each seminar, students also have private tutorials, called conferences, for which they conceive of individualized projects and shape them under the direction of professors. Arts components let students combine history and theory with practice. Painters, printmakers, photographers, sculptors, filmmakers, composers, musicians, choreographers, dancers, actors, and directors work in readily available studios, editing facilities, and darkrooms, guided by accomplished professionals. The secure, wooded campus is 30 minutes from New York City, and the diversity of people and ideas at Sarah Lawrence make it an extraordinary educational environment.

"Sarah Lawrence College no longer uses standardized test scores in the admissions process. This decision reflects our conviction that overemphasis on test preparation can distort results and make the application process inordinately stressful, and that academic success is better predicted by the student's course rigor, their grades, recommendations, and writing ability."

SELECTIVITY

Admissions Rating	**89**
# of applicants	2,727
% of applicants accepted	46
% of acceptees attending	30
# accepting a place on wait list	285
% admitted from wait list	21
# of early decision applicants	204
% accepted early decision	56

FRESHMAN PROFILE

Minimum Paper TOEFL	600
Minimum Computer Based TOEFL	250
Average HS GPA	3.7
% graduated top 10% of class	33
% graduated top 25% of class	70
% graduated top 50% of class	97

DEADLINES

Early decision application deadline	11/15
Early decision notification	12/15
Regular application deadline	1/1
Regular notification	4/1
Nonfall registration?	no

FINANCIAL FACTS

Financial Aid Rating	**91**
Annual tuition	$35,280
Room & Board	$12,152
Required fees	$808
% frosh rec. need-based scholarship or grant aid	45
% UG rec. need-based scholarship or grant aid	45
% frosh rec. need-based self-help aid	48
% UG rec. need-based self-help aid	47
% frosh rec. any financial aid	50
% UG rec. any financial aid	52

SCRIPPS COLLEGE

1030 COLUMBIA AVENUE, MAILBOX #1265, CLAREMONT, CA 91711 • ADMISSIONS: 909-621-8149 • FAX: 909-607-7508

STUDENTS SAY

Academics

With more than 800 undergraduates, the all-women's Scripps College "truly provides a small-college experience" with "an atmosphere that is vibrant, challenging, and conducive not only to learning but also to out-of-class academic discussion." Thanks to the school's membership in the Claremont Consortium (composed of Scripps, Harvey Mudd, McKenna, Pitzer, and Pomona), Scripps also offers "the amazing resources of a bigger school, including excellent faculty, tons of course options, and competitive athletics." Scripps specializes in "teaching students to be independent, intelligent, thoughtful women who are interested in improving both themselves and their world." A feminist perspective informs many classes; one student writes, "We're learning about feminism and being detoxed of the common view that it is evil or man-hating, which is truly liberating and fun to experience." Another jokes, "If you don't come out of here a hard-boiled feminist who still enjoys dressing up for tea, we've done something wrong." Central to any Scripps education is the core program, which is "basically a three-semester humanities course. It is excellent, and it makes for a well-rounded student." Students also love "how everyone takes Core I together, because of the community it creates [during the] freshman year." In addition to these opportunities, Scripps also "has a great off-campus study program, and students are encouraged to study in a foreign country."

Life

Attending Scripps "is like being at a resort," students tell us, because "It's always sunny, the food is great," and "The dorms are incredibly spacious and comfortable." In fact, the entire campus is "exquisite. Even if you wake up in a bad mood, once you step outside and see the beauty of the trees and gardens and fountains, everything seems a little better." Life here is relatively quiet during the week, when "Everyone works hard during the day and then studies or does homework at night." For a break, students often drop by "the Motley, the student-run coffeehouses, where there are always a bunch of people studying, chatting, or just enjoying the great drinks and snacks they serve there." On Thursdays and weekends, "There are always campus parties that are fun to drop by." Most of the parties take place on the campuses of the other 4 C's "because they have more lenient drinking policies, and Scripps generally prefers to keep its campus quiet and clean." These parties "are really fun and take place every weekend; some are large, some small. Many of them are themed parties, and people dress up in costumes. People get pretty into it, and that's fun." Students see hometown Claremont as "not all that thrilling, but it's safe and has nice restaurants and a farmer's market every Sunday, so sometimes it's nice to walk into town with friends." Students note that "the Metrolink train system has a stop that is a 10-minute walk from campus. [It] makes several stops in Claremont every day and travels straight into downtown LA."

Student Body

"Scripps has two stereotypes: the blond Barbie princess and the raging feminist," and while students grudgingly admit that "there is some validity" to the stereotypes, "Most of the students are in fact mild-mannered and [have] fairly studious habits." One student writes, "You can find anyone from the most outspoken social activist to the quietest bookworm, from the artsy type to the scientist. All Scripps women are extremely multifaceted, and you cannot possibly put them in one category." Women here tend to be "very hardworking, givers instead of takers, thoughtful, motivated, approachable, and impressive."

FINANCIAL AID: 909-621-8275 • E-MAIL: ADMISSION@SCRIPPSCOLLEGE.EDU • WEBSITE: WWW.SCRIPPSCOLLEGE.EDU

ADMISSIONS

Very important factors considered include: Academic GPA, alumni/ae relation, application essay, character/personal qualities, class rank, extracurricular activities, first generation, interview, racial/ethnic status, recommendation(s), rigor of secondary school record, standardized test scores, talent/ability, volunteer work, work experience. *Important factors considered include:* Geographical residence. SAT or ACT required; TOEFL required of all international applicants. High school diploma is required, and GED is accepted. *Academic units required:* 4 English, 3 math, 3 science, 3 foreign language, 3 social studies. *Academic units recommended:* 4 English, 4 math, 4 science, 4 foreign language, 4 social studies and history.

The Inside Word

Applicants to Scripps won't encounter any admissions formulas or standardized test minimums. Admissions Officers aim to establish a diverse and talented freshman class and do so by evaluating a variety of factors. Serious candidates should give equal time to each facet of their application. Strong writing skills and intellectual curiosity are viewed as essential qualities in successful applicants.

FINANCIAL AID

Students should submit: FAFSA, CSS/Financial Aid PROFILE, Noncustodial PROFILE, Business/Farm Supplement, verification worksheet, parent and student Federal Income Tax Returns. The Princeton Review suggests that all financial aid forms be submitted as soon as possible after January 1. *Need-based scholarships/grants offered:* Pell Grant, SEOG, state scholarships/grants, private scholarships, the school's own gift aid, Federal Work-Study. *Loan aid offered:* FFEL Subsidized Stafford, FFEL Unsubsidized Stafford, FFEL PLUS, Federal Perkins Loan, college/university loans from institutional funds. Applicants will be notified of awards on or about April 1. Federal Work-Study Program available. Institutional employment available. Off-campus job opportunities are good.

FROM THE ADMISSIONS OFFICE

"At Scripps, we believe that learning involves much more than amassing information. The truly educated person is one who can think analytically, communicate effectively, and make confident, responsible choices. Scripps classes are small (the average class size is 15) so that they foster an atmosphere where students feel comfortable participating, testing old assumptions, and exploring new ideas. Our curriculum is based on the traditional components of a liberal arts education: a set of general requirements in a wide variety of disciplines including foreign language, natural science, and writing; a multicultural requirement; a major that asks students to study one particular field in depth; and a variety of electives that allows considerable flexibility. What distinguishes Scripps from other liberal arts colleges is an emphasis on interdisciplinary courses.

"First-year applicants for Fall 2008 must submit results of the new SAT or the ACT. SAT Subject Tests are not required."

SELECTIVITY

Admissions Rating	96
# of applicants	1,873
% of applicants accepted	45
% of acceptees attending	26
# accepting a place on wait list	148
% admitted from wait list	2
# of early decision applicants	108
% accepted early decision	40

FRESHMAN PROFILE

Range SAT Critical Reading	630–730
Range SAT Math	620–700
Range ACT Composite	27–30
Minimum Paper TOEFL	600
Minimum Computer Based TOEFL	250
Average HS GPA	4.06
% graduated top 10% of class	75
% graduated top 25% of class	95
% graduated top 50% of class	100

DEADLINES

Early decision application deadline	11/1
Early decision notification	12/15
Regular application deadline	1/1
Regular notification	4/1
Nonfall registration?	yes

APPLICANTS ALSO LOOK AT
AND OFTEN PREFER

Occidental College, University of California—Berkeley, University of Southern California, Wellesley College

AND SOMETIMES PREFER

Barnard College, Bryn Mawr College, Claremont McKenna College, Pomona College, Stanford University, University of California—Los Angeles, Vassar College

FINANCIAL FACTS

Financial Aid Rating	97
Annual tuition	$33,506
Room & Board	$10,100
Books and supplies	$800
Required fees	$194
% frosh rec. need-based scholarship or grant aid	42
% UG rec. need-based scholarship or grant aid	41
% frosh rec. need-based self-help aid	33
% UG rec. need-based self-help aid	37
% frosh rec. any financial aid	57
% UG rec. any financial aid	61

SEATTLE UNIVERSITY

ADMISSIONS OFFICE, 900 BROADWAY, SEATTLE, WA 98122-4340 • ADMISSIONS: 206-296-2000 • FAX: 206-296-5656

STUDENTS SAY

Academics

Seattle University is a midsize Jesuit university "dedicated to growth, not only educational but also spiritual, as well as the overall well-being of the person." Issues of "community and social justice in a complex world" permeate the curriculum here, "pushing students to reevaluate their presuppositions about the world in a just and humane manner." For example, "Community-service hours are actually a requirement with specific required freshman-level courses. This is helpful to freshmen, because it gets them to experience at least one aspect of Seattle's community." Academically, SU "is very strong and very challenging" with "time-consuming homework," but "with services like the Writing Center, Math Lab, and professors who check their e-mail even more regularly than the students themselves, it's not hard to find the resources you need to produce quality work." Standout departments include Public Affairs, Criminal Justice, Civil Engineering, Business, English, Psychology, and a nursing program that "rigorously prepares students to be dependable, altruistic nurses who will be leaders in the community." Across disciplines, "small class sizes and personal attention to one's education and career development" as well as "high-quality professors who get to know individual students and focus entirely on each student's learning" define the SU academic experience.

Student Life

Seattle University "is located on one of the liveliest streets in Seattle," and that naturally has a huge impact on students' lives here. After all, "Seattle is one of the best playgrounds a college student could ever ask for," so, "if there's not something going on at the campus, such as an international dinner, formal, game competition between dorms, or BBQ," then "There's always something to do downtown." "Within walking distance of the campus students can find handfuls of amazing restaurants, small venues for concerts, the Seattle Center, movie theaters, and coffee shops. The possibilities are endless." A little farther afield, students can access "professional sports, art, music, beautiful buildings, and a lot of nature. Not too big and definitely not small, Seattle is a very diverse city in many aspects." On campus, "Many of us like to attend school sporting events. There are generally parties afterwards, and also just about every weekend." There are "also lots of clubs and activities on campus," such as "social, political, and cultural clubs that meet once a week on a weeknight and offer activities such as movie nights, casino nights, club nights, guest speakers, camping and snowboarding trips, as well as an annual 'showcase' of sorts including student-organized dinner and entertainment." For a quieter evening, "The residence halls and the student center offer community rooms to watch TV, play video games, or shoot pool."

Students

The typical SU student "would be described in terms of attitude, not any particular look. A typical student is balanced, having a desire to do well in whatever he or she tackles, but especially wherever his or her passion lies. Nearly all students are involved in some organization, club, or volunteer effort in order to make sure that they maintain a connection to the needs of the greater global reality and outside community." The population is "pretty diverse," with "a lot of international students," a "large gay population," and "quite a few nontraditional [over age 25] students" in the mix. Despite the fact that SU is a Jesuit school, "all religions you can think of are present here." Different groups "tend to mesh very well. The diversity is a wonderful tool for shaping us as students." Asians and Latinos account for the lion's share of the racial diversity here.

FINANCIAL AID: 206-296-2000 • E-MAIL: ADMISSIONS@SEATTLEU.EDU • WEBSITE: WWW.SEATTLEU.EDU

ADMISSIONS

Very important factors considered include: Academic GPA, application essay, recommendation(s), rigor of secondary school record, standardized test scores. *Important factors considered include:* Character/personal qualities, extracurricular activities, first generation, talent/ability, volunteer work. *Other factors considered include:* Alumni/ae relation, class rank, geographical residence, interview, level of applicant's interest, racial/ethnic status, state residency, work experience. SAT or ACT required; TOEFL required of all international applicants. High school diploma is required, and GED is accepted. *Academic units required:* 4 English, 3 math, 2 science (2 science labs), 2 foreign language, 3 social studies, 2 academic electives. *Academic units recommended:* 4 science (3 science labs), 4 social studies.

The Inside Word

Seattle University requires all students to declare their intended areas of study on their applications. Candidates should research their prospective major because the academic demands here do vary. Because this is a Jesuit school, Admissions Officers tend to value community service. Those who demonstrate significant commitment to volunteering will find themselves at an advantage, as will those who convey a relatively clear sense of their academic and career goals.

FINANCIAL AID

Students should submit: FAFSA. The Princeton Review suggests that all financial aid forms be submitted as soon as possible after January 1. *Need-based scholarships/grants offered:* Pell Grant, SEOG, state scholarships/grants, private scholarships, the school's own gift aid. *Loan aid offered:* Direct Subsidized Stafford, Direct Unsubsidized Stafford, Direct PLUS, Federal Perkins Loan, Federal Nursing Loan. Applicants will be notified of awards on or about March 21.

FROM THE ADMISSIONS OFFICE

"Seattle University provides an ideal environment for motivated students interested in self-reliance, awareness of different cultures, social justice, and the fulfillment that comes from making a difference. Our urban setting promotes the development of leadership skills and independence as well as providing a variety of opportunities for students to apply what they learn through internships, clinical experiences, and volunteer work. It is an environment that allows us to 'connect the mind to what matters.'

"Our academic offerings are designed to provide leadership opportunities as well as to develop global awareness and enable graduates to serve society through a demanding liberal arts and sciences foundation. In the Jesuit tradition, we teach our students how to think, not what to think. Professional undergraduate offerings include highly respected schools of business, nursing, and science and engineering, as well as career-oriented liberal arts programs such as creative writing, journalism, communications, and criminal justice.

"While located in the center of the city, Seattle University is a true residential campus, including students from 48 states and territories and 76 different nations. Washington State has designated the campus as an 'official backyard sanctuary' for its striking landscaping and environmentally conscious practices—several buildings enjoy official 'green' designations, and the student-run recycling program continually receives national recognition. Additionally, Seattle University is proud of its distinction as the most ethnically diverse institution in the Northwest—all students are valued and respected for their individual strengths, experiences, and worth.

"Pending the results of an examination into the validity of the Writing portion of the new SAT, Seattle University will continue to accept the old SAT and will use the scores from Critical Reading and Math sections to determine placement. In lieu of the SAT, students may also take the ACT (with the Writing component)."

SELECTIVITY

Admissions Rating	88
# of applicants	4,532
% of applicants accepted	65
% of acceptees attending	27
# accepting a place on wait list	258
% admitted from wait list	2

FRESHMAN PROFILE

Range SAT Critical Reading	530–640
Range SAT Math	520–630
Range SAT Writing	510–620
Range ACT Composite	22–27
Minimum Paper TOEFL	520
Minimum Computer Based TOEFL	190
Average HS GPA	3.56
% graduated top 10% of class	32
% graduated top 25% of class	64
% graduated top 50% of class	93

DEADLINES

Regular application deadline	2/1
Regular notification	rolling
Nonfall registration?	yes

APPLICANTS ALSO LOOK AT

AND OFTEN PREFER
Gonzaga University, University of Washington, Western Washington University

AND SOMETIMES PREFER
Santa Clara University, University of Portland, University of San Diego

AND RARELY PREFER
Pacific Lutheran University, University of Puget Sound, University of San Francisco

FINANCIAL FACTS

Financial Aid Rating	85
Annual tuition	$22,905
Room & Board	$7,158
Books and supplies	$1,215
% frosh rec. need-based scholarship or grant aid	34
% UG rec. need-based scholarship or grant aid	35
% frosh rec. need-based self-help aid	45
% UG rec. need-based self-help aid	45
% frosh rec. any financial aid	88
% UG rec. any financial aid	76

SETON HALL UNIVERSITY

ENROLLMENT SERVICES, 400 SOUTH ORANGE AVENUE, SOUTH ORANGE, NJ 07079 • ADMISSIONS: 973-761-9332 • FAX: 973-275-2040

CAMPUS LIFE
Quality of Life Rating	**66**
Fire Safety Rating	**98**
Type of school	private
Affiliation	Roman Catholic
Environment	village

STUDENTS
Total undergrad enrollment	4,951
% male/female	45/55
% from out of state	26
% from public high school	70
% live on campus	44
% African American	11
% Asian	6
% Caucasian	51
% Hispanic	11
% international	1
# of countries represented	71

SURVEY SAYS . . .
Small classes
Great computer facilities
Great library
Diverse student types on campus
College radio is popular
Student publications are popular
Lots of beer drinking
(Almost) everyone smokes

ACADEMICS
Academic Rating	**77**
Calendar	semester
Student/faculty ratio	14:1
Profs interesting rating	72
Profs accessible rating	72
% profs teaching	
UG courses	75
% classes taught by TAs	4
Most common	
lab size	10–19 students
Most common	
reg class size	10–19 students

MOST POPULAR MAJORS
communications studies/speech
communication and rhetoric
criminal justice/safety studies
nursing/registered nurse training
(ASN, BSN, MSN, RN)

STUDENTS SAY

Academics
Named after Saint Elizabeth Ann Seton, Seton Hall is a Catholic university dedicated to "shaping students into servant leaders by enriching the mind, heart, and spirit." Servant leaders are people "who help to change the world" by offering their talents to the improvement of the community, as did the person for whom the university is a namesake. Professors are at the forefront of this intellectual, emotional, and spiritual enrichment, and students say "You won't find better anywhere." "They are always willing to meet with you outside of class and will do anything to help." Professors in the specialty Schools of Diplomacy, Nursing, Education, and Business receive especially high marks. Although students in the honors program "get the best professors" and benefit from "discussion-based classes," all students enjoy "small class sizes" in which "questions are always welcome." Students are much less enthusiastic about the "very conservative" administration, which for many is a "typical bureaucracy that could be improved but could also be much, much worse." Despite the administration's overall conservatism, it has fully embraced certain forms of progress. "One of Seton Hall's greatest strengths is probably its student technology program where every incoming student is issued a laptop that they can use anywhere on campus thanks to wireless Internet."

Life
As one student explains, "Life in general here is what happens at most colleges." "During the week everyone is stressed and a lot of work gets done." On the weekends, students spend their "free time watching movies, attending on-campus events, going to parties, hanging out, and exploring New York." With fewer than half of the students living on campus, Seton Hall is "very much a commuter school." A lot of students come for class and head home afterwards. Even among resident students, "Seton Hall is a suitcase school," which means "a lot of the Jersey kids go home on the weekends." Still, there are "plenty of things to do for those who stay on campus." "The Greek population is relatively small but is highly visible." Students enjoy "a lot of frat parties on the weekends" as well as "drive-in movies" and "dance lessons." Additionally, "extracurricular activities abound" with many students playing "intramural and intercollegiate sports." Even with all these options, students often "hop on the train" and "go into New York City for fun" which can make the campus feel "deserted on the weekends."

Student Body
While the typical student is "probably Catholic" and from "local towns in New Jersey or New York," diversity is "highly valued" on campus, with many students from "different backgrounds, religious beliefs, sexual orientation, everything." Most students manage to "mix in and feel like they're part of the student body." One student warns, however, that there is "very little tolerance for certain groups," especially gay students who are "targets of active discrimination by the university." While many students think the administration "does not handle GLBT issues well," those who are GLBT have "great support from the rest of the SHU community." Students describe themselves as "friendly" and "pretty motivated," conversant in everything from "political and historical issues to fashion." SHU students concentrate on their "work during the week" and "enjoying themselves on the weekend." As one student sums up, "Most students are just average people" with a "broad variance in personalities and interests."

FINANCIAL AID: 973-761-9332 • E-MAIL: THEHALL@SHU.EDU • WEBSITE: WWW.SHU.EDU

ADMISSIONS

Very important factors considered include: Academic GPA, application essay, recommendation(s), rigor of secondary school record, standardized test scores. *Important factors considered include:* Extracurricular activities, volunteer work, work experience. *Other factors considered include:* Character/personal qualities, class rank, interview, talent/ability. SAT or ACT required; ACT with Writing component required. TOEFL required of all international applicants. High school diploma is required, and GED is accepted. *Academic units required:* 4 English, 3 math, 1 science, 2 foreign language, 2 social studies, 4 academic electives.

The Inside Word

Students looking for a good school with solid Catholic roots should consider Seton Hall. Decent grades in college preparatory courses coupled with strong recommendations will net an acceptance for most students. Applicants with above-average marks are often recipients of scholarship money. The university's close proximity to New York allows for myriad educational, internship, and entertainment opportunities.

FINANCIAL AID

Students should submit: FAFSA. The Princeton Review suggests that all financial aid forms be submitted as soon as possible after January 1. *Need-based scholarships/grants offered:* Pell Grant, SEOG, state scholarships/grants, private scholarships, the school's own gift aid. *Loan aid offered:* FFEL Subsidized Stafford, FFEL Unsubsidized Stafford, FFEL PLUS, Federal Perkins Loan, state loans. Applicants will be notified of awards on a rolling basis beginning or about March 1. Federal Work-Study Program available. Institutional employment available. Off-campus job opportunities are good.

FROM THE ADMISSIONS OFFICE

"As the oldest and largest diocesan university in the United States, Seton Hall University is committed to providing its students with a diverse environment focusing on academic excellence and ethical development. Outstanding faculty, a technologically advanced campus, and a values-centered curriculum challenge Seton Hall students. Through these things and the personal attention students receive, they are prepared to be leaders in their professional and community lives in a global society. Seton Hall's campus offers students up-to-date facilities, including an award-winning library facility opened in 1994 and the state-of-the-art Kozlowski Hall, which opened in 1997. The university has invested more than $25 million in the past 5 years to provide its students and faculty with leading-edge information technology. The Mobile Computing Program is widely recognized as one of the nation's best. In 1999 and 2000, Seton Hall was ranked as one of the nation's 'Most Wired Universities' by *Yahoo! Internet Life* magazine. Recent additions to Seton Hall's academic offerings include the School of Diplomacy and International Relations and a number of dual-degree health sciences programs, including physical therapy, physician assistant, and occupational therapy.

"Freshmen who enter Seton Hall University in Fall 2008 are required to submit the Writing component on either the SAT or ACT. However, this Writing test will be used for a correlation study only and will not be used for admission or scholarship decisions."

SELECTIVITY

Admissions Rating	81
# of applicants	5,365
% of applicants accepted	77
% of acceptees attending	25

FRESHMAN PROFILE

Range SAT Critical Reading	480–590
Range SAT Math	500–600
Minimum Paper TOEFL	550
Minimum Computer Based TOEFL	213
Average HS GPA	3.15
% graduated top 10% of class	28
% graduated top 25% of class	60
% graduated top 50% of class	88

DEADLINES

Regular notification	rolling
Nonfall registration?	yes

APPLICANTS ALSO LOOK AT

AND OFTEN PREFER
New York University, Pennsylvania State University—University Park, Villanova University, William Paterson University

AND SOMETIMES PREFER
Fairfield University, Fordham University, Rider University, University of Connecticut

AND RARELY PREFER
Hofstra University, Monmouth University (NJ), Ramapo College of New Jersey, St. Bonaventure University

FINANCIAL FACTS

Financial Aid Rating	72
Annual tuition	$22,770
Room & Board	$10,466
Required fees	$1,950
% frosh rec. need-based scholarship or grant aid	54
% UG rec. need-based scholarship or grant aid	38
% frosh rec. need-based self-help aid	45
% UG rec. need-based self-help aid	45
% frosh rec. any financial aid	91
% UG rec. any financial aid	86

SEWANEE—THE UNIVERSITY OF THE SOUTH

735 UNIVERSITY AVENUE, SEWANEE, TN 37383-1000 • ADMISSIONS: 931-598-1238 • FAX: 931-538-3248

CAMPUS LIFE

Quality of Life Rating	88
Fire Safety Rating	60*
Type of school	private
Affiliation	Episcopal
Environment	rural

STUDENTS

Total undergrad enrollment	1,491
% male/female	48/52
% from out of state	78
% from public high school	52
% live on campus	94
% in (# of) fraternities	70 (11)
% in (# of) sororities	68 (6)
% African American	4
% Asian	2
% Caucasian	89
% Hispanic	3
% Native American	1
% international	2
# of countries represented	22

SURVEY SAYS . . .

Small classes
No one cheats
Campus feels safe
Frats and sororities dominate social
scene
Lots of beer drinking
Hard liquor is popular
(Almost) everyone smokes

ACADEMICS

Academic Rating	94
Calendar	semester
Student/faculty ratio	11:1
Profs interesting rating	97
Profs accessible rating	98
% profs teaching UG courses	100
% classes taught by TAs	0
Most common lab size	10–19 students
Most common reg class size	10–19 students

STUDENTS SAY
Academics

Among the "storied traditions" at Sewanee—The University of the South, the most prominent is the Order of Gownsmen, a student honor society whose members wear gowns to class "to recognize Sewanee's ties with the English universities of Oxford and Cambridge [and] keep our reputation high and our school a comfortable place," students tell us. As at many Southern schools, tradition is the cement that holds the community together. The bricks and mortar are the academics—"by far the greatest strength of Sewanee. Classes are challenging and stimulating at all colleges, but at Sewanee, learning is alive. You don't just take a course; you develop relationships with a preeminent member in the field: your professors." The "Emphasis on active learning and incredible student-faculty interaction is probably Sewanee's greatest, and most often overlooked, strength," students tell us. The heavy workload here is "focused on producing excellent communicators. No matter the major or area of discipline, all professors demand that their students be able to write well when communicating their ideas." One student observes, "Professors are amazing: engaging students outside of the classroom by arranging field trips, outdoor activities, and dinners at their houses. They are tireless in devoting attention to willing students and know us very well. Therefore, they expect much out of us and push us to excel, by encouraging study abroad, writing recommendations for summer internships, and supporting research." Grading here can be tough; "A C-plus at Sewanee would be an A anywhere else," many concur.

Life

"Sewanee is beautiful," students agree, telling us that "there are caves, streams, and mountains on campus, and on top of it all are beautifully ornate academic buildings that are modeled after Oxford's. The campus is 10,000 acres in all, giving you tons of places to explore." Sewanee's massive grounds serve as a magnet for outdoorsy types, and the school does its best to accommodate them. One student writes, "We have an awesome outdoor program that organizes and sponsors hiking, caving, climbing, bicycling, canoeing, skydiving, and snowshoeing trips." While "There are so many things to do here on campus for fun, both dry and with alcohol," most students drink recreationally on a regular basis. "Considering there is no cable and cell phones are practically forbidden, everyone turns to alcohol," explains one student. Undergrads point out that "people do a lot of work during the week—I practically live in the library during the week, as do many students here—but starting Thursday night, the students do a complete turnaround. The party scene is alive and thriving here at Sewanee." Frat parties are the center of the action. "Our Greek system is different from most schools," students explain. "We do not live in the houses, and all parties are open."

Student Body

Sewanee is "largely Episcopalian, and the overwhelming majority of students are Christian. This is, of course, to be expected considering the religious affiliation of the school." Most here "love the outdoors, love to have a good time, and know when to study." Undergrads report, "Although Sewanee is taking steps to attract a more diverse student body, the majority of students here are White Southerners." Preppy is still the predominant look on campus; "You will never see as many popped collars, polo insignias, pearl necklaces, seersucker suits, or bow ties as you will see at around campus at The University of the South," observes one student. Not everyone here is happy about the school's "slow, but detectable" progress toward diversity; some worry that Sewanee's beloved traditions will disappear as its core demographic loses preeminence. Their worries seem premature, at least for the immediate future.

SEWANEE—THE UNIVERSITY OF THE SOUTH

FINANCIAL AID: 931-598-1312 • E-MAIL: COLLEGEADMISSION@SEWANEE.EDU • WEBSITE: WWW.SEWANEE.EDU

ADMISSIONS

Very important factors considered include: Academic GPA, recommendation(s), rigor of secondary school record. *Important factors considered include:* Application essay, character/personal qualities, extracurricular activities, standardized test scores, volunteer work, work experience. *Other factors considered include:* Alumni/ae relation, class rank, first generation, geographical residence, interview, level of applicant's interest, racial/ethnic status, talent/ability. SAT or ACT required; ACT with Writing component required. TOEFL required of all international applicants. High school diploma is required, and GED is not accepted. *Academic units required:* 4 English, 2 math, 2 science (2 science labs), 2 foreign language, 1 social studies, 1 history. *Academic units recommended:* 4 English, 4 math, 4 science (3 science labs), 4 foreign language, 2 social studies, 2 history.

The Inside Word

The Admissions Office at Sewanee is very personable and accessible to students. Its staff includes some of the most well-respected admissions professionals in the South, and it shows in the way they work with students. Despite a fairly high acceptance rate, candidates who take the admissions process here lightly may find themselves disappointed. Applicant evaluation is too personal for a lackadaisical approach to succeed.

FINANCIAL AID

Students should submit: FAFSA, institution's own financial aid form, student and/or parent Federal Income Tax Returns if applicable. The Princeton Review suggests that all financial aid forms be submitted as soon as possible after January 1. *Need-based scholarships/grants offered:* Pell Grant, SEOG, state scholarships/grants, private scholarships, the school's own gift aid. *Loan aid offered:* FFEL Subsidized Stafford, FFEL Unsubsidized Stafford, FFEL PLUS, Federal Perkins Loan, state loans, college/university loans from institutional funds, private alternative loans. Applicants will be notified of awards on or about April 1.

FROM THE ADMISSIONS OFFICE

"Sewanee is consistently ranked among the top tier of national liberal arts universities. Sewanee is committed to an academic curriculum that focuses on the liberal arts as the most enlightening and valuable form of undergraduate education. Founded by leaders of the Episcopal church in 1857, Sewanee continues to be owned by 28 Episcopal dioceses in 12 states. The university is located on a 10,000-acre campus atop Tennessee's Cumberland Plateau between Chattanooga and Nashville. The university has an impressive record of academic achievement—25 Rhodes scholars and 26 NCAA postgraduate scholarship recipients have graduated from Sewanee.

"Sewanee will require all applicants for Fall 2008 to take the new SAT or the ACT with the Writing test. We will consider previous scores in Math and Critical Reading from previous administrations of the SAT when calculating a student's highest composite score, but students are required to take the new SAT."

SELECTIVITY

Admissions Rating	**90**
# of applicants	1,932
% of applicants accepted	71
% of acceptees attending	30
# accepting a place on wait list	172
% admitted from wait list	16
# of early decision applicants	168
% accepted early decision	51

FRESHMAN PROFILE

Range SAT Critical Reading	570–670
Range SAT Math	560–650
Range SAT Writing	570–668
Range ACT Composite	25–29
Minimum Paper TOEFL	550
Minimum Computer Based TOEFL	220
Average HS GPA	3.63
% graduated top 10% of class	42
% graduated top 25% of class	71
% graduated top 50% of class	94

DEADLINES

Early decision application deadline	11/15
Early decision notification	12/15
Regular application deadline	2/1
Regular notification	4/1
Nonfall registration?	no

APPLICANTS ALSO LOOK AT

AND OFTEN PREFER
The University of North Carolina at Chapel Hill, Washington and Lee University

AND SOMETIMES PREFER
Davidson College, Vanderbilt University, Wake Forest University

AND RARELY PREFER
Rhodes College, University of Georgia, The University of Tennessee at Knoxville

FINANCIAL FACTS

Financial Aid Rating	**94**
Annual tuition	$30,438
Room & Board	$8,780
Books and supplies	$800
Required fees	$222
% frosh rec. need-based scholarship or grant aid	38
% UG rec. need-based scholarship or grant aid	45
% frosh rec. need-based self-help aid	28
% UG rec. need-based self-help aid	33

SIENA COLLEGE

515 LOUDON ROAD, LOUDONVILLE, NY 12211 • ADMISSIONS: 518-783-2423 • FAX: 518-783-2436

CAMPUS LIFE

Quality of Life Rating	**80**
Fire Safety Rating	**60***
Type of school	private
Affiliation	Roman Catholic
Environment	town

STUDENTS

Total undergrad enrollment	3,156
% male/female	44/56
% from out of state	12
% live on campus	78
% African American	2
% Asian	4
% Caucasian	85
% Hispanic	4
% international	1
# of countries represented	10

SURVEY SAYS . . .

Small classes
Great library
Students love Loudonville, NY
Frats and sororities are unpopular or
nonexistent
Lots of beer drinking

ACADEMICS

Academic Rating	**82**
Calendar	semester
Student/faculty ratio	14:1
Profs interesting rating	80
Profs accessible rating	84
% profs teaching UG courses	100
% classes taught by TAs	0
Most common lab size	10–19 students
Most common reg class size	20–29 students

MOST POPULAR MAJORS

biology/biological sciences
marketing/marketing management
psychology

STUDENTS SAY

Academics

The Franciscan tradition "is all about community," and, at Siena College, a small school with "a strong Franciscan atmosphere," students benefit from a friendly community in which "there is always someone to lend a helping hand." That someone may be a professor, a tutor, or, on occasion, a Rollerblading friar in robes. No matter whose hand is extended, however, "Every student really has a lot of opportunities to get any amount of personal academic attention or other scholastic opportunities that they want." Biology and other premedical disciplines are highly regarded, and students especially love the Siena College–Albany Medical College Program, a joint acceptance program that focuses on humanities and community service. In addition, the school's many business undergrads feel their program, which is enhanced by a loyal alumni base that helps newly minted grads quickly find jobs, is the school's "greatest strength." Regardless of discipline, Siena "Teachers know who you are and do not just consider you a number, as opposed [how it is at] larger colleges and universities." An honors program offers "even smaller classes, preferential registration, and seminars" to those seeking an extra challenge.

Life

For many students, recreation time at Siena means it's time for a beer or two, and lately that's become a point of contention with the administration. Students tell us that the administration, in its effort to crack down on underage drinking, has instituted security checkpoints at the townhouses (where upperclassmen live and, in previous years, had hosted parties) and limits on the amount of alcohol allowed in the rooms of students over 21. Security can be aggressive, we're told, to the point that more than one undergraduate told us that students sometimes feel "like prisoners." Though this has driven the drinking crowd off campus to nearby clubs and the bars of Albany, on-campus drinking still occurs, but it's more often of the pre-gaming or small-quiet-party variety. The campus still bustles during the week, however, as "Most people are involved in clubs" and at least "one sport, whether intramural or intercollegiate." Other diversions include a school-sponsored bus that takes students to the Crossgates Mall, which "is pretty large and houses a bunch of amazing stores," and "a whole strip of dining-out places." Still, an English major admits, "If you don't drink, I can see where weekends would be boring, especially in the winter." The school does sponsor activities on campus designed "to draw students away from the drinking scene," but "There is often a stigma about the 'coolness' of these events."

Student Body

There "isn't much diversity" on the Siena campus, where it seems just about everyone "is from an upper-middle-class Catholic family from Long Island" or "upstate New York." There are some who don't fit the mold, but not many; students speculate that they're mostly nontraditional or international students. Minority students tend to "stick together, but all seem well-liked." Many students "are involved either in D1 athletics, intramural teams, or clubs and Student Senate activities"; students in these groups tend to party together on the weekends "and generally create a strong group of friends easily." While there's a solid contingent of folks at Siena who "drink, party, and hardly ever study," there are also students, particularly in the sciences, who work hard but "don't socialize much outside of their departments, due to the nature of their program."

SIENA COLLEGE

FINANCIAL AID: 518-783-2427 • E-MAIL: ADMIT@SIENA.EDU • WEBSITE: WWW.SIENA.EDU

ADMISSIONS

Very important factors considered include: Academic GPA, rigor of secondary school record. *Important factors considered include:* Recommendation(s), standardized test scores. *Other factors considered include:* Alumni/ae relation, application essay, character/personal qualities, class rank, extracurricular activities, first generation, interview, level of applicant's interest, racial/ethnic status, talent/ability, volunteer work, work experience. SAT or ACT required; ACT with Writing component required. TOEFL required of all international applicants. High school diploma is required, and GED is accepted. *Academic units required:* 4 English, 3 math, 3 science (3 science labs), 1 social studies, 2 history. *Academic units recommended:* 4 English, 4 math, 4 science (4 science labs), 3 foreign language, 1 social studies, 3 history.

The Inside Word

Siena's draw is still primarily regional, with the vast majority of students arriving from in state. Standards aren't especially high; the admit rate says as much about the applicant pool as it does about the school's selectivity. Expect to meet higher standards if you indicate an interest in the School of Science, as it is the gateway to the school's desirable premedical programs. The school does applicants a favor here—substandard students stand little chance of surviving the school's science regimen.

FINANCIAL AID

Students should submit: FAFSA, state aid form. The Princeton Review suggests that all financial aid forms be submitted as soon as possible after January 1. *Need-based scholarships/grants offered:* Pell Grant, SEOG, state scholarships/grants, private scholarships, the school's own gift aid, Siena Grants, St. Francis Community Grants. *Loan aid offered:* FFEL Subsidized Stafford, FFEL Unsubsidized Stafford, FFEL PLUS, Federal Perkins Loan. Applicants will be notified of awards on or about April 1.

FROM THE ADMISSIONS OFFICE

"Siena is a coeducational, independent liberal arts college with a Franciscan tradition. It is a community where the intellectual, personal, and social growth of all students is paramount. Siena's faculty calls forth the best Siena students have to give—and the students do the same for them. Students are competitive, but not at each other's expense. Siena's curriculum includes 23 majors in three schools—liberal arts, science, and business. In addition, there are over a dozen pre-professional and special academic programs. With a student/faculty ratio of 14:1, class size ranges between 15 and 35 students. Siena's 152-acre campus is located in Loudonville, a suburban community within two miles of the New York State seat of government in Albany. With 15 colleges in the area, there is a wide variety of activities on weekends. Regional theater, performances by major concert artists, and professional sports events compete with the activities on the campus. Within 50 miles are the Adirondacks, the Berkshires, and the Catskills, providing outdoor recreation throughout the year. Because the capital region's easy, friendly lifestyle is so appealing, many Siena graduates try to find their first jobs in upstate New York.

"Freshman applicants must submit the SAT or ACT with the Writing component."

SELECTIVITY	
Admissions Rating	86
# of applicants	5,094
% of applicants accepted	55
% of acceptees attending	25
# accepting a place on wait list	327
% admitted from wait list	23
# of early decision applicants	169
% accepted early decision	23

FRESHMAN PROFILE	
Range SAT Critical Reading	500–580
Range SAT Math	520–620
Range ACT Composite	23–26
Minimum Paper TOEFL	550
Minimum Computer Based TOEFL	213
Average HS GPA	3.58
% graduated top 10% of class	23
% graduated top 25% of class	60
% graduated top 50% of class	92

DEADLINES	
Early decision application deadline	12/1
Early decision notification	12/15
Regular application deadline	3/1
Regular notification	3/15
Nonfall registration?	yes

APPLICANTS ALSO LOOK AT
AND OFTEN PREFER
Providence College, Villanova University
AND SOMETIMES PREFER
Fairfield University, Fordham University, Loyola College in Maryland, Marist College, The University of Scranton
AND RARELY PREFER
Le Moyne College, Sacred Heart University, State University of New York—College at Oneonta, State University of New York—New Paltz, State University of New York—University at Albany

FINANCIAL FACTS	
Financial Aid Rating	74
Annual tuition	$22,510
Room & Board	$8,875
Books and supplies	$900
Required fees	$175
% frosh rec. need-based scholarship or grant aid	66
% UG rec. need-based scholarship or grant aid	65
% frosh rec. need-based self-help aid	56
% UG rec. need-based self-help aid	53
% frosh rec. any financial aid	84
% UG rec. any financial aid	84

SIMMONS COLLEGE

300 THE FENWAY, BOSTON, MA 02115 • ADMISSIONS: 617-521-2051 • FAX: 617-521-3190

STUDENTS SAY

Academics

At Simmons College, its all-female, grade-conscious setting demonstrates that "the girls are here to learn." A senior admits, "It might sound cheesy, but the school is really about helping students find their voice." Professors facilitate this process by "treating everyone with respect, dignity, and compassion." Students feel their teachers are "actually on our side, ready to help with almost anything." Extensive office hours and prompt e-mail responses indicate professors' high level of accessibility. "When you find an amazing professor, you can be sure that s/he is available to you in a big way," writes a senior. The Political Science, International Relations, and Communications Departments rank high with students, while the nursing and physical therapy programs benefit from proximity to some of the nation's top hospitals. "When I look out my window, I see Beth Israel Deaconess Medical Center, and one block down are the rest of the great hospitals in the Longwood Medical Area." This practical training bridges academic work and professional preparation. "All of my professors in the nursing program have wanted me to succeed and have advised me in my career choices." A few departments, such as Music and Psychology, could use a few more faculty members to cover class demand. Complaints surface regarding Culture Matters (officially the "Multidisciplinary Core Course"), a class required of all first-year students. But in most classes, students notice a payoff. "I've seen an amazing improvement in my writing, class participation, and overall attention to detail in my reading." The school places "a high premium on making sure everyone feels comfortable," so that education can be a personal experience. "By the time we graduate, we're far more self-confident."

Life

Be warned: "This is a learning environment, not a place to party or make out with the newest meat from MIT." It's true that on-campus life can feel like "a bizarre combination of a nunnery and Sesame Street." Entertainment veers toward that sleepover-party image of single-sex institutions, complete with "pajamas, movies, and drinks." If Simmons were located in the boonies, the regimen of knitting, Ms. Pac-Man, political rallies, and field hockey could get old. But it's in the middle of Boston, a "huge college-oriented city" that beckons with Newbury Street shopping, hip coffee shops, Red Sox games, and the male/female ratio of the real world. "The school buys bulk discounted tickets to plays and musicals and even the ballet." Participation in the Colleges of Fenway Consortium links the school to its neighbors, though some students seem to have thought before they enrolled that Simmons would host more coed events. Students like coming home to Simmons as much as they like getting away. "It always feels like a safe and secure place to study after a long weekend out." A fair number of entering students seem to experience a rough adjustment period, but grow to love the school after getting accustomed and involved.

Student Body

Simmons women see themselves as open-minded, overachieving feminists who are "just as engaging at a party as [they are] in the classroom." Students routinely take on crazy class hours, club leadership positions, and multiple majors. Recently, the vibe of the school has started to shift "from being all about grades to being more about community." The small, liberal student body accepts lesbianism readily—"You become very accustomed to same-sex relationships"—but "Republicans or Yankees fans might want to tread carefully." Many student activists organize around political issues of gender, race, and class. They note a divide between students "on a first-name basis with every Financial Aid Officer and those whose parents can afford a small island in the Pacific." They are also sensitive to the fact that diversity is lacking. However, a junior points out, "With each incoming class, Simmons becomes more and more diverse." Ultimately, students cultivate "solidarity around being a woman," whether that woman is moneyed Cape Cod stock or a gender-bending punk.

SIMMONS COLLEGE

FINANCIAL AID: 617-521-2001 • E-MAIL: UGADM@SIMMONS.EDU • WEBSITE: WWW.SIMMONS.EDU

ADMISSIONS

Very important factors considered include: Academic GPA, rigor of secondary school record. *Important factors considered include:* Application essay, character/personal qualities, class rank, recommendation(s), standardized test scores. *Other factors considered include:* Extracurricular activities, interview, talent/ability, volunteer work, work experience. SAT or ACT required; TOEFL required of all international applicants. High school diploma or equivalent is not required. *Academic units required:* 4 English, 3 math, 3 science, 3 foreign language, 3 social studies, 3 history. *Academic units recommended:* 4 English, 4 math, 3 science, 4 foreign language, 4 social studies, 3 history.

The Inside Word

Most of the best women's colleges in the country are in the Northeast, including those Seven Sister schools (roughly the female equivalent of the formerly all-male Ivies) that remain women's colleges. The competition for students is intense, and although Simmons is a strong attraction for many women, there are at least a half-dozen competitors who draw the better students away. For the majority of applicants there is little need for anxiety while awaiting a decision. Its solid academics, Boston location, and bountiful scholarship program make Simmons well worth considering for any student opting for a women's college.

FINANCIAL AID

Students should submit: FAFSA. Regular filing deadline is March 1. The Princeton Review suggests that all financial aid forms be submitted as soon as possible after January 1. *Need-based scholarships/grants offered:* Pell Grant, SEOG, state scholarships/grants, private scholarships, the school's own gift aid. *Loan aid offered:* FFEL Subsidized Stafford, FFEL Unsubsidized Stafford, FFEL PLUS, Federal Perkins Loan, state loans, college/university loans from institutional funds. Applicants will be notified of awards on or about March 15.

FROM THE ADMISSIONS OFFICE

"Simmons believes passionately in an 'educational contract' that places students first and helps them build successful careers, lead meaningful lives, and realize a powerful return on their investment. Simmons honors this contract by delivering a quality education and measurable success through singular approach to professional preparation, intellectual exploration, and community orientation.

"Simmons is a 100-year-old university in Boston, with a tradition of providing women with a collaborative environment that stimulates dialogue, enhances listening, catalyzes action, and spurs personal and professional growth.

"Simmons College accepts both the ACT and SAT. Students who enroll in September 2007 and thereafter are required to submit the SAT or the ACT with Writing. Additionally, if English is not your native language a TOEFL is required."

SELECTIVITY

Admissions Rating	86
# of applicants	2,537
% of applicants accepted	59
% of acceptees attending	29
# accepting a place on wait list	8

FRESHMAN PROFILE

Range SAT Critical Reading	510–610
Range SAT Math	500–590
Range ACT Composite	22–27
Minimum Paper TOEFL	560
Minimum Computer Based TOEFL	220
Average HS GPA	3.19
% graduated top 10% of class	26
% graduated top 25% of class	59
% graduated top 50% of class	92

DEADLINES

Regular application deadline	2/1
Regular notification	4/15
Nonfall registration?	yes

APPLICANTS ALSO LOOK AT

AND OFTEN PREFER
Boston University, Mount Holyoke College, Smith College

AND SOMETIMES PREFER
Boston College, Emmanuel College, Northeastern University, University of New Hampshire, University of Vermont

AND RARELY PREFER
Massachusetts College of Pharmacy & Health Science, Suffolk University, University of Massachusetts—Amherst

FINANCIAL FACTS

Financial Aid Rating	62
Annual tuition	$25,914
Room & Board	$10,710
Books and supplies	$960
Required fees	$809
% frosh rec. need-based scholarship or grant aid	59
% UG rec. need-based scholarship or grant aid	61
% frosh rec. need-based self-help aid	63
% UG rec. need-based self-help aid	61
% frosh rec. any financial aid	74
% UG rec. any financial aid	70

SIMON'S ROCK COLLEGE OF BARD

84 ALFORD ROAD, GREAT BARRINGTON, MA 01230 • ADMISSIONS: 413-528-7312 • FAX: 413-528-7334

CAMPUS LIFE

Quality of Life Rating	**86**
Fire Safety Rating	**60***
Type of school	private
Environment	village

STUDENTS

Total undergrad enrollment	368
% male/female	43/57
% from out of state	80
% live on campus	85
% African American	7
% Asian	4
% Caucasian	58
% Hispanic	6
% Native American	1
% international	4

SURVEY SAYS . . .

Small classes
Athletic facilities are great
Campus feels safe
Frats and sororities are unpopular or
nonexistent
(Almost) everyone smokes

ACADEMICS

Academic Rating	**98**
Calendar	semester
Student/faculty ratio	8:1
Profs interesting rating	99
Profs accessible rating	97
% profs teaching UG courses	100
% classes taught by TAs	0
Most common lab size	10–19 students
Most common reg class size	10–19 students

MOST POPULAR MAJORS

cell/cellular biology and histology
creative writing
psychology

STUDENTS SAY

Academics

Simon's Rock, "the only college in the country that is specifically designed for students of high school age who are ready for college," offers "brilliant and creative kids a combination of a lot of freedom and a lot of very demanding work so that they can begin college early and move forward with their lives earlier. It's the perfect environment for kids who think outside the box." Students at the Rock are given a challenging curriculum; one student jokingly describes the approach as "do as you please, and also 400 pages of reading." Undergrads report that "the average student spends more than 7 hours on homework a night and writes at least one six- to ten-page paper a week." In return for their hard work, students receive "up-close and personal attention of teachers who care about you and are not afraid to tell you when you've screwed up," and who are also "more than willing to set up tutorials and even arrange courses that match your academic interests, regardless of how off-the-wall they may be." Slightly more than half the students at Simon's Rock stick around for 2 years, long enough to earn an associate's degree, and then transfer to a larger school. Those who remain here enter the Upper College through "a self-selection process that tends to weed out the people who aren't as serious about the work they want to do. While the Lower College students can be, from time to time, indolent pot-smokers, by and large the juniors and seniors are extremely serious students."

Life

Simon's Rock is located "on top of a mountain in the middle-of-nowhere New England," with the closest town "a mile and a half away." Those who make the trek to town are rewarded with "yummy burritos, groceries, thrift-store shopping and a rad toy store." Because of the school's remote locale, "Students have to make their own fun," and they do so in a variety of ways: "Lots of kids meditate. Lots of kids ride bikes, fence, play soccer, go to the rock wall, or otherwise work out." Others "watch lots of movies, hang out with friends, and play intellectual games," and still others "go to one of the many swimming holes around here." Those with cars (or those who have friends with cars) are most likely to be completely satisfied; they point out that "we're only an hour from Northampton, where there's everything from lectures to concerts, and we also get to live in a nice, quiet New England town." They also note that "going to New York City and Boston is a breeze, and that's what most upperclassmen do on the weekends." Those who are campus-bound, however, caution that "if you're not a nature person, you might not be as happy here as [you would be] somewhere more urban."

Student Body

Who attends Simon's Rock? "Those [students] who are frustrated with the social and academic limitations of high school" are the school's target market, and they are mostly the ones who find their way here. One such student explains, "Simon's Rock is an exceptionally self-selecting institution. Most of us are atypical because if we weren't, we would not be at Simon's Rock." Undergrads "are very smart, or at least smart enough to realize the conformity and uselessness of high school" and "are either very studious or very artistic, or caught somewhere in the middle." Some see Simon's Rock as "'nerd camp' all over again. From neon hair to preppy-looking science students, the Simon's Rock type is that there isn't one." Contrary to popular perception, "We're not all communist beat poets majoring in Movement Studies. Yeah, we have lots of vegetarian liberal kids in sandals from Vermont, but they [also] carry 3.3 GPAs and head our Community Counsel and Fencing Club."

SIMON'S ROCK COLLEGE OF BARD

FINANCIAL AID: 413-528-7297 • E-MAIL: ADMIT@SIMONS-ROCK.EDU • WEBSITE: WWW.SIMONS-ROCK.EDU

ADMISSIONS

Very important factors considered include: Application essay, character/personal qualities, interview, recommendation(s), rigor of secondary school record, talent/ability. *Important factors considered include:* Academic GPA, class rank, level of applicant's interest. *Other factors considered include:* Alumni/ae relation, extracurricular activities, first generation, racial/ethnic status, standardized test scores, volunteer work, work experience. TOEFL required of all international applicants. High school diploma or equivalent is not required. *Academic units recommended:* 2 English, 2 math, 2 science (1 science lab), 2 foreign language, 2 social studies, 2 history.

The Inside Word

The application process at Simon's Rock is highly personalized. The school's unique composition calls for Admissions Officers to thoroughly assess candidates and evaluate whether the college will be a good fit. Prospective students must be extremely motivated and thrive in intellectual environments. They also need to demonstrate a high degree of maturity and an ability to work independently. Officers tend to focus on personal statements, recommendations, and interviews.

FINANCIAL AID

Students should submit: FAFSA, CSS/Financial Aid PROFILE, Business/Farm Supplement, parent and student Federal Income Tax Returns/Federal Verification Worksheet. The Princeton Review suggests that all financial aid forms be submitted as soon as possible after January 1. *Need-based scholarships/grants offered:* Pell Grant, SEOG, state scholarships/grants, private scholarships, the school's own gift aid. *Loan aid offered:* FFEL Subsidized Stafford, FFEL Unsubsidized Stafford, FFEL PLUS, Federal Perkins Loan, state loans, alternative educational loans. Applicants will be notified of awards on a rolling basis beginning or about April 15. Federal Work-Study Program available. Institutional employment available. Off-campus job opportunities are good.

FROM THE ADMISSIONS OFFICE

"Simon's Rock is dedicated to one thing: To allow bright, highly motivated students the opportunity to pursue college work leading to the AA and BA degrees at an age earlier than our national norm.

"Simon's Rock College of Bard will accept either the new SAT or the old SAT (administered prior to March 2005 and without a Writing component), as well as the ACT with or without the Writing component."

SELECTIVITY

Admissions Rating	**90**
# of applicants	204
% of applicants accepted	84
% of acceptees attending	74

FRESHMAN PROFILE

Range SAT Critical Reading	560–690
Range SAT Math	530–680
Range ACT Composite	25–30
Minimum Paper TOEFL	550
Minimum Computer Based TOEFL	200
Average HS GPA	3.36
% graduated top 10% of class	60
% graduated top 25% of class	82
% graduated top 50% of class	94

DEADLINES

Regular application deadline	5/31
Regular notification	rolling
Nonfall registration?	yes

FINANCIAL FACTS

Financial Aid Rating	**87**
Annual tuition	$34,804
Room & Board	$9,260
Books and supplies	$1,000
Required fees	$530
% frosh rec. need-based scholarship or grant aid	51
% UG rec. need-based scholarship or grant aid	39
% frosh rec. need-based self-help aid	47
% UG rec. need-based self-help aid	43
% frosh rec. any financial aid	78
% UG rec. any financial aid	71

SKIDMORE COLLEGE

815 NORTH BROADWAY, SARATOGA SPRINGS, NY 12866-1632 • ADMISSIONS: 518-580-5570 • FAX: 518-580-5584

CAMPUS LIFE
Quality of Life Rating	**88**
Fire Safety Rating	**60***
Type of school	private
Environment	town

STUDENTS
Total undergrad enrollment	2,726
% male/female	40/60
% from out of state	69
% live on campus	82
% African American	2
% Asian	7
% Caucasian	69
% Hispanic	4
% Native American	1
% international	2
# of countries represented	53

SURVEY SAYS . . .
Students love Saratoga Springs, NY
Great off-campus food
Dorms are like palaces
Frats and sororities are unpopular or nonexistent

ACADEMICS
Academic Rating	**92**
Calendar	semester
Student/faculty ratio	9:1
Profs interesting rating	85
Profs accessible rating	89
% profs teaching UG courses	100
% classes taught by TAs	0
Most common lab size	10–19 students
Most common reg class size	10–19 students

MOST POPULAR MAJORS
business administration/management
English language and literature
fine arts and art studies
psychology

STUDENTS SAY

Academics

"Creative thought matters" is Skidmore's slogan, and students here echo it frequently enough to convince us that it's more than your standard college hype; nearly one in five undergrads major in the visual or performing arts. Skidmore also boasts "great science programs," a "superb" English Department, and an "excellent" business program. The combined effect produces "a haven for inquisitive, artsy, liberal-minded students looking for a place to get a good education with minimal pretentiousness." Arts students laud the school's "great artistic community, populated by so many musicians, artists, actors, and dancers who are all passionate about what they do. This leads to collaboration in and outside of schoolwork, making it a great place to develop as an artist." Undergrads in more traditional liberal arts and sciences disciplines love the "opportunities for real work"—such as working as a "lab assistant for research projects" or "in local schools"—and "the very enthusiastic professors who are passionate about their work." Those for whom Skidmore is a fit feel it represents the "perfect balance between structure and freedom."

Life

Students tell us that Skidmore's Saratoga Springs location is one of the best things about the school. "The town is great," a senior raves. "The nightlife is fantastic, internships and volunteer opportunities abound, you have access to the Adirondacks and all of the best ski sites, it's a great place for friends and family to visit . . . everyone loves the place. Most students end up spending a summer or two in Saratoga just so they can enjoy everything about it without being distracted by studies." On campus, life is "very relaxed, and there is generally little pressure on students to do anything. However, the campus is a very involved one and there are countless extracurricular clubs and events going on at any point." Many students "get drunk and go to parties on the weekend," often at upperclassmen's houses, but "It is really easy to find other activities to participate in if partying isn't your scene. There are tons of events every night and lots of people who don't make partying their number one choice." These activities include "tons of campus concerts, performances, and shows" produced by the campus' glut of artists and performers.

Student Body

"Artistic/liberal kids" and "business major/athletic kids" form the two most conspicuous and readily identifiable populations on the Skidmore campus; one student explains, "You can usually tell who is who by the way they dress." While those two groups do "make a large part of the student body," undergrads point out that "there are all types of students that are not in those categories, or lie somewhere in between the two." For example, "We have kids who double major in business and art, athletes who are in the orchestra—you can be anyone you want to be and be accepted as an individual and as a part of the Skidmore community." Indeed, "The student body as a whole is extremely open-minded to diversity. There are a number of LGBT students who are strongly supported by the student body." "Although there is not a large amount of ethnic diversity," one student reports, "I have never seen a student of a different ethnicity be discriminated against, or even heard another student make any racist statement[s]." Are Skidmore students entirely free of prejudice? No, not entirely; one student explains, "The only discrimination I have seen here is against Republicans. Skidmore is extremely liberal, and I would say it is pretty hard to fit in here with extremely conservative beliefs."

FINANCIAL AID: 518-580-5750 • E-MAIL: ADMISSIONS@SKIDMORE.EDU • WEBSITE: WWW.SKIDMORE.EDU

ADMISSIONS

Very important factors considered include: Rigor of secondary school record. *Important factors considered include:* Academic GPA, application essay, character/personal qualities, class rank, extracurricular activities, recommendation(s), talent/ability, volunteer work, work experience. *Other factors considered include:* Alumni/ae relation, first generation, geographical residence, interview, racial/ethnic status, standardized test scores. SAT or ACT required; SAT Subject Tests recommended. TOEFL required of all international applicants. High school diploma is required, and GED is accepted. *Academic units recommended:* 4 English, 4 math, 4 science (3 science labs), 4 foreign language, 4 social studies.

The Inside Word

Skidmore remains a fallback option for Northeastern kids who don't get into their top choices. Admits are very bright kids and a successful applicant must present the Admissions Office with a fairly compelling picture. You'll receive friendly, personalized assistance from the Admissions Office here, especially if you communicate a strong desire to attend Skidmore.

FINANCIAL AID

Students should submit: FAFSA, CSS/Financial Aid PROFILE. Regular filing deadline is January 15. The Princeton Review suggests that all financial aid forms be submitted as soon as possible after January 1. *Need-based scholarships/grants offered:* Pell Grant, SEOG, state scholarships/grants, the school's own gift aid. *Loan aid offered:* FFEL Subsidized Stafford, FFEL Unsubsidized Stafford, FFEL PLUS, Federal Perkins Loan. Applicants will be notified of awards on or about April 1.

FROM THE ADMISSIONS OFFICE

"Launched in 2005, Skidmore's First-Year Experience (FYE) is a year-long academic, co-curricular, and residential initiative that immediately engages each first-year student with a faculty mentor-advisor, with 14 other students in an innovative Scribner Seminar, and with the entire college community through a series of artistic, cultural, and social events. FYE's centerpiece, 50 distinctive seminars—ranging from the human colonization of space to lessons learned from Hurricane Katrina to British national identity—requires each student to participate actively and creatively in his or her own learning. Seminar instructors function as faculty mentor-advisors for their 15 students, and provide curricular and co-curricular perspectives not only on the specific seminar topic but on the liberal arts in general. In most cases, students live in residence halls in close proximity to classmates from their seminar.

"In terms of skills and habits of mind, seminar participants will learn to distinguish among and formulate the types of questions asked by different disciplines; read critically and gather and interpret evidence; consider and address complexities and ambiguities; recognize choices, examine assumptions, and take a skeptical stance; formulate conclusions based upon evidence; and communicate those conclusions orally and in writing. These are the fundamentals for academic excellence.

"The First-Year Experience is just the beginning of the expectation that students will creatively craft an experience leading to intensive work in a major field of study, often via a double major or major and minor, supplemented by a semester abroad, collaborative research with a faculty member, and internships. It is also a singular manifestation of Skidmore's commitment to the belief that 'Creative Thought Matters'—that every life, career, and endeavor is made more profound with creative ability at its core.

"Applicants for Fall 2008 are required to take the SAT or the ACT with the Writing section. We recommend that students provide scores for two SAT Subject Test examinations."

SELECTIVITY

Admissions Rating	93
# of applicants	6,652
% of applicants accepted	39
% of acceptees attending	10
# accepting a place on wait list	877
% admitted from wait list	1
# of early decision applicants	448
% accepted early decision	58

FRESHMAN PROFILE

Range SAT Critical Reading	580–680
Range SAT Math	580–670
Range ACT Composite	25–29
Minimum Paper TOEFL	590
Minimum Computer Based TOEFL	243
Average HS GPA	3.31
% graduated top 10% of class	49
% graduated top 25% of class	82
% graduated top 50% of class	96

DEADLINES

Early decision application deadline	11/15
Early decision notification	12/15
Regular application deadline	1/15
Regular notification	4/1
Nonfall registration?	yes

APPLICANTS ALSO LOOK AT

AND OFTEN PREFER
Boston College, Colby College, Wesleyan University

AND SOMETIMES PREFER
Connecticut College, New York University, Syracuse University

AND RARELY PREFER
Ithaca College, University of Vermont, Wheaton College (MA)

FINANCIAL FACTS

Financial Aid Rating	93
Annual tuition	$34,224
Room & Board	$9,556
Books and supplies	$1,000
Required fees	$470
% frosh rec. need-based scholarship or grant aid	40
% UG rec. need-based scholarship or grant aid	41
% frosh rec. need-based self-help aid	40
% UG rec. need-based self-help aid	41
% frosh rec. any financial aid	40
% UG rec. any financial aid	40

SMITH COLLEGE

SEVEN COLLEGE LANE, NORTHAMPTON, MA 01063 • ADMISSIONS: 413-585-2500 • FAX: 413-585-2527

STUDENTS SAY

Academics

"Fantastic academics" that demand "insane amounts of studying and work" have always been the signature feature of a Smith education, and the women who attend this elite Northeastern school wouldn't have it any other way. One student explains, "Classes are so incredibly challenging, you work your [butt] off to succeed, but you do it because the professors are so great and because the work is interesting." With no core requirements to fulfill, Smithies "can spend much more time taking classes they are interested in. It makes you feel like you are getting more out of your college education." So, too, do professors who "really care and are willing to explain, discuss, re-explain, and work with you until you have a solid grasp of the material." An "amazing library" is among Smith's many resources; what students can't find here in the library or course catalog, they can easily seek out at one of the other member schools in the Five College Consortium (Amherst, Mount Holyoke, Hampshire, and UMass); shuttle buses carry students among the different campuses. As one student sums up, Smith is "unabashedly a women's college, devoted to providing incredible education and opportunities to women from around the globe."

Life

Smith undergrads adore the school's unique housing system, under which "students live in a beautiful nineteenth-century house with 40 of their closest friends." Almost all of the "amazing" dorms "have hardwood floors and big windows" and typically include "dining rooms with kitchen staffs." The system not only allows students to manage their stressful academics in comfort, but also provides them with a ready support network of peers. The houses are just one of many traditions that unite the Smith community; Friday afternoon tea is another. One student reports, "The kitchen staff bakes cookies and all sorts of pastries, and it's a nice time to unwind after the week. We also have candlelight dinner every Thursday night, and dinner is served family style as opposed to buffet." Extracurricular life at Smith tends to be on the quiet side, and students approve; one writes, "Being at Smith, you get the best of all worlds. Parties here tend to be smaller, lower-key events, but having the Five College connection you get your choice of any party you'd want. Go to UMass for frats and big dance parties. Go to Hampshire for a more chill, laid-back vibe. Go to Amherst for something a little more formal." The campus also hosts regular "dances, poetry readings, movies, lectures, cultural events, you name it." Hometown Northampton, "just a 5-minute walk from campus," also shoulders some of the burden. The town "is full of extremely unique stores, boutiques, indie movie theaters, concert venues, bars, coffeehouses, and restaurants."

Student Body

If people who "use the word 'hegemony' in everyday conversation" and who cherish "freedom from the oppressive heteronormative patriarchy"—or even know what that means—sound like your kind of folks, you may be a Smith woman. Smithies are "typically politically active, love to learn, and champion about four different causes. They are quirky and dorky but love to go out and have a good time. And they want to save the world." The crusading can occasionally be overbearing—"Smith students can be vicious when defending their own beliefs and ideas and attacking those who disagree with them," warns one woman—but overall, students regard one another as "caring" and "supportive." Like hometown Northampton, "Smith is a very gay-friendly environment"—students report that there are "a lot of lesbians" on campus, and "quite a few 'boys.'" Straight undergrads think "It's important to stress how easy it is to meet guys. Many hetero women are scared to come here because they believe the stereotype about Smith being solely a haven for man-hating lesbians. It really is not true."

FINANCIAL AID: 413-585-2530 • E-MAIL: ADMISSION@SMITH.EDU • WEBSITE: WWW.SMITH.EDU

ADMISSIONS

Very important factors considered include: Academic GPA, character/personal qualities, recommendation(s), rigor of secondary school record. *Important factors considered include:* Application essay, class rank, extracurricular activities, interview, standardized test scores, talent/ability. *Other factors considered include:* Alumni/ae relation, first generation, racial/ethnic status, volunteer work, work experience. SAT or ACT required; TOEFL required of all international applicants. High school diploma or equivalent is not required. *Academic units recommended:* 4 English, 3 math, 3 science (3 science labs), 3 foreign language, 2 history.

The Inside Word

Don't be fooled by the relatively high acceptance rate at Smith (or at other top women's colleges). The applicant pool is small and highly self-selected, and it's fairly tough to get admitted. Only women who have taken the most challenging course loads in high school and achieved at a superior level will be competitive.

FINANCIAL AID

Students should submit: FAFSA, CSS/Financial Aid PROFILE, Noncustodial PROFILE, Business/Farm Supplement. Regular filing deadline is February 1. The Princeton Review suggests that all financial aid forms be submitted as soon as possible after January 1. *Need-based scholarships/grants offered:* Pell Grant, SEOG, state scholarships/grants, the school's own gift aid. *Loan aid offered:* Direct Subsidized Stafford, Direct Unsubsidized Stafford, FFEL PLUS, Federal Perkins Loan, state loans, college/university loans from institutional funds. Applicants will be notified of awards on or about April 1. Federal Work-Study Program available. Institutional employment available. Off-campus job opportunities are excellent.

FROM THE ADMISSIONS OFFICE

"Smith students choose from 1,000 courses in more than 50 areas of study. There are no specific course requirements outside the major; students meet individually with faculty advisers to plan a balanced curriculum. Smith programs offer unique opportunities, including the chance to study abroad, or at another college in the United States, and a semester in Washington, DC. The Ada Comstock Scholars Program encourages women beyond the traditional age to return to college and complete their undergraduate studies. Smith is located in the scenic Connecticut River valley of western Massachusetts near a number of other outstanding educational institutions. Through the Five College Consortium, Smith, Amherst, Hampshire, and Mount Holyoke colleges and the University of Massachusetts enrich their academic, social, and cultural offerings by means of joint faculty appointments, joint courses, student and faculty exchanges, shared facilities, and other cooperative arrangements. Smith is the only women's college to offer an accredited major in engineering; it's also the only college in the country that offers a guaranteed paid internship program ("Praxis").

"Smith requires either the SAT or the ACT. Scores from older versions of the SAT (pre-March 2005 version) and the ACT are acceptable."

SELECTIVITY

Admissions Rating	95
# of applicants	3,427
% of applicants accepted	53
% of acceptees attending	37
# accepting a place on wait list	286
% admitted from wait list	6
# of early decision applicants	212
% accepted early decision	78

FRESHMAN PROFILE

Range SAT Critical Reading	580–700
Range SAT Math	560–670
Range SAT Writing	640–730
Range ACT Composite	25–29
Minimum Paper TOEFL	600
Minimum Computer Based TOEFL	250
Average HS GPA	4.0
% graduated top 10% of class	61
% graduated top 25% of class	91
% graduated top 50% of class	100

DEADLINES

Early decision application deadline	11/15
Early decision notification	12/15
Regular application deadline	1/15
Regular notification	4/1
Nonfall registration?	no

APPLICANTS ALSO LOOK AT

AND OFTEN PREFER
Brown University

AND SOMETIMES PREFER
Wellesley College

AND RARELY PREFER
Mount Holyoke College

FINANCIAL FACTS

Financial Aid Rating	95
Annual tuition	$32,320
Room & Board	$10,880
Books and supplies	$600
Required fees	$238
% frosh rec. need-based scholarship or grant aid	59
% UG rec. need-based scholarship or grant aid	59
% frosh rec. need-based self-help aid	58
% UG rec. need-based self-help aid	58
% frosh rec. any financial aid	66
% UG rec. any financial aid	65

SONOMA STATE UNIVERSITY

1801 EAST COTATI AVENUE, ROHNERT PARK, CA 94928 • ADMISSIONS: 707-664-2778 • FAX: 707-664-2060

STUDENTS SAY

Academics

Californians seeking a first-rate public-school education that allows them to "take a step back from the fast pace of the city without taking away the fun and activities" look to Sonoma State University, a rural campus that is "very relaxing and beautiful"—but also close enough to San Francisco and Sacramento to benefit from the activities these cities offer. Standout programs here include the Hutchins School of Liberal Studies, which offers interdisciplinary instruction that fosters "cross-disciplinary development of critical-thinking abilities" (many Hutchins students ultimately pursue teaching degrees); a "wonderful" psychology program; a business program that "is very well put together, with very helpful, good teachers"; and "excellent health care and science majors," including a unique environmental management and design program. Students love the fact that the small size of the school allows for "a very personal connection between the student and the professor." Size constraints conspire to make it "harder to get the classes you need," however, and this causes some frustration. Respondents report that "many students take more than 4 years to graduate" because of these limitations. Great funding for the library, on the other hand, means that "it's the best you'll find anywhere, thanks to a donation from *Peanuts* cartoonist Charles Schulz."

Life

The "laid-back and beautiful campus" of Sonoma State "can be too quiet for some people, but for the general population, it is a place to relax and get some peace in their busy schedules." Students who "want a place where you can hear a pin drop, view the stars, and breathe actual air rather than LA smog" will feel most at home here. The downside of all this tranquility is that accompanying it is sometimes a "lack of school spirit. Back in the 1990s we had a football team. No more, and some of us feel like we're really missing out. These days, if you go to any game on campus you will see fewer than 100 students." Even the "amazing lacrosse team" can't draw much of a crowd here. Hometown Rohnert Park "is about an hour from San Francisco," but there's also much to be said for closer destinations. Sonoma County "is full of beautiful hillsides that make for great hiking. The beach is a 40-minute drive west, and many students venture out that way when weather permits." Campus housing "is great; we live in apartments instead of rooms," and with the school "currently focusing on renovating old buildings as well as adding new facilities (a music center and a recreation center, for example)," the campus promises to improve even more in coming years.

Student Body

"The typical student at SSU is a young White female," undergrads here report, estimating that "probably two-thirds of the students are women." Many students can be described as "hippie types, very in tune with the environment and very natural in appearance. Very relaxed, mostly liberal, and left-wing." Those outside the majority demographic "can appear socially removed," but "It seems like everyone can find a niche." SSU has "very few minority students, though that percentage has increased slowly over the years" as "The administration has reached out to city kids as well as minority kids, thus integrating more diversity into the university."

FINANCIAL AID: 707-664-2389 • E-MAIL: ADMITME.@SONOMA.EDU • WEBSITE: WWW.SONOMA.EDU

ADMISSIONS

Very important factors considered include: Rigor of secondary school record, standardized test scores. *Important factors considered include:* Geographical residence, racial/ethnic status, state residency. SAT or ACT required; TOEFL required of all international applicants. High school diploma is required, and GED is accepted. *Academic units required:* 4 English, 3 math, 2 science (1 science lab), 2 foreign language, 1 history, 3 academic electives, 1 visual/performing arts, 1 U.S. government.

The Inside Word

Sonoma State's admissions philosophy can be summed up in one word: objectivity. Standardized test scores and GPAs are the overriding factors. Assuming they meet the minimum standards, applicants are guaranteed an acceptance letter. Students should take a moment to peruse the requirements as some of the more popular majors stipulate higher grades.

FINANCIAL AID

Students should submit: FAFSA. The Princeton Review suggests that all financial aid forms be submitted as soon as possible after January 1. *Need-based scholarships/grants offered:* Pell Grant, SEOG, state scholarships/grants, private scholarships, the school's own gift aid. *Loan aid offered:* Direct Subsidized Stafford, Direct Unsubsidized Stafford, Direct PLUS, Federal Perkins Loan. Applicants will be notified of awards on a rolling basis beginning or about April 15.

FROM THE ADMISSIONS OFFICE

"Sonoma State University occupies 275 acres in the beautiful wine country of Sonoma County, in Northern California. Located at the foot of the Sonoma hills, the campus is an hour's drive north of San Francisco and centrally located between the Pacific Ocean to the west and the wine country to the north and east. SSU is deeply committed to the teaching of the liberal arts and sciences. The campus has earned a national reputation as a leader in integrating the use of technology into its curriculum. Within its 32 academic departments, SSU awards bachelor's degrees in 41 areas of specialization and master's degrees in 14 areas. In addition, the university offers a joint master's degree in mathematics with San Francisco State University. The campus ushered in the twenty-first century with the opening of a new library and technology center, the Jean and Charles Schulz Information Center.

"All freshmen applicants are required to provide SAT or ACT scores. Fall 2008 applicants are encouraged to take the new SAT or the ACT. In addition, students may submit scores from the old (before March 2005) SAT, and we will use their best scores from either test."

SELECTIVITY

Admissions Rating	**60***
# of applicants	10,398
% of applicants accepted	69
% of acceptees attending	21

FRESHMAN PROFILE

Range SAT Critical Reading	450–550
Range SAT Math	450–560
Range ACT Composite	18–23
Minimum Paper TOEFL	500
Minimum Computer Based TOEFL	173
Average HS GPA	3.23

DEADLINES

Regular application deadline	1/31
Regular notification	rolling
Nonfall registration?	yes

FINANCIAL FACTS

Financial Aid Rating	**75**
Annual in-state tuition	$0
Annual out-of-state tuition	$10,170
Room & Board	$8,465
Books and supplies	$1,314
Required fees	$3,648
% frosh rec. need-based scholarship or grant aid	12
% UG rec. need-based scholarship or grant aid	23
% frosh rec. need-based self-help aid	12
% UG rec. need-based self-help aid	25
% frosh rec. any financial aid	26
% UG rec. any financial aid	37

SOUTHERN METHODIST UNIVERSITY

PO BOX 750181, DALLAS, TX 75275-0181 • ADMISSIONS: 214-768-0103 • FAX: 214-768-2507

STUDENTS SAY
Academics
Southern Methodist University seeks "to challenge and develop students intellectually and socially in order to provide a fulfilling higher education." Others agree that students here are "making valuable connections that can serve [them] well in the working world." They "work hard and play hard" so it's all about finding balance between "making the grades and having fun." Good news for grads: Future opportunities abound as "You won't struggle to find a job because of SMU's outstanding reputation in the Dallas market. Its strong name has also branched out into the greater South. Most of the alums are very successful, and they seek out SMU students." The school works its magic most effectively in such popular disciplines as business, advertising, pre-law, and premedical study; its Meadows School of Performing Arts is home to "an incredible music program" and equally strong programs in dance, theater, arts administration, and advertising. Students are keen to brag that SMU professors "go above and beyond their duties" and are always "looking after your best interests." Combine this with a "great administration" that "really strives to stay in touch with their students and uses their feedback to make beneficial changes." SMU's Dallas address means "there are a lot of ways to get involved in the community or resources for your career path." As one student explains, "My school does a great job at helping students decide what they want out of their future and assisting them on making it possible."

Life
"School is hard," notes one student, "but you make it through somehow" thanks to "parties, movies, clubs, bars, [and a] very Greek" campus. In fact, the typical student is described as "sporting a Greek affiliation" (and they don't mean the nationality). The Greeks serve as the nexus of social life and account for a large "sense of community" among students. In short, writes one Greek student, "We run this place. Everyone who is anyone is in it. Tailgating wouldn't happen without us. Homecoming wouldn't happen without us." Togas aside, SMU's "beautiful" campus garners even more accolades. "It is definitely the prettiest campus in Texas, and one of the greatest in the South," says a student. Beyond campus awaits Dallas, where "There is always a party going on, whether it is downtown or at a local bar. Because of the location (in upscale Highland Park), bars are always new and safe with the best DJs. There are more places to eat near SMU than anywhere I have ever been."

Student Body
First, let's address the stereotypes. The typical SMU student is described largely as "upper-class, White, and wealthy—though looks can be deceiving." That said, many note that SMU could use "more diversity" and "Atypical students can feel left out." Another student claims that the school has "a huge mix of students" though "you have to look hard." One unifying factor? All things "Dixie." "Every student here seems to know the words to Dixie," explains a student. "You'll see Rebel flags alongside Texas flags in all the dorm rooms. But it's more of a statement of the genteel Southern style of living people appreciate. Everyone is Republican . . . and very conservative." Though many agree that a majority of students "come from high-income households," SMU is a "dynamic community" that manages "to offer something for everyone. You just have to find your niche."

FINANCIAL AID: 214-768-2058 • E-MAIL: UGADMISSION@SMU.EDU • WEBSITE: WWW.SMU.EDU/ADMISSION

ADMISSIONS

Very important factors considered include: Academic GPA, application essay, class rank, recommendation(s), rigor of secondary school record, standardized test scores. *Important factors considered include:* Character/personal qualities, extracurricular activities, talent/ability, volunteer work, work experience. *Other factors considered include:* Alumni/ae relation, first generation, interview, level of applicant's interest. SAT or ACT required; TOEFL required of all international applicants. High school diploma is required, and GED is not accepted. *Academic units required:* 4 English, 3 math, 3 science (2 science labs), 2 foreign language, 1 social studies, 2 history. *Academic units recommended:* 4 English, 4 math, 4 science (3 science labs), 3 foreign language, 2 social studies, 3 history.

The Inside Word

With a potent combination of high-caliber academics, Texan weather, and classic architecture, admissions standards at SMU have been steadily rising over the last decade, meaning that securing a seat here is getting more and more competitive. Solid high school grades and a roster of activities will usually do the trick, but keep in mind that performing arts majors must audition. Interestingly, all other applicants, regardless of declared major, are listed as "pre-majors" to the Dedman College of Humanities and Sciences.

FINANCIAL AID

Students should submit: FAFSA, CSS/Financial Aid PROFILE, Noncustodial PROFILE, Business/Farm Supplement. The Princeton Review suggests that all financial aid forms be submitted as soon as possible after January 1. *Need-based scholarships/grants offered:* Pell Grant, SEOG, state scholarships/grants, private scholarships, the school's own gift aid. *Loan aid offered:* FFEL Subsidized Stafford, FFEL Unsubsidized Stafford, FFEL PLUS, Federal Perkins Loan, state loans, college/university loans from institutional funds. Applicants will be notified of awards on a rolling basis beginning or about March 15. Federal Work-Study Program available. Institutional employment available. Off-campus job opportunities are good.

FROM THE ADMISSIONS OFFICE

"SMU students balance challenging academic programs with a total campus experience that enables them to choose their own path of achievement. Small classes ensure that students receive personal attention. Classes are taught by professors who are dedicated to teaching undergraduates while producing new knowledge, enriching the classroom. Students also have access to visiting dignitaries ranging from former presidents to Nobel laureates. Reflecting its student-centered focus, SMU is one of the few universities to have a voting student member on its Board of Trustees. Internships, community service, student research opportunities, and study abroad programs abound. SMU also offers a thriving honors program and one of the top merit scholarship programs in the nation. More than 400 arts events each year add a special vitality to campus life, and nearly 200 student organizations provide opportunities for leadership. SMU welcomes a diverse student body from every state and over 90 countries; 72 percent of students receive some form of financial aid. Graduates attend some of the best graduate and professional schools in the nation. They find promising career opportunities through SMU's close ties with Dallas, a center of commerce and culture and gateway to the global community.

"SMU requires either the ACT or SAT. Assessment of written communication skills remains an important component of the SMU application review process. To that end, it is recommended that applicants use every opportunity, including the ACT or SAT, to display their writing skills in the application process."

SELECTIVITY

Admissions Rating	89
# of applicants	7,648
% of applicants accepted	54
% of acceptees attending	33
# accepting a place on wait list	437
% admitted from wait list	23

FRESHMAN PROFILE

Range SAT Critical Reading	560–650
Range SAT Math	580–670
Range SAT Writing	550–650
Range ACT Composite	24–29
Minimum Paper TOEFL	550
Minimum Computer Based TOEFL	213
Average HS GPA	3.50
% graduated top 10% of class	35
% graduated top 25% of class	70
% graduated top 50% of class	91

DEADLINES

Regular application deadline	3/15
Regular notification	rolling
Nonfall registration?	yes

APPLICANTS ALSO LOOK AT

AND OFTEN PREFER
University of Southern California, Vanderbilt University

AND SOMETIMES PREFER
Trinity University, Tulane University, University of Miami, The University of Texas at Austin

AND RARELY PREFER
Baylor University, Texas Christian University, University of Arizona, University of Colorado—Boulder

FINANCIAL FACTS

Financial Aid Rating	80
Annual tuition	$27,400
Room & Board	$10,825
Books and supplies	$800
Required fees	$3,480
% frosh rec. need-based scholarship or grant aid	24
% UG rec. need-based scholarship or grant aid	29
% frosh rec. need-based self-help aid	27
% UG rec. need-based self-help aid	32
% frosh rec. any financial aid	82
% UG rec. any financial aid	65

SOUTHWESTERN UNIVERSITY

ADMISSIONS OFFICE, PO BOX 770, GEORGETOWN, TX 78627-0770 • ADMISSIONS: 512-863-1200 • FAX: 512-863-9601

CAMPUS LIFE

Quality of Life Rating	**86**
Fire Safety Rating	**88**
Type of school	private
Affiliation	Methodist
Environment	town

STUDENTS

Total undergrad enrollment	1,277
% male/female	41/59
% from out of state	7
% from public high school	82
% live on campus	78
% in (# of) fraternities	28 (4)
% in (# of) sororities	31 (4)
% African American	3
% Asian	5
% Caucasian	79
% Hispanic	13
% Native American	1

SURVEY SAYS . . .

Small classes
No one cheats
Great computer facilities
Great library
Career services are great
Students are friendly
Campus feels safe

ACADEMICS

Academic Rating	**88**
Calendar	semester
Student/faculty ratio	10:1
Profs interesting rating	94
Profs accessible rating	93
% profs teaching	
UG courses	100
% classes taught by TAs	0
Most common	
lab size	fewer than 10 students
Most common	
reg class size	10–19 students

MOST POPULAR MAJORS

business administration/
management
communications studies/speech
communication and rhetoric
psychology

STUDENTS SAY

Academics

At this liberal arts university of nearly 1,300 undergrads, students extol the accessibility of Southwestern's professors and administrators. "The teachers and administrators are so easy to get in touch with it's silly," writes a freshman. Another first-year boasts: "I love how approachable everyone is. I've had lunch with the president twice." The flip side to having professors who "give out their home phone numbers" and "take the time to get to know you" is increased accountability: Professors also "require attendance" at their classes. A political science major describes the academic experience as "rigorous but rewarding." Southwestern challenges its students "academically, intellectually, and personally—inside and outside of the classroom," writes a junior. As a result, students benefit from "a lot of intellectual conversation"—but also feel the burden of "lots of homework." While students may grumble a little about the hours they log in the library, they assure us that "graduate schools and employers know that Southwestern produces good graduates, so the hard work is well worth it." They boast that undergrads have the opportunity "to participate in scholarship and actual research." Some students mention that they'd like to see "more options for class offerings." These gripes aside, students are overall quite content; in the words of a senior: "Southwestern has been an overwhelmingly positive experience."

Life

Georgetown, "a sleepy Texas town north of Austin," is the home of Southwestern University. "Small and historical," Georgetown feels to some undergrads like a "retirement community," with "little to offer college students after 10:00 P.M." The town of Round Rock, just "a few miles away," brings a bit more excitement, but the real action takes place in Austin. "Austin's only about 30 minutes away," and this is where students go to find "urban-related activities" such as "shows, readings, concerts, or food." On campus, nightlife consists of fraternity parties, which take place on weekends and on Wednesday nights (at "Study Break" events). Additionally, the Student Activities Office plans concerts and film nights for the weekends. The students who aren't involved in Greek life like to "hang out at someone's apartment, go into Austin, [or] drive home for the weekend." Outdoor activities are also popular at Southwestern; if you're looking to play Ultimate Frisbee, "There is generally a game . . . going on 24/7." Another popular pastime is hitting up The Cove, an on-campus student facility, "which has pool tables, food, BYOB on some nights, foosball, shuffle puck, a fireplace, comfy chairs, and tables where students can hang out." Still, students groan that they "need more things to do on campus." "There are a lot of different organizations and events," though boredom does drive some students to leave town on the weekends. Those who do stick around know there's one place they can always go: "It is normal for the library to have students studying on Friday and Saturday nights."

Student Body

Southwestern prides itself on being a "friendly" place, and as such, "people all get along extremely well" and "respect others' views." The undergrad population here is "very politically active," including vocal extremes ranging from "White Republican Christians" to "liberal tree-huggers," as one sophomore puts it. Many observe that Southwestern has a number of students of "upper-middle-class backgrounds" who hail from Texas. One common thread among all students, in the words of a freshman, is that "everybody here is 'the geek' . . . meaning 'smart kid compared to the rest of the posse.' We have the gorgeous preppy geeks, athletic jock geeks, philosophical genius geeks, writer geeks, math geeks, everything." What the school lacks, students say, is "racial diversity." "There are very few minority students on campus," laments a senior. And with a clear majority of women on campus, female students say that "at times," they "feel a little boy-starved." Overall, students feel "comfortable" here; one freshman writes: "I personally am an atypical student, and I fit in fine."

FINANCIAL AID: 512-863-1259 • E-MAIL: ADMISSION@SOUTHWESTERN.EDU • WEBSITE: WWW.SOUTHWESTERN.EDU

ADMISSIONS

Very important factors considered include: Academic GPA, application essay, class rank, recommendation(s), rigor of secondary school record, standardized test scores. *Important factors considered include:* Alumni/ae relation, character/personal qualities, extracurricular activities, first generation, geographical residence, interview, level of applicant's interest, racial/ethnic status, talent/ability, volunteer work, work experience. SAT or ACT required; ACT with Writing component required. TOEFL required of all international applicants. High school diploma is required, and GED is accepted. *Academic units required:* 4 English, 4 math, 3 science (2 science labs), 2 foreign language, 2 social studies, 2 history. *Academic units recommended:* 4 English, 4 math, 4 science (2 science labs), 3 foreign language, 2 social studies, 2 history.

The Inside Word

Southwestern is one of the best "sleepers" in the nation. Admissions standards are high, but they would be even more so if more people knew of this place. Academic excellence abounds, the administration is earnest and helpful, and the school has attracted national recognition. If you could thrive in a small-town, close-knit environment, Southwestern definitely deserves a look.

FINANCIAL AID

Students should submit: FAFSA. Regular filing deadline is March 1. The Princeton Review suggests that all financial aid forms be submitted as soon as possible after January 1. *Need-based scholarships/grants offered:* Pell Grant, SEOG, state scholarships/grants, private scholarships, the school's own gift aid. *Loan aid offered:* FFEL Subsidized Stafford, FFEL Unsubsidized Stafford, FFEL PLUS, Federal Perkins Loan, state loans, college/university loans from institutional funds. Applicants will be notified of awards on a rolling basis beginning or about March 25.

FROM THE ADMISSIONS OFFICE

"On the outskirts of Texas's vibrant capital city of Austin is Southwestern University, the state's first institution of higher learning. Southwestern is committed to helping students achieve personal and professional success as well as a passion for lifelong learning. The Paideia Program, funded in 2002 by an $8.5 million grant, is a distinctive new option for select students beginning the sophomore year that provides opportunities to compare, contrast, and integrate knowledge and skills gained in various areas of study. In addition to their regular studies, students work with the same Paideia professor over a 3-year period in seminar groups of ten. They work to discover the powerful connections between Southwestern's rigorous academic experience and the dynamic programs available outside the classroom—through leadership, service, intercultural learning, and collaborative research or creative works. All Southwestern students discover that a premier liberal arts education leads to high acceptance rates into prestigious graduate and professional programs and careers right out of college. Southwestern is today what it has always been: a highly personal liberal arts experience that equips students with the strengths they need to develop fulfilling lives.

"Southwestern University will accept both the old and new SAT score formats. The Writing component of the new SAT will be considered in a comprehensive manner, along with overall academic record, application essay, extracurricular activities, recommendations, and a personal interview."

SELECTIVITY

Admissions Rating	88
# of applicants	1,955
% of applicants accepted	65
% of acceptees attending	27
# accepting a place on wait list	26
% admitted from wait list	50
# of early decision applicants	95
% accepted early decision	76

FRESHMAN PROFILE

Range SAT Critical Reading	555–670
Range SAT Math	560–665
Range ACT Composite	23–29
Minimum Paper TOEFL	570
Minimum Computer Based TOEFL	230
% graduated top 10% of class	50
% graduated top 25% of class	85
% graduated top 50% of class	99

DEADLINES

Early decision application deadline	11/1
Early decision notification	12/1
Regular application deadline	2/15
Regular notification	4/1
Nonfall registration?	yes

APPLICANTS ALSO LOOK AT

AND OFTEN PREFER
Rice University, Trinity University

AND SOMETIMES PREFER
Rhodes College, Texas A&M University—College Station, Tulane University, The University of Texas at Austin, Vanderbilt University

AND RARELY PREFER
Austin College, Baylor University, Southern Methodist University, Texas Christian University

FINANCIAL FACTS

Financial Aid Rating	86
Annual tuition	$25,740
Room & Board	$8,710
Books and supplies	$1,000
% frosh rec. need-based scholarship or grant aid	54
% UG rec. need-based scholarship or grant aid	50
% frosh rec. need-based self-help aid	49
% UG rec. need-based self-help aid	46
% frosh rec. any financial aid	82
% UG rec. any financial aid	84

SPELMAN COLLEGE

350 SPELMAN LANE, SOUTHWEST, ATLANTA, GA 30314 • ADMISSIONS: 404-270-5193 • FAX: 404-270-5201

CAMPUS LIFE

Quality of Life Rating	71
Fire Safety Rating	60*
Type of school	private
Environment	metropolis

STUDENTS

Total undergrad enrollment	2,284
% male/female	0/100
% from out of state	70
% from public high school	84
# of sororities	4
% African American	98
% international	1
# of countries represented	18

SURVEY SAYS . . .

Small classes
Lab facilities are great
Campus feels safe
Frats and sororities dominate social scene
Student government is popular
Very little drug use

ACADEMICS

Academic Rating	78
Calendar	semester
Student/faculty ratio	11:1
Profs interesting rating	68
Profs accessible rating	63
% profs teaching UG courses	100
% classes taught by TAs	0
Most common lab size	20–29 students
Most common reg class size	20–29 students

MOST POPULAR MAJORS
political science and government
psychology

STUDENTS SAY

Academics

Dr. Beverly Tatum promised Spelman College students "nothing less than the best" when she became president of the school in 2002, and according to undergrads here, she's delivered on that promise. The women who attend this Historically Black College report that the school succeeds in "instilling in the minds of young Black women that anything is possible" through a "superb and rigorous academic experience" and a "focus on empowering the total self. As a Black woman at a Black school, you never feel intimidated or like an outcast." The curriculum reinforces Black identity—"classes like 'African Diaspora and the World' change not only how you think, but who you are as a person," students report—alongside traditional academic disciplines. Academically, Spelman excels in many areas. Premed sciences are among the school's strong suits; one undergrad writes, "If you want a stronghold for women interested in the sciences, come to Spelman. It seems like everyone I talk to is a science major (although we do have a good amount of women's studies, political science, and economics majors)." For programs not offered on campus, students can take advantage of Spelman's membership in the Atlanta University Center, "the largest consortium of Black colleges in the nation," in order to take classes and utilize resources at three other schools nearby. An added benefit of the consortium is that "during the day, Spelman almost looks like a coed college due to cross registration," allowing students the benefit of both single-sex education and coeducation.

Life

"Spelman is a place that fulfills all of your academic and social needs," students tell us, observing that "Even while going to class and the library, you are sure to [see] someone you know to help ease the stress of studying. The campus also provides great social events. Every Friday, for example, Spelman has Market Friday, where off-campus vendors and student groups set up booths." Students also "hang out on the Strip, the area between our neighbors Morehouse and Clark Atlanta, where you will find a lot of people at any given time." Mostly, though, students like to spend their free time enjoying Atlanta, "a great city to go to school in. Museums, theater, and sports are probably the most popular major events in the area. Many music artists and other celebrities flock to Atlanta for concerts and special events as well." A "trusty-dusty, if rarely on time, AUC shuttle takes students to clubs and other places of interest. There's also the local transit system (MARTA), which you can take to the mall, clubs, theaters, restaurants, Underground Atlanta, and anywhere else in the Atlanta and Metro area." Students tell us that the Spelman campus is "small but absolutely beautiful." Facilities, however, need an upgrade. One undergrad writes, "There is no air conditioning in over half of the dorms. There are just some basic things that must improve."

Student Body

The Black women who attend Spelman "are from everywhere: the West, Midwest, East Coast, South, and 19 other countries. We do have a few students of other ethnic groups as well, and it's not like they fade into the woodwork; everyone is friendly to them, and they participate in class and play sports and do everything that the 'typical' version of a Spelman student would do." Some here "are from an upper-income household, and many came from predominantly White communities looking to experience an HBCU [Historically Black College or University]." Students can be "very opinionated and enjoy expressing those opinions," as evidenced in 2004 by a high-profile controversy over a planned campus visit by rap artist Nelly; one student observes, "As a whole, Spelman women are politically and socially aware and are active people who make it their business to cause change. We are politically active, and we do a lot of community service here, go into the community to tutor students, build homes—everything."

FINANCIAL AID: 404-270-5212 • E-MAIL: ADMISS@SPELMAN.EDU • WEBSITE: WWW.SPELMAN.EDU

ADMISSIONS

Very important factors considered include: Academic GPA, application essay, character/personal qualities, rigor of secondary school record, standardized test scores. *Important factors considered include:* Extracurricular activities, recommendation(s). *Other factors considered include:* Alumni/ae relation, class rank, first generation, geographical residence, level of applicant's interest, volunteer work, work experience. SAT or ACT required; TOEFL required of all international applicants. High school diploma is required, and GED is accepted. *Academic units required:* 4 English, 3 math, 3 science (2 science labs), 2 foreign language, 3 social studies, 2 history, 2 academic electives. *Academic units recommended:* 4 English, 4 math, 4 science (3 science labs), 4 foreign language, 4 social studies, 3 history, 2 academic electives.

The Inside Word

No Historically Black College in the country has a better graduation rate or a more competitive admissions process than Spelman, and on top of this, application totals were up 25 percent last season. Successful candidates show strong academic records with challenging course loads and solid grades. Applicant evaluation is very personal; it is quite important to show depth of character and social consciousness.

FINANCIAL AID

Students should submit: Institution's own financial aid form, CSS/Financial Aid PROFILE. The Princeton Review suggests that all financial aid forms be submitted as soon as possible after January 1. *Need-based scholarships/grants offered:* Pell Grant, SEOG, state scholarships/grants, private scholarships, the school's own gift aid, United Negro College Fund. *Loan aid offered:* FFEL Subsidized Stafford, FFEL Unsubsidized Stafford, FFEL PLUS.

FROM THE ADMISSIONS OFFICE

"As an outstanding Historically Black College for women, Spelman strives for academic excellence in liberal arts education. This predominantly residential private college provides students with an academic climate conducive to the full development of their intellectual and leadership potential. The college is a member of the Atlanta University Center consortium, and Spelman students enjoy the benefits of a small college while having access to the resources of the other three participating institutions. The purpose extends beyond intellectual development and professional career preparation of students. It seeks to develop the total person. The college provides an academic and social environment that strengthens those qualities that enable women to be self-confident as well as culturally and spiritually enriched. This environment attempts to instill in students both an appreciation for the multicultural communities of the world and a sense of responsibility for bringing about positive change in those communities.

"Applicants for Fall 2008 are required to submit standardized test scores from an appropriate venue (i.e. ACT, TOEFL, SAT). The highest composite score will be used in admissions decisions. Writing scores from either the SAT or ACT will not be taken into consideration in the admission process."

SELECTIVITY

Admissions Rating	91
# of applicants	5,428
% of applicants accepted	36
% of acceptees attending	29
# of early decision applicants	200
% accepted early decision	30

FRESHMAN PROFILE

Range SAT Critical Reading	500–590
Range SAT Math	480–570
Range ACT Composite	20–24
Minimum Paper TOEFL	500
Minimum Computer Based TOEFL	250
Average HS GPA	3.58
% graduated top 10% of class	32
% graduated top 25% of class	71
% graduated top 50% of class	94

DEADLINES

Early decision application deadline	11/1
Early decision notification	12/15
Regular application deadline	2/1
Regular notification	4/1
Nonfall registration?	no

APPLICANTS ALSO LOOK AT

AND OFTEN PREFER
Georgia Institute of Technology

AND SOMETIMES PREFER
Clark Atlanta University, Florida A&M University, Hampton University, Howard University, Tuskegee University

AND RARELY PREFER
Emory University, University of Georgia, University of Maryland—College Park

FINANCIAL FACTS

Financial Aid Rating	79
Annual tuition	$14,470
Room & Board	$8,750
Books and supplies	$1,150
Required fees	$2,535
% frosh rec. need-based scholarship or grant aid	61
% UG rec. need-based scholarship or grant aid	57
% frosh rec. need-based self-help aid	82
% UG rec. need-based self-help aid	75
% frosh rec. any financial aid	82
% UG rec. any financial aid	75

ST. BONAVENTURE UNIVERSITY

PO Box D, St. Bonaventure, NY 14778 • Admissions: 716-375-2400 • Fax: 716-375-4005

STUDENTS SAY

Academics

One rough translation of the Italian *buona ventura* is "the good journey," and this has become the operant metaphor for an education at St. Bonaventure University, a small Franciscan university in upstate New York. One undergraduate here reports, "Since I've begun 'the good journey,' I've found that every professor I've ever encountered is the most down-to-earth person who would do anything in order for you to earn the grade you desire." Indeed, students here agree that "the professors are really caring and are here because they love their jobs and they love the students." Undergrads are especially excited about the journalism program, pointing out that "a lot of the mass communications faculty have years of experience in the job place, which is helpful." Historically, they've been generally less enthusiastic about Clare College, the university division through which Bona administers its challenging and Catholic core curriculum. Notes a typical student, "Clare College is a little too demanding for the 100-level courses and required courses it offers, but overall it is something that the school prides itself on, and I feel privileged to have gone through it." Part of the problem with Clare is the disconnect between its admirable goal of broad intellectual inquiry and most students' desire to focus on career-related subjects; one student observes, "Sometimes the atmosphere on campus reflects a lack of concern over educational studies, and it feels as though people often forget that they are at a liberal arts school." Those who "get it" praise Bona's efforts to "provide a broad education about the world while also providing that very precise education about your major and learning values at the same time."

Life

Bona is "in the middle of nowhere, and it's freezing outside for about 70 percent of the school year," so students "do the same thing anyone else would do under the circumstances; we drink with friends." Students agree that Bona is "definitely a party school. While on-campus parties are tough to pull off, there is a party off campus every night. Almost anyone can get into the local bars and there are many houses off campus that have triple keggers nightly." Bona undergrads also tell us that "besides partying, our school offers many programs and clubs that you can participate in. Many students go up to Mt. Irenaeus for a relaxing and spiritual weekend. There are always floor programs going on and there is a club for each major, which take field trips." The radio station is very popular; college sports are big, too. Bona has "tons of intramural sports that are fun to participate in. Every semester there are a few tournaments of various sports where you can arrange to have you and friends on a team together. It is fun just to be social."

Student Body

"Most students are White, Catholic, and come from middle-class families" at Bona, and while "there are not many atypical students, those who are fit in fine, thanks to our Franciscan values." Many "live within 2 hours of campus" and have bonded with the school—usually through its sports teams—long before attending the school. One student writes, "If you go anywhere off campus wearing your Bona gear, someone is likely to yell, 'Go Bonas' at you. It's an instant bond." Most here "have both party-animal and Catholic tendencies," although there are some who lean more toward the former. Most everyone here "is interested in, and usually active in, some sort of sport."

FINANCIAL AID: 716-375-2528 • E-MAIL: ADMISSIONS@SBU.EDU • WEBSITE: WWW.SBU.EDU

ADMISSIONS

Very important factors considered include: Academic GPA, character/personal qualities, interview, recommendation(s), rigor of secondary school record. *Important factors considered include:* Application essay, extracurricular activities, level of applicant's interest, standardized test scores, talent/ability, volunteer work. *Other factors considered include:* Alumni/ae relation, class rank, first generation, work experience. SAT recommended; ACT recommended. SAT or ACT required; TOEFL required of all international applicants. High school diploma is required, and GED is accepted. *Academic units required:* 4 English, 3 math, 3 science, 2 foreign language, 4 social studies. *Academic units recommended:* 4 English, 3 math, 3 science (3 science labs), 2 foreign language, 4 social studies.

The Inside Word

St. Bonaventure is a safety for many students applying to more selective Catholic universities, but it does a good job of enrolling a sizable percentage of its admits. Most solid students needn't worry about admission; even so, candidates who rank St. Bonnie as a top choice should still submit essays and interview.

FINANCIAL AID

Students should submit: FAFSA, institution's own financial aid form, state aid form. The Princeton Review suggests that all financial aid forms be submitted as soon as possible after January 1. *Need-based scholarships/grants offered:* Pell Grant, SEOG, state scholarships/grants, private scholarships, the school's own gift aid. *Loan aid offered:* FFEL Subsidized Stafford, FFEL Unsubsidized Stafford, FFEL PLUS, Federal Perkins Loan, college/university loans from institutional funds. Applicants will be notified of awards on a rolling basis beginning or about April 1.

FROM THE ADMISSIONS OFFICE

"The St. Bonaventure University family has been imparting the Franciscan tradition to men and women of a rich diversity of backgrounds for more than 130 years. This tradition encourages all who become a part of it to face the world confidently, respect the earthly environment, and work for productive change in the world. The charm of our campus and the inspirational beauty of the surrounding hills provide a special place where growth in learning and living is abundantly realized. The Richter Student Fitness Center, scheduled to be completed in 2004, will provide all students with state-of-the-art facilities for athletics and wellness. Academics at St. Bonaventure are challenging. Small classes and personalized attention encourage individual growth and development for students. St. Bonaventure's nationally known Schools of Arts and Sciences, Business Administration, Journalism/Mass Communication, and Education offer majors in 31 disciplines. The School of Graduate Studies also offers several programs leading to the master's degree.

"Applicants for Fall 2008 can submit scores from either the old or new SAT, as well as the ACT. For students who have taken both versions, the best composite score from either the old or new SAT will be used. The Biology Subject Test is required only for students applying to one of our Dual Admission medical programs."

SELECTIVITY

Admissions Rating	72
# of applicants	1,730
% of applicants accepted	86
% of acceptees attending	32

FRESHMAN PROFILE

Range SAT Critical Reading	480–570
Range SAT Math	470–570
Range ACT Composite	19–23
Minimum Paper TOEFL	550
Minimum Computer Based TOEFL	213
Average HS GPA	3.13
% graduated top 10% of class	11
% graduated top 25% of class	31
% graduated top 50% of class	68

DEADLINES

Regular application deadline	4/15
Regular notification	rolling
Nonfall registration?	yes

APPLICANTS ALSO LOOK AT
AND OFTEN PREFER
Providence College, State University of New York at Geneseo, Villanova University
AND SOMETIMES PREFER
Ithaca College, Le Moyne College, Niagara University, Siena College, State University of New York—University at Buffalo
AND RARELY PREFER
Syracuse University

FINANCIAL FACTS

Financial Aid Rating	81
Annual tuition	$21,650
Room & Board	$7,760
Books and supplies	$650
Required fees	$865
% frosh rec. need-based scholarship or grant aid	73
% UG rec. need-based scholarship or grant aid	71
% frosh rec. need-based self-help aid	60
% UG rec. need-based self-help aid	59

ST. JOHN'S COLLEGE (MD)

PO BOX 2800, ANNAPOLIS, MD 21404 • ADMISSIONS: 410-626-2522 • FAX: 410-269-7916

CAMPUS LIFE

Quality of Life Rating	89
Fire Safety Rating	94
Type of school	private
Environment	town

STUDENTS

Total undergrad enrollment	518
% male/female	54/46
% from out of state	84
% from public high school	61
% live on campus	80
% African American	2
% Asian	2
% Caucasian	89
% Hispanic	2
% Native American	0
% international	1
# of countries represented	9

SURVEY SAYS . . .

Class discussions encouraged
No one cheats
Registration is a breeze
Frats and sororities are unpopular or nonexistent
Lots of beer drinking
(Almost) everyone smokes

ACADEMICS

Academic Rating	96
Calendar	semester
Student/faculty ratio	8:1
Profs interesting rating	98
Profs accessible rating	89
% profs teaching UG courses	100
% classes taught by TAs	0
Most common reg class size	10–19 students

MOST POPULAR MAJORS

liberal arts and sciences studies and humanities

STUDENTS SAY

Academics

"The only elective at St. John's College is your choice to attend," explains one student. "From there on out, the program will teach you everything you thought you knew." That's because the entire curriculum at SJC is required, a 4-year survey of intellectual history that "starts at the beginning (ancient Greece) and works its way through the years to modern times. Starting from Euclidian geometry, we end up at relativity. Starting at Aristotelian biology, we end up at quantum mechanics and genetics. The school teaches you that you can only learn where you are by understanding where you have been." Classes here "are all discussion-based; there are no lectures, and classes are never larger than 20 students." Faculty members are referred to as "tutors" rather than professors; they must teach every subject in the curriculum and primarily "serve as guides to learning and add to the discussion. They are, as Socrates says, midwives to ideas." Tutors "come from a wide variety of deeply academic backgrounds, but their specializations have little to do with our curriculum. In the classroom, they are glorified students, as puzzled as the rest of us." The result is "an unbelievable academic community" in which "Philosophy is not a game, but rather a crucial guide for living." St. John's is the perfect place for those "ready to confront history's original thinkers directly" and those who want to "teach themselves how to think, how to read and digest information, and how to appreciate the beauty of the written word."

Life

"Class discussions often spill into out-of-class venues" at St. John's, where "On a beautiful sunny day you'll be struck by the vast numbers of people reading outside on the lawns, benches, chairs, and steps of the quad, front, and back campus." There's a rhythm to life on this campus: "Monday and Thursday nights are largely taken up by seminar (all students have seminar 8:00–10:00 P.M.), and though there is often drinking, hanging out on the quad, and animated discussion afterwards, there isn't much in the way of organized activity." However, "Every other Saturday night from 10:30 P.M. until 2:00 A.M. there are waltz parties, which consist mostly of swing dancing, though waltz, polka, and tango are also played." Also, "The college Film Society shows movies almost every Saturday night." A student group called Reality "organizes occasional non-waltz parties such as Oktoberfest, a Halloween Party, and a weekend of debauchery at the end of the year." Student organizations include a theater group, a chorus, an orchestra, a society called Melee that "battles with swords made of plastic piping wrapped in foam," a group called Mabel the Swimming Wonder Monkey that "watches bad movies and mocks them," and a sizable Christian Fellowship. The highlight of the year, according to most, is the fall croquet match against the Naval Academy. Some here tell us they never leave campus; others report that "trips to Baltimore and Washington are frequent, as well as small groups of students going to concerts."

Student Body

St. John's students report "a definite feeling among students that we've all been Johnnies all our lives, but just didn't have a name for it before." The community here is tight, both because it "is fairly self-selecting, so that most students who come here are invested in their education and self-improvement," and also because "We have a common ground that unites us in the shared curriculum. We're not fragmented by major." An "egalitarian intramural sports program that does not exclude any students and the lack of fraternities and politically partisan groups" also helps. This eclectic group includes "students who graduated at the top of their class in high school, some at the bottom, and some who left high school to come to college."

ST. JOHN'S COLLEGE (MD)

FINANCIAL AID: 410-626-2502 • E-MAIL: ADMISSIONS@SJCA.EDU • WEBSITE: WWW.SJCA.EDU

ADMISSIONS

Very important factors considered include: Application essay. *Important factors considered include:* Character/personal qualities, recommendation(s), rigor of secondary school record. *Other factors considered include:* Academic GPA, alumni/ae relation, class rank, extracurricular activities, first generation, interview, racial/ethnic status, standardized test scores, talent/ability. TOEFL required of all international applicants. High school diploma is required, and GED is accepted. *Academic units required:* 3 math, 2 foreign language. *Academic units recommended:* 4 English, 4 math, 3 science (3 science labs), 4 foreign language, 2 social studies, 2 history.

The Inside Word

St. John's has one of the most personal admissions processes in the country. The applicant pool is highly self-selected and extremely bright, so don't be fooled by the high acceptance rate—every student who is offered admission deserves to be here. Candidates who don't give serious thought to the kind of match they make with the college and devote serious energy to their essays are not likely to be successful.

FINANCIAL AID

Students should submit: FAFSA, CSS/Financial Aid PROFILE, Noncustodial PROFILE, state aid form, Business/Farm Supplement. The Princeton Review suggests that all financial aid forms be submitted as soon as possible after January 1. *Need-based scholarships/grants offered:* Pell Grant, SEOG, state scholarships/grants, the school's own gift aid. *Loan aid offered:* FFEL Subsidized Stafford, FFEL Unsubsidized Stafford, FFEL PLUS, Federal Perkins Loan, college/university loans from institutional funds. Applicants will be notified of awards on a rolling basis beginning or about December 1.

FROM THE ADMISSIONS OFFICE

"The purpose of the admission process is to determine whether an applicant has the necessary preparation and ability to complete the St. John's program satisfactorily. The essays are designed to enable applicants to give a full account of themselves. They can tell the committee much more than statistical records reveal. Previous academic records show whether an applicant has the habits of study necessary at St. John's. Letters of reference, particularly those of teachers, are carefully read for indications that the applicant has the maturity, self-discipline, ability, energy, and initiative to succeed in the St. John's program. St. John's attaches little importance to 'objective' test scores, and no applicant is accepted or rejected because of such scores.

"St. John's College does not require the results of standardized tests, except in the case of international students, homeschooled students, and those who will not receive a high school diploma. Results of the ACT or SAT are sufficient for these students."

SELECTIVITY

Admissions Rating	84
# of applicants	426
% of applicants accepted	81
% of acceptees attending	44

FRESHMAN PROFILE

Range SAT Critical Reading	650–760
Range SAT Math	580–680
Minimum Paper TOEFL	600
Minimum Computer Based TOEFL	250
% graduated top 10% of class	28
% graduated top 25% of class	57
% graduated top 50% of class	87

DEADLINES

Regular notification	rolling
Nonfall registration?	no

APPLICANTS ALSO LOOK AT

AND OFTEN PREFER
Swarthmore College, The University of Chicago, University of Virginia

AND SOMETIMES PREFER
Kenyon College, Oberlin College, Reed College, Smith College

AND RARELY PREFER
Bard College

FINANCIAL FACTS

Financial Aid Rating	91
Annual tuition	$36,342
Room & Board	$8,684
Books and supplies	$280
Required fees	$250
% frosh rec. need-based scholarship or grant aid	54
% UG rec. need-based scholarship or grant aid	59
% frosh rec. need-based self-help aid	63
% UG rec. need-based self-help aid	59
% frosh rec. any financial aid	63
% UG rec. any financial aid	59

ST. JOHN'S COLLEGE (NM)

1160 CAMINO CRUZ BLANCA, SANTA FE, NM 87505 • ADMISSIONS: 505-984-6060 • FAX: 505-984-6162

STUDENTS SAY

Academics

To have any sort of serious discussion about the academic experience of students at St. John's College, one must begin with an understanding of "the Program," which, in a nutshell, is a guided tour through the high points of Western thought. Students actually read the books other people consider doorstops and grapple with primary texts straight from the big thinkers of history. "I thought I knew what a number was, but then I began to study Euclid. I thought I knew what freedom was, but then I read Herodotus," writes one typical undergrad. At St. John's, it is more important to learn "how we arrived at the facts" than the facts themselves. This is radical intellectualism for students who've always dreamed of "a double major in philosophy and math with a triple minor in history of science, history of music, and history of language." The professors, called tutors, are considered "more experienced learners" rather than fonts of knowledge, and they serve to focus all of the paradigm deconstruction, worldview disruption, and interdisciplinary connection. Tutors routinely teach outside of their field of expertise, "so they learn with us." Students recognize the luxury of having such "brilliant, dedicated, understanding, and inspiring" guides to "aggressively critique our arguments." For this experiment in erudition to work, however, students "have to show a great deal of integrity." Everyone arrives at class with scribbles in the margins and an open mind. Slackers are shunned for "harming the class dynamic and cooperative learning process." Above all, students want to learn to think and communicate lucidly. The rigorous subject matter hands them the heaviest weights for all the cerebral workouts necessary to achieving such a goal. At a place where "Education is an end and not a means," the right kind of minds— quick, receptive, and reflective—may experience true "transformation."

Life

A first-year "Johnnie" assures prospective applicants, "There are things to do other than the Program." Typically those include "reading lighter material [or] simply making each other laugh." Students value the idea of balance in their lives and take frequent breaks to practice Brazilian jiu-jitsu, drum up a game of Go, throw some pottery, dust off the cello, or learn to tango. Hiking the nearby trails or gazing at the stars gives students the chance to ponder beauty and the cosmos directly and revive their brains with some fresh air. One freshman likes to "walk out [the] back door to the top of a mountain with friends and watch the sunset." The small population limits the number of community-organized activities, but "People still pursue their interests on their own." An upperclassman writes, "I've been able to direct or codirect at least one play every year since I started here, including freshman year." Students resist the incomplete image of St. John's "either as a geek preserve or drug haven. We're neither." Though "The average Johnnie likes jazz, beer, and hedonism" almost as much as books, all drunken conversation ultimately relates back to the pursuit of truth.

Student Body

A senior emphasizes, "It is important to understand what a tiny, tiny campus we have. You will have your boyfriend in class, your ex in class, your ex's new girlfriend in class, and you need to be able to separate out your emotional involvement, or someone's going to call you on it." Outsiders have "exaggerated the bizarre, cultlike qualities" in the past; students are quick to clarify, "It's an open, loving, dysfunctional family and not a closed, bitter one." Also, not all of these misfits fit the bleary-eyed, borderline-insane reputation surrounding the school. "There are very grounded people with regular schedules of sleeping, eating, and thinking nonphilosophical things." Despite the liberal political leanings of the student body, "This isn't really a good place for wandering hippie types who subscribe to a pluralist philosophy of absolute tolerance." People either "like to learn, like to think, like to work very hard, or some combination of those."

FINANCIAL AID: 505-984-6058 • E-MAIL: ADMISSIONS@MAIL.SJCSF.EDU • WEBSITE: WWW.SJCSF.EDU

ADMISSIONS

Very important factors considered include: Application essay, character/personal qualities, interview, talent/ability. *Important factors considered include:* Extracurricular activities, recommendation(s), rigor of secondary school record. *Other factors considered include:* Class rank, standardized test scores, volunteer work, work experience. TOEFL required of all international applicants. High school diploma or equivalent is not required. *Academic units required:* 3 math, 2 foreign language. *Academic units recommended:* 4 English, 4 math, 3 science (3 science labs), 3 foreign language, 2 social studies, 2 history.

The Inside Word

Self-selection drives this admissions process—over one-half of the entire applicant pool each year indicates that St. John's is their first choice, and half of those admitted send in tuition deposits. Even so, no one in admissions takes things for granted, and neither should any student considering an application. The admissions process is highly personal on both sides of the coin. Only the intellectually curious and highly motivated need apply.

FINANCIAL AID

Students should submit: FAFSA, CSS/Financial Aid PROFILE, Noncustodial PROFILE, Business/Farm Supplement. The Princeton Review suggests that all financial aid forms be submitted as soon as possible after January 1. *Need-based scholarships/grants offered:* Pell Grant, SEOG, state scholarships/grants, private scholarships, the school's own gift aid. *Loan aid offered:* FFEL Subsidized Stafford, FFEL Unsubsidized Stafford, FFEL PLUS, Federal Perkins Loan, college/university loans from institutional funds. Applicants will be notified of awards on a rolling basis beginning or about December 1. Federal Work-Study Program available. Institutional employment available. Off-campus job opportunities are excellent.

FROM THE ADMISSIONS OFFICE

"St. John's appeals to students who value good books, love to read, and are passionate about discourse and debate. There are no lectures and virtually no tests or electives. Instead, classes of 16–20 students occur around conference tables where professors are as likely to be asked to defend their points of view as are students. Great books provide the direction, context, and stimulus for conversation. The entire student body adheres to the same, all-required arts and science curriculum. Someone once said, 'A classic is a house we still live in,' and at St. John's, students and professors alike approach each reading on the list as if the ideas it holds were being expressed for the first time—questioning the logic behind a geometrical proof, challenging the premise of a scientific development, or dissecting the progression of modern political theory as it unfolds.

"As of this book's publication, St. John's College (NM) did not have information available about their policy regarding the new SAT."

SELECTIVITY

Admissions Rating	86
# of applicants	318
% of applicants accepted	83
% of acceptees attending	44

FRESHMAN PROFILE

Range SAT Critical Reading	650–750
Range SAT Math	580–670
Range ACT Composite	28–31
Minimum Paper TOEFL	550
Minimum Computer Based TOEFL	213
% graduated top 10% of class	17
% graduated top 25% of class	54
% graduated top 50% of class	77

DEADLINES

Regular notification	rolling
Nonfall registration?	yes

APPLICANTS ALSO LOOK AT

AND OFTEN PREFER
Deep Springs College, Stanford University

AND SOMETIMES PREFER
Bard College, Claremont McKenna College, Rice University, The University of Chicago

AND RARELY PREFER
Grinnell College, Oberlin College, Whitman College

FINANCIAL FACTS

Financial Aid Rating	96
Annual tuition	$34,306
Room & Board	$8,270
Books and supplies	$275
Required fees	$200
% frosh rec. need-based scholarship or grant aid	67
% UG rec. need-based scholarship or grant aid	64
% frosh rec. need-based self-help aid	68
% UG rec. need-based self-help aid	64

ST. JOHN'S UNIVERSITY

8000 UTOPIA PARKWAY, QUEENS, NY 11439 • ADMISSIONS: 718-990-2000 • FAX: 718-990-5728

STUDENTS SAY

Academics

Like its hometown of Queens, NY, St. John's moves inexorably forward without forgetting its history and traditions. The school's administration is committed to constantly "updating the university's facilities." Recent improvements include "a state-of-the-art athletic training facility and revamped cafeterias." In addition, the school distributes "brand-new laptops to all incoming students" and has "done a tremendous job of implementing technology throughout the campus," which "is completely wireless except for a few athletic fields and parking lots." On the traditions side of the balance, the school recently built "a beautiful brand-new, free-standing church" and maintains "a lot of policies and politics opposed by typical college students . . . [such as] the visitor policies in the dorms." Regarding academics, the university offers some amazing opportunities such as the Institute for Writing Studies and the "Discover the World" program. When it comes to classroom experience, "Professors are professors. Like [at] any school, some are better than others." Students report that "the experience you have at St. John's really depends on what you do with it. Don't take a professor just because he/she is easy— chances are that means they suck! If you are self-motivated . . . you will find challenging professors." Big-picture people will see that St. John's offers "a quality private education" and, in many instances, a "generous" financial aid package that translates to an overall "low cost."

Life

Historically, St. John's has been known as "basically a school for commuters." According to many students, it still is. They argue that because "There aren't many on-campus students," "On the weekends this place is a ghost town." Others counter that "Recently there has been an amazing effort" by the school's Residence Life Department "to bring back campus life," an effort which includes posting "weekly calendars informing us about campus events and activities." For those who prefer off-campus activities in their spare time, the school helps to make that possible, too. There are "shuttles that can take us into the city [aka Manhattan, to those outside New York City] and on weekends . . . to the mall." In addition, the "school runs programs to see Broadway shows for free." Even without the school's help, however, New York is at students' fingertips; almost everything the city has to offer "is just a subway ride away." "Clubs, sports events, parties, restaurants"—you name it, NYC's got it, and St. John's students sample it. The faithful will be happy to know that "St. John's makes it easy to incorporate a spiritual life with an academic one." For the altruistic, there are "community-service initiatives galore."

Student Body

Because it is "located in Queens, the most diverse place on Earth," it's no surprise that St. John's itself is "very, very diverse." Though "everyone gets along exceptionally well," getting along well doesn't equal total integration. There are "major ethnic lines" at St. John's, and each "ethnic group tends [to] hang around with itself, a sight typical of New York in general." Yet students' external differences belie intangible similarities. Many students may be the first in their family to attend college, so a strong work ethic is pervasive. Everyone "wants to achieve something greater than their parents." The second major similarity stems from the first: As students here generally have many responsibilities outside of their schoolwork, it makes sense that "the typical St. John's student is a commuter."

FINANCIAL AID: 1-888-9-STJOHNS • E-MAIL: ADMISSIONS@STJOHNS.EDU • WEBSITE: WWW.STJOHNS.EDU

ADMISSIONS

Very important factors considered include: Academic GPA, standardized test scores, *Important factors considered include:* class rank, recommendation(s), rigor of secondary school record. *Other factors considered include:* Alumni/ae relation, application essay, character/personal qualities, extracurricular activities, first generation, interview, talent/ability, volunteer work, work experience. SAT or ACT required; TOEFL required of all international applicants. High school diploma is required, and GED is accepted. *Academic units required:* 4 English, *Academic units recommended:* 3 math, 2 science (2 science labs), 2 foreign language, 2 history, 1 academic elective.

The Inside Word

The admissions process at St. John's doesn't include many surprises. High school grades and standardized test scores are undoubtedly the most important factors though volunteer work and extracurricular activities are also highly regarded. What is surprising is that this Catholic university doesn't consider religious affiliation at all when making admissions decisions; there are students of every religious stripe here (see the "Student Body" section).

FINANCIAL AID

Students should submit: FAFSA. The Princeton Review suggests that all financial aid forms be submitted as soon as possible after January 1. *Need-based scholarships/grants offered:* Pell Grant, SEOG, state scholarships/grants, private scholarships, the school's own gift aid. *Loan aid offered:* FFEL Subsidized Stafford, FFEL Unsubsidized Stafford, FFEL PLUS, Federal Perkins Loan. Applicants will be notified of awards on a rolling basis beginning or about March 15.

FROM THE ADMISSIONS OFFICE

"Founded by the Vincentian Fathers in 1870, St. John's offers a residential college experience in dynamic New York City. Students pursue more than 100 programs in the arts, sciences, business, education, pharmacy, and allied health. Professors are renowned scholars, 90 percent of whom hold a PhD or comparable degree. Consider these benefits you'll find at St. John's:

- Utilize our state-of-the-art wireless network—one reason why St. John's is the only New York–area university in *Intel's* top 10 'Most Unwired Colleges.'

- Gain a global perspective with the cultural explorations available through our amazing 'Discover the World' program—a dynamic semester living and learning in other lands.

- Build your writing skills with personal support offered students of all majors through our new Institute for Writing Studies.

- Visit museums, see plays, and make New York City your 'living textbook' through our unique 'Discover New York' core course.

- Boost your science knowledge through unique courses like 'Methods of Scientific Inquiry'—and our campus-wide, $20 million upgrade in science facilities.

- Get real-world experience by having a positive impact on others through St. John's extensive Academic Service-Learning offerings.

"St. John's has three residential New York City campuses: our 105-acre Queens campus; our wooded Staten Island campus; and our award-winning Manhattan campus. Graduate centers are located in Oakdale, NY, and Rome, Italy.

"Applicants present a Writing section score when SAT or ACT scores are submitted. While no minimum score on this portion of either exam is required, the Admission Committee may review and evaluate student essays within the context of the admission process or for assessment purposes."

SELECTIVITY
Admissions Rating	79
# of applicants	25,594
% of applicants accepted	59
% of acceptees attending	22
# accepting a place on wait list	74
% admitted from wait list	53

FRESHMAN PROFILE
Range SAT Critical Reading	470–580
Range SAT Math	480–610
Minimum Paper TOEFL	500
Minimum Computer Based TOEFL	173
Average HS GPA	3.2
% graduated top 10% of class	14
% graduated top 25% of class	41
% graduated top 50% of class	74

DEADLINES
Nonfall registration?	yes

APPLICANTS ALSO LOOK AT AND OFTEN PREFER
City University of New York—Baruch College, City University of New York—Queens College, State University of New York—Stony Brook University

AND SOMETIMES PREFER
Hofstra University, Pace University, State University of New York at Binghamton

AND RARELY PREFER
Siena College, St. Bonaventure University

FINANCIAL FACTS
Financial Aid Rating	70
Annual tuition	$26,200
Room & Board	$12,070
Books and supplies	$1,000
Required fees	$640
% frosh rec. need-based scholarship or grant aid	73
% UG rec. need-based scholarship or grant aid	70
% frosh rec. need-based self-help aid	60
% UG rec. need-based self-help aid	64
% frosh rec. any financial aid	98
% UG rec. any financial aid	94

ST. LAWRENCE UNIVERSITY

PAYSON HALL, CANTON, NY 13617 • ADMISSIONS: 315-229-5261 • FAX: 315-229-5818

CAMPUS LIFE

Quality of Life Rating	84
Fire Safety Rating	87
Type of school	private
Environment	village

STUDENTS

Total undergrad enrollment	2,145
% male/female	48/52
% from out of state	53
% from public high school	68
% live on campus	99
% in (# of) fraternities	6 (1)
% in (# of) sororities	20 (4)
% African American	3
% Asian	2
% Caucasian	71
% Hispanic	3
% Native American	1
% international	5
# of countries represented	42

SURVEY SAYS . . .
Small classes
Great computer facilities
Great library
Athletic facilities are great
Everyone loves the Saints
Lots of beer drinking

ACADEMICS

Academic Rating	91
Calendar	semester
Student/faculty ratio	11:1
Profs interesting rating	93
Profs accessible rating	88
% profs teaching UG courses	98
% classes taught by TAs	0
Most common lab size	10–19 students
Most common reg class size	10–19 students

MOST POPULAR MAJORS
economics
English language and literature
psychology

STUDENTS SAY

Academics

Described by one student as a "hidden jewel tucked away in the tundra of the North Country," St. Lawrence University offers a "unique liberal arts education" to prospective undergraduates. Two things that "really stand out" at this small university are the "study abroad programs and the First-Year Program (FYP)." FYP is one of the oldest living-learning programs in the country and all first-year students are required to participate, which "helps strengthen skills and better prepares students for their next 3 years in college." Moreover, nearly 50 percent of the student body "participates in the study abroad programs offered" at some point during their time here. According to one student, "The professors are the best asset of St. Lawrence . . . they are very knowledgeable, and they love what they teach." Classes emphasize "critical thinking and writing," and "Professors are always there for students." Many students "form long-lasting friendships with their professors." Despite the university's small size there are "many class offerings," and students praise a "wonderful president" who leads a "very accessible" administration.

Life

Students at St. Lawrence "work hard [and] play harder!" Most students "socialize frequently" through a variety of outlets, from "theme parties [and] midnight breakfasts" to hanging out at "local bars." Although the surrounding area is "fairly void of cultural experiences," many students participate in "outdoor trips to the accessible Adirondacks or to cosmopolitan Montreal or Ottawa . . . all of which are between 1 to 2 and a half hours away from campus." The university makes "a lot of the accessories for these [outdoor] activities available for little or no upfront price." In addition, "There is always something happening at the student center for those who might prefer a more low-key night, like free movies." Most students "enjoy attending collegiate athletics, especially hockey" with "more than 60 percent of students involved with some sport." All of this contributes to a "very energetic atmosphere" on campus where there is "always an event to watch or participate in." Some students see the relatively isolated location of St. Lawrence as a blessing because it "forces students to form tighter bonds than at schools in cities where there is easy access to many different activities."

Student Body

The typical student at St. Lawrence is "very preppy" and "comes from the New England area." Here, "The guys are called 'Larrys' and the girls are 'Muffies,'" but "Most personalities do not fit the 'snobby preppy' stereotype." Many students qualify as "outdoorsy" types and there are "quite a few jocks." While students acknowledge a "lack of diversity" on campus, they say this is "slowly improving." Even though there are "not many atypical students"—"students all in black or with several piercings"—those who deviate from the "popped collar" and "Vera Bradley bag" trends "fit in regardless." While one student warns that some St. Lawrence students can be "very cliquey" and "difficult to approach," most students describe themselves as "friendly, enthusiastic, and open-minded." Typical or not, an SLU student is primarily "dedicated to academics and is very involved outside of the classroom." "Be it sports or other clubs, SLU students rarely spend time just sitting in their dorm rooms doing nothing."

FINANCIAL AID: 315-229-5265 • E-MAIL: ADMISSIONS@STLAWU.EDU • WEBSITE: WWW.STLAWU.EDU

ADMISSIONS

Very important factors considered include: Academic GPA, application essay, character/personal qualities, recommendation(s). *Important factors considered include:* Class rank, extracurricular activities, interview, racial/ethnic status, rigor of secondary school record. *Other factors considered include:* Alumni/ae relation, first generation, geographical residence, level of applicant's interest, standardized test scores, talent/ability, volunteer work, work experience. TOEFL required of all international applicants. High school diploma is required, and GED is accepted. *Academic units recommended:* 4 English, 4 math, 4 science, 4 foreign language, 2 social studies, 2 history.

The Inside Word

Despite facing stiff competition from many regional competitors, St. Lawrence University has managed to increase its application numbers over the past several years. Because it's increasingly selective, candidates must post decent grades in challenging courses if they hope to be accepted. The Admissions Committee appreciates the time each student puts into his or her application and recognizes those efforts by having three different counselors read each one. The school is a great choice for students looking to attend a small college in the Northeast.

FINANCIAL AID

Students should submit: FAFSA, institution's own financial aid form, Noncustodial PROFILE, Federal Income Tax Returns/W-2s. Regular filing deadline is February 15. The Princeton Review suggests that all financial aid forms be submitted as soon as possible after January 1. *Need-based scholarships/grants offered:* Pell Grant, SEOG, state scholarships/grants, the school's own gift aid. *Loan aid offered:* FFEL Subsidized Stafford, FFEL Unsubsidized Education, FFEL PLUS, Federal Perkins Loan, college/university loans from institutional funds, Gate Student Loan Program. Applicants will be notified of awards on or about March 30. Federal Work-Study Program available. Institutional employment available. Off-campus job opportunities are limited.

FROM THE ADMISSIONS OFFICE

"In an ideal location, St. Lawrence is a diverse liberal arts learning community of inspiring faculty and talented students guided by tradition and focused on the future. The students who live and learn at St. Lawrence are interesting and interested; they enroll with myriad accomplishments and talents, as well as desire to explore new challenges. Our faculty has chosen St. Lawrence intentionally because they know that there is institutional commitment to support great teaching. They are dedicated to making each student's experience challenging and rewarding. Our graduates make up one of the strongest networks of support among any alumni body and are ready, willing, and able to connect with students and help them succeed.

"Which students are happiest at St. Lawrence? Students who like to be actively involved. Students who are open-minded and interested in meeting people with backgrounds different from their own. Students who value having a voice in decisions that affect them. Students who appreciate all that is available to them and cannot wait to take advantage of both the curriculum and the co-curricular options. Students who want to enjoy their college experience and are able to find joy in working hard.

"You can learn the facts about us from this guidebook: We have about 2,000 students; we offer more than 30 majors; the average class size is 16 students; a great new science center is open as of 2007; close to 50 percent of our students study abroad; and we have an environmental consciousness that fits our natural setting between the Adirondack Mountains and St. Lawrence River. You must visit, meet students and faculty, and sense the energy on campus to begin to understand just how special St. Lawrence University is.

"Beginning with applications for entry in Fall 2006, the submission of standardized test scores (SAT or ACT) is optional. Students must indicate on the St. Lawrence Common Application supplement which scores, if any, they wish to have considered in the application process. "

SELECTIVITY	
Admissions Rating	89
# of applicants	3,192
% of applicants accepted	59
% of acceptees attending	33
# accepting a place on wait list	110
% admitted from wait list	15
# of early decision applicants	183
% accepted early decision	81

FRESHMAN PROFILE	
Range SAT Critical Reading	550–640
Range SAT Math	550–640
Range SAT Writing	540–630
Range ACT Composite	25–28
Minimum Paper TOEFL	600
Minimum Computer Based TOEFL	250
Average HS GPA	3.49
% graduated top 10% of class	33
% graduated top 25% of class	67
% graduated top 50% of class	91

DEADLINES	
Early decision application deadline	11/15
Early decision notification	12/15
Regular application deadline	2/15
Regular notification	3/30
Nonfall registration?	yes

APPLICANTS ALSO LOOK AT

AND OFTEN PREFER
Dartmouth College, Middlebury College, Williams College

AND SOMETIMES PREFER
Bowdoin College, Colby College, Colgate University

AND RARELY PREFER
Denison University, Gettysburg College, Hobart and William Smith Colleges

FINANCIAL FACTS	
Financial Aid Rating	87
Annual tuition	$35,375
Room & Board	$9,060
Required fees	$225
% frosh rec. need-based scholarship or grant aid	62
% UG rec. need-based scholarship or grant aid	64
% frosh rec. need-based self-help aid	56
% UG rec. need-based self-help aid	60
% frosh rec. any financial aid	80
% UG rec. any financial aid	82

ST. MARY'S COLLEGE OF MARYLAND

ADMISSIONS OFFICE, 18952 EAST FISHER ROAD, ST. MARY'S CITY, MD 20686-3001 • ADMISSIONS: 240-895-5000 • FAX: 240-895-5001

CAMPUS LIFE

Quality of Life Rating	**90**
Fire Safety Rating	**73**
Type of school	public
Environment	rural

STUDENTS

Total undergrad enrollment	1,892
% male/female	43/57
% from out of state	17
% from public high school	77
% live on campus	80
% African American	9
% Asian	4
% Caucasian	81
% Hispanic	5
% international	1
# of countries represented	34

SURVEY SAYS . . .
Small classes
Students are friendly
Campus feels safe
Low cost of living
Students are happy
Frats and sororities are unpopular or nonexistent

ACADEMICS

Academic Rating	**87**
Calendar	semester
Student/faculty ratio	12:1
Profs interesting rating	89
Profs accessible rating	93
% profs teaching UG courses	100
% classes taught by TAs	0
Most common lab size	10–19 students
Most common reg class size	10–19 students

MOST POPULAR MAJORS
economics
political science and government
psychology

STUDENTS SAY

Academics
As the state's public honors college (it's "not a Catholic college," clarifies one junior), St. Mary's College of Maryland offers its 1,892 undergrads the work-intensive, personalized education of a private school at public-school prices—a fact that regularly places the college among the "best buys" in higher education. Students describe the professors as "really awesome people" who are "passionate about their area of focus," and extol their "willingness to help or even just talk with students outside class time." "You're almost always on a first-name basis with them and have their home phone numbers and e-mail addresses," boasts one double major. While "Not every professor is going to be absolutely fantastic," we see many variations of the refrain: "The professors rock!" While SMCM's administration receives an array of kudos, it also takes a few knocks. A diplomatic junior writes that though administration members "do their best" to maintain dialogue with students, they're often "too removed from the concerns of the students." Because of an enrollment increase a couple of years ago, students in the past have occasionally grumbled about "understaffed" departments, "temporary professors," or "a shortage of classes." Since we last surveyed students, St. Mary's has reported that it is increasing the number of its faculty, so this problem should be greatly diminished. Construction, most likely a result of such growth, grates on many students' nerves—but such are the (temporary) growing pains of small colleges trying to bulk up. Overall, students seem content, describing their education as "challenging but stimulating" and their workload as "heavy." One sophomore writes, "I have learned, laughed, and worked like crazy . . . but it's all been worth it." A final piece of advice for prospective students: "Take a lot of AP classes and do well on the AP exams . . . this will help you place out of a number of general education requirements that are not nearly as strong as many other classes."

Life
Because the "beautiful" SMCM campus lies along the St. Mary's River in the heart of Maryland's Chesapeake Bay region, water sports and other outdoor recreational activities are inescapable here. "You can take out boats, kayaks, etc. just by presenting your student ID," boasts a junior. "Calvert Cliffs is just down the road, too, which is a pretty awesome place to hike." The campus location clearly has its benefits. But "We live in the boonies," admits a sophomore. SMCM is "not located near any big cities or areas that have a lot of off-campus activities" (historic St. Mary's City adjoins the campus; and Washington, DC is a 2-hour drive)—so students rely on campus life to keep them busy. There's "a lot of political activism," "widespread environmental interest," a "wealth of clubs and recreational opportunities," popular athletic programs on the intramural, club, and varsity levels, and, of course, classes to keep these undergrads well occupied. Although some say they drink on weekends, they're quick to add that there are "a lot of students" who don't "party/drink" and that there is "little or no pressure to drink if you're not into it." Overall, the students "lead pretty balanced lives." "Everyone here is all about having fun," says a junior, "but [they] are really serious about getting their work done too."

Student Body
Students describe their classmates as "open," "down-to-earth," "laid-back," and write that the only attribute "typical" of a Seahawk is uniqueness. In the cafeteria, "you can witness a girl wearing Abercrombie & Fitch sitting with a farm girl, a goth, a hippie, and they are all hysterically laughing." Another thing you'll notice in the cafeteria: SMCM has a "large vegan/vegetarian population." Students are "on the whole more likely to be liberal," and at SMCM, "closed-minded behavior is usually not taken well by most students." Students are so trusting of each other that "No one locks any doors on campus . . . Knocking is just not a St. Mary's thing to do!" If undergrads could shake a magic wand, they'd like to see SMCM become more "ethnically diverse." "The school is made up of mostly White, higher-income-level kids," says a senior. That said, everyone is "accepted and accepting."

FINANCIAL AID: 240-895-3000 • E-MAIL: ADMISSIONS@SMCM.EDU • WEBSITE: WWW.SMCM.EDU

ADMISSIONS

Very important factors considered include: Academic GPA, application essay, rigor of secondary school record. *Important factors considered include:* Recommendation(s), standardized test scores. *Other factors considered include:* Alumni/ae relation, character/personal qualities, class rank, extracurricular activities, first generation, talent/ability, volunteer work. SAT or ACT required; SAT and SAT Subject Tests or ACT recommended. SAT Subject Tests recommended, TOEFL required of all international applicants. High school diploma is required, and GED is accepted. *Academic units required:* 4 English, 3 math, 3 science (2 science labs), 3 social studies, 7 academic electives.

The Inside Word

There are few better choices than St. Mary's for better-than-average students who are not likely to get admitted to one of the top 50 or so colleges in the country. It is likely that if funding for public colleges is able to stabilize, or even grow, that this place will soon be joining the ranks of the best. Now is the time to take advantage, before the academic expectations of the Admissions Committee start to soar.

FINANCIAL AID

Students should submit: FAFSA. Regular filing deadline is March 1. The Princeton Review suggests that all financial aid forms be submitted as soon as possible after January 1. *Need-based scholarships/grants offered:* Pell Grant, SEOG, state scholarships/grants, private scholarships, the school's own gift aid. *Loan aid offered:* FFEL Subsidized Stafford, FFEL Unsubsidized Stafford, FFEL PLUS, Federal Perkins Loan. Applicants will be notified of awards on or about April 1. Federal Work-Study Program available. Institutional employment available. Off-campus job opportunities are good.

FROM THE ADMISSIONS OFFICE

"St. Mary's College of Maryland occupies a distinctive niche and represents a real value in American higher education. It is a public college, dedicated to the ideal of affordable, accessible education but committed to quality teaching and excellent programs for undergraduate students. The result is that St. Mary's offers the small college experience of the same high caliber usually found at prestigious private colleges, but at public college prices. Designated by the state of Maryland as 'a public honors college,' one of only two public colleges in the nation to hold that distinction, St. Mary's has become increasingly attractive to high school students. Admission is very selective.

"For freshman Fall 2008, applicants must take the new version of the SAT, but students may submit scores from the old (prior to March 2005) SAT, and admissions will use the student's best scores from either test. The ACT with the Writing section is also accepted."

SELECTIVITY

Admissions Rating	**90**
# of applicants	2,255
% of applicants accepted	56
% of acceptees attending	34
# accepting a place on wait list	126
% admitted from wait list	10
# of early decision applicants	169
% accepted early decision	54

FRESHMAN PROFILE

Range SAT Critical Reading	570–680
Range SAT Math	560–660
Minimum Paper TOEFL	550
Minimum Computer Based TOEFL	250
Average HS GPA	3.5
% graduated top 10% of class	41
% graduated top 25% of class	78
% graduated top 50% of class	96

DEADLINES

Early decision application deadline	12/1
Early decision notification	12/31
Regular application deadline	1/15
Regular notification	4/1

APPLICANTS ALSO LOOK AT AND SOMETIMES PREFER

Dickinson College, Gettysburg College

AND RARELY PREFER

McDaniel College, Washington College

FINANCIAL FACTS

Financial Aid Rating	**84**
Annual in-state tuition	$9,973
Annual out-of-state tuition	$20,307
Room & Board	$8,855
Books and supplies	$1,000
Required fees	$2,016
% frosh rec. need-based scholarship or grant aid	17
% UG rec. need-based scholarship or grant aid	19
% frosh rec. need-based self-help aid	17
% UG rec. need-based self-help aid	19
% frosh rec. any financial aid	59
% UG rec. any financial aid	61

ST. OLAF COLLEGE

1520 St. Olaf Avenue, Northfield, MN 55057 • Admissions: 507-646-3025 • Fax: 507-646-3832

CAMPUS LIFE

Quality of Life Rating	**99**
Fire Safety Rating	**75**
Type of school	private
Affiliation	Lutheran
Environment	village

STUDENTS

Total undergrad enrollment	2,993
% male/female	44/56
% from out of state	42
% from public high school	84
% live on campus	96
% African American	1
% Asian	5
% Caucasian	84
% Hispanic	2
% international	1
# of countries represented	18

SURVEY SAYS . . .

Great food on campus
Great library
Students are happy
Very little drug use
Very little hard liquor

ACADEMICS

Academic Rating	**94**
Calendar	4-1-4
Student/faculty ratio	13:1
Profs interesting rating	91
Profs accessible rating	91
% profs teaching UG courses	100
% classes taught by TAs	0
Most common lab size	20–29 students
Most common reg class size	10–19 students

MOST POPULAR MAJORS
biology/biological sciences
English language and literature
mathematics

STUDENTS SAY
Academics

St. Olaf College is well known for its music programs, but there's much more to this school than its ensembles and soloists. According to undergrads, St. Olaf is "very strong from a liberal arts perspective," and a top institution for "fine arts, math, [and] sciences." It's this thorough slate of offerings that attracts top students of all talents, including, of course, musicians; one writes, "This was the only place where I could get a conservatory-level music education, take classes from internationally known composers, get a great liberal arts background, and play on good athletic teams. People here are really well rounded." Students also love the school's "amazing study abroad opportunities; most of the student body travels abroad at some point. Having a short January term makes it easy even for people with busy academic or sporting schedules." Most of all, Oles cherish the hominess of their campus, rhapsodizing about professors "who invite a 90-piece orchestra over to their house for dinner" and similar communal touchstone experiences. One student notes, "I think that everyone here feels a special connection with the campus, whether it's from the beautiful limestone buildings, the autumn colors that blanket the campus, or the oh-so-tasty chocolate-chip-cookie-smell that wafts over from the local Malt-o-Meal factory. I look around during various seasons and think, 'How am I so lucky to get to experience this?' It truly is magnificent, except, of course, during that inevitable 2-week period in January when the windchill stays constant at an average of about ⁻20F and it's too cold even to snow."

Life

"Campus life is centered on campus, not in the town of Northfield," students say, because "While Northfield is an extremely nice town, we just don't get off campus much. Being on a hill creates what we call the St. Olaf Bubble—it's not the real world." It's also not a dull world. The school "has plenty of stuff going on. The student government brings in many activities—concerts, free movies, speakers—and it's not too hard to find something to do or someone to hang out with." Students here "tend to be active in some kind of organization. Many are in music groups (so many that my non-musical friend has officially designated herself 'audience member'), and there are also many political groups/special interest groups (Amnesty International, Habitat for Humanity, Democracy Matters, College Arts for Social Change, etc.). The presence of Christianity is also widely felt; there are several groups like FCA and Intervarsity, weekly Bible studies, and daily chapel." Students explain that "because most of the student body lives on campus all 4 years, we have a very close student body. This makes it a lot of fun to go to the bars in town, or just to the room next door to hang out." As you might expect, "Music is huge here. For example, Christmas Festival: 500 students, 1 month, 2 hours of music on the program, and thousands of people competing for tickets. It's awesome."

Student Body

Oles are "hardworking and intelligent, very social and helpful, [and] a little sick of all the people talking about how blond, Norwegian, etc. we are. It is just not that true. Yes, we are mostly White, and maybe for people from other areas of the country, it seems very blond. But that is just Minnesota for you. Minnesotans are blonder and more Norwegian than in other states." Many here "are extremely political, and although the college leans towards the left, we have an extremely vocal right side as well." Regardless of politics, undergraduates are socially conscious; the school "has a great volunteer network on campus, in the local community, and worldwide." Oles are serious about their schoolwork and have a genuine curiosity about intellectual subjects; they "have critical minds and never hesitate to contribute to a discussion or a critique." Most "are working toward graduate school, medical school, law school, or business school."

FINANCIAL AID: 507-646-3019 • E-MAIL: ADMISSIONS@STOLAF.EDU • WEBSITE: WWW.STOLAF.EDU

ADMISSIONS

Very important factors considered include: Academic GPA, application essay, rigor of secondary school record. *Important factors considered include:* Character/personal qualities, extracurricular activities, recommendation(s), standardized test scores, talent/ability. *Other factors considered include:* Alumni/ae relation, class rank, first generation, geographical residence, interview, level of applicant's interest, racial/ethnic status, religious affiliation/commitment, state residency, volunteer work, work experience. SAT or ACT required; TOEFL required of all international applicants. High school diploma is required, and GED is accepted. *Academic units required:* 4 English, 2 math, 2 science (1 science lab), 2 foreign language, 1 social studies, 1 history, 2 academic electives. *Academic units recommended:* 4 English, 4 math, 4 science (2 science labs), 4 foreign language, 2 social studies, 2 history, 4 academic electives.

The Inside Word

St. Olaf truly deserves a more national reputation; the place is a bastion of excellence and has always crossed applications with the best schools in the Midwest. Despite its lack of widespread recognition, it is a great choice. Candidates benefit from the relative anonymity of the college through an admissions process that, while demanding, isn't as tough as other colleges of St. Olaf's caliber.

FINANCIAL AID

Students should submit: FAFSA, CSS/Financial Aid PROFILE, St. Olaf Noncustodial Parent Statement. Regular filing deadline is April 15. The Princeton Review suggests that all financial aid forms be submitted as soon as possible after January 1. *Need-based scholarships/grants offered:* Pell Grant, SEOG, state scholarships/grants, private scholarships, the school's own gift aid. *Loan aid offered:* FFEL Subsidized Stafford, FFEL Unsubsidized Stafford, FFEL PLUS, Federal Perkins Loan, Federal Nursing Loan, state loans, college/university loans from institutional funds. Applicants will be notified of awards on a rolling basis beginning or about March 1. Federal Work-Study Program available. Off-campus job opportunities are fair.

FROM THE ADMISSIONS OFFICE

"With 3,000 students, St. Olaf College, a residential campus in Northfield, Minnesota, combines a leading liberal arts experience with the dynamic energy of a small university. Forty-four academic majors, 27 intercollegiate sports, a world-renowned music program, and a nationally recognized commitment to international study help this college of the Lutheran church fulfill its mission to develop mind, body, and spirit. St. Olaf leads the nation in the number of graduates who have earned a PhD in theology/religion and in mathematics. Its rigorous academic program has produced three Rhodes scholars and over 50 Fulbright scholars in the past decade.

"As of this book's publication, St. Olaf College did not have information available about their policy regarding the new SAT."

SELECTIVITY

Admissions Rating	92
# of applicants	3,529
% of applicants accepted	65
% of acceptees attending	35
# accepting a place on wait list	186
# of early decision applicants	112
% accepted early decision	88

FRESHMAN PROFILE

Range SAT Critical Reading	580–700
Range SAT Math	590–700
Range ACT Composite	25–30
Minimum Paper TOEFL	550
Minimum Computer Based TOEFL	213
Average HS GPA	3.67
% graduated top 10% of class	51
% graduated top 25% of class	83
% graduated top 50% of class	99

DEADLINES

Early decision application deadline	11/1
Early decision notification	12/1
Regular notification	rolling
Nonfall registration?	no

APPLICANTS ALSO LOOK AT AND SOMETIMES PREFER

Carleton College, Gustavus Adolphus College, Luther College, University of Minnesota—Twin Cities, University of Wisconsin—Madison

FINANCIAL FACTS

Financial Aid Rating	97
Annual tuition	$30,600
Room & Board	$7,900
Books and supplies	$900
% frosh rec. need-based scholarship or grant aid	64
% UG rec. need-based scholarship or grant aid	65
% frosh rec. need-based self-help aid	64
% UG rec. need-based self-help aid	65
% frosh rec. any financial aid	83
% UG rec. any financial aid	81

STANFORD UNIVERSITY

UNDERGRADUATE ADMISSION, OLD STUDENT UNION 232, STANFORD, CA 94305-3005 • ADMISSIONS: 650-723-2091 • FAX: 650-723-6050

STUDENTS SAY

Academics

Considered by many as the West Coast's one-man answer to the Ivy League, Stanford offers "a mix of incredible academics and a laid-back atmosphere" that many exceptional applicants choose over the likes of Harvard, Princeton, and Yale. That "laid-back" thing is significant. "Despite the fact that Stanford is academically rigorous and demanding, Stanford students very rarely get depressed," undergrads agree. "Sure, it gets stressful at times, but you learn to deal." The "downright fabulous" members of the student body and "the great weather" might provide some potent coping mechanisms, but the faculty really helps to make "Stanford a very well-balanced university." Professors are "interested in getting to know students personally," so much so that they "literally beg students to attend office hours." Of course, this is a very prestigious, research-driven university with a wide range of departments and faculty, which means that not every professor is going to hold a student's hand. Academics in the larger departments can be "very impersonal for a private school." Outgoing or aloof, Stanford's professors are lauded as "the foremost minds in their fields. You take classes from people who write the textbooks that everyone else uses." Along these lines, a sophomore tells us, "My freshman year I was able to take classes from a former Secretary of Defense, the Chairman of the Joint Chiefs, a Pulitzer Prize–winning author, and a Nobel Prize–winning physicist." The in-class opportunities are supplemented by frequent visits to campus by "leaders in the fields of literature, music, science, and statesmanship."

Life

It's true that Stanford students "work hard," but they "play hard, too." At Stanford, playing hard comes in various forms. One prominent form, of course, is partying. On any given Friday (or Saturday) night, "You can find most students heading out to one of the many parties that are held around campus." Others choose to hit "local bars/clubs, and, on occasion, [ride] into San Francisco" for the city's nightlife. Given the "perfect" weather, it's hardly surprising that undergrads also like to take it outdoors for a good time. "Running, swimming, and sunbathing are some of the more common outdoor activities," but "hiking, biking, surfing, and road-tripping in the beautiful California scenery" have their share of enthusiasts, too. As you're probably starting to realize, this is an athletic student body. And because "Almost all Stanford sports teams are nationally ranked," sports events of all sorts—even "the less popular sports"—draw plenty of fans to the bleachers. If all of this isn't enough, the university's undergrads have literally hundreds of organizations to choose from, ranging from the Arabesque Middle Eastern Dance Club to the Quiz Bowl Club. "Most students are used to being leaders in some regard," explains a junior. "This lends itself to a very active student body, but often there are more new clubs and activities than there are people to fill them." Though students tend to be "very busy," the overriding feeling, again, is "laid-back."

Student Body

"If there is any one thing that typifies a Stanford student, it is that they all fit the 'duck' analogy. That is, calm on top, but *busy, busy* underneath." Considering its achievements, there's a certain "modesty" that runs through this student body. Nobody toots their own horn. Nobody acts like they're overwhelmed. Nobody lets on that they're trying really, really hard to clean up in their classes. But these students are "very driven, even if they don't say so and pretend it's not true." The truth is that these undergrads are a "multifaceted, multitalented [group who] are always stressed about academics." Many different backgrounds and experiences are represented at Stanford. "You would never know that he or she spoke fluent German, wrote a novel, or went to the Olympics," a student says of his classmates. "Despite all their accomplishments, they are really down-to-earth and very chill." A senior sums it up best: "We have it all: academics, athletics, myriad activities, gorgeous California weather, and chill California personalities."

FINANCIAL AID: 650-723-3058 • E-MAIL: ADMISSION@STANFORD.EDU • WEBSITE: WWW.STANFORD.EDU

ADMISSIONS

Very important factors considered include: Academic GPA, application essay, character/personal qualities, class rank, extracurricular activities, recommendation(s), rigor of secondary school record, standardized test scores, talent/ability. *Other factors considered include:* Alumni/ae relation, first generation, geographical residence, racial/ethnic status, volunteer work, work experience. SAT or ACT required; SAT Subject Tests recommended; ACT with Writing component required. High school diploma is required, and GED is accepted. *Academic units recommended:* 4 English, 4 math, 3 science (3 science labs), 3 foreign language, 2 social studies, 1 history.

The Inside Word

Not only is Stanford a pinnacle of academic excellence but, among the nation's ultraselective universities, it is one of the most compassionate toward students, both those who attend and those who aspire to attend. It isn't easy for an Admissions Staff to be warm and caring when your reputation is based in part on how many candidates you say no to. In our opinion, Stanford is the best of the best in this regard. Students who haven't devoted themselves to excellence in the same fashion that Stanford itself has are not likely to meet with success in gaining admission.

FINANCIAL AID

Students should submit: FAFSA, CSS/Financial Aid PROFILE. The Princeton Review suggests that all financial aid forms be submitted as soon as possible after January 1. *Need-based scholarships/grants offered:* Pell Grant, SEOG, state scholarships/grants, private scholarships, the school's own gift aid. *Loan aid offered:* FFEL Subsidized Stafford, FFEL Unsubsidized Stafford, FFEL PLUS, Federal Perkins Loan, GATE Loans. Applicants will be notified of awards on a rolling basis beginning or about April 3. Federal Work-Study Program available. Institutional employment available. Off-campus job opportunities are excellent.

FROM THE ADMISSIONS OFFICE

"Stanford looks for distinctive students who exhibit energy, personality, a sense of intellectual vitality and extraordinary impact outside the classroom. While there is no minimum grade point average, class rank, or test score one needs to be admitted to Stanford, the vast majority of successful applicants will be among the strongest students (academically) in their secondary schools. The most compelling applicants for admission will be those who have thus far achieved state, regional, national, and international recognition in their academic and extracurricular areas of interest.

"Stanford currently accepts the Common Application as its exclusive application for admission. In addition to the on-line version of the Common Application, all applicants must submit an on-line Stanford-specific supplement to be considered for admission. The on-line supplement allows candidates to: detail information about an experience they find intellectually engaging; write a note to their freshman year roommate sharing a personal experience they have had; and explain why they feel Stanford is a good fit for them.

"While the SAT or ACT is required for admission, SAT subject tests are not required (and only recommended). AP scores are also not required but may be influential in admission decisions and can be used for placement/credit purposes if an applicant decides to enroll."

SELECTIVITY

Admissions Rating	99
# of applicants	22,333
% of applicants accepted	11
% of acceptees attending	67

FRESHMAN PROFILE

Range SAT Critical Reading	660–760
Range SAT Math	680–780
Range SAT Writing	660–760
Range ACT Composite	28–33
Average HS GPA	4.3
% graduated top 10% of class	89
% graduated top 25% of class	98
% graduated top 50% of class	100

DEADLINES

Regular application deadline	1/1
Regular notification	4/1
Nonfall registration?	no

APPLICANTS ALSO LOOK AT

AND OFTEN PREFER
Harvard College

AND SOMETIMES PREFER
Massachusetts Institute of Technology,
Princeton University, Yale University

AND RARELY PREFER
California Institute of Technology,
University of California—Berkeley

FINANCIAL FACTS

Financial Aid Rating	93
Annual tuition	$32,994
Room & Board	$10,367
Books and supplies	$1,290
% frosh rec. need-based scholarship or grant aid	42
% UG rec. need-based scholarship or grant aid	43
% frosh rec. need-based self-help aid	25
% UG rec. need-based self-help aid	30
% UG rec. any financial aid	77

STATE UNIVERSITY OF NEW YORK AT BINGHAMTON

PO BOX 6000, BINGHAMTON, NY 13902-6001 • ADMISSIONS: 607-777-2171 • FAX: 607-777-4445

CAMPUS LIFE

Quality of Life Rating	63
Fire Safety Rating	73
Type of school	public
Environment	town

STUDENTS

Total undergrad enrollment	11,523
% male/female	52/48
% from out of state	14
% from public high school	87
% live on campus	56
% in (# of) fraternities	8 (22)
% in (# of) sororities	9 (17)
% African American	5
% Asian	14
% Caucasian	47
% Hispanic	7
% international	7
# of countries represented	99

SURVEY SAYS . . .
Great computer facilities
Great library
Diverse student types on campus
Campus feels safe
Students are happy
Student publications are popular
Lots of beer drinking
Hard liquor is popular
(Almost) everyone smokes

ACADEMICS

Academic Rating	75
Calendar	semester
Student/faculty ratio	20:1
Profs interesting rating	64
Profs accessible rating	62
% profs teaching UG courses	90
% classes taught by TAs	9
Most common lab size	20–29 students
Most common reg class size	20–29 students

MOST POPULAR MAJORS
biology/premed
business administration/
management
English
engineering
politics/pre-law
psychology

STUDENTS SAY
Academics
Branded as Binghamton University, SUNY Binghamton is "a top-rate school that's way more competitive than most private schools in the Northeast, and you get it at a state school price," students here report. Undergrads tell us that "your quality of education really depends on what school you will be in," adding that BU boasts "a good management program," a "strong science department, especially in biology, psychology, and the premed programs," a "very strong political science program offering a popular major called politics, philosophy, and law that yields high law school acceptance rates," and "engineering and nursing programs that give the students what they need." Workloads also vary by school, from "killer math and science classes" and "very hard classes in the special schools (engineering, management, and nursing)," to "everything else, which is okay though still competitive." Similarly, professors can range from good to bad, from the requisite "science professors so caught up in their own research they seem to see teaching as an annoying obligation" and "math TAs who do not speak English" to "social science teachers who really care" and "management professors who demand the best and in return, pass along their industry connections." For most students, the administration is either a whipping boy or an afterthought.

Life
Just about everyone at BU agrees that "Binghamton is not the most exciting city in the world. Many would argue that the only reason the town is still around after almost all of the big employers packed up and left is the university." How this affects student life varies; some look at the town and conclude that "there are not many places that students can go. There are bars, frats, and movies, and these places get old quick." Others discover "some little gems in Binghamton, such as galleries on Washington Street, the Art Mission, and the Lost Dog Cafe for local music and a nice break from the bars." It's the same story on campus; many students say that "there is so much to do on campus, but most people are too lazy to explore the different clubs and activities. I feel bad for the students who are missing out on the wide array of on-campus activities, because I know so many of them waste their time drinking either in their dorm rooms or at frat parties." Students "who wish to remain sober have Late Nite Binghamton, which offers free music, movies, drinks, and others games and/or crafts every night on the weekends." Things may perk up here in the future; school spirit is on the rise because "We've recently moved up to Division I in the NCAA."

Student Body
As you might expect at a school with more than 10,000 undergrads, "There is a wide array of students at Binghamton University." Their ranks include "many students from down in Long Island, New York City, and the suburbs," as well as "students from upstate New York." Upstate students tell us, "It is very easy to feel a little alienated because upstate is regarded as heinously uncool by the downstaters and also because a lot of students arrive with a whole network of friends already in place." While geographic diversity is limited mostly to the different regions of New York State, "There is plenty of ethnic diversity here. The Black and Latino Student Unions are both very active groups on campus. The Hillel is also very active as there is a large Jewish population. Asian students make up a large minority. Different groups do not necessarily interact, but there is no tension among groups, either."

STATE UNIVERSITY OF NEW YORK AT BINGHAMTON

FINANCIAL AID: 607-777-2428 • E-MAIL: ADMIT@BINGHAMTON.EDU • WEBSITE: WWW.BINGHAMTON.EDU

ADMISSIONS

Very important factors considered include: Academic GPA, rigor of secondary school record, standardized test scores. *Important factors considered include:* Application essay, extracurricular activities, first generation, recommendation(s), volunteer work. *Other factors considered include:* Alumni/ae relation, character/personal qualities, class rank, geographical residence, level of applicant's interest, racial/ethnic status, state residency, talent/ability, work experience. SAT or ACT required; ACT with Writing component required. TOEFL required of all international applicants. High school diploma is required, and GED is accepted. *Academic units required:* 4 English, 3 math, 2 science, 3 foreign language, 2 social studies. *Academic units recommended:* 4 math, 4 science, 3 foreign language, 3 history.

The Inside Word

Binghamton's admissions process is highly selective but fairly simple. Candidates go through a process that considers an applicant's grades, course selections, and SAT or ACT results. Out-of-state enrollment is small for a public university of Binghamton's reputation, but the university's enrollment management strategy includes enhancing efforts to recruit students from farther afield.

FINANCIAL AID

Students should submit: FAFSA, state aid form. The Princeton Review suggests that all financial aid forms be submitted as soon as possible after January 1. *Need-based scholarships/grants offered:* Pell Grant, SEOG, state scholarships/grants, private scholarships, the school's own gift aid. *Loan aid offered:* Direct Subsidized Stafford, Direct Unsubsidized Stafford, FFEL PLUS, Federal Perkins Loan, Federal Nursing Loan, college/university loans from institutional funds. Applicants will be notified of awards on a rolling basis beginning or about March 15. Federal Work-Study Program available. Institutional employment available. Off-campus job opportunities are excellent.

FROM THE ADMISSIONS OFFICE

"SUNY Binghamton has established itself as the premier public university in the Northeast, because of our outstanding undergraduate programs, vibrant campus culture, and committed faculty. Students are academically motivated, but there is a great deal of mutual help as they compete against the standard of a class rather than each other. Faculty and students work side by side in research labs or on artistic pursuits. Achievement, exploration, and leadership are hallmarks of a Binghamton education. Add to that a campus wide commitment to internationalization that includes a robust study abroad program, cultural offerings, languages and international studies, and you have a place where graduates leave prepared for success.

"Students applying for freshman admission for Fall 2008 are required to take the new version of the SAT (or the ACT with the Writing section). SAT Subject Test scores are not required for admission."

SELECTIVITY

Admissions Rating	**93**
# of applicants	25,001
% of applicants accepted	43
% of acceptees attending	24
# accepting a place on wait list	664
% admitted from wait list	15

FRESHMAN PROFILE

Range SAT Critical Reading	570–650
Range SAT Math	610–690
Range ACT Composite	26–31
Minimum Paper TOEFL	550
Minimum Computer Based TOEFL	213
Average HS GPA	3.7
% graduated top 10% of class	49
% graduated top 25% of class	84
% graduated top 50% of class	98

DEADLINES

Regular notification	4/1
Nonfall registration?	yes

APPLICANTS ALSO LOOK AT
AND OFTEN PREFER
Columbia University, Cornell University, University of Pennsylvania
AND SOMETIMES PREFER
New York University, Pennsylvania State University—University Park, Rensselaer Polytechnic Institute, University of Maryland—College Park, University of Michigan—Ann Arbor
AND RARELY PREFER
Fordham University, Rutgers, The State University of New Jersey—New Brunswick, State University of New York at Geneseo, State University of New York—Stony Brook University, University of Rochester

FINANCIAL FACTS

Financial Aid Rating	**84**
Annual in-state tuition	$4,350
Annual out-of-state tuition	$10,610
Room & Board	$8,588
Books and supplies	$800
Required fees	$1,560
% frosh rec. need-based scholarship or grant aid	38
% UG rec. need-based scholarship or grant aid	40
% frosh rec. need-based self-help aid	40
% UG rec. need-based self-help aid	43
% frosh rec. any financial aid	79
% UG rec. any financial aid	69

STATE UNIVERSITY OF NEW YORK AT GENESEO

ONE COLLEGE CIRCLE, GENESEO, NY 14454-1401 • ADMISSIONS: 716-245-5571 • FAX: 716-245-5550

CAMPUS LIFE

Quality of Life Rating	**70**
Fire Safety Rating	**85**
Type of school	public
Environment	village

STUDENTS

Total undergrad enrollment	5,358
% male/female	41/59
% from out of state	1
% from public high school	81
% live on campus	56
% in (# of) fraternities	9 (9)
% in (# of) sororities	13 (12)
% African American	2
% Asian	6
% Caucasian	76
% Hispanic	3
% international	3
# of countries represented	30

SURVEY SAYS . . .

Students are friendly
Campus feels safe
Low cost of living
Students are happy
Lots of beer drinking
Hard liquor is popular
(Almost) everyone smokes

ACADEMICS

Academic Rating	**76**
Calendar	semester
Student/faculty ratio	19:1
Profs interesting rating	72
Profs accessible rating	71
% profs teaching	
UG courses	100
% classes taught by TAs	0
Most common	
reg class size	20–29 students

MOST POPULAR MAJORS

biology/biological sciences
business administration/
management
elementary education and teaching

STUDENTS SAY

Academics

Forget every preconception you have about state schools or the SUNY system. SUNY Geneseo bucks nearly every expectation; a small teaching-oriented school on a beautiful campus, "Geneseo is the epitome of college life. The people, the classes, the area, and the campus life are ideal for students coming from every different background, just as long as they are looking to grow as a person and a student." One undergrad gushes, "This is a great school with many opportunities and 'extras' for a great price. Many of the private schools I looked at didn't have half the programs or clubs that Geneseo offers." Although small, Geneseo is big enough to "offer many different majors and is strong in those majors," especially when it comes to the sciences. Professors here "are extremely dedicated to undergraduate learning and are always willing to help (with a few exceptions, of course)." Most have impressive credentials, too. One student writes, "My first year here, one of my professors had worked as a United Nations Advisor, and another had previously run for Congress. Geneseo is a place where you can learn from people who have had real-life experience in their fields." To "stimulate the students' interests," most professors "require a lot of group work and class discussion. They are very accessible and do their best to notify students about due dates, study tips, and resources (which they provide an ample supply of) outside of class through e-mails, office hours, or review sessions." Students note that "TAs don't teach lecture classes. Sometimes they teach labs, but even then they're closely monitored by professors."

Life

"Geneseo is in the middle of nowhere, so we make our own fun," students tell us, adding that "while there are many jokes about cow tipping, you'll have a hard time finding someone who's actually done it." To keep students engaged, "The clubs and organizations on campus are constantly putting on events. It is very easy to get involved because there is a club for everyone. Geneseo often hosts guest lecturers and has interesting scholarly events." There are also "some awesome shows put on by the Theater and Music Departments. And all of the events on campus are either free or very low cost." Intramural sports are popular, too, with "broomball being a favorite for everyone," and intercollegiate hockey games that "are well-attended and can be a lot of fun." There's a lively party scene here, but there is also "a large number of students who don't drink at all [and] a new program called 'Late Knight,' which provides alcohol-free entertainment on weekend nights." When all else fails, Geneseo's hills draw plenty of thrill-seekers. "You see a lot of students sledding in the winter or mud sliding in the spring." Another draw is the great outdoors at Letchworth State Park, which "is just a few minutes away by car, and is a great place to hike, picnic, or camp. Many students also bring bikes and ride around the campus and surrounding countryside on weekends." Why not? The surrounding Genesee Valley "is really nice and the sunsets are amazing." When big-city distraction is a necessity, Rochester is not too far away.

Student Body

"Students at Geneseo work really hard; the library is always packed, [but] we also like to have fun and get involved. Everyone I know is part of at least one student organization." Most here "come from Rochester, Buffalo, New York City, or Long Island," and their ranks include "preppy people, people who study, people who are religious, gays, minorities, everything. What's amazing is how people get along so well." Even if the gender scale has a bit of a tilt to it: Nearly two out of three students are female. "Boys, obviously, do exist at Geneseo," writes one woman, "but the lack of males is sort of a running joke among the students." "Minority students are few and far between," but the school does have "a very active Asian population, with an Asian theater group among the cultural organizations."

STATE UNIVERSITY OF NEW YORK AT GENESEO

FINANCIAL AID: 716-245-5731 • E-MAIL: ADMISSIONS@GENESEO.EDU • WEBSITE: WWW.GENESEO.EDU

ADMISSIONS

Very important factors considered include: Rigor of secondary school record, standardized test scores. *Important factors considered include:* Academic GPA, application essay, extracurricular activities, racial/ethnic status, recommendation(s), talent/ability. *Other factors considered include:* Character/personal qualities, class rank, volunteer work. SAT or ACT required; TOEFL required of all international applicants. High school diploma is required, and GED is accepted. *Academic units recommended:* 4 English, 4 math, 4 science, 4 foreign language, 4 social studies.

The Inside Word

Geneseo is the most selective of SUNY's 13 undergraduate colleges and more selective than three of SUNY's university centers. No formula approach is used here. Expect a thorough review of both your academic accomplishments (virtually everyone here graduated in the top half of their high school classes) and your extracurricular/personal side. Admissions standards are tempered only by a somewhat low yield of admits who enroll; this keeps the admit rate higher than it might otherwise be.

FINANCIAL AID

Students should submit: FAFSA, state aid form. Regular filing deadline is February 15. The Princeton Review suggests that all financial aid forms be submitted as soon as possible after January 1. *Need-based scholarships/grants offered:* Pell Grant, SEOG, state scholarships/grants, private scholarships, the school's own gift aid. *Loan aid offered:* FFEL Subsidized Stafford, FFEL Unsubsidized Stafford, FFEL PLUS, Federal Perkins Loan, state loans, alternative loans. Applicants will be notified of awards on a rolling basis beginning or about March 15.

FROM THE ADMISSIONS OFFICE

"Geneseo has carved a distinctive niche among the nation's premier public liberal arts colleges. Founded in 1871, the college occupies a 220-acre hillside campus in the historic Village of Geneseo, overlooking the scenic Genesee Valley. As a residential campus—with nearly two-thirds of the students living in college residence halls—it provides a rich and varied program of social, cultural, recreational, and scholarly activities. Geneseo is noted for its distinctive core curriculum and the extraordinary opportunities it offers undergraduates to pursue independent study and research with faculty who value close working relationships with talented students. Equally impressive is the remarkable success of its graduates, nearly one-third of whom study at leading graduate and professional schools immediately following graduation.

"For Fall 2008, SUNY Geneseo will use either SAT or ACT test results in the admission selection process. The SAT Writing test result will not be used. SAT Subject Test results are not required but will be considered if the applicant submits the test results."

SELECTIVITY

Admissions Rating	94
# of applicants	9,043
% of applicants accepted	41
% of acceptees attending	29
# accepting a place on wait list	930
% admitted from wait list	2
# of early decision applicants	309
% accepted early decision	48

FRESHMAN PROFILE

Range SAT Critical Reading	600–670
Range SAT Math	620–680
Range ACT Composite	27–29
Minimum Paper TOEFL	525
Minimum Computer Based TOEFL	197
Average HS GPA	3.8
% graduated top 10% of class	54
% graduated top 25% of class	89
% graduated top 50% of class	99

DEADLINES

Early decision application deadline	11/15
Early decision notification	12/15
Regular application deadline	1/15
Regular notification	rolling
Nonfall registration?	yes

APPLICANTS ALSO LOOK AT

AND OFTEN PREFER
Colgate University, Cornell University, Vassar College

AND SOMETIMES PREFER
Boston College, State University of New York at Binghamton, Trinity College (CT), University of Rochester

AND RARELY PREFER
Nazareth College of Rochester, State University of New York—Stony Brook University, Syracuse University

FINANCIAL FACTS

Financial Aid Rating	89
Annual in-state tuition	$4,350
Annual out-of-state tuition	$10,610
Room & Board	$7,788
Books and supplies	$800
Required fees	$1,210
% frosh rec. need-based scholarship or grant aid	31
% UG rec. need-based scholarship or grant aid	37
% frosh rec. need-based self-help aid	34
% UG rec. need-based self-help aid	39
% frosh rec. any financial aid	70
% UG rec. any financial aid	75

STATE UNIVERSITY OF NEW YORK—PURCHASE COLLEGE

ADMISSIONS OFFICE, 735 ANDERSON HILL ROAD, PURCHASE, NY 10577 • ADMISSIONS: 914-251-6300 • FAX: 914-251-6314

CAMPUS LIFE

Quality of Life Rating	64
Fire Safety Rating	60*
Type of school	public
Environment	town

STUDENTS

Total undergrad enrollment	3,480
% male/female	46/54
% from out of state	20
% live on campus	69
% African American	9
% Asian	4
% Caucasian	57
% Hispanic	10
% international	2
# of countries represented	21

SURVEY SAYS . . .

Frats and sororities are unpopular or nonexistent
Musical organizations are popular
Student publications are popular
Lots of beer drinking
(Almost) everyone smokes

ACADEMICS

Academic Rating	78
Calendar	semester
Student/faculty ratio	15:1
Profs interesting rating	78
Profs accessible rating	66
% profs teaching	
UG courses	100
% classes taught by TAs	1
Most common	
lab size	10–19 students
Most common	
reg class size	fewer than 10 students

MOST POPULAR MAJORS
liberal arts and sciences/
liberal studies
psychology
visual and performing arts

STUDENTS SAY

Academics

Purchase College is the SUNY system's answer to the region's many high-priced conservatories and arts schools set within a public liberal arts and sciences college. Rhode Island School of Design, students here don't feel they're getting shorted. On the contrary, they laud the teachers with professional experience (the school's proximity to New York City helps here) who "are caring, inspirational, and focused." They also appreciate the fact that access to Purchase's School of Liberal Arts and Sciences provides "a diverse curriculum" with a greater liberal arts focus than you'll find at most arts schools. Of course, they also love how they're "paying state tuition for a school full of ex-Ivy League teachers who were all too eccentric for Ivy schools, so now they teach at Purchase!" The school's more conventional liberal arts and science offerings notwithstanding, Purchase is primarily "an artistic community." Peer "work in the dance, music, photography, film, art, and acting conservator[ies] is amazing, and it is wonderful to be able to experience the work of these students." Classes tend to be small "with a heavy emphasis on writing skills." Students "are usually well-read and prepared for discussion," and, because "Class sizes are not too large," they "are able to contribute to both the structure of the class and the content." Outside the creative arts, Purchase excels in psychology, journalism, premed, biology, and creative writing.

Life

"Campus activities are amazing" at Purchase, a result of the art school/proximity-to-New York combo, which helps bring "nationally recognized figures in the arts to speak on a regular basis, including Art Speigelman and Tony Kushner. There are also free shows several days a week performed by excellent indie bands like My Brightest Diamond and Gregory and the Hawk" as well as numerous events featuring student performances, such as "Fall Ball, a major campus event [that] features a drag show performed by students. Given that many people who dance or sing are in one of the conservatories, it's very entertaining." And then there's New York City, "just a 40-minute train ride away" and "the most popular destination for entertainment." When students "plan on doing something special, [they] plan on going there for the weekend." Purchase has the requisite college parties, but "Excessive drinking is probably far less common at Purchase than at a more frat-oriented school." Students tend to keep very busy with schoolwork, especially those in the conservatories, who "spend a great deal of time practicing and studying."

Student Body

At Purchase, "many students who would be stereotyped as 'freaks' are not that freaky." This group includes "the 'artsy' type who has "green hair" and "piercings" and is "blatantly alternative to pop culture." Such students "comprise a good half of the student population," and, as a result, "they make everyone else considered 'normal' look weird." That being said, the student body here is "extremely diverse." There's "an outspoken gay community and a ton of different ethnicities." Because of the school's "urban feel, racism is virtually obsolete, and there is no hostility towards those of different sexual orientations." "Most everyone finds [his or her] niche at Purchase." In all areas, students "like to dive deep into their interests . . . Purchase is where the dancers, musicians, actors, visual artists, liberal arts and science majors, etc. are all interacting with one another to create a really interesting group of students."

STATE UNIVERSITY OF NEW YORK—PURCHASE COLLEGE

FINANCIAL AID: 914-251-6350 • E-MAIL: ADMISSIONS@PURCHASE.EDU • WEBSITE: WWW.PURCHASE.EDU

ADMISSIONS

Very important factors considered include: Academic GPA, application essay, talent/ability. *Important factors considered include:* Standardized test scores. *Other factors considered include:* Character/personal qualities, extracurricular activities, interview, recommendation(s), rigor of secondary school record. SAT recommended; SAT or ACT required; TOEFL required of all international applicants. High school diploma is required, and GED is accepted.

The Inside Word

About one-third of Purchase College undergraduates enroll in the School of the Arts. All must undergo some type of audition or portfolio review to gain admission; this is the most important piece of the application. Traditional application components—such as high school transcript, test scores, and personal essay—are also considered, but do not figure as prominently. Applicants to the School of Liberal Arts and Sciences undergo a more conventional application review.

FINANCIAL AID

Students should submit: FAFSA, state aid form. The Princeton Review suggests that all financial aid forms be submitted as soon as possible after January 1. *Need-based scholarships/grants offered:* Pell Grant, SEOG, state scholarships/grants, private scholarships, the school's own gift aid. *Loan aid offered:* FFEL Subsidized Stafford, FFEL Unsubsidized Stafford, FFEL PLUS, Federal Perkins Loan. Applicants will be notified of awards on a rolling basis beginning or about March 1. Federal Work-Study Program available. Institutional employment available. Off-campus job opportunities are excellent.

FROM THE ADMISSIONS OFFICE

"At Purchase College, you're encouraged to 'Think Wide Open.' The campus combines the energy and excitement of professional training in the performing and the visual arts with the intellectual traditions and spirit of discovery of the humanities and sciences. A Purchase College education emphasizes creativity, individual accomplishment, openness, and exploration. It culminates in a senior research or creative project that may focus on civic engagement or interdisciplinary work to become an excellent springboard to a career or to graduate or professional school. The Conservatories of Art and Design, Dance, Music, and Theatre Arts and Film that make up the School of the Arts deliver a cohort-based education with apprenticeships and other professional opportunities in nearby New York City.

"You'll find a unique and engaging atmosphere at Purchase, whether you are a student in the arts, humanities, natural sciences, or social sciences. You choose among a wide variety of programs, including arts management, journalism, creative writing, environmental science, new media, dramatic writing, premed, pre-law, and education. You'll attend performances by your friends, see world-renowned artists on stage at the Performing Arts Center, and experience the artworks on display in the Neuberger Museum of Art (one of the largest campus art museums in the country)—all without leaving campus. The new student services building, along with an enhanced student services website, is making Purchase a lot more user-friendly for its students.

"Admissions requirements vary with each program in the college and can include auditions, portfolio reviews, essays, writing samples, and interviews.

"In addition to individual program requirements, Purchase College requires SAT or ACT scores to complete your application. You can apply on line through the college website at www.purchase.edu/admissions."

SELECTIVITY
Admissions Rating	83
# of applicants	7,366
% of applicants accepted	30
% of acceptees attending	31
# of early decision applicants	26
% accepted early decision	42

FRESHMAN PROFILE
Range SAT Critical Reading	510–620
Range SAT Math	480–590
Minimum Paper TOEFL	550
Minimum Computer Based TOEFL	213
Average HS GPA	3.04
% graduated top 10% of class	10
% graduated top 25% of class	32
% graduated top 50% of class	72

DEADLINES
Early decision application deadline	11/1
Early decision notification	12/5
Regular application deadline	7/15
Regular notification	5/1
Nonfall registration?	yes

APPLICANTS ALSO LOOK AT
AND OFTEN PREFER
New York University, The Juilliard School
AND SOMETIMES PREFER
Brandeis University, Carnegie Mellon University, State University of New York—Stony Brook University
AND RARELY PREFER
Emerson College, Hofstra University

FINANCIAL FACTS
Financial Aid Rating	66
Annual in-state tuition	$4,350
Annual out-of-state tuition	$10,610
Room & Board	$9,028
Books and supplies	$1,500
Required fees	$1,359
% frosh rec. any financial aid	78
% UG rec. any financial aid	77

STATE UNIVERSITY OF NEW YORK—STONY BOOK UNIVERSITY

OFFICE OF ADMISSIONS, STONY BROOK, NY 11794-1901 • ADMISSIONS: 631-632-6868 • FAX: 631-632-9898

CAMPUS LIFE
Quality of Life Rating	61
Fire Safety Rating	60*
Type of school	public
Environment	town

STUDENTS
Total undergrad enrollment	14,639
% male/female	50/50
% from out of state	4
% from public high school	90
% live on campus	52
% in (# of) fraternities	1 (15)
% in (# of) sororities	1 (18)
% African American	9
% Asian	22
% Caucasian	35
% Hispanic	9
% international	5
# of countries represented	100

SURVEY SAYS . . .
Class discussions are rare
Great computer facilities
Great library
Diverse student types on campus
Lots of beer drinking
(Almost) everyone smokes

ACADEMICS
Academic Rating	71
Calendar	semester
Student/faculty ratio	17:1
Profs interesting rating	61
Profs accessible rating	62
% profs teaching UG courses	88
Most common lab size	20–29 students
Most common reg class size	20–29 students

MOST POPULAR MAJORS
biology/biological sciences
business administration/
management
psychology

STUDENTS SAY

Academics

Stony Brook University "is a great place for ambitious, focused students who actually want to learn something" at a "great research university in which classes are challenging and interesting." Nearly half the undergraduates here pursue traditionally punishing majors such as biology, computer science ("one of the best undergraduate computer science programs," according to at least one student), and engineering. The school also boasts "a strong marine biology program," a popular undergraduate business program, and a solid selection of liberal arts majors. Students in the science and tech majors describe the school as "challenging but worth it," noting that "the sciences here are amazing. Now that I'm interviewing for medical schools, I'm seeing just how highly they think of Stony Brook's undergraduate science programs!" Professors are accomplished and, while "They can be boring, they know what they're teaching like the back of their hand. They will be very helpful in office hours, as long as you ask questions that show them you're trying." As at similar schools, "The only thing you have to watch out for, occasionally, is getting a professor who does not speak English well; that can cause some problems!" Students have "plenty of research opportunities" here, which is another plus. Stony Brook's administration "may consist of nice people, but it's pretty poorly organized. When there is some sort of paperwork involved, nothing ever goes right the first time around. Also, nothing is convenient, and you'll usually have to go in circles to get something done." Most students find the difficulties worth enduring and focus instead on how the school delivers "a great education for a reasonable price."

Life

"Life at Stony Brook depends on whom you surround yourself with," students tell us. While "a lot of students complain that there's nothing to do on campus," others counter that "the problem is that students aren't willing to put in the effort to find those activities." One undergrad explains, "There are many activities in campus life. However, you won't be aware of them at all if you don't . . . look them up. There are a lot of places where you can go play sports, and most dorms have places to play pool, Ping-Pong, or just watch TV." The school is home to "lots of student clubs with something for everyone" and Division I intercollegiate athletic teams, but "No one goes to athletic games. It's really depressing as a pep band member to play to a dead crowd." The situation isn't helped by the fact that "many people go home on the weekends, and this leads to the university feeling empty on Saturday and Sunday." Hometown Stony Brook "is basically suburban. It is not the best college town. There are a few clubs and bars in the area that some students go to on Thursday nights. However, you have to have a car to get there. . . . If I want to have fun, I generally have to go into the city [NYC]. The city is about 2 hours away by train."

Student Body

The typical student at Stony Brook University "is a middle-class Long Island or Queens kid of Jewish, East Asian, or Indian background." Minority populations are large across a broad demographic range; the school is home to many who are "either Asian, African American, or Hispanic and very, very liberal." Subpopulations "tends to stick to themselves. . . . The atypical students are probably quite miserable at Stony Brook. There is definitely a very Long Island high school–like atmosphere," in part because "over 50 percent of the students are commuters" and in part because the student body is so large. One student writes, "All students fit in, but the student body is often impersonal, and it is very difficult to develop lasting friendships and relationships as a result."

STATE UNIVERSITY OF NEW YORK—STONY BROOK UNIVERSITY

FINANCIAL AID: 631-632-6840 • E-MAIL: ENROLL@STONYBROOK.EDU • WEBSITE: WWW.STONYBROOK.EDU

ADMISSIONS

Very important factors considered include: Rigor of secondary school record, standardized test scores. *Important factors considered include:* Class rank. *Other factors considered include:* Alumni/ae relation, application essay, character/personal qualities, extracurricular activities, interview, recommendation(s), talent/ability, volunteer work, work experience. SAT or ACT required; SAT Subject Tests recommended, ACT with Writing component required. TOEFL required of all international applicants. High school diploma is required, and GED is accepted. *Academic units required:* 4 English, 3 math, 3 science, 2 foreign language, 4 social studies. *Academic units recommended:* 4 math, 4 science, 3 foreign language.

The Inside Word

Liberal arts and social science candidates with above-average grades and test scores should encounter little difficulty gaining entry to SUNY Stony Brook. Students in technical fields (engineering, applied mathematics, computer science), in business, and in music must clear some higher hurdles. You can indicate "undecided" for your major on your application, but know that this does not guarantee you entry into these more competitive majors; you'll still have to meet the admissions requirements when you finally declare a major.

FINANCIAL AID

Students should submit: FAFSA. Regular filing deadline is March 1. The Princeton Review suggests that all financial aid forms be submitted as soon as possible after January 1. *Need-based scholarships/grants offered:* Pell Grant, SEOG, state scholarships/grants, the school's own gift aid. *Loan aid offered:* FFEL Subsidized Stafford, FFEL Unsubsidized Stafford, FFEL PLUS, Federal Perkins Loan. Applicants will be notified of awards on a rolling basis beginning or about March 1.

FROM THE ADMISSIONS OFFICE

"Stony Brook is ranked one of the 150 best universities worldwide in the *London Times'* Higher Education Supplement—placing Stony Brook in the top 2 percent of all universities in the world. For the second year in a row, *Kiplinger's Personal Finance* has ranked Stony Brook one of the "100 Best Values" among public universities. And *U.S. News & World Report* has ranked Stony Brook among the top 100 best national universities and among the top 50 public national universities. The *Wall Street Journal* has ranked us eighth in the nation among public institutions placing students in the elite graduate schools in medicine, law, and business. Our graduates include the leader of the Imaging Team for the Cassini mission to Saturn, the president of Stanford University, a Pulitzer Prize–winning investigative journalist for the *Washington Post*, a Grammy Award–winning performer with the Metropolitan Opera Company, and more than 100,000 others.

"Situated on 1,100 wooded acres on the North Shore of Long Island, Stony Brook offers more than 100 majors and minors for undergraduates, a thriving research environment, and a dynamic first-year experience in one of six small undergraduate communities."

"Guaranteed campus housing for all 4 years, students enjoy outstanding recreational facilities that include a new stadium, modern student activities center, and indoor sports complex. In addition, the Staller Center for the Arts offers spectacular theatrical and musical performances throughout the year."

"We invite students who possess both intellectual curiosity and academic ability to explore the countless exciting opportunities available at Stony Brook.

"Freshmen applying for admission to the university for Fall 2008 are required to take the SAT (or the ACT with the Writing section). SAT Subject Test scores in Math and one other area of the student's choice are recommended, but not required."

SELECTIVITY

Admissions Rating	**60**
# of applicants	21,292
% of applicants accepted	47
% of acceptees attending	27

FRESHMAN PROFILE

Range SAT Critical Reading	510–610
Range SAT Math	570–670
Minimum Paper TOEFL	550
Minimum Computer Based TOEFL	213
Average HS GPA	3.6

DEADLINES

Regular notification	2/1
Nonfall registration?	yes

APPLICANTS ALSO LOOK AT
AND OFTEN PREFER

Boston University, City University of New York—Hunter College, Cornell University

AND SOMETIMES PREFER

Pennsylvania State University—University Park, Rutgers, The State University of New Jersey—New Brunswick, Syracuse University, University of Connecticut

AND RARELY PREFER

Adelphi University, Hofstra University, Saint John's University

FINANCIAL FACTS

Financial Aid Rating	**64**
Annual in-state tuition	$4,350
Annual out-of-state tuition	$10,610
Room & Board	$8,394
Books and supplies	$900
Required fees	$1,281
% frosh rec. need-based scholarship or grant aid	52
% UG rec. need-based scholarship or grant aid	51
% frosh rec. need-based self-help aid	41
% UG rec. need-based self-help aid	42
% frosh rec. any financial aid	75
% UG rec. any financial aid	68

STATE UNIVERSITY OF NEW YORK—UNIVERSITY AT ALBANY

OFFICE OF UNDERGRAD ADMISSIONS, 1400 WASHINGTON AVE., ALBANY, NY 12222 • ADMISSIONS: 518-442-5435 • FAX: 518-442-5383

STUDENTS SAY

Academics

Is SUNY Albany (UAlbany to those in the know) the perfect-sized school? Many here think so. Students describe it as "a big school numbers-wise that feels small." Notes one student, "It has a very broad range of quality academic programs, which is very important for an undecided senior in high school." Another adds, "If you know what you want and are motivated, the sky is the limit." The school exploits its location in the state capital to bolster programs in political science, criminal justice, and business, and it "offers internship opportunities to college students that very few schools can." Other standout departments include psychology, Japanese studies, mathematics, and many of the hard sciences. Professors here vary widely in quality, but a surprising number "are receptive, active, and engaging"—in other words, "a lot more accessible than I would have thought for a school this big." Teachers are especially willing to "go out of their way to help students who are interested in learning, come to class regularly, and care about their academic work." The administration, as at most state-run schools, "is basically an over-bloated bureaucracy. Students are sent from department to department in each of their endeavors. It is advisable to avoid [the] administration if at all possible."

Life

There are three distinct social orbits on the Albany campus. Some students take the initiative "by joining one of the many clubs or groups or getting involved with the student government." Others "party for a good time," telling us that "any night of the week you can find people to go out to the bars and clubs with you" and that "the average night ends between 2:30–4:00 A.M." Both of these groups are likely to tell you that "there is a lot to do in Albany and the surrounding area," including "a great arts district, tons of awesome restaurants, museums, [and] a state park." A third, sizable group primarily complains about the cold weather, and asserts that "there's nothing to do in Albany." The school works to excite these students with "fun programs and entertainers who come to the campus. We have had a series of comedians, rappers/singers, guests from MTV and VH1, authors, political figures, musical performances, sporting events, spirit events, and many other things around campus." School spirit is on the rise among all groups, we're told. The reason? "This year our basketball team began winning, and everyone came out of the woodwork to support them—it was really a great thing to see."

Student Body

Undergrads here believe that the student body is very diverse in terms of ethnicity and also in terms of personality type; one student observes, "You have your motivated students [who] get good grades, are involved, and get amazing jobs in NYC after college. Then you have your unmotivated kids [who] complain, don't go to class, and blame a bad grade on the professor (when really it is because they crammed the night before and didn't go to class)." Geographically, the school is less diverse. Nearly everyone is a New York State resident, with many coming from "downstate New York"—Long Island, New York City, and Westchester County. There's a fair amount of upstate kids as well, and "a lot of people have certain stereotypes in their heads when they first come to Albany. The Long Islander has his idea about the upstater and vice versa. After a few weeks, though, people see that these aren't always true. I think people from anywhere get along pretty well." The international students, who form a small but noticeable contingent, "tend to keep to themselves," perhaps "due to a culture or language barrier." About one-quarter of the campus population is Jewish.

STATE UNIVERSITY OF NEW YORK—UNIVERSITY AT ALBANY

FINANCIAL AID: 518-442-5757 • E-MAIL: UGADMISSIONS@ALBANY.EDU • WEBSITE: WWW.ALBANY.EDU

ADMISSIONS

Very important factors considered include: Academic GPA, character/personal qualities, class rank, rigor of secondary school record, standardized test scores. *Important factors considered include:* Application essay, recommendation(s). *Other factors considered include:* Alumni/ae relation, extracurricular activities, first generation, geographical residence, talent/ability, volunteer work, work experience. SAT or ACT required; ACT with Writing component required. TOEFL required of all international applicants. High school diploma is required, and GED is accepted. *Academic units required:* 4 English, 2 math, 2 science (2 science labs), 1 foreign language, 3 social studies, 2 history, 4 academic electives. *Academic units recommended:* 4 math, 3 science (3 science labs), 3 foreign language.

The Inside Word

In November 2006, *The Wall Street Journal* noted a growing trend among students who, in the past, had limited their postsecondary options to high-end private schools: More such students, the paper reported, have broadened their vision to include prestigious state schools such as SUNY Albany. The driving force, unsurprisingly, is economic. In the event of an unlikely decline in the cost of private education, expect admissions at schools like UAlbany to grow more competitive in coming years.

FINANCIAL AID

Students should submit: FAFSA; New York state residents should apply for TAP online at TapWeb.org. Regular filing deadline is April 15. The Princeton Review suggests that all financial aid forms be submitted as soon as possible after January 1. *Need-based scholarships/grants offered:* Pell Grant, SEOG, state scholarships/grants. *Loan aid offered:* FFEL Subsidized Stafford, FFEL Unsubsidized Stafford, FFEL PLUS, Federal Perkins Loan. Applicants will be notified of awards on a rolling basis beginning or about March 15. Federal Work-Study Program available. Institutional employment available. Off-campus job opportunities are excellent.

FROM THE ADMISSIONS OFFICE

"Increasing numbers of well-prepared students are discovering the benefits of study in UAlbany's nationally ranked programs and are taking advantage of outstanding internship and employment opportunities in Upstate New York's 'Tech Valley.' The already strong undergraduate program is being further enhanced by the recently established Honors College, a university-wide program for ambitious students. Building upon the long-standing success of the University Scholars Program, the Honors College offers enhanced honors courses and co-curricular options including honors housing.

"Ten schools and colleges, including the nation's first College of Nanoscale Science and Engineering, offer bachelor's, master's, and doctoral programs to more than 12,000 undergraduates and 5,000 graduate students. An award-winning advisement program helps students take advantage of all these options by customizing the undergraduate experiences. More than two-thirds of Albany graduates go on for advanced degrees, and acceptance to law and medical school is above the national average.

"Student life on campus includes 200 clubs, honor societies, and other groups, and 19 Division I varsity teams. With 19 other colleges in the region, Albany is a great college town, adjacent to the spectacular natural and recreational centers of New York and New England.

"Freshmen are awarded over $800,000 in merit scholarships each year and nearly three-quarters of our students receive financial aid. Plus, *Kiplinger's Personal Finance* ranks us in the nation's 'Top 50 for Excellence and Affordability.'

"All applicants must submit either the new SAT or the ACT with Writing component."

SELECTIVITY

Admissions Rating	**83**
# of applicants	18,689
% of applicants accepted	56
% of acceptees attending	23
# accepting a place on wait list	360

FRESHMAN PROFILE

Range SAT Critical Reading	520–600
Range SAT Math	540–620
Minimum Paper TOEFL	550
Minimum Computer Based TOEFL	213
Average HS GPA	3.3
% graduated top 10% of class	15
% graduated top 25% of class	50
% graduated top 50% of class	90

DEADLINES

Regular application deadline	3/1
Regular notification	rolling
Nonfall registration?	yes

FINANCIAL FACTS

Financial Aid Rating	**74**
Annual in-state tuition	$4,350
Annual out-of-state tuition	$10,610
Room & Board	$8,604
Books and supplies	$1,000
Required fees	$1,589
% frosh rec. need-based scholarship or grant aid	52
% UG rec. need-based scholarship or grant aid	50
% frosh rec. need-based self-help aid	48
% UG rec. need-based self-help aid	46
% frosh rec. any financial aid	61
% UG rec. any financial aid	60

STATE UNIVERSITY OF NEW YORK—UNIVERSITY AT BUFFALO

15 CAPEN HALL, BUFFALO, NY 14260-1660 • ADMISSIONS: 716-645-6900 • FAX: 716-645-6411

STUDENTS SAY

Academics

Offering "more academic programs per dollar than any other university in the state," SUNY Buffalo (UB for short) "is about choices. You can choose many different . . . combinations of academics and social activities with the support in place." Students brag that UB's "Programs are all of the highest quality, translating [into] a best-value education for students." The School of Engineering and Applied Science in particular "is well respected" and "works with corporate partners in a variety of ways that range from joint-research ventures to continuing education to co-op work arrangements for our students." Other stand-out offerings include: pharmacy, physical therapy, a popular business and management school "that is ranked highly," "a solid undergrad and grad architecture program," and "one of the top nursing programs in the state." Of course, a school with this much to offer is bound to be large, making it "easy not to attend class and fall through the cracks, so one must be self-motivated to do well." Administrative tasks are occasionally Kafkaesque, with "a lot of red tape to go through to get anything done. I feel like a pebble being kicked around when trying to get support or services," notes one student. Many students point out that support services and contact with professors improves during junior and senior years when students are pursuing their majors and forging stronger relationships within their departments.

Life

UB is divided into two campuses. Traditionally, South Campus in Northeast Buffalo has been where "the parties are," though students say, "It's much less safe than North Campus," which is located in the suburban enclave of Amherst. The recent closing of several bars near South Campus has made it less of a party destination than it was in years past; these days many students report going to downtown Buffalo "to go clubbing." Students living on North Campus describe it as "its own little city. We have food services, our own bus system, a highway, even our own zip codes. If you know how to play, North Campus is just as much fun as Main Street [which runs by South Campus]; you just need to know where to go." The North Campus, which features "a lake and a nice bike path for when you want to escape from the hectic [atmosphere]" of academic life, is the more populous of the two; the inter-campus bus system is "convenient," although a car is preferred. Students tell us that "between all of the clubs and organizations, the Office of Student Life, athletics, and the Student Association, there is always something to do" on campus. The school's Division I sports teams "are a big hit around here. Even if we are the worst in the division, we still cheer hard and go crazy for our guys and girls." Those who explore Buffalo extol its "amazing art and music scene."

Student Body

Because of UB's size, "You can find just about every kind of person there is here. Everyone has a place in this large and diverse student population." As one student notes, "Although the typical student is of traditional college age, there really isn't a 'typical' student—the student body is very diverse in terms of religion, ethnicity, nationality, age, gender, and orientation. 'Atypical' students fit in well because of the diversity of the student population." Another student adds, "There are a lot of foreign and minority students, to the point that the actual 'majority' is the minority here at UB." Geographically, UB draws "from urban areas, rural areas, NYC, Long Island, and most every country in the world." As a state school, "A lot of the students are from New York State, but with differing areas of the state, there are many different types of students."

STATE UNIVERSITY OF NEW YORK—UNIVERSITY AT BUFFALO

FINANCIAL AID: 866-838-7257 • E-MAIL: UB-ADMISSIONS@BUFFALO.EDU • WEBSITE: WWW.BUFFALO.EDU

ADMISSIONS

Very important factors considered include: Class rank, rigor of secondary school record, standardized test scores. *Other factors considered include:* Application essay, character/personal qualities, extracurricular activities, geographical residence, racial/ethnic status, recommendation(s), talent/ability, volunteer work, work experience. SAT or ACT required; ACT with Writing component required. TOEFL required of all international applicants. High school diploma is required, and GED is accepted. *Academic units recommended:* 4 English, 3 math, 3 science, 3 foreign language, 4 social studies.

The Inside Word

As students point out, UB "is famous for its architecture, nursing, and pharmacy school[s]"; as such, it makes sense that "those majors are a harder to get into." In fact, admissions standards at UB have grown more demanding across all programs in recent years. Despite the school's large applicant pool, it takes a close look at applications, searching for evidence of special talents and experiences that will enrich campus life.

FINANCIAL AID

Students should submit: FAFSA. The Princeton Review suggests that all financial aid forms be submitted as soon as possible after January 1. *Need-based scholarships/grants offered:* Pell Grant, SEOG, state scholarships/grants, private scholarships, the school's own gift aid, Federal Nursing Scholarship. *Loan aid offered:* Direct Subsidized Stafford, Direct Unsubsidized Stafford, Direct PLUS, Federal Perkins Loan, Federal Nursing Loan, college/university loans from institutional funds. Applicants will be notified of awards on a rolling basis beginning or about February 1.

FROM THE ADMISSIONS OFFICE

"The University at Buffalo (UB) is among the nation's finest public research universities—a learning community where you'll work side by side with world-renowned faculty, including Nobel, Pulitzer, National Medal of Science, and other award winners. As the largest, most comprehensive university center in the State University of New York (SUNY) system, UB offers more undergraduate majors than any public university in New York or New England. With opportunities for joint degrees and combined 5-year bachelor's and master's degrees, you'll be free to chart an academic course that meets your individual goals—you can even design your own major. Our unique University Honors and University at Buffalo Scholars scholarship programs offer an enhanced academic experience, including opportunities for independent study, advanced research, and specialized advisement. The university is committed to providing the latest information technology—and is widely considered to be one of the most wired universities in the country. UB also places a high priority on offering an exciting campus environment. With nonstop festivals, Division I sporting events, concerts, and visiting lecturers, you'll have plenty to do outside of the classroom. We encourage you and your family to visit campus to see UB up close and in person. Our Visit UB campus tours and presentations are offered year-round.

"Freshman applicants for Fall 2008 must take the new SAT (or the ACT with Writing component)."

SELECTIVITY

Admissions Rating	**85**
# of applicants	18,207
% of applicants accepted	56
% of acceptees attending	31
# accepting a place on wait list	363
% admitted from wait list	27
# of early decision applicants	551
% accepted early decision	74

FRESHMAN PROFILE

Range SAT Critical Reading	520–610
Range SAT Math	550–640
Range ACT Composite	24–28
Minimum Paper TOEFL	550
Minimum Computer Based TOEFL	213
Average HS GPA	3.1
% graduated top 10% of class	24
% graduated top 25% of class	62
% graduated top 50% of class	94

DEADLINES

Early decision application deadline	11/1
Early decision notification	12/15
Regular notification	rolling
Nonfall registration?	yes

FINANCIAL FACTS

Financial Aid Rating	**81**
Annual in-state tuition	$4,350
Annual out-of-state tuition	$10,610
Room & Board	$8,086
Books and supplies	$795
Required fees	$1,616
% frosh rec. need-based scholarship or grant aid	35
% UG rec. need-based scholarship or grant aid	33
% frosh rec. need-based self-help aid	52
% UG rec. need-based self-help aid	50
% frosh rec. any financial aid	67
% UG rec. any financial aid	75

STEPHENS COLLEGE

1200 EAST BROADWAY, BOX 2121, COLUMBIA, MO 65215 • ADMISSIONS: 800-876-7207 • FAX: 573-876-7237

STUDENTS SAY

Academics

A small women's college located in the lively college town of Columbia, Missouri, Stephens College is characterized by its intensive liberal arts programs and supportive learning environment. A junior enthuses, "Academics at Stephens are great. Teachers are always available outside of class and the classes are usually challenging and interesting enough to keep students motivated to work hard!" Professors are "completely willing to help in any way, but they also expect a lot from their students," adds a senior. Stephens offers more than 50 majors, of which performing and applied arts (such as theater and fashion design) are among the most popular. Students sing the praises of their major programs, many noting Stephens's strong commitment to hands-on education, alumni networking, and leadership opportunities. A sophomore attests, "Stephens has one of the best fashion design schools in the country. The teachers are highly knowledgeable, and the alumnae network is extensive." Similarly, "The theater program here is unlike any other because we have great alumnae connections and everything we do is hands-on. The students even run their own theater (Warehouse) right next to the Stephens Theater." Students also tell us that "all of the administration is very approachable," often noting in particular the efforts of friendly President Libby.

Life

Ask almost any Stephens undergrad and she will tell you that "the greatest strength of Stephens College is its close community." Stephens women go out of their way to support campus activities and events; for example, "The theater productions and dance productions are wildly popular. They are always on the verge of being sold out." Off campus, Columbia, Missouri (also home to the University of Missouri), is a boisterous college town, boasting "lots of little shops and restaurants, and, of course, tons of bars." Come the weekend, many Stephens women make a beeline for the coed parties at Mizzou. Others "enjoy shopping in the District downtown, hanging out at the Artisan (a coffee shop with live music), and going to concerts at the Blue Note." Many students mention that the campus facilities need a face-lift; even so, they agree that residential life is particularly agreeable at Stephens, in large part because the school offers almost every student a spacious, private dorm room. A junior jokes, "I expect my first studio apartment in New York will be about half the size of my current dorm room." Pet-lovers take note: "Another perk about Stephens is that students are allowed to bring pets! The 'pet floor' program has been very successful. Girls really enjoy having their cat or dog with them at college."

Student Body

Stephens College tends to attract "hardworking, dedicated, and ambitious" young women, most of whom hail from middle-class families in the Midwest. A freshman tells us, "Typically, the students here are average Midwestern girls, and at times there are girls from the coasts who mix things up a bit." "We are not incredibly diverse," adds one junior, "but there are some minorities here on campus." There is a general homogeneity of interests among the students as well, with many gravitating toward similar majors and extracurricular activities. A freshman reports, "There are a lot of theater/dance/fashion majors," so students in other majors can feel like "a bit of a minority. You usually spend time with those in your major since you are in so many classes with them." Stephens undergrads assure us, however, that every student, no matter what her background, fits in on this friendly campus. As one junior attests, "The Stephens community is incredibly accepting and friendly, making it very easy for any student, typical or atypical, to fit in well."

FINANCIAL AID: 573-876-7106 • E-MAIL: APPLY@WC.STEPHENS.EDU • WEBSITE: WWW.STEPHENS.EDU

ADMISSIONS

Very important factors considered include: Application essay, character/personal qualities, recommendation(s), rigor of secondary school record, standardized test scores. *Important factors considered include:* Extracurricular activities, talent/ability. *Other factors considered include:* Class rank, interview, volunteer work, work experience. TOEFL required of all international applicants. High school diploma is required, and GED is accepted. *Academic units recommended:* 4 English, 2 math, 2 science, 2 foreign language, 2 social studies.

The Inside Word

Stephens offers its students a great deal of personal attention—and this extends to its applicants, as well. Character holds significant weight at this college, so expect essays and recommendations to be thoroughly assessed. Weaker candidates who are deemed to have academic promise will most likely find themselves admitted under probationary guidelines. Stephens's impressive yield rate attests to its appeal to prospective students.

FINANCIAL AID

Students should submit: FAFSA. The Princeton Review suggests that all financial aid forms be submitted as soon as possible after January 1. *Need-based scholarships/grants offered:* Pell Grant, SEOG, state scholarships/grants, private scholarships, the school's own gift aid. *Loan aid offered:* FFEL Subsidized Stafford, FFEL Unsubsidized Stafford, FFEL PLUS, Federal Perkins Loan. Applicants will be notified of awards on a rolling basis beginning or about March 1.

FROM THE ADMISSIONS OFFICE

"Historically committed to meeting the changing needs of women, Stephens College engages students in an innovative educational experience that focuses on pre-professional fields and the performing arts and is grounded in the liberal arts. Graduates of Stephens are career-ready women of distinction who are connected through a supportive network of alumnae across the world, confident in themselves, and inspired by our tradition of the 10 ideals as core values that enrich women's lives.

"The women's college setting offers to its students stimulating classroom discussion and close interaction with professors and peers. Bridging theory and application, students engage in hands-on learning opportunities (education majors in our on-campus children's laboratory school and theater in Iowa, for example) as well as internship experiences in their first year of study. The Stephens campus is within walking distance of a thriving downtown, shared by more than 26,000 students at area colleges and universities."

As of this book's publication, Stephens College did not have information available about their policy regarding the new SAT.

SELECTIVITY

Admissions Rating	85
# of applicants	633
% of applicants accepted	76
% of acceptees attending	51

FRESHMAN PROFILE

Range SAT Critical Reading	540–610
Range SAT Math	480–580
Range ACT Composite	21–26
Minimum Paper TOEFL	550
Minimum Computer Based TOEFL	213
Average HS GPA	3.50
% graduated top 10% of class	21
% graduated top 25% of class	67
% graduated top 50% of class	93

DEADLINES

Regular notification	rolling
Nonfall registration?	yes

APPLICANTS ALSO LOOK AT
AND SOMETIMES PREFER
University of Missouri—Columbia
AND RARELY PREFER
Butler University

FINANCIAL FACTS

Financial Aid Rating	76
Annual tuition	$20,500
Room & Board	$7,975
Books and supplies	$1,000
% frosh rec. need-based scholarship or grant aid	64
% UG rec. need-based scholarship or grant aid	54
% frosh rec. need-based self-help aid	62
% UG rec. need-based self-help aid	58
% frosh rec. any financial aid	98
% UG rec. any financial aid	83

STEVENS INSTITUTE OF TECHNOLOGY

CASTLE POINT ON HUDSON, HOBOKEN, NJ 07030 • ADMISSIONS: 201-216-5194 • FAX: 201-216-8348

STUDENTS SAY

Academics

Students at the Stevens Institute of Technology tell us time and again that "Stevens' reputation amongst some of the world's best employers is outstanding." This leads to a "high job placement [rate] and great starting salaries," which, for many, are the primary charms of this small Hoboken school. Engineering disciplines claim about two-thirds of all Stevens undergraduates, and "a huge number participate in the co-op program," which "allows students a break from the theoretical nonsense while putting it to use." In this program, "students spend 5 years getting their undergraduate degree [while] work[ing] three semesters at a company getting experience and pay." That's three semesters of work on top of a 156-credit program that awards a "Bachelor's of Engineering, not [a] Bachelor's of Science in engineering. (We are one of [fewer] than half a dozen schools in the country to offer [it].)" It's a calendar that is not for the faint of heart, since it means a freshman "can have eight classes in [his or her] first semester." Stevens also delivers in mathematics and the sciences; students in the latter area brag that Stevens "always gets a high percent[age] of students accepted . . . to medical school." As at most tech and science schools, students here complain that, while "The professors are very intelligent," "Sometimes we get professors who are unable to communicate the material." This is often attributed to professors whose first language is not English; some say it's "50/50" whether you'll be able to understand your professor. Even so, most agree that "the juice is worth the squeeze . . . you'll get a good job" if you graduate.

Life

Stevens is situated in the town of Hoboken, NJ, which is "located right on the doorstep of New York City." Hoboken boosters believe that "there is simply no better spot in the world to have a college." In truth, this small town close to the capital of the world pleases multiple tastes: "Those that don't enjoy the city are quite content in Hoboken, [and] the more city-slicker-type students feel very at home with the Manhattan skyline as a backdrop." Because the train to New York City is only "a 7-minute walk from campus," it's easy for students to touch as well as look. Despite its great location, Stevens' "highly demanding" academics play the largest role in student life, which is driven by the ebb and flow—usually the latter—of course work. Nevertheless, "Students are very involved [on] campus. Whether it [is] a sports team or Greek life, the vast majority of students do at least one extracurricular activity." Stevens boasts "a very good Division III athletic program," and its teams "have been getting larger fan turnouts" in recent years. Students tell us that there's also "no lack of parties and alcohol [at] this school. You can count on a party every Thursday." A 3:1 male/female ratio drives some male students off campus in search of companionship.

Student Body

Like most tech schools, Stevens "is a nerd school, no doubt about it." It's home to many students who are "very smart but lacking social skills," preferring to "play World of Warcraft in their rooms or watch anime on a Friday night." Students point out that you'll also find "musicians, theater junkies, sports fanatics, and bookworms" on campus. And "just about everybody here has a secret hobby or talent you would have never thought of." In addition, Stevens also has a substantial number of international students—many of whom are "Indian or Asian"—and "lots of minorities" who boost the diversity factor. On the downside, students tend to be very cliquish and "don't associate with each other outside of class" unless they are part of "the group."

FINANCIAL AID: 201-216-5194 • E-MAIL: ADMISSIONS@STEVENS.EDU • WEBSITE: WWW.STEVENS.EDU

ADMISSIONS

Very important factors considered include: Academic GPA, application essay, character/personal qualities, extracurricular activities, interview, recommendation(s), rigor of secondary school record, standardized test scores, volunteer work, work experience. *Important factors considered include:* Class rank, talent/ability. *Other factors considered include:* Alumni/ae relation. SAT or ACT required; TOEFL required of all international applicants. High school diploma is required, and GED is not accepted. *Academic units required:* 4 English, 4 math, 3 science (3 science labs). *Academic units recommended:* 4 science (4 science labs), 2 foreign language, 2 social studies, 2 history, 4 academic electives.

The Inside Word

Stevens is among the most desirable "second tier" engineering/science/math schools; its location and cachet with employers guarantee that. It's a good choice for those who can't get through the door at MIT or Caltech but who are nonetheless extremely smart and unafraid of hard work. Such students will find the Stevens Admissions Office quite sympathetic to their applications.

FINANCIAL AID

Students should submit: FAFSA. The Princeton Review suggests that all financial aid forms be submitted as soon as possible after January 1. *Need-based scholarships/grants offered:* Pell Grant, SEOG, state scholarships/grants, private scholarships, the school's own gift aid. *Loan aid offered:* Direct Subsidized Stafford, Direct Unsubsidized Stafford, Direct PLUS, FFEL Subsidized Stafford, Federal Perkins Loan, state loans, Signature Loans, TERI Loans, NJ CLASS, CitiAssist. Applicants will be notified of awards on a rolling basis beginning or about March 30. Federal Work-Study Program available. Off-campus job opportunities are excellent.

FROM THE ADMISSIONS OFFICE

"Founded in 1870 as the first American college to devote itself exclusively to engineering education based on scientific principles, Stevens Institute of Technology is a prestigious independent university for study and research. In 2004, Stevens was ranked by the Princeton Review as one of the nation's 'Most Entrepreneurial Campuses' for having tailored their undergraduate business and technology curricula to encourage young entrepreneurs, providing them with the training and guidance they need to start their own businesses. In 2006, Stevens was ranked among the nation's top-20 'Most Wired Campuses' by *PC Magazine* and the Princeton Review.

"At the undergraduate level, Stevens' broad-based education leads to prestigious degrees in business, science, computer science, engineering, or humanities. Research activities are vital to the university's educational mission, thus Stevens attracts world-renowned faculty to complement its exceptional on-campus facilities. In addition, Stevens maintains an honor system that has been in existence since 1908. Stevens' more than 1,800 undergraduates come from more than 42 states and 65 countries, creating a diverse, dynamic environment. Stevens also boasts an outstanding campus life—students will find more than 150 student organizations and 25 NCAA Division III athletics teams.

"Stevens requires the SAT or ACT for all applicants. We recommend that all students take SAT Subject Tests to show their strength in English, math, and a science of their choice. Accelerated premed and pre-dentistry applicants must take the SAT as well as two SAT Subject Tests in Math (Level I or II), and Biology or Chemistry. Accelerated law applicants must take two SAT Subject Tests of their choice."

SELECTIVITY

Admissions Rating	**93**
# of applicants	2,278
% of applicants accepted	54
% of acceptees attending	39
# accepting a place on wait list	34
% admitted from wait list	59
# of early decision applicants	211
% accepted early decision	65

FRESHMAN PROFILE

Range SAT Critical Reading	540–650
Range SAT Math	620–710
Minimum Paper TOEFL	550
Minimum Computer Based TOEFL	213
Average HS GPA	3.7
% graduated top 10% of class	53
% graduated top 25% of class	82
% graduated top 50% of class	96

DEADLINES

Early decision application deadline	11/15
Early decision notification	12/15
Regular application deadline	2/15
Regular notification	4/1
Nonfall registration?	no

APPLICANTS ALSO LOOK AT

AND OFTEN PREFER
Carnegie Mellon University, Cornell University, Massachusetts Institute of Technology, Princeton University

AND SOMETIMES PREFER
Johns Hopkins University, Lehigh University, New York University

AND RARELY PREFER
Drexel University, New Jersey Institute of Technology, Rensselaer Polytechnic Institute, Rutgers, The State University of New Jersey—New Brunswick/Piscataway

FINANCIAL FACTS

Financial Aid Rating	**72**
Annual tuition	$33,300
Room & Board	$10,500
Books and supplies	$900
Required fees	$1,800
% frosh rec. need-based scholarship or grant aid	58
% UG rec. need-based scholarship or grant aid	54
% frosh rec. need-based self-help aid	57
% UG rec. need-based self-help aid	56
% frosh rec. any financial aid	83
% UG rec. any financial aid	76

SUFFOLK UNIVERSITY

EIGHT ASHBURTON PLACE, BOSTON, MA 02108 • ADMISSIONS: 617-573-8460 • FAX: 617-742-4291

STUDENTS SAY

Academics

"A small classroom university in the heart of a big city," Boston's Suffolk University "is small enough that you actually recognize students from their pictures in the admissions booklets [and] big enough to attract national speakers like George Bush Sr." It's also a school with a huge international component, thanks to its campuses in Madrid, Spain, and Dakar, Senegal and "a unique partnership with Charles University in Prague," all of which "provide students an easy opportunity to study abroad without the usual hassle of all the paperwork." Academic life on the home campus "includes "down-to-earth professors" who "are always available outside of class and are very helpful" and the Balloti Learning Center, which "offers extra help to students who want or need it." Make no mistake: Academics are "incredibly student oriented" here—"The student and [his or her] concerns come first." Top programs include psychology, government, history, and sociology, which "offers concentrations in criminology and law or health and human services as opposed to just a general major."

Life

Suffolk lacks a traditional sprawling suburban campus. Simply put, Suffolk students know they ain't in Kansas any more! The university consists of a collection of buildings located in swanky Beacon Hill, literally steps from Boston Common and the Public Gardens. So, if you're a city lover you my have just found heaven! Suffolk students are quick to point out that their urban existence can make some feel "disconnected" compounded by the fact that many students choose to live off campus. One commuter writes, "It's sometimes difficult for me to join in some of the activities that they have going on at the school." Even so, many here are satisfied with the status quo; they'll skip the conventional campus activities and the rah-rah campus unity, preferring to spend their free time enjoying the city of Boston. "Most people have lots of friends [at] other schools" and the prevalence of fun activities in Boston such as "movies at the Museum of Fine Arts" and "local concerts." Undergrads agree that "drinking is definitely a huge part of Suffolk," and "Being 21 in Boston or having a good fake ID makes it a much better time. What you lose in the lack of campus, you gain with the city."

Student Body

Suffolk's overseas ties draw a large international population to the Boston campus, to the point that "in some classes, almost half of the students are foreign-born. Interacting with students from different backgrounds or cultures isn't an option—it's a daily occurrence. In my international business classes it leads to fascinating discussions because, rather than read about business in different cultures, we have firsthand experiences." Most of the American student body comes from Boston and the surrounding area; while "The majority [are] pretty run-of-the mill products of Massachusetts suburbia, the minority is pretty eclectic." This minority includes "art-school hipsters" and a "relatively large gay community." Each group also features "a lot of spoiled rich kids" who use "Boston as their playground." Students report that there "isn't a real strong sense of community, unless you live in the dorms" (about one in five does).

FINANCIAL AID: 617-573-8470 • E-MAIL: ADMISSION@SUFFOLK.EDU • WEBSITE: WWW.SUFFOLK.EDU

ADMISSIONS

Very important factors considered include: Academic GPA, rigor of secondary school record. *Important factors considered include:* Application essay, class rank, standardized test scores. *Other factors considered include:* Alumni/ae relation, character/personal qualities, extracurricular activities, first generation, geographical residence, interview, level of applicant's interest, recommendation(s), talent/ability, volunteer work, work experience. SAT or ACT required; TOEFL required of all international applicants. High school diploma is required, and GED is accepted. *Academic units required:* 4 English, 3 math, 2 science (1 science lab), 2 foreign language, 1 social studies, 1 history, 4 academic electives. *Academic units recommended:* 4 English, 4 math, 3 science (1 science lab), 3 foreign language, 1 social studies, 1 history, 4 academic electives.

The Inside Word

Suffolk is unapologetic about its mission to provide access and opportunity to college bound students. That said, test scores and high school GPA requirements are average. Applicants who are borderline based on straight numbers should make their case to the Admissions Office directly.

FINANCIAL AID

Students should submit: FAFSA, institution's own financial aid form. Regular filing deadline is March 1. The Princeton Review suggests that all financial aid forms be submitted as soon as possible after January 1. *Need-based scholarships/grants offered:* Pell Grant, SEOG, state scholarships/grants, private scholarships, the school's own gift aid. *Loan aid offered:* Direct Subsidized Stafford, Direct Unsubsidized Stafford, Direct PLUS, Federal Perkins Loan. Applicants will be notified of awards on a rolling basis beginning or about March 1.

FROM THE ADMISSIONS OFFICE

"Ask any student, and they'll tell you: The best thing about Suffolk is the professors. They go the extra mile to help students to succeed. Suffolk faculty members are noted scholars and experienced professionals, but first and foremost, they are teachers and mentors. Suffolk's faculty is of the highest caliber. Ninety-four percent of the faculty hold PhDs. Suffolk maintains a 13:1 student/faculty ratio with an average class size of 19.

"The university was selected by *U.S. News'* 2005 edition as one of 'America's Best Colleges.' It was also selected as one of the 'Best 201 Colleges' by the *Best 201 Colleges for the Real World* (2001/2002), and was chosen as one of *Barron's Best Buys in College Education.* Career preparation is a high priority at Suffolk. Many students work during the school year in paid internships, co-op jobs, or work-study positions. Suffolk has an excellent job placement record. More than 94 percent of recent graduates are either employed or enrolled in graduate school at the time of graduation.

"The university's academic programs emphasize quality teaching, small class size, real-world career applications, and an international experience. There are more than 30 study abroad sites available to students. The undergraduate academic program offers more than 70 majors and 1,000 courses.

"We require applicants to submit the SAT with the essay score or the ACT taken with the Writing component. Standardized tests are used for both placement and assessment. International students may submit any of the following tests for admission: the TOEFL or ELPT, IELTS, CPE, CAE, and FCE. The role of standardized testing is still a secondary role when considering admission to the university. The candidate's grades and the overall strength of curriculum are primary factors in the admission decision."

SELECTIVITY

Admissions Rating	71
# of applicants	7,106
% of applicants accepted	83
% of acceptees attending	22
# accepting a place on wait list	38
% admitted from wait list	8

FRESHMAN PROFILE

Range SAT Critical Reading	440–550
Range SAT Math	450–550
Range SAT Writing	450–560
Range ACT Composite	19–23
Minimum Paper TOEFL	525
Minimum Computer Based TOEFL	197
Average HS GPA	2.95
% graduated top 10% of class	9
% graduated top 25% of class	29
% graduated top 50% of class	68

DEADLINES

Regular application deadline	3/1
Regular notification	rolling
Nonfall registration?	yes

FINANCIAL FACTS

Financial Aid Rating	67
Annual tuition	$24,170
Room & Board	$13,360
Required fees	$195
% frosh rec. need-based scholarship or grant aid	53
% UG rec. need-based scholarship or grant aid	50
% frosh rec. need-based self-help aid	57
% UG rec. need-based self-help aid	54
% frosh rec. any financial aid	68
% UG rec. any financial aid	63

SUSQUEHANNA UNIVERSITY

514 UNIVERSITY AVENUE, SELINSGROVE, PA 17870 • ADMISSIONS: 570-372-4260 • FAX: 570-372-2722

STUDENTS SAY

Academics

Susquehanna University, a Lutheran-affiliated institution situated in central Pennsylvania, boasts "a great teacher-to-student ratio and a close-knit community that comes from having only 2,000 students on campus." The size of the school, students here tell us, "allows you to try many new and different things that you would miss out on at a bigger university" and "makes us a little community where you know so many people. You get to know your professors very well, feel extremely comfortable going to see them outside of class, and get the attention and help that you need." Students report that SU's business program "is wonderful and challenging." The music, writing, and arts programs here also earn students' praise, while natural science programs benefit from "lots of opportunities for undergraduate research." Students also appreciate the school's "amazing dedication in finding us internships and jobs" and how SU "encourages us to study abroad and in different specialty programs to learn as much as we can in different environments." The school is looking to the future with building initiatives. The music and arts building was finished 3 years ago and new athletic fields were created 2 years ago. The campus center (and cafeteria) were being renovated over summer 2005. Additionally, the Science Department is reportedly working on plans for a second science building. Spring 2006 is slated for the grand opening of SU's new social space, Trax, which will feature a dance floor, DJ booth, game area, bar, performance stage, and outdoor patio." One student observes, "The university is continually improving in both aesthetics and in the quality of education."

Life

"Extracurricular activities are very strong" at SU. Students tell us that "there is a great network of volunteer organizations that work on campus and throughout the local area, from on-campus recycling to mentoring at the middle school. Club sports are also strong," as are the school's Division III intercollegiate athletics. Greek life is also big, with approximately one in four students pledging. Campus organizations "offer a variety of events like movies, spring weekend parties, and different social events." And because the school is small, "You can be involved with a lot of different activities at the same time." The high level of campus activity is necessary, because hometown Selinsgrove "is a nice small town, but it has nothing in the way of entertainment and girls, and the mall sucks—so stock up before you get here." Many students address the boredom of rural seclusion by partying hard, a situation the administration has tried to address recently with predictable results: Plenty of students complain that they "expected a college and instead . . . got a babysitting service." Undergrads here also gripe that the school is currently overcrowded, with a lot of "forced triples" in freshman dorms. They report that those renovations are coming along "slowly, so we'll see what it will look like in the future."

Student Body

"Susquehanna, located in rural central Pennsylvania, undoubtedly lacks diversity," students write. "The average student is of one of two varieties: White, middle-class, Pennsylvania farm children or White, upper-middle-class kids from in or around New York City." Those from the area "often leave on weekends, especially during freshman year, which is annoying because it makes it hard to get to know them." SU undergrads know how to "strike the balance between academics with extracurricular activities. We are involved in athletics, community service, religious groups, and Greek life." Undergrads note "the presence of certain cliques here; for instance, music and drama production, sorority girls, sports teams, frats, etc. However, these groups are not set in stone, and many people have many different friends in numerous cliques." Most students here "dress preppy and carry cell phones," but "There is always someone dressed in sweats or pajamas, too. There are also some atypical students who wear goth or bohemian-style clothing, but that doesn't usually seem to affect how they fit in."

FINANCIAL AID: 570-372-4450 • E-MAIL: SUADMISS@SUSQU.EDU • WEBSITE: WWW.SUSQU.EDU

ADMISSIONS

Very important factors considered include: Academic GPA, rigor of secondary school record. *Important factors considered include:* Application essay, character/personal qualities, class rank, extracurricular activities, interview, recommendation(s), standardized test scores, talent/ability, volunteer work, work experience. *Other factors considered include:* Alumni/ae relation, first generation, geographical residence, level of applicant's interest, racial/ethnic status, religious affiliation/commitment, state residency. TOEFL required of all international applicants. High school diploma is required, and GED is accepted. *Academic units required:* 4 English, 3 math, 3 science (2 science labs), 2 foreign language, 1 social studies, 1 history, 2 academic electives. *Academic units recommended:* 4 English, 4 math, 4 science (3 science labs), 4 foreign language, 4 social studies, 1 history, 4 academic electives.

The Inside Word

Susquehanna is about as low profile as universities come in the age of MTV. Getting in is made easier by the serious competition the university faces from numerous like institutions in the region, some with significantly better reputations.

FINANCIAL AID

Students should submit: FAFSA, CSS/Financial Aid PROFILE, Business/Farm Supplement. Regular filing deadline is May 1. The Princeton Review suggests that all financial aid forms be submitted as soon as possible after January 1. *Need-based scholarships/grants offered:* Pell Grant, SEOG, state scholarships/grants, private scholarships, the school's own gift aid. *Loan aid offered:* FFEL Subsidized Stafford, FFEL Unsubsidized Stafford, FFEL PLUS, Federal Perkins Loan, college/university loans from institutional funds. Applicants will be notified of awards on a rolling basis beginning or about February 15.

FROM THE ADMISSIONS OFFICE

"Students tell us they are getting a first-rate education and making the connections that will help them be competitive upon graduation. Our size makes it easy for students to customize their 4 years here with self-designed majors, internships, volunteer service, research, leadership opportunities, and rewarding off-campus experiences. Many academic programs are interdisciplinary, meaning that you learn to make connections between different fields of knowledge, which will help make you an educated citizen of the world. A high percentage of students do internships at such sites as Morgan Stanley, Cable News Network, Estee Lauder, and Bristol-Myers Squibb. More than 90 percent of our graduates go on for advanced degrees or get jobs in their chosen field within six months of graduation. There are also more than 100 student organizations on campus, which provide lots of opportunity for leadership and involvement in campus life. The campus is known for its beauty and is a few blocks from downtown Selinsgrove and about a mile from shopping and movie theaters at the Susquehanna Valley Mall.

"Susquehanna will consider a student's top standardized test score (SAT or ACT) when evaluating their application. Students are also encouraged to consider SU's alternative to standardized tests, the Write Option. Under the Write Option, a student may submit two graded writing samples instead of SAT or ACT scores."

SELECTIVITY

Admissions Rating	79
# of applicants	2,292
% of applicants accepted	79
% of acceptees attending	30
# accepting a place on wait list	135
% admitted from wait list	4
# of early decision applicants	173
% accepted early decision	77

FRESHMAN PROFILE

Range SAT Critical Reading	530–610
Range SAT Math	520–620
Minimum Paper TOEFL	550
Minimum Computer Based TOEFL	213
% graduated top 10% of class	32
% graduated top 25% of class	64
% graduated top 50% of class	92

DEADLINES

Early decision application deadline	11/15
Early decision notification	12/15
Regular notification	rolling
Nonfall registration?	yes

APPLICANTS ALSO LOOK AT

AND OFTEN PREFER
Bucknell University, Franklin & Marshall College, Lafayette College, Villanova University

AND SOMETIMES PREFER
Dickinson State University, Gettysburg College, Muhlenberg College, Pennsylvania State University—University Park

AND RARELY PREFER
Elizabethtown College, Lebanon Valley College, Lycoming College

FINANCIAL FACTS

Financial Aid Rating	78
Annual tuition	$27,300
Room & Board	$7,600
Books and supplies	$750
Required fees	$320
% frosh rec. need-based scholarship or grant aid	65
% UG rec. need-based scholarship or grant aid	64
% frosh rec. need-based self-help aid	55
% UG rec. need-based self-help aid	53
% frosh rec. any financial aid	92
% UG rec. any financial aid	92

SWARTHMORE COLLEGE

500 COLLEGE AVENUE, SWARTHMORE, PA 19081 • ADMISSIONS: 610-328-8300 • FAX: 610-328-8580

STUDENTS SAY

Academics

Swarthmore College, a school that is "as intense and stimulating as it claims to be," suits students who prefer "an emphasis on learning because it's fun and interesting rather than learning to get a job." One undergrad writes, "A lot of what unifies its student body is the fact that, whether we're pursuing a degree in engineering or we're planning on writing the next Great American Novel, we're all passionate and devoted to something." Swatties love that "Swarthmore is amazingly flexible. The requirements are very limited, allowing you to explore whatever you are interested in and change your mind millions of times about your major and career path. If they don't offer a major you want, you can design your own with ease." Professors also earn raves: They're "genuinely interested in giving the students the best academic experience possible" and "challenge students to become knowledgeable in so many areas yet force them to create their own thoughts." Best of all, they come to Swarthmore to teach undergraduates, meaning that "here you can interact with A-list professors straight out of high school. At other universities I'd be lucky to interact one-on-one with professors of similar stature in my third year of graduate school." Students also think you should know that "the school has a lot of money and is very generous with spending it on undergrads, as there isn't anyone else to spend it on."

Life

"There is a misconception that Swarthmore students do nothing but study," students tell us. "While we certainly do a lot of it, we still find many ways to have fun." Though there "isn't a lot to do right in the area surrounding Swarthmore," "With a train station on campus, Philly is very accessible." Most students, however, find no need to leave campus on a regular basis: "The campus provides for us all that we need, and we rarely make it out to Philly," one content freshman writes. On-campus activities "are varied, and there is almost always something to do on the weekend. There are student musical performances, drama performances, movies, speakers, and comedy shows," as well as "several parties every weekend, with and without alcohol, and a lot of pre-partying with friends." For many, things that are the most fun are "the low-key events, just hanging out with friends, talking about classes, or playing in the snow." One student sums up, "While it is tough to generalize on the life of a Swarthmore student, one word definitely applies to us all: busy. All of us are either working on extracurriculars, studying, or fighting sleep to do more work."

Student Body

Students are "not sure if there is a typical Swattie," but suspect that "the defining feature among us is that each person is brilliant at something. Maybe dance, maybe quantum physics, maybe philosophy; each person here has at least one thing that [he or she does] extraordinarily well." There's also "a little bit of a nerd in every one of us—much more in some than in others. The people are all truly genuine, though, and everyone tends to get along well. We're all a little idiosyncratic: When anything that you might call eccentric, or maybe even a little weird at Swat occurs, the typical reaction is, 'That is so Swarthmore!'" A Swattie "tends to have a tremendously hectic life because he or she joins organizations for which he or she holds a passion, and then has 28 hours of work to accomplish in a 24-hour day." Swatties also tend to be "politically left-wing. One says, "If you are not left-wing it is more difficult, but still possible, to fit in—you just have to expect a lot of debate about your political . . . views.""

FINANCIAL AID: 610-328-8358 • E-MAIL: ADMISSIONS@SWARTHMORE.EDU • WEBSITE: WWW.SWARTHMORE.EDU

ADMISSIONS

Very important factors considered include: Academic GPA, application essay, character/personal qualities, class rank, recommendation(s), rigor of secondary school record. *Important factors considered include:* Extracurricular activities, standardized test scores. *Other factors considered include:* Alumni/ae relation, first generation, geographical residence, interview, level of applicant's interest, racial/ethnic status, talent/ability, volunteer work, work experience. SAT and SAT Subject Tests or ACT with Writing component required. High school diploma or equivalent is not required.

The Inside Word

Competition for admission to Swarthmore remains fierce, as the school consistently receives applications from top students across the country. With numerous qualified candidates, prospective students can be assured that every aspect of their applications will be thoroughly evaluated. While there might not be a typical admit, successful applicants have all proven themselves intellectually curious, highly motivated, and creative-minded.

FINANCIAL AID

Students should submit: FAFSA, institution's own financial aid form, CSS/Financial Aid PROFILE, Noncustodial PROFILE, state aid form, Business/Farm Supplement, Federal Income Tax Returns, W-2 statements, year-end paycheck stub. Regular filing deadline is February 15. The Princeton Review suggests that all financial aid forms be submitted as soon as possible after January 1. *Need-based scholarships/grants offered:* Pell Grant, SEOG, state scholarships/grants, private scholarships, the school's own gift aid. *Loan aid offered:* FFEL Subsidized Stafford, FFEL Unsubsidized Stafford, FFEL PLUS, Federal Perkins Loan, state loans, college/university loans from institutional funds. Applicants will be notified of awards on or about April 1.

FROM THE ADMISSIONS OFFICE

"Swarthmore is a highly selective college of liberal arts and engineering, located near Philadelphia and enrolling a student body of approximately 1,500. A college like no other, Swarthmore is private, yet open to all regardless of financial need; American, yet decidedly global in outlook and diversity, drawing students from around the world and all 50 states; small, yet with the financial strength to offer students and faculty generous resources to push their own and the world's understanding of disciplines from Arabic to plasma physics, from microbiology to dance, from engineering to art history. An institution that celebrates the life of the mind, Swarthmore gives students of uncommon intellectual ability the knowledge, insight, skills, and experience to become leaders for the common good.

"Applicants must submit either the new SAT plus two SAT Subject Tests or the ACT with Writing component. Scores from older versions of the SAT (pre-March 2005 version) and the ACT are acceptable. For the old SAT, scores must be submitted with the results of three SAT Subject Tests, one of which must be the Writing test."

SELECTIVITY

Admissions Rating	98
# of applicants	4,852
% of applicants accepted	19
% of acceptees attending	40
# of early decision applicants	425
% accepted early decision	37

FRESHMAN PROFILE

Range SAT Critical Reading	660–770
Range SAT Math	660–760
Range SAT Writing	650–760
Range ACT Composite	28–34
% graduated top 10% of class	83
% graduated top 25% of class	89
% graduated top 50% of class	100

DEADLINES

Early decision application deadline	11/15, 1/2
Early decision notification	12/15, 2/15
Regular application deadline	1/2
Regular notification	4/1
Nonfall registration?	no

FINANCIAL FACTS

Financial Aid Rating	98
Annual tuition	$32,912
Room & Board	$10,300
Books and supplies	$1,048
Required fees	$320
% frosh rec. need-based scholarship or grant aid	49
% UG rec. need-based scholarship or grant aid	49
% frosh rec. need-based self-help aid	47
% UG rec. need-based self-help aid	47
% frosh rec. any financial aid	49
% UG rec. any financial aid	52

Sweet Briar College

PO Box B, Sweet Briar, VA 24595 • Admissions: 434-381-6142 • Fax: 434-381-6152

STUDENTS SAY
Academics

"A traditional all-girl's school providing exceptional educational opportunities on one of the most beautiful campuses in the nation," Sweet Briar is a tiny liberal arts college that "allows women to do it all; it provides a rigorous academic program as well as a flourishing co-curricular life" that includes "activities and leadership opportunities." A "prestigious riding program" attracts many who want to make equestrian pursuits a part of their academic experience. The small campus is another enticing feature, making it possible "to become involved in any and all aspects of campus life, whether it be academic, social, physical, or extracurricular," while also facilitating "the support of the professors." The faculty here "may not live up to the publishing powerhouses," explains one student, "but they are some of the best teachers with whom I have ever interacted. The small size of the school lends to a very close-knit community, even with the professors, deans, and president." Sweet Briar is strong in education, with a Masters of Arts in Teaching (MAT) program enhanced by "an on-campus kindergarten and preschool, so students interested in being teachers can get teaching experience their first year." Fine arts and social sciences are also popular choices here. The small-school setting is not without its drawbacks; there are problems with course availability ("The courses I would like to enroll in are not offered," writes one student), and limited funding means that the school still needs to "bring many of the buildings up to date and work on getting the campus completely wireless." Students say those problems are worth enduring for the personal attention they receive; "From the administration to the professors, these professionals devote countless hours to being accessible to students and allowing the school to run as an institution for its pupils."

Life

Life at Sweet Briar "is firmly established in traditions. This is one of the most attractive features of the college: The many traditions that build a strong sense of community, whether it be convocation, lantern bearing, step singing, or the many tap clubs active on campus." Socially, the campus "is fairly quiet most of the time. There are a couple of parties a week, but most of the partying (especially on the weekend) is done off campus" at schools like UVA and Hampden-Sydney. Students say "This is not a bad thing," as it allows them to "have our fun and not deal with the mess." The surrounding area is also quiet, as the school "is in a very rural area." Students stay busy during the week; "A lot of girls over-commit themselves to clubs and sports." The school's legendarily beautiful campus continues to live up to its reputation; one student writes, "This is my fourth year at Sweet Briar, and the campus still takes my breath away every morning when I wake up. It's exquisite."

Student Body

Writes one eloquent Sweet Briar student: "Many people stereotype the students at Sweet Briar College. Being a women's college in Southern Virginia allows some to believe us all to be Southern belles interested solely in getting an MRS. We're portrayed as those girls in pink with pearls and ribbons. This, however, could not be further from the truth." While there are some on campus who might fit that stereotype, they are "strongly overpowered" by those who don't. Besides being different from the assumed stereotype, students are also varied among themselves. One students says, "My friends and I, a group of our class leaders, are a random and eclectic group. Our one common trait is that each of us has a little bit of strangeness that we love about ourselves." Another student agrees, "In reality, we are diverse. Many of us do not wear pearls and not all of us ride horses, but we all share an enthusiasm for our academics." The college works to bring many different types of people together, "and each person is respected for her own unique characteristics."

FINANCIAL AID: 434-381-6156 • E-MAIL: ADMISSIONS@SBC.EDU • WEBSITE: WWW.SBC.EDU

ADMISSIONS

Very important factors considered include: Academic GPA, rigor of secondary school record. *Important factors considered include:* Application essay, class rank, interview, recommendation(s), standardized test scores. *Other factors considered include:* Alumni/ae relation, character/personal qualities, extracurricular activities, first generation, talent/ability, volunteer work, work experience. SAT or ACT required; ACT with Writing component required. TOEFL required of all international applicants. High school diploma is required, and GED is accepted. *Academic units required:* 4 English, 3 math, 3 science (2 science labs), 2 foreign language, 3 social studies. *Academic units recommended:* 4 English, 4 math, 4 science (3 science labs), 4 foreign language, 4 social studies.

The Inside Word

A tiny applicant pool allows Sweet Briar to consider each application closely. The school looks not only for evidence of academic achievement and ability but also for "fit" with the school. How well will you fit into/fill out the Sweet Briar community? How well can the school deliver quality academics in your areas of interest? (A school this small can't provide in-depth instruction in every discipline, after all.) These are the questions that will determine your admissions status as Sweet Briar, especially if your test scores and/or high school grades are borderline.

FINANCIAL AID

Students should submit: FAFSA, state aid form. Regular filing deadline is March 1. The Princeton Review suggests that all financial aid forms be submitted as soon as possible after January 1. *Need-based scholarships/grants offered:* Pell Grant, SEOG, state scholarships/grants, private scholarships, the school's own gift aid. *Loan aid offered:* Direct Subsidized Stafford, Direct Unsubsidized Stafford, Direct PLUS, Federal Perkins Loan, college/university loans from institutional funds. Applicants will be notified of awards on a rolling basis beginning or about March 1. Federal Work-Study Program available. Institutional employment available. Off-campus job opportunities are fair.

FROM THE ADMISSIONS OFFICE

"The woman who applies to Sweet Briar is mature and far-sighted enough to know what she wants from her college experience. She is intellectually adventuresome, more willing to explore new fields, and more open to challenging her boundaries. Sweet Briar attracts the ambitious, confident woman who enjoys being immersed not only in a first-rate academic program, but in a variety of meaningful activities outside the classroom. Our students take charge and revel in their accomplishments. This attitude follows graduates, enabling them to compete confidently in the corporate world and in graduate school.

"Applicants to Sweet Briar College should take either the SAT or the ACT with the Writing component, and request from the appropriate testing company that an official copy of the test score be sent to Sweet Briar."

SELECTIVITY

Admissions Rating	82
# of applicants	585
% of applicants accepted	80
% of acceptees attending	40
# of early decision applicants	63
% accepted early decision	92

FRESHMAN PROFILE

Range SAT Critical Reading	510–640
Range SAT Math	470–595
Range SAT Writing	500–600
Range ACT Composite	21–26
Minimum Paper TOEFL	550
Minimum Computer Based TOEFL	213
Average HS GPA	3.4
% graduated top 10% of class	24
% graduated top 25% of class	55
% graduated top 50% of class	88

DEADLINES

Early decision application deadline	12/1
Early decision notification	12/15
Regular application deadline	2/1
Regular notification	3/15
Nonfall registration?	yes

APPLICANTS ALSO LOOK AT

AND OFTEN PREFER
The College of William & Mary, Mount Holyoke College

AND SOMETIMES PREFER
Agnes Scott College, University of Virginia

AND RARELY PREFER
Hollins University, Randolph College

FINANCIAL FACTS

Financial Aid Rating	90
Annual tuition	$24,470
Room & Board	$10,040
Books and supplies	$600
Required fees	$275
% frosh rec. need-based scholarship or grant aid	53
% UG rec. need-based scholarship or grant aid	42
% frosh rec. need-based self-help aid	49
% UG rec. need-based self-help aid	39
% frosh rec. any financial aid	93
% UG rec. any financial aid	91

SYRACUSE UNIVERSITY

201 TOLLEY, ADMINISTRATION BUILDING, SYRACUSE, NY 13244 • ADMISSIONS: 315-443-3611 • FAX: 315-443-4226

STUDENTS SAY

Academics

Syracuse University "is very strong academically" and boasts "some of the nation's top programs" in a broad range of disciplines. Students are especially bullish on the "prestigious" S. I. Newhouse School of Public Communications, which "has some amazing professors who have worked out in the field and are eager to share all of their experiences with their students," as well as the School of Architecture, "an energetic, sleepless journey of collaboration and individuality in an amazingly cool atmosphere" (although some complain that the school's downtown location leaves it feeling isolated from the rest of the campus). SU's programs in advertising, art, business, music, political science, engineering, and the life sciences also earn plaudits from undergraduates. Best of all, students say, SU delivers the benefits of "both large schools and small schools," which means it can offer the ability "to concentrate in an area while also taking a variety of other classes that do not have to be within your major or college," as well as plenty of research faculty who put "SU at the front of [the] material" and "professors who are always available to meet during office hours [or] by appointment." One undergrad sums it up: "SU is big enough to have a wealth of resources but small enough so that you always fit in." Another adds, "SU is about academics and preparing us as best as possible for our future careers, along with a little bit of men's basketball."

Life

Students tell us that "the social life at Syracuse is the epitome of the great American college experience. Local bars, frats, and house parties are all popular. Partying takes place from Thursday through Sunday, and close friendships are easily cultivated during the recovery period in between." However, it's important to note that "the school is great about providing other activities" as well. "You don't need to drink to find something fun to do at night or on weekends." "People climb trees on the quad, go rock climbing on the weekends, [and] take ballet classes. We're notorious for our frat parties, but, at the same time, the library is packed every Saturday night." "The student union also provides free movies on weekends, and there are loads of speakers, concerts, and cultural events throughout the week." Of course, SU sports "are huge"—"Syracuse Basketball is going to win the national championship!" Students are mixed on the city of Syracuse. Some tell us "It's pretty much dead" and "The weather sucks," while others aver that "upstate New York is a great location with lots of outdoor activities, unless you hate sub-Arctic climates."

Student Body

While SU undergrads report that a typical peer would be "fashionable," "wealthy," and "trend-driven," they also point out that "there are also tons of students who don't fit that description." Indeed there are upstate, out-of-state, and international students in addition to an abundance from Long Island and New Jersey. While the student body includes "a large frat/sorority presence," there's also a fair share of "neo-hippies." Although SU's student population appears homogenous to some, other students say "[This] seems to be proven wrong on many occasions. For example, the guy living next to me is from St. Thomas. I have friends from all over the world. . . . All religions, sexual orientations, and ethnic groups are strongly represented."

SYRACUSE UNIVERSITY

FINANCIAL AID: 315-443-1513 • E-MAIL: ORANGE@SYR.EDU • WEBSITE: WWW.SYRACUSE.EDU

ADMISSIONS

Very important factors considered include: Academic GPA, application essay, character/personal qualities, class rank, level of applicant's interest, recommendation(s), rigor of secondary school record, standardized test scores. *Important factors considered include:* Extracurricular activities, interview, talent/ability, volunteer work, work experience. *Other factors considered include:* alumni/ae relation, first generation, racial/ethnic status. SAT or ACT required; ACT with Writing component required. TOEFL required of all international applicants. High school diploma is required, and GED is accepted. *Academic units required:* 4 English, 3 math, 3 science (3 science labs), 2 foreign language, 3 social studies, 5 academic electives. *Academic units recommended:* 4 English, 3 math, 3 science (3 science labs), 3 foreign language, 3 social studies, 5 academic electives.

The Inside Word

Syracuse University is divided into nine colleges, and applicants apply to the college in which they are interested. Most colleges make specific requirements of applicants (for example: a portfolio, an audition, or specific high school course work) in addition to SU's general admissions requirements. Applicants are allowed to indicate a second and third choice—you may still gain admission even if you don't get into your first-choice program.

FINANCIAL AID

Students should submit: FAFSA, CSS/Financial Aid PROFILE, Noncustodial PROFILE, Business/Farm Supplement. Regular filing deadline is February 1. The Princeton Review suggests that all financial aid forms be submitted as soon as possible after January 1. *Need-based scholarships/grants offered:* Pell Grant, SEOG, state scholarships/grants, the school's own gift aid. *Loan aid offered:* FFEL Subsidized Stafford, FFEL Unsubsidized Stafford, FFEL PLUS, Federal Perkins Loan. Applicants will be notified of awards on or about April 1. Federal Work-Study Program available. Institutional employment available. Off-campus job opportunities are good.

FROM THE ADMISSIONS OFFICE

"Syracuse University provides a dynamic learning environment with a focus on scholarship in action, a university where excellence is connected to ideas, problems, and professions in the world. Students at Syracuse University focus on interactive, collaborative, and interdisciplinary learning while choosing their course of study from myriad options; architecture, liberal arts, education, engineering, human services and health professions, information studies, management, public communications, and visual and performing arts. Almost half of undergraduates study abroad. SU operates centers in London, Madrid, Florence, Beijing, Hong Kong, and Strasbourg. New facilities continue to expand scholarship in action opportunities for students. The new 160,000-square-foot Whitman School of Management building is a state-of-the-art facility for all management students. SU's warehouse in downtown Syracuse is currently home to the architecture program and provides the kind of flexible space that is ideal for the design studios. The newly renovated Tolley Building, one of the treasured icons of the campus, is the home of our new Center for the Public and Collaborative Humanities. The innovative and student-focused Newhouse Public Communications Center III, opening in Fall 2007, houses research centers, a high-tech convergence lab, and meeting rooms for student activities, among other facilities. A $107 million Life Sciences Complex will open in the Fall of 2008 and promote interdisciplinary research and education, signaling a new era in scientific research and teaching.

"A distinction of the SU education is the breadth of opportunity combined with individualized attention. Our student/faculty ratio is 12:1, and average class size is 27 students. Only 3 percent of all classes have more than 100 students. Outside the classroom, students are encouraged to immerse themselves in organizations and to take advantage of the cultural and entertainment opportunities available in the city of Syracuse.

"Freshman applicants for Fall 2008 will be required to take the new SAT (or ACT with the Writing component). The new SAT Critical Reading and Math sections will be used in the admissions decisions, since they differ from the old version."

SELECTIVITY

Admissions Rating	92
# of applicants	19,744
% of applicants accepted	51
% of acceptees attending	30
# accepting a place on wait list	1,543
% admitted from wait list	12
# of early decision applicants	821
% accepted early decision	71

FRESHMAN PROFILE

Range SAT Critical Reading	550–650
Range SAT Math	570–680
Range ACT Composite	24–29
Minimum Paper TOEFL	560
Minimum Computer Based TOEFL	217
Average HS GPA	3.6
% graduated top 10% of class	45
% graduated top 25% of class	78
% graduated top 50% of class	97

DEADLINES

Early decision application deadline	11/15
Early decision notification	12/30
Regular application deadline	1/1
Regular notification	3/1
Nonfall registration?	yes

APPLICANTS ALSO LOOK AT AND SOMETIMES PREFER

Boston University, Cornell University, New York University, Pennsylvania State University—University Park, University of Maryland—College Park

FINANCIAL FACTS

Financial Aid Rating	87
Annual tuition	$28,820
Room & Board	$10,420
Books and supplies	$1,234
Required fees	$1,145
% frosh rec. need-based scholarship or grant aid	54
% UG rec. need-based scholarship or grant aid	52
% frosh rec. need-based self-help aid	50
% UG rec. need-based self-help aid	50
% frosh rec. any financial aid	72
% UG rec. any financial aid	72

TEMPLE UNIVERSITY

1801 NORTH BROAD STREET, PHILADELPHIA, PA 19122-6096 • ADMISSIONS: 215-204-7200 • FAX: 215-204-5694

CAMPUS LIFE

Quality of Life Rating	77
Fire Safety Rating	98
Type of school	public
Environment	metropolis

STUDENTS

Total undergrad enrollment	24,070
% male/female	45/55
% from out of state	22
% from public high school	83
% live on campus	20
% in (# of) fraternities	1 (13)
% in (# of) sororities	1 (12)
% African American	18
% Asian	9
% Caucasian	58
% Hispanic	3
% international	3
# of countries represented	137

SURVEY SAYS . . .

Great computer facilities
Great library
Athletic facilities are great
Diverse student types on campus
Great off-campus food
Lots of beer drinking
(Almost) everyone smokes

ACADEMICS

Academic Rating	76
Calendar	semester
Student/faculty ratio	17:1
Profs interesting rating	68
Profs accessible rating	73
Most common lab size	20–29 students
Most common reg class size	10–19 students

MOST POPULAR MAJORS

biology/biological sciences
elementary education and teaching
psychology

STUDENTS SAY

Academics

Students find "very broad choices in classes and majors" within Temple's 12 schools offering undergraduate academic programs. They also find various levels of classroom intimacy, as "class sizes range from about five students up to 200 depending on level and honors." These broad options are a consequence of the school's large enrollment. Another consequence is the fact that "most professors here have a huge number of students to take care of," which means "A student can get lost easily in the numbers." Due to that reality, students who take the initiative are the ones who do best here: "Temple is a great example of a university where you get out what you put in. If you work hard then you will be recognized and succeed." This is not to say that professors are deaf to their students' needs. On the contrary, "Professors are very accessible and genuinely want to help you learn, but you will be working for that A; don't expect it to be handed to you." The academic environment "is intellectually challenging. Due to the diverse nature of both the faculty and student body, professors usually challenge us to assimilate disparate cultural views and to affirm or change our own views of other cultures."

Administratively, "Every Temple student, at one time, has gotten the 'Temple run-around.' In other words, because the school is so big, sometimes finding the exact person you need to talk to is impossible due to limited office hours and [the fact] that the Temple staff has very limited knowledge of other Temple services." Students appreciate the fact that "the technology is outstanding" at Temple, but complain that the school "needs to build more on-campus housing for students." "After sophomore year you are no longer able to live in dorms," and "The surrounding area is not known for having abundant off-campus housing options."

Life

As you consider Temple, keep in mind its hometown: "This is Philly. There are always things to do. There are plenty of museums and historical tours, there are many places to shop, and the food is so diverse and tasty—there is always something new to try." What's more, "There are subway stops at each end of the campus, so it's a breeze to get to Center City." But you don't have to travel far to socialize: "There are a few college bars just steps away from campus which have gotten extremely popular recently." You don't even have to leave campus if you don't want to. "We go to the bars here (there are two on campus); the SAC has food and the new Student Center has everything you could want," writes one satisfied student. "Frats and sororities are pretty unpopular on the whole," however, so "Temple isn't a bona fide party school."

Student Body

The "student body is so diverse," it often feels to students as if "There is a little of everything at Temple University": "From goth to preppy, from European to Asian, from straight male to transsexual, Temple has it all." "Students come from so many diverse backgrounds; no common denominator among them can really be found." This diversity might be "the reason why all students feel welcome here." It also "makes it a great place to learn and live. It's a full cultural experience." If you absolutely had to describe a typical student, you might say that "most students here care about their grades, and you will find lots of people in the library studying at early hours in the morning at finals time."

FINANCIAL AID: 215-204-8760 • E-MAIL: TUADM@TEMPLE.EDU • WEBSITE: WWW.TEMPLE.EDU

ADMISSIONS

Very important factors considered include: Academic GPA, class rank, rigor of secondary school record. *Important factors considered include:* Standardized test scores. *Other factors considered include:* Alumni/ae relation, application essay, character/personal qualities, extracurricular activities, recommendation(s), talent/ability, volunteer work, work experience. SAT or ACT required; ACT with Writing component required. TOEFL required of all international applicants. High school diploma is required, and GED is accepted. *Academic units required:* 4 English, 3 math, 2 science (1 science lab), 2 foreign language, 2 social studies, 1 history, 1 academic elective. *Academic units recommended:* 4 English, 4 math, 3 science (2 science labs), 2 foreign language, 2 social studies, 2 history, 3 academic electives.

The Inside Word

Temple's distinguished reputation and urban environment make the university a good choice for many students, especially Pennsylvania residents. Admissions Officers are fairly objective about their approach to application assessment: They tend to focus principally on GPA, class rank, and test scores. There are no minimum requirements, though, so students who show potential in more subjective arenas should make sure they convey their accomplishments in their applications.

FINANCIAL AID

Students should submit: FAFSA. The Princeton Review suggests that all financial aid forms be submitted as soon as possible after January 1. *Need-based scholarships/grants offered:* Pell Grant, SEOG, state scholarships/grants, private scholarships, the school's own gift aid, Federal Nursing Scholarship. *Loan aid offered:* FFEL Subsidized Stafford, FFEL Unsubsidized Stafford, FFEL PLUS, Federal Perkins Loan, Federal Nursing Loan, college/university loans from institutional funds. Applicants will be notified of awards on a rolling basis beginning or about February 15. Federal Work-Study Program available. Institutional employment available. Off-campus job opportunities are excellent.

FROM THE ADMISSIONS OFFICE

"Temple combines the academic resources and intellectual stimulation of a large research university with the intimacy of a small college. The university experienced record growth in attracting new students from all 50 states and over 125 countries: up 60 percent in 3 years. Students choose from 125 undergraduate majors. Special academic programs include honors, learning communities for first-year undergraduates, co-op education, and study abroad. Temple has seven regional campuses, including Main Campus and the Health Sciences Center in historic Philadelphia, suburban Temple University, Ambler, and overseas campuses in Tokyo and Rome. Main Campus is home to the Tuttleman Learning Center, with 1,000 computer stations linked to Paley Library. New in 2006, our Tech Center has over 600 computer workstations, 100 laptops, and a Starbucks. The Liacouras Center is a state-of-the-art entertainment, recreation, and sports complex that hosts concerts, plays, trade shows, and college and professional athletics. It also includes the Independence Blue Cross Student Recreation Center, a major fitness facility for students now and in the future. Students can also take advantage of the new Student Fieldhouse. The university has constructed two new dorms, built to meet an unprecedented demand for main campus housing.

"Applicants for Fall 2008 are required to take the new version of the SAT (or the ACT with Writing), but students may submit scores from the old SAT as well. The best Verbal and Math scores from either test will be considered."

SELECTIVITY
Admissions Rating	82
# of applicants	18,140
% of applicants accepted	60
% of acceptees attending	36

FRESHMAN PROFILE
Range SAT Critical Reading	490–590
Range SAT Math	500–600
Range SAT Writing	480–580
Range ACT Composite	20–25
Minimum Paper TOEFL	527
Minimum Computer Based TOEFL	197
Average HS GPA	3.26
% graduated top 10% of class	18
% graduated top 25% of class	50
% graduated top 50% of class	88

DEADLINES
Regular application deadline	4/1
Regular notification	rolling
Nonfall registration?	yes

APPLICANTS ALSO LOOK AT
AND OFTEN PREFER
Lehigh University, Pennsylvania State University—University Park, University of Pennsylvania, University of Pittsburgh—Pittsburgh Campus
AND SOMETIMES PREFER
Drexel University, New York University, Rutgers, The State University of New Jersey—New Brunswick, Saint Joseph's University (PA), Villanova University
AND RARELY PREFER
Gettysburg College, LaSalle University, West Chester University of Pennsylvania, Widener University

FINANCIAL FACTS
Financial Aid Rating	78
Annual in-state tuition	$9,680
Annual out-of-state tuition	$17,724
Room & Board	$8,230
Books and supplies	$800
Required fees	$500
% frosh rec. need-based scholarship or grant aid	67
% UG rec. need-based scholarship or grant aid	64
% frosh rec. need-based self-help aid	57
% UG rec. need-based self-help aid	56
% frosh rec. any financial aid	87
% UG rec. any financial aid	88

TEXAS A&M UNIVERSITY—COLLEGE STATION

ADMISSIONS COUNSELING, COLLEGE STATION, TX 77843-1265 • ADMISSIONS: 979-845-3741 • FAX: 979-847-8737

CAMPUS LIFE
Quality of Life Rating	93
Fire Safety Rating	60*
Type of school	public
Environment	city

STUDENTS
Total undergrad enrollment	36,580
% male/female	52/48
% from out of state	3
% live on campus	25
% in (# of) fraternities	6 (33)
% in (# of) sororities	12 (23)
% African American	3
% Asian	4
% Caucasian	79
% Hispanic	12
% Native American	1
% international	1
# of countries represented	125

SURVEY SAYS . . .
Great computer facilities
Great library
Athletic facilities are great
Students are friendly
Everyone loves the Aggies
Student publications are popular

ACADEMICS
Academic Rating	72
Calendar	semester
Student/faculty ratio	20:1
Profs interesting rating	71
Profs accessible rating	78
% profs teaching UG courses	75
% classes taught by TAs	25
Most common lab size	20–29 students
Most common reg class size	20–29 students

MOST POPULAR MAJORS
biological and physical sciences
multi/interdisciplinary studies
operations management and
supervision

STUDENTS SAY
Academics
"The excellence of a great research university filled with many traditions and the warm hospitality of a safe, small town" are the hallmarks of a Texas A&M education. United by the school's hallowed traditions, undergrads at this agriculture and engineering powerhouse "are the most fiercely loyal people to the school and other Aggies," and they can't stop bragging about how great their academic and extracurricular lives are. One student writes, "During the college search, I always heard about colleges looking for 'the well-rounded student.' Texas A&M's strength is being a 'well-rounded university,'" particularly for those interested in veterinary science, agricultural science, construction and engineering, business, and life sciences. Most departments hold students to "very high standards"; as one student puts it, "At Texas A&M University, students generally get what they give. An A is well earned, an F is deserved." Another adds, "Classes are extremely hard, but the Aggie ring is worth more this way." That ring provides access to "the Aggie network," alumni of A&M who "help make a lot of things possible," especially "finding a job. I've heard stories of some people getting hired at the sight of their Aggie ring." With A&M "taking many steps, especially in the past few years, to really make A&M an even stronger university and research institution"—including "hiring a lot of new faculty," and "construction of new facilities on campus"—there are now more reasons than ever to love being an Aggie. How great is it? Ultimately you have to find out for yourself, because "From the outside looking in, you can't understand it, and from the inside looking out, you can't explain it!"

Life
A&M "is rich in tradition such as the Twelfth Man, Muster, Silvertaps, Reveille, 'Howdy,' the Corps of Cadets, Elephant Walk, and Maroon Out, just to name a few." If you're already familiar with these terms, you probably know how deeply they permeate campus life. Others should check out the school's website to learn more about them; how you feel about the traditions will strongly impact how much you enjoy life at A&M. Aggies tend to be enthusiastic about sports, both attending games and participating in club, intramural, and pickup games. Although social activities are bound to be extremely diverse at a campus this large, many students here tell us that Northgate, a "row of bars and restaurants off the north side of campus," is the place to go; live music ("Texas country music is real big at A&M"), drinks, and dancing are all on the menu. Hometown College Station "is a small city, so there aren't many activities available off-campus, but the city is at the crossroads to the three major areas in Texas: Houston, Dallas–Fort Worth, and the Austin–San Antonio area. Weekend trips to these areas are fairly common."

Student Body
While "It is true that there is a very large Caucasian population at TAMU," there are also "large numbers of Middle Eastern, Asian, and Hispanic students" as well, providing a good deal of diversity on campus. It's Texas, and it's not Austin, so it should come as no surprise that A&M students tend to be politically conservative. Some point out that "conservative students are probably the most vocal, making it appear our school is more conservative [than it is]. From my experience, most students place themselves in the middle of left and right, making informed decisions when it comes to politics." Many here "are involved in student organizations and have a good social life as well." About 5 percent of the student body participates in the Corps of Cadets, "a senior military academy within the university." One cadet tells us that he and his peers "are the most visible people on campus and live with a structured military lifestyle."

FINANCIAL AID: 979-845-3236 • E-MAIL: ADMISSIONS@TAMU.EDU • WEBSITE: WWW.TAMU.EDU

ADMISSIONS

Very important factors considered include: Academic GPA, class rank, extracurricular activities, rigor of secondary school record, standardized test scores, state residency, talent/ability. *Important factors considered include:* Application essay, volunteer work, work experience. *Other factors considered include:* Character/personal qualities, first generation, geographical residence, recommendation(s). SAT or ACT required; ACT with Writing component required. TOEFL required of all international applicants. High school diploma is required, and GED is accepted. *Academic units required:* 4 English, 3 math, 3 science (2 science labs), 2 foreign language, 2 social studies, 1 history. *Academic units recommended:* 4 English, 3 math, 3 science (2 science labs), 2 foreign language, 2 social studies, 1 history, 1 computer course.

The Inside Word

Texas A&M uses some cut-and-dried admissions criteria: Students graduating in the top 10 percent of a recognized public or private high school in the state of Texas are automatically in; all they have to do is get their applications in on time. Applicants in the top quarter of their graduating class who have a combined SAT Math/Critical Reading score of 1300 (minimum score of 600 in each component) are also automatically in, as are such students who earn a composite ACT score of 30 (minimum 27 on the Math and English sections). All other applications are deemed "Review Admits" to be sorted through by the Admissions Committee.

FINANCIAL AID

Students should submit: FAFSA, institution's own financial aid form, Financial Aid Transcripts (for transfer students). The Princeton Review suggests that all financial aid forms be submitted as soon as possible after January 1. *Need-based scholarships/grants offered:* Pell Grant, SEOG, state scholarships/grants, private scholarships, the school's own gift aid. *Loan aid offered:* FFEL Subsidized Stafford, FFEL Unsubsidized Stafford, FFEL PLUS, Federal Perkins Loan, state loans, college/university loans from institutional funds. Applicants will be notified of awards on or about March 15. Off-campus job opportunities are excellent.

FROM THE ADMISSIONS OFFICE

"Established in 1876 as the first public college in the state, Texas A&M University has become a world leader in teaching, research, and public service. Located in College Station in the heart of Texas, it is centrally situated among three of the country's 10 largest cities: Dallas, Houston, and San Antonio. Texas A&M is ranked nationally in these four areas: enrollment (seventh in enrollment, 45,380 for Fall 2006); enrollment of top students (sixteenth in number of new National Merit Scholars for Fall 2005); value of research (sixteenth with $457 million in 2004); and endowment ($5.1 billion as of 2006).

"Freshman applicants for Fall 2008 are required to take the new SAT or the ACT. We will not accept scores from the old SAT. We will use the applicant's best single testing date score in decision-making."

SELECTIVITY

Admissions Rating	83
# of applicants	17,410
% of applicants accepted	77
% of acceptees attending	59
# accepting a place on wait list	1,278
% admitted from wait list	83

FRESHMAN PROFILE

Range SAT Critical Reading	520–630
Range SAT Math	560–660
Range SAT Writing	500–610
Range ACT Composite	23–28
Minimum Paper TOEFL	550
% graduated top 10% of class	46
% graduated top 25% of class	77
% graduated top 50% of class	90

DEADLINES

Regular application deadline	2/1
Regular notification	rolling
Nonfall registration?	yes

APPLICANTS ALSO LOOK AT

AND OFTEN PREFER
Rice University

AND SOMETIMES PREFER
Baylor University, Louisiana State University, Texas Tech University, The University of Texas at Austin

AND RARELY PREFER
Southern Methodist University, Stephen F. Austin State University

FINANCIAL FACTS

Financial Aid Rating	82
Annual in-state tuition	$4,371
Annual out-of-state tuition	$12,621
Room & Board	$7,660
Books and supplies	$1,280
Required fees	$2,595
% frosh rec. need-based scholarship or grant aid	34
% UG rec. need-based scholarship or grant aid	29
% frosh rec. need-based self-help aid	22
% UG rec. need-based self-help aid	25

TEXAS CHRISTIAN UNIVERSITY

OFFICE OF ADMISSIONS, TCU BOX 297013, FORT WORTH, TX 76129 • ADMISSIONS: 817-257-7490 • FAX: 817-257-7268

STUDENTS SAY

Academics

Texas Christian University is a small private university affiliated with the Disciples of Christ Church. TCU is "highly respected in Texas," which creates "strong" opportunities for "postgrad jobs or further education." This suits the "career-oriented student body" as does "the location in a large city with lots of future job connections and opportunities." Many TCU students pursue business-related majors through the "top-ranked" Neeley School of Business. TCU's advertising program is "one of the best in the nation," and the university also boasts a "great School of Education," an "excellent premedical program," and a "great social work program." In fact, "The school has many different highly ranked programs, which is appealing to students who can't decide on a major." Students appreciate TCU's commitment to developing "ethical leaders" and love the fact that TCU "has a small-campus feel, but offers all the opportunities . . . you would expect to find on a large campus." Since "The vast majority of all departments give the students at least two semesters of working or internship opportunities," almost all TCU students graduate with real-world experience. TCU's professors "know your name" and "care about you as an individual." They "are more than willing to meet with you outside of class" as long as you show "a substantial amount of effort in class."

Life

According to one student, "The two most popular things at TCU are the Greek life and the football team (when they are winning)." Many students survive happily outside the Greek system, but the divide between Greeks and independents is clearly visible. As one student explains, "Greek life is huge," and if you're not in a Greek organization, "Most all of your friends are other non-Greek people as well." For this reason, campus life can be "very clique-oriented" and can lead to a feeling of "two social classes, which really prevents any real student unity." Fortunately, TCU offers "a very wide variety of activities" outside of Greek life. Many students "are into student government and the campus newspaper (*The Skiff*)," and "There are always events taking place, from theater to music to sports." Since the school is located in a major metropolitan area, "Much of the activity takes place off campus." Students enjoy a "big outpouring of support from the community," and Fort Worth and Dallas offer an "abundance of things to do and places to go," including "great bars, clubs, restaurants, and theaters."

Student Body

The typical TCU student is "frat-tastic: Girls wear a polo shirt, designer jeans, and the latest trendy handbag. The guys are similar, minus the handbag." Most tend to be "White, upper-middle-class, and good-looking" and "usually from the South." Not everyone fits this mold, though. Students point out that "with such a big Greek concentration here, it seems that everyone is rich, shallow, and snobby, but that just tends to be the people you notice." TCU "emphasizes diversity," and all students "manage to find an organization or a group to fit into." Fitting in, however, is relative: "If you're not Greek at TCU, you're nothing, in many people's opinions." Moreover, students from a "lower-income family" may find that they "fit in all right, but aren't accepted into the 'highest' social circles because they can't afford the parties." Overall, TCU students describe themselves as "friendly, easygoing," with a "fun-loving character," and "very fashionable."

FINANCIAL AID: 817-257-7858 • E-MAIL: FROGMAIL@TCU.EDU • WEBSITE: WWW.TCU.EDU

ADMISSIONS

Very important factors considered include: Academic GPA, application essay, character/personal qualities, class rank, recommendation(s), rigor of secondary school record, standardized test scores. *Important factors considered include:* Extracurricular activities, geographical residence, level of applicant's interest, racial/ethnic status, religious affiliation/commitment, talent/ability, volunteer work, work experience. *Other factors considered include:* Alumni/ae relation, first generation, interview. SAT or ACT required; ACT with Writing component recommended. TOEFL required of all international applicants. High school diploma is required, and GED is not accepted. *Academic units required:* 4 English, 3 math, 3 science, 2 foreign language, 3 social studies, 2 academic electives. *Academic units recommended:* 4 English, 4 math, 4 science, 4 foreign language, 4 social studies, 4 academic electives.

The Inside Word

Admissions Counselors at TCU make sure they consider a variety of factors before making admit decisions—students are rarely discounted because they are weak in one particular category. That said, most acceptance letters go to well-rounded applicants. As most TCU students are Texas residents, those applying from out of state are at a slight advantage in the admissions process.

FINANCIAL AID

Students should submit: FAFSA. Regular filing deadline is May 1. The Princeton Review suggests that all financial aid forms be submitted as soon as possible after January 1. *Need-based scholarships/grants offered:* Pell Grant, SEOG, state scholarships/grants, private scholarships, the school's own gift aid, Federal Nursing Scholarship. *Loan aid offered:* FFEL Subsidized Stafford, FFEL Unsubsidized Stafford, FFEL PLUS, Federal Perkins Loan, Federal Nursing Loan, state loans. Applicants will be notified of awards on a rolling basis beginning or about March 1.

FROM THE ADMISSIONS OFFICE

"TCU is a major teaching and research university with the feel of a small college. The TCU academic experience includes small classes with top faculty; cutting-edge technology; a liberal arts and sciences core curriculum; and real-life application though faculty-directed research, group projects, and internships. While TCU faculty members are recognized for research, their main focus is on teaching and mentoring students. The friendly campus community welcomes new students at Frog Camp before classes begin, where students find three days of fun meeting new friends, learning campus traditions, and serving the community. Campus life includes 200 clubs and organizations, a spirited NCAA Division I athletics program, and numerous productions from professional schools of the arts. More than half of the students participate in a wide array of intramural sports, and about 35 percent are involved in Greek organizations, including ones emphasizing ethnic diversity as well as the Christian faith. The historic relationship to the Christian Church (Disciples of Christ) means that instead of teaching a particular viewpoint, TCU encourages students to consider and follow their own beliefs. The university's mission—to educate individuals to think and act as ethical leaders and responsible citizens in a global community—influences everything from course work to study abroad to the way Horned Frogs act and interact. From National Merit Scholars to those just now realizing their academic potential, TCU attracts and serves students who are learning to change the world.

"TCU will accept either the SAT or the ACT (with or without the Writing component) in admission and scholarship processes. The Writing sections will be considered alongside the TCU application essay."

SELECTIVITY

Admissions Rating	82
# of applicants	11,691
% of applicants accepted	48
% of acceptees attending	30
# accepting a place on wait list	550
% admitted from wait list	39

FRESHMAN PROFILE

Range SAT Critical Reading	520–620
Range SAT Math	540–640
Range ACT Composite	23–28
Minimum Paper TOEFL	550
Minimum Computer Based TOEFL	213
% graduated top 10% of class	32
% graduated top 25% of class	64
% graduated top 50% of class	93

DEADLINES

Regular application deadline	2/15
Regular notification	4/1
Nonfall registration?	yes

FINANCIAL FACTS

Financial Aid Rating	78
Annual tuition	$22,980
Room & Board	$7,120
Books and supplies	$810
Required fees	$48
% frosh rec. need-based scholarship or grant aid	33
% UG rec. need-based scholarship or grant aid	37
% frosh rec. need-based self-help aid	29
% UG rec. need-based self-help aid	38
% frosh rec. any financial aid	73
% UG rec. any financial aid	72

THOMAS AQUINAS COLLEGE

10000 NORTH OJAI ROAD, SANTA PAULA, CA 93060 • ADMISSION: 800-634-9797 • FAX: 805-525-9342

CAMPUS LIFE
Quality of Life Rating	98
Fire Safety Rating	74
Type of school	private
Affiliation	Roman Catholic
Environment	rural

STUDENTS
Total undergrad enrollment	351
% male/female	50/50
% from out of state	58
% from public high school	19
% live on campus	99
% Asian	3
% Caucasian	78
% Hispanic	6
% Native American	1
% international	8
# of countries represented	8

SURVEY SAYS . . .
Class discussions encouraged
No one cheats
Students are friendly
Students are very religious
Frats and sororities are unpopular or nonexistent
Very little drug use

ACADEMICS
Academic Rating	98
Calendar	semester
Student/faculty ratio	11:1
Profs interesting rating	98
Profs accessible rating	99
% profs teaching UG courses	100
% classes taught by TAs	0
Most common	
reg class size	10-19 students

STUDENTS SAY

Academics

"This is not a normal university or college," writes a Thomas Aquinas undergraduate—and she knows what she's talking about. TAC "has no majors or minor degrees available." It doesn't use textbooks, and professors—called "tutors"—don't give lectures. So what shape does education take at this tiny, Catholic college? Well, "The college's curriculum is an integrated liberal arts program based primarily on the study of the Great Books." A junior clarifies, "The Great Books . . . are those books that have shaped the entire history of Western thought." During their 4 years, students meet in seminars to discuss readings in a variety of subjects, including "grammar, logic, rhetoric, arithmetic, geometry, music, astronomy . . . science, and philosophy. All of these discussions are ordered towards the highest science, theology." The seminars are small, and class participation is expected. Another twist in the TAC approach is that "everyone here takes the same classes," freshman through senior year. (On this note, prospective transfer students should be aware that "no transfer credits are accepted" because TAC's Bachelor's in Liberal Arts can't be earned without taking the full 4-year curriculum.) These undergrads praise the "true love of learning shown by both the students and the professors," and tell us that professors not only "guide" them in class, but hang out with them afterwards. "It is not uncommon for them to take a group of students out to dinner or host them in their homes," writes a junior.

Life

What do students at TAC think about in their free time? Well, they ponder the usual questions, like, "What is life? Why are we here? What makes the heavens move? Can you prove that God exists?" In general, writes a senior, "Life at Thomas Aquinas College is focused around the academic program," which means that the questions spurred in class regularly carry into Friday and Saturday nights. "According to that [academic] focus," continues the senior, "there are social activities, such as optional classes, designed to directly complement the classes. Official campus parties, such as formal dances and banquet dinners, are also in line with this focus. Off-campus activities, whether it be drinking in the woods or going to the opera, also complement the program." In addition, "Students often go hiking in Los Padres National Forest," which picks up at the edge of campus. "Santa Barbara is close," and Los Angeles isn't too far either, each offering its own satisfying distractions. One junior writes, "We love getting off campus to go see movies, operas, plays, LA Philharmonic performances, the Getty, Huntington Gardens and Library, beaches . . . or the local Blockbuster." Students do have a few complaints about campus life. For instance, "The school's policies concerning conduct, dress code, and rules of residence tend to be rather stringent." Also, "The school is so small [that] it doesn't have the sports facilities, or the clubs and groups that most other colleges have."

Student Body

"This is a Catholic college, and it's proud of its Catholic identity." Approximately 10 percent of the students are non-Catholic. In addition, "A large majority is politically conservative, and a large majority is Caucasian." The student body also includes a noticeable number of "homeschoolers from large families." What these students all have in common is that they are "very serious about their faith and their intellectual life." This lust for learning is something that TAC undergrads are very proud of. "The typical student at TAC has a zeal for seeking truth," writes a student who walked away from more than 3 years of mechanical engineering training at another university after reading the college's founding document. But these students aren't just serious bookworms. They're gabby and social, with a particular itch for dancing— "swing, folk, and ballroom" being the favorites.

FINANCIAL AID: 800-634-9797 • E-MAIL: ADMISSIONS@THOMASAQUINAS.EDU • WEBSITE: WWW.THOMASAQUINAS.EDU

ADMISSIONS

Very important factors considered include: Application essay, character/personal qualities, level of applicant's interest, recommendation(s), rigor of secondary school record, standardized test scores. *Important factors considered include:* Academic GPA, religious affiliation/commitment. *Other factors considered include:* Class rank, extracurricular activities, interview, talent/ability, volunteer work, work experience. SAT or ACT required; TOEFL required of all international applicants. High school diploma is required, and GED is accepted. *Academic units required:* 4 English, 3 math, 2 foreign language, 2 history. *Academic units recomended:* 4 English, 4 math, 3 science, (2 science labs), 2 foreign language, 2 history, 3 academic electives.

The Inside Word

Thomas Aquinas' unique curriculum helps distinguish the small college within the field of higher education, and many interested students cite the school's academic philosophy as one of its chief attractors. TAC professors demand that their students demonstrate intellectual curiosity and enthusiasm, and candidates must display the same level of scholarly zest. The college maintains a rolling admissions policy; however, openings fill quickly, so it is best to get applications in early.

FINANCIAL AID

Students should submit: FAFSA, institution's own financial aid form, state aid form, Federal Income Tax Returns, Noncustodial Parent Statement. The Princeton Review suggests that all financial aid forms be submitted as soon as possible after January 1. *Need-based scholarships/grants offered:* Pell Grant, state scholarships/grants, private scholarships, the school's own gift aid. *Loan aid offered:* FFEL Subsidized Stafford, FFEL Unsubsidized Stafford, FFEL PLUS, college/university loans from institutional funds, Canadian student loans. Applicants will be notified of awards on a rolling basis beginning or about January 1. Off-campus job opportunities are fair.

FROM THE ADMISSIONS OFFICE

"Thomas Aquinas College holds with confidence that the human mind is capable of knowing the truth about reality. The college further holds that living according to the truth is necessary for human happiness, and that truth is best comprehended through the harmonious work of faith and reason. The intellectual virtues are understood to be essential, and the college considers the cultivation of those virtues the primary work of Catholic liberal education.

"The academic program designed to achieve this goal is comprehensive and unified—and it includes no textbooks or lecture classes. In every course—from philosophy, theology, mathematics, and science to language, music, literature and history—students actually read the greatest written works in those disciplines, both ancient and modern: Homer, Plato, Aristotle, Augustine, Aquinas, Newton, Maxwell, Einstein, the Founding Fathers of the American republic, Shakespeare and T. S. Eliot, to name a few. Instead of attending lecture classes, students gather in small tutorials, seminars, and laboratories for Socratic-style discussions.

"One mark of the program's success is the variety of professions and careers that graduates enter. Nearly half attend graduate and professional schools in a wide array of disciplines; among them, philosophy, theology, law, and the sciences are most often chosen.

"SAT or ACT (Writing component encouraged) scores are required, and the essays written for these tests are reviewed by the Admission Committee. However, scores in Critical Reading and Math (SAT) and English and Mathematics (ACT) are more central in the consideration of a student's application."

SELECTIVITY

Admissions Rating	92
# of applicants	207
% of applicants accepted	83
% of acceptees attending	60
# accepting a place on wait list	47
% admitted from wait list	57

FRESHMAN PROFILE

Range SAT Critical Reading	600–740
Range SAT Math	570–660
Range ACT Composite	25–29
Minimum Paper TOEFL	570
Minimum Computer Based TOEFL	230
Average HS GPA	3.44
% graduated top 10% of class	75
% graduated top 25% of class	75
% graduated top 50% of class	100

DEADLINES

Regular notification	rolling
Nonfall registration?	no

APPLICANTS ALSO LOOK AT AND SOMETIMES PREFER

Benedictine College, Christendom College, Franciscan University of Steubenville, The Catholic University of America, University of Dallas

FINANCIAL FACTS

Financial Aid Rating	99
Annual tuition	$20,400
Room & Board	$6,600
Books and supplies	$450
% frosh rec. need-based scholarship or grant aid	60
% UG rec. need-based scholarship or grant aid	60
% frosh rec. need-based self-help aid	69
% UG rec. need-based self-help aid	67
% frosh rec. any financial aid	69
% UG rec. any financial aid	68

TRANSYLVANIA UNIVERSITY

300 NORTH BROADWAY, LEXINGTON, KY 40508-1797 • ADMISSIONS: 859-233-8242 • FAX: 859-233-8797

CAMPUS LIFE

Quality of Life Rating	**88**
Fire Safety Rating	**98**
Type of school	private
Affiliation	Disciples of Christ
Environment	city

STUDENTS

Total undergrad enrollment	1,117
% male/female	59/41
% from out of state	18
% from public high school	85
% live on campus	77
% in (# of) fraternities	50 (4)
% in (# of) sororities	50 (4)
% African American	2
% Asian	2
% Caucasian	87
% Hispanic	2

SURVEY SAYS . . .

Small classes
Athletic facilities are great
Frats and sororities dominate social scene
Lots of beer drinking

ACADEMICS

Academic Rating	**89**
Calendar	4-4-1
Student/faculty ratio	13:1
Profs interesting rating	92
Profs accessible rating	91
% profs teaching UG courses	100
% classes taught by TAs	0
Most common lab size	10–19 students
Most common reg class size	10–19 students

MOST POPULAR MAJORS
biology/biological sciences
business/commerce
psychology

STUDENTS SAY

Academics

Transylvania University "prides itself in its rich history, academic excellence, personable campus, and friendly environment." Students rave about the school's strong sense of community; as one student notes, "Professors, administration, and the students are always including each other in activities." Another student adds, "The professors are always available, and I never feel badly about going and asking them questions. They seem to like seeing students all the time." Undergrads report that "academics are tough, and studying is definitely a must. But classes are fun and small, allowing for you to have lots of individual attention." The school also offers resources such as a writing center and a number of tutoring programs, which students describe as "very helpful." The university also has an "excellent premedical program" with "an awesome acceptance rate into medical school." Students also say that the "Education Department is fantastic," and also rave about the "great science program." The administration is "highly aware of student opinions and genuinely cares about and reacts to student needs and wants." In case any administrators are reading, several undergrads suggested that "the dorms could all use a face-lift."

Life

"Work hard, play hard" is the credo by which most Transylvania students abide. As one undergrad explains, "Student life at Transylvania is almost as busy as the course work. There is always something going on, from Greek functions to cafeteria themes to concerts and movie nights." Campus is located in downtown Lexington, Kentucky, "a great city that's not too big or small." In the city, students have access to "tons of restaurants, bars, and a nice mall. There is a Starbucks down the street. A favorite hangout is the Atomic Cafe, a cool restaurant and bar with yummy food." On campus, Transylvania "has awesome facilities where we can work out or play games (such as the William T. Young Campus Center and the Clive M. Beck Athletic and Recreational Center), and the school is always willing to listen to our suggestions." The Student Activities Board "normally has something happening every month, such as on-campus concerts, carnivals, or movie nights." Greek life is also alive and well at Transylvania. As one student explains, "Greeks do not have 'houses.' We are a wet campus. Most of the partying goes on right here in the halls on campus. People who take things to extremes get in trouble."

Student Body

Transylvania students are "highly motivated, serious about school, friendly, [and] very involved in campus activities." More than half of the students go Greek, but "The campus and student body are both small enough that Greeks hang out with non-Greeks often." As one undergrad notes, "Students should not feel obligated to join a fraternity or sorority just to fit in." The Transylvania student body is "not very diverse," but students "are accepting of differences, especially race, gender, and sexual orientation." Undergrads report that the student body as a whole "promotes and encourages diversity." The school's small size creates a very close-knit environment. "At Transylvania, you want to see the plays because you know people in them," one undergrad explains. "You want to go to sporting events because you can support your friends. Walking to class, tons of people say 'hi' to you because they actually know you!"

FINANCIAL AID: 859-233-8239 • E-MAIL: ADMISSIONS@TRANSY.EDU • WEBSITE: WWW.TRANSY.EDU

ADMISSIONS

Very important factors considered include: Academic GPA, rigor of secondary school record, standardized test scores. *Important factors considered include:* Application essay, class rank, extracurricular activities, recommendation(s). *Other factors considered include:* Alumni/ae relation, character/personal qualities, geographical residence, interview, talent/ability, volunteer work, work experience. SAT or ACT required; TOEFL required of all international applicants. High school diploma is required, and GED is accepted. *Academic units required:* 4 English, 3 math, 3 science, 2 social studies. *Academic units recommended:* 4 English, 4 math, 4 science, 2 foreign language, 2 social studies, 1 history, 1 academic elective.

Inside Word

Applicants who become successful students at TU have the wherewithal to rise to challenging academic demands and the discipline to do so in an ethical fashion. If you're looking for a place to disappear into an ocean of faces, try the University of Kentucky down the road.

FINANCIAL AID

Students should submit: FAFSA. Regular filing deadline is March 1. The Princeton Review suggests that all financial aid forms be submitted as soon as possible after January 1. *Need-based scholarships/grants offered:* Pell Grant, SEOG, state scholarships/grants, private scholarships, the school's own gift aid. *Loan aid offered:* FFEL Subsidized Stafford, FFEL Unsubsidized Stafford, FFEL PLUS, Federal Perkins Loan, college/university loans from institutional funds. Applicants will be notified of awards on a rolling basis beginning or about March 15. Federal Work-Study Program available. Off-campus job opportunities are excellent.

FROM THE ADMISSIONS OFFICE

"Bright, highly motivated students choose Transylvania for our personal approach to learning and our record of success in preparing them for rewarding careers and fulfilling lives. They attend small classes (many have fewer than 10 students) with highly qualified professors (no teaching assistants) and tackle faculty-directed student research projects in intriguing subjects like neurotransmitters and receptors, computer animation, and local Hispanic culture. Transylvania graduates have won prestigious scholarships and distinguished themselves at highly selective graduate and professional schools.

"Transylvania students consider the world their classroom. They enjoy May term travel courses studying the ancient polis in Greece, language and culture in France, and tropical ecology in Hawaii. Study abroad takes them to Germany, England, Japan, Mexico, and other destinations for a summer, a semester, or a year.

"You'll find Transylvania, a small college, nestled in a big city. Transylvania students soak up the advantages of Lexington, Kentucky, with its population of 260,000, numerous internships and job opportunities, and lots of entertainment. On campus, we have more than 50 co-curricular activities, and 16 varsity teams competing in NCAA Division III.

"While Transylvania is the nation's sixteenth-oldest college and proud of its rich history, its commitments to the exploration of a variety of disciplines, to intellectual inquiry, and to critical thinking have never been more relevant than in today's rapidly changing twenty-first-century world.

"Applicants for Fall 2008 are not required to submit Writing scores from the ACT or the SAT."

SELECTIVITY

Admissions Rating	87
# of applicants	1,335
% of applicants accepted	82
% of acceptees attending	28

FRESHMAN PROFILE

Range SAT Critical Reading	540–660
Range SAT Math	520–650
Range ACT Composite	23–28
Minimum Paper TOEFL	550
Minimum Computer Based TOEFL	213
Average HS GPA	3.56
% graduated top 10% of class	41
% graduated top 25% of class	73
% graduated top 50% of class	96

DEADLINES

Regular application deadline	2/1
Regular notification	3/15
Nonfall registration?	yes

APPLICANTS ALSO LOOK AT AND OFTEN PREFER

Miami University, Vanderbilt University

AND SOMETIMES PREFER

Centre College, University of Kentucky

FINANCIAL FACTS

Financial Aid Rating	81
Annual tuition	$20,120
Room & Board	$6,850
Books and supplies	$750
Required fees	$830
% frosh rec. need-based scholarship or grant aid	71
% UG rec. need-based scholarship or grant aid	62
% frosh rec. need-based self-help aid	53
% UG rec. need-based self-help aid	49
% frosh rec. any financial aid	99
% UG rec. any financial aid	98

TRINITY COLLEGE (CT)

300 SUMMIT STREET, HARTFORD, CT 06016 • ADMISSIONS: 860-297-2180 • FAX: 860-297-2287

STUDENTS SAY

Academics

Connecticut's Trinity College "offers a rare combination of high academic standards, a balanced political climate, intense athletic competitiveness/participation, awesome financial aid" and, last but not least, "a huge party scene," prompting some students to opine that "Trinity offers the most even balance of academics (amazing professors, room to find your niche) and social life" among U.S. colleges. Here, "Monday through Thursday everyone goes to class, studies, and gets their work done," but, "Come the weekend, people let loose and party just as hard as they study." Weekdays offer "a great learning experience that provides ample opportunities," thanks in part to the school's small size (which means undergraduates have opportunities for research), a faculty staffed by "brilliant and caring" professors who "prioritize teaching above publishing," and a library that is "nothing less than phenomenal." Students also appreciate Trinity's urban setting, noting that "the city of Hartford [is used] as a valuable learning tool" and pointing out that, unlike "the majority of top liberal arts schools . . . [where] internship opportunities are limited, Trinity offered me the opportunity [for] many hands-on experiences." This may be particularly true if your field of interest is politics (Trinity's "location in a capital city means lots of opportunities for political internships," explains one student). Other standout departments include English (both literature and creative writing), Engineering, Theater, French, and the interdisciplinary program in human rights.

Life

For many Trinity undergrads, "The fraternities dominate the weekend social scene," and because these groups can be "fairly elitist" when it comes to allowing people into their late-night soirees, "Sometimes it's hard to find something to do." Other students take a broader view of campus life. Such students tell us that new groups are "gaining social power," among them "The Fred (named after late professor Fred Pfiel)," which hosts "open mic evenings, nonalcoholic competitions, [and] theme nights," among other events. They also call out Trinity's Cinestudio, "one of the best on-campus student-run movie theaters in the country." While campus theater, orchestra, a cappella, and chamber groups have limited participation, their performances are often well attended by the student body. Students note that "everything is available on campus so there is minimal effort to find things off campus," especially since students generally agree that "the school is located in a very dangerous part of Hartford, leaving close, walking-distance off-campus options almost nil." Those who have cars "often travel to nicer parts of Hartford or other Connecticut towns." One student observes, "Hartford, Connecticut is not as bad as people make it out to be. It has a lot to offer as long as you are willing to leave campus. There are some great restaurants and lots of shows to go to. Don't let yourself get stuck on campus every weekend."

Student Body

"Despite admissions' efforts, Trinity is still characterized by the New England boarding-school grad in polos and pink pants," undergrads here tell us, although some assert that "what many see as the typical student is actually a minority." Still, "The picture that immediately comes to mind is a blond, blue-eyed girl buying Coach . . . with daddy's money." Adding some diversity is "a growing population of 'Wesleyan-types,' who probably got rejected from our fellow Connecticut school. There's [been] an influx of intelligent, down-to-earth people at Trinity who are passionate about a lot more than getting wasted Thursday through Sunday." Students tend to be "over-wired" when not in class, attached to a "cell phone, IM, computer, [or] iPod, and therefore socially awkward or impolite. . . . In class, they are overachievers, very articulate and competitive. Most spend an impressive amount of time studying."

FINANCIAL AID: 860-297-2046 • E-MAIL: ADMISSIONS.OFFICE@TRINCOLL.EDU • WEBSITE: WWW.TRINCOLL.EDU

ADMISSIONS

Very important factors considered include: Rigor of secondary school record. *Important factors considered include:* Application essay, character/personal qualities, class rank, extracurricular activities, interview, racial/ethnic status, recommendation(s), standardized test scores, talent/ability. *Other factors considered include:* Alumni/ae relation, geographical residence, volunteer work, work experience. SAT or ACT required; ACT with Writing component recommended. High school diploma is required, and GED is accepted. *Academic units required:* 4 English, 3 math, 2 science (2 science labs), 2 foreign language, 2 history.

The Inside Word

Students describe Trinity as "the home of Yale rejects," an appraisal that accurately characterizes the school's rep as an Ivy safety (if not the actual makeup of the student body). The school's high price tag ensures that a large percentage of the student body is made up of wealthy prepsters, but the school does offer generous financial aid packages to top candidates who can't afford the hefty price of attending. The school would love to broaden its student demographic, so competitive minority students should receive a very receptive welcome here.

FINANCIAL AID

Students should submit: FAFSA, CSS/Financial Aid PROFILE, Noncustodial PROFILE, Federal Income Tax Returns. Regular filing deadline is February 1. The Princeton Review suggests that all financial aid forms be submitted as soon as possible after January 1. *Need-based scholarships/grants offered:* Pell Grant, SEOG, state scholarships/grants, private scholarships, the school's own gift aid. *Loan aid offered:* Direct Subsidized Stafford, Direct Unsubsidized Stafford, Direct PLUS, FFEL Subsidized Stafford, FFEL Unsubsidized Stafford, FFEL PLUS, Federal Perkins Loan, college/university loans from institutional funds. Applicants will be notified of awards on or about April 1.

FROM THE ADMISSIONS OFFICE

"An array of distinctive curricular options—including an interdisciplinary neuroscience major and a professionally accredited engineering degree program, a unique Human Rights Program, a tutorial college for selected sophomores, a Health Fellows Program, and interdisciplinary programs such as the Cities Program, Interdisciplinary Science Program, and InterArts—is one reason record numbers of students are applying to Trinity. In fact, applications are up 80 percent over the past 5 years. In addition, the college has been recognized for its commitment to diversity; students of color have represented approximately 20 percent of the freshman class for the past 4 years, setting Trinity apart from many of its peers. Trinity's capital city location offers students unparalleled 'real-world' learning experiences to complement classroom learning. Students take advantage of extensive opportunities for internships for academic credit and community service, and these opportunities extend to Trinity's global learning sites in cities around the world. Trinity's faculty is a devoted and accomplished group of exceptional teacher-scholars; our 100-acre campus is beautiful; Hartford is an educational asset that differentiates Trinity from other liberal arts colleges; our global connections and foreign study opportunities prepare students to be good citizens of the world; and our graduates go on to excel in virtually every field. We invite you to learn more about why Trinity might be the best choice for you.

"Students applying for admission for the entering class of Fall 2008 may submit the following testing options: SAT, ACT with Writing, or three SAT Subject Tests."

SELECTIVITY

Admissions Rating	**94**
# of applicants	5,343
% of applicants accepted	43
% of acceptees attending	27
# accepting a place on wait list	430
# of early decision applicants	368
% accepted early decision	69

FRESHMAN PROFILE

Range SAT Critical Reading	600–690
Range SAT Math	610–700
Range SAT Writing	600–700
Range ACT Composite	27–29
% graduated top 10% of class	54
% graduated top 25% of class	83
% graduated top 50% of class	98

DEADLINES

Early decision application deadline	11/15
Early decision notification	12/15
Regular application deadline	1/1
Regular notification	4/1
Nonfall registration?	no

APPLICANTS ALSO LOOK AT

AND OFTEN PREFER
Amherst College, Harvard College, Tufts University, University of Pennsylvania, Yale University

AND SOMETIMES PREFER
Middlebury College, Wesleyan University

AND RARELY PREFER
Boston University, Colgate University, Connecticut College

FINANCIAL FACTS

Financial Aid Rating	**98**
Annual tuition	$33,440
Room & Board	$8,970
Books and supplies	$900
Required fees	$1,690
% frosh rec. need-based scholarship or grant aid	36
% UG rec. need-based scholarship or grant aid	38
% frosh rec. need-based self-help aid	28
% UG rec. need-based self-help aid	33
% frosh rec. any financial aid	33
% UG rec. any financial aid	41

TRINITY UNIVERSITY (TX)

ONE TRINITY PLACE, SAN ANTONIO, TX 78212 • ADMISSIONS: 210-999-7207 • FAX: 210-999-8164

STUDENTS SAY

Academics

"The academics are very strong no matter the major you choose" at Trinity University, a tiny powerhouse of a university located deep in the heart of Texas. The school's "very rigorous undergraduate programs" all include a wide-ranging common curriculum requiring students to master writing, mathematical, computer, and foreign language skills. All students must also fulfill requirements in six areas of knowledge (called Fundamental Understandings in the course catalog). Students tell us that "the broad requirements of the curriculum make for a great base. You can still complete your area of study, all the while learning things you never thought you would, taking classes in subjects you are interested in, but don't necessarily coincide with classes in your major." Those who come here should arrive prepared to log serious hours in the library; one student writes, "No matter what major you decide to pursue, you better believe that there will be work involved." Professors help students meet the challenge; they're "always available, largely brilliant, and willing to discuss damn near anything with a student one-on-one." Undergrads also appreciate that their professors "are open to letting students help with their research projects." Other assets include "an absolutely amazing study abroad program" and an endowed lecture series that is "known for bringing in very influential people as guest speakers. In the past few years we have had John Glenn, Rudy Giuliani, Queen Noor, and Brit Hume." Another student reports, "Tonight they had this woman from the Iraqi Governing Council in an auditorium that sat maybe 250. I can't tell you how many world leaders I've asked questions to."

Life

"The greatest strength of Trinity," students tell us, "is that it is wonderfully located in the middle of San Antonio, yet it feels like you're in the Hill Country." Here it is easy "to study and concentrate on work," but the school also "has a strong sense of community," one reinforced by the "collective cursing of students hiking up Cardiac Hill to get to class from the dorms." Trinity's otherwise "beautiful campus with great architecture" is encircled by "a great city, where there's always something to do, from going to the movies to great restaurants to the Riverwalk to local rodeos . . . pretty much anything you could want to do is available here." Many choose to stick around campus. Trinity requires on-campus residence for the first 3 years, which many students like, citing again that "sense of community that most other campuses don't have." Extracurricular opportunities "are huge, especially intramural sports and student organizations." The Greek scene "is also big, but going Greek is not necessary to be considered 'cool' and not necessary to have good social life." Parties are frequent, but "Trinity's campus is dry, so parties are held off campus." The "terrific Division III athletic teams" here "struggle for support," with the exception of the men's soccer team, "which was number one in the nation in 2003."

Student Body

"You know that kid who makes the rather intelligent off-hand comments in your government and English classes?" queries one Trinity undergrad. "Well, they all go to Trinity. That isn't to say we're all loudmouths, but we're all pretty academic minded." Indeed, "Everyone was one of the 'smart kids' in high school. Even the football players at Trinity are smart, and even the 'cool people' here are just a little nerdy. Everyone studies." While "Most here are from a Southern, somewhat elite background, not all students are like that, and you can definitely find students of all types." One student writes, "While Trinity isn't all rich White kids, there are a few of them, and while they don't exhibit any elitism or anything, they just view the world in a different way and sometimes their cultural ignorance can get kind of old." Trinity's minority population "consists largely of persons with Hispanic and Asian ethnicity. There are a fair number of these students, but African Americans are largely unaccounted for on campus."

TRINITY UNIVERSITY (TX)

FINANCIAL AID: 210-999-8315 • E-MAIL: ADMISSIONS@TRINITY.EDU • WEBSITE: WWW.TRINITY.EDU

ADMISSIONS

Very important factors considered include: Academic GPA, character/personal qualities, class rank, rigor of secondary school record, standardized test scores. *Important factors considered include:* Application essay, extracurricular activities, recommendation(s), talent/ability. *Other factors considered include:* Alumni/ae relation, first generation, geographical residence, interview, level of applicant's interest, state residency, volunteer work, work experience. SAT recommended; ACT recommended; SAT or ACT required; TOEFL required of all international applicants. High school diploma is required, and GED is accepted. *Academic units required:* 4 English, 3 math, 3 science (2 science labs), 2 foreign language, 3 social studies. *Academic units recommended:* 4 English, 3 math, 3 science (2 science labs), 3 foreign language, 3 social studies, 3 academic electives.

The Inside Word

There is no disputing that Trinity attracts an academically excellent student body. For this reason alone, above-average students who need significant financial assistance in order to attend college should definitely consider applying. There is no question that it's an extremely capable student body and that there are significant benefits to be derived from attending.

FINANCIAL AID

Students should submit: FAFSA. Regular filing deadline is April 1 with a preference deadline of February 15. The Princeton Review suggests that all financial aid forms be submitted as soon as possible after January 1. *Need-based scholarships/grants offered:* Pell Grant, SEOG, state scholarships/grants, private scholarships, the school's own gift aid. *Loan aid offered:* FFEL Subsidized Stafford, FFEL Unsubsidized Stafford, FFEL PLUS, Federal Perkins Loan, state loans, college/university loans from institutional funds. Applicants will be notified of awards on April 1. Federal Work-Study Program available. Institutional employment available. Off-campus job opportunities are good.

FROM THE ADMISSIONS OFFICE

"Three qualities separate Trinity University from other selective, academically challenging institutions around the country. First, Trinity is unusual in the quality and quantity of resources devoted almost exclusively to its undergraduate students. Those resources give rise to a second distinctive aspect of Trinity—its emphasis on undergraduate research. Our students prefer being involved over observing. With superior laboratory facilities and strong, dedicated faculty, our undergraduates fill many of the roles formerly reserved for graduate students. With no graduate assistants, our professors often go to their undergraduates for help with their research. Finally, Trinity stands apart for the attitude of its students. In an atmosphere of academic camaraderie and fellowship, our students work together to stretch their minds and broaden their horizons. For quality of resources, for dedication to undergraduate research, and for the disposition of its student body, Trinity University holds a unique position in American higher education.

"Students applying for admission must submit either the ACT or the SAT (both the new and the old version are acceptable). The highest composite test scores from one or multiple dates are evaluated. The SAT Writing section and ACT Writing component are not required, but may be reviewed if submitted."

SELECTIVITY

Admissions Rating	**91**
# of applicants	3,899
% of applicants accepted	61
% of acceptees attending	28
# accepting a place on wait list	143
% admitted from wait list	25
# of early decision applicants	52
% accepted early decision	63

FRESHMAN PROFILE

Range SAT Critical Reading	580–680
Range SAT Math	610–690
Range ACT Composite	26–31
Minimum Paper TOEFL	600
Minimum Computer Based TOEFL	250
Average HS GPA	3.5
% graduated top 10% of class	46
% graduated top 25% of class	79
% graduated top 50% of class	97

DEADLINES

Early decision application deadline	11/1
Early decision notification	12/15
Regular application deadline	2/1
Regular notification	4/1
Nonfall registration?	yes

APPLICANTS ALSO LOOK AT

AND OFTEN PREFER
Rice University, The University of Texas at Austin

AND SOMETIMES PREFER
Texas Christian University, Vanderbilt University, Washington University in St. Louis

AND RARELY PREFER
Rhodes College, Texas A&M University—College Station

FINANCIAL FACTS

Financial Aid Rating	**85**
Annual tuition	$23,136
Room & Board	$8,194
Books and supplies	$900
Required fees	$995
% frosh rec. need-based scholarship or grant aid	43
% UG rec. need-based scholarship or grant aid	38
% frosh rec. need-based self-help aid	34
% UG rec. need-based self-help aid	34
% frosh rec. any financial aid	85
% UG rec. any financial aid	74

TRUMAN STATE UNIVERSITY

McCLAIN HALL 205, 100 EAST NORMAL, KIRKSVILLE, MO 63501 • ADMISSIONS: 660-785-4114 • FAX: 660-785-7456

CAMPUS LIFE
Quality of Life Rating	82
Fire Safety Rating	75
Type of school	public
Environment	village

STUDENTS
Total undergrad enrollment	5,410
% male/female	42/58
% from out of state	22
% from public high school	80
% live on campus	48
% in (# of) fraternities	31 (18)
% in (# of) sororities	22 (11)
% African American	4
% Asian	2
% Caucasian	85
% Hispanic	2
% Native American	1
% international	3
# of countries represented	42

SURVEY SAYS . . .
Small classes
Lab facilities are great
Great computer facilities
Great library
Students are friendly
Campus feels safe
Low cost of living
Students are happy

ACADEMICS
Academic Rating	81
Calendar	semester
Student/faculty ratio	16:1
Profs interesting rating	79
Profs accessible rating	88
% profs teaching UG courses	99
% classes taught by TAs	2
Most common lab size	fewer than 10 students
Most common reg class size	20–29 students

MOST POPULAR MAJORS
biology/biological sciences
business administration/
management
psychology

STUDENTS SAY

Academics

Students who attend Truman State University are convinced that "Truman is one of the best public schools in Missouri, demanding high-level thinking" from undergrads. Students praise TSU's "very strong academic program" with a mandatory liberal arts sequence that "gives students the opportunity to take classes that we would otherwise be unable to take. I can take science, art, history, or several foreign languages. It is wonderful to not be confined to one area." While "Some students see taking a lot of classes that are not directly related to one's major program as a bad thing," the majority recognize that it "helps to diversify our knowledge and to make us more well-rounded individuals. Furthermore, sometimes these classes lead you to realize you are more interested in certain areas than you originally thought." Add "helpful teachers and great study abroad and leadership opportunities" to the mix, and you can see how "Truman gives students the complete education that will make them competitive in the job market and graduate school [admissions]." Students tell us that Truman excels in education ("the best teacher preparation program in the state, if not the region," brags one student), biology, and equine science, among other areas. In all disciplines, "Professors do as much as they can to make themselves accessible, and are always open to an office visit or an e-mail from students if they have a question," and, perhaps best of all, "Truman is a great deal financially."

Life

TSU's small hometown of Kirksville "is not exactly the cultural hub of the Midwest," but the school works hard "to keep students from being bored. The Student Activities Board brings in comedians and bands, and other organizations host events for students like mixers, trivia nights, movie nights, and a cappella concerts." One undergrad explains, "Even though Truman is in a small town, there is plenty to do. The difference is that you don't look so much for something to do, as for someone to do something with. Exploring and wandering around town and the surrounding areas are pretty common activities, as are road trips, and small get-togethers any night of the week." And, "Like most colleges, we party," although "In most cases partying is not excessive and doesn't interfere with schoolwork." TSU students enjoy "a solid Greek presence that doesn't dominate campus life. In other words, your social life will not be over if you don't join a fraternity or sorority." This is true in part because "There are tons of organizations at Truman, and if the one you want doesn't exist, all you need is about six students and a constitution to start your own. Religious—especially Christian—organizations are pretty popular." For road trips, "Columbia is also a quick hour and a half south for [students seeking] more variety than a small town like Kirksville can offer."

Student Body

The "studious" undergrads of TSU include "a lot of overachievers who excel in and out of the classroom." Truman students "are here to learn. Sure, students go to parties, but Truman is not what I'd call a 'party school.' Many people choose alternative ways of having fun." Most here are "Midwesterners, White, and from middle-class or upper-middle-class families." One student confides, "The rumor is that a third of Truman's campus is from St. Louis, White, and Catholic. Fortunately, religiosity isn't so much an 'in-your-face' issue. Students on the whole get along very well across racial, gender, ethnic, age, and major/minor interests." Another undergrad adds, "We joke about the lack of diversity on our campus, but diversity does exist, and everyone seems to get along really well. Furthermore, everyone seems more than willing to open up to other cultures and religions and to learn more about them." A "surprisingly large number of international students" help bump non-White demographics upward.

TRUMAN STATE UNIVERSITY

FINANCIAL AID: 660-785-4130 • E-MAIL: ADMISSIONS@TRUMAN.EDU • WEBSITE: WWW.TRUMAN.EDU

ADMISSIONS

Very important factors considered include: Academic GPA, class rank, rigor of secondary school record, standardized test scores. *Important factors considered include:* Application essay. *Other factors considered include:* Alumni/ae relation, character/personal qualities, extracurricular activities, first generation, geographical residence, level of applicant's interest, racial/ethnic status, state residency, talent/ability, volunteer work, work experience. SAT or ACT required; TOEFL required of all international applicants. High school diploma is required, and GED is accepted. *Academic units required:* 4 English, 3 math, 3 science (2 science labs), 2 foreign language, 3 social studies, 1 fine arts. *Academic units recommended:* 4 math, 1 fine arts.

The Inside Word

Students looking to take advantage of Truman State's educational opportunities and low price tag had better hit the books. As the school's profile continues to rise, competition for admission increases. Applicants with high class rank and strong test scores will be given the most consideration. Candidates will find it to their benefit to apply early, as the decision is nonbinding.

FINANCIAL AID

Students should submit: FAFSA, institution's own financial aid form. The Princeton Review suggests that all financial aid forms be submitted as soon as possible after January 1. *Need-based scholarships/grants offered:* Pell Grant, SEOG, state scholarships/grants, private scholarships, the school's own gift aid. *Loan aid offered:* FFEL Subsidized Stafford, FFEL Unsubsidized Stafford, FFEL PLUS, Federal Perkins Loan, Federal Nursing Loan, state loans, college/university loans from institutional funds, alternative loans. Applicants will be notified of awards on a rolling basis beginning or about April 1. Federal Work-Study Program available. Institutional employment available. Off-campus job opportunities are good.

FROM THE ADMISSIONS OFFICE

"Truman's talented student body enjoys small classes where undergraduate research and personal interaction with professors are the norm. Truman's commitment to providing an exemplary liberal arts and sciences education with nearly 200 student organizations and outstanding internship and study abroad opportunities allows students to compete in top graduate schools and the job market.

"Students applying for Fall 2008 admission to Truman State University can submit scores from both versions of the SAT, as well as the ACT. The best scores from either test will be considered. The Writing section is not currently required for admission to Truman."

SELECTIVITY
Admissions Rating	89
# of applicants	4,337
% of applicants accepted	81
% of acceptees attending	39

FRESHMAN PROFILE
Range SAT Critical Reading	550–680
Range SAT Math	540–660
Range ACT Composite	25–30
Minimum Paper TOEFL	550
Minimum Computer Based TOEFL	213
Average HS GPA	3.78
% graduated top 10% of class	51
% graduated top 25% of class	83
% graduated top 50% of class	98

DEADLINES
Regular application deadline	3/1
Regular notification	rolling
Nonfall registration?	yes

APPLICANTS ALSO LOOK AT
AND OFTEN PREFER
Saint Louis University, University of Missouri—Columbia, Washington University in St. Louis
AND SOMETIMES PREFER
Missouri State University, University of Illinois at Urbana-Champaign
AND RARELY PREFER
Illinois State University, Illinois Wesleyan University, University of Iowa

FINANCIAL FACTS
Financial Aid Rating	89
Annual in-state tuition	$5,970
Annual out-of-state tuition	$10,400
Room & Board	$5,570
Books and supplies	$900
Required fees	$122
% frosh rec. need-based scholarship or grant aid	19
% UG rec. need-based scholarship or grant aid	17
% frosh rec. need-based self-help aid	33
% UG rec. need-based self-help aid	36
% frosh rec. any financial aid	98
% UG rec. any financial aid	97

TUFTS UNIVERSITY

BENDETSON HALL, MEDFORD, MA 02155 • ADMISSIONS: 617-627-3170 • FAX: 617-627-3860

CAMPUS LIFE

Quality of Life Rating	85
Fire Safety Rating	88
Type of school	private
Environment	town

STUDENTS

Total undergrad enrollment	4,982
% male/female	49/51
% from out of state	75
% from public high school	60
% live on campus	75
% in (# of) fraternities	15 (11)
% in (# of) sororities	4 (3)
% African American	6
% Asian	13
% Caucasian	58
% Hispanic	6
% international	8
# of countries represented	67

SURVEY SAYS . . .

Great computer facilities
Great library
Great off-campus food
Campus feels safe
Students are happy
Student publications are popular
Lots of beer drinking

ACADEMICS

Academic Rating	93
Calendar	semester
Student/faculty ratio	7:1
Profs interesting rating	87
Profs accessible rating	84
% profs teaching UG courses	100
% classes taught by TAs	1
Most common lab size	10–19 students
Most common reg class size	10–19 students

MOST POPULAR MAJORS

economics
English language and literature
international relations and affairs

STUDENTS SAY

Academics

Tufts University boasts a "small-campus feel," a "globally recognized" reputation, and "engaging," "personable" faculty. Professors here "know what they are talking about" and "seem to go out of their way to make themselves accessible." These very same professors, however, "flood" students "with tons of work." Lower-level classes can be huge on occasion, but upper-level classes are "small and well-focused." The "transparent" administration tends "to grapple with technology and change" but it is "incredibly helpful" and very well liked, despite "militant political correctness." "President Bacow will generally respond to any e-mail sent to him by a student within about 20 minutes." Academically, while you can choose from a massive number of stellar majors in the liberal arts and engineering, Tufts is probably best known for its "very strong" science programs (especially premed) and its prestigious international relations programs. "Tufts is internationalism," declares one student. "From the Music Department's ethnomusicology [major] to the Political Science Department's international relations major, every facet of Tufts, both in and out of the classroom, revolves around thinking globally." Studying abroad "is highly encouraged"; about 40 percent of students take advantage of awesome study abroad programs in a host of exotic locales including an "amazing" summer program in the Alps.

Life

At Tufts, the campus is "gorgeous," "The food is incredible," and course work is time-consuming, so it's no surprise that social life is basically centered on campus. Students here "know each other." "It's a nice feeling," an undergrad ventures, but "If you want to be anonymous, Tufts is not for you." The "fabulous extracurricular opportunities" include "a daily paper, a dozen student magazines," and "countless service and activism organizations." In addition, a vast array of large-scale, free campus events helps to keep students entertained. While "Drinking is very popular on the weekends," undergrads report that "there is not always a party guaranteed on a Friday or Saturday night, which is unthinkable at bigger schools." When there is one, it can seem as if "The campus police break everything up." This may be why "As you get older and you meet more people, you begin to go to more parties and social events off of campus," a more seasoned student tells us. Many feel that the surrounding town of Medford leaves a lot to be desired, but fortunately, "You have the greatest college city in the nation a subway ride away" if "you get tired [of] the Tufts scene." It should be noted, however, that public transportation into Boston takes "like an hour (counting waiting)." "We're not in Boston," cautions one student. "Don't let the admissions folks fool you."

Students

Some students tell us that Tuft's reputation as a haven for the "Ivy League reject" is accurate. Others vehemently disagree. "The Tufts Ivy complex is over," argues one student. "Anyone here could get into Cornell!" Students describe themselves as "genuinely nice," "painfully liberal," and "very goal-oriented." They are "laid-back" and only "competitive with themselves." One undergrad asserts, "The typical student here is very intelligent and ambitious, but they don't want you to think that." Another adds, "They get their work done so they can have fun too." Ethnic diversity is notable; traditionally underrepresented minorities on campus have a strong presence. However, "People tend to separate into their little cliques after first semester and rarely interact with other people." "Almost all Tufts students are rich" as well. "The frustrating thing is not the lack of ethnic diversity, but the lack of socioeconomic diversity," an English major writes. This student body features "a lot of smart kids in Lacoste polos who are looking to save the world" (or, at least, "convince others they are looking to save to world") and a lot of "preppy," "Louis V. bag," "North Face fleece," "big sunglasses," "rich kids." There are also "the stoners, the die-hard partiers, the activists, the coffeehouse philosophers," and a slew of "obscenely wealthy international kids."

FINANCIAL AID: 617-627-2000 • E-MAIL: ADMISSIONS.INQUIRY@ASE.TUFTS.EDU • WEBSITE: WWW.TUFTS.EDU

ADMISSIONS

Very important factors considered include: Rigor of secondary school record. *Important factors considered include:* Academic GPA, application essay, character/personal qualities, class rank, extracurricular activities, recommendation(s), standardized test scores, talent/ability, volunteer work, work experience. *Other factors considered include:* Alumni/ae relation, first generation, geographical residence, interview, racial/ethnic status. SAT and SAT Subject Tests or ACT required; ACT with Writing component required. TOEFL required of all international applicants. High school diploma is required, and GED is accepted. *Academic units recommended:* 4 English, 3 math, 2 science, 3 foreign language, 2 history.

The Inside Word

The admissions process is rigorous. With an acceptance rate hovering not much over 25 percent and average SAT section scores in the low 700s, you'll need to demonstrate fairly extraordinary academic accomplishments and submit a thorough and well-prepared application in order to get admitted to Tufts. On the bright side, Tufts is still a little bit of a safety school for aspiring Ivy Leaguers. Since many applicants who also get into an Ivy League school will pass on Tufts, it has spots for "mere mortals" at the end of the day.

FINANCIAL AID

Students should submit: FAFSA, CSS/Financial Aid PROFILE, Noncustodial PRO-FILE, Business/Farm Supplement, parent and student Federal Income Tax Returns. Regular filing deadline is February 15. The Princeton Review suggests that all financial aid forms be submitted as soon as possible after January 1. *Need-based scholarships/grants offered:* Pell Grant, SEOG, state scholarships/grants, private scholarships, the school's own gift aid. *Loan aid offered:* FFEL Subsidized Stafford, FFEL Unsubsidized Stafford, FFEL PLUS, Federal Perkins Loan, state loans, college/university loans from institutional funds. Applicants will be notified of awards on or about April 1. Federal Work-Study Program available. Institutional employment available. Off-campus job opportunities are good.

FROM THE ADMISSIONS OFFICE

"Tufts University, on the boundary between Medford and Somerville, sits on a hill overlooking Boston, five miles northwest of the city. The campus is a tranquil New England setting within easy access by subway and bus to the cultural, social, and entertainment resources of Boston and Cambridge. Since its founding in 1852 by members of the Universalist church, Tufts has grown from a small liberal arts college into a nonsectarian university of over 7,000 students. By 1900 the college had added a medical school, a dental school, and graduate studies. The university now also includes the Fletcher School of Law and Diplomacy, the Graduate School of Arts and Sciences, the School of Veterinary Medicine, the School of Nutrition, the Sackler School of Graduate Biomedical Sciences, and the Gordon Institute of Engineering Management.

"Applicants for Fall 2008 are required to submit scores (including the Writing assessment) from either the SAT or ACT. If an applicant submits the SAT, SAT Subject Tests are also required (candidates for the School of Engineering are encouraged to submit Math Level II and either Chemistry or Physics)."

SELECTIVITY

Admissions Rating	**98**
# of applicants	15,295
% of applicants accepted	27
% of acceptees attending	31
# of early decision applicants	1,321
% accepted early decision	32

FRESHMAN PROFILE

Range SAT Critical Reading	670–740
Range SAT Math	670–740
Range SAT Writing	660–740
Range ACT Composite	29–32
Minimum Paper TOEFL	300
Minimum Computer Based TOEFL	100
% graduated top 10% of class	83
% graduated top 25% of class	95
% graduated top 50% of class	99

DEADLINES

Early decision application deadline	11/1
Early decision notification	12/15
Regular application deadline	1/1
Regular notification	4/1
Nonfall registration?	no

FINANCIAL FACTS

Financial Aid Rating	**93**
Annual tuition	$33,906
Room & Board	$9,770
Books and supplies	$800
Required fees	$824
% frosh rec. need-based scholarship or grant aid	34
% UG rec. need-based scholarship or grant aid	35
% frosh rec. need-based self-help aid	34
% UG rec. need-based self-help aid	35
% frosh rec. any financial aid	38
% UG rec. any financial aid	38

TULANE UNIVERSITY

6823 St. Charles Avenue, New Orleans, LA 70118 • Admissions: 504-865-5731 • Fax: 504-862-8715

STUDENTS SAY

Academics

In 2005, Hurricane Katrina sent Tulane students on a forced semester in exile, and when they returned in January 2006 they learned that the university was consolidating schools and deleting departments in an effort to deal with its post-hurricane economic situation. For most schools, this move would have been a death sentence. Tulane, however, is not most schools; it is uniquely Tulane, "the ultimate work-hard, play-hard school" whose strong academics and laid-back approach make it the place where all the "cool smart kids" go, a place that inspires the type of student devotion rarely found at schools that lack powerhouse sports programs. Student after student praises the school's recovery efforts, observing that "Tulane's administration brought us through Katrina and is helping New Orleans through this time as well," and that "in post-Katrina New Orleans, the professors who have returned are the ones who really want to be here and really have a desire to help students learn." Katrina has actually strengthened students' allegiance to the school; as one put it, "This is the most amazing, out-of-this-world place to be—a college experience that no other school could top. And we know it because we experienced other schools during [the] Hurricane Katrina [hiatus]." The Tulane academic experience is distinguished by small classes, mostly "10 to 20 students," "one of the best study abroad programs in the country," and, of course, New Orleans, the "best city in the country," which allows Tulane to offer "a one-of-a-kind out-of-classroom experience." Standout programs include premed, business, economics, architecture, and exercise and sports science.

Life

Tulane students love New Orleans—and love to explore it—a city full of "art galleries and museums," "amazing" shopping on Magazine Street, "family-owned restaurants in the uptown area," "touristy" places in the French Quarter, and "a lot [of] different bars near campus." The city also boasts Audubon Park, "a really fun place to get exercise or spend some time," and, of course, an "unparalleled music scene." None of this, however, stops "about 30 percent of the campus" from getting involved in Greek life, or "most students" from getting involved "in at least two student organizations." In addition, "community service [and] volunteer work," always "very popular at Tulane," have become "especially popular post-Katrina." Those concerned about safety—New Orleans has traditionally had one of the higher crime rates in the nation—should note that "Tulane is located in a major city, but not in downtown New Orleans." By all accounts, campus security does "an excellent job of making sure campus is secure, and students have the opportunity to be escorted anywhere." As an added bonus, "The weather is nice—you can wear flip flops year round."

Student Body

The typical Tulane student "is serious about academics, but isn't holed up in the library all the time." Similar to students at other big-city schools, Tulane undergrads tend to be "self-reliant, motivated, [and] forward looking." They point out that the school is "one of the most geographically diverse schools in the country," observing that "75 percent of the students come from more than 500 miles away. . . . In my eight-person suite there are two girls from Boston, one from New York, one from Texas, one from Baton Rouge, one from Florida, and I'm from Chicago. It's great!" Diversity is further represented in the "tons of very large, very active, very vocal groups on campus for every minority, including ethnicities, political beliefs, religious beliefs, and sexual orientation[s]. Everyone here manages to find [his or her] own little niche." A strong Jewish Studies program helps Tulane draw one of the largest Jewish student populations in the South; about 25 percent of the student body is Jewish.

FINANCIAL AID: 504-865-5723 • E-MAIL: UNDERGRAD.ADMISSION@TULANE.EDU • WEBSITE: WWW.TULANE.EDU

ADMISSIONS

Very important factors considered include: Class rank, rigor of secondary school record, standardized test scores. *Important factors considered include:* Application essay, character/personal qualities, recommendation(s). *Other factors considered include:* Alumni/ae relation, extracurricular activities, interview, talent/ability, volunteer work, work experience. SAT or ACT required; ACT with Writing component required. TOEFL required of all international applicants. High school diploma is required, and GED is accepted. *Academic units required:* 4 English, 3 math, 3 science (3 science labs), 2 foreign language, 3 social studies. *Academic units recommended:* 4 English, 4 math, 4 science (3 science labs), 3 foreign language, 3 social studies, 3 academic electives.

The Inside Word

If you thought Hurricane Katrina would dampen students' enthusiasm for Tulane, think again; the school received nearly 21,000 applications for the class of 2010—a school record. Competition will be further stiffened by the university's decision to reduce future incoming classes by 10 percent. Part of the university's restructuring involves the elimination of some academic programs—before you apply you should check to make sure that your areas of interest are still being served.

FINANCIAL AID

Students should submit: FAFSA, CSS/Financial Aid PROFILE, Noncustodial PROFILE, Business/Farm Supplement. Regular filing deadline is February 1. The Princeton Review suggests that all financial aid forms be submitted as soon as possible after January 1. *Need-based scholarships/grants offered:* Pell Grant, SEOG, state scholarships/grants, private scholarships, the school's own gift aid. *Loan aid offered:* FFEL Subsidized Stafford, FFEL Unsubsidized Stafford, FFEL PLUS, Federal Perkins Loan. Applicants will be notified of awards on a rolling basis beginning or about February 1. Federal Work-Study Program available. Institutional employment available. Off-campus job opportunities are good.

FROM THE ADMISSIONS OFFICE

"With 6,000 full-time undergraduate students in five schools, Tulane University offers the personal attention and teaching excellence traditionally associated with small colleges together with the facilities and interdisciplinary resources found only at major research universities. Following Hurricane Katrina, the university underwent a spectacular renewal: renovating facilities and restructuring academic programs. The opportunities for students to be involved in the rebirth of New Orleans offer an experience unavailable at any other place, at any other time.

"Tulane is committed to undergraduate education. Senior faculty members teach most introductory and lower-level courses, and 74 percent of the classes have 25 or fewer students. The close student-teacher relationship pays off. Tulane graduates are among the most likely to be selected for several prestigious fellowships that support graduate study abroad. Founded in 1834 and reorganized as Tulane University in 1884, Tulane is one of the major private research universities in the South.

"The Tulane campus offers a traditional collegiate setting in an attractive residential neighborhood, which suffered minimal damage after Hurricane Katrina.

"Tulane University will accept the new SAT or the old SAT (administered prior to March 2005 and without a Writing component). For students submitting an ACT score, the ACT with the Writing component is required."

SELECTIVITY

Admissions Rating	94
# of applicants	17,572
% of applicants accepted	45
% of acceptees attending	21
# accepting a place on wait list	2,337
# of early decision applicants	207
% accepted early decision	39

FRESHMAN PROFILE

Range SAT Critical Reading	628–725
Range SAT Math	603–700
Range ACT Composite	28–32
Minimum Paper TOEFL	550
Minimum Computer Based TOEFL	213
Average HS GPA	3.6
% graduated top 10% of class	59
% graduated top 25% of class	75
% graduated top 50% of class	100

DEADLINES

Early decision application deadline	11/1
Early decision notification	12/15
Regular application deadline	1/15
Regular notification	4/15
Nonfall registration?	no

APPLICANTS ALSO LOOK AT

AND OFTEN PREFER
Duke University, Emory University, Vanderbilt University

AND SOMETIMES PREFER
Florida State University, Northwestern University, The University of Texas at Austin, Washington University in St. Louis

AND RARELY PREFER
Rollins College, Skidmore College, Southern Methodist University, University of Richmond

FINANCIAL FACTS

Financial Aid Rating	88
Annual tuition	$28,900
Room & Board	$7,925
Books and supplies	$800
Required fees	$2,310
% frosh rec. need-based scholarship or grant aid	47
% UG rec. need-based scholarship or grant aid	39
% frosh rec. need-based self-help aid	29
% UG rec. need-based self-help aid	29
% frosh rec. any financial aid	92
% UG rec. any financial aid	91

TUSKEGEE UNIVERSITY

OLD ADMINISTRATION BUILDING, SUITE 101, TUSKEGEE, AL 36088 • ADMISSIONS: 334-727-8500 OR 800-622-65311 • FAX: 334-727-4402

CAMPUS LIFE

Quality of Life Rating	**61**
Fire Safety Rating	**60***
Type of school	private
Environment	rural

STUDENTS

Total undergrad enrollment	2,420
% male/female	45/55
% from out of state	59
% live on campus	55
% in (# of) fraternities	6 (5)
% in (# of) sororities	5 (6)
% African American	78
% international	1
# of countries represented	86

SURVEY SAYS . . .

Small classes
Students are friendly
Students don't like Tuskegee, AL
Low cost of living
Everyone loves the Golden Tigers
Frats and sororities dominate social
scene
Musical organizations are popular
Student government is popular

ACADEMICS

Academic Rating	**72**
Calendar	semester
Student/faculty ratio	12:1
Profs interesting rating	65
Profs accessible rating	61
% profs teaching UG courses	100
% classes taught by TAs	0
Most common reg class size	10-19
students	

MOST POPULAR MAJORS

electrical, electronics, and
communications engineering
veterinary medicine (DVM)

STUDENTS SAY

Academics

A sense of history pervades Tuskegee's "beautiful" campus in eastern Alabama, and that's fitting; "Tuskegee is the only HBCU [Historically Black College or University] named by Congress as a National Historic Site." Undergrads here generally sense there is something about "the legacy and good name of Tuskegee University that can propel a student forward." That good name derives mainly from people knowing that if you are a student at Tuskegee, "No one is doing the work for you." Academics are "challenging" here, with "excellent engineering and vet programs," setting especially high standards. Given these demands, students appreciate that "class sizes are small, only slightly larger than the average high school class at times," so it is easy to get to know one's professors. Speaking of professors, they "are not only good teachers, they are also very good mentors." They "want you to succeed" and they prove their dedication by making themselves "available whenever we need them, even if it is 10:00 in the evening." The administration is an entirely different story. Let's just say that "if you can learn to deal with the administrative staff at this school, you will be able to handle anyone in the real world with class and grace." The biggest gripe from the students is that "registration is a hassle. It just doesn't run smoothly at all."

Life

About halfway between Montgomery and Auburn, off I-85, lies the sleepy little town of Tuskegee. "It's a great study environment" because "there are very few distractions." Many students believe "The closest place to go for fun is at least 20 minutes away, and a car is needed. It's in another city and no campus transportation is given." That other city is Auburn, where "You can always mingle with the Auburn University students," go "bowling, or do a little shopping." For those heading in the other direction, there actually is a school shuttle that goes to "Wal-Mart in Montgomery and a small mall." If they stay in Tuskegee, "To have fun, students typically go to local clubs, frat or sorority parties, or have house parties." In addition, "Music is played on the Yard sometimes and SGA arranges all sorts of student activities, such as fashion shows, basketball tournaments, concerts, and game nights." Film buffs appreciate that "a lot of school clubs have movie nights and show really great movies. Even some dorms have movie nights." There are also activities for more wholesome types. For example, "If you like to go to church, they have a lot of church functions." Even with the all these options, some Tuskegee students still say, "Life is boring except for football games." To put it mildly, the "football team is overwhelmingly supported here."

Student Body

"As an HBCU, Tuskegee's student population is composed almost completely of African Americans, though students come from all over, even as far away as Alaska and California." Some report that "the typical student is someone who has a good work ethic and cares a lot about getting the most [he or she] can out [of his or her] school experience"; others note that undergrads prefer "to hurry up and get their degree and live their life and have all the fun they can have." They are "outgoing, smart, and easy to get along with." They also "are very laid-back and rarely cause trouble, unless it's a special occasion (Halloween, Thanksgiving, homecoming, etc.)." Some undergrads offer that "the only atypical students that attend would be Caucasian students who are enrolled in the veterinary school. They have voiced that they come to school just for an education and not to have fun, so they stick together and go to class."

FINANCIAL AID: 334-727-8210 OR 800-416-2831 • E-MAIL: ADMI@TUSKEGEE.EDU • WEBSITE: WWW.TUSKEGEE.EDU

ADMISSIONS

Very important factors considered include: Academic GPA, class rank, recommendation(s), rigor of secondary school record, standardized test scores, talent/ability. *Important factors considered include:* Alumni/ae relation, character/personal qualities. *Other factors considered include:* Application essay, extracurricular activities, first generation, geographical residence, interview, state residency, volunteer work, work experience. SAT or ACT required; TOEFL required of all international applicants. High school diploma is required, and GED is accepted. *Academic units required:* 4 English, 3 math, 2 science, 3 social studies, 4 academic electives.

The Inside Word

Tuskegee presents its students with a myriad of opportunities for discovery and research. Therefore, Admissions Counselors seek applicants who have proven themselves successful in the classroom and are eager to tackle further academic challenges. To gain that coveted acceptance letter, candidates will need a minimum GPA of 3.0 and composite ACT score of 21. Requirements for both the nursing and engineering programs differ slightly from the requirements for other majors. Prospective students interested in either field should investigate the specific criteria.

FINANCIAL AID

Students should submit: FAFSA, institution's own financial aid form, CSS/Financial Aid PROFILE. The Princeton Review suggests that all financial aid forms be submitted as soon as possible after January 1. *Need-based scholarships/grants offered:* Pell Grant, SEOG, state scholarships/grants, private scholarships, the school's own gift aid, United Negro College Fund, Federal Nursing Scholarships. *Loan aid offered:* Direct Subsidized Stafford, Direct Unsubsidized Stafford, Direct PLUS, FFEL Subsidized Stafford, FFEL Unsubsidized Stafford, FFEL PLUS, Federal Perkins Loan, Federal Nursing Loan, state loans, college/university loans from institutional funds.

FROM THE ADMISSIONS OFFICE

"Tuskegee University, located in central Alabama, was founded in 1881 under the dynamic and creative leadership of Booker T. Washington. As a state-related, independent institution, Tuskegee offers undergraduate and graduate programs in five major areas: The College of Agriculture, Environmental, and Natural Sciences; the College of Engineering, Architecture, and Physical Sciences; the College of Business and Information Sciences; the College of Liberal Arts and Education; and the College of Veterinary Medicine, Nursing, and Allied Health. Substantial research and service programs make Tuskegee University an effective comprehensive institution, geared towards preparing tomorrow's leaders today.

"First-year applicants must take the SAT or ACT; the SAT is preferred. International Applicants must complete the TOEFL. Nursing applicants must complete the National League of Nursing exam."

SELECTIVITY

Admissions Rating	**80**
# of applicants	1,931
% of applicants accepted	81
% of acceptees attending	45

FRESHMAN PROFILE

Range SAT Critical Reading	390-500
Range SAT Math	380-490
Range ACT Composite	17-21
Minimum Paper TOEFL	500
Minimum Computer Based TOEFL	173
Average HS GPA	3.0
% graduated top 10% of class	20
% graduated top 25% of class	59
% graduated top 50% of class	100

DEADLINES

Regular notification	rolling
Nonfall registration?	yes

APPLICANTS ALSO LOOK AT

AND OFTEN PREFER
Clark Atlanta University,
AND SOMETIMES PREFER
Alabama A&M University, Florida A&M University, Hampton University, Howard University, Spelman College
AND RARELY PREFER
Alabama State University, Auburn University, The University of Alabama at Tuscaloosa

FINANCIAL FACTS

Financial Aid Rating	**84**
Annual tuition	$14,150
Room & Board	$6,783
Books and supplies	$949
Required fees	$465
% frosh rec. need-based scholarship or grant aid	66
% UG rec. need-based scholarship or grant aid	66
% frosh rec. need-based self-help aid	51
% UG rec. need-based self-help aid	49
% frosh rec. any financial aid	
% UG rec. any financial aid	

UNION COLLEGE (NY)

GRANT HALL, SCHENECTADY, NY 12308 • ADMISSIONS: 518-388-6112 • FAX: 518-388-6986

STUDENTS SAY

Academics

Immersing a bunch of engineers and premeds in an accelerated trimester calendar should be a formula for a high-stress campus, but somehow Union College manages to keep the situation under control. A highly capable student body helps, as does, perhaps, the availability of quality liberal arts classes to intersperse among the science- and math-heavy classes; as one student puts it, "There aren't too many schools that do a good job combining engineering with liberal arts, [but it's] important if you actually want to communicate with people." In fact, many students here believe Union is actually an "excellent liberal arts school with a solid footing in the hard sciences—I wasn't sure exactly what I wanted to do with my life after graduation, [and] Union gave me a myriad of options." Those options include not only "great Science and Engineering Department[s]" but also strong programs in economics, political science, and psychology, all taught by top-notch professors. An economics major writes, "I was really amazed and pleasantly surprised when I saw the caliber of the professors here. They are all interested in their particular field of research, and their enthusiasm in the classroom rubs off on the students and makes for interesting and fun-filled learning exercises." Students even love the trimester system, which "allows a normal course load of only three classes a term." Some feel this allows for "lots of free time." Others caution, "The amount of work is increased, and in addition we must complete courses in only 10 weeks as opposed to the normal 12 to 14. By nature, Union is an accelerated school."

Life

For as long as anyone can remember, the Greeks have dominated the social scene at Union College, and while the frats are still "a big scene on the weekends (30–40 percent of campus is involved in Greek life)," the school is increasing attempts to provide more alternatives. The 2004 creation of seven Minerva Houses—each incoming student is assigned to one—represents the most significant effort; the houses are intended "to provide a nonexclusive (i.e., [non-]Greek) space for students to live and work." It's too early to deem this experiment a success or failure, although almost everyone here has an opinion one way or another. Some report that the Minervas are "a great idea" that are "slowly gaining popularity and momentum," while others see them as "creat[ing] tension over the distribution of funds" or, worse yet, "rapidly becoming small [frat-like] cliques themselves. For example, almost the entire Ultimate Frisbee team lives in Orange House." There's no disagreement over the city of Schenectady; everyone agrees it is less than ideal, and worse, there is "nothing to do." General consensus is that fun means "staying on campus and drinking" or "maybe an excursion to Albany (20 minutes away) for a concert." Campus perks up whenever the hockey team plays, as "Hockey games are huge events here"; football also draws a crowd. While students concede that drinking is big at Union, they also report that "there are other options for students. Every weekend at least one Minerva has to hold an event, [and] there are speakers, lecturers, movies, [and] performances. We always have a lot going on!"

Student Body

While "You can find a variety of people at Union," students say there is definitely "a typical Union student," who can be described as "preppy, Northeastern, [and] middle- to upper-class." By all accounts, you'll find "a lot of athletes, a lot of frat boys," and a lot of students who "wear Polo and Abercrombie" here. Atypical students are those who "find their place on campus in the Minerva House activities and clubs such as Women's Union, Black Student Union, performing arts groups, the college's radio station—WRUC, Ultimate Frisbee, and others." The "terribly cliquish nature of the social scene makes it difficult to provide a decent analysis of individual students."

UNION COLLEGE (NY)

FINANCIAL AID: 518-388-6123 • E-MAIL: ADMISSIONS@UNION.EDU • WEBSITE: WWW.UNION.EDU

ADMISSIONS

Very important factors considered include: Academic GPA, rigor of secondary school record. *Important factors considered include:* Character/personal qualities, class rank, extracurricular activities, recommendation(s), talent/ability. *Other factors considered include:* Alumni/ae relation, application essay, first generation, geographical residence, interview, level of applicant's interest, racial/ethnic status, standardized test scores, state residency, volunteer work, work experience. TOEFL required of all international applicants. High school diploma is required, and GED is not accepted. *Academic units required:* 4 English, 3 math, 2 science (2 science labs), 2 foreign language, 1 social studies, 1 history. *Academic units recommended:* 4 English, 4 math, 4 science (4 science labs), 4 foreign language, 2 social studies, 2 history.

The Inside Word

Hoping to produce world-historical progeny some day? Attending Union College may improve your odds; the school is alma mater to Franklin D. Roosevelt's father and Winston Churchill's grandfather. Craft your application package carefully here. Since Union does not require standardized test scores, there is no need to submit these scores unless they strengthen your application.

FINANCIAL AID

Students should submit: FAFSA, CSS/Financial Aid PROFILE, state aid form, Business/Farm Supplement, Noncustodial PROFILE. Regular filing deadline is February 1. The Princeton Review suggests that all financial aid forms be submitted as soon as possible after January 1. *Need-based scholarships/grants offered:* Pell Grant, SEOG, state scholarships/grants, private scholarships, the school's own gift aid. *Loan aid offered:* FFEL Subsidized Stafford, FFEL Unsubsidized Stafford, FFEL PLUS, Federal Perkins Loan, college/university loans from institutional funds. Applicants will be notified of awards on or about April 1.

FROM THE ADMISSIONS OFFICE

"'Breadth' and 'flexibility' characterize the Union academic program. Whether the subject is the poetry of ancient Greece or the possibilities of developing fields such as nanotechnology, Union students can choose from among nearly 1,000 courses—a range that is unusual among America's highly selective colleges. Students can major in a single field, combine work in two or more departments, or even create their own organizing-theme major. Undergraduate research is strongly encouraged, and more than half of Union's students take advantage of the college's extensive international study program.

"Admission to Union is merit based and driven by years of academic success. Union seeks students with excellent academic credentials. Those credentials are primarily transcripts. Submission of SAT and ACT scores are optional except for the law and medicine programs. Please check Union.edu/Admissions for details."

SELECTIVITY

Admissions Rating	95
# of applicants	4,373
% of applicants accepted	43
% of acceptees attending	30
# accepting a place on wait list	306
% admitted from wait list	8
# of early decision applicants	309
% accepted early decision	77

FRESHMAN PROFILE

Range SAT Critical Reading	550–650
Range SAT Math	580–670
Range ACT Composite	24–29
Minimum Paper TOEFL	600
Minimum Computer Based TOEFL	250
Average HS GPA	3.5
% graduated top 10% of class	64
% graduated top 25% of class	84
% graduated top 50% of class	98

DEADLINES

Early decision application deadline	11/15
Early decision notification	12/15
Regular application deadline	1/15
Regular notification	4/1
Nonfall registration?	no

APPLICANTS ALSO LOOK AT

AND OFTEN PREFER
Colby College, Colgate University

AND SOMETIMES PREFER
Hamilton College, Lafayette College, Skidmore College

AND RARELY PREFER
Rensselaer Polytechnic Institute, University of Rochester

FINANCIAL FACTS

Financial Aid Rating	95
Comprehensive fee	$44,043
Books and supplies	$450
% frosh rec. need-based scholarship or grant aid	60
% UG rec. need-based scholarship or grant aid	48
% frosh rec. need-based self-help aid	45
% UG rec. need-based self-help aid	42
% frosh rec. any financial aid	59
% UG rec. any financial aid	62

UNITED STATES AIR FORCE ACADEMY

2304 CADET DRIVE, SUITE 2500, USAF ACADEMY, CO 80840-5025 • ADMISSIONS: 719-333-2520 • FAX: 719-333-3012

CAMPUS LIFE
Quality of Life Rating	78
Fire Safety Rating	60*
Type of school	public
Environment	metropolis

STUDENTS
Total undergrad enrollment	4,524
% male/female	82/18
% from out of state	94
% live on campus	100
% African American	4
% Asian	8
% Caucasian	78
% Hispanic	7
% Native American	2
% international	1

SURVEY SAYS . . .
Small classes
No one cheats
Lab facilities are great
Great computer facilities
Great library
Athletic facilities are great
Career services are great
Campus feels safe
Frats and sororities are unpopular or
nonexistent
Very little drug use

ACADEMICS
Academic Rating	99
Calendar	semester
Student/faculty ratio	8:1
Profs interesting rating	88
Profs accessible rating	99
% profs teaching	
UG courses	100
% classes taught by TAs	0
Most common	
reg class size	10–19 students

MOST POPULAR MAJORS
business administration/
management
engineering
social sciences

STUDENTS SAY

Academics

If the prospect of "seemingly impossible academic demands" piled atop "mentally and physically demanding experiences, such as military free-fall parachute training, combat survival, and evasion training" appeals to you, you may well be United States Air Force Academy material. The academy "challenges every student on every level" in its pursuit of "building officers who want to serve in the United States Air Force." Students warn that "this is not school, it is work. The training is intense and sometimes demands more hours than there are in a day." The payoff, of course, is a commission as an Air Force officer at graduation, accompanied by a really cool skill set. As one student puts it, "The experiences gained at USAFA cannot be found at any other school—skydiving, internships at national labs, flying programs, emphasis on leadership and character development, etc." Another adds, "This school's academic programs are one of a kind. I was given the opportunity to manage a $150,000 program that involves directing 16 other seniors toward a final event at the end of the year where we will launch a rocket to space off the coast of California." Students tell us that academy professors "are very tough on us, and the curriculum itself is hard, but professors understand that as cadets we are required to do more than just study for quizzes and write papers. Therefore, most of our instructors are very understanding, and they try to make this place run as smoothly as possible. There are always exceptions, but that is all they are: Exceptions to the rule!"

Life

"Life is incredibly busy" at the Air Force Academy. "If it isn't schoolwork, then you are working out or working on military duties. There is free time, but it is limited and often best used doing schoolwork." It's often not possible for students to leave campus to have fun; one student explains, "As a freshman, you have a certain number of passes to go out. Plus, it's possible to be restricted. If you are on probation (for failing academics, athletics, conduct, or honor), you cannot leave [without permission]." Those who can't get passes "are forced to come up with other ways to have fun. Others really love to sleep, and then there are those who are obsessed with the weight room and the athletic facilities." Life becomes a little easier as you rise through the ranks. Upperclassmen look forward to "getting out into the town to see a movie or go to dinner. Of course, skiing and snowboarding are popular too." Students should note that underage "Drinking on campus is unheard of these days; it's illegal and tightly enforced. Drinking off campus is the norm."

Student Body

Air Force cadets tend to be "self-motivated, highly ambitious achievers"; "type-A personalities who don't go looking for extra work but make sure that any job assigned to them is done well." Students observe that "cadets are fairly similar; we have a small student body, and service academies generally attract people with the same kind of views." They tend to be "from conservative backgrounds." Exchange cadets and midshipmen from other academies and international students add some diversity, bringing "representatives of 40 different countries and nearly all ethnic and racial backgrounds to campus." Common personality types range from "type-A athlete" to the "type-A nerd" to "everyone else, who tries to balance academics, athletics, and military training without getting overburdened." Many students claim that your average cadet "is a bit cynical," but "The guy who's yelling at you on Monday is the guy loaning you his car on Saturday." The low number of females makes for a very interesting social environment, and the military aspect also limits how "atypical" anyone can actually be here.

E-MAIL: RR_WEBMAIL@USAFA.AF.MIL • WEBSITE: WWW.USAFA.AF.MIL

ADMISSIONS

Very important factors considered include: Character/personal qualities, interview, rigor of secondary school record, standardized test scores. *Important factors considered include:* Academic GPA, application essay, class rank, extracurricular activities, talent/ability, volunteer work, work experience. *Other factors considered include:* Alumni/ae relation, recommendation(s). SAT or ACT required; ACT with Writing component required. *Academic units recommended:* 4 English, 4 math, 4 science (4 science labs), 2 foreign language, 3 social studies, 3 history.

The Inside Word

The Air Force Academy promises a demanding 4 years, and the fainthearted need not apply. Due to the arduous nature of the school, it's no wonder that applicants face stringent requirements right at the outset. Aside from an excellent academic record, successful candidates need to be physically fit. They also must win a nomination from their congressperson. Honor is a valued quality at the academy, and Admissions Officers will only accept those with the strength of character and determination necessary to succeed at one of the country's most elite institutions.

FINANCIAL AID

The Princeton Review suggests that all financial aid forms be submitted as soon as possible after January 1.

FROM THE ADMISSIONS OFFICE

"Applicants for Fall 2008 are required to take the new SAT (or the ACT with the Writing section), but students may submit scores from the old SAT or ACT as well, and will use the student's best scores from either test. "

SELECTIVITY

Admissions Rating	96
# of applicants	9,296
% of applicants accepted	19
% of acceptees attending	77

FRESHMAN PROFILE

Range SAT Critical Reading	580–668
Range SAT Math	610–690
Average HS GPA	3.86
% graduated top 10% of class	50
% graduated top 25% of class	81
% graduated top 50% of class	98

DEADLINES

Regular application deadline	1/31
Regular notification	rolling
Nonfall registration?	no

APPLICANTS ALSO LOOK AT AND SOMETIMES PREFER

United States Coast Guard Academy, United States Merchant Marine Academy, United States Military Academy, United States Naval Academy

FINANCIAL FACTS

Financial Aid Rating	60*
Annual in-state tuition	$0*
Annual out-of-state tuition	$0*

*Tuition covered by full scholarship.

United States Coast Guard Academy

31 MOHEGAN AVENUE, NEW LONDON, CT 06320-8103 • ADMISSIONS: 800-883-8724 • FAX: 860-701-6700

STUDENTS SAY

Academics

The United States Coast Guard Academy "brings together a diverse group of people dedicated to a common goal and teaches them how to live and work together to become leaders and to truly function as a team. We all live in the same building, eat the same meals, and go through the same training." If learning "personal discipline and how to balance a lot of responsibility with a heavy class load" sounds appealing to you—and you like the sea—then the CGA may be the right fit for you. Benefits include a free education ("although you put in enough mandatory extracurricular work to work your way though a normal college"), a "guaranteed job for 5 years after you graduate," and "incredible summer training programs that include all-expenses-paid trips (on Coast Guard ships) to places like Hawaii, Alaska, and Bermuda." Students can choose from only eight majors (the majority of which have the word "engineering" in them somewhere), and much of the course work here is required. "Every cadet has to take mandatory classes of Calculus I and II, Chemistry I and II, Physics I and II, Morals and Ethics, World and American Government, Criminal Justice, Health, Static Engineering Design, Basic Naval Architecture, English and Literature, Introduction to Electrical Engineering, and Macroeconomics, before and while we are taking our major-area classes. We all leave here very well-rounded." While professors "are tough and push us hard," students enjoy "an incredible support network of teachers, students, mentors, coaches, and staff that take an integral role in helping us to achieve our personal and professional goals in and out of the Coast Guard."

Life

"Life is very regimented" at CGA, as students "all live in the same building, wake up at the same time, attend formations, and eat together." The experience "is a mix of military training, academics, and other activities. The first year is all about indoctrination. You will carry about 20-plus credit hours, military work (duty and always having your uniform and room ready for inspection), and required activity credits." Even after the first year, "We are not given many of the freedoms that most college students have. We aren't allowed to go out on weeknights, and the rest of our liberty is restricted." As a result, cadets report, "When we are given the opportunity to go out or go on vacation, we go hard." The strict regulations work for some students, but others "become cynical by the time they have become seniors. Sometimes I regret not experiencing the kind of life that normal college students get to have." Stress relievers include club sports, which "are incredible considering the size of the school." Days out enjoying "the picturesque New England setting" and trips to New York City and Boston also help.

Student Body

"Because of the uniform, there is no discrimination like the petty discrimination of cliques in high school" at CGA. "We are shipmates, no matter where you were from or what you were like in your previous life as a civilian." One student explains, "Since we know we'll be working together for the rest of our military careers, people treat others with the utmost respect. There is no cheating, no stealing, no lying. If someone says they'll do something, they will." Most students are "A-type personalities" who "come from backgrounds in which [they] have always excelled academically, socially, and athletically. Atypical students are those who miss one or more of those traits." One cadet warns, "Atypical students quickly become typical students. We make sure of that!" Those who cannot fit the mold "do not perform well or are discharged."

UNITED STATES COAST GUARD ACADEMY

E-MAIL: ADMISSIONS@USCGA.EDU • WEBSITE: WWW.USCGA.EDU

ADMISSIONS

Very important factors considered include: Academic GPA, character/personal qualities, class rank, extracurricular activities, rigor of secondary school record, standardized test scores. *Important factors considered include:* Application essay, recommendation(s), talent/ability. *Other factors considered include:* Alumni/ae relation, interview, level of applicant's interest, volunteer work, work experience. SAT or ACT required; ACT with Writing component required. TOEFL required of all international applicants. High school diploma is required, and GED is accepted. *Academic units required:* 4 English, 4 math, 3 science (3 science labs).

The Inside Word

The Coast Guard is the smallest service academy, regarded by many as a well-kept secret. Just like the other military service academies, admission is highly selective. Candidates must go through a rigorous admissions process that includes a medical exam and physical fitness evaluation. Those who pass muster join a very proud service. If you're a woman and thinking about a service academy, be aware that the Corps of Cadets at the Coast Guard Academy is 30 percent women!

FINANCIAL AID

The Princeton Review suggests that all financial aid forms be submitted as soon as possible after January 1.

FROM THE ADMISSIONS OFFICE

"Founded in 1876, the United States Coast Guard Academy enjoys a proud tradition of graduating leaders of character. The academy experience melds academic rigor, leadership development, and athletic participation to prepare you to graduate as a commissioned officer. Character development of cadets is founded on the core values of honor, respect, and devotion to duty. You build friendships that last a lifetime, study with inspiring professors in small classes, and train during the summer aboard America's tall ship *Eagle*, as well as the service's ships and aircraft. Top performers spend their senior summer traveling on exciting internships around the nation and overseas. Graduates serve for 5 years and have unmatched opportunities to attend flight school and graduate school, all funded by the Coast Guard.

"Appointments to the Academy are based on a selective admissions process; Congressional nominations are not required. Your leadership potential and desire to serve your country are what counts. Our student body reflects the best America has to offer—with all its potential and diversity!

"Applicants for Fall 2008 are required to take the new SAT (or the ACT with the Writing section), but students may submit scores from the old SAT or ACT as well, and will use the student's best scores from either test."

SELECTIVITY

Admissions Rating	96
# of applicants	1,633
% of applicants accepted	24
% of acceptees attending	70

FRESHMAN PROFILE

Range SAT Critical Reading	570–670
Range SAT Math	610–680
Range ACT Composite	25–29
Minimum Paper TOEFL	560
Minimum Computer Based TOEFL	220
Average HS GPA	3.76
% graduated top 10% of class	50
% graduated top 25% of class	90
% graduated top 50% of class	99

DEADLINES

Regular application deadline	3/1
Regular notification	rolling
Nonfall registration?	no

FINANCIAL FACTS

Financial Aid Rating	60*
Annual in-state tuition	$0*
Annual out-of-state tuition	$0*

*Tuition covered by full scholarship.

UNITED STATES MERCHANT MARINE ACADEMY

OFFICE OF ADMISSIONS, KINGS POINT, NY 11024-1699 • ADMISSIONS: 516-773-5391 • FAX: 516-773-5390

CAMPUS LIFE

Quality of Life Rating	63
Fire Safety Rating	60*
Type of school	public
Environment	village

STUDENTS

Total undergrad enrollment	1,007
% male/female	86/14
% from out of state	87
% from public high school	70
% live on campus	100
% African American	2
% Asian	3
% Caucasian	90
% Hispanic	5
% international	2
# of countries represented	3

SURVEY SAYS . . .

Small classes
Career services are great
Lousy food on campus
Low cost of living
Frats and sororities are unpopular or nonexistent
Very little drug use

ACADEMICS

Academic Rating	75
Calendar	trimester
Student/faculty ratio	11:1
Profs interesting rating	61
Profs accessible rating	70
Most common lab size	10–19 students
Most common reg class size	10–19 students

MOST POPULAR MAJORS

engineering
naval architecture and marine engineering
transportation and materials moving services

STUDENTS SAY

Academics

"Producing the highest caliber of professional mariners in terms of character and ability" is what it's all about at the federally funded United States Merchant Marine Academy. The USMMA is not a carefree experience; the workload is intense ("17 to 25 hours per week in class," students estimate), because a year spent at sea means students "have to fit 4 years of college into the 3 years we are physically on campus." This time spent at sea, however, is "what sets Kings Point [USMMA] apart. Sea year teaches midshipmen how to study independently and work in an adult environment, and it gives us a global perspective." One midshipman notes, "The training that the students get while out at sea is second to none in learning about engineering, navigation, and business." Another thing that makes the hard work worthwhile is the prospect of "incredible options when you graduate." One student explains, "We can become officers in any branch of the military, including the NOAA [National Oceanic and Atmospheric Administration] and Coast Guard. We can sail merchant ships or go into shore-side engineering and management careers. We can go to grad school with a stipend from the government. And the alumni network is unbelievable. Aside from all of that, we graduate having worked in our chosen field and sailed in almost every sea on Earth," and visited "maybe a dozen different countries." Graduates of USMMA walk away with "one of the top maritime educations that can be found in the world."

Life

Life at USMMA is rugged and highly regimented. It's especially difficult for first-year students (called "plebes"), who "are on lockdown most of the time" and "who clean everything. Rather than having a janitor service for the barracks, the plebes clean, and if cleaning isn't done well, we get in trouble with the upperclassmen." While many underclassmen jokingly compare the plebe experience to being "in jail," they also praise the way the experience of being a plebe molds character; as one student states, "Plebes have horrible lives to begin with. However, the structure and environment develop great leaders and provide a solid foundation for success." All students participate in a daily regimen of reveille, morning inspection, colors, classes, muster, more classes, and drills. Upperclassmen, on the other hand, enjoy "more liberty and spend a lot of time off campus, either in Great Neck (the town nearest us) or in New York City." USMMA midshipmen appreciate "the many opportunities for student leadership; every student is required to be a team leader for a room of plebes [during] sophomore year, every junior is required to hold a petty officer position to a student senior officer for at least a trimester, and every senior holds an officer position for at least half of senior year." Students also praise the way academy life presents "various ways to challenge oneself physically, mentally, and emotionally" and to expand one's horizons. One student sums up, "It's a full schedule, but it's fulfilling. I have personally been to Japan, China, Germany, England, New Zealand, Antarctica, Belgium, and up and down the East and West Coasts of the United States."

Students

The stereotypical USMMA student "is a conservative White male, often—but not always—from a military background." Women and students of color are in the minority at USMMA. Regardless of race or sex, however, all students "share a common love for the United States and a desire to serve it admirably." Beyond love for their country, what ties students together is the shared experience: "At USMMA there is a bond that is formed during Indoc [the 2-week indoctrination program], and there is a sense of pride in being a Kings Pointer." Because of "the close bonds developed, race and geographical origin are nonissues among the student body." Or, as another student puts it, "Shared pain makes most people fit in just fine."

UNITED STATES MERCHANT MARINE ACADEMY

FINANCIAL AID: 516-773-5295 • E-MAIL: ADMISSIONS@USMMA.EDU • WEBSITE: WWW.USMMA.EDU

ADMISSIONS

Very important factors considered include: Character/personal qualities, rigor of secondary school record, standardized test scores. *Important factors considered include:* Application essay, class rank, extracurricular activities, geographical residence, recommendation(s), talent/ability. *Other factors considered include:* Interview, racial/ethnic status, state residency, volunteer work, work experience. SAT or ACT required; TOEFL required of all international applicants. High school diploma is required, and GED is not accepted. *Academic units required:* 4 English, 3 math, 3 science (1 science lab), 8 academic electives. *Academic units recommended:* 4 English, 4 math, 4 science (2 science labs), 2 foreign language, 4 social studies.

The Inside Word

Prospective midshipmen face demanding admission requirements. The USMMA assesses scholastic achievement, strength of character, and stamina (applicants must meet specific physical standards). Candidates must also be nominated by a proper nominating authority, typically a state representative or senator.

FINANCIAL AID

Students should submit: FAFSA, institution's own financial aid form. Regular filing deadline is May 1. The Princeton Review suggests that all financial aid forms be submitted as soon as possible after January 1. *Need-based scholarships/grants offered:* Pell Grant, private scholarships. *Loan aid offered:* FFEL Subsidized Stafford, FFEL Unsubsidized Stafford, FFEL PLUS. Applicants will be notified of awards on a rolling basis beginning or about January 31. Off-campus job opportunities are poor.

FROM THE ADMISSIONS OFFICE

"What makes the U.S. Merchant Marine Academy different from the other federal service academies? The difference can be summarized in two phrases that appear in our publications. The first: 'The World Is Your Campus.' You will spend a year at sea—a third of your sophomore year and two-thirds of your junior year—teamed with a classmate aboard a U.S. merchant ship. You will visit an average of 18 foreign nations while you work and learn in a mariner's true environment. You will graduate with seafaring experience and as a citizen of the world. The second phrase is 'Options and Opportunities.' Unlike students at the other federal academies, who are required to enter the service connected to their academy, you have the option of working in the seagoing merchant marine and transportation industry or applying for active duty in the Navy, Coast Guard, Marine Corps, Air Force, or Army. Nearly 25 percent of our most recent graduating class entered various branches of the armed forces with an officer rank. As a graduate of the U.S. Merchant Marine Academy, you will receive a Bachelor of Science degree, a government-issued merchant marine officer's license, and a Naval Reserve commission (unless you have been accepted for active military duty). No other service academy offers so attractive a package.

"Freshman applicants for the academic year starting in July 2008 must take the new SAT or the ACT with the Writing component. Students may still submit scores from older SAT or ACT tests that did not include a writing/essay component. For homeschooled students, we recommend they also submit scores from SAT Subject Tests in Chemistry and/or Physics."

SELECTIVITY

Admissions Rating	94
# of applicants	1,797
% of applicants accepted	21
% of acceptees attending	77
# accepting a place on wait list	212
% admitted from wait list	1

FRESHMAN PROFILE

Range SAT Critical Reading	570–690
Range SAT Math	590–670
Range ACT Composite	25–31
Minimum Paper TOEFL	550
Minimum Computer Based TOEFL	213
Average HS GPA	3.6
% graduated top 10% of class	26
% graduated top 25% of class	64
% graduated top 50% of class	96

DEADLINES

Early decision application deadline	11/1
Early decision notification	12/31
Regular application deadline	3/1
Regular notification	rolling
Nonfall registration?	no

APPLICANTS ALSO LOOK AT

AND OFTEN PREFER
United States Naval Academy

AND SOMETIMES PREFER
United States Air Force Academy, United States Coast Guard Academy, United States Military Academy

AND RARELY PREFER
Maine Maritime Academy, Massachusetts Maritime Academy, State University of New York—Maritime College

FINANCIAL FACTS

Financial Aid Rating	98
Annual in-state tuition	$0*
Annual out-of-state tuition	$0*
Required fees	$2,606
% frosh rec. need-based scholarship or grant aid	15
% UG rec. need-based scholarship or grant aid	5
% frosh rec. need-based self-help aid	15
% UG rec. need-based self-help aid	8

*Tuition covered by full scholarship.

UNITED STATES MILITARY ACADEMY

600 THAYER ROAD, WEST POINT, NY 10996-1797 • ADMISSIONS: 845-938-4041 • FAX: 845-938-3021

CAMPUS LIFE
Quality of Life Rating	71
Fire Safety Rating	83
Type of school	public
Environment	village

STUDENTS
Total undergrad enrollment	4,231
% male/female	85/15
% from out of state	92
% from public high school	86
% live on campus	100
% African American	6
% Asian	7
% Caucasian	77
% Hispanic	7
% Native American	1
% international	1
# of countries represented	35

SURVEY SAYS . . .
Small classes
No one cheats
Great computer facilities
Great library
Athletic facilities are great
Career services are great
Campus feels safe
Frats and sororities are unpopular or nonexistent
Very little drug use

ACADEMICS
Academic Rating	98
Calendar	semester
Student/faculty ratio	7:1
Profs interesting rating	89
Profs accessible rating	98
% profs teaching UG courses	100
% classes taught by TAs	0
Most common lab size	10–19 students
Most common reg class size	10–19 students

MOST POPULAR MAJORS
economics
history
political science and government

STUDENTS SAY

Academics

A United States Military Academy education "is not easy and not always fun, but it is a great experience to be proud of," and one that is designed "to educate tomorrow's world leaders." Don't come to West Point expecting the typical college experience. As one student explains, "The military atmosphere makes everything different. Teachers are usually commissioned Army officers and strict discipline is maintained within the classroom at all times. Disciplinary actions ensure that students turn in assignments on time, arrive to class on time, and do not miss class." Also, USMA uses "the Thayer method" of education, under which "Cadets are required to teach themselves the material before coming to class and then spend class time clarifying what was self-taught the night before." Though some find the system "unrealistic," most agree that "it is not really enjoyable to endure, but it does help foster individual academic responsibility." It also contributes to the sense that USMA "give you 28 hours of things to do in a 24-hour day." Expect to be "busy," but know that "every teacher makes an explicit point of stating that any help that a cadet needs will be given. If you want to do well here and are willing to work for it, the path is available for you to do so." Take heart; though the program "is as grueling as can be for the first 2 years," you'll find that in the final 2 years "You have a lot more time to do what you want to do."

Life

"Life at West Point is very regimented" and "Just about every hour of every day is busy." As one student puts it, "West Point tries to make sure that we have little free time and are always doing something (physical, academic, or military)." Another adds that there is "not much room for fun." "Physical fitness is a big part of every student's life," as "West Point has corps-wide physical testing events. From the APFT (Army Physical Fitness Test) to the infamous and dreaded IOCT (Indoor Obstacle Course Test), this place will make you stay in shape or get rid of you." In order to leave campus overnight, students need a pass. "During the first year, you are only guaranteed one pass to leave a semester, but everyone is allowed to go on trip sections, plebes included. Plebes are also allowed to go to the mall, visit sponsors' houses, play sports, and go to their own club to hang out—all without having to take pass." Also, "Passes are awarded for grades, physical fitness, attitude, special activities, etc." So as long as you are a "good person" and "take care of your business," the school is "more than happy to reward you and let you get off post for the weekend." Cadets love to "go to New York City on the weekend." Fitness doesn't end with the school day as many "enjoy the thrill of the outdoors and taking things to the extreme."

Student Body

Being a military school, it should come as no surprise that things as USMA are "uniform." "Most students are the same," notes a senior. They're "intelligent, athletic, honest, and committed to serving in the Army." And while it is a coed institution, expect a greater number of "male students." Gender aside, students are "very alike as far as life goals and ambitions . . . all are very intellectual and bring their own views to the school." There are "a lot of type-A personalities" here, all "prepared to do anything and everything to be the best." However, some find that the school "still has a long way to go" in terms of "ethnic diversity." But being part of "The Long Gray Line" comes with a "unifying, competitive spirit" that "levels the playing field" for these "soldiers and students."

FINANCIAL AID: 845-938-3516 • E-MAIL: ADMISSIONS@USMA.EDU • WEBSITE: WWW.USMA.EDU

ADMISSIONS

Very important factors considered include: Academic GPA, application essay, character/personal qualities, class rank, extracurricular activities, recommendation(s), rigor of secondary school record, standardized test scores, talent/ability. *Important factors considered include:* Geographical residence, interview, level of applicant's interest, racial/ethnic status, volunteer work. *Other factors considered include:* Alumni/ae relation, state residency, work experience. SAT or ACT required. High school diploma is required, and GED is accepted. *Academic units recommended:* 4 English, 4 math, 4 science (2 science labs), 2 foreign language, 3 social studies, 1 history, 3 academic electives.

The Inside Word

America's military academies experienced an increase in applicants after 9/11. They've been experiencing a similar drop in applications as the Iraq War continues, although it should be noted that the academies believe factors other than the war explain the drop. Regardless, fewer applicants means less competition, but it's still plenty tough to get into West Point. You have to begin the process in your junior year in order to get the requisite nomination. You'll need to excel in school to have a prayer; you'll also need to get into great physical condition to survive the vetting process.

FINANCIAL AID

The Princeton Review suggests that all financial aid forms be submitted as soon as possible after January 1. *Need-based scholarships/grants offered:* All cadets are on active duty as members of the United States Army and receive an annual salary of approximately $10,148. Room and board, medical and dental care is provided by the U.S. Army. A one-time deposit of $2,900 is required upon admission.

FROM THE ADMISSIONS OFFICE

"As a young man or woman considering your options for obtaining a quality college education, you may wonder what unique aspects the United States Military Academy has to offer. West Point offers one of the most highly respected, quality education programs in the nation. A West Point cadetship includes a fully funded 4-year college education. Tuition, room, board, medical, and dental care are provided by the U.S. Army. As members of the armed forces, cadets also receive an annual salary of more than $8,880. This pay covers the cost of uniforms, books, a personal computer, and living incidentals. By law, graduates of West Point are appointed on active duty as commissioned officers.

"Since its founding nearly two centuries ago, the Military Academy has accomplished its mission by developing cadets in four critical areas: intellectual, physical, military, and moral-ethical—a 4-year process called the 'West Point Experience.' Specific developmental goals are addressed through several fully coordinated and integrated programs.

"A challenging academic program that consists of a core of 31 courses provides a balanced education in the arts and sciences. This core curriculum establishes the foundation for elective courses that permit cadets to explore in greater depth a field of study or an optional major. All cadets receive a Bachelor of Science degree, which is designed specifically to meet the intellectual requirements of a commissioned officer in today's army.

"The physical program at West Point includes both physical education classes and competitive athletics. Every cadet participates in an intercollegiate, club, or intramural-level sport each semester. This rigorous physical program contributes to the mental and physical fitness that is required for service as an officer in the army.

"Applicants are required to take the new SAT (or the ACT with the Writing component). Students may also submit scores from the old SAT or ACT, and their best scores will be used regardless of test date."

SELECTIVITY

Admissions Rating	**96**
# of applicants	10,778
% of applicants accepted	14
% of acceptees attending	77

FRESHMAN PROFILE

Range SAT Critical Reading	570–670
Range SAT Math	600–690
Range ACT Composite	21–36
Average HS GPA	3.75
% graduated top 10% of class	48
% graduated top 25% of class	77
% graduated top 50% of class	94

DEADLINES

Regular application deadline	2/28
Regular notification	rolling
Nonfall registration?	no

APPLICANTS ALSO LOOK AT AND OFTEN PREFER

United States Air Force Academy, United States Naval Academy

FINANCIAL FACTS

Financial Aid Rating	**60***
Annual in-state tuition	$0*
Annual out-of-state tuition	$0*

*Tuition covered by full scholarship.

UNITED STATES NAVAL ACADEMY

117 DECATUR ROAD, ANNAPOLIS, MD 21402 • ADMISSIONS: 410-293-4361 • FAX: 410-295-1815

STUDENTS SAY

Academics

The United States Naval Academy "produces leaders, not just people with book knowledge" through a grueling academic and physical ordeal that forges graduates who are "strong morally, mentally, and physically, able to cope in any place that they are put, and able to overcome any obstacle that lies in their way." This "nonstop competition from start to finish [instills] discipline, time management, and dedication," as well as "great moral and ethical values" in midshipmen. All students receive a full scholarship, but no one here would tell you she or he is getting a free ride." "Academics are extremely hard" because, in large part, "There is very little time to do your work, with the military aspect taking up a great deal of time." The USNA offers a "solid curriculum" reinforced by small classes ("Even freshmen-level courses never exceed 21 students per class"), tremendous resources ("We have the money to access all kinds of amazing things"), and a solid faculty ("I take classes from a former Chairman of the Joint Chiefs of Staff and other respected professionals"). One student sums up: "This school sets and maintains a standard unimaginable at other colleges and universities, and the feeling of accomplishment at the end of the day is hard to beat."

Life

"Every midshipman may complain at one time or another about many aspects of life at the Naval Academy, but, overall, I believe it is what we want," notes one student at the USNA. "We did not come here for an easy experience. We came here to be the best. And the administration, officers, and professors expect exactly that from us." Be forewarned that "your first year will be extremely hard here," as "Plebe year is something that you'll have to experience in order to believe." For plebes, "Life is as restricted as it gets, short of prison. No music and movies, and you can only go out on Saturdays. We have mandatory drill, training, and physical exercise, along with student and military chains of command that restrict weekend liberty and what clothes we can wear, among other things." Throughout all 4 years, students "do an enormous amount of professional training, from summer training cruises to character development and leadership classes," and they "work out all the time." Campus recreation includes extracurricular activities "of every size and description"; when they get liberty ("You get more each year"), students head to Annapolis or to other nearby campuses. "For fun, there are about 10 bars within walking distance, for those of age." Students agree it's a rough life, but "Even the people who say they hate it rarely ever leave. There's nothing like being in King Hall (our dining hall) with 4,000 other midshipmen banging crab mallets on the table during the annual fall Crab Feast, or walking into Memorial Hall late at night and reading the names of graduates that have died in combat and remembering that 'they have set the course.'"

Student Body

"Contrary to what one might expect, there is a tremendous variety of students" at the United States Naval Academy. "They come from all over the country and many different socioeconomic classes and walks of life. No one can tell what kind of financial background you have; we all wear the same uniform, get the same pay, and get, in effect, full scholarship and free room and board." Many "were high school athletes who lettered in two or more varsity sports while having a 3.9 GPA in classes," the type of people who "excelled at almost everything they tried their hand at in high school and continue to excel at USNA." Despite the diversity of backgrounds, "There are almost [no] students who are atypical, because this is not an environment hospitable to them."

ADMISSIONS

Very important factors considered include: Application essay, character/personal qualities, class rank, extracurricular activities, interview, level of applicant's interest, recommendation(s), rigor of secondary school record, standardized test scores. *Important factors considered include:* Talent/ability. *Other factors considered include:* Alumni/ae relation, first generation, geographical residence, racial/ethnic status, volunteer work, work experience. SAT or ACT required; TOEFL required of all international applicants. High school diploma or equivalent is not required. *Academic units recommended:* 4 English, 4 math, 2 science (1 science lab), 2 foreign language, 2 history, 1 introductory computer and typing course.

The Inside Word

It doesn't take a genius to recognize that getting admitted to the USNA requires true strength of character; simply completing the arduous admissions process is an accomplishment worthy of remembrance. Those who have successful candidacies are strong, motivated students, and leaders in both school and community. Perseverance is an important character trait for anyone considering the life of a midshipman—the application process is only the beginning of a truly challenging and demanding experience.

FINANCIAL AID

Although the United States Naval Academy does not require students to complete a financial aid form, the Princeton Review suggests that all financial aid forms be submitted as soon as possible after January 1.

FROM THE ADMISSIONS OFFICE

"The Naval Academy offers you a unique opportunity to associate with a broad cross-section of the country's finest young men and women. You will have the opportunity to pursue a 4-year program that develops you mentally, morally, and physically as no civilian college can. As you might expect, this program is demanding, but the opportunities are limitless and more than worth the effort. To receive an appointment to the academy, you need 4 years of high school preparation to develop the strong academic, athletic, and extracurricular background required to compete successfully for admission. You should begin preparing in your freshman year and apply for admission at the end of your junior year. Selection for appointment to the academy comes as a result of a complete evaluation of your admissions package and completion of the nomination process. Complete admissions guidance may be found at www.usna.edu.

"SAT results from tests prior to March 2005 and ACT results from tests prior to February 2005 will be used by the Naval Academy, and no conversion of scores is necessary due to compatibility of old and new scoring systems."

SELECTIVITY

Admissions Rating	96
# of applicants	10,746
% of applicants accepted	14
% of acceptees attending	81
# accepting a place on wait list	85
% admitted from wait list	21

FRESHMAN PROFILE

Range SAT Critical Reading	560–670
Range SAT Math	600–700
Minimum Paper TOEFL	200
% graduated top 10% of class	54
% graduated top 25% of class	81
% graduated top 50% of class	96

DEADLINES

Regular application deadline	1/31
Regular notification	rolling
Nonfall registration?	no

APPLICANTS ALSO LOOK AT

AND OFTEN PREFER
Duke University, Harvard College, United States Air Force Academy, University of Virginia

AND SOMETIMES PREFER
Georgia Institute of Technology, Massachusetts Institute of Technology, Pennsylvania State University—University Park, United States Military Academy

AND RARELY PREFER
Boston University, Purdue University—West Lafayette, St. John's College (MD)

FINANCIAL FACTS

Financial Aid Rating	60*
Annual in-state tuition	$0*
Annual out-of-state tuition	$0*
Books and supplies	$1,000

*Tuition covered by full scholarship.

THE UNIVERSITY OF ALABAMA AT TUSCALOOSA

Box 870132, Tuscaloosa, AL 35487-0132 • Admissions: 205-348-5666 • Fax: 205-348-9046

CAMPUS LIFE

Quality of Life Rating	**85**
Fire Safety Rating	**73**
Type of school	public
Environment	city

STUDENTS

Total undergrad enrollment	19,237
% male/female	47/53
% from out of state	24
% from public high school	90
% live on campus	29
% in (# of) fraternities	20 (21)
% in (# of) sororities	26 (31)
% African American	11
% Asian	1
% Caucasian	84
% Hispanic	2
% Native American	1
% international	1
# of countries represented	83

SURVEY SAYS . . .

Great library
Athletic facilities are great
Everyone loves the Crimson Tide
Frats and sororities dominate social scene
Lots of beer drinking
Hard liquor is popular

ACADEMICS

Academic Rating	**76**
Calendar	semester
Student/faculty ratio	19:1
Profs interesting rating	80
Profs accessible rating	80
% profs teaching UG courses	71
% classes taught by TAs	11
Most common lab size	20–29 students
Most common reg class size	10–19 students

MOST POPULAR MAJORS

biology/biological sciences
finance
nursing/registered nurse training
(ASN, BSN, MSN, RN)

STUDENTS SAY

Academics

"Tradition and excellence" go hand in hand at the University of Alabama's flagship Tuscaloosa campus. Combining an atmosphere of "Southern charm with a modern and certainly enriching education," 'Bama offers the best of all worlds to students seeking a "student-centered research university with a rich tradition of academic, athletic, and community excellence where any student can find peers with common interests, enhance his or her knowledge base, and forge friendships that will last a lifetime." Students agree that UA is "a first-rate public university," and that "with 18,000 students and tons of majors and student organizations, this place can be about whatever you want it to be." Standout programs include business, accounting, dance, nutrition and dietetics, social work, communication and information science, and nursing. Honors students praise the administration for offering "strong support" and "incredible research opportunities" to program participants. In many areas, professors are "top researchers or writers in their fields" who "go out of their way to help you with whatever you need." UA also offers "a wide range [of] opportunities for hands-on experience. The colleges work with students to place them in internships that will allow them to grow and learn about their field, and also make contacts for future employment."

Life

Greek life and Crimson Tide football are the twin pillars of UA life. Undergrads report that "UA has a really strong Greek system, so the sororities and fraternities are very present around campus, and they're pretty impressive." The Greeks may be impressive, but they are not monolithic; as one undergrad points out, "The Greeks do pretty much decide the SGA [student government] and homecoming, but they don't control all the clubs or honor societies." Football is the more universal force; it "encompasses the entire campus. Life during football season revolves around football. The vast majority of the students support and enjoy it." The social life of the campus cycles around the season; "During football season, weekends consist of band parties on Fridays, games on Saturdays followed by parties, and recovering on Sundays." Beyond frats and pigskins, "Life on campus is up to the particular students. If they want to fit in, they party with the party kids. If they are not typical party people, they can find others to spend time with doing whatever they feel is fun." With such a large student body, clubs abound: "There is interest in every possible subject under the sun; chances are that no matter what interest a student holds, there are at least half a dozen other students on campus with the same interest."

Student Body

Most UA students are "easygoing, with plenty of Southern hospitality," and have a "very balanced approach between study and social life." While some students feel that "student culture here puts a great deal of pressure on students to fit into the mold that has dominated this campus for so long," and others claim that the campus is "not as integrated as it could be," still others praise the university for embracing diversity among the student body. As one student states, it's true that "[many] students at the University of Alabama are White, middle- to upper-class kids from the South. They tend to come from traditional families, and a lot are religious. [But] the university is increasing diversity." Undergrads report that "minority groups tend to find a great deal of support and develop much pride here, and they experience very little criticism." The student body is also "far more ideologically diverse than most people would like to think; there is a myth that the university is overrun with [those on the] far right, but this is simply not true; there is a wide representation of political views among the student body."

THE UNIVERSITY OF ALABAMA AT TUSCALOOSA

FINANCIAL AID: 205-348-6756 • E-MAIL: ADMISSIONS@UA.EDU • WEBSITE: WWW.UA.EDU

ADMISSIONS

Very important factors considered include: Academic GPA, rigor of secondary school record, standardized test scores. *Important factors considered include:* Class rank. *Other factors considered include:* Alumni/ae relation, application essay, character/personal qualities, extracurricular activities, first generation, interview, recommendation(s), talent/ability, volunteer work, work experience. SAT or ACT required; TOEFL required of all international applicants. High school diploma is required, and GED is accepted. *Academic units required:* 4 English, 3 math, 3 science (2 science labs), 1 foreign language, 3 social studies, 1 history, 5 academic electives. *Academic units recommended:* 4 English, 3 math, 3 science (2 science labs), 1 foreign language, 3 social studies, 1 history, 5 academic electives.

The Inside Word

The University of Alabama at Tuscaloosa relies heavily on objective data in the application process. Admission is not highly competitive, and applicants with satisfactory grades and modest test scores are likely to be accepted.

FINANCIAL AID

Students should submit: FAFSA. The Princeton Review suggests that all financial aid forms be submitted as soon as possible after January 1. *Need-based scholarships/grants offered:* Pell Grant, SEOG, state scholarships/grants, private scholarships, the school's own gift aid, Federal Nursing Scholarship. *Loan aid offered:* Direct Subsidized Stafford, Direct Unsubsidized Stafford, Direct PLUS, Federal Perkins Loan, college/university loans from institutional funds. Applicants will be notified of awards on a rolling basis beginning or about April 1.

FROM THE ADMISSIONS OFFICE

"Since its founding in 1831 as the first public university in the state, the University of Alabama has been committed to providing the best, most complete education possible for its students. Our commitment to that goal means that as times change, we sharpen our focus and methods to keep our graduates competitive in their fields. By offering outstanding teaching in a solid core curriculum enhanced by multimedia classrooms and campus-wide computer labs, the University of Alabama keeps its focus on the future while maintaining a traditional college atmosphere. Extensive international study opportunities, internship programs, and cooperative education placements help our students prepare for successful futures. Consisting of 11 colleges and schools offering 220 degrees in more than 100 fields of study, the university gives its students a wide range of choices and offers courses of study at the bachelor's, master's, specialist, and doctoral levels. The university emphasizes quality and breadth of academic opportunities and challenging programs for well-prepared students through its Honors College, including the University Honors Program, International Honors Program, and Computer-Based Honors Programs and Blount Undergraduate Initiative (liberal arts program). Twenty-four percent of undergraduates are from out of state, providing an enriching social and cultural environment.

"Applicants for the 2008 freshmen class may submit either the new SAT or the old SAT (administered before March 2005). For those students electing to take the ACT test, the Writing component is not required for admission to the University of Alabama."

SELECTIVITY

Admissions Rating	85
# of applicants	12,513
% of applicants accepted	70
% of acceptees attending	50

FRESHMAN PROFILE

Range SAT Critical Reading	500–630
Range SAT Math	500–630
Range ACT Composite	21–27
Minimum Paper TOEFL	500
Minimum Computer Based TOEFL	173
Average HS GPA	3.4
% graduated top 10% of class	39
% graduated top 25% of class	54
% graduated top 50% of class	79

DEADLINES

Regular notification	rolling
Nonfall registration?	yes

APPLICANTS ALSO LOOK AT
AND OFTEN PREFER
Duke University, Florida State University, University of Georgia, University of Tennessee—Knoxville, Vanderbilt University
AND SOMETIMES PREFER
Auburn University, Louisiana State University, Samford University, Tulane University

FINANCIAL FACTS

Financial Aid Rating	74
Annual in-state tuition	$5,754
Annual out-of-state tuition	$16,670
Room & Board	$6,468
Books and supplies	$300
% frosh rec. need-based scholarship or grant aid	16
% UG rec. need-based scholarship or grant aid	19
% frosh rec. need-based self-help aid	27
% UG rec. need-based self-help aid	31
% frosh rec. any financial aid	68
% UG rec. any financial aid	74

UNIVERSITY OF ARIZONA

PO Box 210040, Tucson, AZ 85721-0040 • Admissions: 520-621-3237 • Fax: 520-621-9799

CAMPUS LIFE

Quality of Life Rating	68
Fire Safety Rating	60*
Type of school	public
Environment	metropolis

STUDENTS

Total undergrad enrollment	28,013
% male/female	47/53
% from out of state	33
% from public high school	90
% live on campus	20
% in (# of) fraternities	10 (25)
% in (# of) sororities	11 (20)
% African American	3
% Asian	6
% Caucasian	65
% Hispanic	16
% Native American	2
% international	3
# of countries represented	124

SURVEY SAYS . . .

Great computer facilities
Great library
Everyone loves the Wildcats
Frats and sororities dominate social scene
Student publications are popular
Lots of beer drinking
Hard liquor is popular

ACADEMICS

Academic Rating	70
Calendar	semester
Student/faculty ratio	18:1
Profs interesting rating	63
Profs accessible rating	62
% profs teaching UG courses	78
% classes taught by TAs	22
Most common lab size	10–19 students
Most common reg class size	10–19 students

MOST POPULAR MAJORS

elementary education and teaching
political science and government
psychology

STUDENTS SAY

Academics

Students at the University of Arizona enjoy that sought-after combination of reasonable tuition and solid reputation, and they know it. "I can't believe the diversity of academic opportunities and relatively low cost of education and living," gushes a junior. The academic rigor surprises some admitted students, who report, "It's definitely harder than I expected it to be." Overall, students agree that "it is a great learning environment." Despite it being a "large campus," the "friendly" professors "try very hard to make learning fun and interesting." Another student concurs, "The professors all have available time in which you can go see them and are happy to see you." Undergraduates find their instructors "very understanding [and] highly skilled in their fields." Teaching assistants "who work with classes are almost always really passionate, energetic, and ambitious." However, when it comes to the administration, students are evenly split between decrying it for "canceling classes and important programs while pouring more money into weight rooms for their athletes," and praising it for being "helpful and friendly" while trying "their hardest to answer questions accurately and forward you to the right person." Either way, one student notes that while the administration is typically "ready with answers to your questions, you sort of have to stumble your way through" early on. Bigger is not always better to some in Tucson. One undergraduate writes, "I just wish classes were smaller, so it would be easier to learn."

Life

Any description of the "beautiful" University of Arizona would not be complete without tribute to the "constant party" that animates the campus. "For the 21-and-over crowd the bars near campus are packed almost 7 days a week," says a junior. That said, at the end of the day people are here for school so despite the "party all the time" lore, they "don't lose sight of their academic goals." Active Greek chapters generate a steady flow of "great parties and date dashes." Students agree that "Tucson is an amazing place" and "There is an immense amount of things to do . . . but you have to make an effort to find new things." After classes, most converge on Fourth Avenue ("where the bars are," along with restaurants and movie theaters). Currently, local Tucson residents are working with the U of A to address rowdy house parties; however, everyone unites around Wildcat basketball. "The team is always awesome," notes one student. Students appreciate "the near-perfect weather most of the year." When it's snowy—in the mountains, that is—"some people go up to Mt. Lemon and go skiing or snowboarding." Students also take advantage of other "outdoor recreation opportunities, like hiking and mountain biking," but some feel that there isn't "much to do without a car." For most, though, the continually good weather is enough and they spend their time accordingly "sunbathing and people-watching outside while they study to pass exams."

Student Body

When you break it down, the U of A population sorts into "all types: athletes, nerds, Greeks, hippies, [and] preppies." Students can choose a "sun-bleached, name-brand, party" crowd or the "laid-back, more academically minded" scene. A typical student "loves sports, loves our teams, and loves to party." Many note the "large amount of Greek/Greek-esque people," explaining that while "there does seem to be a mold . . . it is possible to find a niche." All things considered, students are "friendly, outgoing, and accepting of a lot of different people." In addition, "The school also hosts a visible "population of out-of-staters." The student body includes "students of all backgrounds, religions, ethnicities, and incomes" who coexist in a "very open, accepting, and friendly environment." One undergraduate says of his colleagues, "While some are well-rounded, passionate, intelligent individuals, the vast majority, socially speaking, seem to be stuck somewhere between middle school and high school." Regardless, "It's a relatively large campus so it's not hard to find someone [who] shares your common interests."

FINANCIAL AID: 520-621-1858 • E-MAIL: APPINFO@ARIZONA.EDU • WEBSITE: WWW.ARIZONA.EDU

ADMISSIONS

Very important factors considered include: Academic GPA, rigor of secondary school record. *Other factors considered include:* Application essay, character/personal qualities, class rank, extracurricular activities, first generation, geographical residence, interview, racial/ethnic status, recommendation(s), standardized test scores, state residency, talent/ability, volunteer work. SAT or ACT recommended. High school diploma is required, and GED is accepted. *Academic units required:* 4 English, 4 math, 3 science (3 science labs), 2 foreign language, 1 social studies, 1 history, 1 fine art. *Academic units recommended:* 4 English, 4 math, 3 science (3 science labs), 2 foreign language, 2 social studies, 1 history, 1 fine art.

The Inside Word

The sun never sets for an Arizona resident—particularly if they're applying to the University of Arizona and have a solid academic record. The university currently offers "assured admission" for freshmen applicants. This essentially guarantees all applicants immediate admission provided they have fulfilled the following requirements, as detailed on the school's website: They must be "an Arizona resident, attend a regionally accredited high school, rank in the top 25 percent of their class, and have no course work deficiencies as prescribed by the Arizona Board of Regents."

FINANCIAL AID

The Princeton Review suggests that all financial aid forms be submitted as soon as possible after January 1. *Need-based scholarships/grants offered:* Pell Grant, SEOG, state scholarships/grants, private scholarships, the school's own gift aid, Federal Nursing Scholarship. *Loan aid offered:* FFEL Subsidized Stafford, FFEL Unsubsidized Stafford, FFEL PLUS, Federal Perkins Loan, Federal Nursing Loan, college/university loans from institutional funds. Federal Work-Study Program available. Institutional employment available. Off-campus job opportunities are good.

FROM THE ADMISSIONS OFFICE

"Surrounded by mountains and the dramatic beauty of the Sonoran Desert, the University of Arizona offers a top-drawer education in a resort-like setting. Some of the nation's highest-ranked departments make their homes at this oasis of learning in the desert. In addition to producing cloudless sunshine 350 days per year, the clear Arizona skies provide an ideal setting for one of the country's best astronomy programs. Other nationally rated programs include nursing, sociology, management information systems, anthropology, creative writing, and computer and aerospace engineering. The university balances a strong research component with an emphasis on teaching—faculty rolls include Nobel and Pulitzer Prize winners. Famous Chinese astrophysicist and political dissident Fang Lizhi continues his landmark studies here; he now teaches physics to undergraduates. The wealth of academic choices—the university offers 118 majors—is supplemented by an active, progressive campus atmosphere; conference-winning basketball, softball, and football teams; and myriad recreational opportunities.

"As of this book's publication, the University of Arizona did not have information available about their policy regarding the new SAT."

SELECTIVITY

Admissions Rating	**83**
# of applicants	16,609
% of applicants accepted	80
% of acceptees attending	45

FRESHMAN PROFILE

Range SAT Critical Reading	490–600
Range SAT Math	500–630
Range ACT Composite	20–26
Average HS GPA	3.36
% graduated top 10% of class	34
% graduated top 25% of class	62
% graduated top 50% of class	87

DEADLINES

Regular notification	rolling
Nonfall registration?	yes

APPLICANTS ALSO LOOK AT

AND OFTEN PREFER
University of California—Irvine,
University of Washington,

AND SOMETIMES PREFER
Ohio University—Athens, University of California—Santa Barbara, University of California—Los Angeles, University of Colorado—Boulder, University of Wisconsin—Madison

AND RARELY PREFER
Arizona State University at the Tempe Campus, Baylor University, Northern Arizona University

FINANCIAL FACTS

Financial Aid Rating	**64**
Annual in-state tuition	$4,594
Annual out-of-state tuition	$14,800
Room & Board	$7,850
Books and supplies	$816
Required fees	$172
% frosh rec. need-based scholarship or grant aid	33
% UG rec. need-based scholarship or grant aid	34
% frosh rec. need-based self-help aid	18
% UG rec. need-based self-help aid	26

UNIVERSITY OF ARKANSAS—FAYETTEVILLE

232 Silas Hunt Hall, Fayetteville, AR 72701 • Admissions: 479-575-5346 • Fax: 479-575-7515

CAMPUS LIFE

Quality of Life Rating	84
Fire Safety Rating	60*
Type of school	public
Environment	town

STUDENTS

Total undergrad enrollment	14,350
% male/female	50/50
% from out of state	21
% from public high school	95
% live on campus	29
% in (# of) fraternities	18 (15)
% in (# of) sororities	20 (11)
% African American	4
% Asian	3
% Caucasian	81
% Hispanic	3
% Native American	2
% international	2
# of countries represented	103

SURVEY SAYS . . .

Great library
Athletic facilities are great
Students love Fayetteville, AR
Everyone loves the Razorbacks
Frats and sororities dominate social
scene
Lots of beer drinking

ACADEMICS

Academic Rating	73
Calendar	semester
Student/faculty ratio	17:1
Profs interesting rating	71
Profs accessible rating	72
% profs teaching	
UG courses	96
% classes taught by TAs	27
Most common	
lab size	10–19 students
Most common	
reg class size	20–29 students

MOST POPULAR MAJORS

elementary education and teaching
finance
marketing/marketing management

STUDENTS SAY

Academics

"Football, beer, business, Greek life, research and development, and all things Southern are the way of life" at the University of Arkansas—Fayetteville, a school that, "like most universities, is exactly what each student makes it out to be. It can be an academic haven or a party paradise. Whichever route a student chooses, Fayetteville and the university offer plenty of tools to ensure success." For those pursuing academics, there are the "many science departments that have top-notch research going on" as well as the popular and well-funded Sam Walton College of Business. U of A also boasts "a well-known engineering program," "an excellent Bachelor of Science in Nursing program," a "great creative writing program," and an honors program "that is keen on postgraduate activities and works hard to help students put forth strong applications for graduate school and postgraduate fellowships." No matter what you study here, prepare for an administration that "is a giant, cumbersome bureaucracy. It is impossible to deal with anyone directly about problems related to course credit, tuition, scholarships, etc." On the plus side, "There are tons of scholarships for study abroad and grad school."

Life

"There are a lot of activities on the U of A campus," with "over 250 student organizations and sports clubs providing something for almost everyone. And it is really easy to get involved." The campus also offers "a lot of social opportunities," including "free entertainment several times per month, such as live bands, free food, etc. There's Friday Night Live almost every Friday night, and many students participate in that. The residence halls also host parties for Halloween, Mardi Gras, and other events." During the fall, "Razorback football games dominate." "Not only are students hyped up for football games but the entire town revolves around the university, so it becomes citywide excitement! Parties are everywhere!" Hometown Fayetteville "is a great town to find things to do" and "is the kind of town where you can walk everywhere, so there's really no need for a car. Dickson Street is adjacent to campus and is full of bars, restaurants that serve many different types of food, live music every night, etc. On the weekends it borders on insanity! There is also an arts center, lots of great coffee shops, eclectic stores, and a nice downtown square within a quarter mile of Dickson Street." As if all that weren't enough, "Outdoor activities abound here in northwestern Arkansas; we're in the Boston Mountains, the most rugged part of the Ozark Highlands, and you can go rock climbing, mountain biking, whitewater kayaking, canoeing, fishing, and hunting in the 2-plus- million-acre Ozark National Forest, which is close by." "The weather in northern Arkansas is warm year-round" so "Even winter is quite mild" here.

Student Body

"Most of the kids at U of A are just good, down-home Southerners." Many "take 12 to 15 hours a semester, work part-time, and still manage to have active social lives." Students say they "want to have their weekends free to relax, not work on schoolwork. We work hard, but we want to have fun too." U of A undergrads "are generally pretty friendly. When you walk around campus people might say hi to you even if they don't know you." There is some diversity here, due in part to the international students: "You can hear several different languages just by walking in the student union," undergrads tell us. "Everyone here loves the Razorbacks," and that love unites the student body. The "huge division between Greeks and non-Greeks" occasionally tests that unity.

UNIVERSITY OF ARKANSAS—FAYETTEVILLE

FINANCIAL AID: 479-575-3806 • E-MAIL: UOFA@UARK.EDU • WEBSITE: WWW.UARK.EDU/ADMISSIONS

ADMISSIONS

Very important factors considered include: Academic GPA, class rank, rigor of secondary school record, standardized test scores. *Other factors considered include:* Alumni/ae relation, character/personal qualities, extracurricular activities, geographical residence, recommendation(s), state residency, talent/ability, volunteer work, work experience. SAT or ACT required; TOEFL required of all international applicants. High school diploma is required, and GED is accepted. *Academic units required:* 4 English, 4 math, 3 science (2 science labs), 3 social studies, 2 academic electives. *Academic units recommended:* 2 foreign language.

The Inside Word

The admissions policy at the University of Arkansas—Fayetteville is straightforward. Applicants are guaranteed entrance as long as they meet published GPA requirements and standardized test minimums. Students who do not meet these requirements should not panic. They may still be admitted after an individualized review. As is the case with most rolling admissions policies, candidates will find it in their best interest to apply early. Those who do will have priority for both housing and orientation.

FINANCIAL AID

Students should submit: FAFSA. The Princeton Review suggests that all financial aid forms be submitted as soon as possible after January 1. *Need-based scholarships/grants offered:* Pell Grant, SEOG, state scholarships/grants, private scholarships, the school's own gift aid. *Loan aid offered:* FFEL Subsidized Stafford, FFEL Unsubsidized Stafford, FFEL PLUS, Federal Perkins Loan, state loans, college/university loans from institutional funds, alternative loans. Applicants will be notified of awards on or about April 1.

FROM THE ADMISSIONS OFFICE

"The University of Arkansas aims to become one of the top 50 public research universities, fueled by a historic $300 million gift received entirely in cash in March 2003 from the Walton Family Charitable Support Foundation. The largest gift ever to a public university, it established and endowed an undergraduate honors college and provides financial support to nearly 2,000 students. In 2004, the U of A provided more than $250,000 to support undergraduate research and more than $350,000 for study abroad. In 2005, the U of A completed a successful $1 billion campaign.

"The U of A's growing academic stature is exemplified by student accomplishment. Since 1990 U of A undergraduates have won 30 Goldwater Scholarships; 12 have been recognized by the *USA Today* All-USA College Academic Team; 16 have received National Science Foundations graduate fellowships; 10 have received Fulbright scholarships; 11 have received British Marshall scholarships; six have received Truman scholarships; five have received Udall scholarships; three have received Madison scholarships; three have received Tylenol scholarships; and one has received a Rhodes scholarship. All students who attend the U of A benefit from a range of choice in 208 academic programs; and yet, as research universities go, U of A is on the small side. The student/faculty ratio is 17:1, which allows students to receive individual attention from faculty. The university is located in Fayetteville, a small city on the beautiful Ozark Plateau. It's friendly, safe, diverse, and offers awesome recreational opportunities, a robust economy, vibrant cultural life, and a moderate climate. In 2004, a Washington, DC, nonprofit group named it one of the most livable communities in the United States.

"The University of Arkansas—Fayetteville will accept either the new SAT or the old SAT (administered prior to March 2005 and without a Writing component), as well as the ACT with or without the Writing component."

SELECTIVITY
Admissions Rating	**86**
# of applicants	8,443
% of applicants accepted	68
% of acceptees attending	48

FRESHMAN PROFILE
Range SAT Critical Reading	510–630
Range SAT Math	530–650
Range SAT Writing	510–640
Range ACT Composite	22–28
Minimum Paper TOEFL	550
Minimum Computer Based TOEFL	213
Average HS GPA	3.6
% graduated top 10% of class	32
% graduated top 25% of class	61
% graduated top 50% of class	88

DEADLINES
Regular application deadline	8/15
Regular notification	rolling
Nonfall registration?	yes

FINANCIAL FACTS
Financial Aid Rating	**73**
Annual in-state tuition	$4,590
Annual out-of-state tuition	$12,724
Room & Board	$6,522
Books and supplies	$956
Required fees	$1,218
% frosh rec. need-based scholarship or grant aid	22
% UG rec. need-based scholarship or grant aid	24
% frosh rec. need-based self-help aid	25
% UG rec. need-based self-help aid	31
% frosh rec. any financial aid	71
% UG rec. any financial aid	67

UNIVERSITY OF CALIFORNIA—BERKELEY

110 SPROUL HALL #5800, BERKELEY, CA 94720-5800 • ADMISSIONS: 510-642-3175 • FAX: 510-642-7333

STUDENTS SAY

Academics

"Prestige" and "opportunity" often popped up in students' descriptions of University of California—Berkeley, a school universally acknowledged as one of the top research institutions in the nation. Incoming undergrads here know they've been admitted to an academic mecca, home to "many Nobel laureates" and "an extremely challenging, top-notch educational experience." Students say that the faculty here, "even the lecturers, are simply amazing. Faculty members are renowned researchers with world-class recognitions and awards. The lecturers are major executives and/or experts in the relevant industries; they truly enrich the Berkeley education by bringing into light the life applications of the disciplines they teach." Opportunities for undergraduate research "are abundant, and with some effort, just about anyone who's actively looking for a job (research or not) on campus can find one." Students warn that nothing comes easy here. "Be prepared to fight every inch of the way, because this is not a school where a professor will take you by the hand and lead you to the promise[d] land," writes one student. Another observes, "Academically, Berkeley is harder than it looks . . . [professors] do not inflate grades, so if you score the mean, you will get a B-minus/C-plus in the class." A huge school, Berkeley allows students access to "an amazing number and variety of courses" and "teaches them to fend for themselves," but also means that "you have to learn things the hard way, which isn't always nice."

Life

"Life's tough at Berkeley" because "classes are generally very unforgiving, so students don't find much time to do anything other than study." When students can break free of the books, a world of options awaits them, both on campus and off. Undergrads tell us that "most of us start our day walking through Sproul Plaza getting news from every other group on campus, whether it be a movie playing in Wheeler, or a general meeting or someone coming to speak." Students participate in "hundreds of student organizations" and "really show their school spirit with regards to athletics; our football games are always packed with rowdy fans." For those seeking one, there's a lively party scene; one student reports, "On every Tuesday, Thursday, Friday, and Saturday night, you can bet there will be a host of different fraternity and sorority parties, in addition to co-op and house parties. Many of the Greek parties take place at clubs or bars in the city, and the location is always rented out exclusively for the students. On any other night of the week, there are local bars and clubs that are always fun." Then there's Berkeley with its "amazing variety of restaurants" and trips to San Francisco. Yet despite the many social opportunities, many students tell us they don't feel especially connected to the Berkeley social scene. One undergrad explains, "Students live up to hours away via car or BART, since high rent prices in the city of Berkeley force many out of the city's limits. If kids don't find a niche in some group or activity, they end up completely lost for a social life."

Student Body

"There is no typical student" at this school of 23,000 undergraduates, Berkeley students insist. "If you walk into a lecture hall and you had to group people into what 'crowd' they were in high school, it would be near impossible," explains one student. "Not only are there the jocks, the sorority girls, the band geeks, and the drama nerds, there are also the 'save-the-tree-frog, legalize-marijuana businesspeople' and the 'squirrel-fishing, classical-music-club-committee, soccer fanatics.' The only one thing that most of these kids have in common is that they are all ridiculously smart." The school has a large minority population, but "African Americans are underrepresented, as are Latinos. Diversity seems to be defined as a lack of Whites, but you can hardly call a student population wherein 40 percent of its members are Asian 'diverse.'" Because "Nobody at UC—Berkeley is going to take your hand to help you find your own path," Berkeley students "must forge their own road by critically analyzing and thinking independently," and therefore "grow intellectually at an alarming rate."

FINANCIAL AID: 510-642-6442 • E-MAIL: OUARS@UCLINK.BERKELEY.EDU • WEBSITE: WWW.BERKELEY.EDU

ADMISSIONS

Very important factors considered include: Academic GPA, application essay, rigor of secondary school record, state residency. *Important factors considered include:* Character/personal qualities, extracurricular activities, standardized test scores, talent/ability, volunteer work, work experience. *Other factors considered include:* First generation, geographical residence. SAT or ACT required; SAT Subject Tests required; ACT with Writing component required. TOEFL required of all international applicants. High school diploma is required, and GED is accepted. *Academic units required:* 4 English, 3 math, 2 science (2 science labs), 2 foreign language, 2 social studies, 2 history, 1 academic elective, 1 visual or performing arts. *Academic units recommended:* 4 English, 4 math, 3 science (3 science labs), 3 foreign language, 2 social studies, 2 history, 1 academic elective, 1 visual or performing arts.

The Inside Word

Berkeley is the most selective campus of the UC system. There is little room for deviation in any applicant's academic profile, and out-of-state students find the going even tougher, with available spaces few and far between.

FINANCIAL AID

Students should submit: FAFSA, state aid form. Regular filing deadline is March 2. The Princeton Review suggests that all financial aid forms be submitted as soon as possible after January 1. *Need-based scholarships/grants offered:* Pell Grant, SEOG, state scholarships/grants, private scholarships, the school's own gift aid. *Loan aid offered:* Direct Subsidized Stafford, Direct Unsubsidized Stafford, Direct PLUS, Federal Perkins Loan, college/university loans from institutional funds. Applicants will be notified of awards on or about April 15. Federal Work-Study Program available. Institutional employment available. Off-campus job opportunities are excellent.

FROM THE ADMISSIONS OFFICE

"One of the top public universities in the nation and the world, the University of California—Berkeley offers a vast range of courses and a full menu of extracurricular activities. Berkeley's academic programs are internationally recognized for their excellence. Undergraduates can choose one of 100 majors. Thirty-five departments are top ranked, more than any other college or university in the country. Access to one of the foremost university libraries enriches studies. There are 23 specialized libraries on campus and distinguished museums of anthropology, paleontology, and science.

"All applicants must take the ACT Assessment plus the new ACT Writing Test or the new SAT Reasoning Test. In addition, all applicants must take two SAT Subject Tests in two different subject areas. If a Math SAT Subject Test is chosen by the applicant, he/she must take the Math Level II exam (Math 1 is not acceptable)."

SELECTIVITY

Admissions Rating	97
# of applicants	41,750
% of applicants accepted	24
% of acceptees attending	42

FRESHMAN PROFILE

Range SAT Critical Reading	580–710
Range SAT Math	620–740
Range SAT Writing	590–710
Minimum Paper TOEFL	550
Minimum Computer Based TOEFL	213
% graduated top 10% of class	98
% graduated top 25% of class	100
% graduated top 50% of class	100

DEADLINES

Regular application deadline	11/30
Regular notification	3/31
Nonfall registration?	yes

APPLICANTS ALSO LOOK AT

AND OFTEN PREFER
Stanford University

AND SOMETIMES PREFER
University of California—Los Angeles

AND RARELY PREFER
University of California—Santa Barbara, University of California—Davis, University of California—San Diego, University of California—Santa Cruz

FINANCIAL FACTS

Financial Aid Rating	87
Annual in-state tuition	$0
Annual out-of-state tuition	$19,068
Annual out-of-state fees	$8,937
Annual in-state fees	$8,385
Room & Board	$13,074
Books and supplies	$1,326
% frosh rec. need-based scholarship or grant aid	44
% UG rec. need-based scholarship or grant aid	45
% frosh rec. need-based self-help aid	40
% UG rec. need-based self-help aid	39

UNIVERSITY OF CALIFORNIA—DAVIS

178 MRAK HALL, DAVIS, CA 95616 • ADMISSIONS: 530-752-2971 • FAX: 530-752-1280

STUDENTS SAY

Academics

UC—Davis may be best known for its "tremendous life sciences division." One student writes, "This campus claims to have more biology majors than any other campus in the U.S. and I believe it." Students tout "the undergraduate research opportunities" as "perhaps the greatest in the nation," but they are quick to point out that there's more to UC—Davis than just the hard sciences. "It's not all just biology and chemistry courses," writes a human development major. "Because I branched out a little, I was able to experience far more than the average biology major. Everything I'm learning is interconnecting in ways I didn't think about before." Students find their professors to be "friendly" and "interesting." "While every once in a while you get a bad egg," a senior writes, "the majority [of faculty] are very good." Undergrads agree that while "most of the professors are very accessible, you need to make the first move." As at most schools, the upper-level courses highlight the academic experience. Advancing to upper classes also opens up "opportunities to get involved in internships here and abroad." At all levels, "UC—Davis offers a challenging curriculum that effectively prepares us for advanced degrees, while also teaching us the importance of arranging our schedule to accommodate our demanding schoolwork."

Life

"Many of the students are very environment-friendly" at UC—Davis, and they love to take advantage of "all the outdoor activities you can sign up for, like hiking, backpacking, camping, and ski trips. Going for walks along the arboretum or picnics at Putah Creek are nice, especially during the spring, when there are ducks everywhere. Seriously, they're all over campus." Students also appreciate the "mass recycling programs for every kind of waste—including food waste—and the use of reusable containers and cups that is encouraged in all dining facilities." Hometown Davis "is a small town that closes down around 9:00 or 10:00 P.M., even on weekends. If you want a nice small town with friendly people, then this is the place for you. But if you are looking for nightlife, then maybe a more urban environment would be better." It's good to note that the student body is large enough to sustain a fairly active campus, with regular movies, a hopping intramural sports program, and "lots of performances at the top-notch Mondavi Center for the Performing Arts, [varying] from operas and ballets to gospel singers and nude dance troupes." College sports promise to become more popular in the future, as "We're moving up to Division I, which is super-promising."

Student Body

UC—Davis is home to over 23,000 undergraduates, so "No matter where you go on campus, you're bound to find someone you can totally relate to in the same room, and someone else who's the complete opposite." Demanding academics and the Northern California setting mean that "we're a school of dedicated students who are relatively mellow and not too rowdy. It is a good environment for going to college." The typical undergrad here is "either White or Asian in ethnicity, at least a little religious, [and] initially wanted to go to another school (Davis was their second choice)."

UNIVERSITY OF CALIFORNIA—DAVIS

FINANCIAL AID: 530-752-2390 • E-MAIL: FRESHMANADMISSIONS@UCDAVIS.EDU • WEBSITE: WWW.UCDAVIS.EDU

ADMISSIONS

Very important factors considered include: Academic GPA, rigor of secondary school record, standardized test scores. *Important factors considered include:* Application essay, character/personal qualities, extracurricular activities, first generation, talent/ability. *Other factors considered include:* State residency, volunteer work, work experience. SAT Reasoning Test or ACT with Writing component required; SAT Subject Tests required. TOEFL required of all international applicants if native language and language of instruction are not English. High school diploma is required, and GED is accepted. *Academic units required:* 4 English, 3 math, 2 science (2 science labs), 2 foreign language, 2 social studies, 1 academic elective, 1 visual and performing arts. *Academic units recommended:* 4 English, 4 math, 3 science (3 science labs), 3 foreign language, 2 social studies, 1 academic elective, 1 visual and performing arts.

The Inside Word

California's discontinuation of affirmative action in the UC admission process has created much uncertainty regarding the future of candidate selection in the system. A higher percentage of students are admitted to Davis than to Berkeley or UCLA, but don't forget that the UC system in general is geared toward the best and brightest of California's high school students.

FINANCIAL AID

Students should submit: FAFSA, state aid form. The Princeton Review suggests that all financial aid forms be submitted as soon as possible after January 1. *Need-based scholarships/grants offered:* Pell Grant, SEOG, state scholarships/grants, private scholarships, the school's own gift aid. *Loan aid offered:* Direct Subsidized Stafford, Direct Unsubsidized Stafford, Direct PLUS, Federal Perkins Loan, college/university loans from institutional funds. Applicants will be notified of awards on a rolling basis beginning or about March 15.

FROM THE ADMISSIONS OFFICE

"UC—Davis is characterized by a distinguished faculty of scholars, scientists, and artists, a treasured sense of community, and dedication to innovative teaching, research, and public service. Students follow a philosophy of learning, discovery, and engagement. Their involvement in academic, leadership and honors programs, as well as internships, education abroad, and research, typify the undergraduate experience. Students can earn degrees in more than 100 majors, interact with the university's professional schools through select minor programs, and receive pregraduate advising in nearly any field imaginable.

"The friendly, supportive nature of the campus and Davis community also defines the undergraduate experience. UC—Davis offers its active student body more than 450 student organizations, NCAA Division I athletics, and stunning cultural, academic, and recreational facilities such as the Mondavi Center for the Performing Arts, the Genome Center, and the Activities and Recreation Center.

"UC—Davis also provides many resources to help undergraduates build social and career networks before they graduate, so they're well connected by the time they don their cap and gown. Within one year following graduation, 95 percent of June 2003 baccalaureate degree recipients were working full time or were studying for or had completed a postgraduate degree.

"Freshman applicants are required to take the ACT with the Writing component or the SAT, as well as two SAT Subject Tests in two different subject areas."

SELECTIVITY

Admissions Rating	94
# of applicants	32,635
% of applicants accepted	68
% of acceptees attending	25

FRESHMAN PROFILE

Range SAT Critical Reading	500–630
Range SAT Math	560–670
Range ACT Composite	23–29
Minimum Paper TOEFL	550
Minimum Computer Based TOEFL	213
Average HS GPA	3.70
% graduated top 10% of class	95
% graduated top 25% of class	100
% graduated top 50% of class	100

DEADLINES

Regular application deadline	11/30
Regular notification	3/15
Nonfall registration?	no

APPLICANTS ALSO LOOK AT

AND OFTEN PREFER
University of California—Berkeley, University of California—Los Angeles, University of California—San Diego

AND SOMETIMES PREFER
California Polytechnic State University—San Luis Obispo, University of California—Santa Barbara

AND RARELY PREFER
University of California—Riverside, University of California—Merced

FINANCIAL FACTS

Financial Aid Rating	73
Annual in-state tuition	$0
Annual out-of-state tuition	$26,984
Room & Board	$11,239
Books and supplies	$1,514
Required fees	$8,299
% frosh rec. need-based scholarship or grant aid	46
% UG rec. need-based scholarship or grant aid	46
% frosh rec. need-based self-help aid	39
% UG rec. need-based self-help aid	41
% frosh rec. any financial aid	46
% UG rec. any financial aid	59

UNIVERSITY OF CALIFORNIA—LOS ANGELES

405 HILGARD AVENUE, BOX 951436, LOS ANGELES, CA 90095-1436 • ADMISSIONS: 310-825-3101 • FAX: 310-206-1206

STUDENTS SAY
Academics
"UCLA is about discovering what direction you want to go in life and then taking the initiative, and the wealth of opportunities, to go out and do it," students at this large, prestigious state school tell us. The benefits of size and tremendous resources mean that "there's just so much to do for everyone" here. One student explains, "I'm an engineering student, but I wanted to go to a school where I could get a great engineering education while also having opportunities to take part in other programs. Here I can take engineering classes and also explore ancient Greece, [the] biology of cancer, and several other fascinating classes through the general education requirements." For those in the sciences, "There are many chances to do research here. Being a research university, the professors and administration often stress the importance and the benefits of research. The benefits include recognition and scholar awards as well as grants and an edge over other students when applying for graduate school." The academic experience at UCLA "can be highly independent. Professors are not always the best teachers. They're mostly concerned with their research, and many treat teaching as a second priority. That's not to say that there aren't amazing professors who inspire you to learn; there are plenty. And although classes (especially science classes) are large, there are plenty of services for helping students with studies." Students have help sorting professorial gems from duds through "the professor review website, which is absolutely amazing. I pick classes based on what it says because it is pretty accurate." Students warn that UCLA "is really competitive because the school is full of overachievers" and that "the quarter schedule strangles the syllabus for time."

Life
"UCLA is a great place to have free time," students report, because "There are endless possibilities as to what to do; no one can ever get bored. Out of all of the schools in California, you would be hard pressed to find a better combination of social life, academics, and food in one place. Not to mention [the fact that] you're bordered by Bel Air, Beverly Hills, Santa Monica, and Westwood. It's pretty hard to top that." Westwood is a student favorite, an area "filled with lots of good restaurants that are generally affordable for college students. There are a huge amount of theaters, movie theaters, and stand-up joints in the local area, and it is easy to get free tickets on campus to many shows." Westwood is also "the main place where people go and party, pre-party, or after-party. People are focused on school but are also ready to party." Greater Los Angeles offers the beach, "lots of free sneaks of upcoming films and talks by actors and directors about their work," and numerous other diversions. On campus "There are tons of ways to get involved. The campus newspaper and musical theater program are both amazing and very professional. Frat and apartment parties are also very popular on campus." One student sums up: "If someone is not happy at UCLA, then they are not happy with their own life. It's not the school."

Student Body
"There are around 35,000 students at UCLA, so it is hard to describe the 'average' student," as the school is home to "top athletes, nonstop partiers, bookworms—any type of person you could imagine." Most are "well-prepared and serious about success at UCLA. It's hard to get into this school, so students' high school prep was indeed rigorous and weeded out" "less serious" applicants. Most respondents agree that while the student body can "be very cliquish," UCLA is diverse—"and not just ethically diverse; it is also religiously and socially diverse." Some complain that "African Americans are underrepresented" but otherwise laud the school for its ability to draw students of all backgrounds.

UNIVERSITY OF CALIFORNIA—LOS ANGELES

FINANCIAL AID: 310-206-0400 • E-MAIL: UGADM@SAONET.UCLA.EDU • WEBSITE: WWW.UCLA.EDU

ADMISSIONS

Very important factors considered include: Academic GPA, application essay, rigor of secondary school record, standardized test scores. *Important factors considered include:* Character/personal qualities, extracurricular activities, talent/ability, volunteer work, work experience. *Other factors considered include:* First generation, geographical residence. SAT or ACT required; SAT Subject Tests required; ACT with Writing component required. TOEFL required of all international applicants. High school diploma is required, and GED is accepted. *Academic units required:* 4 English, 3 math, 2 science (2 science labs), 2 foreign language, 2 history, 1 academic elective, 1 visual and performing arts. *Academic units recommended:* 4 English, 4 math, 3 science (3 science labs), 3 foreign language, 2 history, 1 academic elective, 1 visual and performing arts.

The Inside Word

A powerhouse within the California system, UCLA has its applicants face a stringent and comprehensive assessment. Each application is evaluated within the context of three categories: academics, personal achievement, and life challenges, and each is reviewed by multiple Admissions Officers. Academic success is a must for any serious contender and enrollment in honors and Advanced Placement courses is highly recommended. Additionally, officers pay close attention to level of commitment in regards to extracurricular activities.

FINANCIAL AID

Students should submit: FAFSA. The Princeton Review suggests that all financial aid forms be submitted as soon as possible after January 1. *Need-based scholarships/grants offered:* Pell Grant, SEOG, state scholarships/grants, private scholarships, the school's own gift aid, United Negro College Fund, Federal Nursing Scholarship, National Merit Scholarship. *Loan aid offered:* FFEL Subsidized Stafford, FFEL Unsubsidized Stafford, FFEL PLUS, Federal Perkins Loan, Federal Nursing Loan, state loans, college/university loans from institutional funds. Applicants will be notified of awards on or about March 15. Federal Work-Study Program available. Off-campus job opportunities are good.

FROM THE ADMISSIONS OFFICE

"Undergraduates arrive at UCLA from throughout California and around the world with exceptional levels of academic preparation. They are attracted by our acclaimed degree programs, distinguished faculty, and the beauty of a park-like campus set amid the dynamism of the nation's second-largest city. UCLA's highly ranked undergraduate programs incorporate cutting-edge technology and teaching techniques that hone the critical-thinking skills and the global perspectives necessary for success in our rapidly changing world. The diversity of these programs draws strength from a student body that mirrors the cultural and ethnic vibrancy of Los Angeles. Generally ranked among the nation's top half-dozen universities, UCLA is at once distinguished and dynamic, academically rigorous and responsive.

"All applicants must take the ACT plus Writing or the SAT Reasoning Test. In addition, all applicants must take two SAT Subject Tests in two different subject areas. (If a Math SAT Subject Test is chosen by the applicant, he/she must take the Math Level II exam.)"

SELECTIVITY

Admissions Rating	98
# of applicants	47,317
% of applicants accepted	26
% of acceptees attending	39

FRESHMAN PROFILE

Range SAT Critical Reading	570–690
Range SAT Math	610–720
Range SAT Writing	590–700
Range ACT Composite	24–30
Minimum Paper TOEFL	550
Minimum Computer Based TOEFL	220
Average HS GPA	4.14
% graduated top 10% of class	97
% graduated top 25% of class	100
% graduated top 50% of class	100

DEADLINES

Regular application deadline	11/30
Regular notification	rolling
Nonfall registration?	no

FINANCIAL FACTS

Financial Aid Rating	83
Annual in-state tuition	$6,141
Annual out-of-state tuition	$24,825
Room & Board	$12,415
Books and supplies	$1,485
Required fees	$381
% frosh rec. need-based scholarship or grant aid	52
% UG rec. need-based scholarship or grant aid	51
% frosh rec. need-based self-help aid	37
% UG rec. need-based self-help aid	39

UNIVERSITY OF CALIFORNIA—RIVERSIDE

1138 HINDERAKER HALL, RIVERSIDE, CA 92521 • ADMISSIONS: 951-827-3411 • FAX: 951-827-6344

STUDENTS SAY
Academics
Unlike many of its larger UC peers, "UC—Riverside has all the advantages of being a smaller campus: Classes are smaller, and professors are friendly and helpful." Small classes give students the opportunity to get acquainted with their professors and other faculty members, and the school places great emphasis on attending office hours." The premedical sciences are a particular strength at UCR; other popular majors include biology/biological sciences, business administration, and psychology. (Riverside is "one of only two UCs [Berkeley is the other] with an undergrad business administration program"). Across departments, "The professors are very knowledgeable in their fields and expect students to be equally knowledgeable." In addition to assigning rigorous course work, "The faculty also encourages internships and research. Many students also take up a minor or second major." Aside from internships, undergrads here benefit from "the great variety of opportunities, which include education abroad programs, interuniversity programs, postgrad programs, and two great libraries."

Life
Life at Riverside can be "very calm, and the school's atmosphere in general is very quiet." One contributor to this sense of calm is the fact that many students commute to school. "We are not a huge party school," students admit, but "There is always a party to go to if that's what you're into." Although the city of Riverside has "very little to offer in the way of entertainment," students compensate by joining various clubs and student organizations, including sororities and fraternities, which have a noticeable presence on campus. The school also offers "countless events, including free movie screenings, concerts, academic discussion forums, plays, and trips." Popular campus hangouts include "a great rec center," "the student commons," and "a campus movie theater, where some of our classes are held." Students seem to agree, however, that "intercollegiate sports need more student support." Those with cars leave campus relatively frequently on the weekends, finding plenty to do outside of town; one student explains, "Within an hour's drive you can ski in the mountains, go sunbathing at the beach, visit a major theme park, or even hang out in Hollywood for a day."

Student Body
UCR is "one of the most diverse campuses in the UC system"; one thing that makes the school unique is its particularly "large population of Asian students," who constitute a plurality of the student body. As a result of the diversity on campus, the school "has very few 'typical' students." One respondent writes, "I believe that anyone could find a group of friends here because there are so many different types of people going to this school." Students praise the school's "clubs and organizations" for "uniting differences and providing forums for the expression and understanding of these differences." As a result of this unity, "UCR is a very sociable campus, and it seems like everyone, no matter [what] gender, ethnicity, or sexual orientation, is accepted and feels welcomed."

UNIVERSITY OF CALIFORNIA—RIVERSIDE

FINANCIAL AID: 951-827-3878 • E-MAIL: UGADMISS@UCR.EDU • WEBSITE: WWW.UCR.EDU

ADMISSIONS

Very important factors considered include: Academic GPA, first generation, rigor of secondary school record, standardized test scores. *Other factors considered include:* Application essay, state residency. SAT or ACT required; SAT Subject Tests required; ACT with Writing component required. TOEFL required of all international applicants. High school diploma is required, and GED is accepted. *Academic units required:* 4 English, 3 math, 2 science (2 science labs), 2 foreign language, 2 history, 2 academic electives. *Academic units recommended:* 4 math, 3 science (3 science labs), 3 foreign language.

The Inside Word

Formulas are the foundation of the UC—Riverside admission process. Applicants who meet GPA and standardized test minimums should have no problems gaining acceptance. There is a priority filling period so students should apply as early as possible.

FINANCIAL AID

Students should submit: FAFSA, state aid form. Regular filing deadline is March 2. The Princeton Review suggests that all financial aid forms be submitted as soon as possible after January 1. *Need-based scholarships/grants offered:* Pell Grant, SEOG, state scholarships/grants, private scholarships, the school's own gift aid. Included in state scholarships/grants above. *Loan aid offered:* Direct Subsidized Stafford, Direct Unsubsidized Stafford, Direct PLUS, Federal Perkins Loan. Applicants will be notified of awards on a rolling basis beginning or about March 1. Federal Work-Study Program available. Institutional employment available. Off-campus job opportunities are excellent.

FROM THE ADMISSIONS OFFICE

"The University of California—Riverside offers the quality, rigor, and facilities of a major research institution, while assuring its undergraduates personal attention and a sense of community. Academic programs, teaching, advising, and student services all reflect the supportive attitude that characterizes the campus. Among the exceptional opportunities are the UC—Riverside/UCLA Thomas Haider Program in Biomedical Sciences, which provides an exclusive path to UCLA's Geffen School of Medicine; the University Honors Program; an extensive undergraduate research program; UC's only undergraduate degree program in business administration in Southern California; and UC's only bachelor's degree in creative writing. More than 250 student clubs and organizations and a variety of athletic and arts events give students a myriad of ways to get involved and have fun.

"All applicants must take the ACT Assessment plus Writing Test or the SAT Reasoning Test. In addition, all applicants must take two SAT Subject Tests in two different subject areas. If students choose the Math SAT Subject Test, they must take the Math Level II exam."

SELECTIVITY

Admissions Rating	**91**
# of applicants	19,982
% of applicants accepted	83
% of acceptees attending	18

FRESHMAN PROFILE

Range SAT Critical Reading	440–560
Range SAT Math	470–610
Range SAT Writing	450–570
Range ACT Composite	18–23
Minimum Paper TOEFL	550
Minimum Computer Based TOEFL	220
Average HS GPA	3.43
% graduated top 10% of class	94
% graduated top 25% of class	100
% graduated top 50% of class	100

DEADLINES

Regular application deadline	11/30
Regular notification	rolling
Nonfall registration?	no

FINANCIAL FACTS

Financial Aid Rating	**79**
Annual in-state tuition	$0
Annual out-of-state tuition	$18,684
Room & Board	$10,200
Books and supplies	$1,700
Required fees	$6,591
% frosh rec. need-based scholarship or grant aid	55
% UG rec. need-based scholarship or grant aid	55
% frosh rec. need-based self-help aid	51
% UG rec. need-based self-help aid	47
% frosh rec. any financial aid	80
% UG rec. any financial aid	70

UNIVERSITY OF CALIFORNIA—SAN DIEGO

9500 GILMAN DRIVE, 0021, LA JOLLA, CA 92093-0021 • ADMISSIONS: 858-534-4831 • FAX: 858-534-5723

CAMPUS LIFE
Quality of Life Rating	**72**
Fire Safety Rating	**60***
Type of school	public
Environment	metropolis

STUDENTS
Total undergrad enrollment	20,679
% male/female	48/52
% from out of state	3
% live on campus	33
% in (# of) fraternities	10 (19)
% in (# of) sororities	10 (14)
% African American	1
% Asian	39
% Caucasian	32
% Hispanic	11
% international	3
# of countries represented	70

SURVEY SAYS . . .
Great computer facilities
Campus feels safe
Intercollegiate sports are unpopular
or nonexistent
Great off-campus food

ACADEMICS
Academic Rating	**80**
Calendar	quarter
Student/faculty ratio	19:1
Profs interesting rating	63
Profs accessible rating	64
% classes taught by TAs	10
Most common lab size	20–29 students
Most common reg class size	10–19 students

MOST POPULAR MAJORS
economics
microbiology
political science and government

STUDENTS SAY
Academics

The University of California—San Diego is "a great research facility" that "is all about science," a place where premedical students benefit from "outstanding biological sciences and chemistry programs," and earth sciences and environmental systems programs capitalize on affiliation with the Scripps Institute of Oceanography. The school's hard-science focus means that "for the vast majority of UCSD students, school is all about studying." A quarterly academic calendar ratchets up the academic pressure and leaves precious little time to goof off. While some here report that the "Dedicated faculty are always accessible and willing to help and guide you," many caution that "in many of the hard sciences, there's a massive concentration on research. It really does take preference over the quality of teaching in many courses. Lots of professors would rather spend their entire lives in their labs and never have to speak to a single student. That needs to change." Students outside the hard sciences occasionally feel neglected. "I sometimes feel as if there aren't as many resources for us," writes one social science major. "I've been able to do research, but students who are in the sciences seem to be offered a lot more resources [such as] grad school info sessions and extracurricular opportunities." On the plus side, San Diego is home to many businesses that dovetail with UCSD's specializations, so there are "many opportunities for internships here. They prepare you well for work experience in your major." UCSD's six-college system is also seen as an asset, "allowing students the advantages of a large research university and the feel of a small university within their [individual] colleges."

Life

"You'll read articles saying that UCSD students are generally unhappy and don't get out and do as much stuff as folks at other campuses, and there's a deal of truth to that," students tell us, adding that "it's mostly the individual fault of each person. There's lots to do, but no one will push you out the door." While "UCSD is in one of the best locations for off-campus fun, many people spend hours upon hours studying. The classwork is hard, and focus is necessary to succeed." But the opportunities are not lacking. True, UCSD lacks a Greek Row, and strict enforcement of residential regulations makes on-campus partying difficult. The absence of a football team and "the lackluster nature of our other teams" means that "UCSD students are generally uninterested in UCSD sports" and have "very little school spirit." Still, some students adamantly oppose the stereotype that the school is "socially dead." One student writes, "The best part of UCSD is that if you want to study, you can study; if you want to party, you can do that too, but the two never impinge on one another." To find a party, "All it takes is asking around or even going online." Hometown La Jolla may be a "swanky area," but it is "not friendly to students." Still, students recognize that there are "so many recreational activities in San Diego, and lots of students love the beach." One undergrad sums up, "Life here is pretty decent, as long as you're willing to leave campus on the weekends for fun. I love to go to the beach and surf, snorkel, kayak . . . anything that gets me outside. And this [retreat from campus] is necessary; on the weekends, the campus dies."

Student Body

The stereotypical UCSD student "is a science nerd with the big backpack and glasses, who's just not into the social scene." He or she is the type of kid "you'd find at the campus shuttle stop at nine o'clock on a Saturday night, reading his textbook with a flashlight." Such students "don't have enough fun," we're told, and "are very focused on grades." But not all the students are like this—it's just that the students who defy the stereotype are likely, according to one respondent, to be "non-science majors." "The school is really diverse," contends one student; in particular, there is a large contingent of Asian students. According to at least one respondent, the homosexual community is welcomed: "We have about 10 different queer clubs on campus."

FINANCIAL AID: 858-534-4480 • E-MAIL: ADMISSIONSINFO@UCSD.EDU • WEBSITE: WWW.UCSD.EDU

ADMISSIONS

Very important factors considered include: Academic GPA, application essay, character/personal qualities, rigor of secondary school record, standardized test scores, state residency, talent/ability, volunteer work. *Important factors considered include:* Extracurricular activities. *Other factors considered include:* Work experience. SAT or ACT required; SAT and SAT Subject Tests or ACT required; ACT with Writing component required. TOEFL required of all international applicants. High school diploma is required, and GED is accepted. *Academic units required:* 4 English, 3 math, (2 science labs), 2 foreign language, 2 history, 1 academic elective, 1 visual and performing arts. *Academic units recommended:* 4 English, 4 math, (3 science labs), 3 foreign language, 2 history, 1 academic elective, 1 visual and performing arts.

The Inside Word

While not as lauded as Berkeley or UCLA, UCSD is quickly earning its place as one of the gems of the UC system. It continues to distinguish itself in a number of ways, including its individualized approach to admissions. Although Admissions Officers do implement a formula, they factor in extracurricular pursuits and personal experiences. Applicants will need to be strong in all areas if they hope to attend UCSD.

FINANCIAL AID

Students should submit: FAFSA, state aid form. Regular filing deadline is June 1. The Princeton Review suggests that all financial aid forms be submitted as soon as possible after January 1. *Need-based scholarships/grants offered:* Pell Grant, SEOG, state scholarships/grants, private scholarships, the school's own gift aid. *Loan aid offered:* FFEL Subsidized Stafford, FFEL Unsubsidized Stafford, FFEL PLUS, Federal Perkins Loan, college/university loans from institutional funds, alternative loans. Applicants will be notified of awards on a rolling basis beginning or about March 15.

FROM THE ADMISSIONS OFFICE

"UCSD is recognized for the exceptional quality of its academic programs: a recent Johns Hopkins study rated UCSD faculty first nationally among public institutions in science; *U.S. News & World Report* rates UCSD seventh in the nation among state-supported colleges and universities; Kiplinger's '100 Best Values in Public Colleges' ranks UCSD tenth in the nation. UCSD ranks fifth in the nation and first in the University of California system for the amount of federal research dollars spent on research and development; and the university ranks tenth in the nation in the excellence of its graduate programs and the quality of its faculty, according to the most recent National Research Council college rankings.

"All applicants must take the ACT Assessment plus the new ACT Writing Test or the new SAT Reasoning Test. In addition, all applicants must take two SAT Subject Tests in two different subject areas. (If a Math SAT Subject Test is chosen by the applicant, he/she must take the Math Level II exam.)"

SELECTIVITY

Admissions Rating	**96**
# of applicants	43,586
% of applicants accepted	49
% of acceptees attending	21

FRESHMAN PROFILE

Range SAT Critical Reading	540–660
Range SAT Math	600–700
Range ACT Composite	23–29
Minimum Paper TOEFL	550
Average HS GPA	3.9
% graduated top 10% of class	99
% graduated top 25% of class	100
% graduated top 50% of class	100

DEADLINES

Regular application deadline	11/30
Regular notification	rolling
Nonfall registration?	yes

APPLICANTS ALSO LOOK AT
AND OFTEN PREFER
University of California—Berkeley,
University of California—Los Angeles
AND SOMETIMES PREFER
California Polytechnic State University—
San Luis Obispo, Stanford University,
University of California—Davis
AND RARELY PREFER
San Diego State University

FINANCIAL FACTS

Financial Aid Rating	**75**
Annual in-state tuition	$6,685
Annual out-of-state tuition	$23,961
Room & Board	$9,657
Books and supplies	$2,504
Required fees	$540
% frosh rec. need-based scholarship or grant aid	51
% UG rec. need-based scholarship or grant aid	46
% frosh rec. need-based self-help aid	46
% UG rec. need-based self-help aid	42
% frosh rec. any financial aid	87
% UG rec. any financial aid	84

UNIVERSITY OF CALIFORNIA—SANTA BARBARA

OFFICE OF ADMISSIONS, 1210 CHEADLE HALL, SANTA BARBARA, CA 93106-2014 • ADMISSIONS: 805-893-2881 • FAX: 805-893-2676

CAMPUS LIFE
Quality of Life Rating	89
Fire Safety Rating	60*
Type of school	public
Environment	city

STUDENTS
Total undergrad enrollment	18,210
% male/female	45/55
% from out of state	4
% from public high school	87
% live on campus	31
% in (# of) fraternities	4 (18)
% in (# of) sororities	7 (19)
% African American	3
% Asian	16
% Caucasian	52
% Hispanic	19
% Native American	1
% international	1
# of countries represented	112

SURVEY SAYS . . .
Great library
Athletic facilities are great
Students are happy
Student publications are popular
Lots of beer drinking
Hard liquor is popular

ACADEMICS
Academic Rating	82
Calendar	quarter
Student/faculty ratio	17:1
Profs interesting rating	74
Profs accessible rating	78
Most common lab size	20–29 students
Most common reg class size	10–19 students

MOST POPULAR MAJORS
cell/cellular biology and
anatomical sciences
economics
psychology

STUDENTS SAY

Academics

"Don't believe all the hype," students at the University of California—Santa Barbara say, meaning the hype about UCSB being nothing but a hard-core party school. Undergrads want you to know that "UCSB is a serious academic institution" with "outstanding academics" and "opportunities to participate in high-level scientific research," though it "also happens to be the most beautiful place in the world in which to be stressed out." Five Nobel laureates (including three in physics) pepper the faculty, and, "Because this school is [mainly] undergraduates, real professors teach you. . . . My ECON 1 professor was President Reagan's national economic adviser and created Reaganonomics. That is pretty cool." UCSB is most highly regarded in the sciences. The university's Marine Science Institute facilities provide "invaluable fieldwork and lab experience with top-notch biologists," and the school's multiple nanotechnology centers are "revolutionary." Programs in physics and material sciences are also highly regarded. Intro-level lectures can be "gargantuan," but students point out that though "It is easy to complain that the lectures are huge and that it is hard to get into classes," the experience here "all depends on the amount of effort you put in. There is always help if you choose to seek it." One undergrad agrees, "There are hundreds of academically challenging classes and amazingly talented teachers at UCSB, but it is up to the students to go out and make the most of their academic experience. Nothing is handed to us." UCSB has done a good job of moving administrative tasks online: "Grades, registration, communication, transcripts . . . it's all done on the computer. Financial aid is automatically deposited into my account. There really isn't a need to stand in line for services because you don't need to, but if you do they're generally helpful."

Life

"Life here is very chill. I mean that in the best way," a UCSB student reports, adding, "People aren't freaking out about classes or stressing out. People just do their work and then go hang out at the beach" or "in IV (Isla Vista, the local, mostly student community)." A sophomore brags that "everything I need is on campus or nearby in Isla Vista. I hardly ever need to go off campus or drive anywhere." The beach is a constant temptation; as one student points out, "UCSB is on the beach . . . literally. As I'm writing this survey, I'm looking out my dorm window and seeing the ocean, just feet from my building." Surfing, swimming, and sunbathing are all big, as are "hiking up to the waterfalls, rock climbing, spearfishing, kayaking, scuba diving, [and] beach volleyball." Most parties take place in Isla Vista, where "17,000 19-to-21-year-olds are all jam-packed into this six-tenths-of-a-square-mile community, so you can imagine how the parties are. . . . Every night is wild, but, obviously, Friday and Saturday nights are the craziest." For some, Isla Vista "can get boring, because it's the same party every weekend," but for others, it never grows old. Downtown Santa Barbara "is beautiful and perfect for nights out, movies, or an outing."

Student Body

The "stereotype of 'beautiful beach kids' does exist," writes one student, who notes that "I have heard the joke that UCSB is the only UC that requires a head shot in the application. However, there are all types of students that attend the school, and anyone can and does find their niche." Undergrads here are generally "more laid-back and less stressed out about school" than most college kids and "take school seriously, but also know how to enjoy their youth." They are typically "very athletic and in shape. They love the outdoors." Oddly, students perceive their campus as "pretty White" even though Chicano, Latino, and Asian populations are relatively high; their perception suggests a campus on which students of different backgrounds don't often intermix.

UNIVERSITY OF CALIFORNIA—SANTA BARBARA

FINANCIAL AID: 805-893-2432 • E-MAIL: APPINFO@SA.UCSB.EDU • WEBSITE: WWW.UCSB.EDU

ADMISSIONS

Very important factors considered include: Academic GPA, application essay, standardized test scores. *Important factors considered include:* Character/personal qualities, extracurricular activities, rigor of secondary school record, talent/ability. *Other factors considered include:* First generation, state residency, volunteer work, work experience. SAT or ACT required; SAT and SAT Subject Tests or ACT required; ACT with Writing component required. TOEFL required of all international applicants. High school diploma is required, and GED is accepted. *Academic units required:* 4 English, 3 math, 2 science (2 science labs), 2 foreign language, 2 social studies, 1 history, 1 academic elective, 1 visual and performing arts. *Academic units recommended:* 4 math, 3 science (3 science labs), 3 foreign language.

The Inside Word

UCSB received over 40,000 freshman applications for the 2006–2007 year, an increase of about 10 percent over the previous year. With that sort of volume, you can't expect personalized treatment from the Admissions Office; admissions decisions are based on the numbers, plus a quick look at extracurriculars, awards, and honors.

FINANCIAL AID

Students should submit: FAFSA. Regular filing deadline is March 2. The Princeton Review suggests that all financial aid forms be submitted as soon as possible after January 1. *Need-based scholarships/grants offered:* Pell Grant, SEOG, state scholarships/grants, private scholarships, the school's own gift aid. Work-study is also available as need-based aid. *Loan aid offered:* Direct Subsidized Stafford, Direct Unsubsidized Stafford, Direct PLUS, FFEL PLUS, Federal Perkins Loan, college/university loans from institutional funds. Applicants will be notified of unofficial aid eligibility starting April 1. Applicants are notified of their official aid eligibility on a rolling basis beginning or about May 15.

FROM THE ADMISSIONS OFFICE

"The University of California—Santa Barbara is a major research institution offering undergraduate and graduate education in the arts, humanities, sciences and technology, and social sciences. Large enough to have excellent facilities for study, research, and other creative activities, the campus is also small enough to foster close relationships among faculty and students. The faculty numbers more than 900. A member of the most distinguished system of public higher education in the nation, UC—Santa Barbara is committed equally to excellence in scholarship and instruction. Through the general education program, students acquire good grounding in the skills, perceptions, and methods of a variety of disciplines. In addition, because they study with a research faculty, they not only acquire basic skills and broad knowledge but also are exposed to the imagination, inventiveness, and intense concentration that scholars bring to their work. UCSB is one of 62 members of the prestigous Association of American Universities.

"All applicants must take the ACT Assessment plus the new ACT Writing Test or the new SAT Reasoning Test. In addition, all applicants must take two SAT Subject Tests in two different subject areas. (If a Math SAT Subject Test is chosen by the applicant, he/she must take the Math Level II exam.)"

SELECTIVITY

Admissions Rating	**95**
# of applicants	39,854
% of applicants accepted	53
% of acceptees attending	19

FRESHMAN PROFILE

Range SAT Critical Reading	530–650
Range SAT Math	540–660
Range ACT Composite	22–28
Minimum Paper TOEFL	500
Minimum Computer Based TOEFL	173
Average HS GPA	3.74
% graduated top 10% of class	96
% graduated top 25% of class	98
% graduated top 50% of class	100

DEADLINES

Regular application deadline	11/30
Regular notification	3/15
Nonfall registration?	yes

APPLICANTS ALSO LOOK AT

AND OFTEN PREFER
University of California—Berkeley,
University of California—Los Angeles,
University of California—San Diego

AND SOMETIMES PREFER
University of California—Davis

AND RARELY PREFER
California Polytechnic State University—
San Luis Obispo, University of
California—Santa Cruz

FINANCIAL FACTS

Financial Aid Rating	**78**
Annual in-state tuition	$0
Annual out-of-state tuition	$18,168
Room & Board	$11,178
Books and supplies	$1,505
Required fees	$7,277
Books and supplies	$1,505
% frosh rec. need-based scholarship or grant aid	40
% UG rec. need-based scholarship or grant aid	38
% frosh rec. need-based self-help aid	33
% UG rec. need-based self-help aid	35
% frosh rec. any financial aid	64
% UG rec. any financial aid	58

UNIVERSITY OF CALIFORNIA—SANTA CRUZ

ADMISSIONS, COOK HOUSE, 1156 HIGH STREET, SANTA CRUZ, CA 95064 • ADMISSIONS: 831-459-4008 • FAX: 831-459-4452

STUDENTS SAY

Academics

The University of California—Santa Cruz offers one of the nation's best combinations of "research and education in a comfortable environment" and is, by all accounts "a great place to live and study!" Students attribute their enthusiasm to an "incredibly beautiful" campus, "intelligent, eloquent, and easily accessible professors," academics that are "impressive and challenging," and people who are "happy, open-minded, and a little bit crazy." This school is best suited to those who can motivate themselves in a "chill" environment, the sort of student whose motto might be "There's no point in learning if you're too stressed to enjoy it." The sciences are "world class" at UCSC. The Biology Department is "heading the Human Genome Project," and the Astrophysics Department is "ranked third in the country." The school also boasts "one of the finest engineering programs in the UCs," as well as "a great marine biology program." While the "Professors all do research," what sets them apart from those at the typical research-driven university is that "they really care about teaching" and are "very accessible." As one student sums up, "There are a lot of opportunities offered at UCSC in terms of internships, research opportunities, job opportunities, and networking because of the . . . faculty. It's the people who make this place valuable."

Life

Students say, "There really is a ton to do" in the area surrounding UCSC, "especially if you like being outdoors." Thanks to the sprawling, lush campus, students don't even have to leave school grounds to "explore caves, climb a huge tree in the forest, or walk or bike or jog." With their campus located "right on the coast" students "love to go to the beach for fun" and "A lot of students also take up surfing." The party scene on and off campus consists of "mostly decentralized, smaller parties, due to the near-absence of fraternities and sororities." It also includes "a lot of drug use" that is limited to "specific locations" and "easy to avoid" for abstaining students. Since Santa Cruz is a "small city," students "have to be inventive" when it comes to finding entertainment. Many students cite a "fun nightlife" with a "number of clubs and bars that cater mostly to the younger crowd." There are also "lots of galleries" in Santa Cruz for students who are into art. Ambitious students "may head to San Jose or San Francisco on the weekend for a more rowdy bar or club scene." Both cities are "readily accessible via public transportation."

Student Body

True to UCSC's reputation, there is certainly a "plethora" of "hippie types who climb trees and walk around barefoot" on campus, but they don't crowd out "the intensely athletic students, intellectuals, computer geeks, surfers, punks, preps" and more. As one student explains, "Every kind of person attends UCSC, but I believe we're all united [in] our desire to chill out and have a good time with each other." Being different is "truly embraced and encouraged" here. Politically, students tend to be "very liberal" and sometimes "not willing to hear other opinions." Some students are more committed to their beliefs than others, and there's "plenty of half-hearted activism" on campus. Politics aside, UCSC students are generally "very sociable and considerate." Meat eaters should take note that there is "a relatively large vegetarian/vegan population" on campus.

FINANCIAL AID: 831-459-2963 • E-MAIL: ADMISSIONS@UCSC.EDU • WEBSITE: WWW.ADMISSIONS.UCSC.EDU

ADMISSIONS

Very important factors considered include: Academic GPA, application essay, rigor of secondary school record, standardized test scores, state residency. *Important factors considered include:* Character/personal qualities, class rank, extracurricular activities, first generation, geographical residence, talent/ability. *Other factors considered include:* Volunteer work, work experience. SAT or ACT required; SAT and SAT Subject Tests or ACT required; ACT with Writing component required. TOEFL required of all international applicants. High school diploma is required, and GED is accepted. *Academic units required:* 4 English, 3 math, 2 science (2 science labs), 2 foreign language, 1 social studies, 1 history, 1 academic elective, 1 visual or performing arts. *Academic units recommended:* 4 English, 4 math, 3 science (3 science labs), 3 foreign language, 1 social studies, 1 history, 1 academic elective, 1 visual or performing arts.

The Inside Word

UC—Santa Cruz's admissions process can be summed in one word—formula. If prospective students meet the requirements, only then will they be eligible to receive an acceptance letter. Weaker candidates will be reassured to learn that officers award points for a variety of special circumstances, including improvement in academic performance, geographic location, and achievement in special projects. UCSC's acceptance rate belies the high caliber of applicants it regularly receives.

FINANCIAL AID

Students should submit: FAFSA, Regular filing deadline is March 2. The Princeton Review suggests that all financial aid forms be submitted as soon as possible after January 1. *Need-based scholarships/grants offered:* Pell Grant, SEOG, state scholarships/grants, private scholarships, the school's own gift aid. *Loan aid offered:* Direct Subsidized Stafford, Direct Unsubsidized Stafford, Direct PLUS, Federal Perkins Loan. Applicants will be notified of awards on a rolling basis beginning or about April 1. Federal Work-Study Program available. Off-campus job opportunities are excellent.

FROM THE ADMISSIONS OFFICE

"Since its founding in 1965, UC—Santa Cruz has earned a national reputation as a campus devoted to excellence in undergraduate teaching, graduate study and research, and professional education. Its academic plan and physical design combine the advantages of a small-college setting with the intensive research and academic strengths traditional to the University of California. At UC—Santa Cruz, undergraduate courses are taught by the same faculty who conduct cutting-edge research. In a national survey of more than 60 elite research universities by the Association of American Universities, UC—Santa Cruz ranked fifteenth for students in all disciplines whose bachelor's degrees led to doctorates. The campus is growing selectively and is investing half a billion dollars in new and improved infrastructure.

"All applicants must take the ACT Assessment plus the new ACT Writing Test or the new SAT Reasoning Test. In addition, all applicants must take two SAT Subject Tests in two different subject areas. (If a Math SAT Subject Test is chosen by the applicant, he/she must take the Math Level II exam.)"

SELECTIVITY

Admissions Rating	93
# of applicants	24,534
% of applicants accepted	80
% of acceptees attending	17

FRESHMAN PROFILE

Range SAT Critical Reading	500–630
Range SAT Math	520–640
Range SAT Writing	510–620
Range ACT Composite	22–28
Minimum Paper TOEFL	550
Minimum Computer Based TOEFL	220
Average HS GPA	3.51
% graduated top 10% of class	96
% graduated top 25% of class	100
% graduated top 50% of class	100

DEADLINES

Regular application deadline	11/30
Regular notification	rolling
Nonfall registration?	yes

APPLICANTS ALSO LOOK AT

AND OFTEN PREFER
Stanford University, University of California—Berkeley, University of California—Los Angeles

AND SOMETIMES PREFER
University of California—Santa Barbara, University of California—Davis, University of California—San Diego

AND RARELY PREFER
San Francisco State University, San Jose State University, University of California—Riverside

FINANCIAL FACTS

Financial Aid Rating	78
Annual in-state tuition	$0
Annual out-of-state tuition	$18,168
Room & Board	$11,805
Books and supplies	$1,395
Required fees	$7,017
% frosh rec. need-based scholarship or grant aid	42
% UG rec. need-based scholarship or grant aid	41
% frosh rec. need-based self-help aid	41
% UG rec. need-based self-help aid	40

UNIVERSITY OF CENTRAL FLORIDA

PO Box 160111, ORLANDO, FL 32816-0111 • ADMISSIONS: 407-823-3000 • FAX: 407-823-5625

Academics

With its "great Engineering and Computer Science Departments, through which many undergraduates can get hands-on experience in their field via research," the University of Central Florida is a school "so career oriented that non-declared majors are practically corralled into 'Career Exploration' camps." And yet this is hardly a cutthroat, high-pressure school; on the contrary, students extol UCF's "laid-back attitude. We may not be as highly regarded as an Ivy League school, but there are amazing things going on here that don't require enormous amounts of pressure. You'll do well because you want to, not because your school's reputation mandates it." Those "amazing things" occur not only in the aforementioned disciplines, but also in hospitality management, mass communications, education, and business. The liberal and fine arts, on the other hand, "need to have more money allocated to them" and suffer in comparison to their more career-driven academic counterparts. To mitigate the drawbacks of big-school impersonality, UCF offers a number of personalizing services. "Every large lecture class has a 'SI' (supplemental Instruction) where there is a student who previously passed the class with an A, who also provides free tutoring." In addition, "There is a large Student Academic Resource Center where students can go for free tutoring in any subject." UCF undergrads also benefit from "awesome technology on campus and in the classroom. The whole campus is wired with wireless Internet. There is a strong emphasis on technology, and when a department is funded well, it is extremely well funded. Corporate partnerships are big here."

Life

Even though "UCF is really large," you "don't have to feel like you're lost in the mix" here because "There's a place for everyone, and the school, student government, and campus activities board make it easy to find it." Undergrads boast that "there is something to do almost every night of the week on campus. There is almost every imaginable intramural sport, and there is quite a bit to do off campus as well." The area surrounding the school features "lots of restaurants and places to shop. Students can go to movie theaters, bowling alleys, parks, and even campus-organized events" in their free time. Then there's downtown Orlando, "which is great, and the UCF SGA is adept at exploiting the local resources (e.g., Universal Studios and the rest of International Drive)." The city has a decent nightlife, with "a large segment of young/professional/hip people living in Orlando and populating the bars and clubs." Ask students how life here could improve and most will mention the football team, which went 0–11 in 2004. "Many students joke that we are a drinking school with a football problem," cracks one student, adding quickly that "we still have pride, and those games are still very well attended." Undergrads would also love to see the constant on-campus construction come to an end. One writes, "A joke around campus is that UCF stands for 'Under Construction Forever,' and it's true. Our school mascot should be the crane because there is so much construction. The campus looks great, though, and we have many nice new facilities."

Student Body

One student describes the UCF student body so neatly we have to include her entire survey response. She writes, "The typical student? You are talking about a campus with 45,000 students; there is no possible way to describe a typical student. There is a vast difference among students not only between the different schools (business, health and public affairs, communication, hospitality, engineering, arts and sciences, etc.), but also within the schools themselves. You have students who have always been at UCF, transfer students, and nontraditional students. We mix so well that one cannot really tell who is who. Of course you can always pick out the athletic students (a huge group) and the Greeks, but mostly, everyone gets along pretty well on campus. And if you don't get along with someone, it is pretty easy to hide among 45,000 other people."

FINANCIAL AID: 407-823-2827 • E-MAIL: ADMISSION@MAIL.UCF.EDU • WEBSITE: WWW.UCF.EDU

ADMISSIONS

Very important factors considered include: Academic GPA, rigor of secondary school record, standardized test scores. *Important factors considered include:* Application essay. *Other factors considered include:* Alumni/ae relation, character/personal qualities, class rank, extracurricular activities, geographical residence, interview, level of applicant's interest, recommendation(s), state residency, talent/ability, volunteer work, work experience. SAT or ACT required; ACT with Writing component required. TOEFL required of all international applicants. High school diploma is required, and GED is accepted. *Academic units required:* 4 English, 3 math, 3 science (2 science labs), 2 foreign language, 3 social studies, 4 academic electives.

Inside Word

Over the past decade, UCF has been making a concerted effort to increase its admissions profile, and, by and large, it has been successful, as the acceptance rate keeps going down while the test scores and average GPAs of newly enrolled students keep ticking up. That means it's virtually nipping at the heels of cross-state rivals Florida State University and University of Florida in terms of selectivity. As is the case at many state schools, it's all a numbers game here; students aren't required to interview or submit essays. It's also worth noting that when calculating your GPA, which is a very important criterion for admission, the Admissions Committee weights honors, AP, dual enrollment, and International Baccalaureate academic classes more heavily than regular classes.

FINANCIAL AID

Students should submit: FAFSA. Regular filing deadline is June 30. The Princeton Review suggests that all financial aid forms be submitted as soon as possible after January 1. *Need-based scholarships/grants offered:* Pell Grant, SEOG, state scholarships/grants, private scholarships, the school's own gift aid, university scholarships and grants. *Loan aid offered:* FFEL Subsidized Stafford, FFEL Unsubsidized Stafford, FFEL PLUS, Federal Perkins Loan. Applicants will be notified of awards on a rolling basis beginning or about March 15.

FROM THE ADMISSIONS OFFICE

"The University of Central Florida offers competitive advantages to its student body. We're committed to teaching, providing advisement, and academic support services for all students. Our undergraduates have access to state-of-the-art wireless buildings, high-tech classrooms, research labs, web-based classes, and an undergraduate research and mentoring program.

"Our Career Services professionals help students gain practical experiences at NASA, schools, hospitals, high-tech companies, local municipalities, and the entertainment industry. With an international focus to our curricula and research programs, we enroll international students from 126 nations. Our study abroad programs and other study and research opportunities include agreements with 98 institutions and 36 countries.

"UCF's 1,415-acre campus provides a safe and serene setting for learning, with natural lakes and woodlands. The bustle of Orlando lies a short distance away: the pro sport teams, the Kennedy Space Center, film studios, Walt Disney World, Universal Orlando, Sea World, and sandy beaches are all nearby.

"Applicants for Summer 2008 and beyond are required to take the new version of the SAT (or the ACT with the writing section), but we will allow students to submit scores from the old SAT or ACT as well, and will use the student's best scores from either test."

SELECTIVITY

Admissions Rating	89
# of applicants	24,345
% of applicants accepted	52
% of acceptees attending	53
# accepting a place on wait list	410

FRESHMAN PROFILE

Range SAT Critical Reading	520–610
Range SAT Math	540–640
Range SAT Writing	500–590
Range ACT Composite	22–27
Minimum Paper TOEFL	550
Minimum Computer Based TOEFL	213
Average HS GPA	3.57
% graduated top 10% of class	35
% graduated top 25% of class	77
% graduated top 50% of class	93

DEADLINES

Regular application deadline	5/1
Regular notification	rolling
Nonfall registration?	yes

FINANCIAL FACTS

Financial Aid Rating	69
Annual in-state tuition	$3,492
Annual out-of-state tuition	$17,017
Room & Board	$8,000
Books and supplies	$888
Required fees	$10
% frosh rec. need-based scholarship or grant aid	21
% UG rec. need-based scholarship or grant aid	26
% frosh rec. need-based self-help aid	17
% UG rec. need-based self-help aid	25
% frosh rec. any financial aid	93
% UG rec. any financial aid	80

THE UNIVERSITY OF CHICAGO

1101 EAST FIFTY-EIGHTH STREET, ROSENWALD HALL, SUITE 105, CHICAGO, IL 60637 • ADMISSIONS: 773-702-8650 • FAX: 773-702-4199

CAMPUS LIFE

Quality of Life Rating	**83**
Fire Safety Rating	**60***
Type of school	private
Environment	metropolis

STUDENTS

Total undergrad enrollment	4,790
% male/female	50/50
% from out of state	78
% from public high school	63
% in (# of) fraternities	(11)
% in (# of) sororities	(4)
% African American	4
% Asian	13
% Caucasian	48
% Hispanic	8
% international	7
# of countries represented	59

SURVEY SAYS . . .

No one cheats
Lab facilities are great
Great computer facilities
Great library
Athletic facilities are great
Students love Chicago, IL

ACADEMICS

Academic Rating	**99**
Calendar	quarter
Student/faculty ratio	6:1
Profs interesting rating	81
Profs accessible rating	81
Most common lab size	10–19 students
Most common reg class size	10–19 students

MOST POPULAR MAJORS

biology/biological sciences
economics
English language and literature

STUDENTS SAY

Academics

"Dedication to enriching the 'life of the mind' is palpable" at the "incomparable" The University of Chicago. It is home to "the best Economics Department in the country" and one of the best (and most monstrously ugly) main libraries on earth. Chicago students believe that "no university offers a better academic experience," and there is "an unexpectedly vibrant school spirit that comes not from athletics, but [a] shared academic involvement." Undergraduates must complete an intense, "interdisciplinary" core curriculum that "teaches them how to think about literature and philosophy and science." The Core is "rigorous" and "You will spend about a third of your time here on it. But it's [also] fantastic, and you come out an incredibly well-rounded thinker with opinions on a wide variety of subjects." Naturally, "Courses are tough." "Once you're out of the fire," though, "You realize how much more enriched you've become intellectually, with respect [as] to how to learn and . . . knowledge itself." Professors at Chicago "are the best in the world" and are "real celebrities in their fields of study," but they "make every effort to help every student who asks." Still, "there are duds." "Not everyone with the intelligence to do amazing research is capable of teaching." The "incredibly supportive" administration "takes pains to engage the entire campus in a sort of collective, community-wide conversation. . . . They bring in all sorts of speakers, allow student groups almost absolute freedom, and are very supportive of student initiatives."

Life

The quarter system "makes for a particularly fast-paced" schedule. "We wear t-shirts that say U of C: Where fun comes to die, and we're proud of it," explains a first-year student. "Don't come here if you don't plan to work very hard," an economics major warns. "We spend a large chunk of our time studying and should be studying much of the time that we are not." However, according to one student, "As much as a lot of people complain about the extremely rigorous academics at this school, we all secretly love it or we wouldn't be here." And "contrary to popular belief," students "certainly do know how to have fun." There are "concerts, plays, movies," and "tons of truly brilliant events on campus." Students also spend a lot of time "just talking" with "fascinating" classmates "who can hold their own on any topic under the sun." "The frat party scene is not much at all compared to other schools, but it's still there. Room parties with extended friends and random people from the building are usually more popular." While "scorn for the lovely neighborhood" surrounding the campus is "exceedingly common," downtown Chicago is "very accessible." The city "is a huge asset and resource," "whether it's for an internship," "a night out," or "just a day away from campus."

Student Body

Students at Chicago are "intense," "opinionated," "engaged with the world around them," and "somewhat zany." "Most everyone has a quirk," a senior reports, "like the center on the football team who's really into Dungeons & Dragons." Without question, "the popular stereotype" of the Chicago student is "a nerdy, socially awkward person." Living up to the hype are an abundance of students "religiously dedicated to academic performance" and "a bunch of strange people," "usually clutching some fantastic book." However, "There aren't as many extremely strange and nerdy students as there have been in the past." "A portion of the student body at the U of C [are] actually talented, cool, and (gasp!) attractive." "There are loads of people that are fascinating," a sophomore writes. There are "artists, communists, fashionistas, activists," and even "some who aren't posing at all." "Everyone who is at The University of Chicago considers themselves at the best possible university," concludes one student. "It's a self-selecting group," and most people are "happy to be here." Chicago students "look down on other schools, particularly the Ivies."

FINANCIAL AID: 773-702-8666 • WEBSITE: WWW.UCHICAGO.EDU

ADMISSIONS

Very important factors considered include: Application essay, character/personal qualities, recommendation(s), rigor of secondary school record, talent/ability. *Important factors considered include:* Academic GPA, class rank, extracurricular activities, volunteer work. *Other factors considered include:* Alumni/ae relation, first generation, interview, level of applicant's interest, racial/ethnic status, standardized test scores, work experience. SAT or ACT required; TOEFL required of all international applicants. High school diploma or equivalent is not required. *Academic units recommended:* 4 English, 4 math, 4 science, 3 foreign language, 2 social studies, 2 history.

The Inside Word

The University of Chicago is home to the "Uncommon Application" and essay topics such as, *"Don't play what's there, play what's not there." Miles Davis. Discuss.* That's right: People here dwell on deep thoughts and big ideas. In your application you'll need to demonstrate outstanding grades in the tough courses; really high standardized test scores; and, most of all, that you will fit in with a bunch of thinkers. Think really hard before you write your three essays and try to say really intelligent things during your interview. Under no circumstances whatsoever should you even consider missing the interview.

FINANCIAL AID

Students should submit: FAFSA, institution's own financial aid form, CSS/Financial Aid PROFILE, Noncustodial PROFILE, Business/Farm Supplement. Regular filing deadline is February 1. The Princeton Review suggests that all financial aid forms be submitted as soon as possible after January 1. *Need-based scholarships/grants offered:* Pell Grant, SEOG, state scholarships/grants, private scholarships, the school's own gift aid. *Loan aid offered:* FFEL Subsidized Stafford, FFEL Unsubsidized Stafford, FFEL PLUS, Federal Perkins Loan. Applicants will be notified of awards on or about April 15.

FROM THE ADMISSIONS OFFICE

"The University of Chicago is a place where talented young people—writers, politicians, activists, artists, mathematicians, and scientists—come to learn in a setting that rewards interesting thought and prizes initiative and creativity. Chicago is also a place where collegiate life is urban, yet friendly and open, and free of empty traditionalism and snobbishness. Chicago is the right choice for students who know that they would thrive in an intimate classroom setting. Classes at Chicago are small, emphasizing discussion with faculty members whose research is always testing the limits of their chosen fields. Students at U of Chicago take chances—delighting professors when they pursue a topic on their own for the fun of it, or display an articulate voice in papers and in discussion. Their good times include the normal collegiate good times—a highly successful Division III sports program, small but active Greek life, 35 student theatrical productions a year, a rich musical life—and the extraordinary opportunities a major city offers our students, who enjoy the politics, music, theater, commerce, architecture, neighborhood life of Chicago.

"Applicants are asked to submit either the SAT or the ACT. Chicago does not require the SAT Subject Tests. The ACT may be taken without the optional Writing section."

SELECTIVITY

Admissions Rating	98
# of applicants	9,538
% of applicants accepted	38
% of acceptees attending	34
# accepting a place on wait list	888
% admitted from wait list	1

FRESHMAN PROFILE

Range SAT Critical Reading	670–770
Range SAT Math	650–760
Range ACT Composite	28–33
Minimum Paper TOEFL	600
Minimum Computer Based TOEFL	250
Average HS GPA	3.89
% graduated top 10% of class	80
% graduated top 25% of class	97
% graduated top 50% of class	100

DEADLINES

Regular application deadline	1/2
Regular notification	4/1
Nonfall registration?	no

APPLICANTS ALSO LOOK AT

AND OFTEN PREFER
Columbia University, Harvard College, Northwestern University, University of Pennsylvania, Yale University

AND SOMETIMES PREFER
Cornell College, University of California—Berkeley, Washington University in St. Louis

AND RARELY PREFER
Georgetown University, New York University

FINANCIAL FACTS

Financial Aid Rating	94
Annual tuition	$33,336
Room & Board	$10,608
Books and supplies	$1,000
Required fees	$669
% frosh rec. need-based scholarship or grant aid	47
% UG rec. need-based scholarship or grant aid	45
% frosh rec. need-based self-help aid	38
% UG rec. need-based self-help aid	39
% frosh rec. any financial aid	59
% UG rec. any financial aid	56

UNIVERSITY OF CINCINNATI

OFFICE OF ADMISSIONS, PO BOX 210091, CINCINNATI, OH 45221-0091 • ADMISSIONS: 513-556-1100 • FAX: 513-556-1105

CAMPUS LIFE

Quality of Life Rating	64
Fire Safety Rating	94
Type of school	public
Environment	metropolis

STUDENTS

Total undergrad enrollment	19,217
% male/female	49/51
% from out of state	11
% live on campus	20
% in (# of) fraternities	NR (23)
% in (# of) sororities	NR (10)
% African American	12
% Asian	3
% Caucasian	77
% Hispanic	2
% international	1
# of countries represented	124

SURVEY SAYS . . .

Great computer facilities
Great library
Diverse student types on campus
Everyone loves the Bearcats
Lots of beer drinking
Hard liquor is popular
(Almost) everyone smokes

ACADEMICS

Academic Rating	70
Calendar	quarter
Student/faculty ratio	14:1
Profs interesting rating	64
Profs accessible rating	64
Most common reg class size	20-29 students

MOST POPULAR MAJORS

communications studies/speech
communication and rhetoric
marketing/marketing management
psychology

STUDENTS SAY

Academics

You can't generalize about the undergraduate experience at the University of Cincinnati. At this large public school, "Each college within the university is like a different world," creating a distinct academic and social experience for students in every program. A junior explains, "The best part about UC is that you get to enroll in a smaller college for your major studies, whether it's CCM [College-Conservatory of Music] for music, DAAP for art, or Arts and Sciences for psychology, so you get the feel of a smaller college while still having all the resources a large university has to offer." On that note, UC can be a challenge. One junior warns, "At UC, it's pretty well known that students attending the best programs will be dedicating their lives to their studies. I am at CCM and I spend my life in a practice room. Sometimes I am at school for 13 to 14 hours a day." But the hard work pays off. UC, says another student, "will satisfy those looking to get a great education and the opportunities to build a great resume filled with experience through the school's co-op program."

Life

With active programs in the arts, it's unsurprising that "there are many different types of performances at CCM, ranging from orchestra, dance, . . . choir, [and] theater." In addition, "Basketball and football games are widely attended." Aside from athletics, "the biggest social draw for people at UC is the Greek scene," and many students enjoy a good party. However, a sophomore tells us that "in general, after the freshman year, everyone is focused on doing work and reaching goals. People seem content just hanging out when there's time, relaxing and watching a movie." In fact, students say there isn't much enthusiasm for campus social events, though the school "is trying to make campus a place to hang out on evenings and weekends." An optimistic senior shares, "UC is nicknamed 'Under Construction,' as the campus is always changing. Many new facilities [have been] added, like a movie theater, student recreation center, new restaurants, and even shopping!" Even so, "Cincinnati is a great backdrop for a college town," offering "many places to shop, museums, and other cultural things to do."

Student Body

Attracting students from the Cincinnati area, across the United States, and throughout the world, University of Cincinnati boasts a largely diverse student body. A senior shares, "There is a broad range of ethnicities, religions, backgrounds, and even sexual orientations. I really enjoy interacting with students from other parts of the U.S. and from other countries." In addition, UC attracts a sizable population of older students, who add another dimension to the campus community. One senior reports, "There are a good deal of older classmates who have full-time jobs and families. There [is] also a large amount of commuters that make for a different type of college." While it would be difficult to generalize about this diverse population, most say there is a consistently friendly vibe on the UC campus. A junior insists, "No student is the same at UC, but the typical student is friendly and willing to lend a hand or hang out if you approach them." Another adds, "There are lots of artsy kids and lots of engineers. Somehow we manage to get along."

FINANCIAL AID: 513-556-1000 • E-MAIL: TRANSFER@UC.EDU • WEBSITE: WWW.ADMISSIONS.UC.EDU

ADMISSIONS

Very important factors considered include: Academic GPA, class rank, personal statement, rigor of secondary school record. *Other factors considered include:* Extracurricular activities. SAT or ACT required; ACT with Writing component required. High school diploma is required, and GED is accepted. *Academic units required:* 4 English, 3 math, 2 science, 2 foreign language, 2 social studies, 2 academic electives. *Academic units recommended:* 4 math, 3 science, 1 history.

The Inside Word

One of the University of Cincinnati's greatest strengths is that it provides a small-college atmosphere within a large university setting. Each school maintains some autonomy, and this extends to admissions policies. Requirements vary among programs and candidates will need to do their research before completing their applications. Competitive programs tend to fill up rather quickly, so interested students should submit their materials as early as possible.

FINANCIAL AID

Students should submit: FAFSA. The Princeton Review suggests that all financial aid forms be submitted as soon as possible after January 1. *Need-based scholarships/grants offered:* Pell, SEOG, state scholarships/grants, private scholarships, the school's own gift aid, Federal Nursing Scholarships. *Loan aid offered:* Direct Subsidized Stafford, Direct Unsubsidized Stafford, Direct PLUS, FFEL Subsidized Stafford, FFEL Unsubsidized Stafford, FFEL PLUS, Federal Perkins Loan, Federal Nursing Loan, state loans, college/university loans from institutional funds. Applicants will be notified of awards on a rolling basis beginning or about March 10. Federal Work-Study Program available. Institutional employment available. Off-campus job opportunities are excellent.

FROM THE ADMISSIONS OFFICE

"Remarkable architecture, park-like open spaces, engaging student tour guides, and a welcoming Admissions Staff make the University of Cincinnati a must-visit destination. UC campus has been transformed over the past 10 years and is drawing national and international attention for blending student life, learning, research, and recreation in a unique urban environment.

"Freshman application materials include high school transcripts, test scores, a personal statement, and a list of co-curricular activities. Some academic programs require additional materials.

"Sign up for a visit, become a Bearcat VIP, and apply online at Admissions.uc.edu. Information about all UC majors is linked from the website. We also have Tuesday-night online chat sessions for students and parents. Nothing beats a visit, however, for assessing how well you'll fit in here.

"Either the SAT or ACT is required for students applying to bachelor's degree programs; the ACT Writing component is required. SAT Subject Tests are not required."

SELECTIVITY

Admissions Rating	**78**
# of applicants	10,741
% of applicants accepted	76
% of acceptees attending	39

FRESHMAN PROFILE

Range SAT Critical Reading	490-600
Range SAT Math	510-630
Range SAT Writing	470-590
Range ACT Composite	21-27
Minimum Paper TOEFL	515
Average HS GPA	3.35
% graduated top 10% of class	21
% graduated top 25% of class	45
% graduated top 50% of class	77

DEADLINES

Regular application deadline	9/1
Regular notification	rolling
Nonfall registration?	yes

FINANCIAL FACTS

Financial Aid Rating	**65**
Annual in-state tuition	$7,896
Annual out-of-state tuition	$22,419
Room & Board	$8,286
Books and supplies	$1,185
Required fees	$1,503
% frosh rec. need-based scholarship or grant aid	26
% UG rec. need-based scholarship or grant aid	24
% frosh rec. need-based self-help aid	20
% UG rec. need-based self-help aid	18
% frosh rec. any financial aid	82
% UG rec. any financial aid	75

UNIVERSITY OF COLORADO—BOULDER

552 UCB, BOULDER, CO 80309-0552 • ADMISSIONS: 303-492-6301 • FAX: 303-492-7115

CAMPUS LIFE

Quality of Life Rating	86
Fire Safety Rating	89
Type of school	public
Environment	city

STUDENTS

Total undergrad enrollment	26,165
% male/female	53/47
% from out of state	31
% live on campus	26
% in (# of) fraternities	7 (15)
% in (# of) sororities	10 (12)
% African American	2
% Asian	6
% Caucasian	78
% Hispanic	6
% Native American	2
% international	1
# of countries represented	115

SURVEY SAYS . . .

Great computer facilities
Great library
Athletic facilities are great
Students love Boulder, CO
Great off-campus food
Students are happy
Everyone loves the The Colorado
Buffaloes
Lots of beer drinking
Hard liquor is popular

ACADEMICS

Academic Rating	68
Calendar	semester
Student/faculty ratio	16:1
Profs interesting rating	73
Profs accessible rating	73
% profs teaching	
UG courses	88
% classes taught by TAs	10
Most common	
lab size	20–29 students
Most common	
reg class size	10–19 students

MOST POPULAR MAJORS

English language and literature
physiology
psychology

STUDENTS SAY

Academics

The University of Colorado—Boulder serves everyone from the most committed undergraduates to those who live by the motto "Skis and C's get degrees." The differences among students are many at this large research institution, but everyone agrees on one thing: The place is drop-dead gorgeous. Even those who tout at length the "opportunities to take classes and participate in graduate courses as an undergraduate, often in renowned academic departments" and the "chances for students to get published, receive grants, and develop relationships with prestigious faculty" can't help appreciating the fact that "the skiing and snowboarding are the best here." As one student puts it, CU provides students with plenty of resources "to pursue what they want (whether that be skiing, music, partying, or just about any outdoor activity imaginable) while also receiving a first-class education." CU is also "a top engineering school" that has "great programs in the sciences and a strong commitment to scientific advancement"; the architecture, journalism and mass communications, and aerospace programs are also held in high esteem by students. Since the school is large there are many available academic choices; some here complain, however, that the school's "core curriculum is overwhelming. It's very hard to take classes that you want outside of your major because the requirements are too specific and too many. This contributes in a major way to the fact that it is not uncommon at all for students to graduate in more than 4 years."

Life

CU has endured its fair share of negative publicity in recent years. A football recruiting scandal and a radical professor who exercised his right to free speech to outrageous effect generated headlines, and the alcohol-related death of an underclassman added a tragic exclamation point. Students tell us that "Boulder needs to find a way to get itself out of the spotlight, because despite how wonderful it is, the media find a way of highlighting its problems, and that seems to be all that anyone knows about us, especially outside of Colorado." There is, of course, so much more to life at CU; sure, "There are parties going on all the time where people can drink, but that is not all that CU has to offer. There are [also] hundreds of clubs that students participate in, along with a lot of fun intramural sports." Intercollegiate football remains huge, the scandal notwithstanding. The Greek scene, though, has taken a bigger hit; these days "'The Hill (the campus' largest social scene) is heavily guarded by police, and the Greek system is under constant scrutiny." As a result, "House and dorm parties are becoming very popular." The best options for fun, though, are off campus, where "You can head up to the mountains to ski or snowboard, catch a concert at one of the many local music venues (from small clubs to Red Rocks), go to Denver (for free with your student pass), go camping, hang out on Pearl Street, or just sit at one of the many coffee shops in the city of Boulder."

Student Body

There is a sense that "Most students are from upper-middle-class to upper-class families and are supported heavily by their parents," at CU, although with a student population of more than 25,000 "there are also plenty of students who are not from wealthy families." While "There is not much ethnic diversity" here, there are all types of people, from "liberals, conservatives, vegetarians, self-proclaimed nerds and computer geeks, hippies, jocks, savvy business students, poets, writers, [and] artists" to "scientists, partiers, and introverts. There is a group here for anyone." While not all students are "focused academically," those who are find many who share their interests. An interesting bit of trivia: "Almost everybody has an iPod," several students observe.

UNIVERSITY OF COLORADO—BOULDER

FINANCIAL AID: 303-492-5091 • E-MAIL: APPLY@COLORADO.EDU • WEBSITE: WWW.COLORADO.EDU

ADMISSIONS

Very important factors considered include: Academic GPA, class rank, rigor of secondary school record, standardized test scores. *Important factors considered include:* Application essay, character/personal qualities, first generation, racial/ethnic status, recommendation(s), state residency. *Other factors considered include:* Alumni/ae relation, extracurricular activities, geographical residence, level of applicant's interest, talent/ability, volunteer work, work experience. SAT or ACT required; TOEFL required of all international applicants. High school diploma is required, and GED is accepted. *Academic units required:* 4 English, 3 math, 3 science (2 science labs), 3 foreign language, 3 social studies, 1 history, 1 geography.

The Inside Word

Applicants who meet specific standardized test and GPA requirements are guaranteed acceptance to University of Colorado—Boulder. CU makes provisions, however, for candidates who don't meet those requirements but demonstrate academic potential. With nearly a third of the student body from out of state, CU boasts far more geographic diversity than most state schools.

FINANCIAL AID

Students should submit: FAFSA; Federal Income Tax Returns. The Princeton Review suggests that all financial aid forms be submitted as soon as possible after January 1. *Need-based scholarships/grants offered:* Pell Grant, SEOG, state scholarships/grants, private scholarships, the school's own gift aid. *Loan aid offered:* Direct Subsidized Stafford, Direct Unsubsidized Stafford, Direct PLUS, Federal Perkins Loan, college/university loans from institutional funds, private lenders. Applicants will be notified of awards on a rolling basis beginning or about February 1. Federal Work-Study Program available. Institutional employment available. Off-campus job opportunities are excellent.

FROM THE ADMISSIONS OFFICE

"The University of Colorado at Boulder is a place of beauty and academic prominence at the foot of the Rocky Mountains. A sense of vitality and curiosity fills the campus, and yet it's comfortable and relaxed. It's a place you can be yourself and let your imagination soar.

"We have programs for you if you seek leadership training, research experience, academic honors, international experience (one in four graduates has studied abroad), community involvement, and more. The Undergraduate Academy gives exceptionally talented and intellectually committed students the opportunity to expand their education outside the classroom, build a sense of community, and help prepare for postgraduate opportunities. Residential academic programs (RAPS) in several halls provide undergraduates with shared learning and living experiences.

"Getting involved is easy at CU—Boulder. If you are interested in student government, clubs, athletics, recreation, Greek life, volunteer work, theater, dance, film, exhibits, planetarium shows, or concerts, you will find them here.

"To find out if CU—Boulder is the place for you, we encourage you to visit. Contact the Office of Admissions, or take a virtual tour at www.colorado.edu/prospective.

"The University of Colorado at Boulder requires either SAT or ACT scores for admissions; the Writing tests are currently not used in making decisions. SAT scores from tests taken before March 2005 are accepted for consideration. SAT Subject Test scores are not required."

SELECTIVITY

Admissions Rating	80
# of applicants	18,173
% of applicants accepted	88
% of acceptees attending	36

FRESHMAN PROFILE

Range SAT Critical Reading	520–630
Range SAT Math	540–650
Range ACT Composite	23–28
Minimum Paper TOEFL	500
Minimum Computer Based TOEFL	173
Average HS GPA	3.53
% graduated top 10% of class	23
% graduated top 25% of class	54
% graduated top 50% of class	90

DEADLINES

Regular application deadline	1/15
Regular notification	rolling
Nonfall registration?	yes

APPLICANTS ALSO LOOK AT
AND OFTEN PREFER
Arizona State University at the Tempe Campus, Stanford University, University of California—Santa Cruz
AND SOMETIMES PREFER
San Diego State University, University of Arizona, University of Miami, University of Wisconsin—Madison
AND RARELY PREFER
University of Utah, University of Wyoming

FINANCIAL FACTS

Financial Aid Rating	87
Annual in-state tuition	$4,554
Annual out-of-state tuition	$22,450
Room & Board	$8,300
Books and supplies	$1,698
Required fees	$1,089
% frosh rec. need-based scholarship or grant aid	22
% UG rec. need-based scholarship or grant aid	21
% frosh rec. need-based self-help aid	36
% UG rec. need-based self-help aid	31
% frosh rec. any financial aid	63
% UG rec. any financial aid	52

UNIVERSITY OF CONNECTICUT

2131 HILLSIDE ROAD, UNIT 3088, STORRS, CT 06268-3088 • ADMISSIONS: 860-486-3137 • FAX: 860-486-1476

CAMPUS LIFE
Quality of Life Rating	**69**
Fire Safety Rating	**87**
Type of school	public
Environment	town

STUDENTS
Total undergrad enrollment	16,006
% male/female	49/51
% from out of state	30
% from public high school	87
% live on campus	71
% in (# of) fraternities	7 (15)
% in (# of) sororities	7 (10)
% African American	5
% Asian	7
% Caucasian	70
% Hispanic	5
% international	1
# of countries represented	109

SURVEY SAYS . . .
Great library
Everyone loves the Huskies
Intramural sports are popular
Student publications are popular
Lots of beer drinking
Hard liquor is popular

ACADEMICS
Academic Rating	**73**
Calendar	semester
Student/faculty ratio	17:1
Profs interesting rating	63
Profs accessible rating	69
% profs teaching	
UG courses	77
% classes taught by TAs	23
Most common	
lab size	20–29 students
Most common	
reg class size	10–19 students

MOST POPULAR MAJORS
biological sciences
nursing/registered nurse training
political science
psychology

STUDENTS SAY

Academics

The hardy students of University of Connecticut recognize that a UConn education "is based on a solid foundation of research and academics" and a pedagogical approach that "promotes learning in and out of the classroom," although that's not to say that there's not a contingency that are "all about partying, having a good time, and doing the least amount of studying possible." UConn is large enough to offer "a wide range of great majors," including programs at the "fantastic School of Business," the "well-known Education Department," and "a solid engineering school with a unique biomedical engineering major." In most areas, UConn "networks to provide students [with] millions of opportunities for students to expand in academics, self, and even careers," including "great internships." The school "does a great job of publicizing these opportunities, as well. We are a big icon of the state, and we keep our prestige." Thanks to the "UConn 2000" and "UConn Twenty-first Century" initiatives, the campus "is improving drastically with a $2.3-billion construction program designated to refurbishing (and adding onto) nearly every building on campus." As is the case at many large state schools, "The success of a UConn student's education is really a matter of personal responsibility. Introductory classes tend to be large and very impersonal, so it is up to the individual to do well." Bureaucratic tasks such as registration "can be a real pain," and "the class enrollment process is very confusing and difficult to use," but overall, students speak warmly of their interactions with administrators. "While usually you have to go through a middleman to get to the administration, it is possible to voice your concerns," sums up a satisfied student.

Life

UConn is located in Storrs, which "is pretty much in the middle of nowhere." It seems especially so to students without cars, of whom there are quite a few (those with wheels can take advantage of Hartford and, occasionally, Boston). Some students feel this predicament "forces us to go out and party simply because there is nothing better to do." Others point out that "people go out a lot, yeah, and there's often alcohol involved, but there are many interesting and fun things to do here for those who don't like that kind of stuff. For instance, there are UConn Late Nights in Student Union at which students can just hang out, meet new people, play games, and have fun. There are also interesting lectures given by guest speakers at the Dodd Research Center, and movie nights and concerts. Since I've been here I've seen Dave Chappelle, Kanye West, NAS, Busta Rhymes, Lewis Black, and more perform." Those eager to join clubs and organizations will also find many to accommodate them here. And then there are the intercollegiate sports. "Basketball and football games are always a blast!" undergraduates assure us (the men's and women's hoops squads are both perennial national contenders).

Student Body

Students report that the typical UConn undergraduate "is a Connecticut resident"—but after that, "it is so hard to generalize a student population of nearly 15,000." Sure, "A lot of students are very similar in appearance" because "They are from in-state, and a lot of the same trends are prevalent. But there are plenty of students who do not follow this stereotype, and everyone fits in fine." Many feel that UConn is "a fantastic representation of the Northeast in all respects," especially the "actively involved, down-to-earth, [and] pretty friendly" student body. The party animal is a vanishing breed here (though the speed at which he or she is vanishing is open to debate); one student explains, "UConn has had its reputation as a drinking school for many years. And every year, the number of students who come here specifically to party and drink declines."

FINANCIAL AID: 860-486-2819 • E-MAIL: BEAHUSKY@UCONN.EDU • WEBSITE: WWW.UCONN.EDU

ADMISSIONS

Very important factors considered include: Academic GPA, class rank, rigor of secondary school record, standardized test scores, talent/ability. *Important factors considered include:* Application essay, character/personal qualities, extracurricular activities, first generation, racial/ethnic status, recommendation(s), volunteer work. *Other factors considered include:* Alumni/ae relation, geographical residence, level of applicant's interest, state residency, work experience. SAT or ACT required; SAT or ACT with Writing component required. TOEFL required of all international applicants. High school diploma is required, and GED is accepted. *Academic units required:* 4 English, 3 math, 2 science (2 science labs), 2 foreign language, 2 social studies, 3 academic electives. *Academic units recommended:* 3 foreign language.

The Inside Word

Similar to most large, public institutions, UConn focuses primarily on quantifiable data such as grades, class rank, and test scores when making admit decisions. Connecticut residents who demonstrate significant academic achievement stand a good chance of being admitted, though the acceptance rate has decreased significantly over the past few years. Candidates are advised to apply early as the school has a rolling admissions policy and applications are considered on a space-available basis.

FINANCIAL AID

Students should submit: FAFSA. The Princeton Review suggests that all financial aid forms be submitted as soon as possible after January 1. *Need-based scholarships/grants offered:* Pell Grant, Academic Competitiveness Grant, National SMART Grant, SEOG, state scholarships/grants, private scholarships, the school's own gift aid. *Loan aid offered:* FFEL Subsidized Stafford, FFEL Unsubsidized Stafford, FFEL PLUS, Federal Perkins Loan. Applicants will be notified of awards on a rolling basis beginning or about March 1. Federal Work-Study Program available. Institutional employment available. Off-campus job opportunities are good.

FROM THE ADMISSIONS OFFICE

"Thanks to a $2.3-billion construction program that is impacting every area of university life, the University of Connecticut provides students a high-quality and personalized education on one of the most attractive and technologically advanced college campuses in the United States. Applications are soaring nationally as an increasing number of high-achieving students from diverse backgrounds are making UConn their school of choice. From award-winning actors to governmental leaders, students enjoy an assortment of fascinating speakers each year, while performances by premier dance, jazz, and rock musicians enliven student life. Our beautiful New England campus is convenient and safe, and most students walk to class or ride university shuttle buses. State-of-the-art residential facilities include interest-based learning communities and honors housing as well as on-campus suite-style and apartment living. Championship Division I athletics have created fervor known as Huskymania among UConn students.

"Freshman applicants seeking admittance for Fall 2008 are required to submit official score reports from the new SAT or ACT with Writing component."

SELECTIVITY

Admissions Rating	88
# of applicants	19,778
% of applicants accepted	51
% of acceptees attending	32
# accepting a place on wait list	1,660
% admitted from wait list	23

FRESHMAN PROFILE

Range SAT Critical Reading	530–630
Range SAT Math	560–660
Range ACT Composite	23–27
Minimum Paper TOEFL	550
Minimum Computer Based TOEFL	213
% graduated top 10% of class	38
% graduated top 25% of class	81
% graduated top 50% of class	98

DEADLINES

Regular application deadline	2/1
Regular notification	rolling
Nonfall registration?	yes

APPLICANTS ALSO LOOK AT

AND OFTEN PREFER
Boston College, Boston University, University of Delaware, University of Maryland—College Park, Villanova University

AND SOMETIMES PREFER
Northeastern University, Pennsylvania State University—University Park, Providence College, Syracuse University

AND RARELY PREFER
Rutgers, The State University of New Jersey—New Brunswick, University of Massachusetts—Amherst, University of New Hampshire, University of Rhode Island, University of Vermont

FINANCIAL FACTS

Financial Aid Rating	72
Annual in-state tuition	$6,816
Annual out-of-state tuition	$20,760
Room & Board	$8,850
Books and supplies	$726
Required fees	$2,026
% frosh rec. need-based scholarship or grant aid	39
% UG rec. need-based scholarship or grant aid	37
% frosh rec. need-based self-help aid	36
% UG rec. need-based self-help aid	37
% frosh rec. any financial aid	50
% UG rec. any financial aid	48

UNIVERSITY OF DALLAS

1845 EAST NORTHGATE DRIVE, IRVING, TX 75062 • ADMISSIONS: 972-721-5266 • FAX: 972-721-5017

CAMPUS LIFE
Quality of Life Rating	82
Fire Safety Rating	93
Type of school	private
Affiliation	Roman Catholic
Environment	city

STUDENTS
Total undergrad enrollment	1,137
% male/female	44/56
% from out of state	44
% from public high school	45
% live on campus	62
% African American	1
% Asian	6
% Caucasian	67
% Hispanic	17
% international	1
# of countries represented	12

SURVEY SAYS . . .
Small classes
No one cheats
Students are friendly
Students are very religious
Frats and sororities are unpopular or nonexistent
(Almost) everyone smokes

ACADEMICS
Academic Rating	85
Calendar	semester
Student/faculty ratio	11:1
Profs interesting rating	91
Profs accessible rating	90
% profs teaching UG courses	100
% classes taught by TAs	0
Most common lab size	fewer than 10 students
Most common reg class size	20–29 students

MOST POPULAR MAJORS
biology/biological sciences
business administration/
management
English language and literature

STUDENTS SAY

Academics

For many of the students at this small Catholic school in the Dallas suburbs, the University of Dallas is all about the core curriculum, an integrated survey of Western civilization's great texts and ideas. The Core gobbles up nearly half the credits required to graduate—but few complain about this. On the contrary, most students choose UD precisely because of its reverence for the classics. One observes, "Where else can you find students discussing casually over lunch, as if were the most normal thing in the world, Plato's *Republic*, the concept of divine love in Dante's *Commedia*, or the effects of the French Revolution on modern society?" The other cornerstone of a UD education is the sophomore-year Rome program, through which "about 85 percent of all students" enjoy "an altogether amazing experience" at UD's private campus just outside the city of Rome, Italy. The semester abroad "includes a 5-day guided tour of Italy's famous cities, an 8-day excursion through Greece, and then a 10-day period during which students are allowed [to go] wherever they want. Everyone says that they come back as a family and continue to miss being there for the rest of their lives." One senior gushes, "The Rome semester was probably the single best experience of my life." Both in Rome and stateside, UD classes are "small and very discussion oriented," and professors are "brilliant and concerned with their students—not just helping them do well in the class, but [also] helping them become better people." Students praise UD's humanities offerings, but some feel that "science majors are often put on the back burner."

Life

"I thought it was just a marketing technique when the school kept talking about how important the community is," writes one UD undergrad, "but I've come to know that it is all true." Students unite for "school-sponsored events every week with music or karaoke," "movie nights and cooking nights in the dorms," "weekend parties at the apartments across the street (which are usually pretty controlled; people drink, but there is rarely any binge drinking or drug use)," "Thank God It's Thursday, which celebrates the start of the weekend in the Rathskellar, the on-campus bar," and other special events. An event called Charity Week "is one of the highest points of the year. It helps get the freshmen involved with the campus while reuniting the junior class after being split in two their sophomore year for the Rome semester. It raises money for various organizations and is a week of fun and relaxation." Among the athletic teams, rugby and women's soccer both "draw a large crowd." Students agree that their campus "is not very pretty" and note that "you don't go to UD for the architecture," but also observe that "in the spring, when the trees blossom, it is very beautiful." Because "The campus is really rather isolated" in the suburbs, "You need access to a car in order to survive at UD. There are lots of places to go in Dallas and Fort Worth; you just need a way to get to them."

Student Body

UD's core curriculum attracts serious-minded students who "really think about things. The Core exposes us to philosophy and literature and history, and when you go through that, you can't help but find life more interesting." Many bring a conservative Catholic perspective to their studies, but "a lot of non-Catholics still enjoy this school a great deal." Some are quite religious, others less so; one student writes, "A very small group of students are sometimes so engaged in their religion they wear it like a shiny badge of righteousness, so you might think the school is full of these people, but it is not." For many, coming to UD becomes a family affair; one undergrad explains, "The first person in the family goes to UD, and gets everyone else hooked as well, so all of their younger siblings end up going to UD; several professors know or teach entire families over the years."

UNIVERSITY OF DALLAS

FINANCIAL AID: 972-721-5266 • E-MAIL: UGADMIS@UDALLAS.EDU • WEBSITE: WWW.UDALLAS.EDU

ADMISSIONS

Very important factors considered include: Academic GPA, application essay, character/personal qualities, recommendation(s), rigor of secondary school record, standardized test scores. *Important factors considered include:* Talent/ability. *Other factors considered include:* Alumni/ae relation, class rank, extracurricular activities, first generation, interview, level of applicant's interest, volunteer work, work experience. SAT or ACT required; ACT with Writing component required. TOEFL IELTS or SAT required of all international applicants. High school diploma is required, and GED is accepted. *Academic units required:* 4 English, 3 math, 3 science, 3 social studies, 4 academic electives. *Academic units recommended:* 4 English, 4 math, 3 science, 3 foreign language, 4 social studies, 4 academic electives, 2 art/drama.

The Inside Word

The University of Dallas is a school deeply rooted in Catholic principles. Its unique academic program couples a classic liberal arts education with the pursuit of moral and intellectual virtues. The Admissions Team gives each applicant careful consideration, endeavoring to find candidates likely to benefit from and contribute to the school environment. Scholarship is especially valued, as students at UD are expected to be immersed in their studies and always ready to engage in a philosophical debate.

FINANCIAL AID

Students should submit: FAFSA. The Princeton Review suggests that all financial aid forms be submitted as soon as possible after January 1. *Need-based scholarships/grants offered:* Pell Grant, SEOG, state scholarships/grants, private scholarships, the school's own gift aid. *Loan aid offered:* FFEL Subsidized Stafford, FFEL Unsubsidized Stafford, FFEL PLUS, Federal Perkins Loan, state loans. Applicants will be notified of awards on a rolling basis beginning or about March 15.

FROM THE ADMISSIONS OFFICE

"Quite unabashedly, the curriculum at the University of Dallas is based on the supposition that truth and virtue exist and are the proper objects of search in an education. The curriculum further supposes that this search is best pursued through an acquisition of philosophical and theological principles on the part of a student and has for its analogical field a vast body of great literature—perhaps more extensive than is likely to be encountered elsewhere—supplemented by a survey of the sweep of history and an introduction to the political and economic principles of society. An understanding of these subjects, along with an introduction to the quantitative and scientific worldview and a mastery of a language, is expected to form a comprehensive and coherent experience, which, in effect, governs the intellect of a student in a manner that develops independence of thought in its most effective mode.

"Students applying for admission for Fall 2008 are required to take the SAT Reasoning Test or the ACT with Writing Assessment."

SELECTIVITY

Admissions Rating	87
# of applicants	876
% of applicants accepted	85
% of acceptees attending	42

FRESHMAN PROFILE

Range SAT Critical Reading	560–690
Range SAT Math	540–650
Range SAT Writing	540–660
Range ACT Composite	24–29
Minimum Paper TOEFL	550
Minimum Computer Based TOEFL	213
Average HS GPA	3.6
% graduated top 10% of class	41
% graduated top 25% of class	71
% graduated top 50% of class	88

DEADLINES

Regular application deadline	8/1
Regular notification	rolling
Nonfall registration?	yes

APPLICANTS ALSO LOOK AT

AND OFTEN PREFER
Southern Methodist University, University of Notre Dame

AND SOMETIMES PREFER
Austin College, Texas Christian University, Trinity University

AND RARELY PREFER
Loyola University—New Orleans, Saint Louis University, Spring Hill College, Texas A&M University—College Station, The University of Texas at Austin

FINANCIAL FACTS

Financial Aid Rating	79
Annual tuition	$21,819
Room & Board	$7,615
Books and supplies	$1,500
Required fees	$1,448
% frosh rec. need-based scholarship or grant aid	62
% UG rec. need-based scholarship or grant aid	60
% frosh rec. need-based self-help aid	50
% UG rec. need-based self-help aid	48
% frosh rec. any financial aid	97
% UG rec. any financial aid	94

UNIVERSITY OF DAYTON

300 COLLEGE PARK, DAYTON, OH 45469-1300 • ADMISSIONS: 937-229-4411 • FAX: 937-229-4729

STUDENTS SAY
Academics
"Academically challenging yet unpretentious, casual yet fun as hell," the University of Dayton is a midsize Catholic school that "is all about community: community when we study, community when we party, community when we are doing service, community when we pray. There are so many opportunities to build community and be accepted in the community here." Both academics and service "are taken very seriously" at UD. One undergrad notes, "You earn what you deserve. As long as you work hard, and your teachers can see that, you won't have a problem." Top programs include "a great premed program," "a wonderful Engineering Department," "an amazing teacher education program," and an "awesome business school" that includes the Davis Center for Portfolio Management, a "student-run fund that invests more than $3 million of the university's endowment." The number of options is unusual for an institution with such a small-school feel; students describe UD as "small enough that you get to know people very well, and you are always seeing someone you know, yet big enough that there are always new people to meet."

Life
"Community is probably the first word that comes to the majority of the student body's minds," agree most of the students we surveyed at UD. While it may "sound really cheesy," undergrads insist that "everyone is family here" and that "you are welcome from the very moment you step onto campus." Nowhere is this more apparent than in the student neighborhood, in which "Porch sitting is a must on sunny days." One student explains, "Porches are symbolic of UD. Everyone sits out on their porch. It's one huge neighborhood where everyone is welcome to party or to chill. And when we party, everyone leaves their door wide open for anyone to come." Campus organizations at UD "sponsor great weekend events," such as "trips to Chicago and Cincinnati, free movies, cookouts, arts and crafts, flag football games, cornhole (a horseshoe-like game played with cloth bags filled with corn) tournaments, comedy tours, karaoke, and retreats." And let's not forget Dayton basketball, "the gem of the community." True to its Marianist tradition, UD also has "the largest campus ministry in the country. We help both the local and global community with things ranging from one-time service days to immersion trips and even an entire year of service." Beyond campus, things get a little less idyllic. "Dayton as a city needs to improve," students say, noting the fact that "UD is neighboring a poverty-stricken area."

Student Body
The typical UD student is "semireligious, overly friendly, welcoming, and accepting of the few diverse students who are here." He or she also "loves UD basketball, community service, beer, and most of all, holding the door for the person behind them." That final attribute is "all part of the Marianist tradition. Complete strangers help each other all the time, and everyone says hi to one another." The UD "look" is casual, as "the average UD student can be found wearing jeans, a UD hoodie, and flip-flops or Birkenstock clogs. Most students are laid-back, down-to-earth, and fun, yet they know how to get down to business and study." Because of the school's Catholic focus, "The majority of students are Catholic, and some students who are not Catholic feel that the university incorporates too much religion in service-type activities. They fit in among the students but may feel left out when it comes to service and retreat activities because there is a heavy Catholic emphasis."

FINANCIAL AID: 937-229-4311 • E-MAIL: ADMISSION@UDAYTON.EDU • WEBSITE: WWW.UDAYTON.EDU

ADMISSIONS

Very important factors considered include: Academic GPA, rigor of secondary school record. *Important factors considered include:* Class rank, standardized test scores, talent/ability. *Other factors considered include:* Alumni/ae relation, application essay, character/personal qualities, extracurricular activities, first generation, interview, racial/ethnic status, recommendation(s), volunteer work, work experience. SAT or ACT required; TOEFL required of all international applicants. High school diploma is required, and GED is accepted. *Academic units required:* 2 units of foreign language are required for admission to the College of Arts and Sciences. *Academic units recommended:* 4 English, 3 math, 2 science, 3 social studies, 4 academic electives.

The Inside Word

University of Dayton is an excellent option for students who want to attend a Catholic university but don't meet the stringent criteria of a Georgetown or Notre Dame. UD gives equal weight to all academic factors—e.g., class rank, GPA—on the application. Candidates who demonstrate a modicum of success in the classroom and intellectual promise will most likely be accepted.

FINANCIAL AID

Students should submit: FAFSA. The Princeton Review suggests that all financial aid forms be submitted as soon as possible after January 1. *Need-based scholarships/grants offered:* Pell Grant, SEOG, state scholarships/grants, private scholarships, the school's own gift aid. *Loan aid offered:* FFEL Subsidized Stafford, FFEL Unsubsidized Stafford, FFEL PLUS, Federal Perkins Loan, GATE. Applicants will be notified of awards on or about March 31. Federal Work-Study Program available. Institutional employment available. Off-campus job opportunities are good.

FROM THE ADMISSIONS OFFICE

"The University of Dayton is a Catholic leader in higher education. We offer the resources and diversity of a comprehensive university and the attention and accessibility of a small college.

"More than 70 challenging academic programs are offered in the College of Arts and Sciences and the Schools of Business Administration, Education and Allied Professions, Engineering, and Law. Classes are small—27 students on average. Our more than 800 full-time and part-time faculty are committed to teaching undergraduate students and involving them in their research projects.

"The University of Dayton Research Institute ranks second in the nation in the amount of materials research performed annually. Technology-enhanced learning and the student computer initiative ensure students gain expertise in the tools that will prepare them for the future. All university-owned housing is fully wired for direct high-speed Internet access, and a wireless network covers several academic buildings, the student union, library, outdoor plazas, and residential buildings.

"Recent campus construction provides a modern home for the university's cutting-edge academic programs. New facilities include ArtStreet, Marianist Hall, and the Science Center. Open in January 2006, a new fitness and recreation complex, the RecPlex, provides 130,000 square feet of space for classrooms, courts, a natatorium, offices, and other recreational facilities.

"A strong sense of community is a hallmark feature of the university; a dual emphasis on leadership and service contributes to students' participation in more than 170 clubs and organizations. Division I intercollegiate athletics, and club and intramural sports, are also popular.

"Students applying for Fall 2008 admission may provide scores from either version of the SAT, or the ACT. Scores from the new Writing component will be collected but will not be used for admission purposes for 2008. The highest composite scores from either test will be used in admissions decisions."

SELECTIVITY

Admissions Rating	81
# of applicants	9,045
% of applicants accepted	79
% of acceptees attending	25
# accepting a place on wait list	16
% admitted from wait list	100

FRESHMAN PROFILE

Range SAT Critical Reading	510–620
Range SAT Math	530–650
Range ACT Composite	23–28
Minimum Paper TOEFL	523
Minimum Computer Based TOEFL	193
Average HS GPA	3.48
% graduated top 10% of class	22
% graduated top 25% of class	49
% graduated top 50% of class	80

DEADLINES

Regular notification	rolling
Nonfall registration?	yes

APPLICANTS ALSO LOOK AT

AND OFTEN PREFER
University of Notre Dame

AND SOMETIMES PREFER
John Carroll University, Marquette University, Miami University, Saint Louis University, The Ohio State University—Columbus

AND RARELY PREFER
Ohio University—Athens, Purdue University—West Lafayette, University of Cincinnati, Xavier University (OH)

FINANCIAL FACTS

Financial Aid Rating	87
Annual tuition	$24,880
Room & Board	$7,600
Books and supplies	$1,299
Required fees	$1,070
% frosh rec. need-based scholarship or grant aid	53
% UG rec. need-based scholarship or grant aid	58
% frosh rec. need-based self-help aid	55
% UG rec. need-based self-help aid	66
% frosh rec. any financial aid	77
% UG rec. any financial aid	82

UNIVERSITY OF DELAWARE

ADMISSIONS OFFICE, 116 HULLIHEN HALL, NEWARK, DE 19716-6210 • ADMISSIONS: 800-422-5867 • FAX: 302-831-6905

CAMPUS LIFE

Quality of Life Rating	**75**
Fire Safety Rating	**60***
Type of school	public
Environment	town

STUDENTS

Total undergrad enrollment	15,211
% male/female	42/58
% from out of state	60
% from public high school	80
% live on campus	47
% in (# of) fraternities	12 (15)
% in (# of) sororities	12 (15)
% African American	5
% Asian	4
% Caucasian	83
% Hispanic	4
% international	1
# of countries represented	100

SURVEY SAYS . . .

Great computer facilities
Great library
Great off-campus food
Students are happy
Lots of beer drinking
Hard liquor is popular

ACADEMICS

Academic Rating	**80**
Calendar	4-1-4
Student/faculty ratio	12:1
Profs interesting rating	73
Profs accessible rating	78
% profs teaching UG courses	95
% classes taught by TAs	5
Most common lab size	10–19 students
Most common reg class size	10–19 students

MOST POPULAR MAJORS
biology/biological sciences
elementary education and teaching
psychology

STUDENTS SAY

Academics

The University of Delaware is in the midst of major institutional changes: A new president took the reins in July 2007, and a new class registration system was implemented in 2006. Regarding the former, students are delighted. Because the new president is the former Dean of the Wharton School of Business, undergraduates are hopeful that he will "do wonders for our prestige." Regarding the latter, they couldn't be more displeased. "Registration is a nightmare," making it "near impossible to get the exact schedule you want." Between those two extremes, respondents to our survey describe a middle-of-the-road academic experience. Take professors, for example. Some "are experts in their fields and are excellent at teaching," while others "are purely there for research," or "have no clue how to teach a class." While most may be "genuinely interested in meeting with students and talking about the class material," "They won't hunt you down" to make sure you're getting it. In other words, there is a willingness to help "as long as the student takes the initiative." The same can be said of the administration. Students generally consider it to be of "average quality." It "can be a pain with some administrative tasks (financial aid, anything that involves going to student services), but it's probably par for the course." In a departure from their typically balanced assessments of UD, undergrads maintain an exceptionally positive view of their school's "absolutely beautiful" campus and its "phenomenal" study abroad program.

Life

Student life at UD is characterized by the timeless effort "to balance partying and studying." During the week, which runs from Sunday through Wednesday, "Life usually remains centered around studies." "You will find the libraries [and] computer labs filled," and "Quiet hours are enforced." For many, working out is part of their weekday work regimen: "A lot of people enjoy going to the gym." Come Thursday, however, "Those with good schedules start going out." "Parties are what everyone looks for," especially house parties, and they are reportedly in abundant supply. Those who aren't into drinking but want to stay on campus can take advantage of "a movie theater right on campus that show[s] fairly current movies for only $3." The SCPAB (Student-Centered Programming Advisory Board) also "books some pretty good musicians and comedians." Many students "hang out on Main Street," which "intersects campus" and includes "endless restaurants, the bookstores, a bowling alley, and a movie theater." Because "the campus is close to Baltimore, DC, and Philly, road trips to museums and other universities [are] always possible."

Student Body

Budding psychologists take note: Undergrads here report a collective "tunnel vision," and it's focused on "success." According to a junior, "Most of us come from upper-middle-class homes and won't be satisfied with anything less than what we already have." As a means to an end, "Academics are important." But only so much—course work "won't stop anyone from going out," an international relations major reports. Geographically, students mainly hail "from the New Jersey, Delaware, Maryland, and Pennsylvania region." Sartorially, "People care what they look like" and those "who have money flaunt it by what they wear." Temperamentally, people are "relaxed, friendly, and generally very approachable." There are very few categories UD students can be sorted into, but an in-state/out-of-state divide exists. Students "from Delaware are not considered as smart as those not from Delaware because it is easier for them to get in," and there is also a widespread perception that those from in-state "are not as well off financially."

FINANCIAL AID: 302-831-8761 • E-MAIL: ADMISSIONS@UDEL.EDU • WEBSITE: WWW.UDEL.EDU

ADMISSIONS

Very important factors considered include: Academic GPA, rigor of secondary school record, state residency. *Important factors considered include:* Application essay, character/personal qualities, extracurricular activities, recommendation(s), standardized test scores, talent/ability, volunteer work, work experience. *Other factors considered include:* Alumni/ae relation, class rank, first generation, geographical residence, interview, level of applicant's interest, racial/ethnic status. SAT or ACT required; SAT Subject Tests recommended; ACT with Writing component required. TOEFL required of all international applicants. High school diploma is required, and GED is accepted. *Academic units required:* 4 English, 3 math, 3 science (2 science labs), 2 foreign language, 2 social studies, 2 history, 2 academic electives. *Academic units recommended:* 4 English, 4 math, 4 science (3 science labs), 4 foreign language, 2 social studies, 2 history, 2 academic electives.

Inside Word

It's rare that a flagship state university enrolls more students from out of state than in state, but the University of Delaware does. It is situated near many more-populous states on the East Coast which makes it a viable and desirable alternative for those states' residents. The school is sensitive to this fact, and in-state students will find admission to UD significantly easier than out-of-state students will.

FINANCIAL AID

Students should submit: FAFSA. Regular filing deadline is March 15. The Princeton Review suggests that all financial aid forms be submitted as soon as possible after January 1. *Need-based scholarships/grants offered:* Pell Grant, SEOG, state scholarships/grants, private scholarships, the school's own gift aid. *Loan aid offered:* Direct Subsidized Stafford, Direct Unsubsidized Stafford, Direct PLUS, Federal Perkins Loan, Federal Nursing Loan. Applicants will be notified of awards on or about March 15. Federal Work-Study Program available. Institutional employment available.

FROM THE ADMISSIONS OFFICE

"The University of Delaware is a major national research university with a long-standing commitment to teaching and serving undergraduates. It is one of only a few universities in the country designated as a land-grant, sea-grant, urban-grant, and space-grant institution. The academic strength of this university is found in its highly selective honors program, nationally recognized Undergraduate Research Program, study abroad opportunities on all seven continents, and its successful alumni, including three Rhodes Scholars since 1998. The University of Delaware offers the wide range of majors and course offerings expected of a university but in spirit remains a small place where you can interact with your professors and feel at home. The beautiful green campus is ideally located at the very center of the East Coast 'megacity' that stretches from New York City to Washington, DC. All of these elements, combined with an endowment approaching $1 billion and a spirited Division I athletics program, make the University of Delaware a tremendous value.

"Freshman applicants for Fall 2008 are required to take the SAT Reasoning Test (or the ACT with the Writing section). If a student takes the new SAT more than once, the best individual scores from each test taken will be combined. Two SAT Subject Tests are recommended for applicants to the University Honors Program."

SELECTIVITY

Admissions Rating	92
# of applicants	21,930
% of applicants accepted	47
% of acceptees attending	31
# accepting a place on wait list	1,237
% admitted from wait list	48

FRESHMAN PROFILE

Range SAT Critical Reading	540–640
Range SAT Math	560–660
Range SAT Writing	540–650
Range ACT Composite	23–28
Minimum Paper TOEFL	550
Minimum Computer Based TOEFL	213
Average HS GPA	3.6
% graduated top 10% of class	39
% graduated top 25% of class	80
% graduated top 50% of class	98

DEADLINES

Regular application deadline	1/15
Regular notification	3/15
Nonfall registration?	yes

FINANCIAL FACTS

Financial Aid Rating	80
Annual in-state tuition	$6,980
Annual out-of-state tuition	$17,690
Room & Board	$7,366
Books and supplies	$800
Required fees	$760
% frosh rec. need-based scholarship or grant aid	26
% UG rec. need-based scholarship or grant aid	24
% frosh rec. need-based self-help aid	29
% UG rec. need-based self-help aid	28

UNIVERSITY OF DENVER

University Hall, Room 110, 2197 South University Boulevard, Denver, CO 80208 • Admissions: 303-871-2036 • Fax: 303-871-3301

STUDENTS SAY

Academics

A little under half of the University of Denver's (DU) undergraduates pursue degrees in business. This pre-MBA focus contributes substantially to the university's overall character. Students are, for the most part, diligent workers focused on obtaining a successful career. That's not to suggest that students pursuing majors other than business receive the short shrift at DU. The university also excels in pre-law studies, music, and communications. In fact, students brag that "there is ample funding for all the departments at DU, and therefore undergrads have incredible opportunities to pursue serious academic projects. A dedicated student can get an education equal to that of a student at any top university." While there's a wide range of opinions regarding the workload—some students describe it as "intense," others find it "super easy"—most agree that "the fact that the school is small benefits everyone. Teachers and students form relationships and work together when in the classroom. Teachers also meet students at The Pub (the on-campus restaurant) for study sessions." Students tell us DU "makes it easy and affordable for anyone to study abroad."

Life

The University of Denver offers "tons of different organizations to participate in. DU Programs Board, the Greek system, DU Alpine Club, and Student Government are just a few of the on-campus activities offered." Unfortunately, most of these activities do not inspire the majority of undergraduates. "In the winter, the campus empties out on the weekends as students head to the mountains to ski and [snow]board," undergrads report. Students also frequent the "nearby Cherry Creek district for dinner and a movie." Because "The campus is officially dry," a good amount of drinking occurs off campus, frequently at the "great neighborhood bars located one to three blocks from campus." Students always return to campus for sporting events, however, especially for games featuring "the great hockey team," which won the NCAA championship in 2004 and 2005. Students also love to take advantage of the Ritchie Center, "a great sports facility [for working out] that is gorgeous and free to students." As one undergraduate puts it, "With a stunning campus and 300 days of sunshine in Denver, you can't go wrong!"

Student Body

Students say DU is the "perfect size to meet new people all the time, but [also] to run into people you know every time you walk across campus." At a school where "Everyone is friendly" and "smile[s] at each other walking to class," undergrads feel this is a boon to their overall experience. While students report a noticeable contingent of undergrads "from affluent backgrounds [who are] trendy and party a lot," they also tell us there are "many students [who] are more interested in academics [and] other areas of student life. These students are also quite easy to find, and fit in just as well." Intellectual interests at DU tend to be "very career- and goal-oriented." One student wryly notes that DU is not the place to find students who "go to coffee shops to discuss Kafka or talk politics in the dining hall." The university does, however, have a considerable jock population. Students "enjoy being outdoors (anything from a snowball fight to a marathon run to speed skiing)" and "like to work out [and] participate in athletics."

FINANCIAL AID: 303-871-4020 • E-MAIL: ADMISSION@DU.EDU • WEBSITE: WWW.DU.EDU/ADMISSION

ADMISSIONS

Very important factors considered include: Academic GPA, character/personal qualities, interview, rigor of secondary school record, standardized test scores. *Important factors considered include:* Application essay, extracurricular activities, level of applicant's interest, recommendation(s), talent/ability, volunteer work, work experience. SAT or ACT required; TOEFL required of all international applicants. High school diploma is required, and GED is accepted. *Academic units recommended:* 4 English, 4 math, 4 science (2 science labs), 3 foreign language, 2 social studies, 2 history.

The Inside Word

Any good student will find getting admitted to Denver to be a fairly straightforward process.

FINANCIAL AID

Students should submit: FAFSA. Regular filing deadline is March 1. The Princeton Review suggests that all financial aid forms be submitted as soon as possible after January 1. *Need-based scholarships/grants offered:* Pell Grant, SEOG, state scholarships/grants, private scholarships, the school's own gift aid. *Loan aid offered:* Direct Subsidized Stafford, Direct Unsubsidized Stafford, Direct PLUS, FFEL Subsidized Stafford, FFEL Unsubsidized Stafford, FFEL PLUS, Federal Perkins Loan, college/university loans from institutional funds. Federal Work-Study Program available. Institutional employment available. Off-campus job opportunities are excellent.

FROM THE ADMISSIONS OFFICE

"Founded in 1864, the University of Denver offers an educational experience characterized by adventurous learning and innovative mentoring from a caring faculty. Our undergraduate students come from all across the United States and from more than 80 countries to study in an environment that nurtures potential and passion. The Hyde Interview requirement provides all applicants the opportunity to give a voice to their application while assisting DU with admission decisions.

"DU is continually developing educational initiatives that help students prepare for an ever-changing world. Among our offerings: residence-based learning communities that provide extracurricular and co-curricular programming in particular areas; a grant program for students that funds everything from research to creative endeavors; and hundreds of internship opportunities that put students in laboratories, corporate offices, government agencies, and cultural settings. In addition, one of the signature offerings is the Cherrington Global Scholars program which allows students to study abroad at the same cost of a term at DU. More than 70 percent of DU students study abroad at some point in their years in school—which ranks DU second nationally among doctoral and research institutions for percentage of students participating.

"DU's 125-acre campus, located in a quiet residential neighborhood, is eight miles from downtown Denver and a half-hour's drive from the Rocky Mountain foothills. DU students enjoy an active lifestyle with plenty of opportunities to enjoy recreation in the Rockies, cheer on one of the city's many professional sports teams, or explore the city's lively arts and entertainment scene. Many DU students partake in these activities by using the new light rail system, an above-ground train that is free to all DU students. There is a station conveniently located on our campus and provides students a great mode of transportation for a variety of purposes such as entertainment, internships, and jobs in the Denver area.

"Applicants may submit either version of the ACT or SAT."

SELECTIVITY

Admissions Rating	87
# of applicants	4,656
% of applicants accepted	73
% of acceptees attending	33
# accepting a place on wait list	275
% admitted from wait list	4

FRESHMAN PROFILE

Range SAT Critical Reading	530–640
Range SAT Math	540–650
Range ACT Composite	23–28
Minimum Paper TOEFL	525
Minimum Computer Based TOEFL	193
Average HS GPA	3.58
% graduated top 10% of class	35
% graduated top 25% of class	67
% graduated top 50% of class	92

DEADLINES

Regular application deadline	1/15
Regular notification	3/15
Nonfall registration?	yes

APPLICANTS ALSO LOOK AT AND OFTEN PREFER

Colorado College, Colorado State University, University of Colorado—Boulder

AND SOMETIMES PREFER

Boston University, University of Puget Sound, University of Vermont

FINANCIAL FACTS

Financial Aid Rating	72
Annual tuition	$31,428
Room & Board	$8,697
Required fees	$804
% frosh rec. need-based scholarship or grant aid	44
% UG rec. need-based scholarship or grant aid	42
% frosh rec. need-based self-help aid	39
% UG rec. need-based self-help aid	37
% frosh rec. any financial aid	85
% UG rec. any financial aid	79

UNIVERSITY OF FLORIDA

201 CRISER HALL, BOX 114000, GAINESVILLE, FL 32611-4000 • ADMISSIONS: 352-392-1365 • FAX: 352-392-3987

STUDENTS SAY

Academics

"It is often joked that we only pay tuition so we can have a football team," one University of Florida student writes, but in fact UF provides "a quality education from the state's oldest and most prestigious university" as well as top-flight football to its undergraduates. "The University of Florida is about finding out if you have what it takes to distinguish yourself from 35,000 other intelligent, talented people. It's a reality check." It also provides "tremendous" "networking opportunities." A robust alumni network over 300,000 strong adds to the possibilities, and some undergrads to assert that, in addition to providing a top-notch education, UF delivers "a career in the future." Stand-out programs include engineering, premed, and journalism. While the school "has its share of boring, unapproachable professors," the "vast majority" are "available to help students throughout the week." In fact, both professors and teaching assistants "are easy to access," as they have "set office hours" that are "made very apparent to students." UF's administration "is not too bad, although there is so much red tape to get through that getting anything accomplished is likely to take half the semester." Students appreciate that most administrative tasks can be accomplished "over the computer."

Life

"You can tell that students at UF like to have fun," undergrads here agree, and fortunately for them the opportunities are ample. There is "a lot of stuff to do on campus," and if partying is your thing, there are "37 fraternity/sorority houses" and "an ample number of clubs to check out" in downtown Gainesville. The Student Union also hosts "a bunch of different activities" and "shows recent movies in [its] theater, long before they come out on DVD." Then, of course, there's Gator athletics. "Almost everybody here is crazy about our sports teams, and team spirit is really high," students tell us. One writes, "Sports, both intramural and intercollegiate, are very important. This is one of the main reasons people are drawn to UF." Greater Gainesville "offers enough things to do" that "not being Greek does not hamper one's social life." Indeed, Gainesville "is a true college town—everything is catered to the UF student." For outdoor enthusiasts, "There is a recreational lake that is university-owned, [and] students can go swim, boat, fish, or BBQ [for free]." UF is also located "within 2 hours" of the beach and "under 2 hours" from "theme parks in Orlando." Students here are "always willing to drive the distance" to "away football games within the SEC (Southeastern Conference)."

Student Body

The UF student body conjures to mind the "Greek macho man" and the "Barbie blonde" for many, but with undergrad enrollment around 35,000, "it's hard to define the typical student" here. While the "large, sprawling campus" is home to "more students than can be observed," even a perfunctory glance reveals "all kinds—jocks, Greeks, religious, political, nonreligious, out-of-staters, international people, intense athletes, and everything in between." Some here tell us that "the typical student falls into one of two categories. Either the student is a know-it-all who graduated with an IB diploma and had a 4.0, or [he or she] is a slacker who somehow got into UF and now doesn't take anything seriously except partying." Because of UF's size, "There's a place for everyone to fit in, whether your thing is knitting, rugby, or video games."

ADMISSIONS

SAT or ACT required; ACT with Writing component required. High school diploma is required, and GED is accepted. *Academic units required:* 4 English, 3 math, 3 science (2 science labs), 2 foreign language, 3 social studies.

The Inside Word

Students from low-income families take note: The University of Florida, in an effort to increase enrollment of minority and economically disadvantaged students, has introduced the Florida Opportunity Scholars program, which fully covers 4 years of educational costs for qualifying students (annual family income must not exceed $40,000). If you fit the bill, you should apply; you may be rewarded with a free education at a prestigious school.

FINANCIAL AID

Students should submit: FAFSA. The Princeton Review suggests that all financial aid forms be submitted as soon as possible after January 1. *Need-based scholarships/grants offered:* Pell Grant, SEOG, state scholarships/grants, private scholarships, the school's own gift aid. *Loan aid offered:* Direct Subsidized Stafford, Direct Unsubsidized Stafford, Direct PLUS, Federal Perkins Loan, college/university loans from institutional funds. Applicants will be notified of awards on a rolling basis beginning or about April 1. Federal Work-Study Program available. Institutional employment available. Off-campus job opportunities are fair.

FROM THE ADMISSIONS OFFICE

"University of Florida students come from more than 100 countries, all 50 states, and every one of the 67 counties in Florida. Nineteen percent of the student body is comprised of graduate students. Approximately 3,000 African American students, 4,000 Hispanic students, and 2,300 Asian American students attend UF. Ninety percent of the entering freshmen rank above the national mean of scores on standard entrance exams. UF consistently ranks near the top among public universities in the number of new National Merit and Achievement scholars in attendance.

"The new SAT (or ACT with Writing component) is required for all applicants for 2006 and beyond. The old SAT (or ACT tests taken without Writing) will not be accepted. Sub scores (Critical Reading and Math only) on the new SAT will be mixed/matched with other new SAT sub scores to achieve the highest score."

SELECTIVITY

Admissions Rating	**60***
# of applicants	21,151
% of applicants accepted	57
% of acceptees attending	60
# of early decision applicants	4481
% accepted early decision	50

FRESHMAN PROFILE

Range SAT Critical Reading	570–670
Range SAT Math	590–690
Range ACT Composite	25–29
Average HS GPA	3.9
% graduated top 10% of class	85
% graduated top 25% of class	90
% graduated top 50% of class	97

DEADLINES

Early decision application deadline	10/1
Early decision notification	12/1
Regular application deadline	1/17
Nonfall registration?	yes

FINANCIAL FACTS

Financial Aid Rating	**82**
Annual in-state tuition	$3,206
Annual out-of-state tuition	$17,791
Room & Board	$6,590
Books and supplies	$920
% frosh rec. need-based scholarship or grant aid	21
% UG rec. need-based scholarship or grant aid	24
% frosh rec. need-based self-help aid	18
% UG rec. need-based self-help aid	25
% frosh rec. any financial aid	97
% UG rec. any financial aid	84

UNIVERSITY OF GEORGIA

TERRELL HALL, ATHENS, GA 30602 • ADMISSIONS: 706-542-8776 • FAX: 706-542-1466

CAMPUS LIFE
Quality of Life Rating	85
Fire Safety Rating	82
Type of school	public
Environment	city

STUDENTS
Total undergrad enrollment	25,055
% male/female	43/57
% from out of state	11
% from public high school	81
% live on campus	27
% in (# of) fraternities	21 (35)
% in (# of) sororities	25 (24)
% African American	6
% Asian	6
% Caucasian	83
% Hispanic	2
% international	1
# of countries represented	131

SURVEY SAYS . . .
Student publications are popular
Frats and sororities dominate social scene
Students love Athens, GA
Lots of beer drinking
Hard liquor is popular
Great food on campus
Everyone loves the Bulldogs

ACADEMICS
Academic Rating	73
Calendar	semester
Student/faculty ratio	18:1
Profs interesting rating	75
Profs accessible rating	65
% profs teaching	
UG courses	83
% classes taught by TAs	17
Most common	
reg class size	20–29 students

MOST POPULAR MAJORS
art/art studies
biology/biological sciences
psychology

STUDENTS SAY
Academics

The opportunity to "get an unbelievable education at an even more incredible price" figures prominently into students' choices to attend the University of Georgia. The state's HOPE scholarship program (for Georgia residents who attend college in-state) has helped to make the already low tuition and fees even more affordable for most students. Georgia undergraduates say that UGA "is about working hard and playing hard" but always "maintaining a balance between the two." One student claims UGA "is the type of school you see in the movies, the sun is always shining and everyone is always having a great time." Along with such cinematic scenery, students enjoy "the resources provided by the school, such as the new Student Learning Center, which houses innumerable computers," and the "wide range of majors offered, with challenging programs of study that can launch a student into a promising future." Classes are taught by "professors who are generally very knowledgeable and know the subject." With over 25,000 undergraduates, "UGA is a big state school, and you have to be somewhat aggressive to stand out from the crowd. I believe that UGA is as challenging as you want to make it. You can take honors courses and do research, or you can coast without attending too many classes." Ambitious students should head straight for the honors classes, which "are smaller, taught by more experienced faculty members, and more open to class discussion and hands-on learning."

Life

"People think Athens is a party town and that everyone goes downtown, which is pretty much true," one student admits. However, this is as far from a bad thing since downtown Athens is, according to students, "hands-down the world's best college town, whether you go to the bars or not. The music scene is awesome, the restaurants are fantastic and unique, and, of course, the bars are the place to be on weekends and Thursday nights." As one student puts it, "There's a saying in Georgia: 'If you lead a good life and say your prayers, when you die you'll go to Athens.' And it is 100 percent true." Besides going to the ubiquitous downtown, students "go to football games, hang out downtown during the day—coffee shops, shopping, restaurants, or go to shows at the many venues." The Greek scene and Dawgs After Dark, the university's late Friday-night programming, round out the campus social scene. During the day, students love to "work out (the Ramsey Fitness Center is always a place to go because it has exercising, racquetball, and swimming to choose from), play intramurals, or go camping, kayaking, and hiking." Politics play a large role in many students' lives. Reportedly "The College Republicans is the largest group on campus."

Student Body

The typical UGA student "is White, from the Atlanta area, middle- to upper-class and mostly mainstream in dress and music style." A surprising number "look as though they were cut [with] a cookie-cutter mold. They dress the same, have the same hairstyle, and generally drive SUVs." However, students report that diversity is on the upswing, particularly the "Black population is growing" and "There are small subsections of people which contribute to the music and art scene in Athens." One student writes, "If you're not a rich kid from metro Atlanta, you'll have a harder time fitting in here. You just have to look a bit harder but you'll find someone with whom you have much in common." Because Athens "is a music town," students observe, "There are a lot of indie rock types and even a bigger hippie-jam band scene." Students also tell us that "it is hard to be nationally diverse with the HOPE scholarship in effect in Georgia . . . but we could use more out-of-state students on this campus."

FINANCIAL AID: 706-542-6147 • E-MAIL: UNDERGRAD@ADMISSIONS.UGA.EDU • WEBSITE: WWW.UGA.EDU

ADMISSIONS

Very important factors considered include: Academic GPA, rigor of secondary school record. *Important factors considered include:* Standardized test scores. *Other factors considered include:* Application essay, character/personal qualities, extracurricular activities, recommendation(s), talent/ability, volunteer work, work experience. SAT or ACT required; ACT with Writing component required. TOEFL required of all international applicants. High school diploma is required, and GED is accepted. *Academic units required:* 4 English, 4 math, 3 science (2 science labs), 2 foreign language, 3 social studies. *Academic units recommended:* 4 English, 4 math, 3 science (2 science labs), 3 foreign language, 1 social studies, 2 history, 1 academic elective.

The Inside Word

The main reason so many Georgians stay in Georgia ain't the weather (though that's nice too), it's the HOPE Scholarship Program. This program is open to Georgia residents who graduate from high school with a 3.0 average GPA, with the provision they maintain a 3.0 GPA in college. The scholarship pays for tuition and most other school-related fees. At the end of the day, it's the one time you can feel good about buying a losing lottery ticket as HOPE is funded solely through the Georgia Lottery.

FINANCIAL AID

Students should submit: FAFSA. The Princeton Review suggests that all financial aid forms be submitted as soon as possible after January 1. *Need-based scholarships/grants offered:* Pell Grant, SEOG, state scholarships/grants, private scholarships, the school's own gift aid. *Loan aid offered:* Direct Subsidized Stafford, Direct Unsubsidized Stafford, Direct PLUS, Federal Perkins Loan, state loans, college/university loans from institutional funds. Applicants will be notified of awards on a rolling basis beginning or about May 15.

FROM THE ADMISSIONS OFFICE

"The University of Georgia offers students the advantages and resources of a top public research university, including a wide range of majors and exceptional academic facilities such as the 200,000-square-foot Student Learning Center. At the same time, UGA provides opportunities more common to smaller, private schools, such as first-year seminars led by distinguished faculty and learning communities that connect students with similar academic interests. As the academic quality of the student body continues to climb, the university is committed to challenging students in the classroom and beyond, with increased emphasis on undergraduate research, service-learning, and study abroad. UGA students taking advantage of such offerings find themselves well positioned to compete with the best undergraduates in the country, as evidenced by their recent string of successes in winning Rhodes, Marshall, and other major scholarships.

"The UGA campus, considered one of the most beautiful in the nation, adjoins vibrant downtown Athens. Renowned for its local music scene, Athens is also a center for the performing and visual arts, thanks in part to UGA's popular School of Music and School of Art. Sports—from football to gymnastics—are also a major attraction, with UGA teams perennially ranked among the best in the country.

"To experience the excitement of UGA, most prospective students visit campus, a 90-minute drive northeast of the Atlanta airport. See the Admissions website (www.admissions.uga.edu) to sign up for a tour with the Visitors Center, view the weekday schedule of admissions information sessions, and find application details."

"Applicants for first-year admission will be required to submit either the SAT or ACT. Students submitting only the ACT must also submit the optional ACT Writing Test."

SELECTIVITY

Admissions Rating	92
# of applicants	15,924
% of applicants accepted	58
% of acceptees attending	55
# accepting a place on wait list	421
% admitted from wait list	88

FRESHMAN PROFILE

Range SAT Critical Reading	560–660
Range SAT Math	570–660
Range SAT Writing	550–650
Range ACT Composite	24–29
Minimum Paper TOEFL	550
Minimum Computer Based TOEFL	213
Average HS GPA	3.76
% graduated top 10% of class	48
% graduated top 25% of class	84
% graduated top 50% of class	98

DEADLINES

Regular application deadline	1/15
Regular notification	rolling
Nonfall registration?	no

APPLICANTS ALSO LOOK AT

AND OFTEN PREFER
Florida State University, Georgia Institute of Technology, The University of North Carolina at Chapel Hill, University of Virginia, Wake Forest University

AND SOMETIMES PREFER
College of Charleston, Emory University, Georgia Southern University, Georgia State University, Mercer University—Atlanta, Vanderbilt University

AND RARELY PREFER
Auburn University, Clemson University, Tulane University, The University of Alabama at Tuscaloosa, University of South Carolina—Columbia

FINANCIAL FACTS

Financial Aid Rating	79
Annual in-state tuition	$3,892
Annual out-of-state tuition	$16,968
Room & Board	$6,848
Books and supplies	$800
Required fees	$1,072
% frosh rec. need-based scholarship or grant aid	27
% UG rec. need-based scholarship or grant aid	22
% frosh rec. need-based self-help aid	15
% UG rec. need-based self-help aid	18
% frosh rec. any financial aid	28
% UG rec. any financial aid	26

UNIVERSITY OF HAWAII—MANOA

2600 CAMPUS ROAD, QLCSS, ROOM 001, HONOLULU, HI 96822 • ADMISSIONS: 808-956-8975 • FAX: 808-956-4148

STUDENTS SAY

Academics

The prime location is undoubtedly the chief allure of the University of Hawaii—Manoa. How could it not be? The school, after all, is situated on an island paradise. There's a lot more than fabulous weather and world-class surfing to recommend UHM, though. Students here tout the "excellent technology and the incredible amount of opportunities and programs available," including solid (and site-appropriate) offerings in marine biology, oceanography, geology, and travel industry management. There's also the school's affordability. Tuition rates are low not only for Aloha State natives but also for the majority of out-of-state students who enjoy a reduced tuition rate under the Western Undergraduate Exchange program. Students also love the "fantastic learning assistance centers, great libraries," and the amount of attention lavished on selected studies and honors students. What they dislike are the burdensome curricular requirements: "It's insane. All the unnecessary requirements mean that almost no student can graduate in 4 years," complains one student, as well as the administration's "laid-back aloha spirit, which is no way to run a premier research institution. It gets them into a lot of messes," as in 2004–2005 when the school came up so short on housing that it had to put students in Waikiki hotels.

Life

"Life here is all about the location," students at UHM agree, adding that "it's great that I can study near the ocean and the city because I can go wherever I want in minutes." A convenient bus system (which, some warn, is "a little expensive") takes those without cars where they need to go, though "Hardly anyone is in a hurry around here." In keeping with a laid-back, local style that pervades the campus, "Dress is casual, usually flip-flops and board shorts" and students "typically go to class in the mornings, head to the beach in the afternoon, and drink and socialize in the evenings." One student sums it up by saying, "It is hard work all week and a tropical vacation every weekend. Stress levels drop the moment you land on this island." Parties occur most frequently in off-campus apartments—there are "absolutely no social fraternities or sororities at UH" and on-campus housing is scarce—or, for students over 21, in "a couple of good bars down the street." Undergrads report that "the UH campus is one of the best party spots on the island, or so says a newspaper survey," but add, "There are plenty of activities that do not involve alcohol as well: hiking, going to the beach, paddling, seeing concerts, visiting various museums and historical sites, and going to plays or the opera." Because so many students commute, the campus itself tends to gets neglected ("The facilities are fairly old and they could use updating"), and student life can be a little slow on weekends—except when the football team plays at home. As one student explains, "Football players are gods here. Hawaii does not have professional sports teams, so UH football players take their place. If you're coming to UH to play football, your college social life is set."

Student Body

"White kids are actually the minority for once," at UHM, whose students are "a mixture of students from the mainland U.S. and local White, Asian, and Pacific Islander students." Many point out that "Hawaii has been, for most of its history as a part of the U.S., a liberal state tolerant to all religious, political, sexual, ethnic diversities." Some, however, warn that "Whites who aren't from the islands can have a tough time fitting in." There's also a lack of unanimity on the bookworm demographic here. Some tell us that "Hawaii is half and half—half 'study nonstop' and half 'don't know what studying means.'" Others, however, feel that "while there's a handful of students who have ambitious career objectives are focused on studying, the typical student is focused mainly on the beach or going to the clubs. Not that there is anything wrong with having fun, but the typical student is a 24/7 partier."

UNIVERSITY OF HAWAII—MANOA

FINANCIAL AID: 808-956-7251 • E-MAIL: AR-INFO@HAWAII.EDU • WEBSITE: WWW.UHM.HAWAII.EDU

ADMISSIONS

Very important factors considered include: Academic GPA, rigor of secondary school record, standardized test scores. *Important factors considered include:* State residency. *Other factors considered include:* Application essay, class rank, extracurricular activities, geographical residence, interview, recommendation(s), talent/ability. SAT or ACT required; ACT with Writing component required. TOEFL required of all international applicants. High school diploma is required, and GED is accepted. *Academic units required:* 4 English, 3 math, 3 science (1 science lab), 3 social studies, 4 academic electives. *Academic units recommended:* 2 foreign language.

The Inside Word

A 2.8 high school GPA meets the university's minimum standards for admission. Though preference is given to state residents for admission, in practice there's room for just about any better-than-average student in the freshman class here.

FINANCIAL AID

Students should submit: FAFSA. The Princeton Review suggests that all financial aid forms be submitted as soon as possible after January 1. *Need-based scholarships/grants offered:* Pell Grant, SEOG, state scholarships/grants, private scholarships, the school's own gift aid, Federal Nursing Scholarship. *Loan aid offered:* FFEL Subsidized Stafford, FFEL Unsubsidized Stafford, FFEL PLUS, Federal Perkins Loan, Federal Nursing Loan, state loans, college/university loans from institutional funds, Nursing Faculty Loan. Applicants will be notified of awards on or about April 1. Federal Work-Study Program available. Institutional employment available. Off-campus job opportunities are good.

FROM THE ADMISSIONS OFFICE

"Students applying for admission for Fall 2008 must submit scores from the new SAT or ACT, including Writing component. Scores from tests without Writing will not be considered. Students who take the new SAT or the ACT more than once will have their best scores considered for admission."

SELECTIVITY

Admissions Rating	**84**
# of applicants	6,167
% of applicants accepted	68
% of acceptees attending	42

FRESHMAN PROFILE

Range SAT Critical Reading	480–580
Range SAT Math	510–610
Range ACT Composite	21–25
Minimum Paper TOEFL	500
Minimum Computer Based TOEFL	173
Average HS GPA	3.41
% graduated top 10% of class	29
% graduated top 25% of class	60
% graduated top 50% of class	91

DEADLINES

Regular application deadline	5/1
Regular notification	rolling
Nonfall registration?	yes

FINANCIAL FACTS

Financial Aid Rating	**73**
Annual in-state tuition	$5,136
Annual out-of-state tuition	$14,400
Room & Board	$7,185
Books and supplies	$1,145
Required fees	$203
% frosh rec. need-based scholarship or grant aid	27
% UG rec. need-based scholarship or grant aid	26
% frosh rec. need-based self-help aid	20
% UG rec. need-based self-help aid	23
% frosh rec. any financial aid	44
% UG rec. any financial aid	41

UNIVERSITY OF IDAHO

IDAHO ADMISSIONS OFFICE, PO BOX 444264, MOSCOW, ID 83844-4264 • ADMISSIONS: 208-885-6326 • FAX: 208-885-9119

CAMPUS LIFE
Quality of Life Rating	**72**
Fire Safety Rating	**60***
Type of school	public
Environment	town

STUDENTS
Total undergrad enrollment	8,636
% male/female	55/45
% from out of state	26
% from public high school	90
# of fraternities	18
# of sororities	8
% African American	1
% Asian	2
% Caucasian	84
% Hispanic	5
% Native American	1
% international	2

SURVEY SAYS . . .
Great computer facilities
Great library
Athletic facilities are great
Frats and sororities dominate social scene
Lots of beer drinking
Hard liquor is popular

ACADEMICS
Academic Rating	**72**
Calendar	semester
Student/faculty ratio	18:1
Profs interesting rating	70
Profs accessible rating	68
% profs teaching UG courses	82
% classes taught by TAs	15
Most common lab size	10–19 students
Most common reg class size	20–29 students

MOST POPULAR MAJORS
elementary education and teaching
mechanical engineering
psychology

STUDENTS SAY

Academics

A little college in the "middle of nowhere," the University of Idaho isn't your average public university. While huge lectures and inaccessible administrators beleaguer other state schools, the affordable price tag at Idaho comes with a friendly and intimate academic environment. Indeed, the school's major strength is that it offers "a wide range of classes while still remaining personal enough for one-on-one learning." At Idaho, "The teachers prefer [that] you call them by first name," and "Professors are always willing to help if you show an interest in your work." As one student explains, "University of Idaho has top-ranked professors in the nation in their field. I believe they chose to teach here . . . because of [the] community, students, and friendly atmosphere." Despite their generally glowing reviews, Idaho students note that "some of our departments are short on funds," which "puts pressure on department heads to meet educational goals of students with fewer instructors than are necessary." Most students feel that "administrators are trying their best to provide quality education while trying to recuperate from past debts." Some students would also prefer to see a little more academic rigor infused into the programs. As one student explains, "The classes I've taken were challenging but not too ridiculously demanding in terms of busy work."

Life

Located in the teensy town of Moscow, "Drinking and studying are the main activities" at the University of Idaho. For the diligent, "The small-town atmosphere provides a great student environment." Many other students, however, "are highly involved in Greek life and other activities on campus," producing a lively campus atmosphere and a thriving party scene. While Moscow may be "a small town with little going on," students agree that "for its size, the party scene is awesome." For students who are not into the Greek scene, the beautiful campus and close-knit community foster a number of other recreational opportunities, including several highly active community-service organizations. As one student affirms, "University of Idaho is known as a party school and we can live up to that, but we study, attend cultural events, and are active in our communities, in addition to our beer drinking." Students say that the university "always provides things to do from . . . sporting events and theater shows" to "intramural sports, rock climbing, and . . . movies at the student union building." Located in beautiful rural Idaho, many students say that "most of the fun in Moscow consists of outdoor recreation."

Student Body

U of I draws the majority of its students from the surrounding areas, attracting, "chill North Idahoans" with a mix of "other spices." Given this breakdown, it's no surprise that at University of Idaho, "most are White, as is our state as a whole." A freshman details, "Typical students at Idaho are from middle-class/upper-middle-class, White homes." Another student adds, "I think there is a lot of diversity as far as types of people, but there could be more ethnic diversity." While there are few minorities, you'll find every personality type "from cowboys to cosmopolitan city residents" on campus. Generally speaking, "Most of the campus is very social" and students describe their classmates as "outgoing" and "friendly."

FINANCIAL AID: 208-885-6312 • E-MAIL: ADMAPPL@UIDAHO.EDU • WEBSITE: WWW.UIDAHO.EDU

ADMISSIONS

Very important factors considered include: Rigor of secondary school record, standardized test scores. SAT or ACT required; TOEFL required of all international applicants. High school diploma is required, and GED is accepted. *Academic units required:* 4 English, 3 math, 3 science (1 science lab), 1 foreign language, 2 social studies, 1 academic elective.

The Inside Word

The University of Idaho's straightforward approach to admissions is a welcome change for students completing more involved applications. In a way that's typical of large, public universities, Admissions Officers arrive at decisions based upon high school GPA and test scores. Most applicants are admitted and welcome the opportunity to attend a strong school at an affordable price.

FINANCIAL AID

Students should submit: FAFSA. The Princeton Review suggests that all financial aid forms be submitted as soon as possible after January 1. *Need-based scholarships/grants offered:* Academic Competitiveness Grant, Pell Grant, National SMART Grant, SEOG, state scholarships/grants, private scholarships, the school's own gift aid. *Loan aid offered:* Direct Subsidized Stafford, Direct Unsubsidized Stafford, Direct PLUS, Federal Perkins Loan, college/university loans from institutional funds. Applicants will be notified of awards on or about March 30. Off-campus job opportunities are good.

FROM THE ADMISSIONS OFFICE

"The University of Idaho combines the best of both worlds. We are the major research university in the state of Idaho and the state's land grant university, and [we provide] a safe, residential environment. Moscow's small size and the supportive surrounding community provide the ideal atmosphere for a total learning experience.

"Students applying for admission into the Fall 2008 entering class are required to take either the SAT or the ACT. Both the new and the old test scores will be accepted. The Writing Test is not required from the ACT. SAT Subject Test scores are not used for admission purposes."

SELECTIVITY

Admissions Rating	78
# of applicants	4,324
% of applicants accepted	80
% of acceptees attending	47

FRESHMAN PROFILE

Range SAT Critical Reading	480–600
Range SAT Math	490–620
Range SAT Writing	460–560
Range ACT Composite	20–26
Minimum Paper TOEFL	525
Minimum Computer Based TOEFL	193
Average HS GPA	3.36
% graduated top 10% of class	20
% graduated top 25% of class	45
% graduated top 50% of class	77

DEADLINES

Regular application deadline	8/1
Regular notification	rolling
Nonfall registration?	yes

APPLICANTS ALSO LOOK AT

AND SOMETIMES PREFER
Boise State University, Utah State University

AND RARELY PREFER
Idaho State University

FINANCIAL FACTS

Financial Aid Rating	76
Annual in-state tuition	$4,200
Annual out-of-state tuition	$13,800
Room & Board	$5,696
Books and supplies	$1,388
% frosh rec. need-based scholarship or grant aid	32
% UG rec. need-based scholarship or grant aid	37
% frosh rec. need-based self-help aid	45
% UG rec. need-based self-help aid	50
% frosh rec. any financial aid	55
% UG rec. any financial aid	56

UNIVERSITY OF ILLINOIS AT URBANA-CHAMPAIGN

901 WEST ILLINOIS STREET, URBANA, IL 61801 • ADMISSIONS: 217-333-0302 • FAX: 217-333-9758

CAMPUS LIFE

Quality of Life Rating	78
Fire Safety Rating	77
Type of school	public
Environment	city

STUDENTS

Total undergrad enrollment	30,721
% male/female	53/47
% from out of state	7
% from public high school	75
% live on campus	50
% in (# of) fraternities	22 (60)
% in (# of) sororities	23 (36)
% African American	7
% Asian	12
% Caucasian	67
% Hispanic	7
% international	5
# of countries represented	120

SURVEY SAYS . . .
Great library
Everyone loves the Fighting Illini
Frats and sororities dominate social scene
Student publications are popular
Lots of beer drinking
Hard liquor is popular

ACADEMICS

Academic Rating	75
Calendar	semester
Student/faculty ratio	17:1
Profs interesting rating	68
Profs accessible rating	69
% profs teaching UG courses	70
% classes taught by TAs	26
Most common lab size	20–29 students
Most common reg class size	20–29 students

MOST POPULAR MAJORS
cell/cellular and molecular biology
political science and government
psychology

STUDENTS SAY

Academics

The "big, boisterous, and bureaucratic" University of Illinois at Urbana-Champaign provides a solid range of top-rate programs at a bargain-basement price. Business and engineering are among the best-known and most popular programs here; also highly touted are offerings in agriculture, animal sciences, psychology, accounting, and architecture. The liberal arts generally fare less well, although they, too, are not without their strengths. Students warn that "this school is academically strong across the board. The standards for grades are high, there are very few easy A's, and yes, they will fail you." Intro classes are especially tough and are "good at weeding out the students who do not belong at this university. There is a lot of work, although it's not too overwhelming." Despite the school's considerable size, professors and administrators here earn wide praise. One student writes, "I think everyone is professional and academic. It surprises me that a large school can be run like a small one." Another agrees, "Keeping in mind that there are roughly 29,000 undergraduates, the school's administrators do a decent job of keeping everything together." And the school's size certainly has its benefits; one undergrad notes, "There are so many opportunities to get involved and so many opportunities to build connections and work with professors."

Life

Students at the U of Illinois "like to study but also have a good time," which is code, it seems, for drinking with friends. One student explains, "Going to school in the middle of cornfields leaves little to do for fun that doesn't involve drinking"; however, the school is looking to improve upon this with the addition of a new Campus Recreation Center and Illinites activities nights. Doing so is no problem, "since you only have to be 19 to enter bars and the same age to bartend. The Greek population is sizable; one frat boy notes, "Illinois is a Greek campus. Most people who are socially adept are associated with a house. Because I'm Greek, I see this as a positive, but I can see how non-Greeks would hate us." Non-Greeks immerse themselves in "the various other subcultures that can be seen throughout campus. You have those people who are interested in politics, others in sports, human rights groups, that sort of thing." Undergrads also enjoy "Frisbee or football throwing in the quad" and "watching movies on the Quad at night (Quad Cinema) in the fall, which is definitely a blast. It is kind of like a drive-in, without the cars." And despite the pitiful state of the football team, "Football tailgating is always popular. When you go to a top party school with a bottom 25 football team, what else is there to do on Saturday mornings?"

Student Body

While "Most students seem to be White upper-middle-class suburbanites from metropolitan Chicago," "There are many people that contradict that stereotype and "Diversity isn't really a problem." You'll see more than your fair share of "super-skinny sorority girls and buffed-up frat boys" here—the type who "go to class in pajamas, but out to the bars all decked out"—but you'll also find lots of minorities and "a lot of students from foreign countries, such as China, Taiwan, Korea, Turkey, and the United Arab Emirates." Undergrads report that "students here at U of I are typical Midwesterners with the joyful addition of international students." If you're looking for the outliers, know that "they can be found in the living-learning communities. The LLCs are really nice because they contain both your average White suburbanite and your atypical person and provide a wonderful place for intellectual stimulation and expansion. LLCs rock!"

UNIVERSITY OF ILLINOIS AT URBANA-CHAMPAIGN

FINANCIAL AID: 217-333-0100 • E-MAIL: ADMISSIONS@OAR.UIUC.EDU • WEBSITE: WWW.UIUC.EDU

ADMISSIONS

Very important factors considered include: Academic GPA, application essay, class rank, rigor of secondary school record, standardized test scores. *Important factors considered include:* Character/personal qualities, extracurricular activities, first generation, talent/ability, volunteer work, work experience. *Other factors considered include:* Geographical residence, racial/ethnic status, state residency. SAT or ACT required; ACT with Writing component recommended. TOEFL required of all international applicants. High school diploma is required, and GED is accepted. *Academic units required:* 4 English, 3 math, 2 science (2 science labs), 2 foreign language, 2 social studies, 2 academic electives.

The Inside Word

Few candidates are deceived by Illinois's relatively high acceptance rate; the university has a well-deserved reputation for expecting applicants to be strong students, and those who aren't usually don't bother to apply. Despite a jumbo applicant pool, the Admissions Office reports that every candidate is individually reviewed, which deserves mention as rare in universities of this size.

FINANCIAL AID

Students should submit: FAFSA. The Princeton Review suggests that all financial aid forms be submitted as soon as possible after January 1. *Need-based scholarships/grants offered:* Pell Grant, SEOG, state scholarships/grants, private scholarships, the school's own gift aid, United Negro College Fund. *Loan aid offered:* Direct Subsidized Stafford, Direct Unsubsidized Stafford, Direct PLUS, Federal Perkins Loan, college/university loans from institutional funds, alternative loans. Applicants will be notified of awards on a rolling basis beginning or about March 15.

FROM THE ADMISSIONS OFFICE

"The campus has been aptly described as a collection of neighborhoods constituting a diverse and vibrant city. The neighborhoods are of many types: students and faculty within a department; people sharing a room or house; the members of a professional organization, a service club, or an intramural team; or simply people who, starting out as strangers sharing a class or a study lounge or a fondness for a weekly film series, have become friends. And the city of this description is the university itself—a rich cosmopolitan environment constructed by students and faculty to meet their educational and personal goals. The quality of intellectual life parallels that of other great universities, and many faculty and students who have their choice of top institutions select Illinois over its peers. While such choices are based often on the quality of individual programs of study, another crucial factor is the 'tone' of the campus life that is linked with the virtues of Midwestern culture. There is an informality and a near-absence of pretension, which, coupled with a tradition of commitment to excellence, creates an atmosphere that is unique among the finest institutions.

"Applicants for Fall 2008 are recommended to take the new SAT or the ACT with the Writing section, but we will allow students to submit scores from the old version (prior to March 2005) of the SAT or ACT. Though strongly recommended, the Writing section of the ACT is not required."

SELECTIVITY

Admissions Rating	90
# of applicants	22,367
% of applicants accepted	65
% of acceptees attending	50
# accepting a place on wait list	601
% admitted from wait list	9

FRESHMAN PROFILE

Range SAT Critical Reading	540–670
Range SAT Math	620–740
Range ACT Composite	25–30
Minimum Paper TOEFL	550
Minimum Computer Based TOEFL	213
% graduated top 10% of class	55
% graduated top 25% of class	96
% graduated top 50% of class	99

DEADLINES

Regular application deadline	1/2
Regular notification	12/15
Nonfall registration?	no

APPLICANTS ALSO LOOK AT

AND OFTEN PREFER
Northwestern University, University of Michigan—Ann Arbor

AND SOMETIMES PREFER
Indiana University—Bloomington, University of Iowa, University of Wisconsin—Madison, Washington University in St. Louis

AND RARELY PREFER
Illinois State University, Purdue University—West Lafayette

FINANCIAL FACTS

Financial Aid Rating	79
Annual in-state tuition	$7,042
Annual out-of-state tuition	$21,128
Room & Board	$7,716
Books and supplies	$1,000
Required fees	$1,674
% frosh rec. need-based scholarship or grant aid	25
% UG rec. need-based scholarship or grant aid	26
% frosh rec. need-based self-help aid	31
% UG rec. need-based self-help aid	32
% frosh rec. any financial aid	40
% UG rec. any financial aid	38

UNIVERSITY OF IOWA

107 CALVIN HALL, IOWA CITY, IA 52242 • ADMISSIONS: 319-335-3847 • FAX: 319-333-1535

CAMPUS LIFE
Quality of Life Rating	87
Fire Safety Rating	78
Type of school	public
Environment	city

STUDENTS
Total undergrad enrollment	19,915
% male/female	47/53
% from out of state	37
% from public high school	90
% live on campus	30
% in (# of) fraternities	7 (16)
% in (# of) sororities	12 (13)
% African American	2
% Asian	3
% Caucasian	80
% Hispanic	2
% international	1
# of countries represented	57

SURVEY SAYS . . .
Great computer facilities
Students love Iowa City, IA
Great off-campus food
Everyone loves the Hawkeyes
Lots of beer drinking
Hard liquor is popular

ACADEMICS
Academic Rating	74
Calendar	semester
Student/faculty ratio	15:1
Profs interesting rating	63
Profs accessible rating	71
% profs teaching UG courses	100
Most common lab size	20–29 students
Most common reg class size	10–19 students

MOST POPULAR MAJORS
communications studies/speech
communication and rhetoric
English language and literature
psychology

STUDENTS SAY
Academics
"Strong academics in a variety of fields," including "excellent research programs in numerous disciplines for those who desire a more research-oriented curriculum," are the foundation of University of Iowa's success—but they're not the entire picture. There's also the "high-tech and fast-paced campus," the "great assistance centers such as the Writing Center, minority centers, and the Career Center," and of course the "wonderful social opportunities," all of which "really contribute to the overall experience of an undergraduate." UI's stellar departments are myriad: Programs in creative writing, English, health sciences (bolstered by the presence of no fewer than three hospitals on campus), speech pathology and audiology, engineering, journalism, and pharmacology all earn students' raves, and that's just the tip of the iceberg. While the quality of teaching here "varies greatly amongst departments," "Almost all professors really do care about how each of their students does. They really stress their availability outside of class for all students to get help if it is needed." Ambitious students should note that "honors classes are available, and professors are open and excited about students who want to go above and beyond." Prospective students should be forewarned, however, that "as with any state-run organization, the school is plagued with bureaucratic process."

Life
"Life at Iowa can be whatever you make it," students at this massive university agree. "If you want to get wild and crazy on the weekends, you can." According to one undergrad, the "gazillion house parties or the trillion bars on campus" make the UI party scene "like a mini-Cancún." On the other hand, "If you like to lay low, you can hit the theater performances at Hatcher or play a few games of basketball," or "Catch a historically significant foreign film playing somewhere for free, or see important movers on the international stage giving speeches on the next big global issue." The point is, there's more to do here than party; as one student puts it, "Contrary to popular belief, not everyone on this campus drinks. There are many residence hall–sponsored activities like swing dances, dorm parties, barbecues, tug-of-war. [The school] tries to do something every weekend." One activity does unite the student body; nearly everyone here is "football crazy," with tailgates and the game both deemed "must-attend" events. Iowa City loves the football team as much as the students do, and students reciprocate by loving the city, which they describe as "the perfect college town" that offers "many social activities, restaurants, and coffee shops geared toward college students." Students also appreciate the fact that Iowa City "is a haven for Democrats, minorities, homosexuals, and others not generally accepted in the Midwest."

Student Body
"As far as the state of Iowa goes, this community is ethnically diverse and very welcoming of people with different religious viewpoints and sexual orientations," students at UI report, but they also remind us that nevertheless, "This school is located in Iowa, so most of the students are White and have Christian backgrounds." This "very liberal" school does, however, include its fair share of "hicks from Iowa and rich kids from Chicago," with some international students in the mix. With nearly 20,000 students, it's impossible to describe the typical UI student, but that didn't stop people from trying. One undergrad writes, "A typical student at the UI is pretty much an average young adult who likes to hang out, go to football games, and go to parties. There are some atypical students—those who are very religious, don't drink, or are punks. Even though they may be 'atypical,' there is still room for them here. Everyone finds a niche."

FINANCIAL AID: 319-335-1450 • E-MAIL: ADMISSIONS@UIOWA.EDU • WEBSITE: WWW.UIOWA.EDU

ADMISSIONS

Very important factors considered include: Academic GPA, class rank, rigor of secondary school record, standardized test scores. *Other factors considered include:* Character/personal qualities, recommendation(s), state residency, talent/ability. SAT or ACT required; ACT with Writing component recommended. TOEFL required of all international applicants. High school diploma is required, and GED is accepted. *Academic units required:* 4 English, 3 math, 3 science, 2 foreign language, 3 social studies. *Academic units recommended:* 4 foreign language.

The Inside Word

While the application process at University of Iowa is fairly formulaic and impersonal, candidates do have the luxury of knowing what to expect. Admission is automatically granted to applicants who meet secondary school course requirements and class rank and entrance exam minimums. The cut-offs are fairly high, and Iowa typically nets a strong crop of talented students. Out-of-state applicants, as well as candidates applying to the engineering school, face even tougher standards.

FINANCIAL AID

Students should submit: FAFSA, institution's own financial aid form. The Princeton Review suggests that all financial aid forms be submitted as soon as possible after January 1. *Need-based scholarships/grants offered:* Pell Grant, SEOG, state scholarships/grants, private scholarships, the school's own gift aid. *Loan aid offered:* Direct Subsidized Stafford, Direct Unsubsidized Stafford, Direct PLUS, Federal Perkins Loan, Federal Nursing Loan, college/university loans from institutional funds. Applicants will be notified of awards on a rolling basis beginning or about March 4.

FROM THE ADMISSIONS OFFICE

"The University of Iowa has outstanding programs in the creative arts, notably the Iowa Writers' Workshop and the world-renowned International Writing Program. It also has strong programs in business, communication studies, journalism, English, engineering, political science, and psychology, and was the birthplace of the discipline of speech pathology and audiology. It offers excellent programs in the basic health sciences and health care programs, led by the top ranked College of Medicine and the closely associated University Hospitals and Clinics.

"The University of Iowa will accept either the new SAT or the old SAT (administered prior to March 2005 and without a Writing component), as well as the ACT with or without the Writing component."

SELECTIVITY

Admissions Rating	82
# of applicants	14,350
% of applicants accepted	83
% of acceptees attending	36
# accepting a place on wait list	149
% admitted from wait list	95

FRESHMAN PROFILE

Range SAT Critical Reading	520–650
Range SAT Math	540–670
Range ACT Composite	23–27
Minimum Paper TOEFL	530
Minimum Computer Based TOEFL	197
Average HS GPA	3.56
% graduated top 10% of class	23
% graduated top 25% of class	54
% graduated top 50% of class	93

DEADLINES

Regular application deadline	4/1
Regular notification	rolling
Nonfall registration?	yes

APPLICANTS ALSO LOOK AT

AND OFTEN PREFER
Northwestern University, University of Illinois at Urbana-Champaign

AND SOMETIMES PREFER
Drake University, Grinnell College, Indiana University—Bloomington, Iowa State University, University of Northern Iowa

AND RARELY PREFER
Cornell College, Illinois State University, University of Missouri—Rolla

FINANCIAL FACTS

Financial Aid Rating	92
Annual in-state tuition	$5,373
Annual out-of-state tuition	$18,548
Room & Board	$6,912
Books and supplies	$840
Required fees	$917
% frosh rec. need-based scholarship or grant aid	29
% UG rec. need-based scholarship or grant aid	27
% frosh rec. need-based self-help aid	37
% UG rec. need-based self-help aid	38
% frosh rec. any financial aid	81
% UG rec. any financial aid	80

UNIVERSITY OF KANSAS

OFFICE OF ADMISSIONS & SCHOLARSHIPS, 1502 IOWA STREET, LAWRENCE, KS 66045 • ADMISSIONS: 785-864-3911 • FAX: 785-864-5017

CAMPUS LIFE

Quality of Life Rating	**89**
Fire Safety Rating	**85**
Type of school	public
Environment	city

STUDENTS

Total undergrad enrollment	20,979
% male/female	50/50
% from out of state	23
% live on campus	22
% in (# of) fraternities	13 (23)
% in (# of) sororities	16 (16)
% African American	4
% Asian	4
% Caucasian	82
% Hispanic	4
% Native American	1
% international	3
# of countries represented	111

SURVEY SAYS . . .
Great library
Athletic facilities are great
Great off-campus food
Everyone loves the Jayhawks
Student publications are popular
Lots of beer drinking

ACADEMICS

Academic Rating	**74**
Calendar	semester
Student/faculty ratio	20:1
Profs interesting rating	77
Profs accessible rating	78
% profs teaching	
UG courses	98
% classes taught by TAs	17
Most common	
lab size	10–19 students
Most common	
reg class size	20–29 students

MOST POPULAR MAJORS
biology/biological sciences
psychology

STUDENTS SAY

Academics

"Strong in traditions, both sports and academics," the University of Kansas (KU to those in the know) is "paradise for sports fans, academicians, liberals, and partiers alike." Students stress that KU provides "the full college experience" through "many amazing research opportunities, supportive faculty, and strong academics, as well as a great social scene." KU boasts a wealth of solid programs, including an "amazing hands-on architecture program," a "fantastic journalism program," a highly reputed program in speech language and hearing, a "good nursing school," and solid science departments. As one student sees it, "My school can offer an Ivy League education to those who are willing to be the best they can be." No matter what discipline you pursue, "The price is amazing for everything that you receive. The buildings, the classrooms, the technology, the campus . . . and the location were all what I was looking for." While KU's class sizes "can be a bit overwhelming," professors "are interested in seeing their students succeed and make themselves readily available to students," and "discussions or labs help make [the large lectures] bearable." Those seeking a more intimate academic experience should consider the honors program; "The people who run it are all super-nice and helpful, and the honors classes themselves are much smaller and more discussion-based, which lets the students think more and become better friends."

Life

"Tradition is a big strength" of KU life. "Singing the alma mater and reciting the Rock Chalk chant before games and other events is awesome," students tell us. For many, "Life revolves around basketball from November to April." Reports one undergrad, "Going to games is great. I've never experienced anything like [it]. I love sitting in the student section. The energy radiating off of everyone is amazing. Camping out in line on the day of basketball games will be one of my greatest memories. You gotta love KU basketball." If you don't, though, you needn't despair, because "Lawrence offers a great downtown with bars, clubs, shops, coffeehouses, and music. There's always something to do, even if you're not 21." The town has "a big music scene, and bands like Pat Green, James Blunt, and Mat Kearney have played numerous shows. Smaller indie-rock bands come through as well. Liberty Hall downtown hosts concerts and projection movies, and the student union always brings in acts like Ben Folds or other celebrities." There's an active party scene on and off campus; according to one undergrad, "The majority of us bust our [butts] during the week, and party the weekend away. There are a lot of places for students to go on weekends to forget about how [crappy] their week was."

Student Body

KU students tell us there are "a lot of fraternity and sorority types at our school, and they're very active on (and off) campus," but there's also "a large number of alternative, indie, and minority students present, and they all fit into a niche as well. Overall, I would say it's a very pleasant coexistence between the two types of people," as "Most people are really easygoing and enjoy getting to know people who are different from them." Demographically, KU is made up of "pretty much plain-vanilla Midwestern college students." They're among the most liberal in the state, but, one student quips, "That isn't saying much, seeing as it is Kansas." However, "Most everyone here is very open-minded and willing to accept people for who they are." As one student puts it, "Nothing surprises me anymore. When I first came to KU it was interesting to see same-sex couples, rocker guys, and girls with their collars popped walking around the same campus. Now, it's just life."

FINANCIAL AID: 785-864-4700 • E-MAIL: ADM@KU.EDU • WEBSITE: WWW.KU.EDU

ADMISSIONS

Very important factors considered include: Academic GPA, class rank, rigor of secondary school record, standardized test scores. SAT or ACT required. High school diploma is required, and GED is accepted. *Academic units required:* 4 English, 3 math, 3 science, 3 social studies, 1 computer technology. *Academic units recommended:* 4 English, 4 math, 3 science, 2 foreign language, 3 social studies, 1 computer technology.

The Inside Word

KU can process your application to its College of Liberal Arts and Sciences or its School of Engineering (architecture program excluded) in 48 hours. In-state students can be admitted to the College of Liberal Arts and Sciences if they achieve a 21/980 on the ACT/SAT (writing section excluded) or earn at least a 2.0 on the Kansas Board of Regents curriculum. Out-of-state students need a 24/1090 or at least a 2.5 on the board curriculum. No matter where you're from, a top-third high school class rank will do the trick. The School of Engineering requires a minimum 28/640 ACT/SAT Math section score for out-of-state students. In-state students need a minimum Math score of 22/540.

FINANCIAL AID

Students should submit: FAFSA. Regular filing deadline is March 1. The Princeton Review suggests that all financial aid forms be submitted as soon as possible after January 1. *Need-based scholarships/grants offered:* Pell Grant, SEOG, state scholarships/grants, private scholarships, the school's own gift aid. *Loan aid offered:* Direct Subsidized Stafford, Direct Unsubsidized Stafford, Direct PLUS, Federal Perkins Loan, college/university loans from institutional funds. Applicants will be notified of awards on a rolling basis beginning or about April 1.

FROM THE ADMISSIONS OFFICE

"The University of Kansas has a long and distinguished tradition for academic excellence. Outstanding students from Kansas and across the nation are attracted to KU because of its strong academic reputation, beautiful campus, affordable cost of education, and contagious school spirit. KU provides students extraordinary opportunities in honors programs, research, internships, and study abroad. The university is located in Lawrence (40 minutes from Kansas City), a community of 80,000 regarded as one of the nation's best small cities for its arts scene, live music, and historic downtown.

"Students applying for Fall 2008 admission may provide scores from either version of the SAT, as well as the ACT. KU will look at the total score of the Math and the Critical Reading (Verbal) section of the exam for admission purposes."

SELECTIVITY

Admissions Rating	**82**
# of applicants	10,240
% of applicants accepted	77
% of acceptees attending	53
# accepting a place on wait list	202
% admitted from wait list	47

FRESHMAN PROFILE

Range ACT Composite	22–28
Average HS GPA	3.4
% graduated top 10% of class	28
% graduated top 25% of class	55
% graduated top 50% of class	88

DEADLINES

Regular application deadline	4/1
Regular notification	rolling
Nonfall registration?	yes

FINANCIAL FACTS

Financial Aid Rating	**74**
Annual in-state tuition	$5,513
Annual out-of-state tuition	$14,483
Room & Board	$5,747
Books and supplies	$750
Required fees	$640
% frosh rec. need-based scholarship or grant aid	25
% UG rec. need-based scholarship or grant aid	26
% frosh rec. need-based self-help aid	35
% UG rec. need-based self-help aid	33
% frosh rec. any financial aid	81
% UG rec. any financial aid	61

UNIVERSITY OF KENTUCKY

100 FUNKHOUSER BUILDING, LEXINGTON, KY 40506 • ADMISSIONS: 859-257-2000 • FAX: 859-257-3823

STUDENTS SAY

Academics

The University of Kentucky in Lexington is "all about making a name for yourself by preparing for and getting involved in future career goals while having fun and enjoying what college is all about." "Making a name for yourself" here requires distinguishing yourself in a crowd of over 18,000 undergraduates; daunting as that sounds, students tell us it can be done. "Getting involved in future career goals" is easy enough, given the "great selection of courses and majors" available. Kentucky offers undergraduate degrees in 12 of its 19 divisions; choices include the College of Agriculture (with popular majors in animal science, agricultural economics, and hospitality management), the College of Business and Management, the College of Education, the College of Engineering, the College of Communications and Information Studies (advertising, journalism, and library science), and the College of Arts and Sciences (biology, history, and political science). Students here laud the "impressive teaching staff, dedicated to enhancing student knowledge and teaching students about the future." UK's brand-new library "is also quite amazing. It is the perfect place to go study because usually the dorms can be a bit too distracting." All told, go-getters willing to take initiative will find that UK offers "a safe and fun atmosphere where you have unlimited opportunities to get involved at a reasonable price."

Life

"Everyone is a Wildcat" at UK, because "UK has tremendous sports programs and big fans all around the United States." Men's basketball fans "are among the craziest in the nation," and students "would be football fanatics if our team would win a game every now and then." "Because UK is dry, most parties are held off campus," so social life for many revolves around the off-campus Greek houses where "There is always a party going on, but you have to be a part of a fraternity or sorority to really know about it and attend." Some students report that "there are a lot of nonalcoholic parties in the dorms that might be crazier than the alcoholic parties," although others advise, "It's better to live off campus because the residence halls are pretty bad (except for the new ones), the meal plan is awful, and everything off campus is a lot cheaper." Hometown Lexington "is a great city with much to do and lots of opportunities. It offers many different clubs, bars, and restaurants that college students can go to as well as horse racing. All of these venues have a 'College Day' where students get discounts." One sophomore warns, however, that "small-town students can become distracted by the lights of the city."

Student Body

"The typical UK student has a Southern accent, likes to party, and often shops at J. Crew," but, "As the undergraduate population is about 18,000, there are a lot of people who do not fit that description." True, one of the most common "types"—or at least the most conspicuous one—are the "beautiful people, the hot girls and guys who roam the campus and dress up to go to class." But for every "collar-popping, stuck-up frat boy" there is also "your typical country Kentucky boy, boots and all." What you won't find many of at UK are "liberals—they are few and far between—and the type of atypical student with wild hair colors or other style extremes." Most here "lean right politically, but generally the student body is apathetic." School spirit is rampant, so much so that "on an average day, one in three students will have some sort of UK clothing on."

FINANCIAL AID: 859-257-3172 • E-MAIL: ADMISSION@UKY.EDU • WEBSITE: WWW.UKY.EDU

ADMISSIONS

Very important factors considered include: Academic GPA, rigor of secondary school record, standardized test scores. *Other factors considered include:* Alumni/ae relation, application essay, character/personal qualities, class rank, extracurricular activities, first generation, geographical residence, interview, racial/ethnic status, recommendation(s), talent/ability, volunteer work. SAT or ACT required; TOEFL required of all international applicants. High school diploma is required, and GED is accepted. *Academic units required:* 4 English, 3 math, 3 science, 2 foreign language, 3 social studies, 5 academic electives, 2 fine or performing arts, 0.5 health, and 0.5 physical education. *Academic units recommended:* 4 English, 4 math, 4 science, 2 foreign language, 3 social studies, 3 academic electives, 2 fine or performing arts, 0.5 health, and 0.5 physical education.

The Inside Word

The University of Kentucky's admissions team is about as objective as they come. If you have the GPA, class rank, and test scores, you'll in all likelihood be welcomed into the Wildcat community. The university is continually looking to improve its selectivity, so hitting the books is a must if you want to be a serious contender.

FINANCIAL AID

Students should submit: FAFSA. Regular filing deadline is February 15. The Princeton Review suggests that all financial aid forms be submitted as soon as possible after January 1. *Need-based scholarships/grants offered:* Pell Grant, SEOG, state scholarships/grants, private scholarships, the school's own gift aid. *Loan aid offered:* Direct Subsidized Stafford, Direct Unsubsidized Stafford, Direct PLUS, FFEL Subsidized Stafford, FFEL Unsubsidized Stafford, FFEL PLUS, Federal Perkins Loan, state loans, college/university loans from institutional funds. Applicants will be notified of awards on or about April 1. Federal Work-Study Program available.

FROM THE ADMISSIONS OFFICE

"The University of Kentucky offers you an outstanding learning environment and quality instruction through its excellent faculty. Of the 1,892 full-time faculty, 98 percent hold the doctorate degree or the highest degree in their field of study. Many are nationally and internationally known for their research, distinguished teaching, and scholarly service to Kentucky, the nation, and the world. UK's scholars (students, faculty, and alumni) have been honored by Nobel, Pulitzer, Rhodes, Fulbright, Guggenheim, and Grammy awards, and most recently the Metropolitan Opera and the Marshall Foundation. Yet, with a student/teacher ratio of only 17:1, UK faculty are accessible and willing to answer your questions and discuss your interests.

"UK will accept either version of the SAT. The new Writing sections of the ACT and SAT will not be used in the admission process. ACT and SAT score requirements will remain the same as the new score will not be figured into the total score used for admission consideration."

SELECTIVITY

Admissions Rating	79
# of applicants	10,024
% of applicants accepted	81
% of acceptees attending	41

FRESHMAN PROFILE

Range SAT Critical Reading	490–610
Range SAT Math	500–630
Range ACT Composite	22–27
Minimum Paper TOEFL	527
Minimum Computer Based TOEFL	197
Average HS GPA	3.48
% graduated top 10% of class	23
% graduated top 25% of class	50
% graduated top 50% of class	79

DEADLINES

Regular application deadline	2/15
Regular notification	rolling
Nonfall registration?	yes

APPLICANTS ALSO LOOK AT

AND OFTEN PREFER
Centre College, Indiana University—Bloomington, Miami University, Transylvania University

AND SOMETIMES PREFER
Bellarmine University, Eastern Kentucky University, University of Louisville, The University of Tennessee at Knoxville, Western Kentucky University

AND RARELY PREFER
Florida State University, Purdue University—West Lafayette, The Ohio State University—Columbus, University of Florida, University of Illinois at Urbana-Champaign

FINANCIAL FACTS

Financial Aid Rating	84
Annual in-state tuition	$6,510
Annual out-of-state tuition	$13,790
Room & Board	$5,560
Books and supplies	$800
Required fees	$794
% frosh rec. need-based scholarship or grant aid	20
% UG rec. need-based scholarship or grant aid	24
% frosh rec. need-based self-help aid	26
% UG rec. need-based self-help aid	29
% frosh rec. any financial aid	40
% UG rec. any financial aid	38

UNIVERSITY OF LOUISIANA AT LAFAYETTE

PO DRAWER 41210, LAFAYETTE, LA 70504 • ADMISSIONS: 337-482-6457 • FAX: 337-482-6195

CAMPUS LIFE

Quality of Life Rating	84
Fire Safety Rating	88
Type of school	public
Environment	city

STUDENTS

Total undergrad enrollment	14,623
% male/female	43/57
% from out of state	4
% from public high school	70
% live on campus	12
% in (# of) fraternities	3 (10)
% in (# of) sororities	5 (9)
% African American	19
% Asian	2
% Caucasian	72
% Hispanic	2
% international	1
# of countries represented	94

SURVEY SAYS . . .

Great library
Students are friendly
Diverse student types on campus
Students get along with local community
Students love Lafayette, LA
Great off-campus food
(Almost) everyone smokes

ACADEMICS

Academic Rating	66
Calendar	semester
Student/faculty ratio	25:1
Profs interesting rating	71
Profs accessible rating	71
% profs teaching	
UG courses	100
Most common	
reg class size	20–29 students

MOST POPULAR MAJORS

business administration/
management
general studies
nursing/registered nurse training
(ASN, BSN, MSN, RN)

STUDENTS SAY

Academics

At the "medium-sized" University of Louisiana at Lafayette—in "the heart of Cajun country"—many students feel "under the shadow" of their mammoth cousin, LSU. We really don't know why. UL Lafayette offers "serious bang for your buck"; tremendously generous grant and scholarship programs and out-of-state fee waivers make UL Lafayette one of the best bargains in the country. Programs in "education, computer science, and engineering" are "ranked as some of the best in the nation." The nursing program is the "third largest" in the country and "one of the best" anywhere. "Seasoned" and "overwhelmingly helpful" professors are "friendly, fun" and "honestly interested in having you learn." "The experience has been absolutely wonderful academically," gushes a senior. "In over 120 hours of course study, I cannot remember hav[ing] one bad professor." Other students disagree; they remember a "couple of bad apples." A perennial complaint among students at UL Lafayette is that many professors from other countries "cannot be understood by the students." The administration is generally unpopular. "The bureaucracy is ridiculous," reports a general studies major. "The university is run like an out-of-date chicken farm," adds a finance major. "No one knows the answer to anything" and "Getting financial aid in a timely manner is a real problem." Students are generally very satisfied, though. "My overall college experience at University of Louisiana at Lafayette has been terrific," asserts a junior. "I would recommend this college to anyone."

Life

UL Lafayette's "beautiful campus" is "full of big trees and handsome Southern architecture." Unfortunately, "It always floods when it rains," some "lousy buildings" "need updating," and the parking situation is just "painful." Nevertheless, "School spirit is really high." "Football games are huge events," and Lafayette is, by all accounts, a "great" college town. "Believe me," swears a wide-eyed first-year student, "it is an experience." The Strip "is right by campus" and "lined with numerous bars and clubs." "Most people," however, "congregate downtown," where it's "almost like Bourbon Street in New Orleans." The local music scene is hopping, and festivals are frequent, including a very large International Music Festival and a gigantic Mardi Gras celebration. If partying isn't your bag, or if you get sick of it, Lafayette also offers an "abundance of coffee shops" and "numerous art venues." "There is so much history and culture in Louisiana" that, frankly, it's hard to "ever be bored or without something fun to do on any day of the week," and you can find "great food anywhere." "If you're looking for a good, inexpensive college education that is packed with good food, cold beer, and excitement, look no further than UL Lafayette."

Student Body

Students at UL Lafayette are "friendly and fun" and "always seem to be in a good mood." They have "Southern flair with a little bit of our Cajun cayenne," a marketing major quips. They're also "very strongly rooted in their religions"; in that regard, "Catholic conservatives" seem to predominate. Many "are from the surrounding area of Acadiana," "lower- to upper-middle class," and "receive some financial support from [their] parents." Many also "have part-time job[s]." Beyond that, "There are many different types of people" and "Everyone seems to get along together." One undergrad reports, "Our campus includes a very diverse group of students from various religious and racial backgrounds." There are also "a few oddballs" who "try to get themselves noticed by the way they dress and their eccentric hair." For the most part, however, "Everyone blends in." "No one really points out or harasses other students here at UL Lafayette, unless that student happens to be wearing LSU paraphernalia."

FINANCIAL AID: 337-482-6506 • E-MAIL: ADMISSIONS@LOUISIANA.EDU • WEBSITE: WWW.LOUISIANA.EDU

ADMISSIONS

Very important factors considered include: Academic GPA, class rank, rigor of secondary school record, standardized test scores. *Other factors considered include:* State residency. SAT or ACT required; TOEFL required of all international applicants. High school diploma is required, and GED is accepted. *Academic units required:* 4 English, 3 math, 3 science, 2 foreign language, 2 social studies, 1 history, 1 academic elective.

The Inside Word

UL Lafayette is still a fallback school for many applicants. You are pretty much guaranteed admission if you carry an ACT score of at least 18 and complete a basic college-prep high school curriculum with a GPA of 2.5 or better. If your numbers are a little lower, you can submit an essay and some other credentials for possible admission through UL Lafayette's Admission by Committee. It should be noted, however, that Admission by Committee is limited to 7 percent of each incoming class.

FINANCIAL AID

Students should submit: FAFSA, institution's own financial aid form. The Princeton Review suggests that all financial aid forms be submitted as soon as possible after January 1. *Need-based scholarships/grants offered:* Pell Grant, SEOG, state scholarships/grants, private scholarships, the school's own gift aid, Federal Nursing Scholarship. *Loan aid offered:* FFEL Subsidized Stafford, FFEL Unsubsidized Stafford, FFEL PLUS, Federal Perkins Loan, Federal Nursing Loan. Applicants will be notified of awards on a rolling basis beginning or about April 1. Federal Work-Study Program available. Institutional employment available. Off-campus job opportunities are good.

FROM THE ADMISSIONS OFFICE

"The University of Louisiana at Lafayette offers students from throughout the United States and more than 90 countries strong academic training and personal enrichment opportunities in a friendly, comfortable, student-centered environment. UL Lafayette students are taught, mentored, and advised by some of the brightest and most accomplished faculty members in the United States. Although UL Lafayette offers more than 100 programs of study and the research opportunities, internship possibilities, and facilities of a major research-intensive university, average class size is approximately the same as that at many high schools and smaller higher education institutions.

"UL students receive a good deal of individual attention and support—both personal and academic—from faculty and staff.

"A wide range of cultural, recreational, and social activities are available on and off campus, including more than 150 campus organizations and clubs, NCAA Division I and intramural athletics, a state-of-the-art aquatic center, a thriving arts scene, a wide range of live music venues, shopping, a great variety of excellent restaurants, theaters, the second largest Mardi Gras in the nation, and an international music festival. In fact, *Utne Reader* magazine selected the city of Lafayette as Louisiana's 'Most Enlightened Town.'

"Our relatively low tuition and generous financial aid and scholarship programs, including an out-of-state tuition waiver for qualified students, make UL Lafayette one of the most affordable universities in the nation.

"Students who have completed the required college preparatory core curriculum in high school may qualify for admission on the basis of a combination of their high school cumulative grade point average and ACT or SAT scores. Writing scores are not required."

SELECTIVITY

Admissions Rating	74
# of applicants	7,140
% of applicants accepted	73
% of acceptees attending	56

FRESHMAN PROFILE

Range ACT Composite	19–25
Minimum Paper TOEFL	525
Minimum Computer Based TOEFL	195
Average HS GPA	3.2
% graduated top 10% of class	14
% graduated top 25% of class	38
% graduated top 50% of class	72

DEADLINES

Regular notification	rolling
Nonfall registration?	yes

FINANCIAL FACTS

Financial Aid Rating	69
Annual in-state tuition	$3,382
Annual out-of-state tuition	$8,962
Room & Board	$3,770
Books and supplies	$1,000
Books and supplies	$1,000
% frosh rec. need-based scholarship or grant aid	47
% UG rec. need-based scholarship or grant aid	42
% frosh rec. need-based self-help aid	24
% UG rec. need-based self-help aid	33
% frosh rec. any financial aid	87
% UG rec. any financial aid	72

UNIVERSITY OF MAINE

5713 CHADBOURNE HALL, ORONO, ME 04469-5713 • ADMISSIONS: 207-581-1561 • FAX: 207-581-1213

STUDENTS SAY

Academics

Combine cheap in-state tuition with top programs, and it's easy to understand why not too many University of Maine students are in any rush to leave the warm embrace (which is at a premium in chilly Maine) of their college after 4 sweet years. Engineering is tops here, but exciting majors like new media, marine science, and landscape horticulture draw their fair share of undergraduates too. For those who fear the anonymity of a public school, UM undergrads swear that "it's not overwhelmingly huge." General education classes can be large and impersonal, but a math major writes, "Most of my classes for the past 2 years have been 20 people, many under 10. I can actually go to my professors with questions on homework, class, or career." Another undergrad adds, "I have always received attention when I needed it, even in classes of 300-plus." One student who is taking advantage of the tutoring program writes that, thanks to the one-on-one time, "I am now receiving 100s on my tests and quizzes." The administration generally makes a good impression on students from the get-go by "setting up meetings with the first-year students to get to know them and to establish a communication line. If anyone has questions, answers are a phone-call, visit, or e-mail away."

Life

Word on the street is that "people here know how to recreate." Take, for example, flowing pumpkin ale at Oktoberfest, mud volleyball along with campus beautification (in lieu of classes) on Maine Day, and the school-sponsored bonfire celebrating the Red Sox pennant in 2004, which, we are told, "was genius, as it kept the excited student body from doing any damage and gave us all an outlet for our celebratory energy." The Division I athletic teams, hockey in particular, draw a rabid following. "When you say Maine Black Bears, you say all." On the weekends, "You can go dancing or drinking at the Bear Brew, which [is] almost always packed on Thursdays." Greek life "is slowly getting a better reputation thanks to the fraternities and sororities changing policies and extending out into the community." After the night's revelries are over, kids grab a few hours of sleep before waking in the morning to hike off any hangovers on the extensive network of trails near the campus. There's a lot of alcohol-less cheer to be had at UM too; plenty of people appreciate that "6 nights out of the week, somewhere on campus you can find free fun that does not involve alcohol or sports." That means karaoke, comedians, movies in the main lecture hall, board games, and open-mic nights. "There's even a knitting club."

Student Body

The University of Maine's undergraduate population includes a colorful array of more than 8,000 characters: "boozers, stoners, foresters, adventurers, businessmen, and the straight-up Mainers." Just what is a "straight-up Mainer?" The answer depends on whom you ask. Most here agree, though, that he isn't so welcoming to out-of-state folks. That shouldn't upset too many people, though, as only about 15 percent of students hail from beyond the borders of The Pine Tree State. Still, according to students, "every type of person is represented in the student body in some way." A visible goth contingent mingles with hacky-sacking hippies and anime enthusiasts. Against the backdrop of "White backhill hicks," the "African American athletes from Massachusetts and hockey players from New York or Canada" do stand out. Still, "You can wear what you want, say what you want, think what you want, and it's accepted." Students tend to form cliques "made up of high school friends or people from your area"; in such a small state, people always seem connected by "three or fewer degrees of separation."

FINANCIAL AID: 207-581-1324 • E-MAIL: UM-ADMIT@MAINE.EDU • WEBSITE: WWW.UMAINE.EDU

ADMISSIONS

Very important factors considered include: Academic GPA, class rank, rigor of secondary school record, standardized test scores. *Important factors considered include:* Application essay, recommendation(s). *Other factors considered include:* Character/personal qualities, extracurricular activities, geographical residence, interview, state residency, talent/ability, volunteer work, work experience. SAT or ACT required; TOEFL required of all international applicants. High school diploma is required, and GED is accepted. *Academic units required:* 4 English, 3 math, 2 science (2 science labs), 2 foreign language, 2 social studies, 4 academic electives, 1 physical education (for education majors). *Academic units recommended:* 4 English, 4 math, 4 science (3 science labs), 2 foreign language, 3 social studies, 1 history, 4 academic electives, 1 physical education (for education majors).

The Inside Word

The University of Maine is much smaller than most public flagship universities, and its admissions process reflects this; it is a much more personal approach than most others use. Candidates are reviewed carefully for fit with their choice of college and major, and the committee will contact students regarding a second choice if the first doesn't seem to be a good match. Prepare your application as if you are applying to a private university.

FINANCIAL AID

Students should submit: FAFSA. The Princeton Review suggests that all financial aid forms be submitted as soon as possible after January 1. *Need-based scholarships/grants offered:* Pell Grant, SEOG, state scholarships/grants, private scholarships, the school's own gift aid. *Loan aid offered:* FFEL Subsidized Stafford, FFEL Unsubsidized Stafford, FFEL PLUS, Federal Perkins Loan, state loans. Applicants will be notified of awards on a rolling basis beginning or about March 15.

FROM THE ADMISSIONS OFFICE

"The University of Maine offers students a wide array of academic and social programs, including clubs, organizations, professional societies, and religious groups. We strive to help students feel welcome and to provide opportunities for them to become an integral part of the campus community. Visit our beautiful campus and become better acquainted with this community. Take a guided campus tour and learn about campus facilities, services and technologies, and living and dining. Our student tour guides give a firsthand view of the Black Bear experience. During your visit, meet with faculty and admission staff to learn more about your program of interest and our academic climate. The University of Maine's commitment to educational excellence and community building will be evident when you visit our campus!

"Students applying for admission are required to submit official scores from either the SAT or ACT. For Fall 2008, we will be looking primarily at the Critical Reading and Mathematics scores on the SAT and will not require the ACT Writing component. UMaine will use the best scores from either test."

SELECTIVITY

Admissions Rating	**78**
# of applicants	5,702
% of applicants accepted	80
% of acceptees attending	39
# accepting a place on wait list	N/A
% admitted from wait list	N/A

FRESHMAN PROFILE

Range SAT Critical Reading	480–590
Range SAT Math	490–600
Range ACT Composite	20–25
Minimum Paper TOEFL	530
Minimum Computer Based TOEFL	197
Average HS GPA	3.25
% graduated top 10% of class	22
% graduated top 25% of class	52
% graduated top 50% of class	86

DEADLINES

Regular notification	rolling
Nonfall registration?	yes

APPLICANTS ALSO LOOK AT

AND OFTEN PREFER
University of New Hampshire, University of Southern Maine, University of Vermont

AND SOMETIMES PREFER
University of Connecticut, University of Maine Farmington, University of Massachusetts—Amherst, University of Rhode Island

FINANCIAL FACTS

Financial Aid Rating	**76**
Annual in-state tuition	$5,970
Annual out-of-state tuition	$16,920
Room & Board	$7,125
Books and supplies	$700
Required fees	$1,494
% frosh rec. need-based scholarship or grant aid	53
% UG rec. need-based scholarship or grant aid	49
% frosh rec. need-based self-help aid	55
% UG rec. need-based self-help aid	56
% frosh rec. any financial aid	76
% UG rec. any financial aid	61

UNIVERSITY OF MARY WASHINGTON

1301 COLLEGE AVENUE, FREDERICKSBURG, VA 22401 • ADMISSIONS: 540-654-2000 • FAX: 540-654-1857

STUDENTS SAY

Academics

After a rapid growth of their graduate programs, the University of Mary Washington upgraded to university status in 2004, but despite the new moniker, little has changed for traditional undergraduates, who continue to receive a demanding, personalized education on UMW's Fredericksburg campus. They tell us that Mary Washington remains "a school with excellent academic programs." Students sometimes balk at "so many core requirements" but appreciate the university's strong offerings in history, education, psychology, English, and the life sciences. Just as important, the school's honor code will continue to "permeate the campus and underlie everything; you trust everyone, so you are nicer to people. People leave their purses, backpacks, and cell phones unattended for hours and nothing is stolen. Most people leave their doors unlocked. It goes way beyond not cheating in the classroom. There is a constant foundation of trust." Undergrads here will rarely see the graduate students and the nontraditional undergraduates seeking professional training, who now attend the school's second campus (the College of Graduate and Professional Studies in Stafford County.

Life

The pace of life at UMW is "pretty relaxed, [with] a lot of small activities that go on [but] no Greek life" to create a happening party scene. It's the kind of place where "After a while students find their niche," whether it be with a clique of friends or an extracurricular organization, "and, if not, they transfer." How easily students find their comfort zone depends largely on how they perceive hometown Fredericksburg. Some praise its "great downtown shopping area completely devoid of chain shops; instead you get a mom-and-pop feel and really cute stores [and] great restaurants." Others feel the city is "pretty dead," telling us that "downtown Fredericksburg is historic and quaint, but not exactly the stuff of which college entertainment dreams are made." Without a Greek scene, parties tend to be pretty small, because larger ones get "broken up by the cops almost immediately." Some students cope by heading elsewhere whenever possible; Washington, DC, Richmond, Virginia Beach, and Charlottesville are all potential weekend destinations. Then there are the outdoorsy types, grateful that "a 2-hour drive to Shenandoah provides days of hiking, biking, climbing, and camping, and even skiing in the winter."

Students

With a slightly heavier female-to-male ratio, UMW continues to have a slightly more estrogen-laced campus, its switch to coeducation over 30 years ago notwithstanding. Your standard-issue UMW woman is "majoring in a liberal art, education, or historic preservation, or even possibly a mixture . . . lives on campus, but goes home a lot, and balances her out-of-class time by either studying, hanging out with friends, or playing a sport." She's also likely to be a conservative from Virginia or Maryland—although "We have a lot of students from New England and New York"—and the type of preppy who wears Abercrombie & Fitch, American Eagle, or [clothes from] other clothing stores that capitalize on people feeling like they need to fit in." The guys are "split between the studious and athletic," and are less likely to be as serious about their schoolwork. UMW is home to "very few minorities (especially African Americans and Hispanics), but they generally fit in." The school "has a strong Christian population . . . but non-Christians don't feel pressured because there are plenty of non-Christians as well."

FINANCIAL AID: 800-468-5614 • E-MAIL: ADMIT@UMW.EDU • WEBSITE: WWW.UMW.EDU

ADMISSIONS

Very important factors considered include: Academic GPA, class rank, rigor of secondary school record, standardized test scores. *Important factors considered include:* Application essay, character/personal qualities, extracurricular activities, volunteer work. *Other factors considered include:* Alumni/ae relation, racial/ethnic status, recommendation(s), state residency, talent/ability, work experience. SAT or ACT required; TOEFL required of all international applicants. High school diploma is required, and GED is accepted. *Academic units required:* 4 English, 3 math, 3 science (3 science labs), 2 social studies, 2 history. *Academic units recommended:* 4 English, 4 math, 4 science (4 science labs), 4 foreign language, 2 social studies, 2 history.

The Inside Word

It's hard to beat small, selective public colleges like Mary Washington for quality and cost, and more and more students are discovering this. The admissions process is very selective and, with the exception of preferential treatment for Virginia residents, functions in virtually the same manner as small private college Admissions Committees do. Students who are interested need to focus on putting their best into all aspects of the application.

FINANCIAL AID

Students should submit: FAFSA. Regular filing deadline is March 1. The Princeton Review suggests that all financial aid forms be submitted as soon as possible after January 1. *Need-based scholarships/grants offered:* Pell Grant, SEOG, state scholarships/grants, private scholarships, the school's own gift aid. *Loan aid offered:* FFEL Subsidized Stafford, FFEL Unsubsidized Stafford, FFEL PLUS, Federal Perkins Loan. Applicants will be notified of awards on or about April 15.

FROM THE ADMISSIONS OFFICE

"Among institutions of higher learning in Virginia, the University of Mary Washington stands alone. We have distinctive academic programs, a breathtakingly beautiful campus, a sharp and diverse student body, and a unique sense of friendship and camaraderie that make the university very special. In fact, we have one of the best combinations of strong academics, personal attention, low cost, and impressive graduate school and job placement of any school in the country. Our students come from all over the country and the world, and are instructed by a faculty that considers teaching its primary objective—research and publishing come second. Committed to providing a well-rounded liberal arts and sciences education, the university offers its students the opportunity to pursue individual or collaborative research projects. Supportive faculty and more than $186,000 in student research funds annually make ours one of the most ambitious undergraduate research programs in the country. There are 17 residence halls on the Mary Washington campus with a university-owned apartment complex located adjacent to the main campus. The 'Apartments at UMW' provide the opportunity for 350 junior and senior students to experience apartment-style living while enjoying the amenities of on-campus living. Recently, the Jepson Executive Alumni Center, a new fitness center, and an indoor tennis facility were added to the university landscape.

"Applicants are required to submit official results of either the old or new SAT, or the ACT. The highest scores will be used in admissions decisions. In addition, we recommend that applicants submit results of two or more SAT Subject Tests of each applicant's choosing."

SELECTIVITY

Admissions Rating	89
# of applicants	4,287
% of applicants accepted	70
% of acceptees attending	31
# accepting a place on wait list	195
% admitted from wait list	55

FRESHMAN PROFILE

Range SAT Critical Reading	580–670
Range SAT Math	560–640
Range ACT Composite	25–29
Minimum Paper TOEFL	550
Minimum Computer Based TOEFL	230
Average HS GPA	3.67
% graduated top 10% of class	38
% graduated top 25% of class	74
% graduated top 50% of class	96

DEADLINES

Regular application deadline	2/1
Regular notification	4/1
Nonfall registration?	yes

APPLICANTS ALSO LOOK AT

AND OFTEN PREFER
The College of William & Mary, University of Virginia

AND SOMETIMES PREFER
James Madison University, University of Richmond

AND RARELY PREFER
George Mason University, Longwood University

FINANCIAL FACTS

Financial Aid Rating	61
Annual in-state tuition	$6,084
Annual out-of-state tuition	$15,964
Room & Board	$6,242
Books and supplies	$900
% frosh rec. need-based scholarship or grant aid	37
% UG rec. need-based scholarship or grant aid	36
% frosh rec. need-based self-help aid	41
% UG rec. need-based self-help aid	43
% frosh rec. any financial aid	57
% UG rec. any financial aid	59

UNIVERSITY OF MARYLAND—BALTIMORE COUNTY

1000 HILLTOP CIRCLE, BALTIMORE, MD 21250 • ADMISSIONS: 410-455-2291 • FAX: 410-455-1094

STUDENTS SAY

Academics

The University of Maryland—Baltimore County is primarily known as a great "science and engineering school" with superb "research opportunities"—but this justly earned reputation tells only part of the story. Many here report that "the humanities are wonderful," even though some concede that they "are not very well funded or respected." Offerings here are enhanced by the "focus on research. There are so many opportunities for students to learn the latest tidbits of up-to-date research done on campus and to work with professors for credit." "The professors seem to be a mixed bag," getting reviews that range from "very inspiring" and "excellent" to "crappy" and "awful," with some falling "in the middle." Students here enjoy "really great opportunities for internships. The proximity to Washington, DC, and Baltimore provides easy access to jobs other people around the country would love to have." UMBC's career services office also facilitates "great placement opportunities. The methods of getting your resume around in your field of interest are easy and very effective." In all areas, UMBC adheres to an "honors college philosophy of smaller classes and more professor interaction."

Life

Campus life at UMBC has many hurdles to clear. One of the biggest is the campus itself, which students complain "has no atmosphere," griping that "it's just a bunch of buildings" that are "disconnected from the surrounding community." Explains one undergrad, "The campus is not very inviting. . . . There's almost nowhere to relax or study outdoors between classes. The dorms are on the outskirts of campus, [so] the part where classrooms are located is pretty desolate. It's rare to see people socializing, sunbathing, playing Frisbee, etc. on campus between classes." Compounding these problems is the fact that it has "the reputation of being a commuter campus." A growing number of underclassmen—over 70 percent of last year's freshman class—also live on campus, which has bolstered a sense of community at UMBC. There is fun to be had, though. Several students write that "fun at UMBC usually consists of hanging out at the Commons and eating food, playing in the game room, or just relaxing in a friend's dorm room." Some note optimistically that "campus life is improving, especially with the addition of our on-campus bar," and others point out that the Student Events Board (which "tries to give us something cool to do as much as possible") has booked "many great events, such as Dave Chappelle, Good Charlotte, Kanye West, Third Eye Blind, Tracey Morgan, and most recently, Yellowcard." While "There are many students that go out to drink," this is not true of "everyone by any means." While "Most weekends are still pretty much dead here," students can take comfort in the fact that "Baltimore's Inner Harbor is only 5 minutes away."

Student Body

With minorities making up about one-third of the student body, UMBC is a "truly diverse" place. "The diversity is wonderful," writes one junior. "It gives everyone a chance to learn about different cultures, religions, etc." A few students also note that while "The ethnic, religious and ideological diversity on the campus means that most people can find some small set of friends or acquaintances with whom they can comfortably spend what free time they have," it also "contributes to a certain cliquishness . . . which is easily seen by the lack of great interaction between students of different nationalities and races." More than half the students are commuters who "like to go to school and go home." While commuters are "typically poorly integrated into the social fabric of the campus," they aren't totally isolated: they have a "commuter lounge where breakfast is offered for free for commuters on Tuesdays and Thursdays." UMBC's students "try to eke out a social existence however they can. Even those who live on campus, however, are typically mostly dedicated to completing their work, rapidly earning their degrees, and quickly leaving the school."

UNIVERSITY OF MARYLAND—BALTIMORE COUNTY

FINANCIAL AID: 410-455-2387 • E-MAIL: ADMISSIONS@UMBC.EDU • WEBSITE: WWW.UMBC.EDU

ADMISSIONS

Very important factors considered include: Academic GPA, rigor of secondary school record, standardized test scores. *Important factors considered include:* Application essay, class rank, recommendation(s). *Other factors considered include:* Character/personal qualities, extracurricular activities, talent/ability, volunteer work. SAT or ACT required; TOEFL required of all international applicants. High school diploma is required, and GED is accepted. *Academic units required:* 4 English, 3 math, 3 science (2 science labs), 2 foreign language, 2 social studies, 2 history, 4 academic electives. *Academic units recommended:* 4 English, 4 math, 3 science (2 science labs), 2 foreign language, 2 social studies, 2 history, 4 academic electives.

The Inside Word

The State of Maryland seems blessed with several strong, small, public universities in addition to its flagship campus at College Park. UMBC is one of those to watch; its national visibility and admissions standards are on the rise. Strong students are attracted by UMBC's emphasis on academic achievement. As a result, the Admissions Committee has grown to expect evidence of challenging academic course work throughout high school from its candidates, preferably at the honors or AP level. This competitive path will give you the best shot for admission if you're an eager learner looking for a campus where the academic experience is engaging.

FINANCIAL AID

Students should submit: FAFSA. The Princeton Review suggests that all financial aid forms be submitted as soon as possible after January 1. *Need-based scholarships/grants offered:* Pell Grant, SEOG, state scholarships/grants, private scholarships, the school's own gift aid. *Loan aid offered:* FFEL Subsidized Stafford, FFEL Unsubsidized Stafford, FFEL PLUS, Federal Perkins Loan. Applicants will be notified of awards on or about April 1.

FROM THE ADMISSIONS OFFICE

"When it comes to universities, a midsized school can be just right. Some students want the resources of a large community. Others are looking for the attention found at a smaller one. With an undergraduate population of over 9,000, UMBC can offer the best of both. There are always new people to meet and things to do—from Division I sports to more than 170 student clubs. As a research university, we offer an abundance of programs, technology, and opportunities for hands-on experiences. Yet we are small enough that students don't get lost in the shuffle. More than 80 percent of our classes have fewer than 40 students. Among public research universities, UMBC is recognized for its success in placing students in the most competitive graduate programs and careers. Of course, much of the success of UMBC has to do with the students themselves—highly motivated students who get involved in their education.

"Freshman applicants for Fall 2008 are strongly encouraged to take the new SAT or ACT; however, the Admissions Committee will consider scores from the old SAT or ACT if no new scores are available."

SELECTIVITY

Admissions Rating	**85**
# of applicants	5,405
% of applicants accepted	72
% of acceptees attending	37
# accepting a place on wait list	257
% admitted from wait list	50

FRESHMAN PROFILE

Range SAT Critical Reading	520–640
Range SAT Math	560–660
Range SAT Writing	520–620
Range ACT Composite	22–27
Minimum Paper TOEFL	550
Minimum Computer Based TOEFL	220
Average HS GPA	3.56
% graduated top 10% of class	28
% graduated top 25% of class	57
% graduated top 50% of class	87

DEADLINES

Regular application deadline	2/1
Regular notification	2/1
	rolling until 5/1
Nonfall registration?	yes

APPLICANTS ALSO LOOK AT

AND OFTEN PREFER
Johns Hopkins University, Virginia Tech

AND SOMETIMES PREFER
Pennsylvania State University—University Park, University of Delaware, University of Maryland—College Park, University of Virginia

AND RARELY PREFER
Salisbury University, St. Mary's College of Maryland, Towson University

FINANCIAL FACTS

Financial Aid Rating	**76**
Annual in-state tuition	$8,914
Annual out-of-state tuition	$17,354
Room & Board	$8,810
Books and supplies	$1,100
% frosh rec. need-based scholarship or grant aid	36
% UG rec. need-based scholarship or grant aid	36
% frosh rec. need-based self-help aid	38
% UG rec. need-based self-help aid	42
% frosh rec. any financial aid	72
% UG rec. any financial aid	57

UNIVERSITY OF MARYLAND—COLLEGE PARK

MITCHELL BUILDING, COLLEGE PARK, MD 20742-5235 • ADMISSIONS: 800-422-5867 • FAX: 301-314-9693

STUDENTS SAY

Academics

The University of Maryland—College Park is a major research institution and students see this as a mixed blessing. Undergrads gain exposure to world-class scholars doing cutting-edge work in their fields. Unfortunately, some of those same professors would rather be doing their research or teaching graduate students instead of delivering an introductory lecture to freshmen. One student warns, "These professors are paid to research and told they have to teach. Many of them don't have teaching degrees and obviously have no idea how to teach." While the problem is most pronounced in the sciences and mathematics, it is by no means universal; even in the aforementioned areas, students report some "amazing" teachers among the duds. Still, most here note that, at UMD, "You are responsible for your own education. No one will hold your hand as they did in high school." Some believe this "prepares you for the real world. You are a number, but that make[s] you try harder to stand out." Those hoping for a warmer and fuzzier education need not abandon hope, provided they can gain admission to the "living-learning programs—i.e., Honors, College Park Scholars, [and] Civicus," which all "provide opportunities for smaller classes and meeting people." College Park's many outstanding programs include the "amazing journalism program" and strong departments in education, engineering, political science, criminology, and business.

Life

The Big Three of campus life at UMD are "Greek life," "bars and/or house parties," and "football games"—both "tailgating and attending." But with "tons of things to do" here, there's more than just "a lot of parties" at College Park. According to one student, the campus "is like its own little town. We have a movie theater, tons of dorms, a huge gym, athletic fields, convenience stores, many restaurants, a bowling alley—all on campus!" UMD students also enjoy hundreds of student groups and an active intramural scene. While a student could easily fill his or her hours with campus activities, the more adventurous take frequent advantage of the school's proximity to Washington, DC, which students confirm "is not a boring city—it has a fantastic nightlife and a great subway/metro system. It's easy to get around." The city of Baltimore is also easily reached by rail. It's not surprising that many here feel that UMD's location is a big strength."

Student Body

"The great thing about a big public university is that there's no such thing as the typical student," explains a sophomore. "Lots of Jews, Catholics, African Americans, Muslims—it's a very nice melting pot," confirms a junior. UMD's College Park campus also hosts "a good mix of returning [i.e., nontraditional] students" who "seem to add to the environment." Undergrads here report that "it's common to see students of every race and background in a discussion class." When classes are finished, however, "Many students socialize and interact" only "within their 'clique,' whether it be religious, cultural, etc." While it is impossible to define a typical student on a campus this large, undergrads spot the following trends: Maryland students usually have "tons of Maryland shirts, sweatpants, and hoodies," "were in the top quarter of their high school," and "take classes seriously," but also "love to support the football and basketball teams. They party pretty hard on weekends, but buckle down when Sunday comes."

UNIVERSITY OF MARYLAND—COLLEGE PARK

FINANCIAL AID: 301-314-9000 • E-MAIL: UM-ADMIT@UMD.EDU • WEBSITE: WWW.MARYLAND.EDU

ADMISSIONS

Very important factors considered include: Academic GPA, rigor of secondary school record, standardized test scores. *Important factors considered include:* Application essay, class rank, first generation, recommendation(s), state residency, talent/ability. *Other factors considered include:* Alumni/ae relation, character/personal qualities, extracurricular activities, geographical residence, racial/ethnic status, volunteer work, work experience. SAT or ACT required; ACT with Writing component required. TOEFL required of all international applicants. High school diploma is required, and GED is accepted. *Academic units required:* 4 English, 3 math, 3 science (2 science labs), 2 foreign language, 3 social studies. *Academic units recommended:* 4 math.

The Inside Word

Many state schools make admissions decisions based on little more than the high school transcript and standardized test scores. University of Maryland is not one of these schools; the College Park Admissions Office also considers (in descending order of importance): essay, extracurricular activities, counselor/teacher recommendations, and responses to its short-answer questions. Don't give any of these application components short shrift; admissions are competitive, and each needs to be strong in order for you to have a decent shot.

FINANCIAL AID

Students should submit: FAFSA. The Princeton Review suggests that all financial aid forms be submitted as soon as possible after January 1. *Need-based scholarships/grants offered:* Pell Grant, SEOG, state scholarships/grants, private scholarships, the school's own gift aid. *Loan aid offered:* FFEL Subsidized Stafford, FFEL Unsubsidized Stafford, FFEL PLUS, Federal Perkins Loan. Applicants will be notified of awards on a rolling basis beginning or about April 1.

FROM THE ADMISSIONS OFFICE

"Commitment to excellence, to diversity, to learning—these are the hallmarks of a Maryland education. As the state's flagship campus and one of the nation's leading public universities, Maryland offers students and faculty the opportunity to come together to explore and create knowledge, to debate and discover our similarities and our differences, and to serve as a model of intellectual and cultural excellence for the state and the nation's capital. With leading programs in engineering, business, journalism, architecture, and the sciences, the university offers an outstanding educational value.

"University of Maryland—College Park will require the new SAT Reasoning Test. For students submitting an ACT score, the ACT with the Writing component is required."

SELECTIVITY

Admissions Rating	94
# of applicants	23,546
% of applicants accepted	44
% of acceptees attending	38

FRESHMAN PROFILE

Range SAT Critical Reading	570–680
Range SAT Math	600–710
Minimum Paper TOEFL	575
Minimum Computer Based TOEFL	232
Average HS GPA	3.89
% graduated top 10% of class	50
% graduated top 25% of class	83
% graduated top 50% of class	99

DEADLINES

Regular application deadline	1/20
Regular notification	4/1
Nonfall registration?	yes

APPLICANTS ALSO LOOK AT

AND OFTEN PREFER
Cornell University

AND SOMETIMES PREFER
New York University

AND RARELY PREFER
University of Maryland—Baltimore County

FINANCIAL FACTS

Financial Aid Rating	67
Annual in-state tuition	$6,566
Annual out-of-state tuition	$20,005
Room & Board	$8,562
Books and supplies	$1,002
Required fees	$1,340
% frosh rec. need-based scholarship or grant aid	23
% UG rec. need-based scholarship or grant aid	26
% frosh rec. need-based self-help aid	25
% UG rec. need-based self-help aid	28
% frosh rec. any financial aid	71
% UG rec. any financial aid	60

University of Massachusetts—Amherst

University Admissions Center, Amherst, MA 01003-9291 • Admissions: 413-545-0222 • Fax: 413-545-4312

CAMPUS LIFE

Quality of Life Rating	**63**
Fire Safety Rating	**86**
Type of school	public
Environment	town

STUDENTS

Total undergrad enrollment	19,299
% male/female	51/49
% from out of state	18
% from public high school	90
% live on campus	62
% in (# of) fraternities	4 (20)
% in (# of) sororities	4 (13)
% African American	3
% Asian	6
% Caucasian	60
% Hispanic	3
% international	1
# of countries represented	98

SURVEY SAYS . . .

Great library
Students aren't religious
Students love Amherst, MA
Great off-campus food
Student publications are popular
Lots of beer drinking
Hard liquor is popular

ACADEMICS

Academic Rating	**68**
Calendar	semester
Student/faculty ratio	18:1
Profs interesting rating	64
Profs accessible rating	64
% profs teaching	
UG courses	88
% classes taught by TAs	13
Most common	
lab size	20–29 students
Most common	
reg class size	20–29 students

MOST POPULAR MAJORS

biological and physical sciences
communications studies/speech
communication and rhetoric
psychology

STUDENTS SAY

Academics

It's all about "finding out where you fit in" at the large University of Massachusetts—Amherst, where students say the experience is "all what you make of it: If you want to party, there is one available to you almost every night. However, it is not difficult to get your work done and be successful." A pre-law student notes, "[You] can just slide by, [but] academics are challenging if [you] wants to get all A's or [are] taking honors courses." Academics are especially demanding in the engineering program, the hard sciences, the sports management program ("one of the oldest and best in the country"), and at the Isenberg School of Management. As at many big schools, "It is easy to not go to class because they are so large, although many teachers now use PRS [a handheld wireless interactive remote unit] which quizzes you and is a method of [taking] attendance during each class." Unlike many major research institutions, UMass—Amherst has a surprising number of professors who "show a passion for teaching. I have yet to see a professor who just teaches for money," a sports management major reports. By all accounts, "More than half of the professors are awesome." Students agree that "UMass—Amherst has countless opportunities for one to get involved and improve his or her leadership and responsibilities."

Life

"There is so much to do on campus here that you rarely have to leave the school to find something," students report, pointing out that, in addition to attending one of the school's ubiquitous sporting events, "You can go ice skating on campus, go to a play, see bands play, see a movie, etc." Are you sitting down? "Most of these things are also free of charge, or available for a reduced fee." When the weather permits, "Numerous people are outside doing some sort of activity, whether it's playing catch, playing a sport with a bunch of people, or just laying out in the sun. In the Southwest Residential area, there is a horseshoe that people call Southwest Beach because on nice days it is packed with hundreds of people." If you're into parties, "There is something going on every night of the week somewhere." However, "It is more than possible to stay in on a Friday night, do your laundry, and watch a movie with friends. Parties are available, but not required." To clarify: "Drinking is big here, but not totally out of control like some say. Off campus is an entirely different concept. The townhouses and off-campus apartments have been known to hold parties of over 1,200 people. Those can be a little intense." Hometown Amherst provides "great restaurants and shows." Northampton and Holyoke, both close by, are "good place[s] to go shopping."

Student Body

"There is no such thing as a typical student at UMass—Amherst." An undergraduate population of over 19,000 makes that impossible; however, students do seem to fall into a few readily identified groups. There are "plenty of students who are here strictly for academics," "people who are here for the party scene," and "a lot of people who came here for academics but fell into the party scene." Most learn to balance fun and work; those who don't exit long before graduation. Students also "tend to fit the mold of their residence," undergrads tell us. One student writes, "Southwest houses students of mainstream culture. Students there can be seen wearing everything from UMass—Amherst sweats to couture. Students in Central (especially Upper Central) tend to be the 'hippie' or 'scene' type kid[s]. Northeast houses . . . the more reserved types. Orchard Hill typically houses the more quiet types as well. . . . The kids in Sylvan are those who couldn't get into their first-choice dorm and "spend their time . . . wishing that they lived somewhere else."

UNIVERSITY OF MASSACHUSETTS—AMHERST

FINANCIAL AID: 413-545-0801 • E-MAIL: MAIL@ADMISSIONS.UMASS.EDU • WEBSITE: WWW.UMASS.EDU

ADMISSIONS

Very important factors considered include: Academic GPA, rigor of secondary school record. *Important factors considered include:* Standardized test scores. *Other factors considered include:* Application essay, character/personal qualities, class rank, extracurricular activities, first generation, geographical residence, level of applicant's interest, racial/ethnic status, recommendation(s), state residency, talent/ability, volunteer work, work experience. SAT or ACT required; ACT with Writing component recommended. TOEFL required of all international applicants. High school diploma is required, and GED is accepted. *Academic units required:* 4 English, 3 math, 3 science (2 science labs), 2 foreign language, 2 social studies, 2 academic electives.

The Inside Word

University of Massachusetts—Amherst requires applicants to identify a first-choice and a second-choice major; admissions standards are tougher in the school's most prestigious programs (such as engineering, business, communications and journalism, economics, computer science, and sports management). It is possible to be admitted for your second-choice major but not your first; it is also possible to be admitted as an "undeclared" student if you fail to gain admission via your chosen majors. You can transfer into either major later, although doing so will require you to excel in your freshman and sophomore classes.

FINANCIAL AID

Students should submit: FAFSA. The Princeton Review suggests that all financial aid forms be submitted as soon as possible after January 1. *Need-based scholarships/grants offered:* Pell Grant, SEOG, state scholarships/grants, private scholarships, the school's own gift aid. *Loan aid offered:* Direct Subsidized Stafford, Direct Unsubsidized Stafford, Direct PLUS, Federal Perkins Loan, state loans. Applicants will be notified of awards on a rolling basis beginning or about April 1.

FROM THE ADMISSIONS OFFICE

"The University of Massachusetts—Amherst is the largest public university in New England, offering its students an almost limitless variety of academic programs and activities. Nearly 100 majors are offered, including a unique program called Bachelor's Degree with Individual Concentration (BDIC) in which students create their own program of study. The outstanding full-time faculty of over 1,100 includes novelist John Wideman, Pulitzer Prize–winners Madeleine Blais and James Tate, National Medal of Science–winner Lynn Margulis, and nine members of the prestigious National Academies. Students can take courses through the honors program and sample classes at nearby Amherst, Hampshire, Mount Holyoke, and Smith Colleges at no extra charge. First-year students participate in the Freshmen Year Experience with opportunities to explore every possible interest through residential life.

"The university's extensive library system is the largest at any public institution in the Northeast. The Center for Student Development brings together more than 200 clubs and organizations, fraternities and sororities, multicultural and religious centers. The campus completes in NCAA Division I sports for men and women, with teams winning national recognition. Award-winning student-operated businesses, the largest college daily newspaper in the region, and an active student government provide hands-on experiences. About 5,000 students a year participate in the intramural sports program. The picturesque New England town of Amherst offers shopping and dining, and the ski slopes of western Massachusetts and southern Vermont are close by.

"SAT or ACT scores are required for admission to the university. The school takes a holistic view of the student's application package, and considers these scores as only part of the evaluation criteria. Additionally, any Advanced Placement, Honors, and SAT Subject Test scores are considered when reviewing each applicant. Three consecutive years of increased applications has made admission more selective."

SELECTIVITY

Admissions Rating	**83**
# of applicants	22,451
% of applicants accepted	71
% of acceptees attending	26
# accepting a place on wait list	290
% admitted from wait list	41

FRESHMAN PROFILE

Range SAT Critical Reading	510–620
Range SAT Math	530–640
Minimum Paper TOEFL	550
Minimum Computer Based TOEFL	213
Average HS GPA	3.46
% graduated top 10% of class	23
% graduated top 25% of class	58
% graduated top 50% of class	94

DEADLINES

Regular application deadline	1/15
Regular notification	rolling
Nonfall registration?	yes

APPLICANTS ALSO LOOK AT AND OFTEN PREFER
Boston College, Boston University, Tufts University

AND SOMETIMES PREFER
Northeastern University, Syracuse University, University of Connecticut

AND RARELY PREFER
Quinnipiac University, University of Hartford, University of Rhode Island

FINANCIAL FACTS

Financial Aid Rating	**72**
Annual in-state tuition	$1,714
Annual out-of-state tuition	$9,937
Room & Board	$6,517
Books and supplies	$1,000
Required fees	$7,881
% frosh rec. need-based scholarship or grant aid	32
% UG rec. need-based scholarship or grant aid	39
% frosh rec. need-based self-help aid	36
% UG rec. need-based self-help aid	46
% frosh rec. any financial aid	67
% UG rec. any financial aid	73

UNIVERSITY OF MIAMI

OFFICE OF ADMISSION, PO BOX 248025, CORAL GABLES, FL 33124-4616 • ADMISSIONS: 305-284-4323 • FAX: 305-284-2507

CAMPUS LIFE

Quality of Life Rating	**96**
Fire Safety Rating	**81**
Type of school	private
Environment	town

STUDENTS

Total undergrad enrollment	9,741
% male/female	41/59
% from out of state	45
% live on campus	42
% in (# of) fraternities	13 (14)
% in (# of) sororities	13 (10)
% African American	9
% Asian	6
% Caucasian	52
% Hispanic	24
% international	6

SURVEY SAYS . . .

Career services are great
Great library
Athletic facilities are great
Diverse student types on campus
Campus feels safe
Everyone loves the Hurricanes

ACADEMICS

Academic Rating	**86**
Calendar	semester
Student/faculty ratio	13:1
Profs interesting rating	77
Profs accessible rating	80
Most common lab size	10–19 students
Most common reg class size	10–19 students

STUDENTS SAY

Academics

University of Miami students are convinced that their school offers "the perfect blend of academics, athletics, lifestyle, culture, and weather." You probably already know about the "beautiful campus, fabulous climate, and unyielding sense of school spirit" at Miami, but are you aware of "the world-class faculty and innumerable research and internship opportunities across disciplines"? "Academics are the sleeper at UM," undergrads here agree. This "perfect-sized school" offers "a great communication program" as well as solid programs in biology, marine science, film, and business. In all areas, students benefit from "amazing academic resources and a variety of learning tools. Also, internships, internships, internships! Most programs require them now," ensuring that "students of all different fields get hands-on opportunities to gain experience before going out into the 'real world.'" Undergrads also note that "thanks to a low student/teacher ratio in most classes, you can build a relationship with your professors, valuable for future graduate school applications and resume references." While "some students come here merely to party and enjoy the city," others "are extremely dedicated," and are well served by a school "that is working hard to increase the value of the degree for its students."

Life

"Studying doesn't seem like such a chore when you're sitting outside under the sun on a 70 degree day in January," UM undergrads agree, noting with glee that "while students elsewhere are wrapped in blankets trying to stay warm, students at the University of Miami are enjoying beautiful weather year-round." It also helps that "the campus is absolutely breathtaking. I swear, each day I walk to class I have to remind myself it's college, not a resort. It makes it a joy to get out of bed and get to class when you get to stroll past the fountains and under the sun into the air-conditioned environment of knowledge. With patio sets at each school and library, there's no excuse not to open a book. Here we study and enjoy the weather." When it's time to unwind, students hang out by "the lake in the middle of campus surrounded by palm trees" or work out in "the state-of-the-art gym." Hurricanes football is the biggest on-campus draw, and "football season is crazy, especially our week-long homecoming celebration." There are also "lots of free activities" offered by the school. For most students, though, "Social life is primarily focused off campus, at Coconut Grove and South Beach, each filled with clubs, bars, restaurants, shops, and movies."

Student Body

University of Miami has a reputation for being "a rich kid's school," and it's true that "you will see parking lots filled with Beemers and Escalades and shoulders slung with Balenciaga, Louis Vuitton, and Coach and eyes shaded by Versace, D&G, and Chanel glasses to name a few." But it's also true that "University of Miami is one of the most diverse colleges in the nation. One will find all types of ethnicities, religious and political faiths, as well as cultural backgrounds" here. The Hispanic and Latino communities are substantial, and there are "many international students." As one student puts it, "Miami is like living in a public-service announcement: beautiful setting, racially diverse people, [courses] available in other languages. The average student is upper-middle-class, is at least bilingual, studies during the week and goes out Thursday through Saturday, complains about the freezing weather on 65-degree days, and knows how to snag a private study room in the library and what clubs to go to in South Beach."

FINANCIAL AID: 305-284-5212 • WEBSITE: WWW.MIAMI.EDU/ADMISSIONS

ADMISSIONS

Very important factors considered include: Application essay, character/personal qualities, class rank, extracurricular activities, recommendation(s), rigor of secondary school record, standardized test scores, talent/ability. *Important factors considered include:* Alumni/ae relation, volunteer work. *Other factors considered include:* Geographical residence, racial/ethnic status, work experience. SAT or ACT required; TOEFL required of all international applicants. High school diploma is required, and GED is accepted. *Academic units recommended:* 4 English, 4 math, 3 science (2 science labs), 2 foreign language, 3 social studies, 2 history.

The Inside Word

The University of Miami's campaign to overcome its reputation as a "football school" is an unqualified success. Each recent academic year has seen an increase in applications and UM's selectivity is on the rise. The school partially attributes this accomplishment to its alumni and gladly repays them by giving legacies a boost during the admissions process. Of course having a 'Cane for a parent isn't enough; students must demonstrate achievement in arduous classes, intellectual promise, and strong moral character.

FINANCIAL AID

Students should submit: FAFSA. The Princeton Review suggests that all financial aid forms be submitted as soon as possible after January 1. *Need-based scholarships/grants offered:* Pell Grant, SEOG, state scholarships/grants, private scholarships, the school's own gift aid, Federal Nursing Scholarship. *Loan aid offered:* FFEL Subsidized Stafford, FFEL Unsubsidized Stafford, FFEL PLUS, Federal Perkins Loan, Federal Nursing Loan, Signature Loan (Alternative). Applicants will be notified of awards on a rolling basis beginning or about March 15. Federal Work-Study Program available. Institutional employment available. Off-campus job opportunities are excellent.

FROM THE ADMISSIONS OFFICE

"The University of Miami in Coral Gables, Florida, is an innovative private research university in a location unlike any other in the country. Located 10 miles from the vibrant international city of Miami, UM's 9,000 undergraduates come from every state and 114 nations, allowing people of many cultures to challenge and champion each other. Faculty work closely with students, and internships and research experiences are integral to academic life. Students work hard as community volunteers and exert leadership in a range of lively clubs and organizations, including the student-managed TV station, radio station, and newspaper.

"The University of Miami will accept either the new SAT or the old SAT (administered prior to March 2005 and without a Writing component), as well as the ACT with or without the Writing component."

SELECTIVITY

Admissions Rating	95
# of applicants	18,507
% of applicants accepted	42
% of acceptees attending	26
# of early decision applicants	811
% accepted early decision	47

FRESHMAN PROFILE

Range SAT Critical Reading	570–670
Range SAT Math	590–680
Range ACT Composite	25–30
Minimum Paper TOEFL	550
Minimum Computer Based TOEFL	213
Average HS GPA	4.04
% graduated top 10% of class	62
% graduated top 25% of class	88
% graduated top 50% of class	98

DEADLINES

Early decision application deadline	11/1
Early decision notification	12/20
Regular application deadline	2/1
Regular notification	4/15
Nonfall registration?	yes

APPLICANTS ALSO LOOK AT

AND OFTEN PREFER
Duke University

AND SOMETIMES PREFER
Boston University, New York University, University of Southern California, Vanderbilt University

AND RARELY PREFER
Florida State University

FINANCIAL FACTS

Financial Aid Rating	78
Annual tuition	$30,732
Room & Board	$9,334
Books and supplies	$830
Required fees	$556
% frosh rec. need-based scholarship or grant aid	55
% UG rec. need-based scholarship or grant aid	52
% frosh rec. need-based self-help aid	41
% UG rec. need-based self-help aid	43

UNIVERSITY OF MICHIGAN—ANN ARBOR

1220 STUDENT ACTIVITIES BUILDING, ANN ARBOR, MI 48109-1316 • ADMISSIONS: 734-764-7433 • FAX: 734-936-0740

STUDENTS SAY

Academics
"Steeped in academics, brimming with extracurriculars, full of opportunity for internships, happily obsessed with partying and football, and set in a fantastically beautiful city." That's the University of Michigan—Ann Arbor (UM) in a nutshell, its students tell us. Academically, the university's "strong suits are its research and its diverse offerings. You can find any club, any class, any research job you'd like. If you can't? Start it. There's funding available." As at most large universities, "It's hard to imagine a school that provides more academically, politically, and socially than Michigan," but "You have to be motivated. The professors don't plan their days around you. But if you really want something and go after it, for the most part, they want to help you." The reward for your perseverance comes from "tremendous academics. . . . It amazes me that I can take classes with English professors who have won national teaching awards, history classes with professors who are known as experts on the Middle East, and political science classes with professors who have helped develop completely new (and now prevalent) ways to look at world politics." Students warn to expect a "challenge from the rigor of the academics." They say, "Most students come here expecting to be blown away by their classes—and they are." Those who brave the challenge and see their way through to graduation experience another windfall: A great alumni network. Michigan grads "are proud to admit their alma mater and do everything they can to help out students and graduates."

Life
Michigan students tell us that "without classes, life here would be the bomb. There is so much going on every day—games, shows, concerts, parties, volunteering, work, you name it." Athletics have a firm grip on the campus; students describe the intercollegiate teams as "amazing! What other school in the country has very good basketball, football, and hockey teams?" Intramurals are "also huge. Most students are very physically active; the gym's always packed." Campus entertainment offers a lot more than ball games, though. One undergraduate reports, "This year there was the Royal Shakespeare Company's residency on campus and the opportunity to see the Bolshoi Ballet perform for a student discount rate of less than 10 dollars." Students love Ann Arbor, calling it "the best college town in the Midwest," with "lots of little quaint shops, a good shopping mall, hundreds of amazing restaurants, and two movie theaters." Plus, Ann Arbor is a very socially active town. If there's a cause, there's someone at UM fighting for it." Students will put down the protest signs, however, to pick up a beer. As one undergrad explains, "There's always a place to party on the weekend . . . or weekday, whether it be a Greek house, which are ancient and historic houses, or a block party just off campus."

Student Body
"It's amazing how diverse UM is," students tell us, with a population that includes "your run-of-the-mill spoiled, rich kids; the anti-intellectual frat boys and sorority girls; the snobby East Coasters; . . . the creative, individualistic kids; the general musicians (this includes marching-banders and the 'garage band' types); the engineering kids; the stoners; and the general alcoholics." Students report that "this school has a little bit of everything, and there is very little mixing between groups. It's hard to build bridges between social groups here, though certainly possible if you try." While not all students are affluent, the well heeled are among the student body's most conspicuous individuals. One undergraduate writes, "Many students flaunt their wealth, from the frat boy or rich kid that dresses like a Queer Eye for the Straight Guy makeover to the rich girl who walks with a trendy cup of coffee in her right hand and a cell phone in her left."

FINANCIAL AID: 734-763-6600 • WEBSITE: WWW.ADMISSIONS.UMICH.EDU, WWW.FINAID.UMICH.EDU

ADMISSIONS

Very important factors considered include: Rigor of secondary school record. *Important factors considered include:* Application essay, character/personal qualities, recommendation(s), standardized test scores, state residency, talent/ability. *Other factors considered include:* Alumni/ae relation, class rank, extracurricular activities, geographical residence, level of applicant's interest, volunteer work, work experience. SAT or ACT required; ACT with Writing component required. TOEFL required of all international applicants. High school diploma is required, and GED is accepted. *Academic units required:* 4 English, 3 math, 3 science, 2 foreign language, 3 social studies. *Academic units recommended:* 4 English, 4 math, 4 science (1 science lab), 4 foreign language, 3 social studies, 2 history, 2 academic electives.

The Inside Word

Making the cut at Michigan is tough—and it is getting even tougher for out-of-state applicants, though the university definitely wants them in large numbers. There are simply loads of applicants from outside the state. If being a Wolverine is high on your list of choices, make sure you're well prepared, and since Michigan admits on a rolling basis, apply early! Michigan establishes an enormous wait list each year. Controversies surrounding Michigan's approach to affirmative action have resulted in significant changes in the manner in which candidates are evaluated, with greater emphasis now given to aspects of candidates' backgrounds that are not quantified by grades and scores.

FINANCIAL AID

Students should submit: FAFSA, CSS/Financial Aid PROFILE, Noncustodial PROFILE, parent and student 1040. Regular filing deadline is April 30. The Princeton Review suggests that all financial aid forms be submitted as soon as possible after January 1. *Need-based scholarships/grants offered:* Pell Grant, SEOG, state scholarships/grants, private scholarships, the school's own gift aid. *Loan aid offered:* Direct Subsidized Stafford, Direct Unsubsidized Stafford, Direct PLUS, Federal Perkins Loan, Federal Nursing Loan, state loans, college/university loans from institutional funds, Michigan Loan Program, Health Professional Student Loans. Applicants will be notified of awards on a rolling basis beginning or about March 15.

FROM THE ADMISSIONS OFFICE

"Michigan is a place of incredible possibility. Students shape that possibility according to their diverse interests, goals, energy, and initiative. Undergraduate education is in the academic spotlight at Michigan, offering more than 226 fields of study in 11 schools and colleges; more than 150 first-year seminars with 20 or fewer students taught by senior faculty; composition classes of 20 or fewer students; more than 1,200 first- and second-year students in undergraduate research partnerships with faculty; and numerous service learning programs linking academics with volunteerism. Some introductory courses have large lectures, but these are combined with labs or small group discussions where students get plenty of individualized attention. A Michigan degree is one of distinction and promise; graduates are successful in medical, law, and graduate schools all over the nation and world. A year after graduation, more than 95 percent of U-M alumni report that they are in the "next step" of their career—whether that is graduate or professional school, working, or volunteering.

"Students applying as freshmen for Summer 2008 or later will be required to submit the results from the new SAT or ACT (with Writing component). At this time, it has not been determined by the university how the Writing sub score will be integrated into the school's review process."

SELECTIVITY
Admissions Rating	96
# of applicants	25,806
% of applicants accepted	47
% of acceptees attending	44
# accepting a place on wait list	2,776

FRESHMAN PROFILE
Range SAT Critical Reading	580–690
Range SAT Math	630–730
Range ACT Composite	27–31
Minimum Paper TOEFL	570
Minimum Computer Based TOEFL	230
Average HS GPA	3.72
% graduated top 10% of class	90
% graduated top 25% of class	99
% graduated top 50% of class	100

DEADLINES
Regular application deadline	2/1
Regular notification	rolling
Nonfall registration?	yes

APPLICANTS ALSO LOOK AT

AND OFTEN PREFER
Brown University, Duke University, Harvard College, Princeton University, Stanford University, University of Pennsylvania

AND SOMETIMES PREFER
Cornell University, New York University, Northwestern University, University of Notre Dame

AND RARELY PREFER
Pennsylvania State University—University Park

FINANCIAL FACTS
Financial Aid Rating	91
Annual in-state tuition	$9,609
Annual out-of-state tuition	$28,381
Room & Board	$7,838
Books and supplies	$1,002
Required fees	$189
% frosh rec. need-based scholarship or grant aid	26
% UG rec. need-based scholarship or grant aid	26
% frosh rec. need-based self-help aid	49
% UG rec. need-based self-help aid	47

UNIVERSITY OF MINNESOTA—TWIN CITIES

240 WILLIAMSON HALL, 231 PILLSBURY DRIVE SOUTHEAST, MINNEAPOLIS, MN 55455-0213 • ADMISSIONS: 612-625-2008

CAMPUS LIFE

Quality of Life Rating	**78**
Fire Safety Rating	**60***
Type of school	public
Environment	metropolis

STUDENTS

Total undergrad enrollment	28,645
% male/female	47/53
% from out of state	27
% live on campus	22
# of fraternities	32
# of sororities	17
% African American	5
% Asian	10
% Caucasian	79
% Hispanic	2
% Native American	1
% international	2

SURVEY SAYS . . .
Great library
Athletic facilities are great
Students love Minneapolis, MN
Great off-campus food
Student publications are popular

ACADEMICS

Academic Rating	**73**
Calendar	semester
Student/faculty ratio	15:1
Profs interesting rating	65
Profs accessible rating	68
Most common lab size	10–19 students
Most common reg class size	20–29 students

STUDENTS SAY

Academics

At the University of Minnesota—Twin Cities, students love "the opportunities and resources available by being a Big Ten school. We have amazing research, highly awarded faculty, lots of school spirit, internship opportunities, and a high public visibility." It's "up to you to carve your own path" here—no one is going to hold your hand, although, at least, "The advising facilities are excellent and the people who work there really do want to help"—but in return for their independent efforts, students enjoy "sooo many options and opportunities." A "strong medical program," a "great veterinary program," and an "excellent business school" are just some of the many top choices here; explains one student, "There really seems to be something for everyone. For students, that means you can come here not knowing what you want to do with your life, try out a bunch of stuff, and figure it out." The U's location yields some plum benefits, including "access to lots of local businesses, which translates into lots of opportunities after graduation." Students report that "the U does a great job trying to help students obtain enough experience and opportunities to make their post-college life better" through research opportunities and internships. Undergrads also love the "great study abroad and exchange programs."

Life

"The greatest thing about the U is always having something different to do," students tell us. They enumerate their many options: "In Minneapolis–St. Paul, the choices are endless: we've got Twins, Vikings, Timberwolves, and Wild games; Gopher athletics (hockey is huge here); concerts; movie theaters; special events like the St. Paul Winter Carnival; and tons of lakes and parks to visit during the summer. We also have our own separate campus community, where you just have regular old college students hanging out at their house or the bar with friends." The school also has "student groups for every imaginable interest, and if you don't find one you like, you can start your own with five people and $20." Some here feel that "the social life is a little hurting" due to the large, diffuse nature of the student body, and they are glad that the university increased support for the Greek community, "because it helps in centralizing the social scene." Others are good with things as they stand. Just about everyone appreciates the "great infrastructure of tunnels and skyways to get between buildings" and "the wonderful campus bus system, without which it would be impossible to get around this big, spread-out campus." These assets are especially important during the long, cold winters, which definitely put a damper on certain extracurricular activities. "Party-hopping is difficult during the winter because it is so cold outside," one undergrad explains.

Student Body

"Counting undergrad and grad students, there are about 55,000 in total, making the campus is a city to itself," writes one undergrad. There is every type of person here." Another observes, "One good thing about a school this size is that there is a little something for everyone. You can show up to class in sweats or in a suit, with blonde hair or green, and no one will look at you funny. Everyone can find a place here where they will fit in. The only problem you will encounter is that if you meet someone cool, you may never see them again. You really have to make an effort if you want to make new friends." Because of its location, "Nearly everyone is from either Minnesota or Wisconsin" and "There are many Somalis and Hmong among the minority population." The standard outfit here? "Backpack, coat, mittens, and a funny hat."

UNIVERSITY OF MINNESOTA—TWIN CITIES

Fax: 612-626-1693 • FINANCIAL AID: 612-624-1665 • WEBSITE: ADMISSIONS.TC.UMN.EDU

ADMISSIONS

Very important factors considered include: Academic GPA, class rank, rigor of secondary school record, standardized test scores. *Other factors considered include:* Alumni/ae relation, character/personal qualities, extracurricular activities, first generation, geographical residence, racial/ethnic status, talent/ability, volunteer work, work experience. SAT or ACT required; ACT with Writing component required. TOEFL required of all international applicants. High school diploma is required, and GED is accepted. *Academic units required:* 4 English, 3 math, 3 science, 2 foreign language, 3 social studies, 1 history.

The Inside Word

Despite what looks to be a fairly choosy admissions rate, it's the sheer volume of applicants that creates a selective situation at Minnesota. Only those with weak course selections and inconsistent academic records need to work up a sweat over getting admitted.

FINANCIAL AID

Students should submit: FAFSA, institution's own financial aid form. The Princeton Review suggests that all financial aid forms be submitted as soon as possible after January 1. *Need-based scholarships/grants offered:* Pell Grant, SEOG, state scholarships/grants, private scholarships, the school's own gift aid, Federal Nursing Scholarship. *Loan aid offered:* Direct Subsidized Stafford, Direct Unsubsidized Stafford, Direct PLUS, Federal Perkins Loan, Federal Nursing Loan, state loans, college/university loans from institutional funds.

FROM THE ADMISSIONS OFFICE

"The University of Minnesota is one of the nation's top research universities. That means your college experience will be enhanced by world-renowned faculty, state-of-the-art learning facilities, and an unprecedented variety of options (147 majors and thousands of challenging courses).

"Hands-on courses, mentor programs, volunteer opportunities, career counseling, internships, and research opportunities are part of the U of M experience. Plus, our Learning Abroad Center offers one of the nation's largest study abroad programs, with over 300 opportunities in 60 countries: You can study art in Florence, agriculture in Morocco, or development in Kenya.

"You will find rolling green space, historic architecture, and breathtaking views of the Minneapolis skyline and Mississippi river right on campus. With a wealth of cultural, career, social, and recreational opportunities in the Twin Cities, there's no better place to earn your college degree! The Twin Cities metro is home to 18 *Fortune* 500 companies, and a recent survey ranked our area in the nation's top 10 in the 'Bohemian Index' for the concentration of creative people.

"The University of Minnesota is a world-class, Big Ten research university. We offer a fantastic education and prestigious degree at a competitive price. Residents of Minnesota benefit from in-state tuition. Minnesota residents may also qualify for the University of Minnesota Founders Free Tuition Program, which combines federal, state, and University grants to cover 100 percent of tuition and fees. Details and eligibility requirements are at Founders.umn.edu. Residents of Kansas, Michigan, Missouri, Nebraska, North Dakota, South Dakota, Wisconsin, or Manitoba pay tuition rates significantly below nonresident tuition. Last year, we also awarded over $9 million in 4-year scholarship packages.

"Scores from either the ACT or the SAT are required to complete your application."

SELECTIVITY

Admissions Rating	88
# of applicants	24,660
% of applicants accepted	57
% of acceptees attending	38

FRESHMAN PROFILE

Range SAT Critical Reading	540–670
Range SAT Math	580–690
Range ACT Composite	23–28
Minimum Paper TOEFL	550
Minimum Computer Based TOEFL	213
% graduated top 10% of class	39
% graduated top 25% of class	77
% graduated top 50% of class	97

DEADLINES

Nonfall registration?	yes

APPLICANTS ALSO LOOK AT AND OFTEN PREFER

Northwestern University, University of Michigan—Ann Arbor

FINANCIAL FACTS

Financial Aid Rating	83
Annual in-state tuition	$9,173
Annual out-of-state tuition	$20,803
Room & Board	$6,996
Books and supplies	$900
% frosh rec. need-based scholarship or grant aid	37
% UG rec. need-based scholarship or grant aid	34
% frosh rec. need-based self-help aid	42
% UG rec. need-based self-help aid	43

UNIVERSITY OF MISSISSIPPI

145 MARTINDALE, UNIVERSITY, MS 38677 • ADMISSIONS: 662-915-7226 • FAX: 662-915-5869

STUDENTS SAY
Academics

The University of Mississippi (or "Ole Miss," as it is familiarly known) is an institution "steeped in rich traditions" that its students praise for having "great people, a beautiful campus, and a hospitable community." Familial connections and affection for the school's past (which includes graduating "numerous senators and representatives, among them Trent Lott, Thad Cochran, and Roger Wicker") draw many to Ole Miss, but that doesn't mean the school is content to rest on its history. On the contrary, in recent years the school has taken major strides toward "making itself one of America's great public universities." The 1997 establishment of the Croft Institute for International Studies, "recently ranked the second best in the nation by the State Department in the areas of job placement," represents one such step. Another was the 1999 creation of the Lott Leadership Institute; together the two resources "provide unique and challenging fields of study that help distinguish Ole Miss academically." Solid programs in journalism, music, accounting, forensic chemistry, engineering, pharmacy, premedicine, and Southern studies help round out the academic picture. Those who can gain access to the Sally McDonnell Barkesdale Honors College should take advantage of the opportunity; the program "is so strongly supported by the administration and alumni that you can literally eat dinner with 14 other honor students and a visiting senator, and then the next day go talk with a visiting ambassador about opportunities for working with the State Department. Honors College students receive many perks, including the chance to go on a 'ventures' trip to a major city, paid for by the Honors College."

Life

Undergrads at Mississippi are generally a content lot. As one student happily exclaimed, "The school spirit and pride people have at Ole Miss is contagious." Indeed, many undergrads view the university as, "a great Southern school with amazing traditions and great standards that knows how to have a good time." Popular traditions include pregaming in The Grove, "a social setting jam-packed with friends and families all bound by the same values of hospitality and friendship." An "extremely popular" Greek system is another tradition that hasn't lost any steam; for many undergrads, "Most all activities outside of class or studying are centered on Greek life," which includes not only "an enormous amount of drinking and partying," but also "being among the most involved and active people on campus." Hometown Oxford "may be small, but there is always something to do. Oxford has some of the best restaurants in the South. Also, Oxford gets great live music, poetry readings, and famous authors frequently. Lake Sardis is also nearby. Many people go boating on free days."

Student Body

Ole Miss is home to more than 12,000 undergraduates, a size that makes generalizations about the entire population difficult and necessarily imprecise. That said, students here detect an undeniable presence of "students who are pretty wealthy and take pride in that"; this group is personified by the "preppy girl or boy wearing expensive labels and going to school to follow in his or her mom or dad's footsteps." Sums up one undergrad, "Ole Miss students are charming and very social; it is as if everyone has been raised attending cocktail parties and debutante balls forever. We are primarily conservative White Southerners who are unashamed of our Southern culture and heritage who flock to the Oxford campus. Those who fit this mold love Ole Miss; [others] seem to view the Southern elitism as 'snobbery.'" This perceived snobbery may be at least a partial result of the fact that the school is "not very diverse."

FINANCIAL AID: 662-915-7175 • E-MAIL: ADMISSIONS@OLEMISS.EDU • WEBSITE: WWW.OLEMISS.EDU

ADMISSIONS

Very important factors considered include: Academic GPA, rigor of secondary school record. *Important factors considered include:* Class rank, standardized test scores. *Other factors considered include:* Alumni/ae relation, state residency, talent/ability. TOEFL required of all international applicants. High school diploma is required, and GED is accepted. *Academic units required:* 4 English, 3 math, 3 science (3 science labs), 1 foreign language, 1 social studies, 2 history, 1 academic elective. *Academic units recommended:* 4 math, 4 science, 2 foreign language, 2 social studies.

The Inside Word

While Ole Miss offers students tremendous educational opportunities, the university's admissions policies are less than strenuous. Applicants who demonstrate moderate success in college prep curricula will most likely secure admittance.

FINANCIAL AID

Students should submit: FAFSA. The Princeton Review suggests that all financial aid forms be submitted as soon as possible after January 1. *Need-based scholarships/grants offered:* Pell Grant, SEOG, state scholarships/grants, private scholarships, the school's own gift aid. *Loan aid offered:* FFEL Subsidized Stafford, FFEL Unsubsidized Stafford, FFEL PLUS, Federal Perkins Loan, college/university loans from institutional funds. Applicants will be notified of awards on a rolling basis beginning or about April 1. Off-campus job opportunities are good.

FROM THE ADMISSIONS OFFICE

"The flagship university of the state, The University of Mississippi, widely known as Ole Miss, offers extraordinary opportunities through more than 100 areas of study, including programs such as the Sally McDonnell Barksdale Honors College and the Croft Institute for International Studies. UM students are the only public university students in the state who have the opportunity to be tapped by the nation's oldest and most prestigious honor society, Phi Beta Kappa. Strong academic programs and a rich and varied campus life have helped Ole Miss graduate 24 Rhodes Scholars, and 11 Truman Scholars. Since 1998 alone, UM has produced five Goldwater Scholars, a Marshall Scholar, and four Fulbright Scholars.

"The campus is diverse; 32 percent come from other states and countries and 13 percent are African American. Recent significant campus improvements include the $25 million Gertrude Ford Performing Arts Center and the privately funded Paris-Yates Chapel and Peddle Bell Tower. UM ranks thirty-third in the nation among public universities for endowment per student. Ole Miss is home to 20 research centers, including the National Center for Justice and the Rule of Law, which provides training on investigating and prosecuting cybercrime; the William Winter Institute for Racial Reconciliation; and the National Center for Natural Products Research.

"The university is located in Oxford, consistently recognized as a great college town and as a center for writers and other artists. Like Ole Miss, Oxford is modest in size and large in the opportunities it provides residents, offering many of the advantages of a larger place in a friendly and open environment.

"Students applying for Fall 2008 will be allowed to take either version of the SAT and are not required to take the ACT Writing section. The university will not consider the writing section of either exam when evaluating students for admission, but certain specialty programs may request these scores."

SELECTIVITY

Admissions Rating	86
# of applicants	7,771
% of applicants accepted	84
% of acceptees attending	40

FRESHMAN PROFILE

Range SAT Critical Reading	460–580
Range SAT Math	460–590
Range ACT Composite	20–26
Minimum Paper TOEFL	550
Minimum Computer Based TOEFL	213
% graduated top 25% of class	47
% graduated top 50% of class	74

DEADLINES

Regular application deadline	7/20
Regular notification	rolling
Nonfall registration?	yes

FINANCIAL FACTS

Financial Aid Rating	72
Annual in-state tuition	$4,602
Annual out-of-state tuition	$10,566
Room & Board	$5,892
Books and supplies	$1,000
% frosh rec. need-based scholarship or grant aid	21
% UG rec. need-based scholarship or grant aid	26
% frosh rec. need-based self-help aid	20
% UG rec. need-based self-help aid	29
% frosh rec. any financial aid	72
% UG rec. any financial aid	75

UNIVERSITY OF MISSOURI—ROLLA

106 PARKER HALL, ROLLA, MO 65409 • ADMISSIONS: 573-341-4165 • FAX: 573-341-4082

STUDENTS SAY

Academics

Prospective University of Missouri—Rolla students should prepare for "mental boot camp," because hard work is the norm at this engineering, mathematics, science, and business-intensive school. In return for their efforts, UMR undergrads receive an education from "one of the best engineering schools in the country" at state-school prices. While students note that "some classes can be more difficult than anticipated due to the fact that English is not the professor's native tongue" (an issue being addressed internally by the university), they give Rolla professors high marks overall. That's because professors "do a good job of explaining the subjects to the students. Even though the subjects are almost always technical and difficult, they usually try to make sense [of them] and teach well." The "free tutoring sessions available for a variety of courses where the various instructors of that course and other upper-level students from that major help you understand the material" also help a lot. UMR undergrads appreciate the fact that Rolla excels not only in the expected areas of engineering (such as electrical and mechanical engineering), but also in some less common disciplines. A "very good program in ceramic engineering, which is not present at all in most engineering schools," as well as "one of the nation's very few mining engineering degrees," earns students' praise. Students also love the Career Opportunity Center, which "really goes above and beyond to help students find internships and full-time job opportunities and prepare for interviews."

Life

"Students have to dedicate a good portion of their time to studies" at UMR, largely because of the homework-intensive nature of the school's popular engineering programs. During the week, "The mood is all about school. On the weekend, a lot of people still focus on school, but there are a lot of parties and events, especially at the Greek houses." As far as other on-campus diversions are concerned, "Lots of events are planned, such as film screenings, comedians, Broadway plays, music performances, concerts, trivia, and professional meetings." Clubs and organizations "are very common." "You have to make your own fun," possibly a result of the fact that hometown Rolla "is a small hick town with nothing to do: no big sports teams, no shopping, no entertainment, no nice restaurants. It's not the place to be for a city kid." Outdoor enthusiasts find Rolla more accommodating because it "has excellent outdoor possibilities, everything from hiking to camping and skeet shooting. Lots of open federal lands and national forests" add to the outdoorsy appeal. Students add that "we are a little over an hour from St. Louis, Columbia, and Springfield, so if the night is slow, we always have somewhere to go."

Student Body

About 70 percent of UMR students graduate with engineering degrees. As a result, Rolla is characterized by some as "a school of nerds: run by the nerd and for the nerd. Geeks of all looks, smells, and intelligence thrive here." The most antisocial among them are the "computer nerds who play online games all day and have Halo tournaments in their dorms." Others are more outgoing; one undergrad reports, "There are two types of people at UMR: the social people who go out and have fun and get highly involved on campus and the introverts." But fear not: "There are enough fun, normal people on campus to balance out the weird ones." While Rolla is relatively lacking in racial diversity, the school is "geographically diverse, with students from rural areas, big cities, and foreign countries." Gender is another issue: With an almost 3:1 male/female ratio, "girls are often flocked to and very often get a lot of unwanted attention."

FINANCIAL AID: 800-522-0938 • E-MAIL: ADMISSIONS@UMR.EDU • WEBSITE: WWW.UMR.EDU

ADMISSIONS

Very important factors considered include: Academic GPA, class rank, rigor of secondary school record, standardized test scores. *Important factors considered include:* Recommendation(s). *Other factors considered include:* Application essay, character/personal qualities, extracurricular activities, interview, talent/ability, volunteer work, work experience. SAT or ACT required; ACT with Writing component recommended. TOEFL required of all international applicants. High school diploma is required, and GED is accepted. *Academic units required:* 4 English, 4 math, 3 science (1 science lab), 2 foreign language, 3 social studies, 1 fine arts.

The Inside Word

Comparable to other leading public universities, it's a numbers game at University of Missouri—Rolla. Applicants who meet class rank and standardized test cut-offs, as well as distribution requirements, will be granted admission. But don't let the straightforward application process fool you—the university draws a competitive, self-selecting pool of applicants. Candidates will find it to their advantage to apply early.

FINANCIAL AID

Students should submit: FAFSA (not required but strongly recommended). The Princeton Review suggests that all financial aid forms be submitted as soon as possible after January 1. *Need-based scholarships/grants offered:* Pell Grant, SEOG, state scholarships/grants, private scholarships, the school's own gift aid, ROTC (Army and Air Force). *Loan aid offered:* Direct Subsidized Stafford, Direct Unsubsidized Stafford, FFEL PLUS, Federal Perkins Loan, state loans, college/university loans from institutional funds, alternative loans. Applicants will be notified of awards on a rolling basis beginning or about April 1.

FROM THE ADMISSIONS OFFICE

"Widely recognized as one of our nation's best universities for engineering, sciences, computer science, and technology, the University of Missouri—Rolla also offers programs in information science, business, and liberal arts. Personal attention, access to leadership opportunities, research projects, and co-ops and internships mean students are well prepared for the future. A 96 percent career placement rate across all majors and a 90-plus percent placement rate to medical, law, and other professional schools tell the tale; UMR offers a terrific undergraduate experience and value for your money.

"The University of Missouri—Rolla makes individual admission decisions based primarily on each applicant's standardized test scores and class rank or GPA. In the case of borderline admission situations, additional factors may be considered.

"As of this book's publication, the University of Missouri—Rolla did not have information available about their policy regarding the new SAT."

SELECTIVITY

Admissions Rating	85
# of applicants	2,257
% of applicants accepted	90
% of acceptees attending	47

FRESHMAN PROFILE

Range SAT Math	590–720
Range ACT Composite	24–30
Minimum Paper TOEFL	550
Minimum Computer Based TOEFL	213
Average HS GPA	3.59
% graduated top 10% of class	39
% graduated top 25% of class	69
% graduated top 50% of class	92

DEADLINES

Regular application deadline	7/1
Regular notification	rolling
Nonfall registration?	yes

APPLICANTS ALSO LOOK AT
AND OFTEN PREFER
Massachusetts Institute of Technology, Purdue University, Saint Louis University, Truman State University, University of Illinois at Urbana-Champaign, University of Missouri—Columbia, Washington University in St. Louis,
AND SOMETIMES PREFER
Colorado School of Mines, Georgia Institute of Technology, Iowa State University, Purdue University—West Lafayette, University of Iowa

FINANCIAL FACTS

Financial Aid Rating	76
Annual in-state tuition	$6,819
Annual out-of-state tuition	$17,085
Room & Board	$6,185
Books and supplies	$875
Required fees	$1,070
% frosh rec. need-based scholarship or grant aid	55
% UG rec. need-based scholarship or grant aid	45
% frosh rec. need-based self-help aid	41
% UG rec. need-based self-help aid	41

THE UNIVERSITY OF MONTANA—MISSOULA

101 LOMMASSON CENTER, MISSOULA, MT 59812 • ADMISSIONS: 406-243-6266 • FAX: 406-243-5711

CAMPUS LIFE

Quality of Life Rating	86
Fire Safety Rating	92
Type of school	public
Environment	city

STUDENTS

Total undergrad enrollment	11,841
% male/female	47/53
% from out of state	27
% from public high school	44
% live on campus	24
% in (# of) fraternities	6 (5)
% in (# of) sororities	6 (4)
% African American	1
% Asian	1
% Caucasian	83
% Hispanic	2
% Native American	4
% international	3
# of countries represented	74

SURVEY SAYS . . .

Athletic facilities are great
Students are friendly
Students love Missoula, MT
Great off-campus food
Students are happy
Everyone loves the Grizzlies
Lots of beer drinking

ACADEMICS

Academic Rating	67
Calendar	semester
Student/faculty ratio	19:1
Profs interesting rating	70
Profs accessible rating	65
% profs teaching UG courses	99
% classes taught by TAs	9
Most common lab size	20–29 students
Most common reg class size	20–29 students

MOST POPULAR MAJORS

business administration/
management
education
psychology

STUDENTS SAY

Academics

You can enjoy both "the outdoors and a great education" at The University of Montana—Missoula, a school that "is whatever you want it to be. It can be hiking and fishing, tailgating at Griz games and dancing at the Foresters' Ball, earning a great education and experiencing new cultures abroad, or it can be a little bit of everything." While "Some programs are better than others," there are many standouts, including forestry, journalism, business, anthropology, creative writing, pharmacy, physical therapy, music, and premedical programs. Class sizes "are very small for a state university" and the professors, who "come to Missoula to give up the city and enjoy the mountains and outdoors," are "available to students outside of class. They are amazing." Administrators are also accessible; they "maintain contact with the student body. For example, the Dean of the College of Arts and Sciences teaches a seminar class in which the president of the university attends a Q & A session with the students." Opportunities for "internships, TA positions, and work-study jobs are easy to find," leaving students feeling "very prepared to enter the job market." Top candidates should strongly consider the Davidson Honors College, where "Students have a great opportunity for interesting classes and an effective environment."

Life

"While students at UM are serious about school," partying "is also a big deal," as "Missoula students are known for throwing some pretty huge parties, and we sure do know how to have a good time." There's plenty to do besides party, though. Most students "have at least one extracurricular activity. Whether it is theater, intramural sports, or a job, UM students keep themselves busy. Sure, there is a good amount of partying that goes on, but there are also lots of alternatives for those who don't want to participate in such activities." Missoula "has beautiful outdoor recreation opportunities" that, for many, are the school's primary allure. One student explains, "With all of the rafting, rock climbing, hiking, skiing, and fishing, anyone who loves nature will love UM." There's also UM intercollegiate athletics, with a football team "that has made four national championship appearances in 10 years and has won its division 9 years out of 10. Yeah, I'd say we play some pretty good football! Not to mention both our men's and women's basketball teams reached the NCAA playoffs last year; that wasn't bad either." Musical and cultural opportunities around campus "are also outstanding, with concerts, plays, and galleries almost every night," and downtown Missoula "has great restaurants and local shopping. Missoula is like nowhere else in the world."

Student Body

There are "two major group types at Montana." One is the "Carhartt-wearing rancher or logger type." The other is "the hippie type." There are others here as well, and "The beautiful thing about The University of Montana is that there really is no 'typical' student. Walking through campus one would see first a student with dreadlocks down to [his or her] waist and amazing handmade clothing and a minute later see a student wearing dress pants and a button-up shirt. Both fit in to the school and town equally." Most here "enjoy the mountains and being in Montana and have found a place to call their own at The University of Montana." They are generally "easygoing and not trying to fit into a group. People mostly do whatever." The typical student also "probably owns a dog." Undergrads do note that "although we celebrate ethnic diversity, most of the population is White. What we lack in ethnic diversity we make up for in intellectual diversity." Much of the racial diversity that exists here "is achieved through the exchange program."

FINANCIAL AID: 406-243-5373 • E-MAIL: ADMISS@UMONTANA.EDU • WEBSITE: WWW.UMT.EDU

ADMISSIONS

Very important factors considered include: Academic GPA, class rank, rigor of secondary school record, standardized test scores. *Important factors considered include:* Extracurricular activities, talent/ability. *Other factors considered include:* Application essay, recommendation(s). SAT or ACT including Writing portion required; TOEFL required of all international applicants. High school diploma is required, and GED is accepted. *Academic units required:* 4 English, 3 math, 2 science (2 science labs), 3 social studies, 2 history, 2 academic electives; choice of 2 units in foreign language, computer science, visual/performing arts, or vocational education. *Academic units recommended:* 2 foreign language.

The Inside Word

The university operates on a rolling admissions basis, and the admissions game here is relatively straightforward: Decisions are based largely upon numbers. Applicants who enrolled in a college prep curriculum and earned average or better grades should be able to make the grade—especially if they apply earlier in the admissions cycle.

FINANCIAL AID

Students should submit: FAFSA. The Princeton Review suggests that all financial aid forms be submitted as soon as possible after January 1. *Need-based scholarships/grants offered:* Pell Grant, SEOG, Academic Competitiveness Grant, National SMART Grant, state scholarships/grants, private scholarships, the school's own gift aid. *Loan aid offered:* FFEL Subsidized Stafford, FFEL Unsubsidized Stafford, PLUS, Federal Perkins Loans. Applicants will be notified of awards on a rolling basis beginning or about April 1. Federal Work-Study Program available. Institutional employment available.

FROM THE ADMISSIONS OFFICE

"There's something special about this place. It's something different for each person. For some, it's the blend of academic quality and outdoor recreation. The University of Montana ranks fifth in the nation among public institutions for producing Rhodes scholars, and *Outside Magazine* lists Missoula in its 'Top Ten Amazing Places for Outdoor Recreation." For others, it's size—not too big, not too small. The University of Montana is a midsized university in the heart of the Rocky Mountains—accessible in both admission and tuition bills—that produces graduates considered among the best and brightest in the world. It is located in a community that could pass for a cozy college town or a bustling big city, depending on your point of view. There's a lot happening, but you won't get lost. People are friendly and diverse. They come from all over the world to study and learn and to live a good life. They come to a place to be inspired, a place where they feel comfortable yet challenged. Some never leave. Most never want to. For more information, go to http://admissions.umt.edu.

"The University of Montana has adjusted admission requirements to reflect the Writing portion of the SAT. The new admission requirements are available on the UM website at http://admissions.umt.edu."

SELECTIVITY

Admissions Rating	**74**
# of applicants	4,855
% of applicants accepted	96
% of acceptees attending	46

FRESHMAN PROFILE

Range SAT Critical Reading	480–600
Range SAT Math	480–600
Range SAT Writing	470–590
Range ACT Composite	20–25
Minimum Paper TOEFL	500
Minimum Computer Based TOEFL	173
Average HS GPA	3.26
% graduated top 10% of class	16
% graduated top 25% of class	40
% graduated top 50% of class	70

DEADLINES

Regular notification	rolling
Nonfall registration?	yes

FINANCIAL FACTS

Financial Aid Rating	**70**
Annual in-state tuition	$5,142
Annual out-of-state tuition	$14,104
Room & Board	$6,100
Books and supplies	$850
Required fees	$1,402
% frosh rec. need-based scholarship or grant aid	34
% UG rec. need-based scholarship or grant aid	40
% frosh rec. need-based self-help aid	43
% UG rec. need-based self-help aid	49
% frosh rec. any financial aid	82
% UG rec. any financial aid	75

UNIVERSITY OF NEBRASKA—LINCOLN

313 NORTH THIRTEENTH STREET, VAN BRUNT VISITORS CENTER, LINCOLN, NE 68588-0256 • ADMISSIONS: 402-472-2023

STUDENTS SAY
Academics
The University of Nebraska—Lincoln, "a big university" with a "small-town feel," attracts its 17,000-plus undergraduates with a mixture of "academic challenge, pioneering research, vast extracurricular opportunity, overwhelming school spirit, and the best people you'll ever meet, anywhere." Oh, yeah, "and great football." UNL is large enough to offer some pretty unique programs, including a "very good construction management program," biological systems engineering, food science, and "one of the best actuarial science programs in the nation." The school also shines in popular disciplines such as journalism, business, psychology, animal science, and engineering; among the most prestigious options here is the "highly selective J. D. Edwards Honor Program in Computer Science and Management, where students live and attend core classes together in business and computer science topics." In all areas, UNL strives to "provide the best possible educational and career opportunities—including excellent research opportunities and a great study abroad program—to a large student body while maintaining a low student/professor ratio," all "on a limited budget." As at many large schools, students say that you have to grind through lower-level classes but, once you reach the upper-level curricula, "Professors truly care about their students and their academic success. They make themselves available and encourage students to take advantage of office hours not just for homework help, but so they can get to know their students."

Life
"There is basically something going on every day, every night" at or around UNL; "You just have to find it." The campus "is literally three blocks from downtown, where bars line both sides of the streets," and "The old-fashioned downtown, called the Haymarket area, is within walking distance and has numerous restaurants." And when Lincoln seems a bit slow, students know they can "head to Omaha, which is only an hour away. Omaha has the Qwest Center, which brings in names like the Rolling Stones and Dave Matthews Band." Campus life "is obviously centered a lot on the athletic department. It is amazing to see how students and outside fans react to the athletes," observes one student. Intramural sports "or maybe just playing a game of Ultimate Frisbee" is also "a big part of the average college student's life." The Lied Center, located on campus, "is another major draw, with performances from major symphonies to *Stomp!* being the norm." Although "UNL is a dry campus," there is still "a vibrant off-campus party scene, and finding a party isn't too difficult." Participation in a "great Greek system" ensures that students are not only alerted to all the "great parties" but are also plugged into UNL's service community.

Student Body
"The typical Nebraska student has the good ol' Midwestern work ethic, is White," "is fairly conservative and concerned about doing well in school," and "prides himself or herself on being 'moral.'" Many "come from religious Christian backgrounds." Students "who hold liberal views have a tough time completely fitting in with certain groups," but fortunately, "At such a big school you can always find people who are like yourself." That's because "even though a large portion of students come from Nebraska high schools, we have many nontraditional, international, and minority students. You will definitely experience an atmosphere of diverse backgrounds at UNL." There is a noticeable divide on campus between "the stereotypical fraternity/sorority, partying-every-weekend kind of people," who appear to be in the majority, and the "significant minority of people who really take school seriously."

UNIVERSITY OF NEBRASKA—LINCOLN

FAX: 402-472-0670 • FINANCIAL AID: 402-472-2030 • E-MAIL: NUHUSKER@UNL.EDU • WEBSITE: WWW.UNL.EDU

ADMISSIONS

Very important factors considered include: Class rank, standardized test scores. *Important factors considered include:* Rigor of secondary school record. *Other factors considered include:* Academic GPA, first generation, recommendation(s), talent/ability. ACT recommended; SAT or ACT required; TOEFL required of all international applicants. High school diploma is required, and GED is accepted. *Academic units required:* 4 English, 4 math, 3 science (1 science lab), 2 foreign language, 3 social studies. *Academic units recommended:* 1 history.

The Inside Word

Admissions Officers at Nebraska concentrate on applicants' course selections, GPAs, and test scores. Students who have had some success in the classroom make strong candidates as potential future Huskers. A few programs, such as architecture and engineering, have stricter requirements, so applicants should investigate the requirements for their intended fields of study before applying.

FINANCIAL AID

Students should submit: FAFSA. The Princeton Review suggests that all financial aid forms be submitted as soon as possible after January 1. *Need-based scholarships/grants offered:* Pell Grant, SEOG, state scholarships/grants, private scholarships, the school's own gift aid. *Loan aid offered:* Direct Subsidized Stafford, Direct Unsubsidized Stafford, Direct PLUS, FFEL Subsidized Stafford, FFEL Unsubsidized Stafford, FFEL PLUS, Federal Perkins Loan, college/university loans from institutional funds. Applicants will be notified of awards on a rolling basis beginning or about April 1.

FROM THE ADMISSIONS OFFICE

"The University of Nebraska—Lincoln offers one of today's most dynamic college experiences. The university has developed a national reputation for its substantial out-of-state scholarship program. As a result, more students nationwide are finding that the university, with its strength in undergraduate education, its tradition of student engagement, its lively campus atmosphere and its connection to downtown Lincoln, is uniquely suited to provide an enriching student experience. The university delivers on the promise of the friendliness of a private college with major university resources. It is no wonder alumni stay connected years after graduating and thousands of miles from campus.

"Established in 1869, the University of Nebraska—Lincoln has a rich tradition of excellence. Students join more than 200,000 alumni who have made their mark as industry leaders in business, engineering, the arts, journalism, education, and the sciences. A degree from Nebraska opens doors. UN—Lincoln graduates recently interviewed on campus with major national companies like Abercrombie & Fitch, the Central Intelligence Agency (CIA), IBM, Microsoft, Sprint, Target, and The Washington Post. Attending UN—Lincoln also means you will have built-in connections with 116 graduate degree programs, including those in University of Nebraska Law, Dental, and Medical Centers located either on campus or 50 miles east in Omaha.

"Freshmen students seeking admission should either be ranked in the upper one-half of their high school class, or have received an ACT composite score of 20 or higher or an SAT total score of 950 or higher (Critical Reading and Math only; Writing portion not considered)."

SELECTIVITY	
Admissions Rating	77
# of applicants	7,993
% of applicants accepted	73
% of acceptees attending	66

FRESHMAN PROFILE	
Range SAT Critical Reading	510–650
Range SAT Math	530–670
Range ACT Composite	22–28
Minimum Paper TOEFL	525
Minimum Computer Based TOEFL	193
% graduated top 10% of class	25
% graduated top 25% of class	53
% graduated top 50% of class	83

DEADLINES	
Regular application deadline	5/1
Regular notification	rolling
Nonfall registration?	yes

FINANCIAL FACTS	
Financial Aid Rating	80
Annual in-state tuition	$5,928
Annual out-of-state tuition	$15,378
Room & Board	$6,523
Books and supplies	$942
Required fees	$1,128
% frosh rec. need-based scholarship or grant aid	36
% UG rec. need-based scholarship or grant aid	34
% frosh rec. need-based self-help aid	30
% UG rec. need-based self-help aid	34
% frosh rec. any financial aid	41
% UG rec. any financial aid	41

UNIVERSITY OF NEW HAMPSHIRE

FOUR GARRISON AVENUE, DURHAM, NH 03824 • ADMISSIONS: 603-862-1360 • FAX: 603-862-0077

CAMPUS LIFE
Quality of Life Rating	**68**
Fire Safety Rating	**81**
Type of school	public
Environment	village

STUDENTS
Total undergrad enrollment	11,523
% male/female	43/57
% from out of state	43
% from public high school	75
% live on campus	57
% in (# of) fraternities	4 (8)
% in (# of) sororities	5 (5)
% African American	1
% Asian	2
% Caucasian	85
% Hispanic	2
% international	1
# of countries represented	37

SURVEY SAYS . . .
Great library
Athletic facilities are great
Frats and sororities
dominate social scene
Lots of beer drinking
Hard liquor is popular

ACADEMICS
Academic Rating	**71**
Calendar	semester
Student/faculty ratio	17:1
Profs interesting rating	63
Profs accessible rating	64
% profs teaching UG courses	89
% classes taught by TAs	1
Most common lab size	20–29 students
Most common reg class size	10–19 students

MOST POPULAR MAJORS
business administration/
management
English language and literature
psychology

STUDENTS SAY

Academics

"University of New Hampshire captures the social appeal every student wants and provides every academic opportunity he or she needs," students at this midsize state university agree. With "so many students and majors it is impossible not to find some activity or major to interest you." UNH allows students to pursue their ambitions as aggressively as they like. Some choose to take advantage of the "excellent nursing and nutrition programs," "the awesome business school," "a great education program," "strong departments in music and computer science," an "incredible aggie school," and "one of the best programs for marine biology on the East Coast." These students tout the "excellent internships and study abroad programs" available here, as well as the "great research opportunities. The business kids are always working on outside projects, and every class I have had has ended with some type of individual research project. There are tons of opportunities for research grants from your sophomore year on. . . . The list is endless." Others pursue an "all play, no work" option, cruising through with a carefully chosen curriculum of easy courses. The presence of this latter group partly accounts for the perception that "UNH is really underrated academically." Undergrads warn that the school "lacks a personal touch at times, but in general, it works well for a university of its size."

Life

"The social scene is great" at UNH, where "The Greek system is strong and very involved in the campus community," and "there are also numerous sports clubs, intramurals, and other groups to get involved in." Undergrads generally "like to party, and the opportunities are plentiful. Along with UMass we're probably the place to go and party if you're going to school in the New England region." One student observes, "Life is all about going to class in sweats and getting dressed up to drink. Classes later in the day are preferred and drinking isn't reserved just for the weekends; it's a week-long ordeal." While some here pride themselves on their partying prowess, others are not impressed; one writes, "I'm from the South, so I've seen what partying is really like at state schools like Georgia and Tennessee. UNH kind of pales in comparison." No one disputes UNH's primacy in college hockey, though; the men's team "is practically an annual participant in the Frozen Four. It's hard not to get caught up in the excitement of the UNH hockey season." The campus also plays host to "constant theatrical productions, comedians, fairs, and sports. Every weekend movies are playing for 2 bucks in the MUB (Memorial Union Building); they range from *Star Wars* to sneak previews of movies that aren't in theaters yet." Outdoor enthusiasts enjoy "at least one student-led hiking/biking/kayaking/rock-climbing/canoeing/sky-diving trip per week, organized by the Outing Club." The nearby White Mountains ensure "great skiing," while the charming oceanfront town of Portsmouth and the Kittery Outlets in Maine mean great dining and shopping is just down the road.

Student Body

"Since we are a state university in New England, sort of in the center of the region, our demographics generally reflect that of New England itself," explains one UNH undergrad. Undergrads "are pretty run-of-the-mill, with a lot of them being local suburban kids from Concord and Manchester. There are some extremes—the hippies, the preps, the hicks, the nerds, the wannabe gangstas—but overall, there is not too much diversity at UNH. Just a lot of average Joes." The student body includes "a lot of jock types. Athletics in all forms (varsity, club, and intramurals) is huge."

FINANCIAL AID: 603-862-3600 • E-MAIL: ADMISSIONS@UNH.EDU • WEBSITE: WWW.UNH.EDU

ADMISSIONS

Very important factors considered include: Academic GPA, class rank, rigor of secondary school record. *Important factors considered include:* Recommendation(s). *Other factors considered include:* Alumni/ae relation, application essay, character/personal qualities, extracurricular activities, first generation, geographical residence, racial/ethnic status, standardized test scores, state residency, talent/ability, volunteer work, work experience. SAT or ACT required; ACT with Writing component required. TOEFL required of all international applicants. High school diploma is required, and GED is accepted. *Academic units required:* 4 English, 3 math, 3 science (3 science labs), 2 foreign language, 3 social studies. *Academic units recommended:* 4 English, 4 math, 3 science (3 science labs), 3 foreign language, 3 social studies, 1 academic elective.

The Inside Word

New Hampshire's emphasis on academic accomplishment in the admissions process makes it clear that the Admissions Committee is looking for students who have taken high school seriously. Standardized tests take as much of a backseat here as is possible at a large public university.

FINANCIAL AID

Students should submit: FAFSA. Regular filing deadline is February 1. The Princeton Review suggests that all financial aid forms be submitted as soon as possible after January 1. *Need-based scholarships/grants offered:* Pell Grant, SEOG, state scholarships/grants, private scholarships, the school's own gift aid, Veterans Educational Benefits. *Loan aid offered:* FFEL Subsidized Stafford, FFEL Unsubsidized Stafford, FFEL PLUS, Federal Perkins Loan, state loans, college/university loans from institutional funds. Applicants will be notified of awards on a rolling basis beginning or about March 1. Federal Work-Study Program available. Institutional employment available. Off-campus job opportunities are excellent.

FROM THE ADMISSIONS OFFICE

"The University of New Hampshire is an institution best defined by the students who take advantage of its opportunities. Enrolled students who are willing to engage in a high quality academic community in some meaningful way, who have a genuine interest in discovering or developing new ideas, and who believe in each person's obligation to improve the community they live in typify the most successful students at UNH. Undergraduate students practice these three basic values in a variety of ways: by undertaking their own, independent research projects, by collaborating in faculty research, and by participating in study abroad, residential communities, community service, and other cultural programs.

"University of New Hampshire will require all high school graduates to submit results from the new SAT or the ACT (with the Writing component). The Writing portions will not be used for admissions decisions during the first 2–3 admissions cycles. Students graduating from high school prior to 2006 can submit results from the 'old' SAT or ACT. The UNH admissions process does not require SAT Subject tests."

SELECTIVITY

Admissions Rating	**79**
# of applicants	13,991
% of applicants accepted	67
% of acceptees attending	33

FRESHMAN PROFILE

Range SAT Critical Reading	500–600
Range SAT Math	510–620
Minimum Paper TOEFL	550
Minimum Computer Based TOEFL	213
% graduated top 10% of class	20
% graduated top 25% of class	61
% graduated top 50% of class	97

DEADLINES

Regular application deadline	2/1
Regular notification	4/15
Nonfall registration?	yes

APPLICANTS ALSO LOOK AT

AND OFTEN PREFER
University of Connecticut, University of Massachusetts—Amherst, University of Vermont

AND SOMETIMES PREFER
Boston University, Northeastern University, Providence College, University of Rhode Island

AND RARELY PREFER
Boston College, Syracuse University, University of Maine

FINANCIAL FACTS

Financial Aid Rating	**74**
Annual in-state tuition	$8,240
Annual out-of-state tuition	$20,690
Room & Board	$7,584
Books and supplies	$1,500
Required fees	$2,161
% frosh rec. need-based scholarship or grant aid	38
% UG rec. need-based scholarship or grant aid	35
% frosh rec. need-based self-help aid	54
% UG rec. need-based self-help aid	54
% frosh rec. any financial aid	84
% UG rec. any financial aid	78

UNIVERSITY OF NEW MEXICO

OFFICE OF ADMISSIONS, PO BOX 4895, ALBUQUERQUE, NM 87196-4895 • ADMISSIONS: 505-277-2446 • FAX: 505-277-6686

STUDENTS SAY

Academics

The University of New Mexico "offers a strong academic community with all of its many research opportunities [for] a bargain price," students at this large state university tell us. Excellent graduate programs in law, business, and medicine exert a trickle-down effect on the undergraduate divisions. Explains one undergrad, "We have one of the top 10 law schools and medical schools in the nation right now, and the undergraduate programs that lead into those schools want to make sure that at least some of their students get accepted and decide to attend one of these graduate programs." Students also praise UNM's offerings in pharmacy, psychology, architecture, anthropology, engineering, and sociology. With this many options, "Even if you don't know what you want, you are bound to find something that you love." Students may find that something through UNM's interesting freshman-year options, which include courses designed to get students up to speed in writing, math, and research skills; freshman learning communities, a pair of team-taught interdisciplinary classes; and freshman interest groups, theme-based seminars that allow students to delve a little deeper into one of their core curriculum requirements. For top-ranked students, UNM's University Honors Program places students in small, seminar-style classes with an intensive focus on writing and reading.

Life

"Campus life can be as full of activities as one wants it to be" at UNM. A large student population means there are always plenty of extracurricular options. Sizeable commuter and nontraditional populations, on the other hand, ensure that many students aren't interested in them, as they visit campus only to attend classes. Commuters do appreciate the university's addition of a new Student Union building, "with three floors that include a movie theater, pool tables, computer labs, art studios, tons of food options, and many ballrooms and conference rooms. Lots of students hang out in the SUB in between classes." For residents and those who live close by, "There is always something going on, whether it's a dance show, a movie on the field, a cultural event, a sporting event, or any other casual activity. There are also a lot of opportunities for community service projects and political activism." Everyone gets behind UNM's "amazing athletics," embraced as enthusiastically by the city of Albuquerque as by UNM students. Basketball has a huge fan base here, while football draws tailgaters regardless of the quality of the team. Because UNM's campus is officially dry, "Many students choose to go to local bars and downtown Albuquerque where there are many bars in one area" to socialize. Most students agree that there's much fun to be had in Albuquerque, "a fairly large city with frequent cultural activities (Zozobra, Balloon Fiesta, State Fair) that are really fun and interesting, especially if you are from out of state and haven't experienced them before."

Student Body

"UNM has students from all walks of life," which isn't so surprising given its undergraduate population of nearly 20,000. Many are nontraditional, are "roughly 25 years old, approach studies from a very practical perspective, and work a full-time job or close to it to pay for school." One undergrad observes, "Because of its many nontraditional students, the school can sometimes feel too old or too young. UNM needs to work on integrating all students and finding activities that allow all age groups to interact" (though any such efforts may be hampered by the fact that "most students are commuters, who are solely focused on earning their degree"). With "many Hispanic, Native American, Anglo, and other students," UNM is "extremely diverse." Notes one student, "There are so many different ethnicities here that racial discrimination really isn't an issue."

FINANCIAL AID: 505-277-2041 • E-MAIL: APPLY@UNM.EDU • WEBSITE: WWW.UNM.EDU

ADMISSIONS

Very important factors considered include: Academic GPA, rigor of secondary school record. *Important factors considered include:* Class rank, standardized test scores. *Other factors considered include:* Application essay, character/personal qualities, extracurricular activities, first generation, recommendation(s), volunteer work, work experience. SAT or ACT required; ACT with Writing component recommended. TOEFL required of all international applicants. High school diploma is required, and GED is accepted. *Academic units required:* 4 English, 3 math, 2 science (1 science lab), 2 foreign language, 1 social studies, 1 history.

The Inside Word

UNM's rolling admissions process is quite typical of large public universities. Consideration is based nearly entirely on courses, grades, and test scores, though recommendations can sometimes help a candidate. Solid average students should encounter no difficulty in gaining an offer of admission.

FINANCIAL AID

Students should submit: FAFSA. The Princeton Review suggests that all financial aid forms be submitted as soon as possible after January 1. *Need-based scholarships/grants offered:* Pell Grant, SEOG, state scholarships/grants, private scholarships, the school's own gift aid, United Negro College Fund, Federal Nursing Scholarship. *Loan aid offered:* Direct Subsidized Stafford, Direct Unsubsidized Stafford, Direct PLUS, Federal Perkins Loan, Federal Nursing Loan, state loans, college/university loans from institutional funds. Applicants will be notified of awards on a rolling basis beginning or about April 15.

FROM THE ADMISSIONS OFFICE

"The University of New Mexico is a major research institution nestled in the heart of multicultural Albuquerque on one of the nation's most beautiful and unique campuses. Students learn in an environment graced by distinctive Southwestern architecture, beautiful plazas and fountains, spectacular art and a national arboretum . . . all within view of the 10,000-foot Sandia Mountains. At UNM, diversity is a way of learning with education enriched by a lively mix of students being taught by a world-class research faculty that includes a Nobel laureate, a MacArthur Fellow, and members of several national academies. UNM offers more than 225 degree programs and majors and has earned national recognition in dozens of disciplines, ranging from primary care medicine and clinical law to engineering, photography, Latin American history, and intercultural communications. Research and the quest for new knowledge fuels the university's commitment to an undergraduate education where students work side by side with many of the finest scholars in their fields.

"The university will continue to accept SAT or ACT scores, but does not require the Writing component at this time. The SAT Critical Reading portion will be used with the SAT Math to be considered in any admission decision based on formula. The use of ACT composite remains unchanged. These requirements are subject to change."

SELECTIVITY

Admissions Rating	**78**
# of applicants	7,134
% of applicants accepted	74
% of acceptees attending	59

FRESHMAN PROFILE

Range SAT Critical Reading	470–600
Range SAT Math	470–590
Range ACT Composite	19–25
Minimum Paper TOEFL	520
Minimum Computer Based TOEFL	190
Average HS GPA	3.33
% graduated top 10% of class	21
% graduated top 25% of class	45
% graduated top 50% of class	79

DEADLINES

Regular application deadline	6/15
Nonfall registration?	yes

FINANCIAL FACTS

Financial Aid Rating	**60***
Annual in-state tuition	$4,360
Annual out-of-state tuition	$17,823
Room & Board	$6,590
Books and supplies	$856

UNIVERSITY OF NEW ORLEANS

AD 103, LAKEFRONT, NEW ORLEANS, LA 70148 • ADMISSIONS: 504-280-6595 • FAX: 504-280-5522

STUDENTS SAY

Academics

The University of New Orleans is "recovering at a snail's pace since Hurricane Katrina," but continues to provide "an equal opportunity for all people to get a superior education at an affordable price." You'll find a "diverse community of students" and "some of the best academics in the country." Classes are "challenging," "rewarding," and "offered at a variety of times, so it is easier for working students to attend class," but there are few bells and whistles. UNO "is geared to get students an education and doesn't fool around with extras." While "It is easy to get in" to UNO, it can be "hard to get out." "Classes are not easy." "UNO is for hard workers," a computer science major asserts. "It isn't an escalator for rich people to send their spoiled kids like the other schools in New Orleans." Faculty members are "accessible," "dedicated," and "extremely knowledgeable." They "have had extensive careers" and retain "good connections to the real world." Students note, however, that the bad professors are "really bad." Also, "since the hurricane," UNO has shut down "many programs," and many academic services "are only a fraction of what they were." UNO still excels in many areas including engineering and naval architecture. Business and hotel, restaurant, and tourism administration are strong as well. There is also a "great jazz program."

Life

"Hurricane Katrina has left our campus a mess," warns a junior. "UNO is getting back to normal, but it will be awhile before it will get better." "Areas of campus are still not rebuilt" and the campus was "a hideous sprawl" even before the storm. While "More people are living on campus" now, UNO remains "primarily a commuter campus." Students here are "almost completely focused on academics." Generally, when classes end, students "leave ASAP." "Job opportunities for college students are pretty good" and "Most students work either full- or part-time." "The overall experience at UNO is a very independent one," an English major reports. "There are clubs and organizations in which to be involved," but "It is hard to get people involved in extracurricular activities." "If you want a college life, you must join a fraternity or sorority or some type of group on campus," a business major ventures. On the plus side, UNO boasts a "world-class" gym, and, of course, the "amazing" city of New Orleans is still brimming "with a lot of opportunity." "It's New Orleans. My god!" exclaims a junior. The campus is "less than 10 minutes to the French Quarter." "There's so much to do" and the food "is unmatched anywhere." "We live in a city that is immersed in culture and entertainment, so fun is not too hard to find," says a senior. "You can find an open bar at any time of any day, but it isn't impossible to find a quiet spot and work out some math."

Student Body

UNO boasts "an eclectic assortment of students" who are "very serious" about academics, yet "very friendly." "Many different ethnic and social backgrounds" are represented here and it's definitely not "a regular 'all-American' college." "Because the school is a commuter school, the student population is made up mostly of local folks," observes an anthropology major. "But that doesn't stop the school from being extremely diverse." "Classmates range from high school grads to grandparents." "It's just a big gumbo of people," a sophomore writes. "The typical student" at UNO is probably "mid-20s, working full- or part-time while attending classes, [and] living off-campus in New Orleans." "I think the typical student at UNO is one who is excited to be in college, often entering or returning to college after spending some time in the workforce," a political science major reports. Many students are "married, have kids, and live in the suburbs" and many are "making a second or third try at college." In recent years, though, "the contingency of on-campus, fresh-out-of-high-schoolers" has grown by "leaps and bounds."

FINANCIAL AID: 504-280-6603 • E-MAIL: ADMISSIONS@UNO.EDU • WEBSITE: WWW.UNO.EDU

ADMISSIONS

Very important factors considered include: Academic GPA, class rank, rigor of secondary school record, standardized test scores. *Other factors considered include:* Geographical residence, recommendation(s), state residency. SAT or ACT required; TOEFL required of all international applicants. High school diploma is required, and GED is accepted. *Academic units required:* 4 English, 3 math, 3 science, 2 foreign language, 1 social studies, 2 history, 1 academic elective, 1 computer literacy or science (0.5 units required).

The Inside Word

Admission is straightforward here. Complete a basic college-bound high school curriculum with a GPA of at least 2.5, get at least an 18 on your ACT, or graduate in the top 25 percent of your high school class. Nontraditional students who don't want to pay the exorbitant prices of the more well-known private universities in New Orleans can find their niche at UNO; if you are 25 or older, the only requirement for admission is a legitimate high school diploma or a GED.

FINANCIAL AID

Students should submit: FAFSA, institution's own financial aid form. The Princeton Review suggests that all financial aid forms be submitted as soon as possible after January 1. *Need-based scholarships/grants offered:* Pell Grant, SEOG, state scholarships/grants, private scholarships, the school's own gift aid. *Loan aid offered:* FFEL Subsidized Stafford, FFEL Unsubsidized Stafford, FFEL PLUS, Federal Perkins Loan, college/university loans from institutional funds. Applicants will be notified of awards on a rolling basis beginning or about April 20.

FROM THE ADMISSIONS OFFICE

"The University of New Orleans returned to its Lakefront campus in Spring 2006 with a full array of academic programs and an enhanced student life program, which includes a cybercafé, campus bar, first-run movies, and a host of exciting student activities. Damage from Hurricane Katrina was limited in scope, and campus facilities are expected to be fully operational for the Fall 2008 semester. A new residence hall, complete with private suite-style bedrooms, is expected to open in Fall 2007."

"The university will serve as a central player in the rebuilding of one of America's most unique and diverse cities. Many academic offerings will focus on the aftermath of the natural disaster and provide students with a living laboratory to address these issues across many disciplines. UNO embraces its mission by providing the best educational opportunities for undergraduate and graduate students, conducting world-class research, and serving a diverse and cultured community in critical areas. UNO's most outstanding offerings include a doctoral program in conservation biology, providing training in the most advanced molecular biological techniques; the largest U.S. undergraduate program in Naval Architecture and Marine Engineering; a leading jazz studies program; one of the top five film programs in the country; and the only graduate arts administration program in the Gulf South.

"UNO will use the total score from the Critical Reading/Verbal and Math sub sections of both the old and new SAT or the composite score for the ACT. The Writing components of the ACT and SAT will be used for placement purposes, but not for admission purposes, at the current time."

SELECTIVITY
Admissions Rating	74
# of applicants	2,522
% of applicants accepted	77
% of acceptees attending	52

FRESHMAN PROFILE
Range SAT Critical Reading	450–610
Range SAT Math	480–620
Range ACT Composite	20–24
Minimum Paper TOEFL	525
Minimum Computer Based TOEFL	195
Average HS GPA	3.11
% graduated top 10% of class	14
% graduated top 25% of class	33
% graduated top 50% of class	66

DEADLINES
Regular application deadline	8/20
Regular notification	rolling
Nonfall registration?	yes

APPLICANTS ALSO LOOK AT AND OFTEN PREFER
Louisiana State University

FINANCIAL FACTS
Financial Aid Rating	61
Annual in-state tuition	$3,292
Annual out-of-state tuition	$10,336
Room & Board	$4,734
Books and supplies	$1,250
Required fees	$518
% frosh rec. need-based scholarship or grant aid	35
% UG rec. need-based scholarship or grant aid	36
% frosh rec. need-based self-help aid	21
% UG rec. need-based self-help aid	31

THE UNIVERSITY OF NORTH CAROLINA AT ASHEVILLE

CPO #2210, 117 LIPINSKY HALL, ASHEVILLE, NC 28804-8510 • ADMISSIONS: 828-251-6481 • FAX: 828-251-6482

STUDENTS SAY

Academics

The centerpiece of any University of North Carolina at Asheville education is a core curriculum, known here as Integrative Liberal Studies (or ILS for short). ILS consumes a substantial portion of students' time; for many, it is the single most important reason for choosing to attend UNCA. ILS includes a number of introductory writing and humanities courses as well as Topical Clusters, which require students "to integrate the same topic through different disciplines, looking at one subject first from, for example, a natural science perspective, then studying it from a social science perspective." The curriculum also requires Intensives—that is, classes designed to strengthen basic academic skills (e.g., writing, research) while broadening students' intellectual horizons. The sum effect of ILS is to "put a lot of emphasis on thought, on thinking for yourself and deeper than most, and becoming involved in those things that are important to you." Offers one undergrad, "The liberal arts atmosphere allows a student to explore a number of different avenues for his or her future, and to decide, based on that exploration, what it is that he or she wants to do with his or her future. UNC Asheville is about finding yourself." Throughout ILS, major studies, and electives, UNCA undergrads enjoy "smaller classes that usually help with one-on-one assistance" and "dedicated professors who are passionate about their jobs." All of these assets "translate into a private liberal arts education at a public school price," undergrads happily note.

Life

North Carolina may be a red state, but it has its blue enclaves. Asheville, a "nice and progressive city," is certainly one of them. The community, students note, is an "artsy town nestled in the mountains" that hosts plenty of shows (including a big annual jam-band festival), "many wonderful restaurants, especially of the ethnic and vegetarian variety," and "lots of old-time music and contra dancing." The surrounding mountains provide "lots of outdoor recreation opportunities," with hiking, mountain biking, and kayaking among the most popular options. The area's many assets help compensate for the sense among some that "life on campus can get pretty routine at times." Then there are those who enthusiastically tout the merits of campus life; one such student writes, "Some people think it's boring, but I love it. There are basketball games, soccer games, and other sports. There are intramurals [in which] everyone is allowed to play. All the dorms have hall socials and study breaks with free food and games. There are parties for NFL games and other sports. Frisbee is a big thing on campus. A lot of people, including me, love to just hang out on the quad in the center of campus." And why not, since "the campus is beautiful, a great place to take your laptop out on the quad on a nice day and write a paper, or just take a walk in the botanical gardens."

Student Body

"There is a slogan that students made up that describes the student body perfectly" at UNCA, and that slogan is, "'Don't be bashful, it's Asheville.' Anything goes within the student body." One student observes, "Both UNCA and Asheville have a lot of 'atypical' people: a lot of hippies, punks, people with tattoos/piercings, artists, actors, musicians, and writers. It's sort of a running joke that you don't get your Asheville card unless you're some sort of oddball." The large hippie contingent brings "lots of activities such as dancing down at the drum circle on Friday nights." But hippies by no means dominate. The school is also home to "an increasing number of folks who lean toward 'prep'" as well as "your people who come from small mountain towns and who think that Asheville is a big city. They tend to be very religious." UNCA also has "many nontraditional [i.e., older] students." Even though UNCA "has a reputation of being very liberal, and there are many liberal students on campus," there are also "a lot of conservative students, as well." Undergrads assure us that "regardless of how students look, they are all very friendly, intelligent, and willing to speak to one another."

ADMISSIONS

Very important factors considered include: Academic GPA, class rank, rigor of secondary school record. *Important factors considered include:* Standardized test scores. *Other factors considered include:* Alumni/ae relation, extracurricular activities, first generation, geographical residence, interview, racial/ethnic status, recommendation(s), state residency, talent/ability, volunteer work, work experience. SAT or ACT required; ACT with Writing component required. TOEFL required of all international applicants. High school diploma is required, and GED is not accepted. *Academic units required:* 4 English, 4 math, 3 science (1 science lab), 2 foreign language, 1 social studies, 1 history. *Academic units recommended:* 4 academic electives.

The Inside Word

UNC Asheville provides a sound public education in a small campus atmosphere and an increasing number of students are setting their sights on it each year. In kind, the school works diligently to create a diverse student body and thoroughly analyzes each application it receives. Although selectivity is rising, candidates who demonstrate reasonable academic success and a variety of extracurricular activities should be able to secure admittance.

FINANCIAL AID

Students should submit: FAFSA. The Princeton Review suggests that all financial aid forms be submitted as soon as possible after January 1. *Need-based scholarships/grants offered:* Pell Grant, SEOG, state scholarships/grants, private scholarships, the school's own gift aid. *Loan aid offered:* Direct Subsidized Stafford, Direct Unsubsidized Stafford, Direct PLUS, Federal Perkins Loan, state loans, college/university loans from institutional funds. Applicants will be notified of awards on a rolling basis beginning or about March 15.

FROM THE ADMISSIONS OFFICE

"If you want to learn how to think, how to analyze and solve problems on your own, and how to become your own best teacher, a broad-based liberal arts education is the key. UNC Asheville focuses on undergraduates, with a core curriculum covering humanities, language and culture, arts and ideas, and health and fitness. Students thrive in small classes, with a faculty dedicated first of all to teaching. The liberal arts emphasis develops discriminating thinkers, expert and creative communicators with a passion for learning. These are qualities you need for today's challenges and the changes of tomorrow.

"The University of North Carolina at Asheville will require the new SAT Reasoning Test. For students submitting an ACT score, the ACT with the Writing component is required."

SELECTIVITY

Admissions Rating	83
# of applicants	2,654
% of applicants accepted	71
% of acceptees attending	30

FRESHMAN PROFILE

Range SAT Critical Reading	530–640
Range SAT Math	520–630
Range SAT Writing	510–620
Range ACT Composite	22–26
Minimum Paper TOEFL	550
Minimum Computer Based TOEFL	213
Average HS GPA	3.7
% graduated top 10% of class	18
% graduated top 25% of class	56
% graduated top 50% of class	96

DEADLINES

Regular application deadline	2/15
Regular notification	3/24
Nonfall registration?	yes

FINANCIAL FACTS

Financial Aid Rating	79
Annual in-state tuition	$2,172
Annual out-of-state tuition	$12,297
Room & Board	$5,880
Books and supplies	$850
Required fees	$1,710
% frosh rec. need-based scholarship or grant aid	34
% UG rec. need-based scholarship or grant aid	39
% frosh rec. need-based self-help aid	22
% UG rec. need-based self-help aid	33
% frosh rec. any financial aid	62
% UG rec. any financial aid	59

THE UNIVERSITY OF NORTH CAROLINA AT CHAPEL HILL

JACKSON HALL 153A, CAMPUS BOX #2200, CHAPEL HILL, NC 27599 • ADMISSIONS: 919-966-3621 • FAX: 919-962-3045

STUDENTS SAY

Academics

The University of North Carolina at Chapel Hill "is so well rounded," according to students who make their case by pointing to the "very highly recognized academics, sports, and quality students who are here to get a great education and have fun doing it." With a typically Southern approach, UNC "creates a very balanced atmosphere to live in. The workload isn't so overwhelming that you can't go out and do anything. . . . It makes for a good place to live because people aren't always stressed out." Undergrads report that "you won't find a better combination of quality, cost, and environment for any student specifically interested in undergraduate programs in business, journalism, or education," and that "the humanities and social sciences have a huge presence here" as well. The sciences aren't too shabby either; in fact, pretty much across the board "The academic life is very rigorous" and professors "are not only educated in their fields but have life experiences that add to the flavor of their courses." Many students warn that academic advising is a weak point; one student reports, "We have complicated requirements for majors and . . . sometimes students end up taking classes that don't count toward their major. Or, they end up not realizing they had to take a particular class until senior year." The constitution of the state of North Carolina keeps UNC's in-state tuition rates very low; some out-of-state students complain that the cost of this guarantee falls disproportionately to them.

Life

"UNC has a great nightlife" with plenty of options. Franklin Street, the main drag of Chapel Hill, runs along one side of the campus and "has tons of restaurants," "packed bars," and college-oriented shopping. "Students from Duke and NC State will often come party on Franklin Street" because it's the most student-friendly stretch in the Triangle. The campus offers "tons of clubs and organizations—more than 600—so there is plenty of stuff to do." The dorms "are wonderful, and there is always something going on," although "Dorm parties are hard to pull off on South Campus, where most of the freshmen live. Just about anything goes on North Campus, though." The active Greek scene also provides plenty of party options; GDIs note that "it's really easy to have a social life and be an independent." But what truly binds the campus are the Tar Heel athletic teams, with the men's basketball team paramount among them. One student reports, "People look forward to basketball season more than anything. The rivalries are intense" and the quality of play is excellent. The Atlantic Coast Conference is arguably the NCAA's strongest in basketball. Students also enjoy a "beautiful campus" and great weather; one student observes, "One of the most relaxing things to do is to sit outside on the grass in the quad studying in the 70 degree weather and sun in November."

Student Body

By state policy, native Tar Heels must make up 82 percent of each incoming undergraduate class at UNC, so "The typical student is a North Carolina resident." Out-of-state students "blend seamlessly into this mix, and are often the ones to take the helm of leadership opportunities." Undergraduates here "are very involved, whether it's in the Greek scene, the religious scene, playing intramural sports, or starting their own club. Philanthropic involvement is also high." Students typically "are academically oriented but aren't dominated by it. You can't 'feel' midterms in the air, as you can at other schools." You'll "find every stereotype represented here: The J. Crew snob, the polo shirt and sunglass-wearing frat boy, the emo/punk rocker, the Southern belle, etc." The most apparent stereotypes, though, are "the ones who look like they stepped out of the Carolina catalogue, sporting Carolina-blue laptop bags, polo shirts, and sneakers." UNC is liberal by Southern standards, although no one would ever confuse a UNC undergrad for a Reed College or Wesleyan University student.

THE UNIVERSITY OF NORTH CAROLINA AT CHAPEL HILL

FINANCIAL AID: 919-962-8396 • E-MAIL: UADM@EMAIL.UNC.EDU • WEBSITE: WWW.UNC.EDU

ADMISSIONS

Very important factors considered include: Academic GPA, application essay, character/personal qualities, class rank, extracurricular activities, recommendation(s), rigor of secondary school record, standardized test scores, state residency, talent/ability. *Important factors considered include:* Alumni/ae relation, first generation, racial/ethnic status, volunteer work, work experience. SAT or ACT with Writing component required. TOEFL required of all international applicants. High school diploma is required, and GED is not accepted. *Academic units required:* 4 English, 4 math, 3 science (1 science lab), 2 foreign language, 2 social studies, 2 academic electives, 1 U.S. history. *Academic units recommended:* 4 English, 4 math, 4 science (1 science lab), 4 foreign language, 3 social studies.

The Inside Word

UNC's admissions process is highly selective. North Carolina students compete against other students from across the state for 82 percent of all spaces available in the freshman class; out-of-state students compete for the remaining 17 percent of the spaces. State residents will find the admissions standards high, and out-of-state applicants will find that it's one of the hardest offers of admission to come by in the country.

FINANCIAL AID

Students should submit: FAFSA, CSS/Financial Aid PROFILE. The Princeton Review suggests that all financial aid forms be submitted as soon as possible after January 1. *Need-based scholarships/grants offered:* Pell Grant, SEOG, state scholarships/grants, private scholarships, the school's own gift aid. *Loan aid offered:* FFEL Subsidized Stafford, FFEL Unsubsidized Stafford, FFEL PLUS, Federal Perkins Loan, state loans, college/university loans from institutional funds, alternative loans. Applicants will be notified of awards on a rolling basis beginning or about March 15.

FROM THE ADMISSIONS OFFICE

"One of the leading research and teaching institutions in the world, UNC Chapel Hill offers first-rate faculty, innovative academic programs, and students who are smart, friendly, and committed to public service. Students take full advantage of extensive undergraduate research opportunities, a study abroad program with programs on every continent except Antarctica, and 600-plus clubs and organizations. We offer all this in Chapel Hill, one of the greatest and most welcoming college towns anywhere.

"Carolina's commitment to excellence, access, and affordability is reflected in premier scholarships, such as the prestigious Morehead and Robertson Scholarships, as well the Carolina Covenant, a landmark program that enables students from low-income families to graduate from Carolina debt-free. We invite you to visit—talk with our professors, attend a class, spend time with some students, and walk across the campus on which public education was born.

"All freshman applicants are required to submit an SAT or an ACT Writing component score. If students took the SAT or ACT before the Writing section was offered, the SAT with the writing section or ACT plus Writing score is still required. While test scores are important, our holistic review process includes other important factors such course work, grades, and extracurricular activities."

SELECTIVITY

Admissions Rating	97
# of applicants	19,728
% of applicants accepted	34
% of acceptees attending	57
# accepting a place on wait list	1,000
% admitted from wait list	27

FRESHMAN PROFILE

Range SAT Critical Reading	590–690
Range SAT Math	610–700
Range SAT Writing	580–680
Range ACT Composite	25–30
Minimum Paper TOEFL	600
Minimum Computer Based TOEFL	250
Average HS GPA	4.37
% graduated top 10% of class	76
% graduated top 25% of class	96
% graduated top 50% of class	99

DEADLINES

Regular application deadline	1/15
Regular notification	1/31, 3/31
Nonfall registration?	no

APPLICANTS ALSO LOOK AT
AND SOMETIMES PREFER
Duke University, University of Virginia
AND RARELY PREFER
North Carolina State University, Wake Forest University

FINANCIAL FACTS

Financial Aid Rating	93
Annual in-state tuition	$3,455
Annual out-of-state tuition	$18,103
Room & Board	$6,846
Books and supplies	$1,000
Required fees	$1,578
% frosh rec. need-based scholarship or grant aid	32
% UG rec. need-based scholarship or grant aid	32
% frosh rec. need-based self-help aid	14
% UG rec. need-based self-help aid	18
% frosh rec. any financial aid	65
% UG rec. any financial aid	58

THE UNIVERSITY OF NORTH CAROLINA AT GREENSBORO

1400 SPRING GARDEN STREET, GREENSBORO, NC 27402-6170 • ADMISSIONS: 336-334-5243 • FAX: 336-334-4180

STUDENTS SAY

Academics

Students describe The University of North Carolina at Greensboro as "about a half-and-half commuter school with great specialized programs and schools such as nursing, education, dance, and music." Undergrads here praise the "high quality of education at a significantly reduced rate, while having the smaller classes allowing closer bonds between faculty and students" than one could reasonably expect for the tuition charged. The key here is the faculty; "UNCG places a big emphasis on having great teachers. There are some duds, but overall, more of them are fantastic than anything else." The school excels in some off-the-beaten-path areas; programs in exercise and sports science, deaf education, and human development and family studies all receive enthusiastic praise from current students. Undergrads also love the "opportunities that are given to network with businesses and people outside of campus" and the "great internships" the school helps them find. Nontraditional students appreciate the "great support system for adult students." As the school's reputation continues to improve, some here worry that this "historically moderate-sized university where student well-being was the first priority . . . will change into a large research university where the focus is raising more and more money instead of concentrating on what is really best for students." One undeniable upside of the school's increased stature is that "you feel like you are respected in the community when you tell someone that you are a student at UNCG."

Life

UNCG is conveniently located "a mile from downtown and close to surrounding schools: Guilford College, NC A&T, Greensboro College, Elon, UNC, NC State." One student observes, "With six colleges around UNCG, a metropolis of 250,000-plus (1.1 million in the metro area), and access within a 3-hour drive to both beaches and mountains, there is always something to do." On campus "UNCG makes it easy for anyone and everyone to fit in and feel included. Through clubs, students have the ability to offer ideas and have them implemented. There's also intramural sports and free events." The high-profile arts programs on campus yield some wonderful cultural opportunities. "The Weatherspoon Museum of Art is amazing at showcasing the most modern American art and keeps this provincial little town on its toes," writes one artist. A performing arts student adds, "There are wonderful concerts and plays and lectures here. It's a great cultural center and you can always have something to do as long as you look for it." Intercollegiate athletics, students tell us, "are not as popular as they could be, even though they are often ranked nationally, or at least ranked in the conference." Many here feel the addition of a football team (the school has none) would change that; "It would really bring the school spirit up," opines one undergrad. The school's many commuters warn that "parking is horrendous. Prepare to get here an hour before class if you want to find a space on time."

Student Body

UNCG is a big school with "many people from all walks of life, social/cultural backgrounds, etc. The university promotes cultural diversity and acceptance and tolerance of people of different backgrounds." One student reports, "One minute you see a bunch of music majors talking about how much Bach has affected their life and the next minute, you see a bunch of sorority girls discussing the Gap. Mainly, I have observed that sorority girls stick together, jocks stick together, etc." Two in three students are female, and there is a widespread perception that "many of the males are either married or gay. The straight young chill male is a minority here." As at many state schools, "About half of the students at UNCG came here to party. The other half consists of hardworking students who are generally frustrated with the slacker mentality in a lot of our classes. This is less of a problem once you get past the intro-level lectures."

THE UNIVERSITY OF NORTH CAROLINA AT GREENSBORO

FINANCIAL AID: 336-334-5702 • E-MAIL: UNDERGRAD_ADMISSIONS@UNCG.EDU • WEBSITE: WWW.UNCG.EDU

ADMISSIONS

Very important factors considered include: Academic GPA, rigor of secondary school record. *Important factors considered include:* Standardized test scores. *Other factors considered include:* Recommendation(s). SAT or ACT required; ACT with Writing component required. TOEFL required of all international applicants. High school diploma is required, and GED is not accepted. *Academic units required:* 4 English, 4 math, 3 science (1 science lab), 2 foreign language, 1 social studies, 1 history.

The Inside Word

UNCG has yet to gain much attention outside of regional circles so, at least for the moment, gaining admission is not particularly difficult. The usual public university considerations apply; expect the Admissions Office to focus on grades and test scores, and not much else. Out-of-staters will find a much smoother path to admission here than at Chapel Hill and will still be within reasonable reach of internship and career possibilities in the Research Triangle.

FINANCIAL AID

Students should submit: FAFSA. The Princeton Review suggests that all financial aid forms be submitted as soon as possible after January 1. *Need-based scholarships/grants offered:* Pell Grant, SEOG, state scholarships/grants, private scholarships, the school's own gift aid. *Loan aid offered:* FFEL Subsidized Stafford, FFEL Unsubsidized Stafford, FFEL PLUS, Federal Perkins Loan, college/university loans from institutional funds. Applicants will be notified of awards on a rolling basis beginning or about March 15. Federal Work-Study Program available. Institutional employment available. Off-campus job opportunities are good.

FROM THE ADMISSIONS OFFICE

"UNCG is committed to helping students discover how they can make their mark in the world. Exceptional teaching and first-rate academic programs provide a solid learning foundation. Hands-on experiences in internships, leadership opportunities, and service-learning programs prepare students to take on the challenges of the twenty-first century. Students can broaden their experience by taking advantage of one of the most extensive and affordable study abroad programs in the country. The Lloyd International Honors College offers a genuinely unique opportunity for talented students in any major to benefit from an enriched and supportive intellectual life with a global perspective. UNCG's ideal size and supportive campus environment enable students to excel as individuals while discovering how they can have an impact on the larger community. Students get connected through more than 180 student organizations, intramural, club and intercollegiate sports, Greeks, outdoor adventures, residential colleges, and a friendly Southern city that quickly starts to feel like home.

"Freshmen applicants must submit at least one SAT or ACT score (including the Writing component)."

SELECTIVITY

Admissions Rating	82
# of applicants	9,905
% of applicants accepted	49
% of acceptees attending	50

FRESHMAN PROFILE

Range SAT Critical Reading	460–570
Range SAT Math	480–570
Range SAT Writing	450–560
Minimum Paper TOEFL	550
Minimum Computer Based TOEFL	213
Average HS GPA	3.51
% graduated top 10% of class	14
% graduated top 25% of class	43
% graduated top 50% of class	86

DEADLINES

Regular application deadline	3/1
Regular notification	rolling
Nonfall registration?	yes

FINANCIAL FACTS

Financial Aid Rating	71
Annual in-state tuition	$2,308
Annual out-of-state tuition	$13,576
Room & Board	$5,513
Books and supplies	$1,314
Required fees	$1,505
% frosh rec. need-based scholarship or grant aid	31
% UG rec. need-based scholarship or grant aid	31
% frosh rec. need-based self-help aid	39
% UG rec. need-based self-help aid	43
% frosh rec. any financial aid	66
% UG rec. any financial aid	62

UNIVERSITY OF NORTH DAKOTA

PO Box 8135, Grand Forks, ND 58202 • Admissions: 800-225-5863 • Fax: 701-777-4857

CAMPUS LIFE

Quality of Life Rating	78
Fire Safety Rating	65
Type of school	public
Environment	town

STUDENTS

Total undergrad enrollment	10,376
% male/female	54/46
% from out of state	49
% from public high school	92
% live on campus	28
% in (# of) fraternities	9 (13)
% in (# of) sororities	7 (7)
% African American	1
% Asian	1
% Caucasian	91
% Hispanic	1
% Native American	3
% international	2
# of countries represented	63

SURVEY SAYS . . .

Great computer facilities
Athletic facilities are great
Students are friendly
Everyone loves the Fighting Sioux
Lots of beer drinking
Hard liquor is popular

ACADEMICS

Academic Rating	67
Calendar	semester
Student/faculty ratio	18:1
Profs interesting rating	67
Profs accessible rating	66
% profs teaching UG courses	90
Most common lab size	20–29 students
Most common reg class size	20–29 students

MOST POPULAR MAJORS

airline/commercial/professional pilot
and flight crew
nursing/registered nurse training
(ASN, BSN, MSN, RN)
psychology

STUDENTS SAY

Academics

Outside of its home state, the University of North Dakota is best known for an aviation program that "is recognized as the best by most airlines and companies." Students note that "the aviation department is constantly changing and including advanced technology in the training. Most schools only teach you rules, while here at UND through the use of 360- and 260-degree sims [simulators], you get practical work experience. (The sims are designed to be exactly like what the FAA will use to train and evaluate you.)" But natives of the Peace Garden State (yes, that is North Dakota's official nickname) know that there's more to UND than flying and landing airplanes. There are also the "great programs in nursing, law, accounting, and forensic science," "the only meteorology program in the area," "a physical therapy program with a good reputation," and "an awesome honors program." In fact, "UND is just a great school to go to if you want lots of academic options." Students do, however, observe that "as with most public universities of this size, the classes are kind of hit or miss when it comes to the teaching skills of your professor. Some classes are excellent, others subpar. As far as class difficulty [is concerned], it is about as hit or miss as your professor." Large classes also provide students with a degree of "anonymity."

Life

"If you can stand the winter months, the University of North Dakota is a nice campus that is full of friendly people and good times," but prospective students should be forewarned that during the winter, "This seems like the coldest campus in the country." During the long winter, "The college hockey team is the biggest attraction. The hockey arena is one even NHL teams wish they could have. Hockey is everything around here." Otherwise, "Most people resort to indoor activities either at the gym, movies, bars, or clubs. During warmer months, many students go outside to play Ultimate Frisbee, baseball, football, and sand volleyball." All year round, students like to unwind with a beer or three: "A lot of people drink between 2 and 4 days out of the week," observes one respondent. Another remarks, "Grand Forks, North Dakota, offers a small-town atmosphere, as well as the small-town need for creativity when trying to find entertainment. The relative lack of entertainment perpetuates the use of alcohol. The proportion of fraternities and sororities per student is extremely high." Plenty of students tell us that they don't drink and still manage to occupy their time with "movies, hanging out with friends, camping, and hunting."

Student Body

According to one senior, "most UND students come from small towns and haven't been exposed to much." The aviation program counters the trend by "drawing in students from all 50 states and multiple countries." One undergrad notes, "If you're from out of state, everyone says, 'You're aviation, right?'" Because "this is Scandinavian country, many students are White, blonde, and have blue eyes." Most are "serious in terms of school, conservative in terms of politics, and somewhat religious." The typical student, we're told, is also "bundled in a wool parka freezing his or her butt off walking to class, grimacing in pain just because it is so cold."

FINANCIAL AID: 701-777-3121 • E-MAIL: ENROLSER@SAGE.UND.NODAK.EDU • WEBSITE: WWW.UND.EDU

ADMISSIONS

Very important factors considered include: Academic GPA, standardized test scores. *Other factors considered include:* Class rank, rigor of secondary school record. SAT or ACT required; TOEFL required of all international applicants. High school diploma is required, and GED is accepted. *Academic units required:* 4 English, 3 math, 3 science (3 science labs), 3 social studies. *Academic units recommended:* 1 foreign language.

The Inside Word

UND's loose admissions standards belie the national reputation it has earned. Akin to most state schools, it's all about meeting GPA and standardized test minimums. The lack of subjective criteria makes for a relatively painless application process, and a majority of students are admitted.

FINANCIAL AID

Students should submit: FAFSA. The Princeton Review suggests that all financial aid forms be submitted as soon as possible after January 1. *Need-based scholarships/grants offered:* Pell Grant, SEOG, state scholarships/grants, private scholarships, the school's own gift aid, Federal Nursing Scholarship. *Loan aid offered:* FFEL Subsidized Stafford, FFEL Unsubsidized Stafford, FFEL PLUS, Federal Perkins Loan, Federal Nursing Loan, alternative commercial loans. Applicants will be notified of awards on or about May 15.

FROM THE ADMISSIONS OFFICE

"More than 10,000 students come to the University of North Dakota each year, from every state in the nation and more than 60 countries. They're impressed by our academic excellence, more than 190 programs, our dedication to the liberal arts mission, and alumni success record. Nearly all of the university's new students rank in the top half of their high school classes, with about half in the top quarter. As the oldest and most diversified institution of higher education in the Dakotas, Montana, Wyoming, and western Minnesota, UND is a comprehensive teaching and research university. Yet the university provides individual attention that may be missing at very large universities. UND graduates are highly regarded among prospective employers. Representatives from more than 200 regional and national companies recruit UND students every year. Our campus is approximately 98 percent accessible.

"Students applying for admission to UND are required to take either the ACT or SAT unless they are older than 25. The ACT Writing component is not a requirement for admission, and SAT results considered include only the Math and Verbal sections."

SELECTIVITY

Admissions Rating	78
# of applicants	3,698
% of applicants accepted	74
% of acceptees attending	70

FRESHMAN PROFILE

Range ACT Composite	20–25
Minimum Paper TOEFL	525
Minimum Computer	
Based TOEFL	195
Average HS GPA	3.37
% graduated top 10% of class	16
% graduated top 25% of class	41
% graduated top 50% of class	76

DEADLINES

Regular notification	rolling
Nonfall registration?	yes

APPLICANTS ALSO LOOK AT AND OFTEN PREFER

Minnesota State University—Moorhead, Saint Cloud State University, University of Minnesota Duluth, University of Minnesota—Twin Cities, University of Wisconsin—Madison

AND SOMETIMES PREFER

Concordia College (MN), Minot State University, University of Minnesota—Crookston

FINANCIAL FACTS

Financial Aid Rating	80
Annual in-state tuition	$4,786
Annual out-of-state tuition	$12,780
Room & Board	$5,085
Books and supplies	$800
Required fees	$1,006
% frosh rec. need-based	
scholarship or grant aid	20
% UG rec. need-based	
scholarship or grant aid	24
% frosh rec. need-based	
self-help aid	47
% UG rec. need-based	
self-help aid	49
% frosh rec. any financial aid	78
% UG rec. any financial aid	76

UNIVERSITY OF NOTRE DAME

220 MAIN BUILDING, NOTRE DAME, IN 46556 • ADMISSIONS: 574-631-7505 • FAX: 574-631-8865

STUDENTS SAY

Academics

Notre Dame has many traditions, including a "devotion to undergraduate education" that you might not expect from a school with such an athletic reputation. Professors here are, by all accounts, "wonderful": "Not only are they invested in their students," they're "genuinely passionate about their field of study," "enthusiastic and animated in lectures," and "always willing to meet outside of class to give extra help." Wary that distance might breed academic disengagement, they ensure that "large lectures are broken down into smaller discussion groups once a week to help with class material and . . . give the class a personal touch." For its part, "The administration tries its best to stay on top of the students' wants and needs." They make it "extremely easy to get in touch with anyone." Like the professors, they try to make personal connections with students. For example, "Our president (a priest), as well as both of our present presidents emeritus, make[s] it a point to interact with the students in a variety of ways—teaching a class, saying mass in the dorms, etc." Overall, "while classes are difficult," "Students are competitive against one another," and "It's necessary to study hard and often, [but] there's also time to do other things."

Life

Life at Notre Dame is centered on two things: "residential life" and "sports." The "Dorms on campus provide the social structure" and supply undergrads with "tons of opportunities" "to get involved and have fun." "During the school week" students "study a lot, but on the weekends everyone seems to make up for the lack of partying during the week and go[es] crazy." The school "does not have any frats or sororities, but campus is not dry, and drinking/partying is permitted within the residence halls." The administration reportedly tries "to keep the parties on campus due to the fact that campus is such a safe place and they truly do care about our safety." In addition to dorm parties, "virtually every student plays some kind of sport [in] his/her residence hall, and the dorms are really competitive in the Interhall Sport System." Intercollegiate sports, to put it mildly, "are huge." "If someone is not interested in sports upon arrival, he or she will be by the time he or she leaves." "Everybody goes to the football games, and it's common to see 1,000 students at a home soccer game." Beyond residential life and sports, "religious activities," volunteering, "campus publications, student government, and academic clubs round out the rest of ND life."

Student Body

Undergrads at Notre Dame report that "the vast majority" of their peers are "very smart" "White kids from upper- to middle-class backgrounds from all over the country, especially the Midwest and Northeast." The typical student "is a type-A personality that studies a lot, yet is athletic and involved in the community. They are usually the outstanding seniors in their high schools," the "sort of people who can talk about the BCS rankings and Derrida in the same breath." Additionally, something like "85 percent of Notre Dame students earned a varsity letter in high school." "Not all are Catholic" here, though most are, and it seems that most undergrads "have some sort of spirituality present in their daily lives." Never known as a very diverse place, "ND is slowly improving in diversity concerning economic backgrounds, with the university's policy to meet all demonstrated financial need." As things stand now, those who "don't tend to fit in with everyone else hang out in their own groups made up by others like them (based on ethnicity, sexual orientation, etc.)."

FINANCIAL AID: 574-631-6436 • E-MAIL: ADMISSIO.1@ND.EDU • WEBSITE: WWW.ND.EDU

ADMISSIONS

Very important factors considered include: Rigor of secondary school record. *Important factors considered include:* Academic GPA, alumni/ae relation, application essay, character/personal qualities, class rank, extracurricular activities, recommendation(s), standardized test scores, talent/ability, volunteer work. *Other factors considered include:* First generation, level of applicant's interest, racial/ethnic status, religious affiliation/commitment, work experience. SAT or ACT required; TOEFL required of all international applicants. High school diploma is required, and GED is not accepted. *Academic units required:* 4 English, 3 math, 2 science, 2 foreign language, 2 social studies, 3 academic electives. *Academic units recommended:* 4 English, 4 math, 4 science, 4 foreign language, 4 social studies.

The Inside Word

Notre Dame is one of the most selective colleges in the country. Almost everyone who enrolls is in the top 10 percent of their graduating class and possesses test scores in the highest percentiles. But, as the student respondents suggest, strong academic ability isn't enough to get you in here. The school looks for students with other talents, and seems to have a predilection for athletic achievement. Legacy students get a leg up but are by no means assured of admission.

FINANCIAL AID

Students should submit: FAFSA, CSS/Financial Aid PROFILE, Noncustodial PROFILE, Business/Farm Supplement, signed Federal Income Tax Returns and W-2 forms (may be requested on individual basis), student Federal Income Tax Returns. Regular filing deadline is February 15. The Princeton Review suggests that all financial aid forms be submitted as soon as possible after January 1. *Need-based scholarships/grants offered:* Pell Grant, SEOG, state scholarships/grants, private scholarships, the school's own gift aid, Alumni Club Scholarships. *Loan aid offered:* FFEL Subsidized Stafford, FFEL Unsubsidized Stafford, FFEL PLUS, Federal Perkins Loan. Privately funded student loan. Applicants will be notified of awards on or about April 1.

FROM THE ADMISSIONS OFFICE

"Notre Dame is a Catholic university, which means it offers unique opportunities for academic, ethical, spiritual, and social service development. The First Year of Studies program provides special assistance to our students as they make the adjustment from high school to college. The first-year curriculum includes many core requirements, while allowing students to explore several areas of possible future study. Each residence hall is home to students from all classes; most will live in the same hall for all their years on campus. An average of 93 percent of entering students will graduate within 5 years.

"Scores from either the old or new SAT are accepted. The highest Verbal score and the highest Math score from either test will be accepted; the Writing component score is not required. The ACT is also accepted (with or without Writing component) in lieu of the SAT."

SELECTIVITY

Admissions Rating	98
# of applicants	12,796
% of applicants accepted	27
% of acceptees attending	58
# accepting a place on wait list	605

FRESHMAN PROFILE

Range SAT Critical Reading	600–720
Range SAT Math	630–740
Range SAT Writing	580–710
Range ACT Composite	31–33
Minimum Paper TOEFL	600
Minimum Computer Based TOEFL	250
% graduated top 10% of class	85
% graduated top 25% of class	97
% graduated top 50% of class	100

DEADLINES

Regular application deadline	12/31
Regular notification	4/10
Nonfall registration?	no

APPLICANTS ALSO LOOK AT

AND OFTEN PREFER
Princeton University, Stanford University

AND SOMETIMES PREFER
Cornell University, Duke University, Georgetown University, Northwestern University

AND RARELY PREFER
Boston College, University of Illinois at Urbana-Champaign, University of Michigan—Ann Arbor

FINANCIAL FACTS

Financial Aid Rating	95
Annual tuition	$32,900
Room & Board	$8,730
Books and supplies	$850
Required fees	$507
% frosh rec. need-based scholarship or grant aid	51
% UG rec. need-based scholarship or grant aid	46
% frosh rec. need-based self-help aid	41
% UG rec. need-based self-help aid	41

UNIVERSITY OF OKLAHOMA

1000 ASP AVENUE, NORMAN, OK 73019-4076 • ADMISSIONS: 405-325-2252 • FAX: 405-325-7124

STUDENTS SAY
Academics
The University of Oklahoma "prides itself on the leadership and ingenuity of its students," a number of whom credit the school's president, David Boren, with transforming OU "from well known in the state of Oklahoma to well known across the nation" in the past decade. Students call their academic experiences at OU "exceptional"—both in and out of the classroom. "We are encouraged to get not only a great academic base but also life experiences, through lab research, internships, and campus leadership positions." Not to be eclipsed by the famous meteorology department, the business and drama programs are starting to get attention as well. When it comes to teaching, some students see "a clear distinction between two types of professors: those who have been here forever and have tenure (they're boring and don't really 'teach'), and new professors, who have real-life experience and give students a feel for what the real world is like." More often than not, we read that the professors are "very helpful and knowledgeable." An economics student boasts that after e-mailing homework assignments to a calculus professor, she "received the answers back promptly." Undergrads wish the school would address the "definite need for more professors and more classes for the ever-growing number of students here at OU." A handful also gripes about having to jump through bureaucratic hoops; writes an all-too experienced senior: "There's a lot of standing in lines for everything." That said, many students find the administration members "available and helpful." Those in the honors program experience "a wonderful dynamic. It's nice to be at a big university but still get to take small, discussion-centered classes." One content sophomore writes, "I believe I am getting not only a great education, but also meeting people who make huge impressions in my life."

Life
To some, OU has a party school reputation, perhaps made possible by its "huge Greek population" (in total, OU offers 49 fraternities and sororities). A senior notes that "there are plenty of things to do on OU's campus besides partying," and students repeatedly point out that Greeks "work hard to co-program with various events and encourage members to attend activities out of their regular spectrum." For example, "In my sorority," writes one senior, "we have different groups come over for dinner and exchanges." This "ongoing process" of increasing interaction among all factions is starting to pay off in some campus wide participation. A senior recounts how OU started "a one-day community-service project called the Big Event that now, in its sixth year, attracts nearly one in every four students." The student union sponsors free new-release movies "just about every Friday night," and the Campus Activities Council organizes "free events like Homecoming, Howdy Week, pep rallies, and concert series (including the Dixie Chicks)." People call the town of Norman, 15 miles from Oklahoma City, "pretty bland to say the least," though it does have a museum, dollar theater, and popular 1950s-style diner. Of course, students and Norman locals come together in their undying love of Sooner football, packing the stadium to see the team and the talented marching band all through the fall.

Student Body
Most students hail from Oklahoma or Texas, and several comment that "you definitely feel the Bible Belt" at OU. Students describe typical classmates as "conservative"; however, in the words of a sophomore, "Most people here are not judgmental, at least openly, and tend to either ignore or respect foreign views and beliefs." In this welcoming group, "If you were to go to a football game by yourself and sit in the middle of the student section, everyone would give you a high five and yell along with you while you were there." One student observes a shift in his classmates: "People are still always talking about what they are doing that night; but surprisingly, students are starting to get more serious about school, which I think is really good."

FINANCIAL AID: 405-325-4521 • E-MAIL: ADMREC@OU.EDU • WEBSITE: WWW.OU.EDU

ADMISSIONS

Very important factors considered include: Academic GPA, class rank, rigor of secondary school record, standardized test scores. *Other factors considered include:* Application essay, recommendation(s), state residency, SAT or ACT required; TOEFL required of all international applicants. High school diploma is required, and GED is accepted. *Academic units required:* 4 English, 3 math, 2 science (2 science labs), 2 social studies, 1 history, 3 academic electives. *Academic units recommended:* 3 foreign language, 1 computer science.

The Inside Word

It's plain from the approach of Oklahoma's evaluation process that candidates needn't put much energy into preparing supporting materials for their applications. This is one place that is going to get you a decision pronto—your numbers will call the shots.

FINANCIAL AID

Students should submit: FAFSA. The Princeton Review suggests that all financial aid forms be submitted as soon as possible after January 1. *Need-based scholarships/grants offered:* Pell Grant, SEOG, state scholarships/grants, private scholarships, the school's own gift aid, United Negro College Fund. *Loan aid offered:* FFEL Subsidized Stafford, FFEL Unsubsidized Stafford, FFEL PLUS, Federal Perkins Loan, Federal Nursing Loan, college/university loans from institutional funds. Applicants will be notified of awards on a rolling basis beginning or about March 15. Federal Work-Study Program available. Institutional employment available. Off-campus job opportunities are excellent.

FROM THE ADMISSIONS OFFICE

"Ask yourself some significant questions. What are your ambitions, goals, and dreams? Do you desire opportunity, and are you ready to accept challenge? What do you hope to gain from your educational experience? Are you looking for a university that will provide you with the tools, resources, and motivation to convert ambitions, opportunities, and challenges into meaningful achievement? To effectively answer these questions you must carefully seek out your options, look for direction, and make the right choice. The University of Oklahoma combines a unique mixture of academic excellence, varied social cultures, and a variety of campus activities to make your educational experience complete. At OU, comprehensive learning is our goal for your life. Not only do you receive a valuable classroom learning experience, but OU is also one of the finest research institutions in the United States. This allows OU students the opportunity to be a part of technology in progress. It's not just learning, it's discovery, invention, and dynamic creativity, a hands-on experience that allows you to be on the cutting edge of knowledge. Make the right choice and consider the University of Oklahoma!

"Both versions of the SAT (or ACT) will be used when considering freshman applicants for admission. The new Writing component of either test is not required of students and is not used in determining admission to the university. The student's best composite score from any one test will be used."

SELECTIVITY

Admissions Rating	83
# of applicants	7,471
% of applicants accepted	91
% of acceptees attending	49
# accepting a place on wait list	993
% admitted from wait list	98

FRESHMAN PROFILE

Range ACT Composite	23–28
Minimum Paper TOEFL	550
Minimum Computer Based TOEFL	213
Average HS GPA	3.6
% graduated top 10% of class	35
% graduated top 25% of class	68
% graduated top 50% of class	92

DEADLINES

Regular application deadline	4/1
Regular notification	rolling
Nonfall registration?	yes

FINANCIAL FACTS

Financial Aid Rating	83
Annual in-state tuition	$3,006
Annual out-of-state tuition	$11,295
Room & Board	$6,863
Books and supplies	$1,099
Required fees	$2,104
% frosh rec. need-based scholarship or grant aid	11
% UG rec. need-based scholarship or grant aid	18
% frosh rec. need-based self-help aid	38
% UG rec. need-based self-help aid	37
% frosh rec. any financial aid	78
% UG rec. any financial aid	74

UNIVERSITY OF OREGON

1217 UNIVERSITY OF OREGON, EUGENE, OR 97403-1217 • ADMISSIONS: 541-346-3201 • FAX: 541-346-5815

CAMPUS LIFE

Quality of Life Rating	**83**
Fire Safety Rating	**68**
Type of school	public
Environment	city

STUDENTS

Total undergrad enrollment	16,282
% male/female	47/53
% from out of state	22
% from public high school	90
% live on campus	22
% in (# of) fraternities	7 (15)
% in (# of) sororities	8 (8)
% African American	2
% Asian	6
% Caucasian	76
% Hispanic	4
% Native American	1
% international	5
# of countries represented	87

SURVEY SAYS . . .
Great library
Athletic facilities are great
Everyone loves the Ducks
Political activism is popular

ACADEMICS

Academic Rating	**73**
Calendar	quarter
Student/faculty ratio	18:1
Profs interesting rating	71
Profs accessible rating	77
% profs teaching UG courses	100
% classes taught by TAs	21
Most common lab size	20–29 students
Most common reg class size	20–29 students

MOST POPULAR MAJORS
business administration
journalism
psychology

STUDENTS SAY

Academics

For applicants looking for "a good balance of fun and studies," the University of Oregon offers top programs in journalism, sports marketing, business, architecture, and education in a laid-back academic atmosphere. Within these popular disciplines, "Demand is so high for classes that even as an upper-level student with significant credits and course work, I have had trouble getting into classes," says a journalism student. Those looking to cruise through college "can skim by with B's and C's in the social sciences," but departments like biochemistry "weed out the drifters and demand a lot of work." Across disciplines, professors exude "a jovial attitude" from the lectern, and students will occasionally "go to an independent film in a small group with a professor or talk politics with them over dinner." One junior recalls, "I did not think that I would get the love and caring behavior that I have received from teachers by going to a big university." Participants in the Clark Honors College feel like they're "attending a small liberal arts school within a larger university" and tout the opportunities for "small classes with heated discussions" and interaction with top faculty. On the downside, "especially for science majors, the rigid Honors College requirements cut into time that could be well spent elsewhere." While some see U of O as simply a "decent education at a decent price," most feel challenged "to become well-rounded thinkers and educated, active participants in the world."

Life

Throw together "hippies, conservatives, sick parties, and rain like no other," and you've got a decent picture of Oregon life. The large Greek system paired with the "typical student who goes to most of their classes and does most of their work but likes partying a lot" accounts for a well-lubricated social scene. However, some students maintain that it's "not nearly the party school that a lot of the California beach and Arizona schools are." Whether students want to have a pint at the local brewpub, talk politics at "a small, international party with yummy food," or rage on at "huge dance parties with hundreds of people," a destination awaits them. On this "very athletic campus," students like to hit the "amazing workout facilities and intramural fields" during the week and spend the weekends camping, hiking, surfing, skiing, and rock climbing. Many also turn out to cheer on the Ducks in Pac-10 action. The "sweet little hippie town" of Eugene, home to many a WTO protester, offers an "extremely fun downtown area that's a different experience from what most college kids are used to." According to a junior, "It is easy to become an active citizen and enjoy the great cultural benefits of the area if one is willing to put in the effort to explore."

Student Body

Most students feel challenged to summarize their 16,282 classmates, since "a very eclectic vibe" pervades the campus. Overall, "U of O is a very liberal school within a very liberal community. As a whole, the area is very accepting of people from different backgrounds." Various subgroups thrive within the university "with their own student organizations and cultures," but the hippies make the reputation. Some believe "The problem is that the hippies get the press and are so outlandish that the majority of students are overlooked." Another student clarifies, "The hippie population is present—and there are probably more here than at other schools—but there are also plenty of people who are not," and are able to "break away from that mold." U of O students, mostly from in-state or somewhere on the West coast, maintain their idealism and an "interest in learning how and where they can make an impact in the world." They ponder questions like "Why are we here? What is our purpose?" which too often lead to, "Why should we bother studying for our history final when we'll all eventually die anyway?"

FINANCIAL AID: 541-346-3211 • E-MAIL: UOADMIT@OREGON.UOREGON.EDU • WEBSITE: WWW.UOREGON.EDU

ADMISSIONS

Very important factors considered include: Rigor of secondary school record. *Important factors considered include:* Academic GPA. *Other factors considered include:* Application essay, class rank, extracurricular activities, first generation, geographical residence, interview, racial/ethnic status, recommendation(s), standardized test scores, state residency, talent/ability, volunteer work, work experience. SAT or ACT required; SAT or ACT with Writing component required. TOEFL required of all international applicants. High school diploma is required, and GED is accepted. *Academic units required:* 4 English, 3 math, 2 science, 2 foreign language, 3 social studies. *Academic units recommended:* 1 science lab, 2 additional units in required college preparatory areas.

The Inside Word

Oregon's admissions process is essentially a formula; it's not likely that anything beyond your grades, rank, and tests will play much of a part in getting you admitted.

FINANCIAL AID

Students should submit: FAFSA. The Princeton Review suggests that all financial aid forms be submitted as soon as possible after January 1. *Need-based scholarships/grants offered:* Pell Grant, SEOG, state scholarships/grants, private scholarships, the school's own gift aid. *Loan aid offered:* Direct Subsidized Stafford, Direct Unsubsidized Stafford, Direct PLUS, Federal Perkins Loan, college/university loans from institutional funds. Applicants will be notified of awards on a rolling basis beginning or about April 15.

FROM THE ADMISSIONS OFFICE

"Many of the UO's over 125 academic programs are internationally recognized for academic excellence. The College of Education and individual departments in architecture, chemistry, economics, English, psychology, molecular biology, biochemistry, physics, and neuroscience all rank among the top 10 in the United States. The UO's School of Journalism and Communication and the College of Business rank in the top 20 in the United States. Eugene is the classic U.S. college town, small enough to bike across, but large enough to offer cafés, clubs, and culture. The UO is located in a vast outdoor recreation area, with hundreds of miles of bike paths and hiking trails inside the city limits. With the Pacific Ocean an hour to the west and the Cascade Mountains an hour to the east, you'll have surfing, skiing, snowboarding, river-rafting, and rock-climbing areas close to home. The UO has been recognized by the American Council on Education as one of the country's leaders in internationalization. Over 14 percent of UO students study abroad in more than 70 countries around the world. You'll attend classes alongside students from all 50 states and 87 countries. At the University of Oregon, you'll live the university motto, "Minds Move Mountains." Whether you want to change a community, a law, or one person's mind, the UO will provide you with all the inspiration and resources you'll need to succeed.

"Applicants for Fall 2008 are required to take the new version of the SAT with the writing component, or the ACT with the Writing section. Students may submit additional test scores from the old version of the SAT (prior to March 2005) or ACT in addition to the new SAT scores, and the student's best test scores will be used."

SELECTIVITY

Admissions Rating	79
# of applicants	10,821
% of applicants accepted	88
% of acceptees attending	36

FRESHMAN PROFILE

Range SAT Critical Reading	488–606
Range SAT Math	500–611
Minimum Paper TOEFL	500
Minimum Computer Based TOEFL	173
Average HS GPA	3.5
% graduated top 10% of class	23
% graduated top 25% of class	56
% graduated top 50% of class	89

DEADLINES

Regular notification	rolling
Nonfall registration?	yes

APPLICANTS ALSO LOOK AT

AND OFTEN PREFER
University of California—Santa Barbara, University of California—Berkeley, University of California—Davis, University of Southern California

AND SOMETIMES PREFER
University of Puget Sound, University of Washington, Willamette University

AND RARELY PREFER
Oregon State University, University of Arizona, University of Colorado—Boulder, University of Portland, Washington State University

FINANCIAL FACTS

Financial Aid Rating	66
Annual in-state tuition	$4,341
Annual out-of-state tuition	$16,755
Room & Board	$7,827
Books and supplies	$900
Required fees	$1,497
% frosh rec. need-based scholarship or grant aid	16
% UG rec. need-based scholarship or grant aid	21
% frosh rec. need-based self-help aid	29
% UG rec. need-based self-help aid	33
% frosh rec. any financial aid	60
% UG rec. any financial aid	60

UNIVERSITY OF THE PACIFIC

3601 PACIFIC AVENUE, STOCKTON, CA 95211 • ADMISSIONS: 209-946-2211 • FAX: 209-946-2413

STUDENTS SAY

Academics

Many at University of the Pacific believe that "science is the driving force at Pacific" and that "accelerated programs in pharmacy and dentistry" are what bring many of the brightest students in the country here. "Many people who have been also accepted by other prestigious schools choose Pacific over these for the accelerated programs." This assessment correctly identifies Pacific's strengths in the sciences, but it doesn't give the rest of the university its due. Pacific's School of International Studies, for example, "is one of six in the nation—and the only one that requires undergraduates to go abroad." The Conservatory of Music is "great and very welcoming," the Sports Sciences Department offers a popular 5-year BA/MBA (as well as a unique sports management program), and the engineering program "provides individual attention and a successful co-op program that helps you to come out of college with experience in the real world." The school has a lot to offer in the way of programs, and in every area, "Pacific is completely for and about the students. You don't feel like you're just a number here. The professors learn your name (even in a lecture situation), and you have access to speak with any professor, dean, or even the president of the university." Furthermore, students proclaim, "You're guaranteed to get the classes you need to graduate in 4 years."

Life

"Student life on campus is good" at Pacific, with "over 120 clubs for student groups. We are [also] encouraged to start our own clubs if we feel that something is missing." Greek life "is pretty active and has a positive reputation." Partying is fairly widespread. "Despite the dry-campus policy, the Greeks get up to plenty of mischief," undergrads assure us. Hometown Stockton "may not exactly be the top destination of some students," but it's not as bad as some guidebooks make it out to be. In recent years, "Stockton has cleaned up downtown, adding new restaurants, a movie theater, and new bars and clubs. A new baseball park for the minor league Stockton Ports and a new arena for hockey, indoor soccer and arena football have just been built." While crime "tends to be a problem in Stockton," most of the trouble "is centralized to one bad area. The surrounding neighborhood around the school is safe, as is the north part of town." Stockton also provides access to "many great nearby state parks," and is "not too far away from San Francisco." Pacific's sports teams, the Pacific Tigers, are "always very exciting to watch. Most of the students are very excited to see games and always bring a lot of school spirit."

Student Body

University of the Pacific "is a melting pot." "This is a pretty diverse campus, and most people here are very accepting of everyone." That said, the typical student, one undergrad tells us, "is from a higher-income household from Southern California or the Bay Area, clean cut, and dressed conservatively." There are, however, "plenty of atypical students," including "a large number of athletes, performance artists, musicians, artists, and engineers" to supplement "the largely professionally driven population." Outside of the high-profile programs, there are a number of students who "just want to have a good time," we're told. In fact, many feel that the campus splits between "those who are extremely motivated to achieve their academic and professional goals" and "those who are here to party and waste time until they become 'adults.'"

FINANCIAL AID: 209-946-2421 • E-MAIL: ADMISSIONS@PACIFIC.EDU • WEBSITE: WWW.PACIFIC.EDU

ADMISSIONS

Very important factors considered include: Rigor of secondary school record. *Important factors considered include:* Academic GPA, application essay, extracurricular activities, first generation, recommendation(s), standardized test scores. *Other factors considered include:* Alumni/ae relation, character/personal qualities, class rank, geographical residence, level of applicant's interest, racial/ethnic status, talent/ability, volunteer work, work experience. SAT or ACT required; SAT and SAT Subject Tests or ACT recommended. SAT Subject Tests recommended; TOEFL required of all international applicants. High school diploma is required, and GED is accepted. *Academic units recommended:* 4 English, 3 math, (2 science labs), 2 foreign language, 3 social studies, 3 academic electives, 1 fine/performing arts.

The Inside Word

Pacific wages a fierce battle for applicants amongst its California counterparts and this results in a deceptively high acceptance rate. While the Admissions Team considers a variety of factors, a challenging course load is most important. It is highly advantageous for interested students to enroll in honors and Advanced Placement classes.

FINANCIAL AID

Students should submit: FAFSA. The Princeton Review suggests that all financial aid forms be submitted as soon as possible after January 1. *Need-based scholarships/grants offered:* Pell Grant, SEOG, state scholarships/grants, private scholarships, the school's own gift aid. *Loan aid offered:* Direct Subsidized Stafford, Direct Unsubsidized Stafford, Direct PLUS, FFEL Subsidized Stafford, FFEL Unsubsidized Stafford, FFEL PLUS, Federal Perkins Loan, Direct Graduate/Professional PLUS Loans. Applicants will be notified of awards on a rolling basis beginning or about March 15.

FROM THE ADMISSIONS OFFICE

"One of the most concise ways of describing the University of the Pacific is that it is 'a major university in a small college package.' Our 3,400 undergraduates get the personal attention that you would expect at a small, residential college. But they also have the kinds of opportunities offered at much larger institutions, including more than 90 majors and programs; hundreds of student organizations; drama, dance, and musical productions; 16 NCAA Division I athletic teams; and two dozen club and intramural sports. We offer undergraduate major programs in the arts, sciences and humanities, business, education, engineering, international studies, music, pharmacy, and health sciences. Some of the unique aspects of our academic programs include the following: We have the only independent, coed, nonsectarian liberal arts and sciences college located between Los Angeles and central Oregon; we have the only undergraduate professional school of international studies in California—and it's the only one in the nation that actually requires you to study abroad; we have the only engineering program in the West that requires students to complete a year's worth of paid work experience as part of their degree; our Conservatory of Music focuses on performance but also offers majors in music management, music therapy, and music education; and we offer several accelerated programs in business, dentistry, dental hygiene, education, law, engineering, and pharmacy. Our beautiful New England–style main campus is located in Stockton (population: 289,800) and is within 2 hours or less of San Francisco, Santa Cruz, Yosemite National Park, and Lake Tahoe.

"SAT Subject Tests recommended: Mathematics, Chemistry (natural science majors only)."

SELECTIVITY

Admissions Rating	88
# of applicants	4,976
% of applicants accepted	69
% of acceptees attending	25
# accepting a place on wait list	30

FRESHMAN PROFILE

Range SAT Critical Reading	500–620
Range SAT Math	540–670
Range SAT Writing	500–610
Range ACT Composite	22–27
Minimum Paper TOEFL	475
Minimum Computer Based TOEFL	150
Average HS GPA	3.46
% graduated top 10% of class	42
% graduated top 25% of class	72
% graduated top 50% of class	93

DEADLINES

Regular notification	3/15
Nonfall registration?	yes

APPLICANTS ALSO LOOK AT AND SOMETIMES PREFER

California Polytechnic State University—San Luis Obispo, University of California—Berkeley, University of California—Davis, University of California—Los Angeles, University of Southern California

FINANCIAL FACTS

Financial Aid Rating	75
Annual tuition	$26,920
Room & Board	$8,700
Books and supplies	$1,314
Required fees	$430
% frosh rec. need-based scholarship or grant aid	63
% UG rec. need-based scholarship or grant aid	63
% frosh rec. need-based self-help aid	59
% UG rec. need-based self-help aid	60
% frosh rec. any financial aid	65
% UG rec. any financial aid	65

UNIVERSITY OF PENNSYLVANIA

ONE COLLEGE HALL, PHILADELPHIA, PA 19104 • ADMISSIONS: 215-898-7507 • FAX: 215-898-9670

STUDENTS SAY

Academics

The University of Pennsylvania is perhaps best known for its Wharton School of Business ("the number-one undergraduate business program in the country," students claim), but this Ivy League institution "is strong in all divisions, a fact that one can take advantage of very easily through dual degree programs across schools." Wharton, the engineering school and science programs "require students to study a lot, as the courses move fast and cover a lot of material," while "Students in the college studying liberal arts don't have it as bad." With a world-class faculty in nearly all disciplines, "Penn offers access to the best and brightest minds in the world, people who are always willing and available to discuss any topic, whether or not you are enrolled in one of their classes." Students tell us that "among the Ivies, Penn seems to be the most career-oriented, as fewer students here are on the academia track than at other schools. Many students take jobs right out after graduation rather than go to graduate school, and Penn does an excellent job of placing these students." Indeed, "A very large number of students grab the country's most prestigious jobs for undergrads: investment banking, consulting, and private equity." As at many large schools, "The administration tends to feel a bit remote to most students" and "The school can be a little bureaucratic, with little communication among administrative departments."

Life

There's a common arc to most students' extracurricular lives during their 4 years at Penn. When they first arrive they stick close to campus. "The social scene for most freshmen consists of frat parties, period," explains one student. As they get older, "They leave the bubble of campus and explore more of Philadelphia. There are a lot of awesome places in the city in terms of the nightlife, but you can't really get in unless you're of age." Options abound both on and off campus; one student notes, "Having Center City (and many bars/clubs/activities) just 20 blocks away is a plus, though there is also tons to do on campus as well." Campus options include "parties, theater, a cappella shows, sporting events, guest lectures, sketch comedy, movie showings, etc." Students point out that "Penn's campus is located in West Philly, which doesn't have the best reputation, but the campus itself is a vast improvement from the local area and security is a moderate concern." They also note that "for being a city school, Penn's campus is so nice, it looks more like a plush suburban park. . . . Walking down Locust Walk (the main artery of campus) one can always see people stopping to say hello to their fellow students, student groups handing out fliers promoting an event or trying to draw attention to an issue, students enjoying an outdoor lunch while sitting at one of the many benches or tables set up outside, or standing in line at one of the lunch trucks (a staple of any Penn student's diet)."

Student Body

"There are distinct stereotypes for each of the four undergraduate schools" at Penn—brainy engineer, ambitious Wharton student, artsy college kid, hard-working nurse—although "generally students from all four schools interact quite smoothly." The student body includes "a surprising number of very religious people, including some staunch Christians and many Jews. There are far fewer agnostics and atheists than you would expect." Penn is known among the Ivies as the school where students unwind most enthusiastically. "Everyone at Penn is very stressed out, all the time, which is why most people have to let loose on the weekend," explains one student. Another adds, "The average Penn student is a thinker and a drinker. Everybody studies really hard all week long and lets loose on the weekends at wild parties. But the students are also insanely smart. On our first day, the Dean asked everyone to stand up in the auditorium who had been valedictorian. The number of people who stood up almost scared me to death."

UNIVERSITY OF PENNSYLVANIA

FINANCIAL AID: 215-898-1988 • E-MAIL: INFO@ADMISSIONS.UGAO.UPENN.EDU • WEBSITE: WWW.UPENN.EDU

ADMISSIONS

Very important factors considered include: Academic GPA, character/personal qualities, recommendation(s), rigor of secondary school record, talent/ability. *Important factors considered include:* Application essay, extracurricular activities, first generation, standardized test scores. *Other factors considered include:* Alumni/ae relation, class rank, geographical residence, interview, level of applicant's interest, racial/ethnic status, volunteer work, work experience. SAT and SAT Subject Tests or ACT required; ACT with Writing component required. TOEFL required of all international applicants. High school diploma or equivalent is not required. *Academic units recommended:* 4 English, 4 math, 4 science, 4 foreign language, 2 social studies, 2 history.

The Inside Word

After a small decline three cycles ago, applications are once again climbing at Penn—the fourth increase in 5 years. The competition in the applicant pool is formidable. Applicants can safely assume that they need to be one of the strongest students in their graduating class in order to be successful.

FINANCIAL AID

Students should submit: FAFSA, institution's own financial aid form, CSS/Financial Aid PROFILE, Noncustodial PROFILE, Business/Farm Supplement, parents' and student's most recent Federal Income Tax Returns. The Princeton Review suggests that all financial aid forms be submitted as soon as possible after January 1. *Need-based scholarships/grants offered:* Pell Grant, SEOG, state scholarships/grants, private scholarships, the school's own gift aid. *Loan aid offered:* FFEL Subsidized Stafford, FFEL Unsubsidized Stafford, FFEL PLUS, Federal Perkins Loan, Federal Nursing Loan, college/university loans from institutional funds, supplemental third party loans guaranteed by institution. Applicants will be notified of awards on or about April 1.

FROM THE ADMISSIONS OFFICE

"The nation's first university, the University of Pennsylvania, had its beginnings in 1740, some 36 years before Thomas Jefferson, Benjamin Franklin (Penn's founder), and their fellow revolutionaries went public in Philadelphia with incendiary notions about life, liberty and the pursuit of happiness. Today, Penn continues in the spirit of the Founding Fathers, developing the intellectual, discussion-oriented seminars that comprise the majority of our course offerings, shaping innovative new courses of study, and allowing a remarkable degree of academic flexibility to its undergraduate students.

"Penn is situated on a green, tree-lined, 260-acre urban campus, four blocks west of the Schuylkill River in Philadelphia. The broad lawns that connect Penn's stately halls embody a philosophy of academic freedom within our undergraduate schools. Newly developed interdisciplinary programs fusing classical disciplines with practical, professional options enable Penn to define cutting-edge academia in and out of the classroom. Students are encouraged to partake in study and research that may extend into many of the graduate and professional schools. As part of our College House system, Penn's Faculty Masters engage students in academic and civic experience while leading residential programs that promote an environment where living and learning intersect around the clock.

"Penn students are part of a dynamic community that includes a traditional campus, a lively neighborhood, and a city rich in culture and diversity. Whether your interests include artistic performance, community involvement, student government, athletics, fraternities and sororities, or cultural and religious organizations, you'll find many different options. Most importantly, students at Penn find that their lives in and out of the classroom compliment each other and are full, interesting and busy. We invite you to visit Penn in Philadelphia. You'll enjoy the revolutionary spirit of the campus and city.

"Penn requires either the new SAT plus two SAT Subject Tests (in different fields) or the ACT. Scores from older versions of the SAT (pre-March 2005 version) and the ACT are acceptable. For the old SAT, scores must be submitted with the results of three SAT Subject Tests, one of which must be the writing test."

SELECTIVITY
Admissions Rating	99
# of applicants	20,483
% of applicants accepted	18
% of acceptees attending	66
# accepting a place on wait list	1,494
% admitted from wait list	2
# of early decision applicants	4120
% accepted early decision	29

FRESHMAN PROFILE
Range SAT Critical Reading	650–740
Range SAT Math	680–770
Range SAT Writing	650–740
Range ACT Composite	29–33
Minimum Paper TOEFL	600
Minimum Computer Based TOEFL	250
Average HS GPA	3.83
% graduated top 10% of class	94
% graduated top 25% of class	99
% graduated top 50% of class	100

DEADLINES
Early decision application deadline	11/1
Early decision notification	12/15
Regular application deadline	1/1
Regular notification	4/1
Nonfall registration?	no

APPLICANTS ALSO LOOK AT
AND OFTEN PREFER
Harvard College, Stanford University, Yale University
AND SOMETIMES PREFER
Brown University, Columbia University, Duke University
AND RARELY PREFER
Cornell University, Georgetown University, Northwestern University

FINANCIAL FACTS
Financial Aid Rating	94
Annual tuition	$30,598
Room & Board	$9,804
Books and supplies	$900
Required fees	$3,558
% frosh rec. need-based scholarship or grant aid	40
% UG rec. need-based scholarship or grant aid	41
% frosh rec. need-based self-help aid	44
% UG rec. need-based self-help aid	44
% frosh rec. any financial aid	62
% UG rec. any financial aid	55

UNIVERSITY OF PITTSBURGH—PITTSBURGH CAMPUS

4227 FIFTH AVENUE, FIRST FLOOR, ALUMNI HALL, PITTSBURGH, PA 15260 • ADMISSIONS: 412-624-7488 • FAX: 412-648-8815

CAMPUS LIFE

Quality of Life Rating	89
Fire Safety Rating	85
Type of school	public
Environment	city

STUDENTS

Total undergrad enrollment	16,796
% male/female	49/51
% from out of state	15
% live on campus	47
% in (# of) fraternities	10 (18)
% in (# of) sororities	9 (11)
% African American	9
% Asian	4
% Caucasian	81
% Hispanic	1
% international	1
# of countries represented	43

SURVEY SAYS . . .
Great computer facilities
Great library
Athletic facilities are great
Great off-campus food
Students are happy
Everyone loves the Panthers
Student publications are popular
Lots of beer drinking

ACADEMICS

Academic Rating	80
Calendar	semester
Student/faculty ratio	16:1
Profs interesting rating	69
Profs accessible rating	79
Most common lab size	20–29 students
Most common reg class size	10–19 students

MOST POPULAR MAJORS
business/marketing
English
social sciences

STUDENTS SAY

Academics

The University of Pittsburgh "is the perfect-sized institution," a place with "all the benefits of a large urban university, including research, internships, and lots of amazing experiences," but also small enough "that people truly have a chance to make a name for themselves on campus. You can't go 5 minutes without bumping into someone you know here." Many departments stand out; all medical fields benefit from the school's affiliation with the renowned research-oriented University of Pittsburgh Medical Center; and programs in dentistry, pharmacology, physical therapy, neuroscience, and biology are all considered outstanding. Programs in engineering, business, and the liberal arts are also noteworthy. Students appreciate the fact that "professors here are all very accessible and really want their students to learn and understand their courses. They are willing to work with the students to [help them] achieve better grades and enhance the learning experience." Opportunities to study abroad abound, and undergrads "can often find study-abroad programs that are cheaper for them than their tuition would have been."

Life

Pitt is located in Oakland, a "really nice location relative to downtown Pittsburgh and the surrounding neighborhoods." Thanks to "the school's arrangement" with the city of Pittsburgh, "every Pitt student gets free city busing," a perk that allows and encourages undergrads to explore the city. Further such encouragement comes in the form of PittArts, a program that "heavily subsidizes cultural events in the city. When Broadway shows come to Pittsburgh, you can get tickets for $10, a dinner at an Italian restaurant, and free transportation downtown. They also offer free lectures, operas, and symphonies." No wonder students tell us that "Pittsburgh is a college city, one that really caters to students. Bigger cities may offer more renowned acts coming through, or more famous museums, but in Pittsburgh we can actually afford to experience them!" The campus is also busy, with "many campus organizations," "free movies in the Union, student performances on campus, lectures (Maya Angelou came recently)"; these offer students lots of opportunities to socialize. Pitt athletics are also popular, with basketball and football drawing the biggest crowds. All of these options "make socializing easier and less alcohol-centric. While there is a lot of drinking on campus, it is just as easy and socially acceptable to sit down to coffee."

Student Body

A "very diverse population" of 16,796 undergraduates virtually guarantees that "everyone is bound to meet someone whom he or she would have never met staying in his or her hometown." The school has "over 450 organizations, and all those groups provide a place for students to come and be their own people in a group they feel comfortable with." Highly competitive admissions mean that "kids here are definitely intelligent and have a lot going for them." They're not just brainiacs, though—in fact, Pitt students "like to have a good time too, not just going out to parties. Many students really take advantage of the free admission to numerous museums and free city busing to visit the many neighborhoods of Pittsburgh." The most dedicated students here, our respondents report, can be found in the medical sciences (neuroscience, chemistry, and biology) as well as in some of the humanities (writing, literature, philosophy).

UNIVERSITY OF PITTSBURGH—PITTSBURGH CAMPUS

FINANCIAL AID: 412-624-7488 • E-MAIL: OAFA@PITT.EDU • WEBSITE: WWW.PITT.EDU

ADMISSIONS

Very important factors considered include: Academic GPA, class rank, rigor of secondary school record. *Important factors considered include:* Standardized test scores. *Other factors considered include:* Application essay, character/personal qualities, extracurricular activities, first generation, geographical residence, racial/ethnic status, recommendation(s), talent/ability, volunteer work, work experience. SAT or ACT required. TOEFL required of all international applicants. High school diploma is required, and GED is not accepted. *Academic units required:* 4 English, 3 math, 3 science (3 science labs), 1 foreign language, 1 social studies, 4 academic electives. *Academic units recommended:* 4 math, 4 science, 3 foreign language, 3 social studies, 2 history.

The Inside Word

With the overwhelming number of applications Pitt receives, it's no wonder its Admissions Counselors rely on numbers. Comparable to its public university brethren, the school makes admit decisions based mostly on secondary school records and test scores. Applicants who provide transcripts laced with honors classes, Advanced Placement classes, and solid grades should be accepted.

FINANCIAL AID

Students should submit: FAFSA, along with Pitt's Financial Aid Application supplement. The filing deadline for the supplement for new students is June 1. The Princeton Review suggests that all financial aid forms be submitted as soon as possible after January 1. *Need-based scholarships/grants offered:* Pell Grant, SEOG, state scholarships/grants, private scholarships, the school's own gift aid. *Loan aid offered:* FFEL Subsidized Stafford, FFEL Unsubsidized Stafford, FFEL PLUS, Federal Perkins Loan, Federal Nursing Loan, college/university loans from institutional funds. Applicants will be notified of awards on a rolling basis beginning or about March 15. Federal Work-Study Program available. Off-campus job opportunities are excellent.

FROM THE ADMISSIONS OFFICE

"The University of Pittsburgh is one of 62 members of the Association of American Universities, a prestigious group whose members include the major research universities of North America. There are nearly 400 degree programs available at the 16 Pittsburgh campus schools (two offering only undergraduate degree programs, four offering graduate degree programs, and ten offering both) and four regional campuses, allowing students a wide latitude of choices, both academically and in setting and style, size and pace of campus. Programs ranked nationally include philosophy, history and philosophy of science, chemistry, economics, English, history, physics, political science, and psychology. The University Center for International Studies is ranked one of the exemplary international programs in the country by the Council on Learning.

"Freshman applicants for Fall 2008 are required to submit SAT or ACT test results. All testing should preferably be completed by fall of your senior year for September admission. We strongly recommend that you take the SAT or ACT at least once as a junior and once as a senior."

SELECTIVITY

Admissions Rating	**88**
# of applicants	18,195
% of applicants accepted	56
% of acceptees attending	34
# accepting a place on wait list	149
% admitted from wait list	65

FRESHMAN PROFILE

Range SAT Critical Reading	560–660
Range SAT Math	570–660
Range ACT Composite	24–29
Minimum Paper TOEFL	550
Minimum Computer Based TOEFL	213
% graduated top 10% of class	43
% graduated top 25% of class	80
% graduated top 50% of class	98

DEADLINES

Regular notification	rolling
Nonfall registration?	yes

APPLICANTS ALSO LOOK AT

AND OFTEN PREFER
Boston University, Carnegie Mellon University, New York University, University of Pennsylvania, Virginia Tech

AND SOMETIMES PREFER
Pennsylvania State University—University Park, University of Delaware, University of Maryland—College Park

AND RARELY PREFER
Duquesne University, Indiana University of Pennsylvania, Slippery Rock University of Pennsylvania, Temple University

FINANCIAL FACTS

Financial Aid Rating	**77**
Annual in-state tuition	$11,368
Annual out-of-state tuition	$20,686
Room & Board	$7,800
Books and supplies	$1,000
Required fees	$770
% frosh rec. need-based scholarship or grant aid	35
% UG rec. need-based scholarship or grant aid	34
% frosh rec. need-based self-help aid	40
% UG rec. need-based self-help aid	44

UNIVERSITY OF PUGET SOUND

1500 NORTH WARNER STREET, TACOMA, WA 98416-1062 • ADMISSIONS: 253-879-3211 • FAX: 253-879-3993

CAMPUS LIFE

Quality of Life Rating	**88**
Fire Safety Rating	**72**
Type of school	private
Environment	city

STUDENTS

Total undergrad enrollment	2,531
% male/female	42/58
% from out of state	69
% from public high school	76
% live on campus	62
% in (# of) fraternities	20 (4)
% in (# of) sororities	18 (4)
% African American	3
% Asian	9
% Caucasian	75
% Hispanic	3
% Native American	1

SURVEY SAYS . . .
Small classes
No one cheats
Great library

ACADEMICS

Academic Rating	**92**
Calendar	semester
Student/faculty ratio	11:1
Profs interesting rating	94
Profs accessible rating	96
% profs teaching UG courses	90
% classes taught by TAs	0
Most common lab size	10–19 students
Most common reg class size	10–19 students

MOST POPULAR MAJORS
business administration/
management
English language and literature
psychology

STUDENTS SAY

Academics

Set "in the shadows of the Cascades" and just down the road from Washington State's Commencement Bay, the University of Puget Sound "offers a strong (and getting stronger) liberal arts education." A junior explains, "We are a very student-centered school," which means that teaching is top priority for this highly qualified faculty. Not only are professors "intelligent, well versed, [and] articulate," they're also concerned about the well-being of their students. "Many professors want to have conversations about what is going on in your life," writes a senior. "They make this school." So does the strong allotment of academic offerings. Students point to the Asian studies, biology, international political economy, and music offerings as the crème de la crème. You won't find the standard "huge lecture classes" at UPS; "Even intro-level lectures have maybe 30 people in them." Despite the friendly atmosphere in class, professors tend to set high expectations for their students. "Coasting by on natural ability doesn't work anymore," warns a senior. Opinions of the administration vary, but most find it to be "caring and supportive of the students. If you have an idea, they say go for it." Students are hoping that the new president of the university will help put the place on the map. As a psychology major puts it, "The university is academically strong, but needs to be recognized for that across the country, not just in the Pacific Northwest."

Life

Whether you're a city slicker or a rugged outdoorsman, UPS's location ensures you'll find something to satisfy your interests. Seattle is a short drive away and has everything from pro sports teams to world-class art exhibits. With beaches, the Sound, the Cascades, and the Olympic Rain Forest all nearby, outdoor enthusiasts are never at a loss for adventure. "Outdoor interests are really popular, [including] Ultimate Frisbee, soccer, biking, and hiking." "Athletics are huge," too, and with 21 varsity teams, 14 intramural sports, and three club sports, athletes have plenty of opportunities to flex their muscles. Sports aside, "There are tons of activities (presentations, volunteer opportunities, meetings, movies, talks, concerts, and clubs) every night of the week." In total, UPS offers about 75 student clubs, and "Most people are involved in a ton of groups." When they're not involved in parties, that is. "There are always plenty going on, either at Greek houses or in other nearby campus houses." But beware, warns an undergrad: "The administration can have a Gestapo-esque feel when it comes to parties and drinking on campus." Nonetheless, some students line up at the keg, while others fill the seats for the popular "one-dollar movies" on campus. Regardless of what you're doing, "If you're not doing anything in the evening, you're either lazy or antisocial . . . or dead."

Student Body

"There are three groups of students" at UPS, according to a senior: "(1) the preppies, (2) the hippies, (3) the Hawaiians." Among groups (1) and (2), you're likely to find "a lot of 'trustafarians' and rich kids." There's no doubt that liberalism rules the roost here, which causes one junior to note that "the least accepted student organization is, ironically, the Republican Majority." But political differences—or any differences, for that matter—don't cause irreparable rifts in this student body. According to a sophomore, "Everyone gets along extremely well, no matter what gender, religion, race, ethnicity, [or] social class. UPS has a great atmosphere that I sincerely appreciate." Another classmate adds, "Overall, students are accepting and curious about other beliefs. And students here are open-minded." They're open-hearted, as well. Many students reported participating in community service.

FINANCIAL AID: 800-396-7192 • E-MAIL: ADMISSION@UPS.EDU • WEBSITE: WWW.UPS.EDU

ADMISSIONS

Very important factors considered include: Academic GPA, rigor of secondary school record, standardized test scores. *Important factors considered include:* Alumni/ae relation, application essay, character/personal qualities, extracurricular activities, racial/ethnic status, recommendation(s), talent/ability. *Other factors considered include:* Class rank, first generation, interview, level of applicant's interest, volunteer work, work experience. SAT or ACT required; ACT with Writing component recommended. TOEFL required of all international applicants. High school diploma is required, and GED is accepted. *Academic units recommended:* 4 English, 4 math, 4 science (4 science labs), 3 foreign language, 3 social studies, 3 history, 1 fine/visual/performing arts.

The Inside Word

The University of Puget Sound is on the right track with its willingness to supply students with detailed information about how the selection process works. If universities in general were more forthcoming about candidate evaluation, college admission wouldn't be the angst-ridden exercise that it is for so many students. All students are aware that their academic background is the primary consideration of every Admissions Committee. How they are considered as individuals remains mysterious. At Puget Sound, it is clear that people mean more to the university than its freshman profile and that candidates can count on a considerate and caring attitude before, during, and after the review process.

FINANCIAL AID

Students should submit: FAFSA. The Princeton Review suggests that all financial aid forms be submitted as soon as possible after January 1. *Need-based scholarships/grants offered:* Pell Grant, SEOG, state scholarships/grants, private scholarships, the school's own gift aid. *Loan aid offered:* FFEL Subsidized Stafford, FFEL Unsubsidized Stafford, FFEL PLUS, Federal Perkins Loan. Applicants will be notified of awards on a rolling basis beginning or about March 15. Federal Work-Study Program available. Institutional employment available. Off-campus job opportunities are excellent.

FROM THE ADMISSIONS OFFICE

"For over 100 years, students from many locations and backgrounds have chosen to join our community. It is a community committed to excellence—excellence in the classroom and excellence in student organizations and activities. Puget students are serious about rowing and writing, management and music, skiing and sciences, leadership and languages. At Puget Sound you'll be challenged—and helped—to perform at the peak of your ability.

"Applicants are required to submit the SAT or the ACT. For the foreseeable future, Puget Sound will record the SAT or ACT Writing component score, but will not require it as a part of a completed freshman admission application."

SELECTIVITY

Admissions Rating	90
# of applicants	5,231
% of applicants accepted	65
% of acceptees attending	20
# accepting a place on wait list	132
% admitted from wait list	25
# of early decision applicants	158
% accepted early decision	91

FRESHMAN PROFILE

Range SAT Critical Reading	575–690
Range SAT Math	570–660
Range SAT Writing	550–660
Range ACT Composite	25–29
Minimum Paper TOEFL	550
Minimum Computer Based TOEFL	213
Average HS GPA	3.55
% graduated top 10% of class	39
% graduated top 25% of class	73
% graduated top 50% of class	98

DEADLINES

Early decision application deadline	11/15
Early decision notification	12/15
Regular application deadline	2/1
Regular notification	4/1
Nonfall registration?	yes

APPLICANTS ALSO LOOK AT

AND OFTEN PREFER

Pomona College, Stanford University, Washington University in St. Louis

AND SOMETIMES PREFER

Colorado College, Lewis & Clark College, University of Washington, Whitman College, Willamette University

AND RARELY PREFER

Albertson College of Idaho, Gonzaga University, Linfield College, Whitworth College

FINANCIAL FACTS

Financial Aid Rating	79
Annual tuition	$31,700
Room & Board	$8,265
Books and supplies	$800
Required fees	$360
% frosh rec. need-based scholarship or grant aid	56
% UG rec. need-based scholarship or grant aid	58
% frosh rec. need-based self-help aid	44
% UG rec. need-based self-help aid	48
% frosh rec. any financial aid	88
% UG rec. any financial aid	90

UNIVERSITY OF REDLANDS

1200 EAST COLTON AVENUE, REDLANDS, CA 92373 • ADMISSIONS: 909-335-4074 • FAX: 909-335-4089

CAMPUS LIFE

Quality of Life Rating	**82**
Fire Safety Rating	**77**
Type of school	private
Environment	town

STUDENTS

Total undergrad enrollment	2,310
% male/female	43/57
% from out of state	29
% live on campus	67
% in (# of) fraternities	5 (5)
% in (# of) sororities	8 (5)
% African American	2
% Asian	6
% Caucasian	58
% Hispanic	11
% international	2
# of countries represented	16

SURVEY SAYS . . .
Small classes
Lab facilities are great
Great computer facilities
Athletic facilities are great
Students are happy

ACADEMICS

Academic Rating	**86**
Calendar	4-4-1
Student/faculty ratio	11:1
Profs interesting rating	86
Profs accessible rating	83
% profs teaching UG courses	100
% classes taught by TAs	0
Most common lab size	10–19 students
Most common reg class size	10–19 students

MOST POPULAR MAJORS
business administration/
management
liberal arts and sciences studies and
humanities
psychology

STUDENTS SAY

Academics

The University of Redlands is essentially two undergraduate programs in one. Through the College of Arts and Sciences (CAS), the majority of students follow a relatively conventional undergraduate curriculum, declaring majors and meeting the related requirements in order to graduate. About 200 students take a more independent approach through the Johnston Center for Integrative Studies, "where students who are accepted can create their own major with the help of their professors." These Johnston students write contracts for their courses and receive narrative evaluations of their work (rather than letter grades). This structure "allows students to learn in a way that is the most efficient for each individual." Because Johnston is a residential community, "Everyone works together to strengthen their education," much to the delight of participants. But regardless of the track they choose, Redlands undergrads enjoy a "personable, student-oriented" school that's "just small enough to have incredible personal attention, yet large enough to still see different people almost every day." Students also appreciate a study abroad program that "is strongly emphasized and encouraged. If there's anywhere in the world that you've had an interest in going—for a month or semester to a year—the University of Redlands is the perfect place to do it. Many students go to Austria because it's a wonderful program, and all your credits transfer when you come back." Redlands excels in a number of areas, including business, music, creative writing, and biology, but they don't do it without a bit of sweat. Undergrads warn, "The academics at Redlands are demanding; I find myself reading, writing, and studying with extremely high degrees of intensity."

Life

Redlands is close to a lot of great places, but the town of Redlands itself "isn't much," students say. A number of them use the nickname "Dead Lands" to sum up their attitude, and a freshman gripes that "we can't just go into town to read at a coffee shop because there is no town!" So while "There's not much to do if you don't have a car," for the automobile-enabled, "Everything is within an hour: the beach, LA, Palm Springs, and the mountains. Trips to the desert in Joshua Tree National Park are also common. Many people like to snowboard or ski in Big Bear in the winter." This nature-rich setting attracts outdoorsy types, and unsurprisingly Redlands "has a very involved outdoor activities group on campus that takes students kayaking, rock climbing and backpacking to destinations throughout the country." The Redlands campus "is beautiful for its Roman-style buildings and pillars, especially in the winter with the snow-capped mountains in the background," and it stays reasonably busy for a school of Redland's size. "Usually, there's something happening on campus, whether it's a philosophical discussion, a screening of a movie, karaoke night, or a basketball game." Still, "On weekends, most people end up drinking and going to parties," which the school frowns upon. Students wish the administration would be "a little more relaxed when it comes to party scenes. It seems like everyone is always getting in trouble. And even the frats have to be really careful and always have huge fines."

Student Body

Because of the CAS/Johnston academic fault line at Redlands, "The school is somewhat divided," with "ultra-liberal Johnston students who meander about the campus on long boards, leaving behind a perpetual smell of hemp and patchouli" on one side, and "more conservative Abercrombie-wearing NCAA athletes, Greeks, and California-skater types" on the other. The CAS student body also includes "math/science geeks, the philosophy brains, the artists and musicians, the business people, and the whimsical lit majors," about half of whom "regard the Johnston kids with complete suspicion and mistrust," in part because some of the Johnston kids seem to look down on the CAS majority. Johnston undergrads are known for being drawn to "a high-energy community of creativity, inhibition, and at times, spurts of college randomness. They are notorious for doing strange things!"

FINANCIAL AID: 909-335-4047 • E-MAIL: ADMISSIONS@REDLANDS.EDU • WEBSITE: WWW.REDLANDS.EDU

ADMISSIONS

Very important factors considered include: Academic GPA, character/personal qualities, recommendation(s), rigor of secondary school record, talent/ability. *Important factors considered include:* Application essay, standardized test scores. *Other factors considered include:* Alumni/ae relation, extracurricular activities, first generation, geographical residence, interview, racial/ethnic status, volunteer work, work experience. SAT or ACT required; ACT with Writing component recommended. TOEFL required of all international applicants. High school diploma is required, and GED is accepted. *Academic units required:* 4 English, 3 math, 2 science (1 science lab), 2 foreign language, 2 social studies. *Academic units recommended:* 4 English, 4 math, 3 science (1 science lab), 3 foreign language, 2 social studies, 1 history.

The Inside Word

The University of Redlands is a solid admit for any student with an above average high school record. Candidates who are interested in pursuing self-designed programs through the University's Johnston Center will find the admissions process to be distinctly more personal than it generally is; the center is interested in intellectually curious, self-motivated students and puts a lot of energy into identifying and recruiting them.

FINANCIAL AID

Students should submit: FAFSA, state aid form, GPA Verification Form for California Residents. The Princeton Review suggests that all financial aid forms be submitted as soon as possible after January 1. *Need-based scholarships/grants offered:* Pell Grant, SEOG, state scholarships/grants, private scholarships, the school's own gift aid. *Loan aid offered:* FFEL Subsidized Stafford, FFEL Unsubsidized Stafford, FFEL PLUS, Federal Perkins Loan, college/university loans from institutional funds. Applicants will be notified of awards on or about February 28. Federal Work-Study Program available. Off-campus job opportunities are fair.

FROM THE ADMISSIONS OFFICE

"We've created an unusually blended curriculum of the liberal arts and pre-professional study because we think education is about learning how to think and learning how to do. For example, our environmental studies students have synthesized their study of computer science, sociology, biology, and economics to develop an actual resource management plan for the local mountain communities. Our creative writing program encourages internships with publishing or television production companies so that when our graduates send off their first novel, they can pay the rent as magazine writers. We educate managers, poets, environmental scientists, teachers, musicians, and speech therapists to be reflective about culture and society so that they can better understand and improve the world they'll enter upon graduation.

"First-year students applying for admission for Fall 2008 are required to submit the results of either the SAT or the ACT. We do not require the Writing section of either test. Students may also submit scores from the old SAT (prior to March 2005) or ACT and the student's best scores from either test will be used."

SELECTIVITY

Admissions Rating	88
# of applicants	3,480
% of applicants accepted	65
% of acceptees attending	27

FRESHMAN PROFILE

Range SAT Critical Reading	540–630
Range SAT Math	540–630
Range ACT Composite	22–26
Minimum Paper TOEFL	550
Minimum Computer Based TOEFL	213
Average HS GPA	3.58
% graduated top 10% of class	37
% graduated top 25% of class	67
% graduated top 50% of class	94

DEADLINES

Regular application deadline	4/1
Regular notification	rolling
Nonfall registration?	yes

APPLICANTS ALSO LOOK AT

AND OFTEN PREFER
Occidental College

AND SOMETIMES PREFER
Chapman University, Loyola Marymount University, Pitzer College, University of San Diego, Whittier College

AND RARELY PREFER
University of California—Riverside

FINANCIAL FACTS

Financial Aid Rating	87
Annual tuition	$28,476
Room & Board	$9,360
Books and supplies	$1,300
Required fees	$300
% frosh rec. need-based scholarship or grant aid	65
% UG rec. need-based scholarship or grant aid	67
% frosh rec. need-based self-help aid	60
% UG rec. need-based self-help aid	63
% frosh rec. any financial aid	91
% UG rec. any financial aid	90

UNIVERSITY OF RHODE ISLAND

14 UPPER COLLEGE ROAD, KINGSTON, RI 02881-1391 • ADMISSIONS: 401-874-7100 • FAX: 401-874-5523

CAMPUS LIFE

Quality of Life Rating	**64**
Fire Safety Rating	**81**
Type of school	public
Environment	village

STUDENTS

Total undergrad enrollment	11,542
% male/female	44/56
% from out of state	39
% live on campus	40
% in (# of) fraternities	10 (11)
% in (# of) sororities	9 (9)
% African American	5
% Asian	2
% Caucasian	75
% Hispanic	5

SURVEY SAYS . . .
Great library
Great off-campus food
Students are happy
Student publications are popular
Lots of beer drinking
Hard liquor is popular
(Almost) everyone smokes

ACADEMICS

Academic Rating	**63**
Calendar	semester
Student/faculty ratio	19:1
Profs interesting rating	61
Profs accessible rating	61
% profs teaching	
UG courses	N/A
% classes taught by TAs	N/A
Most common	
lab size	10–19 students
Most common	
reg class size	20–29 students

MOST POPULAR MAJORS
communication studies
human development and
family studies
nursing
psychology

STUDENTS SAY

Academics

In square miles, Rhode Island is the smallest of the 50 states, but at the University of Rhode Island, a large-scale academic experience is offered to the school's 10,000-plus undergrads. Popular majors include psychology, communication studies, pharmacy, and human development and family studies, and "Most professors go out of their way to help their students." A junior in the communications studies programs appreciates that, "Professors actually know what they're talking about. They've had out-of-the-classroom experience and have held jobs in the fields they're teaching. It's reassuring to know that what I'm learning will still be applicable once I leave my classroom." A student in the Political Science Department confirms, "There are some amazing professors that really get you thinking, but others are not so passionate." We've also heard several rumblings from students who've struggled "to understand the professor due to a lack of the English language." Among this community of pre-professional students, though, most feel that they're receiving a strong, vocation-minded education at "a good price." As one student says, URI is all about "preparing students for the real world." In the meantime, students wrangle with an administration that "puts meaning to the quote, 'In the land of the blind, the man with one eye leads.'" "Registering for classes can be a huge pain, [and] the Internet system is terrible."

Life

The Oliver Watson House—the oldest building at URI—was built around 1796, and when students reflect on the relatively dry campus here (students 21+ can drink in their room), they feel as if they're living back in the era of Oliver Watson himself. "Campus liquor rules are very strict," sighs one student. "Everyone goes home on the weekends [because] there isn't much going on." Those who stick around "are here to party," and head to off-campus ragers or cruise into nearby Providence or Newport. If you find the parties, says a sophomore, the "Social life at URI can be a lot of sloppy fun." Even if that's not your scene, students assure us there's "a peaceful, friendly environment [on a] beautiful campus" with opportunities to satisfy a range of tastes. Make an effort to "get involved, and it's a great place to be." Upwards of 80 campus organizations are offered, and the new, state-of-the-art Ryan Center hosts entertainment and athletic events. The school "definitely takes care of their athletes," and athletics are serious business around here. The Rhode Island Rams' men's basketball team makes a fair share of headlines, and a sophomore asserts, "The ice hockey club team is the best in the nation!" Aside from the "horrific" parking situation—the many students who commute have been known "to skip class because there are literally no spots to park"—students find that life at URI is pretty good; many of them say they chose the school for its beach locale. As one Rhode Island native yelps, "RI born! RI die!"

Student Body

The majority of URI's student body comes from Rhode Island—attracted by the close proximity to home and the nice in-state price—though Massachusetts, New Jersey, Connecticut, and New York contribute noteworthy numbers to the population, too. One student gripes that "local RI students come with their friends from high school and they aren't really interested in making new friends," but at least there's "a mixture of students socioeconomically." Among this mix, "Many students are extremely involved in campus life, but there are still those who are apathetic and refuse to do anything outside of themselves." The majority of URI students are "White and middle-class," and one senior warns that "ethnic groups do not mix. People here tend to hang out with people who look and act like they do." But this tendency, of course, is not law. A business administration major sums up his experience by saying, "At URI you can enjoy the best of what college life has to offer."

UNIVERSITY OF RHODE ISLAND

FINANCIAL AID: 401-874-9500 • E-MAIL: URIADMIT@ETAL.URI.EDU • WEBSITE: WWW.URI.EDU/ADMISSIONS

ADMISSIONS

Very important factors considered include: Rigor of secondary school record. *Important factors considered include:* Academic GPA, application essay, class rank, standardized test scores. *Other factors considered include:* Alumni/ae relation, character/personal qualities, extracurricular activities, first generation, geographical residence, level of applicant's interest, racial/ethnic status, recommendation(s), state residency, talent/ability, volunteer work, work experience. SAT or ACT required; ACT with Writing component required. TOEFL required of all international applicants. High school diploma is required, and GED is accepted. *Academic units required:* 4 English, 3 math, 2 science (1 science lab), 2 foreign language, 2 social studies, 5 academic electives.

The Inside Word

Any candidate with solid grades is likely to find the university's Admissions Committee to be welcoming. The yield of admits who enroll is low and the state's population small. Out-of-state students are attractive to URI because they are sorely needed to fill out the student body. Students who graduate in the top 10 percent of their class are good scholarship bets.

FINANCIAL AID

Students should submit: FAFSA. The Princeton Review suggests that all financial aid forms be submitted as soon as possible after January 1 with a priority deadline of March 1. *Need-based scholarships/grants offered:* Pell Grant, SEOG, state scholarships/grants, private scholarships, the school's own gift aid. *Loan aid offered:* Direct Subsidized Stafford, Direct Unsubsidized Stafford, Direct PLUS, Direct Graduate PLUS, Federal Perkins Loan, Federal Nursing Loan, state loans, college/university loans from institutional funds. Applicants will be notified of awards on a rolling basis beginning on or about March 31. Federal Work-Study Program available. Institutional employment available. Off-campus job opportunities are good.

FROM THE ADMISSIONS OFFICE

"Outstanding freshman candidates for Fall 2008 admission with a minimum SAT score of 1150 (combined Critical Reading and Math) or ACT composite score of 25 who rank in the top third of their high school class are eligible to be considered for a Centennial Scholarship. These merit-based scholarships range up to full tuition and are renewable each semester if the student maintains full-time continuous enrollment and a 3.0 average or better. In order to be eligible for consideration, all application materials must be received in the Admission Office by the December 17, 2007 early action deadline. Applications are not considered complete until the application fee, completed application, official high school transcript, list of senior courses, personal essay, and SAT or ACT scores are received.

"If a student is awarded a Centennial Scholarship, and his or her residency status changes from out-of-state to regional or in-state, the amount of the award will be reduced to reflect the reduced tuition rate.

"The SAT Math and Critical Reading scores are used for admission evaluation and Centennial Scholarship consideration. The Writing score is not currently used for admission evaluation or Centennial Scholarship consideration."

SELECTIVITY

Admissions Rating	**79**
# of applicants	13,497
% of applicants accepted	74
% of acceptees attending	29
# accepting a place on wait list	266

FRESHMAN PROFILE

Range SAT Critical Reading	490–585
Range SAT Math	510–610
Minimum Paper TOEFL	550
Minimum Computer Based TOEFL	213
Average HS GPA	3.12
% graduated top 10% of class	21

DEADLINES

Regular application deadline	2/1
Regular notification	rolling
Nonfall registration?	yes

APPLICANTS ALSO LOOK AT

AND OFTEN PREFER
Brown University, Northwestern University, University of Connecticut, University of Massachusetts—Amherst, University of New Hampshire

AND SOMETIMES PREFER
Boston College, Providence College, Quinnipiac University

AND RARELY PREFER
Carnegie Mellon University, Occidental College, University of Maryland—Baltimore County

FINANCIAL FACTS

Financial Aid Rating	**70**
Annual in-state tuition	$5,656
Annual out-of-state tuition	$19,356
Room & Board	$8,466
Books and supplies	$1,000
Required fees	$2,068
% frosh rec. need-based scholarship or grant aid	49
% UG rec. need-based scholarship or grant aid	53
% frosh rec. need-based self-help aid	48
% UG rec. need-based self-help aid	48
% frosh rec. any financial aid	72
% UG rec. any financial aid	63

UNIVERSITY OF RICHMOND

28 WESTHAMPTON WAY, RICHMOND, VA 23173 • ADMISSIONS: 804-289-8640 • FAX: 804-287-6003

STUDENTS SAY

Academics

With a strong liberal arts core that integrates a "great business school and equally strong leadership school" and "amazing and challenging premed programs," the University of Richmond serves well a student population that "knows that after college they will go to med, law, or grad school and end up with a high-paying job." Undergrads tell us that UR "is the perfect size. It's small enough where it's easy to get involved in lots of different things and to play a leadership role in that group. However, you always have plenty of options and are constantly meeting new people." The school "encourages undergraduate research, both in the sciences and in other fields, and most appealing is that students are often paid for their research," although the benefits to students' resumes aren't half bad either. Classes are "challenging, and the workload can be difficult," but "Professors tend to be understanding" and "really do care about their students." Undergrads love the academics, although many complain that the required writing-intensive, first-year course "is a pain that many students find annoying and pointless." Some here warn that due to the size of the school, "There are a limited number of classes offered. Especially in the less-popular departments, interesting classes that were in the catalogue were hardly offered and were almost impossible to get into for underclassmen." Support systems are strong; they include "academic advisors to ensure that the student is getting a quality education with opportunities to do internships and study abroad," "an effective Career Development Center," "speech, writing and academic skills centers (all excellent)," "free tutoring," and "a great alumni network."

Life

UR's coordinate system divides men and women into coordinate colleges: Richmond for men, Westhampton for women. Students dine and attend classes together and share some student organizations, but they function under separate governance systems. The benefits of this system include "great leadership opportunities for tons of men and women." Many here complain, though, that the system "makes dating on campus difficult. It makes relationships between men and women (whether intimate or just friends) awkward and unlike real life." The problem is exacerbated by the fact that "there aren't enough common get-together spaces for men and women. We need a space to hang out that is not just a mediocre dorm lounge." The Greek houses help; students report that "the fraternity scene is central to the culture of the school, almost at the exclusion of every other weekend activity." Students might take greater advantage of their proximity to a big city except that "it is very difficult to go anywhere without a car because the university as well as the city has limited public transportation." One student explains, "This campus is located near a great city that many students never explore, outside of bars." Perhaps students stick so close to school because it's just so beautiful; everyone here agrees that "our campus is quite obviously one of the most gorgeous in the world. Everything from the lake and gazebo to the architecture of the buildings is breathtaking."

Student Body

UR, most students agree, "is extremely preppy, with a lot of very wealthy students. It is also very fraternity/sorority-oriented. If you aren't in one of those groups, it is definitely harder to find close friends because the school is so small." Harder, but not impossible; notes one outsider, "There is a decided proportion of students who don't fit this mold, who are easy to find and certainly fit in, but if you are one of this latter group, it may seem on occasion as though you are starring in 'Operation J. Crew Invasion.'" Most students "live, eat, study, and party on campus; they enjoy a sense of belonging here. Everyone you pass waves, nods, smiles or says 'hello,' even if you've never met them before. Walking to class can really put you in a good mood, no matter how late you were up cramming for a test."

UNIVERSITY OF RICHMOND

FINANCIAL AID: 804-289-8438 • E-MAIL: ADMISSIONS@RICHMOND.EDU • WEBSITE: WWW.RICHMOND.EDU

ADMISSIONS

Very important factors considered include: Academic GPA, rigor of secondary school record. *Important factors considered include:* Application essay, character/personal qualities, class rank, standardized test scores, talent/ability. *Other factors considered include:* Alumni/ae relation, extracurricular activities, first generation, geographical residence, racial/ethnic status, recommendation(s), state residency, volunteer work, work experience. SAT or ACT required; TOEFL required of all international applicants. High school diploma is not required, and GED is accepted. *Academic units required:* 4 English, 3 math, 2 science (2 science labs), 2 foreign language, 2 history. *Academic units recommended:* 4 English, 4 math, 4 science (4 science labs), 4 foreign language, 4 history.

The Inside Word

While SAT Subject Tests are no longer required, the SAT Writing section has replaced this requisite and is considered equally important. There does appear to be an effort to look at the candidate's record carefully and thoroughly. Course of study, high school performance, and test scores are the most important parts of your application; however, Richmond also makes sure that all files are read at least three times before a final decision has been rendered.

FINANCIAL AID

Students should submit: FAFSA, institution's own financial aid form. Regular filing deadline is February 25. The Princeton Review suggests that all financial aid forms be submitted as soon as possible after January 1. *Need-based scholarships/grants offered:* Pell Grant, SEOG, state scholarships/grants, private scholarships, the school's own gift aid. *Loan aid offered:* Direct Subsidized Stafford, Direct Unsubsidized Stafford, Direct PLUS, Federal Perkins Loan. Applicants will be notified of awards on or about April 1.

FROM THE ADMISSIONS OFFICE

"The University of Richmond combines the characteristics of a small college with the dynamics of a large university. The unique size, beautiful suburban campus, and world-class facilities offer students an extraordinary mix of opportunities for personal growth and intellectual achievement. At Richmond, students are encouraged to engage themselves in their environment. Discussion and dialogue are the forefront of the academic experience, while research, internships, and international experiences are important components of students' co-curricular lives. The university is committed to providing undergraduate students with a rigorous academic experience, while integrating these studies with opportunities for experiential learning and promoting total individual development. The university also places a high value on diversity and believes in taking full advantage of the rich benefits of learning in a community of individuals from varied backgrounds.

"The University of Richmond requires either the SAT or the ACT. We do not preference either test. We evaluate all three sections of the SAT (Critical Reading, Math, and Writing); the Writing section of the ACT is optional. If multiple tests are submitted, the Admission Committee considers those results which are most favorable to the applicant. We do not require or recommend SAT Subject Tests."

SELECTIVITY

Admissions Rating	**94**
# of applicants	5,414
% of applicants accepted	46
% of acceptees attending	31
# accepting a place on wait list	712
% admitted from wait list	1
# of early decision applicants	268
% accepted early decision	68

FRESHMAN PROFILE

Range SAT Critical Reading	590–670
Range SAT Math	600–680
Range SAT Writing	590–680
Range ACT Composite	27–30
Minimum Paper TOEFL	550
Minimum Computer Based TOEFL	213
Average HS GPA	3.48
% graduated top 10% of class	53
% graduated top 25% of class	84
% graduated top 50% of class	97

DEADLINES

Early decision application deadline	11/15
Early decision notification	12/15
Regular application deadline	1/15
Regular notification	4/1
Nonfall registration?	no

APPLICANTS ALSO LOOK AT

AND OFTEN PREFER
The College of William & Mary, The University of North Carolina at Chapel Hill, University of Virginia

AND SOMETIMES PREFER
Boston College, Duke University, Georgetown University, Vanderbilt University, Wake Forest University

AND RARELY PREFER
Bucknell University, Lafayette College

FINANCIAL FACTS

Financial Aid Rating	**95**
Annual tuition	$30,040
Room & Board	$7,200
Books and supplies	$1,050
% frosh rec. need-based scholarship or grant aid	41
% UG rec. need-based scholarship or grant aid	34
% frosh rec. need-based self-help aid	36
% UG rec. need-based self-help aid	31
% frosh rec. any financial aid	65
% UG rec. any financial aid	69

UNIVERSITY OF SAN DIEGO

5998 ALCALA PARK, SAN DIEGO, CA 92110-2492 • ADMISSIONS: 619-260-4506 • FAX: 619-260-6836

CAMPUS LIFE
Quality of Life Rating	88
Fire Safety Rating	71
Type of school	private
Affiliation	Roman Catholic
Environment	metropolis

STUDENTS
Total undergrad enrollment	4,946
% male/female	40/60
% from out of state	36
% from public high school	56
% live on campus	46
% in (# of) fraternities	16 (4)
% in (# of) sororities	23 (6)
% African American	2
% Asian	8
% Caucasian	68
% Hispanic	13
% Native American	1
% international	2
# of countries represented	40

SURVEY SAYS . . .
Small classes
Lab facilities are great
Students love San Diego, CA
Great off-campus food
Campus feels safe

ACADEMICS
Academic Rating	83
Calendar	4-1-4
Student/faculty ratio	15:1
Profs interesting rating	85
Profs accessible rating	85
% profs teaching	
UG courses	100
% classes taught by TAs	0
Most common	
lab size	10–19 students
Most common	
reg class size	30–39 students

MOST POPULAR MAJORS
business administration/
management
communications studies/speech
communication and rhetoric
psychology

STUDENTS SAY
Academics

Approximately one in three undergraduates major in business, management, or marketing at the University of San Diego, a small, prestigious, Catholic school perched on the Pacific Ocean's edge. But there's a whole lot more to a USD education than prepping for a successful corporate career. All undergraduates here must complete the demanding general education requirements that ensure a "values-based education for everyone. You not only learn about Plato's *Republic*, but also how its themes are relevant to our sociopolitical situation today in this country and around the world. There is exploration beyond the here and now and spiritual adventure here." Adding to that sort of experience is USD's community service-learning, which "provides opportunities for community relations and student 'hands-on experience' in different fields (sociology, psychology, political science)." USD also offers solid, popular programs in communications, psychology, and education. Smaller departments like engineering and the sciences earn praise, too, the latter which benefits from "a great facility with brand-new labs." Undergrads in all departments embrace the small school environment in which "Professors know you by name and expect you to be in class and doing your work." USD professors "are enthusiastic and you can tell they love teaching at a small school rather than a huge state university." And just so you know, they expect a lot from their students. One student cautions: "This school is very academically challenging and you have to work hard for your grades. The results, though, are more satisfying because you actually did work hard and put in the effort and you learned something."

Life

"USD is a place where you can be in an engaging and stimulating class one minute, and 5 minutes later you're sitting on the beach with your friends," writes one student, summing up the near-idyllic situation here. "To be able to study and surf at the same time: that's what college is about!" USD students love their campus, which is "beautiful and immaculate. The grounds are perfectly kept at all times, and the architecture is gorgeous. Just being here will make you happy and [keep you] wanting to learn." They're also crazy for the "awesome weather," the "great opportunities to get involved, and the tremendous resources to become a leader on campus, if you have the personal drive to take on the challenge." Most of all, they love San Diego, "one of the coolest, most interactive cities in the world. Along with its beaches, babes, nightlife, and abundant outdoor activities, San Diego is a multicultural epicenter, attracting all kinds of different people." Undergrads recommend the Gaslamp District for fun and food, Mission Beach for the ocean, La Jolla and Fashion Valley for shopping, and Tijuana for wild weekends. About the only thing USD undergrads don't love is the school's public safety policy, which is "very strict. Every week numerous people are written up for not only drinking but even for being in the presence of alcohol. It is as if they have to fill a quota of how many people they write up each weekend." As a result, "There are not many things to do on campus on the weekend. It can get pretty boring if you're stuck there."

Student Body

USD's student body "has the general Southern California 'feeling,' meaning that pretty much everyone is laid-back and easygoing." Many here "come from very affluent families. They drive the best, wear the best, and just have the best of everything. All the girls dress the same," decking themselves out in a tank top, a miniskirt, Ugg boots, and a Louis Vuitton bag. Some observers add that "there are a good number of atypical students at USD, very down-to-earth students with caring and fun personalities. Virtually anyone can find a comfortable group of friends to surround them." Students point out that "even though the campus is pretty religious, almost everyone is accepting of the PRIDE organization. Also, the organizations for minority groups are extremely active on campus (even though the school is not very diverse)."

FINANCIAL AID: 619-260-4514 • E-MAIL: ADMISSIONS@SANDIEGO.EDU • WEBSITE: WWW.SANDIEGO.EDU/ADMISSIONS/UNDERGRADUATE

ADMISSIONS

Very important factors considered include: Academic GPA, rigor of secondary school record, standardized test scores. *Important factors considered include:* Application essay, character/personal qualities, class rank, extracurricular activities, talent/ability, volunteer work. *Other factors considered include:* Alumni/ae relation, first generation, racial/ethnic status, recommendation(s), religious affiliation/commitment, work experience. SAT or ACT required; ACT with Writing component required. TOEFL required of all international applicants. High school diploma is required, and GED is accepted. *Academic units required:* 4 English, 3 math, 3 science (2 science labs), 2 foreign language, 3 social studies. *Academic units recommended:* 4 English, 4 math, 4 science (3 science labs), 3 foreign language, 4 social studies.

The Inside Word

Applicants to the University of San Diego will find a unique place with a remarkable amount of diversity in its 4,000-plus student population. Academically, the school offers a solid liberal arts core with close interaction between professors—all in one of the most livable cities anywhere. Solid test scores and high schools grades should be a given for applicants.

FINANCIAL AID

Students should submit: FAFSA. Regular filing deadline is February 20. The Princeton Review suggests that all financial aid forms be submitted as soon as possible after January 1. *Need-based scholarships/grants offered:* Pell Grant, SEOG, state scholarships/grants, private scholarships, the school's own gift aid. *Loan aid offered:* FFEL Subsidized Stafford, FFEL Unsubsidized Stafford, FFEL PLUS, Federal Perkins Loan, college/university loans from institutional funds, nonfederal loan programs. Applicants will be notified of awards on a rolling basis beginning or about March 1. Federal Work-Study Program available. Institutional employment available. Off-campus job opportunities are good.

FROM THE ADMISSIONS OFFICE

"Looking at the University of San Diego is easy on the eyes. But really seeing our true character demands a little work.

"It is easy to focus on the obvious: the incredible beauty of the campus, the region's unparalleled climate and livability, long lists of recreational and co-curricular opportunities, the vitality of students walking through the central plaza, or even the obvious expressions of USD's Catholic character. But to focus on the superficial would be misleading.

"While the beach is nearby, USD is a serious academic institution. While the campus is stunning, the people make the difference. More than 10,000 candidates vie for 1,100 freshman openings. But to see the 'average' freshman as a 3.8 GPA or a 1220 SAT score would miss the person. Each is unique—selected on expressions of diversity, leadership, service, talent, and essential human character. Faculty, too, are rigorously screened. USD draws over 100 candidates for every faculty opening, and this screening goes well beyond their lists of publications or the names on their diplomas. To challenge and inspire, they bring innovative approaches to undergraduate research, experiential learning, and faculty mentoring.

"While often compared to much larger institutions, USD seeks to be recognized for undergraduate teaching and residential learning. In comparison to schools of similar character, USD's academic offerings are truly impressive; a small sample includes marine biology, environmental studies, Latino studies, communication studies, e-commerce, and professional programs in engineering, business, and education, each of which complements a rigorous liberal arts base. New facilities demonstrate this diversity, including a state-of-the-art science center, the Kroc Institute for Peace and Justice, and the Jenny Craig Sports Pavilion.

"Freshman applicants must submit scores from the new SAT or the ACT exam with Writing. Scores on the previous exams will not be considered. As always, these scores will be used in conjunction with many other factors; in particular, the student's grade point average, curriculum, extra curricular activities, and letters of recommendation."

SELECTIVITY

Admissions Rating	92
# of applicants	10,048
% of applicants accepted	46
% of acceptees attending	24
# accepting a place on wait list	373
% admitted from wait list	67

FRESHMAN PROFILE

Range SAT Critical Reading	530–630
Range SAT Math	550–650
Range ACT Composite	23–28
Minimum Paper TOEFL	550
Minimum Computer Based TOEFL	213
Average HS GPA	3.74
% graduated top 10% of class	43
% graduated top 25% of class	78
% graduated top 50% of class	97

DEADLINES

Regular application deadline	3/1
Regular notification	4/15
Nonfall registration?	yes

APPLICANTS ALSO LOOK AT

AND OFTEN PREFER
University of Southern California
AND SOMETIMES PREFER
University of California—San Diego
AND RARELY PREFER
Santa Clara University

FINANCIAL FACTS

Financial Aid Rating	75
Annual tuition	$32,300
Room & Board	$10,960
Books and supplies	$1,380
Required fees	$264
% frosh rec. need-based scholarship or grant aid	50
% UG rec. need-based scholarship or grant aid	45
% frosh rec. need-based self-help aid	44
% UG rec. need-based self-help aid	44
% frosh rec. any financial aid	77
% UG rec. any financial aid	68

UNIVERSITY OF SAN FRANCISCO

2130 FULTON STREET, SAN FRANCISCO, CA 94117 • ADMISSIONS: 415-422-6563 • FAX: 415-422-2217

STUDENTS SAY

Academics

"Educating minds and hearts to change the world," the Jesuit-led University of San Francisco "prides itself in its dedication to social justice." As one student puts it, "The underlying spiritual mission of the school is really positive, and it integrates itself into our course work in the form of a strong community-service ethic." Although small, USF offers a breadth of options typical of a larger university, including a business school that "provides a great education for those who want to work in San Francisco and the Bay area" and that arms "students with an ethical approach to business"; a nursing program with excellent clinicals that "allow you to schmooze all the right people even before you graduate"; and "a plethora of global awareness programs and seminars." Given the university's location, "There are so many opportunities to take advantage of: internships, research experience, and so forth that might not be readily available" in a smaller city. Classes at USF are often "75 percent lecture, with the last 25 percent of the class reserved for discussion," which students use with enthusiasm. Core requirements include "one class in each of a variety of subject areas (science, math, history, literature, philosophy, and theology) in order to give students a solid liberal arts background." Students may circumvent these requirements by entering the Saint Ignatius Institute, a "Great Books program" that is also "a great community." Another plus: "A high percentage of our student body studies abroad at some point, usually in their junior year. There are so many options for studying abroad!"

Life

"Nestled in a quiet spot of a bustling city," the USF campus is "amazing. You could stay around here your entire college career and never know there was a big city around you. Yet it's close to shops, restaurants, and all the other advantages of urban living, just a few blocks off Golden Gate Park." The campus itself is "small but gorgeous. Every morning as you walk to class, there is the beautiful St. Ignatius Church, big redwood trees, a sprawling grass lawn, gorgeous landscaping, and, often, the fog rolling out in the distance." Just beyond the campus gates, of course, is one of America's great cities. As one student notes, "The best thing about USF is that it's in the middle of San Francisco! And the school definitely takes advantage of that." For recreation, undergrads "can just take the bus and in 5 minutes, we're walking along popular Haight Street. Everything is accessible." The only downside: "The Bay area is incredibly expensive, and the cost can hamper the ability to have fun as a student." Oddly enough, the allure of the big city dampens campus life. "There's not much school spirit here," undergrads tell us, manifested in "the lack of a collective backing of sports on campus."

Student Body

"The student body at USF is like a scaled-down version of the people you will meet in San Francisco, [with] plenty of stylish students, the type who wear heels, miniskirts, and tube tops to an 8:00 A.M. class. One only needs to perch on a bench outside the cafeteria to see all the goths, punks, divas, slackers, jocks, prepsters, and wanna-be-prepsters." Most here "have a passionate interest in something. Almost no one is apathetic. Many people have music as their passion, while others have acting, community service, dancing, writing, and athletics." A large number "are concerned with the political and social affairs on all levels: Local, national, and international, [and] although USF may be a conservative Jesuit school at the core, the generally liberal attitude of San Francisco is heavily reflected in the student body." With "a wide variety of feeder schools, including internationally," USF is "incredibly diverse." It suffers, however, from a dearth of straight men. One woman explains, "There's a high female to male ratio in the freshman class, and we've figured it's much, much higher when you factor out the guys in relationships and gay guys."

FINANCIAL AID: 415-422-6303 • E-MAIL: ADMISSION@USFCA.EDU • WEBSITE: WWW.USFCA.EDU

ADMISSIONS

Very important factors considered include: Academic GPA, recommendation(s), rigor of secondary school record, standardized test scores. *Important factors considered include:* Application essay, class rank. *Other factors considered include:* Alumni/ae relation, character/personal qualities, extracurricular activities, interview, racial/ethnic status, talent/ability, volunteer work. SAT or ACT required; ACT with Writing component required. TOEFL required of all international applicants. High school diploma is required, and GED is accepted. *Academic units recommended:* 4 English, 3 math, 2 science (2 science labs), 2 foreign language, 3 social studies, 6 academic electives; 1 chemistry and 1 biology or physics is required of nursing and science applicants.

The Inside Word

The Admissions Committee at USF is not purely numbers focused. They'll evaluate your full picture here, using your academic strengths and weaknesses along with your personal character strengths, essays, and recommendations to assess your suitability for admission. It's matchmaking. If you fit well in the USF community, you'll be welcome.

FINANCIAL AID

Students should submit: FAFSA. The Princeton Review suggests that all financial aid forms be submitted as soon as possible after January 1. *Need-based scholarships/grants offered:* Pell Grant, SEOG, state scholarships/grants, private scholarships, the school's own gift aid, Federal Nursing Scholarship. *Loan aid offered:* Direct Subsidized Stafford, Direct Unsubsidized Stafford, Direct PLUS, FFEL PLUS (FFEL Loans are for graduate students only), Federal Perkins Loan, Federal Nursing Loan, college/university loans from institutional funds. Applicants will be notified of awards on a rolling basis beginning or about April 1. Federal Work-Study Program available. Institutional employment available. Off-campus job opportunities are excellent.

FROM THE ADMISSIONS OFFICE

"The University of San Francisco has experienced a significant increase in applications for admission over the past 5 years. This has made the application evaluation process more challenging. Ultimately, it gives those who read the applications the opportunity to find applicants who can make the most of the university's academic opportunities, location in San Francisco, and its mission to educate minds and hearts to change the world. Community outreach and service to others, along with academic excellence are characteristics that help distinguish those offered admission.

"Applicants for Fall 2008 are required to take the new SAT Reasoning test (or the ACT with the Writing section). The Writing sections will be used for advising and placement purposes. SAT Subject Test scores will also be accepted. If scores from both the old and new SAT are submitted, the higher of the scores will be used."

SELECTIVITY

Admissions Rating	83
# of applicants	7,105
% of applicants accepted	72
% of acceptees attending	21

FRESHMAN PROFILE

Range SAT Critical Reading	510–620
Range SAT Math	500–620
Range ACT Composite	21–26
Minimum Paper TOEFL	550
Minimum Computer Based TOEFL	213
Average HS GPA	3.47
% graduated top 10% of class	21
% graduated top 25% of class	59
% graduated top 50% of class	91

DEADLINES

Regular notification	rolling
Nonfall registration?	yes

APPLICANTS ALSO LOOK AT

AND OFTEN PREFER
Santa Clara University, University of California—Berkeley, University of California—Davis, University of Southern California

AND SOMETIMES PREFER
Loyola Marymount University, Saint Mary's College of California, University of California—Santa Cruz

AND RARELY PREFER
Boston College, Fordham University

FINANCIAL FACTS

Financial Aid Rating	71
Annual tuition	$30,840
Room & Board	$10,730
Books and supplies	$900
Required fees	$340
% frosh rec. need-based scholarship or grant aid	48
% UG rec. need-based scholarship or grant aid	47
% frosh rec. need-based self-help aid	50
% UG rec. need-based self-help aid	50

UNIVERSITY OF SCRANTON

800 Linden Street, Scranton, PA 18510-4699 • Admissions: 570-941-7540 Fax: 570-941-5928

CAMPUS LIFE

Quality of Life Rating	83
Fire Safety Rating	91
Type of school	private
Affiliation	Roman Catholic/Jesuit
Environment	city

STUDENTS

Total undergrad enrollment	3,946
% male/female	43/57
% from out of state	51
% from public high school	55
% live on campus	53
% African American	2
% Asian	2
% Caucasian	82
% Hispanic	5

SURVEY SAYS . . .

Small classes
Great computer facilities
Great library
Frats and sororities are unpopular or nonexistent
Lots of beer drinking

ACADEMICS

Academic Rating	82
Calendar	semester
Student/faculty ratio	11:1
Profs interesting rating	81
Profs accessible rating	83
% profs teaching UG courses	98
% classes taught by TAs	0
Most common lab size	10–19 students
Most common reg class size	10–19 students

MOST POPULAR MAJORS

communications studies/speech communication and rhetoric
elementary education and teaching
marketing/marketing management

STUDENTS SAY

Academics

With "an outstanding record for admission to graduate programs, not only in law and medicine but also in several other fields," the University of Scranton is a good fit for ambitious students seeking "a Jesuit school in every sense of the word. If you come here, expect to be challenged to become a better person, to develop a strong concern for the poor and marginalized, and to grow spiritually and intellectually." The school manages to accomplish this without "forcing religion upon you, which is nice." Undergraduates also approve of the mandatory liberal-arts-based curriculum that "forces you to learn about broader things than your own major." Strong majors here include "an amazing occupational therapy program, [an] excellent special education program," business, and biology. "This is a great place for premeds and other sciences," students agree. While the workload can be difficult, "a tutoring center provides free tutoring for any students who may need it, and also provides work-study positions for students who qualify to tutor." Need more help? Professors "are extremely accessible. They will go to any lengths to help you understand material and do well," while administrators "are here for the students, and show that every day inside and outside of the classroom." Community ties here are strong; as one student points out, "The Jesuits live in our dorms, creating an even greater sense of community, because we don't view them as just priests, we view them as real people who can relate on our level."

Life

"There is a whole range of activities to do on the weekends" at University of Scranton, including "frequent trips, dances, and movies that are screened for free." Students tell us that "the school and student organizations provide plenty of options, such as retreats, talent shows, and other various activities." There are also "many intramurals to become involved in, and the varsity sports (specifically the women's) are very successful." Furthermore, "Being a Jesuit school, social justice issues are huge. They are taught in the classroom, and students spend a lot of time volunteering." Hometown Scranton is big enough to provide "movie theaters, two malls, parks, a zoo, a bowling alley, and a skiing/snowboarding mountain." In short, there are plenty of choices for the non-partier at Scranton; the many we heard from in our survey reported busy extracurricular schedules. But those seeking a party won't be disappointed here, either. Scranton undergrads "party a lot, but they balance it with studying. Parties are chances to go out, see people, dance, and drink if you want." You "can find a party any time of day, 7 days a week" here, usually with a keg tapped and pouring. Few here feel the party scene is out of hand, however; a typical student writes, "It's very different than at schools with Greek systems. It is a lot more laid-back, and all about everyone having a good time."

Students

While "the typical Scranton student is White, Catholic, and from the suburbs," students hasten to point out that "within this sameness, there is much diversity. There are people who couldn't care at all about religion, and there are people who are deeply religious. Even in the Catholic atmosphere of the school, the school only requires that you learn about Catholicism as it stands. Theology classes . . . are prefaced with the idea that 'You do not have to believe this!'" Undergrads here are generally "friendly and welcoming. Cliques are pretty much nonexistent, and anyone who would be classified as 'popular' is only considered so because they are extremely friendly, outgoing, and seek out friendships with as many people as possible." Students tend to be on the Abercrombie-preppy side, with lots of undergrads of Italian, Irish, and Polish descent.

FINANCIAL AID: 570-941-7700 • E-MAIL: ADMISSIONS@SCRANTON.EDU • WEBSITE: WWW.SCRANTON.EDU

ADMISSIONS

Very important factors considered include: Academic GPA, class rank, rigor of secondary school record, standardized test scores. *Important factors considered include:* Extracurricular activities. *Other factors considered include:* Alumni/ae relation, application essay, character/personal qualities, interview, level of applicant's interest, recommendation(s), talent/ability, volunteer work, work experience. SAT or ACT required; TOEFL required of all international applicants. High school diploma is required, and GED is accepted. *Academic units required:* 4 English, 3 math, 1 science, 2 foreign language, 2 social studies. *Academic units recommended:* 4 English, 4 math, 2 science, 2 foreign language, 3 social studies.

The Inside Word

Admission to Scranton gets harder each year. A steady stream of smart kids from the Tristate Area keeps classes full and the admit rate low. Successful applicants will need solid grades and test scores. As with many religiously affiliated schools, students should be a good match philosophically as well.

FINANCIAL AID

Students should submit: FAFSA. The Princeton Review suggests that all financial aid forms be submitted as soon as possible after January 1. *Need-based scholarships/grants offered:* Pell Grant, SEOG, state scholarships/grants, private scholarships, the school's own gift aid. *Loan aid offered:* FFEL Subsidized Stafford, FFEL Unsubsidized Stafford, FFEL PLUS, Federal Perkins Loan, Federal Nursing Loan. Applicants will be notified of awards on a rolling basis beginning or about March 1. Federal Work-Study Program available. Institutional employment available. Off-campus job opportunities are good.

FROM THE ADMISSIONS OFFICE

"A Jesuit institution in Pennsylvania's Pocono Northeast, the University of Scranton is known for its outstanding academics, state-of-the art campus', and exceptional sense of community. Founded in 1888, the university offers more than 80 undergraduate and graduate academic programs of study through four colleges and schools.

"For 13 consecutive years, *U.S. News & World Report* has named Scranton among the top-10 master's universities in the North. For the past 3 years, Scranton has also been among the 'Great Schools as a Great Price' in the 'Universities—Master's in the North' category. The Princeton Review included Scranton among *The Best 361 Colleges* in the nation for the past 5 years. For 4 consecutive years, *USA Today* included Scranton students on its 'All-U.S.A. College Academic Teams' list. In 2005, Scranton was the only college in Pennsylvania and the only Jesuit university to have a student named to the first academic team. In other national recognition, Kaplan counted Scranton among the nation's '369 Most Interesting Colleges' and was also listed among the 247 colleges in the nation included in the ninth edition of *Barron's Best Buys in College Education*.

"Known for the remarkable success of its graduates, Scranton is listed among the 'Top Producers' of Fulbright awards for American students in the October 20, 2006, issue of *The Chronicle of Higher Education*.

"Freshman applicants for Fall 2008 are required to take the SAT or ACT exam. The writing scores will not be considered in the admissions decision process. Students are encouraged to apply early for admission and can do so online with no application fee at Scranton.edu/apply."

SELECTIVITY

Admissions Rating	**85**
# of applicants	6,777
% of applicants accepted	70
% of acceptees attending	21
# accepting a place on wait list	301
% admitted from wait list	18

FRESHMAN PROFILE

Range SAT Critical Reading	510–600
Range SAT Math	510–610
Minimum Paper TOEFL	500
Minimum Computer Based TOEFL	173
Average HS GPA	3.33
% graduated top 10% of class	26
% graduated top 25% of class	62
% graduated top 50% of class	90

DEADLINES

Regular application deadline	3/1
Regular notification	rolling
Nonfall registration?	yes

APPLICANTS ALSO LOOK AT AND OFTEN PREFER

Fairfield University, Saint Joseph's University (PA), University of Delaware, Villanova University

AND SOMETIMES PREFER

Fordham University, Loyola College in Maryland, Pennsylvania State University—University Park

FINANCIAL FACTS

Financial Aid Rating	**71**
Annual tuition	$25,638
Room & Board	$10,224
Books and supplies	$1,000
Required fees	$300
% frosh rec. need-based scholarship or grant aid	63
% UG rec. need-based scholarship or grant aid	62
% frosh rec. need-based self-help aid	57
% UG rec. need-based self-help aid	57
% frosh rec. any financial aid	82
% UG rec. any financial aid	85

UNIVERSITY OF SOUTH CAROLINA—COLUMBIA

UNIVERSITY OF SOUTH CAROLINA, COLUMBIA, SC 29208 • ADMISSIONS: 803-777-7700 • FAX: 803-777-0101

CAMPUS LIFE
Quality of Life Rating	75
Fire Safety Rating	81
Type of school	public
Environment	city

STUDENTS
Total undergrad enrollment	18,648
% male/female	45/55
% from out of state	11
% live on campus	40
% in (# of) fraternities	14 (18)
% in (# of) sororities	15 (14)
% African American	13
% Asian	3
% Caucasian	71
% Hispanic	2
% international	1
# of countries represented	108

SURVEY SAYS . . .
Great library
Athletic facilities are great
Everyone loves the Fighting Gamecocks
Frats and sororities dominate social scene
Student publications are popular
Lots of beer drinking
Hard liquor is popular

ACADEMICS
Academic Rating	64
Calendar	semester
Student/faculty ratio	17:1
Profs interesting rating	69
Profs accessible rating	70
% profs teaching UG courses	72
% classes taught by TAs	23
Most common lab size	20–29 students
Most common reg class size	20–29 students

MOST POPULAR MAJORS
business administration/management
experimental psychology
public relations/image management

STUDENTS SAY
Academics

With a large in-state population and a proud football tradition, "The University of South Carolina is all about pride—in academics, athletics, and in life." Undergrads at this large research university embrace the entire USC experience, bragging of "an awesome mix of challenging academics and social activities." As at most large state universities, your academic experience at USC "is what you make of it. You can blow off your classes and get by, or you can dive in and try and learn as much as you want to." A few students warn that "most departments are more research oriented than education oriented. The philosophy is that research pays the bills, not the students, and therefore more emphasis should be placed on research." Even so, the academic experience is not an impersonal one; on the contrary, professors "will do everything they can to help you out with any problem, personal or academic. The people here are amazing. A stranger is as likely to be friendly and helpful as your best friend." Students tell us that USC excels in business, mathematics, nursing, education, technology, library service, journalism, psychology, and hotel, restaurant, and tourism management. One USC booster sums up: "The University of South Carolina offers the complete student experience: A variety of student organizations and student activities, a great nightlife in the state capital, challenging classes taught by great professors, and opportunities for research—all within a great environment on a beautiful campus."

Life

USC "is a fun place," especially for sports fans, as life here "mostly revolves around football and basketball. Everyone's always talking about the upcoming game or what next season is going to hold. There's a great sense of school pride." Undergrads proudly assert that "USC is probably the best college for tailgating. Football game days are so fun!" But students don't need a sporting event to have a good time; on the contrary, "Many people party every weekend (beginning Thursday nights)." When they do, "A lot of people hang out in Five Points"—which "offers many nightlife and dining options for college students"—"or the Vista"—which is similar to Five Points, but a bit more upscale. Aesthetes have plenty of options as well; on campus "The Koger Center for the Arts brings [in] great performers every year," while the city's Colonial Center "offers big concerts . . . from Elton John to Jimmy Buffett." Other Columbia highlights include "a very nice zoo" as well as plenty of options for hunting and fishing within 25 miles of the city. Beyond the immediate vicinity, "the mountains are an hour away and so is the beach. A weekend in Charleston, shopping in Charlotte, [and] going to the mountains in NC [North Carolina]" are excursions "you hear about every weekend (when there's not a football game going on)."

Student Body

With an undergraduate student body of over 18,000, USC is home to "so many different types of people . . . involved in so many different activities." When pressed to describe a typical student, undergrads identify "a fun-loving football fan who is a business student or a bio major," and explain that "most students are Southerners who come from a similar Christian, suburban background (although not all remain in that mindset)." However, students also report that USC is home to a "diverse minority and international communities" who "are becoming more and more recognized by the rest of the students." One undergrad sums up: "There isn't a typical student at USC, [but] there are different . . . group[s] that students could be classified into. There are the frat guys and the sorority girls; the good ol' boys who love to hunt and fish; the debutantes [who] are only here to get a MRS degree; the Northerners who came down to USC and had no idea what they were getting themselves into; and then there are the athletes, who pretty much interact only with other athletes."

UNIVERSITY OF SOUTH CAROLINA—COLUMBIA

FINANCIAL AID: 803-777-8134 • E-MAIL: ADMISSIONS-UGRAD@SC.EDU • WEBSITE: WWW.SC.EDU

ADMISSIONS

Very important factors considered include: Academic GPA, rigor of secondary school record, standardized test scores. *Other factors considered include:* Application essay, character/personal qualities, extracurricular activities, talent/ability. SAT or ACT required. TOEFL required of all international applicants. High school diploma is required, and GED is accepted. *Academic units required:* 4 English, 3 math, 3 science (3 science labs), 2 foreign language, 2 social studies, 1 history, 4 academic electives, 1 physical education or ROTC.

The Inside Word

Students tell us that "the admissions process at USC is very fair. The school takes everything into consideration." This is good news for applicants with spotty high school transcripts or poor standardized test scores. Others need not worry—the school bulletin reports that applicants with a B average in college preparatory courses and SAT section scores between 550 and 600 "are normally competitive for admission."

FINANCIAL AID

Students should submit: FAFSA. The Princeton Review suggests that all financial aid forms be submitted as soon as possible after January 1. *Need-based scholarships/grants offered:* Pell Grant, SEOG, state scholarships/grants, private scholarships, the school's own gift aid, United Negro College Fund, Federal Nursing Scholarship, USC Opportunity Grant—Institutional competitive merit awards available to qualified applicants. *Loan aid offered:* FFEL Subsidized Stafford, FFEL Unsubsidized Stafford, FFEL PLUS, Federal Perkins Loan, Federal Nursing Loan. Applicants will be notified of awards on or about April 1. Federal Work-Study Program available. Institutional employment available. Off-campus job opportunities are good.

FROM THE ADMISSIONS OFFICE

"In just 6 years, the number of annual undergraduate applicants to USC has doubled, making it more critical than ever for students to meet the university's priority application deadline. The University of South Carolina's national prominence in academics and research activities also has increased. USC is one of only 62 public research institutions to earn a designated status of 'very high research activity' by the Carnegie Foundation. As early as their freshman year, undergraduates are encouraged to compete for research grants. As South Carolina's flagship institution, USC offers more than 350 degree programs. Over 27,000 students seek baccalaureate, masters, or doctoral degrees. USC is known for its top-ranked academic programs, including its international business and exercise science programs—both rated number one nationally. Other notable programs include chemical and nuclear engineering; health education; hotel, restaurant, and tourism; marine science; law; medicine; nursing; and psychology, among others. USC is recognized for its pioneering efforts in freshman outreach. Its honors college is one of the nation's best, offering an Ivy League–caliber education at state college costs. USC offers student support in such areas as career development, disability services, pre-professional planning, and study abroad.

"On campus, students enjoy a state-of-the-art fitness center, an 18,000-seat arena, an 80,000-seat stadium, and nearly 300 student organizations. Off campus, South Carolina's world-famous beaches and the Blue Ridge Mountains are each less than a 3-hour drive away. The University of South Carolina is located in the state's capital city, making it a great place for internships and job opportunities.

"Because admissions criteria and deadlines are likely to change from year to year, it is important to check for the latest information at SC.edu/admissions.

"Applicants are required to take the Writing section of the SAT (or ACT) for any tests taken after March 2005. We will use the highest scores from either test for evaluation purposes."

SELECTIVITY

Admissions Rating	**87**
# of applicants	13,946
% of applicants accepted	63
% of acceptees attending	42
# accepting a place on wait list	511
% admitted from wait list	8

FRESHMAN PROFILE

Range SAT Critical Reading	520–620
Range SAT Math	540–640
Range ACT Composite	23–28
Minimum Paper TOEFL	550
Minimum Computer Based TOEFL	213
Average HS GPA	3.9
% graduated top 10% of class	29
% graduated top 25% of class	63
% graduated top 50% of class	93

DEADLINES

Regular application deadline	12/1
Regular notification	rolling
Nonfall registration?	yes

APPLICANTS ALSO LOOK AT
AND OFTEN PREFER
The University of North Carolina at Chapel Hill
AND SOMETIMES PREFER
Clemson University
AND RARELY PREFER
Wake Forest University

FINANCIAL FACTS

Financial Aid Rating	**76**
Annual in-state tuition	$7,408
Annual out-of-state tuition	$19,836
Room & Board	$6,520
Books and supplies	$838
Required fees	$400
% frosh rec. need-based scholarship or grant aid	32
% UG rec. need-based scholarship or grant aid	41
% frosh rec. need-based self-help aid	34
% UG rec. need-based self-help aid	40
% frosh rec. any financial aid	95
% UG rec. any financial aid	82

THE UNIVERSITY OF SOUTH DAKOTA

414 EAST CLARK, VERMILLION, SD 57069 • ADMISSIONS: 605-677-5434 • FAX: 605-677-6323

CAMPUS LIFE

Quality of Life Rating	**69**
Fire Safety Rating	**60***
Type of school	public
Environment	village

STUDENTS

Total undergrad enrollment	5,751
% male/female	39/61
% from out of state	26
% from public high school	90
% live on campus	31
% in (# of) fraternities	15 (8)
% in (# of) sororities	9 (4)
% African American	1
% Asian	1
% Caucasian	88
% Hispanic	1
% Native American	2

SURVEY SAYS . . .

Small classes
Great computer facilities
Great library
Frats and sororities dominate social
scene
Lots of beer drinking
Hard liquor is popular
(Almost) everyone smokes

ACADEMICS

Academic Rating	**72**
Calendar	semester
Student/faculty ratio	15:1
Profs interesting rating	73
Profs accessible rating	70
% profs teaching	
UG courses	97
% classes taught by TAs	3
Most common	
lab size	20–29 students
Most common	
reg class size	10–19 students

MOST POPULAR MAJORS

business administration/
management
psychology

STUDENTS SAY

Academics

Tucked into the southeast corner of its home state, The University of South Dakota provides both in- and out-of-state students with "a quality education at an exceptionally affordable price." With highly touted offerings in media, law, political science, business, and pre-health majors, The U "is all about preparing students for their future careers. The school puts a heavy emphasis not only on the material, but also on how it applies to real-life situations, as opposed to a merely academic abstraction." Students apply their learning across subjects through the school's IdEA (Interdisciplinary Education and Action) program. Required of all undergraduates, IdEA consists of nine course credits in thematically linked subject areas (e.g., Global Health, Wealth and Justice in America, and Living a Life of Leadership are three of the six areas), participation in co-curricular events and activities (like giving presentations or attending exhibitions), and an Action project (such as service-learning, research, or creative activity). With fewer than 6,000 undergraduates, The U can offer an unusual amount of student-teacher interaction for a state university; one undergrad writes, "All of my professors have an open-door policy and are usually very willing to work with students outside of the classroom."

Life

The Vermillion campus of The U is "typical" of a smaller state university, with "parties, coffee shops, bar hopping, frats, and sororities" as well as "organizations for virtually anything you can think of, from sports to self-defense, to art to GLBA." During the week, the campus buzzes with activity. One student reports, "The fine arts college regularly has art shows and theatrical performances. The Dakota Dome is host to any number of sporting events [and has] a full gym, pool, tennis, and racquetball courts available to students." Weekends are another matter, however (except when the Division II Coyotes football squad is playing at home). Many here report that USD is "a backpack school [since] there's nothing to keep us here on the weekends." The countryside surrounding Vermillion is a paradise for hunters, fishers, and campers, but others find the town "incredibly boring. It has a Hy-Vee and a Pamida. That's basically it, except for the small shops downtown. There's a bowling alley and several bars. Not much to do for underage students." To the town's credit, it is "supportive and proud of the university. There are few businesses that don't offer discounts for students and hang banners for the sports activities, and the recent addition of Wal-Mart is sure to improve things." Problem is, it just isn't very much fun, so students road trip to Sioux Falls or Sioux City when they can, or they simply head home once classes are done.

Student Body

Many U students "are from small communities from the Midwest (mainly South Dakota and surrounding states), [and are] blonde or brunette, Caucasian, blue- or brown-eyed, [and] have Germanic or Norwegian names." Students are "good to one another and friendly for the most part. We are pretty interested in our university, and even more so in our friends." The school has a growing population of nontraditional students, as well as a "small percentage of students from Africa, Europe, and other continents, countries, and states on exchange programs." One undergrad writes, "Virtually every Midwesterner has a grandparent or great aunt who still doesn't speak English fluently since they immigrated to the U.S., so attitudes against immigrants are hard to find. Perhaps the only thing we wonder is why anyone would be willing to come here and deal with our harsh winters!" The university is "one of the most liberal places in South Dakota," so "Most atypical students fit right in. Alternate sexual orientation is becoming increasingly accepted, for example."

FINANCIAL AID: 605-677-5446 • E-MAIL: ADMISS@USD.EDU • WEBSITE: WWW.USD.EDU

ADMISSIONS

Very important factors considered include: Academic GPA, class rank, rigor of secondary school record, standardized test scores. *Other factors considered include:* Alumni/ae relation, application essay, character/personal qualities, extracurricular activities, geographical residence, racial/ethnic status, recommendation(s), state residency, talent/ability, volunteer work, work experience. SAT or ACT required; SAT and SAT Subject Tests or ACT required. TOEFL required of all international applicants. High school diploma is required, and GED is accepted. *Academic units required:* 4 English, 3 math, 3 science (3 science labs), 3 social studies, 1 fine arts. *Academic units recommended:* 4 English, 4 math, 4 science (3 science labs), 2 foreign language, 3 social studies, 1 fine arts.

The Inside Word

Given the relatively small numbers of high school graduates coming from South Dakota's high schools each year, the university's rolling admission policy is nearly open admission, though admissions standards increase in 2007. Solid college-prep students should encounter no trouble in gaining admission.

FINANCIAL AID

Students should submit: FAFSA. The Princeton Review suggests that all financial aid forms be submitted as soon as possible after January 1. *Need-based scholarships/grants offered:* Pell Grant, SEOG, private scholarships, the school's own gift aid, Federal Nursing Scholarship. *Loan aid offered:* FFEL Subsidized Stafford, FFEL Unsubsidized Stafford, FFEL PLUS, Federal Perkins Loan, Federal Nursing Loan, college/university loans from institutional funds. Applicants will be notified of awards on a rolling basis beginning or about March 1.

FROM THE ADMISSIONS OFFICE

"The University of South Dakota is the perfect fit for students looking for a smart educational investment. The U is South Dakota's only designated liberal arts university and is consistently rated among the top doctoral institutions in the country. Annually, The U awards scholarships to more than 800 first-year students, and over 80 percent of U students receive some form of financial aid through grants, loans, and work-study jobs.

"U students earn the nation's most prestigious scholarships. Our quality of teaching and research prepares students to pursue their passions all over the world, at institutions such as Columbia, Johns Hopkins, The University of Chicago, and beyond. Thirty-eight U students have been awarded prestigious Fulbright, Rhodes, National Science Foundation, Boren, Truman, Udall, Jack Kent Cooke, and Goldwater scholarships and grants for graduate study. Personal attention from our award-winning faculty and our welcoming environment makes students feel right at home.

"As the flagship liberal arts institution in South Dakota, The University of South Dakota—founded in 1862—has long been regarded as a leader in the state and the region. Notable undergraduate and postgraduate alumni include journalist Ken Bode, author and former news anchor Tom Brokaw, writer and Emmy Award–winner Dorothy Cooper Foote, U.S. Senator Tim Johnson, *USA Today* Founder Al Neuharth, and U.S. Senator John Thune.

"Applicants for Fall 2008 are not required to take the new writing test for either SAT or ACT. USD recommends taking the ACT over the SAT. Students who wish to send their SAT scores will have their scores converted to ACT scores for placement and scholarship consideration."

SELECTIVITY

Admissions Rating	74
# of applicants	3,044
% of applicants accepted	86
% of acceptees attending	43

FRESHMAN PROFILE

Range SAT Critical Reading	460–580
Range SAT Math	470–620
Range ACT Composite	20–25
Minimum Paper TOEFL	550
Minimum Computer Based TOEFL	213
Average HS GPA	3.27
% graduated top 10% of class	11
% graduated top 25% of class	32
% graduated top 50% of class	69

DEADLINES

Regular notification	rolling
Nonfall registration?	yes

APPLICANTS ALSO LOOK AT

AND OFTEN PREFER
Minnesota State University—Mankato, University of Nebraska—Lincoln

AND SOMETIMES PREFER
Augustana College (SD), South Dakota State University

AND RARELY PREFER
Dakota State University, Mount Marty College, Northern State University

FINANCIAL FACTS

Financial Aid Rating	85
Annual in-state tuition	$2,690
Annual out-of-state tuition	$7,569
Room & Board	$4,964
Books and supplies	$750
Required fees	$2,690
% frosh rec. need-based scholarship or grant aid	23
% UG rec. need-based scholarship or grant aid	28
% frosh rec. need-based self-help aid	52
% UG rec. need-based self-help aid	57
% frosh rec. any financial aid	93
% UG rec. any financial aid	88

UNIVERSITY OF SOUTH FLORIDA

4202 East Fowler Avenue, SVC-1036, Tampa, FL 33620-9951 • Admissions: 813-974-3350 • Fax: 813-974-9689

CAMPUS LIFE

Quality of Life Rating	**79**
Fire Safety Rating	**60***
Type of school	public
Environment	metropolis

STUDENTS

Total undergrad enrollment	33,580
% male/female	41/59
% from out of state	3
% from public high school	95
% live on campus	12
% in (# of) fraternities	8 (16)
% in (# of) sororities	6 (22)
% African American	12
% Asian	6
% Caucasian	65
% Hispanic	12
% international	2
# of countries represented	158

SURVEY SAYS . . .

Great library
Athletic facilities are great
Diverse student types on campus
Great off-campus food
Student publications are popular

ACADEMICS

Academic Rating	**72**
Calendar	semester
Student/faculty ratio	19:1
Profs interesting rating	72
Profs accessible rating	73
% profs teaching UG courses	83
% classes taught by TAs	17
Most common lab size	20–29 students
Most common reg class size	20–29 students

MOST POPULAR MAJORS

curriculum and instruction
marketing/marketing management
social sciences

STUDENTS SAY

Academics

It is an exciting time to be a part of the community of the University of South Florida, "an up-and-coming public university that is just about to make [its] mark." Founded in 1956, a sense of freshness and opportunity still permeates the college. "As a relatively young school, we are still growing and forming our own personality," writes a senior. "New traditions are continually being created, and school spirit is growing." Academically, students praise the premed program as well as psychology, engineering, communication, and environmental science. If you can get into it, undergrads recommend the Honors College, which "is run very smoothly, with great teachers who are easily accessible and helpful, classes that are small and interesting, and privileges that other students don't get (like early registration for classes)." Even in large lecture courses, professors are reputed to be intelligent, friendly, and available outside the classroom. As USF is a respected educational pillar of the Tampa Bay community, students can easily translate academics into career and internship opportunities in the city. "I had the opportunity to work with companies in the area on projects such as alternative buses, methane microturbine generators and solar cells," writes one senior. While some complain that "the administration is shaky," well-leveraged technology, like the university's website, which "is a thing of beauty and makes almost all personal contact unnecessary," helps USF keep up with the needs of more than 33,000 undergraduates.

Life

On the huge and social campus of USF, there is truly something for everyone. For example, "If it's comic books that tickle your fancy, we have a club for that; if it's surfing, we have a club for that too." While the vast majority of undergraduates commute to USF, there is a surprisingly strong sense of campus community, and many students participate in clubs, sports, and social groups. In addition "There are music concerts almost every weekend on and off campus and new movies on Wednesdays on the lawn on campus." In particular, many undergrads believe that "the Marshall Center is a great place for students, especially those under 21, to hang out; there is always something going on in there, like bands, tournaments, and get-togethers." As "The weather is great . . . outdoor activities are very popular," making it easy to "play beach volleyball right outside my dorm room." Also, "Since Tampa is a large community, many students find lots to do off campus," such as attending sporting events, or going to shows at Busch Gardens. And be aware that "Ybor City, a historic-district-turned-night-clubbing-district, is a very popular night spot for college students." USF is "definitely a major party school," and "Greek life is very prominent." A sophomore avers, "The weekends consist mainly of parties . . . weekdays consist of much of the same . . . plus some classes."

Student Body

The University of South Florida draws students who are "young, older, middle-aged, skinny, average, overweight, bald, hairy, Black, White, or tan." We assume this means the place is diverse. A not-so-literal senior clarifies: "Everyone here is from different walks of life and everyone here is open to it, accepts it, and loves it." Undergrads generally describe their classmates as friendly and studious, and they tell us that at a school of more than 33,000, "You can always find somewhere to fit in." Some would like to see more interaction between ethnic groups outside of class, but in class, "Most of the students are highly intelligent and contribute to class discussions, putting [forth] a different perspective on issues." Even nontraditional students feel comfortable within the undergraduate community. "I find it amazing that as an older student, I don't feel cut off from the events on campus," writes one senior.

FINANCIAL AID: 813-974-4700 • WEBSITE: WWW.USF.EDU

ADMISSIONS

Very important factors considered include: Academic GPA, rigor of secondary school record, standardized test scores. *Important factors considered include:* Class rank, talent/ability. *Other factors considered include:* Application essay, character/personal qualities, extracurricular activities, first generation, geographical residence, recommendation(s), state residency, volunteer work, work experience. SAT or ACT required; ACT with Writing component required. TOEFL required of all international applicants. High school diploma is required, and GED is accepted. *Academic units required:* 4 English, 3 math, 3 science (2 science labs), 2 foreign language, 3 social studies, 3 academic electives.

The Inside Word

A traditional college-prep high school course load is required for admission to USF. Beyond making sure that you complete all prerequisite classes, however, keep two other things in mind when applying to USF. First, admissions decisions are made on a rolling basis, so the earlier one applies, the better his or her chance of acceptance since there are more unfilled seats early in the admissions cycle. Second, Advanced Placement (AP) and International Baccalaureate (IB) classes are looked upon favorably in the Admissions Office here, so if your school offers them, load up on them and do well.

FINANCIAL AID

Students should submit: FAFSA. The Princeton Review suggests that all financial aid forms be submitted as soon as possible after January 1. *Need-based scholarships/grants offered:* Pell Grant, SEOG, state scholarships/grants, private scholarships, the school's own gift aid. *Loan aid offered:* FFEL Subsidized Stafford, FFEL Unsubsidized Stafford, FFEL PLUS, Federal Perkins Loan, college/university loans from institutional funds. Applicants will be notified of awards on or about March 15.

FROM THE ADMISSIONS OFFICE

"Big Town. Big Gown. Big East. Located in the Tampa Bay area, USF is recognized as one of the nation's top metropolitan research universities.

"One of the most distinguishing features of USF is the Honors College. The college has a specially designed honors major, as well as a Research Scholars Program that is offered to students who have demonstrated excellent scholarship potential and who are interested in an intensive research experience. Admission to the Honors College and Research Scholars Program is based on university admissions requirements.

"As students begin the application process, they need to become familiar with USF's admission requirements. Admission is based on the strength of an applicant's high school background, including the degree of difficulty of courses selected, record of academic achievement, and SAT or ACT scores. USF also takes into account the student's profile and special talents in and outside of the classroom.

"Students are encouraged to use academic electives to better enhance their preparation for entrance into a selected major. USF also encourages students with talent in music, art, dance, and theater to balance their high school experience with advanced courses in the visual and performing arts.

"It's always a great time to visit USF. Campus tours, information sessions, and tours of the residence halls are offered daily and the first Saturday of each month. Reservations are strongly encouraged.

"Freshman and lower-level transfer applicants to USF who graduate from high school in 2006 or later are required to submit official results from either the SAT Reasoning Test or the ACT test with Writing."

SELECTIVITY

Admissions Rating	87
# of applicants	22,462
% of applicants accepted	51
% of acceptees attending	39

FRESHMAN PROFILE

Range SAT Critical Reading	500–600
Range SAT Math	510–610
Range SAT Writing	470–570
Range ACT Composite	22–26
Minimum Paper TOEFL	550
Minimum Computer Based TOEFL	213
Average HS GPA	3.61
% graduated top 10% of class	27
% graduated top 25% of class	64
% graduated top 50% of class	94

DEADLINES

Regular application deadline	4/15
Regular notification	rolling
Nonfall registration?	yes

APPLICANTS ALSO LOOK AT

AND OFTEN PREFER
University of Florida

AND SOMETIMES PREFER
Florida State University, University of Central Florida

FINANCIAL FACTS

Financial Aid Rating	63
Annual in-state tuition	$3,416
Annual out-of-state tuition	$16,115
Room & Board	$7,180
Books and supplies	$800
% frosh rec. need-based scholarship or grant aid	20
% UG rec. need-based scholarship or grant aid	29
% frosh rec. need-based self-help aid	13
% UG rec. need-based self-help aid	20
% frosh rec. any financial aid	68
% UG rec. any financial aid	78

UNIVERSITY OF SOUTHERN CALIFORNIA

700 CHILDS WAY, LOS ANGELES, CA 90089-0911 • ADMISSIONS: 213-740-1111 • FAX: 213-740-6364

STUDENTS SAY

Academics

When students insist that "TROJAN PRIDE" is always in capital letters, you know you're in for a school that is "the epitome of what a college should be—amazing professors, friendly, intelligent students, school work during the week/parties on the weekend, beautiful campus, and most of all, TROJAN PRIDE!" A fellow student concurs, "Once a Trojan, always a Trojan. School spirit is by far this school's greatest strength." However, there are those that are bothered "that USC is often perceived as a football school" and would prefer to be recognized for "the fact that USC is academically strong in so many diverse fields." The school's "interdisciplinary approach to academics" and focus on the "hands-on learning experience, which brings professors and administrators (most of whom are required to teach an undergraduate course, including our president) together with students on a regular basis," are all popular among the student body. Best of all—as far as the many career-minded undergraduates are concerned—USC is the school that keeps on giving long after graduation because "USC is all about the connections. Our alumni network is amazing, and the alumni are so successful."

Life

Students note that while "It used to be that the neighborhood around USC shut down on weekends, and that downtown was seedy. But there's been a real renaissance in these neighborhoods, and more and more students choose to live on and near campus and spend weekends here." Now, there are "more restaurants, more museums, more theater, etc. than ever before, and even burgeoning cafes." That said, being "in a large city," "Much of the 'student life' is off campus." USC undergraduates tell us that "LA is a Trojan's playground, if you don't mind driving to get there." One student reports that "usually we find someone with a car and go into Santa Monica or Beverly Hills and shop and eat dinner or go to the movies." However, students are happy to report that "USC is quickly transitioning into a fully residential university." Also, "The just-completed Galen Center sports facility adds a lot of prestige to the neighborhood. It's the new home of USC basketball and serves as a large and modern venue for entertainment events." For the toga-inclined, "Almost all Greek houses are located on one street. It is famous for its parties on Thursday nights because campus dies down on Friday." Students are also "very involved in collegiate sports (especially football)" and on-campus lectures and movie showings. One undergraduate writes, "There's always an advance screening somewhere that you get handed tickets to on the way to class."

Student Body

"There is a huge mix of students at USC," undergraduates tell us. "You have everything from rich daddy's girls to minority students from the poorest LA neighborhoods on scholarships." The campus has always been renowned for its "beautiful people;" however, this focus distracts from the "significant foreign population" and "everything from jocks to eggheads to overachievers to artsy types." It's worth noting that "fraternities and sororities are also a major part of the student body whether you're involved in them directly or not." According to the Irvine Quarterly, USC culls more than one-quarter of its enrollment from families in the bottom third of annual income. Also mixed in among California's future business elite are "students in creative fields such as cinema, architecture, and music, a group of atypical students who happen to be a large percentage of the population, so there's a great mixing of the whole spectrum of people."

FINANCIAL AID: 213-740-1111 • E-MAIL: ADMITUSC@USC.EDU • WEBSITE: WWW.USC.EDU

ADMISSIONS

Very important factors considered include: Academic GPA, application essay, recommendation(s), rigor of secondary school record, standardized test scores. *Important factors considered include:* Extracurricular activities, talent/ability. *Other factors considered include:* Alumni/ae relation, character/personal qualities, class rank, first generation, interview, racial/ethnic status, volunteer work, work experience. SAT or ACT required; ACT with Writing component required. High school diploma is required, and GED is not accepted. *Academic units required:* 4 English, 3 math, 2 science (2 science labs), 2 foreign language, 2 social studies, 3 academic electives. *Academic units recommended:* 4 English, 4 math, 3 science (3 science labs), 3 foreign language, 3 social studies, 3 academic electives.

The Inside Word

With the temperate climate and location, it's no surprise that many USC students stay in Los Angeles after graduation. But there's another reason behind this—the school is the largest private employer in the city. Thanks to this, many students find jobs with their alma mater and while the economic powerhouse that it has become nurtures the surrounding environment, making a good location all the more enviable and viable with every dollar spent.

FINANCIAL AID

Students should submit: FAFSA, CSS/Financial Aid PROFILE, parent and student Federal Income Tax Returns with all schedules and W-2s. USC Non-filing Forms for those not required to file. The Princeton Review suggests that all financial aid forms be submitted as soon as possible after January 1. *Need-based scholarships/grants offered:* Pell Grant, SEOG, state scholarships/grants, private scholarships, the school's own gift aid. *Loan aid offered:* FFEL Subsidized Stafford, FFEL Unsubsidized Stafford, FFEL PLUS, Federal Perkins Loan, credit-ready and credit-based loans. Applicants will be notified of awards on a rolling basis beginning or about March 15 Federal Work-Study Program available. Institutional employment available. Off-campus job opportunities are excellent.

FROM THE ADMISSIONS OFFICE

"One of the best ways to discover if USC is right for you is to walk around campus, talk to students, and get a feel for the area both as a place to study and a place to live. If you can't visit, we hold admission information programs around the country. Watch your mailbox for an invitation, or send us an e-mail if you're interested.

"Freshman applicants are required to submit a standardized Writing exam. We will accept either the new SAT or the ACT with its optional Writing section."

SELECTIVITY

Admissions Rating	**98**
# of applicants	33,979
% of applicants accepted	25
% of acceptees attending	32

FRESHMAN PROFILE

Range SAT Critical Reading	630–720
Range SAT Math	650–740
Range SAT Writing	640–720
Range ACT Composite	28–32
Average HS GPA	3.71
% graduated top 10% of class	86
% graduated top 25% of class	97
% graduated top 50% of class	100

DEADLINES

Regular application deadline	1/10
Regular notification	4/1
Nonfall registration?	yes

APPLICANTS ALSO LOOK AT

AND OFTEN PREFER
Stanford University, University of Pennsylvania

AND SOMETIMES PREFER
New York University, Northwestern University, University of California—Berkeley, University of California—Los Angeles

AND RARELY PREFER
Johns Hopkins University, University of California—San Diego, Vanderbilt University, Washington University in St. Louis

FINANCIAL FACTS

Financial Aid Rating	**97**
Annual tuition	$33,314
Room & Board	$10,144
Books and supplies	$750
Required fees	$578
% frosh rec. need-based scholarship or grant aid	34
% UG rec. need-based scholarship or grant aid	39
% frosh rec. need-based self-help aid	39
% UG rec. need-based self-help aid	43
% frosh rec. any financial aid	72
% UG rec. any financial aid	68

THE UNIVERSITY OF TENNESSEE AT KNOXVILLE

320 STUDENT SERVICE BUILDING, CIRCLE PARK DRIVE, KNOXVILLE, TN 37996-0230 • ADMISSIONS: 865-974-2184

CAMPUS LIFE

Quality of Life Rating	**71**
Fire Safety Rating	**89**
Type of school	public
Environment	city

STUDENTS

Total undergrad enrollment	20,298
% male/female	49/51
% from out of state	14
% live on campus	34
% in (# of) fraternities	13 (20)
% in (# of) sororities	19 (18)
% African American	9
% Asian	3
% Caucasian	85
% Hispanic	2
% international	1
# of countries represented	106

SURVEY SAYS . . .

Great library
Athletic facilities are great
Great off-campus food
Everyone loves the Volunteers
Intramural sports are popular
Frats and sororities
dominate social scene
Student publications are popular
Lots of beer drinking
Hard liquor is popular

ACADEMICS

Academic Rating	**68**
Calendar	semester
Student/faculty ratio	15:1
Profs interesting rating	62
Profs accessible rating	62
% profs teaching	
UG courses	74
% classes taught by TAs	11
Most common	
lab size	20–29 students
Most common	
reg class size	20–29 students

MOST POPULAR MAJORS

English language and literature
political science and government
psychology

STUDENTS SAY

Academics

Academics at the University of Tennessee at Knoxville can be as challenging as you want to make them, students here tell us. This "great institution [offers] ample opportunity for leadership development, involvement, and travel to conferences." The school "has the money to provide top facilities, and they have done so and continue to upgrade facilities." The school also offers "all kinds of majors," including "the best undergraduate engineering program in the state, [a] good journalism program, [and] exceptional Business and Communications Departments." Professors are accomplished and "tend to be really supportive if you are willing to try." Students also report that "there is consistent support for improvement in academic performance through various tutorial programs and extra study sessions that are often available from professors and teaching assistants." The only caveat is that some students here care a lot more about football and parties than academics. "These undergraduates seek mediocre grades and an average experience, and the school lays out a path for them with little, if any, obstacle." At the other end of the spectrum, a few students wish that more were demanded of them academically, claiming, "You'd have to try to flunk out of UT" but this problem will hopefully be curbed by the recent opening of the Student Success Center, a one-stop shop for student services. Those seeking the most rigorous program available should apply to the honors program, which provides "excellent assistance in all academic endeavors." Students warn that UT is administratively challenged and does little to assist students.

Life

"Weekends are when the biggest events occur" at UT, and "Weekends start on Wednesday here, and end on Monday," which means lots of big events, both on and off campus. The biggest of all, without question, is Volunteer football: "Everyone comes together on Saturdays, as the student body, faculty, staff, alumni, and fans all unite in high spirits and pride," students tell us. While football is king, "The whole athletic program at UT is second to none. Not only is the football team consistently ranked in the Top 25 each season, but the women's basketball team has consistently made it to the Final Four in recent years." Intramurals are almost as big and almost as fiercely fought as the intercollegiate games; "Everything is a big deal, there is no casual game," writes one undergrad. Athletics may be first at UT, but for many undergrads partying runs a close second. "The drinking starts at dusk and doesn't end 'til dawn" at the school's many house parties and Greek parties. Students over 21 hit "the Strip," where there are "lots of bars." Younger students can't join them, however, because "The police have gotten really hard on fake IDs." The twin allures of athletics and partying leads students to opine that "Knoxville is a drinking town with a serious football problem." Life isn't just booze and ballgames, though. "We are in the Bible Belt, so religious activities like Campus Crusade are highly attended and interesting," students tell us. The university is also home to a wide range of student clubs and organizations.

Student Body

UT's student body "avidly practices Southern politeness and Republicanism, since most of us were raised in the South. . . . There is no such thing as a serious atmosphere, and usually the most threatening arguments involve people in a drunken discussion of football." Students are "extremely friendly," to the point that "if you're walking down the road at night, people will say, 'Are you looking for a party? Come to ours.'" There's a sense among some that UT has a "homogenous population of White, Southern, middle- to upper-class, BMW-driving, Abercrombie & Fitch–wearing conservatives," with a few "nerds, video gamers, and just plain weird dudes" thrown in for good measure. But "In a public school of 20,000 people, there is no such thing as a typical student. There are all types here, and everyone finds a group of people they connect with," even "Yankees who are teased for their accent." Many here agree: "We could definitely use improvement in the area of diversity, not only ethnically, but also socially and ideologically, though the university is taking strides to increase its minority population through scholarships and programming."

FAX: 865-974-1182 • FINANCIAL AID: 865-974-3131 • E-MAIL: ADMISSIONS@UTK.EDU • WEBSITE: WWW.UTK.EDU

ADMISSIONS

Very important factors considered include: Academic GPA, rigor of secondary school record, standardized test scores. *Other factors considered include:* Alumni/ae relation, application essay, character/personal qualities, class rank, extracurricular activities, first generation, geographical residence, level of applicant's interest, racial/ethnic status, recommendation(s), state residency, talent/ability. SAT or ACT required; TOEFL required of all international applicants. High school diploma is required, and GED is accepted. *Academic units required:* 4 English, 3 math, 2 science (1 science lab), 2 foreign language, 1 social studies, 1 history, 1 visual or performing arts.

The Inside Word

The university takes in a jumbo freshman class and has to use a fairly straightforward approach to getting these kids admitted. Standards are the same for out-of-state applicants as for in-state, but the school's mix of in-state/out-of-state students is firm, since it is set by policy of the Board of Trustees.

FINANCIAL AID

Students should submit: FAFSA, Academic College Scholarship Application. The Princeton Review suggests that all financial aid forms be submitted as soon as possible after January 1. *Need-based scholarships/grants offered:* Pell Grant, SEOG, state scholarships/grants, private scholarships, the school's own gift aid, Federal Nursing Scholarship. *Loan aid offered:* FFEL Subsidized Stafford, FFEL Unsubsidized Stafford, FFEL PLUS, Federal Perkins Loan, college/university loans from institutional funds. Applicants will be notified of awards on a rolling basis beginning or about March 15. Federal Work-Study Program available. Off-campus job opportunities are good.

FROM THE ADMISSIONS OFFICE

"The University of Tennessee at Knoxville is the place where you belong if you're interested in outstanding resources and unlimited opportunities to foster your personal and academic growth. Nine colleges offer more than 110 majors to students from all 50 states and 106 foreign countries. More than 400 clubs and organizations on campus offer opportunities for fun, challenge, and service. UTK is a place where students take pride in belonging to a 200-year-old tradition and celebrate the excitement of 'the Volunteer spirit.' We invite you to explore the many advantages UTK has to offer.

"Freshman applicants to the University of Tennessee are required to submit ACT or SAT scores. The essay is not required."

SELECTIVITY

Admissions Rating	87
# of applicants	12,372
% of applicants accepted	74
% of acceptees attending	46

FRESHMAN PROFILE

Range SAT Critical Reading	520–630
Range SAT Math	530–640
Range ACT Composite	23–28
Minimum Paper TOEFL	523
Minimum Computer Based TOEFL	193
Average HS GPA	3.6
% graduated top 10% of class	41
% graduated top 25% of class	68
% graduated top 50% of class	91

DEADLINES

Priority application deadline	11/1
Regular application deadline	2/1
Regular notification	January and March
Nonfall registration?	yes

APPLICANTS ALSO LOOK AT

AND OFTEN PREFER

Auburn University, East Tennessee State University, Tennessee Technological University

AND SOMETIMES PREFER

Clemson University, University of South Carolina—Columbia, Vanderbilt University

AND RARELY PREFER

The University of Alabama at Tuscaloosa, University of Mississippi, Virginia Tech

FINANCIAL FACTS

Financial Aid Rating	71
Annual in-state tuition	$5,072
Annual out-of-state tuition	$16,338
Room & Board	$6,358
Books and supplies	$1,288
Required fees	$792
% frosh rec. need-based scholarship or grant aid	43
% UG rec. need-based scholarship or grant aid	35
% frosh rec. need-based self-help aid	22
% UG rec. need-based self-help aid	28
% frosh rec. any financial aid	45
% UG rec. any financial aid	43

THE UNIVERSITY OF TEXAS AT AUSTIN

PO Box 8058, Austin, TX 78713-8058 • Admissions: 512-475-7440 • Fax: 512-475-7475

CAMPUS LIFE
Quality of Life Rating	88
Fire Safety Rating	60*
Type of school	public
Environment	metropolis

STUDENTS
Total undergrad enrollment	36,241
% male/female	48/52
% from out of state	4
% live on campus	19
% in (# of) fraternities	9 (26)
% in (# of) sororities	13 (22)
% African American	4
% Asian	17
% Caucasian	57
% Hispanic	17
% international	4
# of countries represented	127

SURVEY SAYS . . .
Career services are great
Great library
Athletic facilities are great
Students love Austin, TX
Everyone loves the Longhorns
Student publications are popular
Lots of beer drinking
Hard liquor is popular

ACADEMICS
Academic Rating	76
Calendar	semester
Student/faculty ratio	18:1
Profs interesting rating	70
Profs accessible rating	63
% profs teaching UG courses	100
Most common lab size	10–19 students
Most common reg class size	10–19 students

MOST POPULAR MAJORS
biology/biological sciences
liberal arts—undeclared
government

STUDENTS SAY

Academics

The University of Texas at Austin is one of the largest universities in the nation, with more than 50,000 students (undergraduate plus grad), and the school "really capitalizes on its size and funds" with "so many libraries, its state-of-the-art technology, and student programs galore," as well as "tons of opportunities to get involved in research." The school poses near-limitless options for undergrads willing to seek them out; one writes, "You can plan your college experience exactly as you want it. Basically the attitude is: If you can fit it in in 4 years and you meet the prerequisites, go for it. And if they don't offer what you want, figure out how to take it and it's yours." As one student puts it, "Academically, UT is what you make of it. If you want to register for courses that are challenging (but worth it) you can. If you want to register for easy-A courses, you can do that too." Of course, "It is easy to get lost in the shuffle" at a school this big, and "When you run into a problem, dealing with the bureaucracy can be difficult and frustrating." Fortunately, "For a school of this size, UT runs pretty well." Professors here are often surprisingly good and engaged, although "Students often have to take the initiative because the professors don't have the time to seek out every student individually." A course instructor survey system allows students to check other students' ratings of professors online; there are also "tons of teaching awards at UT as incentives to focus on that aspect," and they seem to be doing the job.

Life

Lots of self-respecting cities have smaller populations than UT, but they're not surrounded by "the coolest college town that ever existed," so, as you might imagine, "There is so much available to do here that fits the bill for just about anyone." The campus hosts "a huge college scene that translates into lots of parties (and drinking) every weekend, from the Greek houses to off-campus houses, apartments, co-ops, etc." "Football games and other sporting events are also a lot of fun," and the "900-plus registered student organizations" allow undergrads to explore any and all extracurricular interests. Beyond campus is the capital of Texas, a city that "never sleeps. If you can't find anything to do in Austin, you're crazy." Students report that "restaurants are very popular—you can get the best Tex-Mex in the world here," and "Sixth Street is very big with the older students, as it hosts bar after bar and an interesting scene. It's like Austin's version of Bourbon Street," right down to the "tons of concerts; this city is the live music capital of the world." Outdoor enthusiasts also "have lots to do, with the many hike and bike trails in and around Austin. Barton Springs and Zilker Park are favorites for natural recreation. Most UT students love to be outside enjoying the sunshine, be it playing sports, exercising, horseback riding, studying, reading, tanning or just lounging." Don't have a car? Don't worry; "The public transportation is readily available."

Student Body

"There's really no typical student at UT" due to the school's enormous size and the diversity of its home state. One student writes, "It would be really hard to not fit in. In fact, even if you're a left-handed vegetarian lesbian who wants to be an astronaut, there are probably enough people like you to start the 3,000th club on campus. I guess out of over 50,000 students, your odds are pretty good" of finding multiple kindred spirits. UT "is known as the 'liberal' school in Texas, and we do have a large GLBT population, as well as the 'Austin-type' bohemian culture. Of course we have our fair share of cute Texas blondes and frat boys, so a typical student could be any or all of the above."

FINANCIAL AID: 512-475-6282 • WEBSITE: WWW.UTEXAS.EDU

ADMISSIONS

Very important factors considered include: Class rank, rigor of secondary school record. *Important factors considered include:* Application essay, extracurricular activities, standardized test scores, talent/ability, volunteer work, work experience. *Other factors considered include:* Academic GPA, character/personal qualities, first generation, geographical residence, level of applicant's interest, racial/ethnic status, recommendation(s), state residency. SAT or ACT required; ACT with Writing component required. TOEFL required of all international applicants. High school diploma is required, and GED is accepted. *Academic units required:* 4 English, 3 math, 2 science, 2 foreign language, 3 social studies, 2 academic electives. *Academic units recommended:* 4 math, 3 science, 3 foreign language, 1 fine arts.

The Inside Word

Top faculty and super facilities draw a mega-sized applicant pool to UT, as does Longhorn football. Texas wants top athletes in each entering class, to be sure. But it also seeks students who are well qualified academically, and it gets loads of them. Both the university and Austin are thriving intellectual communities; Austin has the highest per capita book sales of any city in the United States. Many students continue on to grad school without ever leaving, which is understandable—it's hard to spend any time without developing an affinity for the school and the city.

FINANCIAL AID

Students should submit: FAFSA. The Princeton Review suggests that all financial aid forms be submitted as soon as possible after January 1. *Need-based scholarships/grants offered:* Pell Grant, SEOG, state scholarships/grants, private scholarships, the school's own gift aid, Federal Nursing Scholarship. *Loan aid offered:* FFEL Subsidized Stafford, FFEL Unsubsidized Stafford, FFEL PLUS, Federal Perkins Loan, state loans. Applicants will be notified of awards on a rolling basis beginning or about March 15. Off-campus job opportunities are fair.

FROM THE ADMISSIONS OFFICE

"For more than 120 years, students from all over the world have come to The University of Texas at Austin to obtain a first-class education. Recognized for research, teaching, and public service, the university boasts more than 130 undergraduate academic programs, more than 350 study-abroad programs, outstanding student services, cultural centers, and volunteer and leadership opportunities designed to prepare students to make a difference in the world. Along with its nationally ranked athletic programs, the university's spirit is enhanced by cultural, artistic, and scientific opportunities that help to make Austin one of the most inviting destinations in the country. The Performing Arts Center hosts plays, Austin's opera and symphony, and visiting musical and dance groups. Students access more than 8 million volumes in the university's 17 libraries and study prehistoric fossils at the Texas Memorial Museum, Renaissance and Baroque paintings in the Blanton Museum, original manuscripts at the Ransom Center, and life in the 1960s at the Lyndon B. Johnson Library and Museum.

"Each year the university enrolls about 50,000 students from richly varied ethnic and geographic backgrounds. Every day graduates contribute to the world community as volunteers, teachers, journalists, artists, engineers, business leaders, scientists, and lawyers. With world-renowned faculty, top-rated academic programs, successful alumni, and such an enticing location, it's no surprise that The University of Texas at Austin ranks among the best universities in the world.

"Freshman applicants must submit official scores from the new version of the SAT or the ACT with the optional Writing exam. SAT Subject Test scores are required only for applicants to the College of Engineering who need to submit scores to meet the Math Readiness Requirement."

SELECTIVITY

Admissions Rating	92
# of applicants	23,502
% of applicants accepted	57
% of acceptees attending	56

FRESHMAN PROFILE

Range SAT Critical Reading	530–660
Range SAT Math	570–690
Range SAT Writing	520–640
Range ACT Composite	23–29
Minimum Paper TOEFL	550
Minimum Computer Based TOEFL	213
% graduated top 10% of class	73
% graduated top 25% of class	95
% graduated top 50% of class	99

DEADLINES

Regular application deadline	2/1
Regular notification	rolling
Nonfall registration?	yes

FINANCIAL FACTS

Financial Aid Rating	91
Annual in-state tuition	$7,630
Annual out-of-state tuition	$20,364
Books and supplies	$800
% frosh rec. need-based scholarship or grant aid	54
% UG rec. need-based scholarship or grant aid	47
% frosh rec. need-based self-help aid	54
% UG rec. need-based self-help aid	52
% frosh rec. any financial aid	84
% UG rec. any financial aid	74

UNIVERSITY OF TORONTO

315 BLOOR STREET WEST, TORONTO, ON M5S1A3 • ADMISSIONS: 416-978-2190 • FAX: 416-978-7022

CAMPUS LIFE
Quality of Life Rating	73
Fire Safety Rating	60*
Type of school	public
Environment	metropolis

STUDENTS
Total undergrad enrollment	59,350
% male/female	44/56
% from out of state	4
% live on campus	23
% international	8
# of countries represented	160

SURVEY SAYS . . .
Career services are great
Great computer facilities
Great library
Diverse student types on campus
Students love Toronto, ON
Great off-campus food

ACADEMICS
Academic Rating	61
Calendar	2 terms (1 fall, 1 winter); 2 summer terms
Student/faculty ratio	26:1
Profs interesting rating	62
Profs accessible rating	61
Most common reg class size	10–19 students

MOST POPULAR MAJORS
general studies
liberal arts and sciences/liberal studies

STUDENTS SAY
Academics
One of Canada's premier universities, the University of Toronto offers world-class academic programs in a thriving, cosmopolitan setting. With faculty members "on the cutting edge of research in their fields," students agree, "The best of the best are teaching here, and it shows. You feel smarter every day just from listening to the lectures presented." The school capitalizes on its location in the center of Toronto: "The city and the university draw on each other in a variety of ways—clinical opportunities and research flow in both directions." On top of that, industrious undergrads tell us, "The libraries and other research facilities here are excellent and contribute much to the overall academic experience." With over 40,000 undergraduates, class sizes run large, especially in the first year. However, students reassure us that "after that, the class sizes drop off drastically to normally between 20 to 100 students," and "The teaching assistants and lab coordinators are really helpful and work with personal questions whenever necessary, so you're not left in the dark." Even so, those looking for an intimate and supportive academic environment might not find a good fit at U of T, as "The general attitude is one of professionalism, and very little mercy." A hearty sophomore declares, "The University of Toronto prepares its students for the real world—only the strong survive, and you're on your own to make things happen."

Life
When they aren't hitting the books, University of Toronto students enjoy life in "one of the coolest cities in North America." With an open campus that is fully integrated into the city's vibrant downtown, students benefit from the fact that "the Royal Ontario Museum is on campus, a ton of pubs and art galleries are within walking distance, and a nightlife to suit just about any type of person" can be found in Toronto. Many students also mention Toronto's art and cultural festivals, bustling ethnic markets, and extensive culinary options. A senior jokes, "It would be possible to eat at a different restaurant every day for the entire duration of my degree, and it's a challenge I only wish I could afford to take." When it comes to campus life, many students feel that the school's spirit and unity is negatively affected by the large number of commuter students who, "just run home after every class to study." Others insist that there are plenty of social and recreational opportunities for those willing to look. A junior elucidates, "Getting involved here takes some research in terms of navigating the over 300 clubs and endless academic/research opportunities, but once I did some searching, I found several places where I fit in well and have fun." For those who live on campus, sororities and fraternities help nurture social bonds, and "Most of the residential colleges have tons of events, from campus-wide capture the flag to movie nights" to "tons of intramural sports."

Student Body
At this large public school, the demographics on campus reflect those of surrounding Toronto, "one of the most diverse cities around." As one junior puts it, "Truly, one of the only things it can be said that all students here have in common is an excellent academic record prior to university. Beyond that, anything goes: There are huge variances in race, religion, sexual orientation, academic focus, postgraduate aspirations, socioeconomic background, disability, nationality, athleticism, and community involvement." A freshman chimes in, "On my floor alone there are kids from at least 10 different countries and, even with the different cultures, we have blended together to make a big family." Most students say it's relatively easy to find a social group among like-minded individuals, despite the school's impressive size and diversity. According to one senior, "Most students will find a niche where they feel comfortable; there's a place for everyone."

FINANCIAL AID: 416-978-2190 • E-MAIL: ADMISSIONS.HELP@UTORONTO.CA • WEBSITE: WWW.UTORONTO.CA

ADMISSIONS

Very important factors considered include: Class rank, rigor of secondary school record, standardized test scores. SAT Subject Tests required; TOEFL required of all international applicants. High school diploma is required, and GED is accepted.

The Inside Word

The University of Toronto is one of Canada's premier public universities and one of the top research institutions in the world. Needless to say, gaining admission to the college is no easy feat. The process is rather objective, however, and applicants with solid numbers are likely candidates for acceptance. Candidates should be aware that qualifications vary from program to program; and as an international student you'll have more paperwork to file. U.S. students can apply for financial assistance from the U.S. Federal Family Education Program (FFELP). The University of Toronto is a recognized postsecondary institution for Federal Stafford Loans. All applicants are automatically considered for admission scholarships.

FINANCIAL AID

Students should submit: The Princeton Review suggests that all financial aid forms be submitted as soon as possible after January 1.

FROM THE ADMISSIONS OFFICE

"The University of Toronto is committed to being an internationally significant research university with undergraduate, graduate, and professional programs of study.

"Students educated at U.S. schools should present good scores on the SAT or ACT examinations. Students must present the Writing component for both tests. Applicants must also present at least three SAT Subject Tests scores or AP scores in subjects appropriate to their proposed area of study. Those seeking admission to science or business/commerce programs are strongly advised to complete AP Calculus AB or BC or IB Mathematics.

"Scores below 500 on any part of the SAT Reasoning or Subject Tests are not acceptable. While many of our programs require higher scores, students normally present scores of at least 1700 out of a possible 2400 on the SAT and 26 on the ACT."

SELECTIVITY

Admissions Rating	60*
# of applicants	60,099
% of applicants accepted	66
% of acceptees attending	33

FRESHMAN PROFILE

Minimum Paper TOEFL	600
Minimum Computer Based TOEFL	250
Average HS GPA	3.0

DEADLINES

Regular application deadline	3/1
Regular notification	rolling
Nonfall registration?	no

FINANCIAL FACTS

Financial Aid Rating	60*
In-province tuition	$3,727–$6,324
Out-of-province tuition	$3,727–$6,324
International tuition	$14,318–$16,107
Room & Board	$10,792
Books and supplies	$1,050
Required fees	$700

THE UNIVERSITY OF TULSA

600 SOUTH COLLEGE AVENUE, TULSA, OK 74104 • ADMISSIONS: 918-631-2307 • FAX: 918-631-5003

CAMPUS LIFE
Quality of Life Rating	**98**
Fire Safety Rating	**80**
Type of school	private
Affiliation	Presbyterian
Environment	metropolis

STUDENTS
Total undergrad enrollment	2,830
% male/female	50/50
% from out of state	36
% from public high school	78
% live on campus	60
% in (# of) fraternities	21 (6)
% in (# of) sororities	23 (9)
% African American	7
% Asian	2
% Caucasian	65
% Hispanic	4
% Native American	4
% international	9
# of countries represented	63

SURVEY SAYS . . .
Small classes
Great computer facilities
Athletic facilities are great
Students are friendly
Students are happy

ACADEMICS
Academic Rating	**88**
Calendar	semester
Student/faculty ratio	11:1
Profs interesting rating	94
Profs accessible rating	96
% profs teaching UG courses	100
% classes taught by TAs	4
Most common lab size	20–29 students
Most common reg class size	10–19 students

MOST POPULAR MAJORS
business administration/
management
marketing/marketing management
mechanical engineering

STUDENTS SAY

Academics

The University of Tulsa is one of the sleeper gems of the Great Plains, a private school large enough to house numerous top-flight programs but small enough to facilitate one-on-one instruction provided in a homey atmosphere. TU is justly recognized for its excellent offerings in computer science, athletic training, and for its "incredible engineering program with a focus on undergraduate research." Students tell us the school is uniformly solid across all popular departments, and that "because of the smaller graduate programs, undergrads get the experiences that only grad students get at larger state schools or seriously research-driven universities." All students here complete the cross-disciplinary Tulsa curriculum that one student says "has been incredible in helping me learn to think in a variety of ways, and connect thoughts across curricula. In every one of my classes, I think back to what I've been learning in another class and that adds to my understanding of my overall education." While "classes are quite strenuous, [a] friendly and helpful atmosphere—with tutoring for all students who need help—and lots of study groups" help students to survive the demanding workload. As for the teachers, "TU professors can be top-notch or so-so. Some of them need to work on their teaching skills. Despite that, every teacher seems to genuinely care about his students, is readily accessible, encourages his students to get involved, and demands quality. If you get out of a class with an A here, you will know the material."

Life

"In general, academics come first for most students" at TU, "but many students enjoying unwinding on the weekends by going out to local bars (to hear several popular local bands), or heading to a nearby party." The Greek houses are popular party destinations, but so, too, are dorm rooms, off-campus apartments, and greater Tulsa, where "There is a burgeoning bar and nightclub scene downtown." The party scene is happening without getting out of hand, students tell us. One undergrad explains, "TU is pretty laid-back in my opinion because they trust us to be adults, and we haven't abused their confidence so far." Athletic events—and the "amazing" facilities that host them—draw big crowds too. "The football team improved greatly in 2005, winning the C-USA Championship and the Liberty Bowl, and our basketball team has high hopes this year. Most of our other sports have always done well and have great attendance, such as soccer." Intramurals and recreational sports are "very big; on any given afternoon there are multiple pick-up games of soccer, football, basketball going on around campus." Campus clubs and organizations are also active, with strong enrollment in religious and service organizations. As a bonus, "The new administration of the student government decided they wanted to really create things to do around campus, so now there are events on campus almost every night." So, what's the downside? "It is so small we call it Tulsa High School. Everyone knows everyone's business."

Student Body

There are "kids from all over the world" at TU, making it "really neat to walk down the sidewalk because you see so many different kids, each with their own beliefs and morals. We all come from different backgrounds, from Christian to Jewish to Muslim to atheist and everything in between." International students provide most of the diversity, as the majority of Americans are "White Christians from Oklahoma, Texas, Missouri, and Arkansas [who are] usually reasonably well off." A freshman from California says she had a bit of "culture shock. The fried food and the popularity of football freaked me out at first. But the Oakies take you in." Nearly everyone is "very serious and passionate about what we are studying. Most of us were in the top 20 percent of our high school class and work very hard in school."

THE UNIVERSITY OF TULSA

FINANCIAL AID: 918-631-2526 • E-MAIL: ADMISSION@UTULSA.EDU • WEBSITE: WWW.UTULSA.EDU

ADMISSIONS

Very important factors considered include: Academic GPA, character/personal qualities, class rank, interview, rigor of secondary school record, standardized test scores. *Important factors considered include:* Application essay, extracurricular activities, level of applicant's interest, recommendation(s), talent/ability. *Other factors considered include:* Alumni/ae relation, first generation, racial/ethnic status, volunteer work, work experience. SAT or ACT required; TOEFL required of all international applicants. High school diploma is required, and GED is accepted. *Academic units recommended:* 4 English, 4 math, 3 science (2 science labs), 2 foreign language, 2 social studies, 2 history, 1 fine arts/humanities elective.

The Inside Word

TU is a university with solid academic offerings, a strong sense of community, lots of student-faculty interaction, and attainable admission standards. The school's commitment to undergrads is clear. One of TU's most impressive programs, The Tulsa Undergraduate Research Challenge (TURC), allows undergrads to complete research along with faculty.

FINANCIAL AID

Students should submit: FAFSA, institution's own financial aid form. The Princeton Review suggests that all financial aid forms be submitted as soon as possible after January 1. *Need-based scholarships/grants offered:* Pell Grant, SEOG, state scholarships/grants, private scholarships, the school's own gift aid. *Loan aid offered:* FFEL Subsidized Stafford, FFEL Unsubsidized Stafford, FFEL PLUS, Federal Perkins Loan. Merit-based academic scholarships are based on school record, test scores, and interview (optional); no additional application form required. Performance scholarships available are based on music and theater auditions. Applicants will be notified of awards on a rolling basis beginning or about March 15. Federal Work-Study Program available. Institutional employment available. Off-campus job opportunities are good. Ninety-five percent of undergraduates receive financial aid: need-based, merit, or both.

FROM THE ADMISSIONS OFFICE

"The University of Tulsa is a private university with a comprehensive scope. Students choose from more than 80 majors offered through three undergraduate colleges—Arts and Sciences, Business Administration, and Engineering and Natural Sciences. Their curriculum can be customized with collaborative research, joint BS/MBA and BA/law degree programs, and an honors program, among other options. Professors are equally committed to teaching undergraduates and to scholarly research. This results in extraordinary individual achievement, as demonstrated by the nationally competitive scholarships TU students have won since 1995: 38 Goldwater scholars, 8 Truman scholars, 5 Udall scholars, and 4 Marshall scholars. Since 1994 campus life has benefited from more than $35 million in new student apartments and residence hall renovations. Over 160 registered clubs, organizations, special interest groups, and intramural and recreational sports exist on campus as well as 6 fraternities and 9 sororities. The 8,300-seat Reynolds Arena is home to the standout Golden Hurricane NCAA Division I men's basketball team, campus events, and concerts. A 40-acre sports complex includes a student fitness center and indoor tennis center that will host the 2008 NCAA Division I Men's and Women's tennis finals. An outdoor adventure freshman orientation program launches an entire first-year experience dedicated to developing students' full potential.

"Applicants for Fall 2008 term are required to submit the SAT or ACT. The Writing component is not required. For admission and scholarship consideration, the best composite score of submitted tests will be used."

SELECTIVITY

Admissions Rating	**90**
# of applicants	2,720
% of applicants accepted	76
% of acceptees attending	32
# accepting a place on wait list	112
% admitted from wait list	85

FRESHMAN PROFILE

Range SAT Critical Reading	530–690
Range SAT Math	540–690
Range ACT Composite	23–30
Minimum Paper TOEFL	500
Minimum Computer Based TOEFL	173
Average HS GPA	3.7
% graduated top 10% of class	59
% graduated top 25% of class	79
% graduated top 50% of class	94

DEADLINES

Regular notification	rolling
Nonfall registration?	yes

APPLICANTS ALSO LOOK AT

AND OFTEN PREFER
Oklahoma State University, Saint Louis University, Southern Methodist University, Texas Christian University, University of Oklahoma

AND SOMETIMES PREFER
Baylor University, Trinity University, Tulane University, Washington University in St. Louis

AND RARELY PREFER
Texas A&M University—College Station, University of Kansas, University of Missouri—Columbia

FINANCIAL FACTS

Financial Aid Rating	**89**
Annual tuition	$21,690
Room & Board	$7,504
Books and supplies	$1,200
Required fees	$80
% frosh rec. need-based scholarship or grant aid	19
% UG rec. need-based scholarship or grant aid	24
% frosh rec. need-based self-help aid	39
% UG rec. need-based self-help aid	40
% frosh rec. any financial aid	96
% UG rec. any financial aid	90

UNIVERSITY OF UTAH

201 SOUTH 1460 EAST, ROOM 250 S, SALT LAKE CITY, UT 84112 • ADMISSIONS: 801-581-7281 • FAX: 801-585-7864

CAMPUS LIFE

Quality of Life Rating	78
Fire Safety Rating	90
Type of school	public
Environment	city

STUDENTS

Total undergrad enrollment	21,249
% male/female	56/44
% from out of state	16
% from public high school	93
% live on campus	12
% in (# of) fraternities	1 (8)
% in (# of) sororities	1 (7)
% African American	1
% Asian	5
% Caucasian	81
% Hispanic	5
% Native American	1
% international	2
# of countries represented	119

SURVEY SAYS . . .

Great computer facilities
Great library
Students are very religious
Students love Salt Lake City, UT
Great off-campus food
Campus feels safe
Students are happy

ACADEMICS

Academic Rating	66
Calendar	semester
Student/faculty ratio	14:1
Profs interesting rating	69
Profs accessible rating	61
% profs teaching UG courses	64
% classes taught by TAs	11
Most common lab size	10–19 students
Most common reg class size	20–29 students

MOST POPULAR MAJORS
economics
mass communications/media studies
political science and government

STUDENTS SAY

Academics

The University of Utah ('the U' to students and supporters) "provides the highest quality education at the lowest possible price in the state of Utah" as well as "the closest thing to a liberal education in the state," according to undergrads here. If Utah is your destination of choice and affordability is a top priority, the U has a good deal to offer. It helps, though, if you are enterprising. "You really have to take care of yourself," one student writes, "and you have to approach the instructors." Because this is primarily a research institution, sometimes "Professors lack teaching ability and make up for it in their research, which isn't always the greatest for us students." On the other hand, research attracts heavy hitters; one student writes, "Many of the instructors have other responsibilities in the community (i.e., politicians and lawyers), making them excellent professors." Some students even brag of personalized classroom experiences and say professors "strive to help us understand the material, rather than move on with the syllabus." One student notes, "Some classes are very, very good, especially upper-division and honors classes." Another student continues that sentiment by saying, "The education here really is top-notch, tons of opportunities for undergraduate research." Students also say the administration generally knows what it is doing. Administrators "are always looking out for the good of the students [and are] very dedicated to education, leadership, and diversity."

Life

"You can't beat our geography," the U undergrads insist, asking "How many other schools are on the top of huge snow-capped mountains?" Cradled by the majestic Wasatch Mountains, Utah's location is indeed spectacular. It also provides easy access to a range of outdoor sports. "The mountains right by the school are awesome for biking, hiking, or skiing," writes one student. Campus life, unfortunately, doesn't provide the same thrills, in large part because "This is a commuter school, so it can be hard to get the same interaction as you get at schools with large residential populations." (According to the university, only about 2,300 of the 21,000-plus students live in the dorms and campus apartments.) Most of the commuters, unfortunately, "don't have time or resources to return to campus several times a week for meetings or other activities." The result? Very little school spirit or social life, though a "relatively small, but notable frat scene" does keep students entertained on campus. Still, most turn elsewhere—that elsewhere being Salt Lake City. Those who do won't be disappointed, though they probably won't be thrilled, either. One student writes, "Salt Lake isn't the greatest college town, but [the university] is located near malls, restaurants, movie theaters, and bars." By most accounts, the social pulse at the U and in town is pretty chaste, a reflection, students say, of the state's Latter Day Saints (LDS) values.

Student Body

University of Utah "is not very diverse," and "The typical student is a member of the LDS faith and conservative." Still, "If you go looking for it you can find almost any group you want" at this school of over 20,000 undergraduates where "The atypical students tend to gravitate toward one another regardless of their other differences." The vast majority here "come from a middle-class, Mormon, white-bread home, but people are very friendly, and minority groups fit in easily," writes one student. Another student agrees, "Students are generally accepting of anyone, regardless of race or religion." A sizeable international population mixes things up a bit; "Walking across campus, you will hear four or five different languages." A large nontraditional student body (i.e., people who are married and/or attend part-time) means that Utah truly "gets people from all walks of life."

FINANCIAL AID: 801-581-6211 • E-MAIL: FAWIN1@SA.UTAH.EDU • WEBSITE: WWW.UTAH.EDU

ADMISSIONS

Very important factors considered include: Academic GPA, rigor of secondary school record, standardized test scores. *Important factors considered include:* Talent/ability. *Other factors considered include:* Class rank, extracurricular activities, interview, racial/ethnic status, recommendation(s). ACT recommended; SAT or ACT required; SAT and SAT Subject Tests or ACT required. TOEFL required of all international applicants. High school diploma is required, and GED is accepted. *Academic units required:* 4 English, 2 math, 3 science (2 science labs), 2 foreign language, 1 history, 4 academic electives.

The Inside Word

Utah is another state in which low numbers of high school grads keep selectivity down at its public flagship university. Admission is based primarily on the big three: Course selection, grades, and test scores; if you have a 3.0 GPA or better and average test scores, you're close to a sure bet for admission.

FINANCIAL AID

Students should submit: FAFSA, institution's own financial aid form. The Princeton Review suggests that all financial aid forms be submitted as soon as possible after January 1. *Need-based scholarships/grants offered:* Pell Grant, SEOG, state scholarships/grants, private scholarships, the school's own gift aid. *Loan aid offered:* FFEL Subsidized Stafford, FFEL Unsubsidized Stafford, FFEL PLUS, Federal Perkins Loan, Federal Nursing Loan, college/university loans from institutional funds, private alternative loans. Applicants will be notified of awards on a rolling basis beginning or about April 15. Federal Work-Study Program available. Institutional employment available. Off-campus job opportunities are excellent.

FROM THE ADMISSIONS OFFICE

"The University of Utah is a distinctive community of learning in the American West. Today's 28,000 students are from every state and 119 foreign countries. The U has research ties worldwide, with national standing among the top comprehensive research institutions. The U offers majors in 73 undergraduate and 94 graduate subjects. Nationally recognized honors and undergraduate research programs stimulate intellectual inquiry. Undergraduates collaborate with faculty on important investigations. The U's intercollegiate athletes compete in the NCAA Division I Mountain West Conference. The men's basketball team has been nationally ranked for several years, as have our women's gymnastics and skiing teams. The U's location in Salt Lake City provides easy access to the arts, theater, Utah Jazz basketball, and hockey. Utah's Great Outdoors—skiing, hiking, and five national parks—are nearby. The university was the site for the opening and closing ceremonies and the Athletes Village for the 2002 Winter Olympic Games.

"Residential Living has greatly expanded the opportunity for students to live on campus with a new and wide variety of housing. Heritage Commons, located in historic Fort Douglas on campus, consists of 21 newly constructed buildings, including three residence hall–style facilities, which accommodate more than 2,500 students.

"Applicants are required to submit ACT scores. SAT scores are also accepted, although ACT scores are preferred. Students are urged to take the ACT near the end of their junior year or early in the senior year of high school."

SELECTIVITY

Admissions Rating	79
# of applicants	6,770
% of applicants accepted	84
% of acceptees attending	42

FRESHMAN PROFILE

Range SAT Critical Reading	500–630
Range SAT Math	500–640
Range SAT Writing	560–670
Range ACT Composite	21–27
Minimum Paper TOEFL	500
Minimum Computer Based TOEFL	173
Average HS GPA	3.52
% graduated top 10% of class	23
% graduated top 25% of class	50
% graduated top 50% of class	82

DEADLINES

Regular application deadline	4/1
Regular notification	rolling
Nonfall registration?	yes

FINANCIAL FACTS

Financial Aid Rating	68
Annual in-state tuition	$4,019
Annual out-of-state tuition	$13,902
Room & Board	$5,604
Books and supplies	$1,080
Required fees	$690
% frosh rec. need-based scholarship or grant aid	22
% UG rec. need-based scholarship or grant aid	28
% frosh rec. need-based self-help aid	19
% UG rec. need-based self-help aid	28
% frosh rec. any financial aid	29
% UG rec. any financial aid	38

UNIVERSITY OF VERMONT

194 SOUTH PROSPECT STREET, BURLINGTON, VT 05401-3596 • ADMISSIONS: 802-656-3370 • FAX: 802-656-8611

STUDENTS SAY

Academics

Quality of life issues are important to most University of Vermont undergrads; when discussing their reasons for choosing UVM, they're as likely to cite the "laid-back environment," the "proximity to skiing facilities," the "great parties," and their "amazing" hometown of Burlington as they are to mention the academics. But, students remind us, "That doesn't mean that there are not strong academics [at UVM]." On the contrary, UVM is made up of several well-established colleges and offers "a wide variety of majors." "You can jump around between majors, and then leave with a recognized diploma in hand for something you love to do." Students single out the business school, the "top-notch" education program, the Psychology Department, premedical sciences, and "the amazing animal science program" for praise, and are especially proud of The Rubenstein School of Natural Resources, home to UVM's environmental science majors; they tell us it "is a great college that feels like it's much smaller, [more] separate, and just cozier than the rest of the school." No matter which discipline, "You get out what you put in." "Teachers are readily available and are willing to help you do well in your classes. They encourage you to get help if you need it and are enthusiastic about what they teach. It's all there; you just have to take advantage of it." The size of the university, we're told, is just right; UVM is "a moderately large school," and it allows undergrads "to feel at home while still offering just about any activity possible."

Life

"UVM is known to be a party school," and "Even though the university has cracked down on drinking (they made it a dry campus this year), it hasn't actually changed much." Indeed, students tell us that one can find "a good balance of having fun and academics" at UVM, "but it's tough, because there's always a party going on somewhere." Students who want to dodge the party scene will find "There is always something" happening in Burlington. The town has "lots of wonderful restaurants, a few movie theaters, a rockin' music scene, several bars, some dancing, and various environmental and social activities downtown." "On campus, there is typically at least one university-sponsored event each night, including interesting lectures, movies, games, or social events." Students love outdoor activities: "When it snows, it's very popular to go to the ski resorts around here and ski or snowboard for the day. When it's still warm out, going to the waterfront and swimming in Lake Champlain is popular too." UVM is an intercollegiate hockey powerhouse, and "In the fall and winter, hockey games are huge social events." They're so popular "that you have to get tickets to them the Monday before the game, or they will be sold out!"

Student Body

There's a "great variety of students" at UVM "because it's a big university," undergrads report, but they also note that "students at UVM are mostly White" and that there's "a lot of money at this school." While the most prevalent UVM archetype is "the guitar-loving, earth-saving, relaxed hippie" who "care[s] strongly about the environment" and "social justice," the student body also includes "your athletic types, your artsy people, and a number of other groups" including "vocal LGBTQ and ALANA populations" who, "though they usually hang out in their own groups," "are also active in all sorts of clubs across campus." Not surprisingly, there are many "New England types," "potheads," and "snow bums." Students report they "pretty much get along well with everyone." They either come here loving the outdoors or learn to love the outdoors by the time they leave.

UNIVERSITY OF VERMONT

FINANCIAL AID: 802-656-3156 • E-MAIL: ADMISSIONS@UVM.EDU • WEBSITE: WWW.UVM.EDU

ADMISSIONS

Very important factors considered include: Rigor of secondary school record. *Important factors considered include:* Academic GPA, application essay, character/personal qualities, class rank, standardized test scores, state residency. *Other factors considered include:* Alumni/ae relation, extracurricular activities, first generation, geographical residence, interview, level of applicant's interest, racial/ethnic status, recommendation(s), talent/ability, volunteer work, work experience. SAT or ACT required; ACT with Writing component required. TOEFL required of all international applicants. High school diploma is required, and GED is accepted. *Academic units required:* 4 English, 3 math, 2 science (1 science lab), 2 foreign language, 3 social studies.

The Inside Word

UVM is a very popular choice among out-of-state students, whom the school welcomes; over half the student body originates from outside of Vermont. While admissions standards are significantly more rigorous for out-of-staters, solid candidates (B-plus/A-minus average, about a 600 on each section of the SAT) should do fine here. The school assesses applications holistically, meaning students who are weak in one area may be able to make up for it with strengths or distinguishing skills and characteristics in other areas.

FINANCIAL AID

Students should submit: FAFSA. The Princeton Review suggests that all financial aid forms be submitted as soon as possible after January 1. *Need-based scholarships/grants offered:* Pell Grant, SEOG, state scholarships/grants, private scholarships, the school's own gift aid, Federal Nursing Scholarship. *Loan aid offered:* FFEL Subsidized Stafford, FFEL Unsubsidized Stafford, FFEL PLUS, Federal Perkins Loan, Federal Nursing Loan, college/university loans from institutional funds. Applicants will be notified of awards on a rolling basis beginning or about March 15.

FROM THE ADMISSIONS OFFICE

"The University of Vermont blends the close faculty-student relationships most commonly found in a small liberal arts college with the dynamic exchange of knowledge associated with a research university. This is not surprising, because UVM is both. A comprehensive research university offering nearly 100 undergraduate majors and extensive offerings through its Graduate College and College of Medicine, UVM is one of the nation's premier public research universities. UVM prides itself on the richness of its undergraduate experience. Distinguished senior faculty teach introductory courses in their fields. They also advise not only juniors and seniors, but also first- and second-year students, and work collaboratively with undergraduates on research initiatives. Students find extensive opportunities to test classroom knowledge in field through practicums, academic internships, and community service. More than 100 student organizations (involving 80 percent of the student body), 20 Division I varsity teams, 15 intercollegiate club and 14 intramural sports programs, and a packed schedule of cultural events fill in where the classroom leaves off.

"Applicants for the entering class of Fall 2008 class and beyond are required to take the new version of the SAT, or the ACT with the Writing section, and must submit official test scores. SAT Subject Tests are neither required nor recommended for the admission application."

SELECTIVITY

Admissions Rating	**83**
# of applicants	17,731
% of applicants accepted	65
% of acceptees attending	19
# accepting a place on wait list	1,050
% admitted from wait list	5

FRESHMAN PROFILE

Range SAT Critical Reading	530–630
Range SAT Math	540–640
Range ACT Composite	22–27
Minimum Paper TOEFL	550
Minimum Computer Based TOEFL	213
% graduated top 10% of class	23
% graduated top 25% of class	62
% graduated top 50% of class	95

DEADLINES

Regular application deadline	1/15
Regular notification	3/31
Nonfall registration?	yes

FINANCIAL FACTS

Financial Aid Rating	**73**
Annual in-state tuition	$9,832
Annual out-of-state tuition	$24,816
Room & Board	$7,642
Books and supplies	$900
Required fees	$1,492
% frosh rec. need-based scholarship or grant aid	48
% UG rec. need-based scholarship or grant aid	48
% frosh rec. need-based self-help aid	45
% UG rec. need-based self-help aid	46
% frosh rec. any financial aid	85
% UG rec. any financial aid	72

UNIVERSITY OF VIRGINIA

OFFICE OF ADMISSION, PO BOX 400160, CHARLOTTESVILLE, VA 22906 • ADMISSIONS: 434-982-3200 • FAX: 434-924-3587

CAMPUS LIFE

Quality of Life Rating	83
Fire Safety Rating	75
Type of school	public
Environment	city

STUDENTS

Total undergrad enrollment	14,676
% male/female	45/55
% from out of state	28
% from public high school	74
% live on campus	44
% in (# of) fraternities	30 (31)
% in (# of) sororities	30 (16)
% African American	8
% Asian	10
% Caucasian	64
% Hispanic	4
% international	5
# of countries represented	124

SURVEY SAYS . . .

Career services are great
Great library
Athletic facilities are great
Everyone loves the Cavaliers,
Wahoos, Hoos
Student publications are popular
Lots of beer drinking

ACADEMICS

Academic Rating	98
Calendar	semester
Student/faculty ratio	15:1
Profs interesting rating	80
Profs accessible rating	78
% classes taught by TAs	16
Most common lab size	10–19 students
Most common reg class size	10–19 students

MOST POPULAR MAJORS

commerce
economics
psychology

STUDENTS SAY

Academics

It's all about balance at the University of Virginia: The balance "between public and private, large research university and small liberal arts college, tradition and progress, and work and play." Here at "Mr. Jefferson's University" the influence of the school's founder is paramount; the school "promotes a Jeffersonian spirit of learning in various aspects of student life," and this creates a cohesive community. In the spirit of one of democracy's greatest proponents, "a surprising amount of the school's administration is left to the students. For example, I think in the 1990s students lobbied for more study space, so Clemons Library was born. Also, honor code offenses and the like are handled by student-run bodies." Academically, UVA "demands a lot [from] students. Expectations of hard work—much less excellence—are high. If you do not study or do work outside of class, you will fall behind fast." In return for their hard work, undergrads gain access to "unlimited opportunity for hands-on experience. Study abroad and research opportunities are encouraged, and funding is always available. And you can tailor your courses to desired interests." Students particularly appreciate that these perks come at a public-school price. Standout programs include premedical study, business, politics, architecture (Jefferson's influence again!), environmental science, and biomedical engineering.

Life

Students at UVA are "very serious about academics and research, but also very much into extracurriculars and social life." Greek organizations "are huge at UVA," and Greek parties are the destination of choice for most freshmen and sophomores. Third- and fourth-years, on the other hand, "usually go to the bars located on the corner" when they want a little weekend rest and relaxation. There are also plenty of other options available; downtown Charlottesville "offers a wealth of opportunities, ranging from movies to concerts to shopping." Many students immerse themselves in student governance, which "permeates everything from the Resident Staff program to intramural sports to every club, publication, and organization. Students have the power to decide what gets done, and are challenged to make UVA a better place for having them as students." There's also UVA football, for which the campus basically grinds to a halt; one student explains, "Game day is devoted to dressing up, pre-game socializing, going to the game to socialize, and then after-game parties." Students also love to take advantage of the many options offered by the Shenandoah Valley, including "apple-picking at Carter's Mountain, hiking at Humpback Rock, and taking a Sunday drive around the beautiful surrounding county. Shenandoah National Park is only 30 minutes away from campus and offers a wealth of outdoor activities." UVA's grounds—please do not use the term "campus" here—are among the nation's loveliest.

Student Body

UVA is "a place where smart kids get together and are excited about learning. That doesn't mean it's a bunch of nerds, however. The intelligence of the average UVA student is masked under cheering at football games, drinking at parties, working out, and doing whatever else we find fun. Being smart is just an accepted fact here. We do our work [and] then go party." One undergrad remarks, "There is no typical student. The campus is big enough that there are lots of people you don't know, but you can [also] run into friends constantly. There's a strong Greek presence, so the typical student might be classified as preppy. There are a lot of average, blend-in type of students, as well, and lots of athletes." While one student warns potential undergrads not to "expect their lavish dream of collegiate social diversity to play out on UVA's campus," most agree that "because of the wide range of groups on grounds, all students are able to find their niche, and there are a lot of niches at UVA. You're pretty much guaranteed not to be the only person around who has a particular interest, hobby, or belief. That's the blessing of a big school."

FINANCIAL AID: 434-982-6000 • E-MAIL: UNDERGRADADMISSION@VIRGINIA.EDU • WEBSITE: WWW.VIRGINIA.EDU

ADMISSIONS

Very important factors considered include: Academic GPA, alumni/ae relation, class rank, first generation, racial/ethnic status, recommendation(s), rigor of secondary school record, state residency. *Important factors considered include:* Application essay, character/personal qualities, extracurricular activities, standardized test scores, talent/ability. *Other factors considered include:* Geographical residence, volunteer work, work experience. SAT, or ACT with Writing Test required; SAT Subject Tests strongly recommended. TOEFL required of all international applicants. High school diploma is required, and GED is accepted. *Academic units required:* 4 English, 4 math, 2 science, 2 foreign language, 1 social studies. *Academic units recommended:* 5 math, 4 science, 5 foreign language, 4 social studies.

The Inside Word

As one of the premier public universities in the country, UVA holds its applicants to high standards. While Admissions Officers don't set minimum requirements, all viable candidates have stellar academic records. Intellectual ability is imperative and prospective students are expected to have taken a rigorous course load in high school. Applicants should be aware that geographical location and legacies hold significant weight, as Virginia residents and children of alums are given preference.

FINANCIAL AID

Students should submit: FAFSA, institution's own financial aid form. The Princeton Review suggests that all financial aid forms be submitted as soon as possible after January 1. *Need-based scholarships/grants offered:* Pell Grant, SEOG, state scholarships/grants, private scholarships, the school's own gift aid. *Loan aid offered:* Direct Subsidized Stafford, Direct Unsubsidized Stafford, Direct PLUS, Federal Perkins Loan, Federal Nursing Loan, college/university loans from institutional funds. Applicants will be notified of awards on or about April 5.

FROM THE ADMISSIONS OFFICE

"Admission to competitive schools requires strong academic credentials. Students who stretch themselves and take rigorous courses (honors-level and Advanced Placement courses, when offered) are significantly more competitive than those who do not. Experienced Admission Officers know that most students are capable of presenting superb academic credentials, and the reality is that a very high percentage of those applying do so. Other considerations, then, come into play in important ways for academically strong candidates, as they must be seen as 'selective' well as academically competitive.

"SAT scores are preferred. The ACT test will also be accepted if the optional ACT Writing Test is also taken. It is strongly recommended that applicants take two SAT Subject Tests of the applicant's choice."

SELECTIVITY

Admissions Rating	97
# of applicants	16,086
% of applicants accepted	37
% of acceptees attending	51
# accepting a place on wait list	1,915
% admitted from wait list	4

FRESHMAN PROFILE

Range SAT Critical Reading	600–710
Range SAT Math	620–720
Range SAT Writing	610–710
Range ACT Composite	26–31
Minimum Paper TOEFL	600
Minimum Computer Based TOEFL	250
Average HS GPA	4.07
% graduated top 10% of class	88
% graduated top 25% of class	97
% graduated top 50% of class	100

DEADLINES

Regular application deadline	1/2
Regular notification	4/1
Nonfall registration?	no

APPLICANTS ALSO LOOK AT

AND OFTEN PREFER
The College of William & Mary, Duke University

AND SOMETIMES PREFER
Cornell University, Georgetown College, Harvard College, Notre Dame College, Pennsylvania State University—Lehigh Valley, Princeton University, The University of North Carolina at Chapel Hill, Virginia Tech, Yale University

FINANCIAL FACTS

Financial Aid Rating	94
Annual in-state tuition	$8,035
Annual out-of-state tuition	$26,135
Room & Board	$6,909
Books and supplies	$1,000
% frosh rec. need-based scholarship or grant aid	20
% UG rec. need-based scholarship or grant aid	20
% frosh rec. need-based self-help aid	16
% UG rec. need-based self-help aid	18
% frosh rec. any financial aid	51
% UG rec. any financial aid	45

UNIVERSITY OF WASHINGTON

1410 NORTHEAST CAMPUS PARKWAY, 320 SCHMITZ BOX 355840, SEATTLE, WA 98195-5840 • ADMISSIONS: 206-543-9686

CAMPUS LIFE
Quality of Life Rating	**80**
Fire Safety Rating	**91**
Type of school	public
Environment	metropolis

STUDENTS
Total undergrad enrollment	25,469
% male/female	49/51
% from out of state	86
% live on campus	17
% in (# of) fraternities	12 (30)
% in (# of) sororities	11 (18)
% African American	3
% Asian	27
% Caucasian	53
% Hispanic	4
% Native American	1
% international	3

SURVEY SAYS . . .
Great computer facilities
Great library
Athletic facilities are great
Students love Seattle, WA
Great off-campus food

ACADEMICS
Academic Rating	**77**
Calendar	quarter
Student/faculty ratio	11:1
Profs interesting rating	69
Profs accessible rating	69
Most common lab size	20–29 students
Most common reg class size	20–29 students

MOST POPULAR MAJORS
economics
political science and government
psychology

STUDENTS SAY
Academics
University of Washington enthusiasts, of whom there are many, believe "It's impossible to spend a day on campus and not fall in love with this school. It offers everything to everyone: diverse and respected programs, good climate, good location, and a student population that is informed enough to give a damn about the world around them." "Independent research and intellectual initiative are encouraged" at UW, where "professors are surprisingly accessible," especially to those who "show the interest to approach them." One student reports, "Most of the professors are excellent teachers who want to make sure you are learning and understanding the material. Most are also very passionate about the subject they teach and make it a great learning experience." UW's strengths include "some of the top graduate programs in the nation," an "amazing premed program associated with one of the top hospitals in the country," a "cheap, big, good engineering program," and computer-related offerings strengthened by "a lot of financial benefits from our relationship with Microsoft." UW students also profit from "an amazing library program. Not only is it huge, but the main library, Suzallo, is beautiful. It looks like something straight out of a Harry Potter movie—it's gorgeous." Administration is typically labyrinthine, but students see the glass as half full. One writes, "Considering the budget crisis in this country, they are doing a phenomenal job with the balancing act."

Life
Students can find "pretty much everything and anything at the UW," and though "nothing is widely advertised or known about, if you do some looking you'll find Ultimate Frisbee groups, 'boffers' staging medieval warfare at the campus center using Nerf bats, intramural sports played at three levels (beginner, intermediate, and advanced), clubs for every interest and hobby, honor societies, and activist groups all over the political spectrum. There are even two unofficial campus newspapers in addition to the UW-sponsored paper." Greek life, with its "non-stop parties," "is huge" on campus, and "Students regularly attend the gym, especially since there are a number of things to do there aside from your basic cardio and lifting." Aesthetically, "The campus is beautiful: clean and green with lots of grassy spaces to hang out, study, or just enjoy the odd sunny day." While life on campus is extremely active, the surrounding city of Seattle is even more so. Near campus, "People go to the Avenue, the road next to campus with funky stores and good restaurants, or U Village, the shopping center with more mainstream/nice stores." Beyond these destinations, "There is plenty to do around town, and with the great bus system, there is absolutely no need for a vehicle. Within the city, there are amazing restaurants, concerts, movie previews, Broadway plays, etc." The city also provides access to excellent outdoor options. "We are close to the mountains, so people who love to ski or board in the winter and hike during summer are really close. We basically live on two lakes, so lake activities like boating are really accessible," explains one undergrad.

Student Body
"Being such a huge school, there are people of every single type at UW," but "most fall into either the coffee-drinking indie-rock group or the engineering or medical majors who spend 8 years or more in college." Whether you're one, both, or neither, "Because of the sheer size of the campus, there is a niche for everybody, and there is bound to be somebody just like you—be [it] that nerd, jock, foreign, or hippie." That might be why "Even though the school is socially and ethnically diverse, groups tend to stick together in cliques." Undergrads tend to be left-coast friendly and "laid-back," "sport a larger than average number of piercings" and are, "for the most part, liberals and Democrats—but there are still UWCR (UW College Republicans) and the LaRouche campaigners." The student body has a definite look of "Northwest fashion" to them. One student notes, "Some friends of mine joke that the UW 'starter pack' includes a North Face jacket, a Nalgene water bottle, and an iPod."

FAX: 206-685-3655 • FINANCIAL AID: 206-543-6101 • E-MAIL: ASKUWADM@U.WASHINGTON.EDU • WEBSITE: WWW.WASHINGTON.EDU

ADMISSIONS

Very important factors considered include: Academic GPA, application essay, rigor of secondary school record. *Important factors considered include:* Character/personal qualities, extracurricular activities, first generation, standardized test scores, talent/ability, volunteer work, work experience. *Other factors considered include:* State residency. SAT or ACT required; ACT with Writing component required. High school diploma or equivalent is not required. *Academic units required:* 4 English, 3 math, 2 science (1 science lab), 2 foreign language, 3 social studies. *Academic units recommended:* 4 English, 4 math, 3 science (3 science labs), 3 foreign language, 4 social studies, 1 history, 1 fine arts.

The Inside Word

Like the other five public colleges in Washington, UW uses an admissions index (AI) as part of its initial review of applications, taking into account the student's GPA, as well as combined SAT or composite ACT scores, course selection, personal statements, and essays. A student whose qualifications exceed expectations in all of these areas may be a "turbo admit"; all other applications receive an intensive review, which evaluates evidence of academic rigor in the student's curriculum, a challenging senior year, academic awards, personal statement, school and community activities, educational and economic disadvantage, personal adversity, grade trends, special talents in the arts, and cultural awareness. UW notes the importance of these qualitative factors as it moves away from AI-driven decisions.

FINANCIAL AID

Students should submit: FAFSA. The Princeton Review suggests that all financial aid forms be submitted as soon as possible after January 1. *Need-based scholarships/grants offered:* Pell Grant, SEOG, state scholarships/grants, private scholarships, the school's own gift aid. *Loan aid offered:* Direct Subsidized Stafford, Direct Unsubsidized Stafford, Direct PLUS, Federal Perkins Loan, Federal Nursing Loan, college/university loans from institutional funds. Applicants will be notified of awards on or about April 1. Federal Work-Study Program available. Institutional employment available.

FROM THE ADMISSIONS OFFICE

"Are you curious about everything, from comet dust to computer game design, salmon to Salman Rushdie, ancient Rome to the atmospherics of Mars? Do you seek the freedom to chart your own course—and work on breakthrough research? Are you ready to cheer on the Division I Huskies and spend your weekends sea kayaking? Would you like to walk to class on a 700-acre stunning, ivy-covered campus, yet be only 15 minutes from downtown Seattle? If the answers are yes, then the University of Washington may be the place for you. Offering more than 140 majors and 450 student organizations, the UW is looking for students who are both excited about the vast academic and social possibilities available to them and eager to contribute to the campus' cultural and intellectual life.

"We encourage you to take advantage of every opportunity in the application, especially the personal statement and activities summary, to tell us why Washington would be good fit for you and how you will contribute to the freshman class.

"Freshman applicants to the University of Washington are required to submit scores from either the new SAT or ACT (with the Writing component)."

SELECTIVITY

Admissions Rating	93
# of applicants	15,923
% of applicants accepted	67
% of acceptees attending	46
# accepting a place on wait list	465
% admitted from wait list	44

FRESHMAN PROFILE

Range SAT Critical Reading	530–650
Range SAT Math	570–670
Range ACT Composite	23–28
Average HS GPA	3.69
% graduated top 10% of class	82
% graduated top 25% of class	96
% graduated top 50% of class	100

DEADLINES

Regular application deadline	1/15
Regular notification	rolling
Nonfall registration?	yes

APPLICANTS ALSO LOOK AT

AND OFTEN PREFER
University of Southern California

AND SOMETIMES PREFER
Seattle University, University of Oregon, Western Washington University

AND RARELY PREFER
University of Colorado—Boulder, University of Puget Sound, Washington State University

FINANCIAL FACTS

Financial Aid Rating	76
Annual in-state tuition	$5,985
Annual out-of-state tuition	$17,592
Room & Board	$8,001
Books and supplies	$945
Required fees	$507
% frosh rec. need-based scholarship or grant aid	27
% UG rec. need-based scholarship or grant aid	33
% frosh rec. need-based self-help aid	21
% UG rec. need-based self-help aid	38

UNIVERSITY OF WISCONSIN—MADISON

716 LANGDON STREET, MADISON, WI 53706-1481 • ADMISSIONS: 608-262-3961 • FAX: 608-262-7706

CAMPUS LIFE

Quality of Life Rating	89
Fire Safety Rating	74
Type of school	public
Environment	city

STUDENTS

Total undergrad enrollment	28,462
% male/female	47/53
% from out of state	31
% live on campus	26
% in (# of) fraternities	9 (26)
% in (# of) sororities	8 (11)
% African American	3
% Asian	6
% Caucasian	85
% Hispanic	3
% Native American	1
% international	4
# of countries represented	110

SURVEY SAYS . . .

Great library
Athletic facilities are great
Students love Madison, WI
Great off-campus food
Everyone loves the Badgers
Student publications are popular
Lots of beer drinking
Hard liquor is popular

ACADEMICS

Academic Rating	81
Calendar	semester
Student/faculty ratio	13:1
Profs interesting rating	70
Profs accessible rating	72
% classes taught by TAs	20
Most common lab size	10–19 students
Most common reg class size	10–19 students

MOST POPULAR MAJORS

biology/biological sciences
English language and literature
political science and government

STUDENTS SAY

Academics

"Choices are the biggest asset at the University of Wisconsin—Madison," where "We have every major under the sun, every kind of club, every kind of person, every kind of activity you can imagine. All you have to do is get out there and find what's right for you." The university is especially strong in "research, research, and research, along with any undergrad programs that lead into some type of research," such as engineering and the sciences. The business program is also "among the best in the country" with "state-of-the-art facilities and equipment." Some students outside these disciplines caution, "UW could improve by putting more emphasis on the arts and humanities rather than always relying on UW as a 'research' school. Facilities for the humanities and social sciences need improvement." Undergrads also tell us that "at times, due to the sheer size, the university can feel a little impersonal. You have to grab the bull by the horns and get yourself involved because nobody is going to do it for you." Those in large lecture classes "spend more time with their TAs than the actual professors teaching the courses," which isn't necessarily a bad thing. "Professors' lectures can be hard to follow," writes a biology major, "but discussion sections led by TAs help to clarify information from the lecture and allow more one-on-one attention." One student advises, "Overall the school runs surprisingly smoothly, but the way in which things are organized makes it essential that you have a good relationship with your advisor, so you know what the heck to do as far as taking the right classes to earn a degree. It can be confusing."

Life

UW's hometown of Madison, most agree, "is the perfect spot for anyone hoping for a small-town atmosphere while being a part of a large-campus lifestyle." One undergrad writes, "If you take the time to look into some of the options, you'll never get bored. But if you're looking for a relaxing day, Madison is great for that, too. Just take a walk through its beautiful setting." The city is "especially great in the warm months. At any given time, walk down State Street and you will pass an inordinate number of diners and unique stores, a good number of homeless people—many of whom the students have nicknames for—musicians showing off their talents, a bunch of food vendors, some Christian dude preaching and reading parts of the Bible to everyone who walks by, a group of atheists yelling at him, and a bunch of other people advertising protests and student organizations." All year round "The access to government, politics, and history is perfect for any liberal arts major." On campus, UW "has a group to represent every segment of the population. There are groups here for every race, religion, gender, sexual orientation, political affiliation, and anything else you could think of. A campus center helps people to find volunteer opportunities." Intercollegiate athletics are huge. Reports one student, "Our level of enthusiasm for multiple sports cannot be beat. We don't suck up to just one sport because we don't have to." Another student agrees, "One of the most fun things at our school is our Badger game days. There's nothing like getting up at 9:00 A.M. to drink before an 11:00 A.M. football game. The streets are lined with parties and blasting music by early morning."

Student Body

According to the undergrads we contacted, "One of the greatest strengths of Madison is the people themselves. Madison draws a wide array of people with one thing in common and that is their talent. Not just academic talent—although that is prevalent—but talents that extend in all directions and make meeting people every day an exciting thing to do." It is "easy to find people you are compatible with here, both because of the size of the student population and the many interest groups you can join." With over 28,000 undergrads, UW "has people of every ethnic, social, economic, and religious background. You can always find someone to relate to."

FINANCIAL AID: 608-262-3060 • E-MAIL: ONWISCONSIN@ADMISSIONS.WISC.EDU • WEBSITE: WWW.WISC.EDU

ADMISSIONS

Very important factors considered include: Academic GPA, class rank, rigor of secondary school record. *Important factors considered include:* Application essay, standardized test scores, state residency. *Other factors considered include:* Alumni/ae relation, character/personal qualities, extracurricular activities, first generation, interview, level of applicant's interest, racial/ethnic status, recommendation(s), talent/ability, volunteer work, work experience. SAT or ACT required; ACT with Writing component required. TOEFL required of all international applicants. High school diploma is required, and GED is accepted. *Academic units required:* 4 English, 3 math, 3 science, 2 foreign language, 3 social studies, 2 academic electives. *Academic units recommended:* 4 English, 4 math, 4 science, 4 foreign language, 4 social studies, 2 academic electives.

The Inside Word

Wisconsin has high expectations of its candidates, and virtually all of them relate to numbers. Though not at the top tier of selectivity and not quite entirely admissions by formula, UW does look at each application individually.

FINANCIAL AID

Students should submit: FAFSA, institution's own financial aid form. The Princeton Review suggests that all financial aid forms be submitted as soon as possible after January 1. *Need-based scholarships/grants offered:* Pell Grant, SEOG, state scholarships/grants, private scholarships, the school's own gift aid. *Loan aid offered:* FFEL Subsidized Stafford, FFEL Unsubsidized Stafford, FFEL PLUS, Federal Perkins Loan, Federal Nursing Loan, state loans. Applicants will be notified of awards on a rolling basis beginning or about April 1.

FROM THE ADMISSIONS OFFICE

"UW—Madison is the university of choice for some of this country's (and the world's) best and brightest. Our freshman class has an average ACT score of 27.5 and an average SAT of 1260. Over half come from the top 10 percent of their high school class, and nearly 95 percent come from the top quarter.

"These factors combine to make admission to UW—Madison both competitive and selective. We consider academic record, course selection, strength of curriculum (honors, AP, IB, etc.), grade trend, class rank, results of the ACT and/or SAT, and non-academic factors. We do not have a prescribed minimum test score, GPA, or class rank criteria. Rather we admit the best and most well-prepared students—students who have challenged themselves and who will contribute to Wisconsin's strength and diversity—for the limited space available.

"Each application is personally reviewed by our admission counselors. Admission decisions are made within 6 weeks of the time when an applicant's admission file is complete. A complete file includes the application for admission, application fee, official high school transcript, and official test score report(s). Supplemental application materials may include a personal statement and letters of recommendation.

"We practice rolling admissions and applications are accepted beginning September 15. For full consideration for fall and summer terms, complete applications must be received by February 1. The deadline for the spring term is October 1. Applications received after these deadlines will be considered on a space-available basis.

"Starting in Fall 2008, all freshman applicants must submit results from either the new SAT or the ACT with the Writing component. Students who took either test before February 2005 must take at least one of the exams again in order to provide a Writing score and be eligible for admission."

SELECTIVITY

Admissions Rating	93
# of applicants	22,816
% of applicants accepted	58
% of acceptees attending	42

FRESHMAN PROFILE

Range SAT Critical Reading	560–670
Range SAT Math	610–710
Range SAT Writing	570–670
Range ACT Composite	26–30
Minimum Paper TOEFL	550
Minimum Computer Based TOEFL	213
Average HS GPA	3.67
% graduated top 10% of class	58
% graduated top 25% of class	93
% graduated top 50% of class	100

DEADLINES

Regular application deadline	2/1
Regular notification	rolling
Nonfall registration?	yes

APPLICANTS ALSO LOOK AT

AND OFTEN PREFER
Marquette University, University of Illinois at Urbana-Champaign, University of Michigan—Ann Arbor, University of Minnesota—Twin Cities

AND SOMETIMES PREFER
Northwestern University, University of Colorado—Boulder, University of Wisconsin—La Crosse, University of Wisconsin—Eau Claire, University of Wisconsin—Milwaukee

FINANCIAL FACTS

Financial Aid Rating	71
Annual in-state tuition	$6,730
Annual out-of-state tuition	$20,730
Room & Board	$6,920
Books and Supplies	$890
% frosh rec. need-based scholarship or grant aid	17
% UG rec. need-based scholarship or grant aid	20
% frosh rec. need-based self-help aid	23
% UG rec. need-based self-help aid	27

UNIVERSITY OF WYOMING

DEPARTMENT 3435, 1000 EAST UNIVERSITY AVENUE, LARAMIE, WY 82071 • ADMISSIONS: 307-766-5160 • FAX: 307-766-4042

STUDENTS SAY

Academics

"Large enough to offer big-school opportunities to all students but small enough that those opportunities are not competitive," the University of Wyoming optimizes the advantages of its midsize status. The university attracts enough students to host a wide range of strong majors, including those with wide appeal (biology, education, pharmacy, nursing, criminal justice), as well as those aimed at more idiosyncratic populations (rangeland ecology and wasteland management; textiles and merchandising; and, "one of the very few agricultural economics programs in the nation"). At the same time, the school has been able to keep class sizes manageable and student-teacher interaction frequent. Unfortunately, some students feel that although UW has mandatory advising, some students feel that "it sucks. It seems like any person can sign up for any class." On the whole, the secret to the university's success, we're told, is that "UW is well funded. This means there are a lot of extracurricular opportunities available to everyone. Every day I hear about some amazing program that is looking for applicants . . . summer drawing classes in India, research opportunities on a glacier in Alaska, language study in Peru, field trips to natural gas fields and conservation ranches, and the list goes on. It also means that tuition isn't too high—another plus." Add to the mix "phenomenal research opportunities [and] classrooms constantly under a state of upgrade to integrate the latest technologies and teaching aids" and you'll understand why so many here give UW an unqualified thumbs-up.

Life

Numerous "outdoor events lie at the students' fingertips" at UW where, thanks to the proximity of the "beautiful Snowy Mountains," undergrads regularly enjoy high-quality "skiing, snowboarding, camping, hiking, canoeing, rock climbing, hunting, and fishing." In fact, many choose the school primarily for its myriad outdoor opportunities; those who do either have a high tolerance for cold weather or grow greatly disappointed in their choice. For those who prefer to keep warm indoors, UW has "a lot of activities affiliated with the school and off campus. There are over 100 different student life organizations, so if you are looking to get involved you most certainly can." Wyoming often hosts "free activities, like comedy nights, concerts, and film festivals," too. Best of all, "students get in free to all sporting events, and Wyoming fans are crazy. We almost always storm the field when we win a football game." Basketball, volleyball, and soccer are also "really popular during their respective seasons." Hometown Laramie "is a small town, so people tend to think the only thing you can do here is drink. However, there are many volunteer services and research opportunities here that other schools don't have." There are also plenty of opportunities to tie one on, with "lots of house parties" and "Fort Collins (home to Colorado State University) and its hopping club scene only 45 minutes away." For students who crave big-city life, "Denver is only a couple hours [away]."

Student Body

Sometimes the clichés are true: there is indeed a "large population of truck-driving, rifle shooting, rodeoing, snoose-spitting, belt-buckle-wearing ranch kids" at UW. There are, however, also a lot of students who don't fit that mold. Undergrads point out that Laramie's size means you can "easily get to know every corner of the town and campus." It is also "by far the most liberal city in the state, by virtue of the university," and that "there were as many Kerry bumper stickers as Bush stickers here in 2004." Students also point out that all factions here share a common trait: "Basically, Wyomingites don't want to be told what to do. If either Republicans or Democrats tell them what to do, they will be pissed." Accordingly, most here "adopt a live-and-let-live attitude, respect each others' views, and mind their own business, creating a remarkably tolerant atmosphere." A large nontraditional population—from older students to those with families—"fits in fairly well." In fact, "Everyone fits in here, as long as they don't care that there isn't a mall in town!"

FINANCIAL AID: 307-766-2116 • E-MAIL: WHY-WYO@UWYO.EDU • WEBSITE: WWW.UWYO.EDU

ADMISSIONS

Very important factors considered include: Academic GPA, rigor of secondary school record, standardized test scores. *Important factors considered include:* Level of applicant's interest. *Other factors considered include:* Application essay, character/personal qualities, extracurricular activities, interview, recommendation(s), state residency, talent/ability. SAT or ACT required; TOEFL required of all international applicants. High school diploma is required, and GED is accepted. *Academic units required:* 4 English, 3 math, 3 science (3 science labs), 3 cultural context electives (recommended: 3 behavioral or social sciences, 3 visual or performing arts, 3 humanities or earth/space sciences). *Academic units recommended:* 4 English, 4 math, 4 science (3 science labs), 2 foreign language, 3 cultural context electives (recommended: 3 behavioral or social sciences, 3 visual or performing arts, 3 humanities or earth/space sciences).

The Inside Word

The admissions process at Wyoming is fairly formula-driven. State residents need a minimum 2.75 high school GPA to gain admission. Nonresidents have to have a 3.0 GPA. That and some solid test scores will open the door to the university.

FINANCIAL AID

Students should submit: FAFSA. The Princeton Review suggests that all financial aid forms be submitted as soon as possible after January 1. *Need-based scholarships/grants offered:* Pell Grant, SEOG, state scholarships/grants, private scholarships, the school's own gift aid. *Loan aid offered:* FFEL Subsidized Stafford, FFEL Unsubsidized Stafford, FFEL PLUS, Federal Perkins Loan. Applicants will be notified of awards on or about March 15. Off-campus job opportunities are good.

FROM THE ADMISSIONS OFFICE

"The University of Wyoming and the town of Laramie are relatively small, affording students the opportunity to get the personal attention and develop a close rapport with their professors. They can easily make friends and find peers with similar interests and values. Over 200 student organizations offer students a great way to get involved and encourage growth and learning. Couple the small size with a great location, and you have a winning combination. Laramie sits between the Laramie and Snowy Range Mountains. There are numerous outdoor activities in which one can participate. Furthermore, the university works hard to attract other great cultural events. Major-label recording artists come to UW as well as some of today's great minds. In all, the University of Wyoming is a great place to be because of its wonderful blend of small town atmosphere with 'big city' activities.

"The University of Wyoming requires first-time, incoming freshmen to submit scores from either the ACT or SAT. The Writing component of the ACT and SAT is not required, but is reviewed if submitted. Scores from either the new or old SAT are accepted."

SELECTIVITY

Admissions Rating	85

FRESHMAN PROFILE

Minimum Paper TOEFL	525
Minimum Computer Based TOEFL	197

DEADLINES

Regular application deadline	8/10
Regular notification	rolling
Nonfall registration?	yes

FINANCIAL FACTS

Financial Aid Rating	72
Annual in-state tuition	$2,820
Annual out-of-state tuition	$9,360
Room & Board	$6,861
Books and supplies	$1,200
Required fees	$696
% frosh rec. need-based scholarship or grant aid	54
% UG rec. need-based scholarship or grant aid	48
% frosh rec. need-based self-help aid	35
% UG rec. need-based self-help aid	45

URSINUS COLLEGE

URSINUS COLLEGE, ADMISSIONS OFFICE, COLLEGEVILLE, PA 19426 • ADMISSIONS: 610-409-3200 • FAX: 610-409-3662

CAMPUS LIFE
Quality of Life Rating	88
Fire Safety Rating	85
Type of school	private
Environment	metropolis

STUDENTS
Total undergrad enrollment	1,565
% male/female	48/52
% from out of state	38
% from public high school	61
% live on campus	97
% in (# of) fraternities	17 (7)
% in (# of) sororities	28 (7)
% African American	7
% Asian	4
% Caucasian	75
% Hispanic	3
% international	1
# of countries represented	24

SURVEY SAYS . . .
Small classes
Lab facilities are great
Athletic facilities are great
Lots of beer drinking

ACADEMICS
Academic Rating	94
Calendar	semester
Student/faculty ratio	12:1
Profs interesting rating	88
Profs accessible rating	87
% profs teaching UG courses	100
% classes taught by TAs	0
Most common lab size	10–19 students
Most common reg class size	fewer than 10 students

MOST POPULAR MAJORS
biology/biological sciences
economics
psychology

STUDENTS SAY

Academics

Ursinus College is justly renowned for its Biology and Chemistry Departments. The school's graduates—about one in eight proceed to medical school—boast an impressive 90-plus percent acceptance rate with medical programs. A program this successful, of course, does a good job of winnowing out any slackers, which explains why "Ursinus has many 'ex-biology' students as well as biology students." Those who survive the ordeal benefit from "some of the best chemistry and biology labs around, where really interesting research is being done by undergraduate students and professors. It's nice to have that opportunity, rather than giving up all the research opportunities to graduate students." "Passionate" professors who "care about you and your education" are very accessible to students, as well as an "administration that runs smoothly." A laptop for every student is also part of the deal. Ursinus isn't exclusively about premeds, either. In fact, just as many graduates go on to law school, thanks to "strong humanities programs, especially in history, politics, philosophy, and religion." A brand-new performing arts center that will open in April 2005, promising a flowering of music, dance, and theater on campus. In all areas, "Ursinus College does a great job at preparing its students for future education or jobs by focusing on independent learning, discussions, and providing a ton of learning resources."

Life

"Ursinus is all about having a great learning atmosphere while at the same time providing a place for sports and many other kinds of social events where one can get a true and complete liberal arts education," undergraduates here agree. Even the overworked premeds occasionally find time to work out, play on a team, participate in a student organization, and attend the occasional frat party, we're told. "Greek organizations run the social life and all the big parties" at Ursinus, with about one-third of all students pledging. At the same time, there are "both registered and unregistered parties every weekend," so there's always a party for unaffiliated students to attend. Students like to drink—beer pong is a popular pastime—and smoke herb, but will point out that "while Ursinus College students do party very hard, they are reasonably responsible about it. The college has very loose rules which allow students to make up for the difficult academics with an active social life, while still being held responsible for their actions." For those who abjure intoxication, "There are usually plenty of nonalcoholic activities on campus to attend like movies, concerts, etc." Just don't expect much from Collegeville (yes, the town's real name) other than a Dunkin' Donuts. That's why when students leave campus, they usually head to Philly about half an hour away. A bus or train can "get you to the hot spots of the city," although automobile is the preferred mode of transportation.

Students

The "motivated and ambitious" undergraduates of Ursinus "have a desire to succeed, but also want to have a good time while in college." Many "are White and from the middle to upper classes of society," but students claim that Ursinus "has a larger minority component than most liberal arts colleges in the this area." Students note, however, that "the typical student at Ursinus is generally very well rounded. There are no typical 'jocks' because so many people play sports, and there are no typical 'nerds' because a lot of the same kids excelling in the playing fields are excelling in the classroom as well." In the past, Ursinus has had a large preppy population ("Most of the kids want to be Abercrombie models"), but these days it's starting to attract "a lot of students who have different tastes." "We're a good-looking school," says one. A senior describes her school as "one huge clique. Students here may not be diverse in ethnicity, but they are at least diverse in their interests." Undergrads report approvingly that "the tolerant atmosphere on campus is rather amazing. The Gay-Straight Alliance, for example, is a vivacious group coming up with a lot of activities that involve the whole campus."

FINANCIAL AID: 610-409-3600 • E-MAIL: ADMISSIONS@URSINUS.EDU • WEBSITE: WWW.URSINUS.EDU

ADMISSIONS

Very important factors considered include: Class rank, extracurricular activities, rigor of secondary school record. *Important factors considered include:* Academic GPA, alumni/ae relation, application essay, racial/ethnic status, recommendation(s), standardized test scores, talent/ability, volunteer work, work experience. *Other factors considered include:* Character/personal qualities, first generation, geographical residence, interview, level of applicant's interest. TOEFL required of all international applicants. High school diploma is required, and GED is not accepted. *Academic units required:* 4 English, 3 math, 1 science (1 science lab), 2 foreign language, 1 social studies, 5 academic electives. *Academic units recommended:* 4 math, 3 science, 4 foreign language, 3 social studies.

The Inside Word

The admission process at Ursinus is very straightforward; about 70 percent of those who apply get in. Grades, test scores, and class rank count for more than anything else, and unless you are academically inconsistent, you'll likely get good news.

FINANCIAL AID

Students should submit: FAFSA, institution's own financial aid form, CSS/Financial Aid PROFILE. Regular filing deadline is February 15. The Princeton Review suggests that all financial aid forms be submitted as soon as possible after January 1. *Need-based scholarships/grants offered:* Pell Grant, SEOG, state scholarships/grants, private scholarships, the school's own gift aid. *Loan aid offered:* FFEL Subsidized Stafford, FFEL Unsubsidized Stafford, FFEL PLUS, Federal Perkins Loan, college/university loans from institutional funds, Ursinus Gate First Marblehead Loans. Applicants will be notified of awards on or about March 15. Federal Work-Study Program available. Institutional employment available. Off-campus job opportunities are excellent.

FROM THE ADMISSIONS OFFICE

"Located a half-hour from center-city Philadelphia, the college boasts a beautiful 168-acre campus that includes the Residential Village (renovated Victorian-style homes that decorate the Main Street and house our students) and the nationally recognized Berman Museum of Art. Ursinus is a member of the Centennial Conference, competing both in academics and in intercollegiate athletics with institutions such as Dickinson, Franklin & Marshall, Gettysburg, and Muhlenberg. The academic environment is enhanced with such fine programs as a chapter of Phi Beta Kappa, an early assurance program to medical school with the Medical College of Pennsylvania, and myriad student exchanges both at home and abroad. A heavy emphasis is placed on student research—an emphasis that can only be carried out with the one-on-one attention Ursinus students receive from their professors.

"Ursinus will continue to ask applicants for writing samples—both a series of application essays and a graded high school paper. Pending further examination, the Writing portion of the new SAT will not initially affect admissions decisions."

SELECTIVITY

Admissions Rating	**89**
# of applicants	4,408
% of applicants accepted	47
% of acceptees attending	20
# accepting a place on wait list	200
% admitted from wait list	82
# of early decision applicants	397
% accepted early decision	31

FRESHMAN PROFILE

Range SAT Critical Reading	560–680
Range SAT Math	540–660
Range ACT Composite	22–28
Minimum Paper TOEFL	500
Minimum Computer Based TOEFL	173
% graduated top 10% of class	47
% graduated top 25% of class	75
% graduated top 50% of class	93

DEADLINES

Early decision application deadline	1/15
Regular application deadline	2/15
Regular notification	4/15
Nonfall registration?	yes

APPLICANTS ALSO LOOK AT
AND OFTEN PREFER
Brown University, Haverford College, Johns Hopkins University, Princeton University, Swarthmore College

AND SOMETIMES PREFER
Dickinson College, Franklin & Marshall College, Gettysburg College, Villanova University

FINANCIAL FACTS

Financial Aid Rating	**89**
Annual tuition	$33,200
Room & Board	$7,600
Books and supplies	$1,000
% frosh rec. need-based scholarship or grant aid	78
% UG rec. need-based scholarship or grant aid	80
% frosh rec. need-based self-help aid	78
% UG rec. need-based self-help aid	80
% frosh rec. any financial aid	78
% UG rec. any financial aid	80

VALPARAISO UNIVERSITY

KRETZMANN HALL, 1700 CHAPEL DRIVE, VALPARAISO, IN 46383 • ADMISSIONS: 219-464-5011 • FAX: 219-464-6898

CAMPUS LIFE

Quality of Life Rating	**74**
Fire Safety Rating	**79**
Type of school	private
Affiliation	Lutheran
Environment	town

STUDENTS

Total undergrad enrollment	2,904
% male/female	48/52
% from out of state	64
% from public high school	80
% live on campus	64
% in (# of) fraternities	26 (9)
% in (# of) sororities	20 (6)
% African American	4
% Asian	2
% Caucasian	85
% Hispanic	3
% international	2
# of countries represented	49

SURVEY SAYS . . .

Small classes
No one cheats
Great library
Students are friendly

ACADEMICS

Academic Rating	**85**
Calendar	semester
Student/faculty ratio	12:1
Profs interesting rating	78
Profs accessible rating	82
% profs teaching UG courses	100
% classes taught by TAs	0
Most common lab size	10–19 students
Most common reg class size	10–19 students

MOST POPULAR MAJORS

atmospheric sciences and meteorology
nursing/registered nurse training (ASN, BSN, MSN, RN)
psychology

STUDENTS SAY

Academics

Valparaiso's brand-new Christopher Center library complex stands as a shiny monument to the university's dedication to academics. Once freshmen get through the Valpo core curriculum, they choose from a host of strong major programs, with nursing, and biology specifically called out quite often. Nearly all students agree that professors "put the human, caring relationship first, rather than the teacher-pupil, formal relationship." In addition to conducting tutoring sessions and study groups, professors extend holiday invitations, make appearances at non-academic events, and call students to check on them when they're sick. The administration also demonstrates dedication to enriching the undergraduate experience. Check this out: "During my year abroad, I received a scholarship for which I didn't even apply. I had complained to the International Studies Director about money, and he went to bat for me. The next month, without my knowing it, I began to receive a monthly scholarship from a foreign government! That shows the kind of support I've gotten." The less optimistic see the administration as "hopelessly anachronistic [or] stuffy and conservative." Ultimately, however, students support the school's "high morals and standards." Governed by an honor code, cheating has all but disappeared on this campus of 3,000 undergraduates. With the combination of mental and spiritual enrichment as the goals of a Valpo education, it's hardly surprising that "the main focus is academics."

Life

It's pretty easy to guess which things are encouraged and discouraged at Valpo. For example: chapel good, kegs bad. Dorm visitation privileges between men and women are restricted, and the campus is officially dry. Also, this school is not kidding around when it comes to enforcement. "The police are really strict. They should focus more on keeping students safe, [rather] than busting everyone for alcohol." Despite these deterrents, many students drink, enough so that "we think of ourselves as 'The Lutheran Party School.'" Many students mention the activities common to other sober campuses: scavenger hunts, comedians, late-night bingo, sledding on lunch trays, and Mario Kart 64 tournaments. Caffeine addicts with a conscience gather over Fair Trade coffee at the popular coffee shop in the library. Everyone turns out for the Union Board's annual major concert and "to watch Homer Drew coach the Crusader basketball team" to sweet victory. When the campus and small-town life start to feel like they're closing in, students head to Chicago or the beaches at Indiana Dunes.

Student Body

The Valpo population largely comprises White, studious, middle-class students forever flashing that famously genuine Valpo smile. Some students say that "most of the people here believe in the Bible and follow the guidelines set forth in [it]," but others claim that "less than half of the students could be described as 'religious' by any stretch of the imagination." Amid this mix of Lutherans and Catholics, lapsed or practicing, students generally agree that they have not "personally experienced any problems due to religious differences." A senior tells us, "You do not have to be a Lutheran or believe in God to enjoy Valpo." Overall, the campus tends to be conservative, but "There is a very visible population of student Democrats and politically aware activists." The Office of Multicultural Programs "is doing a lot to bring more culture to campus, and minority organizations have decent clout on campus." A business student says, "Minorities here are, in fact, scarce, so we find ourselves fighting ignorance, and it just gives us a reason for being here." Sexual orientation, described as "a sore point," seems to be the last frontier of tolerance. "I was really disappointed to find out that all of the notices about National Coming Out Week were vandalized," writes a freshman. Another student cites the ongoing dialogue as a positive aspect of campus life, pointing out that "it is rare, in a university setting, that those who disagree morally with homosexuality would actually be allowed to speak."

VALPARAISO UNIVERSITY

FINANCIAL AID: 219-464-5015 • E-MAIL: UNDERGRAD.ADMISSIONS@VALPO.EDU • WEBSITE: WWW.VALPO.EDU

ADMISSIONS

Very important factors considered include: Academic GPA, rigor of secondary school record. *Important factors considered include:* Class rank, extracurricular activities, standardized test scores, talent/ability. *Other factors considered include:* Alumni/ae relation, application essay, character/personal qualities, first generation, interview, level of applicant's interest, racial/ethnic status, recommendation(s), religious affiliation/commitment, volunteer work. SAT or ACT required; ACT with Writing component required. TOEFL required of all international applicants. High school diploma is required, and GED is accepted. *Academic units required:* 4 English, 3 math, 2 science (2 science labs), 3 social studies, 3 academic electives. *Academic units recommended:* 4 English, 4 math, 3 science (3 science labs), 2 foreign language, 3 social studies, 3 academic electives.

The Inside Word

Valparaiso admits the vast majority of those who apply, but candidates should not be overconfident. Places like this fill a special niche in higher education and spend a good deal of time assessing the match a candidate makes with the university, even if the expected better-than-average high school record is present. Essays and extracurriculars can help you get admitted if your transcript is weak.

FINANCIAL AID

Students should submit: FAFSA. The Princeton Review suggests that all financial aid forms be submitted as soon as possible after January 1. *Need-based scholarships/grants offered:* Pell Grant, SEOG, state scholarships/grants, private scholarships, the school's own gift aid. *Loan aid offered:* Direct Subsidized Stafford, Direct Unsubsidized Stafford, Direct PLUS, Federal Perkins Loan, college/university loans from institutional funds. Applicants will be notified of awards on a rolling basis beginning or about March 1. Federal Work-Study Program available. Institutional employment available. Off-campus job opportunities are good.

FROM THE ADMISSIONS OFFICE

"Valpo provides students a blend of academic excellence, social experience, and spiritual exploration. The concern demonstrated by faculty and administration for the total well-being of students reflects a long history as a Lutheran-affiliated university.

"All first-time students from the high school graduating class of 2008 must submit an SAT or ACT score with the new Writing component with their application. If they previously took the SAT or ACT without the Writing portion, they must take the test again."

SELECTIVITY

Admissions Rating	**85**
# of applicants	3,785
% of applicants accepted	89
% of acceptees attending	23

FRESHMAN PROFILE

Range SAT Critical Reading	500–620
Range SAT Math	520–650
Range SAT Writing	490–610
Range ACT Composite	22–28
Minimum Paper TOEFL	550
Minimum Computer Based TOEFL	213
Average HS GPA	3.43
% graduated top 10% of class	35
% graduated top 25% of class	67
% graduated top 50% of class	93

DEADLINES

Regular application deadline	8/15
Regular notification	rolling
Nonfall registration?	yes

APPLICANTS ALSO LOOK AT

AND OFTEN PREFER
Indiana University—Bloomington, Purdue University—West Lafayette

AND SOMETIMES PREFER
Bradley University, Butler University, Marquette University

AND RARELY PREFER
Loyola University—Chicago, University of Illinois at Urbana-Champaign

FINANCIAL FACTS

Financial Aid Rating	**81**
Annual tuition	$23,200
Room & Board	$6,640
Books and supplies	$1,000
Required fees	$800
% frosh rec. need-based scholarship or grant aid	71
% UG rec. need-based scholarship or grant aid	67
% frosh rec. need-based self-help aid	54
% UG rec. need-based self-help aid	55
% frosh rec. any financial aid	98
% UG rec. any financial aid	95

VANDERBILT UNIVERSITY

2305 WEST END AVENUE, NASHVILLE, TN 37203 • ADMISSIONS: 615-322-2561 • FAX: 615-343-7765

CAMPUS LIFE

Quality of Life Rating	**88**
Fire Safety Rating	**99**
Type of school	private
Environment	metropolis

STUDENTS

Total undergrad enrollment	6,330
% male/female	48/52
% from out of state	83
% from public high school	57
% live on campus	83
% in (# of) fraternities	34 (19)
% in (# of) sororities	50 (12)
% African American	8
% Asian	6
% Caucasian	67
% Hispanic	5
% international	2
# of countries represented	55

SURVEY SAYS . . .

Students love Nashville, TN
Great off-campus food
Students are happy
Frats and sororities dominate social scene
Student publications are popular
Lots of beer drinking
Hard liquor is popular

ACADEMICS

Academic Rating	**94**
Calendar	semester
Student/faculty ratio	9:1
Profs interesting rating	84
Profs accessible rating	83
Most common lab size	10–19 students
Most common reg class size	10–19 students

MOST POPULAR MAJORS

engineering science
psychology
sociology

STUDENTS SAY

Academics

The word "balance" pops up a lot in students' descriptions of Vanderbilt University. Most often it's used to describe the amalgamation of "high academic standards" and "myriad" "social, service, and leadership opportunities" that characterizes so many students' experiences here. It is also used to describe the school's well-balanced mix of academic strengths; no surprise there, as Vandy excels in such diverse areas as premedicine, engineering, mathematics, sociology, psychology, and education. Sometimes the word refers to the balance between the "big city" benefits of Nashville—which include not only a world-class music scene but also "great opportunities for jobs, internships, [and] service"—and Vandy's "campus feel." In whatever context, students' numerous references to balance are a testimony to their comfort and satisfaction with the Vanderbilt experience. Undergrads here report a convivial atmosphere that takes away "a lot of the pressure" created by the "academically rigorous" curriculum. Professors "are generally good teachers who make themselves available through prompt responses to e-mail and through office hours," while administrators "are very accessible—you can see them in their office or spot them walking through campus"; the chancellor has been sighted "everywhere from plays to the dining hall to frat parties." Fellow students "aren't competitive and are constantly helping each other."

Life

Vanderbilt's campus life is "stimulating, challenging, [and] fun." "There is always something going on," a sophomore reports. Greek life is "a very large part of Vanderbilt's social scene," as most "Fraternity parties are open to everyone." These parties "rival no other," and they "always have bands or themes or activities, so it's not just a crowd of people getting drunk." But there's more than the just the Greek scene for students to participate in; students tout "clubs for every interest, sports for every level of ability," and "student theater every night of the week." Students also tell us that "Christian and other religious organizations are a big part of Vanderbilt campus life" and that "service organizations are really important at Vanderbilt, and the majority of students are involved in volunteer work in the Nashville community." As for intercollegiate sports, "Attending sporting events is popular, though I wouldn't go so far as to say everyone is a devoted fan." Just about everyone has nice things to say about hometown Nashville. One student writes, "Nashville is a great place to live—there is always something going on. Centennial Park is right across the street; it's a great place to study, walk, or hang out. Downtown has an awesome party scene" that, of course, includes lots of live music. One student adds, "The weather is a pretty nice perk too."

Student Body

"Vanderbilt has come a long way from the stereotypical Southern, wealthy, White student," undergrads here assure us, noting that "there are students from all over the country." While there is "definitely still a strong presence of Polo-clad fraternity guys and sorority girls, the image of Vanderbilt has become so much more than that and now encompasses students from different ethnicities, religions, and geographical regions." Today, the glue that binds the student body is that "everyone is involved." It seems like every student has at least one passion that [he or she] pursue[s] actively on campus or off campus. Everyone is in at least one student organization. No one here is only about academics." Students also tend to be "religious," "very approachable, and friendly, [and] passionate about their studies."

FINANCIAL AID: 615-322-3591 • E-MAIL: ADMISSIONS@VANDERBILT.EDU • WEBSITE: WWW.VANDERBILT.EDU

ADMISSIONS

Very important factors considered include: Academic GPA, class rank, extracurricular activities, rigor of secondary school record, standardized test scores. *Important factors considered include:* Application essay, recommendation(s). *Other factors considered include:* Character/personal qualities, first generation, interview, racial/ethnic status, talent/ability, volunteer work, work experience. SAT or ACT required; SAT Subject Tests with Writing component recommended. TOEFL required of all international applicants. High school diploma is required, and GED is not accepted. *Academic units required:* 4 English, 3 math, 2 science (2 science labs), 2 foreign language, 2 social studies. *Academic units recommended:* 4 English, 4 math, 4 science (4 science labs), 4 foreign language, 4 social studies.

The Inside Word

Vanderbilt received 25 percent more early decision applications for the 2006–2007 academic year than it did for the previous academic year, and as a result, competition has increased for those spaces. Still, if you consider early decision here (or anywhere, for that matter), remember that you will not learn about financial aid until long after you've received your binding decision.

FINANCIAL AID

Students should submit: FAFSA, CSS/Financial Aid PROFILE, Noncustodial PROFILE. The Princeton Review suggests that all financial aid forms be submitted as soon as possible after January 1. *Need-based scholarships/grants offered:* Pell Grant, SEOG, state scholarships/grants, private scholarships, the school's own gift aid. *Loan aid offered:* FFEL Subsidized Stafford, FFEL Unsubsidized Stafford, FFEL PLUS, Federal Perkins Loan, Federal Nursing Loan, college/university loans from institutional funds, Undergrad Education Loan. Applicants will be notified of awards on or about April 1. Federal Work-Study Program available. Institutional employment available.

FROM THE ADMISSIONS OFFICE

"Vanderbilt is one of a very small number of colleges that makes a dual promise: Applications are considered without regard for financial need (need-blind), and every admitted U.S. applicant's demonstrated financial need will be fully met. Early decision applicants who submit the CSS PROFILE at the time of application will be provided with a provisional award of need-based financial aid.

"Exceptional accomplishment and high promise in some field of intellectual endeavor are essential. The student's total academic and non-academic record is reviewed in conjunction with recommendations and personal essays. For students at the Blair School of Music, the audition is a prime consideration.

"Living on campus is a crucial element of the Vanderbilt experience. With the opening of the new Freshman Commons in the Fall of 2008, all students will be expected to live on campus for all 4 years.

"The Vanderbilt undergraduate experience is often described as uniquely balanced. Students are encouraged to participate in a broad spectrum of campus organizations (over 350) among an increasingly diverse population including approximately 25 percent students of color in the class of 2010. This diversity is also evident from recent survey data which reveals that Vanderbilt first-year students self-identify almost equally as liberal, conservative, or moderate. Recent additions to campus include the Schulman Center for Jewish Life, a newly renovated Black Cultural Center, and the Studio Arts Building.

"Freshman applicants for Fall 2008 are required to submit Writing scores from the new SAT or ACT as part of their application."

SELECTIVITY

Admissions Rating	98
# of applicants	12,189
% of applicants accepted	34
% of acceptees attending	39

FRESHMAN PROFILE

Range SAT Critical Reading	630–730
Range SAT Math	650–740
Range SAT Writing	630–710
Range ACT Composite	28–32
Minimum Paper TOEFL	570
% graduated top 10% of class	79
% graduated top 25% of class	95
% graduated top 50% of class	99

DEADLINES

Early decision application deadline	11/1
Early decision notification	12/15
Regular application deadline	1/3
Regular notification	4/1
Nonfall registration?	no

APPLICANTS ALSO LOOK AT

AND OFTEN PREFER
Cornell University, Georgetown University, Princeton University, University of Notre Dame, University of Virginia

AND SOMETIMES PREFER
Dartmouth College, Duke University, Emory University, Northwestern University, Wake Forest University

AND RARELY PREFER
Boston College, Rhodes College, Southern Methodist University, Tulane University, Washington University in St. Louis

FINANCIAL FACTS

Financial Aid Rating	96
Annual tuition	$34,414
Room & Board	$11,446
Books and Supplies	$1,140
Required Fees	$864
% frosh rec. need-based scholarship or grant aid	42
% UG rec. need-based scholarship or grant aid	38
% frosh rec. need-based self-help aid	26
% UG rec. need-based self-help aid	26

VASSAR COLLEGE

124 RAYMOND AVENUE, POUGHKEEPSIE, NY 12604 • ADMISSIONS: 845-437-7300 • FAX: 845-437-7063

CAMPUS LIFE

Quality of Life Rating	**80**
Fire Safety Rating	**89**
Type of school	private
Environment	town

STUDENTS

Total undergrad enrollment	2,379
% male/female	40/60
% from out of state	73
% from public high school	65
% live on campus	95
% African American	5
% Asian	9
% Caucasian	75
% Hispanic	6
% international	5
# of countries represented	43

SURVEY SAYS . . .

Small classes
Great library
Frats and sororities are unpopular or
nonexistent

ACADEMICS

Academic Rating	**98**
Calendar	semester
Student/faculty ratio	8:1
Profs interesting rating	91
Profs accessible rating	88
% profs teaching	
UG courses	100
% classes taught by TAs	0
Most common	
lab size	10–19 students
Most common	
reg class size	10–19 students

MOST POPULAR MAJORS

English language and literature
political science and government
psychology

STUDENTS SAY

Academics

Vassar College "is a great place to explore your options" because "There's no real core curriculum. All you need in the way of requirements are one quantitative class and one foreign language credit. Plus, one-quarter of your credits must be outside of your major." This approach, students agree, "really encourages students to think creatively and pursue whatever they're passionate about, whether that be medieval tapestries, neuroscience, or unicycles. Not having a core curriculum is great because it gives students the opportunity to delve into many different interests." So much academic freedom might be a license to goof off at some schools; here, however, students "are passionate learners who participate in both academic and extracurriculars with all their might." Most of these "smart hippies with books in hand discussing feminism and politics and last night" don't need curricular requirements to compel them to take challenging courses. Vassar excels in the visual and performing arts—the "Drama Department is huge" —as well as in English, psychology, history, life sciences, and natural sciences. In all disciplines, "Profs here are mostly great teachers, and they're teachers first. Since there are no grad students here, undergrads are the top priority, and it shows in the one-on-one interactions you have with your teachers."

Life

"Life is campus-centered" at Vassar, in large part because hometown Poughkeepsie "does not offer much in the way of entertainment. The campus provides most of the weekend activities." One undergrad observes, "It's unfortunate but not rare for people to graduate from Vassar knowing nothing about Poughkeepsie other than where the train station to New York City is." The sojourn to New York, alas, is a relatively "expensive endeavor for weekly entertainment; it's about $30 round-trip, and that doesn't include doing stuff once you get there." Fortunately, "There is a huge array of things to do every night on campus. Comedy shows, improv, an incredibly wide array of theater productions" —including "several shows a year and three student groups devoted to drama"—four comedy groups, five a cappella groups," and interesting lectures create numerous opportunities to get out of the dorms at night." Provided you "pay attention to all the events e-mails Vassar sends out, you can usually find something random, fun, and free to do on a slow afternoon or weekday night." Weekends, on the other hand, "are completely different. If you don't drink or like being in situations where drinking/recreational drugs are involved, you'll probably have a dead social life." It's "not a wild, enormous party scene like at a state school" here, but rather one that occurs "earlier in the night, and in smaller groups of people." Vassar's self-contained social scene illustrates "something called the 'Vassar Bubble,' which means that you see the same people every day. You are so cut off from the world that sometimes it's difficult to keep up with current events."

Student Body

"There are common labels that get placed on people at Vassar," including "'hippie,' 'hipster,' and 'pretentious,' and to a degree, the labels are accurate." Vassar is a comfortable respite for "indie-chic students who revel in obscurity, some socially awkward archetypes, and some prep school pin-ups with their collars popped. But the majority of kids on campus are a mix of these people, which is why we mesh pretty well despite the cliques that inevitably form." What nearly everyone shares is "an amazing talent or something that they passionately believe in" and "far-left politics, with no desire or intention to try to understand any political view even slightly left of center. Most of them are pretty nice people, though."

FINANCIAL AID: 845-437-5230 • E-MAIL: ADMISSIONS@VASSAR.EDU • WEBSITE: WWW.VASSAR.EDU

ADMISSIONS

Very important factors considered include: Rigor of secondary school record. *Important factors considered include:* Academic GPA, application essay, character/personal qualities, class rank, extracurricular activities, recommendation(s), standardized test scores. *Other factors considered include:* Alumni/ae relation, first generation, geographical residence, interview, level of applicant's interest, racial/ethnic status, talent/ability, volunteer work, work experience. SAT and SAT Subject Tests or ACT required; ACT with Writing component recommended. TOEFL required of all international applicants. High school diploma is required, and GED is accepted. *Academic units required:* 4 English, 4 math, 4 science (3 science labs), 3 foreign language, 2 social studies, 2 history, 4 academic electives. *Academic units recommended:* 4 English, 4 math, 4 science (3 science labs), 4 foreign language, 4 social studies, 2 history.

The Inside Word

With acceptance rates hitting record lows, stellar academic credentials are a must for any serious Vassar candidate. Importantly, the college prides itself on selecting students that will add to the vitality of the campus; once Admissions Officers see that you meet their rigorous scholastic standards, they'll closely assess your personal essay, recommendations, and extracurricular activities. Indeed, demonstrating an intellectual curiosity that extends outside the classroom is as important as success within it.

FINANCIAL AID

Students should submit: FAFSA, institution's own financial aid form, CSS/Financial Aid PROFILE, Noncustodial PROFILE, state aid form, Business/Farm Supplement. Regular filing deadline is February 1. The Princeton Review suggests that all financial aid forms be submitted as soon as possible after January 1. *Need-based scholarships/grants offered:* Pell Grant, SEOG, state scholarships/grants, private scholarships, the school's own gift aid. *Loan aid offered:* Federal Perkins Loan, loans for noncitizens with need. Applicants will be notified of awards on or about March 30. Federal Work-Study Program available. Institutional employment available. Off-campus job opportunities are fair.

FROM THE ADMISSIONS OFFICE

"Vassar presents a rich variety of social and cultural activities, clubs, sports, living arrangements, and regional attractions. Vassar is a vital, residential college community recognized for its respect for the rights and individuality of others.

"Candidates for admission to the Class of 2012 at Vassar must submit either the SAT Reasoning Test and two SAT Subject Tests taken in different subject fields, or the ACT exam (the optional ACT writing component is recommended)."

SELECTIVITY

Admissions Rating	**97**
# of applicants	6,075
% of applicants accepted	30
% of acceptees attending	37
# accepting a place on wait list	450
% admitted from wait list	11
# of early decision applicants	586
% accepted early decision	43

FRESHMAN PROFILE

Range SAT Critical Reading	660–740
Range SAT Math	640–710
Range ACT Composite	29–31
Minimum Paper TOEFL	600
Minimum Computer Based TOEFL	250
Average HS GPA	3.7
% graduated top 10% of class	67
% graduated top 25% of class	93
% graduated top 50% of class	100

DEADLINES

Early decision application deadline	11/15
Early decision notification	12/15
Regular application deadline	1/1
Regular notification	4/1
Nonfall registration?	no

APPLICANTS ALSO LOOK AT

AND OFTEN PREFER
Brown University, Yale University

AND SOMETIMES PREFER
Columbia University, New York University, Wesleyan University

AND RARELY PREFER
Skidmore College, Union College (NY)

FINANCIAL FACTS

Financial Aid Rating	**97**
Annual tuition	$35,520
Room & Board	$8,130
Books and supplies	$860
Required fees	$510
% frosh rec. need-based scholarship or grant aid	48
% UG rec. need-based scholarship or grant aid	45
% frosh rec. need-based self-help aid	48
% UG rec. need-based self-help aid	46
% frosh rec. any financial aid	55
% UG rec. any financial aid	55

VILLANOVA UNIVERSITY

800 LANCASTER AVENUE, VILLANOVA, PA 19085-1672 • ADMISSIONS: 610-519-4000 • FAX: 610-519-6450

STUDENTS SAY

Academics

"An exceptional and well-known business program" with particular strengths in finance and commerce attracts nearly a quarter of the undergraduate student body at Villanova University, a prestigious Augustinian school located in the suburbs of Philadelphia. "Employers look to employ Nova graduates" because they know they've studied with "professors who bring real-world experience to the classrooms" and have benefited from "an awesome internship program." Students here are not just business wonks; the school's "rigorous core curriculum" "emphasizes a solid foundation in liberal arts and creative thinking," thereby "developing the whole person through ethical learning." The ethical learning component here "goes far beyond the classroom," as "Participation in service programs (some of the largest in the country), involvement with extracurricular groups, and strong programs established by the university (such as learning communities), are a perfect complement to the excellent development that takes place inside the classroom." Engineering is another area in which Nova students enjoy "an incredible program" with "great facilities." Across the board, "Class sizes are small, and even in a bigger lecture atmosphere, groups are broken up once a week for discussion." Beyond this, "Villanova provides its students with a very high level of technology: access to wireless internet, webmail, and class websites."

Life

At Villanova, "You will work hard Sunday through Wednesday, have fun Thursday through Saturday, and on Sunday you will donate your time to a good cause." Academics, Nova athletics (especially men's basketball), and clubs keep students busy right up until Thursday evening, at which point "People are ready to party, so they either hop on the train to Philly, go to the local bars on the Main Line, or catch a ride to a fraternity party." (Because "There are no frat houses or team houses on campus," all parties "are off campus, and tickets often need to be purchased for as much as $30 the week before. Buses are taken to and from, or you have to know someone to get in. It is a huge hassle for an underclassman, but it's worth the effort.") For many, Sundays are dedicated to church and service. Semester breaks are often also devoted to service: "For fall, winter, and spring break our school runs trips to different parts of the world. Habitat for Humanity trips take place within the United States and allow students to build a house while interacting with the community, strengthening their faith, and creating amazing friendships. Mission trips travel outside of the United States to Mexico, South America, Africa, etc. These trips open the eyes and broaden the minds of those who go on them."

Student Body

"Villanova has the stereotype of White, preppy, private schooled, rich kids." It may be true that, at first glance, what one sees here is "a lot of outgoing, wealthy, well-kept, suburban students who look like they graced the cover of the newest J. Crew magazine and are currently shooting a Crest ad." It's worth noting, however, that "appearances are deceiving. There are plenty of people who do not fit this stereotype." Those schooled in the nuances of Villanova demographics tell us that "there are actually two typical types of students at Villanova. One type consists of preppy, White, rich kids. The other type of student is the one who's interested in community service. There are many students who care a great deal about others and will participate in any activity that allows them to do so." This student is quick to point out, however, that "this is not to say that these groups do not sometimes overlap."

VILLANOVA UNIVERSITY

FINANCIAL AID: 610-519-4010 • E-MAIL: GOTOVU@VILLANOVA.EDU • WEBSITE: WWW.VILLANOVA.EDU

ADMISSIONS

Very important factors considered include: Academic GPA, class rank, rigor of secondary school record, standardized test scores. *Important factors considered include:* Application essay, character/personal qualities, extracurricular activities, recommendation(s), talent/ability, volunteer work, work experience. *Other factors considered include:* Alumni/ae relation, first generation, geographical residence, level of applicant's interest, racial/ethnic status, state residency. SAT or ACT required; ACT with Writing component required. TOEFL required of all international applicants. High school diploma is required, and GED is accepted. *Academic units required:* 4 English, 4 math, 4 science (2 science labs), 2 foreign language, 2 academic electives. *Academic units recommended:* 4 English, 4 math, 4 science (3 science labs), 4 foreign language, 2 academic electives.

The Inside Word

While not as competitive as some of its Catholic brethren, Villanova's growing reputation makes it a strong choice for capable and accomplished students. The university gives equal weight to most facets of the application, and candidates are expected to do the same. Applicants should be aware that admissions criteria vary slightly among Villanova's schools. Students who opt to apply early action also must contend with more arduous standards.

FINANCIAL AID

Students should submit: FAFSA, institution's own financial aid form. Regular filing deadline is February 7. The Princeton Review suggests that all financial aid forms be submitted as soon as possible after January 1. *Need-based scholarships/grants offered:* Pell Grant, SEOG, state scholarships/grants, private scholarships, the school's own gift aid. *Loan aid offered:* FFEL Subsidized Stafford, FFEL Unsubsidized Stafford, FFEL PLUS, Federal Perkins Loan, Federal Nursing Loan. Applicants will be notified of awards on or about April 1. Federal Work-Study Program available. Institutional employment available. Off-campus job opportunities are excellent.

FROM THE ADMISSIONS OFFICE

"The university is a community of persons of diverse professional, academic, and personal interests who in a spirit of collegiality cooperate to achieve their common goals and objectives in the transmission, the pursuit, and the discovery of knowledge. Villanova attempts to enroll students with diverse social, geographic, economic, and educational backgrounds. Villanova welcomes students who consider it desirable to study within the philosophical framework of Christian Humanism. Finally, this community seeks to reflect the spirit of St. Augustine by the cultivation of knowledge, by respect for individual differences, and by adherence to the principle that mutual love and respect should animate every aspect of university life."

—*Villanova University Mission Statement*

"Freshman applicants to Villanova University are required to submit scores from either the new SAT or ACT with Writing component. "

SELECTIVITY

Admissions Rating	**95**
# of applicants	12,913
% of applicants accepted	43
% of acceptees attending	30
# accepting a place on wait list	2,034
% admitted from wait list	2

FRESHMAN PROFILE

Range SAT Critical Reading	570–670
Range SAT Math	610–700
Range SAT Writing	570–670
Range ACT Composite	27–30
Minimum Paper TOEFL	550
Minimum Computer Based TOEFL	213
Average HS GPA	3.72
% graduated top 10% of class	51
% graduated top 25% of class	88
% graduated top 50% of class	97

DEADLINES

Regular application deadline	1/7
Regular notification	4/1
Nonfall registration?	no

APPLICANTS ALSO LOOK AT

AND OFTEN PREFER
Georgetown University, University of Notre Dame

AND SOMETIMES PREFER
Boston College, College of the Holy Cross

AND RARELY PREFER
Fairfield University, Loyola College in Maryland, Providence College

FINANCIAL FACTS

Financial Aid Rating	**72**
Annual tuition	$33,000
Room & Board	$9,560
Books and supplies	$950
Required fees	$580
% frosh rec. need-based scholarship or grant aid	44
% UG rec. need-based scholarship or grant aid	39
% frosh rec. need-based self-help aid	46
% UG rec. need-based self-help aid	40
% frosh rec. any financial aid	68
% UG rec. any financial aid	63

VIRGINIA POLYTECHNIC INSTITUTE AND STATE UNIVERSITY (VIRGINIA TECH)

UNDERGRADUATE ADMISSIONS, 201 BURRUSS HALL, BLACKSBURG, VA 24061 • ADMISSIONS: 540-231-6267 • FAX: 540-231-3242

STUDENTS SAY

Academics

Students at tech schools don't typically brag about their quality of life, but then again, Virginia Polytechnic Institute and State University, otherwise known as Virginia Tech, is not your typical tech school. Here, students happily discover that they don't have to forfeit "a variety of exciting extracurricular activities" that include "a football program that takes priority for all but the most dedicated students" in order "to achieve an excellent education." Programs in engineering, architecture, agricultural science, and forestry "are all national leaders in their areas" at VT, while the "outstanding" business program offers "top-notch access to occupations in the field through the efforts of the department." Throughout this large school, undergrads are "continually surprised by the genuine interest the faculty and instructors take in students and their education. Open office doors, beyond just the posted office hours, e-mail communication, and openness to accept undergraduate students in graduate course work and as researchers in labs demonstrate not only how committed VT teachers are, but also how optimistic they are of students' success." About one in five students here pursues engineering, a degree that "provides a mixture of practical and theoretical teaching in the classes, experimental labs, a design capstone" and "a cooperative education program that places great value on applying knowledge in the real world."

Life

Virginia Tech may be located "in the middle of nowhere," but students don't seem to mind, because "The people you meet and the cozy town of Blacksburg can be so much fun. Being part of the Hokie nation is really special." School spirit is high, driven by a football team that "is king in Blacksburg. It's hard not to be excited about football when you are tailgating with friends and seeing 60,000 people pack the stadium." While most students here struggle with heavy workloads, they still manage to enjoy themselves. "You can always find people outside playing volleyball or basketball, or using the drill field for games of pickup soccer and football" at Tech, and lots of students exploit the "perfect location for outdoor activities." According to one undergrad, "Within 30 minutes from campus, you can be hiking on the Appalachian Trail, floating down the New River, picnicking in the Jefferson National Forest, or listening to live old-time music at the Floyd Country Store on Friday nights." Shopping isn't quite as convenient: "The good local shopping is about 30 minutes away," students tell us. When it's time to kick loose, "Apartment parties are a big thing at Virginia Tech, and beer pong is almost as popular as football. There are plenty of party animals here, if that's your thing, but it's also pretty easy to find people who know how to have fun without getting drunk." Many of those people dedicate themselves to "the more than 500 student organizations on campus." When small-town life starts to feel to restrictive, "Roanoke is just down the road and offers malls and movie theaters."

Student Body

Virginia Tech's "large student body makes it easy to find many people that have the same interests and are able to become good friends." The unifying thread on campus is "that we are all proud Hokies. While everyone has their differences, we come together as a united campus. The students here are awesome!" There are, of course, "a lot of nerdy engineering boys" as well as "a corps of cadets" at VT, but "There are not many minority students on campus other than the international ones." The population shows a strong bias toward northern Virginia: "Some days it seems as if 25,000 kids from northern Virginia descended on a tiny mountain town," writes one student.

VIRGINIA POLYTECHNIC INSTITUTE AND STATE UNIVERSITY (VIRGINIA TECH)

FINANCIAL AID: 540-231-5179 • E-MAIL: VTADMISS@VT.EDU • WEBSITE: WWW.VT.EDU

ADMISSIONS

Very important factors considered include: Academic GPA, rigor of secondary school record, standardized test scores. *Other factors considered include:* Alumni/ae relation, character/personal qualities, extracurricular activities, first generation, geographical residence, racial/ethnic status, recommendation(s), state residency, talent/ability, volunteer work, work experience. SAT or ACT required; ACT with Writing component required. TOEFL required of all international applicants. High school diploma is required, and GED is accepted. *Academic units required:* 4 English, 3 math, 2 science (2 science labs), 1 social studies, 1 history, 4 academic electives. *Academic units recommended:* 4 math, 3 science, 3 foreign language.

The Inside Word

Students interested in Virginia state schools are advised to consider Tech. Although not as competitive as UVA or William & Mary, Tech is a well-regarded institution offering a great education at bargain prices. Admissions decisions tend to be based upon numbers and statistics. While there are no established cut-offs, the primary focus is on grades, strength of schedule, GPA, and test scores.

FINANCIAL AID

Students should submit: FAFSA. The Princeton Review suggests that all financial aid forms be submitted as soon as possible after January 1. *Need-based scholarships/grants offered:* Pell Grant, SEOG, state scholarships/grants, private scholarships, the school's own gift aid, cadet scholarships/grants. *Loan aid offered:* Direct Subsidized Stafford, Direct Unsubsidized Stafford, Direct PLUS, Federal Perkins Loan, college/university loans from institutional funds. Applicants will be notified of awards on a rolling basis beginning or about March 30. Federal Work-Study Program available. Off-campus job opportunities are excellent.

FROM THE ADMISSIONS OFFICE

"Virginia Tech offers the opportunities of a large research university in a small-town setting. Undergraduates choose from more than 70 majors in 7 colleges, including nationally ranked architecture, business, forestry, and engineering schools, as well as excellent computer science, biology, and communication studies, and architecture programs. Technology is a key focus, both in classes and in general. All first-year students are required to own a personal computer, each residence hall room has Ethernet connections, and every student is provided e-mail and Internet access. Faculty incorporate a wide variety of technology into class, utilizing chat rooms, online lecture notes, and multimedia presentations. The university offers cutting-edge facilities for classes and research, abundant opportunities for advanced study in the honors program, undergraduate research opportunities, study abroad, internships, and cooperative education. Students enjoy more than 600 organizations which offer something for everyone. Tech offers the best of both worlds—everything a large university can provide and a small-town atmosphere.

"Fall 2008 freshman applicants must take the new SAT or ACT with Writing section unless they are satisfied with SAT or ACT scores received prior to March 2005. We will use the highest scores from any SAT or ACT test scores submitted."

SELECTIVITY

Admissions Rating	89
# of applicants	19,046
% of applicants accepted	66
% of acceptees attending	40
# accepting a place on wait list	1,115
% admitted from wait list	11
# of early decision applicants	2496
% accepted early decision	49

FRESHMAN PROFILE

Range SAT Critical Reading	530–630
Range SAT Math	570–660
Range SAT Writing	530–620
Range ACT Composite	23–27
Minimum Paper TOEFL	550
Minimum Computer Based TOEFL	207
Average HS GPA	3.74
% graduated top 10% of class	38
% graduated top 25% of class	81
% graduated top 50% of class	98

DEADLINES

Early decision application deadline	11/1
Early decision notification	12/15
Regular application deadline	1/15
Regular notification	4/1
Nonfall registration?	yes

APPLICANTS ALSO LOOK AT

AND OFTEN PREFER
James Madison University, University of Virginia

AND SOMETIMES PREFER
Virginia Commonwealth University

AND RARELY PREFER
The College of William & Mary, The University of North Carolina at Chapel Hill

FINANCIAL FACTS

Financial Aid Rating	70
Annual in-state tuition	$5,772
Annual out-of-state tuition	$17,980
Room & Board	$4,932–$6,236
Books and supplies	$1,067
Required fees	$1,625–$1,795
% frosh rec. need-based scholarship or grant aid	28
% UG rec. need-based scholarship or grant aid	25
% frosh rec. need-based self-help aid	28
% UG rec. need-based self-help aid	29
% frosh rec. any financial aid	36
% UG rec. any financial aid	34

WABASH COLLEGE

PO Box 352, 301 West Wabash Avenue, Crawfordsville, IN 47933 • Admissions: 765-361-6225 • Fax: 765-361-6437

STUDENTS SAY

Academics

Undertaking higher education at Wabash College entails a lot of "thinking about what it means to be a man, challenging current definitions, and graduating as a gentleman." Students feel comfortable in the traditional academic framework that encourages responsible action and critical thinking. A junior history major believes, "The all-male environment makes us more open to frank discussion of issues that would not be raised at a large coed school." The Science, Language, Math, and Economics Departments rank highly, while courses in the speech, psychology, and history programs are considered lightweight. Rather than "spoon-feed" their students, professors employ "the Socratic Method, meaning that they drill you on what you read the night before to make sure you are prepared for class." Faculty members retain their authority while routinely participating in campus clubs and sporting events alongside their students. A chemistry major says, "I have been to the home of every professor in my department," and all freshmen are invited to the president's house soon after their arrival. These rapport-building interactions create an environment where "crime, insubordination, and plagiarism are almost nonexistent." Graduates are released into the real world cushioned with alumni contacts and career placement support. "I knew there was not another school in the Midwest that would take care of me the way Wabash College does."

Life

Life at Wabash is governed by the Gentleman's Rule, which basically says, "Don't be an idiot," trusting students to define "idiot" for themselves. "Everyone enjoys freedom to an amazing extent but also knows where the limits are." New rules are starting to appear, however, rankling students who think "It's only going to create more rebellion." Wabash loves a good tradition, particularly of the gladiatorial variety. The Monon Bell Game against DePauw is officially the "oldest football rivalry west of the Alleghenies." Fraternities also perpetuate long-standing, testosterone-fueled intramural competition. "We are constantly pitted against each other for some type of honor that has been around since forever. Your fraternity's honor is on the line." Though Greek bonds run deep at Wabash, "independent men" insist they lead a viable social life too. The weekly books/booze cycle dictates "from Sunday to Thursday, we study like monastic initiates. On the weekends, we're as libertine as any Bohemian." At times, the line blurs: "It is the weirdest thing. A bunch of guys will be drinking and all of a sudden a political or religious debate breaks out." Students also spend time "writing for the newspaper, editing a student journal, playing collegiate sports, learning a musical instrument, writing and reciting poetry, or acting in a theater production." And why shouldn't they? "Wabash has a lot of money" to fund any student's interest or whim.

Student Body

Despite ongoing efforts to diversify the student body, Wabash remains "a monochromatic sea of Indiana WASPs." That said, tolerance and open-mindedness are considered part of being a gentlemanly Indiana WASP. "I'm a practicing Buddhist myself, and even though there are many students who feel very strongly about their own faith, never once have I felt that a student or professor was judging me because my faith was different than theirs." Universal school identification trumps even the most contentious dividing line of all: "While the cracks at his masculinity from those who know nothing of Wabash may have chafed him, a Wabash man accepts homosexuals as members of the same grand school." Several students comment that African American students "create their own close-knit community." All Wabash men relate to each other based on shared interests in studies and career, politics, social events, and community service, as well as "a common feeling of invincibility among us."

FINANCIAL AID: 765-361-6370 • E-MAIL: ADMISSIONS@WABASH.EDU • WEBSITE: WWW.WABASH.EDU

ADMISSIONS

Very important factors considered include: Academic GPA, class rank, rigor of secondary school record. *Important factors considered include:* Character/personal qualities, extracurricular activities, interview, recommendation(s), standardized test scores, talent/ability. *Other factors considered include:* Alumni/ae relation, application essay, first generation, geographical residence, level of applicant's interest, racial/ethnic status, volunteer work, work experience. SAT or ACT required; TOEFL required of all international applicants. High school diploma is required, and GED is accepted. *Academic units recommended:* 4 English, 4 math, 2 science (2 science labs), 2 foreign language, 2 social studies, 2 history.

The Inside Word

Wabash is one of the few remaining all-male colleges in the country, and like the rest it has a small applicant pool. The pool is highly self-selected, and the academic standards for admission, while selective, are not particularly demanding. However, Wabash is tough to graduate from—don't consider it if you aren't prepared to work.

FINANCIAL AID

Students should submit: FAFSA, CSS/Financial Aid PROFILE, Noncustodial PROFILE, Federal Income Tax Returns and W-2 statements. Regular filing deadline is March 1. The Princeton Review suggests that all financial aid forms be submitted as soon as possible after January 1. *Need-based scholarships/grants offered:* Pell Grant, state scholarships/grants, private scholarships, the school's own gift aid. *Loan aid offered:* FFEL Subsidized Stafford, FFEL Unsubsidized Stafford, FFEL PLUS, college/university loans from institutional funds. Applicants will be notified of awards on or about March 31. Institutional employment available. Off-campus job opportunities are good.

FROM THE ADMISSIONS OFFICE

"Wabash College is different—and distinctive—from other liberal arts colleges. Different in that Wabash is an outstanding college for men only. Distinctive in the quality and character of the faculty, in the demanding nature of the academic program, in the farsightedness and maturity of the men who enroll, and in the richness of the traditions that have evolved throughout its 174-year history, Wabash is preeminently a teaching institution, and fundamental to the learning experience is the way faculty and students talk to each other—with mutual respect for the expression of informed opinion. For example, students who collaborate with faculty on research projects are considered their peers in the research—an esteem not usually extended to undergraduates. The college takes pride in the sense of community that such a learning environment fosters. But perhaps the single most striking aspect of student life at Wabash is personal freedom. The college has only one rule: 'The student is expected to conduct himself at all times, both on and off the campus, as a gentleman and a responsible citizen.' Wabash College treats students as adults, and such treatment attracts responsible freshmen and fosters their independence and maturity.

"For students applying for admission into the Fall 2008 entering class, Wabash will accept either the new version of the SAT or the old version; the same policy applies for the ACT. Wabash will use the student's best scores from either examination, and will accept the SAT or ACT Writing portions in place of an essay. Wabash does not require SAT Subject Tests."

SELECTIVITY

Admissions Rating	90
# of applicants	1,319
% of applicants accepted	51
% of acceptees attending	40
# accepting a place on wait list	59
% admitted from wait list	7
# of early decision applicants	47
% accepted early decision	74

FRESHMAN PROFILE

Range SAT Critical Reading	510–620
Range SAT Math	560–653
Range SAT Writing	500–610
Range ACT Composite	22–28
Minimum Paper TOEFL	550
Minimum Computer Based TOEFL	213
Average HS GPA	3.67
% graduated top 10% of class	39
% graduated top 25% of class	73
% graduated top 50% of class	96

DEADLINES

Early decision application deadline	11/15
Early decision notification	12/15
Regular notification	rolling
Nonfall registration?	no

APPLICANTS ALSO LOOK AT

AND OFTEN PREFER
Indiana University—Bloomington, Purdue University—West Lafayette

AND SOMETIMES PREFER
Butler University, DePauw University, Hanover College

AND RARELY PREFER
Franklin College, Miami University

FINANCIAL FACTS

Financial Aid Rating	99
Annual tuition	$24,342
Room & Board	$7,064
Books and supplies	$700
Required fees	$450
% frosh rec. need-based scholarship or grant aid	81
% UG rec. need-based scholarship or grant aid	70
% frosh rec. need-based self-help aid	63
% UG rec. need-based self-help aid	57
% frosh rec. any financial aid	93
% UG rec. any financial aid	88

WAGNER COLLEGE

ONE CAMPUS ROAD, STATEN ISLAND, NY 10301-4495 • ADMISSIONS: 718-390-3411 • FAX: 718-390-3105

CAMPUS LIFE
Quality of Life Rating	**73**
Fire Safety Rating	**72**
Type of school	private
Affiliation	Lutheran
Environment	metropolis

STUDENTS
Total undergrad enrollment	1,941
% male/female	38/62
% from out of state	59
% live on campus	77
% in (# of) fraternities	8 (5)
% in (# of) sororities	11 (4)
% African American	6
% Asian	2
% Caucasian	78
% Hispanic	6
% international	1
# of countries represented	7

SURVEY SAYS . . .
Small classes
Theater is popular
Lots of beer drinking
Hard liquor is popular

ACADEMICS
Academic Rating	**79**
Calendar	semester
Student/faculty ratio	13:1
Profs interesting rating	74
Profs accessible rating	78
% profs teaching UG courses	100
Most common lab size	fewer than 10 students
Most common reg class size	10–19 students

MOST POPULAR MAJORS
biology/biological sciences
business administration/
management
psychology

STUDENTS SAY

Academics

In theory, the Wagner Plan for the Practical Liberal Arts educates free thinkers who can also pay the rent. Required senior-year internships and active volunteering programs mean "a head start on post-graduation plans." First-year learning communities incorporate experiential learning, creative expression, interdisciplinary connections, and frequent trips to the "classroom of New York City." A freshman writes, "They force you to look at the way two subjects relate to each other in a new way." Some people think the 4-year-old program still needs to work out a few kinks. "It is difficult for students to have confidence in what they are doing if there is no one to encourage them," an English major writes, referring to the self-guided assignments. Theater is a big thing here, too, but even with its liberal and fine arts focus, Wagner manages to also attract students interested in health professions with top nursing and physician's assistant programs. Regardless of major, writing skills are emphasized. "If you don't like doing papers, this is not the place for you. Even the dance classes have tons of them assigned," students warn. Professors are said to be available for academic advice, problem solving, or casual conversation. Reviews of the efficacy of the administration are mixed, but one sage senior adds some helpful context, noting that "since coming to Wagner the administration has gotten better (more involved) and the professors are still about the same (sometimes you get old, boring ones; other times you get good, interesting ones). The more I've gotten involved on campus, the better my experience has been as a whole,"—advice that a student at any college could employ to good effect.

Life

Visually, imagine "a classic TV high school"—a large, well-endowed, private high school—and you've got Wagner College. Students relish their dorm-room views of the skyline of Lower Manhattan and make frequent trips to "the greatest metropolis on Earth." One grumpy junior points out that Wagner is "supposedly close to NYC," but cites the time it takes to get to the Staten Island ferry, ride it, and hop the subway to midtown to argue to the contrary. Commuters mingle with residents, though on-campus students maintain that they "have more fun living the ultimate college life." Nighttime hours are typically reserved for social activities, sometimes involving alcohol, rather than sleeping, resulting in a culture prone to cat-napping. Other popular activities include movie nights, hanging out at the coffeehouse, and using open studio space for ceramics and sculpture. The annual Wagnerstock festivities bring barbecues, bands, and booths. With only 20 percent Greek participation, it's up to the "theater people" to throw the risqué theme parties, like "Schoolgirls and Professors." Most students report that they love the Wag's acceptance of diverse groups. "It's a melting pot next to the biggest melting pot of them all—NYC." Students at Wagner are the first to admit they love to gripe when opportunity presents itself, but underneath the East Coast attitude, they admit, "We're spoiled here."

Student Body

Pull a Wagner student from the crowd and you'll typically find wrinkled clothes, flip flops, and dark circles under the eyes. A senior psychology major sees everyone as "White, young, and skinny." Others are quick to note that there is no typical Wagner student: "Everyone here is an individual—and not in a weird way." A vocal percentage of Wagner kids "dream of making it on Broadway," and this show-tune-humming theater contingent does feel some animosity from the jocks. "Ultimately, they all get along pretty well. Just don't ask different categories to sit together in the dining hall." Single straight women complain about "a really low ratio of guys to girls" and the fact that "a lot of the guys here are gay." A small-town transplant writes, "Wagner has really opened my eyes to the issues facing the homosexual community." The college's "commitment to teaching us to accept diversity" seems to be working.

FINANCIAL AID: 718-390-3183 • E-MAIL: ADMISSIONS@WAGNER.EDU • WEBSITE: WWW.WAGNER.EDU

ADMISSIONS

Very important factors considered include: Academic GPA, class rank, rigor of secondary school record, standardized test scores. *Important factors considered include:* Application essay, extracurricular activities, interview, recommendation(s). *Other factors considered include:* Character/personal qualities, level of applicant's interest, talent/ability, volunteer work, work experience. SAT or ACT required; TOEFL required of all international applicants. High school diploma is required, and GED is accepted. *Academic units required:* 4 English, 3 math, 2 science (1 science lab), 2 foreign language, 1 social studies, 3 history, 6 academic electives.

The Inside Word

Wagner has profited in recent years from a renewed interest in urban colleges. In other words, don't take the application process too lightly. Applicants are met with a college Admissions Staff dedicated to finding the right students for their school. Wagner's pioneering efforts in experiential learning for all students make its recent resurgence well earned.

FINANCIAL AID

Students should submit: FAFSA, institution's own financial aid form. The Princeton Review suggests that all financial aid forms be submitted as soon as possible after January 1. *Need-based scholarships/grants offered:* Pell Grant, SEOG, state scholarships/grants, private scholarships, the school's own gift aid. *Loan aid offered:* FFEL Subsidized Stafford, FFEL Unsubsidized Stafford, FFEL PLUS, Federal Perkins Loan, Federal Nursing Loan. Applicants will be notified of awards on or about March 1.

FROM THE ADMISSIONS OFFICE

"At Wagner College, we attract and develop active learners and future leaders. Wagner College has received national acclaim (*Time* magazine, American Association of Colleges and Universities) for its innovative curriculum, The Wagner Plan for the Practical Liberal Arts. At Wagner, we capitalize on our unique geography; we are a traditional, scenic, residential campus, which happens to sit atop a hill on an island overlooking lower Manhattan. Our location allows us to offer a program that couples required off-campus experiences (experiential learning), with 'learning community' clusters of courses. This program begins in the first semester and continues through the senior capstone experience in the major. Fieldwork and internships, writing-intensive reflective tutorials, connected learning, 'reading, writing, and doing': At Wagner College our students truly discover 'the practical liberal arts in New York City.'

"Applicants for Fall 2008 are required to take the current version of the SAT, or the ACT with the Writing section."

SELECTIVITY

Admissions Rating	88
# of applicants	2,862
% of applicants accepted	59
% of acceptees attending	32
# accepting a place on wait list	85
% admitted from wait list	11
# of early decision applicants	130
% accepted early decision	50

FRESHMAN PROFILE

Range SAT Critical Reading	540–640
Range SAT Math	540–640
Range SAT Writing	520–630
Range ACT Composite	24–27
Minimum Paper TOEFL	550
Minimum Computer Based TOEFL	217
Average HS GPA	3.52
% graduated top 10% of class	18
% graduated top 25% of class	69
% graduated top 50% of class	92

DEADLINES

Early decision application deadline	1/1
Early decision notification	1/15
Regular application deadline	2/15
Regular notification	3/1
Nonfall registration?	yes

APPLICANTS ALSO LOOK AT

AND OFTEN PREFER
Fairfield University, New York University

AND SOMETIMES PREFER
Drew University, Fordham University, Hobart and William Smith Colleges, Muhlenberg College

AND RARELY PREFER
Manhattan College, Marist College, Quinnipiac University

FINANCIAL FACTS

Financial Aid Rating	82
Annual tuition	$29,400
Room & Board	$8,900
Books and supplies	$701
% frosh rec. need-based scholarship or grant aid	69
% UG rec. need-based scholarship or grant aid	52
% frosh rec. need-based self-help aid	44
% UG rec. need-based self-help aid	40
% frosh rec. any financial aid	95
% UG rec. any financial aid	89

WAKE FOREST UNIVERSITY

Box 7305, Reynolda Station, Winston-Salem, NC 27109 • Admissions: 336-758-5201 • Fax: 336-758-4324

CAMPUS LIFE

Quality of Life Rating	76
Fire Safety Rating	88
Type of school	private
Environment	city

STUDENTS

Total undergrad enrollment	4,313
% male/female	49/51
% from out of state	74
% from public high school	65
% live on campus	70
% in (# of) fraternities	34 (14)
% in (# of) sororities	50 (9)
% African American	6
% Asian	5
% Caucasian	84
% Hispanic	2
% Native American	1
% international	1

SURVEY SAYS . . .

Small classes
Great computer facilities
Great library
Everyone loves the Demon Deacons
Frats and sororities dominate social scene
Lots of beer drinking
Hard liquor is popular

ACADEMICS

Academic Rating	90
Calendar	semester
Student/faculty ratio	10:1
Profs interesting rating	85
Profs accessible rating	85
% profs teaching UG courses	100
% classes taught by TAs	0
Most common lab size	10–19 students
Most common reg class size	10–19 students

MOST POPULAR MAJORS

business administration/management
communications studies/speech communication and rhetoric
political science and government

STUDENTS SAY

Academics

"Our nickname, 'Work Forest,' applies," caution undergraduates at Wake Forest University, a private school that offers "the perfect combination of small college atmosphere with big university opportunities." "You have to put a lot of effort into your work" in this "tough atmosphere" where "The BS-ing that got you A's in high school will get you a C-minus at the most." Students agree, however, that although the workload is "sometimes excessive," it's worth it for the "incredible academic experience" and the "tremendous opportunities" it creates for a student body "anxious to get ahead in the world." Technology is another of the school's strengths; at Wake, "Each student is given a computer and printer at the beginning of their freshman and junior years, and technology aides are available in every dorm to assist students [with] computer or network problems." As for the workload, many here say it's tough but manageable and point out that "the administration and professors are accessible and willing to talk through difficult assignments or reevaluate things when given the students' perspectives." One undergrad sums it up perfectly: "Though everyone will find something to complain about, the truth is that Wake is amazing. Everyone has school spirit, everyone cares about the school, the professors care about the students, the campus is drop-dead gorgeous, and the people are just mad cool."

Life

"Frat parties are wildly popular" at Wake Forest; they occur "both on and off campus," and "are open to everyone." You "can find a party that serves alcohol pretty much any night of the week," although most students are too busy with schoolwork to maintain that type of social schedule. "When Wake students aren't partying or studying, sports are huge," as "Everyone goes out to football and basketball games. Intramurals are also very popular and some (such as flag football) are extremely competitive." Students are split over the appeal of Winston-Salem. Naysayers, who are in the majority, complain that "there isn't much to do in Winston-Salem other than the usual: mall, movies, clubs, and on-campus events. Most students aren't culturally interested in the activities that Winston-Salem has to offer. The town isn't for teenagers but for families." These students also feel that "it's unfortunate that the school is located in a residential area with no easily accessible commercial districts." Others insist that "Winston-Salem is a gold mine of opportunities . . . film festivals, art shows, theater performances, a great mall. Wake students always complain about Winston-Salem, but there is plenty of fun stuff to do if you look for it. And the downtown [area] is absolutely gorgeous." Quaint Reynolda Village, which is within walking distance of campus, offers some upscale shopping as well as an art museum.

Student Body

Wake has earned its reputation as a preppy haven; most students here seem to be "skinny, White, and conservative in [their] political views. They wear polos with popped collars—Vera Bradley bags, Sperry's, etc. roam the campus." One student observes, "Wake Forest can change your fashion style or habits because of the lack of variety. When I say 'variety' I don't mean the different colors of Ralph Lauren Polos." There is, however, "a growing and vocal liberal population." Left-leaning subgroups, "such as the gay and lesbian population, which is not only growing but finding better acceptance here," are expanding. There is even "a little more variety with respect to body shapes," and not everyone is rail thin on campus anymore. Racial minorities, however, "are still few and far between." Wake is home to "a small, very committed Christian population," but "most students are still sleeping in on Sunday mornings. Wake has a struck a strange balance between its Baptist heritage and the increasingly secular culture."

WAKE FOREST UNIVERSITY

FINANCIAL AID: 336-758-5154 • E-MAIL: ADMISSIONS@WFU.EDU • WEBSITE: WWW.WFU.EDU

ADMISSIONS

Very important factors considered include: Academic GPA, application essay, character/personal qualities, class rank, rigor of secondary school record, standardized test scores. *Important factors considered include:* Extracurricular activities, recommendation(s), talent/ability. *Other factors considered include:* Alumni/ae relation, first generation, geographical residence, interview, level of applicant's interest, racial/ethnic status, religious affiliation/commitment, state residency, volunteer work. SAT or ACT required; ACT with Writing component required. TOEFL required of all international applicants. High school diploma is required, and GED is accepted. *Academic units required:* 4 English, 3 math, 1 science, 2 foreign language, 2 social studies. *Academic units recommended:* 4 English, 4 math, 4 science, 4 foreign language, 4 social studies.

The Inside Word

Wake Forest's considerable application numbers afford Admissions Officers the opportunity to be rather selective. In particular, Admissions Officers remain diligent in their matchmaking efforts—finding students who are good fits for the school—and their hard work is rewarded by a high yield rate. Candidates will need to be impressive in all areas to gain admission, since all areas of their applications are considered carefully. A relatively large number of qualified students find themselves on Wake Forest's wait list.

FINANCIAL AID

Students should submit: FAFSA, CSS/Financial Aid PROFILE, Noncustodial PROFILE, state aid form. Regular filing deadline is March 1. The Princeton Review suggests that all financial aid forms be submitted as soon as possible after January 1. *Need-based scholarships/grants offered:* Pell Grant, SEOG, state scholarships/grants, private scholarships, the school's own gift aid. *Loan aid offered:* FFEL Subsidized Stafford, FFEL Unsubsidized Stafford, FFEL PLUS, Federal Perkins Loan, state loans, college/university loans from institutional funds, private alternative loans. Applicants will be notified of awards on or about April 1.

FROM THE ADMISSIONS OFFICE

"Wake Forest University has been dedicated to the liberal arts for over a century and a half; this means education in the fundamental fields of human knowledge and achievement. It seeks to encourage habits of mind that ask why, that evaluate evidence, that are open to new ideas, that attempt to understand and appreciate the perspective of others, that accept complexity and grapple with it, that admit error, and that pursue truth.

"Wake Forest is among a small, elite group of American colleges and universities recognized for their outstanding academic quality. It offers small classes taught by full-time faculty—not graduate assistants—and a commitment to student interaction with those professors. Students are provided ThinkPad computers and color printer/scanner/copiers. Classrooms and residence halls are fully networked. Wake Forest maintains a need-blind admissions policy by which qualified students are admitted regardless of their financial circumstances.

"Applicants for Fall 2008 are required to submit scores from the SAT Reasoning Test and/or the ACT plus Writing. SAT Subject Tests are strongly recommended for students planning to apply for merit-based scholarships."

SELECTIVITY
Admissions Rating	95
# of applicants	7,341
% of applicants accepted	43
% of acceptees attending	36
# of early decision applicants	719
% accepted early decision	43

FRESHMAN PROFILE
Range SAT Critical Reading	690–610
Range SAT Math	710–710
Minimum Paper TOEFL	600
Minimum Computer Based TOEFL	250
% graduated top 10% of class	62
% graduated top 25% of class	88
% graduated top 50% of class	98

DEADLINES
Early decision application deadline	11/15
Early decision notification	12/15
Regular application deadline	1/15
Regular notification	4/1
Nonfall registration?	yes

APPLICANTS ALSO LOOK AT AND SOMETIMES PREFER
Duke University, The University of North Carolina at Chapel Hill, University of Virginia, Vanderbilt University

FINANCIAL FACTS
Financial Aid Rating	81
Annual tuition	$32,040
Room & Board	$8,800
Books and supplies	$850
Required fees	$100
% frosh rec. need-based scholarship or grant aid	37
% UG rec. need-based scholarship or grant aid	33
% frosh rec. need-based self-help aid	27
% UG rec. need-based self-help aid	28

WARREN WILSON COLLEGE

PO Box 9000, Asheville, NC 28815-9000 • Admissions: 828-771-2073 • Fax: 828-298-1440

STUDENTS SAY

Academics

The centerpiece of a Warren Wilson education is the Triad program, which "integrates work, service, and academics" by requiring all students to complete "15 hours of work every week on campus" and "100 hours of service before graduation" in addition to their course work. The goal is "to create students who look at the big picture, and see that there is a world outside of themselves." Students say it generally works: "Integrating work, service, and academics seems to bring about some sort of personal utopia," declares one undergrad. The work opportunities arise from the 1,100-acre campus, which includes a farm; students learn "blacksmithing, cooking, farming, being a writing tutor, maintaining the trails, and painting," but must also "be prepared to scrub toilets or wash dishes in the dining hall." One undergrad jokes, "WWC really stands for 'We Work Constantly.'" WWC's best academic programs piggyback on the Triad concept. "Programs in environmental education and sustainable agriculture are excellent," and "In science labs it's great to be able to walk outside and explore the campus or take a hike and find 90 percent of the plants and animals you were talking about in class." It's not all agriculture and technology, though; students tell us that "creative writing is an important program here." As is the case at many small schools, "Teachers are more than willing to meet you outside of class. They understand we have a life outside of the classroom, and they are willing to set up times to meet with you." Students appreciate the fact that their professors "are paid to teach. The school couldn't care less if they ever write a book. And there are no TAs."

Life

"Because of the work program, time is not as abundant here as it may be at other schools," WWC undergrads caution. The workload is substantial, as undergrads "run the campus. We do the landscaping, the cooking, the cleaning, the bike repair, the building, the gardening, and the farming. You can't be lazy here." Undergrads still manage to carve enough time out of their schedules to enjoy "excellent programs and activities such as fencing, dancing, climbing, hiking, camping, kayaking, herbal classes, and cooking." One student writes, "Many students have a surprisingly good-natured interest in dorky things like bird watching, contra dancing, and pot-lucks, a unanimous love of tubing down a flooded river," and "walking around the trails here and taking advantage of the campus beauty." As one student puts it, "When you first see the campus nestled in the mountains with the cows grazing in the field, it takes your breath away." Two times a year WWC throws a 'Bubba,' a party "held in a cow pasture and chaperoned by faculty and staff. There are t-shirt sales to fund the kegs and nonalcoholic treats and refreshments for underage partygoers. It all centers around a big bonfire where 150 or so people stand around, talking, laughing, and generally have a good time." Nearby Asheville "is pretty awesome" for the occasional escape from campus. Some even consider it "the Paris of the mountains, with plenty of things to do downtown."

Student Body

The typical WWC undergrad "likes good organic wholesome food, a good local brew and bluegrass on a starry night, is health conscious but smokes hand-rolled cigarettes, dresses in work clothes but accessorizes, recycles, doesn't watch TV, and knows some botanical-ornithological basics." To put it more simply: "This place is a haven for hippies and very left-wing people." Other types pepper the student body, including "surfers, farmers, and punks, some people with dreadlocks, others with dyed hair. A small portion of the population has facial piercings and tattoos." But overall, "People here are just like people anywhere else. Yeah, there are the hippies, but just like any school there are a wide variety of personalities. If you are interested in this school in the first place, chances are you will fit right in."

FINANCIAL AID: 828-298-3325 • E-MAIL: ADMIT@WARREN-WILSON.EDU • WEBSITE: WWW.WARREN-WILSON.EDU

ADMISSIONS

Very important factors considered include: Application essay, character/personal qualities, interview, rigor of secondary school record, standardized test scores, volunteer work, work experience. *Important factors considered include:* Class rank, recommendation(s). *Other factors considered include:* Alumni/ae relation, extracurricular activities, state residency, talent/ability. SAT or ACT required; TOEFL required of all international applicants. High school diploma is required, and GED is accepted. *Academic units required:* 4 English, 3 math, 2 science (2 science labs), 3 history. *Academic units recommended:* 2 foreign language.

The Inside Word

At Warren Wilson College, one's sense of social commitment is as vital to the admissions process as one's high school transcript—the college desires students who are actively engaged in their communities. Admissions Officers are interested in applicants who seek to make connections and understand how to apply what they learn in the classroom to outside projects and activities.

FINANCIAL AID

Students should submit: FAFSA, institution's own financial aid form. The Princeton Review suggests that all financial aid forms be submitted as soon as possible after January 1. *Need-based scholarships/grants offered:* Pell Grant, SEOG, state scholarships/grants, private scholarships, the school's own gift aid. *Loan aid offered:* FFEL Subsidized Stafford, FFEL Unsubsidized Stafford, FFEL PLUS, Federal Perkins Loan, college/university loans from institutional funds. Applicants will be notified of awards on a rolling basis beginning or about March 2.

FROM THE ADMISSIONS OFFICE

"This book is *The Best 366 Colleges*, but Warren Wilson College may not be the best college for many students. There are 3,500 colleges in the U.S., and there is a best place for everyone. The 'best college' is one that has the right size, location, programs, and above all, the right feel for you, even if it is not listed here. Warren Wilson College may be the best choice if you think and act independently, actively participate in your education, and want a college that provides a sense of community. Your hands will get dirty here, your mind will be stretched, and you'll not be anonymous. If you are looking for the traditional college experience with football and frats and a campus-on-a-quad, this probably is not the right place. However, if you want to be a part of an academic community that works and serves together, this might be exactly what you are looking for.

"Students applying for Fall admission should provide results of the SAT or ACT."

SELECTIVITY

Admissions Rating	**80**
# of applicants	840
% of applicants accepted	74
% of acceptees attending	36
# of early decision applicants	58
% accepted early decision	83

FRESHMAN PROFILE

Range SAT Critical Reading	550–670
Range SAT Math	510–620
Range SAT Writing	530–630
Range ACT Composite	22–27
Minimum Paper TOEFL	550
Average HS GPA	3.45
% graduated top 10% of class	18
% graduated top 25% of class	35
% graduated top 50% of class	78

DEADLINES

Early decision application deadline	11/15
Regular application deadline	2/28
Regular notification	2/1
Nonfall registration?	yes

APPLICANTS ALSO LOOK AT

AND OFTEN PREFER
Earlham College

AND SOMETIMES PREFER
The Evergreen State College

AND RARELY PREFER
Antioch College, Arizona State University at the Tempe Campus, Guilford College

FINANCIAL FACTS

Financial Aid Rating	**73**
Annual tuition	$21,384
Room & Board	$6,700
Books and supplies	$870
Required fees	$300
% frosh rec. need-based scholarship or grant aid	45
% UG rec. need-based scholarship or grant aid	43
% frosh rec. need-based self-help aid	49
% UG rec. need-based self-help aid	50

WASHINGTON COLLEGE

300 WASHINGTON AVENUE, CHESTERTOWN, MD 21620 • ADMISSIONS: 410-778-7700 • FAX: 410-778-7287

STUDENTS SAY

Academics

Students say that "individualized attention" is the greatest strength of Chestertown, Maryland's Washington College (WC). The small size of this liberal arts school "allows everyone, including professors and the administration, to get to know [students] both inside and outside of the classroom." WC places a strong emphasis on writing and literature and has a well-respected creative writing program; every year, the school awards the Sophie Kerr Prize to one graduating senior. According to the school's website, the honor is "the largest undergraduate prize in the nation. Last year's prize was worth over $60,000." Students rave about WC's Rose O'Neill Literary House, a Victorian home that serves as the hub of the school's literary activities. Undergrads also applaud WC's "great psych program [and] excellent record of placement into medical schools," and they appreciate the academic freedom that the small school allows them. "You can develop and design your own major and independent research projects, from biology to drama to sociology," one student explains. Furthermore, "The professors are amazing; there is plenty of opportunity to meet with them and to further discuss any issues in class. They are wonderful at helping students advance their careers in their chosen fields. Often they take their students' research to conferences and seminars." The administration is described as "fairly accessible." One student says, "Sometimes, it would be helpful if they allowed students to have more of a voice in school decisions."

Life

Students describe Chestertown as "rural, small, quaint, and beautiful." The town features "one movie theater and two pizza places. You have to make your own entertainment. For a lot of students, this means drinking a lot, but the more creative kids find other ways to keep themselves busy." Students who crave urban entertainment take road trips. "It is an hour and a half drive to Washington, DC and Philadelphia. Annapolis and Baltimore are nearby (an hour or so), as are Newark and Dover (both in Delaware)." Students who choose to stay on and around campus enjoy "watching plays, working out in the gym, swimming, or playing games in the student center. Musicians or comedians come every now and then, and the school invites many speakers, including famous figures such as Howard Dean, Robert Novak, and James Carville." Many students "take advantage of WC's rural surroundings by either taking part in water sports on the river, horseback riding, biking, or just exploring backcountry roads." Students also "party at off-campus houses or at dorms," but they don't necessarily classify WC as a party school. One undergrad explains, "There aren't many big, raging parties on a regular basis, but there are preplanned events that get rather large."

Student Body

WC students are "driven to succeed but know how to relax and have fun." The bulk of the student body "appears to be White, upper-middle-class jocks, Greeks, and yuppies in training," one student says, "but there is a good-sized underground with diverse interests from diverse backgrounds." Another student contributes, "We have several individuals on campus who are not very traditional in their choice of dress or behavior, but I don't believe that they're treated any differently because of it." Many students complain that the school lacks ethnic diversity, but other students point out that "a significant percentage of the student population is international, including a number of students from Japan." WC's gay community "is able to be extremely open about their preferences and no one really bothers them." One student adds, "Since WC is a liberal arts college, there is an easy mix of different types of students. All of the groups easily intermingle and are friendly across campus. It is a very genuine and pleasant mix of students."

FINANCIAL AID: 410-778-7214 • WEBSITE: HTTP://ADMISSIONS.WASHCOLL.EDU

ADMISSIONS

Very important factors considered include: Academic GPA, interview, rigor of secondary school record. *Important factors considered include:* Class rank, level of applicant's interest, standardized test scores. *Other factors considered include:* Alumni/ae relation, application essay, character/personal qualities, extracurricular activities, first generation, geographical residence, racial/ethnic status, recommendation(s), state residency, talent/ability, volunteer work, work experience. SAT or ACT required. High school diploma is required, and GED is accepted. *Academic units required:* 4 English, 3 math, 3 science (2 science labs), 2 foreign language, 2 social studies. *Academic units recommended:* 4 English, 4 math, 4 science (3 science labs), 4 foreign language, 4 social studies.

The Inside Word

Though Washington's acceptance rate hovers just under 60 percent, the statistic belies the competitive nature of the applicants. Prospective students who view WC as one of their top choices should do themselves a favor and complete their application ahead of the prescribed deadline. Preference is granted to those who submit by February 1. Interviews are also highly recommended and those who decline the opportunity will be putting themselves at a disadvantage.

FINANCIAL AID

Students should submit: FAFSA, institution's own financial aid form. The Princeton Review suggests that all financial aid forms be submitted as soon as possible after January 1. *Need-based scholarships/grants offered:* Pell, SEOG, state scholarships/grants, private scholarships, the school's own gift aid. *Loan aid offered:* FFEL Subsidized Stafford, FFEL Unsubsidized Stafford, FFEL PLUS, Federal Perkins, college/university loans from institutional funds. Applicants will be notified of awards on a rolling basis beginning or about March 15. Federal Work-Study Program available. Institutional employment available. Off-campus job opportunities are good.

FROM THE ADMISSIONS OFFICE

"We tell our students, 'Your revolution starts here,' because the person who graduates from Washington College is not the same one who matriculated 4 years earlier, and because through your experiences here, you will be empowered and emboldened to change the world. Your education reflects the maxims of our founder, George Washington: The strength of America's democracy depends on the success of students like you to evolve as a critical and independent thinker, to persevere in the face of challenge, to assume the responsibilities and privileges of informed citizenship. That's where we come in, providing a truly personalized education that tests—and stretches—the limits of each student's talents and potentials. We reach beyond the classroom to create challenges and opportunities that expand your brainpower and creativity through collaborative research with faculty, through independent and self-directed study, and through the rigor of creating a senior project that demonstrates the power of a maturing intellect. All this happens in a wonderfully distinct setting—in historic Chestertown, on the Chester River, amid the ecological bounty of Maryland's Chesapeake Bay—that helps define who we are and that will shape your own college experience.

"Washington College requires either SAT or ACT scores. There is no minimum SAT/ACT cut-off score for admission. However, the middle 50 percent of accepted applicants have SAT scores in the 1050 to 1250 range. The average SAT (Critical Reading and Math) score for enrolled freshmen is 1150 (24 for ACT)."

SELECTIVITY

Admissions Rating	**87**
# of applicants	2,134
% of applicants accepted	60
% of acceptees attending	25
# accepting a place on wait list	235
% admitted from wait list	15
# of early decision applicants	41
% accepted early decision	80

FRESHMAN PROFILE

Range SAT Critical Reading	510-620
Range SAT Math	510-610
Range SAT Writing	520-610
Range ACT Composite	20-25
Average HS GPA	3.40
% graduated top 10% of class	37
% graduated top 25% of class	70
% graduated top 50% of class	94

DEADLINES

Early decision application deadline	11/15
Early decision notification	12/15
Regular application deadline	3/1
Regular notification	rolling
Nonfall registration?	yes

FINANCIAL FACTS

Financial Aid Rating	**90**
Annual tuition	$31,570
Room & Board	$6,790
Required fees	$590
% frosh rec. need-based scholarship or grant aid	36
% UG rec. need-based scholarship or grant aid	43
% frosh rec. need-based self-help aid	27
% UG rec. need-based self-help aid	32
% frosh rec. any financial aid	79
% UG rec. any financial aid	85

WASHINGTON & JEFFERSON COLLEGE

OFFICE OF ADMISSIONS, 60 SOUTH LINCOLN STREET, WASHINGTON, PA 15301 • ADMISSIONS: 888-W-AND-JAY OR 724-223-6025

CAMPUS LIFE

Quality of Life Rating	70
Fire Safety Rating	90
Type of school	private
Environment	village

STUDENTS

Total undergrad enrollment	1,505
% male/female	54/46
% from out of state	25
% from public high school	80
% live on campus	88
% in (# of) fraternities	32 (6)
% in (# of) sororities	42 (4)
% African American	3
% Asian	1
% Caucasian	88
% Hispanic	1

SURVEY SAYS . . .

Small classes
Great computer facilities
Everyone loves the Presidents
Frats and sororities dominate social scene
Lots of beer drinking
Hard liquor is popular

ACADEMICS

Academic Rating	84
Calendar	4-1-4
Student/faculty ratio	12:1
Profs interesting rating	81
Profs accessible rating	85
% profs teaching UG courses	100
% classes taught by TAs	0
Most common lab size	10-19 students
Most common reg class size	10-19 students

MOST POPULAR MAJORS

biology/biological sciences
business administration/
management
English language and literature

STUDENTS SAY

Academics

"High academic standards" and small class sizes, coupled with a student body made up of individuals "very serious about their education" leads to a lot of hard work and accountability for the undergrads of Washington & Jefferson College. While many choose the college for its strong programs in the sciences and the liberal arts, every major at W&J is reportedly difficult. The college's friendly professors, administrators, and staff, however, do their best to help students to succeed and "make you feel as comfy as possible." Despite the heavy workload, students describe W&J as a "fun, challenging, and nurturing environment" where students are truly mentored and supported by the faculty and staff. As one freshman writes, "The professors are amazing. They are always there whenever you are struggling, confused, or just want to talk. Even the administration is available to chat!" While the quality of the academic program is undisputed, some students gripe about the high costs of this private school. In particular, students tell us that "the Financial Aid Department needs some work." Commenting on this state of affairs, a freshman jokes that the college might consider changing its motto to "providing the best education possible for the most amount of money."

Life

When considering student life at W&J, a junior offers this 1980s analogy: "It's like a mullet: business in the front, party in the back." Indeed, students say that W&J is the place to go for both a "good education and a good time," as the friendly student body is as social as it is studious. On campus, "People are busy with sports, clubs, and fraternities/sororities"; athletics are also particularly popular with students. A sophomore writes, "Our school is all about education . . . and after education comes sports." During the weekend, the W&J campus comes alive with parties. "After a hard week of stressful classes, most of the people here drink," writes a student. However, undergraduates reassure us that there are "no crazy state school–style parties" at W&J, and most students prioritize books over booze. As one sophomore reports, "I like to drink and party on the weekends, but get my homework done during the week." Whether you like the W&J social life or not, you're stuck with it, as undergraduates are required to live on campus.

Student Body

On the whole, this small campus is home to "nice, studious, involved, and athletic" undergrads, most of whom take their education very seriously. Almost all students claim to be "hard workers" and generally describe their classmates as intelligent and motivated, but the similarities don't end there. A junior reports that "everyone is pretty typical—White, upper-middle-class American. We have very few minorities." Another confesses, "The majority of students are cookie-cutter images of each other. There is very little individuality on this campus." Even so, students claim that their classmates are generally accepting and friendly, even if there are very few students who don't fit in. A junior writes, "Everyone gets along no matter what they look like; a benefit to a small campus." In fact, students insist that W&J, "works like a small community; everyone helps everyone."

WASHINGTON & JEFFERSON COLLEGE

FAX : 724-223-6534 • FINANCIAL AID: 724-223-6019 • E-MAIL: ADMISSION@WASHJEFF.EDU • WEBSITE: WWW.WASHJEFF.EDU

ADMISSIONS

Very important factors considered include: Academic GPA, application essay, class rank, interview, recommendation(s), rigor of secondary school record. *Important factors considered include:* Character/personal qualities, extracurricular activities, standardized test scores. *Other factors considered include:* Alumni/ae relation, geographical residence, level of applicant's interest, racial/ethnic status, state residency, talent/ability, volunteer work. SAT or ACT required; TOEFL required of all international applicants. High school diploma is required, and GED is accepted. *Academic units required:* 3 English, 3 math, 1 science, 2 foreign language, 6 academic electives.

The Inside Word

In a reflection of the students they aim to admit, Washington & Jefferson College takes a well-rounded approach to admissions. Academic record, class rank, personal statement, and extracurricular activities are all thoroughly evaluated. Most prospective students work diligently to secure admittance. The lucky applicants who receive a fat letter in the mail are welcomed into a distinctive community that promises to broaden their horizons and prepare them for a successful future.

FINANCIAL AID

Students should submit: FAFSA. The Princeton Review suggests that all financial aid forms be submitted as soon as possible after January 1. *Need-based scholarships/grants offered:* Pell, SEOG, state scholarships/grants, private scholarships, the school's own gift aid, Academic Competitiveness Grant and National SMART Grant. *Loan aid offered:* FFEL Subsidized Stafford, FFEL Unsubsidized Stafford, FFEL PLUS, Federal Perkins, college/university loans from institutional funds. Applicants will be notified of awards on a rolling basis beginning or about March 1.

FROM THE ADMISSIONS OFFICE

"There is a palpable sense of momentum and energy at Washington & Jefferson. Enrollment has grown significantly over the past 5 years. Additional faculty members have been hired, and academic programs have been added and expanded to accommodate the increased enrollment. The student-centered teaching and learning community that has always distinguished W&J remains our top priority. It is no surprise that 100 percent of our graduates who took the bar exam passed in 2006, or that 90 percent of our graduates recommended for medical and law school are admitted. The college has added almost $75 million dollars in new facilities since 2002, including two new residence halls, ten theme-based residential houses, new athletic facilities, a state-of-the-art technology center, and the Howard J. Burnett Center, which houses our programs in accounting, business, economics, education, entrepreneurial studies, and modern languages. Construction on a new $30 million science facility is scheduled to begin within the next 2 years. Despite an almost fourfold increase in applications in this time, the Admission Staff remains committed to reviewing each application individually. Our students are balanced, goal oriented, active, engaged and involved and we look for evidence of these traits in prospective students. We encourage students to use every aspect of the application process to demonstrate that they possess these qualities. If you are looking to become part of an institution that is constantly changing for the better and that will be an even better place by the time you graduate, then we encourage you to consider W&J.

"Students applying for Fall 2008 must submit scores from the SAT (or ACT). It is not required that they take the new version of the SAT (or the ACT with the Writing section). We will allow students to submit scores from either version of the SAT (or ACT) and will use the student's best scores from either test."

SELECTIVITY

Admissions Rating	**89**
# of applicants	5,591
% of applicants accepted	36
% of acceptees attending	22
# accepting a place on wait list	35
% admitted from wait list	23

FRESHMAN PROFILE

Range SAT Critical Reading	500-600
Range SAT Math	520-620
Range ACT Composite	22-26
Minimum Paper TOEFL	500
Minimum Computer Based TOEFL	267
Average HS GPA	3.36
% graduated top 10% of class	30
% graduated top 25% of class	65
% graduated top 50% of class	94

DEADLINES

Early decision application deadline	12/1
Early decision notification	12/15
Regular application deadline	3/1
Regular notification	rolling
Nonfall registration?	yes

FINANCIAL FACTS

Financial Aid Rating	**71**
Annual tuition	$27,680
Room & Board	$7,602
Books and supplies	$800
Required Fees	$400
% frosh rec. need-based scholarship or grant aid	67
% UG rec. need-based scholarship or grant aid	62
% frosh rec. need-based self-help aid	69
% UG rec. need-based self-help aid	63
% frosh rec. any financial aid	99
% UG rec. any financial aid	96

WASHINGTON AND LEE UNIVERSITY

LETCHER AVENUE, LEXINGTON, VA 24450-0303 • ADMISSIONS: 540-458-8710 • FAX: 540-458-8062

STUDENTS SAY

Academics

Students tell us that Washington and Lee offers "the best conservative liberal arts education money can buy," highlighting two qualities that have long defined the W&L experience: conservatism and money. The school is no mere holding pen for the trust-fund set; on the contrary, more than half the school's graduates find careers in business and management or law, placing them among the world's active movers and shakers. Students here endure "a rigorous academic environment" with "absolutely no grade inflation." The curriculum includes "a very strict general education requirement that gives a broad-based liberal arts education, so that our degree is held in high regard." An "extensive and active" alumni network is just one of the payoffs for enduring the grind; close student-faculty relations, which allow one student to brag: "I've got 15 [professors] I could call on to write me personal recommendations for grad school," is another. Undergrads love the honor code because it "really creates a close-knit community." A more cynical sophomore quips, "You can leave your laptop lying around and no one will steal it . . . maybe it's because of the honor code . . . maybe [it's] because everyone has his own." Standout programs here include journalism, premed, and the aforementioned business and management.

Life

"Work hard, party hard" is more than a cliché at Washington and Lee. Students take their schoolwork very seriously here, but, once the books are packed away, they are ready to cut loose. Undergrads tell us that, at W&L, "There is never a dead night. Never." Most students gravitate toward the "huge frat parties" with "each frat trying to outdo the other" for "the recruitment of freshmen males." These parties all provide free alcohol. Those who don't drink report that "activities are limited." The Student Activities Organization "sponsors alternative events and activities" such as intramural sports, "but many of the games get cancelled because of teams forfeiting" (due to an insufficient number of players, we assume). Still, "Movie and game night in the commons area is really enjoyable, as well as the few parties that advertise to not serve alcohol (very under-attended, but still fun)." Hometown Lexington offers little relief, as, after dark, "The entire town literally shuts down and Domino's is the only source of night food other than the school cafe." Outdoors lovers, take note: The W&L campus is "beautiful, summer and winter, and is a wonderful environment to work in." "On a nice spring afternoon, students can be found sunning on the Colonnade, tubing the Maury River, or sitting out on the rocks at Goshen. We'll hike House Mountain or go fly fishing on any of the rivers around us."

Student Body

The "country-club Southerner" has long been the poster student for Washington and Lee, and students tell us that the image still reigns supreme. Here, the typical girl "is gorgeous with nice hair (often blonde), good skin, in shape (everyone here works out a lot), and always dressed nicely. Pearls, skirts, sundresses, and bright colors dominate. And guys, they are the typical frat guys: shaggy hair, baseball caps, khaki shorts, polos, Rainbows." The typical student also "has little or no financial burden and can pay for our tuition without financial aid." Yet there are also "strong and growing minority populations and an ongoing dialogue about ways to diversify the school." One student observes, "This school is making a very visible effort to be seen as a 'school located in the South' and not a 'Southern school.' And, honestly, outside of the pastels and it being a little more conservative/religious than your average elite liberal arts college, it really isn't that distinctively Southern." Atypical students, though "highly recognizable when seen mostly due to the nonconformist clothing they wear," still "fit in because small class size[s] and the overall small campus size promote interaction."

FINANCIAL AID: 540-463-8715 • E-MAIL: ADMISSIONS@WLU.EDU • WEBSITE: WWW.WLU.EDU

ADMISSIONS

Very important factors considered include: Character/personal qualities, class rank, extracurricular activities, rigor of secondary school record, standardized test scores. *Important factors considered include:* Interview, recommendation(s). *Other factors considered include:* Alumni/ae relation, application essay, geographical residence, racial/ethnic status, state residency, talent/ability, volunteer work, work experience. SAT or ACT required; SAT Subject Tests required. TOEFL required of all international applicants. High school diploma or equivalent is not required. *Academic units required:* 4 English, 3 math, 1 science (1 science lab), 3 foreign language, 1 social studies, 1 history, 4 academic electives. *Academic units recommended:* 4 math, 3 science, 4 foreign language, 2 history.

The Inside Word

Washington and Lee offers two separate rounds of early decision: A November 15 deadline with a December 22 notification and a January 21 deadline with an February 1 notification. Note that early decision acceptance is binding; if accepted, you will be expected to withdraw all other applications. The upside here is that the school is more lenient in assessing borderline applications during the early decision process.

FINANCIAL AID

Students should submit: FAFSA, CSS/Financial Aid PROFILE, Noncustodial PROFILE, Business/Farm Supplement. Regular filing deadline is February 9. The Princeton Review suggests that all financial aid forms be submitted as soon as possible after January 1. *Need-based scholarships/grants offered:* Pell Grant, SEOG, state scholarships/grants, private scholarships, the school's own gift aid. *Loan aid offered:* FFEL Subsidized Stafford, FFEL Unsubsidized Stafford, FFEL PLUS, Federal Perkins Loan, college/university loans from institutional funds. Applicants will be notified of awards on or about April 6. Federal Work-Study Program available. Institutional employment available. Off-campus job opportunities are fair.

FROM THE ADMISSIONS OFFICE

"Washington and Lee University is a small, private, liberal arts institution located in the beautiful Shenandoah Valley, in Lexington, Virginia. The nation's ninth-oldest university, W&L has been touched and shaped by major men, women, and moments in U.S. history. Today, W&L enjoys national appeal, with undergraduates representing 46 states and 47 countries. Small classes, state-of-the-art facilities, and outstanding teachers combine to prepare W&L students for success in both graduate school and the workplace. Professors are committed to mentoring their students in and out of the classroom, often forming lifelong relationships in the process. Over 90 percent of faculty hold earned doctoral or terminal degrees and remain active researchers in their chosen fields. W&L's curriculum offers unique breadth among the nation's leading undergraduate colleges, boasting such majors as accounting, business, engineering, journalism, and public policy, in addition to the traditional arts and sciences. Interdisciplinary courses are common at W&L and employ the latest technology and research techniques. The fully accredited Williams School of Commerce, Economics, and Politics and the nationally ranked School of Law afford undergraduates with remarkable opportunities more typically found in comprehensive research universities. Student autonomy is a hallmark of a W&L education and the student-run honor system yields high expectations that students internalize and live out in a community of trust. With exams not proctored and facilities open 24/7, this pervasive trust engenders a commitment to honor and civility that continues to inform students' decisions well beyond graduation. "High school graduates of 2008 will have four options for fulfilling testing requirements: new SAT plus two SAT Subject exams in unrelated areas; old SAT plus three SAT Subject Tests, one of which must be in Writing; new ACT with essay plus two SAT Subject exams in unrelated areas; old ACT plus three SAT Subject exams, one of which must be in Writing."

SELECTIVITY

Admissions Rating	**98**
# of applicants	4,215
% of applicants accepted	27
% of acceptees attending	39
# accepting a place on wait list	351
% admitted from wait list	19
# of early decision applicants	921
% accepted early decision	38

FRESHMAN PROFILE

Range SAT Critical Reading	660–730
Range SAT Math	650–730
Range ACT Composite	28–31
% graduated top 10% of class	81
% graduated top 25% of class	98
% graduated top 50% of class	100

DEADLINES

Early decision application deadline	11/15
Early decision notification	12/22
Regular application deadline	1/15
Regular notification	4/1
Nonfall registration?	no

APPLICANTS ALSO LOOK AT

AND OFTEN PREFER
Duke University, University of Virginia

AND SOMETIMES PREFER
The College of William & Mary, Davidson College, Georgetown University, The University of North Carolina at Chapel Hill

AND RARELY PREFER
Rhodes College, University of Georgia, University of Richmond, Vanderbilt University, Wake Forest University

FINANCIAL FACTS

Financial Aid Rating	**92**
Annual tuition	$27,960
Room & Board	$7,225
Books and supplies	$1,500
Required fees	$675
% frosh rec. need-based scholarship or grant aid	31
% UG rec. need-based scholarship or grant aid	27
% frosh rec. need-based self-help aid	13
% UG rec. need-based self-help aid	14

WASHINGTON STATE UNIVERSITY

370 LIGHTY STUDENT SERVICES, PULLMAN, WA 99164-1067 • ADMISSIONS: 888-468-6978 • FAX: 509-335-4902

CAMPUS LIFE

Quality of Life Rating	**73**
Fire Safety Rating	**80**
Type of school	public
Environment	town

STUDENTS

Total undergrad enrollment	16,489
% male/female	48/52
% from out of state	8
% from public high school	88
% live on campus	33
% in (# of) fraternities	15 (23)
% in (# of) sororities	18 (16)
% African American	3
% Asian	6
% Caucasian	72
% Hispanic	4
% Native American	1
% international	6
# of countries represented	82

SURVEY SAYS . . .

Great library
Athletic facilities are great
Everyone loves the Cougars
Frats and sororities dominate social scene
Lots of beer drinking
Hard liquor is popular

ACADEMICS

Academic Rating	**67**
Calendar	semester
Student/faculty ratio	14:1
Profs interesting rating	65
Profs accessible rating	67
% profs teaching UG courses	84
% classes taught by TAs	8
Most common reg class size	20–29 students

MOST POPULAR MAJORS

education
mass communications/media studies
nursing/registered nurse training
(ASN, BSN, MSN, RN)

STUDENTS SAY

Academics

"A moderately large research university with some very good programs," Washington State University delivers quality and value in a pleasant small-town environment to Washington residents and out-of-state students alike. The Edward R. Murrow School of Communications is among WSU's major drawing cards; the university also boasts a veterinary program "that is one of the leading programs in the nation," a business school whose offerings include a "great MIS program," a "very good agriculture program," solid offerings in plant sciences, zoology, and molecular biosciences, and programs in material science and engineering in which "Students have good contact with professors." In fact, throughout the university professors are typically "extremely accessible and work very well with the students. My math professor even plays basketball with all the students at our state-of-the-art rec center every week." As at any school, "When you get a bad professor, look out, but fortunately the majority of professors at WSU are good and want you to do well." Even the administration, often the whipping boy of students at large state schools, earns mostly good marks; one undergrad writes, "The administration, the criticisms of some students notwithstanding, is actually working hard to improve the school's quality, which is noticeable and appreciated." Some even report sensing that "staff actually cares about you as a person, and not just as another random number who pays $20,000 a year. They care about my success, and I appreciate that."

Life

"The weekends are thriving" at WSU, where some head to small house parties while others beat a path to Greek Row, a popular destination. One student writes, "Every night of the weekend (and sometimes during the week) there is a party you can go to. . . . People over 21 go to one of the three bars near campus around 11:00 P.M. and can dance and drink the rest of the night. I love the party scene at WSU, it's a great way to meet friends and potential interests." Some contend that "if you don't like to party, options are a bit limited," but others point to a broad range of athletic events ("Student camaraderie is outstanding at basketball and football games!") and extracurriculars as alternate options. Hometown Pullman "is tiny, with only 25,000 people, of whom 20,000 are students." Many here relish the environment, pointing out that "it is such a small community, you know it is safe to walk around by yourself at night" and noting that "while some people complain about boredom here, they usually are not very social. With 16,000-plus undergraduates you have to lock yourself in your room to not find something to do."

Students

"It's hard to define a typical student" at WSU, as "There are a lot of students from rural areas of Washington and quite a few from suburban areas" along with a fair share of "rich White kids from Seattle." Students tell us that "it's definitely not a yuppie school. Most people are down to earth and lean a little conservative politically," but there's a substantial liberal population as well. Most important, "Most of these people are very tolerant, so there is no real worry about expressing your beliefs and being attacked for them." Minorities "are definitely outnumbered on campus, but the school has numerous cultural events to encourage diversity and to get everyone to interact. The largest ethnic groups on campus (after Caucasian) include Hawaiian, Asian, Hispanic, and African American." One minority student reports, "All in all, it's not hard to fit in here. Students are extraordinarily friendly, and the guys constantly open doors for the ladies, or vice versa. Little things like that indicate how fun, friendly, and welcoming people are here."

WASHINGTON STATE UNIVERSITY

FINANCIAL AID: 509-335-9711 • E-MAIL: ADMISS2@WSU.EDU • WEBSITE: WWW.WSU.EDU

ADMISSIONS

Very important factors considered include: Academic GPA, standardized test scores. *Important factors considered include:* Application essay, recommendation(s), rigor of secondary school record. *Other factors considered include:* Extracurricular activities. SAT or ACT required; ACT with Writing component required. TOEFL required of all international applicants. High school diploma is required, and GED is accepted. *Academic units required:* 4 English, 3 math, 2 science (1 science lab), 2 foreign language, 3 social science (1 history), 1 academic elective. *Academic units recommended:* 4 English, 4 math, 2 science (1 science lab), 2 foreign language, 1 academic elective.

The Inside Word

The huge number of applications WSU must process each year should leave Admissions Officers little time to consider anything other than grades, quality of curriculum, and standardized test scores. Yet WSU also encourages applicants to submit a personal statement and, presumably, takes the time to read them. Herein lies your chance to make up for an inconsistent high school record or less-than-optimal test scores. Make the most of your opportunity.

FINANCIAL AID

Students should submit: FAFSA. The Princeton Review suggests that all financial aid forms be submitted as soon as possible after January 1. *Need-based scholarships/grants offered:* Pell Grant, SEOG, state scholarships/grants, private scholarships, the school's own gift aid. *Loan aid offered:* FFEL Subsidized Stafford, FFEL Unsubsidized Stafford, FFEL PLUS, Federal Perkins Loan, Federal Nursing Loan. Applicants will be notified of awards on a rolling basis beginning or about April 15.

FROM THE ADMISSIONS OFFICE

"At Washington State University, you work side by side with nationally renowned faculty who help you succeed. Many academic programs rank among the nation's best. Programs are designed to give you real-world experience through internships, community service, in-depth labs, and study-abroad experiences. Plus, many disciplines encourage you to participate in faculty research or conduct your own. If you have top grades and a passion for learning, the highly acclaimed Honors College challenges you with interdisciplinary studies, rich classroom discussions, and research opportunities.

"The campus forms the heart of a friendly college town where faculty and peers help you achieve your greatest potential. More than 200 campus organizations connect you with others who share your interests and empower you to build leadership skills. Year after year, employers return to campus seeking Washington State University graduates and regard them as the best prepared in the state.

"In addition to the Pullman campus, WSU has three nonresidential urban campuses in Spokane, the TriCities (Richland), and Vancouver.

"The priority date to apply for admission and the deadline to apply for scholarships is January 31. For your candidacy to be considered, you must complete the high school core curriculum and provide official scores from the new SAT or the ACT with the Writing Test (with both assessment and writing components completed during the same sitting). If you graduated from high school before 2006, you may provide scores from either the old or new SAT or ACT examinations. We also encourage you to deliver a strong personal statement (essay)."

SELECTIVITY
Admissions Rating	83
# of applicants	9,314
% of applicants accepted	77
% of acceptees attending	40

FRESHMAN PROFILE
Range SAT Critical Reading	480–590
Range SAT Math	500–610
Minimum Paper TOEFL	520
Minimum Computer Based TOEFL	190
Average HS GPA	3.45
% graduated top 10% of class	38
% graduated top 25% of class	62
% graduated top 50% of class	91

DEADLINES
Regular notification	rolling
Nonfall registration?	yes

FINANCIAL FACTS
Financial Aid Rating	72
Annual in-state tuition	$5,432
Annual out-of-state tuition	$15,072
Room & Board	$6,890
Books and supplies	$912
Required fees	$1,015
% frosh rec. need-based scholarship or grant aid	22
% UG rec. need-based scholarship or grant aid	32
% frosh rec. need-based self-help aid	38
% UG rec. need-based self-help aid	43
% frosh rec. any financial aid	73
% UG rec. any financial aid	72

WASHINGTON UNIVERSITY IN ST. LOUIS

CAMPUS BOX 1089, ONE BROOKINGS DRIVE, ST. LOUIS, MO 63130-4899 • ADMISSIONS: 314-935-6000 • FAX: 314-935-4290

STUDENTS SAY

Academics

Students at Washington University find Ivy-caliber academics free of psychotic premeds or other bothersome nerds. A sophomore in the humanities says, "A lot of great students decide to come here because you can be serious about academics yet laid-back." The strong Science Departments support their students in terms of research opportunities and pre-professional advising but bury them with the workload. In other words, "You'll definitely learn chemistry, but your grade might reflect the opposite." Advisors in every department come well armed with information. A sophomore writes, "For every class I've ever asked about, my advisor has had a story or a piece of advice." Incoming students balk at the arts and sciences "cluster" system, but an upperclassman assures that "once you get a sense of what they want, it's not too tough to get your distribution requirements done." Faculty members and students genuinely enjoy their time together and choose to extend their classroom relationship. "I just finished a 5-hour class dinner at my professor's house—we didn't want to leave!" writes one student. "She always has her class over at the end of the semester to eat, have fun, and discuss our final papers. What more could you want?" Alas, not everyone sings similar praise. One in six students attends the engineering school, where you're wise to "research your professors, as some only care about their research." These gripes find audience during the free-lunch Dean's Forums, though taking action is another issue. The school's leadership, "dignified, but willing to smile," is getting serious about Washington's reputation and ranking, and "this has led to a concerted effort to eliminate the more relaxed atmosphere of the school." For now, the low-stress attitude remains. "People here are smart, there's no doubt, but there's also a common goal to make it fun and a willingness to take breaks . . . often."

Life

Washington life strikes a balance of "great academics, good sports, a medium size, yummy food, a breathtaking campus, nice dorms, friendly people, and financial assistance." Students here are "extremely bright" and believe they have brains to spare if they decide to drink their weekends away. Though management has started down "a path to make the campus dry," undergrads are currently able to "break into a philosophical or political debate in the middle of a game of beer pong." Casual hanging out or dining with friends break up the party scene. "Often I'll come back to my dorm and find half of my floor doing something together, whether it's playing a game or helping each other study for exams." The campus abuts two idyllic student-friendly areas: the Loop, for cute shops, ethnic restaurants, and independent movies, and Forest Park, with its free museums, zoo, and science center. Students consider the park, which is 500 acres larger than Manhattan's Central Park, their "front yard" and make frequent use of the skating rink, paddleboats, and shade trees. More than 200 student organizations, ranging from club sports to community service groups, benefit from a whopping shared budget of more than $2 million each year.

Student Body

Washington hosts a student population roughly "one-third Jewish, one-third Catholic, and the rest are Protestant, Buddhist, Muslim, or don't care." Most people come from New Jersey or New York, but shed their East Coast intensity upon arrival in the Midwest. The majority espouses strong leftist views and backs them up with political involvement. "Everyone is pretty passionate about something, and that's inspiring," says a first-year. Different groups interact easily, as students attest: "My boyfriend is Black, my best friends are Korean and half Indian, and I am a White woman." Though many Washington students come from boatloads of money, people observe "no segregation between the haves and the have-nots." A junior emphasizes, "This is a very rich school, but most people aren't in your face about their wealth." The average Washington student isn't used to being average, but these "over-committed, fun-loving, high school all-stars" still coexist with "very little animosity or competitiveness."

FINANCIAL AID: 888-547-6670 • E-MAIL: ADMISSIONS@WUSTL.EDU • WEBSITE: WUSTL.EDU

ADMISSIONS

Very important factors considered include: Academic GPA, application essay, character/personal qualities, class rank, extracurricular activities, recommendation(s), rigor of secondary school record, standardized test scores, talent/ability, volunteer work, work experience. *Other factors considered include:* Alumni/ae relation, first generation, interview, level of applicant's interest, racial/ethnic status. SAT or ACT required; TOEFL required of all international applicants. High school diploma is required, and GED is accepted. *Academic units recommended:* 4 English, 4 math, 4 science (4 science labs), 2 foreign language, 4 social studies, 4 history.

The Inside Word

The fact that Washington U. doesn't have much play as a nationally respected car-window decal is about all that prevents it from being among the most selective universities. In every other respect—that is, in any way which really matters—this place is hard to beat and easily ranks as one of the best. No other university with as impressive a record of excellence across the board has a more accommodating admissions process. Not that it's easy to get in here, but lack of instant name recognition does affect Washington's admission rate. Students with above-average academic records who are not quite Ivy material are the big winners. Marginal candidates with high financial need may find difficulty; the admissions process at Washington U. is not need-blind and may take into account candidates' ability to pay if they are not strong applicants.

FINANCIAL AID

Students should submit: FAFSA, CSS/Financial Aid PROFILE, Noncustodial PROFILE, student and parent Federal Income Tax Returns (or signed waiver if there is no tax return). Regular filing deadline is February 15. The Princeton Review suggests that all financial aid forms be submitted as soon as possible after January 1. *Need-based scholarships/grants offered:* Pell Grant, SEOG, state scholarships/grants, private scholarships, the school's own gift aid, United Negro College Fund, Academic Competitiveness Grant, National SMART Grant. *Loan aid offered:* FFEL Subsidized Stafford, FFEL Unsubsidized Stafford, FFEL PLUS, Federal Perkins Loan, state loans, college/university loans from institutional funds. Applicants will be notified of awards on or about April 1. Federal Work-Study Program available. Institutional employment available. Off-campus job opportunities are excellent.

FROM THE ADMISSIONS OFFICE

"Washington University students learn in a flexible academic atmosphere that encourages them to cross disciplines, taking courses in any of our five undergraduate divisions: Arts and Sciences, Architecture, Art, Business, and Engineering. We also offer graduate programs in these divisions as well as law; medicine, including occupational therapy and physical therapy; and social work. This interdisciplinary environment allows students to study alongside other academically talented students from across the country and around the world in any subject that interests them. Through research projects that start as early as the freshman year, students can participate with our world-class faculty in the creation of knowledge. This academic exploration takes place in a supportive, friendly community that provides the resources to ensure success. Outside the classroom, students participate in nearly 200 activities, including community service and multicultural groups; musical, dance, and theater groups; fraternities and sororities; intramural sports; student government; and literary groups. We invite you to visit Washington University any time to experience these outstanding opportunities firsthand.

"Applicants for Fall 2008 are required to submit scores from either the SAT or ACT test. Applicants who submit scores from the ACT test may submit with or without the Writing component."

SELECTIVITY

Admissions Rating	99
# of applicants	22,251
% of applicants accepted	21
% of acceptees attending	32

FRESHMAN PROFILE

Range SAT Critical Reading	670–750
Range SAT Math	700–780
Range ACT Composite	30–33
Minimum Paper TOEFL	550
Minimum Computer Based TOEFL	213
% graduated top 10% of class	95
% graduated top 25% of class	100
% graduated top 50% of class	100

DEADLINES

Early decision application deadline	11/15
Early decision notification	12/15
Regular application deadline	1/15
Regular notification	4/1
Nonfall registration?	no

APPLICANTS ALSO LOOK AT

AND OFTEN PREFER
Harvard College, Princeton University, Stanford University, University of Pennsylvania, Yale University

AND SOMETIMES PREFER
Cornell University, Duke University, Northwestern University, The University of Chicago

AND RARELY PREFER
Emory University, Tulane University, University of Michigan—Ann Arbor, University of Rochester

FINANCIAL FACTS

Financial Aid Rating	98
Annual tuition	$34,500
Room & Board	$11,252
Books and supplies	$1,160
Required fees	$1,024
% frosh rec. need-based scholarship or grant aid	39
% UG rec. need-based scholarship or grant aid	42
% frosh rec. need-based self-help aid	32
% UG rec. need-based self-help aid	32
% frosh rec. any financial aid	40
% UG rec. any financial aid	42

WEBB INSTITUTE

298 CRESCENT BEACH ROAD, GLEN COVE, NY 11542 • ADMISSIONS: 516-671-2213 • FAX: 516-674-9838

CAMPUS LIFE

Quality of Life Rating	**98**
Fire Safety Rating	**76**
Type of school	private
Environment	village

STUDENTS

Total undergrad enrollment	87
% male/female	80/20
% from out of state	76
% from public high school	80
% live on campus	100
% Asian	1
% Caucasian	95
% Hispanic	2

SURVEY SAYS . . .

Small classes
No one cheats
Career services are great
Campus feels safe
Frats and sororities are unpopular or
nonexistent
Very little drug use

ACADEMICS

Academic Rating	**95**
Calendar	semester
Student/faculty ratio	8:1
Profs interesting rating	72
Profs accessible rating	99
% profs teaching UG courses	100
% classes taught by TAs	0
Most common reg class size	20–29 students

STUDENTS SAY

Academics

Offering a full-tuition scholarship to every student and boasting a "100 percent placement rate in grad schools and careers," Long Island's Webb Institute would be the ideal school for everyone, but for one catch: only one major, naval architecture and marine eengineering, is available here. For the "shipbuilders of tomorrow," though, Webb is a dream come true—a "rigorously academic experience tempered by a spirit of cooperation amongst the students and professors who are always willing to help out." Like most engineering schools, Webb demands a lot from its students; one writes, "This school is about keeping a positive attitude in the face of long days and nights of plentiful and difficult work." That task is made easier by the fact that students and faculty form "a tight-knit community with strong social bonds. It is not competitive amongst the students, which makes the overall academic experience good." Webb professors "are readily available and often hold review sessions outside of class hours," and while "some introductory professors just don't know how to teach, all courses important to the major are taught by knowledgeable and good professors." Administrators are "readily available and responsive to suggestions, [and] because our school is run on an honor code, the administration has little to do with the overall social lives of the students. So in essence the students run the school." One engineer concludes, "For the major they offer, it's the best school in the world. The professors are great, the other students are great, and overall the school is great."

Life

"The class load is brutal" at Webb Institute, and "Schoolwork has a tendency to take over everything," including leisure time. "We get hours of homework each night," students explain, "so we have to work together and make homework fun in order to survive." All students live together, too, in a remodeled mansion on a 26-acre beachfront estate. As a result, "You get to know your classmates very well because you spend all day with them. All of the classes intermingle a lot too." Webb engineers "joke that we function on our own time zone here. We stay up until 2:00 or 3:00 A.M. regularly, but classes don't start until 9:00 A.M., so we sleep later than the rest of the Eastern Seaboard too." When students can muster some spare time, they enjoy typical college fun. One student reports, "There are many school-sponsored parties every semester, as well as a pub, a TV room, and game room in the main building. Watching movies is pretty popular, as well as video games. Also, there are annual white-water rafting and ski trips. Basketball and other sports are played pretty often, just for fun." Because the administration "is very strict about drinking on campus," students head to the local pub or travel into New York City when they feel the need to tie one on. "One must make every effort possible to go to New York City, an easy one-hour train ride away," students insist.

Student Body

"All of the students are very hardworking" at Webb, because "If you're not then you won't stay for very long." There are "two types of students at Webb: those who are bookworms and study all the time and are always working, and those who do the work when needed but also enjoy themselves on campus by playing sports or going out and having a good time." As at most engineering schools, most students are male; atypical of engineering schools, nearly all students are White. "We're all nerdy White boys, except for the few nerdy White girls," sums up one student, adding that "minority students aren't social outcasts or anything like that. We don't care what you look like; we care what's going on inside and upstairs. We treat each other with mutual respect."

FINANCIAL AID: 516-671-2213 • E-MAIL: ADMISSIONS@WEBB-INSTITUTE.EDU • WEBSITE: WWW.WEBB-INSTITUTE.EDU

ADMISSIONS

Very important factors considered include: Academic GPA, character/personal qualities, class rank, interview, rigor of secondary school record, standardized test scores. *Important factors considered include:* Extracurricular activities, level of applicant's interest, recommendation(s). *Other factors considered include:* Talent/ability, volunteer work, work experience. SAT required; SAT Subject Tests required. High school diploma is required, and GED is not accepted. *Academic units required:* 4 English, 4 math, 2 science (2 science labs), 2 social studies, 4 academic electives.

The Inside Word

Let's not mince words; admission to Webb is mega-tough. Webb's Admissions Counselors are out to find the right kid for their curriculum—one that can survive the school's rigorous academics. The applicant pool is highly self-selected because of the focused program of study: naval architecture and marine engineering.

FINANCIAL AID

Students should submit: FAFSA. Regular filing deadline is July 1. The Princeton Review suggests that all financial aid forms be submitted as soon as possible after January 1. *Need-based scholarships/grants offered:* Pell Grant, state scholarships/grants, private scholarships, the school's own gift aid. *Loan aid offered:* FFEL Subsidized Stafford, FFEL Unsubsidized Stafford, FFEL PLUS. Applicants will be notified of awards on or about August 1. Off-campus job opportunities are fair.

FROM THE ADMISSIONS OFFICE

"Webb, the only college in the country that specializes in the engineering field of naval architecture and marine engineering, seeks young men and women of all races from all over the country who are interested in receiving an excellent engineering education with a full-tuition scholarship. Students don't have to know anything about ships, they just have to be motivated to study how mechanical, civil, structural, and electrical engineering come together with the design elements that make up a ship and all its systems. Being small and private has its major advantages. Every applicant is special and the President will interview all entering students personally. The student/faculty ratio is 8:1, and since there are no teaching assistants, interaction with the faculty occurs daily in class and labs at a level not found at most other colleges. The college provides each student with a high-end laptop computer. The entire campus operates under the Student Organization's honor system that allows unsupervised exams and 24-hour access to the library, every classroom and laboratory, and the shop and gymnasium. Despite a total enrollment of between 70 and 80 students and a demanding workload, Webb manages to field six intercollegiate teams. Currently more than 60 percent of the members of the student body play on one or more intercollegiate teams. Work hard, play hard and the payoff is a job for every student upon graduation. The placement record of the college is 100 percent every year.

"Freshman applicants must take the new SAT. In addition, students may submit scores from the old SAT (before March 2005), and the best scores from either test will be used. We also require scores from two SAT Subject Tests: Math Level I or II and either Physics or Chemistry."

SELECTIVITY

Admissions Rating	**97**
# of applicants	90
% of applicants accepted	34
% of acceptees attending	77
# of early decision applicants	31
% accepted early decision	39

FRESHMAN PROFILE

Range SAT Critical Reading	650–700
Range SAT Math	700–770
Range SAT Writing	630–690
Average HS GPA	3.9
% graduated top 10% of class	69
% graduated top 25% of class	100

DEADLINES

Early decision application deadline	10/15
Early decision notification	12/15
Regular application deadline	2/15
Regular notification	3/15–4/30
Nonfall registration?	no

APPLICANTS ALSO LOOK AT

AND OFTEN PREFER
United States Coast Guard Academy,
United States Naval Academy

AND SOMETIMES PREFER
The Cooper Union for the Advancement
of Science and Art, Virginia Tech

AND RARELY PREFER
State University of New York—Maritime
College, University of Michigan—Ann
Arbor

FINANCIAL FACTS

Financial Aid Rating	**88**
Annual tuition	*$0
Room & Board	$9,000
Books and supplies	$750
% frosh rec. need-based scholarship or grant aid	5
% UG rec. need-based scholarship or grant aid	2
% frosh rec. need-based self-help aid	23
% UG rec. need-based self-help aid	10
% frosh rec. any financial aid	40
% UG rec. any financial aid	33

*Tuition covered by full scholarship.

WELLESLEY COLLEGE

BOARD OF ADMISSION, 106 CENTRAL STREET, WELLESLEY, MA 02481-8203 • ADMISSIONS: 781-283-2270 • FAX: 781-283-3678

CAMPUS LIFE
Quality of Life Rating	95
Fire Safety Rating	83
Type of school	private
Environment	town

STUDENTS
Total undergrad enrollment	2,215
% male/female	0/100
% from out of state	89
% from public high school	64
% live on campus	97
% African American	6
% Asian	26
% Caucasian	47
% Hispanic	7
% international	8
# of countries represented	79

SURVEY SAYS . . .
Small classes
Dorms like palaces
Great library
Diverse student types on campus
Very little hard liquor
Great computer facilities

ACADEMICS
Academic Rating	98
Calendar	semester
Student/faculty ratio	9:1
Profs interesting rating	99
Profs accessible rating	98
% profs teaching UG courses	100
% classes taught by TAs	0
Most common lab size	10–19 students
Most common reg class size	10–19 students

MOST POPULAR MAJORS
biology/neuroscience
economics/political science
English language and literature
psychology

STUDENTS SAY

Academics

Wellesley College, "a small liberal arts institution with the intimacy of a family and the academic excellence of a top-rank university," provides its "all-female" student body with "an excellent education to make women independent individuals" while "preparing ambitious women to succeed in the professional world." This elite school located just outside Boston offers "undergraduate research opportunities, close relationships with professors, a suburban environment," and much more. One student explains, "Wellesley has everything I was looking for. It was a small, liberal arts school in New England with small class sizes, excellent professors, and an amazing reputation. I also appreciated the culture within the student body, the dedicated alumnae network, and the academic challenge." "Class work is rigorous" at Wellesley as teachers here "have incredibly high expectations," "But there are lots of resources available to help you if you need it," not the least of which are professors who "hold a large amount of office hours and even provide you with their home phone numbers and cell phone numbers in case you have any questions, whether about the class, the assignment, or life. The dedication of the Wellesley community is what I find to be stand out about the school." Spending part of junior year abroad is a staple of a Wellesley education. One student reports that "over 50 percent of Wellesley students travel abroad." Indeed, at home or abroad Wellesley offers "unlimited opportunities" and "takes the steps necessary" to help young women "realize [their] potential."

Life

At Wellesley, "the focus is all on academics," especially during the week. "You won't see students partying here on weekdays! Instead, you'll find students attending lectures, or discussing the news or issues on campus and what homework they have." The school's "close-knit atmosphere and location" make for an "unbelievably rich" college experience. While it's true that "there are no males around, at least not to the degree that there would be on a co-ed campus," students see this as a benefit. A freshman says, "This simply makes me focus more on what I'm really at college for: To get the most out of the educational opportunities available to me. In class, I am able to focus wholeheartedly on the subject matter, which is sometimes more difficult to do if there's a cute guy sitting in the class with me who is looking at me or whom I like." When it's time to chill, "Students attend cultural shows and plays on campus but mostly head into Boston." Social connections in this city dictate that eventually "Everyone ends up knowing someone else who goes to school in Boston and from that person, develops an additional social network in the city. This gives students a much-needed break on weekends from the often stressful Wellesley environment."

Students

Students describe the typical Wellesley undergrad (aka "Wendy Wellesley) as "an overachiever balancing two majors, 10 extracurricular activities, and several volunteer jobs." She is "passionate, hardworking, and wants to have an impact on the world around her." One student notes that "strong personalities," "diverse" individuals, and a "large range of interests" do not "allow the existence of absolutely typical students." Though "trends do occur," the "common denominator" among students is their "commitment to academic excellence." Beyond these traits, "Students are extremely diverse—ethnically, geographically, and socioeconomically. Because students come from so many backgrounds, no students are truly in the minority, and it is therefore easy for anyone to fit in."

FINANCIAL AID: 781-283-2360 • E-MAIL: ADMISSION@WELLESLEY.EDU • WEBSITE: WWW.WELLESLEY.EDU

ADMISSIONS

Very important factors considered include: Application essay, character/personal qualities, high school transcript, recommendation(s), rigor of secondary school record, standardized test scores. *Important factors considered include:* Class rank, extracurricular activities. *Other factors considered include:* Alumni/ae relation, first generation, geographical residence, interview, level of applicant's interest, racial/ethnic status, talent/ability, volunteer work, work experience. SAT and SAT Subject Tests or ACT required; ACT with Writing component required. High school diploma or equivalent is not required. *Academic units recommended:* 4 English, 4 math, 3 science (2 science labs), 4 foreign language, 4 social studies, 4 history.

The Inside Word

As the number of women's colleges diminishes—*The New York Times* recently reported that the U.S. now has only about 60 all-women's schools, down from over 300 in the 1960s—competition for admission to the remaining single-sex institutions stiffens. Wellesley has always been an elite institution, but it grows ever more so as its number of competitors for top women students shrinks. If you submit your application materials to Wellesley by November 1, the school will provide you with an early evaluation, giving you some idea of your chances for admission.

FINANCIAL AID

Wellesley's admission process is 'need-blind' for U.S. citizens and permanent residents, which means that the college admits students without regard for their family's ability to pay. *Students should submit:* FAFSA, institution's own financial aid form, CSS/Financial Aid PROFILE, Noncustodial PROFILE, Business/Farm Supplement, parents' and student's Federal Income Tax Returns and W-2s. The Princeton Review suggests that all financial aid forms be submitted as soon as possible after January 1, which is also the deadline for early decision applicants. *Need-based scholarships/grants offered:* Pell Grant, SEOG, state scholarships/grants, the school's own gift aid. *Loan aid offered:* FFEL Subsidized Stafford, FFEL Unsubsidized Stafford, FFEL PLUS, Federal Perkins Loan, state loans, college/university loans from institutional funds. Applicants will be notified of awards on or about April 1. Federal Work-Study Program available. Off-campus job opportunities are excellent, and is available for students admitted off the wait list.

FROM THE ADMISSIONS OFFICE

"Ranked fourth among liberal arts and sciences colleges according to the 2006 *U.S. News & World Report* survey, and widely acknowledged as the nation's best women's college, Wellesley College provides students with numerous opportunities on campus and beyond. With a long-standing commitment to and established reputation for academic excellence, Wellesley offers more than 1,000 courses in 53 established majors and supports 180 clubs, organizations, and activities for its students. The college is easily accessible to Boston, a great city in which to meet other college students and to experience theater, art, sports, and entertainment. Considered one of the most diverse colleges in the nation, Wellesley students hail from 79 countries and all 50 states.

"As a community, we are looking for students who possess intellectual curiosity: the ability to think independently, ask challenging questions, and grapple with answers. Strong candidates demonstrate both academic achievement and an excitement for learning. They also display leadership, an appreciation for diverse perspectives, and an understanding of the college's mission to educate women who will make a difference in the world.

"SAT and SAT Subject Tests or ACT with Writing component required. Two SAT Subject Tests required, one of which should be quantitative (Math or Science). We strongly recommend that students planning to apply early decision complete the tests before the end of their junior year and no later than October of their senior year."

SELECTIVITY

Admissions Rating	97
# of applicants	3,974
% of applicants accepted	36
% of acceptees attending	41
# accepting a place on wait list	395
% admitted from wait list	3
# of early decision applicants	236
% accepted early decision	55

FRESHMAN PROFILE

Range SAT Critical Reading	660–750
Range SAT Math	650–720
Range SAT Writing	660–740
Range ACT Composite	29–31
% graduated top 10% of class	85
% graduated top 25% of class	98
% graduated top 50% of class	100

DEADLINES

Early decision application deadline	11/1
Early decision notification	12/15
Regular application deadline	1/15
Regular notification	4/1
Nonfall registration?	no

FINANCIAL FACTS

Financial Aid Rating	98
Annual tuition	$32,384
Room & Board	$10,216
Books and supplies	$800
Required fees	$688
% frosh rec. need-based scholarship or grant aid	53
% UG rec. need-based scholarship or grant aid	58
% frosh rec. need-based self-help aid	47
% UG rec. need-based self-help aid	54
% frosh rec. any financial aid	56
% UG rec. any financial aid	60

WELLS COLLEGE

ROUTE 90, AURORA, NY 13026 • ADMISSIONS: 315-364-3264 • FAX: 315-364-3227

STUDENTS SAY

Academics

Most Wells students enrolled expecting an education designed to "form a strong community and strong female leaders." Not surprisingly, the college's recent decision to admit men and the arrival of its first coed class have left the student body with mixed feelings toward the administration. "The deans and the president are not straightforward in their interaction[s] with students," writes a senior. "They say one thing but do another, with seemingly little interest as to the desires of the students." A more even-handed student tells us, "Although [the] administration has proven to be not fully trustworthy in the information conveyed to students regarding Wells going coed, they have been accessible for dialogue on the matter, as well as for personal concerns." Students unite in praise of the school's honor code, which rewards responsibility with freedom—"Students are allowed to take exams out of the classroom and leave it in the[ir] professor's office when they're done." They also enjoy "one-on-one relationships" with professors who "are often upset if you don't come to their office hours to bug them" and "will approach you after [class] if they think you did well or saw that you were unprepared." With "highly rigorous" academics, extensive study abroad opportunities, and a "very interesting and very rare" book arts center, we predict Wells will continue to attract students into its coed halls.

Life

The Wells existence "can be summarized in one word: isolation." Hometown Aurora mostly shuts down by 8:00 P.M. One student warns: "If you are from NYC, you may be culture shocked" when you find yourself spending "Friday and Saturday nights doing homework." Besides the farms and barns, "There's a bar where the entire senior class congregates on Fridays, a wickedly expensive inn, and a pizza place." Students tell us that at Wells "The most fun comes from the traditions: The Even/Odd rivalry, Junior Blast, Freshman Elves . . . these are really what give Wells its fabulous life." Civilization, meaning malls and other college students, lies 45 minutes away in Ithaca, but some people prefer to stay put, swimming in Cayuga Lake, sledding down Student Union hill, exploring the local cemetery, and involving themselves with campus organizations. Spontaneous games of "hallway soccer," "wine and Cheez-Its" parties, and trips to the 24-hour Wal-Mart are also common. Students emphasize the luxury of "the safe space we have here. You can walk back to your dorm across campus at 3:00 A.M. alone and your biggest worry is bumping into the campus skunk." However, that might not hold true during dining hours: "I was told I was going to get the 'freshman 15,'" a student writes. "Whoever said that never ate in my school's dining hall."

Student Body

With only about 470 undergrads, "Everyone knows everyone else" at Wells. So it's fortunate that, despite a lingering resentment over the administration's decision to go coed, most students are tolerant of their new male peers. One student explains, "There were a lot of protests over it [2 years ago], but the people who were in those protests left that to [2 years ago] and they treat the guys great." As a male student was elected freshman class president in 2005–2006, it would seem that male students have been fully integrated into the Wells community. One male student, however, offers a different perspective: "Guys have been discriminated against here, but that's [to be] expected. Over time this will fade. I think there is more anger at the girls who are here because of the guys than anger at the guys themselves!" Regardless of gender, Wells students are outspoken, with "politics, establishing fair trade with poor countries, [and] women's studies" common topics of conversation. The liberal students tend to dominate this discussion: "It's generally assumed that whoever goes to the school is either a feminist or a Democrat."

FINANCIAL AID: 315-364-3289 • E-MAIL: ADMISSIONS@WELLS.EDU • WEBSITE: WWW.WELLS.EDU

ADMISSIONS

Very important factors considered include: Academic GPA, extracurricular activities, recommendation(s), rigor of secondary school record, standardized test scores. *Important factors considered include:* Application essay, interview. *Other factors considered include:* Alumni/ae relation, character/personal qualities, class rank, level of applicant's interest, talent/ability, volunteer work, work experience. SAT or ACT required; TOEFL required of all international applicants. High school diploma is required, and GED is accepted. *Academic units required:* 4 English, 3 math, 2 science (2 science labs), 1 social studies, 3 history, 2 academic electives. *Academic units recommended:* 4 math, 3 science (3 science labs), 2 foreign language, 2 social studies, 2 history, 3 academic electives, 2 music, art, computer science.

The Inside Word

Wells is engaged in that age-old admissions game called matchmaking. There are no minimums or cutoffs in the admissions process here. But don't be fooled by the high admit rate. The Admissions Committee will look closely at your academic accomplishments, but also gives attention to your essay, recommendations, and extracurricular pursuits. The committee also recommends an interview; we suggest taking them up on it.

FINANCIAL AID

Students should submit: FAFSA, CSS/Financial Aid Profile (for early decision applicants only). The Princeton Review suggests that all financial aid forms be submitted as soon as possible after January 1. *Need-based scholarships/grants offered:* Pell Grant, SEOG, state scholarships/grants, private scholarships, the school's own gift aid. *Loan aid offered:* FFEL Subsidized Stafford, FFEL Unsubsidized Stafford, FFEL PLUS, Federal Perkins Loan. Applicants will be notified of awards on a rolling basis beginning or about March 1. Federal Work-Study Program available. Institutional employment available. Off-campus job opportunities are fair.

FROM THE ADMISSIONS OFFICE

"Wells College believes the twenty-first century needs well-educated individuals with the ability, self-confidence, and vision to contribute to an ever-changing world. Wells offers an outstanding classroom experience and innovative liberal arts curriculum that prepares students for leadership in a variety of fields, including business, government, the arts, sciences, medicine, and education. By directly connecting the liberal arts curriculum to experience and career development through internships, off-campus study, study abroad, research with professors, and community service, each student has an ideal preparation for graduate and professional school as well as for the twenty-first century.

"Wells College requires freshman applicants to submit scores from the old or new SAT. Students may also choose to submit scores from the ACT (with or without the Writing component) in lieu of the SAT."

SELECTIVITY

Admissions Rating	**84**
# of applicants	1,075
% of applicants accepted	71
% of acceptees attending	23
# of early decision applicants	15
% accepted early decision	73

FRESHMAN PROFILE

Range SAT Critical Reading	510–610
Range SAT Math	490–590
Range ACT Composite	20–26
Minimum Paper TOEFL	550
Minimum Computer Based TOEFL	213
Average HS GPA	3.5
% graduated top 10% of class	26
% graduated top 25% of class	61
% graduated top 50% of class	93

DEADLINES

Early decision application deadline	12/15
Early decision notification	1/15
Regular application deadline	3/1
Regular notification	4/1
Nonfall registration?	no

APPLICANTS ALSO LOOK AT

AND OFTEN PREFER
Hobart and William Smith Colleges, Mount Holyoke College, Smith College

AND SOMETIMES PREFER
Alfred University, Bryn Mawr College, Colgate University, Hamilton College, Ithaca College, State University of New York at Binghamton, State University of New York at Geneseo, Syracuse University

AND RARELY PREFER
Elmira College, Le Moyne College

FINANCIAL FACTS

Financial Aid Rating	**78**
Annual tuition	$15,580
Room & Board	$7,800
Books and supplies	$700
Required fees	$1,200
% frosh rec. need-based scholarship or grant aid	83
% UG rec. need-based scholarship or grant aid	76
% frosh rec. need-based self-help aid	80
% UG rec. need-based self-help aid	75
% frosh rec. any financial aid	90
% UG rec. any financial aid	89

WESLEYAN COLLEGE

4760 FORSYTH ROAD, MACON, GA 31210-4462 • ADMISSIONS: 478-757-5206 • FAX: 912-757-4030 • 800-447-6610

CAMPUS LIFE

Quality of Life Rating	89
Fire Safety Rating	60*
Type of school	private
Affiliation	Methodist
Environment	city

STUDENTS

Total undergrad enrollment	546
% male/female	0/100
% from out of state	13
% from public high school	81
% live on campus	76
% African American	32
% Asian	3
% Caucasian	50
% Hispanic	3
% international	10
# of countries represented	22

SURVEY SAYS . . .

Small classes
No one cheats
Students are friendly
Diverse student types on campus
Different types of students interact
Campus feels safe

ACADEMICS

Academic Rating	90
Calendar	semester
Student/faculty ratio	10:1
Profs interesting rating	90
Profs accessible rating	90
% profs teaching UG courses	100
% classes taught by TAs	0
Most common lab size	fewer than 10 students
Most common reg class size	10–19 students

MOST POPULAR MAJORS

business administration
communications
biology/chemistry
psychology
education

STUDENTS SAY

Academics

"You may be tired and overwhelmed" by the workload at Wesleyan College, a tiny liberal arts school for women noted for "giving exceptional women exceptional education at an affordable price," but "You will love every minute here," especially if "participating in lots of traditions" appeals to you. Fewer than 600 women attend the school, which is "so small that classes are usually under 20 students and are only taught by professors, never by teaching assistants. Every class can be discussion based, and most are." Wesleyan professors "are all very down-to-earth and helpful. They're available when you need them, and they are always eager for everyone to participate in class discussions." That availability is important, because "The academics are pretty intense," a fact that makes it easy to fall behind. The intensity also means that students leave feeling "really prepared for whatever lies ahead." Fortunately, "The staff really helps the students, especially with easing them into their first year with facilities like the Academic and Writing Centers." Students single out the Departments of English, Music, and Business for praise. The administration, they say, is accessible but "doesn't always run efficiently."

Life

Campus life at Wesleyan College revolves around homework and sisterhood. The former is the result of academic rigor; the latter, a Wesleyan tradition in which "Each class has its own colors and its own mascot. We have class rivalries, but in a good way, and compete in class sports and other competitions." Sisterhood activities "are the main focus" of extracurricular life. Enrichment activities known as "convos" (short for "convocations") are also important; students are required to attend 10 per year. Otherwise, campus life is relatively quiet, with the peace occasionally punctuated by a "campus wide event like homecoming or the Spring Dance." Drinking and drugs are strictly prohibited on the campus, and "Being under the influence on campus is not taken lightly. There are parties, but they're underground." Students occasionally venture out to the clubs, movie theaters, and coffee shops off campus, but most agree that "there's not really a lot to do in Macon." Many also feel quite comfortable on campus, where the accommodations are top-notch. The "Dorms are very spacious and comfortable," and the grounds are "extremely beautiful and relaxing. It is nice to sit by the lake and watch the ducks." The only fly in the soup is the food, which is described by more than a few as "horrible." Adding insult to injury, some students gripe about dining hall hours; one writes: "The cafeteria is open for about an hour for each meal time, and that's it, although the school does work with students and departments that have scheduling problems. "

Student Body

For such a small student body, Wesleyan College has "an extremely diverse campus in terms of race, color, national origin, sexual orientation, musical tastes, and whatnot, and everybody fits in extraordinarily well." "Over 30 countries" are represented among the school's approximately 600 students, and the African American population here is substantial (at over 25 percent). All students enjoy "a great atmosphere of respect where we are able to learn about many different cultures, religions, and beliefs." Women here tend to keep busy. They "are usually on their way to their next activity. What you eventually realize here is that everyone has something in common with someone else. It could be classes, it could be a hobby, it could be a club, or it could be that you are roommates, but regardless, there is always someone to hang out with." Many are enthusiastic about the school's traditions; they are "into the sisterhood, the class cheers, the pep rallies, the works. Others, though, are totally uninterested in the sisterhood stuff and just focus on studies."

FINANCIAL AID: 800-447-6610 • E-MAIL: ADMISSION@WESLEYANCOLLEGE.EDU • WEBSITE: WWW.WESLEYANCOLLEGE.EDU

ADMISSIONS

Very important factors considered include: Rigor of secondary school record. *Important factors considered include:* Application essay, character/personal qualities, class rank, extracurricular activities, recommendation(s), standardized test scores, talent/ability, volunteer work. *Other factors considered include:* Alumni/ae relation, interview, work experience. SAT or ACT required; TOEFL required of all international applicants. High school diploma is required, and GED is accepted. *Academic units required:* 4 English, 3 math, 3 science (2 science labs), 2 foreign language, 3 social studies. *Academic units recommended:* 4 English, 4 math, 4 science (3 science labs), 4 foreign language, 4 social studies, 2 academic electives.

The Inside Word

As a small school tucked away in Georgia, Wesleyan doesn't garner as large an applicant pool as a school of its caliber should. The college still manages to attract some talented students, however, and good candidates need to be academically competitive. A majority of students come from the region, so applicants who represent some geographic diversity might be at a slight advantage.

FINANCIAL AID

Students should submit: FAFSA, institution's own financial aid form, state aid form. Regular filing deadline is June 30. The Princeton Review suggests that all financial aid forms be submitted as soon as possible after January 1. *Need-based scholarships/grants offered:* Pell Grant, SEOG, state scholarships/grants, private scholarships, the school's own gift aid. *Loan aid offered:* FFEL Subsidized Stafford, FFEL Unsubsidized Stafford, FFEL PLUS, Federal Perkins Loan, college/university loans from institutional funds, CitiAssist, Wells FARGO, Collegiate Loans, Key Alternative Loans. Applicants will be notified of awards on a rolling basis beginning or about March 1. Federal Work-Study Program available. Off-campus job opportunities are good.

FROM THE ADMISSIONS OFFICE

"Mention the term 'women's college' and most people envision ivy-covered towers in the Northeastern U.S. However, Wesleyan College in Macon, Georgia was founded in 1836 as the first college in the world chartered to grant degrees to women. Today it is recognized as one of the nation's most diverse and affordable selective 4-year liberal arts colleges. Students value the college's tradition of service and rigorous academic program renowned for its quality. An exceptional faculty teaches classes in seminar style. A student/faculty ratio of 10:1 ensures that students are known by more than just a grade or a number. The acceptance rate of Wesleyan students into medical, law, business, and other graduate programs is exemplary.

"Undergraduate degrees are offered in 35 majors and 29 minors including self-designed majors and interdisciplinary programs, plus eight pre-professional programs that include seminary, engineering, medicine, pharmacy, veterinary medicine, health sciences, dental, and law. A $12.5 million science center added to the college's offerings for 2007. Master of Arts degrees in education and an accelerated Executive Master of Business Administration program enroll both men and women.

"Beyond the academic, Wesleyan offers a thriving residence life program, NCAA Division III athletics, championship IHSA equestrian program, and meaningful opportunities for community involvement and leadership. The college's beautiful 200-acre wooded campus, along with 30 historically significant buildings, is listed in the National Register of Historic Places as the Wesleyan College Historic District. Wesleyan is nestled in a northern suburb of Macon, the third largest city in the state.

"First-year applicants must take either the SAT or ACT."

SELECTIVITY

Admissions Rating	87
# of applicants	559
% of applicants accepted	53
% of acceptees attending	51
# of early decision applicants	64
% accepted early decision	47

FRESHMAN PROFILE

Range SAT Critical Reading	500–630
Range SAT Math	490–600
Range ACT Composite	21–26
Minimum Paper TOEFL	550
Minimum Computer Based TOEFL	213
Average HS GPA	3.5
% graduated top 10% of class	34
% graduated top 25% of class	57
% graduated top 50% of class	85

DEADLINES

Early decision application deadline	11/15
Early decision notification	12/15
Regular application deadline	8/1
Regular notification	rolling
Nonfall registration?	no

APPLICANTS ALSO LOOK AT
AND SOMETIMES PREFER
Agnes Scott College, Emory University, Mercer University—Macon, University of Georgia
AND RARELY PREFER
Berry College, Florida State University, Rhodes College, University of Florida

FINANCIAL FACTS

Financial Aid Rating	80
Annual tuition	$16,500
Room & Board	$7,600
Books and supplies	$900
% frosh rec. need-based scholarship or grant aid	43
% UG rec. need-based scholarship or grant aid	44
% frosh rec. need-based self-help aid	30
% UG rec. need-based self-help aid	34
% frosh rec. any financial aid	96
% UG rec. any financial aid	91

WESLEYAN UNIVERSITY

STEWART M. REID HOUSE, 70 WYLLYS AVENUE, MIDDLETOWN, CT 06459-0265 • ADMISSIONS: 860-685-3000 • FAX: 860-685-3001

CAMPUS LIFE

Quality of Life Rating	**83**
Fire Safety Rating	**80**
Type of school	private
Environment	town

STUDENTS

Total undergrad enrollment	2,805
% male/female	50/50
% from out of state	92
% from public high school	57
% live on campus	98
% in (# of) fraternities	2 (9)
% in (# of) sororities	1 (4)
% African American	7
% Asian	11
% Caucasian	60
% Hispanic	8
% international	6
# of countries represented	48

SURVEY SAYS . . .

No one cheats
Great library
Athletic facilities are great
Students are friendly
Political activism is popular

ACADEMICS

Academic Rating	**96**
Calendar	semester
Student/faculty ratio	9:1
Profs interesting rating	89
Profs accessible rating	81
% profs teaching UG courses	100
% classes taught by TAs	0
Most common lab size	10–19 students
Most common reg class size	10–19 students

MOST POPULAR MAJORS

English language and literature
political science and government
psychology

STUDENTS SAY

Academics

Students at Wesleyan University relish "the immense amount of freedom the school gives you," both in terms of curricular choices ("because of the lack of core curriculum, you can mold each semester however you want: lots of lecture, lots of discussion, a mix") and in extracurricular life (in other words, "Public Safety rarely bothers the students"). The latter may sound like a recipe for a non-stop party, but that's hardly the case at Wesleyan; students here don't see the school as a 24/7 kegger, but rather as "a playground for the most opinionated and social-norm-destroying students of our generation to debate issues that really matter to them." If that suggests a school entirely focused on humanities and social sciences, guess again; Wes "has one of the strongest science programs [of] any of the top liberal arts school[s]. One-quarter of the students major in a science. Since we're in a university, but have very few graduate students, there are tons of opportunities for students to get involved in research. As a sophomore, I was highly involved in a $5 million NIH grant. That's pretty unique and amazing." In all disciplines, "Professors are incredible. They are all as available as they could be to us and more willing to help than I ever expected college professors to be." Those who teach "upper level courses are ridiculously passionate about what they teach, and are usually doing research that is very relevant to their field. At Wesleyan, I always get the sense that I am surrounded by many brilliant minds." A "very active student body . . . frequently tries to make changes in the way that the school is run," and "The administration does a good job [of] working with students to ensure that we all have the most positive experience possible."

Life

The Wesleyan campus is a busy one, replete with club and intercollegiate athletics, frat and house parties, and lots of performances and lectures. One student explains, "The Wes social scene is very much what you want to make it. Want to party? We do have frats (though they're a super-small part of campus life) and house parties. Don't want to party? Go to a play, concert, movie, or just hang out. Not everyone here is partying." Indeed, "There is plenty to keep you occupied" at Wesleyan, including campus politics, as "On this campus there is always some issue being fought or demonstrated against." Students take a strong hand in driving campus life, as "Everything is mostly student-run." "If a Wes student wants something that doesn't currently exist on campus, [he or she] make[s] it happen." Hometown Middletown, while "clearly lacking the resources of a large city," "has lots of opportunities to get involved and feel like a member of the community for four years." A junior reports, "Main Street in Middletown has changed tremendously just in the three years I have been here. Lots of new restaurants, bars, and art galleries have opened."

Student Body

"Passionate" is a word that pops up frequently when Wesleyan undergrads describe their peers, as does "intelligent." In fact, Wesleyan is a magnet for kids who value intellect, not only as a means to good grades and a career, but also as an instrument of self-development. "Everyone is excited about something," undergrads report. Students here are engaged in campus life, meaning that "a lot of things on campus are student-run and a lot of learning takes place outside the classroom due to casual interaction between peers." Demographically speaking, there are "two main molds of a Wesleyan student: The preppy New England kid and the kid . . . that [is] some kind of mix between a hipster and a hippie. Outside of that it's an extremely diverse group of kids who come from all over and have a wide range of interests." Most students here "are liberal and 'alternative.'"

FINANCIAL AID: 860-685-2800 • E-MAIL: ADMISS@WESLEYAN.EDU • WEBSITE: WWW.WESLEYAN.EDU/

ADMISSIONS

Very important factors considered include: Rigor of secondary school record. *Important factors considered include:* Academic GPA, application essay, character/personal qualities, class rank, first generation, racial/ethnic status, recommendation(s), standardized test scores, talent/ability. *Other factors considered include:* Alumni/ae relation, extracurricular activities, geographical residence, interview, volunteer work, work experience. SAT and SAT Subject Tests or ACT required; ACT with Writing component recommended. TOEFL required of all international applicants. High school diploma or equivalent is not required. *Academic units required:* 4 English, 3 math, 3 science, 3 foreign language, 3 social studies. *Academic units recommended:* 4 English, 4 math, 4 science (3 science labs), 4 foreign language, 4 social studies.

The Inside Word

You want the inside word on Wesleyan admissions? Read *The Gatekeepers: Inside the Admissions Process at a Premier College*, by Jacques Steinberg. The author spent an entire admissions season at the Wesleyan Admissions Office; his book is a wonderfully detailed description of the Wesleyan admissions process (which is quite similar to processes at other private, highly selective colleges and universities).

FINANCIAL AID

Students should submit: FAFSA, institution's own financial aid form, CSS/Financial Aid PROFILE, state aid form, Business/Farm Supplement, Noncustodial PROFILE. Regular filing deadline is February 15. The Princeton Review suggests that all financial aid forms be submitted as soon as possible after January 1. *Need-based scholarships/grants offered:* Pell Grant, SEOG, state scholarships/grants, private scholarships, the school's own gift aid. *Loan aid offered:* FFEL Subsidized Stafford, FFEL Unsubsidized Stafford, FFEL PLUS, Federal Perkins Loan, college/university loans from institutional funds. Applicants will be notified of awards on or about April 1.

FROM THE ADMISSIONS OFFICE

"Wesleyan faculty believe in an education that is flexible and affords individual freedom and that a strong liberal arts education is the best foundation for success in any endeavor. The broad curriculum focuses on essential communication skills and analytical abilities through course content and teaching methodology, allowing students to pursue their intellectual interests with passion while honing those capabilities. As a result, Wesleyan students achieve a very personalized but broad education. Wesleyan's Dean of Admission and Financial Aid, Nancy Hargrave Meislahn, describes the qualities Wesleyan seeks in its students: 'Our very holistic process seeks to identify academically accomplished and intellectually curious students who can thrive in Wesleyan's rigorous and vibrant academic environment; we look for personal strengths, accomplishments, and potential for real contribution to our diverse community.'

"Applicants will meet standardized testing requirements one of two ways: by taking the new SAT plus two SAT Subject Tests of the student's choice, or by taking the old SAT plus three SAT Subject Tests (one of which must be Writing)."

SELECTIVITY

Admissions Rating	97
# of applicants	7,242
% of applicants accepted	28
% of acceptees attending	36
# accepting a place on wait list	418
% admitted from wait list	12
# of early decision applicants	665
% accepted early decision	44

FRESHMAN PROFILE

Range SAT Critical Reading	640–750
Range SAT Math	650–730
Range SAT Writing	640–730
Range ACT Composite	28–32
Minimum Paper TOEFL	600
Minimum Computer Based TOEFL	250
Average HS GPA	3.95
% graduated top 10% of class	68
% graduated top 25% of class	91
% graduated top 50% of class	100

DEADLINES

Early decision application deadline	11/15
Early decision notification	12/15
Regular application deadline	1/1
Regular notification	4/1
Nonfall registration?	no

APPLICANTS ALSO LOOK AT

AND OFTEN PREFER

Brown University, Columbia University, Harvard College, Stanford University, Yale University

AND SOMETIMES PREFER

Amherst College, Bowdoin College, Princeton University, Swarthmore College, Williams College

AND RARELY PREFER

Brandeis University, Middlebury College, Oberlin College, Tufts University, Vassar College

FINANCIAL FACTS

Financial Aid Rating	96
Annual tuition	$36,536
Room & Board	$10,130
Books and supplies	$2,410
Required fees	$270
% frosh rec. need-based scholarship or grant aid	41
% UG rec. need-based scholarship or grant aid	45
% frosh rec. need-based self-help aid	44
% UG rec. need-based self-help aid	48
% frosh rec. any financial aid	39
% UG rec. any financial aid	43

WEST VIRGINIA UNIVERSITY

ADMISSIONS OFFICE, PO BOX 6009, MORGANTOWN, WV 26506-6009 • ADMISSIONS: 304-293-2121 • FAX: 304-293-3080

CAMPUS LIFE
Quality of Life Rating	86
Fire Safety Rating	94
Type of school	public
Environment	town

STUDENTS
Total undergrad enrollment	20,590
% male/female	54/46
% from out of state	43
% live on campus	26
% in (# of) fraternities	12 (13)
% in (# of) sororities	13 (10)
% African American	3
% Asian	2
% Caucasian	90
% Hispanic	2
% international	2
# of countries represented	91

SURVEY SAYS . . .
Career services are great
Everyone loves the WV
Mountaineers
Hard liquor is popular
Lots of beer drinking
Great library
Student publications are popular

ACADEMICS
Academic Rating	64
Calendar	semester
Student/faculty ratio	23:1
Profs interesting rating	67
Profs accessible rating	70
Most common lab size	20–29 students
Most common reg class size	20–29 students

MOST POPULAR MAJORS
business administration/
management
engineering
health professions and related
sciences

STUDENTS SAY

Academics
"Awesome academics and great school spirit" (not always in that order) define the WVU experience for many undergraduates here. Whether they're bleeding blue and gold on game day, enjoying the "exceptional partying" around campus, or grinding their way through one of WVU's standout academic programs, Mountaineers constantly "take pride in our school and state." WVU excels in numerous academic areas, including engineering, premedicine, journalism, psychology, forensics, advertising, music, and athletic training; a number of recent facilities upgrades have helped make some of these programs even better. Students here tell us that, although "Professors have hundreds of students," they "are always willing and interested to meet their students individually," and that WVU "Administrators don't hide in their offices; they actively participate in school functions." Undergrads also appreciate "plenty of internship and research opportunities" as well as a "good co-op program." WVU's elite Honors College "is really a great strength" and "is amazing at working with [its] students."

Life
WVU's football program "is one of the best in the country, and every Saturday is a great day," because "the entire state converges on Mountaineer Field to witness some of the best in NCAA football." Students throw themselves completely into the games as well as the "amazing" tailgates. One student notes, "The unity that is created among athletics is unmatched." If your passion for sports is weak, however, there's no reason to despair: At WVU, "There is an organization for everyone. There's a Fall Fest where major bands such as O.A.R. and Cypress Hill play and the school offers food, soda/pop, and beer in a controlled environment. There is a full bowling alley, billiard hall, and arcade in the bottom floor of our Student Union building, along with a full food court. There is a state-of-the-art rec center that receives tremendous use." While there are plenty of beer- and booze-soaked parties for those who are so inclined, there's also an alcohol-free program each weekend called WV Up All Night "where there is fun stuff and movies and comedy shows and games and free food at the student center" (although some warn that many people "get drunk and then go there for the free food"). Other options include the "Christian groups on campus," which "provide fun, safe, and religious activities in place of partying." Hometown Morgantown earns high marks; students praise its "refreshing, slower pace of life" as well as "the 15 bars downtown that are no more than 80 feet from each other." Main Street offers shopping that "caters to many tastes and styles."

Student Body
"There isn't a 'typical student'" at this school of 20,000-plus undergrads, although it seems that "everyone wears gold and blue and fits in fine." Students here detect a "good mix of the country and the city" as well as "a large out-of-state population," and they tell us that "what makes it such a great school is how everyone meshes together." Minorities, however, mesh to a lesser extent; as one student observes, "WVU is 90 percent White, so ethnically diverse students stand out. It's not that they're singled out, but it's just easy to notice [them] around campus. However, there is no discrimination, and everyone gets along well from what I've seen." The student body includes "typical fraternity and sorority students, but there are also so many intellectuals and unique individuals that you see them no matter where you turn." Undergrads are generally "easygoing, friendly, and approachable" and are "involved in club sports, clubs, the arts, residential education, or the Morgantown community."

FINANCIAL AID: 304-293-5242 • E-MAIL: WVUADMISSIONS@ARC.WVU.EDU • WEBSITE: WWW.WVU.EDU

ADMISSIONS

Very important factors considered include: Academic GPA, standardized test scores. *Important factors considered include:* Level of applicant's interest, state residency. *Other factors considered include:* Extracurricular activities, recommendation(s), volunteer work. SAT or ACT required; ACT with Writing component required. TOEFL required of all international applicants. High school diploma is required, and GED is accepted. *Academic units required:* 4 English, 3 math, 3 science (2 science labs), 3 social studies. *Academic units recommended:* 2 foreign language.

The Inside Word

While standards for general admission to WVU are not especially rigorous, you'll find admission to its premier programs to be quite competitive. Admission to the College of Business and Economics, for example, requires a high school GPA of at least 3.75 and an SAT Math score of at least 610. Programs in computer science, education, engineering, fine arts, forensics, journalism, medicine, and nursing all require fairly impressive credentials. If you are not admitted to the program of your choice, you may be able to transfer to it later if your grades are good enough, but it won't be easy.

FINANCIAL AID

Students should submit: FAFSA, state aid form. Regular filing deadline is March 1. The Princeton Review suggests that all financial aid forms be submitted as soon as possible after January 1. *Need-based scholarships/grants offered:* Pell Grant, SEOG, state scholarships/grants, private scholarships, the school's own gift aid. *Loan aid offered:* Direct Subsidized Stafford, Direct Unsubsidized Stafford, Direct PLUS, Federal Perkins Loan, college/university loans from institutional funds. Applicants will be notified of awards on a rolling basis beginning or about March 15.

FROM THE ADMISSIONS OFFICE

"From quality academic programs and outstanding, caring faculty to incredible new facilities and a campus environment that focuses on students' needs, WVU is a place where dreams can come true. The university's tradition of academic excellence attracts some of the region's best high school seniors. WVU has produced 25 Rhodes Scholars, 29 Goldwater Scholars, 18 Truman Scholars, 5 members of *USA Today*'s All-U.S.A. College Academic First Team, and 2 Udall Scholarship winners. Whether your goal is to be an aerospace engineer, reporter, physicist, athletic trainer, opera singer, forensic investigator, pharmacist, or CEO, WVU's 179 degree choices can make it happen. Unique student-centered initiatives include Operation Jump Start, which helps students experience true education extending beyond the classroom. Resident Faculty Leaders live next to the residence halls to mentor students, and WVU Up All Night provides a way to relax and have fun with free food and activities nearly every weekend. The Mountaineer Parents' Club connects more than 13,000 WVU families, and a parents' helpline (800-WVU-0096) leads to a full-time parent advocate. A new Student Recreation Center includes athletic courts, pools, weight/fitness equipment, and a 50-foot indoor climbing wall. Also, a brand-new life sciences building and completely renovated library complex just opened. With programs for studying abroad, a Center for Black Culture and Research, an Office of Disability Services, and a student body that comes from every WV county, 50 states, and 91 different countries, WVU encourages and nurtures diversity. More than $150 million in annual grant funding makes WVU a major research institution where undergraduates can participate. The main campus is one of the safest in the nation, and the area's natural beauty provides chances to ski, bike, hike, and go white-water rafting.

"All applicants beginning with the Fall 2007 class are required to take the new ACT Writing assessment as part of the ACT exam or take the new SAT exam to be considered for admission."

SELECTIVITY

Admissions Rating	74
# of applicants	12,047
% of applicants accepted	92
% of acceptees attending	44

FRESHMAN PROFILE

Range SAT Critical Reading	460–560
Range SAT Math	480–580
Range ACT Composite	20–26
Minimum Paper TOEFL	550
Minimum Computer Based TOEFL	173
Average HS GPA	3.3
% graduated top 10% of class	17
% graduated top 25% of class	40
% graduated top 50% of class	73

DEADLINES

Regular notification	rolling
Nonfall registration?	yes

APPLICANTS ALSO LOOK AT

AND OFTEN PREFER
Pennsylvania State University—University Park, University of Pittsburgh—Pittsburgh Campus, Virginia Tech

AND SOMETIMES PREFER
James Madison University, Marshall University, The Ohio State University—Columbus, University of Maryland—College Park

AND RARELY PREFER
Fairmont State College, Shepherd University, University of Delaware

FINANCIAL FACTS

Financial Aid Rating	77
Annual in-state tuition	$4,476
Annual out-of-state tuition	$13,840
Room & Board	$6,630
Books and supplies	$900
% frosh rec. need-based scholarship or grant aid	34
% UG rec. need-based scholarship or grant aid	37
% frosh rec. need-based self-help aid	33
% UG rec. need-based self-help aid	43
% frosh rec. any financial aid	69
% UG rec. any financial aid	86

WESTMINSTER COLLEGE (PA)

319 SOUTH MARKET STREET, NEW WILMINGTON, PA 16172 • ADMISSIONS: 800-942-8033 • FAX: 724-946-7171

STUDENTS SAY

Academics

At most schools, if your alarm clock doesn't go off the morning of your final exam, you miss the test, fail the class, and enter therapy. Not so for a freshman at Westminster: "I received a phone call from my professor at quarter after nine saying, 'The exam has started! Where are you? Get down here!'" This type of personal attention is the norm at Westminster, where students cite the faculty and administrators as one of the school's greatest assets. "My sister who had just graduated introduced me to the professors in her education major. They hugged me, shook my hand, and treated me like family." Clearly, many of the teachers here "relate well to the students and their needs," cultivating a "personal and comfortable atmosphere in the classroom," which extends outside of class as well. It's not unusual to be invited to a professor's house for a meal; even the president hosts picnics and dinners to get to know the students. A sophomore now majoring in communications was appreciative when "The Dean of Academic Affairs took me under his wing last year because I was undecided." Undergrads aspiring to be doctors one day hope to cash in on the school's exceptional medical school acceptance rates. But they don't complete the premed program easily; these students will tell you that "slacking is not an option." Other top programs include English, business, elementary education, and music. In addition, "The education experience in physics here competes with some of the biggest name schools, even though we lack equipment and opportunity." Overall, the Westminster academic experience aims to "expand your views on the world" and make students "think more clearly and analytically." The Career Center "offers amazing career placements, and they are always willing to help students improve resumes and job skills." A graduating senior sums it up well, saying her school is "loaded with people looking to make each student's life a little easier."

Life

"People think we don't do anything here because our college is located in a small, dry town." Rural New Wilmington shuts down at 7:00 P.M., precluding much excitement "unless an Amish revolt should break out." Most people head to nearby megalopolises Grove City and New Castle "because this town is stuck in 1950." On-campus activities occasionally suffer from low attendance, but movies and sports draw a crowd. Religious students take part in "varied opportunities for Christian fellowship and worship. There are organizations for athletes; Gospel Choir and Praise Band for singers and musicians; and Bible study groups, chapel services, a weekly informal, student-led worship, and weekly Vespers for everyone else." Though the campus is "supposedly dry," students still find a way to drink. "I feel that by following the rules and applying myself to my studies I am in the minority of kids who take college seriously," reports a resident assistant. Several students comment that rivalries between fraternities and tensions between Greeks and independent students have been overemphasized in the past. They claim all groups come together "for fun and philanthropy." A chorus of voices also agree that both the food and the parking situation could use some improvement.

Student Body

Westminster students jump to point out that "things have really improved here in terms of diversity, especially in the past 2 years." For example, "There has been a dramatic spike in the number of open homosexuals and people who support that community. A gay student was even elected as homecoming king." On the other hand, many still complain that the small percentage of minorities is disheartening. Undergraduates separate into straight-laced religious types, rowdy bacchanalian slackers, and a few black-clad "protestors of modern society." Most are Caucasian and come from rural towns in eastern Ohio or Western Pennsylvania—with a few Pittsburgh suburbanites mixed in—and families with money and college degrees. Many respondents emphasize "the interpersonal aspect" of the community—the say-hi-to-everyone culture, rooted in Christian conservative values without being all-the-way religious right.

WESTMINSTER COLLEGE (PA)

FINANCIAL AID: 724-946-7102 • E-MAIL: ADMIS@WESTMINSTER.EDU • WEBSITE: WWW.WESTMINSTER.EDU

ADMISSIONS

Very important factors considered include: Interview, rigor of secondary school record, standardized test scores. *Important factors considered include:* Application essay, character/personal qualities, class rank, recommendation(s). *Other factors considered include:* Alumni/ae relation, extracurricular activities, talent/ability, volunteer work, work experience. SAT or ACT required; TOEFL required of all international applicants. High school diploma is required, and GED is accepted. *Academic units required:* 4 English, 3 math, 2 science (2 science labs), 2 foreign language, 2 social studies, 1 history, 3 academic electives.

The Inside Word

The vast majority of those who apply to Westminster gain admission, but the applicant pool is strong enough to enable the college to weed out those who don't measure up to the solid entering class academic profile. Candidates who are shooting for academic scholarships should play the admissions game all the way and put a solid effort into the completion of their applications.

FINANCIAL AID

Students should submit: FAFSA, institution's own financial aid form. The Princeton Review suggests that all financial aid forms be submitted as soon as possible after January 1. *Need-based scholarships/grants offered:* Pell Grant, SEOG, state scholarships/grants, private scholarships, the school's own gift aid. *Loan aid offered:* FFEL Subsidized Stafford, FFEL Unsubsidized Stafford, FFEL PLUS, Federal Perkins Loan, Resource Loans. Applicants will be notified of awards on a rolling basis beginning or about November 1.

FROM THE ADMISSIONS OFFICE

"Since its founding, Westminster has been dedicated to a solid foundation in today's most crucial social, cultural, and ethical issues. Related to the Presbyterian Church (U.S.A.), Westminster is home to people of many faiths. Our students and faculty, tradition of campus, and small-town setting all contribute to an enlightening educational experience.

"For purposes of admission and merit scholarships Westminster College will evaluate applicants for Fall 2008 using the composite score of the Math and Critical Reading sections of the new SAT or the composite score of the ACT. Westminster will collect new Writing section scores and compare with national percentiles for possible inclusion in admission and scholarship criteria for the future."

SELECTIVITY

Admissions Rating	**79**
# of applicants	1,302
% of applicants accepted	77
% of acceptees attending	36

FRESHMAN PROFILE

Range SAT Critical Reading	480–592
Range SAT Math	480–590
Range ACT Composite	20–25
Minimum Paper TOEFL	550
Minimum Computer Based TOEFL	213
Average HS GPA	3.4
% graduated top 10% of class	20
% graduated top 25% of class	55
% graduated top 50% of class	87

DEADLINES

Early action application deadline	11/15
Early action notification	12/15
Regular application deadline	5/1
Regular notification	rolling
Nonfall registration?	no

APPLICANTS ALSO LOOK AT

AND SOMETIMES PREFER
Duquesne University
AND RARELY PREFER
Allegheny College, Thiel College, Washington & Jefferson College

FINANCIAL FACTS

Financial Aid Rating	**61**
Annual tuition	$25,530
Room & Board	$7,660
Books and supplies	$900
Required fees	$1,000
% frosh rec. need-based scholarship or grant aid	81
% UG rec. need-based scholarship or grant aid	79
% frosh rec. need-based self-help aid	68
% UG rec. need-based self-help aid	65

WESTMINSTER COLLEGE (UT)

1840 SOUTH 1300 EAST, SALT LAKE CITY, UT 84105 • ADMISSIONS: 801-832-2200 • FAX: 801-832-3101

STUDENTS SAY

Academics

There is more than one Westminster College, so let's not get confused. This is the one in the heart of Salt Lake City that's "the only liberal arts college in Utah." "Small class sizes" and "personal attention" abound on this "beautiful campus." Pre-professional programs are strong, particularly in nursing, education, and business. Westminster also offers some of the coolest programs anywhere. During an intense May Term, students take unique courses, such as "Chemistry and Biology of Brewing," or study off campus. You can study aviation in Alaska, for example, or traditional Indian culture—in India. "The May Term trips are a great opportunity" to "learn more about a different country," a junior writes. A semester-long program called Winter at Westminster offers backcountry touring, clinics in bobsledding and Nordic jumping, and camping in a yurt. Back on campus, Westminster's "easily accessible" professors facilitate "fun and interactive" discussions. "All the professors know you on a first-name basis," explains one happy student. "They practically beg you to come to their office hours for help." Views of the administration are mixed. Some students see Westminster as "a well-oiled machine" and its administrators as "genuinely interested in how the students are doing and making sure that any problems are solved as quickly as possible." Other students call the administration "disconnected." "Our science and lab facilities are substandard," a senior writes, but a new science center is planned and the school has spent $1 million in the past year for new, state-of-the-art equipment. "Many programs are under-funded and largely run by adjuncts to save money."

Life

At Westminster, "Life on campus is very dramatic." "Everyone knows everyone else," and "Everyone is involved in everyone else's business." Fortunately, there are numerous reasons for undergrads to get out and about: "Many people are involved with extracurricular activities" and "leadership opportunities" are abundant. The ASWC (Associated Students of Westminster College) also sponsors "many activities each week," including stand-up comics and dances. In addition, "The Music and Theater Department[s] are very popular." Student opinion of the food ranges from "not great" to it "sucks"—"they fry everything." Off campus, "There is a lot to do" around the city and "the state of Utah." The college "is located in the heart of Sugarhouse," one of Salt Lake City's oldest neighborhoods. "Clothes stores, book stores, bars, and restaurants are all within walking distance." "For fun," students "go to a movie or out to dinner," or "bask in the aroma-rich atmospheres of the local coffee shops." While "Many students go to clubs and bars for fun," "This isn't a real big party school." "There is a segment of the student body population that will not party for religious reasons," notes a junior. "Proximity to the beautiful mountains" means that "outdoor activities" abound here. Westminster is only "minutes away from some pretty awesome ski resorts" so skiers and snowboarders can "maximize their time on the slopes." "Utah has the greatest snow on earth," avows a junior.

Students

"Westminster is not religiously affiliated" and many students here "are not religious at all." At the same time, "a large portion" of the student body is "religious and wholesome." "We're in Utah," explains a junior. When asked to describe a typical student, Westminster undergrads offer: "White, middle-class, from Utah, [and] either fresh out of high school or fresh off an LDS [Latter Day Saints] mission." "Most of the students are traditional students" but "There are many people over age 25" as well. The "self-motivated" students here are "very active (and liberal) politically" and "pretty studious." They "tend to be kind of preppy, but you can find hippies." There are "the children of the very rich who are just mediocre and the children of the very poor who are brilliant." "There are not many minorities on campus" and Westminster is "less diverse than the average university," but "more diverse, generally, than the rest of the state." Students from ethnic minorities who are here "seem to integrate well into the social groups on a friendly level."

FINANCIAL AID: 801-832-2500 • E-MAIL: ADMISSION@WESTMINSTERCOLLEGE.EDU • WEBSITE: WWW.WESTMINSTERCOLLEGE.EDU

ADMISSIONS

Very important factors considered include: Academic GPA, rigor of secondary school record. *Important factors considered include:* Application essay, class rank, interview, standardized test scores. *Other factors considered include:* Alumni/ae relation, character/personal qualities, extracurricular activities, geographical residence, recommendation(s), talent/ability. SAT or ACT required; ACT with Writing component recommended. TOEFL required of all international applicants. High school diploma is required, and GED is accepted. *Academic units required:* 4 English, 2 math, 3 science, 2 foreign language, 2 social studies, 1 history, 2 academic electives. *Academic units recommended:* 4 English, 3 math, 3 science, 3 foreign language, 2 social studies, 1 history, 3 academic electives.

The Inside Word

It's not spectacularly difficult to gain admission to Westminster, particularly if you have solid grades and have taken a reasonably broad college-prep curriculum; your high school grades are probably the single biggest admissions factor here; essays are also important. Your standardized test scores, on the other hand, don't need to be out of this world. While almost every student at Westminster is on some kind of scholarship, you should pay special attention to every facet of the application if you are gunning for a lot of free money.

FINANCIAL AID

Students should submit: FAFSA. The Princeton Review suggests that all financial aid forms be submitted as soon as possible after January 1. *Need-based scholarships/grants offered:* Pell Grant, SEOG, state scholarships/grants, private scholarships, the school's own gift aid, United Negro College Fund. *Loan aid offered:* FFEL Subsidized Stafford, FFEL Unsubsidized Stafford, FFEL PLUS, Federal Perkins Loan. Applicants will be notified of awards on or about March 15. Federal Work-Study Program available. Institutional employment available. Off-campus job opportunities are excellent.

FROM THE ADMISSIONS OFFICE

"Founded in 1875, Westminster College is a private, comprehensive, liberal arts college dedicated to students and their learning, and offers one of the most unique learning environments in the country. Located where the Rocky Mountains meet the vibrant city of Salt Lake, Westminster blends classroom learning with experiences derived from its unique location to help students develop skills and attributes critical for success in a rapidly changing world. Impassioned teaching and active learning are the hallmarks of the Westminster experience.

"Each application is read and reviewed individually by an Admissions Counselor who takes into account both level of challenge in course work and grades received. Either the SAT or ACT exam is accepted. Writing ability will be assessed through the Writing sections of the SAT, ACT, application essays, and in some cases, other writing samples such as graded papers. For 2007–2008, the Writing section of the ACT is recommended but not required, and the Writing component of the SAT will be reviewed. However, only the Math and Critical Reading scores will be used for merit scholarship consideration for the 2007–2008 year.

"Westminster College has a rolling application deadline and will accept applications until the class is filled. To be eligible for the widest array of financial aid—and over 97 percent of freshmen receive some financial aid—April 15 is the priority consideration deadline for fall semester, and June 1 is the deadline for on-campus housing applications."

SELECTIVITY

Admissions Rating	81
# of applicants	1,182
% of applicants accepted	79
% of acceptees attending	40

FRESHMAN PROFILE

Range SAT Critical Reading	507–640
Range SAT Math	490–610
Range ACT Composite	21–26
Minimum Paper TOEFL	550
Minimum Computer Based TOEFL	213
Average HS GPA	3.49
% graduated top 10% of class	27
% graduated top 25% of class	53
% graduated top 50% of class	84

DEADLINES

Regular notification	rolling
Nonfall registration?	yes

APPLICANTS ALSO LOOK AT

AND OFTEN PREFER
University of Utah, Utah State University

AND SOMETIMES PREFER
Brigham Young University (UT), Colorado College, Gonzaga University, University of Puget Sound

AND RARELY PREFER
Lewis & Clark College

FINANCIAL FACTS

Financial Aid Rating	85
Annual tuition	$20,640
Room & Board	$6,140
Books and supplies	$1,000
Required fees	$390
% frosh rec. need-based scholarship or grant aid	61
% UG rec. need-based scholarship or grant aid	65
% frosh rec. need-based self-help aid	55
% UG rec. need-based self-help aid	63
% frosh rec. any financial aid	83
% UG rec. any financial aid	85

WHEATON COLLEGE (IL)

501 COLLEGE AVENUE, WHEATON, IL 60187 • ADMISSIONS: 630-752-5005 • FAX: 630-752-5285

STUDENTS SAY

Academics

At Wheaton, ask a faculty member to lunch and the student government will pick up the tab. "Most professors are more than happy to go with you!" The emphasis on teacher-student interaction starts early, since the school likes to see professors put "a lot of effort into the introductory classes. They believe it is their duty to present students with the most engaging education possible." Even established slackers admit that "classes and texts are so stimulating that sometimes I actually want to study." Many students emphasize the workload is heavy with rich content rather than "busy work." Courses are "usually well organized and well taught," making it nearly impossible for students to "name an absolute favorite because there are too many." The Conservatory of Music is especially well known for academic quality. Instructors all around "strive to present information honestly, with the least possible degree of bias, in order to equip students to discover the truth for themselves." Students call the administration "generally knowledgeable and effective, but also overbearing and sometimes paranoid." A senior reports, "They work hard to maintain this holy, Christian atmosphere while often overlooking or neglecting the problems of the school and student body." Still, Wheaton succeeds at its goal of "integrating the Christian faith into all areas of academia with the purpose of making Christian workers who will infiltrate every part of the world and affect it for Christ and his kingdom."

Life

Wheaton life is governed by a community covenant, signed by all, aiming to "control everyone's life so they stay Christian," according to some undergraduate agitators. "While there is some underground smoking and drinking, I would say that it is less than 2 percent of the students who would partake over their 4 years," estimates one student. Entertainment centers more on the wholesome, dorm-based life: raids on brother/sister floors, miniature golf courses set up in the halls, or an innocent game of sardines. The recent legalization of dancing, as long as it's not "immodest, sinfully erotic, or harmfully violent," has spawned a frenzy of square-dancing and swing-dancing events. As far as the "somewhat strange dating scene," most coed events organized by the school are called "a joke." Other students think, "It actually reminds me of a more normalized form of high school dating, one with far less rumor-mongering, fighting, and drama." Many kids avoid the dating scene altogether, spending time at Bible study, staying up late watching movies, talking theology, or immersing themselves in the chaste haven of a philosophy paper on a Friday night. For variety, students can escape to the North Woods campus, explore Chicago, or participate in urban social justice ministries.

Student Body

Wheaton students form "strong social support networks" based mainly on sports teams, dormitory floors, major, or artistic involvement. A senior who had a single room in one of the dorms said of the building, "We treated our small population of 50 guys like a sort of alternative community—not quite monastic though." Christianity operates as the default denominator, to the extent that some students feel "You have to be a Christian here or you won't fit in." At the forefront of the "strictly monocultural" population, we find preppy, type-A, conservative WASPs, who are "obsessed with their GPA and being the perfect Christian." The commonly held concern with social issues has triggered "a recent emphasis on diversity issues and racial relations." A junior says of his peers, "While they are mostly good people, their cultural exposure is close to nil. They tend to believe that all Asians know martial arts, all African Americans can rap well, and that anyone not from the conservative part of the U.S. is weird." A degree of diversity and worldliness comes from students who grew up overseas "either as missionary kids or military brats."

WHEATON COLLEGE (IL)

FINANCIAL AID: 630-752-5021 • E-MAIL: ADMISSIONS@WHEATON.EDU • WEBSITE: WWW.WHEATON.EDU

ADMISSIONS

Very important factors considered include: Academic GPA, application essay, character/personal qualities, recommendation(s), rigor of secondary school record, standardized test scores. *Important factors considered include:* Interview, level of applicant's interest, talent/ability. *Other factors considered include:* Alumni/ae relation, class rank, extracurricular activities, first generation, geographical residence, racial/ethnic status, religious affiliation/commitment, state residency, volunteer work. SAT or ACT required; TOEFL required of all international applicants. High school diploma is required, and GED is accepted. *Academic units recommended:* 4 English, 4 math, 4 science, 3 foreign language, 4 social studies.

The Inside Word

The admissions process at Wheaton is quite rigorous. As at most small colleges, the review of candidates focuses on far more than courses, grades, and test scores. The Admissions Committee will also carefully consider your essays, recommendations, and other indicators of your character as they assess how well suited you are to the campus community. Wheaton limits acceptance to students who profess Christian faith.

FINANCIAL AID

Students should submit: FAFSA, institution's own financial aid form. The Princeton Review suggests that all financial aid forms be submitted as soon as possible after January 1. *Need-based scholarships/grants offered:* Pell Grant, SEOG, state scholarships/grants, the school's own gift aid. *Loan aid offered:* FFEL Subsidized Stafford, FFEL Unsubsidized Stafford, FFEL PLUS, Federal Perkins Loan, college/university loans from institutional funds, alternative loans. Applicants will be notified of awards on a rolling basis beginning or about March 1. Federal Work-Study Program available. Institutional employment available. Off-campus job opportunities are excellent.

FROM THE ADMISSIONS OFFICE

"At Wheaton, we're commited to being a community that fearlessly pursues truth, upholds an academically rigorous curriculum, and promotes virtue. The college takes seriously its impact on society. The influence of Wheaton is seen in fields ranging from government (the former speaker of the house) to sports (two NBA coaches) to business (the CEO of John Deere) to music (Metropolitan Opera National Competition winners) to education (over 40 college presidents) to global ministry (Billy Graham). Wheaton seeks students who want to make a difference and are passionate about their Christian faith and rigorous academic pursuit.

"Fall 2008 applicants are required to submit results from the new SAT, or ACT with Writing section. Wheaton will use the highest of these scores from either test in evaluating a student's application."

SELECTIVITY

Admissions Rating	**95**
# of applicants	2,115
% of applicants accepted	56
% of acceptees attending	49
# accepting a place on wait list	164
% admitted from wait list	64

FRESHMAN PROFILE

Range SAT Critical Reading	610–760
Range SAT Math	610–700
Range SAT Writing	590–700
Range ACT Composite	27–31
Minimum Paper TOEFL	550
Minimum Computer Based TOEFL	213
Average HS GPA	3.73
% graduated top 10% of class	58
% graduated top 25% of class	85
% graduated top 50% of class	98

DEADLINES

Regular application deadline	1/10
Regular notification	4/1
Nonfall registration?	yes

APPLICANTS ALSO LOOK AT
AND SOMETIMES PREFER
Biola University, Gordon College, Grove City College, Northwestern University, Taylor University, Westmont College
AND RARELY PREFER
Cedarville University, Covenant College, Davidson College, St. Olaf College, University of Illinois at Urbana-Champaign, Vanderbilt University

FINANCIAL FACTS

Financial Aid Rating	**78**
Annual tuition	$22,450
Room & Board	$7,040
Books and supplies	$744
% frosh rec. need-based scholarship or grant aid	39
% UG rec. need-based scholarship or grant aid	40
% frosh rec. need-based self-help aid	44
% UG rec. need-based self-help aid	46
% frosh rec. any financial aid	69
% UG rec. any financial aid	68

WHEATON COLLEGE (MA)

OFFICE OF ADMISSION, NORTON, MA 02766 • ADMISSIONS: 508-286-8251 • FAX: 508-286-8271

CAMPUS LIFE
Quality of Life Rating	69
Fire Safety Rating	80
Type of school	private
Environment	village

STUDENTS
Total undergrad enrollment	1,561
% male/female	38/62
% from out of state	67
% from public high school	63
% live on campus	96
% African American	4
% Asian	3
% Caucasian	79
% Hispanic	3
% international	2
# of countries represented	34

SURVEY SAYS . . .
Small classes
Frats and sororities are unpopular or nonexistent

ACADEMICS
Academic Rating	94
Calendar	semester
Student/faculty ratio	12:1
Profs interesting rating	86
Profs accessible rating	85
% profs teaching UG courses	100
% classes taught by TAs	0
Most common lab size	19–22 students
Most common reg class size	25–30 students

MOST POPULAR MAJORS
art studio
economics
English
history
psychology

STUDENTS SAY
Academics
"The greatest strengths of Wheaton are the opportunities that come as a result of being such a small school," students at this New England liberal arts stronghold agree. Those opportunities include "close relationships with faculty, chances to study something independently if the subject is not specifically offered," and the encouragement students receive, "for studying abroad and getting internships, which is really awesome at the undergraduate level." Students get personal-touch treatment from the moment they arrive. Their first academic experience is the First-Year Seminar, "in which students learn to read, write, and study at a college level. It serves as an introductory course for the way most classes will run. The professor of this course will be the student's advisor until that student declares his/her major. . . . Each first-year student is also assigned two upper-class students who serve as mentors to the freshmen, guiding them through their adjustments to college life and answering any questions that need answering. The transition into college life couldn't have been easier because of this program." The personal attention continues right through to graduation and beyond, with help from the exceptional Filene Center, "a career and job placement services office that is the best institution available to students and graduates of Wheaton. It opens many doors for students to obtain internships as well as jobs after college, and from freshman year on they help you build your resume and interests." The school's size also has its drawbacks; "It is very difficult to get into the classes of your choice here, especially if you are a psychology major," warns a student in one of the school's more popular majors.

Life
"Wheaton is cursed by geography," students agree, complaining that hometown Norton "has nothing to offer college students." Couple this with the school's aggressively enforced dry-campus policy and you can see why "Wheaton is a suitcase school. Too many people go home on the weekends, and college shouldn't be like that." Students wish it were otherwise. "You don't get the full experience by going home every weekend," grouses one. On the upside, the school is making efforts to address the situation. One undergrad explains, "The school has tried having dances and more on-campus events, but the reality of it is that campus life over the weekend here will never be fabulous." As a result, students bug out on Fridays, "going into Boston and Providence for dinner or just to hang out." Things are pretty busy during the week, as "There are over [60] student run organizations on campus. Literally, there is something for everybody, and if you don't find a club for you, start one! The process is very easy!" Weekends, however, are a different story. Also, "Athletics are a big part of life here, since such a big proportion of students are athletes." A few students note the benefits of living in quiet seclusion: "Our small, suburban town means that students concentrate on their studies, sans distractions, on a beautiful campus," explains one undergrad.

Student Body
"There are no 'typical' students on campus, unless you count White, upper-middle-class, sweater-and-jeans-wearing, white-teeth-blazing, upstanding men and women," jokes a typical Wheatie. This same student adds that "realistically, we are a predominately wealthy, educated student body whose parents are usually educated as well. We have a pitifully small racial and ethnic population, and those who are diverse tend to group together." A former women's school, Wheaton is still predominantly female. One male observes, "I can't complain about the male to female ratio—62 percent female is 62 percent female no matter how you look at it. The benefits . . . just think about the benefits." Most undergraduates "fall into the category of 'liberal' when it comes to many issues [and] are very intellectually and artistically active. Students are really encouraged to explore their interests and passions here," regardless of the health impact. "Almost 100 percent of the campus exercises regularly, [yet] many students smoke like chimneys."

WHEATON COLLEGE (MA)

FINANCIAL AID: 508-286-8232 • E-MAIL: ADMISSION@WHEATONCOLLEGE.EDU • WEBSITE: WWW.WHEATONCOLLEGE.EDU

ADMISSIONS

Very important factors considered include: Academic GPA, application essay, character/personal qualities, extracurricular activities, first generation, rigor of secondary school record, talent/ability. *Important factors considered include:* Alumni/ae relation, class rank, interview, recommendation(s), volunteer work, work experience. *Other factors considered include:* Geographical residence, level of applicant's interest, racial/ethnic status, standardized test scores, state residency. TOEFL required of all international applicants. High school diploma is required, and GED is accepted. *Academic units recommended:* 4 English, 4 math, 3 science (2 science labs), 4 foreign language, 3 social studies, 2 history.

The Inside Word

Wheaton is to be applauded for periodically re-examining its admissions process; some colleges use virtually the same application process eternally, never acknowledging the fluid nature of societal attitudes and institutional circumstances. Approaches that emphasize individuals, or even their accomplishments, over their numbers are unfortunately rare in the world of college admission, where GPA and SAT reign supreme. Wheaton has an easier time than some colleges in taking this step because it isn't prohibitively selective.

FINANCIAL AID

Students should submit: FAFSA, CSS/Financial Aid PROFILE, Noncustodial PROFILE, Business/Farm Supplement, parent and student Federal Income Tax Returns and W-2s. Regular filing deadline is February 1. The Princeton Review suggests that all financial aid forms be submitted as soon as possible after January 1. *Need-based scholarships/grants offered:* Pell Grant, SEOG, state scholarships/grants, private scholarships, the school's own gift aid. *Loan aid offered:* FFEL Subsidized Stafford, FFEL Unsubsidized Stafford, FFEL PLUS, Federal Perkins Loan, state loans. Applicants will be notified of awards on or about April 1.

FROM THE ADMISSIONS OFFICE

"What makes for a 'best college'? Is it merely the hard-to-define notions of prestige or image? We don't think so. We think what makes college 'best' and best for you is a school that will make you a first-rate thinker and writer, a pragmatic professional in your work, and an ethical practitioner in your life. To get you to all these places, Wheaton takes advantage of its great combinations: a beautiful, secluded New England campus combined with access to Boston and Providence; a high quality, classic liberal arts and sciences curriculum combined with award-winning internship, job, and community-service programs; and a campus that respects your individuality in the context of the larger community. What's the 'best' outcome of a Wheaton education? A start on life that combines meaningful work, significant relationships, and a commitment to your local and global community. Far more than for what they've studied or for what they've gone on to do for a living, we're most proud of Wheaton graduates for who they become.

"Wheaton does not require students to submit the results of any standardized testing. The only exception is the TOEFL for students for whom English is a second language. Students who choose to submit standardized testing may use results from the historic SAT, its revised version, or from the ACT."

SELECTIVITY

Admissions Rating	94
# of applicants	3,614
% of applicants accepted	41
% of acceptees attending	28
# accepting a place on wait list	299
% admitted from wait list	41
# of early decision applicants	206
% accepted early decision	173

FRESHMAN PROFILE

Range SAT Critical Reading	600–680
Range SAT Math	580–670
Range ACT Composite	25–28
Minimum Paper TOEFL	550
Minimum Computer Based TOEFL	213
Average HS GPA	3.5
% graduated top 10% of class	53
% graduated top 25% of class	83
% graduated top 50% of class	99

DEADLINES

Early decision application deadline	11/15
Early decision notification	12/15
Regular application deadline	1/15
Regular notification	4/1
Nonfall registration?	yes

APPLICANTS ALSO LOOK AT

AND OFTEN PREFER
Bates College, Connecticut College

AND SOMETIMES PREFER
Hamilton College, Skidmore College, University of Vermont

AND RARELY PREFER
Boston University, Brandeis University, Clark University

FINANCIAL FACTS

Financial Aid Rating	89
Annual tuition	$36,430
Room & Board	$8,640
Books and supplies	$940
Required fees	$260
% frosh rec. need-based scholarship or grant aid	52
% UG rec. need-based scholarship or grant aid	48
% frosh rec. need-based self-help aid	53
% UG rec. need-based self-help aid	49
% frosh rec. any financial aid	66
% UG rec. any financial aid	63

WHITMAN COLLEGE

345 BOYER AVENUE, WALLA WALLA, WA 99362-2083 • ADMISSIONS: 509-527-5176 • FAX: 509-527-4967

STUDENTS SAY
Academics
With "a tight community that has approachable professors, small class sizes, and a rigorous academic course to prepare well-rounded, well-educated students," Whitman College is a comfortable fit for its "intelligent and passionate" student body. Undergrads here especially appreciate "the great length to which the staff, faculty, and administration go to make sure that we are happy, healthy, and doing well in school. It's a very homey place." The school offers "tons of great study areas and learning facilities to take advantage of, like computer labs in every building and a 24-hour library." Students are particularly impressed with the "strong Biology Department, which offers a great BBMB program (biophysics, biochemistry, molecular biology)." The workload is heavy, and "Some Whitman kids wear themselves thin doing too much. There's almost the social expectation that you will participate in a million activities, have a job, volunteer, have tons of friends, party hard, and—of course—excel academically, which can be really stressful." Most here don't mind, however. In fact, they relish the challenge, which is why they chose Whitman in the first place. "This school demands an intense amount of effort, time, and commitment," writes one senior. "But it pays off socially and academically if you have the motivation." Students also love that they "have a big say in what is going on. We get a voice in choosing the new college president, in reviewing teachers, and even in the admissions process."

Life
Hometown Walla Walla "is cute and quaint, but as far as activities that college students want to do, fairly limited. There's bowling, wheat fields, a movie theater, some good restaurants, and not much more." Some here feel the town is "Whitman's biggest drawback," but many observe that "being in such a small town forces the campus life to be amazing." By most accounts, campus life is just that. One student reports, "There is always a ridiculous amount of things going on on campus. Sometimes the trouble is choosing what you are going to do or having time to do all of the things you are interested in. There are tons of clubs (and some really odd ones, like the Ender's Game Alliance and the Flight Club) to get involved in and lots of musical performances, plays, parties, speakers, etc." As a result, students stick close to home, which is why "The campus here is often referred to as 'The Whitman Bubble.' Often you forget there is a world outside of Whitman just because you are so overwhelmed with all that is here." To break up long nights spent on homework, "Every dorm has a planned study break once a week, in which we do things like finger-paint, have pillow fights, or invite one of the insanely popular a cappella groups to sing to us." Undergrads appreciate that "Whitman is a very green campus and aware of the environment. There are always numerous vegetarian and vegan options in the dining halls."

Student Body
"Everyone is passionate and active about both academics and extracurricular activities," at Whitman, "whether it's music, volunteering, intramural sports, a political group, or something else. People aren't content with just sitting around doing nothing." Undergrads here identify the typical student as "a high middle- to upper-class White kid who grew up near Seattle or Portland," but they also detect "a surprising number of students from lower-income families." There are lots of "granola hippies" here who are "hard workers, environmentally and politically conscious, vegetarian, Birkenstock-wearing, bicycling, happy people." Most here agree that "Whitman needs to work on diversity. There is not enough racial diversity on campus, although the school is working hard to encourage diversity. There are diversity clubs on campus that help minority students and increase awareness about diversity on and off campus." The student body is "heavy on Democrats."

FINANCIAL AID: 509-527-5178 • E-MAIL: ADMISSION@WHITMAN.EDU • WEBSITE: WWW.WHITMAN.EDU

ADMISSIONS

Very important factors considered include: Application essay, character/personal qualities, rigor of secondary school record. *Important factors considered include:* Academic GPA, interview, racial/ethnic status, recommendation(s), standardized test scores, talent/ability. *Other factors considered include:* Alumni/ae relation, class rank, extracurricular activities, first generation, geographical residence, level of applicant's interest, state residency, volunteer work, work experience. SAT or ACT required; ACT with Writing component required. TOEFL required of all international applicants. High school diploma is required, and GED is accepted. *Academic units recommended:* 4 English, 4 math, 3 science (3 science labs), 2 foreign language, 2 social studies, 2 history, 1 arts.

The Inside Word

Whitman's Admissions Committee is to be applauded; any admissions process that emphasizes essays and extracurriculars over the SAT has truly gotten it right. The college cares much more about who you are and what you have to offer if you enroll than it does about what your numbers will do for the freshman academic profile. Whitman is a mega-sleeper. Educators all over the country know it as an excellent institution, and the college's alums support it at one of the highest rates of giving at any college in the nation. Student seeking a top-quality liberal arts college owe it to themselves to take a look.

FINANCIAL AID

Students should submit: FAFSA, CSS/Financial Aid PROFILE. Regular filing deadline is February 1. The Princeton Review suggests that all financial aid forms be submitted as soon as possible after January 1. *Need-based scholarships/grants offered:* Pell Grant, SEOG, state scholarships/grants, private scholarships, the school's own gift aid. *Loan aid offered:* FFEL Subsidized Stafford, FFEL Unsubsidized Stafford, FFEL PLUS, Federal Perkins Loan, state loans, alternative student loans. Applicants will be notified of awards on a rolling basis beginning or about December 20. Federal Work-Study Program available. Institutional employment available.

FROM THE ADMISSIONS OFFICE

"Whitman is a place that encourages you to explore past the boundaries of disciplines because learning and living don't always fall neatly into tidy little compartments. Many students choose Whitman specifically because they're interested in a particular career such as business or engineering but want the well-rounded preparation that only a liberal arts education provides.

"Applicants for Fall 2008 are required to take the new version of the SAT or the ACT with the Writing section, but students may submit scores from the old version of the SAT (prior to March 2005) or ACT as well, and the best scores from either test will be used."

SELECTIVITY

Admissions Rating	**95**
# of applicants	2,740
% of applicants accepted	47
% of acceptees attending	28
# accepting a place on wait list	108
% admitted from wait list	30
# of early decision applicants	157
% accepted early decision	78

FRESHMAN PROFILE

Range SAT Critical Reading	610–720
Range SAT Math	620–690
Range SAT Writing	610–700
Range ACT Composite	28–32
Minimum Paper TOEFL	560
Minimum Computer Based TOEFL	220
Average HS GPA	4.0
% graduated top 10% of class	58
% graduated top 25% of class	89
% graduated top 50% of class	98

DEADLINES

Early decision application deadline	11/15
Early decision notification	12/15
Regular application deadline	1/15
Regular notification	4/1
Nonfall registration?	yes

APPLICANTS ALSO LOOK AT

AND OFTEN PREFER
Carleton College, Pomona College, Reed College, University of California—Berkeley

AND SOMETIMES PREFER
Colorado College, Occidental College, University of Puget Sound, University of Washington

AND RARELY PREFER
Gonzaga University

FINANCIAL FACTS

Financial Aid Rating	**89**
Annual tuition	$30,806
Room & Board	$7,840
Books and supplies	$1,400
% frosh rec. need-based scholarship or grant aid	51
% UG rec. need-based scholarship or grant aid	46
% frosh rec. need-based self-help aid	47
% UG rec. need-based self-help aid	43
% frosh rec. any financial aid	81
% UG rec. any financial aid	86

WHITTIER COLLEGE

13406 PHILADELPHIA STREET, PO BOX 634, WHITTIER, CA 90608 • ADMISSIONS: 562-907-4238 • FAX: 562-907-4870

STUDENTS SAY

Academics

A Whittier College education is a paradigmatic small-school experience, with all its many benefits and occasional drawbacks. Students enthusiastically tell us that "the greatest strength of the school is its small size," which allows for "discussion-based classes that are always taught by a full professor, the freedom to move around on your own and challenge yourself as much as you want, [and] countless opportunities to get involved and explore your interests and talents." It also means professors have time to "genuinely care about their students and their students' success. They wonder why you are not in class and are always open for a knock at their office door and hour-long discussions." One undergrad notes, "We get strong support from the faculty and upperclassman, who help the students with everything from writing papers to organizing schedules to adjusting to life on your own." On the downside, "There's no mega-stadium or brand-new lab equipment. The school was built in the early 1900s, so some of the buildings are old. But you'd be amazed how the teachers make use of everything they have." The school is upgrading facilities whenever it can; one student reports, "We have this brand-spanking-new library facility that is pretty sweet, and an all-new computer lab. Not to mention the Center for Academic Success, which provides free tutoring (very helpful) and has really comfortable beanbags to chill out in." Though in the past students have complained about the administration, the college has made a concerted effort to improve services by adding new staff to the Financial Aid Office and sending out aid packages to students before they leave for summer vacation.

Life

Whittier's size has as powerful an impact on its social life as on its academics. As one student puts it, "The joke on campus is that the school's so small that everyone knows what you did before you even do it." Undergrads report that "campus life seems very calm because it is such a small school, and there aren't that many students. However, that does not mean it's not fun. There are campus events constantly and students participate religiously." There are also "parties just about every night" and lots of "ultra-competitive beer pong" for those so inclined. Non-drinkers in our survey say that, "as easy as it is to find them, it is also just as easy to avoid them." Like Randy Newman, students love LA, "a great place to go to college. Whittier allows you to mix suburban and urban life. You can either stay in Whittier for a movie and dinner, or go to LA for a great concert or a night at the clubs." There's also "Disneyland, Huntington Beach, and Knott's Berry Farm, all just a close drive from school." Best of all, according to many here, "The beaches are only 20 minutes away. Lots of people surf." Nearly all these activities require a car, or a friend with a car; one undergrad warns, "If you don't have a car, prepared to be completely bored on weekends and at a real disadvantage when you need to run errands such as buying food." You won't be completely stranded, though, since "Uptown Whittier is just down the street from school and has a number of shops and restaurants: several great Asian restaurants, Mexican restaurants, BBQ, pizza, burgers, gelato, a Starbucks, and a movie theater along with miscellaneous other shops."

Student Body

A lot of schools brag about the diversity of their student body, but few can match Whittier, where "we have Blacks, Whites, Hispanics, Asians, gays, straights, Christians, Muslims, the poor, and the very rich. The greatest thing is that even with such diversity among such a small school, everyone is extremely friendly, open to new ideas, and accepts people for who they are." Students also vary widely in the degrees of their ambition and curiosity; one undergrad notes, "There are some students that do not take advantage of the opportunities here and make you wonder how they even passed high school. But then we have Marshall and Rhodes Scholar nominees, and a majority of students who have plans for graduate school."

FINANCIAL AID: 562-907-4285 • E-MAIL: ADMISSION@WHITTIER.EDU • WEBSITE: WWW.WHITTIER.EDU

ADMISSIONS

Very important factors considered include: Application essay, rigor of secondary school record. *Important factors considered include:* Academic GPA, character/personal qualities, extracurricular activities, interview, recommendation(s), standardized test scores, talent/ability, volunteer work. *Other factors considered include:* Alumni/ae relation, class rank, first generation, geographical residence, racial/ethnic status, state residency, work experience. SAT or ACT required; ACT with Writing component required. TOEFL required of all international applicants. High school diploma is required, and GED is accepted. *Academic units required:* 3 English, 2 math, 1 science (1 science lab), 2 foreign language, 1 social studies. *Academic units recommended:* 4 English, 3 math, 2 science, 3 foreign language, 2 social studies.

The Inside Word

The Admissions Committee at Whittier subjects each candidate to very close scrutiny and their interest in making good solid matches between candidates and the college is paramount. If Whittier is high on your list, make sure you put forth a serious effort to demonstrate what you want out of the college and what you'll bring to the table in return.

FINANCIAL AID

Students should submit: FAFSA, CSS/Financial Aid PROFILE. Regular filing deadline is June 30. The Princeton Review suggests that all financial aid forms be submitted as soon as possible after January 1. *Need-based scholarships/grants offered:* Pell Grant, SEOG, state scholarships/grants, private scholarships, the school's own gift aid. *Loan aid offered:* Direct PLUS, FFEL Subsidized Stafford, FFEL Unsubsidized Stafford, FFEL PLUS, Federal Perkins Loan, alternative financing loans. Applicants will be notified of awards on a rolling basis beginning or about February 15. Federal Work-Study Program available. Off-campus job opportunities are good.

FROM THE ADMISSIONS OFFICE

"Faculty and students at Whittier share a love of learning and delight in the life of the mind. They join in understanding the value of the intellectual quest, the use of reason, and a respect for values. They seek knowledge of their own culture and the informed appreciation of other traditions, and they explore the interrelatedness of knowledge and the connections among disciplines. An extraordinary community emerges from teachers and students representing a variety of academic pursuits, individuals who have come together at Whittier in the belief that study within the liberal arts forms the best foundation for rewarding endeavor throughout a lifetime.

"Freshman applicants for Fall 2008 must take the new SAT (or the ACT with the Writing component). In addition, students may submit scores from the old SAT (before March 2005) or ACT, and we will use their best scores from either test."

SELECTIVITY

Admissions Rating	**84**
# of applicants	3,089
% of applicants accepted	58
% of acceptees attending	19

FRESHMAN PROFILE

Range SAT Critical Reading	480–590
Range SAT Math	480–590
Range ACT Composite	22–24
Minimum Paper TOEFL	550
Minimum Computer Based TOEFL	230
Average HS GPA	3.12
% graduated top 10% of class	27
% graduated top 25% of class	57
% graduated top 50% of class	88

DEADLINES

Regular notification	rolling
Nonfall registration?	yes

APPLICANTS ALSO LOOK AT

AND OFTEN PREFER
Occidental College, University of Redlands

AND SOMETIMES PREFER
Loyola Marymount University, Pitzer College

AND RARELY PREFER
Chapman University, Claremont McKenna College

FINANCIAL FACTS

Financial Aid Rating	**84**
Annual tuition	$27,906
Room & Board	$8,334
Books and supplies	$800
Required fees	$200
% frosh rec. need-based scholarship or grant aid	54
% UG rec. need-based scholarship or grant aid	55
% frosh rec. need-based self-help aid	59
% UG rec. need-based self-help aid	64
% frosh rec. any financial aid	92
% UG rec. any financial aid	89

WILLAMETTE UNIVERSITY

900 STATE STREET, SALEM, OR 97301 • ADMISSIONS: 503-370-6303 • FAX: 503-375-5363

STUDENTS SAY

Academics

Willamette University is an "academically rigorous," intimate, and "seriously gorgeous" liberal arts school in Oregon. "Outstanding" academic programs include the sciences, a "great focus" on the arts, a popular Japanese Studies Program, and "a highly acclaimed political science program." Across the board, undergrads report "a lot of school work" which includes a first-year seminar and a senior project. On the plus side, "Small class sizes allow lots of discussion and personal attention" and undergraduate research opportunities allow students to work with faculty members on the kinds of projects reserved for grad students at most other schools. Willamette is also "very accommodating for double majors." Professors are, "for the most part, super interesting and exciting." "The really good professors make every single class really enjoyable," are "very involved with students' lives," and are "very responsive to the needs of students." A politics major beams: "I'm only a freshman and I've already had dinner at a professor's house, just like the 'spiel' said." Administrators "seem to slack off in a lot of ways" but, ultimately, they "will help you out with whatever you'd like to pursue." "If you want to start something on campus, there is usually a way."

Life

"The overall ambience" at Willamette is "relaxed and inviting." Students here describe their school as "an oasis of enlightenment" surrounded by a "sketchy" "cultural wasteland" (Salem, Oregon). Intercollegiate and intramural sports are hugely popular here, and the "incredibly strong" track and cross-country programs are especially noteworthy. Quite often "You'll see students reading or relaxing on campus by the stream, or in the field." "Some of the most fun I have is just hanging out with people at random places on campus," adds a sophomore. Willamette does, however, "gear up every now and again for campus activities like our music festival or for a sit-in," explains an anthropology major. While "There are several events that are sponsored by Greeks," frats don't dominate. "If you're in one and know people in them, they're great. If you aren't, then you don't really care." A junior takes a more concerned position: "One of the biggest drawbacks to our school is that the party scene is not very good. The administration is very restrictive with Greek parties, off-campus parties, and other sorts of parties that students try to have." By all accounts, however, "access to outdoor activities" is fantastic. Willamette is "2 hours from the coast" and "2 hours from the mountains." Also, "it's only a 45-minute drive over to Portland" and "a ton of cultural stuff."

Student Body

Undergrads report "a lot of rich kids" at Willamette, and portray "the typical student" as "White," suburban, and "from the Northwest, most likely Oregon." Many students, however, receive "sweet" financial aid packages, and an excellent scholarship program "attracts students from a huge variety of backgrounds." Still, "There are not that many ethnic minorities." Asian students make up the largest minority here, and a fair number hail from Japan "as Willamette has a program with the Tokyo International University." Students at Willamette rate their "interesting, intelligent, genuine, [and] community-oriented" peers as "pretty hard workers" and say "There's a social group for almost everyone—jocks, preps, partiers, nerds; you name it." There are also "outdoorsy" types and "a lot of musicians" here. Conflict between groups is very minimal. "Everyone is accepting . . . so it's not intimidating to meet random people." Politically, Willamette is "extremely liberal." There are plenty of "politically left-wing people who love granola and Howard Dean," though, interestingly, few "real hippies."

FINANCIAL AID: 503-370-6273 • E-MAIL: LIBARTS@WILLAMETTE.EDU • WEBSITE: WWW.WILLAMETTE.EDU

ADMISSIONS

Very important factors considered include: Academic GPA, class rank, recommendation(s), rigor of secondary school record, standardized test scores. *Important factors considered include:* Application essay, character/personal qualities, extracurricular activities, interview, talent/ability. *Other factors considered include:* Alumni/ae relation, first generation, geographical residence, racial/ethnic status, volunteer work, work experience. SAT or ACT required; ACT with Writing component required. TOEFL required of all international applicants. High school diploma is required, and GED is accepted. *Academic units recommended:* 4 English, 4 math, 3 science (3 science labs), 3 foreign language, 1 social studies, 2 history.

The Inside Word

Willamette is a bit of safety school for the Northwest. Although almost 50 percent of the students here graduated in the top 10 percent of their high school classes, test scores are within range for a lot of applicants. The admissions process is pretty standard for a small liberal arts college. Extracurriculars, recommendations, and essays are helpful but, more than likely, your grades will determine your fate.

FINANCIAL AID

Students should submit: FAFSA, CSS/Financial Aid PROFILE (required only for early action applicants—to be filed by Decmber 1). Regular filing deadline is February 1. The Princeton Review suggests that all financial aid forms be submitted as soon as possible after January 1. *Need-based scholarships/grants offered:* Pell Grant, SEOG, state scholarships/grants, private scholarships, the school's own gift aid. *Loan aid offered:* FFEL Subsidized Stafford, FFEL Unsubsidized Stafford, FFEL PLUS, Federal Perkins Loan, state loans, private loans. Applicants will be notified of awards on or about April 1. Federal Work-Study Program available. Institutional employment available. Off-campus job opportunities are fair.

FROM THE ADMISSIONS OFFICE

"The interactions between great teachers and great students are at the heart of the Willamette University experience. Considering that 8 of the past 16 Oregon Professors of the Year (selected by the Council for Advancement and Support of Education) come from our campus, it is no surprise that student surveys overwhelmingly praise 'the quality of education' and 'interactions with faculty' as satisfying attributes of the Willamette experience. To further enhance the strength of the faculty and the opportunities for student-faculty interaction, Willamette is adding 25 new faculty positions over the next 5 years.

"The accomplishments of Willamette graduates help put the quality of the education in perspective. In the past decade, nearly 90 of our students have been awarded competitive, national scholarships and fellowships, including Trumans, Fulbrights, Goldwaters and Watsons. With 20 Peace Corps volunteers currently serving, Willamette ranks in the top 10 for small colleges and universities with the most alumni volunteers.

"On-campus developments this past year include the opening of Kaneko Commons, the first of four residential commons that will transform campus living organizations. Kaneko, much anticipated by the Campus Sustainability Council, was our first LEED-certified 'green' building.

"All freshman applicants for Fall 2008 must submit either the new SAT or the ACT with Writing section."

SELECTIVITY

Admissions Rating	91
# of applicants	2,988
% of applicants accepted	75
% of acceptees attending	21
# accepting a place on wait list	165
% admitted from wait list	52

FRESHMAN PROFILE

Range SAT Critical Reading	580–690
Range SAT Math	580–670
Range ACT Composite	24–30
Minimum Paper TOEFL	550
Minimum Computer Based TOEFL	213
Average HS GPA	3.74
% graduated top 10% of class	47
% graduated top 25% of class	77
% graduated top 50% of class	98

DEADLINES

Regular application deadline	2/1
Regular notification	4/1
Nonfall registration?	yes

APPLICANTS ALSO LOOK AT

AND OFTEN PREFER
Colorado College, Whitman College

AND SOMETIMES PREFER
Lewis & Clark College, University of Oregon, University of Puget Sound

AND RARELY PREFER
Linfield College, Pacific University, Seattle University

FINANCIAL FACTS

Financial Aid Rating	84
Annual tuition	$28,416
Room & Board	$7,000
Books and supplies	$800
Required fees	$170
% frosh rec. need-based scholarship or grant aid	66
% UG rec. need-based scholarship or grant aid	62
% frosh rec. need-based self-help aid	57
% UG rec. need-based self-help aid	56
% frosh rec. any financial aid	94
% UG rec. any financial aid	94

WILLIAM JEWELL COLLEGE

500 COLLEGE HILL, LIBERTY, MO 64068 • ADMISSIONS: 816-415-7511 • FAX: 816-415-5040 • 888-2-JEWELL

CAMPUS LIFE

Quality of Life Rating	**96**
Fire Safety Rating	**89**
Type of school	private
Affiliation	historically Baptist
Environment	town

STUDENTS

Total undergrad enrollment	1,404
% male/female	38/62
% from out of state	20
% from public high school	90
% live on campus	61
% in (# of) fraternities	29 (3)
% in (# of) sororities	31 (4)
% African American	5
% Asian	1
% Caucasian	88
% Hispanic	3
% Native American	1
% international	1
# of countries represented	12

SURVEY SAYS . . .

Small classes
Students are friendly
Students get along with local community
Students love Liberty, MO
Students are happy
Frats and sororities dominate social scene

ACADEMICS

Academic Rating	**91**
Calendar	semester
Student/faculty ratio	12:1
Profs interesting rating	95
Profs accessible rating	90
% profs teaching UG courses	100
% classes taught by TAs	0
Most common lab size	10–19 students
Most common reg class size	fewer than 10 students

MOST POPULAR MAJORS

business administration/management
nursing/registered nurse training (ASN, BSN, MSN, RN)
psychology

STUDENTS SAY

Academics

A freshman majoring in political science reports, "Students at William Jewell College often believe that they are attending one of the top colleges in the Midwest, if not the United States, and receiving an Ivy League-quality education. That may be stretching it a bit, but I don't think that it's too far from the truth." This historically Baptist college offers a "highly selective and extremely intense" Oxbridge Honors Program, which subjects students to instruction English tutorial style. The nursing, music, education, and political science departments draw the most students, though class sizes across disciplines are often kept under 20. Nearly everyone emphasizes how actively welcomed they are made to feel by Jewell administrators. A freshman remembers, "They were so concerned with whether or not I was going to be happy." The president and his wife host a Christmas party complete with snickerdoodles, and professors are known for their "understanding of personal issues." One sophomore writes, "If you have something come up in your life or need a little break for some reason, professors will work with you to help you through." Some students accuse professors of "pushing their beliefs on everyone [or] trying to convert people" religiously and politically. Other undergraduates see just the opposite taking place: "My professors like to spark a conversation then get out of it and let the students hash it out," recounts a chemistry major. Either way, by getting through WJC, "You can't help but be a more informed and complete contributor to the world around you."

Life

Students who arrive expecting an oasis of godly behavior in a heathen world may be disappointed. "I thought it was a Christian School—as it turns out I was wrong." In this semireligious environment, rules may govern visitation, but you can get a beer if you want one. Members of fraternities claim, "It is not your typical party-hard/bad grades Greek life." Watch for the new Greek Strategic Plan to "help all of us become undivided" and present a milder Greek image. A senior reminds readers, "Just because I am a Christian doesn't mean I don't get out and have good, clean fun." Students frequent something called "Worship Jams," as well as on-campus concerts booked by College Union Activities. A freshman's typical evening entails "hanging out in the dorm because we are all broke. We also play a lot of pranks." Off-campus destinations in Liberty include the Corner Bar for drinks or Steak and Shake for late-night eats. For the culturally inclined, the Harriman Arts Program arranges student tickets for ballet and orchestra performances 20 minutes away in Kansas City.

Student Body

The distinctive quality of the Jewell student body is a repeated emphasis on thoughtfulness and self-reflection. "Overall, I live with students who want to use their passions in life to positively change society." Another student adds, "It doesn't matter what it is that you believe, as long as you have looked down every road and sought out every option before reaching a complete and final decision." It seems that Jewell conservatives think the school is too liberal, and vice versa. "We all have some sort of political views and talk about the world and the state of the country." Discussions get interesting because the split is about 50/50 between actively practicing Christians and the Baptists by birth only. The Republican/Democrat line doesn't coincide exactly, but close. An African American student finds it "exhausting being Black here," and many people recognize a need for improved representation "of our pluralistic society." Finally, with a slightly lopsided gender ratio, it sometimes feels more like an all-girls school than a coed one.

WILLIAM JEWELL COLLEGE

FINANCIAL AID: 888-2-JEWELL • E-MAIL: ADMISSION@WILLIAM.JEWELL.EDU • WEBSITE: WWW.JEWELL.EDU

ADMISSIONS

Very important factors considered include: Rigor of secondary school record. *Important factors considered include:* Academic GPA, application essay, character/personal qualities, class rank, extracurricular activities, first generation, level of applicant's interest, recommendation(s), standardized test scores, talent/ability. *Other factors considered include:* Alumni/ae relation, interview, racial/ethnic status, volunteer work, work experience. SAT or ACT required; ACT with Writing component recommended. TOEFL required of all international applicants. High school diploma is required, and GED is accepted. *Academic units required:* 4 English, 3 math, 3 science (1 science lab), 2 foreign language, 3 social studies. *Academic units recommended:* 4 English, 4 math, 3 science (1 science lab), 3 foreign language, 3 social studies, 2 academic electives.

The Inside Word

Admission to William Jewell requires the usual suspects: solid grades and test scores. The college is competitive, but admission is not out of reach for the average student. Once admitted, undergrads benefit from William Jewell's leading efforts in experiential learning.

FINANCIAL AID

Students should submit: FAFSA. The Princeton Review suggests that all financial aid forms be submitted as soon as possible after January 1. *Need-based scholarships/grants offered:* Pell Grant, SEOG, state scholarships/grants, the school's own gift aid. *Loan aid offered:* FFEL Subsidized Stafford, FFEL Unsubsidized Stafford, FFEL PLUS, Federal Perkins Loan, Federal Nursing Loan, nonfederal alternative loans (non-college). Applicants will be notified of awards on a rolling basis beginning or about February 15. Off-campus job opportunities are excellent.

FROM THE ADMISSIONS OFFICE

"'Founded in 1849, William Jewell College offers students an outstanding liberal arts education and a unique focus on cultivating leadership within an environment that values Christian ideals and spiritual growth. Its beautiful campus is perched above the town of Liberty, Missouri, and offers students all the amenities of a beautiful residential campus with exceptional recreational and athletic facilities. The college is just 20 minutes from downtown Kansas City.

"Enrollment stands at approximately 1,400 full-time students. The student body has representation from approximately 36 states and 12 foreign countries. International programs in Europe, Australia, Central and South America, and Asia allow Jewell students to study at some of the world's great universities. The Oxbridge Honors Program, recognized as one of the best study abroad opportunities in the nation, combines British tutorial methods of instruction with opportunities for a year of study in Oxford or Cambridge.

"Jewell continues to earn its reputation as a campus of achievement. Since being named *Time* Magazine's 'Liberal Arts College of the Year' in 2001–2002, the school has seen its students earn one Marshall Scholarship, three Truman Scholarships, and two Goldwater Scholarships. In addition, it has produced a Rhodes Scholar Finalist and its students have landed and two spots on *USA Today*'s All-U.S.A. College Academic Team. The college's Harriman Arts Program is considered the Midwest's premier program in the performing arts. The renowned Pryor Leadership Studies Program allows students to enhance their leadership skills across the curriculum.

"William Jewell College requires students to submit scores from either the ACT or the SAT in order to complete their application for admission. While the college does not require the new Writing section of the ACT or SAT, students are required to submit a separate essay. William Jewell does not require SAT Subject Tests."

SELECTIVITY

Admissions Rating	**88**
# of applicants	1,312
% of applicants accepted	63
% of acceptees attending	30

FRESHMAN PROFILE

Range SAT Critical Reading	520–660
Range SAT Math	500–660
Range ACT Composite	22–28
Minimum Paper TOEFL	550
Minimum Computer Based TOEFL	213
Average HS GPA	3.69
% graduated top 10% of class	38
% graduated top 25% of class	66
% graduated top 50% of class	96

DEADLINES

Regular application deadline	8/15
Regular notification	rolling
Nonfall registration?	yes

FINANCIAL FACTS

Financial Aid Rating	**74**
Annual tuition	$21,400
Room & Board	$5,700
Books and supplies	$650
Required fees	$300
% frosh rec. need-based scholarship or grant aid	71
% UG rec. need-based scholarship or grant aid	64
% frosh rec. need-based self-help aid	50
% UG rec. need-based self-help aid	48
% frosh rec. any financial aid	99
% UG rec. any financial aid	96

WILLIAMS COLLEGE

33 Stetson Court, Williamstown, MA 01267 • Admissions: 413-597-2211 • Fax: 413-597-4052

STUDENTS SAY

Academics

"The academics are quite rigorous—expect to spend 6 hours a day studying—and the professors definitely challenge you" at Williams College, a small liberal arts school in the northwestern corner of Massachusetts. Undergrads insist, however, that "that's what you come here for." A strong campus community makes Williams "a perfect stepping stone from high school to the real world. If you feel you can become obscenely excited at the sight of a purple cow (our mascot); love to get to know professors, classmates and staff on a personal level; and enjoy sports at all, be it as a spectator, athlete, or would-be athlete, Williams is your nirvana." Undergrads assure us that "there's absolutely no place better for an undergraduate to study any of the hard sciences or art history" and that "math, English, economics, and the visual and performing arts are also very strong." Course work "really pushes you to delve deep into the material and encourages original thinking," allowing students "to learn a lot, more maybe than you even think possible." Undergrads are especially enthusiastic about Williams' winter study program, "a month where you take one relatively low-stress class and get to go snowboarding and hang out a lot. My friends and I like to think of it as our reward for having lived through finals." One student says, "Williams combines stellar academics with a beautiful campus, friendly atmosphere, and caring administration that jump to make students as happy as possible. I've never seen a happier group of people in my life."

Life

"Williams is in the middle of some very beautiful, although very isolated, countryside" in Williamstown, which "is not exactly a metropolis." One student reports, "Because Williamstown pretty much closes at 5:00 p.m., the college knows it has to provide all of our entertainment, and it does a pretty great job of it. Movies, plays, concerts, and lectures can be found on campus almost every night of the week, and each weekend a few student organizations get $500 to throw all-campus parties." Athletics occupy the minds of many undergrads; the intercollegiate teams "are particularly strong," "Intramural sports are big, as is just playing for fun," and the surrounding area is especially amenable to outdoor fun. One student notes, "We enjoy the outdoors year round. On a random Friday in October, the president continues a 200-year tradition by declaring it 'Mountain Day'; classes are cancelled and the majority of the student body heads to the top of our mountain to enjoy the fall colors, the outdoors, and each other! In winter, most everyone skis or snowboards at a local ski mountain, 15 minutes away from campus." As one student puts it, "I've never seen so many physically active people in my life. It's actually inspired me to start going to the gym." Williams' strong sense of community receives a boost from the "JA entry system, under which 15 to 25 freshmen live in 'entries' with two 'JAs.' The JAs are basically upperclassmen who volunteer to be cool junior friends to all of the frosh on campus. The entry system eases the transition from high school to college, as you have a core group of friends from the first day of school on." The dorms, we're told, "are awesome, with nice touches that make dorm life very comfortable and noninstitutional."

Student Body

Williams undergrads describe themselves as "exceptionally driven and intelligent, yet not dorky or unsociable." Ephs (pronounced "Eefs," short for the school's founder, Ephraim Williams) "love politics, scientific research, reading," and for some, "getting plastered after a rough week." Because of the school's secluded mountain location, "Students tend to be outdoors types, and sports are big, although we don't have typical college 'jocks.' Everyone participates at their level. The presence of sports on campus means that most students are tremendously motivated, disciplined, and hardworking, not to mention fit." While "There is a bit of segregation between the jocks and the artsy students, there isn't ever any tension" between the two groups.

FINANCIAL AID: 413-597-4181 • E-MAIL: ADMISSION@WILLIAMS.EDU • WEBSITE: WWW.WILLIAMS.EDU

ADMISSIONS

Very important factors considered include: Academic GPA, application essay, recommendation(s), rigor of secondary school record, standardized test scores. *Important factors considered include:* Class rank, extracurricular activities, talent/ability. *Other factors considered include:* Alumni/ae relation, character/personal qualities, first generation, geographical residence, racial/ethnic status, volunteer work, work experience. SAT and SAT Subject Tests or ACT required; ACT with Writing component required. High school diploma or equivalent is not required. *Academic units recommended:* 4 English, 4 math, 3 science (3 science labs), 4 foreign language, 3 social studies.

The Inside Word

As is typical of highly selective colleges, at Williams high grades and test scores work more as qualifiers than to determine admissibility. Beyond a strong record of achievement, evidence of intellectual curiosity, noteworthy non-academic talents, and a noncollege family background are some aspects of a candidate's application that might make for an offer of admission. But there are no guarantees—the evaluation process here is rigorous. The Admissions Committee (the entire Admissions Staff) discusses each candidate in comparison to the entire applicant pool. The pool is divided alphabetically for individual reading; after weak candidates are eliminated, those who remain undergo additional evaluations by different members of the staff. Admission decisions must be confirmed by the agreement of a plurality of the committee. Such close scrutiny demands a well-prepared candidate and application.

FINANCIAL AID

Students should submit: FAFSA, CSS/Financial Aid PROFILE, Noncustodial PROFILE, Business/Farm Supplement, parent and student Federal Income Tax Returns and W-2s. Regular filing deadline is February 1. The Princeton Review suggests that all financial aid forms be submitted as soon as possible after January 1. *Need-based scholarships/grants offered:* Pell Grant, SEOG, state scholarships/grants, private scholarships, the school's own gift aid. *Loan aid offered:* Direct Subsidized Stafford, Direct Unsubsidized Stafford, Direct PLUS, Federal Perkins Loan, college/university loans from institutional funds. Applicants will be notified of awards on or about April 1. Federal Work-Study Program available. Institutional employment available.

FROM THE ADMISSIONS OFFICE

"Special course offerings at Williams include Oxford-style tutorials, where students (in teams of two) research and defend ideas, engaging in weekly debate with a faculty tutor. Annually 30 Williams students devote a full year to the tutorial method of study at Oxford; half of Williams students pursue overseas education. Four weeks of Winter Study each January provide time for individualized projects, research, and novel fields of study. Students compete in 32 Division III athletic teams, perform in 25 musical groups, stage 10 theatrical productions, and volunteer in 30 service organizations. The college receives several million dollars annually for undergraduate science research and equipment. The town offers two distinguished art museums, and 2,200 forest acres—complete with a treetop canopy walkway—for environmental research and recreation.

"For Fall 2008, students are required to submit either the new SAT or the ACT including the optional Writing section. Students may also submit scores from the old SAT and ACT. Applicants should also submit scores from any two SAT Subject Tests."

SELECTIVITY

Admissions Rating	**99**
# of applicants	5,999
% of applicants accepted	19
% of acceptees attending	47
# accepting a place on wait list	506
% admitted from wait list	13
# of early decision applicants	554
% accepted early decision	39

FRESHMAN PROFILE

Range SAT Critical Reading	660–760
Range SAT Math	660–760
Range ACT Composite	29–33
% graduated top 10% of class	90
% graduated top 25% of class	95
% graduated top 50% of class	100

DEADLINES

Early decision application deadline	11/10
Early decision notification	12/15
Regular application deadline	1/1
Regular notification	4/1
Nonfall registration?	no

APPLICANTS ALSO LOOK AT

AND OFTEN PREFER
Harvard College, Massachusetts Institute of Technology, Princeton University, Stanford University, Yale University

AND SOMETIMES PREFER
Amherst College, Brown University, Dartmouth College

AND RARELY PREFER
Carleton College, Colgate University, Hamilton College, Haverford College, Middlebury College

FINANCIAL FACTS

Financial Aid Rating	**99**
Annual tuition	$33,478
Room & Board	$8,950
Books and supplies	$800
Required fees	$222
% frosh rec. need-based scholarship or grant aid	46
% UG rec. need-based scholarship or grant aid	43
% frosh rec. need-based self-help aid	46
% UG rec. need-based self-help aid	43
% frosh rec. any financial aid	47
% UG rec. any financial aid	44

WITTENBERG UNIVERSITY

PO Box 720, Springfield, OH 45501 • Admissions: 800-677-7558 • Fax: 937-327-6379

CAMPUS LIFE

Quality of Life Rating	**82**
Fire Safety Rating	**76**
Type of school	private
Affiliation	Lutheran
Environment	town

STUDENTS

Total undergrad enrollment	1,873
% male/female	44/56
% from out of state	25
% live on campus	85
% in (# of) fraternities	8 (6)
% in (# of) sororities	18 (6)
% African American	6
% Asian	1
% Caucasian	83
% Hispanic	1
% international	2
# of countries represented	23

SURVEY SAYS . . .

Small classes
Lab facilities are great
Students are friendly
Students are happy
Lots of beer drinking

ACADEMICS

Academic Rating	**85**
Calendar	semester
Student/faculty ratio	12:1
Profs interesting rating	92
Profs accessible rating	94
% profs teaching UG courses	100
% classes taught by TAs	0
Most common lab size	10–19 students
Most common reg class size	10–19 students

MOST POPULAR MAJORS

biological and physical sciences
business/commerce
teacher education, multiple levels

STUDENTS SAY

Academics

Often described as "a small university with a family feel," Wittenberg offers the "opportunities and challenges of a large school on a small, close-knit campus," students here report. One satisfied undergrad explains, "Academically, Witt gives me what I wanted in high school but never received: highly focused and intense courses that challenge me but don't destroy the confidence in how I'm handling the class." Witt achieves this happy balance by providing "small classes, accessible faculty, a friendly staff, the personal attention needed to grow as a person and an academic, and a great social scene." Popular programs in biology, political science, and education all rank high here; students also praise the less-popular but equally strong marine and aquatic biology program. Undergrads point out that "since this is a liberal arts school, we are required to take general education courses. Professors are extremely helpful in getting all of your requirements filled, not only for generals but for the intended major." Professors also "all absolutely love to teach, are intrigued by class discussions, and are willing to work with you as an individual student." As a result, "This is definitely not a school where you are only known by your student ID number." The administration is "always open to students' input and ideas" and Witt's learning environment "is one that fosters motivated and high-achieving students."

Life

At Wittenberg, you'll find "the perfect balance of academics and extracurriculars," students agree, reporting that Witt is "a very social campus that is all about hanging out and having a good time." Undergrads "study pretty hard during the week," then "Saturday nights are the party nights because all the athletic teams have parties after their games." That's when "Everyone parties pretty hard, but only if they want to." We're told that most RAs here are willing to let their residents enjoy a party or two, which makes good times easy to come by. Campus life offers "clubs and groups for whatever you are interested in and more," as well as "an awesome Frisbee golf course" and "sororities and frats that are pretty popular." In addition, the school boasts "really strong sports for a Division III school, and we take our athletics pretty seriously." As proof, "we have a lot of students who could play at Division I schools who choose to come here." In 2002–2003, women's teams won championships in field hockey, volley ball, and basketball. Undergrads brag that Witt's campus is "gorgeous all year round; in the spring there are flowers everywhere, and in the fall the trees turn amazing colors." Even so, most agree that it's "nice to get off campus occasionally. The Kuss Performing Arts Center in Springfield brings in great entertainment. There's also putt-putt, movies, restaurants, shopping, and a great bike trail in town. Yellow Springs, a small town only about 20 minutes away, has a great arts theater and quaint shops." Dayton and Columbus "are just down the road for bigger-city entertainment."

Student Body

Witt undergrads "are generally well rounded and have strengths and interests in many areas; arts, politics, athletics, etc. It's not uncommon to find a jock that plays the trumpet and is involved in social awareness organizations." Witt fields 23 intercollegiate teams, which means lots of athletic types mixed among the small student population. "Friendly and outgoing" describe most Witt students, regardless of their interests: "You can't walk to class without seeing 10 people you know and saying "hi" to about 20 more." "Preppy but not over-the-top preppy" is the overwhelming style, and "Many students at Witt are wealthy, and (some are) legacies." Overall, "people are free-spirited and laid-back." They "work hard for their classes but also like to have a good time." There is a sizeable group of very religious students who shun the party scene but enjoy extracurricular life all the same. Students say it is refreshing that at Witt, just about everyone "is proud of the school. When you walk into your class, over three-fourths [of] the students will have on some school apparel."

WITTENBERG UNIVERSITY

FINANCIAL AID: 800-677-7558 • E-MAIL: ADMISSION@WITTENBERG.EDU • WEBSITE: WWW.WITTENBERG.EDU

ADMISSIONS

Very important factors considered include: Application essay, class rank, interview, recommendation(s), rigor of secondary school record, standardized test scores. *Important factors considered include:* Character/personal qualities, extracurricular activities, talent/ability, volunteer work. *Other factors considered include:* Alumni/ae relation, work experience. SAT or ACT required; TOEFL required of all international applicants. High school diploma is required, and GED is not accepted. *Academic units required:* 4 English, 3 math, 3 science (2 science labs), 2 foreign language, 2 history. *Academic units recommended:* 4 English, 4 math, 4 science (2 science labs), 3 foreign language, 3 history.

The Inside Word

Wittenberg's applicant pool is small but quite solid coming off of a couple of strong years. Students who haven't successfully reached an above-average academic level in high school will meet with little success in the admissions process. Candidate evaluation is thorough and personal; applicants should devote serious attention to all aspects of their candidacy.

FINANCIAL AID

Students should submit: FAFSA. The Princeton Review suggests that all financial aid forms be submitted as soon as possible after January 1. *Need-based scholarships/grants offered:* Pell Grant, SEOG, state scholarships/grants, private scholarships, the school's own gift aid. *Loan aid offered:* FFEL Subsidized Stafford, FFEL Unsubsidized Stafford, FFEL PLUS, Federal Perkins Loan, college/university loans from institutional funds. Applicants will be notified of awards on a rolling basis beginning or about March 1.

FROM THE ADMISSIONS OFFICE

"At Wittenberg, we believe that helping you to achieve symmetry demands a special environment, a setting where you can refine your definition of self yet gain exposure to the varied kinds of knowledge, people, views, activities, options, and ideas that add richness to our lives. Wittenberg is a university where students are able to thrive in a small campus environment with many opportunities for intellectual and personal growth in and out of the classroom. Campus life is as diverse as the interests of our students. Wittenberg attracts students from all over the United States and from many other countries. Historically, the university has been committed to geographical, educational, cultural, and religious diversity. With their varied backgrounds and interests, Wittenberg students have helped initiate many of the more than 125 student organizations that are active on campus. The students will be the first to tell you there's never a lack of things to do on or near the campus any day of the week, if you're willing to get involved.

"Wittenberg University requires freshman applicants to submit scores from the old or new SAT. Students may also choose to submit scores from the ACT (with or without the Writing component) in lieu of the SAT."

SELECTIVITY

Admissions Rating	**84**
# of applicants	2,392
% of applicants accepted	82
% of acceptees attending	29
# of early decision applicants	39
% accepted early decision	82

FRESHMAN PROFILE

Range SAT Critical Reading	520–650
Range SAT Math	530–640
Range ACT Composite	22–24
Minimum Paper TOEFL	550
Minimum Computer Based TOEFL	213
Average HS GPA	3.46
% graduated top 10% of class	32
% graduated top 25% of class	62
% graduated top 50% of class	86

DEADLINES

Early decision application deadline	11/15
Early decision notification	12/1
Regular notification	rolling
Nonfall registration?	yes

APPLICANTS ALSO LOOK AT
AND OFTEN PREFER
Miami University
AND SOMETIMES PREFER
Allegheny College, Denison University, Ohio Wesleyan University, The College of Wooster, The Ohio State University—Columbus
AND RARELY PREFER
Capital University, Gettysburg College, Ohio Northern University

FINANCIAL FACTS

Financial Aid Rating	**83**
Annual tuition	$31,400
Room & Board	$7,880
Books and supplies	$800
% frosh rec. need-based scholarship or grant aid	71
% UG rec. need-based scholarship or grant aid	73
% frosh rec. need-based self-help aid	69
% UG rec. need-based self-help aid	69
% frosh rec. any financial aid	99
% UG rec. any financial aid	99

WOFFORD COLLEGE

429 North Church Street, Spartanburg, SC 29303-3663 • Admissions: 864-597-4130 • Fax: 864-597-4147

STUDENTS SAY

Academics

"A great tradition of academic excellence, a good social life, and a community that lasts far beyond graduation" all draw students to Wofford College, a small Southern liberal arts school with "an outstanding biology program" that produces "a high percentage of students accepted into medical and dental school." Pre-law tracks, theology, and business are also reportedly quite strong here. In all areas, "Academics are very, very rigorous," but while "The workload here is heavy most of the time," Wofford never loses sight of its goal to provide "a well-balanced experience that stresses academics and a good, well-rounded education" that includes "community involvement and having fun." Great instructors help; students tell us that "the entire faculty at Wofford College is devoted to helping each and every student succeed. The professors are extremely willing to meet outside of class in order to answer any questions." In addition, Wofford "has a peer tutoring program that is extremely helpful. The program is free to students, and tutors are paid by the school. In short, if ever you find that you're having trouble, there's always someone who can help you get it sorted out." Sums up one undergrad, "Wofford College is a place to call home, where the course work is challenging but enjoyable, and you are known by a name, face, and personality rather than just an ID number."

Life

Imagine the idealized campus of a small, elite Southern college, and you'll have a pretty good mental picture of Wofford, whose campus "looks like a picture out of a movie!" The country club–like setting "is pristine, the grass is green, the buildings are maintained, and trash is something you rarely see." Sports are huge here; Wofford is a Division I school with 17 teams, meaning a good portion of the school's 1,100 students are involved in competitive sports teams. Even bigger, though, is Greek life; students agree that the Greek houses are "the center of campus, not only for the social scene but also as the leaders in the classroom and on-campus organizations." Undergrads warn that "on the weekends, the partying can be pretty intense as people relieve stress from their workload during the week. However, there also are lots of activities for nondrinkers. We have several theaters, a mall, many restaurants, free movie rentals from the library, and other colleges hosting events." Hometown Spartanburg "is a relatively small town that has all the basic stores you could ever need and tons of college appropriate restaurants, but only a select handful of nice places to eat." The school is "situated in an awkward area of Spartanburg. There isn't really anything near to it (within walking distance) except, of course, for the Krispy Kreme. Thank God for Krispy Kreme!" As a result, "We usually go to Greenville (25 minutes away) for most concerts and shopping."

Student Body

There is a definite "Wofford type," students tend to agree. One explains, "The typical student is a preppy kid from South Carolina who drives an SUV, likes music from Alabama to Jimmy Buffet, is a member of a sorority or fraternity, and dreams of being added onto George W. Bush's family tree." He or she is "serious about life and success," was "exceptionally gifted in high school in some area (academics or athletics usually)," and "is looking for a professional degree to use in order to continue on with education or get a job." There are, of course, students who don't fit the mold, however. One such student claims, "At first it can be difficult to acclimate, but being different, it becomes more apparent who is similarly minded, and there is a sort of 'force de resistance' among the atypical students." The school is making things easier for those outside the norm with its living-learning communities, such as "the race relations group and the arts LLC," both of which have promoted better-integrated campus community interactions.

FINANCIAL AID: 864-597-4160 • E-MAIL: ADMISSIONS@WOFFORD.EDU • WEBSITE: WWW.WOFFORD.EDU

ADMISSIONS

Very important factors considered include: Academic GPA, rigor of secondary school record. *Important factors considered include:* Application essay, character/personal qualities, class rank, extracurricular activities, standardized test scores, talent/ability. *Other factors considered include:* Alumni/ae relation, first generation, geographical residence, racial/ethnic status, recommendation(s), volunteer work, work experience. SAT or ACT required; ACT with Writing component required. TOEFL required of all international applicants. High school diploma is required, and GED is accepted. *Academic units recommended:* 4 English, 4 math, (3 science labs), 3 foreign language, 2 social studies, 1 history, 3 academic electives.

The Inside Word

Wofford College distinguishes itself by providing students with an extremely supportive environment. This concern extends to the applications it receives, each of which is given careful consideration. Students who have earned decent grades in challenging courses will find themselves with an opportunity to attend a school that is gaining a reputation as one of the South's premier liberal arts colleges.

FINANCIAL AID

Students should submit: FAFSA. The Princeton Review suggests that all financial aid forms be submitted as soon as possible after January 1. *Need-based scholarships/grants offered:* Pell Grant, SEOG, state scholarships/grants, private scholarships, the school's own gift aid. *Loan aid offered:* FFEL Subsidized Stafford, FFEL Unsubsidized Stafford, FFEL PLUS, Federal Perkins Loan, state loans. Applicants will be notified of awards on or about March 31. Federal Work-Study Program available. Institutional employment available. Off-campus job opportunities are good.

FROM THE ADMISSIONS OFFICE

"Approaching the end of his first year in office in the spring of 2001, Wofford President Benjamin Dunlap (a Rhodes scholar and Harvard PhD) asked the faculty, 'If you had the assurance of sufficient time and institutional support to teach the sort of course you've always dreamed of, what would you do?' In response, using grants from the Andrew Mellon and National Science Foundations, Wofford faculty created approximately 50 new courses and almost a dozen new interdisciplinary course sequences. Some of the new courses are 'learning communities,' the prototype for which was fashioned by a biologist and an English professor on 'the nature and culture of water.' A Spanish language course is taught in conjunction with a Latin American and Caribbean history course and a sociology course featuring fieldwork in the local Hispanic community. Handsomely appointed rooms suitable for meetings, meals, and seminars have been included in an ongoing series of major building projects and renovations to forge even closer relationships between faculty and students. Blessed with a Phi Beta Kappa academic tradition, a nationally ranked program of studies abroad, and an economy of scale that encourages innovation and collaboration among faculty and students, Wofford is positioning itself among the national leaders in redefining the liberal arts. More importantly, however, the college community is vigorously pursuing a goal of educating young leaders who can make connections, cross boundaries, and negotiate a world no longer neatly divided into categories of endeavor.

"Wofford College requires freshman applicants to submit scores from either the old or new SAT. Students may also choose to submit scores from the ACT in lieu of the SAT."

SELECTIVITY

Admissions Rating	**91**
# of applicants	2,089
% of applicants accepted	57
% of acceptees attending	31
# accepting a place on wait list	57
% admitted from wait list	5
# of early decision applicants	537
% accepted early decision	60

FRESHMAN PROFILE

Range SAT Critical Reading	560–670
Range SAT Math	590–680
Range SAT Writing	530–660
Range ACT Composite	22–27
Minimum Paper TOEFL	550
Minimum Computer Based TOEFL	213
% graduated top 10% of class	61
% graduated top 25% of class	83
% graduated top 50% of class	98

DEADLINES

Early decision application deadline	11/15
Early decision notification	12/1
Regular application deadline	2/1
Regular notification	3/15
Nonfall registration?	yes

APPLICANTS ALSO LOOK AT

AND OFTEN PREFER
Wake Forest University
AND SOMETIMES PREFER
Furman University
AND RARELY PREFER
Clemson University, University of South Carolina—Columbia

FINANCIAL FACTS

Financial Aid Rating	**87**
Annual tuition	$27,830
Room & Board	$7,705
Books and supplies	$907
% frosh rec. need-based scholarship or grant aid	53
% UG rec. need-based scholarship or grant aid	52
% frosh rec. need-based self-help aid	22
% UG rec. need-based self-help aid	26
% frosh rec. any financial aid	89
% UG rec. any financial aid	86

WORCESTER POLYTECHNIC INSTITUTE

100 INSTITUTE ROAD, WORCESTER, MA 01609 • ADMISSIONS: 508-831-5286 • FAX: 508-831-5875

CAMPUS LIFE

Quality of Life Rating	85
Fire Safety Rating	82
Type of school	private
Environment	city

STUDENTS

Total undergrad enrollment	2,857
% male/female	74/26
% from out of state	50
% from public high school	66
% live on campus	59
% in (# of) fraternities	29 (11)
% in (# of) sororities	31 (3)
% African American	2
% Asian	6
% Caucasian	79
% Hispanic	4
% international	7
# of countries represented	81

SURVEY SAYS . . .

Lab facilities are great
Great computer facilities
Career services are great
Students are happy
Frats and sororities dominate social
scene

ACADEMICS

Academic Rating	89
Calendar	quarter
Student/faculty ratio	13:1
Profs interesting rating	77
Profs accessible rating	89
% profs teaching	
UG courses	100
% classes taught by TAs	0
Most common	
lab size	20–29 students
Most common	
reg class size	fewer than 10 students

MOST POPULAR MAJORS

computer science
electrical, electronics, and
communications engineering
mechanical engineering

STUDENTS SAY

Academics

Worcester Polytechnic Institute, students boast, "is revolutionary with its approach to teaching," employing a "project-based curriculum that stresses the importance of both theory and practice." Students here must complete three projects, "one relating to humanities, one relating to the impact of technology on society, and a final senior project" that is typically a "group project done in cooperation with industry; i.e., not an 'academic' project." The Project Enhanced Curriculum ensures that students get "real-world industry experience before getting into the real world by applying what you learn in the classroom into projects." Students typically travel abroad to complete at least one of their projects, allowing them to "help another community on the other side of the world." As yet another added bonus, "The projects program looks excellent on your resume." Students also love WPI's quarterly academic calendar. One writes, "If I don't like a class but have to get through it, it's only 7 weeks. If I love the material, I can get out in 7 weeks and jump onto the next class!" Students warn that "the terms are pretty intense and go by so quickly that there is little room for error" but add that "it is very easy to get in touch with the professors after class, and they are very willing to help." A lenient grading system—"You can only receive an A, B, C, or an NR"—reduces the pressure somewhat, although it does little to mitigate the "immense workload." Independent students are especially well suited to WPI, which "fosters a can-do attitude that allows students to pave their own ways, create their own degree programs, and arrange their own degree requirement projects."

Life

"During the week [at WPI], most of the attention is focused on school activities, whether it's homework, clubs, or other extracurriculars," while "on the weekends, people try to relax after the week that has just ended and prepare themselves for the upcoming week." The campus enjoys "a strong sense of community, probably because of the campus set-up. The campus is on a hill, so we are separate from the city, and we are our own community with its own issues, and we deal with issues as a whole." Students tell us that "the Greek life on campus holds a big presence, and it is hard to find other activities to occupy your free time without at least socializing with members of the Greek community." Of the intercollegiate sports, "Basketball is big. The men's team made it to the NCAA Division III national tournament in 2005 and 2006." Because "Worcester isn't the greatest town," students tend to stick close to campus for fun, although "We also make trips to Boston and other better cities," including Hartford and Providence.

Student Body

The WPI student body spans two extremes, from "the students who do not come out of their room and are very nerdy," and those who "are very involved and meet everyone and fit in." One student writes, "WPI is an experiment in social interactions the likes of which the world rarely sees. For every typical frat guy and girl, there's a computer nerd or D&D guru who could write this entire response in COBOL coding for you." Nearly everyone here was "an atypical high school student" who "did very well in high school" while also being "really good in X (where X is a sport, club president, highly active student)." Finally, the "One thing that binds everyone at WPI is their love for technology. Within that major division of technology-loving people, the campus is filled with diverse students."

FINANCIAL AID: 508-831-5469 • E-MAIL: ADMISSIONS@WPI.EDU • WEBSITE: WWW.WPI.EDU

ADMISSIONS

Very important factors considered include: Academic GPA, rigor of secondary school record. *Important factors considered include:* Application essay, character/personal qualities, class rank, extracurricular activities, recommendation(s), standardized test scores. *Other factors considered include:* Alumni/ae relation, geographical residence, interview, level of applicant's interest, racial/ethnic status, talent/ability, volunteer work, work experience. SAT or ACT required; TOEFL required of all international applicants. High school diploma is required, and GED is accepted. *Academic units required:* 4 English, 4 math, 2 science (2 science labs). *Academic units recommended:* 4 science, 2 foreign language, 2 social studies, 1 history.

The Inside Word

WPI's high admission rate is the result of a self-selecting applicant pool; very few people bother to apply here if they don't think they have a good chance of getting in. The relatively low rate of acceptees attending tells you that WPI is a 'safety' or backup choice for students hoping to get into MIT, CalTech, RPI, Case Western, and other top tech schools.

FINANCIAL AID

Students should submit: FAFSA, CSS/Financial Aid PROFILE, Noncustodial PROFILE, parent and student prior year Federal Income Tax Returns. Regular filing deadline is February 1. The Princeton Review suggests that all financial aid forms be submitted as soon as possible after January 1. *Need-based scholarships/grants offered:* Pell Grant, SEOG, state scholarships/grants, private scholarships, the school's own gift aid. *Loan aid offered:* FFEL Subsidized Stafford, FFEL Unsubsidized Stafford, FFEL PLUS, Federal Perkins Loan, state loans, college/university loans from institutional funds. Applicants will be notified of awards on or about April 1.

FROM THE ADMISSIONS OFFICE

"Projects and research enrich WPI's academic program. WPI believes that in these times simply passing courses and accumulating theoretical knowledge is not enough to truly educate tomorrow's leaders. Tomorrow's professionals ought to be involved in project work that prepares them today for future challenges. Projects at WPI come as close to professional experience as a college program can possibly achieve. In fact, WPI works with more than 200 companies, government agencies, and private organizations each year. These groups provide opportunities where students get a chance to work in real, professional settings. Students gain invaluable experience in planning, coordinating team efforts, meeting deadlines, writing proposals and reports, making oral presentations, doing cost analyses, and making decisions.

"Applicants for Fall 2008 are required to take either the new SAT or the ACT (the Writing section is optional). We will allow students to submit scores from the old SAT (prior to March 2005) or ACT as well, and will use the student's best scores from either test. Science and Math SAT Subject Tests are recommended."

SELECTIVITY

Admissions Rating	**92**
# of applicants	4,931
% of applicants accepted	67
% of acceptees attending	24
# accepting a place on wait list	174
% admitted from wait list	16

FRESHMAN PROFILE

Range SAT Critical Reading	560–670
Range SAT Math	640–720
Range SAT Writing	550–640
Range ACT Composite	25–30
Minimum Paper TOEFL	550
Minimum Computer Based TOEFL	213
Average HS GPA	3.7
% graduated top 10% of class	53
% graduated top 25% of class	83
% graduated top 50% of class	99

DEADLINES

Regular application deadline	2/1
Regular notification	4/1
Nonfall registration?	yes

APPLICANTS ALSO LOOK AT

AND OFTEN PREFER
Cornell University, Massachusetts Institute of Technology

AND SOMETIMES PREFER
Boston University, Carnegie Mellon University, Rensselaer Polytechnic Institute, Tufts University

AND RARELY PREFER
Northeastern University, Rochester Institute of Technology, University of Connecticut, University of Massachusetts—Amherst

FINANCIAL FACTS

Financial Aid Rating	**77**
Comprehensive fee	$43,278
Books and supplies	$1,000
% frosh rec. need-based scholarship or grant aid	76
% UG rec. need-based scholarship or grant aid	67
% frosh rec. need-based self-help aid	51
% UG rec. need-based self-help aid	54
% frosh rec. any financial aid	98
% UG rec. any financial aid	93

XAVIER UNIVERSITY OF LOUISIANA

ONE DREXEL DRIVE, BOX 132, NEW ORLEANS, LA 70125-1098 • ADMISSIONS: 504-520-7388 • FAX: 504-520-7941

Academics

Xavier University of Louisiana, the nation's only Historically Black Catholic College or University, excels in a number of areas, most famously in premedical and pharmacy studies. Xavier promotional literature justifiably boasts of its accomplishments in these fields: of all American schools, Xavier confers the most biology and life sciences degrees to African Americans; awards the greatest number of Doctor of Pharmacy degrees to African Americans; and places the most African Americans into medical schools. Given these achievements, it should surprise no one that students here must survive a tough curriculum; "Xavier wears you out so that the real world will not," is how one student puts it. Fortunately, undergrads receive plenty of support from a faculty and staff who "provide a family-like atmosphere for students and lay a strong foundation for those who want to pursue positions of leadership and service." Professors here "are very knowledgeable and know a lot about their subjects. Most of them break material down really well so you can understand complex ideas." They are also "passionate about what they do," exuding an enthusiasm that inspires students. Xavier is also strong in business studies.

Life

To state the obvious, Xavier "is set in the middle of New Orleans, so there is plenty to do." Students tell us that "a lot of first-years do a lot of partying," which explains why close to one in four doesn't return for sophomore year. Those who manage to stick around for the duration tell us that "during the week, everyone is mostly focused on schoolwork. For the weekend, people like to chill at home and watch movies or go out to parties." Since campus policies impose strict restrictions on noise, dorm visitation, and drinking, parties usually occur off campus, either at one of the many other area colleges or at clubs in town. Students also like to "just go to the French Quarter and walk around" or hit the many music clubs and fine eateries that distinguish the Crescent City. Students praise the Student Government's efforts to "provide wonderful activities for students living on and off campus" but tell us that "Xavier could improve on the atmosphere of the campus. Sure, it's an old school, but the grounds could still be more appealing."

Student Body

"Xavier is a Historically Black College, so there is a majority of Black students on campus," students explain, but they also point out that "we do have students of other racial and ethnic backgrounds who also attend." One undergrad observes, "I have personally seen a great interaction with the student population, but there is still some segregation among the students sometimes, which doesn't go unnoticed." The typical Xavier undergrad is "Black, smart, sometimes a little too hard on themselves," and "strives for success and wants to further her education through a graduate/professional program." Undergraduates here are typically studious, occasionally to the point of being "stress worshippers."

XAVIER UNIVERSITY OF LOUISIANA

FINANCIAL AID: 504-520-7517 • E-MAIL: APPLY@XULA.EDU • WEBSITE: WWW.XULA.EDU

ADMISSIONS

Very important factors considered include: Recommendation(s), rigor of secondary school record, standardized test scores. *Important factors considered include:* Class rank. *Other factors considered include:* Alumni/ae relation, application essay, character/personal qualities, extracurricular activities, interview, racial/ethnic status, talent/ability, volunteer work, work experience. SAT or ACT required; TOEFL required of all international applicants. High school diploma is required, and GED is accepted. *Academic units required:* 4 English, 2 math, 1 science, 1 social studies, 8 academic electives. *Academic units recommended:* 4 math, 3 science, 1 foreign language, 2 social studies, 1 history.

Inside Word

This school is a prestigious pipeline for those committed to a career in both natural and hard sciences. Xavier is best known for its identity as a Catholic institution with a predominantly African American student body and its reputation as a great premed school.

FINANCIAL AID

Students should submit: FAFSA. The Princeton Review suggests that all financial aid forms be submitted as soon as possible after January 1. *Need-based scholarships/grants offered:* Pell Grant, SEOG, state scholarships/grants, private scholarships, the school's own gift aid, United Negro College Fund. *Loan aid offered:* Direct Subsidized Stafford, Direct Unsubsidized Stafford, Direct PLUS, FFEL Subsidized Stafford, FFEL Unsubsidized Stafford, FFEL PLUS, Federal Perkins Loan. Applicants will be notified of awards on a rolling basis beginning or about April 1. Federal Work-Study Program available. Institutional employment available. Off-campus job opportunities are good.

FROM THE ADMISSIONS OFFICE

"A message from the SGA President: 'On behalf of the students of Xavier University of Louisiana, it is my pleasure to invite you to consider a college experience that will change and enhance your life forever.

"'Xavier alumni are known across the world for being exceptional doctors and lawyers, educators and journalists, philanthropists, research scientists and the like. Despite the damages to our campus last August from Hurricane Katrina, I can assure you that choosing Xavier is still a great choice indeed.

"'As a senior business administration major with a concentration in finance, and president of the Student Government Association (SGA), I know that Xavier has thoroughly prepared me for my career in corporate America while nurturing me spiritually and socially. True, I never might have imagined attending a school in a city that experienced so much tragedy following Hurricane Katrina. However, with tragedy comes great opportunity to triumph.

"'Since our campus reopened in January 2006 after repairing the hurricane damage, the Xavier family has grown stronger. People in general seem more appreciative of friends, family, and what some might call 'sentimental' values. In a way, Hurricane Katrina may have added to the character of people, and enhanced the very principles this university was founded upon.

"'The university's founder, St. Katharine Drexel, understood the necessity to provide minority students with a quality education—second to none—and the skills needed to be better leaders and involved in service, in order to help build a more just and humane society. What better time than now to become a part of the rebuilding of New Orleans—one of America's most unique cities—while gaining one of the best college educations in the world?'

"SAT and ACT scores are used as a factor in admission decisions at Xavier University of Louisiana. Applicants should take the new SAT or the ACT with Writing component. In addition to being used for admission decisions, the scores and sub scores are used for course placement purposes at Xavier."

SELECTIVITY

Admissions Rating	**78**
# of applicants	4,248
% of applicants accepted	83
% of acceptees attending	28
# accepting a place on wait list	22
% admitted from wait list	23

FRESHMAN PROFILE

Range SAT Critical Reading	440–470
Range SAT Math	430–540
Range ACT Composite	18–24
Minimum Paper TOEFL	550
Average HS GPA	3.06
% graduated top 10% of class	30
% graduated top 25% of class	55
% graduated top 50% of class	83

DEADLINES

Regular application deadline	7/1
Regular notification	4/15
Nonfall registration?	yes

FINANCIAL FACTS

Financial Aid Rating	**66**
Annual tuition	$12,100
Room & Board	$7,100
Books and supplies	$1,000
Required fees	$1,000
% frosh rec. need-based self-help aid	15
% UG rec. need-based self-help aid	73
% frosh rec. any financial aid	84
% UG rec. any financial aid	87

XAVIER UNIVERSITY (OH)

3800 VICTORY PARKWAY, CINCINNATI, OH 45207-5311 • ADMISSIONS: 513-745-3301 • FAX: 513-745-4319

STUDENTS SAY

Academics

Xavier University, a medium-sized Jesuit institution "in the heart of Cincinnati," instills "a real sense of community and social conscience" while still "giving students the needed skills to succeed in all of their life endeavors." Xavier even tosses in a broad liberal arts education for good measure, courtesy of a core curriculum and distribution requirements that include lots of theology, philosophy, English, history, and foreign language. But it's business that many students—one in four, to be more precise—major in here; undergrads tout the "great entrepreneurship program" and XU's "great record" for placing accounting students in graduate schools. XU's nursing program is also "very strong," with "an excellent" "pass rate on the NCLEX," and the education program earns similar plaudits. In all areas, XU offers "relatively small" classes, "which can make it hard when it's time for registration, but when you're in class it's great." Academics are "challenging, but the teachers and administration help make the transition [from high school] smooth and are there whenever you need their help." "Academically, it is nearly impossible to fail," a freshman adds. "There are always tutoring centers and help [is] available for any subject, whenever you need it." The school also "excels at real-world placement. If you want an internship, just ask. There's even a team of people here whose only job is to find internships and co-ops for students." Undergrads also appreciate their classmates' low-key approach; they "care, but are very laid-back in classes."

Life

"Xavier University has a little bit of everything: service projects, strong academics, social events, religious events, weekend trips, and lots of other activities to get involved in." A good number of the aforementioned activities "are put on by [the] Student Activities Council and by student government." Many Xavier students "go to the sporting events," with a heavy focus on the men's basketball team, which "is obviously a huge deal here" (the team was the 2005–2006 Atlantic 10 champion). Students say XU parties "usually don't get too out of control. I've never really heard or experienced any . . . of the typical bad college party experiences," a sophomore reports. They also tell us that "there are few bars around (mainly only one, for upper classmen) so people generally party at houses." Big city living lures some students off campus; Cincinnati "is a great city to go out in—there are areas such as Mt. Adams and Newport that provide entertainment and dining for both college-aged students and young professionals."

Student Body

"I'd say 95 percent of the students at this school are friendly and always willing to meet new people or help you if you have a problem," writes one student, expressing a commonly held perception of Xavier undergrads. Students "spend a lot of time with varieties of people—not just a "clique" or single group of people—[so] it is fairly easy to get to know a large percentage of your classmates, especially the peers in your graduating class." In terms of demographics, "Lots of kids come from suburban areas and went to Catholic schools, so there is a large population of wealthy, religious students." Adding some ethnic diversity are "significant populations of minority students (Black, Asian, international, etc.) who each have [a] strong voice on campus." Alternative culture is hardly found here; one student notes, "It's rare to find a kid with a mohawk unless the rugby team shaved his head. Most kids are clean-cut." An accounting and finance major adds, "There are no real emo/goth kids at this school (thank God)." However, a weekend degree program and night classes draw a substantial nontraditional population to the school.

XAVIER UNIVERSITY (OH)

FINANCIAL AID: 513-745-3142 • E-MAIL: XUADMIT@XAVIER.EDU • WEBSITE: WWW.XAVIER.EDU

ADMISSIONS

Very important factors considered include: Rigor of secondary school record. *Important factors considered include:* Academic GPA, application essay, character/personal qualities, class rank, recommendation(s), standardized test scores. *Other factors considered include:* Alumni/ae relation, extracurricular activities, first generation, level of applicant's interest, talent/ability, volunteer work, work experience. SAT or ACT required; TOEFL required of all international applicants. High school diploma is required, and GED is accepted. *Academic units recommended:* 4 English, 3 math, 3 science, 2 foreign language, 3 social studies, 5 academic electives, 1 health/physical education.

The Inside Word

Above-average students should encounter little difficulty in gaining admission to Xavier. Others may be able to finagle their way in with some elbow grease, credible demonstrations of commitment to academics and Jesuit ideals of service, and a Catholic approach to academics.

FINANCIAL AID

Students should submit: FAFSA. The Princeton Review suggests that all financial aid forms be submitted as soon as possible after January 1. *Need-based scholarships/grants offered:* Pell Grant, SEOG, state scholarships/grants, private scholarships, the school's own gift aid. *Loan aid offered:* FFEL Subsidized Stafford, FFEL Unsubsidized Stafford, FFEL PLUS, Federal Perkins Loan. Applicants will be notified of awards on a rolling basis beginning or about February 15. Federal Work-Study Program available. Institutional employment available. Off-campus job opportunities are excellent.

FROM THE ADMISSIONS OFFICE

"Founded in 1831, Xavier University is the fourth oldest of the 28 Jesuit colleges and universities in the United States. The Jesuit tradition is evident in the university's core curriculum, degree programs and involvement opportunities. Xavier is home to 6,600 total students; 3,800 degree-seeking undergraduates. The student population represents more than 34 states and 50 foreign countries.

"Xavier offers 69 academic majors and concentrations and 42 minors in the Colleges of Arts and Sciences; Business; and Social Sciences, Health, and Education. Most popular majors include business, communication arts, education, psychology, biology, sport management/marketing, and pre-professional study. Other programs of note include University Scholars; Honors AB; Philosophy, Politics, and the Public; Army ROTC, study abroad, academic service-learning, and service fellowship.

"There are over 100 academic clubs, social and service organizations, and recreational sports activities on campus. Students participate in groups such as student government, campus ministry, performing arts, and intramural sports. Xavier is a member of the Division I Atlantic 10 Conference and fields teams in men's and women's basketball, cross-country, track, golf, soccer, swimming, and tennis, as well as men's baseball and women's volleyball.

"Xavier is situated on more than 148 acres in a residential area of Cincinnati, Ohio. The face of Xavier has continued to change with the planned addition of a technology-based learning commons, renovated library and classroom buildings, a new building for the Williams College of Business, a new retail and residential complex, and a new student recreation facility. The additions are part of a $200 million capital campaign and will begin being built in 2008.

"Applicants must submit results from the SAT or ACT. Xavier will accept results from the old or new SAT/ACT and the student's best score(s) from either test will be used. The Writing portion of the SAT/ACT is not required and will not be used in admission and scholarship decisions."

SELECTIVITY
Admissions Rating	87
# of applicants	5,500
% of applicants accepted	72
% of acceptees attending	21
# accepting a place on wait list	141
% admitted from wait list	9

FRESHMAN PROFILE
Range SAT Critical Reading	530–640
Range SAT Math	540–640
Range SAT Writing	510–620
Range ACT Composite	23–29
Minimum Paper TOEFL	530
Minimum Computer Based TOEFL	197
Average HS GPA	3.63
% graduated top 10% of class	33
% graduated top 25% of class	63
% graduated top 50% of class	90

DEADLINES
Regular application deadline	2/1
Regular notification	1/15, 3/15
Nonfall registration?	yes

APPLICANTS ALSO LOOK AT
AND OFTEN PREFER
University of Notre Dame
AND SOMETIMES PREFER
Miami University, The Ohio State University—Columbus, University of Dayton
AND RARELY PREFER
University of Cincinnati

FINANCIAL FACTS
Financial Aid Rating	76
Annual tuition	$23,270
Room & Board	$6,675
Books and supplies	$900
Required fees	$715
% frosh rec. need-based scholarship or grant aid	56
% UG rec. need-based scholarship or grant aid	52
% frosh rec. need-based self-help aid	44
% UG rec. need-based self-help aid	41
% frosh rec. any financial aid	96
% UG rec. any financial aid	96

YALE UNIVERSITY

PO BOX 208234, NEW HAVEN, CT 06520-8234 • ADMISSIONS: 203-432-9316 • FAX: 203-432-9392

CAMPUS LIFE
Quality of Life Rating	94
Fire Safety Rating	60*
Type of school	private
Environment	city

STUDENTS
Total undergrad enrollment	5,303
% male/female	51/49
% from out of state	93
% from public high school	55
% live on campus	88
% African American	8
% Asian	13
% Caucasian	50
% Hispanic	8
% Native American	1
% international	8
# of countries represented	108

SURVEY SAYS . . .
Registration is a breeze
Great library
Musical organizations are popular
Student publications are popular
Theater is popular
Students are happy

ACADEMICS
Academic Rating	95
Calendar	semester
Profs interesting rating	83
Profs accessible rating	83
Most common	
reg class size	10–19 students

MOST POPULAR MAJORS
economics
history
political science and government

STUDENTS SAY

Academics

"There are too many strengths to name" at Yale University, one of the nation's top undergraduate and graduate institutions, but that doesn't stop undergrads here from trying; they identify "the resources, of course, the marvelous professors, and the students themselves" as some of Yale's biggest assets. As one student puts it, "Coming to Yale means that you will be able to do anything you want to do at the highest caliber. They will make it as easy as they can for you to learn what you want." If the experience sounds a little daunting, that's because it is. One undergrad explains, "It's intimidating, Yale University. You feel like you have something to prove. Were you the 'mistake' who got in? You challenge yourself for the sake of learning and for the sake of being the best." (It's comforting to note that "faculty tries to ensure that no one is lost in the wash.") Students' burdens are somewhat lessened by the fact that "you don't really have to deal with the highest levels of the administration, because every residential college has a master (for residential issues) and a dean (for academic issues), who you can easily discuss things with, and who will generally help you take care of things in the most efficient way possible."

Life

Yale is extremely demanding academically, but students here still find time for plenty of extracurricular enrichment and fun. One student reports, "People generally study Monday through Thursday, and oftentimes have extracurriculars in the evenings. On the weekends, people tend to study during the day and go out at night." Undergrads tell us that "art, music, theater, and sports are huge, loved, and well funded, as are organizations such as the *Yale Daily News*, the Slavic Chorus (a cappella is huge here), Just Add Water (a comedy troupe), and the fire-juggling club (best Halloween show in the world!)." The campus also sustains "an absolutely ridiculous amount of theatrical and musical events." Students also love the traditional "Masters' Teas, of which there are several every week, with everyone from the Swiss delegate to the United Nations to Eric Schlosser (author of *Fast Food Nation*) to biomedical engineers coming to share their life experiences over tea and chocolates." Yale's campus is "gorgeous" with "jaw-dropping architecture and awesome dorms and dining halls." While New Haven is not held in especially high regard, students appreciate that "there are some excellent clubs and restaurants in town" and that "the city provides easy access to New York," which can be reached by train in about 90 minutes.

Student Body

While "There is no typical Yale student," most agree that "there are two overarching characteristics that everyone here has been blessed with: talent and motivation." One student notes, "Though we come from different backgrounds and have different interests, it's easy to look around and imagine your classmates being the leaders of the next generation. Professors and peers alike never cease to surprise you and just completely blow you away with their talent and knowledge and personality. Yet at the same time, everyone is down-to-earth. Very few people flaunt their abilities, though they have every right to." Students "tend to have a liberal bent, although any political affiliation (just like any background) is welcomed, and politics carry over from mere discussion into real action: Community programs, public-health advocacy and work, and political campaigns are all vital to campus life." Undergrads are also typically "non-competitive and very supportive of each other academically and socially." One student explains, "If I have to miss lecture, I know that first, I can always e-mail my professor and ask for help, and second, any one of a dozen friends will gladly not only share notes, but also go over them with me to make sure that I understand them." Thanks to need-blind admissions and generous financial aid, "The economic backgrounds of students are very diverse."

FINANCIAL AID: 203-432-2700 • E-MAIL: UNDERGRADUATE.ADMISSIONS@YALE.EDU • WEBSITE: WWW.YALE.EDU/ADMIT

ADMISSIONS

Very important factors considered include: Academic GPA, application essay, character/personal qualities, class rank, extracurricular activities, recommendation(s), rigor of secondary school record, standardized test scores, talent/ability. *Other factors considered include:* Alumni/ae relation, first generation, geographical residence, interview, level of applicant's interest, racial/ethnic status, state residency, volunteer work, work experience. SAT and SAT Subject Tests or ACT required; ACT with Writing component required. TOEFL required of all international applicants. High school diploma or equivalent is not required.

The Inside Word

There is no gray area; Yale is ultra-selective with growing applicant pools each year. And there's nothing to be gained by appealing a denial here—the Admissions Committee considers all of its decisions final. Yale uses a regional review process that serves as a preliminary screening for all candidates, and only the best-qualified, well-matched candidates actually come before the Admissions Committee.

FINANCIAL AID

Students should submit: FAFSA, CSS/Financial Aid PROFILE, Noncustodial PROFILE, Business/Farm Supplement, parent Federal Income Tax Returns. Regular filing deadline is March 1. The Princeton Review suggests that all financial aid forms be submitted as soon as possible after January 1. *Need-based scholarships/grants offered:* Pell Grant, SEOG, state scholarships/grants, private scholarships, the school's own gift aid, United Negro College Fund. *Loan aid offered:* FFEL Subsidized Stafford, FFEL Unsubsidized Stafford, FFEL PLUS, Federal Perkins Loan, state loans, college/university loans from institutional funds. Applicants will be notified of awards on or about April 1.

FROM THE ADMISSIONS OFFICE

"The most important questions the Admissions Committee must resolve are 'Who is likely to make the most of Yale's resources?' and 'Who will contribute significantly to the Yale community?' These questions suggest an approach to evaluating applicants that is more complex than whether Yale would rather admit well-rounded people or those with specialized talents. In selecting a class of 1,300 from approximately 21,100 applicants, the Admissions Committee looks for academic ability and achievement combined with such personal characteristics as motivation, curiosity, energy, and leadership ability. The nature of these qualities is such that there is no simple profile of grades, scores, interests, and activities that will assure admission. Diversity within the student population is important, and the Admissions Committee selects a class of able and contributing individuals from a variety of backgrounds and with a broad range of interests and skills.

"Applicants for the entering class of Fall 2008 may take either version of the SAT. In addition, applicants will be required to take three SAT Subject Tests of their choice. Applicants may take the ACT, with the Writing component, as an alternative to the SAT and SAT Subject Tests."

SELECTIVITY

Admissions Rating	**96**
# of applicants	21,101
% of applicants accepted	9
% of acceptees attending	70

FRESHMAN PROFILE

Range SAT Critical Reading	700–780
Range SAT Math	690–790
Range ACT Composite	31–34
Minimum Paper TOEFL	600
Minimum Computer Based TOEFL	250
% graduated top 10% of class	95
% graduated top 25% of class	4
% graduated top 50% of class	1

DEADLINES

Regular application deadline	12/31
Regular notification	4/1
Nonfall registration?	no

FINANCIAL FACTS

Financial Aid Rating	**96**
Annual tuition	$33,030
Room & Board	$10,020
Books and supplies	$2,700
% frosh rec. need-based scholarship or grant aid	42
% UG rec. need-based scholarship or grant aid	41
% frosh rec. need-based self-help aid	44
% UG rec. need-based self-help aid	42

PART 4

"COW TIPPING IS DEFINITELY PASSÉ HERE."

Our survey has seven questions that allow students to answer in narrative form. We tell students that we don't care *what* they write: If it is "witty, informative, or accurate," we try to get it into this book. We use all the informative and accurate essays to write the "Students Speak Out" sections; below are excerpts from the wittiest, pithiest, and most outrageous narrative responses to our open-ended questions.

LITERARY ALLUSIONS...

"To study at this school is to have infinite control over your destiny: You can crouch in your room like Gregor Samsa transformed into a dung beetle, or you can plunge into the infinite sea of faces that each year flood OSU like a tidal wave."

—A.W., Ohio State University

"The typical student at Chicago is affluent, White, wears intellectual glasses with black plastic frames, reads all the time, and can convincingly argue that the DMV should offer driving tests in Ancient Greek or Coptic."

—Female Freshman, University of Chicago

"'Prosperity unbruised cannot endure a single blow, but a man who has been at constant feud with misfortunes develops a skin calloused by time . . . and even if he falls he can carry the fight upon one knee.' —Seneca on Providence."

— Matthew D.,
University of Connecticut

"Very definitely a love/hate relationship here. This is the level of hell that Dante missed."

—Amy P., Caltech

"The Deep Springs Experience is like working in an atrophy factory. Much of what you do in labor and government is fixing, improving, or replacing what came before you. No matter what frame of reference you use—daily, monthly, or yearly—you still feel like Sisyphus. The joy and value comes in building your muscles on so many different rocks."

—Whet M., Deep Springs College

"Lewd quotes on the bathroom walls, at least, come from great authors."

—Matt J., Simon's Rock College of Bard

"In the cafeteria, the chocolate milk is cheap and delicious. It is also always satisfying. Plus, Seattle University doesn't have my dad, who was always drunk. This is good."

—Anonymous Freshman,
Seattle University

"When students first arrive, they call the Observatory Hill Dining Facility 'O-Hill.' They soon learn to call it 'O-Hell,' because the food here is beyond revolting."

— Greg F.,
University of Virginia

"If I had known that I'd be rooming with roaches and poisoned by the cafeteria staff I would have gone to Wayne State. I really can't complain, though, because I have met my husband here, like my mom did 20 years before."

— M.L.P., Fisk University

"The food here has particularly fancy names, and it seems as though they spend more time thinking of these names than they spend on making decent food."

— Andrew Z., Wheaton College

"If you're looking for gray skies, a gray campus, and gray food, then Albany is the place to be!"

— Michele G.,
SUNY—UNiversity at Albany

"The food isn't that bad, if you don't mind varying shades of brown. On a good day the food on your tray will remind you of the brown paint sampler at your local Sherwin-Williams dealer."

— Rob P., College of the Holy Cross

"You should mention Lil', the lady who has worked in the dining hall for 50 years and who everyone loves. She plays the spoons all the time and runs around."

— Aaron R., Tufts University

"The food needs to improve. Probably everyone says that, but I was told that I was going to get the "freshman 15" . . . well whoever said that never ate in my school's dining hall."

—E.M., Wells College

"In my experience New York is a place that allows people to be anyone they want to be. You can wear a zebra-striped bikini in the middle of winter on a snow-covered street here, and people would hardly look twice"

—Sophomore, Barnard College

"Change the name of UC—Irvine to UC—Newport Beach and we would have more girls."

— Pat M., UC—Irvine

"As this school is located in a tiny Texas town, a favorite activity is called 'rolling.' Rolling entails piling into a car with many drinks and driving the backcountry roads. Very slowly."

— Anonymous, Southwestern University

"Connecticut is a cute state. It's a great place to go to school, but I wouldn't want to live here."

— Claire S., NJ native, Fairfield University

"Binghamton is always gray. The two days a week we have sun, it's beautiful, but otherwise, sunglasses are not a must unless you're an artsy-fartsy pseudo-chic literature and rhetoric/philosophy major."

— Deborah C., SUNY at Binghamton

"Socially, the surrounding area is so dead that the Denny's closes at night."

— Thomas R., UC—Riverside

"The local liquor stores and towing companies make a lot of money."

— Katherine R., University of Rhode Island

"Davis is boring; you need a lot of drugs."

—Anonymous, UC—Davis

"It is definitely important to have a car, as the population of Canton frequently matches our winter temperature. 'Canton gray,' our perennial sky color, is one Crayola missed."

— Daniel R., St. Lawrence University

"Contrary to popular belief, cow tipping is definitely passé here."

— Anonymous, University of Connecticut

"Montreal is the sh*@!"

—Elizabeth R., McGill University

"Fredericksburg is boring if one is not amused by the simple pleasures of existence such as breathing, sleep, and other things."

—Rich W., Mary Washington College

"I love escaping from Claremont. I wish I had a car! Claremont seems to be stuck in a White, bureaucratic, conservative nightmare. I feel cut off from the rest of the world, like I've fallen into Wonderland—the rules of the outside world don't apply here. However, I do feel like I've gotten and am getting a good education."

—Anonymous, Scripps College

"What do we do for fun? Danville is small, so we go on raids to Wal-Mart. It never fails, no matter what time of day or night that you go to Wal-Mart: You will always run into at least two separate groups of people you know. Plus, Wal-Mart is just a cool place to play around in. Where else can you find [everything from] toy footballs and bikes to goofy hats, clothes, shoes? And let me tell you, those aisles make for a good game of hide and seek."

—Anonymous, Centre College

SECURITY...

"Campus security is made up of a bunch of midget high school dropouts with Napoleonic complexes who can spot a beer can from a mile away."

—Anonymous, UC—San Diego

"For fun we try to ski around campus on the snow, but campus safety must feel that we should be smoking weed because they allow that more than outdoor activities."

—Male Junior, Clarkson University

"Public safety here is a joke. The public safety officers are like the Keystone Kops on Thorazine."

—Anonymous, Bryn Mawr College

"No doors are locked here—none—but you have to notice the doorknob."

—Female Senior, Simon's Rock College of Bard

"Sure, our campus is diverse if you call 'diverse' a campus full of White kids looking to make 30 to 50 grand after graduation."

—Joseph M. C., Davidson College

"If you're thinking of applying to MIT, go ahead. Because, believe it or not, most people here are at least as stupid as you are."

—Patrick L., MIT

"The typical student is mostly an easygoing, skirt-wearing, intelligent, procrastinating kid. Although, there [are] of course, many many many variations on this. Not all kids wear skirts. Not all the boys in skirts are straight. Not all the girls in skirts are straight. 'Everybody here looks like Jesus!' was a pretty accurate description from an outsider."

—Amy P., New College of Florida

"Students here mostly get along, and since it is a business school we all have a common goal of being rich."

—Female Sophomore, Babson College

"People who go to school here are all pretty good looking, especially the women. It should be renamed UKB, the University of Ken and Barbie."

—Tony H., Arizona State University

"Wesleyan is not only the 'diversity university' but also the 'controversy university,' the 'fight adversity university,' and the 'if we keep trying we might have some unity' university. We satisfy all types."

—John P., Wesleyan University

"Mt. Holyoke students are friendly and respectful with the exception of the occasions when the entire campus gets PMS."

—Abigail K., Mount Holyoke College

"My roommate's a complete jerk so I spend most of my nights sleeping in the backseat of my truck."

—Ronald G., Arizona State University

"Girls over 5'8", watch out—for some reason, guys here have munchkin blood in them or something."

—Robyn A., Tufts University

"A school can be defined by its graffiti and its level of cleverness. Three-quarters of our school graffiti is pro- or anti- a specific fraternity, with the other one-quarter devoted to homophobic or misogynist theories."

—Matthew E., College of William & Mary

"This is a great university if you're not studying sciences involving animal research, politics, teacher education (certification), or anything that offends any long-haired leftist who's a vegetarian."

—Brock M., University of Oregon

"This school is filled with wealthy, well-dressed egomaniacs who are about as socially conscious as Marie Antoinette."

—Anonymous, Hofstra University

"For self-absorbed artists my peers are all surprisingly good dancers."

—Jackie G., Bennington College

"When you first come here, you think everybody's really strange. Over time, though, you realize everybody is, and so are you. No big deal."

—Josh B., St. John's College

"University of Chicago's reputation is not entirely deserved. It's not true [that] the place is completely full of nerds. It's only partially completely full of nerds."

—David G., University of Chicago

"I have this really big booger in my nose that I can't quite handle. What do I do? Pick it in public and look like a typical Brown freak, or just deal with it?"

—"Optional," Brown University

"Don't let anyone try to tell you that this is a diverse but close-knit atmosphere. The people here are about as diverse as a box of nails."

—Cari L., College of the Holy Cross

"UNH is about as diverse as the NHL."

—Curtis E., University of New Hampshire

"We are cheeseballs but rather enlightened; thus we condescendingly tolerate almost everyone."

—Cache M., Lawrence University

"Denison has attempted to lose the 'rich kid party school' image and expand the diversity of the student body, but now it is becoming the 'I wish this were still a rich kid party school.' There is an awful lot available here, but students seem unmotivated and lazy."

—Anonymous, Denison University

"Most of my peers are narrow-minded morons who seem to live in the 50s. Because of this constant annoyance, the rest of us have a camaraderie that allows us to see how the other half lives."

—Gary A., Louisiana State University

"Everyone here is too smart for their [sic] own good. As one upper-level executive in the Houston area put it, 'The students at Rice know how to make it rain, but they don't know to come in out of it.'"

—John B., Rice University

"My roommate's feet really stink."

—Anonymous, Claremont McKenna

"Kids at Bard are like fish in a fishbowl, no blinking but always hitting the glass."

—Zak V., Bard College

"Sometimes people complain about the lack of student involvement. I think someone should really do something about the apathy at St. Lawrence."

—Bill P., St. Lawrence University

"Bates is so diverse! Yesterday I met somebody from Connecticut!"

—Ellen H., Bates College

"Most are either Bible-thumping, goodie-goodie, White, stuck-up, right-wing, straight-A losers or work-hard, play-harder and party-hardy, willing-to-try-anything cool people."

—Male Sophomore, Colorado School of Mines

"Rose-Hulman is one of the few places where it's safer to leave a $20 bill on your desk than it is to forget to log out of the computer network."

—Zac C., Rose-Hulman Institute of Technology

"We have this typical student stereotype we call 'Wendy Wellesley.' Wendy takes copious notes, is a devoted member of 10 organizations, always has an internship, goes over the page limit on every assignment, takes six classes, goes to all the office hours, triple majors, and is basically diligent, overcommitted, extroverted, overachieving, and energetic (but without a sense of humor or ability to relax)."

—R.D., Wellesley College

"People at F&M are about as original and colorful as the pages of the Encyclopedia Britannica, with different numbers so you can tell them apart, but otherwise arranged much around the same old dull principles."

—Anonymous, Franklin & Marshall College

"I am constantly impressed with the creativity of hell-raisers on campus. One day I walked past the Manor House to find a dozen plastic babies climbing all over the roof! Right before Parents' Weekend, some people hung up signs saying 'Princeton Review reports: "LC students ignore herpes on a regular basis." Please visit the health clinic!'"

—Anonymous, Lewis & Clark College

"I have not met anyone who was horrible."

—Anonymous, University of Maryland—Baltimore County

"Diversity in the female population means different shades of hair color . . . we often joke that Burberry is SMU Sorority Camouflage."

—Male Senior, Southern Methodist University

"The only thing the administration does well is tasks involving what Kenneth Boulding would call 'suboptimization.' Give them something that really doesn't need doing, and it will be accomplished efficiently."

—Dana T.,
University of Minnesota—Twin Cities

"Our Business Office may be the smoothest-running machine since the Pinto!"

—Robert C., University of Dallas

"Despite the best efforts of the administration to provide TCNJ students with an inefficient, cold-hearted, red-tape-infested, snafu-riddled Soviet-style administrative bureaucracy, The College of New Jersey is a pretty decent place to go for a fairly reasonable amount of money."

—Anonymous,
The College of New Jersey

"The Admissions Office tries to make you apply based on, 'Well, we're very old and . . . and . . . well, we look nice. We'll do whatever it takes to make you happy! Really! I mean it. See my honest smile?' If you visit the school, ditch the tour and the gimmicks and talk to the professors."

—Anonymous, Southwestern University

"Our advisors are amazing as well. I have been on a first-name basis with mine since our first e-mail (when I'm not calling her 'the Goddess')."

—Female Freshman, American University

"The administration runs a wonderful school, and the students and teachers have a wonderful school. Fortunately, these are not the same school."

—Male Freshman/Sophomore, Bard College

"Administration is like the stock market, you invest time and money, sometimes you get a return, other times you don't."

—J.W.R., Albertson College of Idaho

"The Bursar's Office and Financial Aid are slightly retarded when it comes to communication. The daily walk between the two offices might have contributed to my not gaining 'the freshman 15.'"

—Brittany R., Wesleyan College

"Columbia is like a fruit truck. It picks up varied and exotic fruits and deposits them rotten at their destination."

—Paul L., Columbia University

"The University of Minnesota is a huge black hole of knowledge. It sucks things into it from far and wide, compressing to the essence. Unfortunately, it is very hard to get anything out of a black hole. What I have managed to eke out has been both rewarding and depressing."

—James McDonald,
University of Minnesota

"The strangest incident I've ever had in class was when one of my journalism profs burnt our tests in the microwave. But he decided to give everyone in the class an A, instead of retesting."

—Ashlea K., Ohio University

"Boulder is the world in a nutshell, served with alfalfa sprouts."

—Glenn H.,
University of Colorado—Boulder

"Going to Northwestern is like having a beautiful girlfriend who treats you like crap."

—Jonathan J. G., Northwestern University

"Unless you are totally committed to science, do not come. Caltech has as much breadth as a Russian grocery store."

—Daniel S., Caltech

"Being at Marlboro is like having a recurring bizarre dream. You're not quite sure what it all means, but it happens a lot. If it stopped you'd probably wonder why, but then you'd just eat breakfast."

—Mark L., Marlboro College

"Life at school is an oxymoron."

—Dave G., UC—Davis

"One other thing I love about NYU: online registration! God bless the NYU Registrar!"

—Timothy A., New York University

"Vassar is like a sexual disease: Once you've accepted it, it's great, but when you realize you've got another three years to put up with it, you go see a medical adviser immediately."

—Henry R., Vassar College

"Vassar is like a big walrus butt: lots of hair, but also very moist."

—Calder M., Vassar College

"I feel that this school is a maze with snakes and bulls. If you live with a raised fist or a raised phallus, it is easy. If you are earthly, bound to do nothing, come."

—Anonymous, University of Oregon

"Getting an education from MIT is like getting a drink from a firehose."

—Juan G., MIT

"[The] Financial Aid Office needs a complete overhaul. An atom bomb would suffice."

—Male Senior, Duquesne University

"My life here is as the torrential rains of Dhamer upon the Yaktong Valley. I bleat like a llama shedding out of season."

—Ronald M., James Madison University

"When I think of W&L in its current state, I'm forced to think of an old, majestic, beautiful chicken running around with it's head cut off."

—Senior, Washington and Lee University

"Intro classes have the consistency of Cheez Whiz: They go down easy, they taste horrible, and they are not good for you."

—Pat T., University of Vermont

"This school was founded by Jesuits . . . . However, I believe that it has been hijacked by yuppie prisses."

—Anonymous, Loyola Marymount University

SEX, DRUGS, ROCK & ROLL...

"This school is no good for people who like art, music, and Sonic Youth. 'Society is a hole.' There's a quote by Sonic Youth."

—Meghan S., Lake Forest College

"Yeah, there aren't any guys, but who doesn't like doing homework on a Saturday night?"

—Nicole C., Wellesley College

"Montreal is the city of festivals. It is the party central of Canada. McGill is located right in the middle of it all."

—Female, McGill University

"UCSB is the only place where U Can Study Buzzed and still ace an exam the next day."

—Tracy B., UC—Santa Barbara

"The university tries to offer activities as an alternative to alcohol on the weekends. Those are not heavily attended. The weekends are for drinking."

—Maura G., Ohio University

"The dances here are a riot because I love watching nerds and intellectuals dance."

—Male Senior, Columbia University

"Beam, Bud, beer, babes—the four essential B's."

—"Jim Beam," Wittenberg University

"When I visited schools, I went to Brown and Northwestern on the same trip. I went to NU on a Wednesday and Thursday night. I partied like a champ. At Brown on Friday, I was invited to two parties (I should be psyched) but they were both for nude people. Augh yuck!"

—Silvy N., Northwestern University

"William & Mary: where you can drink beer and have sex in the same place your forefathers did."

—Adam L., College of William & Mary

"A Denison student might be quoted as saying, 'Life is a waste of time, and time is a waste of life; so get wasted all the time, and have the time of your life.'"

—Katherine H., Denison University

"This campus is an extremely great place to spend 4 college years, but it is still plagued, as all other campuses are—including Christian colleges, with sin. Therefore, this campus needs to come under submission to Jesus Christ."

—Laura D., James Madison University

"I have been around the block, you know, sex, drugs, and rock and roll. . . . I was in a sorority . . . . I tend to sleep around, too, but I basically think like a guy, so guys don't disrespect me. I am very picky in who I sleep with, only the best-bodied, best-looking dudes. They feel privileged, and I give them a hell of a time. I am quite the hottie, and I know it, so anyone who has a problem can just stay away."

—Anonymous, University of South Dakota

"St. Mary's College of Maryland Poem:

We are located on the H2O
We get blazed up whereever we go.
You throw your shoes around the tree
When you lose your virginity.
Parties here are just like heaven,
'Cause we're all boozed up 24/7.
The girls are cute; the guys are hot,
If you open your window you are bound
to smell pot.
If you visit my school I can promise you
this,
You'll get so finagled you'll wake up in   piss."

—Anonymous,
St. Mary's College of Maryland

"People think about math, physics, and sex."

—Freshman,
California Institute of Technology

"For such a small school there is a surprising amount of on-campus activities such as academic speakers, weekend concerts, speed-dating nights, and good sex talks."

—Junior, Colorado College

"The typical Hampshire student is queer—perhaps not in actual sexual orientation, but definitely in attitude."

—Freshman, Hampshire College

"Any campus attempt to provide drug-free entertainment shuts down at 10:20 P.M. to allow plenty of time to be drunk. The general campus motto is 'If you weren't wasted, the night was.'"

—Junior, Lehigh University

"Drug use here is extremely prevalent. People smoke pot everywhere, even outdoors."

—Freshman, New College of Florida

SCHOOL VS. THE "REAL WORLD"...

"College is the best time of your life. Never again will you be surrounded by people the same age as you, free from grown-ups and the threat of working in the real world. Your parents give you money when you ask for it, and all you have to do is learn!"

—Jennifer F., Syracuse University

"Real-life experience in such concepts—alienation, depression, suppression, isolationism, edge of racial tension, apathy, etc.—before the 'real world.'"

—Anonymous, NYU

"When we lose a football game to a college with lower academic standards, we console ourselves by saying that one day they will work for us and then we'll get even!"

—Michael J.,
Sewanee—The University of the South

"Going to Chem. review is like masturbating with sandpaper: It's just a bad idea."

—Robby M.,
California Institute of Technology

SCHOOLS THAT ARE ALL THAT AND A BAG OF CHIPS

"I like Duquesne because it has a mission beyond just educating students—it tries also to educate the heart and soul—and that makes for better students, a better university, and a better world."

—Female Senior, Duquesne University

"For the first time in my life I am allowed to think for myself. . . . This is an environment where one can proclaim in class that Socrates is a bastard and, if able to support the statement, be respected for it."

—Female Freshman,
Simon's Rock College of Bard

"Best ever, dude! Nobody complains if I leave the toilet seat up."

—Derek L., Deep Springs College

"We're small enough that you'll probably hug a significant portion of the population by the time you graduate."

—Male Junior, Bard College

"We play dodge ball at recess and think what it would be like if we could fly."

—Joseph W., Beloit College

"The students here are as diverse as their views and backgrounds. My friends are mostly thespians and lesbians, and they rock!"

—Female Junior, Bennington College

"Stanford is where gorgeous weather meets amazing, intelligent, and laid-back people [who] learn in an environment where the professors are all known worldwide and yet [are] supremely approachable."

—Female, Stanford University

IN CASE YOU WERE WONDERING...

$Drexel = (Content[good] - Schedule[finals] - Tuition)^{[sum(geeks)/sum(jocks)]} + [avg[i,j](sqrt[(geekPos[i] - jockPos[j]).x^2 + (geekPos[i] - jockPos[j]).y^2]) - 200ft] = 8.5/10$

—Male Junior, Drexel University

"I was smart once. I used to sleep. Then I majored in chemical engineering."

— C. C. Smith, Clemson University

"There's about 15 too many classes along the lines of 'Talking Heads: The Politics of Cabbage in Nineteenth Century Guam.'"

—Sarah G., Bennington College

"Classes are hard to get. Usually you have to cheat and just add the class, telling them you are a graduating senior. I've done that for the last three years and it works!"

—Anonymous, UC—Davis

"I am a hermit who enjoys Ramen noodles and skin flicks. In the winter, I sit in a yoga position by a patch of ice on the sidewalk and mock people as they fall. I often bend spoons with my mind."

—Junior, Indiana University of Pennsylvania

"When I'm not trying to free Mumia, experience non-gender orgasm/transgender interpretive dance, contracting any number of venereal diseases, or trying to be hopelessly unique, I obsess to no end in trying to reconcile my existentialist beliefs with paying $30,000 a year to attend this socially legitimizing institution."

—Katherine S., Bard College

"Those who oppose the Dark Lord will be crushed, but those who are its friend will receive rewards beyond the dreams of avarice."

—Anonymous, Sarah Lawrence College

"There is a real problem with moles on this campus; no one is willing to talk about them."

—Alexander D., Bates College

"Bates College is a phallocentric, logocentric, Greco-Roman, linear-rational, ethnocentric, homophobic, patriarchal institution. How's that for a list of catchwords?"

—Stephen H., Bates College

"Could not shake the insatiable urge to milk cows."

—Jacob, Deep Springs College

"Our school is the school of the future and always will be."

—Chuck C., Rhodes College

"To begin, there's an apartment complex on a main road in my college city, and one of the apartments has put up a sign a few times this year that reads 'Honk for a drink.' So anytime someone drives by and honks his/her horn, the guys on the balcony take a swig of beer. I have also heard a story of a guy who turned 21 here, and his buddies had a beer tube made that went from the third floor apartments down to the ground filled with beer for the guy to drink. . . . Someone like me would never survive an ordeal like that, given my stature. Also, because Interstate 81 cuts through our campus, many drunk girls, especially on homecoming, enjoy giving the truck drivers a little peep show either day or night. . . . One of the great things about our school, though, is that we have a bus service called 'Ride with Len.' This man had a relative die from a drunk driver, and so on the weekends he takes to driving a huge bus around our town to take college kids to their prospective [sic] places safely. He has gotten so popular that more buses and drivers have been added. So I'd say that although many people drink here, they drink responsibly."

—Anonymous, James Madison University

"A crust of bread is better than nothing. Nothing is better than true love. Therefore, by the transitive property, a crust of bread is better than true love."

—Jason G., Gettysburg College

"Bentley College has fulfilled all and more of my expectations than I ever imagined."

— Dawn T., Bentley College

"Everyone seems to be really into political correctness, but in the wake of the recent Supreme Court decision, I don't see that lasting very long."

—John R., Birmingham-Southern College

"Sarah Lawrence is a haven of unity and acceptance. Every morning at sunrise the entire campus gathers around the flagpole, holds hands, and sings 'We Are The World.' If you're really lucky, you get to be Dionne Warwick or Willie Nelson. If you show up late you have to be Bob Dylan. But everyone gets free doughnuts, and it's the happiest time of the day for most students. One morning I went hung over and threw up in the middle of the circle. I was so ashamed, but then I looked around at the diverse group of smiling faces from all over the country and the world and suddenly I felt better. I went home and threw up some more, thankful to live in the world of love that is Sarah Lawrence."

—Matt F., Sarah Lawrence College

On the academics/administration: "They think they know a lot but they actually don't know anything, but some of them know that, so they know everything."

—Male Junior, College of the Atlantic

PART 5

INDEXES

INDEPENDENT COUNSELING

There are currently two professional organizations for independent counselors that require professional credential review: Independent Educational Consultants Association (IECA) and National Association for College Admission Counseling (NACAC). Counselors affiliated with both groups provide varied and detailed services to students and families exploring future educational opportunities. Should you consider seeking the services of an independent counselor, I encourage you to visit both the IECA and NACAC websites for up-to-date information and listings.

Sincerely,

Robert Franek

Lead Author, *The Best 366 Colleges*

VP—Publisher

The Princeton Review

IECA—The Independent Educational Consultants Association is a national non-profit professional association of independent consultants.

www.iecaonline.com

NACAC—The National Association for College Admission Counseling is an organization of 9,000 global professionals dedicated to serving students as they make choices in pursuing postsecondary education.

www.nacacnet.org

INDEX OF SCHOOLS

INDEX OF SCHOOLS BY LOCATION

UNITED STATES

INDEX OF SCHOOLS BY COST

Price categories are based on current tuition (out-of-state tuition for public schools) and do not include fees, room, board, transportation, or other expenses.

LESS THAN $15,000

Berea College	90
Brigham Young University (UT)	104
California State University—Stanislaus	116
City University of New York—Brooklyn College	136
City University of New York—Hunter College	138
City University of New York—Queens College	140
College of New Jersey, The	162
College of the Ozarks	164
Colorado State University	172
Deep Springs College	190
Evergreen State College, The	218
Fisk University	222
Flagler College	224
Grove City College	254
Hampton University	266
Howard University	288
Indiana University of Pennsylvania	296
Kansas State University	310
Louisiana State University	326
McGill University	350
Montana Tech of the University of Montana	368
New Mexico Institute of Mining & Technology	380
Salisbury University	454
Sonoma State University	480
Spelman College	486
State University of New York at Binghamton	504
State University of New York at Geneseo	506
State University of New York—Purchase College	508
State University of New York—Stony Brook University	510
State University of New York—University at Albany	512
State University of New York—University at Buffalo	514
Texas A&M University—College Station	532
Truman State University	544
Tuskegee University	550
United States Air Force Academy	554
United States Coast Guard Academy	556
United States Merchant Marine Academy	558
United States Military Academy	560
United States Naval Academy	562
University of Arizona	566
University of Arkansas—Fayetteville	568
University of Hawaii—Manoa	606
University of Idaho	608
University of Kansas	614
University of Kentucky	616
University of Louisiana at Lafayette	618
University of Massachusetts—Amherst	628
University of Mississippi	636
University of Montana—Missoula, The	640
University of New Orleans	648
University of North Carolina at Asheville, The	650
University of North Carolina at Greensboro, The	654
University of North Dakota	656
University of Oklahoma	660
University of South Dakota, The	686
University of Utah	700
University of Wyoming	710
Webb Institute	742
Wesleyan College	748

West Virginia University	752
Xavier University of Louisiana	778

$15,000–$30,000

Agnes Scott College	52
Albertson College	54
Albion College	56
Alfred University	58
Allegheny College	60
American University	62
Arizona State University	66
Auburn University	68
Austin College	70
Barnard College	76
Baylor University	80
Bellarmine University	82
Beloit College	84
Birmingham-Southern College	92
Bradley University	100
Bryant University	108
California Institute of Technology	114
Calvin College	118
Catawba College	126
Catholic University of America, The	128
Centenary College of Louisiana	130
Clarkson University	146
Clemson University	148
Coe College	150
College of the Atlantic	156
College of Charleston	158
College of William & Mary, The	166
Cooper Union	178
Cornell College	180
Creighton University	184
Davidson College	188
Denison University	192
DePaul University	194
DePauw University	196
Duquesne University	206
Eckerd College	208
Elon University	210
Emerson College	212
Eugene Lang College	216
Florida Southern College	226
Florida State University	228
Fordham University	230
Furman University	236
George Mason University	238
Georgia Institute of Technology	244
Gonzaga University	248
Grinnell College	252
Guilford College	256
Gustavus Adolphus College	258
Hampden-Sydney College	262
Hanover College	268
Hendrix College	276
Hillsdale College	278
Hiram College	280
Hofstra University	284
Hollins University	286
Illinois Institute of Technology	290

Robert Franek is a graduate of Drew University and vice president and publisher for The Princeton Review. He has proudly been a part of the company for five years. Robert comes to The Princeton Review with an extensive admissions background. In addition, he owns a walking tour business, leading historically driven, yet not boring, walking tours of his favorite town, New York City!

Tom Meltzer is a graduate of Columbia University. He has taught for The Princeton Review since 1986 and is the author or coauthor of seven Princeton Review titles, the most recent of which is *Illustrated Word Smart*, which Tom cowrote with his wife, Lisa. He is also a professional musician and songwriter. A native of Baltimore, Tom now lives in Hillsborough, North Carolina.

Christopher Maier is a graduate of Dickinson College. During the past five years, he's lived variously in New York City, coastal Maine, western Oregon, central Pennsylvania, and eastern England. Now he's at an oasis somewhere in the Midwestern cornfields—the University of Illinois—where he's earning his MFA in fiction. Aside from writing for magazines, newspapers, and The Princeton Review, he's worked as a radio disc jockey, a helping hand in a bakery, and a laborer on a highway construction crew. He's trying to avoid highway construction these days.

Carson Brown graduated from Stanford University in 1998, and after getting paid too much for working for various Internet companies for several years, sold her BMW and moved to Mexico. She has now overstayed her welcome south of the border and is returning to San Francisco to be responsible and further her career working as a writer and editor.

Julie Doherty is a freelance writer, web designer, and preschool teacher. She lives in Mexico City.

Andrew Friedman graduated in 2003 from Stanford University, where he was a President's Scholar. He lives in New York City.

Counselor Order Form

The Princeton Review

NAME:_____ TITLE:_____

Company or School Name:_____

Billing Address:_____ City:_____ State:_____ Zip Code:_____

Shipping Address: (If different from billing)_____

City:_____ State:_____ Zip Code:_____

Phone:_____ Fax:_____ Email Address:_____

BILLING INFORMATION: *Check one of the following*

❐ Enclosed a check for the sum of:_____

❐ Please send me a bill with a Purchase Order #_____

❐ Please charge my credit card for the sum of:_____

Credit Card # and type:_____ Expiration Date:_____

Name on the Card:_____ Signature:_____ Date:_____

ORDERING INSTRUCTIONS:

The Essential Package includes 1 of each book listed in the Essential Package column. There is no limit to the quantity you may order.

		Essential Package	Single Books	Your Price	Total Price
Your Educator DISCOUNT		30%	15%	15%	
Essential Package Price		$163			$163
TITLE	**ISBN**	Quantity	Quantity		
The Best 366 Colleges, 2008 edition	9780375766213	Included		$18.66	
Complete Book of Colleges, 2008 edition	9780375766206	Included		$22.91	
America's Best Value Colleges, 2008 edition	9780375766015	Included		$16.11	
The Best Northeastern Colleges, 2008 edition	9780375766190	Included		$14.41	
Guide to College Majors, 2008 edition	9780375766374	Included		$17.85	
Taking Time Off	0375763031	Included		$15.26	
Parents' Guide to College Life	9780375764943	Included		$11.86	
The K&W Guide to Colleges for Students with Learning Disabilities and A.D.D., 9th edition	9780375766336	Included		$22.95	
Guiding Teens with Learning Disabilities	9780375766237	Included		$19.51	
Paying for College Without Going Broke (with foreword by former President Bill Clinton)	9780375766305	Included		$17.00	
The Gay and Lesbian Guide to College Life	9780375766237	Included		$11.86	
College Navigator	9780375765834	Included		$11.01	
The Road to College	9780375766176	Included		$11.86	
SUB-TOTAL Books					$

Don't Forget Shipping & Handling

Books: $2.95 for 1, $9.95 for 2 or more

Total (Books and Shipping and Handling)

$_____

Please fax this order form to
    attn: Adam Davis, 212-874-1754
or mail to
    The Princeton Review attn: Adam Davis
    2315 Broadway, New York, NY 10024
Please call or Email with questions
212-874-8282 x1440 or TPRBooks@Review.com

FINDING THE FUNDS:
What you should know about paying for your college education

A year attending a public college on average costs $12,796. Going to a private one will cost you $30,367 per year. Laying down what could be as much as $120,000 if not more over four years is a lot. That's the equivalent of almost 500 iPods, 12,000 movie tickets, or 444,444 packs of instant noodles.

Your parents have a tough job ahead of them. Just about everyone needs some kind of financial assistance. Fortunately, you have many different options, including grants, scholarships, work-study, federal loans, and private loans. Read on to learn about these options and share this with your parents.

OTHER PEOPLE'S MONEY

Scholarships and Grants

These are the best forms of financial aid because they don't have to be paid back. Scholarships are offered to students with unique abilities that the school is seeking to infuse into the student body, such as exceptional talent in music, art, or athletics. However, most scholarships require that you pass and maintain a minimum GPA requirement and some grants may not extend through all four years of your undergraduate education.

Federal grants for undergraduate study include Pell Grants, Federal Supplemental Educational Opportunity Grants (FSEOG), Academic Competitiveness Grants (ACG), and national SMART grants. Pell Grants are the most common type of federal grant awarded to undergraduate students, and form the base upon which supplemental aid from other financing sources may be added. Moreover, Pell Grant recipients receive priority for FSEOG awards, which are provided to students with exceptional financial need, and for National SMART Grants for math and science students.

Academic Competitiveness Grants (ACG) are a brand new kind of grant that began in the 2006–07 academic year. They are for students who have attended secondary school programs that have been qualified by the government as achieving a high standard of academic rigor. As with Federal Supplemental Educational Opportunity Grants, ACG awards are generally provided as a supplement to students already receiving Federal Pell Grants.

Additionally, your state residency or the state where the school you wish to attend is located also opens you up to state-funded grants and scholarships. Remember to check out the state grant application deadlines found on the FAFSA website mentioned below.

Note that as you advance through your undergraduate education, that progress itself makes you eligible for additional federal, state, and private grant and scholarship opportunities.

Maximize your eligibility for free money by completing the Free Application for Federal Student Aid ("FAFSA") online annually at http://www.fafsa.ed.gov. Visit the Department of Education's student aid portal at http://studentaid.ed.gov for the latest information on federal aid available to students like you. According to the National Center for Education Statistics, approximately 63% of all undergraduates receive some form of financial aid. There is approximately $80 billion in federal grants, loans and work-study funds available out there. Even if you don't think you'll qualify, it is worth it to fill out this form.

Work-study

Federal work-study is another way to lessen the burden of college tuition. Work-study is an actual part-time job, with pay of at least the current federal minimum wage—sometimes higher depending on the type of work you do.

Another advantage of federal work-study is that the program can sometimes place you in jobs related to your field of study. So, while you might be able to get equivalent wages working at a local restaurant or retail store, with work-study, you can sometimes gain resume-building experience related to your degree – in a school laboratory or research center, for example.

How much work-study you receive depends on your level of financial need and the funding level provided by your school. Be aware that work-study alone isn't going to be enough to pay for your education. But, it can be a good way to lessen the sting.

LOANS

When scholarships, grants, and work-study don't cover the full cost of attendance, many students take out loans to help out with the rest.

Avoid loans if you can. A loan can best be described as renting money. There's a cost and it may not be an easy cost to bear.

Here's an interesting anecdote. Many students graduate college without knowing what types of loans they received, who the lender was, and how much they owe. The first time many students become aware of the scope of their obligation is when they receive their first bill—six months after graduation.

This is often because students are passive participants in the financial aid process and do not educate themselves or ask questions. Most students receive a list of "preferred lenders" from their financial aid office and simply go with the lender recommended to them. Over the course of the previous year, relationships between financial aid offices and lenders have been called into question by State Attorneys General, the Department of Education and regulators. Financial aid offices in certain cases received revenue from lenders in exchange for being placed on the "preferred lender list." Some schools have even rented out their name and logo for use on loan applications. These practices occur without disclosure to parents and students.

It is important to know that the "preferred lenders" may not offer the best deals on your loan options. While your financial aid office may be very helpful with scholarships and grants, and is legally required to perform certain duties with regard to federal loans, many do not have staff researching the lowest cost options at the time you are borrowing.

Remember that your tuition payment equals revenue for the school. When borrowing to pay tuition, you can choose to borrow from any lender. That means you can shop for the lowest rate. Keep reading. This will tell you how.

TYPES OF LOANS

The federal government and private commercial lenders offer educational loans to students. Federal loans are usually the "first resort" for borrowers because many are subsidized by the federal government and offer lower interest rates. Private loans have the advantage of fewer restrictions on borrowing limits, but may have higher interest rates and more stringent qualification criteria.

Federal Loans
There are three federal loan programs. The Federal Perkins Loan Program where your school lends you money made available by government funds, the Federal Direct Loan Program (FDLP) where the government lends its money directly to students; and the Federal Family Education Loan Program (FFELP) where financial institutions such as MyRichUncle lend their own money but the government guarantees them. While most schools participate in the Federal Perkins Program, institutions tend to favor either the FFELP or FDLP. You will borrow from FFELP or FDLP depending on which program your school has elected to participate in.

The government only lends money directly to you under the Federal Direct Loan Program. Lenders provide loans guaranteed by the federal government in the Federal Family Education Loan program.

The Federal Perkins Loan is a low-interest (5%) loan for students with exceptional need. Many students who do not qualify or who may need more funds can borrow FFELP or FDLP student loans. Under both programs, the Stafford loan is the typical place to start. The Stafford loan program features a fixed interest rate and yearly caps on the maximum amount a student can borrow. Stafford loans can either be subsidized (the government pays the interest while the student is in school) or unsubsidized (the student is responsible for the interest that accrues while in school). Starting July 1, 2007, the maximum amount an independent freshman student can borrow is $7,500.

It is often assumed that the government sets the rate on student loans. The government does not set the rate of interest. It merely indicates the maximum rate lenders can charge. These lenders are free to charge less than the specified rate of 6.8% for Stafford loans. There is also an origination fee of up to 2% dropping to 1.5% on July 1, 2007. In some cases you may also be charged up to a 1% guarantee fee. Any fees will be taken out of your disbursement.

Historically lenders have hovered at the maximum rate because most loans were distributed via the financial aid office whereby a few lenders received most of the loans. The end result was limited competition. At 1,239 institutions, one lender received more than 90% of the number of Stafford loans in 2006.

Certain lenders offer rate reductions, also known as borrower benefits, conditioned on the borrower making a certain number of on-time payments. Unfortunately, it is estimated that 90% of borrowers never qualify for these reductions.

Last year, MyRichUncle challenged this process by launching a price war. The company cut interest rates on Stafford loans and introduced widespread price competition. These interest rate cuts are effective when students enter repayment and do not have any further qualification requirements. In addition, students only lose the rate reduction if they default.

Parents can also borrow a PLUS loan. The Parent PLUS Loan program allows the parents of dependent students to take out loans to supplement the aid packages of their children. The program allows parents to borrow money to cover any cost not already met by the student's financial aid package up to the full cost of attendance. Unlike the Stafford Loan, eligibility for the Parent PLUS loan is not determined by the FAFSA. A parent fills out a loan application and signs a master promissory note. Eligibility is contingent upon whether the parent has an adverse credit history. Adverse credit history is defined as being no more than 90 days delinquent on any debt, having not declared bankruptcy in the last five years, and having not been the subject of a default determination on a foreclosure, a repossession, a tax lien, a wage garnishment, or a write-off of Title IV debt in the last five years.

The maximum rate a lender can charge for Parent PLUS loans is 8.5%. PLUS loans also have an origination fee of up to 3%, and a guarantee fee of up to 1%. Any fees will be taken out of your disbursement.

Your financial aid office is legally required to certify for lenders that you are enrolled and based on your financial aid package, the amount in Federal loans you are eligible to borrow. You are free to choose any lender even if the lender is not on your financial aid office's preferred lender list.

To shop for low cost Federal loans, call a number of lenders before applying to determine their rates and fees. This is an effective approach because your application will not impact the price. Once you are comfortable that you have the lowest cost option, apply and submit the Master Promissory Note to your lender of choice.

Private Loans
Private student loans can make it possible to cover the costs of higher education when other sources of funding have been exhausted. Additionally, when you apply for federal loans, you can borrow up to what your institution has pre-defined as the annual cost of attendance. If your anticipated expenses are above and beyond this pre-defined cost because of your unique needs, it will take a series of appeals before your institution will allow you to borrow more federal loans. Private loans help you meet your true expectation of what you will need financially. Private loans can pay expenses that federal loans can't, such as application and testing fees and the cost of transportation.

When you apply for a private loan, the lending institution will check your credit history including your credit score and determine your capacity to pay back the money you borrow. For individuals whose credit history is less than positive, lenders may require a co-borrower: a credit-worthy individual who also agrees to be accountable to the terms of the loan. While private loans do not have annual borrowing limits, they often have higher interest rates, and interest rate caps are higher than those set by Federal loans. Generally, the loans are variable rate loans, so the interest rate may go up or down, changing the cost.

To shop for a private loan, after you've researched several options, apply to as many of them as you feel comfortable. Once you are approved, compare rates. Pick the lowest cost option.

EXTRA LESSONS

Borrow the minimum
Just because someone is offering to lend you thousands upon thousands of dollars doesn't mean you should necessarily take them up on that offer. At some point, you'll have to repay the debt and you'll have to do it responsibly. Wouldn't it be better to use your money for something more worthwhile to you?

Know your rights

Currently, student lending is an industry that is under heavy scrutiny. It is important, now more than ever, for parents and students to have an active voice and to make educational and financial choices that are right for them. Some schools work with "preferred lenders" when offering federal and private loans. You are not required to choose a loan from one of these lenders if you can find a better offer. With respect to Federal loans the financial aid office has a legislated role which is to certify for the lending institution that you the borrower are indeed enrolled and the amount you are eligible for. They are not legally empowered to dictate your choice of lender and must certify your loan from the lender of your choice. You have the right to shop for and to secure the best rates possible for your loans. Don't get bullied into choosing a different lender, simply because it is preferred by an institution. Instead, do your homework and make sure you understand all of your options.

Know what you want

When it's all said and done, you will have to take a variety of factors into account in order to choose the best school for you and for your future. You shouldn't have to mortgage your future to follow a dream, but you also shouldn't downgrade this opportunity just to save a few bucks.

An out-of-the-box approach

Community colleges are a viable option for those ultimately seeking a four-year degree. Articulation agreements between community colleges and major four-year institutions allow students to complete their general education requirements at community colleges and have them transferred to a four-year institution. If you are really keen on graduating from that fancy four year college of your choice, transferring in from a community college is a cheaper path to getting that same degree. At an average cost of $2,272 per year, it is a thought worth exploring.

MYRICHUNCLE

MYRICHUNCLE
STUDENT LOANS

Call us:
1-800-926-5320

or learn more online:
MYRICHUNCLE.COM

Who we are:

MyRichUncle is a national student loan company offering federal (Stafford, PLUS and GradPLUS) and private loans to undergraduate, graduate, and professional students. MyRichUncle knows that getting a student loan can be a complicated and intimidating process, so we changed it. We believe students are credit-worthy borrowers, and that student loan debt should be taken seriously by borrowers and lenders alike. We propose changes in the student loan industry that will better serve parents, schools, and most importantly, students.

Why it matters:

Your student loan will be your responsibility. When you enter into a loan agreement, you're entering into a long-term relationship with your lender—15 years, on average. The right student loan with the right lender can help you avoid years of unnecessary fees and payments.

What we do:

MyRichUncle pays close attention to the obstacles students face. Removing these obstacles drives everything we do. MyRichUncle discounts federal loan rates at repayment rather than requiring years of continuous payments to earn the discount, which saves you money right from the start. We help you plan ahead, so you can choose the best loans and save.

Our credentials:

MyRichUncle is a NASDAQ listed company. Our symbol is UNCL. In 2006, MyRichUncle was featured in FastCompany Magazine's Fast 50 and in Businessweek's Top Tech Entrepreneurs. MyRichUncle and its parent company, MRU Holdings, are financed by a number of leading investment banks and venture capitalists, including subsidiaries of Merrill Lynch, Lehman Brothers, Battery Ventures and Nomura Holdings.

Our Books Help You Navigate the College Admissions Process

Find the Right School

Best 366 Colleges, 2008 Edition
978-0-375-76621-3 • $21.95/C$27.95

Complete Book of Colleges, 2008 Edition
978-0-375-76620-6 • $26.95/C$34.95

College Navigator
978-0-375-76583-4 • $12.95/C$16.00

America's Best Value Colleges, 2008 Edition
978-0-375-76601-5 • $18.95/C$24.95

Guide to College Visits
978-0-375-76600-8 • $20.00/C$25.00

Get In

Cracking the SAT, 2008 Edition
978-0-375-76606-0 • $19.95/C$24.95

Cracking the SAT with DVD, 2008 Edition
978-0-375-76607-7 • $33.95/C$42.00

Math Workout for the NEW SAT
978-0-375-76433-2 • $16.00/C$23.00

Reading and Writing Workout for the NEW SAT
978-0-375-76431-8 • $16.00/C$23.00

11 Practice Tests for the SAT and PSAT, 2008 Edition
978-0-375-76614-5 • $19.95/C$24.95

12 Practice Tests for the AP Exams
978-0-375-76584-1 • $19.95/C$24.95

Cracking the ACT, 2007 Edition
978-0-375-76585-8 • $19.95/C$24.95

Cracking the ACT with DVD, 2008 Edition
978-0-375-76586-5 • $31.95/C$39.95

Crash Course for the ACT, 3rd Edition
978-0-375-76587-2 • $9.95/C$12.95

Crash Course for the New SAT
978-0-375-76461-5 • $9.95/C$13.95

Get Help Paying for It

How to Save for College
978-0-375-76425-7 • $14.95/C$21.00

Paying for College Without Going Broke, 2008 Edition
978-0-375-76630-5 • $20.00/C$25.00
Previous Edition: 978-0-375-76567-4

Available at Bookstores Everywhere
www.PrincetonReview.com

AP Exams

Cracking the AP Biology Exam,
2006–2007 Edition
978-0-375-76525-4 • $17.00/C$24.00

Cracking the AP Calculus AB & BC Exams,
2006–2007 Edition
978-0-375-76526-1 • $18.00/C$26.00

Cracking the AP Chemistry Exam,
2006–2007 Edition
978-0-375-76527-8 • $17.00/C$24.00

**Cracking the AP Computer Science
A & AB Exams,** 2006–2007 Edition
978-0-375-76528-5 • $19.00/C$27.00

**Cracking the AP Economics (Macro &
Micro) Exams,** 2006–2007 Edition
978-0-375-76535-3 • $17.00/C$24.00

**Cracking the AP English Language and
Composition Exam,** 2006–2007 Edition
978-0-375-76536-0 • $17.00/C$24.00

Cracking the AP English Literature Exam,
2006–2007 Edition
978-0-375-76537-7 • $17.00/C$24.00

**Cracking the AP Environmental
Science Exam,** 2006–2007 Edition
978-0-375-76538-4 • $17.00/C$24.00

Cracking the AP European History Exam,
2006–2007 Edition
978-0-375-76539-1 • $17.00/C$24.00

Cracking the AP Physics B & C Exams,
2006–2007 Edition
978-0-375-76540-7 • $19.00/C$27.00

Cracking the AP Psychology Exam,
2006–2007 Edition
978-0-375-76529-2 • $17.00/C$24.00

Cracking the AP Spanish Exam,
2006–2007 Edition
978-0-375-76530-8 • $17.00/C$24.00

Cracking the AP Statistics Exam,
2006–2007 Edition
978-0-375-76531-5 • $19.00/C$27.00

**Cracking the AP U.S. Government
and Politics Exam,** 2006–2007 Edition
978-0-375-76532-2 • $17.00/C$24.00

Cracking the AP U.S. History Exam,
2006–2007 Edition
978-0-375-76533-9 • $17.00/C$24.00

Cracking the AP World History Exam,
2006–2007 Edition
978-0-375-76534-6 • $17.00/C$24.00

SAT Subject Tests

**Cracking the SAT Biology E/M
Subject Test,** 2007–2008 Edition
978-0-375-76588-9 • $19.00/C$25.00

Cracking the SAT Chemistry Subject Test,
2007–2008 Edition
978-0-375-76589-6 • $18.00/C$22.00

Cracking the SAT French Subject Test,
2007–2008 Edition
978-0-375-76590-2 • $18.00/C$22.00

Cracking the SAT Literature Subject Test,
2007–2008 Edition
978-0-375-76592-6 • $18.00/C$22.00

**Cracking the SAT Math 1 and 2
Subject Tests,** 2007–2008 Edition
978-0-375-76593-3 • $19.00/C$25.00

Cracking the SAT Physics Subject Test,
2007–2008 Edition
978-0-375-76594-0 • $19.00/C$25.00

Cracking the SAT Spanish Subject Test,
2007–2008 Edition
978-0-375-76595-7 • $18.00/C$22.00

**Cracking the SAT U.S. & World History
Subject Tests,** 2007–2008 Edition
978-0-375-76591-9 • $19.00/C$25.00

WE KNOW APPLYING TO COLLEGES IS STRESSFUL.

Why Not Win $1,000 for It?

Yeesh. Everyone around you may be weary of your obsessing over every detail of your (or your child's) college search. You know the angst. Location? Academic reputation? Tuition? Majors? Dream school? Safety school? But we're into this stuff even more than you are—so much so that we've created our College Hopes Survey, an opportunity for you to tell us how your search and application experience is going. Our survey's a heck of a lot shorter than any college app you'll face (it's just 10 questions), and it'll only take about five minutes to complete.

But wait, there's more. We're giving a $1,000 scholarship to one lucky participant (at random). Ten questions. Five minutes. Chance for $1,000 bucks. You do the math.

Complete this form and mail or fax it back to us. Or visit us at *PrincetonReview.com/go/survey* and submit your survey to us online.

In March 2008, we'll post our survey findings on our website, PrincetonReview.com and give one participant the happy news that they've won the $1,000 scholarship. Right about the time you'll be receiving those fat (or not-so-fat) letters from colleges. Hope springs eternal.

Official Rules:

We will conduct a random drawing in March 2008 to select a winner. The winner of the drawing will receive a $1,000 scholarship. Your odds of winning depend upon the number of entries received. If you win, you must redeem the scholarship within twelve months of notification. This promotion is not open to employees of The Princeton Review or Random House and is, of course, void where prohibited by law. All taxes are the sole responsibility of the winners. No purchase necessary: If you choose not to buy this book (big mistake!) or fill out the survey (bad decision!), you may enter this drawing by going to our website at: *www.PrincetonReview.com/go/survey* or by sending a postcard with your name, address, and phone number to The Princeton Review, c/o Robert Franek—College Hopes Survey, 2315 Broadway, New York, New York, 10024-4332. You may also write us to get a listing of the prize winner. By the way, we are not responsible for failures in electronic transmission or lost, misdirected, illegible, or mutilated entries.

The Princeton Review
www.PrincetonReview.com

College Hopes & Worries Survey 2008

Snail mail to Robert Franek, The Princeton Review, 2315 Broadway, New York, NY 10024
or fax to Robert Franek, 212-874-1754 or fill out online at PrincetonReview.com/go/survey

Name _____

Address (optional) _____

City / State / Zip _____

Daytime phone _____

E-mail address _____

I am ____ a parent of a student ____ a student applying to attend college beginning in

____ Fall or Spring 2008 ____ Fall or Spring 2009 ____ Later (indicate year:_____).

1   What would be your "dream" college? What college would you most like to attend (or see your child attend) if chance of being accepted or cost were not an issue?"

_____

2   How many colleges will you (your child) apply to?

____ 1 to 4

____ 5 to 8

____ 9 to 12

____ 13 or more

3   How many colleges do you think you'll visit?

____ 1 to 4

____ 5 to 8

____ 9 to 12

____ 13 or more

____ Don't plan to visit any colleges.

4   What has been, or do you think will be the toughest part of your (your child's) college application experience? (Choose one.)

____ Deciding which colleges to apply to

____ Taking standardized tests such as SAT or ACT

____ Writing college essays and completing applications

____ Deciding which college to attend

5   What do you estimate your (or your child's) college degree will cost, including four years of tuition, room & board, fees, books and other expenses? (Choose one.)

_____ More than $100,000

_____ $75,000 to $100,000

_____ $50,000 to $75,000

_____ $25,000 to $50,000

_____ Less tha $25,000

6   How necessary will financial aid (education loans, scholarships or grants) be to pay for your (your child's) college education? (Choose one.)

_____ Extremely

_____ Very

_____ Somewhat

_____ Not at all

7   What's your biggest concern about applying to or attending college? (Choose one.)

_____ Won't get into first-choice college

_____ Will get into first-choice college, but won't have sufficient funds/financial aid to attend

_____ Will get into a college I (my child) want(s) to attend, but will take on major loan debt to do so

_____ Will attend a college I (my child) may not be happy about

8   How would you gauge your stress level about the college application process? (Choose one.)

_____ Very High

_____ High

_____ Average

_____ Low

_____ Very Low

9   Ideally, how far from home would you like the college you (your child) attends to be? (Choose one.)

_____ 0 to 250 miles

_____ 250 to 500 miles

_____ 500 to 1,000 miles

_____ 1000 miles or more

10   When it comes to choosing which college you (or your child) will attend, which of the following do you think it is most likely to be? (Choose one.)

_____ College with best academic reputation

_____ College with best program for my (my child's) career interests

_____ College that will be the best general fit

_____ College that will be the most affordable